An Index to
Publications
of the
American Jewish Historical Society
Volumes 21-50
[1913-1961]

Prepared by
The American Jewish Historical Society

Introduction by
Jeffrey S. Gurock

CARLSON
Publishing Inc

BROOKLYN, NEW YORK, 1994

The Library of Congress has determined that this title is out of scope for the CIP program. AACR2 cataloging is provided below, courtesy of the State Historical Society of Wisconsin Library.

An index to Publications of the American Jewish Historical Society : volumes 21-50,
    1913-1961 / prepared by the American Jewish Historical Society ; introduction
    by Jeffrey S. Gurock.
    xxii, 439 p. ; 23 cm.
    ISBN 0-926019-76-7
      1. American Jewish Historical Society. 2. Jews—United States—History—
Periodicals—Indexes. 3. Publications of the American Jewish Historical Society—
Indexes. I. American Jewish Historical Society.
E184.J5A52 Index

Typographic design: C. J. Bartelt

Typeface: Adobe Janson Text

Jacket and Case design: Ann Harakawa

Printed on acid-free, 250-year-life paper.

Manufactured in the United States of America.

Contents

Preface

This *Index* to the scholarly journal of the American Jewish Historical Society for the years 1916 to 1961 (Volumes 21 to 50) is intended to provide contemporary readers with convenient access to the rich treasury of articles and reviews published by the Society during those years. Since 1892, *Publications* (in 1962 renamed *American Jewish Historical Quarterly;* in 1978 renamed yet again *American Jewish History*) has provided historians with the knowledge base from which a significant portion of American Jewish scholarship has been written. It is virtually impossible to read a serious scholarly work in American Jewish history without finding reference to one or more articles from *Publications* and its successor titles.

In the introduction to this index which follows, Professor Jeffrey S. Gurock of Yeshiva University, the current Associate Editor of *American Jewish History*, notes that, from its beginning, the Society has pursued the mission of preserving and disseminating evidence of the contributions made by American Jews to world civilization. The journal has served as an outlet for historians of American Jewry whose essays, before the 1950s, could find few if any other journals that would publish their writings.

The Society has since its earliest days attracted a diverse mix of professional scholars, learned amateurs and members of the general public—each with a somewhat different interest in the history of American Jewry. It has been the task of the Society's journal to provide a common ground for the Society's diverse scholarly and lay constituencies. This balancing act has not been simple. For every scholar who has lamented that *Publications'* articles were excessively antiquarian, quaint or popular, one can find a lay member of the Society who complained that the journal was excessively dry and scholarly. This

seems to be the fate—and editorial dilemma—of any journal that must please both a lay and scholarly audience.

The publication of this index would not have been possible without the generous support of a testamentary bequest from Leon J. Obermayer. A prominent Philadelphia attorney, Mr. Obermayer served as President of the American Jewish Historical Society from 1964 to 1967 and as Chairman of its Board of Trustees from 1967 to 1972. Thereafter until his death in 1984 he served as Honorary Chairman of the Board. In 1968, Mr. Obermayer received the Society's Lee M. Friedman Award Medal for his distinguished service to the field of American Jewish history.

The Obermayer bequest is also making possible the Society's publication of a companion index to the present one, which covers Volumes 51 to 80 of *Publications* and its successor titles, as well as the publication of a compendium of Nathan M. Kaganoff's *Judaica Americana* bibliographies published in the journal from 1962 until Kaganoff's passing in 1992. These three reference tools, used together, will prove an essential aid to researchers interested in the facts, stories and analyses—written by the field's leading scholars—that bring American Jewish history into the present.

Michael Feldberg
Executive Director
American Jewish Historical Society
Waltham, Massachusetts
April, 1994

Introduction

Examining a Journal in Transition

This index to *Publications of the American Jewish Historical Society*, covering the years from 1913 to 1961, canvasses a journal whose mission, format and range of contributors changed dramatically in the course of those forty-eight years. This invaluable bibliographic aid begins with Volume 21 of *Publications*, when the goals of those who then wrote American Jewish history were still very much the same as those of the individuals who had founded the Society in 1892.[1]

When it was first founded, collecting and publishing materials "bearing on the history of America" had been one of the explicit objectives of the Society. For example, the first issue of the journal catalogued in this index is titled "The Lyons Collection Volume I" (1913). The family of the late Reverend Jacques Judah Lyons, longtime minister of Congregation Shearith Israel, New York's Spanish-Portuguese synagogue, donated materials to the Society that he had amassed in the 1870s in anticipation of writing a history of Jews in this country. The Lyons archive included such important sources as the earliest extant minute books of the congregation and the 1825 speech of Mordecai Manuel Noah at the cornerstone laying ceremony in Ararat, Noah's utopian Jewish community near Niagara Falls. To this day, the documents in the Lyons Collection, reprinted in *Publications*, inform writing on this period of American Jewish history.

Publications in the 1910s likewise loyally kept up the filiopietistic tradition of the Society's first amateur writers who had used the journal to tell readers about the achievements of previously unrecognized Jewish forebears. Alicia Lindo's 1915 portrayal (Volume 23) of her less-

---

[1] For comparison, see *Index to the Publications of the American Jewish Historical Society, Numbers 1 to 20* (New York, 1914).

than-renowned ancestor David Lindo, a chemist and businessman in the West Indies, was very much within that spirit, and is a good example of this sort of very personal history.

The continued use of history as a subtle weapon against those who would question the Jews' historical contributions to America was yet a third goal or tradition maintained in the 1910s. Back in the 1890s, during an epoch of rising nativism and intensifying social exclusionary anti-Semitism, studies documenting Jews in this country from the very start, or who fought and died to make America what it became, were essential components in Jewish communal defense strategies. Oscar Straus, the Society's first president, probably said it best when he suggested that if it were historically proven that Jews had taken an active part in the discovery of the New World "this fact would be an answer for all time to come to anti-Semitic tendencies in this country."

Predictably, *Publications* first twenty volumes contained much about Columbus' Jewishness, about the "F.F.J.'s" (the First Families of Jewry) or about Jewish heroes in the Revolutionary and Civil War.

Twenty years later, in the 1910s, Jews still felt somewhat insecure in this country and contributors to *Publications* continued to respond to their discomfort through apologetics. They tirelessly investigated how many Jews died on American battlefields from Lexington and Concord to Gettysburg and even in the Spanish-American War. A perusal of our *Index* immediately reveals that articles, notes, documents and broadsides on early American Jews commanded abundant space in almost every edition of the journal. And typically, there was always a historical note or two on a Jew who had performed distinguished military or government service.

The style of apologetics composed in the 1910s also closely resembled that of two decades earlier. The approach of the first cautious defenders had been to extol what Jews had done, while playing down, with studied circumspection, whatever contemporary lessons might be learned from their ancestor's exploits. The intellectual anti-Semitism that moved many to respond was not addressed directly, and contributors stressed what historical studies could do to improve America for all people. So it was in 1914 when the Society's Curator, Leon Huhner, wrote for Volume 22 about the "Jewish Signers to a Patriotic Address

to Congress in 1783," or for Volume 26 (1918) on "Jews in the War of 1812." In the latter piece, Huhner was quick to point out that it was "only by a system of extravagant bounties that a substantial force [of Americans] was brought together at all [but that] . . . Jews, who participated . . . to their honor be it said, practically all of them had volunteered."

Complementing Huhner and his colleague's carefully crafted apologetics, *Publications* promoted, during the 1910s, another more frontal dimension to Jewish defense. The *Index* records that in 1916 *Publications* produced "Jewish Disabilities in the Balkan States . . ." Here the journal and its Society assisted the American Jewish Committee in fighting anti-Semitism overseas. It was the hope of the Society and the Committee—a number of leading members belonged to both groups—that Congressional and State Department officials would read this document and be reminded of America's long-standing commitment to humanitarian diplomacy. The model for this endeavor was the article titled "Jews in the Diplomatic Correspondence of the United States" (Volume 15 of *Publications*) that appeared in 1906. This defense tradition and stratagem long endured. In a format explicitly reminiscent of these efforts, the Society edited, with Committee assistance, "American Intercession on Behalf of Jews in the Diplomatic Correspondence of the United States, 1840-1938" (Volume 36 [1943]).

There certainly was talk within the Society during the 1910s of expanding the scope of *Publications* and its coterie of contributors. In 1902, Society president Cyrus Adler, who served from 1899 to 1921, had already called for the expansion of the scope of *Publications*, beyond its chronicling of Jewish events in the New World, to comprehend all of Jewish history as it related to the American experience. However, a close examination of the contents of the journal, using this *Index* as an aid, reveals that in the 1910s and beyond, with the exception of one special issue (Volume 26 [1918]) explicitly devoted to papers of a "general historical interest," the Society retained a very narrow geographical focus. Indeed, some periods and topics within American Jewish history itself commanded constant attention, while others were virtually ignored. For example, articles on East European Jews in America were totally non-existent for the full twenty-five years between

1913-1939. *Publications* really did not study this aspect of American Jewish history and world Jewish history, in general, until the late 1940s-1950s.

Adler also spoke of a day when there would be university-trained practitioners of the Society's discipline, with professors having a recognized place both within the American academy and the world of Jewish scholarship. But the professionalization of the field would not fully be underway until after World War II. American historians had neither the interest in, nor affinity for, the dispassionate study of minority groups or immigrant history. They focused on military, political and diplomatic history. If anything, the few references to Jews then in the literature bespoke the racist and nativist rhetoric and sentiment of intolerance. Meanwhile, European Jewish scholars evinced little enthusiasm for examining the supposed intellectually-barren saga of a frontier Jewish community in America that did not fit traditional historical patterns. American Jewry by comparison to Europe, had endured few persecutions and produced no great rabbis and scholars and was thus deemed unworthy of sustained consideration. Meanwhile, the few Jews then teaching history in America's colleges correctly perceived that scholarly specialization American Jewish history was a dead end career path. American Jewish history was relegated, by default, through the 1910s and long thereafter, to the province of "amateurs, antiquarians, necrologists and undaunted sentimentalists."

Actually, during the inter-war period, *Publications'* horizons narrowed further as it pursued the single-minded passion of its long-time president, A.S.W. Rosenbach. This collector extraordinaire of rare books headed the Society from 1921 to 1948 and committed his small clan of collaborators to the keeping and publishing of documentary records, and to the presentation of bibliography and primary source materials, even to the exclusion of filiopietism, apologetics and defense activities. Our *Index* quantifies Rosenbach's all-encompassing leadership of the Society as it records several hundred references to his activities, exclusive of the articles, notes, and necrologies and presidential addresses that were printed. No individual came close, during this period, to doing as much on behalf of the Society and for the telling of American Jewish history as Rosenbach saw it. This indefatigable

bibliophile's most enduring historiographical contribution to the discipline was Volume 30 (1926) which devoted itself, in its entirety, to Rosenbach's "An American Jewish Bibliography, being a list of Books and Pamphlets by Jews or Relating to Them Printed in the United States . . . until 1850," an unsurpassed achievement.

Yet, as the Rosenbach years drew to a close, it was clear to those both within and without the Society that, for a generation, *Publications* had taken little cognizance of the gradual evolution of new approaches to the study of American Jewry. The late 1910s-1920s had witnessed the appearance of serious sociological works about the transformation of Jewish life in America. Far less hide-bound than historians, empirical and sympathetic social scientists, especially those who taught or studied in the University of Chicago's Sociology Department, had begun to take careful looks at how immigrants, African-Americans and other minorities tried to integrate into American society. For the Chicago School of sociologists, the American Jewish saga was an intrinsic part of the nation's cultural mosaic.

While this approach to social analysis implicitly advocated assimilation, a new breed of 1920s Jewish communal workers wrote about existing Jewish problems with an emphasis on group persistence and development—what is now called "continuity." Historical sketches and insights often accompanied the descriptive and prescriptive articles that made up Jewish and general sociology of the time. Though still the mainstay of strictly historical writing, Rosenbach's *Publications* was, from then on, no longer alone in speaking about American Jewry's past.

In 1936, the Society's journal began to share its field with *Jewish Social Studies [JSS]*, a publication of the Conference on Jewish Relations. Under the influence of philosopher Morris Raphael Cohen, political scientist Hans Kohn and historian Salo W. Baron, now university-based and Jewish communal researchers could publish their studies in the same journal. Far more methodologically sophisticated than *Publications*, *JSS*'s historical and sociological studies in America were linked up with comparable literature on communities in Europe and Palestine. For someone like Adler, these studies were really a first breakthrough in linking American Jewish and European scholarship.

But to Adler's likely dismay, *Publications* was not the forum for these long hoped for developments.

Publications was likewise not the place where, in the mid-to-late 1930s, the small but growing group of Jewish social scientists published. *Jewish Social Studies* was the first home for these academics, as it was for scholars of modern Jewish life from Central and Eastern Europe who fled to these shores to escape Hitler. A few years later, these same groups of scholars were also writing about the history of their adopted land in two other journals dedicated to Jewish history and modern social science and headed by refugee scholars. In 1938, Dr. Guido Kisch, the distinguished historian of medieval Jewish jurisprudence began editing *Historia Judaica*. And in 1941, YIVO (the Yiddish Scientific Institute) from Vilna that had resettled in New York began communicating with the small indigenous group of American Jewish scholars who wrote in Yiddish, while it brought American Jewish historians and sociologists into contact with wider worlds of modern Jewish scholarship. These were scholarly arenas that Rosenbach's *Publications* never entered.

While there is no record of any Jewish academic/communal worker or any refugee scholar being turned away from the Society, and no scholar was ever formally discouraged from writing about East European Jews, the regnant perception was that the Society was an elite, exclusive organization, shepherded by a sometimes irascible leader who cultivated a clique of writers who ceaselessly examined a narrow set of themes and personalities that interested its small cadre of long-time members.

So disposed and unchanging, by the end of World War II, *Publications* was both out of touch with the growth of interdisciplinary Jewish social studies and was increasingly out of line with the new directions American history was taking. Marcus Lee Hansen had clearly shown the way in a classic set of essays, *The Immigrant in American History* (1940). He argued that to properly understand American Jewish history, the saga of immigration had to be comprehended. Writing without apology or polemic, Hansen underscored not only the contribution but the adaptability of newcomers to the culture of America.

Hansen's call surely did not lead at once to an efflorescence of works on all immigrant groups. Such research required acquaintance

with foreign languages with which most American-trained historians were not familiar. And there was still, "the ill repute which filiopietists lent to this field of inquiry." Nonetheless, with the emergence of Oscar Handlin's work in the 1940s, immigrant historiography began to take its place in the American academy. Both in Handlin's important study of immigrant adjustment, *Boston's Immigrants*, published in 1941, and in his later Pulitzer prize winning saga *The Uprooted*, Handlin followed Hansen's principles, transferred the venue of immigrant study from the frontier to the urban center, and reiterated how the new American could be studied objectively.

While Handlin, who taught at Harvard, was establishing himself and his field, he challenged the American Jewish Historical Society in May, 1948, by helping to convene a conference of twenty-eight scholars from all across the United States to consider ways to upgrade the "low status of writing in American Jewish history." These experts generally agreed that what "passes now for history is an accumulation of details of little consequence, only slightly related either to the real problems of the present or to the real people of the past." They also believed that the AJHS was "the logical agency" to help "shed retrogressive traits that narrow" the field. But that organization, Handlin stressed, with pointed reference to Rosenbach's work and perspective, ". . . will not fill the role unless it undergoes a radical reform. At present it is still bogged down in its own parochial little interests, cut off from the main streams of American intellectual life—for that matter, from the main streams of Jewish intellectual life."

By the end of Rosenbach's period, a new journal appeared that was dedicated specifically to the study of the American Jewish past. In December, 1947, Dr. Nelson Glueck, president of the Hebrew Union College in Cincinnati, authorized Professor Jacob Rader Marcus to establish the American Jewish Archives on his campus. The Archives' mission immediately brought Marcus, who would also soon emerge as a major force in the Society itself, into friendly competition with the AJHS as American Jewry's record keeper. And when the periodical, *American Jewish Archives*, first appeared in June, 1948, *Publications* lost its uniqueness as a historical journal.

It took the initiatives of a new Society president, elected in 1948, and the cooperation of the most distinguished Jewish historian in America to awaken the Society and to begin the transformation of *Publications* from a bastion of antiquarianism to a leader in the modern historical study of the American Jewish experience.

A quick glance at Boston attorney Lee Max Friedman's *Publications* record, which our *Index* ably documents, gives little indication that the new president was attuned to the new types of American Jewish history that scholars were writing about in other journals. Between 1913 and 1947, Friedman wrote more than twenty-five articles, notes and necrologies primarily on Colonial and Early National Jewish themes or on local Boston history. A typical offering was his "Jews in the Vice Admiralty Court of Colonial Rhode Island," published in Volume 37 (1947). And in fact, even as he worked to bring new types of historiography to the journal, he personally continued to write on the traditional themes that interested him. The *Index* informs us that as late as Volume 41 (1951-1952), Friedman was still contributing traditional articles to *Publications* on the early Jewish settlers in South Carolina, or on "A Great Colonial Case and a Great Colonial Lawyer."

And yet while Friedman was the quintessential history "buff" and part of the small inner circle that had long run the Society, it was this seventy-seven year old amateur historian who, in his 1948 inaugural presidential address, essentially commended Hansen-like studies to future Society writers and tacitly acknowledged that, at that moment, *Publications* was not doing its share to advance its field. He openly admitted that the journal neglected the examination of East European Jewish life in America, as it focused heavily on early American Jews.

But Friedman did more than prove that a new Society president was cognizant of developments among American historians. He wanted the doors of *Publications* flung open to a wide range of scholars and scholarship. He promoted this new, broader outlook for *Publications* through a book review section. There, experts from a variety of disciplines were invited to examine works in all areas of American and Jewish history. He likewise made the journal more attractive to scholars by changing *Publications* from an annual, based primarily upon papers read at the yearly meeting, to a more readily approachable quarterly.

These new features appeared in Volume 38 (1948-49), the issue containing Rosenbach's valedictory and Friedman's inaugural speech.

Friedman labored mightily to convince the best historians on American immigration to write for *Publications*. The journal's publication in Volume 40 (1951) of Oscar Handlin's "American Views of the Jews at the Opening of the Twentieth Century," was Friedman's first great coup. And when, in a subsequent issue, Volume 47 (1957) John Higham of Johns Hopkins University published his "Social Discrimination against Jews in America, 1830-1930," *Publications*, could boast that it was the home for two of the essential works on nativism and anti-Semitism in American historiography.

Additionally, Friedman's creation of a distinguished six-man publications committee confirmed the impression that he was highly desirous of moving the Society away from being "a one-man or little group organization." To be sure, some sort of publications group had existed in prior administrations. In the Adler and Rosenbach years, the president, sometimes the curators (Max J. Kohler and Leon Huhner) and the corresponding secretary (for many years, Albert Friedenberg) met on an ad-hoc basis and made decisions on what should appear in print. And if at some time, they were sanctioned as the Society's "editors," the fact is that not until the 1948-1949 editions of the journal were members of a designated Publications Committee enumerated as such in the masthead of *Publications*. Friedman's new, very public committee, included Jacob Marcus, the most knowledgeable historian of American Jewry of the time; Salo Baron of Columbia University; the Jewish Theological Seminary's Alexander Marx; the New York Public Library's Joshua Bloch; Isidor Meyer, Librarian of the Society; and long-time Society friend Maurice Jacobs. This meant that new viewpoints would be heard within the councils of the AJHS. By 1961, the Committee had expanded to include some seventeen academics and a different coterie of concerned lay leaders. Isidor Meyer was designated *Publications'* first official editor in 1950.

But notwithstanding all of these moves and changes, the readiness of Salo Baron to be active in *Publications* was undeniably the Friedman administration's greatest triumph. Though an executive committee member since 1931, the great Viennese-trained occupant of the pres-

tigious Miller Chair of Jewish History at Columbia University had until then not made his considerable talents and influence felt within the journal. Our *Index* shows that in the first decade and one half of his affiliation with the Society, this most prolific of scholars, arguably the greatest Jewish historian of his time, had not published in *Publications*. Baron's involvement with the journal did more than just bring respectability to the Publications Committee. His seminal, fifty page essay (Volume 39 [1950]) coherently and specifically outlined the needs and methods for the ultimate emergence of the study of American Jewry as a major American and Judaic discipline. His prestigious name brought an entire group of his colleagues and students into the ranks of *Publications'* authors.

Our *Index*'s mere listing of Baron's "American Jewish History: Problems and Methods," cannot do justice to the grandeur of a study that not only retold the sorry tale of how scholars had long disdained American Jewish history but patiently outlined how this discipline might garner respect in the academy. Our bibliographical aid can, however, efficiently quantify the degree to which Baron's colleagues, friends and students, in the years immediately following the publication of his pathbreaking piece, looked to *Publications* as an organ for the best, new scientific works. For example, in the very same issue that contained Baron's piece, social scientist Abraham Duker, a regular contributor to *Jewish Social Studies*, offered his own views of the field and made the case that Jewish sociology and social and cultural history had to find a home in *Publications*.

From 1950 to 1955, several other Conference members and YIVO people, all within Baron's intellectual circle, contributed monographic essays and agreed to review books for the journal. The review essays often were concerned with subjects outside of American Jewish history. Sociologists and demographers Charles B. Sherman, Jacob Lestschinsky, and Mark Wischnitzer, political scientist Hans Kohn and historians Bernard D. Weinryb and the highly prolific Zosa Szjakowski, all broadened *Publications* scholarly and geographic horizons. The latter published four articles in *PAJHS* over a two year period (1950-1951) on related aspects of East European migration.

In the 1950s, this journal also attracted some of the best young scholars, some of them students of Baron, historians who are today among the most respected practitioners in the field. Significantly, during these years the study of East European Jewish life came of age in *Publications* as Baronians Abraham J. Karp, Lloyd P. Gartner and Arthur A. Goren and Handlin's prized student, Moses Rischin, among others, published the first fruits of their now classic examinations of the social, political and religious history of the ghetto.

Another Baron disciple, Naomi W. Cohen, arguably today's most prolific and accomplished scholar of American anti-Semitism, published her first piece in *Publications* in 1951, a study of Reform Jewish attitudes towards Zionism. Incidentally, Baron had to have been particularly pleased with Cohen's essay because it had been a winning submission to a 1949 Historical Essay Contest that the Publications Committee initiated and judged "to bring to light hitherto unpublished data of historical value as well as the interpretation of this material." The results of this contest must have also gratified Oscar Handlin since his disciple, Moses Rischin, likewise, placed in the competition.

Baron further professionalized the Society's publications by inaugurating a relationship between the Society and the American Historical Association. Starting in 1954, the AHA authorized a joint session with the Society in its annual meeting. The AJHS' successful relationship with America's most respected historical association brought increased visibility, respect, and quality papers to *Publications.*

The efforts of Jacob Rader Marcus in the 1950s also changed and improved the focus of *Publications.* Though his American Jewish Archives was his first love, he did, like Baron, serve as a president of the Society in the 1950s. (Baron succeeded Friedman in 1952 and stayed on until 1954. Marcus was president between 1955 and 1958.) Marcus also gave direction to the field when he bypassed his own journal and placed two of his most significant research and methodological pieces in the AJHS' publication. Both his "Periodization in American Jewish History" (1958) and his "The Theme in American Jewish History" (1959) limned the contours of the discipline. Our *Index* indicates that during that decade Marcus also published three pieces on Jews in the Colonial and Civil War Periods. These same years also saw his student and

erstwhile associate at the Archives, Bertram W. Korn, write for *Publications*, "Jews and Negro Slavery in the Old South, 1789-1865" (Volume 50 [1961]), the most influential article to date on Jews, slavery and the Civil War. Korn, too, would serve as a Society president (1958-1961), comfortably dividing his loyalties between the Cincinnati and New York-based periodicals.

It remained, however, for the Peekskill Conference of 1954 to bring together all of those who wanted to transform the journal from a pillar of apologetics to a dynamic scholarly organ. This gathering of academics, which Baron would later characterize as probably his proudest moment in "turning the Society around" and setting as its "major emphasis . . . to promote research and publications in the field of American Jewish history writing," attracted over twenty-five Jewish and American historians, Jews and Gentiles, and social scientists from around the nation and the world to ascertain "methods and norms for future research."

Ben Zion Dinur, Professor Emeritus of modern Jewish history at Hebrew University, came from Israel and spoke encouragingly of American Jewish history as a respected Judaica discipline. Distinguished American historians like Allen Nevins of Columbia, Arthur Mann of Smith College, Yale's Rollin G. Osterweis and Robert Ernst of Adelphi University, and literary critic Alfred Kazin also attended the conference. Baron's colleagues, disciples and friends assembled. Marcus spoke on "Letters as a Source of Biography" and Rischin talked about Jews and the American labor movement. Baron student Moshe Davis, who was also a friend of Nevins, co-edited the proceedings of the conference with Isidor S. Meyer, the Society's librarian and *Publications* editor. The "Proceedings of the Conference of Historians" in *Publications* (Volume 46 [1957]) showed all how far the journal—and its discipline—had advanced.

Despite all of these efforts at professionalization, *Publications* was not transformed into a journal exclusively for and by scholars. While apologetics would no longer occupy its pages, traditionalists such as Lee Max Friedman still published their antiquarian articles. Still, as our *Index* for the 1950s verifies, *Publications* carried in the 1950s many articles that interested few academics, but may have captivated general

readers. The same 1950 volume of *Publications* that carried Handlin's study of American anti-Semitism, Cohen's prize winning essay, a Szajkowski study of relations between Germans and East European Jews in Americas and a scholarly treatment of the history of United States government policies on Palestine also contained the story of an early Jew in Detroit and the saga of two American naval expeditions to Palestine in the mid-19th century. There was also room for a necrology of a Jewish former U.S. Senator.

This combination of scholarly studies and historical notes and tales interesting to history buffs and general readers was very apparent, as well, in the juxtaposition of articles in the September, 1953 edition. Rischin's consideration of the early career of Yiddish journalist Abraham Cahan was situated between a note on a colonial silversmith and the first of two pieces on Lincoln's Jewish chiropodist. An addendum to this highly idiosyncratic study of a friend of "the Civil War president [who] served him in several capacities—from toe nail trimmer to espionage agent and political campaigner in the election of 1864"—appeared in December, 1954. That same volume welcomed Abraham J. Karp's very important biography of Rabbi Jacob Joseph as *Publications* devoted the entire March, 1955 issue to this study of immigrant Orthodox Jewish life on the Lower East Side.

During these years, the journal published both scholarly articles and anecdotal pieces because even the Society's most rarefied professors understood that their discipline, almost uniquely, had to serve several different audiences. Though concerned with strengthening and expanding their niche in the academy, this first generation of university practitioners of American Jewish history agreed with Friedman's belief that widespread Jewish public knowledge of American Jewish history—even if sometimes it included learning about a presidential chiropodist—was one essential way of perpetuating group identity against assimilation.

Like his predecessors, the early leaders of the Society, Friedman asserted that history had to have a community service agenda. But the emphasis of this work had now changed from Jewish defense to the preservation of Jewish identity. Even the Peekskill gathering tacitly presumed that while the study of American Jewish history had to

mature within the academy, it also had to play a continued role in Jewish survival and even its defense. Thus, at the Peekskill gathering a former U.S. government official identified "some of the areas of research through which historians and other scholars can contribute to the formulation of immigration policy." He admonished his scholarly colleagues that students of American Jewish history had to be more than passive observers of past trends and careful investigators of historical questions. They could also participate, through their studies, in formulating contemporary public policies.

These two large publication agendas—the promotion of the academic study of American Jewish history and the use of the discipline to advance communal concerns—continued to inform the articles that appeared in the journal beginning with Volume 51 (1962) when *Publications* was renamed the *American Jewish Historical Quarterly*. My essay describing the continuing evolution of these agendas is published as an introduction to *An Index to* AMERICAN JEWISH HISTORICAL QUARTERLY/AMERICAN JEWISH HISTORY, *Volumes 51-80* (Carlson Publishing, Inc., 1994).

Jeffrey S. Gurock
Libby M. Klaperman Professor of Jewish History
Yeshiva University
April, 1994

Sources

Moses Rischin. *An Inventory of American Jewish History*. Cambridge, Mass., 1954.

Jeffrey S. Gurock. *American Jewish History: A Bibliographical Guide*. New York, 1983.

Idem. "From *Publications* to *American Jewish History*: The Journal of the American Jewish Historical Society and the Writing of American Jewish History," *American Jewish History* vol. 81, #2 (Winter, 1993-1994): 153-271.

The Index

A

Aarifi Pasha, 36:45
Aaron, 50:311
Aaron, R., *Pardes Binah*, 22:133; *Pardes Hakmah*, 22:133
Aaron, Benjamin, 50:253
Aaron, Charles I., 28:257
Aaron, David, necrology of, 33:xii
Aaron ben Gershon Abulrabi, 28:156
Aaron, Hart, 21:106, 108, 138, 213; 27:244, 387
Aaron, Henry, 27:51, 58-59
Aaron, Isaac, 29:143-44, 146
Aaron, Israel, address, 39:453; Isaac M. Wise, 40:34
Aaron, Joseph, "Joseph Aaron," 25:122-23; "A Key to the Hebrew Language, and the Science of Hebrew Grammar Explained. (With Points)," 25:122-23; 30:291, 293
Aaron, Louis I., necrology of, 28:xxxii, 257-58
Aaron, Marcus, 28:257
Aaron of Messina, 28:207
Aaron, Moses, *The merchant; a satire*, 35:xvii
Aaron (slave), 28:228
Aarons, Abraham, 26:251; 27:91
Aarons, David, 25:118
Aarons, Elizabeth, 25:118
Aarons, Jacob, 25:118
Aarons, Judah, 26:251
Aaron's Voice, 30:363
Aaronsburgh, *The Aaronsburgh Lottery*, 30:83-84; *Proclamation of Aaronsburgh*, 30:83, 85
Aaronsohn, Aaron, 22:226; 34:243; "Aaron Aaronsohn, Agricultural Explorer," 29:xxix; 31:xii, 197-210; Agricultural Experiment Station, 49:190
Aaronsohn, Alexander, 31:210; 46:488
Aaronsohn, Sara, 31:210
Aaronson (Russian Jew), 47:105, 108

Aaronson, Joseph Moses, 34:56
Aaronson, Moses, *Maatoei Moshe*, 35:xx
Abandana, Raephaell, 23:80
Abarbanel, Benjamin, 26:251; 32:56
Abarbanel, Phineas, 23:27
Abarbanell, Fenetta, 32:56
Abbady, Israel, 26:251-52; 32:56
Abbas, Elissa, 44:248
Abbot, Abiel, *Traits of Resemblance*, 30:116, 118
Abbot, Dodge & Co., 31:137
Abbott, Edith, 34:214
Abbott, F. E., 42:83-84
Abbott, Justice, 31:125
Abbott, Wilbur C., 37:425
Abdul Hamid II, 40:111
Abdullah, Achmed, 35:271-72
Abeal Family, 41:110
Abeal, David, 27:244
Abe Bloch & Co., 23:191
Abecassis, Judah S., 21:213, 215
Abeel, David, *The Missionary Convention at Jerusalem*, 30:320
Abel, Senior, 45:152
Abela, Sarah, 27:244
Abele, Abraham, 22:125
Abeles, 38:197
Abelow, Samuel P., "An Index to the Jewish Encyclopedia, containing references to articles dealing with the history of the Jews in the United States," 22:xiii; Jewish education, 35:62; Brooklyn Jewry, 35:137
Abenacer, Joseph, 33:77
Abenatar, Benjamin, 29:22
Abenatar, David de Abraham, 29:36
Abenatar, Isaac, 27:244; 44:218
Abenatar, Ishac, 44:229
Abenatar, Jacob, 22:170; 44:218
Abenattar, Ishac, 44:229-30

Abenattar, Jacob, 44:227
Abendana, 26:252
Abendana (family name), 48:139
Abendana, Dauid, 42:279, 393
Abendana, Isaque, 42:280, 392-93
Abendana, Ishag, 42:283
Abendana, Israel, 42:279, 393
Abendana, Jacob, 42:278, 393
Abendana, Moseh, 42:279, 393
Abendana, Moses, 33:65
Abendanon, Haim, 21:43
Abendanon, Joseph (Charleston, S.C.), 50:41; (Philadelphia), 27:462; 34:270
Abendanon, Mordecai, 34:270
Abendanon, Rachel, 27:112
Abendblatt, 41:212
Abercrombie, 35:17
Aberdeen, Earl of, 25:15
Abernaca, Joseph, 33:63, 87
Aberson, 39:202-3
Abert, John James, 39:34
Abi Jetomim ve Dayan Almanot, 44:222
Abidan, 33:146
Abie's Irish Rose, 40:357
Abinatar, Isaac, 44:218
Abinu, Jacob b. Abraham, 27:231-32
Abisdid, Isaac, 26:254
Abi Yetomin of Amsterdam, 29:9-10, 15, 22, 27
Aboab family, 42:108, 214, 389
Aboab, Abraham Dejeosua, 42:278, 393
Aboab Cardozo, 42:214
Aboab, David Semach, 32:12
Aboab, Emanuel, 32:56
Aboab, Isaac (Aboab III), 22:118-20; 27:480; 33:55, 87, 100; 34:8-10
Aboab, Jeosuah, 29:21
Aboab, Moseh, 42:278, 393
Aboab, Moses, 26:251
Aboab, Rachel, 29:14
Aboab, Sarah, 22:179; 29:21
Aboab, Semuel Semah, 29:14
Aboaf, Dauid, 42:278, 393
Aboaff, Abraham, 33:77, 97
Aboaff, Jacob (Brazil), 33:65; (N.Y.), 29:43-45, 50
Aboaffe, Abraham, 33:65
Abodah Zara, 22:104
Abof, Isack, 34:8

"Abolitionist Bible," 50:288
Abolitionists, *see*: Slavery
Abondana, Sarah, 34:270-71
Abot de Rabbi Nathan, 25:179-83; 43:195
Abrabanel, 31:178
Abrabanel, Jona, 47:71
Abraham (family name), 35:6
Abraham (slave), 50:173
Abraham, Abraham, necrology of, 22:xii, 199-200
Abraham Adams Ben Ali, 27:58
Abraham Baruch Bar Simcha, 27:78
Abraham Bar David, 27:78
Abraham Ben Esdra, 21:239
Abraham, Chapman, "Chapman Abraham: An Early Jewish Settler in Detroit," 39:470, 40:81-86
Abraham Erlanger Fund, 34:iv
Abraham Ibn Ezra, 28:142, 191; 34:156
Abraham, Fineas, 27:462
Abraham, Isaac, 27:43
Abraham ben Isaac, 22:xxii
Abraham, Israel, 37:392, 415
Abraham, Br. Joseph, 21:42
Abraham, Joseph, Daniel Webster correspondence, 27:507-8
Abraham, Br. Joseph & Michael, 21:44
Abraham, Br. Juda, 21:40, 44
Abraham, Bar Judah, 31:237
Abraham, Leah, 27:395
Abraham, Leizer, 27:395
Abraham, Lewis, 32:121; 34:191; "Lewis Abraham," 32:117-18
Abraham, son of Ligucius, 28:153, 202
Abraham, Magen, 44:92-93
Abraham, Moses, 38:349
Abraham, Woodeard, 40:76
Abraham & Straus, 22:199, 238; 31:272; 38:20
Abraham de Meza, David de, 29:24
Abraham Lincoln Association, 50:379; gift, 34:xxvii
Abraham Lincoln Bookstore, 50:270
Abraham Touro Fund, 38:60
Abrahams, 21:115; 35:5; Lyon collection, 27:315
Abrahams, Abraham (N.Y), 21:51, 53, 55, 63, 74, 79, 81; 27:40; 33:252, 254; National Archives, 47:190

Abrahams, Abraham I., 27:27-28, 51, 150-56, 253, 417; 28:225; 50:46; N.Y. Kosher meat, 25:47; ritual circumcision, 44:58-63
Abrahams, Abraham de Lyon, 27:156
Abrahams, Barnett, 22:201
Abrahams, Bell, 27:78
Abrahams, Charlotte, 27:110
Abrahams, David, 21:55, 60
Abrahams, Edmund H., 31:6; gift, 33:xxxiii
Abrahams, Ema, 21:79
Abrahams, Emanuel, 27:226; 50:41, 46
Abrahams, Gellah (Adolphus), 23:157
Abrahams, Gitla, 27:111
Abrahams, Hannah, 27:110
Abrahams, Hyam, 27:63, 153, 215
Abrahams, I., 27:78
Abrahams, Isaac (Boston), 23:79; (New York), 21:148, 163, 167, 211-12; 22:161-62; 27:41, 51, 54, 60-62, 86, 150, 243, 253, 315, 389; 50:37, 46; kosher meat, 25:52; *The Powers of Chymistry*, 30:119
Abrahams, Isaac, Sr., 27:83
Abrahams, Israel (England), 25:159; 26:245; 29:xx, 3; 34:171, 173; 37:2; address of, 29:xxii-xxvi; "A Bordeaux Subscription," 23:189; communication, 22:xviii; editor, 33:25; *The Glory of God*, 32:xxvi; *Jewish Studies in Memory of Israel Abrahams*, 32:xxvi; "John Quincy Adams and Joseph Hume," 22:177-78; "Johnson of Columbia and the Hebrew Language," 25:xiv, 109-11; "Joseph Aaron," 25:122-23; necrology of, 31:xxiii, 249-50; "A New History of the Jews," 29:xv; *Permanent Values in Judaism*, 32:xxvi
Abrahams, Israel (N.Y.), 21:45, 48, 55
Abrahams, Jacob, 21:63, 162-63, 170, 214-15; 26:238; 27:74, 83-84, 89, 91, 315, 327; 50:41; honored, 27:395-96; Kosher meat, 25:34, 39-40, 46, 49-53, 55, 58, 62
Abrahams, Joseph, 21:58, 63
Abrahams, Joseph (b. Abraham I.), 27:154
Abrahams, Joseph (father of Abraham de Lyon), 27:156
Abrahams, Joseph B., 35:xix; bookplates, 45:192, 215; gift, 35:xx
Abrahams, Judit, 50:41
Abrahams, Leah, 27:110, 122
Abrahams, Lionel, 26:xii-xiii

Abrahams, M., 21:51
Abrahams, Menahem Israel, 27:156
Abrahams, Meyer, 26:254
Abrahams, Moses (Jamaica), 27:42; (N.Y.), 21:55; 27:41, 83, 86, 87, 152
Abrahams, Perla S., 31:5-7
Abrahams, Ralph, 23:87
Abrahams, Robert, 34:ix
Abrahams, Samuel, 27:51, 55, 83, 242
Abrahams, Samuel, Sr., "Court Decisions on the Sunday Laws," 45:264
Abrahams, Sarah, 22:194
Abrahams, Saul, 21:48-49, 51, 55
Abrahams, Simeon, 21:215; 27:252, 515; 37:43
Abrahams, Solomon, 25:52
Abrahams, Susman, 50:36
Abrahams, Mrs. (Boston), 23:87; Lyons collection, 27:103
Abrahams, widow, 21:71
Abrahams, William, 23:87
Abrahamson, Abraham, 32:xxv
Abram, Isaac, 27:51
Abram (slave), 50:173
Abramowicz, Dina, 50:271
Abramowitz, Chayyim, 33:161
Abrams (Niagara), 35:13
Abrams (Philadelphia), 34:101
Abrams, Abraham J., 50:37
Abrams, Charles, 39:242
Abrams, J. S., 47:38
Abrams, Mani, 27:51
Abrams, Moses, 31:135-37, 139, 142, 151-52, 160, 166, 170
Abrams, Moses L., 44:142, 189-92
Abrams, Susman, 50:27
Abrams, widow, 27:97
Abrather, Joseph, 32:61
Abravalla, Rivas, 35:221
Abravanel, Isaac, 28:204, 211; 33:36; 35:221
Abravanel, Isaac I., 28:188
Abravanel, Jarchi Haleri (Halevi), 21:239
Abravanel, Judah (Leo Hebraeus), 28:204
Abriscus, Carsporos, 27:244
Abschach, G., 38:246-47
Abschach, Marquis d', 43:42
Abuafe, Chacham Isake, 42:293
Abudiente, Abraham, 26:251
Abudiente, Gideon, 35:28

Abudiente, Jehuda, 44:218
Abudiente, Joseph, 44:218
Abudiente, Moses, 35:28
Abudiente, Moses Gideon, 35:28
Abudiente, Simson de Rehuel, 35:37
Abyssinia, 50:11
Academia de los Floridos, 29:11, 22
Academic Freedom Study, 47:228
Academy of Fine Arts (Philadelphia), 50:245
Academy of History, 28:274
Academy for Jewish Research, 38:338
Academy of Medicine (Cincinnati), 23:112;
    (Havana), 43:74; (New York), 26:222
Academy of Music (N.Y.), 40:146-47, 150-51,
    153-54, 156, 162, 172; (Philadelphia),
    22:144
Account of Three Jewish Children, An, 30:88
Ach, Abraham, 29:130
Achduth Veshalom Congregation, Fort
    Wayne, 25:151
Acher, Mr., 38:151
Achocado, Alvaro Rodriguez, 31:30
Achrimon, 33:149
Acker, Stephen, 27:326
Acker, Wolvert, 41:120
Ackerman and Co. (San Francisco), 37:45
Ackerman, John, 35:184
Ackerman, Nathan W., and Marie Jahoda,
    Anti-Semitism and Emotional Disorder,
    reviewed, 40:91-93
Acland, P. L. D., 26:120
Acland, Thomas, 26:120
Acohen, Semuel de Selomoh, 29:17
Acost, Joseph D', 26:247
Acosta, Abraham Mendes de, 29:16
Acosta, Benjamin D', 42:307, 309
Acosta, David de, 32:56
Acosta, Joseph D', 21:176, 179
Acosta, Joseph d', 44:205, 211
Acosta, Manuel de, 32:117
Act of Uniformity of 1662, 31:118
Acton, Edward, 31:232; 35:247-48
Acton, Solomon, 23:28
Acts of Trade, 46:28, 31
Adair, James, 39:186
Adam, Alexander, *Roman Antiquities*, 30:282,
    284
Adam, John, 27:331
Adamic, Louis, 38:14; 39:339; 46:369

Adams, Abigail, 27:186, 192; 46:438
Adams Brothers, 46:128
Adams, Charles Follen, 40:326
Adams, Charles Francis, 35:169; 37:186;
    38:326; 42:137
Adams & Co., 44:23
Adams County Court House, 50:350
Adams, David, 34:267
Adams, Franklin Pierce, 35:262
Adams, Hannah, 39:307; *Dictionary of Religion
    and Religious Denominations*, 30:172; *History
    of the Jews*, 30:147-48; 32:37; German
    edition, 22:xxxi, 26
Adams, Henry, 39:200; 40:330; 46:193
Adams, Henry K., 40:134
Adams, Herbert Baxter, 26:1; 28:34,
    "Columbus in Oriental Literature," 33:32
Adams, Isaac, 29:129
Adams, James Truslow, 39:288; 49:254
Adams, John, 35:xvii; anti-Semitism, 38:109,
    119-21, 123, 129-30, 136-37; Bill of
    Rights, 37:14; Great Seal, 41:62; history,
    writing of, 46:180, 438; "Isaac Gomez Jr.
    Correspondence," 37:xxxi, 444-47; and
    Jews, 34:168; "John Adams: Educator,"
    45:58-60; "John Adams Writes a Letter,"
    37:xxxv, 185-201; letter, 43:237; Luis
    Gomez litigation, 23:81; Mordecai Manuel
    Noah, 46:10; "A proposal to improve the
    lotteries of the United States, patented by
    Jacob I. Cohen and signed by President
    Monroe and Vice-President Adams, March
    3, 1825," 33:xviii; *Selections of a Father for
    the Use of His Children*, 37:444-47
Adams, John Quincy, 45:59; conditions of
    Jews, 22:184; and David L. Yulee, 25:12-
    14; Ghent mission, 27:495; immigration,
    34:184; and Joseph Hume, 22:177-78;
    Mordecai M. Noah, 43:180; Joseph P.
    Nones, 46:13; War of
    1812, 26:185, 200
Adams, Maud, 38:318
Adams, Randolph G., 30:vi
Adams, Samuel, 23:84
Adams, S. J., 50:391
Adams, W., 30:277
Adamsky, Isaac, 50:314
Adamsky, Simon, 50:314

Adas Israel Congregation (Fall River),
37:421; (Louisville), 27:524; 30:445-46
Adas Jeshurun Congregation (Utica), 29:135,
47:198
Adath Israel Congregation (Boston), 32:xv,
xx, 45:271; 47:60; Reform Judaism, 44:250-
51; 45:270-71; *Growth and Achievement of
Temple Israel, 1854-1954*, 49:224-25;
(Madison, Indiana), 37:440; *see also:* Israel
Temple, Boston
Adath Jeshurun Congregation (Augusta,
Georgia), 46:191; (Philadelphia), 29:157
Adath Joseph Congregation (St. Joseph,
Missouri), 25:124
Adath Yeshurun Congregation (Syracuse),
38:66
Addams, Jane, 37:442; 41:308; 46:297
Addath Vesholum (Fort Wayne), 29:130
Addison, James Thayer, 35:257
Addison, Joseph, 34:237-38
Addison Gallery of American Art, 42:417
Addee, Alvey Augustus, 33:229; passports and
Russia, 36:245-46, 251-52; Russo-
American Treaty, 41:172
Adelaide Hebrew Congregation (Australia),
35:xx
Adelman, David C., 46:184-85
Adelphic Society (Philadelphia), 27:229
Adelson, Joseph, 48:68
Adenauer, Konrad, 46:351
Adlam, Captain, 35:19
Adler, A., 29:130
Adler, Abraham, 25:174
Adler, Mrs. Abraham, 25:174
Adler, Ahron, 35:87
Adler, Bernhard, 41:259
Adler, Cyrus, 22:ix; 31:1; 34:299; 37:32, 41,
480, and Aaron Aaronsohn, 31:203;
address, 34:250; address of president,
22:xix-xxiv; 26:xxiii-xxvi; 28:xxv; "Adolphus
S. Solomons and The Red Cross," 33:211-
30; Alliance Israélite Universelle, 39:422;
American Academy of Political and Social
Science, delegate to, 29:xii; American
Jewish Committee, 49:190, 193-94, 199-
200; American Jewish Historical Society,
founding of, 43:153; Am. Jewish Yearbook,
Editor, 42:100; American Jews, 39:66; anti-
Semitism, 38:134; appreciation, 28:xxxv;

and A. S. W. Rosenbach, 42:460; Balkans,
Bucharest Peace Conference, 24:84, 86-93;
"The Beginning of Semitic Studies in
America," 33:21; and Bernard Felsenthal,
45:101; Board of Delegates of American
Israelites, 29:76; bookplates, 45:205, 207;
"Catalogue of a Hebrew Library, being the
collection with a few additions of the late
Joshua I. Cohen of Baltimore," 33:23;
"Catalogue of the Leeser Library," 33:23;
Christopher Columbus, 23:103; Civil War,
50:299; "Columbus in Oriental
Literature," 33:32; "Dr. Cyrus Adler's
Contributions to American Jewish
History," 33:xxv, 17-42; editing, 23:vii;
25:vii; 26:vii; 28:vii, 29:vii, 31:vii; 32:iv;
33:vi; "E. N. Adler Ms. Collection,"
45:155; Felsenthal Collection, 45:96, 99-
100, 105-7; finance committee, 29:xi;
Friendenberg works, 35:120, 130, 132-33;
gifts, 22:xxxi, xxxiv; 23:xvii; 25:xv;
28:xxxviii; 29:xiii; 33:xxxiii; 34:xxv; 35:xix;
government publications, 22:xxxv; Granada
trial, 34:173; "Hebrew Instruction in
Philadelphia, 1793," 35:281; and Herbert
Friedenwald, 37:463-65; historiography,
32:130; history, writing of, 41:217-21;
46:194, 431; Isaac Leeser, 48:208, 232,
235; "Jacob H. Schiff, His Life and
Letters," 32:6, 33:31; Jewish elementary
education, 42:15, 36; Jewish Historical
Society of England, 28:xviii-xix; The
Jewish Publication Society of America,
26:x; "Jews in the Diplomatic
Correspondence of the United States,"
24:41; 33:40; Judeans, address to, 26:xx, 1-
10; "Lectures, papers and addresses,"
34:xxv; Lincoln-Hart letters, 38:139;
Lyons papers, 21:x, xii; 27:xix; Martin Van
Buren papers, 22:71; Mesopotamian
project, 47:154, 158, 160-65; National
Archives, 47:193; Nazi anti-Semitism,
36:365-66; necrologies of Ceasar Cone,
26:xiv, 276-77; Charles J. Cohen, 31:xxix,
255-56; Felix M. Warburg, 35:x, 323-25;
Jacob H. Schiff, 28:xxxii, 301-4; Mendes
Cohen, 25:xii, 145-47; Moses R. Walter,
26:xiv, 288-89; Oscar S. Straus, 31:xxiii,
295-97, 40:10, 12; Perry Frankel, 29:xiv,

160-61; necrology of, 37:xii, 451-54; night school, 31:226; passport issue, 36:282-84; Peace Conference, 1919, 43:231; Polish disabilities, 36:148, 152, 155; president, 22:xi, xvi, xxvii; 23:xii; 24:x; 25:xi; 26:xii, xiii, xxx; 28:xiv, xxi, xxv; presides, 22:xiv, xix; 23:ix; 25:ix, xii; 26:ix-xii, xxii-xxxv; 28:vi-xxxv; 32:xxi; prototypes, 35:255; publications committee, 29:xi; "Random notes," 35:xv; recognized, 26:xvii; 29:xvi-xvii, 2; 30:v, 33:8, 16, 37:5, 37:7; "The Relation of Adolphus S. Solomons to the Red Cross," 28:xv; Rumania, 36:135-36; Russia, intervention, 39:67; Russo-American Treaty, 41:178; Schiff biography, 32:xxv; Sebato Morais works, 37:60, 84-85, 92-93; Spanish-American War reports, 22:xxxi; Sunday services question, 42:378, 381; thirty-first annual meeting, committee on, 29:xxvi; "Told in a Coffee House," 33:22; Torah in America, 44:64; "Twenty Years of the American Jewish Historical Society," 22:ix; "The Voice of America on Kishineff," 33:27; writings of, 43:239; Y. M. H. A., 37:234, 236, 306-7; and Aaron M. Margalith, *American Intercession on Behalf of Jews in the Diplomatic Correspondence of the United States, 1840-1938,* 36:3-402; 37:11; and Albert M. Friedenberg, "References to Jews in the Correspondence of John J. Crittenden," 23:vii, xiii, 117-27
Adler, Mrs. Cyrus, 29:166
Adler, David, 47:36, 38, 42, 46
Adler, Elkan N., 27:523; collection, 31:xviii; death, 37:xii; inquisition, 33:30, 34; membership, 22:xxv; necrologies of H.S.Q. Henriques, 31:xxiii, 261-63; Isidore Spielmann, 31:xiii, 290-91; Samuel A. Hirsch, 31:xvi, 263-65
Adler, Felix, 27:389, 42:104; history, writing of, 46:178, 181, 187, 190, 410-11, 418; Joseph Seligman, 41:32-33; N.Y. chief rabbi, 44:159; N.Y. immigrants, 48:57-58, 90; Red Cross, 33:217, 219-21; Reform Judaism, 44:251; Y. M. H. A., 37:258
Adler, Hannah, 50:174
Adler, Henrietta, 27:120
Adler, Henry, 40:23

Adler, Hermann, 24:24; 47:99; necrology of, 22:xii, 200-203
Adler, Isaac, 27:389
Adler, Isaac L., 40:69
Adler, Isac, 41:259
Adler, Jacob (actor), 39:98; 49:106
Adler, Jacob, 47:42-43, 45; 50:167
Adler, Julius, 41:267
Adler, L. Brothers & Co., 40:71
Adler, Lehmann, 41:256
Adler, Liebman, 34:xviii; 40:23; Felsenthal Collection, 45:96, 98, 100, 126
Adler, Line, 45:83, 89
Adler, Louis, 47:38, 46
Adler, Maurice, 29:129
Adler, Mrs. Morton L., 35:xix
Adler, Nathan (Germany), 31:273, 35:191; Israel Baer Kursheedt, 41:289; *Particulars of Murder of Nathan Adler,* 30:458-60, 464
Adler, Nathan Marcus, 22:201; 37:219; 44:129, 183; tribute to, 37:77
Adler, Newbouer & Co., 47:37
Adler, S. & Bro., 47:36
Adler, Samuel (New York), 22:135
Adler, Samuel (rabbi), 37:32; 40:21, 31; 50:94; bookplate, 45:156; Felsenthal Collection, 45:95-96, 99
Adler, Samuel (2), 41:262
Adler, Samuel (Alabama), 50:155
Adler, Sarah, 47:39
Adler, Solomon, 47:36, 38-39, 42, 46
Adler; Schiff v., 25:135
Adler, Selig, "Backgrounds of American Policy Toward Zion," 46:130; "The Buffalo Project: Writing the History of a Medium-Sized Community," 46:158-60; discussant, 50:427; executive council, 49:268; local history, 49:155, 214, 254-59, 263
Adler, Simon, 41:257
Adler, Simon Louis, bookplate, 45:205
Adler, Stella, 35:244
Adler, surname, 37:378
Adler, Victor, 41:211
Adler, Yankel, 40:320
Admetus and Other Poems, 38:266, 268, 270; 45:249
Adolphus, surname, 37:380
Adolphus, Charity, 21:115; 27:329

Adolphus, Ezekiel, 23:157
Adolphus; Franks *v.*, 22:xxxiv
Adolphus, Isaac, 21:79, 88, 92, 93, 111-15,
   117, 121, 150, 211; 27:328-30;
   naturalization, 37:373, 377, 380, 386;
   38:235; will, 23:157
Adolphus, Jacob, 23:157
Adolphus, M. A., 27:120
Adolphus, N., 27:290
Adolphus, Philip, 23:157
"Adolphus S. Solomons and the Red Cross,"
   50:299
Adorno, T. W., Elsie Frenkel-Brunswik,
   Daniel J. Levinson, and R. Nevitt Sanford,
   The Authoritarian Personality, reviewed,
   41:97-104
Adret, Solomon ben Abraham, 22:61, 63-67,
   69
Adrian, Emperor, 21:241
Adrian VI, 28:168-69; 31:16-17, 19
Adrian, Mich., religious observances, 37:36
A. D. Straus & Co., 31:294
Adult Education Council (Chicago), 50:432
Advisory Committee to Jewish Students of
   Columbia University, 49:62
Advisory Committee of the President's
   Council for Fitness of Youth, 50:434
Aeltesten de Kaufmannschaft, 46:99
Affonseca, Balthazer d', 33:65
Africa, liquor traffic, 28:259
After Dark, 40:348
Aga Khan Diamond Jubilee Medal, 49:271
Agassiz, Louis Jean Rudolphe, 42:341
Aggadath Shir ha Shirim, 25:183
Agner, William, 27:244
Agresti, Madame, 33:xxxi
Agresti, O. R., 34:186
Agricola, 46:434
Agricultural colonies, *see*: Colonization
Agricultural School in Jaffa, 39:393
Agriculture, "Aaron Aaronsohn, Agricultural
   Explorer," 29:xxix, 31:vii, 197-210
Agsteribbe, I., 48:262
Agudat Israel, 49:273, 275
Agudat Ovdal Adama, 35:63
Agudath Ben Jacob, Congregation (Fall
   River), 37:421
Agudath Harabbonim, 39:296
Aguila, Antonio de, 23:133

Aguilar, Abraham, 37:332
Aguilar, Ephraim Lopez Pereira d', 35:234
Aguilar, Grace, 30:367, 425; 34:269; Isaac
   Leeser, 48:239; *Sabbath Thoughts and
   Sacred Communings*, 30:451; *The Spirit of
   Judaism*, 30:363-64, 447; writings of,
   43:239
Aguilar, Isaac d', 33:87
Aguilar, Isabel de, 31:21-22, 24-25
Aguilar, Moses Raphael de, 33:55, 100
Aguilar, Mosseh Rel de, 42:280, 393
Aguilar, Mozes Raphael de, 42:236-37, 280
Aguilar, Rebecca, 37:332
Aguillar Free Library, 25:112; 31:275;
   37:225, 289-90
Aguilar Free Library Fund, 40:164
Aguilar Society, 40:165
Aguillar, Emanuel, 27:185
Aguillar, Ephraim de, 27:18
Aguillar, Joseph d', 27:120
Aguillar, Joseph de Moseh, 27:18
Aguillar, Raphael Moses de, 27:480
Agus, Jacob, 47:62, 153, 49:270
Ahabath Achim Congregation (Altoona, Pa.),
   37:34
Ahad Ha'am, 40:374, 44:124, 49:84, 140-41
Ahasuerus, 40:136
Ahavatachim Congregation (Fall River),
   37:421
Ahavath Chased Congregation (New York),
   29:131, 34:303, 37:230, 251, 253, 309, 315
Ahavath Israel Congregation (Liberty, N.Y.),
   37:xxviii; New York City, 29:131; 34:303;
   Y. M. H. A., 37:230, 251, 253, 309, 315
Ahavat Sholom Congregation (New York),
   44:136
Ahin, Bendich, 28:204
Ahlborn, Fannie, 29:166
Ahlborn, Julius, 29:166
Ahmed Arabi Bey, 27:87-91, 97
Ahmed Riza Bey, 47:172
Ahoti Ruhamah, 22:137
Aird, Mr., 27:376
Aisin, Ger, 39:96
Aismar, V., 38:245
Aitz Raanon Synagogue (Rochester), 40:64,
   69
Aix-la-Chapelle, 27:357; Conference of 1818,
   29:154; "The Congress of Aix-la-
   Chapelle," 26:82-94

Akabah, 26:152
Akely, 25:142
Akhund Mullah Abdullah, 36:11
Akiba, R., 43:195
Akron, Ohio, Jewish Center, 37:319; Jewish
   Welfare Fund, contribution, 37:xxvii;
   religious observances, mid-nineteenth
   century, 37:38
Alabama, "Anglo-Jewish Legal Cases,"
   25:136; Claims, Court of Commissioners
   of, 22:229
Alabama Company, 50:332
Alamannus, Elijah, 28:155
Alascar, Joseph de David, 29:18
Alaska, civil rights, 34:220; Jewish local
   history, 49:217
Alatino, Bonajuto, 28:189
Alatinus, Bonaintus, 28:179
Alatinus, Moses, 28:179-80
Alatri, Samuel, 37:76
Albani, Cardinal, 28:190
Albany, N.Y., Jewish Welfare Fund,
   contribution, 37:xxvii; "The Jews in
   Albany, New York, 1655-1914," 49:229;
   "Recorded Transactions of Asser Levy at
   Albany, N.Y.," 26:246-47; religious
   observances, mid-nineteenth century,
   37:36
Albany Argus, 48:150
Albany Daily Advertiser, 43:190
Albany Gazette, 50:10, 14
Albany Hospital, 28:285
Albany Jewish Home Society, 28:285-86
Albany Jewish Social Service, 35:322
Albany Medical College, 35:321
Albemarle, Duke of, 23:26
Alberga, Alexander, 25:116
Alberga, Benjamin, 25:117
Alberga, Judah, 25:116
Albert, King of Belgium, 28:260, 270
Albert, Mrs. Sigmund, 26:281
Albert Temple (Albuquerque), "Recollections
   of Early Days in New Mexico, and the
   Beginning of Temple Albert of
   Albuquerque," 29:xxx
Albertina (Viennese), 48:253
Alberts, Leon N., 45:135
Alberts, Morris Z., 45:135
Albi, Synod of, 28:144

Albo, Joseph, 44:125
Albornoz, Bernardino de, 31:24
Albrecht, Duke, 28:66
Albright, William Foxwell, The Biblical Period,
   reviewed, 40:193; "Israel—Prophetic
   Vision and Historical Fulfillment," 46:130
Albro, John, 27:175
Albu, Solomon, 29:133
Albukerke, Francisco de tada, 33:113
Albuquerque, N.M., "Recollections of Early
   Days in New Mexico, and the Beginning of
   Temple Albert of Albuquerque," 29:xxx
Albuquerque, Isabel de, 23:134
Alby, Ernest, 27:520
Alcharisi, Judah ben Solomon, 38:276
Alcyphron, 44:159
Alden, Timothy, 25:132
Aldrich, Senator, 22:238
Aldrich, Mrs. 28:58
Aleichem, Sholem, 39:112
Aleinikov, N., 38:307
Alencastrensis, Alphonsus, 28:164
Alentius, 28:166
Alewijn, Abraham, 33:50
Alexander, Mr., 36:44
Alexander (Translator), 31:xviii
Alexander I, Czar, 28:114-15; 41:169; 43:172;
   46:9-10; 50:4; disabilities, 36:196-97, 394;
   "The Influence of Lewis Way and Other
   English Missionaries upon Alexander I's
   Treatment of the Jews," 26:116-25;
   29:154; Jewish rights, 26:38, 69, 82, 84-85;
   "The Upward Struggle of the Cause of
   Secular Education in Russian Jewry in the
   Reigns of Alexander I and Nicholas I,"
   28:xv; 29:182
Alexander II, 36:179, 197, 203, 389-90, 392,
   396-97, 401; 41:170; 43:40, 61
Alexander 2d (pope), 21:241
Alexander III (czar), 39:233; 40:233; 41:150;
   43:48, 51; 47:156-57
Alexander IV (pope), 28:142, 145
Alexander VI (pope), 21:241; 28:161-62, 166,
   183
Alexander, Mrs., 27:112
Alexander, A., 29:130
Alexander, Abraham (Charleston, S.C.),
   50:41, 46; (N.Y.), 21:35
Alexander, battle of, 50:265

Alexander, Benjamin, 23:155
Alexander, Cosmus, 23:14
Alexander, David, 31:262
Alexander, David L., 46:98
Alexander, Henry A., "Abraham Phillips,
   U.S.N.," 32:xx, 125-27; gift, 33:xxxii
Alexander, J. A., 50:336
Alexander, James, "A Great Colonial Case
   and a Great Colonial Lawyer: Solomon de
   Medina et al vs. Rene Het et al," 42:71-82,
   213; "James Alexander and the Jews,
   Especially Isaac Emanuel," 35:171-88
Alexander, Joseph, 27:509
Alexander Kohut Memorial Foundation,
   33:21; 34:304; gifts, 34:xxv; 35:xxii
Alexander, Marx, 43:250
Alexander, L. (San Francisco), 37:45
Alexander, Br. Mordy, 21:55
Alexander, Morris (Moritz), 44:161, 190, 192
Alexander, Nathan, 21:45, 68
Alexander Pasha, 24:121
Alexander, Prince of Bulgaria, 24:74, 79
Alexander Bar Salomon, 27:78
Alexander, Solomon Michael, 38:183
Alexander, William, 44:8; 45:51
Alexander the Great, 29:xxiv; Jerusalem,
   26:165, 168-69; Jewish attitude, 22:35
Alfandery, Aharon, 34:293
Alfonso, King of Spain, 29:89
Alfonso V of Aragon, 28:155, 209
Alfonso X, 22:62
Alfred Whital Stern Collection of
   Lincolniana, 50:396
Algeçiras Act, 36:40
Algeçiras Conference, 24:88; 36:36-40;
   "Moroccan Jewish Rights at the Algeçiras
   Conference," 28:xxxiii
Algemeine Encyclopedie, 40:403
Alger, Horatio, Jr., 28:306; 49:7-8; Joseph
   Seligman, 41:28
Algerine War, 26:185
Algerian War, 27:495
Alice (slave), 50:162
Alide, 38:268, 271; 39:327; 45:249, 256
Alien and Sedition acts, 38:121; 46:303
Alien Immigration Commission, 36:133
Ali Pasha, 24:121
A. Lippman & Company, 28:257
Alkalai, Judah, 49:141

Allaire, Alexander, 23:151
Allen family, 41:90
Allen (editor), 43:19
Allen, Captain, 39:6
Allen, Charles Dexter, 45:134
Allen, Mrs. Clarence M. (Bernadine), 50:271,
   274, 291
Allen, Ebenezer, 27:181, 404
Allen, Frederick Lewis, 46:434
Allen and Hallam, 33:176
Allen, Henry S., 49:186-87
Allen, James (R.I.), 37:393-410; (Richmond,
   Va.), 27:506
Allen, Joseph, 49:270
Allen (Allensky), Julian, 39:152-53
Allen, Lewis, 41:93
Allen, Lewis, Jr., 41:88
Allen, Lewis F., 37:441; 46:165
Allen, Michael M., 41:215; 50:290-91; "The
   Diary of Chaplain Michael M. Allen,
   September 1861," 38:347; 39:177-82
Allen, Stephen, 27:467; 30:404
Allen, Susana, 27:181
Allen, Thomas J., 38:332
Allen, William, 26:117
Allen, William (Pittsfield, Mass.), 38:49
Allen, William H., 39:55
Allenby, Edmund H. H., 29:xxiv; 35:254;
   36:68; 43:144
Allerton v. Allerton, 29:150
Allgemeine Zeitung des Judentums, 41:229-30
Alliance Israélite de Maroc, 36:26
Alliance Club (N.Y.), 39:440
Alliance Committee (New York), 39:442
Alliance Israélite Universelle, 26:240; 32:127;
   40:164, 177; Adolf Guttmacher, 25:151;
Alliance Israélite Universelle, Board of
   Delegates of American Israelites, 29:77-78,
   84-86, 89, 92, 96-97, 99, 102, 110, 114-16;
   "The Alliance Israélite Universelle in the
   United States, 1860-1949," 39:389-443;
   American Israelites, 49:22, 25; Argentina
   colonization, 43:40, 42, 52, 64; "The
   Attitude of American Jews to East
   European Jewish Immigration (1881-
   1893)," 40:221-80; East European Jewry,
   49:78; Baltimore, 37:470; Charles L.
   Hallgarien, 31:190; cultural advances,
   28:128-29, 132; East European

immigration, 41:128, 135-36, 140-44, 149, 154-55, 157; emigration or reconstruction, 42:158-88; Ephraim Lederer, 31:276; gift, 25:xvi; Heinrich Graetz, 28:77-78; immigrants, 49:174; Israël Lévi, 37:475; "Jewish Disabilities in Balkans," 24:2, 7, 10, 22, 24, 44, 47-50, 52, 65, 70, 72-74, 78; Joseph ha Kohen Mss., 22:112, 234; "Memorial of Alliance Israélite Universelle of Paris to the Congress of Berlin," 24:105-7; Montefiore Fund, 37:98; night school, 31:226; Oscar B. Teller, 28:310; Paris Conference 1876, 24:29, 35-36, 39; Morocco, 36:40; Persia, 36:18; Roumanian problem, 24:111; 36:113, 116; 45:67, 73, 78; Russian immigrants, 48:42, 85, 96, 117; Russian passport issue, 46:93-94, 98; Sabato Morais, 37:72, 74; Simon Wolf, 47:82; Zionism, 49:188

Alliance Review, The, 39:442

Allied Welfare Appeal, 42:198; (Easton, Pa.), 42:197-98, 202-3

Allievi, Senator, 28:51

Allingham, John Till, *Transformation; or, Love and Law*, 33:174, 194

Allison, A. K., 50:336

Allman, Herbert D., "A unique institution; the history of the National Farm School," 34:xxv

Allon, Gedaliah, 42:317

Almaden Mine, 23:124-25

Almagro, 31:4

Almanzi, Joseph, 37:79; 45:140

Alma-Tadema, Sir Lawrence, 28:27; 35:250

Almeida, Jorge de, 31:28; 37:453

Almeida, Semuel de Castro, 44:229

Almeyda, Abraham, 32:61

Almeyda, David, 32:61

Almeyda, Hana Abigail, 37:338

Almeyda, Jacob, 21:45; 27:244

Almeyda, Jorge de, 33:41

Almosino, Hasday, 21:186; 27:50

Almosnino, Moseh, 29:26

Almund, Rosetta, 33:203

Almy, William E., 27:454

Alonso, Ana, 31:25

Alonso, Hernando, "Hernando Alonso, a Jewish Conquistador with Cortes in Mexico," 31:xxix, 2-4, 8-31

Alonzo (slave), 50:189

Alpena, Mich., religious observances, 37:38

Alper, Michael, 40:54

Alpert, Abraham, 46:77

Alpert, Carl, 40:322, "Two American Naval Expeditions to Palestine, 1848 and 1854," 39:470; 40:281-87

Alsberg, P. A., 50:271

Alsop, John, 27:327

Alsop, Joseph, 27:329

Alstead, Johann Heinrich, 35:150

Altamirano, Licentiate, 31:20

Altaras, Jacques Isaac, 42:159

Altena, 32:10

Altenmuhr, "A Note on Altenmuhr Jews," 49:53-55

Alter, Isaac Meir ben Israel, 35:263

Altfeld, E. M., 35:135; *Jews of Maryland*, 31:xxxiii

Altheimer, Alan J., 50:432

Altheimer, Ben, 29:169

Altmann, Adolf, 22:xviii

Altman (dept. store), 38:20

Altmeier, Löw, 41:256

Altneu Synagogue (Prague), 50:103

Altoona, Pa., religious observances, 37:38

Aluares, David, 42:286

Aluares, Joseph S., 42:280, 393

Alueres, David Baruh, 37:334

Alueres, Rachel, 37:337

Alumni Association of the Hebrew Union College, 25:152

Alumni Bulletin of the University of Virginia, 28:47-48

Alvarado, 27:507

Alvarenga, Isaac de Costa, 28:249

Alvarenga, Isaac Haim Nines, 37:83

Alvarenga, Joseph Abigail Da Costa, 37:337

Alvarenga, Joseph Da Costa, 37:337

Alvarenga, Samuel De Costa, 28:249

Alvares, Abraham, 37:331

Alvares, Abraham Baruh, 37:336

Alvares, Baruh, 37:337

Alvares, Baruh Judith, 32:61

Alvares, David (Brazil), 42:253, 280, 393-93; (Jamaica), 32:61

Alvares, Esther Baruh, 37:331, 340

Alvares, Jacob, 29:38

Alvares, Jacob, Jr., 27:359

Alvares, Judith B., 32:63
Alvares, Mordecai, 37:392
Alvares, Moses, 23:85
Alvares, Mosses Baruch, 42:280, 393
Alvarez, David, 23:28
Alvarez, Francisco, 31:30
Alvarez, Jorge, 31:29
Alvarez, Juan, 22:156
Alvarez, Manuel, 31:29, 31
Alvarez, Maria Harby, 32:46
Alvarez, Moses, 27:198
Alvarez, Mosseh Mendez, 21:11, 20, 23, 25
Alvarez, Pelayo, 31:31
Alvaringa, Joseph da Costa, 23:28
Alveranga, Abraham D. C., 37:342
Amalgamated Clothing Workers of America,
    44:242; 46:241; 49:83
Amalgamated Men's Clothing Workers,
    Jewish Unionism, 41:323, 327, 332, 344
Amar, Isaac, 36:25
Amateur Musical Society, 29:160
Ambler, 28:246
Ambrosius, Moses, 34:175, 44:92-93
Amburgo, Moseh Namiaz de, 42:278, 293,
    395
America First Bulletin, 45:235
America-Israel Society, 47:226
America Judaica, 39:227
Americana, 50:270; *An American Jewish
    Bibliography*, 44:252-54
Americana Catalogue, 50:287
American Academy of Arts and Sciences,
    35:314
American Academy for Jewish Research,
    34:304; 43:250; proceedings of, 33:30-31
American Academy of Ophthalmology and
    Oto-Laryngology, 31:256-57
American Academy of Political and Social
    Sciences, 28:307; 29:xii; Jacob Harry
    Hollander, 37:473
American Advertiser, 21:172
American Aid Societies, 49:181
American Almanack, 35:284
American Anthropological Association,
    46:301
American Antiquarian Society, 25:84;
    centenary, 22:xiv; Cotton Mather, 26:206;
    gifts, 23:xviii; phylactery, 38:49; scripture
    calendar, 32:30

American Anti-Slavery Society, 42:151, 155
American Association for the Advancement of
    Science, 49:165
American Association of the History of
    Medicine, 45:197
American Association for Jewish Education,
    39:263; 40:95, 412; 42:29; 46:152, 168
American Association of the Red Cross,
    Adolphus S. Solomons, 33:213-14, 223-24
American Association for State and Local
    History, 40:413; 46:444-45; 49:155
American Bank of Vincennes, 48:258
American Bar Association, 49:56
American Baron de Hirsch Fund, 28:130
American Bible Society, 35:305
American Biographical Sketch Book, 30:430
American Brotherhood of Israel, Fall River,
    37:421
American Captive; or Siege of Tripoli, 33:174,
    192; 40:347
American Chemical Society, 22:225
American Cities Company, 28:309
American Civil Liberties Union, 45:237
American and Commercial Advertiser, The,
    23:142
American Commission to Negotiate Peace,
    28:259-60
American Committee for Ameliorating the
    Condition of the Russian Refugees
    (Boston), 46:74-77, 80
American Committee for the Protection of
    the Foreign-Born, 45:228
American Commonwealth, 43:160
American Company, 33:173, 175-79, 183
American Council for Judaism, 40:94, 394;
    42:454; 46:281; 48:244, 254
American Economic Association, 28:308;
    37:473
American Economic Committee for
    Palestine, 37:477
American Electro-Chemical Society, 22:225
American Exchange-Irving Trust Company,
    31:272
American Federation of Labor, 42:322; 43:33;
    49:107; history, writing of, 46:223-26, 232,
    258, 291, 299, 302; Jewish unionism,
    41:300, 318-19, 329, 332-36
American and Foreign Anti-Slavery Society,
    42:153

American Federation of Jews from Central Europe, 46:59
American Federation for Polish Jews, 45:232
American Fellowship Committee of the Israel Medical Association (Philadelphia), 45:197
American Foreign Service, 40:110
American Friends of the Hebrew University, 42:460; 49:12
American Hebrew, 32:124; 33:36, 129, 240-41; 50:384; Abram Samuel Isaacs, 31:265; A. M. Friedenberg, 35:116; American Judaism, 42:101; anti-Semitism, 42:348-50; Charles H. Jonas Parole, 42:408; collection, 22:xxxiv; Daniel Peixotto Hays, 29:169; Emma Lazarus, 37:22, 24-28; 39:321; 45:251; 48:276; Evian Conference, 45:229; Felsenthal Collection, 45:103, 122; G. Washington correspondence, 25:113; gift, 33:xxx; Henry Pereira Mendes, 35:318; historiography, 26:30; immigration, 49:185; Jewish labor, 41:210; Jewish question, N.Y., 49:108, 119; Joseph Jacobs, 25:161; Judaism, 28:9; Minnie D. Louis, 29:179; Moses Montefiore, 25:112; N.Y. chief rabbi, 44:143, 150, 160, 169-70, 173; Nissim Behar, 39:425-26; Reform Judaism, 40:385, 393-94; Russian immigrants, 48:122; Sabato Morais, 37:57; Shearith Israel History, 45:66; Solomon Solis-Cohen, 38:338; Spanish-American War, 41:358, 360, 371; Sunday services question, 42:382; Y. M. H. A., 37:239, 256, 261, 289
American Hebrew Association, Y. M. H. A., 37:225, 230-31, 243, 246, 249-59, 261-62, 271, 273, 276, 319
American Hebrew College, 45:95
American Hebrew Publishing Company, 40:331
American Historical Association, 26:xvii-xviii; 39:289, 351; 43:140; 46:466; 48:69; 49:155; Alonzo Howard Clark, 28:266; American Jewish history problems, 39:214, 225; Jewish local historical writing evaluated, 49:213-64; meetings with, 22:xiv, xxv; 23:x; 44:245; 45:128; Vice-Admiralty Court, 37:391
American Historical Review, The, 28:xii, xxix; 47:224; 50:378

American Historical Society, 31:249; Jake Gimbel, 48:259
American Information Service, 46:351
American Israelite, 42:101; Alliance Israélite Universelle, 39:427; British Declaration, 39:453; Daniel Peixotto Hays, 29:169; Des Moines Jewry, 47:208; Easton (Pa.) Jewry, 42:195; Isaac Mayer Wise, 40:20, 24; Lewis Abraham, 32:117; N.Y. chief rabbi, 44:132, 143, 145, 152, 159; Prague Jewry, 50:118; Reform Judaism, 40:368-69, 386-88; Rochester, N.Y. Jewry, 44:237; Russo-American Treaty, 41:182; Sabato Morais, 37:57-58; Spanish-American War, 41:358, 360; Y. M. H. A., 37:250, 254, 265
American Israelites, America and Near East, 36:5, 20, 24, 26, 100; Board of, 37:95-101
American Jew as Patriot, Soldier and Citizen, The, 50:303-4, 307, 315, 406
American Jew in the Civil War, The, Catalogue of the Exhibit of the Civil War Centennial Jewish Historical Commission, 50:277
American Jewish Advocate, 30:387, 389
American Jewish Agricultural Association, 27:160
American Jewish Archives, 39:177, 222; 49:152, 154; Americana, 44:253; Barrak Hays, 45:55; bibliography, 50:69; Civil War, 49:137; 50:263, 267, 270, 272, 274, 287, 306, 315, 362, 384-86, 404, 406; Connecticut Jewry, 38:332; history, writing of, 46:168, 421; Jacob Rader Marcus, 40:53; 50:157, 426; Jewish local history, 49:216, 244, 254, 256, 258, 261; Longfellow and Jews, 45:26; Sephardic records, 44:117-18; southern Jewry, 50:157, 290
American Jewish Cases, "Anglo-Jewish Legal Cases," 25:134-38
American Jewish Chronicle, 49:197
American Jewish Committee, 24:x; 39:110; Alliance Israélite Universelle, 39:439; American Jewish history problems, 39:220, 250; anti-Semitism, 40:91, 101-4, 199; Benjamin Nathan Cardozo, 49:12; bookplate, 45:152, 172, 204; Bucharest Peace Conference, 24:84-93; Bureau of Jewish Statistics, 25:161; 26:xxvii; Ceasar

Cone, 26:276; civil rights, 47:16, 45:152, 172; communal activity, 44:214; communications, 42:463-66; "The Congress versus the Committee: A Crisis in American Judaism, 1903-1922," 45:262; Cyrus Adler, 33:19; 37:452; delegate to, 29:xii; discrimination, 47:194; "The Early Attitude of the American Jewish Committee to Zionism (1906-1922)," 49:188-201; East European Jewry, 49:86; Ephraim Lederer, 31:276; federated Jewry, 48:144; Felix M. Warburg, 35:324; gifts, 33:xxxiii; 34:xxv; 35:xxiii; Herbert Friedenwald, 37:464-66; immigration, 34:216-17; history, writing of, 46:187, 280, 374, 402; Isaac Leeser, 48:228, 236; Jacob Moritz Loeb, 45:211; "Jewish Rights at the Congresses of Vienna (1814-1815), and Aix-la-Chapelle (1818)," 26:vii, xv, 33-125; "The Jews in the Wars of the United States," 26:xxiv, xxv; Julian W. Mack, 37:476; "Louis Marshall," 33:xxx; MacIver Report, 42:320-25, 327-28; Maurice Stern, 28:309; Max James Kohler, 34:298; Mayer Sulzberger, 28:xii; 29:189; 45:204; Morris Loeb, 22:226; Moses R. Walter, 26:289; Oscar S. Straus, 31:296; 40:13; Palestine relief, 36:64; passport issue, 36:364-67; Poland, 36:152; prejudice, 41:97-104; refugees, 45:221-22, 226, 228, 231-33; Rufus Learsi, 44:123; Rumania, 36:134-35; Russo-American Treaty (1832), 36:278, 281-82, 285, 290; 41:178-79; Simon Wolf, 29:204; Sol M. Stroock, 37:479; S. W. Rosendale, 35:322; U.S. diplomatic intercession, 37:11

American Jewish Communal History Series, 44:246; 49:216

American Jewish Communities (1854-1865), map of, 50:277, 353

American Jewish Conference, 45:246

American Jewish Congress, 39:111-12; American Jewish history problems, 39:245; communal activity, 44:214; "The Congress versus the Committee: A Crisis in American Judaism, 1903-1922," 45:262; East European Jewry, 49:86; Edward B. Glick, 48:136; gift, 33:xxx; history, writing of, 46:326; Julian W. Mack, 37:476;

MacIver Report, 42:320-25, 328; Martin A. Meyer, 29:181; passport issue, 36:373-75; Reform Judaism, 40:369; refugees, 45:221, 224, 231-33; Rufus Learsi, 44:123; Women's Division, 39:334; Zionism, 49:191-92, 198

American Jewish Historical Records, 44:246

American Jewish Historical Society, 26:3, 47:200; acquisitions, 22:xxxi-xxxv; American Historical Association, sessions with, 44:245; American Jewish Communal History Series, 44:246; American Jewish historical records, 44:246; "American Jewish Historical Society: Retrospect and Prospects," 41:217-224; anniversary recognized, 26:xii; annual meetings, twentieth, 22:ix-xiii; twenty-first, 22:xiv-xviii; twenty-second, 22:xix-xxx; twenty-third, 23:ix-xviii; twenty-fourth, 25:ix-xvi; twenty-fifth, 26:ix-xii; twenty-sixth, 26:xxiii-xxxv; twenty-seventh, 28:vi-xvi; twenty-eighth, 28:xvii-xxiii; twenty-ninth, 28:xxv-xxxv; thirtieth, 29:xi-xvii; thirty-first, 29:xix-xxxi; thirty-second, 29:xxxiii-xxxvii; thirty-third, 31:xiii-xviii; thirty-fourth, 31:xix-xxv; thirty-fifth, 31:xxvii-xxx; thirty-sixth, 32:ix-xiv; thirty-seventh, 32:xv-xx; thirty-eighth, 33:xi-xviii; thirty-ninth, 33:xix-xxvi; fortieth, 34:ix-xv; forty-first, 35:ix-xvi; forty-second, 37:xxix-xxxi; forty-third, 37:xxxi-xxxiii; forty-fourth, 37:xxxiv-xxxvi; forty-fifth, 38:341-43; forty-sixth, 38:343-45; forty-seventh, 38:345-47; forty-eighth, 39:469-71; forty-ninth, 40:405-7; fiftieth, 41:385-90; fifty-first, 42:413-19; fifty-second, 43:230-38; fifty-third, 44:240-47; fifty-fourth, 45:260-65; fifty-fifth, 46:492-93; fifty-sixth, 47:200-203; fifty-seventh, 48:265-66; fifty-eighth, 49:265-71; fifty-ninth, 50:425-27; B'nai B'rith, 44:244-45; bookplates, 45:164-66; Civil War, 50:263, 267, 269-70, 274, 282-83, 285-86, 291-92, 299-300; 307-10, 314, 345-46, 351, 354, 361, 377, 399; Conference of Historians, 44:245, 247; constitution and by-laws, 25:xii, 219-27; 28:xxii; 45:263-64; dedication of rooms, 32:xxi-xxiii; *Dictionary of American Jewish Biography*, 44:247; executive council

by-laws, 41:389; 42:414; exhibits, 44:244; history essay award, 44:245; Historical Essay Contest, 38:v-vi, 77-78; Historical Information office, 44:244-45; historical records, 38:vii, 99; honorary president, 38:343; Jewish History Week, 44:244; library, 44:244; New England chapter, 44:243; officers, terms of, 41:389; "The Reception by the Judaeans," 26:ix, xv, xvii-xxii; reports of officers, see: annual meetings, ante; research fellowship, 44:246; "A Survey of the *Publications of the American Jewish Historical Society*, and a Plan Suggested for future research," 28:xxxiii; "Thoughts on the Philosophy of American Jewish History," 28:232-36; travelling exhibition, 38:4

American Jewish History, "American Jewish History: Problems and Methods," 39:207-66; "American Jewish History as Reflected in General American History," 39:283-90; "Communal and Social Aspects of American Jewish History," 39:267-82; "Emerging Culture Patterns in American Jewish Life—The Psycho-Cultural Approach to the Study of Jewish Life in America," 39:351-88; "The Jewish Community of Milwaukee, Wisconsin, 1860-1870," 49:242; "Know Thyself—A Program for American Jewish History," 39:337-50; "On the Writing of American Jewish History," 39:303-12; "The Popularization of American Jewish History," 39:313-17; "Religious and Cultural Phases of American Jewish History," 39:291-301; "Resources on American Jewish History at the Library of Congress," 47:179-85, 201; "Resources on American Jewish History in the National Archives," 47:186-95, 201; symposium, 38:346-47; 46:133-446; "The Writing of American Jewish History," 46:493

American Jewish History Center, 46:192; 49:137, 154, 216, 242, 263

American Jewish Joint Distribution Committee, Persia, 36:18; Polish activities, 36:141-47, 162

American Jewish Publication Society, 49:17, 24; Sol Weil, 38:72; Y. M. H. A., 37:229

American Jewish Relief, 31:220

American Jewish Relief Committee, 28:276, 284, 287; 29:198

American Jewish Tercentenary, Abba Eban, address by, 45:6-8; Adlai E. Stevenson, address by, 45:16-19; Dwight D. Eisenhower, address by, 44:67-74; Herbert H. Lehman, "The Search for Ideals, a Program of Action, and Leadership," 45:12-15; Jacob Blaustein, "The Unfolding Future," 45:9-11; Nathan M. Pusey, "America and Jerusalem," 45:1-5; "An Old Faith in the New World: Highlights of Three Hundred Years," 44:210-14, 240; Robert F. Wagner, address by, 44:78-79; "Some of the Tercentenary's Historic Lessons," 44:199-209, 240; Thomas E. Dewey, address by, 44:75-77

American Jewish Tercentenary Committee, 44:244

American Jewish Year Book, 26:9; 33:22; 34:xix; 37:452, 465, 483; 39:230; 42:100; 45:228-29

American Jewry and the Civil War, 50:270, 277, 291-94, 345-46, 348, 350-52

American Jews Annual, 32:118

American Journal of Semitic Languages, 47:219

American Judaica, 50:69; and Hebraica, 50:270

American Labor Party, 41:329

American Labor Union, 48:40

American Law Institute, 49:12

American Law Review, 47:212

American Law School Review, 47:212

American Magazine, 43:34

American Magazine and Monthly Chronicle for the British Colonies, 30:43

American Malting Company, 28:257

American Medical and Philosophical Register, 46:12

American Medical Association, 31:257; 45:189

American Medicine, 38:337

American Mercury, 39:51

American Missionary Association, 50:178

American Mission Schools, 40:5

American Museum of Natural History, 35:325, 46:298

American National Red Cross Relief Committee, 33:216, 221, 222, 224

American Oriental Society, 25:152; 33:19, 32; 40:51

American Party, 49:131

American Philosophical Society, Abraham Simon Wolf Rosenbach, 42:459; Cyrus Adler, 33:22; Henry M. Phillips, 22:144; I. Minis Hays, 23:185-86; James Alexander, 35:172

American Portraits, 48:250

American Protective Association, 40:71, 46:278, 294, 303

American Red Cross, 36:67; 43:253; 50:299; "Adolphus S. Solomons and the Red Cross," 33:211-30; 41:205

American Red Cross Society, 26:xxv

American Relief Administration, 29:185; Poland, 36:148, 153, 155

American Revolution, 22:xxxii, 163-64; 23:184, 189; 26:3, 7, 178-79, 181, 185-86, 189, 190-91, 267; 28:294, 300; 31:45; 39:344-45; 40:85-86, 218-19, 409; 41:123-24, 280, 286-87, 292, 294; 42:337, 349, 429, 438-39, 459; 43:1, 71, 131-32, 135, 162, 199-200, 205, 235; 46:149-50, 180, 190, 269, 381, 424, 435-36, 438; 50:327, 334; "Abraham Simons, A Georgia Patriot of the Revolutionary War," 31:xvii; "Abraham Solomon: A Revolutionary Soldier," 40:76-80; "Barrak Hays: Controversial Loyalist," 43: 231; 45:54-57; "Calendar of the Correspondence of George Washington, Commander in Chief of the Continental Army, with the Continental Congress," 25:113; "Calendar of the Correspondence of George Washington, Commander in Chief of the Continental Army, with the Officers," 25:113; "Captain Abraham Simons of the Georgia Line in the Revolution," 33:231-36; "David Salisbury Franks, a Distinguished Patriot and Officer of the Revolutionary War," 26:xiv; documents, 31:xxxv; "Gleanings of Jewish Interest in American Colonial and Revolutionary History," 25:xiii; "Isaac Moses and his services in the American Revolution," 31:xxiv; "A Jewish Voice for Peace in the War of American Independence, the Life and Writings of Abraham Wagg, 1719-

1803," 31:xiv, 33-75; "Jews Interested in Privateering in America During the Eighteenth Century," 23:vii, 10-11, 163-76; "The Jews of America during the Struggle for Independence," 31:xvii; Jews in, 27:331-32, 345, 388, 494, 496-97; 50:51, 56-58; "The Jews in the Revolutionary War," 31:xxiv; "The Jews in the Wars of the United States," 26:xxiv, xxv, xxvii; "Letter of Jonas Phillips, July 28, 1776, Mentioning the American Revolution and the Declaration of Independence," 25:xiii, 128-31; loyalists, 23:97-100, 166-67; loyalist Jews, 23:97, 99; 40:85; "The Revolutionary Soldiers Buried in the Spruce Street Cemetery, Philadelphia, Pa.," 44:242; Sheftall papers, 37:8; "Simon Nathan's Important Services to the American Cause in the Revolution," 31:xvi; "Some Jewish Loyalists in the American War of Independence," 31:xxiv; 38:81-107; "Some New York Jewish Patriots," 26:237-39; "Some Notes on the Participation of Jews in the American Revolution, 1775-83," 31:xxx; "Some Revolutionary Letters," 25:142-43; "Three Early Letters, 1769-1782," 28:252-54; "Two Letters of Solomon Bush, a Revolutionary Soldier," 23:xiii, 177-78; *see also*: Non-importation Resolutions

American Roumanian Society, 24:11, 24; 29:95; Joseph Seligman, 41:33, 37

American, Samson, 27:389

American Scenic and Historic Preservation Society, 31:77; 38:52

American School of Oriental Research, 33:22; Felix W. Warburg, 36:324; Jerusalem, 40:52

American Social Science Association, 36:398

American Society of Biblical Literature, 43:250

American Society for Meliorating the Conditions of the Jews, 43:177-78; 45:189; Constitution, Etc., 30:188, 205, 207-8, 244, 386, 431-32; "Joseph S. C. F. Frye and the American Society for Meliorating the Condition of the Jews," 28:xxxiii

American Society of Civil Engineers, 26:146

American Society for Jewish Farm Settlement in Russia, 35:324

American Spirit, The, 40:13
American Star, 39:279
American Statistical Association, 37:473
American Steam-Ship Company of
  Philadelphia, 45:83, 89
American Stomach Hospital, Philadelphia,
  29:157
American Surgical Society, 22:220
American Trader's Compendium, 40:126-27
American Unitarian Association, 22:18
American Weekly Magazine, 38:46
American Weekly Mercury, 30:29; 32:113
American Zionist Medical Unit to Palestine,
  36:69-70, 72-73
Americana, Rosenbach collection, 32:xxi
Americanisher Volkskalender, 33:129
Americanization and Americanism, 39:338-
  50, 353ff; 40:367ff; 42:203, 205, 207-10,
  339; 43:35, 147; 44:4, 122, 128, 154, 184;
  45:217-18, 240-41, 243; 46:163, 219-20,
  268-88, 297, 357, 366-403, 405-45;
  48:109, 142-45; 49:88, 120-22, 125-26,
  162-63, 234, 237, 248, 259; history,
  writing of, 46:163, 219-20, 297, 357, 466-
  503
Americo, 22:109-11, 115-16
Ames, Winthrop, 35:257
Amézquita y Soria, Francisco de, 23:135
Am-Haarez, 29:191-92
Amherst, Jeffery, 22:41, 46; 50:124; "Jewish
  Colonial Enterprise in the Light of the
  Amherst Papers (1758-1763)," 35:xv, 1-25
Amity, 48:172
Am Olam, 35:63; 39:237; 43:145; 48:80, 89,
  131
Amory, R. G., 40:120
Amram, David Werner, 28:211; "The Jewish
  Law of Divorce," 33:xxix, xxxii-xxxiii
Amromin, Jerome David, "Jerome David
  Amromin Music and Art Collection,"
  45:214
Amsel, Henry, 41:370
Amsoll, Gutrath, 41:253
Amter, Israel, 50:252
Amtorg Corporation, 45:141
Amuneth Anethem Congregation (Fort
  Wayne), 37:39
Amy, Joshua, 35:291
Amy, Joshua, Jr., 35:291
Amzalak, Moses Bensabat, 33:37

Anarchists, 46:309; 49:81-82, 85
Anche Chesed Congregation, La Crosse,
  Wisconsin, 38:333
Ancker, G. V.; A. Ottolengui *v*., 30:390
Ancona, Jacob d', 29:29
Ancona, Sydenham E., 29:123
Anderson, Alexander, 45:133
Anderson, Doctor, 21:109
Anderson Galleries, 50:403
Anderson, Hurst R., 47:203
Anderson, James Albert, 34:215
Anderson, John, 48:180
Anderson, Marian, 48:10
Anderson, Martin B., 50:81, 95-96
Anderson, Maxwell, 40:357-58
Anderson, Robert, 50:317-18
Anderson, Thomas, 37:442
Andover Academy, 47:15
Andover College, "College Bookplates With
  Hebrew Inscriptions," 45:131-33
Andover-Harvard Theological Library,
  45:134
Andover Theological Seminary, 45:24;
  bookplate, 45:131, 134
Andrada, Abraham da Costa, 29:36
Andrada, Francisca Beringel da, 33:79
Andrada, Isabel de, 31:27
Andrada, Leonor de, 31:27-28
Andrada, Salvador, 34:175
Andrade, 25:112
Andrade, Abraham (France), 41:12
Andrade, Abraham (Curaçao), 44:228-29
Andrade, Abraham da Costa (Curaçao),
  44:227-28
Andrade, Abraham da Costa (Jamaica), 29:36
Andrade, Abraham de David Costa, 44:231
Andrade, Angela da Costa de, 32:56
Andrade, Benjamin Costa, 44:228
Andrade, David, 29:36
Andrade, David Costa, 44:230
Andrade, David DaCosta, 32:56
Andrade, Ishac Hisquiao de, 44:229
Andrade, Jacob Costas, 44:229
Andrade, Jacob de Abraham, 44:231
Andrade, Jacob de Mordechay Israel de,
  44:231
Andrade, Jeudit, 29:36
Andrade, Joseph, 27:79, 243
Andrade, Joseph Da Costa de, 32:56

Andrade, Mordechay, 44:228
Andrade, Salvador d', 21:176-77, 178-79;
   27:379
Andrade, Simon de, 23:134
Andrado, Steven Correa d', 33:118
Andrassy, Gyula, 24:44, 50-51, 64, 66, 120-21
Andre, John, 29:xiii; 46:423
Andrew Freedman Home, 31:271
Andrew, John Albion, 38:174; 42:136
Andrew, Mary, 50:163
Andrews, B., 40:79-80
Andrews, Charles M., 23:92-93, 95-96
Andrews, Edward G., 33:221
Andrews, H. M., 27:120
Andrews, Joseph, 21:162-63; 27:83, 86;
   kosher meat, 25:51-52, 55
Andrews, Judge, 29:149
Andrews, Robert, 28:226
Andrews, Sarah, 27:112
Andrews, Mrs., 21:88
Andros, Edmund, 27:379; 31:93
Andrzejowski, Julius W., 39:162
Angel, 27:91
"Angel Band, The," 33:212
Angel, Myer, 50:164
Angell, James B., 40:7
Angelo, son of Leucius, 28:156
Angers, Pierre Jean David d', 39:10, 42
Angerson, John, 27:244
Angle, Myer, 27:78
Angle, Paul M., 50:271
Anglican Church, 47:176
Anglo-American Committee of Inquiry into
   Palestine, 46:184
Anglo-American Treaty of 1924, 39:332
Anglo-Jewish, "Bibliotheca Anglo-Judaica,"
   25:159
Anglo-Jewish Association, 24:22, 29, 34, 39,
   45-46, 93; 43:64; "Memorandum on the
   Treaty Rights of the Jews of Roumania,"
   24:137-53
Anglo-Jewish Association, American
   Israelites, 29:78, 86, 98-99; Clarence I. De
   Sola, 28:271; East European Jewish
   immigration, 41:131, 154; education,
   39:433; emigration, 42:176; H.S.Q.
   Henriques, 31:262; Kishiney Jews, 34:281;
   Mesopotamian project, 47:170; Morocco,
   36:26; Russian passport issue, 46:94, 97-98

Anglo-Jewish Historical Exhibition (1887),
   22:203; 25:159; 31:290
Anglo-Jewish History, "An Unfamiliar Aspect
   of Anglo-Jewish History," 25:vii, 63-74
Anglo-Jewish Legal Cases, 25:134-38
Anglo-Jewish Press in America, 38:310
Anglo-Jewish West Asian Company, 26:163
Angoff, Charles, 46:62-63
Angola, 46:485; 47:174
Angriff, Der, 36:274
Anho, Francisco Ferinando, 33:115
Ani, 39:101
Anickster, Lesser, 40:69
Anjos, Francisco dos, 43:129
Annals of the Jewish Nation, 30:277
Anne, Queen of England, 22:128; 27:295-96;
   28:231; 30:43
Annulment, 29:151-52
Annunzio, Gabriele, d', "To Moie Ezekiel,"
   28:28-29
Anrouge, Amador d', 33:115
Anschel, Abraham, 41:262
Ansell, A., 23:141
Ansell, Moses, 43:27
Anshe Chesed Congregation, New York,
   27:504; 49:19; "The Americanization of
   the German Jew in New York City prior to
   the Civil War," 37:xxxi; Confirmation
   Exercise, 23:180; formed, 41:228; gift,
   32:xxviii; Hebrew Union College, 40:31;
   Young Men's Association, 37:253, 255-57
Anshe Chesed School, "Source Material on
   the Anshe Chesed School of New York,
   1835-1860," 37:xxxi
Anshe Emet Congregation, Chicago, 45:213
Anshe Emeth Congregation, Albany, 35:321
Ansche Maariv Congregation, Chicago,
   41:250, 46:388, 411
Ansonia and Seymour, Conn., United Jewish
   Welfare Fund, contribution, 37:xxvii
Antelo, 22:145
Anthology of American Poetry, 50:401
Anthon Battalion, 22:xii; 27:160
Anthon, Henry, 26:220
Anthony, Beriah, 35:142
Anthony, L., 29:12
Anthony Street Theater, New York, 33:196
Anti-alienism, 39:106; 42:133-40
Anti-American, 38:1-2

Anti-Defamation, 39:216
Anti-Defamation League, 29:187; 33:189;
38:2; 47:16; Chicago, gift, 35:xxiii; Easton,
Penn., 42:202; MacIver Report, 42:320-25,
328; mis-description of Jews, 34:187
Anti-Semitism, 29:xxiii-xxiv; 33:11-13; 37:8-
10; 38:1, 11; 39:280; 40:199-201; 41:22;
42:110-11; 46:175-76, 183-84, 189, 197-
98, 247, 277, 371-73, 380, 388, 392, 441;
48:200; 50:406-7; and abolition, 42:133,
141-44, 152-53; Alliance Israélite
Universelle, 39:416-17; "American Anti-
Semitism in the Late Nineteenth Century:
A Re-interpretation," 45:262; *The
American Jew: A Zionist Analysis*, reviewed,
47:61-62; American Jewish Committee,
40:91, 101-4, 199; American Jewish history
problems, 39:210, 215-16, 228, 234, 236,
242-45, 260; "American Jewry, The
Refugees and Immigration Restriction
(1932-1942)," 45:219-47; "American
Views of the Jew at the Opening of the
Twentieth Century," 40:323-44; Anatole
Leroy-Beaulieu, 22:223-24; Anti-
Defamation League, 29:187; 33:189; 38:2,
42:202; 47:16; *Anti-Semitism and Emotional
Disorder*, reviewed, 40:91-93; *Anti-
Semitism in Modern France: Vol. I, The
Prologue to the Dreyfus Affair*, reviewed,
41:95-96; "Anti-Semitism and Reaction,
1795-1800," 38:109-37, 343; art world,
28:9; Austria, 50:118; Austria and U.S.
envoy, 36:323-47; *The Authoritarian
Personality*, reviewed, 41:97-104; Benjamin
Nones, 38:109, 132-34, 137; "A Bordeaux
Subscription," 23:189; Brazil, 33:68-76;
brokers, 28:256; Canada, 39:104; Canadian
Jewish Congress, 50:139-41; Catholic
Church, 26:26-27, 31; cemetery vandalism,
42:427-28; Charles L. Hallgarten, 31:190;
Civil War, 49:138, 162; Colorado, 49:218;
Cyrus Adler, 36:365-366; 38:134;
"Disgraceful Acts of a Mob at a Jewish
Funeral in New York, 1743," 31:240-41;
Dorothy Canfield Fisher, 48:247-50, 252;
*Dynamics of Prejudice: A Psychological and
Sociological Study of Veterans*, reviewed,
40:101-4; "An Early English Intervention
on Behalf of Foreign Jewry," 35:xvi, 213-

17; Easton, Pa., 42:204; "Emigration to
America or Reconstruction in Europe,"
42:157-88; England, 25:157-58; ethnic
politics, 50:203, 210, 215, 248; "The
European Aspect of the American-Russian
Passport Question," 46:86-100; European
emigration, 42:209-10; "The Exodus from
Brazil and Arrival at New Amsterdam of
the Jewish Pilgrim Fathers, 1654," 44:80-
97, 255; France, 39:323; George
Washington, 38:120, 133; Georgia,
31:223; Germany, 23:105-8; 37:19; 40:300-
301; 45:221; Germany and U.S.
intercession, 36:348-85; Henry Cohen,
42:452; Hilton-Seligman affair, 41:33-34;
"Historical Outline of Anti-Semitism in
the United States," 32:xiii; Holland and
David Nassy, 22:25-38; "Hon. Oscar S.
Straus' Memoranda Preceding Dispatch of
the Hay Roumanian Note," 24:108-14;
"The Influence of the Russo-American
Treaty of 1832 on the Rights of American
Jewish Citizens," 41:163-94; Isachar
Zacharie, 43:91; Israel Leeser, 48:224-25,
243; Italy, 36:386-88; Jewish cases, 29:151;
"Jewish Disabilities in the Balkan States:
American Contributions Toward Their
Removal, with Particular Reference to the
Congress of Berlin," 24:1-153; 25:xiv;
Jewish local history, 49:230, 248-49;
"Jewish Physicians in Italy: Their Relation
to the Papal and Italian States," 28:xxiii,
133-211; *Jews in the Soviet Union*, reviewed,
42:442-49; Journal of Commerce, 38:309;
*Judith Bensaddi and the Reverend Doctor
Henry Ruffner*, 39:115-42; MacIver report,
42:320-22, 325, 327, 329; Martin
Phillipson, 26:284; Masonry, 43:141; Max
James Kohler, 34:165, 186, 189, 220-33,
250; "Memorandum on the Treaty Rights
of the Jews in Roumania," 24:137-53;
Misdescription of Jews, 34:187; Morocco,
36:19-41; New England, 46:75, 128; New
York Jews, 49:93, 100-103, 114, 127-28,
133; *Niles Weekly Register*, 50:4-6, 14;
nineteenth century, 23:105-8; "Noah's
Ararat Jewish State in Its Historical
Setting," 43:170-91; Oliver Wendell
Holmes, 42:349, 353, 355-57; Palestine,

36:42-95; "Paul Haupt and the Mesopotamian Project, 1892-1914," 47:154-75; Persia, 36:11-18; "Petition of the Roumanian Jews to the Chamber of Deputies, 1872," 24:98-101; phases, 39:300-301; Poland, 39:164; Poland and U.S. intercession, 36:140-67, 389-402; Portugal, 22:112-14, 117-19, 126, 131-32, 155-56, 158, 180-82; Prague, 59:98, 103, 112-15; "Proceedings Relating to the Expulsion of Ezekiel Hart from the House Assembly of Lower Canada," 23:xiv, 43-53; "Reaction of Reform Judaism in America to Political Zionism," 40:361-94; "A Refutation of Anti-Semitism Among American Atheists, 1864: An Episode in the Life of Ernestine L. Rose," 49:268; "Religious and Racial Prejudice in America: An Historical and Psychological analysis with Special Reference to the Jews," 29:xxxvi; "The Revolution of 1848 and the Jewish 'On to America' Movement," 38:185-234, 345; Rochester, N.Y., 40:71; Rufus Learsi, 44:123-24; Rumania, 38:53-56; "Rumania and America, 1873; Leon Horowitz' Rumanian Tour and Its Background," 45:67-92; Rumania and United States intercession, 36:99-139; Russia, 23:98; 42:177; 50:6, anti-Semitic May laws of 1882, 49:162; Isidor Rayner, 40:288-310; *The Russian Jews in America*, 48:28-62, 78:133; U.S. intercession, 36:171-295, 389-402; *In Search of Freedom: A History of American Jews from Czechoslovakia*, reviewed, 39:329-31; "Secretary Hay's Roumanian Note of 1902 and the Peace Conference of Bucharest of 1913," 24:80-97; "A Side Light on Restrictive Covenants," 41:381-84; "Social Discrimination Against Jews in America, 1830-1930," 47:1-33; "Some American Anti-Semitic Publications of the Late 19th Century," 37:xxxv, 421-25; "Something Additional on General Grant's Order Number 11," 40:184-86; southern states, 50:165, 197, 199; Spain, 22:132; 23:130; *Strangers in the Land: Patterns of American Nativism, 1860-1925*, reviewed, 45:217; "Swedenborgian Background of

Thomas Lake Harris' Anti-Semitism," 41:439; Switzerland, 36:299-322; Turkey, 36:3-10; U. S. Grant, 47:80; "Unequal Religious Rights in Maryland Since 1776," 25:vii, 93-107; United States, 33:xxx; 39:359, U.S. constitutional rights, 43:159-69; U.S. diplomatic intercession, 36:xii-xiii; and in Austria, 36:323-47; Germany, 36:348-85; Italy, 36:386-88; Morocco, 36:19-41; Palestine, 36:42-95; Persia, 36:11-18; Poland, 36:140-67, 389-402; Rumania, 36:99-139; Russia, 36:171-295, 389-402; Switzerland, 36:299-322; Turkey, 36:3-10; "Unpublished Canadian State Papers Relating to Benjamin Hart," 23:vii, 137-40
Antieurs, Manuel, 33:119
Antin, Mary, 46:62; "The Promised Land," 22:206; "They Who Knock at Our Gates," 23:xviii
Antiochus IV, 26:165
Antiochus VII, 26:165; "When Did Jerusalem Surrender to Antiochus Sidetes?," 26:xiv, 165-71
Antiquarus, Jacobus, 28:196
Antiques, 45:53
Anti-Tenement Law, 48:52
Antokolski, Mark (1), 28:2
Antokolski, Mark (2), 36:239-40, 398
Anton, Charles E., 45:143
Anton, Karl, 24:74-75, 36:116
Antonia, 26:168
Antonius, Marcus, 38:264
Antony, Allard, 29:44-45
Antunes, David Dias, 32:16
Antunes, Hester, 26:251, 254
Antunes, Joseph, 27:244
Antwerp Aid Society, 41:142
Antwerp Committee, 41:157
Anverson, W., 23:139
Anzeiger, 41:249
Appel, Jacob, 26:183
Appel, John J., 40:205, "Henry Wadsworth Longfellow's Presentation of The Spanish Jews," 45:20-34; " 'A Smile' Said to Have Been Written by Henry Wadsworth Longfellow for *The Israelite:* A Correction," 40:182-83
Appert, Francois, 46:11

Applegate, Joseph, 27:244
Appleton, John, 36:302
Appleton, Nathaniel, Hebrew at Harvard, 22:3, 11, 21; 35:167-68
Appleton's New American Cyclopedia, 48:90
Arabs, and Palestine, 40:313-17; "United States Policies on Palestine," 40:107-18
Aragon, Isabel de, 23:133
Ararat, *see*: Grand Island
Ararij, Solomon, 28:239
Arbeiter Ring, 50:205, 209, 222, 225, 252
Arbeiter Zeitung, 48:131-33
Arbib family, 37:76
Arbib-Costa, Alfonso, 34:248
Archard, député, 41:161
Archer, J. H. L., 37:340-41
Architecture, "The American Synagogue of Today: Its Art and Architecture," 44:242; "The Egyptian Revival In Synagogue Architecture," 41:61-75; "The Sources of the Architectural Historian," 45:265; 46:114-19; *Synagogue Architecture in the United States: History and Interpretation*, reviewed, 46:64-66
Archives Israelites, 26:240
Ardole I, 28:188
Arène, Emmanuel, 41:161
Arent, Albert E., 47:203
Arez Hadashah, 22:137
Argentina, argricultural colony, 38:241; 42:178-82; Baron de Hirsch, 47:158, 160-61, 165; "David Feinberg's Historical Survey of the Colonization of the Russian Jews in Argentina," 43:37-69; immigration, 38:307, 309-10, 313-16; Joseph Fels, 46:483; Russian Jewish press, 39:87-97, 99, 103, 106-7, 113
Argentine project, 36:226
Argosy Gallery, 41:277
Argus, and Greenleaf's Daily Advertiser, 38:117, 127
Arias, Diego Rodriguez, 32:117
Arieli, Jehoshua, 50:271
Arion Society, 40:167
Arizona, Jewish local history, 49:217; Masonry, 22:182
Arje, Abraham, 28:168-69
Arkansas, 48:83; Jewish local history, 49:217; Masonry, 25:114

Arktus, 39:103
Arlington National Cemetery, 28:54, 59-60
Armed Forces Institute of Pathology, Walter Reed Army Medical Center, Washington, D.C., 50:272
Armenia Lodge, No. 97 (I.O.O.F.), 47:46
Armenian Apostolic Church, 46:414
Arminius, 31:175, 177
Armring family, 22:34
Armstrong, Colonel, 26:231
Armstrong, General, 26:179
Armstrong, Joseph Layton, 41:92
Armstrong, Leander A., 50:231
Army and Navy Club of Washington, 28:292
Arnold, Abraham B., 41:249
Arnold, Adolf Löb, 41:267
Arnold, Benedict, 25:113; 27:482; 46:38; David Salisbury Franks, 38:82, 96; *Proclamation*, 30:80-81
Arnold, Bernhard, 41:259
Arnold, Corinne B., necrology of, 32:xvi
Arnold family, 41:88-90
Arnold, Isaac N., 22:100
Arnold, Josef Aron, 41:253
Arnold, Lazarus, 21:215
Arnold, Mayer, 41:93
Arnold of Villanova, 28:146, 207
Arnoldi, G., 23:139
Arnstein, A., 40:242
Arnstein and Eskeles, 26:51
Arnstein family, Vienna, 26:37, 51-52, 66-67, 100
Arnstein, Nathan, 28:103
Arobas, Miriam, 32:56
Aron, Henry, 27:63
Aron, Solomon, 50:41
Arons, David, 43:238
Aronson, Harris, 27:515
Aronson, Wolf, 50:42, 46
Arredendo, Fernando de la Mazo and Son, 25:132
Arrias, Ribca, 25:139
Arrobas, Abigail, 32:56
Arrobas, Lunah, 32:56
Art, "American Jewish Bookplates," 45:129-216; "The American Synagogue of Today: Its Art and Architecture," 44:242; "Art and Artists of Our Time," 26:280; "Chinese Influence in Seventeenth Century Jewish

Silver," 44:8-11; Civil War, 50:381-88; "The Form and Decoration Of Silver *Rimonim*," 45:48-53; *Jewish Artists of the 19th and 20th Centuries*, reviewed, 40:317-21; Jews in art, 32:xxvii; "Moses Jacob Ezekiel," 28:xxii, 1-62; "The Ritual Silver Made by Myer Myers," 43:1-9; silverware, 45:270; Society for the Dissemination of Knowledge of Jewish Art, 31:190

"Artaxerxes," 23:179

Arthur, Chester A., 26:xxv; Red Cross, 33:212-13, 223-24; Russian passports, 36:233; Russo-American Treaty, 41:171

Art Institute of Chicago, 31:251

Artom, Benjamin, 42:440

Artom, Isaac, 37:76

Artom, M., 29:127

Artz, 34:77

Artz, Max, "The Teacher in Talmud and Midrash," 43:194

Aruch Completum, 45:103

Asa, Abraham, 35:305

As a Man Thinks, 40:354-55

As a Mighty Stream, reviewed, 40:201-4

Asavado, Moses Cohen De, 21:123

Asbury, Henry, 44:99-100, 103, 105

Asch, Abraham J., 35:64

Asch, Joseph M., 27:505

Asch, Louis, 29:113

Asch, Morris Joseph, 50:327-28

Asch, Myer, "Colonel Myer Asch and the Centennial Exposition at Philadelphia, 1876," 26:xv

Asch, Shalom, 35:275; 39:103; 43:36; 45:139-40; "The Shalom Asch Collection of Judaica," 45:139, 168; writings of, 43:239

Aschalta di-Geula, 49:273

Ascher, H., 29:131

Ascher, Jacob C., 45:26

Ascoli, David de, 28:174

Ascoli, Graziadio I., 37:76

Ascoli, Raphael E. H., 37:73, 78

Ash, Abraham Joseph, 44:130-31, 133-35, 139, 162

Ash, Mark, 37:257

Ashburton Treaty, 25:14-15

Ashby, Jane, 42:149

Ashe, Isaac, 26:152-53

Ashenheim, Lewis (ed.), *First Fruits of the West*, 30:383; (ed.) *Jewish Monthly Magazine*, 30:383; *On Precipitate Burial Amongst the Jews*, 30:398

Ashenheim, Neville, 37:329

Asher, "The Ashers of Toronto," 26:xv

Asher, Asher, 37:96; 41:141

Asher, Caleb, 30:402

Asher, David, 27:91

Asher from Frankfurt, 27:79

Asher b. Jehiel, 22:61; 25:180

Asher, Michael, 21:23, 29, 34-35, 39-40, 43-44; 23:82; 29:153; 42:336

Asher, Mosche, 26:265

Asher, Rachel, 34:60-64

Asher, Rebecca, 23:150; 34:61

Asher, Rycha, 33:200; 41:286, 290

Ashers, Rebeca, 21:11, 19; 27:122

Asherson, 31:199-200

Ashey, Jacob, 26:183

Ashhurst, John, 30:vi

Ashi, R., 22:67

Ashinsky, Aaron Mordecai, 42:13

Ashley, William, 22:180

Asia and Asiatics, history, writing of, 46:290-92, 297, 303-4, 318-20, 323, 330

Asilva, Moses de, 33:68

Ashkenasi, Aaron Selig, 47:196

Ashkenazi, Bezallel, "The Library of R. Bezallel Ashkenazi traced from his Responsa and his Novellae," 25:178

Ashkenazic Synagogue (Kingston), 37:342

Askin, John, 23:34; 40:85

Askowith, Dora, 28:136; 34:248; "The Earliest Jewish Settlers of Cape Cod," 42:415

Asmonean, The, 26:271; 30:440, 442; 43:144; 48:220; Sabato Morais, 37:57

Asmoneans, 26:170

Asper, Joel F., 42:412

Aspinwall, 23:79

Assaf, Simhah, 43:241

Asseas, Zewi, 39:99

Assenheim, Lewis, 26:271

Asser, Carl, 26:73-74

Asser, M., 29:127

Assevedo, Abraham d', 33:91-93, 102, 109

Assias, Abraham, 27:58

Assisi, Saint Francis, 47:143

Associate, The, 37:285
Associated Charities (El Paso), 35:326
Associated Hebrew Charities, 40:227; 46:393
Associated Jewish Charities (Baltimore), 29:176, 178; 45:198; Chicago, 28:241
Associated Jewish Philanthropies of Boston, 49:149; *Pioneers in Service: The History of the Associated Jewish Philanthropies of Boston*, reviewed, 47:59-60
Associated War Relief Societies, 50:138
Associated Talmud Torahs (Chicago), 42:34; (Philadelphia), 42:35-36
Associated Y. M. H. A.'s of New England, 37:306
Associated Y. W. H. A.'s of New England, 37:284, 306
Association of the Bar, New York, 26:288
Association of American Hebrew Congregations, East European Jewry, 49:87; N.Y. chief rabbi, 44:136, 142-49, 155-56, 161-62, 171, 181, 184-87, 189-98
Association of the American Orthodox Hebrew Congregations, New York chief rabbi, 44:136-49, 155-58, 162-67, 170-74, 177-78, 185-87, 189-98; 49:231
Association Bulletin, 37:237, 246, 255, 257-59; 38:338
Association for Childhood Education, 45:214
Association for Jewish Colonization in the Soviet Union, 38:242
Association of Jewish Immigrants (Philadelphia), 40:237, 239-41, 244; 48:236
Association of Polish Exiles in America, 39:150
Association for Promoting Jewish Settlements in Palestine, 26:147-49
Association of Reform Rabbis (New York), 40:51
Association of Research Libraries, 45:148
Association Review, 37:237-38, 251, 255, 257, 259, 285
Association for State and Local History, 49:155
Assyriology, 39:446, 450, 464-65, 467
Astor, John Jacob, 21:xvi; 27:491
Astor Library, 43:11; 45:203
Astoria, N.Y., Center of Israel, 37:322
Astruc, Elie-Aristide, 24:29-30; 41:161; 42:176

Astruc, R., 29:84
Astruco di Napoli, 28:178
Asylum for Indigent Boys, 27:418
Atchison, Topeka and Santa Fe Railroad, 41:43, 45
Athenaeum, The, 25:162
Atherton, Lewis E., 46:210
Atherton, Percy A., 22:229
Athias (family name), 48:139
Athias, David-Israel, 29:13, 25
Athias, Joseph, 27:279
Athyas, Isaac, 42:391-93
Atias, Dauid, 42:278, 391-93
Atias, David, 42:259, 278, 283-84, 288-92, 391-92; 44:83
Atias, Ishac, 42:225, 258-60, 275, 277, 283-85, 289-90, 292
Atias, Joseph, 42:278, 393
Atkinson, Edward, 43:33
Atlanta Hebrew Orphan Asylum, 29:202, 205; 34:xxii
Atlantic and Danville Railroad, 26:275
Atlantic Monthly, 38:268; 40:413; 43:23; 45:28; 49:105-6
Atlas, Samuel, 40:49
Atlas to Accompany the Official Records of the Union and Confederate Armies, 50:382-83
Atomic Energy Commission, 40:212-13
Atta Troll—A Midsummernight's Dream, 45:252
Attente, Jacob, 32:56
Atwater, John B., 28:267
Aub, Jacob, 29:133; 39:178
Auburn; Johnson *v.*, 29:150
Auckland, Lord, 35:36
Audit Office, London, 23:97
Auerbach, Berthold, 28:100; 29:128; 33:xxxi; 43:58
Auerbach (Utah), 38:333
Auerbach, Ella, Fleishman, "Jewish Settlement in Nebraska," 31:xxx
Auerbach, Helen Hays, 29:169
Aufrecht, L., 40:27, 36
Augsburg Confession, 28:218
Augsburger, Isak, 41:257
Augur, Christopher Columbus, 43:99
August, Thomas P., 27:506
Augusta, Ga., religious observances, 37:36
Augustine, Saint, 47:143

Augustus, 26:168; 28:135; 41:62
Aunt Nanny, 50:168
Aurora, 38:122, 134-35
Auschwitz, 46:441
Austern, Thomas, 47:203
Austin (Kansas), 23:70
Austin, Henry, 41:71
Austin, R. N., 47:38
Austin, San Felipe de, 46:101
Austis, John, 40:216-17
Australia, 47:171, 174; history, writing of, 46:289, 320-21, 323-24; Jewish migration, 41:156, 244, 267; Jews in South Australia, 1836-1936, 35:xx
Australian Jewish Historical Society, 45:261
Austria, 45:227, "An Austro-Hungarian Movement to Encourage the Migration of Jews to America, 1848," 23:187-89; anti-Semitism, 50:118; Balkan disabilities, 24:120-21, 125-26, 142, 144; 26:5, 89, 124; "The Congress of Aix-la-Chapelle," 26:82-94; "Congress of Berlin, 1878," 24:40-41, 44, 46, 50-51, 56, 64, 108; Congress of Vienna, 26:34; "Educational Reforms in Europe in Their Relation to Jewish Emancipation—1778-1919," 28:83-132; expulsion from, 35:213; historiography, 26:27; history, writing of, 46:308, 312, 320, 324, 351, 441; Jewish disabilities in Balkans, 24:19-20, 22, 102, 110, 134; "Jewish Rights at the Congresses of Vienna (1814-1815), and Aix-la-Chapelle (1818)," 26:vii, xv, 33-125; Revolution of 1848, 38:186-87, 190-91, 197; Russian passports, 46:87, 93; U.S. diplomatic intercession, 36:ix, 323-47
Austriacus, 39:107
Austria-Hungary, 38:186, 190-91; East European Jewish migration, 41:139, 141, 178; history, writing of, 46:228, 290, 308
Ausubel, Herman, 39:214
Ausubel, Nathan, 47:181
Auswanderer, 38:192
Authoritarianism, *The Authoritative Personality*, reviewed, 41:97-104
Authors Club, London, 28:261
Autographs, acquisition of, 22:xxxi
L'Autorite, 46:88
Avala, Franzesco, 33:39

Avembenist, Azzachus (Isaac Bendeniste), 28:143
Averroes, 28:201
Avery Institute, 50:178
Avicenna, 28:172
Avignon, 28:191; Synod of, 28:143
Avila, Herman Lopez de, 31:14
Avila, Jehosuah Ys: de, 42:280, 393
Avinoam, Reuben, 50:401
Avukah's Torchbearer, 33:129
Ayala, Francisco Gutierrez Serrano de, 23:133
Aylion, Selomoh de Jacob, 29:25
Ayrolt, Peter, 34:274
Ayrton, Hertha, 35:246
Ayrton, Professor, 35:246
Ayyelet Ahabim, 22:118, 120
Azéno, Michel, 41:152
Azeuedo, Abraham de, 42:281-83, 286-88, 391, 393
Azeuedo, Mosseh de, 42:279, 393
Azevede Cristanos Novos, 31:xxxiii
Azevedo, d' (family name), 48:139
Azevedo, Abraham de (Brazil), 42:225, 260, 275, 277, 281-88, 391, 393; 44:83; 46:47
Azevedo, Abraham de (Hague), 32:20
Azevedo, Benjamin Cohen d', 26:251
Azevedo, Deborah d', 26:256
Azevedo, Emanuel, d', 26:251
Azevedo, Esther d', 50:148
Azevedo, Isaac d', 26:251
Azevedo, Isaac Cohen d', 27:349
Azevedo, Menesah Cohen D', 26:254
Azevedo, Moses Cohen d' (London), 26:252, 256; 27:47; 50:148; "The Sermon Preached in London, 1776, by Rabbi Moses Cohen D'Azevedo on the American Revolution," 31:xxx
Azevedo, Moses Cohen d' (Newport), 27:349
Azevedo, Rachel d', 50:160
Azevedo, Rachel Cohen d', 27:349
Azevedo, Mr. (Virgin Islands), 44:115
Aziel, Nadel, 49:54
Azuby, Abraham, 42:55; 50:41, 46
Azuby, Abraham de Ely, 29:32
Azuby, Daniel, 26:251
Azulaj, Chaim Joseph David, 34:16, 293-94
Azuly, Abraham, 42:237, 241, 256, 258, 279, 390, 393

B

Baa, Enid, 50:148, "The Preservation of the Sephardic Records of the Island of St. Thomas, Virgin Islands," 44:114-19
Baars, 32:14
Babb, James T., 47:124
Babel, Isaac, 46:441
Babin, Moshe, and David C. Kogen, "A Catalogue of the Mayer Sulzberger Papers in the Dropsie College for Hebrew and Cognate Learning," 38:342
Babmut riots, 36:274
Baby, Mr. (Canada), 31:186
Baby, Francois, 23:49-50
Bacharach, Menahem, 31:55
Bacharach, Phaibush Uri, 31:34
Bacharach, R. Elkanan, 31:55
Bache, Benjamin F., 38:121, 135
Bache, Jules S., 46:243
Bache, Richard, 28:226
Bacheler, Origen, *Restoration and Conversion of the Jews*, 30:369
Bacher, Wilhelm, 29:194; 45:101; necrology of, 22:xxviii, 203-6
Bachman, Jacob, 26:183
Bachman, Samuel, 26:183
Bachrach, David, 31:220
Back, Jacques, 37:307
Backer, Jochim Wesselsen, 26:247
Bacon (State Dept.), 36:275
Bacon, John, 30:200
Bacon, Louisa Crowninshield, 42:338
Bacon, Nathaniel, 46:34
Bacon, Roger, 31:264
Bacon, William, 40:77
Baconian Literary Association, 31:188
Bacot, Thomas, 48:181, 185-86, 191
Bad Axe, "The Palestine Colony in Michigan," 29:61-74
Badeau, J., 23:139

Badi, Joseph, *Religion in Israel Today: The Relationship Between State and Religions*, reviewed, 49:272-76
Baeck, Leo, 40:53; 43:195
Baedo, Guido, 28:192
Baehr, George, 42:127-28
Baena, Alfonso de, 45:22, 26
Baer, Fritz, 31:234-35; 47:136; corresponding member, 37:xii; Jews in Christian Spain, 32:xxvii
Baer, Jacob, 26:187
Baer, Judith, 41:259
Baer, Louis, necrology of, 34:ix
Baerman, Wolf, 29:62
Baerwald, Hermann, 41:144-45
Baesa, Joseph, 29:38
Baeza, Cathalina Rodriguez, 29:38
Baeza, David Moses Cardozo, 26:254; 32:11; 34:275
Baeza, Edmund I., 34:276
Baeza, Isaac, 26:254
Baeza, Joshua, 34:276
Bagaijo, Pinhas Mordech, 34:293
Bagdad, Caliphs of, 21:239
Bagdad Railway, 47:165-66, 168, 175
Bagehot, Walter, 41:317-18
Bagehot, William, 46:231
Bagg, Moses M., 47:198
Bahaim, Aaron Moses, 27:91
Bahauya, Rabbanoo, 28:243
Bahia, map, 31:xxxi
Bahlul, Daniel, 38:72
Bail, M., 26:87
Bailby, Léon, 46:90
Bailen, Mr. and Mrs. Samuel L., 45:164
Bailey, 34:101
Bailey, Benjamin, 23:76, 82
Bailey, Gamaliel, 50:173
Bailey, Nathan, 47:203

Bailey, Walter G., 36:156, 159
Bailey, William, 26:176
Bailey-Myers, Theodorus, 26:177
Bainbridge, William, 46:13-14
Bairack, Michael, 44:144
Baiz, Jacob, 49:186
Baiz, Sarah Miriam, 27:111
Baker, Adolph, 29:129
Baker, D. E., 35:230
Baker, Elizabeth, 40:59
Baker, George P., 35:257-58
Baker, Greenebaum, 31:149, 152
Baker and Kilby, 35:22
Baker, M., 35:136
Baker, Newton D., 26:282; 29:159
Baker, Samuel, 41:66
Baker, Turner-Baker papers, 47:189
Baker; Wood v., 29:150
Bakhmetieff, George, 41:182, 187
Balaban, 29:xliii
Balaban, Barney, 38:1; gift, 37:13
Balaban, Z., 48:194
Balatshano, 36:116
Balborda, Samuel d'Isaac Mendes, 29:38
Balch, Emily, 46:128-29
Baldwin, Faith, 35:271-72
Balfour, Arthur J., 28:270; 36:73, 78, 82, 145; 39:204
Balfour Declaration, 36:78, 84, 89, 94; 39:204-5, 332-33, 440, 453; 40:113, 362, 366, 390, 392-94; 46:277; 49:84, 194, 197; 50:139; American Zionism, 45:36, 41-45, 213
Balkan States, 46:290, "Bismarck and Beaconsfield in Their Relations to the Jews," 26:258-59; Board of Delegates of American Israelites, 29:76; Brussels Conference 1872, 24:25-29; Congress of Berlin, 36:112; disabilities, 26:7; "Jewish Disabilities in the Balkan States: American Contributions Toward Their Removal, with Particular Reference to the Congress of Berlin," 24:ix, 1-153; 25:xiv; Joseph Seligman, 41:37-38; London conference, 36:134-36; migration, 44:201, 203, 238; Prague Jews, 50:99
Balkan Wars, 24:83-94
Ballantyne and Constable, 22:58
Ballenger, Mr., 37:42

Ballin, Simon M., 32:119
Ballinger-Pinchot controversy, 47:187
Ballou, Hosea, *Opinions and Phraseology of the Jews*, 30:381
Balmes, Abraham de, 28:202
Balmes, Abram di Mayr de, 28:161, 204
Balmes, Astruc de, 28:160, 204
Balsara, H. F., 34:200
Balson, Dr., 28:210
Balta, *Am Olam* Group, 38:246; riots, 36:208-10
Baltimore, Board of Trade, 25:153; Civil War, 50:278, 301; Colonial congregations, 28:xxvi; "An Estimate of Baltimore's Jewish Population," 29:xxix; "Four Early Jewish Cemeteries at Baltimore," 32:xiii; German Reformed Church, 22:192; history, writing of, 46:189-90, 193, 273, 278, 283; "Jewish Education in Baltimore from its Beginnings until the 1880's," 44:242; Municipal Art Commission, 25:147; Municipal Research Committee, 25:154; necrology of Mendes Cohen, 25:xii, 145-47; New Charter Commission, 25:154; *Niles' Weekly Register*, 50:3-5, 18; "Notes on Early Jewish Settlers of Baltimore," 22:191-95; Peabody Institute, 25:147; religious observances, 37:35; "The Russian Night School of Baltimore," 31:vii, xvii, 225-28; "The Sephardic Congregation of Baltimore," 23:vii, xiv, 141-46; Special Relief Committee, 25:154
Baltimore American, The, 23:143-44
Baltimore Conference, 40:365
Baltimore Education Authority, 49:162
Baltimore Hebrew College and Teachers' Training School, 49:265-71
Baltimore Hebrew Congregation, 22:194; 23:141; 25:99, 151; constitution and by-laws, 30:341; "The Refusal of a Charter to the Baltimore Hebrew Congregation by the Legislature of Maryland," 32:xiii
Baltimore Hebrew Sunday School Association, 23:144-45
Baltimore Jewish Charities, 29:176
Baltimore Jewish College, 31:281
Baltimore, Lord, 25:100
Baltimore Museum of Art, 31:282; 45:198
Baltimore News, 37:473

Baltimore & Ohio Railroad, 25:145-46; 28:301; 31:xxxiv; 41:46; 46:189-90; Masonry, 34:68

Baltimore Orphan Asylum, 29:202

Baltzell, E. Digby, 48:66

Balzac, Honore de, 35:239-40

Bamberg (Utah), 38:333

Bamberger, Abraham, 41:259

Bamberger, Bernard J., 46:62; necrology of Samuel of Schulman, 45:265-67

Bamberger, Caroline, necrology of, 37:xii, 455-57

Bamberger and Company, L., 37:455-56

Bamberger (Dept. Store), 38:20

Bamberger, Elkan, 37:445

Bamberger, Isaac, 40:222

Bamberger, J., 42:172

Bamberger, Jacob F., 40:263; 49:186

Bamberger, L., 29:111, 113

Bamberger, Leopold, 24:27; 45:77, 80-81

Bamberger, Louis, executive council, 31:xxix; 32:xix; 34:xiv; 37:xxxii; gifts, 31:xxxiii; 32:xxviii; 41:287; "Louis Bamberger," 34:xxvi; necrology of, 37:xii, 455-57

Bamberger, Louis, b. Abraham Bamberger, 41:259

Bamberger, Ludwig, 24:16; 28:80; 36:239, 397; 41:234

Bamberger, Matilda, 31:293

Bamberger, Max and Sarah, Seashore Home at Atlantic City, 28:288

Bamberger, S., 22:xxxv

Bamberger, Seligmann Baer, 23:108

Bancker, Christopher, 31:95-96, 99

Banco de Credito Real de Pernambuco, 43:129

Bancroft, Aaron, *Discourse Before Worcester Auxiliary Society*, 30:222

Bancroft, Frederic, 50:171

Bancroft, George, 36:109; 42:457; 46:466; David Yulee, 25:16, 19; Jewish disabilities, 24:21; 36:348, 350-51; Uriah Phillips Levy, 39:14, 24, 34, 51

Bancroft, Hubert Howe, 38:326

Band, Benjamin, *Portland Jewry, Its Growth and Development*, 49:223

Bandann, Grace, 37:470

Bang, Herman J., 35:256

Bangor, Maine, 46:187-89

Bangs, Edward, 40:187

Bangs, Isaac, 40:187

Bank, A. M., 29:163; 45:151

Bank of America, 48:260

Bank of England, 31:35, "Was the Bank of England Protected by a Jew?," 25:111

Bank of New York, 34:xxv

Bank of New York and Trust Company, 38:49

Bank of North America, 27:470

Bank of the United States, N.Y., 46:175

Banker family, 41:110

Banker, Adrian, 27:244

Banking, 46:175, 235, 345, 395, 443; *The Republican Bank*, 30:337, 339; sixteenth century, 22:xxix

Banks, Nathaniel P., 43:72, 81, 83-89, 92, 94-107, 109, 112-15, 119-21, 124; 50:377; Isachar Zacharie, 44:106-13

Banks, Mrs. Nathaniel P., 43:115

Banks Clubs, 43:115

Banners, Rudolph, 34:96

Bannister, Mr., 37:197

Bannister, Jack, 35:235

Bannister, John, 27:451, 452

Bannister, Roger, 46:470-71

Baptists, 47:25, 143; Board of Foreign Missions, 33:234-35

Bar, Benjamin R., 21:10

Bär, Manasse, 41:257

Baranof, M., 50:220

Bar Association of the City of New York, 49:6, 56

Barbados, 22:xxxii; Congregation Mekabetz Nidhe Yisrael, 22:131; 29:xliii; "Documents Relating to the History of the Jews in Jamaica and Barbados in the Time of William III," 22:xxviii; 23:vii, 25-29; "The Early Barbados Connections of the Gomez Family of Philadelphia and New York," 29:xxxvii; "Extracts from Various Records of the Early Settlement of the Jews in Barbados, W.I.," 26:xxxiii, 250-56; Hebrew literature, 22:120-21, 131; "Items from the Old Minute Book of the Sephardic Congregation, of Hamburg, Relating to the Jews of Barbados," 32:114-16; Jewish cemetery, 37:327-28, 459-60; *The Jewish Colonists in Barbados*, 35:xxii,

294; Jews in, 34:275-78; "The Jews in Barbados in 1739. An Attack upon Their Synagogue. Their Long Oath," 22:197-98; "The Jews of Barbados before 1776 and Their Commercial Connections," 32:xiii; Jews' Synagogue, Bridgetown, 22:179; kosher meat shipped to, 22:xxii; "Material relating to the Inquisition, and the Jews of Barbados," 32:xx; "Monumental Inscriptions of Barbados," 33:xxxii; 44:246; Nidchi Israel, *Consecration Service*, 30:284; "A Note on the Jewish Vestry Bill of Barbados," 22:xiii; "Notes from Wills of the Family of Massiah of Barbados," 22:178-80; Sephardic Jews, 29:9-14; Shearith Israel Congregation (N.Y.), 27:215, 245-46, 249, 288, 292, 294, 304, 310, 338, 463-64, 475, 522

Barbados Museum and Historical Society, 34:276-78; 37:460

Barbara Weinstock lectureship in the Morals of Trade, 29:195

Barbary States, 36:3, 20; 40:347; 46:4, 6-7, 13-14; 50:11

Barclay, James T., 39:11

Barclay, Thomas S., 37:442

Bard, Harry, 49:270

Bar-David, Jaap, 50:271

Bardin, William, 37:106-7

Bardos, Moses Mendez, 21:45

Barent, Alexander, 27:8

Barett, Esther (Starr), 27:487

Bargash, Sid Mohamed, 36:31

Barham, Janes, *see*: Marks, Jane

Bar Judah, 21:31

Barker, 31:111, 124

Barker, George P., 30:404

Barker, Jacob, 30:404

Barker, Johnny, 38:133

Barkly & Albot, 43:219

Bar Kochba Rebellion, 37:20-21

Barleben, Hersch, 32:119

Barlow, Joel, 41:4

Bar Mitzvah, 29:264, 371-83

Barnard, Aaron, 27:83

Barnard, Alexander, 27:79

Barnard, Captain, 27:365

Barnard, David, 27:510

Barnard, Edward, 35:11

Barnard, Gen., 39:9

Barnard, Myer, 27:83

Barnard, Samuel, *Polyglot Grammar*, 30:232

Barnard, Thomas, 22:21

Barn-Burners, 30:440

Barned, Levy, 25:117

Barnert, Nathan, 42:378, 382

Barnes, Jos. K., 33:218, 223; 50:328

Barnes, Margaret, 35:262

Barnes, Mrs., 33:196

Barnet, 27:314

Barnet, Abraham, 25:52

Barnet, Abram, 27:79, 83

Barnet, Hadassa, 27:110

Barnet, Lazarus, 27:462

Barnet, Moses, 21:48

Barnet, Sarah, 27:270

Barnet, William, 23:139

Barnett, Arthur, "Records of the Western Synagogue 1761-1832," 33:xxxii

Barnett, Daniel, 22:192

Barnett, L. D., 49:67

Barnett, Lionel D., 42:298, 436

Barnett, R. D., necrology of Wilfred Sampson Samuel, 49:64-69

Barnett, Ralph, 34:206

Barnett, Samuel, 27:271

Barnett, Samuel M., 43:117

Barnett, Samuel & Co., 49:64

Barney, Joshua, 23:170

Barnit, Aaron, 27:68

Barnitz, Jacob, Jr., 26:187

Barns (Judah Monis), 40:119

Barns, Simon, 23:80

Baruh, *see*: Barrow

Barnum, Henry A., 47:79

Barnum, Phineas Taylor, 44:40

Barodet, député, 41:161

Baron, Elias and Minna, Publications Fund, 44:247

Baron, I. M., 42:420

Baron, Joseph L., 33:147

Baron, Laurent, 23:139

Baron, Salo W., 40:407, "American Jewish Communal Pioneering," 43:133-50; "American Jewish History: Problems and Methods," 39:207-66; American Jewish history conference, 46:137-40; Brazil, Jews in, 42:223; church and state, 43:196;

corresponding secretary, 38:346; 39:469;
40:406; 41:387; emigration, 41:238; essay
committee, 38:vi, 78; *Essays in Jewish Life
and Thought, Presented in Honor of Salo
Wittmayer Baron*, 49:230; executive
council, 32:xii; 33:xxv; 37:xxix; 38:342;
44:241; 46:493; 47:201; 48:266; George A.
Kohut Memorial, 34:253; gifts, 33:xxxiii;
35:xxiii; history, writing of, 39:313, 315-
16, 336; 46:348, 443, 445; "Conference
Theme," 46:137-40; Jewish and general
history, 39:288, 290; Jewish Historical
Society of Israel, 41:391; Lee M. Friedman
appreciation, 42:415; Lee Max Friedman
Award Medal, 49:271; "The National State
and the Jew," 32:xii; past president, 50:426;
president, 42:414; 43:230; 44:240-47;
recognized, 44:241; remarks as president,
44:243-47; *A Social and Religious History of
the Jews*, reviewed, 42:313-18; "Some of
the Tercentenary's Historic Lessons,"
44:199-209, 240; "The Study of American
Jewish History: Problems and Methods,"
38:346; Utica, N.Y., 47:198; Vienna,
Jewish question, 34:225; and Jeannette M.
Baron, "Palestinian Messengers in the
United States, 1849-1879," 35:xv;
"Palestinian Relief and American Jewry,
1849-1879," 37:xxix
Baron de Hirsch colony, 43:59-60
Baron de Hirsch Committee, 31:226
Baron de Hirsch Fund, 31:267; 39:250;
46:236; 49:162; agricultural projects,
41:21-22; American Jews and immigration,
40:6, 227-28, 250-51, 255, 259, 330;
Argentina, 38:241, 245; 39:88-89, 103;
43:37-69; Bernard A. Palitz, 29:181-82;
Boston, 46:77, 81; Canada, 39:103; gift,
34:xx; immigrants, 38:310-11, 315, 48:236;
Kohler bibliography, 34:183, 186, 207,
209, 211, 213, 218, 254; Mayer Sulzberger,
29:189; Max James Kohler, 34:298;
Michigan colony, 29:66-68, 72-73; Russian
Jews, 48:111, 113-23; Sabato Morais,
37:77; Y. M. H. A., 37:291, 295, 298
Baron de Hirsch Institute, 50:135; Montreal,
28:271
Baron de Hirsch schools, 42:171

Baron de Hirsch Trade School, 38:311;
39:90, 93
Barondess, Benjamin, 50:271, 274, 396
Barondess, Joseph, 35:64, 252; 50:213;
necrology of, 32:ix-x
Baroway, Aaron, 31:xxxiii; 37:437; 50:43
Baroway, Moses, 36:69; necrology of, 31:xxiii
Baroway, Solomon, 31:226
Barr, Joseph F., 50:260, 270-71, 304; 49:137
Barreros colony, 43:61
Barreto, Francisco, 43:129
Barrett, Jacob, 50:167-68
Barrett, *Life of Lincoln*, 32:xxvi
Barrett, Samuel, 38:150
Barrette, Joan, 33:116
Barretto, Alfero Lepo, 33:113
Barrick, Solomon, 50:41
Barrington, 31:61
Barrios, Daniel Levi de, 29:8, 11, 13, 15, 20,
23, 37-38
Barrios, Daniel Lopes, 37:338
Barrios, Deborah, 29:37
Barrios, Jahacob Henriques de, 29:18-19
Barrios, J. H. de, Junior, 29:18-19
Barrios, Levy Joseph, 32:61
Barrios, Simon Levi de, 29:11
Barron, James, 46:10
Barrow, Baruch, 22:179
Barrow, Daniel, 35:50
Barrow, Emanuel, 25:118
Barrow, Mrs. Eml., 25:118
Barrow, Frances, 37:419
Barrow, John Henry (ed.), *Mirror of
Parliament*, 22:177
Barrow, Joseph, 26:251, 253
Barrow, Judith, 35:51
Barrow, Rebecca, 35:51
Barrow, Roderick, 22:179
Barrow, Sarah, 22:179; 35:31
Barrow, Simon, 26:253
Barrows, Daniel, 35:30
Barru, Daniel, 35:30
Barruch, 23:80
Barruch (Baruch), 35:27
Barruch, Abraham, 35:31
Barruch, Aron, 35:31
Barruch, Rebecca, 35:31
Barruh, Jacob Ysidro, 32:61; 35:31
Barry, John, 23:170

Barry, Philip, 40:357
Barsimson, Jacob, 32:20, 134; 33:199; 34:176; 44:75-76, 91, 93-94, 211; 45:61; "More About Jacob Barsimson, the First Jewish Settler in New York," 29:vii, xiv, 39-52
Barth, Carl G., 41:43, 48
Barth, Pero, 40:83
Bartholdi, Frederic Auguste, 37:17
Bartholdy family, 26:100
Bartholomei, Michel, 36:202
Bartlett, John Russell, 27:445-48; 34:4
Barton, 25:10
Barton, Clara, 26:xxv; 33:212-16, 218, 221, 223-28
Barton, Elizabeth, 27:71
Barton, George A., "George A. Barton Collection," 45:148, 171
Barton, Mrs. George, 45:148
Barton, Stephen E., 33:216, 221
Baruch, Abraham Henrique, 32:56
Baruch, Bernard M., 41:310; 47:190; 48:250; 50:271, 275, 330, 336
Baruch, David, 38:62, 65-67
Baruch, Esther (Massiah), 22:178
Baruch, Isabel, 37:436
Baruch, Jacob (Brazil), 33:65
Baruch, Jacob (Germany), 26:36-37, 45-47, 61, 66, 77
Baruch, Simon, 50:324, 329-30, 366
Baruh, Daniel, 35:30
Baruh, Isaque, 42:278, 393
Baruk, Isaque Moses, 23:27
Barzelay, Simon, 21:23, 33
Barzila, Phillips, 25:112
Barzilai, Salvatore, 28:21
Barzilay, Benjamy, 42:279, 287-89, 392-93
Barzilay, Samuel, 42:280, 283
Bas, 33:61
Basan, David Jacob, 25:115-16
Basan, Deborah, 25:115-16
Basan, Halbert, 25:115
Basan, M., 25:115
Basan, Wallace, 25:116
Basch, Dr., 32:87
Basch, Louis, 38:34
Basedow, 28:91
Basil, St., 28:137
Basinges, Ralph de, 41:383
Basle, Oecumenical Council of, 28:157-58

Basler, Roy P., 50:379
Basnage, Jacob Christian, 26:11
Bass, Bethia, 23:89
Bass, Doctor, 25:143
Bassan, David Jacob, 37:341, 343
Bassan, Jacob, 37:341, 343
Bassan, Judith, 37:343
Bassavilbasso colony, 43:59-60
Bastanho, Manuel Correa, 33:117
Bastianelli, Raphael, 28:58-59
Batavian Petroleum Company, 48:263
Batcheller, George, 47:86
Bateman, Mr., 44:49-50
Bateman, Mrs., 44:49
Bates, Katharine Lee, 35:243
Baton Rouge, La., 48:197, religious observances, mid-nineteenth century, 37:37
Battle Creek, Mich., Jewish Federation, contribution, 37:xxvii
Batty, David, 27:244
Bauer-Mayer, Joanne, 45:215
Baughman, 42:410
Bauland, Moritz, 41:262
Baum, Abraham, 29:113
Baum, Rabbi, 28:286
Baum, J. and Bro. (San Francisco), 37:45
Baumgardt, David, "Dorothy Canfield Fisher: Friend of Jews in Life and Work," 48:245-55, 265
Baumgarten, Eduard, 37:148
Baumgarten, Emanuel, 45:70
Baumgarten, Julius, 50:370, 381
Baumgarten, Morris, 26:248
Baumgarten, Selig, 26:248
Baumgarten, William, 26:248
Bavaria, civil rights, 26:35, 39, 56, 59, 61; education, 28:112; history, writing of, 46:388-89, 404
Bavli, Hillel, 50:271, Masad, 35:xxi, The Modern Renaissance of Hebrew Literature, reviewed, 40:195; "Three Hebrew epics by American Hebrew poets on the American Indian," 35:xv
Baxter, Rev, 30:15
Bayard, 22:151
Bayard, James A., 26:185; 34:251; 46:2
Bayard, N., 26:258

PUBLICATIONS OF THE AMERICAN JEWISH HISTORICAL SOCIETY

Bayard, Thomas Francis, 38:289; Austria, 36:323-41, 343-45; Judah P. Benjamin, 34:251; Palestine, 36:46, 48-51; Russia, 36:214; 40:299
Baylinson, A. S., 31:116
Baylinson; People v., 29:153
Baym, Max I., 39:321, 323-25, 327; "Emma Lazarus' Approach to Renan and Her Essay, 'Renan and the Jews,' " 37:xxxiv, 17-29; "Emma Lazarus and Emerson," 38:261-87; "The Jewish Orientation of Emma Lazarus," 38:346
Baynton and Wharton, 23:13, 15, 18
Bayouk, Judah Moses, 40:248-49, 275-80
Bay Psalm Book, The, 30:v, 1-4; 34:51-52; 35:148; 45:63; 46:181; 47:152
Bayrut, 40:108-10
Bazaine, Marshal, 32:71-72, 75, 81
Bazan, Jorge Jacinto, 32:117
Bazelon, David L., 47:203
Beach, Elias J., 29:168
Beach, Erasmus Darwin, 43:11
Beach, Frank, 48:257
Beach, John, *Three Discourses*, 30:58
Beaconsfield, Lord, *see*: Disraeli, Benjamin
Beadle, Elias Root, 35:306
Beale, James, 27:506
Beall, John Y., "President Lincoln and the Case of John Y. Beall," 32:132
Beals, Ralph L., 46:301
Bean, Louis, 46:346
Bean, William, 42:136
Bear, M., 29:134
Bear, Sol, 27:514
Bear Market, 25:45, 50
Beard, Charles A., 38:110; 46:433
Beard, Daniel Carter, 33:31
Beard, John, 37:401
Beard, Mary R., 38:110
Bearden, Elizabeth Twigg, 38:30, 40
Bearden, Frances, 38:41
Bearden, Marcus D., 38:30
Beatty, David, 31:215
Beau Brummell, 40:354
Beaujeau, M. de, gift, 22:xxxv
Beaumont, Francis, 33:171
Beaumont, Thomas, 31:122
Beaumont and Fletcher, *The Scornful Lady*, 33:171

Beauregard, Pierre Gustave Toutant, 50:314, 342, 382
Beavan, Thomas W. W., 23:156
Beaver, Philip, 40:126
Beaver trade in colonial America, 23:3-8, 10-11, 13, 16, 21
Bebee, Mr., 27:67
Bebee, Samuel, 27:71
Beber, Sam, Distinguished Alumni Award, 50:434
Becher, B., 29:124
Becher, P., 29:134
Beck, John B., 26:221-23
Beck, Karl Isidor, 35:123
Beck, M., 24:82
Beck, T. Romeyn, 26:221, 226
Becker, Abraham G., necrology of, 31:xxiii, 250-52
Becker, Carl Lotus, 39:304
Becker, Daniel, 50:165
Becker, J., 39:178, 180-81
Becker, James, 36:155
Becker, Lavy M., 49:269
Becket, John, 28:226
Becket, T., 37:199
Beckles, John A., 26:252, 254
Beckley, West Virginia, *History of the Beckley Jewish Community (Beckley, West Virginia) and of Congregation Beth El (The Beckley Hebrew Association) (including Raleigh and Fayette Counties, West Virginia) (1895-1955)*, 49:241-42
Beckman, Harry, 35:307
Beckman, Joseph, 29:62, 69
Beckwith, Captain, 26:183
Becx, Mathijs, 33:123-24
Becx, Willem, 33:123-24
Bedard, 23:49
Bedford Charity Case, 31:109, 112, 125
Bedford State Reformatory for Women, 29:168
Beecher family, 42:347
Beecher, Henry Ward, 23:62; 34:178; 38:321; 38:191; 40:5; 41:34; 42:348
Beecher, Lyman, 39:191
Beedleman, Jacob, 41:86
Beef Trust, 47:189
Beekman, 34:119
Beekman family, 41:110

Beekman, Geradus, 21:17; 27:244
Beekman, Henry R., 38:50
Beekman, James, 44:200
Beekman, M., 33:104
Beekman, William, 28:226
Beer, 26:98
Beer, Benjamin, 28:188
Beer, Bernard (Levy), 25:66
Beer, Edith C. (Hellman), 28:260
Beer, Elijah, 28:188
Beer, Esther (Elias), 25:66-69
Beer, George Louis, 46:428, "George Louis
    Beer, A Tribute," 31:xxxi; necrology of,
    28:xxxii, 258-61
Beer, Julius, 28:259
Beer, Mrs. Julius, "George Louis Beer, A
    Tribute," 31:xxxi
Beer, Peter, 28:73, 97
Beer, Sophia, 28:259
Beer, Sorlie, 41:256
Beer, Thomas, 46:434
Beerman, L. I., 42:420
Beermann, H., 37:46
Beers, Henry P., 46:160
Beeston, William, 31:243-44
Beethoven, 39:325
Behar, Nissim (Behar), 39:406-43
Behnken, Marjorie, 50:271
Behrend, 25:65
Behrend, Adajah, 50:328
Behrendt, George S., 46:121
Behrendt, H., 29:130
Behrman, Samuel Nathaniel, 40:359
Beigh, Henry, 37:91
Beilin, A., 50:402
Beilis, Mendel, 36:291
Bein, David, 38:203
Beir, Joseph, 40:65
Beis David Congregation (Fall River), 37:421
Beis Eil Congregation (Los Angeles), 29:130
Belais, Edward, 38:72
Belasco, David, 35:271, 273; 38:318; 40:357-
    59; 45:179, 199
Belasco, Moses, 26:252-54
Belcher, 22:183
Belcher, Jonathan, 22:11; 30:35
Belden, Charles F. D., 30:vi
Belding, Jerard, 27:244
Belez colony, 43:59, 61

Belfone, S., & Co., gift, 34:xxvii
Belgium, 46:93, Central Commission of the
    Israelites, 26:284; civil rights, 26:70, 72-73;
    emancipation, 26:268; Commission for
    Relief, 40:14; "Francis Joseph Grund,"
    26:234-35; George Louis Beer decorated,
    28:260; history, writing of, 46:290, 312,
    320-21; synagogue language, 28:113
Belillos, Joseph Ysrael, 42:278, 393
Belinfante, Cohen, 38:237
Belinfante, Isaac a Cohen, 29:29
Belinfante, Mehir A. Cohen, 26:251; 29:12
Belinfante, Méïr Haïm, 29:12-13
Belinfante, Sadik, 29:12
Belinfante, Sarah, 22:179; 32:56
Belizario, Andrew, 25:117
Belizario, Arthur Wellesley, 25:118
Belizario, Benjamin, 25:117-18
Belizario, Eve, 25:117-18
Belkin, Samuel, 48:265; executive council,
    38:346; 39:470; 42:414; 45:264
Belknap, Jeremy, *Two sermons*, 35:xvii
Bell, Daniel, 46:262, "Jewish Labor History,"
    46:257-60
Bell, John (Dr.), 26:222
Bell, John, 48:150
Bell, Philip, 27:322
Bell, Thomas, 37:395-98, 400, 406
Bellamont, Governor, 31:229-30
Bellamy, 32:49
Bellamy, Edward, 46:477
Bellefeuille, J. L., 23:139
Belles, Beaux and Brains of the 1860's, 50:397
Belle's stratagem, 33:174, 178
Bellevue Hospital, 26:221; 42:114, 119
Bellevue Medical Center, 50:275, 330, 366
Bellomont, Earl of, 27:382
Belmont family, 34:xix, "The Belmont-
    Belmonte Family," 26:xxxiii
Belmont (Schönberg), August, 27:510-13;
    33:216, 221; 34:250; 35:262; 41:27; 47:188;
    50:345, 407; Isachar Zacharie, 43:113;
    "Services rendered by the Seligmans,
    Rothschilds and August Belmont to the
    United States during the Civil War and
    the 'seventies," 33:xxv; Tammany Hall,
    43:31
Belmont, Belle, 29:166
Belmont, Daniel, 42:280, 393

Belmont, Perry, 40:333
Belmonte, Baron de, 22:xii; 31:243-44, 246; 42:461; "Baron de Belmonte's Petition," 38:45-46
Belmonte, Emanuel, 42:461
Belmonte, Francisco Baron Ximenes, 42:461
Belmonte, Ishac Nunnes, 29:16
Belmonte, Jacob, 44:227
Belmonte, Manuel de, 42:461
Belmonte, Manuel Francisco de, 31:29
Beltrami, J. C., *La Découverte des Sources du Mississippi*, 30:222
Bemis, Samuel Flagg, 38:129, 137
Bemvenist, Yosef, 42:280, 393
Bemvenista, Jeuda, 42:280, 393
Ben, Wah, 34:197
Bena Ariezer Synagogue (Rochester), 40:69
Benai David Temple (Rochester), 40:69, 72
Benaja, Leone, 28:173, 203
Benamezegh, Elias, 37:93
Bendann, Grace, 31:225-27
Bendau, David, 27:191
Bendavid, Lazarus, 28:92
Bendell, Herman, 35:320
Bendeniste, Isaac (Azzachus Avembenist), 28:143
Bender, Albert M., "Albert M. Bender and Fine Printing in Northern California," 39:470
Benderly, Samson, 35:62; 37:307; 42:11, 28
Bendove, R. A., 33:165
Benedetti, Salvatore De, 37:78
Benedict VIII, 28:142
Benedict XIII, 28:155
Benedict, Judge, 26:260; 29:149-50
Benedict, Julius, 32:xxviii
Benedict, Marcus, 40:18
Benedictions, "The Origin and Composition of the 18 Benedictions," 31:xxxii
Benedictus, Frances, 26:264
Benedikt, C., 34:256
Benedito, Baron, 38:313-14, 316
Ben-Eliezer, M., 33:145, 150, 157
Bene Israel Congregation (Cincinnati), 25:150; 29:162; 40:25, 46; (New York), 49:19; (Providence), 49:19
Bene Jerushum Congregation (Newark), 49:19; (New York), 21:223; 38:75; 49:19
Benes, Eduard, 50:111

Benet, Stephen Vincent, 48:165
Beneveniste, Moses, 37:387
Benevolent Society of True Sisters, 47:44
Bene Yeshurun Congregation (Cincinnati), 40:20, 22-24
Benfield, Bernard, 26:xiv; death, 37:xii
Benguiat, Hadji Ephraim, 33:21
Ben Gurion, David, 43:144; 46:130; 49:141
Benhacar e Bomdia, Ishac, 42:279, 393
Ben Hur, 40:336
Beni Israel, 21:237
Benisch, Abraham, 26:147
Benja, Doras, 21:108
Benjacob, 22:103
Benjamin (family name), 48:139
Benjamin, Benjamin, 27:151
Benjamin, David, 27:448
Benjamin, Elias, 27:43; 50:38
Benjamin, Eugene S., 34:186
Benjamin, G. B., 22:100
Benjamin, George, 22:194
Benjamin, Gitlah, 27:111
Benjamin, I. J., II, 47:35, 196; 49:39-40, 49; 50:200
Benjamin, Israel Joseph, 34:27
Benjamin, Jacob, 23:63-66, 74-75
Benjamin bar R. Jochanan, R., 21:10
Benjamin, John, 37:419
Benjamin, Joseph, 27:395
Benjamin, Judah P., 22:xxiii; 40:288; 44:118; Attorney General of the Confederacy, 50:319-20; autograph letter, 22:xxxv; bibliography, 50:69; biography, 22:xxxi; Civil War, 29:120; 41:75; 42:139; 50:321-22; and common law, 40:87-88; Crittenden letters, 23:x, 124-25; David Yulee, 25:1, 16; diary, 31:xxxiv; history, writing of, 28:236; 37:425; 44:252; 45:260; Isachar Zacharie, 43:101, 107-9, 113; "Judah P. Benjamin as a Jew," 38:153-71; Judaica, 37:436, 441; Kohler bibliography, 34:176-77, 186, 190, 192, 249, 251; letters, 31:xxxv, xxxiii; 35:xix, 133; papers of, 34:xviii; portrait, 32:xxvi; and slavery, 22:xxxiii; 50:153-54, 181, 191-92, 201; "Some Additional Notes on Judah P. Benjamin," 31:xvi
Benjamin, Levi, 37:449
Benjamin, M. I., 29:133
Benjamin, Meyer, 31:239

Benjamin, Moses, 37:373, 377, 380, 386; 38:235-36
Benjamin, Myer (Newport), 27:198, 350
Benjamin, Myer (New York), 27:151
Benjamin Nones & Co., 47:205
Benjamin, P., 34:xxi
Benjamin, Philip, 44:118
Benjamin, Rabbi, 21:16, 26-28
Benjamin, Rachel, 32:132
Benjamin, Rebecca, 32:56; 44:118
Benjamin, Ruth L., "Marcus Otterbourg, United States Minister to Mexico in 1867," 32:65-98; "Memoir of Marcus Otterbourg, United States Minister to Mexico in 1867," 31:xxiv; 32:xiii; "Petition of Pennsylvania Jews to Council of Censors regarding a Religious Test," 31:xxix
Benjamin, Walter R., 28:252
Benjamin of Tudela, 28:142, 205; 41:25; 45:26
Benjamin on Sales, 40:88
Benner, Thos. S., 37:448
Bennet, 25:118
Bennet, William S., 24:83; 34:200, 203
Bennett, Bishop, 37:441
Bennett, Charles, 27:506
Bennett, Congressman, 26:216
Bennett, David, 50:313
Bennett, James Gordon, 21:229; 30:404; 43:112
Bennett, William, 29:113; 49:186
Bennett, W. Sterndale, 35:240
Bennington Banner, 48:254
Benoth Israel Association, 46:85
Benoth Israel Sheltering Home (Boston), 46:74, 76-77, 82
Benrimo, Barrow, 27:515
Benrimo, Samuel, 27:277
Bensaken, Eleazar, 27:40, 152, 154-55
Bensel, John A., 50:235
Benshiton, W. L., 36:22-25
Ben Sira, 25:184-85, 187
Bensonhurst Jewish Community House (Brooklyn), 37:322
Bensonta, 27:79
Bentham and the Ethics of Today, 48:246
Bentinck, George, 35:254
Bentinck, Henry, 35:254

Bentley, William, 37:441; 38:49; 43:204
Bently & Co., 35:185
Benton (Free State Democratic Party), 23:64
Benton, Thomas H. (Col.) (1842), 22:92
Benton, Thomas Hart, 43:77
Bentura, Charles Cotterel, 37:407
Bentwich, Norman, 34:245; 43:196
Bentwich, Norman de Mattos, 46:99
Bentz, Rachel, 27:277
Benveniste, Mosseh de Daniel, 29:31
Ben-Yehudah, Eliezer, 39:407
Benzadon, Jacob, 27:91
Ben Zaken, Abraham, 27:152
Benzaken, Eleazer, 25:47
Ben Zaken, Jacob, 27:154-55
Ben Zakhar, 39:369
Ben Zenuda, 36:58
Ben Zion, 40:320
Ben Zoma, 43:244
Ben-Zvi, Isaac, 49:170
Berachah we-Shalom Congregation (Surinam), 22:27
Berboza, Balthazar, 33:114
Berboza, Manuel, 33:117
Berboza, Maria, 33:117
Berch, Rose, 46:121
Berdrow, 26:51
Berenson, Bernhard, 35:256-57
Berenson, V., 38:316
Berenstein, Zion, 35:307
Beresford Club, 29:180
Beretto, Philipo Pais, 33:118
Berezoff, Matter of, 29:151
Berg, Dr., 38:35
Berg, Albert A., 42:127
Berg, S., 29:134
Berg Institute of Research, 42:130
Berger, Abraham, 47:216, 220; 50:271
Berger, Doctor, 27:343
Bergheimer, Anna, 41:259
Bergk, J. A., 35:282
Bergman, Mrs., gift, 31:xxxiii
Bergman, Mrs. Alexander, gift, 29:xl
Bergman, Philip, 27:514
Bergman, S., 49:186
Bergmann, Hugo, 50:116
Bergson, Henri, 34:243; 35:263
Bergson, Michael, 35:263

Berith Kodesh Temple (Rochester), 42:371, 374, 383-84; 45:205; 50:82, 84, 90, 95
Berith Shalom Congregation (N.Y.), 49:60
Berith Sholem Congregation (Springfield, Ill.), 37:49
Berk, M. A., History of the Jews, 30:451
Berkeley, 29:137
Berkeley, Bishop, 27:453
Berkeley, George, 25:109
Berkenheimer, A., 39:93
Berkheim, 26:89
Berkovich, 43:56
Berkowicz, Jozef, 39:151
Berkowicz, Leon, 39:151
Berkowitz, Abram, 42:419
Berkowitz, Henry (Alabama), 32:130; (Philadelphia), 41:90; (Wisconsin), 38:333; "Additional Data on the History of Congregation Rodeph Shalom of Philadelphia," 28:xxxiii; Chautauqua Society, 42:4; gift, 28:xl; Hebrew Union College, 40:34; Jewish Chautauqua Society, 48:235; necrology of, 31:xvi, 252-53; Reform Judaism, 48:243
Berkowitz, Isaac Dob, 33:131, 149, 151
Berkowitz, Max E., 31:253
Berkshire, Earl of, 31:119
Berkson, Isaac B., 40:322; book review by, 40:313-17
Berl, Alfred, 39:441
Berle, A. A., "The World Significance of a Jewish State," 28:xl
Berle, Alfred, 43:66, 68
Berlin, conversions, 26:207-9; Jewish emancipation, 26:37, Royal Academy of Fine Arts, 28:4, 7
Berlin Central Committee for Emigration of Russian Jews, 42:180-84, 187-88
Berlin Committee, 49:177
Berlin committee on immigration, 40:229, 242; attitudes to, 41:139, 143ff
Berlin Conference (1869), 42:164, 166
Berlin Conference (1874), 42:175
Berlin Congress of 1878, 24:ix, 1, 16, 24, 39-79, 121-23, 127; 26:30, 156; 36:349; "Bismarck and Beaconsfield in Their Relations to the Jews," 26:258-59; "Memorial of Alliance Israélite Universelle

of Paris to the Congress of Berlin," 24:105-7
Berlin, Ellin, 35:270
Berlin, Hayyim, 44:137, 139, 141
Berlin, Hirsch Leib, 44:143
Berlin, Irving, 35:270; 47:181
Berlin, Isaiah, 33:251
Berlin, Jacob G., 21:214; 25:51, 52; 27:75
Berlin, Meir, 33:152
Berlin, Treaty of, 24:120, 122, 124, 126, 128-29, 131-53; "The Jews of Roumania and the Treaty of Berlin," 24:114-37; "Secretary Hay's Roumanian Note of 1902 and the Peace Conference of Bucharest of 1913," 24:80-97
Berlin, University of, 26:284; 34:303; 45:267
Berliner, A., 28:71, 88, 278-79; 35:209
Berliner, Abraham, 43:244, 246; 45:101
Berliner, Emile, 29:xxvi; necrology of, 32:xvi
Berliner, M., 29:113; 49:186
Berliner, Max, 46:88
Berliner Israelitischen Gemeinde, 43:64
Berlin-Roumanian Committee, 29:109
Berlinger, Hundel, 41:262
Berlinger, Jakob, 41:262
Berlizheimer, Bernhard, 41:262
Berlizheimer, David, 41:262
Berman, 31:139
Berman, Clement, 38:306, 313
Berman, Harold, gift, 35:xxiii; "Nahman Passi, a Sixteenth-Century Turkish Statesman," 29:xxxvi
Berman, Hyman, 49:155, 259-64
Berman, Jeremiah J., 50:280, "Jewish Educational Arrangements in New York City, 1860-1900," 39:470; "Jewish Education in New York, 1860-1900," 49:230; "The Trend in Jewish Religious Observance in Mid-Nineteenth-Century America," 37:xxxiv, 31-53
Berman, Morton, "History of Temple Isaiah Israel, Chicago (1852-1952)," 41:390
Berman, Mr., 43:56
Berman, Nathan, "The German Jewish congregation at Madison, Wis., 1850-1931," 33:xvii
Berman, V., 38:313; 39:89
Bermann, M., 31:200
Bermas, Mr., 31:146

Bermegero, Garcia Gonzalez, 31:26
Bermejo, Juan, 35:222
Bernal, A. I. H., 22:xxiii; 29:130; autographs, 26:xxxv
Bernal, Abraham, 32:64
Bernal, J. I., 37:419
Bernal, Joseph Rodrigues, 29:32
Bernal, Maestre, 22:155
Bernard, Aaron, 27:90
Bernard, Abm., 27:79
Bernard, Alexander, 27:84
Bernard, H. R., 33:236
Bernard, James, 27:352
Bernard, John, 33:183, 191
Bernard, Kenneth A., 50:271
Bernard, Myer, 27:79
Bernard, William S., 46:302, and Carolyn Zeleny and Henry Miller (eds.), *American Immigration Policy: A Reappraisal*, reviewed, 40:98-100
Bernard Mo's, 27:462
Bernardin, Saint of Siena, 28:157
Bernardinus of Feltre, 28:190-91
Bernardson, 27:45
Bernat, Paul, 42:419
Bernays, 29:128
Bernays, Jacob, 50:92
Berned, Esther, 25:117
Berned, Levy, 25:117
Berney, Albert, death, 37:xii; necrology of Jane Friedenwald, 29:xxxvi, 165-67
Bernfeld, Max, 50:238
Bernhard, Mr. (St. Louis), 37:41
Bernhard, L., 29:132
Bernhardt, Sarah, 35:248, 250
Bernheim, Abram C., 45:179, 201-2
Bernheim, B., 37:273
Bernheim, Bernard, necrology, 31:xxiii
Bernheim Brothers, 28:39, 42-43
Bernheim, Carl, 48:58
Bernheim, Chas. L., 40:263; 49:186
Bernheim, Franz, 34:231
Bernheim, H., 29:129
Bernheim, Henry C., 50:394
Bernheim, Isaac W., 37:269-70, 273, 307; 44:1; 49:195, 199; death, 37:xii; Hebrew Union College, 40:44; "History of the Settlement of Jews in Paducah and in the Lower Ohio Valley," 22:xviii; "Story of the

Bernheim family," gift, 33:xxix, xxxii-xxxiii; Zionism, 40:384-85
Bernheimer, 27:121
Bernheimer, Abraham, 41:256
Bernheimer, Adolph, 41:250
Bernheimer, Charles S., 45:177, 192; "Historical Sketch of the Jewish Community of Philadelphia, 1703-1926," 38:342; "The Jewish Population of Cities in the United States," 29:xxxvi; nominating committee, 29:xxxv
Bernheimer, Jacqs. A., 27:389
Bernheimer, Jeanette, 41:256
Bernheimer, Jüttle, 41:253
Bernheimer, Maier, 41:253
Bernstein, Aaron Simcha, 35:54
Bernstein, Bernard, 36:172; 41:165; 46:86
Bernstein, H., "The Truth about the Protocols," 34:xxv
Bernstein, Herman, 34:201, 36:281, 49:108
Bernstein, Hirsch, 33:128, 134; 35:64; 44:125
Bernstein, Isaac, 27:515
Bernstein, Leonard, 47:181-82
Bernstein, Mordecai, "A Note on Altenmuhr Jews," 49:53-55
Bernstein, Morris, 42:420, 422; 46:121, 333
Bernstein, S., 34:238
Bernstein, Simon, 33:149
Bernstein, Theresa F., 47:182
Bernstein, Wladimir, 46:66
Bernstein, Zvi Hirsch, 45:70-72
Bernstorff, 26:57, 82
Bernstorff, Countess, 26:52
Bernton, Harry S., 47:203
Berr, Michel, 26:84
Berrett, James, 26:218
Berretto, Bernardo Velho, 33:114
Berrian, William, 27:317, 382
Berrien, John, 23:157
Berrion family, 41:110
Berrion, John, 27:244
Berry v. Berry, 29:150
Berthelot, 25:121
Berthelot, Capt., 23:43-44, 139
Berthier, 27:77
Bertram, Corneille Bonaventure, 37:186
Bertram, L. J., 37:329
Berwin and Bros., P. (San Francisco), 37:45
Beseglio, R., 28:51

Besnardiere, La, 26:39
Bessarabia, 24:52, 65-66, 122; 36:102, 107
Bessera, Antho. da Rotga, 33:114
Besso, Henry V., 34:293; *Vide e obras de Maimonides*, 35:xxi
Best, Dr., 32:38
Best, C. J., 31:106
Betancour, Laurents Ferera, 33:116
Betanzos, Domingo de, 31:17, 19
Beth Ahabah Synagogue (Richmond), 38:161, 164-65
Beth David Hospital (N.Y.), 49:86
Beth Eil Congregation (Los Angeles), 29:130
Bethel, 35:151
Beth El Congregation (Beckley, West Virginia), *History of the Beckley Jewish Community (Beckley, West Virginia) and of Congregation Beth El (The Beckley Hebrew Association) (including Raleigh and Fayette Counties, West Virginia) (1895-1955)*, 49:241-42; (Detroit), 29:63, 67; 31:269; 40:81; (Fall River), 37:421; (New York City), 29:132; 31:257, 269; 34:168, 189; 39:451; 40:39; 42:104; 44:161, 251; 45:94, 205; 49:19; 50:286; (Utica), 29:135; 47:198
Beth-El Emeth Congregation (Memphis), 50:292; (Philadelphia), 29:133; 41:90; 49:19
Beth El Hebrew Relief Society (Detroit), 29:63
Beth-El Jacob, Congregation (Des Moines), 47:208
Beth-El on Raritan, 27:247
Beth-El Sisterhood (New York), 37:294
Beth El Temple (Buffalo), 46:166; (New York), 37:245, 252-57, 294, 311, 315
Beth Elohim, Congregation (Brooklyn), 29:129
Beth Elohim Congregation (Charleston, S.C.), 21:94, 164, 220; 26:192; 27:40, 463-64; 29:129; 32:42, 50, 127; 37:35; 40:398-99; 43:237; 46:115; 47:129; 48:241; 49:20; 50:285; anniversary, 39:471; George Washington correspondence, 27:221-22, 497; *Hymns for Beth Elohim Congregation*, 30:366; "Jewish Education in Charleston, South Carolina, During the Eighteenth and Nineteenth Centuries," 42:43-70; Joseph Tobias, 49:33, 37; law violations,

39:272; minutes, 27:226-27; *Niles' Register*, 50:13; 1790 community, 50:31-32, 46-47, 52, 55; plantation owners, 50:154, 175; "Two Unknown Historic Candelabra from K. K. Beth Elohim of Charleston, S.C.," 23:xiii, 186-87
Beth Elohim Unveh Shallom (Charleston), 48:177
Beth Emeth, Congregation (Albany), 28:286, 304; 29:180, 194; (Flatbush), 29:151
Beth Emeth Temple, Albany, N.Y., 29:180-94
Bethencourt, L. Cardozo de, 23:189; 37:361; 47:70-71; "Notes on the Spanish and Portuguese Jews in the United States, Guiana, and the Dutch and British West Indies During the Seventeenth and Eighteenth Centuries," 29:vii, xxxvii, 1-38
Beth Hamidrash Anshe Ungarn Congregation (New York), 44:136, 168
Beth Hamidrash Hagadol Congregation (New York), 44:128-98; 49:87
Beth Hamidrash Halchei Yousher, 44:131
Beth Hasholom Congregation (Williamsport, Pa.), 37:34
Beth Israel Association (Boston), 46:85
Beth Israel Bikur Cholim (New York City), 29:132; 49:19
Beth Israel Bikkur Holim, Congregation (New York), 44:176
Beth Israel Congregation (Amsterdam), 31:175; 42:225; (Baltimore), 23:vii, xiv, 141-46; (Hartford), 37:429; 45:146; (Houston), 37:40; (Jackson, Miss.), 29:130; (Louisville), 29:130; (Philadelphia), 30:450; 47:204-5; Hebrew school, 48:76; organization, 48:216; Rosenthal family, 41:198; synagogue architecture, 41:72-74; (New York), 37:504; (Richmond Hill, L.I.), 35:xxiii; (Rochester), 40:66, 69, 72-73; (San Francisco), 41:370; gift, 35:xxiii
Beth Israel Hebrew School (Los Angeles), 33:167
Beth Israel Hospital (Boston), 46:85; (Newark), 37:456; (New York), 35:54, 63; 39:89; 42:103; 47:229; development, 49:80, 116; gift, 34:xxii
Beth Jacob Congregation (Albany), *Order of Consecration Service*, 30:431

Beth Jacob Schools, 40:402-3
Beth Jahacob, 44:222
Beth Jahacob Congregation (Amsterdam), 42:225
Beth Shalome Congregation (Richmond, Va.), 21:xviii, xxiii, 165; 27:488, 497; 38:164-65; 49:19; 50:30-31, 64; J. J. Lyons correspondence, 27:144-45; Levy family, 46:103; organization date, 46:68; synagogue, funds for, 27:232-33
Beth Talmud, 25:179
Beth Zion Temple (Buffalo), 37:295
Bettan, Israel, 40:47
Bettelheim, Dr., 29:107
Bettelheim, A. S., 34:304
Bettelheim, Aaron, 31:219; 45:116
Bettelheim, Bruno, and Morris Janowitz, *Dynamics of Prejudice: A Psychological and Sociological Study of Veterans*, reviewed, 40:101-4
Bettelheim family, 34:xviii
Betterton, W. G., 43:92-95
Betteuile, Dru de, 41:382-83
Bettman, B., 37:263, 269
Bettman, Morris L., 45:157
Bettmann, Abraham, "Dr. Abraham Bettmann, a Pioneer Physician of Cincinnati," 23:vii, 105-16
Bettmann, Bernhard, 40:23, 38, 45
Bettmann, W. A., 23:112
Betts, Frederick J., 25:122
Betts, Samuel R., 30:208-9, 404
Beule, J. C., 39:83
Beuningen, Jonathan van, 44:218
Bevan, Frances Jean, 40:294
Beveridge, Albert Jeremiah, 46:434
Beverwyck, 26:247
Bevis Marks Community, 22:1, 201
Bevis Marks synagogue (London), 26:262; 29:31; 34:276-78; 35:33, 37, 230; 37:467; 40:124; 41:84; 44:9; 45:49-50, 53; 49:67; Charleston, S.C. Congregation, 42:43, 49-52, 55; ritual silver, 43:5-6, 9; Sephardimism, 42:435-36, 439-40
Bexley, Lord, 26:268
Bey of Algiers, 46:4, 6-7, 14
Beyrouth, 26:134
Bezalel School (Jerusalem), 40:319; 45:158
Bezerra, Antho., 33:115

Bezerra, Antonio, 33:80
Beziers, Council of, 28:144
Bialik Hayyim Nachman, 43:239
Bialik Prize, 50:117
Bialystok pogrom, 36:274-75
Bianconi, 24:78
Biba, 28:56-57
Bibb, 23:120
Bible, 46:382, 410; *Bible View of Slavery, A Discourse Delivered at the Jewish Synagogue "B'nai Jeshurun," New York, on the Day of the National Fast, January 4, 1861*, 50:287-88; *Biblia Hebraica*, 30:155-56, 431-32, 443, 451-52; *Prospectus of a Hebrew Bible*, 30:157
Bible reading, 34:229; schools, 42:148; "Anglo-Jewish Legal Cases," 25:137
Bible study, "The Influence of Lewis Way and Other English Missionaries upon Alexander I's Treatment of the Jews," 26:116-25
Biblical Canon, 25:182
Biblical history, 46:439
Biblical Repertory, 35:xx
Bibliographic Society of America, 43:250
Bibliographic Society of London, 35:314
Bibliographies in American History, 46:160
Bibliography, 29:xi; 45:143, 152, 165; 47:184, 218, 221; 48:235; *An American Jewish Bibliography*, 44:252-54; Civil War, 50:268, 401; Ephraim Deinard, 34:154-63; "The Hebrew Periodical Press in America, 1871-1931," 33:127-70; history, writing of, 46:158-60, 162; Max James Kohler, 34:165-258; "A Proposal to the Membership of the American Jewish Historical Society for a New American Jewish Bibliography," 50:68-72; "A Selected Bibliography of the Writings of Albert M. Friedenberg," 35:xiv, 115-37; "Jewish Bibliography, 1640-1850," 30:iii-486
Bibo, Nathan, *see:* Goldenstein, Raphael
Bicheno, James, "Friendly Address to the Jews," 26:129-31; 30:99-101; "The Restoration of the Jews, the Crisis of all Nations," 26:129-31; "Signs of the Times," 26:129-31
Bickart-Sée, Edmond, 46:96

Bicker, Walter, 23:159
Bickley, John, 37:14
Biddle, C. C., 30:200
Biddle, Charles, 43:236
Biddle, Edward, 34:77
Biddle family, 50:244
Biddle, James, 23:19; 50:244
Biddle, N., 28:xxxiv
Bieber, Hugo, 44:114-15
Bien, H., 26:272
Bien, Hermann M., 37:268
Bien, Julius, 29:206; 40:263; 45:99; Civil
  War, 50:371, 381-83; Hebrew Immigrant
  Aid Society, 49:175-76, 186
Biesenthal, S. B., 29:130
Bieu, Mrs., 42:79
Bigart, L., 36:40
Big Divide, The, reviewed, 38:321-22
Bigelow, Bruce Macmillan, "Aaron Lopez,
  Colonial Merchant," 32:xix
Biggs, Joseph L., 32:125
Bigotry, 42:349, 351, 354; 46:294; see also:
  Race prejudice
Bijlsma, Dr., 32:8-9, 21n
Bijur, Nathan, 25:176; 34:207; necrology of,
  33:xii
Bikart, Methilde, 41:253
Bikart, Salomon, 41:253
Bikkure ha-Ittim, 22:130
Bikur Cholim w-Kadisha (New York), 29:132
Bilah; Bat Hisquiau, 21:11
Bilah Bat Hisquian, 31:238
Bilbo, Theodore Gilmore, 49:227
Bilgray, Albert, 39:225
Billers, William, 28:256
Billings, John S., 46:233-37
Billington, Mrs., 23:179
Billington, Ray, 45:217
Bill of Rights, 37:185; 38:1-2, 18; 43:161-64,
  168; 44:208; 46:288; manuscript copy, gift
  of, 37:13
Bills of credit, 34:272-73
Billstein, Nathan, 31:xxxiv
Binder, Abraham W., 40:54; 47:181
Binder, Samuel, 40:244
Bindona, Joseph, 50:123
Bing, Abraham, 23:109, 113
Binger, Carl (forw.), Anti-Semitism and
  Emotional Disorder, reviewed, 40:91-93

Bingham, 22:76
Bingham, John A., 29:201
Bingham, John Armor, 47:78-79
Bingham, Robert W., 36:86
Bingham, Theodore, 50:210-11, 213, 219
Binswanger, Elizabeth Sophia, 31:159
Binswanger, Frank C., 43:238
Binswanger, Isidor, 29:111, 113; 48:226
Binswanger, Mrs. Simon, 28:315
Biogenetics Center, 42:130
Biographical research, 46:446
Biography, 46:135, 399, 400, 420-46
Bird, 31:106
Birje of Amsterdam, 27:244
Birkenheim, B., 43:57
Birmingham, Ala., United Jewish Fund,
  contribution, 37:xxxvii
Birnbaum, Eduard, "Eduard Birnbaum
  Collection," 45:157
Birnbaum, Nathan, 49:141
Birnholz, Freda B., 45:177, 192-94
Birnholz, Marco, 45:193-94, 213
Birnholz, Rose, 45:194
Biro-Bidjan project, 38:242; 39:113
Birobidzhan episode, 42:444
Birongel, Francisco, 33:113
Birrell, Captain, 38:151
Birth, customs with, 39:368-70
Birth, William, 48:15
Bischoffsheim, 29:127
Bischoffsheim, R., 41:161
Bisgyer, Maurice, 47:201, 203
Bishop, Isaac W., 30:404
Bishop, Maria, 46:102
Bishop's College, 50:129
Bismarck, Prince, 24:35, 40-41, 46-47, 50-52,
  56, 59-61, 63-69, 71, 75, 120-21; 36:348-
  49, 351-54, 358, 360; 40:200; "Bismarck
  and Beaconsfield in Their Relations to the
  Jews," 26:258-59; Kohler Bibliography,
  34:222, 235
Bisno, Julius, 46:120-21, 123; 47:201; Civil
  War, 50:271, 275, 345; executive council,
  42:415; 44:241; 50:426; S. Calif. Jewish
  Historical Society, 42:420-21, 423
Bissera, Joan Pessoa, 33:119
Bissera, Manuel Jacoma, 33:117
Bitker, Bruno V., 34:215
Bittleman, Alexander, 50:252

Bi-Weekly Summary of Events of Jewish Interest, 29:171
Bixby, William K., 39:183
Bizerra, Manuel, 33:117
Bizet, Jacques, 35:121, 260
Black, Dr., 22:172
Black, Hugo, 42:357; 43:166
Black Jack, battle of, 23:70, 72-75, 77
Black, Jeremiah S., 38:157
Black, Morris A., 41:316; 46:230
Black, William Henry, 26:147
Blackmar, Judge, 25:135
Black Plague, 28:148-49
Blackstone Memorial, 47:158
Blackstone Petition, 36:42
Blackstone, William, 31:107, 124
Blackstone, William E. (Rev.), 36:42
Blackwell, Montague, 38:88-89
Blackwood, 23:48-49
Blackwood, 26:155
Blagge, Benjamin, 27:250
Blaine, Ephraim, 23:11, 16, 21
Blaine, James A., 40:300, 303; 48:127
Blaine, James G., 23:16; Jewish disabilities, 24:113; 36:32, 34-35, 58, 192-203, 205, 215-25, 354; Russo-American Treaty, 41:169-70; Simon Wolf, 47:82-84, 88, 92
Blair, Mr., 29:55
Blair, F. P., 30:404
Blair, Francis Preston, Sr., 43:112
Blair, Samuel, 38:122
Blake, John B., 39:34, 62, 65
Blake, Nicholas, 35:294
Blake, Sally E., 45:197
Blake, Tucker, 39:62; 43:123
Blake, W. W., 28:250
Blake, William, 32:4
Blakely, Mr., 42:191
Blanberg, Nahum, 22:174
Bland, Michael, 27:450
Blank, L., 38:244
Blank, Sheldon, 40:48
Blankenhorn, 31:207
Blanshard, Paul, 46:277, 279
Blasé, "Diary of a Blasé," 31:xxxi
Blashki, Viva, 49:69
Blasphemy Act (Maryland), 25:99-100, 103-4
Blau, Joel, 31:262; gift, 33:xxxiii

Blau, Joseph L. (ed. and intro.), *Cornerstones of Religious Freedom in America*, reviewed, 40:96-98; (ed.), *Essays in Jewish Life and Thought, Presented in Honor of Salo Wittmayer Baron*, 49:230; "The Maryland 'Jew Bill': A Footnote to Thomas Jefferson's Work for Freedom of Religion," 37:xxxv
Blau, Ludwig, 22:203; 34:13; 43:250
Blaube, Mr., 44:2
Blaustein, David, 35:60; 45:145; 49:120; necrology of, 22:xvii, 206-11
Blaustein, Jacob, "The Unfolding Future," address by, 45:9-11
Blaustein, Joseph Isaac, 48:194
Blaustein, Miriam, 22:210
Blaustein, Morton K., 49:270
Blaxland, G. Cuthbert, 38:290, 292
Blecher, Jacob, 43:59
Bleecker, John, 28:224
Bleeker, Anthony J., 27:228; 39:34
Bleichröder family, 34:20, 25
Bleichroeder, 26:259
Bleichroeder, Gerson von, 24:47, 50-52
Bleichroeder, Julius, 24:25
Blight, 23:120
Blinn, Holbrook, 35:270
Blioch, I. S., "Jean de Bloch (I. S. Blioch), Champion of International Disarmament, Advocate of Russian Jewish Emancipation and Worker for Russian Economic Development," 29:xv; 31:xvii
Bliss, Captain, 27:426-27
Bliss, Leslie E., 30:vi
Bloch, Abe, 35:131; necrology of, 23:xiii, 191
Bloch, Alfred, 45:259
Bloch, Baer-Moses, 47:219
Bloch, David, 26:262
Bloch, Ernest, 47:181-82
Bloch family, 28:264; 34:19; 41:226
Bloch, Gotthilf, 41:262
Bloch, Hirsch Zwi, 34:19
Bloch, Isaac, 29:131
Bloch, Ivan, 43:65
Bloch, Jacob Henry, 34:19; 41:226
Bloch, Jean de, 29:182; 34:249; "Jean de Bloch (I. S. Blioch), Champion of International Disarmament, Advocate of Russian Jewish Emancipation and Worker

for Russian Economic Development,"
29:xv; 31:xvii
Bloch, Joseph S., 34:225
Bloch, Joshua, 30:vi; 37:459; 40:322, 405;
42:112, 467; 49:251; Bible reading, 43:195;
bibliography, 33:131; bookplates, 45:136;
book reviewed by, 42:91-107; (pref.),
*Documentary History of the Jews in the
United States*, reviewed, 42:109-11; editing,
39:iv; essay committee, 38:vi, 78; 39:114a-
b; essay judge, 43:70; executive council,
34:xiv; 35:xiv; 37:xxxiv; "The First Hebrew
Periodical in America," 32:xiii; G.
Washington correspondence, 32:121; gifts,
33:xxxii, xxxiii; 34:xxiii, xxiv; 35:xix; "The
History of the Hebrew Periodical Press in
America," 23:xiii; "Isaac M. Wise on the
Jewish Community of Cincinnati in 1872,"
37:xxxii; "Is Haym Salomon Mentioned in
the Responsa of Aryeh Loeb Ben Hayyim
Breslau?," 33:251; "Isidor Rayner (1850-
1912)," 40:288-310; "Jewish Massacres,"
33:xxx; Kohler Bibliography, 34:249, 253;
"Miscellaneous Notes," 37:xxix;
necrologies of Abram Samuel Isaacs,
31:265-66; Alexander Marx, 43:231, 241-
52; George Alexander Kohut, 34:ix, xv,
303-6; Wilberforce Eames, 35:x, xvi, 312-
15; necrology of, 47:201, 216-22;
nominations committee, 31:xv; 41:387;
42:414; 43:230; *Of Making Many Books*,
reviewed, 43:239-40; (compiler), *The People
and the Book. The Background of Three
Hundred Years of Jewish Life in America*,
reviewed, 45:61-63; presides, 42:415;
45:264; 46:493; "Rabbi N. Streusand and
His Anti-Reform Tract," 37:xxxv;
Recording secretary, 38:346; 39:469;
40:406; 41:388; 42:414; 43:230; "The
Record of Jewish Participation in the
American Armed Forces during World
War I," 37:xxxv; Reform Judaism, 39:451,
465; "Rosa Mordecai's *Recollections of the
First Hebrew Sunday School*," 42:397-406;
vice-president, 44:241; 45:264; 46:492; and
Max J. Kohler, "Jean de Bloch (I. S.
Blioch), Champion of International
Disarmament, Advocate of Russian Jewish

Emancipation, and Worker for Russian
Economic Development," 31:xvii
Bloch, Koppel, 34:19
Bloch, Lazare, 41:146
Bloch, Lazarus, 23:191
Bloch, Louis, 35:120
Bloch, M., and Co., 47:37
Bloch, Maier, 41:254
Bloch, Menachem, 50:271
Bloch, Mina, 41:257
Bloch, Moses, 27:47
Bloch, Necha (Stoch), 47:219
Bloch, Ovsey, 39:106-7
Bloch, Simon, 27:90
Bloch, Simon L., 29:185
Bloch, Solomon ben Ephraim, 35:209
Bloch, Solomon Henry, 34:19
Blochman, Ch., 33:150
Bloch Publishing Company, 46:431; 47:181
Block, Doctor, 27:79
Block, Mr., 37:199
Block, Abraham, 27:45, 76; 35:198
Block, Hanna, 22:195
Block, Jacob (1), 22:193
Block, Jacob (2), 22:195
Block, Jacob W., 50:236
Block, Joseph, 37:270
Block, Judah, 22:195
Block, Levi (1), 22:195
Block, Levi (2), 22:193
Block, Levi (3), 22:195
Block, Lion, 22:195
Block, Louis, 22:182
Block, Lucia R., 50:350
Block, M. S., 22:195
Block, Myer, 22:195
Block, Myer J., 22:194-95
Block, S. S., 22:195
Block, Mrs. Samuel, 28:315
Block, Simon, 21:169; 22:194
Block, Simon, Jr., 27:79
Block, Simon J., 22:195
Blog, Abraham Solomons, 21:121, 131
Bloit, Piero, 25:120
Blommestein, W. E. van, 48:263
Blondheim, David S., 28:251; 45:144, 170
Blondheim, Grace, 49:270
Blood Accusations, 48:217, 224
"Bloody Angle," 50:385

Bloom, Daniel, 23:153
Bloom, E., 29:130
Bloom, Hanna, 28:310
Bloom, Herbert I., 33:42; 42:112; 46:192; books reviewed by, 42:107-9, 214; 47:112-20, 209; 50:73-76; Brazil, Jews in, 42:223, 305; "The Dutch Archives, with Special Reference to American Jewish History," 32:xii, 7-21; *The economic activities of the Jews in Amsterdam in the 18th and 19th centuries*, 35:xxi; "A Study of Brazilian Jewish History 1623-1654, Based Chiefly Upon the Findings of the Late Samuel Oppenheim," 33:xxvi, 43-125
Bloom, Isaac, 40:46
Bloom, Maurice J., "The Gomez House," 40:406; "Early Jewish Associations with West Point," 41:389
Bloom, Sol, 34:xxvii; *Autobiography of Sol Bloom*, reviewed, 38:317-19
Bloom, Solomon, 34:xxv
Bloomfield, Joseph, 35:121
Bloomfield, Lord, 28:119
Bloomfield, Thomas, 33:252
Bloomgarten, Lewis, 29:135
Bloomingdale, Charles, 31:146, 151
Bloomingdale (dept. store), 38:20
Bloore, Stephen, 40:415, "The Jew in American Dramatic Literature (1794-1930)," 40:345-60, 406
Blosz, Karl, 35:120
Bluch family, 27:465
Bluestein, Richard, 40:53
Bluestone, E. M., 49:271
Bluestone, Joseph Isaac, "The Memoirs and Scrapbooks of the Late Dr. Joseph Isaac Bluestone of New York City," 35:xiv, 53-64
Blum, 39:151
Blum, A., 37:40; gift, 23:xviii
Blum, Abraham, necrology of, 29:xiv, 155-56
Blum, David, 41:267
Blum, Fred, 50:271
Blum, Hyman, 40:263
Blum, Isador, 50:43
Blum, Isidor, 22:191; 37:35
Blum, Jakob Josef, 41:254
Blum, Joseph, 31:226
Blum, Leon, 35:260; 40:403

Blum, Marum, 41:257
Blum Pasha (Julius), 47:98
Blum, Robert, 33:240
Blumberg, Lenie, 48:26-27
Blumberg, Meyer, 48:26
Blumenberg, Leopold, 35:120
Blumenfeld, Kurt, 49:141
Blumenfeld, Ralph David, 35:261; 41:249
Blumenfield, David, 41:248-49
Blumenthal, Emil, 50:313
Blumenthal, George, 42:125-26; death, 37:xii
Blumenthal, Joseph, 37:85-86, 92, 268
Blumenthal, L., 21:215
Blumenthal, Lawrence, 38:59, 67
Blumenthal, M., 29:113
Blumenthal, Mark, 38:59, 68; 42:118-19
Blumenthal, Moritz, 41:262
Blumenthal, Solomon, 50:313
Blumenthal, Walter Hart, 34:231, "Alleged Masonic Symbols and Ritual in Aboriginal America," 28:xxiii; "The Black Hand Rock near Newark, Ohio," 28:xxiii; "The Hand Symbol in Aboriginal America and Primitive Palestine," 29:xv; "Henry Phillips on the Yarmouth Petroglyph," 28:xxii-xxiii; "Israelite and Indian: A Parallel or an Identity," 22:xvii; "Mormon Petroglyph at Manti, Utah," 28:xxii; nominations committee, 28:xxxii; "In Old America," gift, 33:xxix, xxxii-xxxiii; "The Old Fancy That Ophir Was in the New World," 29:xxix; "The Sacred Number Seven in Aboriginal America and the Old Testament Heptad," 28:xxxiii; "Samuel Harris on the Dighton Rock Inscription," 28:xxii; "Several Unnoted Writings on the Vagary of the Ten Tribes in America," 28:xxiii
Blumenthal, William E., 42:420; 46:120, 122
Blumenthaler, Esther, 41:262
Blün, Ida, 22:237-39
Blün, Nathan, 22:237
Blunt, 31:121
Blunt, Henry, *Lectures*, 30:332
Bluntschli, Johann Kaspar, 24:97; "Roumania and the Legal Status of the Jews in Roumania," 24:76
B'nai Abraham Congregation (Easton, Pa.), 42:196, 202

B'nai Amoona, 46:65
B'nai Avrihum Congregation (Quincy, Ill.),
29:133
B'nai Benjamin, 46:488
B'nai B'rith, 25:124; 34:270; 39:255; 42:110;
49:188; Adolph Kraus, 50:119; and
Alliance Israélite Universelle, 39:413-20,
425-29; and American Jewish Historical
Society, 44:244-45; Benjamin Franklin
Peixotto, 45:68, 78; Bernhard Felsenthal,
45:95-127; Buffalo lodge, 46:163;
(Canada), 50:141; Civil War committee,
50:263, 267, 270-72, 274, 292, 302, 309,
325-30, 371, 381-82, 405; (Colorado),
49:218; Committee on Jewish Americana,
49:137; communal affairs, 43:141;
development, 49:17, 26; discrimination,
47:15-16; (Easton, Pa.), 42:195, 197, 202;
Federated Jewry, 48:144; gifts, 29:xli,
32:xxvii; 35:xxiii; history, writing of,
46:240-41, 309, 394; Isaac Max Rubinow,
49:91; "Jewish Disabilities in Balkans,"
24:9, 11, 22-23; Jerusalem Lodge, 36:57;
Kishinev Jews, 34:280; Kohler
bibliography, 34:187, 199, 217; MacIver
report, 42:320; Martin A. Marks, 26:282-
83; Martin Zielonka, 35:326; (Memphis),
49:239; (Milwaukee), 47:35, 46-48, 57;
(New Haven), 37:47; (New York), 41:229;
and Odd Fellows, 48:200; Palestine, 29:98;
and refugees, 45:221, 225-26, 232-33, 238,
243; religious liberty statue, 29:106;
(Rochester), 40:66; Sabato Morais, 37:79;
Simon W. Rosendale, 35:322; Simon
Wolf, 47:83; widows and orphans, 48:213;
youth organization, 50:434
B'nai B'rith Congregation (Los Angeles),
46:121-22; (Wilkes-Barre), 49:19
B'nai B'rith Hillel Foundation, 46:124
B'nai B'rith House (Columbus), 37:294
B'nai B'rith, Israel's Herold, 26:273
B'nai B'rith Magazine, 45:224, 226, 228, 231,
236-37, 242-43
B'nai B'rith Manual Training School, 37:291
B'nai B'rith Museum (Washington, D.C.),
49:137
B'nai B'rith News, 29:xliii
B'nai B'rith Orphanage at Erie, 31:298

B'nai B'rith Vocational Service Bureau,
39:237, 244
B'nai Emet Anshe Merimpol Congregation
(New York), 44:136
B'nai Israel Congregation (Cincinnati),
39:446-48, 454; 39:461-64; (New York),
29:132; (Williamson, W. Va.), 37:xxxviii
B'nai Jehudan, Congregation (Kansas City),
31:252
B'nai Jeshurun Congregation (Cincinnati),
28:46; 50:118; (Dayton), 29:130; (Des
Moines), 47:208; (Milwaukee), 47:38-44,
57-58; (Newark), 29:176, 183
B'nai Jeshurun Congregation (N.Y.), 27:99,
109-10, 311, 342-43, 398-99, 504, 517;
31:260; 34:xxi; 35:319; 39:246; 40:188,
399; 45:71; 46:126; building fund, 41:86;
"A Chapter on the Founding of
Congregation B'nai Jeshurun, the Second
Oldest Synagogue in New York," 31:xvi;
Civil War, 50:272, 274, 287, 297;
communal affairs, 43:135-37; early settlers,
42:432, 438; Education Institute, 27:160,
514, 516; first cemetery, 27:270-71; gift,
32:xxviii; history, writing of, 46:384, 387;
Israel Baer Kursheedt, 41:289; Ladies
Hebrew Benevolent Society, 27:123;
Mordecai Manuel Noah, 41:15; 43:171,
179, 191; Mount Sinai Hospital, 42:116
B'nai Jeshurun Educational Institute (N.Y.),
39:43
B'nai Moshe Congregation (Evansville),
38:53, 55
B'nai Shalom Congregation (Chicago), 37:32;
41:390; (Yonkers), 37:40
B'nai Yeshurun Congregation (Cincinnati),
28:290; (Cleveland), 26:282-83; (New
York), 38:58-64, 75
Boardman, Mr., 37:134
Boardman, Mabel T., 33:222, 225, 228
Board of Arbitration, 41:319-21
Board of Charities, District of Columbia,
29:200
Board of Community Relations, 46:165
Board of Delegates of American Israelites,
25:112; 26:xxxiv, 213; 28:283; 29:200-202;
36:20, 24-26, 177; 38:240; 42:168-69, 172-
74; 48:224-28, 230, 236-37, 266; 49:189;
50:170; Alliance Israélite Universelle,

39:389-95, 399-402, 415; American Jews
and immigration, 40:224, 263; "The Board
of Delegates of American Israelites (1859-
1878)," 49:16-32; Brussels Conference
1872, 24:26; Civil War, 49:138; 50:274,
291-92, 297; correspondence, 34:xxi;
diplomatic correspondence, 36:5; final
report, 29:83-116; Hebrew Union College,
40:21; "Jewish Disabilities in Balkans,"
24:3, 8, 11-12, 22; Kohler bibliography,
34:187-88, 199, 210; Montefiore
Testimonial Fund, 37:95-100; Myer S.
Isaacs, 40:141; 1859-1878, paper, 28:xv;
Paris Conference 1876, 24:31-34, 36-39;
proceedings of, 29:xl, xli; religious liberty,
North Carolina, 29:81-82; Rumanian
disabilities, 36:100, 112, 117; symposium,
48:266; Y. M. H. A., 37:233-34, 245, 251,
260-62
Board of Delegates on Civil and Religious
Rights, 40:31, 262; 48:143-44
Board of Delegates of United Hebrew
Orthodox Congregations, 44:131, 188
Board of Deputies of British Jews, 26:254;
29:78, 83, 86, 89, 93, 99; 33:xxxiii; 36:113;
37:95-101; 42:439; 46:97; 49:26, 28
Board of Emigration, 40:235
Board of Guardians for the Relief of the
Jewish Poor (London), 28:248
Board of Jewish Education of Chicago, 42:33
Board of Law Examiners (Pennsylvania),
23:192
Board of Prison Inspectors of Philadelphia,
28:283
Board of Public Education (Philadelphia),
38:337
Board of Survey Associates, Inc., 37:476-77
Board of Visa Appeals, 46:335
Boas, Emil L., 49:186-87
Boas, Franz, 34:248; 42:367; 45:217; 46:300;
49:97
Bobrick, Inspector, 37:176
Bocacio, Agustin, 31:10, 21
Bodenheim, Mr., 31:159
Bodenheim, Maxwell, 35:268-69
Bodenheimer, Emilie, 31:297
Bodenheimer, Jacob, 31:297
Bodenstein, Julius, 35:120
Boder, David P., 46:355

Bodin, Jean, 37:188
Bodin, Vincent, 35:183
Bodleian Library, 25:180; 48:252
Boehm, Adolf, 49:140
Boehm, D., 35:272-73
Boemus, Joan, *Ominium gentium mores leges et
ritus*, 22:111
Boer, Captain, 27:304
Boeresco, H., 24:124-28, 142-45, 150
Boerne Foundation, 31:190
Boerne, Ludwig, 26:36, 46-47, 76, 100
Boernstein, Colonel, 29:123
Bofarull y Sans, Francisco de, 26:23
Bogardus, Mr., 27:316
Bogart, Cornelius, 27:244
Bogart, Elsie Schuyler, 31:241
Bogart family, 41:110
Bogen, B., 39:87-96, 98
Bogen, Boris D., 29:182; 36:143-44, 156, 159;
38:311, 314-15; 40:40
Bogen, Joseph, 37:268
Bogolubov, L., 38:316; 39:89-90
Boheme, La, 47:187
Bohemia, 26:31; 28:101; 46:290; 50:107, 111,
114; "The Autobiography of an Unknown
of the Seventeenth Century: a Picture of
the Condition of the Jews of Bohemia,"
25:xiii; Board of Delegates of American
Israelites, 29:90; Revolution of 1848,
38:187-88, 190-92, 196-97
Bohun, 31:110
Bohun, Edmund, 37:382
Bohn, William E., 41:330
Boie, Heinrich Christian, 37:176
Bois, Captain, 27:303
Boker, George H., 36:109; 40:110
Bokser, Benzion, gift, 34:xxvii
Bolingbroke, Lord, 31:129; 35:203
Bollwan, Israel, 29:130
Bolt, Elidia, 27:244
Bolton, Aquila, 22:190
Bolton, S., 32:30
Bolton Hall, 46:486
Bolton & Laforgue, 22:191
Bomdia, Dauid Leui, 42:279, 393
Bomeisler, Edwin, 31:139, 141, 144, 147-49,
151-53, 160-62, 168
Bomeisler, Eveline, 31:139, 141-42, 154, 160-
61

Bomeisler, Louis, 41:86, 93
Bon, Hiam, 21:58
Bon, Salomon Haim, 27:244
Bonacosa, Jacob, 28:200
Bonaiutus of Spoleto, 28:179-80
Bonan, Simon, 25:42
Bonaparte, *see*: Napoleon Bonaparte
Bonaparte, Jerome, 28:106; 33:189
Bonaparte in England, 33:174, 189-90
Bonar, Andrew A., 22:172; 26:134; and R. M.
  McCheyne, *Narrative of a Mission of Inquiry
  to the Jews*, 30:370, 399
Bonavoglio, Moses Hefez, 28:209
Bond, Francis A., 39:18
Bond, Nathan, 43:204
Bond, Phineas, 25:126-27
Bond, Solomon, 31:238
Bondavin (Bonjudes), 28:210
Bondi, August, 23:63, 66-68, 70-77; 50:285,
  354
Bondi, Herz Emanuel, 23:63
Bondi, Jonah (Jonas), 26:272; 50:301
Bondrop, Edler von, 50:111
Bondy, Maximilian, 26:31; 38:197; 50:111
Bone, Solomon, 21:48
Bonfil, Daniel and Son, 44:234-36
Bonfils, 24:97
Bonham, Milledge Luke, 50:342
Bonheur, Lucien, 39:406
Boniface VIII, 28:146
Boniface IX, 21:241; 28:149-53, 155
Bonilla, Alonso Fernandez de, 31:3, 9, 12, 15,
  18-19, 21-25
Bonilla Revolution, 31:213
Bonilla y San Martin, Adolfo, 28:xiv;
  necrology, 31:xxiii
Bonitto, Aaron Charles, 25:117
Bonitto, Judith, 25:117
Bonitto, Moses, 25:117
Bonitto, Solomon, 37:342
Bonne, Pierre A. de, 23:43, 49-50
Bonnet, Captain, 46:41
Bonns, Henry, 47:36, 42-43, 45-46
Bonta, Johanes, 23:149
Bontecou, Daniel, 23:153
Bontecou, Josephine, 43:12
Bontemantel, Hans, 33:92
Bookbinder, Jack, 47:182
Booker, Armistead, 50:168

Bookman, The, 40:347; 43:23; 45:146
"Book of Prayers for Dew and Rain," 22:122-
  23
Book of the History of Jacob Joseph in New York,
  44:172
Bookplates, 42:415; 50:394-96; "American
  Jewish Bookplates," 45:129-216
Book Publishers Association of Israel, 50:272
Book Sellers Association of Israel, 50:271
Bookstaber, Philip David, 39:458
Boone, Daniel, 23:22; 28:42; 33:4
Boorstin, Daniel J. (ed.), *American Judaism*,
  reviewed, 47:121-23
Booth, Edwin, 22:194
Booth, John Wilkes, 38:320; 41:206; 50:380
Boots, Jan, 32:14
Borah, William E., 49:13
Bordas, A. T., 26:243
Bordeaux, "A Bordeaux Subscription," 23:189
Borden, Gail, 46:11
Borden, Samuel, 26:183
Borgenicht, Louis, 46:255
Borgia, 23:49
Borgo, Pozzo di, 26:51
Borne, Karl Ludwig, 45:252
Borochov, B., 39:112
Borochov, Ber, 46:371; 49:84, *Nationalism and
  the class struggle*, 35:xxii
Borofsky, Samuel H., 46:83
Borovský, Karel Havlí ek, 50:103-4
Borowsky, Samuel J., 33:147
Borrenstein, David, *A bibliography of David
  Borrenstein*, 35:xx
Borres, Judith, 26:251
Bortman, Mark, 41:277, 287; art exhibit,
  42:417-19; Boston, meeting, 42:413;
  "Colonial Merchants: Moses Hayes and
  Michael Gratz and Their Newport
  Ventures," 46:493; curator, 47:200; 48:265;
  executive council, 42:414; 49:268;
  Hendrick's Collection, 49:62; "Paul
  Revere and His Jewish Correspondents,"
  42:415; "Paul Revere and Son and Their
  Jewish Correspondents," 43:199-229;
  treasurer, 43:230; 44:241; 45:264; 46:492
Bosis, Adolfo de, 28:24, 52, 57-61
Bosis, Arturo de, 28:59
Bosis, Bobi de, 28:59
Bosis, Charis de, 28:57

Bosis, Lilian Vernon de, 28:24-26, 55-61
Bosis, Manlio de, 28:59
Bosniak, Jacob, 34:xxvii
Bosqualo, Aaron, 21:117
Boss, Peter, 30:4, 6-7, 10
Boss, Widow, 27:441
Boston, 48:231, Board of Court House
   Commissioners, 22:229; "Boston in
   American Jewish History," 42:333-40; "A
   Chapter in the History of the Jews of
   Boston," 49:225; Civil War, 50:278, 389;
   Common Council, 22:229; discrimination,
   47:18; "Early Jewish Residents in
   Massachusetts," 23:vii, 79-90; "Early Jews
   in Boston," 29:153; "1854—Boston and Its
   Jews," 49:225; *Growth and Achievement,
   Temple Israel, 1854-1954*, reviewed,
   44:250-51; history, writing of, 46:185, 188,
   191-95, 293, 297, 415, 422; 49:226, 247;
   "The Impact of Immigration and
   Philanthropy Upon the Boston Jewish
   Community (1880-1914)," 46:71-85;
   49:225; "Jewish Education in Boston,"
   49:224; Jews in law and medicine, 22:149;
   "Philanthropy and the Rise of the Jewish
   Community of Boston, 1880-1914,"
   44:240; *Pioneers in Service: The History of the
   Associated Jewish Philanthropies of Boston*,
   reviewed, 47:59-60; religious observances,
   mid-nineteenth century, 37:36; school
   committee, 22:229
Boston Association of Ministers, 47:148
Boston Committee, 39:145
Boston *Courier*, 38:174
Boston *Daily Advertiser*, 26:184
Boston Dental College, 22:229
Boston Female Asylum, 27:418
Boston *Herald*, 42:339
Boston Home for Incurables, 22:229
Boston *News Letter*, 37:121
Boston *Pilot*, 46:294
Boston Provident Association, 46:73-74, 78
Boston Public Library, 30:vi; 34:265; 42:413,
   419; 45:206
Boston Sons of Liberty, 37:117
Boston Store, 38:20
Boston Theatre, 33:182-83, 191-93
Boston *Transcript*, 38:160; 43:23; 47:80
Bostonian Society, 45:270

Bostwick, Joseph P., 23:139
Boswell, James, 32:5; 46:434, 467
Bosworth, 31:123
Botany, 23:185
Bote, Der, 26:272
Botelho, Manuel Delmedo, 33:119
Botkin *v.* Miller, 25:134
Botkowsky, Moses, 44:190, 192
Bottigheimer, Ellis, 38:161, 165
Boucher, Jonathan, 46:21
Boucicault, Dion, 40:348-50
Boudin, Louis, 50:224-25
Boudinot, Elias, 22:xxxv, 184; 30:188; 38:49;
   39:186; "Jewish references in the will of
   Elias Boudinot," 33:xvii; "A Letter of
   David Franks to Elias Boudinot," 38:48;
   Star in the West, 30:162-63
Bouilly, Jean Nicolas, *Une Folie, Capt. Beldare*,
   33:191
Boulanger, Georges Ernest Jean Marie, 46:88
Boulions, Ferdinandes Rodrigus, 33:113
Bouquet, Henry, 35:7-9
Bourdages, 23:47-49
Bouret, 31:72
Bourges, Isacq, 33:65
Bourne, 31:106, 113
Bouton, J. W., 27:475
Bouvary, Mrs., 34:143
Bouvé, Clement L., 34:204, 245
Bouvet, Joachim, 49:44
Bowden, Donald Paul, 48:259
Bowder, 34:279
Bowdoin College, 45:23-24, 30
Bowen, Constant, 35:291
Bowen, James, 43:110
Bowen, John (Calif.), 31:147; (R.I.), 35:291
Bowen, Judge (Canada), 25:121-22
Bowers, Claude G., 50:180
Bowers, Claude M., 38:135
Bowler, Metcalf, 35:288-90; 37:108
Bowman, 31:106, 110-11, 113-14
Bowne, 22:77
Bowns & Brown, 31:164
Bowry, Richard, 23:158
Bowry, William, 23:158
Boxer Revolution, 31:212
Boxer, C. R., *The Dutch in Brazil, 1624-1654*,
   reviewed, 47:112-20, 209
Boyd, Esa, 34:46, 48

Boyd, General, 26:175-76, 193
Boyd, Judge, 25:104
Boyd, Julian P., 39:266; "The Function of State and Local Historical Societies with Respect to Manuscripts," 44:247
Boyd, Samuel, 27:242
Boyd, Stephen, 34:36
Boydell, John, 35:285
Boydell, Josiah, 35:284
Boyer, Rich and, 28:313
Boy Scouts of America, 33:31, 45:210, 47:230; gift, 33:xxxiii
Boysset, Charles, 41:161
Brackenridge, Colonel, 26:193
Brackenridge, H. M., 27:518; 30:258
Brackett, Miss, 25:56
Bradford, Mr., 38:281-82
Bradford, Joseph, 23:82; 29:153
Bradford, Col. William, 41:292
Bradford, William (Gov.), 39:452; 42:334; 43:197; 46:23-24, 180; "The Hebrew Words on the Tombstone of William Bradford," 22:xiii, 186-87; "The Hebrew Preface to Bradford's History of the Plymouth Plantation," 38:289-303, 346; "Hebrew Quotations in Bradford's 'Third Dialogue,' " 39:471
Bradford, William (printer), 30:v, 4, 6-7, 10; 42:82; 43:236-37; bookplates, 45:202
Bradford, William, Jr., 23:154
Bradlaugh, 31:113
Bradshaw, George, 28:231
Bradshaw, Samuel Alexander, 26:163; "A Tract for the Times, being a Plea for the Jews," 26:142
Bradstreet, 23:80
Bradstreet, Simon, 30:26
Brady, Matthew, 50:342
Braganza, 29:33
Bragg, Braxton, 38:27; 50:342
Braham (singer), 23:179
Braham, D. D. (newsman), 46:91
Braham, Horace, 35:270
Braid, Abm., 27:326
Brailsford, H. N., 34:223
Brainin, Reuben, 33:131, 147, 149-50, 152, 154; 39:98, 108, 441; 45:181, 208-9
Brampton, Gulielmo, 26:249
Bramson, Leonti, 40:403

Branch, John, 46:11, 15
Brandão, David, 33:77; 44:83
Brandão, Diego Dias, 33:65
Brandão, Gaspar Francisco, 33:77
Brandão, Jacob, 37:339-40
Brandão, Jacob Rodrigues, 29:36
Brandaun, Iael Rodrigues, 29:36
Brandeis (Omaha), 37:443
Brandeis, Adolf, 38:196
Brandeis, Alter, 24:14-15
Brandeis (dept. store), 38:20
Brandeis family, 38:195, 197
Brandeis, Louis D., 38:196; 39:111-12, 330, 346; *Brandeis: A Free Man's Life*, 50:345; Aaron Aaronsohn, 31:209-10; Ballinger-Pinchot Controversy, 47:187; "Brandeis and Scientific Management," 41:41-60; "Cardozo and Brandeis: Modern Sons of Liberty," 44:240; Cardozo appointment, 49:13; common law, 40:88-89; death, 37:xii; Hadassah, 49:167-68; history, writing of, 46:228, 273, 280, 435; Judah P. Benjamin, 38:170; Julian W. Mack, 37:476; Louis Dembitz Brandeis Centennial Medal, 46:492; "Mr. Justice Brandeis: A Law Clerk's View," 46:467-73, 492; and Oliver Wendell Holmes, 42:352-54, 357-58; scientific management, 41:310, 312, 319-20; Zionism, 40:113; 45:37; 46:62; 49:141, 191-93; 50:103, 119-20
Brandeis, Mrs., 46:470
Brandeis Hillel Foundation, 46:493
Brandeis University, 39:335; 45:171, 185; 47:233; Civil War, 50:262, 272, 274, 383, 396; "Judaica and Hebraica Collection in College Libraries," 45:147-48
Brandes (Zionism), 39:110
Brandes, Georg (Morris Cohen) (Danish critic), 35:256, 264
Brandes, G. S. (Westphalia), 32:119
Brandes, J. S. (Westphalia), 32:119
Brandeur, Esther, "Esther Brandeur, an Early Canadian Jewish Convert," 26:xv
Brandia, 23:177
Brandon, Abraham, 22:179; 26:251-52; 32:56
Brandon, Abraham R., 21:220; 27:79, 340
Brandon, Abraham Rodrigues, 26:251, 253; 41:285
Brandon, C. H., 29:19

Brandon, David, 22:179; 26:251
Brandon, David Perayra, 50:160
Brandon, E., 27:107
Brandon, Frederick M., 27:484
Brandon, I., 25:117
Brandon, Isaac, 27:107, 214
Brandon, Isaac B., 27:91
Brandon, Isaac L., 27:343
Brandon, Isaac Lopez, 26:251, 256
Brandon, Isaac Pereirs, 32:63
Brandon, J. L., 27:122
Brandon, Jacob Rodrigues, 21:121
Brandon, Levina, 27:122
Brandon, Levina Reyna Leah, 27:122
Brandon, Moses, 32:56
Brandon, Moses and Isaac, 27:245
Brandon, Pereira Esther, 32:61
Brandon, Pereira Isaac, 32:61
Brandon, Rachel, 27:111
Brandon, Rodrigo Arias, 33:100
Brandon, Ronald, "Fortiter et recte," 34:xxv;
    gift, 34:xxv
Brandon, Sarah, 27:338
Brandon, Sarah Esther, 27:340
Brandon, Stanley, 44:118
"Brandon the Jew," 25:73
Brann, M., 29:191
Brann, Marcus, 43:250; communication,
    22:xviii; gift, 25:xv; necrology of, 28:xxxii,
    261-65
Brannan, 26:193
Brannon, Peter A., 34:267
Brasch, H., 45:261
Brasher, Col., 27:391
Brashor, Isaac, 27:245
Brasilla, Samuel, 23:81
Braslau, Sophie, 48:202, 267; 49:70, 143
Brassavola, 28:189
Bratburd v. Bratburd, 29:149
Bratiano, M., 24:52, 65, 73, 132, 148
Brattel (Brattle), William, 22:22-23
Braude, Henry W., death, 37:xii
Braude, Joseph, 38:306
Braude, Markus, 40:403
Braudo, Vera S., 38:348
Braunstein, Baruch, 34:251
Brav, Ernest A., 29:157
Brav, Hanna, 29:156
Brav, Herman A., necrology of, 29:xiv, 156-
    57

Brav, Isaac, 29:156
Brav, Stanley R., 29:157; "Mississippi
    Incident," 49:227
Bravo, Abm., 27:245
Bravo, Alex, 25:117
Bravo, Alexander, 27:483
Bravo, Benjamin, 32:61, 63; 35:294-95
Bravo, Carlos (Charles), 25:117
Bravo, David, 32:61
Bravo, Sarah, 25:117
Braxton, Carter, 23:11, 176
Braynard, Frank O., "Copper for the
    Savannah of 1818," 48:170-76; 49:62
Brazil, 46:338; "The Classis of Pernambuco,"
    32:xiii; colonization, 39:98, 101, 309;
    Colonization Assn., 38:312; *The Dutch in
    Brazil, 1624-1654*, reviewed, 47:112-20,
    209; "The Exodus from Brazil and Arrival
    in New Amsterdam of the Jewish Pilgrim
    Fathers, 1654," 44:80-97, 255; 49:229;
    Hebrew literature, 22:117-20, 126;
    Inquisition, 33:70; 50:73; "Isaac de Castro,
    Brazilian Jewish Martyr," 47:63-75;
    "Jewish Soldiers in Dutch Brazil (1630-
    1654)," 46:40-50; Jews in, 29:39-42, 45-46,
    48; 31:4; 43:233-34; *Jews in Colonial Brazil*,
    reviewed, 50:73-76; "The Jews of Dutch
    Brazil," 29:xxix; "The Jews of Portugal and
    Brazil," 32:xx; Joseph Fels, 46:482; "The
    Members of the Brazilian Jewish
    Community (1648-1653)," 42:387-95, 416;
    slavery, 47:113-15; "A Study of Brazilian
    Jewish History 1623-1654, Based Chiefly
    Upon the Findings of the Late Samuel
    Oppenheim," 33:xxvi, 43-125; "The
    Synagogue and Cemetery of the Jewish
    Community in Recife, Brazil (1630-
    1654)," 43:127-32
Brazilay, Benjamin, 42:287-89
Brazos de Santiago, 46:103-4
Breakfast Prayer Clubs, 39:370
Bréal, Michel, 41:161
Breasted, James, 27:329
Breck, Samuel, 40:79
Breckenridge, Jew bill in Maryland, 32:xxviii
Breckinridge, Clifton R., 36:237, 240-44,
    247-52, 255-59; 39:69-72, 78-80, 84-85;
    41:172-73
Breckinridge, John C., 48:150; 50:321, 342

Bredero, Hendrik, 34:28, 40
Bredsted, John, 21:41
Breested & Co., 21:18, 24
Brego, Antho. Dias da, 33:113
Bregstone, B., "Chicago and its Jews," 34:xxiv
Bregy, F. Amedee, 31:275
Breier, Eduard, 35:120
Breitenbach, Juliana Regina von, 28:218
Breitschid, Rudolf, 46:95
Bremen, flag case, 36:372-73; Jewish
    emancipation, 26:35, 37, 41, 43-44, 48, 56,
    59-61, 64-65
Bremer, Fredrika, 39:340
Bremer, Joseph, 47:37
Bremer & Morawetz, 47:37
Brenner, Anita, 33:35
Brenner, I. D., 33:146
Brenner, Josephy Chayyim (Hayyim), 33:147,
    156; 49:140
Brenner, Victor D., 45:208; 50:383, 394
Brent, Robert, 48:9
Breslau, Aryeh Loeb, 34:112, "Is Haym
    Salomon Mentioned in the Responsa of
    Aryeh Loeb Ben Hayyim Breslau?,"
    33:251; Pene Aryeh, 35:xx
Breslau, Isadore, 47:203
Breslau Committee, 41:140-41
Breslau Seminary, 28:75-77, 262, 264;
    47:176; 50:88, 91-93
Breslau, University of, 28:72-73, 262; 29:128
Bresselau of Hamburg (Notary), 26:48, 90
Bresslau, Harry, 22:211; 36:357
Bressler, David M., 28:131; 34:199; death,
    37:xii
Brethren of Jacob, Fall River, 37:421
Brett, Catherine, 32:101, 104-6
Brett, Roger, 32:104
Brettschneider, Dr., 28:57-59
Brevard, 29:145
Brevis, J., 35:xxiii
Brevoort, Henry, 28:251; 34:252
Brewer, David J., 35:125
Brewer, Justice, 31:115-16; 34:220
Brewer, Mary, 22:23
Brewster, Mr., 27:391
Brewster, F. Carroll, 23:191; 28:266
Brewster, Judge, 22:99
Bricker, Eliezer, 35:57
Brickner, Balfour, 47:203

Brickner, Isaac M., 42:371
Brickner, Max, 40:70
Brickner, Samuel M., 42:371, 374
Brickner, Walter M., 32:xxviii
Brickner, Mrs. Walter M., 31:5-7; gift,
    31:xxxiv
Bridenbaugh, Carl, 39:183
Bridges, Charles, Exposition of the Book of
    Proverbs, 30:420
Bridges, John, 23:148
Bridges, Julia, 42:147
Bridgeport, Conn., religious observances,
    mid-nineteenth century, 37:36
Bridgetown, Jews in, 34:275-78
Brigham, Clarence S., 30:vi; 38:49
Brigham, Herbert O., 37:153, 163
Bril, I. L., 34:240
Brill, I., 41:233
Brill, Mrs. I. (Nissem), 41:233
Brill, Jechiel, 33:134
Brill, Jehiel, 45:70
Brill, Nathan E., 42:124
Brillant, 38:202
Brinerhof, Jores, 27:245
Brink, 31:124
Brinkerhoff family, 41:110
Brinkmann, Gustav, 26:52
Brinley, Francis, 35:291
Brinley, Jacob William, 27:79
Brinneque, Alexis, 23:139
Brinneque, Jean, 23:139
Brinsley, John, 32:24, 31
Brintnall, Captain, 39:190
Brion, Fredericka, 38:271
Brioschi, Mimi, 28:57
Brisbane, Arthur, 39:428
Brislow, Bruce, 37:438
Britenstool, Hirsch, 40:59
Brith Kodesh Temple (Rochester), 37:36;
    40:60, 63-65, 67-69, 71
B'rith Olam Temple (Rochester), 40:69
Brith Sholom Community Center
    (Bethlehem, Pa.), 37:320
Brith Sholom Congregation (Easton, Pa.),
    42:193-96, 216
British Archaeological Association, 49:68
British Board of Jewish Deputies, 49:188;
    refugees, 49:78
British and Continental Trade Union, 41:317

British and Foreign Bible Society, 26:116-17, 121-22, 124-25
British and German Synagogue, 23:179
British Institute of Industrial Art, 31:291
British Jewish Board of Guardians, 41:156
British Magazine, The, 25:111
British Museum, 25:114, 180; 26:242; 44:91, 96; 49:271
British Public Record Office, 25:128; 38:45
British Records Association, 49:68
British Royal Commission on Alien Immigration, 46:371
British Trade Union Movement, 46:231
British West Indies, "A List of Wills of Jews in the British West Indies, Proved Before 1800," 29:xxx; 32:55-64
Brito, Ferinand Dias de, 33:85
Brito, Francisco de, 33:73, 112
Brito, Isaac Hayyim Abendana de, 22:120-21
Britt, George, 34:251
Britto, Abigail de, 25:139
Britto, Joan Machado de, 33:116
Broadcast Music, Inc., 50:271
Broadhead, G. H., 32:109
Broad Tree Tunnel, 25:145
Broadway Shambles, 25:42
Broches, S., *in miten Tumel*, 35:xxi; "A Chapter in the History of the Jews of Boston," 49:225
Brockholst, Mary, 28:227
Brockman, C. A., *100 Years of Aurora Grata, 1808-1908*, 35:xxi
Brod, Max, 35:271; 50:103, 109, 112, 115-17, 120
Brodski, Abraham, 28:128
Brodski, I., 28:128
Brodsky, H., 44:165-66
Brodsky, H. J., 39:426-27
Brodsky, Louis B., 36:372-73
Brody, David, "American Jewry, the Refugees and Immigration Restriction, 1932-1942," 44:240; 45:219-47
Brody, Fannie M., 39:224; "The Hebrew Periodical Press in America, 1871-1931," 33:127-70
Brody, Mrs. Sol, 43:238
Broeck, Christina Ten, 31:241
Broglie, Maurice de, 26:71-72
Brokers, discrimination, 28:256

Brome, Richard, *The Jewish gentleman*, 33:171
Bromeis, Johann Conrad, 41:70
Bromet, J., 27:145
Bromo, Anto Louis, 33:114
Bromsen, Maury A., 42:90
Bronx Free Synagogue, 33:184
Bronx House, 37:323
Bronx Juvenile Service League, 37:323
Brook, Captain, 28:250
Brook Farm Settlement, 41:21
Brooke, Henry L., 27:506
Brooklyn, N.Y., 46:293, 440; religious observances, mid-nineteenth century, 37:37; Temple Israel, 22:200
Brooklyn College, 44:240
Brooklyn *Eagle*, 44:182
Brooklyn Federation of Jewish Charities, 22:200
Brooklyn Institute of Arts and Sciences, 25:162
Brooklyn Jewish Center, 37:323
Brooklyn Jewish Hospital, 47:229
Brooklyn Museum, 45:210
Brooklyn *Times*, 42:383
Brooklyn Young Men's Hebrew Union, 37:253
Brooks (Utah), 38:333
Brooks & Ball (Boston), 22:228
Brooks, David, 37:104, 107-8, 111
Brooks, Horace, 39:33, 35
Brooks, M., 29:132
Brooks, Walter, 34:219
Broome, Allen, 22:76
Broome, John, 38:127
Brotherhood Week, 46:294
Brothers, Richard, *A Revealed Knowledge of the Prophecies and Times*, 30:101-3, 106-11
Brotier, Gabriel, 49:41, 45-47
Brough, John, 50:293
Brougham, John, 40:348-50
Brougham, Lord Chancellor, 26:268; 31:123, 126-31; 34:228
Broughton, 31:110
Broughton, Samson Shelton, 23:148
Broughton, William, 37:167
Brouillet, Elizabeth McKenney, 45:54
Brouillet, Mary Louise, 45:56
Broun, Heywood, 34:251
Brown (N.Y. Central R.R.), 41:312

Brown, Adam, 50:314
Brown, A. G., 26:215
Brown, Aaron, death, 37:xii
Brown, Brockden, 39:140
Brown, Capt., 39:179
Brown, David (N.Y.), 23:148
Brown, David (Scotland), Palestine and Jews, 26:151-52
Brown, Dorothy Oskern, 50:391
Brown, E. B. M., 39:402
Brown, Esther, 23:148
Brown, Frances, 23:158
Brown, Francis, 29:164
Brown, Frederick, 23:66, 69
Brown, General, 26:175
Brown, George, 23:158
Brown, George T., 50:300
Brown, Gerard, 27:322
Brown, Governor, 25:23
Brown, Helena, 44:2
Brown, Isaac, 50:313
Brown, James Francis, 41:294
Brown, Jane, 27:322
Brown, Jason, 23:70
Brown, John (Harpers Ferry), 38:173; 42:110; 48:150; 50:285, 354; "Some Jewish Associates of John Brown," 23:vii, 55-78
Brown, Mrs. John Nicholas, 50:271-72, 275, 382, 387-88
Brown, John, Jr., 23:66, 70
Brown, John Carter, Library, 30:vi, 46:420
Brown, Joseph, 23:148
Brown, Joseph Emerson, 44:109
Brown, Josias, 23:148
Brown, Moses, 27:431
Brown, Noah, 48:172-73
Brown, Richard, 47:148
Brown, Robert, 23:161
Brown, Saul, 21:xv; 27:175-76; "Saul Brown, the First Hazan in North America, and Benjamin Wolf, the Third Recorded Hazan," 32:xix
Brown, Thomas, *History of Destruction of City and Temple of Jerusalem*, 30:232
Brown, William, *Antiquities of the Jews*, 30:208
Brown University, 22:164, 209; 31:296; 40:4; 49:11; 50:271-72, 391; "Jewish Elements in Brown's Early History," 37:xxx, 135-45;

"Judaica and Hebraica Collection in College Libraries," 45:144-45, 170
Browne, Chauncey, 35:184
Browne, Edward Benjamin Morris, 41:358-60
Browne, G. M., 34:210
Browne, Walter, 30:404
Brownel, Julian, 27:439
Brownel, Widow, 27:440
Browning, Orville Hickman, 42:408-11; 44:102-5
Browning, Mrs. Orville Hickman, 42:410
Browning, Robert, 38:268
Brownings, Elizabeth and Robert, 47:224
Brownlow, William Gannaway, 42:133, 144-45
Brownson, Orestes, 42:86
Bruce, Hubert, 35:270
Bruchado, Gonsalvo Dias, 33:114
Bruck, William W., 46:124
Brucker, W. M., 34:218
Brudno, Ezra S., 35:256-57
Bruenn, Bernard, necrology of, 26:xiv, 275-76
Bruenn, Zacharie, 26:275
Bruere, Robert, 46:470
Brugh, Peter, 42:417
Brugh, Sarah, 42:417
Bruhns, 26:99-100
Brüll, Adolf, 39:451; 45:107
Brumson, 27:79
Brunan family, 25:74
Bruner, Carl, 39:63
Brunn, Flora, 31:253
Brunner, Arnold W., 35:325; necrology of, 31:xxiii, 253-55
Brunner, Rudolph, 28:256
Brunner, Sebastian, 28:78
Bruno, Mathilde, 32:66
Brunschvigg, Léon, 35:260
Brunswick, Laurence, 43:238
Bruslé, Marie Aimee, 48:198
Brussels, International Jewish Conference, 28:132; 29:95, 109
Brussels Committee, 41:141
Brussels Conference of 1872, 24:25-29; 42:173-75; 45:68, 73, 80
Brussels Exhibition, 31:290
Brussels Monetary Conference, 40:333
Brussels, University of, 26:284
Bruyn, Edmund, 25:140-41; 35:307

Bryan, Dr., 39:178
Bryan, William Jennings, 29:174; 36:64-66; 40:333, 341; 41:300; 50:229; Isidor Raynor, 40:228; Oscar S. Straus, 40:14
Bryan, William Lowe, 48:260
Bryant, Captain, 27:354-57
Bryant, Insign, 40:187
Bryant, William, 35:184, 186
Bryant, William Cullen, 33:190; 41:32; 42:348; 43:78; A. S. W. Rosenbach, 42:457; Civil War, 50:389, 391
Bryce, James, 43:160
Brylantowski, Dr., 39:164
Bryt, Captain, 21:39
Buber, Martin, 40:195; 49:141; "Character Change and Social Experiment in Israel," 46:130; "The Human Path," 43:195
Buber, Salomon, 41:145
Bubonic plague, 28:161
Buchacher, Nahum, 33:161
Buchacher, Nathan, 33:166
Buchamp, Mr., 38:47
Buchanan, James, 22:89; David Yulee, 25:16, 20, 24, 27; Emanuel B. Hart, 32:110; Mortara Incident, 37:83; 42:152; Russo-American Treaty, 40:297, 299; 41:163-65; 50:332; Swiss disabilities, 36:302, 313-14
Bucharest, Peace Conference of 1913, 24:2, 92-93; "Secretary Hay's Roumanian Note of 1902 and the Peace Conference of Bucharest of 1913," 24:80-97; Treaty of, 36:349
Buchhalter, Judah, 44:136-38, 141, 155, 158, 160-61, 192
Buchheim, Dr., 45:126
Buchholz & Son, 50:306
Buchholz, Carl August, 26:37, 43, 47-49, 62, 84, 90, 95
Buchman, M., 40:238
Buchner, Adolph, 24:8-9
Buck, Pearl, 39:116
Buck's Stove and Range Co., 47:187
Buckingham, O., 25:77
Buckingham, William Alfred, 37:426
Buckland, Dr., 30:334
Buckland, W. W., 25:182
Buckle, 34:224
Buckle and Monypenny, 35:130, 238; 46:435
Buckle, William, 27:71

Buckmaster (N.Y.), 25:56
Buckmaster, Lord, 31:106, 112
Buckner, Simon Bolivar, 50:342
Budd, Thomas, 30:4, 6-7, 10
Budko, Joseph, 40:318, 320
Buduschnost, 38:242
Buel, 22:73, 75
Bueno, Abraham, 23:149; 33:95, 97
Bueno, Daniel, 26:251
Bueno, David de Daniel Baruh, 29:18
Bueno, John, 32:56
Bueno, Joseph, 23:83, 147-49; 27:39; 28:215; 31:81-83, 90, 93-95, 99, 101-2; 37:328
Bueno, Rachel, 23:149
Buffalo, N.Y., "The Buffalo Project: Writing the History of a Medium-Sized Community," 46:158-59; Civil War, 50:278, 407; history, writing of, 46:158-69, 178, 181, 190, 275; Jewish local history, 49:255-56, 258, 263; religious observances, mid-nineteenth century, 37:36; Y.M.H.A., 37:226
"Buffalo Bill," 43:32
Buffalo Bureau of Jewish Education, 46:163
Buffalo Evening News, 46:161
Buffalo Express, 41:185; 42:383
Buffalo Hebrew Sheltering Home, 46:163
Buffalo Historical Society, 46:161-62
Buffalo Jewish Review, 46:159
Buffalo (N.Y.) Museum, 48:100
Buffalo Patriot-Extra, 43:188
Buffalo Public Library, 46:161, 165
Buford, Colonel, 23:62, 63
Buhler, Kathryn, 43:1, 203
Bukeah, 26:151-52
Bulam Association, 40:126
Buley, R. Carlyle, 46:153
Bulfinch, Charles, 43:201
Bulgaria, 24:120, 122; Bucharest Peace Conference, 24:87, 91-93; civil rights, 24:105-7; "Congress of Berlin, 1878," 24:42, 53-62, 65, 68-71, 73-74, 78-79; disabilities, 29:97; history, writing of, 46:294-95, 308, 320, 324; "Jewish Disabilities in Balkans," 24:2
Bull, 28:175-76
Bull, Caleb, 37:103
Bull, Henry, 37:400
Bull, Joseph, 27:450

Bull, Lieut. Governor, 35:7
Bull Run, 50:324, 370, 381, 395
Bullestrate, 33:61, 97
Bulletin du Comité des Délégations Juives, 29:171
Bulletin of the New York Public Library, 26:242
Bullett, William F., 26:191
Bullimore, George, 35:11
Bullock, Captain, 26:190
Bulova, Joseph, 39:330
Bülow, Bernhard von, 24:35, 49, 51, 65, 121
Bulwer-Lytton, Edward George, 41:88
Bumstead, Thomas, 40:77
Bun, Solomon, 21:44-45, 55
Bunche, Ralph, 39:467
Bund, 39:101; 41:306-7; 42:322; 46:222, 266; Poland, 36:164
Bunker Hill Monument, 26:199-200
Bunker Hill National Monument Association, 43:216
Bunn, Rachel, 23:152
Bunn, Rosa, 31:241
Bunn, Rose, 23:152; 33:209-10
Bunn, Solomon, 23:152; 31:238; 33:210
Buntline, Mrs. Ned, 34:143
Bunzel, 38:197
Burckhard, Max, 35:288
Burd, F., 22:190
Burder, Samuel, *Oriental Customs*, 30:124
Burdoe, Theodore, 34:197
Bureau of Census, 39:229; 47:187; 48:65
Bureau of Corporations, 47:189
Bureau of Immigration and Naturalization, 47:191
Bureau of Indian Affairs, 47:190
Bureau of Jewish Education, 35:62; 42:28
Bureau of Jewish Social Research, 29:xlii, 171; 39:253; 46:163; 48:66
Bureau of Jewish Statistics, 25:161; 26:xxiv, xxvii
Bureau of Pay, Provisions and Clothing (Confederate), 50:332
Burg, A. S., 42:419
Burge, Thomas, 27:175
Burges, Abraham, 27:176
Burges, Miss, 22:40
Burges, R. F., 31:212
Burgess, George (trans.), *Psalms in English*, 30:350

Burgess, John W., 23:55, 70, 76
Burgh, Coenraet, 33:108, 110, 125
Burgos, Abao, 42:279, 393
Burgos, Abraham, 26:251; 27:245
Burgos, Dauid, 42:279
Burgos, Elias, 26:251; 33:97
Burgos, Irmiau, 29:11
Burgos, Isaac, 29:11
Burgos, Jacob de, 29:11
Burgos, Luna, 42:428
Burgos, Mrs. Lunah, 21:37
Burgos, Mordicay, 21:37; 32:56
Burgos, Rebecca, 26:251
Burgoyne, General, 31:44; 40:78
Burgunder, Joseph, 27:514
Burial ceremonies, 39:372-73, *Compendium of Order of Burial Service and Rules for Mourning, K. K. Shearith Israel*, 30:244-45; *Precipitate Burial Amongst the Jews*, 30:398
Burial grounds, 25:135; 29:150; Arlington National Cemetery, 28:54, 59-60; Baltimore, four early cemeteries, 32:xiii; Barbados, 37:327-28, 459-60; "Monumental Inscriptions of Barbados," 33:xxxii; 44:246; Beth-El Emeth Cemetery Association, Philadelphia, 28:269; B'nai Jeshurun, 27:270-71; Boston, 23:82-83; 42:336, 338; Brazil, 42:232, 262; 43:127-30; "The Burial Society at Curaçao in 1783," 22:xii; Charleston, S.C., 41:123; Cuming Street Cemetery, 26:192-93; Jewish cemetery, 31:xxxiii; Chatham Square Burial ground, 22:xxxiv; 26:220; 49:229; Curaçao, 22:xii; 26:240-41; customs at cemeteries, 39:372; early New York Jewish cemeteries, 27:265-78; Easton, Pa., 42:194; Eleventh Street Burying Ground, 21:190-92; *Epitaphs from the Jewish Cemetery in St. Thomas, W. I., 1837-1916. With an Index Compiled from Records in the Archives of the Jewish Community in Copenhagen*, reviewed, 48:138-39; "Four Early Jewish Cemeteries at Baltimore," 32:xiii; Gonzales, Texas, 34:xx; "The Hunt's Bay Jewish Cemetery, Kingston, Jamaica British West Indies," 37:xxx, 327-44; "Is the Cemetery in the New Bowery on the Site Granted by the Dutch in New York in 1656?," 29:xv; "The

Jewish Burial Ground on New Bowery, New York, Acquired in 1682, Not 1656," 31:vii, 77-103; Jewish cemeteries at New York, 22:162; "Monumental Inscriptions of Barbados," 33:xxxii, 44:246; Nevis, B.W.I., 25:149; New Bowery burial ground, 38:52; 40:409; 44:76; Newport, 22:xxxiii; 27:175, 191-210, 215, 413-15; 31:77; 34:173; 45:26-27; New York, 45:2; Oliver Street Cemetery, 27:46, 121-22, 162, 265-74, 278, 299-301, 305-7, 310, 312, 330, 340, 343, 372, 491; Philadelphia, 22:xxxii; 43:235-36; 45:31; 46:3; *Portraits Etched in Stone/ Early Jewish Settlers/ 1682-1831*, 42:425-34; *Precious Stones of the Jews of Curaçao: Curaçaon Jewry, 1656-1957*, reviewed, 47:176-78; Richmond, Va., 50:316; "The Revolutionary Soldier Buried in the Spruce Street Cemetery, Philadelphia, Pa.," 44:242; St. Thomas, W.I., 48:138-39; Salt Lake City, 49:240; Shearith Israel Congregation, 21:xii-xiii, 7-9, 30, 37-38, 65, 119-20, 145, 178-79, 185-93; Long Island cemetery, 27:121-22, 162, 267, 285, 493; "Threat to the Chatham Square Cemetery in the Eighteenth Century," 33:xvii; "Tombstones That Tell a Story: Charleston's Historic Coming Street Cemetery," 50:316; Twenty-first Street Cemetery, N. Y.," 27:120-22, 266-67, 275-78, 284, 493; vandalism, 42:427-28; "What We Learn from the Tombstones in the New Bowery Cemetery," 32:xiii; Woodsville, Miss., 34:xx
Burke, Edmund, 38:85, 91; 46:20-21, 231; 48:11
Burke, Emily, 31:6
Burke, J., 31:182
Burkhard, Andrew, 41:291
Burkhardt, Moses, gift, 35:xix
Burla, Jair, 50:402
Burleson, Edward, 46:107
Burling, Samuel, 23:153
Burling, Thomas, 27:320
Burlington Company, 23:19-20
Burlo, 39:178
Burmania, M. de, 35:215
Burnet (Barbados), 22:198

Burnet, William (Gov.), 23:150; 35:180; 42:76, 80
Burnett, Henry L., 34:194
Burnham, Viscount, 28:xviii
Burnham's Antique Bookshop, 45:212
Burnley, Albert T., 22:xxiii; 23:117-21
Burnley, William, 23:117-20
Burnside, Ambrose Everett, 38:37; 43:81; 48:10
Burnstein, Simon, 47:203
Burr, Aaron, 22:152; 26:221; 38:127
Burrall, Charles, 48:184-92
Burrall, Jonathan, 48:182-83, 189
Burras, George, 27:236
Burravik, I., "The witches," 34:xxiv
Burrill, Joseph, 35:291
Burrough, 35:30
Burroughs, Samuel, 37:168
Burrows, Lawrence, 23:153
Burstein, Simon, 44:178
Burton, 23:34
Burton, Clarence M., 40:84
Bury, John B., 26:14
Busbequius, 37:133
Busch, Ignaz, 38:202
Busch, Isidor, 26:273; 39:159; 45:103; 48:220; Alexander Kohut, 33:239-41; Austro-Hungary migration, 23:187-89; "On to America" movement, 38:186-87, 190-91, 194-96, 221-25, 228-31
Bush, 31:124
Bush, Mr., 34:83, 98
Bush, Abm., 27:245
Bush, George, 30:341; *Anastasis*, 30:399; *Grammar of the Hebrew Language*, 30:300, 332; *Notes on the Book of Genesis*, 30:344; *Questions and Notes Upon the Book of Exodus*, 30:278; *The Valley of Vision*, 30:382
Bush, I., 43:236
Bush, Isaac, 27:245
Bush, Isidor, 47:79-80; Judaica, 37:436, 442-43; Y. M. H. A., 37:263
Bush, Jay, 39:81
Bush, Lewis, 35:120; "Major Lewis Bush: A Correction," 38:346
Bush, Matthias, 21:58; 23:16; 25:113-14; 26:232-34, 236; 27:21; 33:207, 209; 43:235, 237
Bush, Moses, 25:113

Bush, Nathan, 23:175
Bush, Rebecca, 33:202, 207, 210
Bush, Richard, 35:291
Bush, Samuel, 23:175
Bush, Solomon, 27:462; 33:207; 35:120;
    50:39, 46; letter, 43:235; Non-Importation
    Agreement, 26:236; "Solomon Bush's
    Patriotic Action in London in 1789,"
    31:xvi; "Two Letters of Solomon Bush, a
    Revolutionary Soldier," 23:xiii, 177-78
Bushwick, 27:249
Busick, David, 27:335
Busick, Jonas, 27:335
Business Archives Council, 49:68
Business history, 46:210-14; see also:
    Economic history
Business, Jews in, 46:210-14, 237, 250-51,
    255, 379, 398-99
Business letters, records, 46:159, 422
Bustament, Anastasid, 39:12
Butchering, "The Question of the Kosher
    Meat Supply in New York in 1813: with a
    Sketch of Earlier Conditions," 25:vii, xii,
    31-62; kosher butchers, 49:246, 251
Bute, Piero La, 40:83
Buteau, 22:160
Butkowsky, Moses, 35:61; 44:136, 190, 192
Butler, 23:21
Butler, A., 22:190
Butler, Benjamin Franklin, 34:188; 39:1, 10,
    63, 65; 44:106; 49:23; Board of Delegates
    of American Israelites, 29:77, 79; exclusion
    of Jews, 29:117-28, 200; Isachar Zacharie,
    43:84, 87-90, 94; Lives and Opinions of Benj.
    Franklin Butler and Jesse Hoyt, 30:404;
    Myer S. Isaac correspondence, 29:117-28
Butler, Faith, 23:90
Butler, Gen. (Conn.), 39:179
Butler, Jere F., 50:233-34

Butler, John, 32:30
Butler, Nicholas Murray, 49:11; 50:399; "Dr.
    Nicholas Murray Butler on Columbia's
    Jewish Graduates," 37:435
Butler, Pierce, 25:1; 27:497; 28:235; 34:251;
    Judah P. Benjamin biography, 22:xxxi
Butler, William, 23:156
Butler, Mrs., 33:219
Butler (Pa.), Jewish Welfare Fund,
    contribution, 37:xxvii
Buttenwieser, Joseph L., 26:x, xxviii; 28:xx,
    xxxi; 29:xxvii, xxxiv; auditor, 28:xiii; 29:xii
Buttenwieser, L., 29:107
Buttenwieser, Moses, 40:36
Butter and Egg Man, The, 40:354
Butterfield, Margaret, 44:106
Butterworth, Judge, 43:94
Button, Stephen Decatur, 41:73
Butzel, Martin, 40:232-33; "The Palestine
    Colony in Michigan," 29:61-74
Buxbaum, Joseph, 41:259
Buzagale, Moses, 32:56
Byalik, Hayim N., 35:58
Byars, William Vincent, 25:113; 26:232-33;
    death, 37:xii; elected corresponding
    member, 25:ix; gifts, 26:xxxv; 28:xl; "The
    Gratz Papers," 23:vii, xiii, 1-23; 25:119;
    26:xxxiii; "Jacob Myers, a Type of
    American Enterprise," 25:xiv; "Two Great
    American Pioneers—Manuel Lisa and
    Joseph Simon," 22:xxix
Byrne, C. E., 42:454
Byrnes, Robert F., Antisemitism in Modern
    France: Vol I: The Prologue to the Dreyfus
    Affair, reviewed, 41:95-96
Byron, Admiral, 31:61
Byron, Lord George Gordon, 35:238; 37:210;
    41:283; La Profezia di Dante, 30:198
"By the Waters of Babylon," 45:256

C

Cabala, "A Cabalistic MS. from the Library of Judah Monis," 28:xv, 242-45
Cable, Robert, 42:419
Cabot, George, 43:216
Cabral, Isabella, 33:116
Cabral, Joan Pais, 33:116
Cabral, Louis de Mendosa, 33:116
Cadell, T., 37:199
Cadena, Jeronomo, 33:119
Cadet, Lyon, 41:93
Cadillac, Antoine de la Mothe, 40:81
Cadmis, Cornelius, 23:154
Cadmis, Mary, 23:154
Cadwalader, Thomas, 26:181
Caesar, F., 39:95
Caesar, Julius, 21:238; 28:135
Caesar's Column, 40:338, 340
Caetani, Duke of, 28:51-53
Cafiero, Mario J., 50:230
Cafritz, Morris, 47:203
Cahan, Abraham, 22:175; 38:247-48, 305; 44:144; 46:62; 46:127; "Abraham Cahan and the New York *Commercial Advertiser*: A Study in Acculturation," 43:10-36; *Daily Forward*, 40:100; 45:240; ethnic politics, 50:211-12, 215, 224; history, writing of, 46:222, 224; Jewish question, 41:211; 49:105; labor, 41:307, 330; 43:192
Cahen, Isidor, 29:84, 86
Cahen, Louis, 41:161
Cahen, M., 42:57; *Catechism of Religious and Moral Instruction*, 30:382
Cahensly movement, 46:284
Cahmachi, Code of, 24:116
Cahn, Mrs. Eli, 28:315
Cahn, F., 29:134
Cahn, Lazarus, 32:119
Cahnman, Werner J., 50:271
Cahoone and Yates, 37:168

Cahul, 36:102-4, 110
Cairo, 26:134; Genizah at, 25:183-85
Cairoli, 24:126, 144
Calado, 33:44
Calado, Manoel, 43:128
Calatayud, Juan Sanchez de, 31:235
Caldas, Alonso Alvarez de, 31:31
Calder, William F., 36:157
Caldwell, James, 27:376-78
Caldwell, John L., 36:18
Caleb, Isaac von, 39:126, 134
Calendar, "Early English Efforts for Reformation of the Hebrew Calendar," 32:xiii; "The Proposed Scripture Calendar," 32:23-24
Calender, Taylor, 28:xxxiv
Calhero, Antho. Correa, 33:114
Calhoun, John C., 22:83; 23:119; 25:22; 39:344; 41:31; 43:77; 45:56; 49:139
California, 25:23; 38:243; "A California Pioneer: The Letters of Bernhard Marks to Jacob Solis-Cohen (1853-1857)," 44:12-57; Civil War, 50:277, 280, 304, 404; Grand Lodge, Masons, gift, 26:xxxv; history, writing of, 46:189, 192, 290, 314; in 1854, 22:167-69; Jewish local history, 48:217; Land Act, 46:296; "Letters of a California Pioneer," 31:vii, xvii, 135-71; "References to Jews in Harris Newmark's 'Sixty Years in Southern California,'" 26:xiv; *A Report on the Jewish Population of San Francisco, Marin County and the Peninsula, 1959*, reviewed, 50:143-44; Sandlotters, 46:303; school issue, 46:296; slavery, 23:57; "Some California Pioneers," 26:xxxi
California Commission of Charities and Corrections, 29:180
California Hebrew and English Almanac, 30:452

California Historical Society, 42:423
California State Library, 45:149-51, 171
California, University of, 29:180-81, 195; at
  Berkeley, 34:153; 48:256, 259; "Judaica
  and Hebraica Collection in College
  Libraries," 45:143-44; at Los Angeles,
  48:256-57, 259
Calisch, Edward N., 34:249; "Moses Myers of
  Norfolk," 22:xiii; and Max J. Kohler,
  "Some Additional Notes on Judah P.
  Benjamin," 31:xvi
Calish, Meyer, 29:132
Calisher, H. J., 29:133
Calixtus III, 28:159
Call, George W., 25:23
Callender, 23:15
Callender, Robert, 30:71, 77
Calligraphy, 50:385
Callmus, Levi, 26:187
Calloway, Benjamin, 50:20
Calmet, 49:42
Calo, Mark, 21:161
Calo, Moses, 27:23, 26-27
Calonemos, Moses, 21:106
Calvares, Rabbi, 27:185
Calverly, Edmund, 27:175
Calvin, John, 28:90
Calvinists, 26:211-12; Jews in Holland,
  31:175
Calvo, 31:xxxv
Calvo, Abraham, 33:65
Calvo, Hisquiao Mordechay, 22:169-70;
  29:30
Camargo, Juan de, 23:131
Camartho, Luiz, 23:29
Cambden, Lord Chancellor, 25:119-20
Cambel, William, 27:245
Cambell, John, 50:182
Camble, John, 28:228
Cambreleng, Churchill Caldom, 22:80-81
Cambreleng, Stephen, 39:35
Cambreling, C. C., 30:404
Cambridge Historical Journal, 29:154
Cambridge University, 25:157, 182, 185;
  45:31
Camero, Ignatio de, 33:115
Cameron, Simon, 38:25, 36; 48:160, 165
"Cameron Dragoons," 39:177; 50:291, 307
Camerz, Captain, 27:366

Caminha, Alvaro de, 28:214
Caminha, Pedro da Costa, 33:118
Caminho, Antho. Ferdinano, 33:115
Cammeo, Joseph, 37:78
Camondo, A. de, 41:161
Camonha, Francisco Dandrado, 33:112
Camp, E., 29:133
Campa, Emiliano, 31:213
Campanal, 27:413
Campanal, Asher, 21:41, 46-47, 54, 57-58,
  69, 213; 31:237
Campanal family, 40:120
Campanal, Valentine, 21:4, 10, 15-17, 20, 23,
  26-28, 31, 213; 25:43; 31:237
Campanall, 34:8
Campanel, Rachel, 21:69, 89, 91, 93-95, 107,
  109
Campanell, Abraham, 27:176
Campanell, Daniell, 27:176
Campanell, David, 27:176
Campanell family, 42:335
Campanell, Mordecai, 27:175-77, 416, 444;
  "Note on Mordecai Campanell," 29:xxix
Campanero, Diego, 31:23
Camp Bauercrest, 50:431
Campbell (N.Y.), 22:79
Campbell, 28:252
Campbell, Alexander, 48:181, 192
Campbell, Captain, 35:8
Campbell family, 40:120
Campbell, General, 38:88-89
Campbell, John, 23:20-21, 23; "David
  Franks' Interest in Lands in Virginia, in
  1774," 25:119-20
Campbell, Lewis D., 32:73-80, 84-91
Campbell, Mrs. Patrick, 35:267-68
Campbell, Robert, 23:23
Campbell, Samuel, 49:50
Campbell, William, 41:119
Cample, Captain, 40:83
Camp Donor, 50:431
Campe, "Discovery of the New World,"
  22:125
Campenell, David, 23:83
Camp Ilee, 50:431
Camp Modin, 50:431, 434-35
Campo, Rodrigo del, 31:31
Componell, Asher, 23:149
Campos, Mr., 32:81

Campos, Abraham, 21:45
Campos, Abraham de, 29:22
Campos, Aron de, 29:23
Campos, Isaac, pereira of do, 21:23
Campos, Jacob de, 21:43
Campos, Mose, 29:36
Camren, Ann, 49:37
Canada, 26:133; 40:237, 239, 259, 311;
  47:174; "Adolphus Mordecai Hart, of
  Quebec," 25:xiii, 121-22; "The Ashers of
  Toronto," 26:xv; civil rights, 30:295-97;
  "Data on Samuel Jacobs, an Early
  Canadian Jewish Settler," 28:xxxiii; "Early
  Beginnings of Canadian Jewish History,"
  29:xxxvii; "An Early Jewish Merchant of
  Halifax," 25:xiii; "Esther Brandeur, an
  Early Canadian Jewish Convert," 26:xv;
  "The First Jewish Settler of Ottawa,
  Canada," 23:xiv; "Further Data on the
  Hart Family of Three Rivers, Quebec,"
  26:xv; Hart family, 34:xviii; "History of
  Jewish Immigration to Canada (1947-
  1957)," 47:202; "History of the Jews of
  Canada," 31:xxxiv; history, writing of,
  46:182, 192, 238, 274, 289, 326, 422, 425;
  "The Jews of Northern Ontario," 25:xiii;
  "The Levy Family of Canada," 25:xiii;
  "Newman L. Steiner, the First Jewish
  Justice of the Peace in Ontario," 26:xv;
  "Newspaper Comments on the Samuel
  Hart Case," 25:xiii; "The Nordheimers of
  Toronto," 26:xxxi; 100th anniversary of the
  emancipation of the Jews in Canada, 35:xxii;
  "Proceedings Relating to the Expulsion of
  Ezekiel Hart from the House of Assembly
  of Lower Canada," 23:xiv, 43-53; "The
  Rossin Brothers of Toronto, Canada,"
  28:xvi; "Samuel Gradische, an Eighteenth
  Century French Sutler," 25:xiii; "Samuel
  Jacobs, an Early Canadian Jewish
  Merchant," 23:xiv; "Some Aspects of the
  Historical Development of the Canadian
  Jewish Community," 50:121-42; suffrage,
  30:295-97; "A Suit at Law Involving the
  First Jewish Minister in Canada," 31:vii,
  xvii, 181-86; "Two Letters of Aron Hart of
  Three Rivers, 1775 and 1776," 26:257-58;
  "Unpublished Canadian State Papers
  Relating to Benjamin Hart," 23:vii, 137-

40; "Unpublished Documents dealing with
  'the Petition of Certain Israelites of the
  City of Montreal for the Benefit of Public
  Register to Record Births, Deaths,
  Marriages, etc.,' " 28:xvi; "An Unpublished
  Document in the Case of Thomas Coffin
  against Ezekiel Hart, of Three Rivers,
  Province of Quebec," 28:xvi; "An
  Unpublished Letter of Aron Ezekiel Hart,"
  26:xv, 256-57; "Unpublished Reference in
  the Canadian State Papers to Benjamin and
  Samuel B. Hart," 23:xiv; "When did David
  S. Franks Last Leave Canada?," 31:234
Canadian Historical Association, 48:69
Canadian Jewish Archives, 50:125
Canadian Jewish Congress, 50:125, 139-41;
  gifts, 34:xxv; 35:xxiii; resolutions honoring,
  49:265-67, 269
Canadian Jewish History, 49:267, 269-70
Canadian Marine & Commercial Company,
  28:270
Canadian Pacific Railroad, 41:46; 50:128
Canadian Zionists, 28:270
Canby, Edward Richard Sprigg, 43:92
Canchess, Izaque, 42:280, 393
Candelabra, "Two Unknown Historic
  Candelabra from K. K. Beth Elohim of
  Charleston," 23:xiii, 186-87; see also:
  Menorrah
Cane, 40:79
Caneiro de Morais, Francisco, 33:112
Canfield, S. A. Martha, 33:213
Cannibal's Progress, The, 38:120
Cannon, Mary, 23:152
Canon, John, 21:18
Canqui family, 25:74
Cantacuzène, Prince, 36:236-37; 41:171-72
Cantara, Christopher, 37:403
Cantarini, Hayyim Moses (Angelo) ben Isaiah
  Azriel, 28:203
Cantarini, Isaac Hayyim (Vito), 28:203
Cantarini, Judah (Leon) ben Samuel (Simon)
  ha-Kohen, 28:203
Cantarini, Kalonymus Aaron (Clement) ben
  Samuel (Simon) ha-Kohen, 28:203
Canter, David, 27:87, 91, 120
Canter, Hannah, 27:278
Canter, Jacob, 50:41, 47
Canter, Joshua, 27:278, 315

Canterbury, Council of, 28:144
Cantine, Moses I., 30:404
Cantor, 41:4
Cantor, Bernard, 39:334
Cantor, Jacob A., 40:158
Cantor, Reuben, 50:166
Canty & Solomons, 50:41
Canunha, Manuel Rodrigus, 33:117
Capadoce, Aaron, 32:20
Capadoce, Abraham, 32:20
Capadosen, George, 27:30-31
Cape Cod, "The Earliest Jewish Settlers,"
   42:415
Capedose, A. E., 35:xx
Capes, William, 28:89
Caplan, Chayyim, 33:159
Caplan, Isaac, "Rabbi Isaac Caplan
   Collection," 45:163
Capodistrias, Count, 26:51-52, 82, 117
Capon, Charles B., 45:206
Carabajal family, 44:124
Caracas Conference, 44:71
Caradja, John, 24:116
Carathéodory Pasha, 24:58, 60-61, 64
Caravajal, Ana de, 31:30
Caravajal, Baltasar Rodriguez, 31:26
Caravajal, Francisca Nuñez de, 31:26-30
Caravajal, Luis de, 31:27; *Process de Luis
   Caravajal*, 35:xxi
Carb, David, 35:257
Cardazo, Abraham, 32:64
Cardosa, Isaac, 28:199
Cardose, Maniel Rodrigus, 33:47
Cardoso, Dauid, 42:278, 393
Cardoso, Ishac, 47:70-73
Cardoso, Jacob Uziel, 29:15
Cardoso, Michael, 33:66; 50:76
Cardoso, Mose, 37:417
Cardoso, Moses Jesurun, 28:239; 37:335
Cardoso, Sebastian, 32:117
Cardoso, Simeon, 42:279, 393
Cardoza, Aaron, 21:61
Cardoza, Abraham, 27:42
Cardoza, Daniel, 33:77
Cardoza, David N., 50:66
Cardoza, Jacob, 21:47-48
Cardoza, the Jew, 25:74
Cardoza, Moses, 27:42
Cardoze family, 42:108, 214; 48:139

Cardoze, Moise, 44:234
Cardozo, Aaron, 27:151
Cardozo, Aaron N., 50:63, 66
Cardozo, Aboab, 22:171
Cardozo, Abraham H., 26:230
Cardozo, Abraham Rodrigues, 37:419
Cardozo, Adeline, 27:110
Cardozo, Aharon Uziel, 29:15
Cardozo, Albert, 21:215; 27:166, 394
Cardozo, Albert (father, Benjamin N.
   Cardozo), 49:5-6
Cardozo, Albert II, 49:7
Cardozo, Albert Jacob, "A New York
   Election Circular in Hebrew of 1867,"
   34:285-88
Cardozo, Benjamin Nathan, 34:285; 37:203,
   435; 39:346; 40:88-90; 41:310; 42:358;
   46:435, 470; 49:62; 50:177; "Cardozo and
   Brandeis: Modern Sons of Liberty,"
   44:240; "Justice Benjamin Nathan
   Cardozo: His Life and Character," 48:266;
   49:5-15; "Law and Literature," gift,
   33:xxix, xxxii-xxxiii; necrology of Francis
   Déak Pollak, 26:xiv, 286-88
Cardozo, D. A. Jessurun, 42:467; 43:254;
   44:255; book review by, 42:435-41;
   "Growth of the New Sephardic
   Communities in the United States,"
   38:344; "Haym Salomon's Address in the
   Synagogue," 38:344; "The Second
   Immigration of Sephardim to America,"
   44:242
Cardozo, Daniel Aboab, 44:230
Cardozo, Daniel Costa, 29:16
Cardozo, David, 48:12
Cardozo, David Aboab, 44:227
Cardozo, David N., 27:496
Cardozo, David Uziel, 44:228
Cardozo, Elias, 27:151
Cardozo, Eliau Aboab, 42:278, 393
Cardozo, Elizabeth, 49:7
Cardozo, Ellen, 27:111
Cardozo, Ellen (Sister, Benjamin N.), 49:7
Cardozo, Emily, 49:5, 7
Cardozo family, 34:xviii; 35:xviii; 50:253
Cardozo, Francis Lewis, Sr., 50:177-80, 188
Cardozo, Grace, 49:7
Cardozo, Hetty, 27:110
Cardozo, I. N., 21:171

Cardozo, Isaac, 50:177
Cardozo, Isaac N. (N.Y.), 27:120, 253
Cardozo, Isaac N. (Charleston), *Discourse*,
  30:243
Cardozo, Isaac Yeshurun, 37:335
Cardozo, Jacob, 27:245
Cardozo, Jacob de Danl Ahoab, 22:169-70;
  29:30
Cardozo, Jacob N., 32:40; 50:177, 193; *Notes
  on Political Economy*, 30:240; *Oration*,
  30:145
Cardozo, Jehosua, 29:16
Cardozo, Judith, 27:110
Cardozo, Lavinia Abigail, 27:110
Cardozo, Michael H., 21:171, 214
Cardozo, Michael H. (Atty.), 26:230
Cardozo, Moses Jessurun, 23:28
Cardozo, Moses N., 50:164, 182
Cardozo, Mrs. (Savannah), 48:13
Cardozo, Rebecca, 49:5, 7
Cardozo, Salamao, 42:279, 393
Cardozo, Sarah, 27:110
Cardozo, Sarah (Peixotto), 26:230
Cardozo, Thomas Y., 50:179-80, 188
Cardozo, W. Warrick, 50:188
Cardozo, Zipporah, 27:110
Cardozo and Nathan, 49:56
Care, Henry, 32:30
Carey, Henry C., 46:404
Carey, Matthew, 35:285, 287; 46:404
Carey and Hart, 41:88
Carigal, Haim Isaac, 21:115, 22:127-28;
  32:57; 42:342-43; 43:143; 46:431
Carigal, Raphael Haim Ishac, 26:251; 44:223-
  25, 234-36; will, 31:242-43
Carillo, Ana, 23:132
Carillo, Antonio, 23:131-32
Carillo, Gaspar, 23:132
Carillo, Maria Barbara, 23:132
Carillon, Benjamin Cohen, 23:180-82;
  Refutation of Address on Christianity, 23:182;
  Refutation of An Affectionate Address, 30:420;
  " 'The Refutation' of Rabbi B. C. Carillon,
  Jamaica, 1847," 26:xv; *Sermon*, 30:399
Carlebach, S., 26:47-48, 53, 64
Carleton, Guy, 31:234; 38:89; 40:84
Carlisle, Earl of, 23:26; 31:47, 60
Carlotta, 32:68
Carlsbad Conference, 26:89

Carlyle, Thomas, 28:xxxiv; 32:3; 33:17;
  43:238; history, writing of, 46:426, 433-34;
  "Thomas Carlyle and His American
  Publisher, Abraham Hart," 26:xxxi
Carmoly, Eliakim, 28:102; 29:19; *History of
  Jewish Physicians*, 30:399
Carnegie, Andrew, 40:9; 46:437
Carnegie Foundation, 46:301; 50:119
Carnegie Institution of Washington, 22:xxiii;
  23:91, 103; 34:18; gifts, 33:xxxiii; 34:xxvii
Carnegie Museum of Pittsburgh, 48:258
Carnero, Antho. Viera, 33:113
Caro, Georg, 26:15, 25; 35:130; "Gabriel von
  Salamanka," 22:xiii; necrology, 22:xvii,
  211-13
Caro, Joseph, 28:68; 44:197
Caro, Moses, 28:243
Carolina, 26:205; "An Attempted Jewish
  Land Company in Colonial Carolina,"
  44:242
Caron, M., 23:49
Carpeles, Joseph, 34:110, 112-13, 115
Carpeles, Philip, 47:56
Carpeles, Wolf, 34:110, 112
Carpels, Johanan, 48:24
Carpenter, John, 23:158
Carpenter's Hall, 28:xxxix
Carpentier, James S., 29:168
Carpentier, Servatius, 33:121, 123
Carpi, Moses, 28:190
Carr, Caleb, 27:175
Carr, George, 39:65
Carr, Robert, 37:167
Carregal, David, 31:242
Carregal, Hori, 31:242
Carrington, Joseph M., 27:506
Carrion, Alvaro de, 31:30
Carrol, Joseph, 25:116
Carroll, Charles, 31:xxxiii; 46:39, 271
Carroll, John (Bishop), 46:270, 283
Carroll, Thos., 37:449
Carron, Abra, 32:56
Carruth, Jemeima, 22:23-24
Carson, Gerald, 46:167
Carson, Kit, 39:345
Carter, James, 35:291
Carter, Robert, 35:291
Carter, Samuel Powhatan, 38:28-29, 39
Carteret, 29:137

Carteret Book Club, 29:183
Carthagena, Inquisition of, 29:23-25
Carthew, Elizabeth, 23:151
Cartier, George, 23:46, 139
Cartwright, Major, 31:114
Cartwright, Peter, 38:320
Caruallo, Abm., 27:245
Caruthers, William Alexander, 38:331
Carvajal, Antonio Fernandez, 42:437
Carvajal, Lina, 31:4
Carvalho (Baltimore), 48:210
Carvalho (N.Y.), 27:79
Carvalho (teacher), 34:124, 132, 135
Carvalho, Abraham Baruh, 29:22
Carvalho, Antho., 33:113
Carvalho, Clara, 26:255
Carvalho, Daniel Hisquiya, 37:338
Carvalho, David (Jamaica), 32:61; 37:335
Carvalho, David (Philadelphia), 27:464
Carvalho, David N., 23:144
Carvalho, Domingo, 33:115
Carvalho, Emanual Nunez, 21:161-64;
    22:129; 26:252; 27:314, 337; 30:iv; 39:299;
    42:53; 48:72; data on, 27:463-64; *Funeral
    Sermon*, 30:164-65; Gershom M. Seixas
    eulogized, 27:263, 519, 521; *Key to Hebrew
    Tongue*, 30:157, 159-60
Carvalho, Isaac, 32:61
Carvalho, Jan Fernando, 33:112
Carvalho, Jules, 29:84
Carvalho, Julia N., 23:145
Carvalho, Ladesma Da, 32:61
Carvalho, Manoel Lopes da, 22:180-82
Carvalho, Moses Gomes, Jr., 29:19
Carvalho, Pedro, 33:118
Carvalho, Ribca, 29:22
Carvalho, Ribca Nunes, 29:28
Carvalho, Samuel, 32:61
Carvalho, Sarah N., 23:145
Carvalho, Sebastiao, 33:81, 118
Carvalho, Sijmon, 33:118
Carvalho, Solomon Nunes, 23:142-43, 146;
    27:463; 32:40; Civil War, 50:262, 383;
    *Incidents of Travel and Adventures in the Far
    West*, 44:66
Carvalho de Bento Roz, Diago, 33:112
Carvalle, Jacob, 32:56
Carvallo, Abraham, 32:57
Carvallo, Margaret, 32:57
Carvallo, Rachel, 32:57
Carvallo, Rachel Nunez, 32:56
Cary, Mr., 35:203
Caryl, Joseph, 32:30
Casanowicz, Immanuel Moses, 33:21
Casas, Bartolomé de las, 28:35; 38:11
Case, Harold C. "A Cultural Pattern for a
    Better America," 42:413
Caseres, Sarah Gomes de Caseres, 21:34
Caskie, John S., 27:506
Caspe, Abram, 50:237
Casres, Gomes Isaac, 32:61
Casres, Samuel, 27:245
Cass, Lewis, 26:215; 29:90; 36:301, 306-14,
    316-19; 38:166; 43:77
Cassado, Francisco, 33:112
Cassard, Jacques, 42:108, 215
Casse, Germain, 41:161
Cassel, B., *Keidan*, 35:xxi
Cassel, Ernst, 47:165-66, 168-70, 172-74
Cassel, Selig, 28:182; *Juden*, 26:12
Casseres, Benjamin de, 44:227
Casseres, Danl de Dd. Gomez, 22:170
Casseres, Daniel Gomes, 44:229
Casseres, Daniel Gomez, 44:233
Casseres, Dauid Cohen, 42:278, 393
Casseres, Jacob Gomes, 44:230
Casseres, Josiau Ydanha de, 25:138
Casseres, Mosseh de, 22:170, 172; 44:232
Casseres, Samuel de, 22:171
Casseres, Saul Ydanha de, 25:138
Casseres, Semuel de, 44:227, 233
Casseres, Semuel Idanha de, 22:169-70;
    29:30; 44:227-28
Casserez, Josiao de, 44:222
Casserez, Josiao Idanha de, 27:23
Casserez, Saul, 27:23
Casserez, Semuel Idanha de, 25:138
Casserly, Eugene, 41:37
Casserly, Senator, 24:11
Cassuto, Alfonso, "Autos-de-fe Celebrated by
    the Mexican Inquisition, 1648," 32:117;
    "Items from the Old Minute Book of the
    Sephardic Congregation, of Hamburg,
    Relating to the Jews of Barbados," 32:114-
    16; "Material relating to the Mexican
    Inquisition, and the Jews of Barbados,"
    32:xx

Cassuto, J., "Brief Extracts from the Minutes of the Sephardic Congregation of Hamburg (around 1660)," 22:xxix; "Extracts From the Minute-Book of the Portuguese-Jewish Congregation of Hamburg," 23:182-83

Cassuto, Umberto, 26:24; *I Manoscritti Palatini Ebraici*, 35:xxii

Castanha, Gabriel, 33:65; 44:83

Castanha, Hester, 26:251

Castanho, Isaac, 33:55

Castanho, Isaque, 42:278, 393

Castel, Daui, 42:279, 393

Castel-Bianco, Joao Rodrigo de (Amatus Lusitanus), 28:163-65, 172-73, 188, 199

Castelar, Emilio, 33:36-38

Castella, David Nines, 32:57

Castella, Judith, 32:57

Castella, Sarah, 32:56

Castelli, David, 37:93

Castelli, Guiseppe, 28:184

Castello (Rhode Island), 37:402, 405-6

Castello, David (Barbados), 32:56

Castello, David (N.Y.), 34:280

Castello, David Nunes, 26:251

Castello, Elias N., 27:51

Castello, Julia, 27:110

Castello, Moses (Barbados), 32:56

Castello, Moses (N.Y.), 27:57

Castello, Moses N., 27:51

Castello, Rachel, 27:112

Castelnau, General, 32:78

Castilho, 32:10

Castille soap, 27:446

Castillero; United States v., 38:154

Castillo, Edmund, 34:280

Castillo, Severo, 32:96; 47:52

Castle, Curtis H., 36:254

Castle, William R., 35:257

Castle Garden, 40:226, 230

Castlereagh, Viscount, 26:38, 50, 70, 76, 79-80, 82, 124

Castor, 26:167, 169

Castra, Hananel De, 26:251

Castro, *The Portuguese Jews in Amsterdam*, 31:xxxiii

Castro, Abraham de, 47:65

Castro, Abm. Mendes (N.Y.), 21:48

Castro, Abraham Mendes de (Curaçao), 29:29

Castro, Adah de, 44:119

Castro, Alexander de, 50:148

Castro, Benjamin, 27:51, 59

Castro, Daniel, 21:28-29, 31, 33, 41, 43-44, 48, 53, 55, 63

Castro, Daniel Mendes de, 27:245

Castro, David de, 44:119

Castro, David de Mosseh de, 22:170

Castro, de, family, 28:217

Castro, Henry, "Castroville and Henry Castro," 34:xxvii

Castro, Isaac de, 33:96; 50:73; "Isaac de Castro, Brazilian Jewish Martyr," 47:63-75

Castro, Isaac Mendez, 21:48

Castro, Jacob de (Jamaica), 32:61; 37:335

Castro, Jacob de (N.Y.), 21:53, 55, 63; 22:170

Castro, Jacob de (St. Thomas), 50:148

Castro, Jacob de Mosseh de, 44:233-34

Castro, Jacob Osorio de, 23:181

Castro, Lea Mendes de, 29:19

Castro, Morris Fedanque de, 44:119

Castro, Moses Nahamias d', 33:65

Castro, Rachel de, 37:335

Castro, Salomon de, 22:170

Castro, Selomoh de Mosseh de, 44:233

Castro, Sol de, 27:79

Caswell, Governor, 29:143

Caswell-Massey Co., Ltd. (New York), 50:272

Catalog of the Alfred Whital Stern Collection of Lincolniana in the Library of Congress, 50:404

Catalog of the Exhibit of the Civil War Centennial Jewish Historical Commission, 50:277

Catalog of the Exhibit of the Lincoln Sesquicentennial Association of California displayed at the Los Angeles County Museum, 50:404

Catalog of the United States Information Service, Lincoln Exhibition held in Israel, 1959-1960, 50:404

Catarina, 33:87

Cathcart, Lord, 26:124-25

Cather, Willa, 46:127

Catherine of Aragon, 28:170

Catherine of Russia, 39:31

Catherine II, 28:101; 36:194-95, 200, 203; 41:169

Catherine Market, 25:37
Catherwood, 33:24
Catholic Church, 24:55, 58, 72; 34:228, 230;
    50:100, 102; abduction of Edgar Mortara,
    29:77-78; 48:224-25; Anti-Catholicism,
    40:329, 342; Bible study, 26:116; "Cardinal
    Gibbons and His Attitude Toward Jewish
    Problems," 31:vii, 219-24; *The Dutch in
    Brazil, 1624-1654*, reviewed, 47:112-20,
    209; "Hernando Alonso, a Jewish
    Conquistador with Cortes in Mexico,"
    31:xxix, 2-4, 8-31; history, writing of,
    46:213, 242, 246, 250, 264, 268-73, 277,
    279, 282-84, 286-88, 293-95, 315-16, 329,
    404-5, 407, 414, 416, 425; Inquisition,
    33:25, 34, 40-41; "Isaac de Castro,
    Brazilian Jewish Martyr," 47:63-75; Jewish
    historiography, 26:26-27, 31; "Jewish
    Physicians in Italy: Their Relation to the
    Papal and Italian States," 28:xxiii, 133-211;
    Jews and Protestants in Brazil, 33:68-76,
    81, 102; *Jews in Colonial Brazil*, reviewed,
    50:73-76; *Latin America and the Palestine
    Problem*, reviewed, 48:136-37; "Material
    relating to the Inquisition, and the Jews of
    Barbados," 32:xx; North Carolina, 29:140;
    Polish-American Organizations, 39:149,
    162-64
Catholic Sisters of St. Joseph, 33:232
Catholic Sisters of Saint Vincent de Paul
    Hospital, 50:333
Catilo, David Espinoza, 22:123
Catskills, 39:96, 383
Catt, Carrie Chapman, 34:219
Cattahoula Parish, 48:84-85
Catton, Bruce, 50:399
Cattaue, Baron, 47:97
Caumels, Père, 44:115
Causon, Inquisition in France, 32:xxvii-xxviii
Cavarillon, B., 34:128
Cave, Stephen, 47:87
Cavelgantij, Antho, 33:115
Cavelgantij, Manuel, 33:119
Cavillo, E. N., 27:45
Cavis, Curtis Carroll, 38:331
Cavour, Camillo Benso, 28:13
Cavour, Count, 29:127
Cayenne, 22:126-27; 32:15-20; Sephardic
    Jews, 29:19-20

Caylus, Anne Claude Phillippe de Tubiéres
    de, 41:61
Cazalet, Edward, 26:161-63
Cazenovia, New York, assessments, list of,
    25:112
Cazeres, Antonio Dias de, 31:31
Cazeres, Leonor de, 31:31
Cazerez, Samuel de, 23:27
Cazes family, 28:194
Cazot, Jules, 41:161
Cecil, Lord David, 46:434
Cecil, Robert, 36:78-79
Cecord, Petter, 27:245
*Celebrated Case of Fitz John Porter: An
    American Dreyfus Affair, The*, 50:398
Celler, Emanuel, 34:191; 45:227-28, 237;
    "Caleb Cushing and the Proposed
    Readmission of the Jews," 31:xvi
Celsus, 28:136
Cemeteries, *see*: Burial grounds
Ceniselli circus, 36:208
Centennial Exposition, Ohio Valley, 37:451;
    Philadelphia, 1876, 28:297
Center of Research in Entrepreneurial
    History, 46:211
Centinel, The, 22:79
Central Board of Jewish Education, 35:62;
    42:11
Central Bureau for the Settlement of German
    Jews, 49:169
Central Commission of the Israelites of
    Belgium, 26:284
Central Conference of American Rabbis,
    25:152; 28:275; 29:181; 31:252, 270;
    39:253, 259, 296, 453-54, 456, 461-63,
    467; 40:37, 201, 364-66, 368-69, 371, 383-
    84, 390-94; 41:350-61, 367; 42:7, 102, 104;
    45:146, 191, 266-67; 46:276; 47:221;
    50:118; Year Book, 31:xxxiv
Central Islip State Hospital, 34:215
Central Jewish Consistory of France, 46:96
Central Jewish Institute, 28:287
Central-Organ, 38:190-91
Central Park Improvement Company, 32:133
Central Polish Committee (New York),
    39:154-56, 158, 161
Central Relief Committee, 40:312; 49:87-88
Central Synagogue, New York City, 45:199
Century Club (New York), 47:14

Century Magazine, The, 40:335; 45:251, 255
Cera, David, 42:279
Ceshinsky, Binah, 45:162, 174
Chagall, Marc, 40:319-30; 42:433
Chajes, Hirsch Perez, 33:244
Chajes-Preisstiftung, Dr. H. P., 34:304
Chajes, Saul, Theasaurus pseudonymorum,
    34:xxv
Chaldaea, 47:164, 166
Chaloner, John, 27:450
Chaloner, Walter, 35:290-92; 40:75
Chamberlain (London), 31:107
Chamberlain, Daniel H., 50:178
Chamberlain, Henry Cardinal, 28:180
Chamberlain, Houston Stewart, 34:243;
    46:309
Chamberlain, Joseph, 47:166
Chamberlain, Joseph P., 36:369
Chamberlin, 37:133
Chamberlin, Culver P., 39:66
Chamber Music Society (Prague), 50:106
Chambers, Jacob, 25:140
Chambers, Judge, 25:101, 104
Chambrum, Adolphe de, 43:112
Chamosa, Steven Rodrigus, 33:118
Champlin, Christopher, 27:428-29
Champlin, Mrs., 27:245
Champion, Elijah, 37:107; 38:151
Chandler, Howard P., 36:136
Chandler, Lewis Stuyvesant, 50:229-30
Chandler, Walter M., 24:83; "The Jews of
    Roumania and the Treaty of Berlin,"
    24:114-37
Chandler, William E., 39:50
Channcy, Charles, 22:179
Channing, Mr., 35:302
Channing, Edward, 39:287; 49:255
Channing, John, 37:415; 40:75
Channing, Walter, 27:453-54
Channing, William Ellery, 35:202; 37:17;
    38:273-74, 281; 42:344
Chanute, Octave, 25:146
Chapel of Emmanuel, 47:152
Chapin, Howard M., 40:75
Chaplaincies, 29:103-4; 39:265, 437; 40:54;
    42:454; 44:252; 49:22, 138; 50:290;
    bookplates, 45:214-15; chaplaincy rights,
    42:140; Civil War, 38:243, 345; 41:214-15;
    47:194; "The Diary of Chaplain Michael

M. Allen, September 1861," 38:347;
    39:177-82; Isaac M. Wise, 40:186, 41:358,
    360; "Question of Equality: The
    Chaplaincy of Controversy," 50:291;
    Spanish American War, 41:357-58, 360-
    65, 371-72, 376; World War II, 47:231
Chapman, 43:19
Chapman, George, Eastward Hoe, 33:171
Chapman, Guy, 45:258
Chapman, Maria, 50:176
Chapman, Nathan, 31-34
Chapman, Reuben, 50:192
Chapters of Isaac the Scribe, 30:61
Charakteristik/ Abraham Lincolns/ Dargestellt
    in einer/ Trauerpredigt. Gehalten am 19.
    April 1865, von/ Jonas Bondi/ in the
    Synagogue der Gemeinde Poel Zedek,/ Ecke
    29. Street and 8th Avenue,/ New York,/
    50:301
Chardin, Daniel, 28:249-50
Chardin, John, 28:249-50
Chardin, Lady, 28:250
Charif, L., 33:161, 166
Charif (rabbi), 38:308
Charitable Burial Society (Boston), 46:81
Charity Organization Society, 46:166
Charlap, Abraham Hymon, 33:143
Charles, King of Roumania, 22:133; 24:2, 13-
    15, 17, 22, 75, 127, 145; "Congress of
    Berlin, 1878," 24:74-75
Charles, King of Spain, 22:111, 116
Charles, Prince of Roumania, 29:93; 36:100-
    101, 116-17; 45:73
Charles I, Duke of Mantua, 28:193
Charles II, 25:111; 27:487; 31:117-19, 121;
    47:119; 50:128
Charles II, King of England, 29:137; 34:237;
    45:52
Charles II, Duke of Mantua, 28:194
Charles III, 27:471
Charles IV, 28:169
Charles V, 31:13, 174
Charles VI (France), 21:240
Charles VIII, 28:162
Charles of Anjou, 28:206
Charles, Archduke, 27:487
Charleston, S. C., 22:154; 26:185, 188-90,
    233, 252, 254; 48:209, 216-17, 234, 241;
    Bicentennial Committee, 40:398; Burial

Ground, 41:123; Civil War, 50:279, 285-
87, 332, 334, 383, 407; Colonial
congregations, 28:xxvi; Cuming Street
Cemetery, 26:192; De Costa burial
ground, 26:193; early Jews, 25:131;
Hebrew literature, 22:128-29; *The Hebrew
Orphan Society of Charleston, S. C.,
Founded 1801: An Historical Sketch*, 49:238; history,
writing of, 46:156, 177, 185, 270-71, 273,
387, 424, 428, 440; *Hymns for Beth Elohim
Congregation*, 30:366; *Introduction to Reform
Judaism at Charleston, S. C.*, 31:xxxiv;
Jewish Cemetery, 31:xxxiii; "The Jewish
Community of Charleston, S. C., 1750-
1950," 39:471; Jewish Congregation,
25:50; 26:193; and George Washington,
22:xxxi; "Jewish Education in Charleston,
South Carolina, During the Eighteenth
and Nineteenth Centuries," 42:43-70;
"Jewish Education in Charleston, South
Carolina, During the Eighteenth and
Nineteenth Centuries," 49:239; "Jewish
Education in Charleston, S. C., 1750-
1950," 39:471; Jewish history, 39:253-54,
269, 272, 291-92, 344; Jewish local history,
49:260; *The Jews of Charleston: A History of
an American Jewish Community*, 49:237-38;
"Joseph Tobias of Charles Town:
'Linguister,' " 49:33-38; "Records of the
Western Synagogue, 1761-1832," 33:xxxii;
Reformed Society of Israelites, 30:238-39,
243, 268; religious observances, mid-
nineteenth century, 37:35; *Service and
Miscellaneous Prayers Adopted by Reformed
Society of Israelites*, 30:268; "Two Unknown
Historic Candelabra from K. K. Beth
Elohim of Charleston, S. C.," 23:xiii, 186-
87
Charleston College, 40:215
Charleston *Courier*, 32:44
Charlotte, Princess, 26:252; 27:401
Charlotte, Queen, 27:392
Charlotte Temple, 33:180
Charlottesville, Va., religious observances,
mid-nineteenth century, 37:38
Charlton, Mrs., 23:177
Charmes, Gabriel, 38:278
Charsky, Jenny, 45:195
Charter of Privileges (Pennsylvania), 40:97

Chase, 26:252
Chase, Edward M., death, 37:xii
Chase, Ham Alexander, 22:180
Chase, Major, 25:23
Chase, Salmon P., 38:174; 41:27; 43:90-91,
108
Chatard, F. E., 43:74
Chatard, Pierre, 43:74
Chateaubriand, 40:283
Chatham Burial Ground, 22:xxxiv; 26:220;
*Portraits Etched in Stone/ Early Jewish
Settlers/ 1682-1831*, 42:425-34
Chatterton, Thomas, 35:230-31
Chauncy, Charles, 35:151; 47:149
Chautauqua movement, 46:145
Chauves, I., 27:51
Chavas, Abraham, 21:114-15, 213
Chaves, Aron de, 27:245; 44:229
Chaves, Daniel, 27:55
Chaves, Diogo Fernandes, 29:10-11
Chaves, Jeosuah de, 27:245
Chaves, Manoel Nunes, 29:10, 12, 22
Chaves, Mosseh de, 44:228, 230
Chaves, Sarah, 27:245
Chaves, Simon Rodriguez, 29:11
Chavez, Abraham de, 44:227, 230
Chavias *v.* Chavias, 29:151
Cheating Cheaters, 40:354
Cheavitean, 25:3
Chebrah Kahl Adath Kurland, 25:135
Chee, Lee, 34:202
Cheeseborough, John, 48:183
Cheeseman, Samuel, 27:71
Cheesman, John C., 39:34
Cheetham, James, 25:36
Cheefetz, Asa, 47:182
Chemistry, "A Sketch of the Life of David
Lindo," 23:vii, 37-41
Chemists' Club of New York, 22:225
Cherokee Indians, 22:173-74; 23:22; 35:7
Cherrwaud, 27:344
Cherry, Louis I., 50:229
Cherry Street Synagogue, Philadelphia,
42:403
Chertoff, Mordecai, 49:270
Chertok *v.* Chertok, 29:153; 31:xxxiv
Chesapeake & Delaware Ship Canal, 25:146
Chesnutt, Josephine, 34:267-68
Chess, "The Rice Gambit," 25:176

Chess, Checkers and Whist Club, New Orleans, 26:276
Chesterfield, Philip Dormer Stanhope, *Economic della Vita Umana*, 30:232-33
Chesterfield colony, 38:315
Chestnut, James, 50:332
Chestnut Street Theatre, Philadelphia, 33:184, 186, 192, 194-96
Chevra Bikur Cholim, Milwaukee, 47:45
Chevras Nashim Gemilus Chesed, Milwaukee, 47:45
Chev Sholom Congregation (Harrisburg, Pa.), 41:373
Chiang Kai-shek, 44:127
Chicago, Board of Education, 29:187; "Chicago and its Jews," 34:xxiv; *The Chicago Pinkas*, 49:220; Civil War, 50:277, 302, 346, 351, 391, 396, 407; "A Contribution to the History of the Israelites in Chicago," 44:242; Ezekiel statue, 28:35; history, writing of, 46:159, 240, 393, 365, 388, 411, 415, 435; International Exposition, 26:2; 33:21; 39:397; "The Jewish Historical Society of Illinois," 28:xv, 239-41; Jewish local history, 49:243, 246-47, 260; "A Priceless Heritage: The Epic Growth of Nineteenth Century Chicago Jewry," 49:221; religious observances, mid-nineteenth century, 37:36; Socialist Convention, 50:217; "The Yiddish Schools in Chicago," 49:221; "Zionism Comes to Chicago," 49:221
Chicago Camping Association, 50:432
Chicago Conference for Youth, 50:432
Chicago Federation of Synagogues, 29:157
Chicago Hebrew Alliance, 22:210
Chicago Hebrew Institute, 29:157; 37:300; 42:12
Chicago Historical Society, 28:240; Civil War, 50:272, 274, 293, 378, 380
"Chicago Jewish Forum, The," 39:289
Chicago Record-Herald, 41:185
Chicago, Rock Island and Pacific Railroad, 41:50
Chicago Theological College, 50:70
Chicago Tribune, 42:135; 44:102; 47:15
Chicago, University of, 37:476; 40:51, 101; 45:163; 47:22; 49:11
Chicago Woman's Club, 29:159

"Chicago World," 39:397
Chichkine, 39:68-70, 72
"Chief Rabbis of England, The," 22:200, 203
Chiel, Arthur A., 50:271; "Early Jewish Adventures in Canada," 49:270
Child, David Lee, 42:151
Child, Lydia Maria, 42:132, 150-51; "Mrs. Child's Visit to a New York Synagogue in 1841," 38:173-84
Child Adoption Committee, 39:334
Childers, Erskine, 35:36
Childers, H. C. E., 35:36
Childers, Rowlanda, 35:37
Child Labor Association, 28:307
Children of the Ghetto, 40:346
Children of Israel Congregation (Des Moines), 47:208; (Augusta), 46:191
Children's Aid Society (N.Y.), 40:164
Childs, Cromwell, 35:292
Childs, Ozro W., 46:124
"Child's History of the United States, A," 26:280
China, 34:227; 50:13; Board of Delegates of American Israelites, 29:88; "Chinese Influence in Seventeenth Century Jewish Silver," 44:8-11; history, writing of, 46:285, 292, 296-97, 299, 310, 320, 323; Jews in, 29:191; "The Simson-Hirsch Letter to the Chinese Jews, 1795," 49:39-52
Chinese Benevolent Association, 34:196
Chinese Exclusion Act, 34:165, 195-98, 203; 46:310, 333
Chinillo, Azarias, 31:235
Chinillo, Noha, 31:235
Chipkin, Israel S., 35:xviii
Chipman, J. Logan, 36:233
Chipp, Charles W., 25:141
Chippewa, Battle of, 26:182
Chippewa Indians, 23:33, 35
Chishin, Abraham, 43:67
Chisolm, Edward, notice of insult, 32:116
Chisuk Emunah Congregation (Columbus, Indiana), 37:33
Chizuk Amunah Congregation (Baltimore), 29:178; 31:281
Choate, Joseph H., 33:221; 36:127
Cholwell, John, 23:149
Chomsky, Samuel, 42:420

Chovevé Zion, 26:154, 163-64
Chovis, 27:60
Christ, "Moses Jacob Ezekiel," 28:xxii, 1-62
Christian Advocate, 39:138
Christian, Alexander, 49:39-52
Christian Index, 33:234
Christian, Prince, 26:159
Christian IV, King of Denmark, 28:213, 217
Christian VI, 46:10
Christian Ticket (Maryland), 50:20-21
Christian Turkey Persecution, 24:40
Christianity, 39:364; 41:16-19, 21-23; 50:102, 115; "An Affectionate Address, to the Jews of Jamaica on the Great Subject of Christianity," 23:182; Brazil, 33:56-58, 60, 62-63, 69-75, 92; "A Catechism of the Christian Religion," 34:xvii; "The Classis of Pernambuco," 32:xiii; and disabilities, 49:23; "The Doctrine that 'Christianity is a Part of the Common Law,' and its Recent Judicial Overthrow in England, with Particular Reference to Jewish Rights," 31:vii, xvi, 103-34; "An Early American Hebrew-Christian Agricultural Colony" (note), 22:19, 184-86; Ernest Renan, 37:24; *The Grounds of Christianity Examined*, 30:149; "The Hebraic Background of Puritanism," 47:140-53, 200; history, writing of, 46:139, 183, 193, 213, 268-72, 281-82, 297, 382, 405-6, 423, 425, 442, 444; Jewish relationship, 39:239; *Jews in Colonial Brazil*, reviewed, 50:73-76; and Jews in Palestine, 36:47; missionaries, 40:5, 108, 286; National Soldiers Organization, 47:79; *New-England's Spirit of Persecution*, 30:4, 6-7, 10; *Niles' Weekly Register*, 50:5-7, 20; Palestine, claims of Jews for, 36:42; Persian Jews, converts to, 36:11-18; religious freedom, 26:34; Russia and Jewish education, 35:39-51; "Some Final Words on Emma Lazarus," 39:321-27; United States Constitution, 29:104
Christus: A Mystery, 40:182-83; 45:25
Christmas, Lee, 31:213
Christmas and Hanukkah, 39:365-66; 49:163
Christy, Ensign, 35:16
Chrysler's Farm, 26:176
Chrysostom, St. John, 28:137
Chu, Lau, 34:202

Chuck, Zvi Elhanan, 44:136, 140, 146, 161-62, 177
Chumaceiro, Chief Rabbi, 26:241
Chumaceiro, Jacob Mendes, 42:441
Chumaceiro, Joseph H. M., 42:65-66
Church, J., Jr., 50:389
Church, John Hubbard, *The Jewish Polity Overturned*, 30:136
Church, William C., 39:326
Church and State, 39:263; Christianity in the Constitution, 29:104; *Cornerstones of Religious Freedom in America*, reviewed, 40:96-98; Debates in the Jewish Community of 1848, 43:196; history, writing of, 46:138, 198, 272, 405-6; Maryland, 29:105; New Mexico, 37:443; North Carolina, 29:105; Reconstruction Act of 1866, 29:105; "Religious and Cultural Phases of American Jewish History," 39:291-301; Sabato Morais on, 37:65-67, 70, 72; "Unequal Religious Rights in Maryland Since 1776," 25:vii, 93-107
Churchill, Charles Henry, 26:141
Churchill, E. F., 31:118-19
Churchill, Winston, 40:117, 213, 394; 42:73; 44:72
Churchman, Roberts & Co., 31:137
Church of England, 26:131
Church of Scotland, 22:172; 26:134
Churgin, Pinchas, 33:131, 161
Chwolson, Daniel, 34:150; 45:102
Ciano, Galeazzo, 36:386-87
Cibber, Colley, 35:229
Cibot, Pierre-Martial, 49:42, 47-48
Cicero, 28:135
Cigar factories, 46:395; 48:46-47, 51, 124
Cijwin Camps, 50:431
Cincinnati, 47:34; 48:212; Academy of Medicine, 23:112; "Dr. Abraham Bettmann, a Pioneer Physician of Cincinnati," 23:vii, 105-16; Bene Israel Congregation, 25:150; 50:278, 293-95, 310, 329, 389, 393, 407; "Isaac M. Wise on the Jewish Community of Cincinnati in 1872," 37:xxxii; Jewish Welfare Fund, contribution, 37:xxvii; Keren Ami, contribution, 37:xxviii; religious

observances, mid-nineteenth century, 37:35
Cincinnati Art Academy, 28:31
Cincinnati Art Museum, 28:28, 31
Cincinnati Charter Commission, 29:161
Cincinnati City Planning Commission, 28:284
Cincinnati Commercial, 40:184
Cincinnati Enquirer, 39:462
Cincinnati General Hospital, 28:290
Cincinnati Independent, 34:143
Cincinnati Post, 39:462
Cincinnati, University of, 25:151; 28:274; 40:26
Cincinnati Zion College, 49:17
Circumcision, 37:39-44, "A Letter and Memorandum on Ritual Circumcision, 1772," 44:58-63; "The Mohelim of Curaçao and Surinam, and Other Notes," 25:xiii, 138-41; records of by Abraham I. Abrahams, 27:150-56; "Records of a West Indian Mohel," 25:114; rites, 39:369
Cisco, John J., 39:34
Citizen's Bank (N.Y.), 48:124
Citizens' Union, New York, 26:288; 28:307
City and Suburban Homes Company, 28:308
City Club (New York), 26:287
City College of New York, 49:25; "Judaica and Hebraica Collection in College Libraries," 45:142-43
City Gazette of Charleston, 21:229
Civic Forum, New York City, 28:308
Civil rights, 26:6; 34:165, 186, 220-33; 36:119; 38:1-6, 21; Board of Delegates of American Israelites, 49:18-19, 29, 32; "Board of Delegates on Civil and Religious Rights," 48:143-44; Brazil, 33:60; Brussels Conference, 1872, 24:25-29; "Civil Liberties and the Jewish Tradition in Early America," 46:20-39; Claims of Jews to an Equality of Rights, 30:355-56; Conference of Israelites, 24:102-5; "The Congress of Aix-la-Chapelle," 26:82-94; "Congress of Berlin, 1878," 24:40-79; "The Doctrine that 'Christianity is a Part of the Common Law,' and its Recent Judicial Overthrow in England, with Particular Reference to Jewish Rights," 31:vii, xvi, 103-34; "Educational Reforms in Europe in Their

Relation to Jewish Emancipation, 1778-1919," 28:83-132; English Colonies, 49:35; "The First Settlement of the Jews in Newport," 34:1-10; Germany, U.S. intercession, 36:348-85; history, writing of, 46:286, 293; "The Influence of Lewis Way and Other English Missionaries upon Alexander I's Treatment of the Jews," 26:116-25; Italy, U.S. intercession, 36:386-88; "Jewish Rights at the Congresses of Vienna (1814-1815), and Aix-la-Chapelle (1818)," 26:vii, xv, 33-125; John Quincy Adams and Joseph Hume (note on), 22:177-78; Maryland, Bill Respecting Civil Rights and Religious Privileges, 30:216; "Memorandum on the Treaty Rights of the Jews of Roumania," 24:137-53; Morocco, U.S. intercession, 36:19-41; New Netherlands, 21:175-81; "Hon. Oscar S. Straus' Memoranda Preceding Dispatch of the Hay Roumanian Note," 24:108-14; Palestine, U.S. intercession, 36:42-95; Paris Conference 1876, 24:29-39; Persia, U.S. intercession, 36:11-18; "Petition of the Roumanian Jews to the Chamber of Deputies, 1872," 24:98-101; Poland, U.S. intercession, 36:140-67, 389-402; "Regarding the Draft of a System of Legislation for the Jews, July 17, 1809, by Wilhelm von Humboldt," 26:103-15; Rumania, U.S. intercession, 36:6, 99-139; Russia, U.S. intercession, 36:171-295, 389-402; "Satow on Capo d'Istrias," 29:154; "Secretary Hay's Roumanian Note of 1902 and the Peace Conference of Bucharest of 1913," 24:80-97; "Social Discrimination Against Jews in America, 1830-1930," 47:1-33; Speech on Confirmatory Act Abolishing Religious Test, 30:227; Serbia, 36:6; Switzerland, U.S. intercession, 36:299-322; Turkey, U.S. intercession, 36:3-10; "Unequal Religious Rights in Maryland Since 1776," 25:vii, 93-107; U.S. diplomatic intercession in Austria, 36:323-47; Germany, 36:348-85; Italy, 36:386-88; Morocco, 36:19-41; Palestine, 36:42-95; Persia, 36:11-18; Poland, 36:140-67, 389-402; Rumania, 36:99-139; Russia, 36:171-295, 389-402; Switzerland, 36:299-322;

Turkey, 36:3-10; "Unpublished Canadian State Papers Relating to Benjamin Hart," 23:vii, 137-40; "Wilhelm von Humboldt's Relations to the Jews," 26:95-103; William H. Taft, 28:xxxvii

Civil War, 26:7, 194, 230, 248; 28:2, 294; 29:64; 38:243; 39:152-53, 236, 341, 345; 40:191, 282; 49:154-55; 50:263-408; *American Jewry and the Civil War*, reviewed, 41:214-15; Board of Delegates of American Israelites, 29:79; bonds, 31:188-89; Centennial Jewish Historical Commission, 49:137-39, 154-55, 279; Cherry Street Synagogue, 43:236; *The Civil War: Volume I, The American Iliad as Told by Those Who Lived It*, 50:401; *The Civil War: Volume II, The Picture Chronicle of the Events, Leaders, and Battlefields of the War*, 50:401; Civil War Centennial Jewish Historical Commission, 49:137-39; 50:260, 263, 267-68, 270, 405-6; "Civil War in Yiddish Literature," 50:402-3; "The Civil War: The Resurgent Interest of Collectors and Writers," 50:427; Correspondence Between Myer S. Isaacs and Gen. B. F. Butler, 29:117-28; David L. Yulee, 25:23-28; "The Diary of Chaplain Michael M. Allen, September, 1861," 39:177-82; "Divided Loyalties in 1861: The Decision of Major Alfred Mordecai," 48:147-69, 266; Evidence of Business Discrimination in the Civil War Period," 38:342; "From Peddler to Regimental Commander in Two Years: the Civil War Career of Major Louis A. Gratz," 38:2-44, 345; "Henry Mosler, Pictorial Interpreter of the Civil War," 41:389; history, writing of, 46:162, 271, 274, 290, 437; "Isachar Zacharie: Lincoln's Chiropodist," 43:71-126; "Jewish Chaplains during the Civil War," 38:345; Jews in, 29:123, 205; "Jews and Negro Slavery in the Old South, 1789-1865," 50:151-201, 426; Judah P. Benjamin, 38:153-71; "Leopold Karpeles: Civil War Hero," 49:268; "The Lincoln-Hart Correspondence," 38:139-45; Memorial Monument (Salem Fields Cemetery), 50:313; "Services rendered by the

Seligmans, Rothschilds and August Belmont to the United States during the Civil War and the 'seventies," 33:xxv; Simon Wolf, 29:200-201; "Some Jewish Associates of John Brown," 23:vii, 55-78; "Something Additional on General Grant's Order Number 11," 40:184-86

Civil War Centennial Jewish Historical Commission, 50:427

Claiborne, Ala. religious observances, mid-nineteenth century, 37:36

Clancarty, 26:39, 50, 72, 79

Clapp, G. C. & Co., 50:389

Clapp, Moses E., 24:83

Clapp Mission, 40:118

Clara colony, 39:91-92

Clara de Hirsch Home for Working Girls, 29:179; 40:6

Clara de Hirsch School for Girls, 31:227

Clara, Isabel, 31:30

Clarendon, Lord, 24:151; 26:140, 151; 36:310

Clark (N.Y.), 27:391

Clark (newsman), 32:91

Clark, Alonzo Howard, necrology of, 28:xxii, 265-66

Clark, Champ, 41:184

Clark, Charles, 50:336

Clark, Chief Justice, 29:152

Clark, Daniel, 42:143

Clark, George Rogers, 23:12, 21

Clark, James F., 37:163

Clark, Jane Perry, 34:251

Clark, John Bates, 37:471

Clark, Thomas C., 38:1, 3

Clark, Thomas D., 46:210

Clark, William Bell, 47:203

Clark University, 23:95

Clarke, Adam, 30:145; *Compendium on the History of the Jews*, 30:243; *Short History of the Ancient Israelites*, 30:145

Clarke, Jeremiah, 35:291

Clarke, John (Newport), 27:453

Clarke, John (N.Y.), 25:78

Clarke, John H., 26:282

Clarke, Joseph, 27:451

Clarke, L. H., *Report of Trial, Miller vs. Noah*, 30:208-9

Clarke, Mary, 25:78

Clarke, Nathaniel, 35:291

Clarke, Robert Boucher, 26:254
Clarke, Samuel, 23:158
Clarke, Thomas (Barbados), 22:178
Clarke, Thomas, Palestine and Jews, 26:151-52
Clarke, Walter, 27:175
Clarke, Weston, 27:175
Clarkson, 23:18
Clarkson, Matthew (1), 23:159
Clarkson, Matthew (2), 23:174
Clatworthy, John, 34:270
Claude, Anne, 41:61
Claus, Friar, 45:25
Clava, Benjamin Moses, 26:232-34
Clava, Jesaia de, 29:36
Clava, Semuel, 29:36
Clavai, Moses, 25:113
Clay, C. C., Jr., 50:318
Clay, Cassius M., 36:172; 41:166
Clay, Edward, 22:183; 29:141
Clay, Henrietta, 33:3-5; gift, 33:xxix
Clay, Henry, 22:96; 23:124; 25:26, 28; 26:185; 27:495; 28:42; 36:300; 38:166; 43:76; 46:2-3, 9, 13; 49:139
Clay, Mrs. Henry, 25:26
Clay, Thomas Hart, 33:3
Clay, Mrs. Thomas Henry, 29:53-54; 39:466
Clay, Virginia, 25:19, 26
Claypool, David C., 27:228
Clayton Act of 1914, 41:328
Clayton, Daniel, 50:164
Cleanliness, Washington and Mosaic Law, 39:319-20
Clearwater, Alphonso T., "Notes on Jewish silversmiths at the time of the Revolution," 31:xxiv
Clemenceau, Georges E. B., 34:223; 36:165-67; 45:259; 46:89, 96
Clement V, 21:241
Clement VI, 21:241; 28:148
Clement VII, 28:168-70, 192-93, 195
Clement VIII, 28:179-80, 193; 31:174
Clement IX, 28:184
Clement XIV, 37:360
Clement XXIV, 28:186
Clement v. De Rose, 25:135
Clements, William L., Library, 30:vi
Clench, Robert, 30:63
Clerk, Lord Vere Beau, 49:33-34

Clerks Aid Society, 37:46
Clermont, 48:172
Cletherall, James, 50:162
Cleva, Moses, 34:87
Cleveland (Miss.), Consolidated Joint Drive, contribution, 37:xxviii
Cleveland (Ohio), 47:34; 49:257; Civil War, 50:266, 278, 309, 376, 387, 391; "The Inner Life of the Jewish Community," 49:233; Jewish local history, 49:264; "The Relation of Jewish and General Institutional Development," 49:233; religious observances, mid-nineteenth century, 37:36
Cleveland Conference (1855), 45:94; 48:224; 49:17
Cleveland Convention, 45:37-38
Cleveland, Grover, 25:146; 31:272, 295; 36:263, 323, 341, 344-45; 39:71; 40:5, 7-9, 289, 332; 41:179; 48:127; 49:133-34; history, writing of, 46:165, 333, 438
Cleveland Hebrew Observer, 42:383-84
Cleveland Hebrew School and Institute, 33:160
Cleveland, Henry Russell, 45:24
Cleveland Jewish Orphan Asylum, gift, 34:xxii
Cleveland Leader, 42:383
Cleveland, Mrs. (actress), 33:182
Cleveland Orphan Asylum, 29:187
Cleven, E. C., 39:83
C. Levy & Co., 31:164
Clift, John, 48:181
Clingman, Thomas L., 50:295, 357
Clinton, DeWitt, 22:72-74, 76, 79; 25:33, 52, 56, 141; 27:69, 158, 338; 34:133; "A Slave Proclamation of De Witt Clinton," 25:xiii
Clinton, George, 21:xix, 141, 143, 184; 23:152; 27:xvii, 32-35, 245; 35:186; 41:111
Clinton, Henry, 28:253-54; 31:44; 38:98; 45:55
"Clinton Thespians," 33:175
Cloaks & Suits Operators' Union, New York, gift, 35:xxiii
"Cloisters, The," 40:182-83
Clopper, Catherine, 27:28, 39, 71
Clopper, Cornelius, 21:17, 299-300
Clopper, Cornelius, Jr., 27:28-29, 39, 71
Clossy, Samuel, 28:226

Cloth and Clothing, 40:70
Clothiers Association, 40:70
Clothing Industry, 40:61-62, 65, 67; 49:75,
   78, 95; history, writing of, 46:171, 219,
   223, 227-32, 236, 241, 248, 255, 257, 395
Cluckston, Samuel, 27:245
Clyde, William P., 33:221
Coan, Elias, 29:146
Coats, Commodore, 27:357
Cobb, Captain, 36:26, 28
Cobb, Howell, 50:319-20
Cobb, James, *House to be sold*, 33:174, 189
Cobbett, William, 38:121, 129-30
Coblens, Estate of Pauline Einhorn, gift,
   35:xx
Cochran, 35:8
Cochran, Philip, 27:71
Cochran, Thomas C., 46:192; "Business
   History in the Social Sciences," 46:210-14
Cochran, W. C., 39:449
Cockburn, 26:191
Cockran, William Bourke, 45:44
Cocks, Herrocks, 26:153
Coddington, David V. S., 39:62-63, 65
Coddington, J. I., 30:404
Coddington, Jonathan D., 39:34
Coddington, William, 27:175
Cody, William, 43:32
Coelho, Andre, 33:114
Coelho, David Jesurun, 42:279, 392-93
Coelho, David Ysurum, 42:285
Coelho, Duarte de Albuquerque, 46:40
Coen, Jacob, 42:287
Coenraad, Barend, 48:24
Coenraetsen, Hans, 26:247
Coffee, Mr., 23:74
Coffee, Rudolph, 40:371
Coffin, Colonel (Canada), 23:49, 137-40
Coffin, George, 27:390
Coffin, Thomas, 23:44, 49; "An Unpublished
   Document in the Case of Thomas Coffin
   against Ezekiel Hart, of Three Rivers,
   Province of Quebec," 28:xvi
Cogalniceanu (Kogalniceanu), M., 24:36-38,
   52, 65, 73, 101, 117
Cogsdel, Doctor, 27:254
Coggeshall, John, 27:175
Coggeshall, Miss, 27:440
Coggshall, Mr., 38:59, 75

Cogswell, Jonathan, *Hebrew Theocracy*, 30:433
Cohain, Abm., 21:45
Cohalan, Judge, 29:150-51
Cohan, Meyer, 32:12
Cohen, 27:83
Cohen, Miss (Charleston), 27:286
Cohen, Mr. (1), 21:101
Cohen, Mr. (2), 21:160
Cohen (Newport), 27:413
Cohen (New York), 27:30
Cohen (writer), 29:127
Cohen, Mrs., 23:141
Cohen, A., 29:135
Cohen, A. H., 21:167
Cohen, Abraham (Brazil), 33:80, 97, 99-100;
   42:278, 388, 393
Cohen, Abraham (Cayenne), 32:16
Cohen, Abraham (Charleston, S.C.), 32:47
Cohen, Abraham (Georgetown), 47:190;
   50:42, 47, 156, 169; "Abraham Cohen:
   Deputy Postmaster at Georgetown, South
   Carolina (1789-1800)," 48:177-93
Cohen, Abraham (Newport), 27:182-83
Cohen, Abm. (N.Y. 1769), 21:170; 27:55
Cohen, Abraham (N.Y. 1825), 27:315
Cohen, Abraham H. (Lyons Papers), 27:97,
   109, 145, 342
Cohen, Abraham H. (N.Y.), 34:125, 130, 137
Cohen, Abraham ha, 28:168-69
Cohen, Abraham Myers (N.Y.), 21:29, 38, 40,
   42, 49, 51, 55; 23:152; 27:162, 385; 37:373,
   377, 386; 38:235
Cohen, Abraham Myers (Philadelphia),
   30:249
Cohen, Abraham S., 26:272
Cohen, Adolph, 37:42; 44:190
Cohen, Alfred, 43:64-65
Cohen, Alfred M., 34:258; 36:365-66; 37:242,
   266-70, 307; 40:46-47
Cohen, Alonzo, 50:190
Cohen, Andrew, 37:419
Cohen, Aron, 27:51, 242
Cohen, B., 43:140
Cohen, B. M., 27:170
Cohen, Barnet, 27:42
Cohen, Barnet A., 50:154, 180, 189-90
Cohen, Barrow, 48:209
Cohen, Baruch, 27:79
Cohen, Bella, 50:189

Cohen, Ben, 46:124
Cohen, Benedict, 35:307
Cohen, Benjamin, 50:189-90
Cohen, Benjamin Phillip Owens, 50:180,
    189-90
Cohen, Benjamin V., 47:200, 202
Cohen, Bernard, 46:121
Cohen, Bilah, 23:152
Cohen, Boaz, 43:242; "Bibliography of Prof.
    Louis Ginzberg," gift, 34:xxv; "Jacob
    Henriques, Petition," 32:122-23; "A Note
    on Jacob Henriques, of London," 32:xix
Cohen, Captain, 33:95
Cohen, Caroline, "Records of the Myers,
    Hays and Mordecai Families from 1707-
    1923," 22:xxiv
Cohen, Mrs. Casper, 27:111
Cohen, Catharine (Baltimore), 23:145
Cohen, Catherine (N.Y.), 27:110, 167
Cohen, Catherine (Mrs. Samson Isaaks),
    33:203
Cohen, Charity, 27:75
Cohen, Charity Solis, 22:xxii; 28:xxxix
Cohen, Charles, 29:132
Cohen, Charles J., 30:vii; 37:93; "Diary of a
    Blasé," 31:xxxi; executive council, 22:xii,
    xvi, xxvii; 25:xi; 26:xii; 28:xxi, xxii; 29:xxix;
    31:xxix, xxiii; gifts, 25:xv; 28:xxxix; 29:xii;
    31:xxxiii; necrology of, 31:xxix, 255-56;
    necrologies of Emanuel Cohen, 28:xxxii,
    266-68; Ephraim Lederer, 31:xxiv, 275-78
Cohen, Clothilde Florence, 31:255
Cohen, Coleman, 50:314
Cohen, Cother, 27:315
Cohen, Daniel (1737), 21:45, 48, 55
Cohen, Daniel (1827), 27:167
Cohen, Daniel (S.C.), 50:190
Cohen, David, 50:154
Cohen, E. A., 26:212-13
Cohen, Edward, 23:145
Cohen, Mrs. Edward, 38:62; gift, 22:xxxiv;
    "Records of the Myers, Hays and
    Mordecai Families from 1707-1913,"
    22:xxiv
Cohen, Eleanor, 28:xxxviii
Cohen, Eleanor (d. Jacob I.), 27:110, 164, 167
Cohen, Eleanor H., 50:194
Cohen, Eleanor (Mrs. Philip I.), 27:111
Cohen, Eleanor S., gifts, 29:xiii; 31:xxxiii

Cohen, Eleanor Septima, 45:178, 198
Cohen, Elkalah, 33:201, 210
Cohen, Elkalah Myers, 33:205
Cohen, Elkalah Myers (Mrs. Gershom M.
    Seixas), 27:161-62; 35:189
Cohen, Elkaly, 23:152
Cohen, Emanuel (Minnesota), 28:xii; 37:257;
    necrology of, 28:xxxii, 266-68
Cohen, Emanuel (N.Y.), 23:152
Cohen, Emanuel Myers, 21:45, 48
Cohen, Emily, 50:190
Cohen, Emma, 50:190
Cohen, Ephraim, 36:58
Cohen, Esther, 23:152
Cohen, Eugenia, 27:110, 167
Cohen, Ezekiel Odler, 27:83
Cohen family (Baltimore), 23:141;
    (Philadelphia), 22:34
Cohen, Felix S., 38:331; 39:200; 40:95;
    45:226; 46:346
Cohen, Frances, 50:190
Cohen, Gedaliah, 49:270
Cohen, Gedalya, 27:79
Cohen, Gersh L., 21:170
Cohen, Gershom (Charleston), 50:41, 47
Cohen, Gershom (N.Y.), 27:167, 259
Cohen, Gerson, 43:195
Cohen, G. M., 26:273; *The Hebrew Language*,
    30:452
Cohen, G. P., 32:116
Cohen, Grace, 27:111
Cohen; Gratz *vs.*, 30:440-41
Cohen, Hazan, 35:201
Cohen, H. G., 27:79
Cohen, H. H., 27:184
Cohen, H. H. Samuel, 21:139
Cohen, Helen W., 29:206
Cohen, Henry (Jamaica), 25:113
Cohen, Henry (Philadelphia), 31:255; 37:70;
    38:74
Cohen, Henry (Texas), 33:xix-xxvi; 35:221;
    45:146; 50:386; "American Jewish
    historical notes," 31:xxiv; executive
    council, 22:xii, xvi, xxvii; 23:xii; 25:xi;
    28:xiv; 29:xiv; 31:xvi; 32:xii; 33:xxv; 37:xxix;
    38:342; 39:470; 41:388; *The Festival of
    Pentecost*, 30:370-71; gifts, 25:xvi; 32:xxviii;
    34:xx; necrology of, 42:415, 451-55; *One
    hundred years of Jewry in Texas*, 35:xxi

Cohen, Mrs. Henry, 45:146
Cohen, Hermann, 28:80; 43:250
Cohen, Hiah, 23:152
Cohen, Hyman, 26:190
Cohen, I., 29:134
Cohen, I. H., 27:62
Cohen, I. I., 31:xxxiii
Cohen, I. Myers, 21:182
Cohen, I. N., 46:167
Cohen, Inez, 26:287
Cohen, Isaac (Baltimore), 22:194
Cohen, Isaac (Charleston), 27:59, 79, 221
Cohen, Isaac (England), 41:226
Cohen, Isaac (New York), 27:155
Cohen, Isaac A., 34:293
Cohen, Isaac Abraham, 27:79
Cohen, Isaac N., 50:307, 363
Cohen, Israel (Richmond), 50:63
Cohen, Israel, *Contemporary Jewry: A Survey of Social, Cultural, Economic and Political Conditions*, reviewed, 40:401-4; "Jewish Life in Modern Times," 23:xvii
Cohen, Mrs. Israel, 23:141, 145
Cohen, Israel I., 23:141; 41:226
Cohen, Jacob (Charleston), 29:129; 34:115; 50:41, 47, 159, 161, 168
Cohen, Jacob (HIAS), 49:186
Cohen, Jacob (Long Island), 27:387
Cohen, Jacob (Montreal), 50:39, 47
Cohen, Jacob (New Amsterdam), 34:274; 46:27
Cohen, Jacob (New Town), 27:244
Cohen, Jacob (N.Y.) (1), 27:34, 42, 109, 240, 252, 418, 462, 504
Cohen, Jacob (N.Y.) (2), 27:75
Cohen, Jacob (N.Y.) (3), 27:314
Cohen, Jacob (N.Y.) (4), 27:379
Cohen, Jacob (N.Y.) (5), 21:142, 144, 146, 161, 184, 209
Cohen, Jacob (Philadelphia), 34:109-10, 114-15; 43:238; 46:183; 47:188
Cohen, Jacob (St. Thomas), 28:214
Cohen, Jacob (Savannah), 26:190
Cohen, Jacob I. (Baltimore), 23:141, 144-45; 25:99, 107; 45:198
Cohen, Jacob I. (N.Y. 1804), 27:79, 110, 163-64, 167, 466, 489
Cohen, Jacob I. (Penn.), 41:226

Cohen, Jacob I. (Richmond), 26:186; 34:114; 50:63, 162-63; "A proposal to improve the lotteries of the United States, patented by Jacob I. Cohen and signed by President Monroe and Vice-President Adams, March 3, 1825," 33:xviii
Cohen, Jacob I., Jr., 50:22
Cohen, Jacob J., 39:63, 65
Cohen, Jacob Raphael (Montreal), 50:131; "A Suit at Law Involving the First Jewish Minister in Canada," 31:vii, xvii, 181-86
Cohen, Jacob Raphael (Philadelphia), 47:205
Cohen, Jacob Sol, 27:462
Cohen, Jacob Solis, 27:318
Cohen, Jacob & Co., 27:227
Cohen, Jacobs, 29:144
Cohen, Jane, 50:190
Cohen, John, 50:190
Cohen, Joe (N.Y.), 27:79
Cohen, Joseph (Charleston), 31:255
Cohen, Joseph (Lynchburg), 50:163
Cohen, Joseph H. (N.Y.), 35:55
Cohen, Joseph H. (Boston), 42:419
Cohen, Joseph Simon (Pa.), 22:154
Cohen, Joshua, 39:63, 65
Cohen, Joshua Falk b. Mordecai, 39:215
Cohen, Joshua I. (Maryland), 22:xxiv; 23:141; 25:99, 107; 33:23-24, 28, 34:xviii; "Catalogue of a Hebrew Library, being the collection with a few additions of the late Joshua I. Cohen of Baltimore," 33:23
Cohen, Joshua I. (physician), 27:488-90
Cohen, Joshua J., 39:34
Cohen, Josiah, 37:243
Cohen, J. S., 50:164
Cohen, Judah Asher, 27:258
Cohen, Judah G., 27:79
Cohen, Judith, 27:111
Cohen, Jr. and Bros., 47:188
Cohen, Katherine, 22:57
Cohen, Lawrence L., 50:333
Cohen, Lawrence L., Jr., 50:333
Cohen, Levi A., 36:29-30
Cohen & Levy (Charleston), 27:61-62
Cohen, Levy (N.Y. 1785), 21:148-49, 159; 27:41, 43, 51, 253
Cohen, Levy (N.Y.), 35:259
Cohen, Lewis (N.Y.), 21:214; 22:180; 27:261, 305, 486

Cohen, Lewis I. (N.Y. 1800s), 34:126-27
Cohen, Lionel L., 31:291
Cohen, M., 33:201
Cohen, M. I., 27:483
Cohen, M. M., *Notices of Florida*, 30:306-7; *Proceedings of the New-Orleans Commercial Library Society*, 30:312; *Sketch of the Seminole War*, 30:306
Cohen, M. S. (N.Y.), 27:515; 29:132
Cohen, M. S. (Savannah), 29:134
Cohen, Marx, 50:154
Cohen, Marx E., Jr., 50:316
Cohen, Mary, 38:74
Cohen, Mary Ryshpan, 39:201
Cohen, Mathias, 27:182-83
Cohen, Max, 46:235-37
Cohen, Max (Spanish War), 41:377
Cohen, Max (Y. M. H. A.), 37:239, 256, 258
Cohen, Melvin M., 38:15
Cohen, Mendes (Baltimore), 22:194; 33:23-24; 45:198; necrology of, 25:xii, 145-47
Cohen, Mendes (N.Y.), 34:xxii
Cohen, Mendes I., 23:141; 28:251
Cohen, Mendez, 39:63
Cohen, Mendus, 26:186
Cohen, Meyer (1736), 23:151
Cohen, Meyer (1876), 32:121
Cohen, Meyer (Maryland), 37:437
Cohen, Miriam, 27:110, 167
Cohen, Moishe Abraham, *The Life and Times of General Two-Gun Cohen*, reviewed, 44:126-28
Cohen, Mordecai, 50:154
Cohen, Morris Raphael, 38:331; 40:209; 42:354, 357-58; 47:124, 205; *A Dreamer's Journey: The Autobiography of Morris Raphael Cohen*, reviewed, 30:199-201; *Reflections of a Wandering Jew*, reviewed, 40:94-95
Cohen, Moses (Brazil), 33:53
Cohen, Moses (Charleston), 48:177; 50:41
Cohen, Moses (N.Y.), 27:155, 315
Cohen, Moses (Philadelphia), 22:197; "A Famous Family Fight About Real Estate: Gratz *vs.* Cohen," 37:xxxiii, 345-52
Cohen, Moses (Sholam Colony), 23:179; 35:307; 48:100
Cohen, Moses A. (Orthodox congregations), 44:190, 192

Cohen, Moses A. (S.C.), 50:189-90
Cohen, Mosse Bar Jonatan a, 21:33
Cohen, Mosseh, 42:277, 393
Cohen, Myer (1), 21:183
Cohen, Myer (2), 29:206
Cohen, Myer David, 38:338
Cohen, Myer M. (Philadelphia), 27:461
Cohen, Myer M. (N.Y.), 50:63
Cohen, Myers, 37:374, 377
Cohen, N. M., 47:203
Cohen, Naomi Wiener, 40:105, 415; book review by, 40:96-98; "The Reaction of Reform Judaism in America to Political Zionism," 40:361-94
Cohen, Nina (Morais), 28:268
Cohen, Perry, 50:174
Cohen, Philip (Charleston), 22:129; 29:129; 32:37-38, 51
Cohen, Philip (b. Jacob), 27:167
Cohen, Philip I. (Baltimore), 26:186
Cohen, Philip I. (N.Y.), 27:110
Cohen, Philip Melvin, 50:194
Cohen, Rachel, 23:151; 33:210
Cohen, Rachel Adler, 27:45
Cohen, Rachel E., 23:145
Cohen, Ralph, 41:374
Cohen, Rebecca (d. Sam'l Myers), 23:152; 33:203, 210
Cohen, Rebecca (d. Jacob I.), 27:110, 167
Cohen, Rebecca (mother of Jacob I.), 27:167
Cohen, Rebecca (Mrs. Jacob M.), 27:111
Cohen, Rebecca Sarzedas, 50:47
Cohen, Mr. and Mrs. Reginald, 50:271, 274-75, 307, 363
Cohen, Rev., 21:203
Cohen, Richa, 23:152
Cohen, Richea, 33:210
Cohen, Roger S., Jr., 50:271, 275, 341
Cohen, Rose, 23:155
Cohen, Sally, 27:55, 75
Cohen, Samuel (Maryland), 26:186
Cohen, Samuel (N.Y.), 27:515; 38:58
Cohen, Samuel (S.C.), 50:190
Cohen, Samuel A., 27:258
Cohen, Samuel Bar Meyr, 31:236
Cohen, Samuel Myers (N.Y.), 21:4, 6, 11, 14, 26, 38, 42, 213; 23:151-52; 27:122, 384-85; 31:237; 33:201, 206, 209-10; 37:373, 377, 386; 38:235

Cohen, Samuel Myers (Philadelphia), 50:63
Cohen, Sarah, 27:110, 167
Cohen, Sarah M., 27:162
Cohen, Seby, 21:41
Cohen, Semuel A., 29:32
Cohen, Seymour Jay, "The American Yiddish Press during the First World War," 37:xxxii
Cohen, Sheldon, 50:175
Cohen, S. I., "Elements of the Jewish Faith," 22:xxxiii; 30:172-73, 210-11
Cohen, Simon, 25:72, 74
Cohen, Simon Myers, 25:35; 27:74, 83, 86
Cohen, Simon Odler, 27:43
Cohen, Simon P., 50:350
Cohen, Simon R., 41:370
Cohen, Sol, gifts, 35:xxiii
Cohen, Solomon (Atlanta), 50:172, 201
Cohen, Solomon (N.Y.), 27:90
Cohen, Solomon (Savannah), 29:134
Cohen, Solomon (S.C.), 39:42; 48:177, 180; 50:42, 47, 156, 194-95
Cohen, Mrs. Solomon, 48:77
Cohen, Solomon I., 48:72-73
Cohen, Solomon L., 27:486
Cohen, Solomon M., 37:349
Cohen, Solomon Myers, 21:103, 105, 111, 114-16, 118, 121-23, 125, 129-31, 140, 141-46, 148-49, 159, 183, 211; 27:38, 40-41, 51, 54, 61, 70, 253, 274, 461; 50:37, 47
Cohen, Solomon Solis, 29:191; gifts, 26:xxxv; 29:xii
Cohen, Sophia (Andrade), 27:111, 486
Cohen, Susan, 50:190
Cohen, T. Barrett, 42:46
Cohen v. Webb, 26:260
Cohen, William N., 31:257
Cohen, Yeckiel A., 30:445
Cohen, Zacharias, 35:293
Cohen, Zillah Phillips, 38:70
Cohen, Zipporah (N.Y. 1828), 27:110, 167
Cohen, Zipporah, 31:210
Coheno, Samuel, 42:108
Cohen's Bluff, 50:190
Cohens of Maryland, 31:xxxiii
Cohn, Mr., 35:xix
Cohn, Abraham, 50:3-4, 6
Cohn, Adolphe, 35:122
Cohn, Albert, 35:79-80; 42:164, 168; 45:70

Cohn, B., 29:130
Cohn, Deborah, 31:225
Cohn, Elkan, 37:45; 38:320
Cohn, Mr. and Mrs. Eugene, 50:271, 274, 306
Cohn, Fannia, 41:327
Cohn, Franz, 28:77
Cohn, H., 29:130
Cohn, H. and Co. (San Francisco), 37:45
Cohn, Harris J., necrology of, 31:xxiii
Cohn, Haskell, 42:419
Cohn, Helen, 35:320-21
Cohn, Kasper, 42:423
Cohn, L., 29:135
Cohn, Leah, 34:149
Cohn, Leopold, 45:102
Cohn, Louis, 35:320
Cohn, Louis (Salt Lake City), 22:182
Cohn, M., 35:102
Cohn, M. (N.Y.), 44:132
Cohn, M. and Co. (San Francisco), 37:45
Cohn, N. A., 29:134
Cohn, Tobias, 28:199
Cohn, Werner, 48:64
Cohn, Willy, 32:xxviii
Cohnheim, Max, 41:233
Cohn-Wiener, Jews in art, 32:xxvii
Cohon, Mrs., 23:86
Cohon, Samuel S., 40:48, 105; 43:196; 46:63; "The History of the Hebrew Union College," 39:469; 40:17-55; "The History of the Jews in Russia in the 19th Century," 22:xviii
Cohon, Simon, 29:146
Coin's Financial School, 40:333
Coke, Daniel Parker, 38:101
Coke, Lord, 31:109-10, 120, 123-24, 133
Colasa, Belthor, 33:115
Colburn, Henry, 35:238
Colby, Bainbridge, 36:80
Colden, Cadwallader, 42:80; 45:202
Colden, Dr., 35:187
Colden, Governor, 23:155
Cole, Arthur H., 46:211
Cole, Colonel, 23:15
Cole, Cornelius, 41:37
Cole, Edward, 30:77
Cole, George Watson, 30:vi
Cole, Senator, 24:11

Colebrook, Nesbitt and Franks, 26:266
Colebrooke, George, 35:20, 22-23
Colebrooke, James, 35:20, 22-23
Coleman, Byla, 23:152
Coleman, Coleman, 23:152
Coleman (N.Y.), 27:45
Coleman (Alabama); National Jewish
    Hospital for Consumptives *v.*, 25:136
Coleman, Edward D., 30:vii; 33:20, 22, 147,
    251; 34:iv, 72, 75, 280, 297, 305; 37:xi,
    461; 39:75, 78, 83; 43:250; 50:71;
    "American and British Intervention on
    Behalf of Kishinev Jews in 1903," 34:280-
    84; "Benjamin Levy," 34:271-72; "The
    Bible in the English Drama," gift, 33:xxix,
    xxxii-xxxiii, 8; "A Bibliography of the
    Writings of Max James Kohler," 34:xiv,
    165-258; "Bridgetown, Barbados," 34:275-
    78; "David Longworth, American
    Publisher, Friend of the Jews," 35:281-85;
    editing, 34:iv; 35:iv; executive council,
    33:xxv; 34:xiv; gifts, 33:xxxiii; 34:xxiii;
    35:xx; "Jewish Americana," 34:273-75;
    "The Jewish Dead During the 1793 Yellow
    Fever," 35:285-87; "Jewish Merchants and
    Colonial Slave Trade," 34:285; "Jewish
    Prototypes in American and English
    Romans and *Drames* à Clef," 35:xiv, 227-80;
    necrology of, 37:xii, 458-60; "A New York
    Election Circular in Hebrew of 1867,"
    34:258-88; "A New York Première of
    Herzl in 1885," 35:287-88; NOMCOM,
    33:xvi; (notes), 34:265-66; "Plays of Jewish
    Interest on the American Stage, 1752-
    1821," 33:xvii, 171-98; reports of librarian,
    33:xii, xxvii, 8; 34:x, xvi-xxvii; 35:xvii-xxiv;
    "Sarah Abondana," 34:270-71; "A Selected
    Bibliography of the Writings of Albert M.
    Friedenberg," 35:xiv, 115-37; "William
    Dunlap's Jewish Friends," 34:278-80
Coleman, George, *Love Laughs at Locksmiths*,
    33:174, 191
Coleman, Harris, 27:509
Coleman, Isabella, 27:509
Coleman, M. & Co., 37:458
Coleman, William, 22:79, 83; 30:205
Coleridge, Lord, 31:107, 113
Coleridge, Samuel Taylor, 35:239
Colfax, Schuyler, 50:289-90, 355

Colfax Settlement (Denver), 37:296
Colins, 35:203
Colker, Isaac, 27:90
Collected Works of Abraham Lincoln, 50:379
College Bookplates with Hebrew
    Inscriptions, 45:130-34
College of Charity Padre Venancio, 43:130
College fraternities, "The History of
    American Jewish College Fraternities,"
    23:xv
College of the City of New York, 28:286,
    311; 31:271; 39:199-201; 45:205, 210, 267;
    47:22, 78; 49:97; 50:119
College of Jewish Studies, 45:162-63, 185;
    46:365; 49:155
College Libraries, "Judaica and Hebraica
    Collections in College Libraries," 45:134-
    48
College of New Jersey (Princeton), 37:135
College of Heralds, 40:216, 219
College of New York, discrimination, 29:105
College of Pharmacy of the City of New
    York, 29:167
College of Physicians of Philadelphia, 22:232;
    45:197
College of Physicians and Surgeons (N.Y.),
    26:223, 227; 46:12
College of William and Mary, 49:139
Collegiate Institute at Brockport, 50:86, 88
Collens, Antoine, 39:22
Collier, Constance, 35:268
Collier's Weekly, 43:26
Collins, Mr., 31:186
Collins, Abraham, 27:91
Collins, Henry, 27:245
Collins, J. P., 32:99-100
Collitz, Rachel, 48:26
Collmus, Levy, 22:194
Colloredo, Count, 38:195, 233
Colly, Rachel, 21:60
Colman, Benjamin, 22:2-3; 28:242-43; 30:iv;
    35:161-62; 37:441; *Discourse*, 30:21-23, 26;
    Moses a Witness to Our Lord, 30:23
Cologna, Abraham de, 41:12, 14
Colombier, Marie, 35:250
Colomé (Colomer), Antonia, 28:273
Colonial America, "Gleanings of Jewish
    Interest in American Colonial and

Revolutionary History," 25:xiii; Jews in, 26:5-6

Colonial Dames of America, 45:54-55; 48:4

Colonial wars, "The Jews in the Wars of the United States," 26:xxiv, xxv, xxvii

Colonimo y Gurario, Puigeerver, 35:221, 225

Colonization, Adolphe Cremieux Hebrew Farm Colony, 39:396; agricultural colonies, 39:238; 40:244-51, 269, 276-80; 42:158, 180, 182-83; 48:33-35, 37, 44, 78-101; 49:178-79; Alachua, Fla., 25:132-34; Alliance colony, N.J., 38:307, 310; 40:248-50, 276-80; 48:92-97, 99; Argentina, 38:24ff; 39:87ff; 42:178-82; 43:37-69; Arkansas colonies, 48:87-89, 93; Beer Sheba-Colony, 48:87, 93; 49:179; Belez colony, 43:59, 61; Bethlehem Yedudah colony, 38:306-7; 48:85-87, 93; Barreros colony, 43:61; Bassavilbasso colony, 43:59-60; Brazil, 39:98; Canada, 38:314; 39:104; Carmel colony, 38:310; 43:59-60; 48:92, 97-99; Dakota colonies, 38:306-7, 314; "David Feinberg's Historical Survey of the Colonization of the Russian Jews in Argentina," 43:37-69; Devil's Lake agricultural experiment, 49:227; "An Early American Hebrew-Christian Agricultural Colony," 22:184-86; "Further Information Concerning the Jewish Colony 'Shalom' at Yageville in Ulster County, N. Y.," 35:xv, 306-9; "Jewish Agricultural Colonies in the United States," 38:345; 48:87, 93; *A Jewish Agricultural Colony in Louisiana*, 35:xxii; Jewish Colonization Association, 28:129-31; 31:190, 206; 36:226; 38:241, 312, 316; 39:413, 318; 40:254; 42:180-86; 43:37-69; 46:480-81, 483; 47:165-66, 168, 170-71; "The Jewish Colony of Sholam, Ulster County, N. Y., 1838," 23:178-79; Kansas colonies, 48:87, 93; Louisiana, 37:440; 48:83-85, 93; Mesopotamia Project, 47:157-58, 160-69; Paul Haupt and the Mesopotamian Project, 1892-1914," 47:154-75; "Paul Haupt's Plan for Settling Russian Jews in Mesopotamia," 44:242; Michigan colony, 29:66-68, 72-73; Moses Elias Levy's Agricultural Colony in Florida," 25:132-34; "The Palestine Colony in Michigan," 29:vii, xxix, 61-74;

"A Real Estate Record of the Sholam Colony," 25:xiii; Sholam Colony, 25:140-41, 38:xxxi; single tax and colonization, 46:477-80, 483-84; Vandalia colony, 23:18-19; Woodbine Colony, 38:311; 39:89, 95; "Letters of Vladimir Korolenko about Woodbine, New Jersey (1893)," 45:365

Colorado, Jewish local history, 49:218; "The Jewish Physicians of Colorado, Biographic and Bibliographic," 31:xviii

Colovii, Abraham, 37:132

Colquhoun, Peter, *A treatise on the police of the metropolis*, 35:xx

Columbia Boat Club, 28:306

Columbia Club, 29:169; 45:205; 47:13

Columbia College, 21:xvi; 22:152, 156, 162; 27:373-74, 389; 35:205; 45:140; 46:51; "College Bookplates with Hebrew Inscriptions," 45:131, 133, 167, 169

Columbia College Medical School, 26:220-21

Columbia Council School (Pittsburgh), 37:295

Columbia Grammar School, 34:304; 40:3

Columbia Hebrew Sunday School, 50:170

Columbia Religious and Industrial School for Girls, 31:261

Columbia, South Carolina, 50:154, 167, 169-70; religious observances, mid-nineteenth century, 37:37

Columbia University, 22:112; 25:175; 26:220-21, 277; 28:260, 306; 34:153; 37:479; 40:3, 408-9, 411; 41:277; 45:131, 201, 226; 47:16-17, 21, 226; 49:6, 11-12, 25, 97, 257; Committee on advisor to Jewish students, 49:12; "Dr. Nicholas Murray Butler on Columbia's Jewish Graduates," 37:435; gift, 34:xxvii; "Jews in the History of Columbia University," 32:xx; "Johnson of Columbia and the Hebrew Language," 25:109-11; "Judaica and Hebraica Collections in College Libraries," 45:140-41; library, 45:133-34, 167, 169, 185; "Sampson Simson's Bequest to Columbia," 37:xxxiii, 434; "Temple Emanu-El of New York and the Chair in Rabbinical Literature at Columbia 1887," 37:xxxiii

Columbia University Club, 28:261
Columbia World Exposition, 42:3
Columbian College, Ga., 33:235
Columbian Exposition, Chicago, 38:318
Columbian Magazine, 25:114
Columbus, Christopher, 22:105; 23:103, 130;
26:xix-xx; 27:474; 29:xi; 32:xxii, 1; 34:174-
75; 35:223-24; 37:79, 442; 38:16; 40:12-13,
395, 410; 45:63; 46:396; America in
Hebrew literature, 22:101-3, 111-12, 114-
16, 123-25; "Christopher Columbus and
the Participation of the Jews in the
Spanish-Portuguese Discoveries," 33:35;
45:102; "Columbus and the Jews," 29:xxix;
31:234-35; 33:32-39; "Columbus in
Oriental Literature," 33:32; Ezekiel Statue,
28:33-36; Jewish physicians, 22:155; "The
Spanish Argument for the Jewish Origin of
Columbus," 29:xv; Spanish-Jewish origin,
22:xxi
Columbus *Enquirer*, 50:174
Colvelt, Laurens, 31:90
Comanos, Nicholas D., 47:83-84, 93-95, 99
Comb, George, 27:323
Combs, Leslie, 22:97
Comité de Secours pour les Israélites russes,
40:257
"Commentary," 39:290; 42:465
Commerce, "Some New Manuscript Sources
for the Study of Modern Commerce,"
23:95
Commercial Advertiser, The, 21:229; 38:119,
127-28; 43:179, 185; "Abraham Cahan and
the New York Commercial Advertisers: A
Study in Acculturation," 43:10-36
Commercial Dictionary, 40:126-27
Commercial Express, Times, 29:120
Commercial and Notarial Precedents, 40:126-27,
133
Commission of Churches on International
Affairs, 46:359
Commission on Community Interrelations,
42:321
Commission on Immigration and
Naturalization, 46:291
Commission on Information about Judaism,
39:457
Commission on Jewish Education, 39:454,
468; 42:5, 7-9, 41; 45:267

Commission for Relief in Belgium, 40:14
*Committee of Citizens of New York, Friendly to
Literature and Drama*, 33:190
Committee on Commerce and Manufacture,
43:226-28
Committee on Dietary Laws of the United
Synagogue of America, 25:69
Committee on Fair Employment Practice,
47:195
Committee for Industrial Organization,
42:322
Committee on Jewish Americana of the B'nai
B'rith, 49:154
Committee on Jews in Foreign Lands, 40:371
Committee for Plantation Affairs, 49:209
Committees of Safety or of Correspondence,
43:199
Committee of Ten, 34:219
Committee of the National Jewish
Immigration Council, 28:131
Common Law, The, 49:12; "The Doctrine that
'Christianity is a Part of the Common
Law,' and its Recent Judicial Overthrow in
England, with Particular Reference to
Jewish Rights," 31:vii, xvi, 103-4
Commons, John R., 41:303, 312, 337, 342;
46:221, 261
Commonwealth Alms House (Mass.), 46:73
Commonwealth Club of California, 29:180,
197
Commonwealth Securities Co. *v.* West 134th
Street Realty Co., "Anglo-Jewish Legal
Cases," 25:138
Communism, 34:xxiii; 43:193; 49:8, 83;
history, writing of, 46:258, 260, 268, 275,
278, 288, 292, 296, 326-27, 336, 410; *The
Jews and Communism*, reviewed, 50:251-53;
and Zionism, 49:245
Community Relations Council or
Committees, 42:323
Compromise of 1850, 46:276
Comte, August, 48:92; 49:82
Conant, Rev. Dr., 50:81
Conant, Thomas Jefferson, 30:iv; *Defense of
Gesenius' Hebrew Grammar*, 30:421-22;
Exercises in Hebrew Grammar, 40:400;
(trans.), *Hebrew Grammar*, 30:334, 400
Concelho, Balthazar Leitao Vacz, 33:114
Concordia Club, 29:180

Concordia of Munich, 23:112
Concordia Society, 26:212
Conder, Claude Reignier, 26:154-55
Condy, Benjamin, 23:160
Cone, Caesar, necrology of, 26:xiv, 276-77
Cone family, 46:436
Cone, G. Herbert, 32:xix
Cone, Helen, 26:276
Cone, Henry, 40:58
Cone, Herman (Baltimore), 26:276
Cone, Herman (Tenn.), 50:167
Cone, Levi, 29:146
Cone, Spencer H., *Restoration of the Jews*, 30:382
Conegliano, Israel, 28:199-200
Conegliano, Jeremiah (Lorenzo da Ponte), 30:196; 34:179; *Storia Compendiosa*, 30:130, 132
Conegliano, Solomon, 28:199
Confederacy, 47:189, 191; David L. Yulee, 25:22-27; Jewish cemetery (Richmond, Va.), 50:316; Jewish soldiers, 50:314-16; Jews and slavery, 29:125; Judah P. Benjamin, 38:153-71
Confederation of the Rhine, 26:35
Conference of American Rabbis, 40:72
Conference on the Early History of Zionism in America, 49:221
Conference of Historians, 44:245, 247; 47:183
Conference of Israelites, 24:102-5
Conference of Jewish Adjustment in America, 46:374
Conference of Jewish Experience in America, 46:187
Conference on Jewish Relations, 39:201, 290; 40:94; 44:209; 46:363, 365
Conference on Jewish Social Studies, 49:137, 154; 50:263, 267
Conference of Managers of the Associated Jewish Charities, 46:393
Conference on the Writing of American Jewish History, 46:133-446; 47:214
Confirmants Club of the Bronx Free Synagogue, 33:184
Confirmation certificates, St. Thomas, D. W. I., 22:xxviii; "An Early Confirmation Certificate from the Island of St. Thomas, Danish West Indies," 23:180-82

Conger, Mrs. Omar D., 33:213
Congregation of the Children of Israel, 23:151
Congregation "Seekers of Peace," 30:421
Congregationalists, 47:143, 145-46, 149, 152
Congregations of Israel of New York, 44:174
Congress, "The Congressional Debates and Reporters (1889)," 32:134; "David L. Yulee, Florida's First Senator," 25:vii, 1-29; Jewish question in Roumania, 24:8-9, 16-17, 83, 114-15; Jews in, 22:141, 238
Congress of Aix-la-Chapelle, 43:172
Congress of Berlin, 29:85; 41:38
Congress at Brussels, 29:95
Congress Bulletin, 45:231, 235
Congress of the Confederation, 43:162
Congress House, 39:334
Congress of Industrial Organization, 41:329, 332, 334-35, 354; 46:291, 302
Congress of Jewish Women, 29:160
Congress of National Service, 26:xxvii
Congress of Vienna, 26:124; 28:xxxviii, xl, 70; 43:176, 178; 46:9, 366; 49:198
Congressional Globe, 26:216; 38:167
Congreve, William, 35:229; 46:433
Conheim, Herman, 45:39; necrology of, 31:xxix
Conjoint Committee of the Jewish Board of Guardians, 41:156-57
Connecticut, "Anglo-Jewish Legal Cases," 25:135; Civil War, 50:277, 304, 313, 387; history, writing of, 46:152, 295, 314, 422-23; Jewish local history, 49:219; "Notes from the Will of Mordecai Marks, Early Connecticut Merchant, and Genealogical Data Regarding Him and His Family," 29:xvi
Connecticut, University of, "Judaica and Hebraica Collection in College Libraries," 45:145-46
Connelly, Max, 40:354, 357
Connelley, William E., 23:69, 71
Conness, John, 37:43
Connoisseur, The, 44:9; 45:271
Connolly, John, 23:23
Connolly, W., 23:16
Conolly, Captain, 30:408
Conor, Miss, 22:40
Conrad, Ernst, 49:270

Conrad, Gabe, 31:213
Conrad, Janet Rosenfield, 22:229
Consalvi, Cardinal, 26:51-52
Conscientious Objectors, Board of Inquiry, 37:476
Conservative Judaism, 39:259, 279, 297-98, 371-72; 40:361, 401; 43:146; 48:143; 49:232, 251; *American Judaism*, reviewed, 47:121-23; Congregation Schools, 42:20; *Differentiation Features of Orthodox, Conservative and Reform Jewish Groups in Metropolitan Philadelphia*, reviewed, 49:276-78; history, writing of, 46:163, 171, 187; Kashrut, 39:376; *Yahadut Amerika be-Hitpathutah (The Shaping of American Judaism)*, reviewed, 42:91-107
Consistorial and Episcopal Court of London, 38:289
Constantine, 28:137
Constantinople, 26:138, 140, 150-51, 159-60; Conference of Israelites, 24:102-5; Conference of the Powers, 24:29-30, 34, 40, 43, 49-50, 118-19, 122, 138-40; "Memorial of Alliance Israélite Universelle of Paris to the Congress of Berlin," 24:105-7
Contaro, Christopher, 37:402
Contemporary Jewish Record, 45:226
Contemporary Jewry: A Survey of Social, Cultural, Economic and Political Conditions, reviewed, 40:401-4
Content, Moses, 27:110
Content, Simon, 27:105, 110
Continental Army, "Calendar of the Correspondence of George Washington, Commander in Chief of the Continental Army, with the Officers," 25:113; pay for, 22:195-97
Continental Congress, 23:10, 173; 28:254; "Calendar of the Correspondence of George Washington, Commander in Chief of the Continental Army, with the Continental Congress," 25:113; "Jewish Signers to a Patriotic Address to Congress in 1783" (note), 22:196-97
Continental Trade Union movement, 46:231
Contreras, Pedro Moya de, 31:9, 18-21, 23
Convention of 1800, 38:136

Convention of Jewish Societies for Promoting Physical Culture, 49:86
Convention of Paris, "Petition of the Roumanian Jews to the Chamber of Deputies, 1872," 24:98-101
Convention of Reform, 40:201
Conversion, 26:207-8; 27:519-20, 522; 40:119; 50:5-6; "A Cabalistic MS. from the Library of Judah Monis," 28:xv, 242-45; "Cotton Mather and the Jews," 26:xiv, 201-10; Persian Jews, 36:11-18
Conway, G. R. G., 31:2; elected corresponding member, 31:xxvii; gifts, 32:xxv; 33:xxix; "Hernando Alonso, a Jewish Conquistador with Cortés in Mexico," 31:xxix, 2-4, 8-31; *Martinez del Rio*, 35:xxi; *Process de Luis Caravajal*, 35:xxi
Conway, J. H., 27:506
Conway, Moncure D., 35:243; 50:198
Cooch, Mrs. Edward, gift, 35:xxi
Cook, Mathilda V., gift, 35:xviii
Cook, O. F., 31:204, 210
Cook County Bureau of Public Welfare, 50:432
Cooke, Benjamin, 34:118
Cooke, John, 23:79
Cooley, Thomas M., 31:115
Coolidge, Calvin, 35:325; 42:334; 45:205
Coolidge, Mary Roberts, 34:251
Coons, Eva, necrology of, 28:xv, 268-69
Coons, Henry R., 28:269
Coons, Isidor, 28:269
Cooper (editor), 43:15, 19
Cooper, Ashley, 29:137
Cooper, Astley Paston, 43:72-73, 75, 78
Cooper, Captain (England), 27:366; 34:98
Cooper, Captain, 32:79
Cooper, Grey, 28:253-54; 38:98
Cooper Institute, 49:19
Cooper, James Fenimore, 22:175; 41:88; 42:457
Cooper, Mrs. Morris W., 31:268
Cooper, Peter, 41:32
Cooper, William, *The Promised Seed*, 30:110-11, 114-15; 34:xvi
Cooper, William (Col.), 50:384
Cooper Union, 41:27; 45:203; 47:228; 50:271-72, 274, 341
Co-operative League of America, 41:343

Coote, Richard, 38:45-46; 42:461
Copeland, Royal S., 36:368
Copernicus, 22:103
Copland, Aaron, 47:181-82
Copley, John Singleton, 22:47
Copper manufacture, "Copper for the
   Savannah of 1818," 48:170-76; 49:62;
   "Paul Revere and Son and Their Jewish
   Correspondence," 43:199-229
Coralnik, Abraham, 45:152
Corbett, Henry W., 41:36, 40
Corbett, John, 31:94-95
Corbin, Austin, 47:12, 20
Corbin, H. C., 41:377
Corca, Imanuel de Moss. Alvares, 22:170
Corcoran Art Gallery, 28:26-27
Corcos, Aaron, 21:167
Corcos, Aaron Judah, 27:107
Corcos ben Isaac, Tranquillo (Manoah) Vita
   (Hayyim), 28:184
Corcos, Joseph M., 29:50-51; 42:214-15;
   47:176; "Synopsis of the History of the
   Jews of Curaçao," 22:171
Cordier, Henry, 49:41
Cordoba, Pedro de, 31:16
Cordova, 23:131; 27:79; "The de Cordova
   Family in Jamaica," 22:xviii
Cordova, Emanuel de, 50:123
Cordova, Esther De, 25:118
Cordova, Gabriel de, 23:133
Cordova, Gonsalvo de, 28:204
Cordova, Isaac d'Abraham de, 29:36
Cordova, Jacob de, 22:120; 25:118; 27:245;
   50:192
Cordova, Jacob Hayyim, 22:120
Cordova, Jeoshua Hisquiao de, 44:219
Cordova, Jeosuah de, 29:27
Cordova, Joshua de, "Reason and faith,"
   34:xvi
Cordova, Joshua Hezekiah de, 25:114;
   26:242; 27:12-13; 35:311; "Joshua
   Hezekiah de Cordova, Isaac Gomez, Jr.,
   and Jacob Mordecai, Apologetes for
   Judaism," 38:343
Cordova, Joshua Raphael De, 25:118
Cordova, Judah De, 25:117-18
Cordova, Michael De, 25:118
Cordova, Moses de, 21:45; 27:245
Cordova, Moses Raphael de, 22:120

Cordova, Raphael J. De, 40:363
Cordova, R. J. De (Jamaica), 23:182
Cordova, R. J. De (N.Y.), 48:200
Cordozo, I. N., 21:171
Cordwainers' Case, "The Cordwainers' Case
   and Moses Levy," 38:342
Corea, Manuel Alvarez, 44:232
Corel, Andrew Cotter Du, 23:154
Corinaldi, Abraham Henry, 25:115
Corinaldi, Hanah, 25:115
Corinaldi, Horatio, 25:115
Corinaldi, Jacob Portello, 25:115
Corinth, Lovis, 40:320
Corkan, Charles E., 34:239
Corles, Calvin D., 50:382
Cormack, Bartlett, 40:358
Corn, Florence Hays, 29:169
Corneau, Em., 41:161
Cornel, David S., 42:287
Cornell, Nat., 35:181
Cornell, Samuel, 42:417
Cornell, Susannah, 42:417
Cornell University, 22:199; 28:26; 46:149
Cornual, Thomas, 27:245
Cornwallis, 31:48
Coronal, David Senior, 33:55
Coronel, Dauid Senior (1), 42:277, 279, 388,
   392-93
Coronel, Dauid Senior (2), 42:280, 388, 392-
   93
Coronel, Ishac Senior, 42:278, 393
Coronel, Jehosuah Senior, 42:279, 394
Correa, Abraham Alvares, 44:228
Correa, Gil, 44:83
Correa, Jacob Gabai, 42:280, 399
Correa, Joan de Barros, 33:115
Correa, Manuel Alvares, 37:392, 412-13,
   415-16
Correa, Manuel de Mosseh Alvares, 44:231-
   32
Correa, Mordechai Alvarez, 22:171
Correa, Mordy, 27:245
Correa, Mosseh Alvares, 44:229-30
Correa, Mosseh de Manuel de Mosseh
   Alvares, 44:232
Correspondence russe, La, 46:95
Corrigan, Michael Augustine, 46:284
Corrodi, Heinrich, 45:28-29
Cors & Bull, 27:329

Corei, Edward, 46:309
Cortelyou, George B., 24:82
Cortés, "Hernando Alonso, a Jewish Conquistador with Cortés in Mexico," 31:xxix, 2-4, 8-31
Cortez, 32:xxii
Corti, Count, 24:121
Corticos, Daniel de Moseh, 29:28
Cortino, Manuel, 25:89
Cortisos, Abraham, 29:36
Cortissos (Cortiços), Benjamin, 29:24, 28
Cortlandt, Aug. V., 25:91
Cortland family, 40:120
Cortwall, Angel de, 22:178
Corvalo, Benjamin, 23:28
Corvelho, Isaac, 33:95
Corwin, Thomas, 32:67, 69-70; 47:50
Corwine, Brother & Co., 31:137
Cosby, William, 23:150; 42:77
Cosio, Francisco G. de, 33:33
Cosmopolitan, 33:28
Cosmos Club of Washington, 37:473
Costa, De, 31:109, 111-13, 125; 48:139
Costa, Aaron Da, 25:117
Costa, Abraham da, 33:65
Costa, Abraham Mendes de Acosta or da, 29:16
Costa, Abraham Rodriguez da, 25:117
Costa, Abram da, 27:227
Costa, Alberquerque Daniel de, 32:62
Costa, Alexander da, 25:117
Costa, Alvaro du, 28:250
Costa, Amos da, 25:117
Costa, Angela da (Massiah), 22:178
Costa, Aron d'Abraham da, 37:12
Costa, Benjamin Mendes de, 21:11, 20
Costa, Daniel da, 22:179; 25:117; 26:252
Costa, Daniel Mendes da, 32:63
Costa, Daniel Nunes da, 21;5, 7-10, 19, 181
Costa, Daniel Nunez da, 33:253
Costa, Dauid da, 42:278, 394
Costa, David (1), 25:117
Costa, David (2), 25:117-18
Costa, David (3), 25:117
Costa, David (4), 25:118
Costa, David Alfred da, 25:118
Costa, David Rodrigues da, 25:117-18
Costa, Emanuel Mendes de, 35:235
Costa, da, & Farr, 27:245

Costa, Francisco Carnero da, 33:113
Costa, Gaspar Francisco da, 33:80; 44:83
Costa, Gaspar Franco da, 33:65
Costa, H. B. da, 50:175
Costa, Hananel Mendes da, 27:9, 20, 47
Costa, Isaac da (Boston), 38:98-103
Costa, Isaac da (Brazil), 33:77, 88
Costa, Isaac da (Charleston), 50:41, 47
Costa, Isaac da (N.Y.), 21:51, 63, 79, 94, 139, 220; 27:42, 226-27, 462; 41:123
Costa, Isaac da, Jr., 27:226-27
Costa, Isaac da, Sr., 50:47
Costa, Isaac de, *Noble families among Sephardic Jews*, 35:xx
Costa, Isaac Gomez da, 27:58
Costa, Isaac Haim Rod da, 27:245
Costa, Isaac Hananel da, 26:251
Costa, Isaac Mendes da, 32:63
Costa, Ishac Haym Rodrigues da, 25:138
Costa, Ishac Haim Rodrigues da (Curaçao), 44:230
Costa, Jacob da (Barbados), 22:178; 25:118
Costa, Jacob (N.Y.), 21:79
Costa, Jacob da (S.C.), 50:66
Costa, Jacob Mendes da, 44:119
Costa, Jacob Telles da, 29:24-25
Costa, Jahacob Mendez da, 21:11, 14, 20
Costa, Jaspar Ferdinandus da, 33:47
Costa, Jeronimo Nunes da, 33:100
Costa, Jeronimus Nunes da, 33:50
Costa, Jeuda Mosse da, 29:28
Costa, John da, "The Portuguese Inquisition of 1730 with Special Reference to John da Costa, Sometimes Commissary-General of Portugal," 29:xxxvi
Costa, John Mendez da, 28:250
Costa, Jonathan Mendes da, 44:119
Costa, Joseph da (Brazil), 42:278, 287-88, 392, 394
Costa, Joseph da (N.Y.), 29:49
Costa, Lady Reba Mendes da, 32:64
Costa, Louisa da, 25:117
Costa, Luis da, 33:65
Costa, M. da, 26:252
Costa, Manasseh Mendes da, 27:18
Costa, Manuel da (Brazil), 33:87, 119
Costa, Manuel de (N.Y.), 30:33; 35:176
Costa, Manuel Ferera da, 33:116
Costa, Manuel Vaz de, 42:74

Costa, Mattens da, 33:119
Costa, Mattias da, 33:115
Costa, Mary Ann da, 25:117
Costa, Mendes da, 32:8, 14
Costa, Moses Mendes da, 26:251; 37:419
Costa, Moses Nunez da, 27:245
Costa, Mosseh Mendez da, 21:14
Costa, da, Mrs., 27:59
Costa, da, Mrs. J., 48:263
Costa, N. da, 27:1
Costa, Nunes da, 38:236
Costa, Pedro Correa da, 33:117
Costa, Rachel da, 45:186
Costa, Ralph Brandon Da, 25:118
Costa, Ramah Mendes da, 44:119
Costa, Rebecca da (S.C.), 50:66
Costa, Rebecca da (West Indies), 25:117
Costa, Samuel da, 50:41
Costa, Sarah da (Charleston), 50:41, 47
Costa, Sarah da (West Indies), 25:118
Costa, Septimus da, 25:118
Costa, Signor, 27:479
Costa, Uriel da, 29:xiii, 49
Costaforo, 24:26, 28; 36:110-11
Costello, 40:129
Costigan, 40:283
Costo, Vas de David, 32:61
Costrell, Bessie, 34:236
Cotinho, Isaac Henriques, 37:328
Cotinho, Moses Henriques, 27:245
Cotter, Captain, 26:183
Cotton, John, 46:22-23
Cottrel, James, 32:25
Couchman, Stephen, 26:131
Coughlin, Charles E., 45:235
Coulter, E. Merton, 50:179-80
Coulthurst, M., 26:254
Coulton, John, 39:3-4
Coun, James, 33:254
Council of American Hebrew Congregation, 41:178
Council of Anglo-Jewish Association, 46:97
Council Educational Alliance (Cleveland), 37:296
Council of the Four Lands, 26:20
Council House (Albany), 37:296; (New York), 37:296
Council on Jewish Education, 42:36

Council of Jewish Federations and Welfare Funds, 39:253; 42:323; 43:147-47; 44:244; 48:66, 146; 49:154, 217; (Canada), 50:141
Council of Jewish Women, 29:160, 179; 31:259, 288; 37:301
Council of Judaism, 48:254
Council of the League of Rights of Men, 46:97
Council on Library Resources, 48:69
Council of Maryland for 1742, 22:194
Council of National Defense, 29:158-59; 37:476
Council of Social Agencies, 50:432
Council on Social Work Education, 47:232; 50:434
Council of Trade and Plantations, 31:230; 38:45-46; 46:28-29
Council of Young Men's Hebrew and Kindred Associations, 37:284
County Lawyers' Association, New York, 26:288
Courier, Der, 48:132
Courier and Enquirer (New York), 22:82, 86
Courlander, 21:159
Course of Lectures on the Jews, 30:344
Court, Elizah V., 33:254
Court of Appeals (New York), 49:10-12, 14
Court of Arbitration at the Hague, 40:8
Courval, Anthony P. de, 23:139
Courval, Mahor, 23:138-39
Cousinery Brothers, 31:198
Cousins, Robert G., 36:276
Coutinho, Francisco de Souza, 22:30; 33:82, 103; 47:117
Coutinho, Isaac, 28:239
Coutino, Abraham Dias, 25:43
Coutino, Jacob Henriquez, 44:229
Coutino, Moses, 23:27
Coutino, Mosseh Henriquez, 44:229
Couty, Rabba, 26:6; 46:29
Coven, Milton I., 47:202
Cowan, Barnet, 22:162
Cowell, "References to M. M. Noah and A. Phillips 1821-1822, in 'The theatrical life of Joe Cowell Comedian,' written by himself," 33:xvii
Cowen, Alma Desenberg, 29:158
Cowen, Bayard, 29:158

Cowen, Elfrida, 27:xix; "An Interesting
Reference to Warder Cresson," 26:xxxi,
"Judith Salzedo Peixotto," 26:xiv, 249-50;
"Moses Elias Levy's Agricultural Colony
in Florida," 25:132-34; "Moses Elias Levy
(Yulee) of Florida," 25:xii; "A Proselyte
Apostate: A Romance of a Century Ago,"
25:xii; "Some California Pioneers," 26:xxxi
Cowen, Elizabeth, 29:158
Cowen, Israel, Congress of National Service,
26:xxvii; necrology of, 29:xxix, 157-58;
"References to Jews in Harris Newmark's
'Sixty Years in Southern California,' "
26:xiv
Cowen, Julia, 49:64
Cowen, Philip, 22:174; 34:233-34; 37:239,
256; 39:325; 42:102, 348-50; 50:384; gifts,
22:xxxiii; 25:xvi; 26:xxxiii; 32:xxv; 33:xxxiii;
34:xx; "Memories of an American Jew,"
33:27
Cowen, Robert Ernest, 37:439
Cowgill, Mary, 30:200
Cowin, Isaac, 29:146
Cowley, Arthur Ernest, 33:132
Cowley, Hannah, *Belle's stratagem*, 33:174,
178
Cowley, Hannah P., 35:233-34
Cowperthwait, Samuel, 23:159
Cox, Charles C., 27:488
Cox, George, 45:193
Cox, R., 26:117
Cox, Samuel, 48:34
Cox, Samuel S., 24:16-17; 36:233; 41:168,
170
Coxe, Richard S., 39:34
Coxe, Tench, 37:348-49
Cozzens, Charles, 35:291
Cozzens, Mathew, 23:166
Cracow, 26:20
Craeck, Jan, 44:90
Craft, Charles, 27:320
Craft, Jane, 27:320
Crafts, Wilbur F., 31:222
Craig, Henry K., 48:155-63
Craig, James H., 23:49-53; 26:257
Craigie, Mrs., 45:28
Cramer, Harry, 38:73
Cramer, J., 37:419
Cramer, J. B., 37:419

Cranch, Richard, 45:58
Crandall, Edward, 35:270
Crane, Charles R., 36:79
Crane, Frederick E., 49:14
Crane, Judge, 25:135
Crane, Robert Newton, 34:186
Crane, Stephen, 43:12; 46:434
Crane, William M., 39:27, 28, 59
Cranston, Mayor, 27:452-53
Cranston, Walter, 37:418
Crapwell, Edwin, 43:112-13
Croghan, George, 37:347
Crasto, Abraham Mendes de, 21:47-49, 55
Crasto, Antho. de, 33:114
Crasto, Cosmo de, 33:79
Crasto, Daniel de, 21:28-29, 31, 33, 41, 43-
44, 48, 53, 55, 63
Crasto, David de, 44:227-29
Crasto, David de Eliao Namias de, 22:169-
70; 29:30
Crasto, David G., 27:79
Crasto, David Namias de, 44:228
Crasto, Ishac de David Namias de, 44:231
Crasto, Ishac Namias de, 23:183
Crasto, Jacob de, 21:63
Crasto, Jacob de Mordechay de, 44:230
Crasto, Jacob de Mosseh de, 44:232
Crasto, Manoel de, 50:74
Crasto, Mordechay de, 44:228-29, 231
Crasto, Mosse de, 42:279, 394
Crasto, Pedro de, 33:118
Crasto, Raphael Namias de, 22:169-70; 29:30
Crastoz, Moseh Nhemias, 42:279, 394
Crasto, Daniel de, 27:245
Crate, Daniel de, 21:51
Crawford, 22:76, 78; 26:194
Crawford, Charles, 30:83; 46:183; *Essay on the
Propagation of Gospel*, 30:119-20
Crawford, Francis Marion, 28:27; 35:249-50
Crawford, Thomas, 28:27, 62
Crawford, W. H., 30:404
Crawford, William, 39:5-6, 55
Crawley, 32:92-93
Creedmoor State Hospital, 47:216
Creek Agency, 34:267-68
Creelman, James, 41:184-85
Creizenach, Theodor, 35:125
Crémieux, Adolphe, 24:25-26, 47; 29:127;
33:xxxi; 34:249; 35:136; 36:3; 39:396, 403,

425; 40:403; 41:37-38; 42:162-64, 168-69; 43:40; 49:188; Board of Delegates of American Israelites, 29:77, 86, 92, 95, 97, 110; "Jewish Disabilities in Balkans," 24:2, 7, 9, 22; letters, 31:xxxiii; Paris Conference 1876, 24:29-30, 39
Crémieux, Isaac Adolphe, 28:119, 132
Crémieux Association Branch, 39:396
Crémieux colony, 38:241, 248, 305-6; 48:85-87, 93
Cresson, Laura May, gift, 33:xxxii
Cresson, Warder, 26:147, 149; 27:503; 33:xxxii; 35:240; 39:333; 40:287, 363; "An Interesting Reference to Warder Cresson," 26:xxxi; 28:241-42; *Jesus Christ Crucified Afresh*, 30:278-79; "Warder Cresson's 'The Key of David,' 1852," 26:xv
Crevecoeur, J. Hector St. John, 39:349; 46:289
Crevier, Joseph, 23:139
Crimea, 34:150, 155
Crimean War, 23:125; 25:xii; 26:151, 156; Red Cross, 33:212
Crimmins, John D., 33:221
Crimshier, John de, 23:157
Crispijsen, Elbert, 33:121
Cristalar, A. M., 27:510
Critic, 43:23; 45:250
Critic Club of Sacramento, 29:196
Crittenden, John Jordan (Kentucky), 22:xxiii; 28:42; 39:16; "References to Jews in the Correspondence of John J. Crittenden," 23:vii, xiii, 117-27; 35:130
Croce, Benedetto, 50:268
Crockery Board of Trade, 31:272
Crockett and Fickett shipyard, 48:173
Crockett, William, 48:173
Croghan, George, 23:4, 7-9, 11, 13-22; 30:63; 33:4; 35:15
Crohan, Dennis, 30:77
Crohn, Burrill B., 42:216; 50:282; "The Centennial Anniversary of the Mount Sinai Hospital (1852-1952)," 42:113-30; 49:231; "Doctor Israel Moses," 37:xxxii; "History of the Mount Sinai Hospital (1852-1952)," 41:390
Croke, Richard, 28:170
Croker, Richard, 43:31
Croly, George, *Salathiel*, 30:364, 433

Cromartie, M. W., 26:254
Cromelien, David, 27:245, 315
Cromelien, Hetty, 27:286, 289
Cromelien, Rowland, 27:286, 289, 315
Crommelin, 27:105
Crommelin, H., 27:120
Cromwell, Oliver, 26:127; 27:228, 387; 29:xxv, 46-48; 31:116-17, 121, 123, 260; 34:6, 174; 35:118, 148; 37:362; 39:185; 40:124; 42:428, 437; 44:96
Cromwell, Richard, 25:100; 46:36
Cronbach, Abraham, 40:47
Cronson, Bernard, 42:26-28
Crooger, Jon., 21:48
Crookshanks, Jon., 26:249
Cropsey, Judge, 29:150
Crosby, John P., 39:34
Cross, J. C., 26:245
Cross, James, 40:124
Cross, Wilbur L., Library, 45:145
Crossman, Richard, 39:333
Crosta, Daniell D. de, 21:45
Crosta, S. da, 27:63
Crosta, Solomon da, 27:51, 59
Croswell, Edwin, 30:404
Crothers, Governor, 31:221
Crouch, Nathaniel, 31:117; *Eine Reise nach Jerusalem*, 30:92, 94; *Journey to Jerusalem*, 30:97, 100; 35:xix
Crowe, Eyre A., 36:81
Cruger, Henry (?), 38:118
Cruger, Henry, Jr., 35:300
Cruger, John, 25:91
Cruger, John Harris, 22:39
Crugier, Thomas, 34:120
Crum, Bartley, 39:333
Crump, William W., 27:506
Crumpton, Thomas, 33:207
Crusades, 26:128
Cruttwell, Clement, 37:380
Cruz, Ferdinando Mendes, 33:113
Cruz, Manuel Fernando, 33:77-78, 119
Crybbace, Thomas Tully, 26:141-42
Crygier, Simon, 28:226
Cuba, 25:133; 28:238, 290; 41:367-69, 71
Cubucana, 22:111
Cuello, Domingo, 31:28
Cuenca, Maria de, 31:21
Culberson, Charles A., 36:285; 41:180, 189

Cullen, Charles Edmond, 42:180
Cullen, Rosana, 26:278
Cullum, George W., 26:181
Cultural Politics, 50:112
Cultural Zionism, 49:84
Culver, Essae M., 50:271
Cumberland, Richard, 35:234-35; 37:197;
  40:346; *The Fashionable lover*, 33:175; *The
  Jew*, 30:102-5; 33:182
Cumberland Island, 26:192
Cumbther, D. W., 34:267
Cummings, Homer S., 45:222
Cummings, John, 39:32
Cundall, Frank, 23:26, 182; 25:114; 35:130,
  137; communication, 22:xviii; elected
  member, 22:xiv; "Extracts from a Jamaica
  Magazine of 1797 Relating to the Jews,"
  25:xiv; gifts, 22:xxxii, xxxiv; 23:xviii; 25:xv;
  26:xxxiv; 28:xxxix; Jamaican history,
  22:xxxii; "The Migration from Surinam to
  Jamaica," 28:xi; necrology of, 35:x, 311; "A
  Note on Isaac Lopez, a Jamaican
  Minister," 22:xiii; "Michael Leoni,"
  23:179-80; "Note on Michael Leoni,"
  22:xxix; "A rare work by Israel Lopez
  Laguna, the first Jamaican author," 31:xxiv;
  "The Taxation of Jews in Jamaica," 28:xvi;
  238-39; "The Taxing of the Jews in
  Jamaica in the Seventeenth Century,"
  29:xv, 243-47; and Joseph L. Pieterez,
  "Jamaica under the Spaniards," 28:xi; and
  N. Darnell Davis, "Documents Relating to
  the History of the Jews in Jamaica and
  Barbados in the Time of William III,"
  22:xxviii; and N. Darnell Davis and Albert
  M. Friedenberg, "Documents Relating to
  the History of the Jews in Jamaica and
  Barbados in the Time of William III,"
  23:vii, 25-29
Cunha, Andreas Soares da, 33:113
Cunha, Daniel Mendes, 32:64
Cunha, Diego Soares da, 33:112
Cunha, Francisco Soaris da, 33:112
Cunha, Gastao da, 36:81
Cunha, Isaac Rodrigues, 29:50-51
Cunha, Israel da, 33:65
Cunha, Laurens de, 33:116
Cunha, Manuel da, 33:116

Cunha, Xavier da, necrology of, Alberto
  Carlos da Silva, 22:xxviii; 25:148
Cunningham, 25:56
Cunningham, Waddell, 26:269
Curaçao, 22:123; 26:219; 28:216; 29:46, 50;
  "The Burial Society in Curaçao in 1783,"
  22:xii, 169-72; Congregation Mikveh
  Israel, 22:122, 169; Hebra or Burial
  Society, 25:138; "Jewish Education in
  Curaçao," 44:215-36; kosher meat, 25:43;
  "The Mohelim of Curaçao and Surinam,
  and Other Notes," 25:xiii, 138-41;
  "Observations on the Climate and Diseases
  of the Island of Curaçao," 26:221; *Precious
  Stones of the Jews of Curaçao: Curaçaon
  Jewry, 1656-1957*, reviewed, 47:176-78;
  Sephardic Jews, 29:20-31; "Shemah Israel,
  A Magazine of the Reform Movement in
  Curaçao, 1864-1865," 26:xv, 239-41
Curado, Vincent, 33:118
Curator, reports of, 22:x, xxxi-xxxvi; 23:xvii-
  xviii; 25:ix, xv, xvi; 26:x, xxvi, xxxiii-xxv;
  28:xii, xxxvii-xli; 31:xiii, xix, xxvii, xxxi-
  xxxv; 32:x, xvii, xxv-xxxii; 33:vii, xxi, xxvii-
  xxxiii; 34:x, xvi-xxvii; 35:x, xvii-xxiv
Curiel, Abraham, 44:231-32
Curiel, Benjamin, 22:169-70; 29:30
Curiel, Ishac, 25:138
Curiel, Ishac d'Abraham da Silva, 29:28
Curiel, Jacob, 44:228
Curiel, Josseph, 25:138; 44:231
Curiel, Josseph de Isaac, 29:30
Curiel, Jossep de Is., 22:169-70
Curiel, Selomoh de Jacob, 44:231
Curiet, Abraham Moses, 37:83
Curson, Samuel, 25:130
Curtin, Andrew G., 24:122; 29:91; 36:173-74
Curtis, Charles, 45:40
Curtis, George William, 34:169
Curtis, M. B., 40:352
Curtis, Natalie, 41:116-17
Curzon, Lord, 36:80, 82
Cushing, Caleb, 29:89; "Caleb Cushing and
  the Proposed Readmission of the Jews,"
  31:xvi
Cushing, Harvey, 46:434
Cushing, William Barker, 50:333
Cushman, Charlotte, 50:299
Custis, Elija Parke, 46:3

Custodiano, Antonio, 26:248
Cuthbert, J., 23:49
Cuthbert, R., 23:49
Cutler, Mr., 40:304
Cutler, Harry, 36:285; 49:193
Cutter, George W., 38:65
Cutting, Olivia M., 33:222
Cuyler, Philip, 26:268-70
Cuzzins, Captain, 27:182
Cyprus, 26:156; 47:163
Cyrenaica, 46:481; 47:174
Czaykowski, 39:151

Czechoslovakia, *In Search of Freedom: A History of American Jews from Czechoslovakia*, reviewed, 39:329-31; "German Jews of Prague: A Quest for Self-Realization," 50:98-120; history, writing of, 46:286, 312, 320, 324, 368, 412, 425; "The Revolution of 1848 and the Jewish 'On to America' Movement," 38:185-234, 345; State Prize, 50:117; "Woodrow Wilson, the Birth of Czechoslovakia and Congressman Sabath," 38:342
Czechowski, M. B., 39:163-64
Czernitscheff, General, 26:50

D

Dacheröden, Caroline von, 26:97
Dactilus, 28:159
Dagama, Abraham, 42:280, 394
Dagama, Isaac, 23:157-58
Dagama, Sarah (Pinheiro), 23:157-58
Daggett, Windsor P., 40:54
Dahlgren, John Adolphus Bernard, 50:332
Daily Advertiser, The (N.Y.), 38:121; 49:52
Daily Atlas (Milwaukee), 47:49
Daily Dispatch (Richmond), 21:xxiii
Daily Express (New York), 39:136
Daily Gleaner, 37:343
Daily News, 46:92
Daily Tribune, 40:150
Dakotas, 48:83; 49:179
Dakota colonies, 38:306-7, 314
Dakota Indians, "A Hebrew-Dakota
    Dictionary," 42:361-70
Daladier, Edouard, 46:259
Dalberg, Karl von, 26:35, 39, 61
Dalcho, Frederick, 32:52
Dalegao, Jan Viera, 33:119
Dalgado, Francisco Dias, 33:112
Dallas, A. J., 39:12, 59
Dallas, George M., 22:89
Dalmbert, "Historical Sketch of the
    Dalmbert Brothers," 23:xiv
Dalmedo, Paulo, 33:119
D'Almeida, 22:29
Dalsace, Gustave, 41:161
Dalsheimer, Simon, 31:226
Daly, Augustin, 35:233; 40:350-51
Daly, Charles P., 31:81-83, 94, 102-3;
    32:110-11, 130; 34:3, 7, 172, 174, 177, 246,
    256, 299; 43:176; 44:200; "The Settlement
    of the Jews in North America," 22:xxxiii
Damasa, Abm., 27:91
Damascus, 24:88, 94; 28:74, 172

Damascus affair, 22:71; 24:4-5; 26:135-36,
    254-55; 27:115, 520; 29:59; 36:ix; 41:16,
    289; 42:60-61; 47:128; 48:217, 224; 49:17;
    50:13
Damascus meetings, 48:144
Dame, William, 27:415
Dan II, 24:100
Dana, Henry Wadsworth Longfellow,
    38:332; 45:27
Dana, Herman, 42:419
Dance of Death, The, 45:250, 253-54
D'Andrade, David DaCosta, 32:57
Dandrade, Salvador, 44:205; 46:27
Dandrado, Joan Gomez, 33:115
Dandrado, Pedro Dacunha, 33:118
Dandrado, Pedro Dias, 33:117
Daniel, Henry, 27:59-60, 274
Daniel, Samuel, 32:61
Daniel Guggenheim Fund, 47:181
Daniels, Mr., 27:239
Daniels, Alfred B., 26:xxxiii; gift, 22:xxxii
Daniels, Edward S., "Extracts from Various
    Records of the Early Settlement of the
    Jews in the Island of Barbados, W. I.,"
    26:250-56
Daniels, Elias, 27:215
Daniels, Samuel, 27:91
Daniels, Samuel Elias, 26:251-55; 27:215
Daniels, Sophie, 26:255
Danish West Indies, 28:219, 221; 47:193; "An
    Early Confirmation Certificates from the
    Island of St. Thomas, Danish West
    Indies," 23:180-82; "Gabriel Milan, the
    Jewish Governor of St. Thomas," 28:213-
    21
Danne, Julie, 27:277
Danne, Michael, 25:120
Danneberg, M., 27:505
Dannett, Sylvia G. G., 50:271, 275, 396

91

Dano, 32:77, 89
Danon, Ben, 31:198
Dante, 28:147, "Dante: His Jewish
  Connections and Supposed Jewish
  Origin," 29:xxxvi; "Heaven and Hell with
  Special Reference to Dante," 29:xli
Danto, Charles, 29:68
Danubian Principalities, 29:86; 47:193;
  49:28-29; Board of Delegates of American
  Israelites, 29:92-98, 109-11
Danz, Syndic, 26:37, 53, 58
Danziger, Abraham (Lincoln), 37:43
Danziger, Henry, 37:43
Danziger, Isaac (Andrew Johnson), 37:43
Danziger, Jacob (John Conness), 37:43
Danziger, Rev., 27:504
Darby, 23:120
D'Arcy, Rey, 35:268
Darcys, 34:98
Darech Emuno, 38:68
Darius, 50:265
Darkest Russia, 46:95, 99
Darley, J., 33:195
Darmesteter, James, 37:29; 39:321, 323
Darmstadt, George, 50:175
Darmstadt, Joseph, 50:63, 164
Darmstadt, Patty, 50:175
Darmstaedter, Frank J., 41:296; 43:9
Darr, Joseph, 35:141
Dartmoor Prison, 26:294; 39:6-7, 27, 52
Dartmouth College, 38:336-37; 40:407;
  41:49; "College Bookplates with Hebrew
  Inscriptions," 45:131-33
Dartmouth, Lord, 25:119
Darwin, Charles, 42:342, 357
Dashew, Mrs. Jacob, 49:270
Dassevede, Carol, 33:115
Dassevedo, Antonio Paijs, 33:47
Dassevedo, Domingo Carvalho, 33:112
Dassevedo, Domingo Rodrigus, 33:112
Dassevedo, Ferdinand Cortinho, 33:113
Dassevedo, Ignatio Mendes, 33:115
Dassine, Jacob, 33:122
Dasylua, Salamao, 42:278, 394
Daudet, Alphonse, 35:248
Daueiga, Samuel, 42:220, 258, 280, 285, 291-
  93, 392, 394
Daugherty, James, 50:402

Daughters of the American Revolution,
  33:218; 45:54, 198; Israel (Baltimore),
  22:215; 25:151
Daughters of Rebecca, Easton, Pa., 42:202
Daughters of Zion (N.Y.), 49:167
Davenport, E. L., 50:299
Davenport, Mary, 27:321
Davenport, Thomas, 27:319-21
Daveyga, Is, 21:170
Davezac, A., 27:254; *Case on the Contested Seat
  of David Levy*, 30:364-65
David, Aaron Hart, 50:129
David bar Aleazer, 27:91
David, Capt. (1769), 22:40-41, 46-47
David, Charlotte, 27:79
David, David, 29:141
David, Davidson, 22:193
David, Eleazar, 27:76
David, Henry, 41:392; 42:215; history,
  writing of, 46:257, 264-66; "Jewish Labor
  History—A Problem Paper," 46:215-20;
  "The Jewish Unions and Their Influence
  upon the American Labor Movement,"
  41:339-45, 387
David, Hyam, 21:73, 79
David, King, 23:106
David ben Loeb, *Shir Hillulim, Migdal David*,
  22:120
David, Maurice, "Who was Columbus?,"
  33:36-37
David, Moritz, 50:313
David, Mos., 21:160
David ben Moses, 22:115
David, Percy, 50:126
David, Rabbi, 21:114
David, Samuel, 27:76, 79
David, Sigmund, 41:195-203
"David L. Yulee, Florida's First Senator,"
  50:335
David of Palermo, 28:207
David of Paris (sculptor), 27:401
David, the Jew, 31:247
David Horodoker Benevolent Assn., 25:136
Davidovich, D., 39:109
Davidow, 46:86
Davids, David, 28:xxxviii
Davidsohn, 29:xliii
Davidson, B. J., 39:83
Davidson, Cecilia R., 45:244

Davidson, David, 25:117
Davidson, Dr., 27:239
Davidson, Gabriel, 34:243; 39:238; "The
    Palestine Colony in Michigan," 29:vii,
    xxix, 61-74; "The Story of Sholem," 29:xv;
    and Dr. Edward A. Goodwin, "The
    Chaluzim in American Colonization,"
    31:xvii; and Max J. Kohler, "Aaron
    Aaronsohn, Agricultural Explorer,"
    29:xxix; 31:vii, 197-210
Davidson, Israel, 29:xiv; 31:xv; 32:xii; 34:286;
    45:142; death, 37:xii; gift, 35:xviii;
    "Thesaurus of Mediaeval Hebrew Poetry,"
    33:26
Davidson, Jo, 35:266
Davidson, Joseph, 38:63
Davidson, Lewis, 25:117
Davidson Library of Judaica, 45:143, 169
Davidson, Mary, "Descendants of Mary
    Davidson and Col. Isaac Franks," 23:xvii
Davidson, Ralph, 38:63
Davidson, Thomas, 39:201
Davies, Captain, 27:363
Davies, David, 27:105, 519; *Philosophy of the
    Hebrews*, 30:313-14
Davies, Elizabeth, 27:271
Davies, John, 40:169
Davies, John M., 42:115
Davies, Joseph, 27:271
Davies, Lawrence, 33:18
Davies, Lionel, 40:140, 169-70
Davies, Rowland, 27:105
Davies, T., 37:199
Davilla, 37:199
Davis, Mr. (London), 27:79
Davis, Mrs., 25:112
Davis, Alexander, 50:160
Davis, Allan, 35:257-58, 268
Davis, Ansley, 50:173-74, 187
Davis, Bancroft, 33:213
Davis, Benjamin, 50:160, 169, 173-74
Davis, Mrs. Benjamin, 28:240
Davis, Capt. (Civil War), 39:179
Davis, Captain (War of 1812), 26:180
Davis, Charles Augustus, 39:34
Davis, Curtis Carroll, 38:331; 39:206; "Judith
    Bensaddi and the Reverend Doctor Henry
    Ruffner," 39:115-42
Davis, David (Illinois), 44:101

Davis, David (Philadelphia), 33:6
Davis, David B., 38:59
Davis, Eliza, 34:237
Davis, Evan, 23:158
Davis family (London), 27:91
Davis, George, 50:169, 173-74
Davis, Goodman, 33:6
Davis, Helen I., 34:252; "Bret Harte and His
    Jewish Ancestor, Bernard Hart," 32:99-
    111; gift, 32:xxv
Davis, Henry, 27:51
Davis, Henry, Jr., 27:318
Davis, Henry Winter, 40:290
Davis, Israel, 29:134
Davis, James, 28:240; death, 37:xii
Davis, Jefferson, 23:58, 62, 126; 25:23-24, 26,
    28; 29:120-21; 40:88, 145; 43:101, 107,
    109-12; 48:153, 167; 50:316-21, 332, 342,
    365, 386, 407
Davis, Mrs. Jefferson, 38:158
Davis, John, 27:315
Davis, John W., 28:xviii-xix; 34:228; 36:80
Davis, Joseph, 39:159
Davis, Lottie K., 43:198
Davis, Michael, 27:271
Davis, Mrs. Michael M., 26:229
Davis, Miriam Maduro Peixotto, 33:6
Davis, Moses (1), 27:41, 43
Davis, Moses (2), 27:79
Davis, Moses (Westchester), 50:38, 48
Davis, Moshe, 37:15; 38:vi, 78; 39:259; 43:70;
    47:200; 48:266; 49:216, 251; American
    Jewish History conference, 46:35-36, 141-
    42; Civil War, 50:271, 275, 404;
    conference of historians, 44:245, 247;
    "Cyrus Adler and the Peace Conference,
    1919 (on the occasion of the 90th
    anniversary of his birth)," 43:231; *Darkhei
    ha-Yahadut ha-Amerika (Jewish Religious
    Life and Institutions in America: An
    Historical Study)*, reviewed, 43:197-98;
    executive council, 37:xxxvi; 38:342; 39:470;
    42:414; (ed.), *Israel: Its Role in Civilization*,
    reviewed, 46:129-31; "Israel Friedlander's
    'Aspects of Historical Judaism,' " 38:342;
    Jewish Historical Society of Israel, 41:391;
    Jewish local history, 49:263; "Jewish
    Religious Life and Institutions in
    America," reviewed, 40:194-95; "The

Lincoln-Hart Correspondence," 38:139-45; (ed.), *Mordecai M. Kaplan Jubilee Volume*, 43:194-97; necrology of Louis Mayer Rabinowitz, 47:201, 226-29; "A New Direction" on address, 46:141-42; presides, 48:266; "Sabato Morais: A Selected and Annotated Bibliography of His Writings," 37:xxxv, 55-93; vice-president, 45:264; 46:492; 48:265; 49:268; 50:426; writing American Jewish history, 46:135-36, 191-93, 445; *Yahadut Amerika be-Hitpathutah (The Shaping of American Judaism)*, reviewed, 42:91-107

Davis, Nicholas Darnell, 35:130, 132; gift, 22:xxxii; necrology of, 25:xii, 148-49; "Notes from Wills of the Family of Massiah of Barbados," 22:xiii, 178-80; *see also*: Cundall, Frank

Davis, Owen, 35:268

Davis, Rachel Du-Bois, gift, 34:xxv; "The Jews in American Life," 34:xxv

Davis, Rev., 22:24

Davis (David), Richard, 27:39, 70, 299; 31:97-99

Davis, Robert C., 31:211

Davis, Rowland, 21:169

Davis, Solomon, 50:173-74

Davis, Timothy M., 39:62

Davis, William, 22:76

Davis, William A. & Co., 38:123

Davis, W. J., 34:252

Davis Strachan & Co., 25:131

Davison, Mr., 37:408

Davison, C. S., 34:228

Davison, Henry, 27:514

Davison, Sol, 33:xxvi

Daviss, Robert, 40:82

Dawes, Anna Laurens, 47:9

Dawid, Joseph, 39:151

Day, The, 43:192

Day, Benjamin M., 34:215-16

Day, George E., 45:132

Day, Olivia Hotchkiss, 45:132

Day, Thomas, 21:20

Day Missions Library, 45:132

Daye, Stephen, 45:129; *The Bay Psalm Book*, 30:v

Dayton, Daniel, 26:225

Dayton, Jonathan, 39:19, 29

Dazevado, Isaac, 27:185

Dazeveda, Moses Cohen, 44:63; "Moses Cohen Dazavedo," 33:xvii

Deaboab, Joshua, 21:58

Dead Sea Exploration, 40:282-83

Dead Sea Scrolls, 42:317; 46:130

Deaf and Dumb Institute (N.Y.), 27:505; (Philadelphia), 27:370

Dean, John, 27:325

Dean, Samuel, 27:320

Deane, 31:72

Dearborn, General, 26:174

Dearborn Independent, 40:325; 42:320; 47:32

Dearborn Publishing Company *v.* Fitzgerald, 29:150

Deas, George, 50:397

Death and dying, Jewish law re, 27:46-50, 229-30

Debil, 41:146

Deborah, 26:271-73; 36:317; 40:20, 24, 350; 45:103, 126; 48:261; 50:118, 293-95

Deborah Nursery, 44:131

Debs, Eugene, 50:204-5, 211, 215, 220-21, 230

Debtors oath, 35:289

DeCampus, Samuel, 32:57

Decaserez, Abrao, 42:279, 394

Decastro, Joseph, 32:61

Decatur, Stephen, 26:185, 195; 27:495, 497; 39:8; 41:5-6; 46:4, 6-7, 10, 15

Decazes, Duke, 24:35

Decebalus, 24:100

De Chavez family, 42:108, 214

Decker, Benton C., 36:65-66

Declaration of Independence, 27:189; 42:432; 43:162-63; 46:181; 50:243, 246, 396; "Letter of Jonas Phillips, July 28, 1776, Mentioning the American Revolution and the Declaration of Independence," 25:xiii, 128-31

DeCordova family, in Jamaica, 22:xviii; *see also*: Cordova

DeCosta, *see also*: Costa

DeCosta, Alberquerque Daniel, 32:62

Decosta, David da, 32:57

Decosta, Jose, 27:43

Decoster, Ezek, 23:87

Decoster, Mrs., 23:87

Dedirick, Mr., 27:311

Defahr, Abraham, 27:235
Defense Service Act of 1949 (Israel), 49:275
Defontes, Izaque, 42:278, 394
Defosse, Pierre, 23:139
Defriez; Isaac v., 28:246
Deguignes, Joseph, 49:41, 45
Dehaine, Jacob, 37:169
DeHass, F. S., 29:100-101
De Horta, 33:37
Deinard, Ephraim, 22:102, 120; 33:30, 132,
    136-44, 146-48, 150-59; 34:xvii; 35:64;
    39:224; 45:136, 143-45, 149, 151, 154,
    204; 47:180; bibliography, 34:154-63;
    collection, 33:30; "Ephraim Deinard,"
    34:xiv, 149-63
Deinard, Jukuthiel Gerson, 34:149
Dekey, Elizabeth, 27:248
Delancey, James, 40:120
Delancey, Oliver, 40:120; 41:285, 287; 43:132
Delancey, Peter, 38:97
Delancy, General, 27:472
Deland, Margaret, 34:234
Delany, John, 21:193
Delapina, Jacob, 27:114
Delara, Cohen Moses, 32:62
Delattre, député, 41:161
Delaware, Delaware Constitution Sesqui-
    centennial, 35:xxi
Delaware and Hudson Canal, 35:307-9
Delaware and Schuylkill Canal Navigation,
    22:191
Delean, Leah, 32:57
Deleeon, Solomon, 32:61
Deleon, I. Alvares, 34:125, 140
Delesser, Aaron, 37:419
Delgadillo, Diego, 31:11
Delgado, Henrietta, 25:118
Delgado, Mary, 25:117
Delgado, Moses, 25:118
Delieben, Hannah, 23:187
Delieben, Israel, 23:187; 50:31
Delieben, Mrs. (Savannah), 48:13
Delima, Haine, 32:57
Delisser, George, 25:116
Delitzsch, Franz, 26:120; 33:36; Literaturblatt
    des Orients, 22:102
Delivant, Julia, 25:71
Dellon, The Inquisition in Goa, 31:xxxiii
Dellyon, Mathias, 32:57

Delmar, Alexander, 32:39-40
Delmar, Jacob, 32:64
Delmar, Jb., 21:171
Delmar, M., 27:120
Delmar, Sarah, 27:111
Delmedigo, Elijah, 28:197, 207
Deloche, Max, 41:161
Delucena, Abraham, 33:252
Delvalle (family name), 48:139
Delvally, Mrs., 27:91
Delyon, Lebinah, 32:57
Delyon, Moses (N.Y.), 21:51
Delyon, Moses (R.I.), 37:392, 398, 401-3,
    405-6
Delyon, Rachael, 32:57
Demarchena, Abraham, 42:278, 394
Dembitz, Lewis N., 40:28; 42:105; 47:203;
    50:345
Demedina, Jácob, 32:57
DeMedina, Joyce, 32:57
Demercado, Esther, 25:115
Demesquieta, Abraham Buino, 23:29
Demetrius, 26:169
DeMille, Henry Churchill, 40:359
Demilt, Isaac, 21:18
Deming, Sarah, 23:89
Democrat, The, 38:113-14
Democratic Party, 22:229; 41:329; 43:31;
    47:48, 51; 49:114-15; 50:289, 345
Democratic Society (New York), 38:115-17,
    124-25, 132; (Philadelphia), 38:132-37;
    46:3
Democratic Society of Polish Exiles in
    America (Towarzystwo Demokratyczne
    Wygnancow Polskich w Ameryce), 39:150-
    51
Demokrata Polski, 39:154
Demorag, Philip, 35:290
Demtres, William, 31:92-94, 100
DeMyer, Henry, 31:93
Demyre, Nicholas, 31:93
Demyre, William, 31:94, 100
Dendera, Temple of, 41:64
Denham, Edward, 37:343
Denison, George S., 43:90-91
Denmark, 26:57, 136, 219; "Gabriel Milan,
    the Jewish Governor of St. Thomas,"
    28:213-21
Dennie, Joseph, 38:130-32

Dennov, Peter, 43:51
Denton, Daniel, 45:202
Dentecolles, Francois-Xavier, 49:44
Dentz, Fredrik Oudschans, "The Name of
    the Country Surinam as a Family Name:
    The Biography of a Surinam Planter of the
    Eighteenth Century," 48:19-27, 262-64
Denucé, J., 34:266; 35:137
Denver, National Jewish Hospital for
    Consumptives, 25:124; 37:440
Denver Jewish News, 45:195
Denver School of Medicine, 45:195
Deodatus of Nola, 28:169
DePas, *see*: Pas
Depas, Ralph, 27:502-3
Depass, Joseph, 38:332
Depaz, Elias, 26:235; "Memorial of Solomon
    and Elias De Paz on the Capture of their
    Ship in 1728-9 off Jamaica by the
    Spaniards," 26:248-49
Depaz, Solomon, 26:235, "Memorial of
    Solomon and Elias De Paz on the Capture
    of their Ship in 1728-9 off Jamaica by the
    Spaniards," 26:248-49
DePeister, *see*: Peister (Peyster)
Depew, Chauncey M., 29:174; 33:221; 36:43
De peyster, 34:119
Depeza, Abraham, 31:242
Depeza, Moses, 31:242
DePuy, Moses, 35:307
Derby, Lord, 24:34, 104, 112
Derby, Richard, 37:108
Derech Emunch Congregation, Arverne,
    28:287
Dérenbourg, Joseph, 24:30; 41:161; 42:166;
    45:97, 102, 107-9
Deribera, Rodrigo, 23:151
Derkheim, Abram, 50:31
Derkheim, Myer, 50:31
Derrick, David, 50:286-87
Dervall, Rachel, 23:149
Dervall, Samuel, 23:149
Desbrosses, Elias, 28:224, 227; 34:119
Deschanel, Emile, 32:57
Desjardins, Ernest, 41:161
Des Moines, *Jews of Des Moines: The First
    Century*, 47:207; 49:222
Desmons, F., 41:161

De Sola, Abraham (Montreal), 21:xxiv, xxv;
    28:269; 38:72
De Sola, Abram, 28:xxxviii
De Sola, A. D. Meldola, 38:72
De Sola, Arthur, 44:118
De Sola, B., 38:72
De Sola, Bella Maud (Goldsmith), 28:281
De Sola, Clarence I., 25:113; gift, 28:xl;
    necrology of, 28:xxxii, 269-72
De Sola, D. A., 42:426
De Sola, Eliza, 35:316
De Sola, Ester (Joseph), 28:269
De Sola, Francisco, 44:116-18
De Sola, Gershon, 38:72
De Sola, H., 38:72
De Sola, Hannah, "An Early Confirmation
    Certificate from the Island of St. Thomas,
    Danish West Indies," 23:180-82
De Sola, Isaac Haim, 23:180
De Sola, Jacob M., 23:143
De Sola, Meldola, 28:xxxviii
De Sola, Mendola, 35:318; 42:378, 380
De Sola, Raphael Samuel Mendes, "Book of
    Prayers for Dew and Rain," 22:122-23
De Sola, Solomon, 35:xviii
De Sola, Mrs. Solomon, gift, 35:xviii
De Sola, Zipporah (Hoheb), 23:180
Desossa, Mosses, 32:61
Desportes, R. S., 50:330
Désprez, Félix, 24:57, 68-69, 121
Dessau, 28:104
Dessau, Abraham, 29:179
Dessau, Fanny (Zachariah), 29:179
Dessauer, Ernestine, 41:256
Destruction of Jerusalem, The, 30:188
Desuza, Abraham, 32:57
Desuza, Isaac, 32:57
Detmold, William, 42:117
Detorez, Jacob, 23:28
Detorres, Jacob, 32:61
Detroit, "Chapman Abraham: An Early
    Jewish Settler in Detroit," 40:81-86; "Jews
    in Detroit Prior to and Including 1850,"
    49:226; religious observances, mid-
    nineteenth century, 37:36; "The Startling
    Experience of a Jewish Trader During
    Pontiac's Siege of Detroit in 1763," 23:vii,
    xiv, 31-35
Detroit Historical Society, 49:226

Dettelbacher, Pauline, 41:246, 253
Deutch, Rachel, 47:202
Deutsch, Emanuel, 45:121
Deutsch, Gertrude, 31:xxxii
Deutsch, Gotthard, 26:28; 28:vii; 29:xiv;
39:305; 40:36, 38, 44, 48; 45:99, 101, 103;
46:488-89; "Abraham Alexandre Lindo, a
Pioneer American Jewish Publicist,"
25:xiv; "Dr. Abraham Bettmann, a Pioneer
Physician of Cincinnati," 23:vii, 105-16;
"America in Haskalah Literatures," 25:xiv;
"An American Mission to Palestine in
1847," 28:xxiii; communication from,
26:xxx; "The Criticism of Historical
Sources in the Talmud," 22:xviii; gift,
28:xxxviii, xl; "Graetz, the Historian of the
Jews," 26:xxx; "Heinrich Graetz, the
Historian: on the Centenary of his Birth,
October 31, 1917," 28:63-81; "How to Fill
the Gaps in Graetz's History," 28:xxxiii;
regrets of, 28:xvii; "The Talmud as
Source-Material for Jewish History,"
28:xxiii
Deutsche Chemische Gesellschaft, 22:225
Deutsche Hifsverein, 47:170
Deutsch-Israelitische Gemeindebund, 26:284
Deutsches Museum, 37:171
Devès, Paul, 41:161
Devil, 33:174-76
Devil's Lake agricultural experiment, 49:227
Devil's law case, The, 33:178
Devonshire, Duke of, 35:35
Devries, Judah A., 27:228
Devuiere, Batist, 40:83
De Waltoff, D. B., 33:163
Dewees, William P., 46:12
Dewey, George, 40:288; 43:29-30
Dewey, John, 42:342; 49:160
Dewey, Thomas E., "Address of Governor
Thomas E. Dewey," 44:75-77
DeWolf, *see*: Wolf
Deyo, Robert E., 41:124-25
DeYoung, *see*: Young
D'fonsica, Jacob, 32:57
Diable boiteux, 33:176
Dial, The, 50:198
Dias, Abraham, 37:338; 44:228
Dias, Abraham Lopes, 44:229
Dias, Abraham Ysreal, 44:92

Dias, Antonio, 46:40
Dias, David (Brazil), 33:68
Dias, David (Curaçao), 44:227
Dias, David de Jacob Lopes, 44:231
Dias, David Lopes, 44:227
Dias, Henrique, 43:129
Dias, Ishac Lopez, 44:227
Dias, Isaac, 32:57
Dias, Jacob Lopes, 44:228, 230-31
Dias, Lewis, 26:251
Dias, Jh. Lopez, 27:107
Dias, Pasqual, 33:118
Dias, Rachel, 33:87
Dias, Sarah Israel, 32:57
Diaspora, 46:196, 199-200, 206; "The
Beginnings of the Egyptian Diaspora,"
22:xvii
Diaswido, Moses, 32:57
Diaz, Abraham Israel, 42:225, 260, 275, 277-
78, 283-84, 391, 394
Diaz, Antonio de Cazeres, 31:27
Diaz, Armando, 31:214
Diaz, David, 42:222, 225, 260, 275, 277, 281-
82, 391, 394
Diaz, Francisco Lopez, 32:117
Diaz, Isque Fernandez, 23:27
Diaz, Isk, 21:51
Diaz, Jorge, 31:30
Diaz, Juan, 31:23
Diaz, Leonor, 31:28
Diaz, Luis (Barbados), 23:29
Diaz, Luis (Brazil), 33:99
Diaz, Luis (Mexico), 31:31
Diaz, Manuel, 31:29
Diaz, Porfirio, 31:215; 32:76, 86-87, 89-90,
93; 46:483
Diaz, Salo Yzarael Mendez, 42:278, 394
Dibdin, Thomas John, 33:174, 194; *The Jew
and the Doctor*, 30:127, 210; 33:188; *Liberal
opinions*, 33:187; *School for prejudice*, 33:187
Dick (slave), 50:162
Dickarson, 38:151
Dickens, Charles, 32:1; 34:237; 35:244-45;
47:224; 48:85; and Jews, 22:xxxiii
Dickenson, 25:56
Dickenson (actor), 33:193
Dickie, Mr., 27:258
Dickins, 27:413
Dickinson, Ann, 34:120

Dickinson, Charles S., 50:320
Dickinson, Emily, 46:442
Dickstein, Samuel, 45:227-28, 237
Dictionary of American Biography, 50:342, 345, 380-81, 383-84, 387, 397
Dictionary of American Jewish Biography, 44:247; 46:426, 436-37
"Dictionary of American National Biography," 22:x
Diefenbaker, John George, 49:267
Dien, 38:242
Diesendruck, Zevi, 40:48
Diet and dietary laws, 39:x, 362; 41:19, 34; 46:400; 48:233, 240; "New York Chooses a Chief Rabbi," 44:129-98; "The Question of the Kosher Meat Supply in New York in 1813: with a Sketch of Earlier Conditions," 25:vii, xii, 31-62; "Religious and Cultural Phases of American Jewish History," 39:291-301; and traveling man, 25:69
Dietz, August, 50:381
Dietz-Monnin, 41:161
Digges, W. H., 31:137
Dighton Rock, "Samuel Harris on the Dighton Rock Inscription," 28:xxii
Dike, Judge, 25:137; 29:153
Dikeman, John, 28:226
Diller, Captain, 26:183
Dillingham, Edward, 40:187
Dillingham Commission, 50:210
Dilyon, Benjamin, 32:57
Dinah (slave), 50:160
Dinckey, George, 26:183-84
Dingol, Solomon, 48:137
Dinin, Samuel, 42:420; 46:61-62, 120, 122-23
Dinkelspiel and Co., Simon (San Francisco), 37:45
Dinur, Ben Zion, 46:266, 426; 47:183; "American Jewish History in the Light of Modern Jewish History," 46:196-209
Dinwiddie, Robert, 33:173
Diplomatic service, 26:7
Dirck the Swede, 26:247
Dircks, Anna Maria (Tresoria), 37:109
Dircks, Jacob Gerhard, 37:109
Disabilities, 34:186, 220-33; 36:99-139; 39:208-9, 243; 47:193; "Anglo-Jewish Legal Cases," 25:134-38; Balkan States, 24:ix, 1-153; 25:xiv; 41:37-38; "Benjamin

F. Peixotto's Mission to Roumania," 24:1-24; "Bismarck and Beaconsfield in Their Relations to the Jews," 26:258-59; brokers, 28:256; Brussels Conference 1872, 24:25-29; "The Congress of Aix-la-Chapelle," 26:82-94; "The Doctrine that 'Christianity is a Part of the Common Law,' and its Recent Judicial Overthrow in England, with Particular References to Jewish Rights," 31:vii, xvi, 103-34; "An Early English Intervention on Behalf of Foreign Jewry," 35:xvi, 213-17; Germany, U.S. intercession, 36:348-85; "The Influence of Lewis Way and Other English Missionaries upon Alexander I's Treatment of the Jews," 26:116-25; Italy, U.S. intercession, 36:386-88; "Jewish Physicians in Italy: Their Relation to the Papal and Italian States," 28:xxiii, 133-211; "Jewish Rights at the Congresses of Vienna (1814-1815), and Aix-la-Chapelle (1818)," 26:vii, xv, 33-125; Jews' Naturalization Act of 1753, 35:35; Maryland, 26:193; Morocco, U.S. intercession, 36:19-41; "Naturalization Role of Jews of New York (1740-1759)," 37:xxx, 369-89; North Carolina, 29:138, 140; Palestine, U.S. intercession, 36:42-95; Paris Conference 1876, 24:29-39; Persia, U.S. intercession, 36:11-18; Poland, U.S. intercession, 36:140-67, 389-402; "Regarding the Draft of a System of Legislation for the Jews, July 17, 1809, by Wilhelm von Humboldt," 26:103-15; Rumania, U.S. intercession, 36:99-139; Russia, U.S. intercession, 36:171-295, 389-402; Serbia, 36:6; Switzerland, U.S. intercession, 36:299-322; Turkey, U.S. intercession, 36:3-10; U.S. diplomatic intercession in Austria, 36:323-47; Germany, 36:348-85; Italy, 36:386-88; Morocco, 36:19-41; Palestine, 36:42-95; Persia, 36:11-18; Poland, 36:140-67, 389-402; Rumania, 36:99-139; Russia, 36:171-295, 389-402; Switzerland, 36:299-322; Turkey, 36:3-10; "Wilhelm von Humboldt's Relations to the Jews," 26:95-103; William H. Taft, 28:xxxvii; *see also:* Emancipation

Discourse on the Restoration of the Jews, 41:16, 18

"Discovery of the New World," 22:125

Discrimination, 34:186, 220-33; 38:1-6, 156; 43:146; 44:208-9; 45:9-10, 224; 47:127-28, 194, 233; 48:243; "The Abrogation of the Russian-American Treaty of 1832 and the Drafting of the Treaties of 1919 for Protecting Religious and Racial Minorities," 32:xix; *Claims of Jews to an Equality of Rights*, 30:355-56; College of New York, 29:105; "An Early English Intervention on Behalf of Foreign Jewry," 35:xvi, 213-17; "The European Aspect of the American-Russian Passport Question," 46:86-100; "Evidences of Business Discrimination in the Civil War Period," 38:342; history, writing of, 46:252-53, 268, 271-72, 313, 329, 330-31, 336, 401, 416-17; "The Influence of the Russo-American Treaty of 1832 on the Rights of American Jewish Citizens," 41:163-94; (Maryland), *Bill Respecting Civil Rights and Religious Privileges*, 30:216; New Netherlands, 29:39-52; *Persecution of Jews in the East*, 30:350-51; Prague, 50:98-120; "President Roosevelt and the Abrogation of the Russian Treaty of 1832," 32:xix; "Rumania and America, 1873: Leon Horowitz' Rumanian Tour and its Background," 45:67-92; Russia and Isidor Rayner (1850-1912), 40:288-310; "A Side Light on Restrictive Covenants," 41:381-84; "Social Discrimination against Jews in America, 1830-1930," 47:1-33; Speech on Confirmatory Act Abolishing Religious Test, 30:227; *Strangers in the Land: Patterns of American Nativism, 1860-1925*, reviewed, 45:217; "Unequal Religious Rights in Maryland Since 1776," 25:vii; 93-107; U.S. Army Chaplain, 29:103-4

Disinero, Francisco Lopes, 33:112

Diskin, Joseph Duber, 44:137, 141

Dispeck, David ben Joel, 31:268

Dispersed of Judah, Congregation, New Orleans, 35:xviii; 38:64

Displaced persons, 46:294, 303, 312-15, 324, 330, 333, 343, 351-65

D'Israel, L. S., *Talmudic Maxims*, 30:433-34

Disraeli, Benjamin, 24:121; 25:68; 29:xliii, 152; 31:187; 32:1; 33:xxxi; 34:222, 224; 35:120, 237-39, 246, 253-54; 37:21; 40:119, 330; 41:38; 42:440; 45:260; 46:435; Balkan States and Jewish disabilities, 24:24, 41, 45-46, 51, 66, 71, 121; "Bismarck and Beaconsfield in Their Relations to the Jews," 26:258-59; Coningsby, 30:381, 398; *Contarini Fleming*, 30:278; *Henrietta Temple*, 30:312; Palestine restoration, 26:157, 159; *Sybil*, 30:382; *Venetia*, 30:312; *Vivian Grey*, 30:240; *The Young Duke*, 30:269

D'Israeli, Isaac, 22:xxxi; 35:238, 246; 43:239; 45:25; *Amenities of Literature*, 30:353; *Calamities of Authors*, 30:148; *Curiosities of Literature*, 30:96, 284, 291, 300; *The Literary Character*, 30:177; *Miscellanies of Literature*, 30:353; *Narratives Poems*, 30:121; *Quarrels of Authors*, 30:155; *Romances*, 30:121-22

Disraeli Literary Association, 31:293

Dissertation on the New Heavens and Earth, 30:370

Diston, Oliver, 50:389

District of Columbia, 50:280, 304; board of education, 29:200; Jewish local history, 49:220; "Notes of Jewish Interest in the District of Columbia," 26:xiv; 211-18; Sunday Legislation, 26:217-18; "A Supposed Interdenominational Society in 1832," 26:211-13; Washington Hebrew Congressional Charter, 26:213-17

Dittenhoefer, Abram J., 47:77; 50:398

Dittenhoefer, Isaac, 38:348

A Divine Call to the Jews, 30:90-91, 97

Divinsky, Gecob, 38:73

Divorce, 26:259-60; 29:149, 153; 37:51; 44:133, 155-56; 49:87; "Anglo-Jewish Legal Cases," 25:135; Israel, 49:276

Dix, Dorothea Lynde, 50:328

Dix, Henry A., 46:255

Dix, John A., 22:200; 39:14; 43:124; 50:235-36

Dix, Mark H., gift, 33:xxxiii

Dix, Morgan, *see*: Groesbeck, David

Dizdar, Ahmed Agha, 37:220

Djavid Bey, 36:74

Djemal Pasha, 36:67

Dmowski, Roman, 36:150-51
Dnieper Manufacturing Association, 43:69
Dob Pique, Rabbi, 27:99, 338
Dobbin, James C., 40:285
Dobroudja, 24:65, 73, 92
Dobsevage, A. D., 35:64
Dobsevage, I. George, 50:394
Debson, Richard, 37:420
Dr. Herzl Zion Club, 33:146-47
Doctorowitz, J., gift, 35:xxiii
Doctor Plot trials, 50:98
Dr. Reed Cushion Shoe Company, 31:284
Dod, Daniel, 48:175
Dodd, William E., 36:375
Dodge, Cleveland H., 33:221-23
Dodge, G. M., 50:293
Dodge, James M., 41:45-46, 48
Dodsley, J., 37:199
Dodsley, Robert, see: Nathan Ben Saddi
Dodson, Michael and Joseph Stock, Appendix to Lowth's Isaiah, 30:294
Doedens, H., 33:87
Doerr, Noel, 42:305-9
Doesburg, Lambertus, 48:24
Doherty, Beka, The Mount Sinai Hospital, 1852-1952, 49:231
Dohm, C. G., 22:27
Dohm, Christian Wilhelm, 26:41, 48, 83, 85, 88, 95-97, 102; 28:93; 29:19; 34:25; 35:122; 37:173, 175-77; education, 28:84-85, 93-95, 110
Dolgin, Simon A., 46:121
Dolitzky, M. M., 35:64
Doliueyra, Moseh, 42:278, 284, 286, 391, 394
Dolivera, Gonsalvo, 33:118
Dolivera, Joan, 33:116
Dolivera, Maria, 33:119
Domenge, Jean, 49:44-45
Dominiano, 35:222
Domingo de Betanzas, 31:17, 19
Dominguez colony, 39:94
Dominican Republic, iniquities, 31:15
Donald Steamship Lines, 28:270
Donaldson, John, 37:116-17, 119
Doneldson, John, 27:245
Dongan, Governor, 27:379
Dongan, Thomas, 31:89, 91-92
Donnan, Elizabeth, 34:285
Donnelly, Ignatius, 40:338-39, 341, 343

Donnolo, Sabbato ben Abraham, 28:140-41
Donohoe, Michael, 41:187
Donohue, C., 49:187
D'Orce, 38:316
Dordecht club, 22:33, 36
Doria, Andrea, 28:195
Dormido, Daniel, 42:279, 394; 50:76
Dormido, Salomon, 50:76
Dormido, Ysra Lemos, 42:279, 394
Dormitzer, 38:197
Dornbusch, C. E., 50:269, 271
Dorr, Captain, 26:184
Dorris, Jonathan Truman, 50:335
Dorsey, James Owen, 42:367
Dorshay Zedek Congregation, Mobile, 46:117-18
Dorshe Daath Society, 29:157
Dostie, A. P., 43:99
Dostoevski, Feodor Mikhailovich, 50:115
Doswell, Thomas W., 27:506
Dothan, Ala., Jewish Welfare Fund, contribution, 37:xxviii
Deubreva, Ferdinand F., 37:443
Dougherty, John, 32:52
Douglas, Lincoln-Douglas debates, 31:294; 50:346-47, 350
Douglas, Stephen, 23:58; 25:22; 41:233; 44:99, 102, 104; 48:150; 50:346-48
Douglas, William O., 43:161
Douglass, 33:173
Douglass, Frederick, 33:213
Doumergue, Gaston, 46:98
Dounash Ben Labrat, 37:69
Dournovo, 39:72
Dovale, Eliao, 44:233
Dovrede, Gideon, 23:158
Dow, Daniel, A Dissertation on the Sinaitic and Abrahamic Covenants, 30:145-46
Down with the Jews, 37:424
Downey, John G., 46:124
Downing, Thomas, 27:121
Downtown Talmud Torah, 35:62
Doyle(s), 23:63, 69
Doyle, John A., 38:290-91
Drachman, Bernard, 33:132; 34:xvii; 35:64; 37:93; 44:145, 169; gift, 34:xxv; "Looking at America," 34:xxv; The Unfailing Light: Memoirs of an American Rabbi, reviewed, 40:311-13

Drachman, Harry Arizona, 22:182
Drachman, Julian M., 40:313
Drage, Charles, *The Life and Times of General Two-Gun Cohen*, reviewed, 44:126-28
Drago, Abraham (Amsterdam), 32:19, 20
Drago, Abraham (Brazil), 42:280, 394
Drago, Isaac Franco, 42:253, 278, 291-92, 392, 394
Drago, Isack, 32:16
Drago, Isacq Franco, 33:63
Drago, Jacob, 33:88; 42:223, 225, 258, 260, 275, 277, 281-82, 284-87, 292-93, 390, 394
Drago, Manuel Fernandez, 33:53
Drago, Moseh, 42:259, 292, 387, 392, 394
Drago, Moseh Franco, 44:223
Drake, Francis, 32:6
Drake, J., 25:35
Drake, Japser, *see*: Sears, Isaac
Drama, 39:96, 102, 104; 46:348-49; *Alberti*, 30:179, 182-83; *Almachide*, 30:268; *L'Ape Musicale*, 30:268; *Camillus*, 30:290; *Il Don Giovanni*, 30:243; *Dramas, Discourses and Pieces*, 30:334; *Elisa e Claudio*, 30:282, 290; *The Evil Eye*, 30:276; *The Fortress of Sorrento*, 30:136-37; G. Ganguda, 39:104; *The Grecian Captive*, 30:202, 204; *Hadad*, 30:235; Jacob Gordin, 39:102; *The Jew*, 30:102-5; *The Jew and the Doctor*, 30:127, 210; "Jewish Prototypes in American and English *Romans* and *Drames á Clef*," 35:xiv, 227-80; Jewish Theater, 38:308, 311; 39:217, 257-58; *The Maid of Midian*, 30:288-89; *Marion*, 30:205-6; *The Merchant of Venice*, 30:220, 440; *Il Mezenzio*, 30:298; *The Mountain Torrent*, 30:190-91; "A New York Première of Herzl in 1885," 35:287-88; *Le Nozze Di Figaro, Il Don Giovanni, e l'Assur Re d'Ormus*, 30:242-43; "Plays of Jewish Interest on the American Stage, 1752-1821," 33:xvii, 171-98; "Present-day American Jewish drama," 35:xv; "References to M. M. Noah and A. Phillips 1821-1822, in 'The theatrical life of Joe Cowell Comedian, written by himself,'" 33:xvii; *The Rose of Arragon*, 30:202-3; *Sacred Dramas*, 30:83, 86, 112; *She Would Be a Soldier*, 30:185-86; *Shylock*, 47:5; *A Tale of Lexington*, 30:216-17; *The*

Wandering Boys, 30:193, 195; 39:362, 367-68, 388; 48:133; Yiddish theatre, 39:257-58; *Zamira*, 30:304-5
Dramatic literature, Jew in, 40:345-60, 406
Dransfield, Thomas, 50:81
Draper, Helen Fidelia, 33:222
Draper, John, 37:122
Draper, Simon, 39:34
Drascovich, Mr., 50:248-49
Drayton, William Henry, 39:344-45
Draz, Nico, 39:84
Dreben, Helen, 31:221
Dreben, Sam, 35:327; "The Fighting Jew," 31:xiv, 211-17
Dreifus, H., 29:134
Dreifus, Herbert Loeb, 41:373
Dreifuss, Babette, 41:267
Dreifuss, Bessie Hays, 29:169
Dreifuss, Jeremias, 41:267
Dreller, Louis, 47:203
Drexel, Morgan and Company, 48:58
Dreyfous, Joseph, 27:315
Dreyfous, L., 27:120
Dreyfus, Alfred, 22:224; 28:79-80; 34:xix, 165, 223, 228-30; 35:137, 258; 39:95, 409, 416; 40:325; 41:212; 43:32; 45:206; 46:90, 94, 197-98; 48:252; *Antisemitism in Modern France: Vol. I, The Prologue to the Dreyfus Affair*, reviewed, 41:95-96; "Re: The Affaire Dreyfus," 45:258-59; *Zola and the Dreyfus case*, 35:xxi
Dreyfus, Pierre, 35:137
Dreyfus, Robert, 35:260
Dreyfus, Stanley, 40:53
Dreyfuss family (D.C.), 41:373
Dreyfuss, Hayum, 41:267
Drew, 29:69
Drielsma, J. A., 48:23
Droilett, Paul, 23:148
Dropsie, Aaron, 41:87; 47:206
Dropsie family, 41:88-90
Dropsie, Moses Aaron, 28:xxxiv, 283; 29:188-89; 40:10-11; 42:378, 380-81; 43:148; 45:180, 202-3; 47:79, 206; 48:208, 230-31, 236; 50:245, 394
Dropsie College for Hebrew and Cognate Learning, 22:xix, xxviii; 23:103; 25:ix; 26:xxiii, xxxii; 28:xii, xxv, xxxv, 283, 310; 29:xxxiii, xxxvii, 190, 192; 30:vi; 31:xix, xv,

276, 296; 33:18, 25-26, 29; 37:xi, xxxi, 15, 57, 60, 451; 38:139, 143, 163, 343; 39:261-62, 469; 40:10-11, 13; 42:24, 37, 459; 43:157, 250; 44:64, 66; 45:147, 202-4, 207; 47:139, 200, 206, 221, 226; 48:231-32, 236; 50:70, 244-45, 270-72, 274, 296, 301, 394, 402; Board of Delegates of American Israelites, 29:77; Hebrew Union College, 40:49

Droysen, J. G., 36:358

Druck, David, gift, 34:xxv

Drukker, S., 29:134

Drummond, Evan, 35:181, 183-84

Drummond, Joan, 35:184

Drummy, Mary, 23:152

Drumont, 22:223

Drumont, Edouard Adolphe, 25:122; 37:423; 40:325, 329; 41:95-96

Duane, James, 27:470; 45:57

Duane, William, 38:134-35

Duarte, Manuel, 33:117

Duberman, Martin Bauml, "The Congress versus the Committee: A Crisis in American Judaism, 1903-1922," 45:262

Dubester, Henry J., "Resources on American Jewish History at the Library of Congress," 47:179-85, 201

Dubinsky, David, 40:397; 41:329, 335-37, 354; 46:258

Dublin, Frances, "Jewish Colonial Enterprise in the Light of the Amherst Papers (1758-1763)," 35:xv, 1-25

Dublin, Louis I., 46:314, 346

Dublois, Stephen, 35:182

Dubnow, Simon M., 26:20; 28:118; 39:98, 305; 43:156; 47:222

Du-bois, Abraham, 39:184

Dubois, H.-A., 41:161

Du Bois, W. E. B., 38:111; 46:274-75

Dubov, Marcus Hillel, 33:27; "The Hebrew Correspondence Between the Reverend Marcus Hillel Dubov and Secretary of State John Hay," 38:53-56, 342

Dubunckii, Jankel (Leib), 38:73

Dubunckii, Mordecai, 38:73

Dubunckii, Nahum, 38:73

Duchesnay, 23:48

Duchesnel, Dr., 29:59

Duclerc, senateur, 41:161

Dudden, Arthur P., 42:312; "The Single-Tax Zionism of Joseph Fels," 46:474-91, 493

Dudley, Joseph, 23:79

Dudley, Thomas, 42:343

Duenna, The, 23:179; 33:174, 176-77

Duer, Mr., 27:392

Dufaure, M., 24:72

Duff (actor), 33:193

Duffer, C. Z. F., 22:33

Duffie, Archibald, 41:119

Duffield, George, 37:189-97; 43:237

Duffield, Pitts, 43:19, 21

Duffil, Isaac, 37:412, 417

Duffy, Archibold, see: Cambel, William

Duggan, Stephen P., 34:234

Duhalde, Jean-Baptiste, 49:41, 44-45

Duke, Alfred, 39:141

Duke University, 40:51; 46:421

Duker, Abraham G., 39:206, 477; 42:90; 46:63; 49:155, 213-14, 254-56, 258-60; "American Jews and the Polish Insurrection of 1863," 37:xxx; "American Reaction to Zygmunt Krasinski's Anti-Frankist Undivine Comedy in 1948," 41:389; "A Conceptual Framework for the Interpretation of American Jewish History," 44:240; "Efforts of Polish Jews in America in behalf of Poland's Independence before and during the Polish Revolution of 1863," 37:xxxii; "Emerging Culture Patterns in American Jewish Life—The Psycho-Cultural Approach to the Study of Jewish Life in America," 39:351-88; "An Evaluation of Achievement in American Jewish Local Historical Writing," 49:214-53; executive council, 46:493; 49:268; history, writing of, 46:263-64, 404-10, 412, 414; *Jewish Community Relations: An Analysis of the MacIver Report*, reviewed, 42:319-30, 463-66; Jewish Historical Society of Israel, 41:391; "Polish-Jewish Relations in the United States after 1865," 39:470; "Polish Political Emigres in the United States and the Jews, 1833-1865," 38:342; 39:143-67; "The Psycho-Cultural Approach to the Study of Jewish Life in America," 38:347; "The Sale of a Negro Slave in Brooklyn in 1683," 49:229; "Swedenborgian Background of

Thomas Lake Harris' Anti-Semitism," 41:389
Duke's Place Synagogue, London, 42:439
Dulerant, David, 39:151
Dulles, Allen W., 39:332; 45:42
Dulles, John Foster, 44:71
Dumas, Mr., 37:199
Dumas, Alexandre, 37:18
Du Maurier, George, 35:252
Dun, R. G. and Co., 46:235
Dunant, Henri, 33:212
Dunbar, Mr., 35:202
Dunbar, David, 26:231
Dunbar, John R. W. (notes), *History of Jewish Physicians*, 30:399
Dunbar, William, 27:450
Dunbarton House, 48:4
Duncan, 44:102
Duncan, David, 23:21
Duncan, Norman, 43:19, 28
Duncan, Guilhelme, 33:73
Dunckee, Sarah, 27:111
Dunckley, Samuel R., 22:179
Dundas, Brigadier General, 38:88
Dundas, James, 30:77
Dunedin, Lord, 31:106
Dungan, Irvin, 36:233
Dungan, Mahlon, 22:90
Dunham, Daniel, 35:291; 37:167-68
Dunham, David R., 25:10
Dunlap, John, 23:156
Dunlap, William, 33:172-73, 184, 186-90; *Bonaparte in England*, 33:189; *Thirty years ago*, 33:190; "William Dunlap's Jewish Friends," 34:278-80
Dunlop, Lloyd A., 50:379
Dunmore, Governor, 23:22
Dunmore, John Earl of, 25:119
Dunn, James Clement, 36:374
Dunn, Robert, 43:19
Dunn, Thomas, 23:49-50
Dunning, Captain, 26:180
Dunscomb, William E., see: Groesbeck, David
Dunster, D. D., 35:186-87
Dunster, Henry, 35:150
Dunton, Thomas, 35:291
Duplessis, Charles, 23:139

Duponceau, Peter S., 27:524; *Case on the Contested Seat of David Levy*, 30:364-65
Dupont, 23:122
Dupont, conseiller, 41:161
Duport, Adrien, 35:122
Dupuis, Charles Francois, 37:188
Dupuy, John, 23:183
Duque, Samuel, 29:36
Durant Motors, 41:250
Durasse, Jacob, 21:58
Durbin, John Price, 30:277
Dürer, Albrecht, 48:253
Durfee, Joseph, 23:166; 35:291
Durfee, Thomas, 35:290
Durhaim, M., 27:45
Durham, City of; Munick v., 29:152
Durkee, Mr., 48:190-91
Durment, Edmund S., 45:258-59
Durnovo, Ivan, 43:51, 55
Durocher, 23:48-49
Dury, John, 32:30
Duschinsky, Charles, 37:35; gift, 28:xl; "Rabbi David Oppenheimer (1664-1736), and the Acquisition of His Books and MSS. by the Bodleian Library, Oxford," 31:xvi
Duschnes, Elsie, 31:259
Duschnes, Gustave S., 31:259
Dushkin, Alexander, 39:263; gift, 28:xl
Dutch East India Company, 31:175-76; 47:119
Dutch Indies, 32:xxvii
Dutch Israelite Reformed Community, Curaçao, 26:239-40
Dutch West India Company, 27:481; 29:20, 39-40, 43, 47, 49; 34:4-5, 10, 274; 43:233-34; 44:78, 81-82, 205, 219, 248; 46:26-28, 31; Brazil, 46:40-41, 46, 48; *The Dutch in Brazil, 1624-1654*, reviewed, 47:112-20, 209; colony, 21:xiv; "The Jewish Burial Ground on New Bowery, New York, Acquired in 1682, Not 1656," 31:vii, 77-103; "The Jews in St. Eustatius, Dutch West Indies," 31:xvi
Dux, Adolf, 38:208
Dvorsky, 26:31
Dvorsky, Mayer, 47:209; 48:140
Dwight, Edwin Welles, 39:190-92
Dwight, Samuel, 48:183

E

Eager, Bezaleel, 22:23
Eames, Nelson, 35:313
Eames, Phoebe Harriet Crane, 35:313
Eames, Wilberforce, 30:vi, 4, 69; 34:52;
35:148; corresponding member, 34:ix;
"Early English Efforts for Reformation of
the Hebrew Calendar," 32:xiii; Memorial
Volume, 31:xxxiii; necrology of, 35:x, xvi,
312-15; "The Proposed Scripture
Calendar," 32:23-24
Eardley, Baron, 35:36
Earl, Captain, 27:441
Earle, George H., 36:346
"Early American Jewish Portraits and Silver"
(exhibit), 42:413, 416-19
Earnest, Matthias, 27:245
East, Robert A., 38:48
East Asiatic Library of Columbia University,
49:41
East Chicago, Ind., United Jewish Appeal,
37:xxviii
Easterbrook v. Hebrew Ladies Orphan
Society, 25:135
East India Company, 28:250; 31:117; 31:230;
Brazil, 33:46-47, 51, 58, 84
East Indies, "The Gratz Papers," 23:2-3
East New York Sentinel, 35:313
East and West India Companies, 32:8-9
Eastern European Jewry, 50:268, 402-3; "The
Efforts of East European Jewry to
Organize Its Own Community in the
United States," 49:73-89; "The Jewish
Question in New York City (1902-1903),"
49:90-136, 271; periodization of American
Jewish history, 47:127, 129-33
Eastern States Wholesale Society, 41:343
Easton, John, 27:175
Easton, Nicholas, 34:5

Easton, Pa., 50:278; "An American Jewish
Community: Easton, Pennsylvania, on Its
Two Hundredth Anniversary," 42:193-
206; 49:234; Jewish Community Council,
contribution, 37:xxviii; religious
observances, mid-nineteenth century,
37:36; "200th Anniversary of Easton, Pa.,"
41:390
Easton Express, 45:268
Eastward Hoe, 33:171
Eastwood, Rev., 27:339
Eatman, Cyrus, 23:139
Eaton, 23:120
Eaton, Herbert N., *An Hour with the
American Hebrew*, 37:422
Eayres, Isaac, 27:245
Eban, Abba, 46:130; "The American Jewish
Tercentenary," address by, 45:6-8
Ebbinghaus-Killian case, 26:211
Ebeling, Daniel, 37:441
Eber bar Shalomo, 27:408
Ebreo (Jacob Mantino), 28:170-72
Eccles, J. A., 35:257-58
Echo de Paris, L', 46:89
Echo z Polski, 39:157, 160-62
Eck, Ed, 35:307-9
Eck, Johann Maier von, 35:122
Eckert, Henry, 34:77
Eckford, Henry, *Statement Relative to Henry
Eckford*, 30:227, 229-30
Eckman, Julius, 26:271; 38:154-58; 49:21
Eckout, Albert, 47:116
Eckstein, Abraham W., 41:373
Eckstein, David, "The Life of David
Eckstein, American Consul at Amsterdam,
1878-1890," 34:xiv
Eckstein, Isaac, 50:314
Eckstein, Sam, 29:62
Ecole des Chartes, 48:252

Economics, history, writing of, 46:135, 144-45, 170-72, 179-80, 188-90, 202-4, 210-67, 446
Eddy, Spencer, 36:274-77
Edelman, H., *Gedulath Shaul*, 22:132
Edelman, Samuel, 39:332
Edelman, Wolfel, 38:73
Edelmann, Mordecai Isaac, 33:132
Eden, Anthony, 36:86
Eden, William, 31:47, 60
Eden Street Congregation (Baltimore), 23:142-43
Ederhy, David or Jacob, 36:23
Edgar, William (Detroit), 40:86
Edgar, William (Ind.), 30:77
Edict of Toleration of 1649, 25:100
Edinburgh, University of, 22:164
"Edinburgh Reviewer," 25:68
Edinger, Dora, 41:233
Edison, Irving, 45:182, 209
Edison, Thomas A., 32:123
Edmonds, John W., 30:404
Edouart, Auguste, Civil War, 50:296, 312, 316, 335, 345; "Notes on Silhouettes of American Jews by August Edouart and Other Silhouettists," 34:xiv
Edrehi, Isaac, 45:31
Education, 48:214, 225, 229-32; 49:16; aid to students, 29:108; Board of Delegates of American Israelites and Hebrew education, 29:106-8; *Cornerstones of Religious Freedom in America*, reviewed, 40:96-98; "Educational Reforms in Europe in Their Relation to Jewish Emancipation, 1778-1919," 28:83-132; "Hebrew in the Schools of Colonial America," 32:113-14; Henrietta Szold, 49:160-63, 165-66; history, writing of, 46:145-46, 152, 163, 180-81, 249-51, 382-83, 387, 396-97, 404; "The Impact of the American Constitution Upon the Jews of the United States," 43:159-69; "Isaac Leeser and the Jews of Philadelphia: A Study in National Jewish Influence," 48:207-44; Jewish, 40:94-95, 402, 407; "Jewish Education in Baltimore from its Beginnings until the 1880's," 44:242; "Jewish Education in Charleston, South Carolina, During the Eighteenth and Nineteenth Centuries," 42:43-70;

"Jewish Education in Curaçao," 44:215-36; "Jewish Education in New York City," 28:xl; "Jewish Elementary Education in the United States (1901-1950)," 42:1-42; "Jewish Education in the United States (1950-1960)," 49:268; Jewish local history, 49:221, 223-24, 230, 235, 239; "Jewish Parochial Education in New York City," 34:xiv; "The Jewish University Idea in Early American Jewish Education," 29:xxix; Joseph Isaac Bluestone, 35:61-62; "Max Lilienthal's Activities in Russia: New Documents," 35:xv, 39-51; "The Polonies Talmud Torah of New York," 34:123-41; Prussia, 28:70; "The Russian Night School of Baltimore," 31:vii, xvii, 225-28; Shearith Israel Congregation, 27:xvi, 8, 10, 17-18, 51-55, 57, 71, 81-83, 92, 95, 115, 137, 140, 146, 243, 397-98; "Social Discrimination Against Jews in America, 1830-1930," 47:1-33; "The Upward Struggle of the Cause of Secular Education in Russian Jewry in the Reigns of Alexander I and Nicholas I," 28:xv; "The World of Hyman Gratz," 50:241-47; *see also*: Young Men's Hebrew Association
Educational Alliance (Los Angeles), 37:294; (New York), 22:209, 211, 238; 28:300; 31:271, 275; 34:197, 240, 246; 35:62-63, 323; 37:248-49, 274, 290-91, 293, 295, 299, 307, 312, 315, 323; 39:407; 40:164; 45:145; 49:109-13, 115-20
Educational Center (Seattle), 37:296
Educational Convention, 29:111
Educational League (N.Y.), 49:116-19
Edward, King of England, 22:202; 29:xxii; 31:133, 262
Edward VII, King, 26:159
Edwards, Jonathan, 39:186; 47:143; *Language of the Muhhekaneew Indians*, 30:86-87, 120
Edwards, Judge, 25:137
Edwards, Morgan, 37:136
Edwards, Ogden, 25:39, 58
Edwards, Richard, 45:53
Edwards, William H., 36:177, 179
Edwin, David, 30:145
Edzor, John, 40:75
Efron, L., 34:xxiii
Efros, Israel, 43:195

Efreymson, Gustave A., 37:xii
Egbert, James, 27:240
Egelson, Louis I., 32:xxviii
Eger, Akiba, 28:71; 34:16
Eger, David, 29:133
Eggleston, Edward, 34:237
Egmont, Earl of, 34:285
Egypt, 26:137-38, 146-47, 156, 158, 163, 219; 28:251; 29:200; 50:11, 332; "The Beginnings of the Egyptian Diaspora," 22:xvii; *Egypt and the Books of Moses*, 30:374; "Simon Wolf as United States Consul to Egypt," 46:493; 47:76-100
Egypte, L', 47:91
Ehanido, Belthior Manuel, 33:114
Ehrenreich, Levi, 50:313
Ehrlich, Arnold B., 34:303; 40:31; 42:103; 45:70, 140
Ehrman, Sidney M., 45:144
Eichberg, Babbette, 31:193
Eichberger, Maindle, 41:259
Eichberger, Samuel Theodor, 41:256
Eichholz, Adolph, death, 37:12; necrology of Samuel Snellenburg, 29:xxxvi, 185-86
Eichholz, Hannah, 29:186
Eichhorn, Johann Gottfried, 37:186; 49:42, 46
Eichler, M. M., 22:xi, "Cora Wilburn," 22:xii
Eicholt, Jacob, 22:189
Eichtal, Adolphe d', 41:161
Eichtal, Gustave d', 41:161
Eidlitz, 38:197
Eidlitz, Leopold, 46:64
Eights, Jonathan, 26:226
Eilenburg, Eliezer, "Eliezer Eilenburg, a German Jewish Wanderer of the Sixteenth Century," 23:xiii
Einhorn, David, 23:107; 26:273; 31:269-70; 32:xxviii; 34:xxiv, 180, 193, 295; 35:xviii; 40:21, 29, 32, 364; 42:104; 43:146, 148; 45:94-96, 100, 103, 110, 114, 124-25; 48:224-25; 49:21; 50:199; Board of Delegates of American Israelites, 29:79; Civil War, 50:285-86, 354
Einhorn, Mrs. David, 34:180
Einhorn, Julie Ochs, 34:180
Einhorn, Marx, 41:262
Einhorn, Max, 49:97
Einhorn, Moses, 33:165

Einstein, A., 29:134
Einstein, Albert, 37:457; 44:124
Einstein, B., & Co., claim, 31:140
Einstein, Babette (Landauer), 26:277
Einstein, Benjamin Franklin, necrology of, 26:xiv, 277-79
Einstein, Bros. (San Francisco), 37:45
Einstein, Eveline, 41:256
Einstein, Henrietta, 23:76
Einstein, Joseph, 30:421; 48:226
Einstein, Judith (Lewis), 22:228
Einstein, Lewis, 22:227-28
Einstein, Lewis (diplomat), 36:36, 38
Einstein, Rudolph, 26:277
Einstein, S. S., 37:268
Einstein, Therese, 22:228
Einstein Medical Center, 48:234
Einstein & Townsend, 26:278
Einstein, Townsend, Guiterman & Shearn, 26:278
Einziger, Erna, Ellen, 50:273
Eiseman, Charles, 37:266, 268; necrology of, 29:xxxvi, 158-59
Eiseman, I., 29:129
Eisenbaum (Poland), 28:126
Eisenbaum, Antoni, 39:151
Eisenbaum, Michal, 39:151
Eisenberg, Mrs. Benjamin K., 50:426
Eisenberg, Maurice, 37:266, 268-69, 271
Eisenhower, Dwight D., 46:303, 332; 50:434, "Address by President Dwight D. Eisenhower," 44:67-74; "General Dwight D. Eisenhower and the Displaced Jews," 42:415
Eisenlohr, Professor, 22:199
Eisenman, Charles, & Co., 29:158
Eisenmenger, Johann Andreas, 45:29
Eisenschiml, Otto, 41:216; book reviews by, 38:319-21; 41:214-15; Civil War, 50:272, 275, 398-99, 401
Eisenstadt, Benzion, *Anshe haShem b'Arzoth haBrith*, 34:xxv; gift, 34:xxv
Eisenstein, Judah D., 22:117; 32:121; 33:132; 34:56; 37:465; 42:92; 44:146, 185, 197; 45:70, 149
Eisler, Sol. H., 50:238
Eisner, Moris, 39:159
Eisner, Pavel, 50:115
Eisner, Sigmund, necrology, 31:xxiii

El-Arish project, 26:164
Elberfeld *Farbenfabrik*, 29:194
Elbogen, 37:378
Elbogen, Ismar, 28:264; 40:49; 45:147; "The
First Attempt to Form a Union of
American Jewish Congregations,"
37:xxxiii; "The Montefiore Testimonial
Fund and American Israel," 37:xxx, 95-101
Elder, Daniel, 22:179
Elder, Roderick, 22:180
Elders of Zion, Protocols of, 40:323, 344
Eldon, Lord, 31:109, 121, 123, 125
Eldred, Mrs. N., 27:437, 439, 442
Eldridge, Captain, 27:294, 310
Eldridge, Oliver, 37:46
Eleazar b. Samuel, 21:198
Eleazar ben Shammua, 43:248
Eleazer, Levi, 26:254
Eleazer Ben Zakin (Zaken), 21:106, 108, 148-
49, 159
Elections, "The Supposed Disfranchisement
of the Jews in New York After the
Contested Election for Representative in
1737: A History," 29:xxx; "The True Story
of the Relation of the Jews to the
Contested Election for Representative in
New York in 1737," 29:xxxvii
Electric Boat Company, 25:176
Electric Storage Battery Company, 25:176
Electric Vehicle Company, 26:176
Elephantine, "The Jewish Colony of
Elephantine," 22:xiii
Eleventh Street Cemetery, 27:267, 277-78,
313-14, 491
Elfelt, Clare E., 31:273
Elfelt, E. S., 31:157
Elfelt, Edwin, 31:154
Elfelt, Gus, 31:152, 154
Elgin, Lord, 26:156; 27:517
Eliakim ben Jacob, 22:119
Elias, Benjamin, 21:4, 9, 19, 21, 22, 213;
23:151; 31:238; 34:59-60
Elias, Esther, 25:66-69
Elias, Sam, 29:69
Elias the tailor, 25:68
Eliashburg, Mordecai, 43:41
Eliassof, Herman, 28:239; 33:132, 134-38,
140, 142, 147-48, 150, 152; 34:257;
37:172; gift, 26:xxxv

Eliau Ben Araha, 34:293
Eliezer a Cohen, 25:138
Eliezer bar Jehudah, 21:10, 16, 27-29, 31, 33,
41-42, 44, 48
Eliezer br Nethanel, 21:41
Elijah (physician), 28:191
Elijah be'er [Fonte] ben Shabbathai (Elijah di
Sabbato), 28:152-53
Elijah, Jacob, 22:133
Elijah ben Judah, 28:187
Elinus, 28:205
Eliot, Charles W., 32:123; 34:203; 40:406;
41:311; 46:228
Eliot, George, 34:239; 35:246-48; 37:22-23;
38:278; 39:327; *Daniel Deronda* 25:157-58
Eliot, John, 39:186
Elisama, 30:300
Eliza (slave), 50:162
Elizabeth, Queen, 23:93; 32:31; 42:441
Elizabeth, Queen of England, 49:271
Elizabeth II, Queen, 49:267, 271
Elizer, Eleazer, 50:32, 42, 48
Elizer, Elisha, 50:164
Elizer, Isaac, 27:178, 180, 185, 408, 416;
50:26, 36, 48
Elizur, Isaac, 26:245
Eljaszewicz, K., 39:151
Elkan of Boppard, 31:34
Elkan, Ben., 27:79
Elkan, Isak, 41:262
Elkan, Marcus, 27:206; 50:63
Elkan, Moses, 41:256
Elkan, Mrs. Phila, 27:206
Elkan, S., 27:79
Elkin, Belle, 26:255
Elkin, Benjamin, 26:251, 256
Elkin, D., 39:87
Elkin, Israel, 32:64
Elkin, Mozely, 26:254
Elkin, Mozely Isaac, 26:251
Elkin, Nathan, 33:157
Elkind, D., 38:310
Elkins, Mr., 27:430
Elkins Park Temple Center (Philadelphia),
41:91
Elkins, Stephen B., 50:382
Elkins, William M., 35:266
Elkus, Abram I., 34:199, 203, 205-7, 257-58
Elkus, Mrs. Abram I., 26:281

Elkus, Gleason and Proskauer, 47:230
Ella Rosenberg, 33:174, 191-92
Ellenborough, Lord, 40:127
Ellery, William, 37:111
Ellet, Henry S., 50:319, 365
Elley, Frank, 39:20
Ellinger, Abraham, 41:254
Ellinger, J. G., 43:67
Ellinger, Moritz, 29:111, 113, 163; 33:241;
  38:245; 40:225, 246, 257, 263; 48:34, 84-
  85; 49:176-79, 186
Elliot, Andrew, 22:21
Ellis, David A., 37:307; necrology, 32:xvi
Ellis, E., 29:134
Ellis, I., 27:51
Ellis, John, 28:226
Ellis, John W., 48:152-53
Ellis, Josiah, 27:41, 43, 62, 253; kosher meat,
  25:47
Ellis, Max, 48:258
Ellis, Miss, 34:279
Ellis, Myer, 27:79
Ellis Island committee, 34:xix
Ellison, James, American captive; or Siege of
  Tripoli, 33:174, 192; 40:347
Ellmann, L., 29:131
Ellsler, Fanny, 35:240
Ellsworth, Oliver, 37:103
Elmaleh, Leon H., 22:xxvii; 26:xxix; 28:xxxii;
  29:xxxv; 31:xxiii; 37:93; 41:89; necrologies
  of Stanley V. Mastbaum, 28:xv, 292-93;
  William Morris, 31:xvi, 293-84
Elman, Mischa, "Memoirs of Mischa Elman's
  father," 34:xxv
Elman, Saul, gift, 34:xxv; "Memoirs of
  Mischa Elman's father," 34:xxv
Elm Street Synagogue (New York), 40:188-
  89; 50:13; (Paterson), 31:265
Eloise, Grace, 34:xxi
El Paso, "Social Service Endeavor for Jewish
  Soldiers, El Paso, 1916," 26:xxxi
El Paso Herald, 35:327
El Porvenir, 26:239, 241
El Sabada, 35:327
Elsass, Isak, 41:267
Elsberg, Charles A., 34:234; 42:122, 125
Elsbree, Oliver Wendell, 37:443
Elsey (slave), 50:160
Elsner, Simon L., 40:66

Elton, John H., 39:20
Elvert, Christian d', 35:118
Ely, Ezra Stiles, 40:96
Ely, Nathan E., 39:34
Elysium Club, 22:229
Elzaz, Barnett A., 32:39-42; 37:35; 39:253;
  40:218; 41:77; 42:58; 49:260; Jewish
  cemetery, 31:xxxiii; "A Jewish Diary of a
  Voyage from London to Charlestown in
  1776," 31:xvi; "The Jews of South
  Carolina," 32:35, 37; A "Note on Haym
  Salomon," 31:xvii; "The Reformed Society
  of Israelites of Charleston, S. C.," 32:35
Emancipation, 26:6; 39:208, 210; "The
  Alliance Israélite Universelle in the United
  States, 1860-1949," 39:389-443;
  "Benjamin F. Peixotto's Mission to
  Roumania," 24:1-24; "A Bordeaux
  Subscription," 23:189; "Congress of
  Berlin, 1878," 24:40-79; "Educational
  Reforms in Europe in Their Relation to
  Jewish Emancipation, 1778-1878," 26:xxxi;
  "Educational Reforms in Europe in Their
  Relation to Jewish Emancipation, 1778-
  1919," 28:83-132; "Emigration to America
  or Reconstruction in Europe," 42:157-88;
  France, 26:35, 73, 90; "Hugo Grotius and
  the Emancipation of the Jews in Holland,"
  31:xxiv, 173-80; Influence of American
  Precedents and Jewish Patriotism upon
  Jewish Emancipation Abroad," 26:266-68;
  "The Influence of Lewis Way and Other
  English Missionaries upon Alexander I's
  Treatment of the Jews," 26:116-25; "Jean
  de Bloch (I. S. Blioch), Champion of
  International Disarmament, Advocate of
  Russian Jewish Emancipation and Worker
  for Russian Economic Development,"
  29:xv; 31:xvii; "Jewish Disabilities in the
  Balkan States: American Contributions
  Toward Their Removal, with Particular
  Reference to the Congress of Berlin,"
  24:ix, 1-153; 25:xiv; "Jewish Rights at the
  Congresses of Vienna (1814-1815), and
  Aix-la-Chapelle (1818)," 26:vii, xv, 33-125;
  "The Jews of Roumania and the Treaty of
  Berlin," 24:114-37; "Memorandum on the
  Treaty Rights of the Jews of Roumania,"
  24:137-53; "Napoleon and the Jews,"

26:xiv; Paris Conference 1876, 24:29-39; "Regarding the Draft of a Sistem of Legislation for the Jews, July 17, 1809, by Wilhelm von Humboldt," 26:103-15; "The Revolution of 1848 and the Jewish 'On to America' Movement," 38:185-234, 345; Switzerland, 32:xxv; "Switzerland and Jewish Emancipation," 28:xxii; "Wilhelm von Humboldt's Relations to the Jews," 26:95-103

Emanuel, 28:124

Emanuel, Abby, 27:290, 293, 298, 303

Emanuel Cohen Center (Minneapolis), 37:322

Emanuel, David, 35:133

Emanuel, Edwin, 27:293

Emanuel, Ephraim, 29:147

Emanuel, Flora, 27:290, 293-94, 298, 303, 310

Emanuel, Hetty, 27:293

Emanuel, Isaac, 29:147; "Isaac Emanuel," 35:xv; "James Alexander and the Jews, Especially Isaac Emanuel," 35:171-88

Emanuel, Isabel, 27:303

Emanuel, Jesse, 29:147

Emanuel, Joel, 27:293

Emanuel, Joseph, 27:395

Emanuel, Julia di, 31:280

Emanuel, Juliet, 27:293-94

Emanuel, Lafayette Gomez, 27:290, 293, 308

Emanuel, Levi, 29:147

Emanuel, Lewis, 27:315

Emanuel, Michael, 29:147

Emanuel, Miriam, 27:290, 293, 303

Emanuel, Nathan, 27:78-79, 285, 290, 293-94, 298, 302, 304, 315

Emanuel, Arah (nee Gomez), 27:78, 91, 111, 285, 287-88, 290, 293-94, 298, 303, 310

Emanuel (slave), 50:159

Emanu-El Sisterhood (N.Y.), 31:259; 37:294; (San Francisco), 37:295

Emanuel Congregation (Dallas), 34:303; (Milwaukee), 47:43; (New York), 26:240; 28:xvii, xxiii; 29:181; 31:257, 278; 32:xxviii; 33:xii; 34:xxi, 189, 303; 37:233; 38:68; 39:102, 106; 40:21, 163, 212, 363; 41:33, 229-30, 246; 42:101, 105; 44:154, 157, 251; 45:95, 140, 156; 47:198; 48:225; 49:21, 29-30; 50:91, 94; Board of

Delegates of American Israelites, 29:79; Civil War, 50:272, 274, 313; Library of Hebrew and Rabbinical Literature, 45:140; "Temple Emanu-El of New York and the Chair in Rabbinical Literature at Columbia, 1887," 37:xxxiii; (San Bernardino), 34:xxvii; (San Francisco), 26:230; 29:180, 198; 37:36; 41:33, 370; 45:143-44, 170; 46:65; "The Cornerstone Box of the Old Temple Emanu-El of San Francisco: New Light on Pacific Coast Jewry, 1849-1864," 32:xiii-xiv; 50:133

Emanu-El Review, 34:184

Emanuel Temple (New York), 22:xiv, xxvii; 26:240; 27:121, 504; 28:xvii, xxiii; 29:79, 181; 31:257, 278; 32:xxviii; 33:xii; 34:xxi, 189, 303; 37:233, 249, 294-95, 312, 315; 38:68; 39:102, 106; 40:21, 163, 212, 363; 41:33, 229-30, 246; 42:101, 105; 44:154, 157, 251, 257; 45:140, 156, 169; 47:198; 48:225; 49:21, 29-30; 50:91, 94; (Westwood, N.J.), 37:295

Emanu-El Theological Association of New York, The Preparatory School, 40:31-32

Emanuel Theological Seminary Temple (New York), 40:311

Ember, Aaron, 33:20-21; 45:144

Emden, Abraham, 37:374, 381

Emden, Jacob, 45:140

Emek ha-Baka, 22:112

Emergency Aid Committee, Kovno, 42:162-64

Emergency Refugee Shelter at Fort Ontario, 47:192

Emerich, Martin, 41:174

Emerick, Samuel, 27:120

Emerson, 37:133

Emerson, Edith, 38:274

Emerson, Ellen, 38:272-75, 281-84

Emerson, Harrington, 41:43, 45, 48, 312; 46:228

Emerson, Luther O., 50:389, 391

Emerson, Ralph Waldo, 23:55, 62, 76; 37:17; 39:114, 323-27; 42:83-84, 86, 341, 356; 45:33, 253; 46:127-29; "Emma Lazarus and Emerson," 38:261-87; history, writing of, 46:193, 212, 289, 410, 426

Emigrant Aid Society of Massachusetts, 23:59

Emigration, "The Alliance Israélite Universelle in the United States, 1860-1949," 39:389-443; Board of Delegates of American Israelites, 29:101-2; *To Dwell in Safety, The Story of Jewish Migration since 1800*, reviewed, 39:196-98; "Emigration to America or Reconstruction in Europe," 42:157-58; "Jewish Emigration from Wurttemberg to the United States of America (1848-1855)," 41:225-73; "The Kishineff Pogrom and Jewish Emigration to the United States on the Fiftieth Anniversary," 42:415; *Niles' Weekly Register*, 50:9; "Polish Political Emigres in the United States and the Jews, 1833-1865," 39:143-67; "The Revolution of 1848 and the Jewish 'On to America' Movement," 38:185-234, 345; Roumania, 24:25-29, 39

Emigration Commission, 49:180-81

Emigration Conference in Frankfurt (1904), 42:185

Emigration Society, 38:190

Emin, Isaac, 38:246

Emma Lazarus Down Town Club, 40:164

Emmanuel, Isaac Samuel, "Jewish Education in Curaçao," 44:215-36; "New Light on Early American Jewry," 49:229; *Precious Stones of the Jews of Curaçao: Curaçaon Jewry, 1656-1957*, reviewed, 47:176-78

Emmanuel, Samuel, 41:262

Emmerich, Philip, 23:142

Emmett, Christopher J., 46:4

Emmett, T. A., 27:344

Emmich, Z., 37:41

Emory, William Helmsley, 43:99-100

Emott, George, 41:112

Emott, James, 23:154

Empeytaz, 26:120

Employing Printers' Association, 31:286

Encyclopaedia Britannica, 47:219

Encyclopedia Judaica, 34:xviii

Ende, Jacobus van den, 32:14

Endeks, 39:164

Enelow, Hyman G., 29:181; 32:121; 34:193, 254; 39:456, 461; 45:94, 104, 136, 155; gift, 33:xxxii; necrology, 34:ix; Selected works of H. G. Enelow, 35:xx

Enfield, Lord, 24:139

Engel, A., Fr., 48:263

Engel, Dr., 23:188; 38:191, 222-25

Engel, Irving M., communications, 42:463-66

Engel, Mrs. L. H. Surinamer, 48:263

Engelhardt, conseil, 41:161

Engelman, Uriah Zevi, 42:112; book reviews by, 49:276-78; 50:143-44; history, writing of, 46:165, 177, 179, 182, 184, 187; "Jewish Education in Charleston, S.C., 1750-1950," 39:471; "Jewish Education in Charleston, South Carolina, During the Eighteenth and Nineteenth Centuries," 42:43-70; 49:239; "Jewish Education in the United States (1950-1960)," 49:268; *The Jews of Charleston*, reviewed, 40:398-401; "The Jews of Charleston: A History of an American Jewish Community," 49:237-38; "Not by Written Documents Alone," 46:152-57; "Sources of Jewish Statistics," reviewed, 40:196

England, *see:* Great Britain

Englander, A., 38:155

Englander, Henry, 40:43; gifts, 28:xxxviii; 33:xxxiii

Engleman, Morris, 33:xxxiii

English, George Bethune, 35:202-5; *The Grounds of Christianity Examined*, 30:149

English, William, 22:90

English Acts of Trade, 46:28

English Navigation Act, 33:85

Engravers, "Selig Baumgarten," 26:xv, 248

Engs, George, 27:213

Engs, P. W., 27:452

Engs, Samuel, 27:413, 451

Enis, William, 27:440-41

Enlightenment, 38:212-13; 43:182; 46:287; Russia and Jewish education, 35:39-51

Ennery, J., 30:437

Enoch, Samuel, 49:54

Enoch, Simon, 38:75

Enright, Mrs., 39:78

Enriquez, Beatriz, 32:117

Enriquez, Bento, 33:66

Enriquez, Catalina, 31:28, 31

Enriquez, Clara, 31:29, 31

Enriquez, Diego, 31:28

Enriquez, Josepha, 23:134

Enriquez, Micaela, 32:117

Enriquez, Pedro, 31:28

Enriquez, Rafaela, 32:117
Ent, John, 28:226
Entre Rios colony, 39:94
Epean, Mr., 31:43, 58, 67, 75
Ephraim, Madame, 26:38, 52
Ephraim, Veitel-Heine, 35:231
Epistle of Sherira Gaon, 28:65
Eppinger, Isaac, 40:250, 275; 49:186
Eppinger, Solomon, 40:27, 36
Eppstein, 37:378
Eppstein, J. E., 37:171
Eppstein, Julius, 41:253
Epstein, A., 33:162
Epstein, Elias, 40:48
Epstein, I., 29:131
Epstein, Jacob (sculptor), 40:320
Epstein, Jacob (war relief), 31:221
Epstein, Jacob Nahum, 43:241
Epstein, Jakob, 41:262
Epstein, Louis M., 45:163-64
Epstein, M. (England), 28:xviii-xx
Epstein, M. (Fort Wayne), 29:130
Epstein, Melech, 41:342; communication,
    42:215; *Jewish Labor in U. S. A.: An
    Industrial, Political and Cultural History of
    the Jewish Labor Movement, 1882-1914*,
    reviewed, 41:209-14; *Jewish Labor in
    U.S.A.: An Industrial, Political, and Cultural
    History of the Jewish Labor Movement, 1914-
    1952*, reviewed, 43:192-94; *The Jews and
    Communism*, reviewed, 50:251-53
Epstein, Shachno, 50:252
Equal rights, 46:293; "The Influence of the
    Russo-American Treaty of 1932 on the
    Rights of American Jewish Citizens,"
    41:163-94
Ercole I, Duke, 28:188, 191
Ergas, Ralph, 37:419
Erianger, Moses, 26:xix
Erie Canal, 22:76
Erlanger, Abraham, 34:iv; 45:155; necrology
    of, 32:xvi
Erlanger, Abraham L., 35:259; 40:358
Erlanger, Judge, 25:135
Erlanger, Michael, 45:70
Erlanger, Michel, 41:153, 161
Erlanger v. Erlanger, 29:153
Erlich, Jakob, 39:151
Ermell, Charles, 35:35

Ermell, Jane, 35:35
Ernest (violinist), 29:127
Ernst, J. E., 34:190, 192
Ernst, Robert, 46:184, 404, 406-15, 418;
    book review by, 45:217-18; "Concepts of
    Americanism as Reflected in Minority
    Groups," 46:268-88
Erra, Pater, *The Book of Knowledge*, 30:90
Ersch and Gruber, *Encyklopaedie*, 26:12
Erskine, 30:129; 31:106
Erving, George, 39:9
Esco Foundation, 40:314
Esdra, Joseph E., 29:129
Eshner, Augustus A., 38:337
E. Silverman & Co., 47:37
Eskeles family, 26:37, 100
Eslaing, Count d', 31:74
Esler, Jacob, 22:197
Esmit, Adolphe, 28:218-21
Esmit, Nicholas, 28:218, 220
Esmond, Henry Vernon, 40:354
Espana Hebrea, La, 22:xxxiii
Espano, da, 27:91
Espaul, Augustijn de l', 32:20
Espaul, P. de L', 32:20
Esperame, Madam, 40:82
Esperanoa de Israel, 47:71
Espinosa, 31:4
Espinosa, Abraham Nunes de, 32:16, 19
Espinosa, Isaac, 21:60
Espinosa, Ledesma y Aguilar, 23:132
Espriella, Manuel Alvarez, 35:282-84
Esquiline, The, 28:25
Esrogat et Frau, 38:202
Essai sur la colonie du Surinam, 34:xvii
Esseneka, 39:344
Essex County, N.J., *The Essex Story: A History
    of the Jewish Community in Essex County,
    New Jersey*, reviewed, 46:68-69
Essex Institute, 43:72; 44:106, 110
Essrig, Henry, 40:53
Este family, 28:188-90
Esterman, Joseph, 33:132, 150, 152
Esther, Feast of, 40:135-72; scroll of, 45:144,
    210, 213
Esther (slave), 50:162
Estrada, Alonso de, 31:15, 20
"Ethan Brand," 45:20
Ethridge, John, 39:34

Ethical Club (Rochester, N.Y.), 40:69
Ethical Culture movement, 39:278; 42:104;
  44:251; Society for (N.Y.), 37:258; 45:96,
  105; 48:57; (Philadelphia), 46:477
Ethical Record, 45:105
Ets Haim v Hohel Jahacob, 44:221-23
Ettelsohn, Nachman Baer, 33:135
Etten, Esther, 31:285
Ettenheimer, Elias S., 40:66, 239
Etting, 22:189
Etting, Asher, 21:45, 55; 27:245
Etting, Benjamin (N.Y.), 21:103, 105; 23:157
Etting, Benjamin (Philadelphia), 45:201
Etting Cemetery, 31:xxxiii
Etting Collection, 25:113; 34:75; 43:234-35
Etting, Elijah, 34:67; 41:226; 50:60
Etting, Ellen, 28:xxxviii
Etting family, 29:xlii; 41:88-90; 50:29, 244;
  papers of, 23:14-19, 21
Etting, Francis, 22:xxxiii
Etting, Frank Marx, 26:234; 45:179, 200-201;
  50:394
Etting, Gratz, 26:195
Etting, Harriet Marx, 45:201
Etting, Henry, 26:195
Etting, Joseph, 27:55, 57
Etting, Josephine, 23:145
Etting, Moses, 23:157
Etting, Mrs., 28:xxxviii
Etting, Rachel, 21:78; 28:xxxviii; 34:67
Etting, Reuben, 38:339; 50:60
Etting, Richea G., 23:145; 31:xxxii
Etting, S., 27:105
Etting, Samuel, 23:143; 26:186
Etting, Solomon, 22:193; 25:95, 99, 107;
  26:188; 27:63; 28:xxxviii; 37:437; 46:189;
  47:192; 50:21-22, 39, 43, 48; portrait of,
  42:417; "A Shechitah Certificate Issued to
  Solomon Etting in Lancaster, 1782,"
  34:xiv-xv, 66-69
Ettlinger, Jacob, 31:268
Ettlinger, Julia, 40:26
Ettore, General, 28:60
Etz Chayim Temple (Rochester), 40:69
Eudowood Sanitorium, 25:151
Eugenie, Empress, 46:8
Eugenius IV, Pope, 28:156, 158
Eunwitz, Marguerite, 45:205
Eupraxius, 28:141

Eureka Club (Rochester), 40:66-67, 71
European Cooperation Administration,
  41:317; 46:231
Eusebius, 26:167, 171; 37:133
Eustacchio, Bartolomeo, 28:173
Eustachi's New-Yorker Volks-Theater,
  33:184
Eustis, William, 43:204
Eutaw Place Congregation (Baltimore),
  23:143
Eutaw Savings Bank, Baltimore, 25:153
Evans, 22:77
Evans (England), 31:107
Evans, Charles, 30:vi
Evans, F. N., 35:258
Evans, Lewis, 23:4
Evans, T., 37:199
Evans-Gordon, Major, 36:133-34
Evarts, William M., 24:32-34, 36-38, 41;
  29:88, 96, 100; 36:112-17, 177-81, 186,
  188-92, 194, 349; 41:167-68; 44:103;
  Morocco persecutions, 36:24-25, 29-31;
  Rumanian disabilities, 36:8-9
Evening Service of Roshashanah and Kippur,
  30:51-52
Evening Star, 48:15
Everett, Edward, 23:60; 25:14-15; 26:200;
  35:202
Everett, H. Sidney, 36:188
Everett, Silas K., 39:35
Everit, 23:118
Eversley, W., 26:254
Eversly, J. C., 26:254
Everyman in his humour, 33:172
Evian Conference, 45:228-29
Evora Inquisition, 29:17
Ewen, David, 47:181
Ewing, Samuel, 22:57
Exclusion Act (1924), 46:296
Exeter, Council of, 1287, 28:144
Exhibition of Fine Arts, Paris, 31:290
Exhibition of Spanish Art, 31:290
Exhibit of the Civil War Centennial Jewish
  Historical Commission, 50:265, 267
Exhibit on "The American Jew in the Civil
  War," 50:273
Exmouth, Edward Pellew, 46:6
Expatriation, 36:255-56, 259, 280
Extradition Treaty of 1887, 41:185

Eyges, Leon Russell, 22:ix, xi
Eyles, John, 28:256
Eytinge, Rose, 48:202, 267; 49:70, 143
Eytinge, S., 37:449
Ezekiel, Catherine de Castro, 28:2
Ezekiel, Edwin N., 46:103
Ezekiel family, 41:88-90
Ezekiel, Mrs. Gerald A., 50:272, 274, 384
Ezekiel, Henry Clay, 28:3-4, 6, 27, 34, 40, 49
Ezekiel, Henry C., 37:266, 268
Ezekiel, Herbert T., 38:154-56, 161, 165; 46:68; 50:316; and Gaston Lichtenstein, "The History of the Jews of Richmond from 1769 to 1917," 26:xxiv; 49:241
Ezekiel, J., 27:95
Ezekiel, Jacob, 27:145, 236, 506; 28:2; 32:130; 39:449; 40:23, 46
Ezekiel, Joseph, 27:83
Ezekiel, Joseph, Jr., 27:74
Ezekiel, Leah Morena, 27:112
Ezekiel, Mrs. Louis, 28:50
Ezekiel, Mosely, 27:508
Ezekiel, Moses Jacob, 35:250; 39:454, 466; Beethoven, 28:28; Christ in the Tomb, 28:26-

27, 31-32; Christopher Columbus, 28:35; Confederate monument, 28:54; creed of, 50:384; David, 28:27-29, 32; "The Early Congressional Debates and Reporters," 28:xxxix; Ecce Homo, 28:31; "The Ghetto and the Jews of Rome," 28:18; Civil War, 50:295, 342, 374, 383-84; Isaac Mayer Wise, 28:44; Israel, 28:7-8, 10-12, 27-28, 30, 32; Judith, 28:27-29, 32; The Martyr, 28:31; "Moses Jacob Ezekiel," 28:xxii, 1-62; The New South, 28:54-55, 62; photograph of, 50:383; Poe, 28:55-56; Religious Liberty, 28:11-17, 37, 39, 62; religious liberty statue, 29:106, 201; "Sir Moses Ezekiel: A Memoir," 28:xvi; works by, 50:383-84
Ezekiel, N., 29:133
Ezekiel, Naphtali, 27:506
Ezekiel, Philip E., 50:175
Ezekiel, Rebecca, 28:268
Ezekiel, Tobias, 27:76, 120
Ez Hayyim (schools), 43:128; 44:171-72, (Brazil), 42:232, 262, 295

F

Faber, George Stanley, *The Conversion of the Jews*, 30:210; *Dissertation on the Prophecies*, 30:132-33, 147; *View of the Prophecies*, 30:136, 138

Fabri, 32:14

Fabronius, 50:285

Faculty Club, 29:180

Fadi, Aaron, 28:207

Fagen, Melvin M., 46:246

Fagg, Fred D., Jr., 46:124

Fagnani, Charles P., 29:169

Fair American (Young Quaker), 33:179

Fairchild, Charles S., 33:221

Fairchild, David, 31:201, 204, 208, 210

Fairchild, Henry P., 34:214

Fairchild, Henry Pratt, 46:291, 298

Fairchild, Lucius, 36:30-35

Fair employment practices, 39:265; committee on, 47:195

Faires, John W., "Memoir of Rev. John W. Faires," 31:xxxiii

Faires Classical Institute, 31:256

Fairmount Park, 29:201; commissioner of, 22:143-44

Fairmount Park Art Association, 29:xli; 31:256

Falasha State, 43:183

Falcão (Falcon), Mosseh, 29:18

Falk, Joshua, 39:215; 45:63

Falk, Rabbi, 22:202

Falk, S., 37:440

Falk, Samson, 47:39-40, 42, 44, 57

Falk, Solomon Löw, 41:257

Falk, Stanley L., 50:271; "Divided Loyalties in 1861: The Decision of Major Alfred Mordecai," 48:147-69, 266

Falke, Alexander, 50:313

Falkenau, 38:202

Fall of the Spanish American Empire, reviewed, 38:323-25

Falmouth (Henry Moses), 25:67-68

"Falstaff," 40:159

Family, Jewish family and writing history, 46:202, 204, 249; customs, 39:368

Family distress, 33:187

Family Service Association of America, 49:61

Family structure, 39:356, 387-88

Faneuil Hall, 26:200

Fanning, David, 22:188; 29:142-43

Fanny (slave), 50:162

Fano, Jacob, 28:193

Faraj ben Salim, 28:205-7

Farband-Labor Zionist Order, 43:192

Farber, Isaac, 50:174

Faria, Francisco de, 26:xxxiv; 33:112; "Additional Material on Francisco de Faria," 25:xiii, 127-28

Faria, Isa de, 42:278, 394

Faria, Jan, 33:119

Faria in de Stadt, Francisco, 33:119

Faria in de Vergia, Francisco, 33:112

Farissol, Abraham, *Iggeret Or'hoth' Olam*, 22:105

Farley, Phillip P., 50:229-30

Farm and Fireside, 46:490

Farman, Elbert E., 47:85-86

"Farmer's Almanac, The," 34:xiv

Farmers Home Administration, 47:192

Farmer's Register, The, 50:194

Farmer's Weekly Museum, 38:130

Farnesworth, Ellis, 37:199

Faro, Abraham, 42:278, 394

Faro, David Israel, 42:279, 394; 44:93

Faro, Isaac Gabay, 50:253

Faro, Ishac Henriques, 44:223

Farragut, David Glasgow, 28:6; 44:112-13; 48:10

Farras Transportation Company, 28:270
Farrell, James T., 46:127
Farro, Mosseh Vaz, 44:229
Fascism, 36:386-88; 46:292, 327
Fashion, 33:174-75
Fastove, A., 45:184
Father John, of Cronstadt, 36:400
Father Thomas Affair, *see*: Damascus Affair
Fatman, Joseph, 27:514; 30:421
Fatte, Gabriel de la, 27:482
Fauman, Joseph, 46:254-55
Fauman, S. Joseph, 48:67
Faunce, William H. P., 28:xxx
Faure, John P., 33:216-21, 223
Faures, Mr., 27:90
Fauriel, Claude, 38:278
Faust, 45:256
Faust, A. B., 34:184
Fava, Baron, 36:334
Fawcett, Judge, 29:149
Fay, Theodore S., 24:3; 29:90; 36:238, 303-22; 49:28
Fay & Farwells, 31:137
Faya, Aron de La, 42:279, 394
Feast of Esther, *see*: Purim Associations
Feast of Passover, 50:309-11, 400
Fechheimer, A. Lincoln, 40:44
Fechheimer, Goodkind and Co. (San Francisco), 37:45
Fechheimer, S. Marcus, necrology of, 33:xxi
Feder, Mr., 45:80
Federacion Sioniste de Chile, 34:xxv
Federal Theater Project, 47:192
Federal Trade Commission, 46:472; 47:189
Federalists and democracy, 38:109-37
Federated Jewish Charities (Baltimore), 22:215; 25:151, 154; (Boston), 22:229; 49:225
Federation of American Zionists, 35:57-60; 36:64; 38:339; 40:391; 42:100; 45:64, 99, 196; 48:244; 49:84, 166-67, 190-91
Federation of Galician and Bukovinian Jews of America, 49:86
Federation of Jewish Agencies (Philadelphia), 48:234
Federation of Jewish Charities, 31:287; 37:300-301; (Boston), 46:76-77, 81, 84-85; (Cleveland), 29:158; (New York), 28:287; 44:75

Federation of Jewish Historical Societies, 45:262
Federation of Jewish Labor, 48:131-33
Federation of Jewish Organizations, 39:423; 436-37; 49:86
Federation of Jewish Philanthropies, 31:190; (Canada), 50:135, 138; (Pittsburgh), 28:257
Federation of Jewish Philanthropic Societies, 31:271
Federation of Jewish Welfare (Los Angeles), 46:123
Federation of Orthodox Rabbis of America, 33:164
Federation of Polish Jews, 34:191; gift, 35:xxiii
Federation of Roumanian Jews, 49:86
Federation of Russian-Polish Hebrews of America, 49:86
Federation Settlement (New York), 37:295
Federation for the Support of Jewish Philanthropic Institutions, 28:287; 31:259; (New York), 35:323; 42:31
Federations of Charities, Chicago, 42:33
Federations, Jewish Education, 42:30-39
Feibleman, Julian B., 34:xx
Feigel, 38:197
Feigen, S. J., 33:167
Feigin, Samuel I., 45:163
Feilchenfeld, Dr., 22:207
Fein, Isaac M., 49:270; "American Jewish Items in *Niles' Weekly Register*, 1811-1849," 49:268; "Baltimore, Maryland, during the Civil War," 50:427; "Jewish Education in Baltimore from its Beginnings until the 1880's," 44:242; history, writing of, 46:189-90, 193; *Niles' Weekly Register on the Jews*, 50:3-22
Feinberg, D., 38:316
Feinberg, David, 40:403; "David Feinberg's Historical Survey of the Colonization of the Russian Jews in Argentina," 43:37-69
Feiner, Arthur H., 34:215
Feiner, Bernhard, 38:73
Feinerman, Abraham, 40:54
Feingold, Dina, collection, 45:149
Feingold, Marcus, necrology of, 31:xxiii, 256-57
Feingold, Max, 45:149
Feingold, Rose Evelyn, 31:257

Feinman (Urban) v. Feinman, 29:150
Feinsinger, Solomon, 40:48
Feist, Abe, necrology of, 32:xvi
Feldenheimer, Abraham, 41:254
Feldenheimer, Isak, 41:262
Feldenheimer, Josef, 41:257
Feldenheimer, Samson, 41:256
Feldenheimer, Zilli, 41:262
Feldgoise, Samuel S., executive council,
    45:264
Feldman, Abraham J., 35:137; Abraham J.
    Feldman Collection of Judaica, 45:145-46;
    gift, 35:xxiii
Feldman, Ephraim, 40:36, 43
Feldman, Jacob S., The Early Migration and
    Settlement of Jews in Pittsburgh, 1754-1894,
    49:235-36
Feldman, Leon A., "The Jewish Personality
    of the Jewish College Student," 44:242
Feldman, William M., 31:xxxiv
Felicia, Queen, 30:41
Felix Dining Salon, 50:396
Fell, Christopher, 41:112, 119
Fell, Jesse W., 44:101
Fellheimer, Abraham, 41:254
Fellener, August, 41:262
Fellhenner, Louis, 41:262
Fell's Point Congregation, Baltimore, 23:141
Fels, Joseph, 42:312; Foundation, 46:488;
    Fund Commission, 46:487; "The Single-
    Tax Zionism of Joseph Fels," 46:474-91,
    493
Fels, Mr. and Mrs. Joseph, 38:73
Fels, Lazarus, 46:475
Fels, Mary, 46:475-77, 486-88
Fels, Rosina, 38:73
Fels, Samuel, 46:475
Fels, Samuel S., 31:203
Fels, Susannah Freiberg, 46:475
Felsenthal, B., 26:1; 28:239; 32:130; "A
    Sermon by Moses Mendelssohn Printed in
    Philadelphia 130 Years Ago," 30:54
Felsenthal, Barbara, 29:196
Felsenthal, Bernhard, 29:196; 33:39; 34:xx;
    37:59, 85, 87; 40:391; 42:100, 140; 46:202;
    "Jewish Culture and Religious Life in
    America as Reflected in the Felsenthal
    Collection," 44:242; 45:93-127
Felsenthal, Bernhard I., 26:245-46

Felsenthal, Eli B., 28:240
Felsenthal, Emma, gift, 34:xx
Felsenthal, Julius, 22:167-69
Felsh v. Tonkin, "Anglo-Jewish Legal
    Cases," 25:137
Felt, James, 49:151
Felton, Cornelius Conway, 45:21
Feltre, Bernardin de, 28:196
Feltus, H. I., 26:225
Female Hebrew Benevolent Society (New
    York), 27:114; 31:288; (Philadelphia),
    30:233-34, 308-9, 320-21; 48:71-72
Fenno, John, 38:132
Fenno, John Ward, 38:132
Fensterwald Settlement (Nashville), 37:296
Ferber, B., 38:316
Ferber, Edna, 35:261-62; 40:359
Ferdinand, King of Spain, 21:239; 27:474;
    28:209; 35:10, 224; 39:172; expulsion of
    Jews, 33:12
Ferdinand of Aragon, 23:130
Ferdinand I of Naples, 28:191, 204
Ferdinand Vincenzo II, Duke of Mantua,
    28:193
Ferdinand and Isabella, 22:114-15
Ferdinandes, Gaspar, 33:113
Ferea, Sebastian, 33:118
Fereira (Ferreira), Aharon Henriques, 29:16
Fereira, Ishac de Abraham Henriquez, 44:232
Fereirra, Ishac Henriquez, 44:229-30
Ferera, Abraham, 33:87
Ferera, Antho., 33:114
Ferera, Belthor Leitao, 33:114
Ferera, David de, 29:49; 46:35-36
Ferera, Diogo Lopes, 33:112
Ferera, Gasper Dias, 33:73, 89, 118
Ferera, Hilming, 33:115
Fereyra, Ishac de Abm. Henriquez (Gabay),
    22:170
Fergusson, David, 22:xviii; 33:34
Fergusson, James, 46:88
Feria, Bento Massedo, 33:114
Fernandes, Abraham, 25:138
Fernandes, Alexander, 48:23
Fernandes, Antonio dias, auto de fe, 22:180-
    82
Fernandes, Jacob, 37:338
Fernandes, Jacob Nunes, 23:150
Fernandes, Raquel, 37:338

Fernandez family, 29:37
Fernandez, Inez, 31:30
Fernández y González, Francisco, necrology
    of, 26:xxx; 28:272
Fernback, Agnes B., 45:139
Fernberger, Henry, necrology of, 32:xvi
Fernow, Berthold, 37:35; 44:90
Fero v. Fero, 29:150
Ferrara, 28:103, 164, 181, 184, 187-90
Ferrara, David, 27:379
Ferrara, Duke of, 27:279; 28:180
Ferrero, Guglielmo, 37:425
Ferreyra, Ishac Henriques, 25:138
Ferris, Adolphus, 27:277
Ferro, Abraham de David, 29:36
Ferro, Benjamin Vas, 27:245
Ferro, David Silva, 37:377
Ferro (family name), 37:381, 386
Ferro, George da Silva, 33:119
Ferro, Gonzalo Perez, 31:27, 30
Ferro, Ishac Nunes, 29:16
Ferro, Jacob, 21:42, 45; 32:62; 37:373, 375,
    386
Ferro, Jacob, Jr., 21:43; 38:235
Ferro, Jacob Semuel, 44:228
Ferro, Moses, 37:330
Ferrun, Anagram, see: Ruffner, Henry
Fetz, 27:91
Feuchtwanger, Augusta (Levy), 35:xix
Feuchtwanger, Lewis, 35:xix
Feuchtwanger, Mrs. L., 27:111
Feuchtwanger, S., 37:42
Feversham, Flyinghorse, 35:177
Feversham, Lowenstaff, 35:177
Fichhandler, Thomas C., 47:202
Fickett, Francis, 48:173
Fidanque (family name), 48:139
Fidanque, Abm. Haim, 22:170
Fidanque, B. D. Foundation, 44:118
Fidanque, E. Alvin, 44:118
Fidanque, Eliao, 22:170; 44:230
Fidanque, Jacob, 32:115; 44:230
Fidanque, Joseph, 44:227
Fiddler Ed., 35:307-9
Fiddler, Miss, 38:31
Fidelity and Deposit Company, Baltimore,
    26:153-54
Fidus, 39:98
Field, Cyrus W., 36:43

Field, James, 23:139
Field, Marshall, 46:210
Field, Maunsell B., 32:97
Field, Stephen J., 36:234
Fielding, Howard Ioan, 37:188
Fields, Harold, 46:356
Fiertes, Ricardo Los, 34:143
Figaro, Le, 46:89
Figeroa, Dauid de, 42:279, 394
Figl, Leopold, 46:351
Filene, Edward, 46:436
Filene (store), 38:20
Fillmore, Millard, 36:299-300; 38:160, 166
Filtzer, Mrs. E. J., 49:270
Finance Company of Pennsylvania, 25:173
Finberg, Abraham, 47:198
Fine, Alvin I., 40:53
Finesilver, Susskind Moses, 37:42
Fink, Alexander, Jr., 25:50
Fink, Alexander, Sr., 25:50
Fink, John L., 25:48-49
Fink, Mr., 31:146-47, 157-58, 168
Fink, Pauline, 34:212
Finkelstein, Louis, 37:13; 43:195; 47:220;
    48:250; executive council, 37:xxix; 38:342;
    39:470; 42:414; 45:264; gift, 34:xxvii; (ed.),
    *The Jews: Their History, Culture and
    Religion*, reviewed, 40:192-96; necrology of
    Sol M. Stroock, 37:479-80; "The Origin of
    the Synagogue," 31:xvi
Finlay, Hugh, 48:179-80
Finlay, Lord Chancellor, 31:106, 113
Finlay, Mr., 31:186
Finley, John H., 34:232
Finn, James, 26:135, 140; 49:41-48, 52
Finn, Mrs. James, 26:135
Finnigan, Joseph, 25:23, 24
Finucane, James, 46:330
Finzi, 26:133
Finzi family, 28:190
Finzi, Abraham, 26:251, 254-56
Finzi, Judith, 26:255-56
Fiorentino, Salamone, 38:105
Firefly, 48:172
Firkovich, Abraham, 34:150, 154
First Fruits of the West: Bikkure ha-Yam,
    26:271; 30:383
First General Conference of Canadian Jews,
    28:271

First Hebrew Congregation of Berkeley, 29:180
First Pennsylvania Bank and Trust Company, 50:240
First Zionist Congress, 41:22
Firth, Pond & Co., 50:389, 391
Fischel, A., 21:198; 27:124, 261; 38:71
Fischel, Arnold, 40:148; 42:211; 49:22; 50:291-92
Fischell, Dr., 29:103-4, 131
Fischel, Harry, 37:307; gift, 34:xxvii
Fischel, Max, 43:18
Fischer, 38:203
Fischer, Paul, 45:213
Fish (N.Y.), 25:56
Fish, Carl R., 23:102-3
Fish, Hamilton, 25:29; 29:93, 95; 36:105-10, 173-75, 348; 37:435; 40:389; 41:166; 47:78-79; "Jewish Disabilities in Balkans," 24:16-21, 31; "Jonathan Nathan's Letters to Hamilton Fish, 1847-1857," 37:xxxiii; Roumanian problem, 24:110, 112-13
Fish, Hamilton, Jr., 36:83-84, 368; and Zionism, 45:41-44
Fish, Isaac, 29:133
Fish, James, 27:322
Fish, Sidney M., 50:53; *Aaron Levy: Founder of Aaronsburg*, 40:405; "The Ancestral Background and the Early Youth of Barnard and Michael Gratz," 38:344; "The Construction and Dedication of the First Two Synagogue Buildings of Congregation Mickve Israel, Philadelphia (1782 and 1818-1825)," 43:231; "David Franks and Joseph Simon, Commissaries," 39:470; "Early Jewish Religious Functionaries in Pennsylvania, 1742-1790," 40:406; "Illinois and Wabash Land Companies (1773-1823) and their Jewish Stockholders," 41:389; "Jewish Commissaries to the British and Provincial Troops in America during the French and Indian War and Pontiac's Conspiracy," 42:415
Fish, Stuyvesant, 26:220
Fishberg, Maurice, 34:248
Fishblatt, Bilhah, 27:111
Fishell, Dr., 34:170
Fisher, Andrew, 25:50

Fisher, Dorothy Canfield, "Dorothy Canfield Fisher: Friend of Jews in Life and Work," 48:245-55, 265
Fisher, Elena, 27:245
Fisher, Gilbert, 27:326
Fisher, H. D., 38:73
Fisher, Henrick, 33:254
Fisher, James, 27:326
Fisher, James (son, D. Canfield Fisher), 48:249
Fisher, John, 48:249, 254
Fisher, Mykel, 27:242
Fisher, Stanley W., 45:52
Fisher, Thomas, 35:19
Fisher, William, 37:257
Fischoff, 29:126
Fisk, Pliny, 30:188
Fisk, Rev., 22:24
Fisk University, 45:147
Fiske, Clinton B., 41:40
Fiske, John, 34:234; 38:326; 46:127
Fita, Antonia (Colomé), 28:273
Fita, Felix Fidel, 28:273
Fita, Fidel, 26:23
Fita, P. Fidel, 22:xxxiii
Fita y Colomer, Fidel, honorary member, 25:ix; necrology of, 28:xv, 272-74
Fitch, Ashbel P., 22:238
Fitch, Clyde, 40:354
Fitch, Eleazer T., 30:264
Fitch and Engs Co., Newport, 27:211, 213
Fitspatrick, Mary, 39:75
Fitzgerald, 43:30
Fitzgerald; Dearborn Publishing Company v., 29:150
Fitzgerald, F. Scott, 35:268
Fitzgerald, John J., 41:187
Fitzpatrick, Ben, 50:318
Fitzpatrick, Edwin, 26:250
Fitzpatrick, John C., "Calendar of the Correspondence of George Washington, Commander in Chief of the Continental Army, with the Continental Congress," 25:113; "Calendar of the Correspondence of George Washington, Commander in Chief of the Continental Army, with the Officers," 25:113
FitzRandel, Nathaniel, 27:245
Five Jewish Lawyers of the Common Law, 40:87-90

Flaccus, 28:135
Flagg, 22:82
Flagg, Azariah C., 30:404
Flamengo, Jacob Nunes, 27:245
Flamingo, Jacob, 27:289
Flamingo, S., 27:289
Flamingo, Solomon, 27:289
Flanders, Ralph E., 48:255
Flatbush Hebrew Institute, 35:xxiii
Flavin, Martin A., 40:357
Flayderman, Norm, 50:271, 275, 340
Fleckles, Eleazar, 40:18
Flegenheimer, William (1), 50:384-85
Flegenheimer, Dr. William (2), 50:272, 276
Fleisher, Alexander, 37:254
Fleischer, Charles, 39:109; 44:250-51
Fleischman, Doris, 31:xxxii
Fleischman, Ernest M., 45:213
Fleischman, Lawrence A., 50:272, 275, 374, 384
Fleischman, Samuel, necrology of, 31:xvi, 257-58; 34:189; "Plan for World Peace," 31:xxxii
Fleming, John (1820), 21:165
Fleming, John, 42:458
Fletcher, Governor, 49:59
Fletcher, Henry P., 45:40
Fletcher, J. S., 35:264
Fletcher, see: Beaumont
Fleury, Abbé, 30:145
Flexner, Abraham, 39:330; 46:436; 49:97, 271; 50:119; necrology of Louis Bamberger and Caroline Fuld, 37:455-57
Flexner, Simon, 49:271
Fliasnick, Bernard, 50:233-34
Flick, Alexander C., 35:137, 307; History of the state of New York, 35:xx
Flint, Josiah, 32:31
Flint, Margaret A., 50:272
Flint, Timothy, 48:218
Flora (slave), 50:159-60
Florance, Anne, 27:166
Florance, Mrs. Benjamin (Kursheedt), 27:111, 420
Florance family, 27:465; 50:244
Florance, Hadasa, 27:111
Florence, 28:196-97
Florence, Dr., 35:201
Florence, Jacob, 31:xxxiii

Florence, Lewis, 50:169
Florence, Synod of, 28:156
Florence, Theodore J., 29:133
Florence Heller Graduate School for Advanced Studies in Social Welfare, Brandeis University, 50:434
Florentine, Abraham, 38:105-6
Flores, Abm Rodriguez, 21:43
Flores, Isaac, 21:61
Flores, Isaac de Abraham Nunes, 29:36
Flores, Joseph de Ishac Levi, 29:18
Flores, Joseph Levy, 29:18
Flores, Luis Teodoro de, 23:133
Florida, Case on the Contested Seat of David Levy, 30:364-65; Civil War, 50:279-80, 304, 365; "David L. Yulee, Florida's First Senator," 25:vii, 1-29; Jewish local history, 49:220; "Jewish Merchants in Louisiana and West Florida, and the English Expedition to the Illinois in 1764-1765," 29:xvi; "Moses Elias Levy's Agricultural Colony in Florida," 25:132-34; Notices of Florida, 30:306-7; Sketch of the Seminole War, 30:306
Florida Historical Quarterly, 47:224
Florida Railroad, 25:21, 26, 28
Florsheim, Mrs. Louis, 26:xiv; 28:315
Floyd, John B., 25:20; 48:154; 50:310, 342
Fluegel, Maurice, 24:26; 29:92; 39:394-95
Flyinghorse, 35:177
Flying Scud, 40:349
Fly Market, New York, 25:32-33, 45, 50
Flynt, Henry, 22:11; 30:41; 35:166-68; 37:122, 132-33
Foa, Tobias, 35:208
Foard, A. I., 50:331
Foch, Ferdinand, 31:215
Fogel, Herbert, 45:57
Fogg, George G., 36:322
Fogg, Mr., 29:90
Fogh, Sophia, 27:120
Folger, Charles J., 33:213
Folger Library, 39:309
Foligno, F. Gentile da, 28:182
Foligno, Gentile da, 28:202
Folk-lore, 25:162
Folson, Nathaniel S., Prophecies of Daniel, 30:364
Folz, Hans, 35:122

Fonseca, Abaan da, 42:278, 394
Fonseca, Abraham, 21:21
Fonseca, Abraham-Haim Lopez da, 29:21; 42:108, 214
Fonseca, Alvarez de, 28:250
Fonseca, Balthasar de, 33:47, 77, 97; 42:253; 50:78
Fonseca, Beatriz de, 23:134
Fonseca, David de Jacob Lopes da, 44:222
Fonseca, David Lopes da, 42:214
Fonseca, Debora (Massiah), 22:178
Fonseca, Eliau de David de Jacob Lopes da, 44:222
Fonseca (family name), 48:139
Fonseca, Fernandez de, 50:123
Fonseca, Hester Fonseke, 29:15
Fonseca, Isaac de, 22:180
Fonseca, Isaac Aboab da, 29:xliii; 42:219, 223, 235-36, 240-41, 254, 258-59, 274, 281, 290, 293, 387, 390, 392-93; 46:47; 50:73, 76; "Cultural Background of Isaac Aboab da Fonseca: An Analysis of His Library," 45:265
Fonseca, Isaac de (London), 21:29
Fonseca, Ishac da, 29:18
Fonseca, Ishack da, 21:11, 16, 25, 27-28
Fonseca, Jacob, 22:178; 29:18; 32:63
Fonseca, Jacob Lopes de, 22:122; 27:23; 29:29; 44:223, 225
Fonseca, Joas de, 33:65
Fonseca, John de, 33:115
Fonseca, Joseph Nuñez da, see: Nassi, David
Fonseca, Lopez de (Curaçao), 22:171
Fonseca, Lopez de (New York), 38:236
Fonseca, Moses Lopez de, 21:xv, 4, 9, 11, 26, 30-31, 34-36, 208; 23:159; 27:262; 31:237
Fonseca, Mosseh da, 29:18
Fonseca, Pedro de, 31:31
Fonseca, Rachel D., 37:337
Fonseca, Ribca de, 21:16
Fonseca, Samuel Haim Lopez, 22:169
Fonseca, Semuel Haim Lopez, 22:170; 29:30
Fonseca, Tomas de, 31:31
Fonseca, Widow, 21:18-19
Fonsequa, Jacob, 21:9
Fontaney, Jean de, 49:44
Fontes, Diego Nunes, 33:112
Fontes, Francisco Gonsalvos, 33:113
Fool, The, 40:354

Foote (England), 31:113
Foote, Henry, 38:164
Foote, Samuel, *Devil*, 33:175
Forbes, 35:17-18
Forbes, James, 35:259; 40:357
Forbes, William H., 42:367
Forchheimer, Frederick, 23:112, 116
Forchheimer, Meyer, 23:111
Forchheimer, Sara, 23:114
Ford, Henry, 36:383-84; 40:323-34, 360; 42:320; 46:437
Ford Foundation, 46:149-50
Ford, John, 35:228
Ford, Paul Leicester, 35:253
Ford, Standish, 22:190
Ford, Worthington Chauncey, 23:96; "Commerce of Rhode Island, 1726-1800," 25:113
Fordham College, 47:22
Ford-Sapiro Trial, 34:227
Foreest, Cosmo de, 33:115
Foreign Archives Committee, "Report of the Foreign Archives Committee," 23:xiv, 91-103
Foreign Mission School, 39:191
Foreign Policy Association, 36:369
Foreman, Oscar, 28:240
Forest, de la (Consul General), 27:471
Forget-Me-Not, The, 30:433
Forli, Jewish Synod at, 28:154
Form of Daily Prayers, 30:240-42
Form of Service for the Dedication of the Portuguese Hebrew Congregation "Shearith Israel," In West 19th Street, near Fifth Avenue, Consecrated on Wednesday, the 25th Elool, 12th September, 5620 (1860), 50:282
Fornaraki affair, 47:99
Fornberg, K., 39:105, 107
Fornerod, President (Switzerland), 36:309
Forney, J. W., 50:289-90
Forrest, Uriah, 48:8, 14
Forshay, James, 27:326
Forshay, William, 27:326
Forst, Abm., 27:45
Forst, David, 25:113
Forster, 25:7
Forsyth, John, 24:4-5, 94; 34:174; 36:3-5
Fort Chartres, 23:5, 8, 14, 17
Fort Cumberland, 35:23

Fort Delaware, 48:168
Fort Detroit, 40:81
Fort Dobbs, 29:141
Fort Duquesne, 35:2, 17-18
Fort Fredericks, 26:231
Fort Gage, 23:20
Fort George, 26:182
Fort Hendricks, 31:241
Fort Lewis, 35:22
Fort McHenry, 26:186
Fort Monroe, 48:159
Fort Moultrie, 50:317, 382
Fort Necessity, 23:4
Fort Orange, 21:175
Fort Pennsylvania, 50:387
Fort Pitt, 23:5, 13-14, 17-18, 21; 35:8-9, 14, 16, 23
Fort Pulaski, 50:335-38
Fort Sumter, 48:159; 50:317-18, 382
Forte, Nathaniel, 26:254
Fortnightly Club (Rochester, N.Y.), 40:69
Fort Pickens, 48:154
"Fortress of Sorrento, The," 21:229; 41:3
Fortunatae Islands, 22:106
Fortune, 39:236; 45:228; 46:239
Fort Wayne, Ind., 50:277; Achduth Veshalom Congregation, 25:151; religious observances, mid-nineteenth century, 37:37
"Forty-Eighters," 41:231-33; 45:2; 46:290, 388, 475
Forum, The, 25:176
Forverts, 41:307
Forward, 46:397; 47:228; 49:84; 50:205, 208, 211, 215, 218, 223-24
Fosdick, Dorothy, 47:203
Foss, Lukas, 47:182
Foster, J., 28:250
Foster, James, 27:44
Foster, John (1680), 23:83
Foster, John (1760), 34:120
Foster, John G., 43:106, 119
Foster, Mrs. John G., 43:119
Foster, John W., 29:205; 33:223, 225-27; 36:177-204, 227, 229, 236; 41:168-69, 171
Foster, Maj. General, 50:378
Foster, Stephen C., 50:390
Foster, William Z., 41:332
Foster, Solomon, 26:ix

Foster, William, 23:81
Foucher, L. C., 23:45-46, 138
Fould, 29:125-27
Fournier, A., 26:45, 50
Fourth Lantern Oecumenical Council, 28:142
Four Years in Rebel Capitals: An Inside View of Life in the Southern Confederacy from Birth to Death, from the original notes collated in the years, 1861 to 1865, 50:397
Fousset, 41:161
Fowler, Daniel, 41:119
Fowler, Robert Ludlow, 28:247
Fowler, Samuel, 41:119
Fowler, Surrogate, 26:259
Fowlers, Nathaniel, 25:77
Fox, Burton, 25:150
Fox, Charles Edwin, necrology of Henry Berkowitz, 31:xvi, 252-53
Fox, Daniel M., 28:310; 47:79
Fox, Dixon Ryan, 39:287; 46:149
Fox, Edgar, 25:150
Fox, George (1907), 40:377
Fox, George (1674), *A Looking-Glass for the Jews*, 30:80, 82-83
Fox, George L., 45:215
Fox, Joseph, 38:71
Fox, Solomon, necrology of, 25:xii, 149-50
France, 25:5; 26:100, 157, 219; 40:325; *Annals of the Revolution in France*, 30:266; "A Bordeaux Subscription," 23:189; "The Congress of Aix-la-Chapelle," 26:82-94; Congress of Berlin, 24:53, 60-61, 63, 65, 66, 70-71, 108, 115, 151; education, 28:85, 87, 90, 105, 112-13; Federalists and democracy, 38:109-14, 119-29, 136-37; "Francis Joseph Grund," 26:234-35; Inquisition, 32:xxvii-xxviii; Jewish disabilities in Balkans, 24:2, 16, 19, 21-22, 35-36, 43, 49, 102, 110, 121, 125-26, 128, 132, 134, 142, 144; Jewish emancipation, 26:35, 73; Jewish historiography, 26:26, 31; Maximilian, 32:67-72; "Napoleon and the Jews," 26:xiv; Palestine and the Jews, 26:128-31; 36:51, 53, 63, 66-68, 74; "The Participation of Jews in the New York Celebration of the Revolution of 1830 in France," 22:xvii; Russian passports, 46:87-90, 92-98; 47:87-89, 94

France, Anatole, 35:252-53, 258
Francees, Diego Dias, 33:112
Frances, Jan Laurento, 33:116
Francez (s), Joseph, 42:278, 283-85, 289-92, 391-92, 394; 44:82
Franchetti family, 37:76
Franchi, Cardinal, 24:72
Francia, Francis, 35:229, *Trial of Francis Francia*, 35:xx
Francis (actor), 33:182
Francis, Mr., 36:120
Francis I, Austria, 28:115
Francis, Christopher, 27:319
Francis, David R., 36:292-93
Francis, Dr., 26:221; 27:316
Francis, John M., 36:323, 331-35, 338-40
Francis, John W., 30:369
Francis, John Wakefield, 46:12
Francis, Joseph (emperor), 36:336
Francis, King, 28:168
Francis, Lewis, 27:302
Francis, M.A., 48:10
Francisco, Charles, 33:121
Francisco, Gaspar, 33:77
Francisco, Jean, 33:115
Franciz, Joseph, 33:100
Franck, Adolphe, 41:161
Franck, Isaac, 47:201-2; "The Changing American Jewish Community," 46:61
Franck, S. P., 39:408
Franckel, David Hirchel, *Eine Danck-Predigt*, 30:45-46; *A Thanksgiving Sermon*, 30:43-45, 47-49, 51, 53-54
Fränckel, Jonas, 28:76
Frankel, Michael Hirshel, *American Magazine and Monthly Chronicle for the British Colonies*, 30:43
Franckfoort, Abraham, 49:229
Francks, Jacob, 27:416
Franco, 27:83
Franco, Alvarez, 33:53
Franco, Francisco, 48:201
Franco, Isaac, 32:57
Franco, Jacob, 32:57
Franco, Joseph, 29:14
Franco, M., 24:78-79
Franco, Maria, 29:12
Franco, Moseh de Jacob, 27:9
Franco, Moses, 26:251; 32:57

Franco, Nicholas (Bishop of Treves), 28:200
Franco, Solomon, 23:79; 39:342; 42:333-34; 50:253
Franco-British Exhibition, 31:290
Franco-Prussian War, 26:251
Frank, Abraham, 31:234
Frank, Abraham Moses, 41:257
Frank, Adam, 32:xxvi
Frank and Adler, 27:514
Frank, Benjamin, 28:215; 31:229, 230
Frank, Bertha Rayner, 31:226; 40:294; necrology of, 22:xxviii, 213-18
Frank case, 40:323-24
Frank, Fr., 28:113
Frank family, 49:6
Frank of France, 29:127
Frank, Heinrich Moses, 41:257
Frank, Henriette, necrology of, 29:xxix, 159-60
Frank, Henry L., 28:240; 29:159; necrology of, 31:xxiii
Frank, Henry S., Memorial Synagogue (Philadelphia), 25:175
Frank, Isaac, 47:205
Frank, Jacob (1) (Philadelphia), 28:255-56
Frank, Jacob (2) (Philadelphia), 41:282, 285-87
Frank, Jacob (fur dealer), 37:442
Frank, Julius J., necrology of, 33:xiii
Frank, Mrs. Julius J., "The Jewish Encyclopedia," 33:xxxi
Frank, Lawrence P., 42:420, 422; 46:120-22
Frank, Leo M., 35:276; 42:355-56; 31:223
Frank, Leopold, 41:262
Frank, Louis M., 37:455
Frank, Rayner, Loan Fund, 22:217
Frank, Robert, 42:128
Frank, S., 41:144
Frank, Samuel Leon, 22:214, 216; Hospital, 22:217
Frank, Waldo D., 35:275-76; 47:62; "Our America," 34:xxiii
Frankel, 39:197
Frankel, Aaron Hirsch, 35:64
Frankel, Bernard L., 43:238
Frankel, David (New York), 43:250; 45:141
Frankel, David (Westphalia), 28:106
Frankel, Herbert, 50:272, 274, 292
Frankel, Jacob, 42:211; 50:292

Frankel, Lee K., address, comment on,
34:188; auditor, 26:x, xxviii; 28:xiii, xx,
xxxi; 29:xii, xxvii, xxxiv; 31:xiii, xx, xxvii;
32:xi; letters, 31:xxxiii; Louis Marshall
portraits, 33:xxxi; necrology of, 33:xiii
Frankel, N., 38:310
Frankel, Perry, necrology of, 29:xiv, 160-61
Frankel, Robert, 50:292
Frankel, Zacharias, 28:262-63; 42:93; 50:91,
96
Frankel, Zechariah, 28:72, 75-76; 39:208;
40:18
Frankenberg, Abraham von, 35:122
Frankenheimer, Mrs. Samuel (Helen), 29:196
Frankenthal, Max, 50:385-86
Frankfort Conference, 40:364
Frankfort-on-the-Main, 26:68, 86; 28:104;
"The Congress of Aix-la-Chapelle," 26:82-
94; Diet at and Jewish question, 26:55-57,
59-60, 62-64, 66, 68, 75, 78-81, 88-89;
Jewish emancipation, 26:35-37, 43, 45-47,
53-55, 57, 59-62, 69, 74-81, 124
Frankfurt, Moses ben Mendel, 22:125
Frankfurter, Felix, 39:346; 46:435; 48:250;
American Jewish Committee, 49:193; anti-
semitism, 38:170; church-state, 40:97;
executive council, 40:406; 41:388; 42:414;
honorary member, 43:230; labor, 34:244;
41:310; 47:190, 203; Oliver Wendell
Holmes, 42:354-55, 358; Palestine, 36:73-
76
Frankfurter, Naftaili, 50:91
Frankfurter, Veit, 41:262
Frankfurter Zeitung, 40:400
Frankl, Ludwig August, 23:188; 38:225; "On
to America" movement, 38:186, 191, 222-
25
Frankl, P. F., 25:179-80
Franklin, 35:187
Franklin, A. E., 35:xxi
Franklin, Andrew, The Wandering Jew; or,
Love's masquerade, 33:174, 185
Franklin and Armfield, 50:172
Franklin, Benjamin, 22:49; 25:65; 31:63, 72;
34:274; 38:4-5, 82; 40:2; 46:212; 47:205,
139; American Philosophical Society,
35:172; "Benjamin Franklin's 'Parable on
Brotherly Love,' " 37:xxxv, 147-52; B. F.
Epstein, 26:277; David Franks, 49:208;

Gratz family, 23:7, 14; 33:4; 37:347;
letters, 43:235-36; 45:62, 131; Mickve
Israel Congregation, 21:xvi; 42:257; Rufus
Isaacs, 40:89; Solomon Solis-Cohen,
38:338; U.S. Great Seal, 41:62; Masonry,
23:xvii
Franklin, David, 37:254-55
Franklin, Ernestine P., 33:184
Franklin & Hall, 35:188
Franklin, Hyman, 50:313
Franklin, John, 25:20
Franklin, Leo M., 40:392-93
Franklin, Moses Joshua, 38:71
Franklin, Temple, 49:208
Franklin, Thomas, 27:245
Franklin, Thomas, Jr., 23:159
Franklin, Walter, 27:245; 41:111
Franklin, William, 23:15, 19-20; 30:77
Franklin Institute in Philadelphia, 22:139;
38:4; 48:74
Franklin Library, 41:2
Franks, 21:xv, xvi; 23:167; 35:182; 37:380
Franks, A. A., 42:419
Franks, Aaron (br. Jacob), 21:24; 25:79
Franks, Aaron (br. Moses), 26:264-65
Franks, Aaron (London), 27:472; 35:186;
37:419
Franks, Abigail (Mrs. Abraham) (London),
25:75; 26:261-63, 265-66
Franks, Abigail (Bilha Abigail bat Mosche
Asher), 26:265
Franks, Abigail (Mrs. Jacob) (1), 22:39-40
Franks, Abigail (Mrs. Jacob) (2), 25:78-79;
27:460; 37:116
Franks, Abigail, tombstone inscription,
28:xxxix
Franks, Abraham (1) (London), 21:24; 25:75-
77; 26:260-63, 265-66
Franks, Abraham (2), 27:264
Franks, Abraham (3) (br. Moses Franks),
26:264-65
Franks, Abraham (4), 27:376
Franks, Abraham (Philadelphia), 34:101
Franks, Abraham (Quebec), 31:234
Franks, Benjamin, 26:264-65; "Benjamin
Franks, Merchant, and Captain Kidd,
Pirate," 29:xxxvi; 31:229-34
Franks, Bilha Abigail, 35:286; 41:285-87
Franks' clan, 35:4, 17, 20-22

Franks, David (1), 21:45, 53, 63, 102; 25:79
Franks, David (2), 37:419
Franks, David (3), 46:423
Franks, David (4) (Philadelphia), 22:xxxv, 39;
26:232-33, 235-36; 27:460, 472; 28:253-
54; 30:71, 77; 33:4, 253; 34:80, 83, 285;
35:18, 20-22, 24, 286; "David Franks as an
Insurance Broker, 1757 and 1758," 26:xxxi,
268-70; "David Franks and George
Washington in 1758," 31:235-36; "David
Franks' Interest in Lands in Virginia,"
25:xiii, 119-20; "David Franks, Jew,
Merchant, and Suspected Tory," 44:242;
"David Franks and Joseph Simon,
Commissaries," 39:470; directory, 50:63;
Gratz Bros., 23:5, 13, 15-17, 20, 97;
25:113, 125-26; 37:347-48; "A Letter of
David Franks, dated 1778, as Commissary
of Prisoners, etc.," 26:xxxi; "A Letter of
David Franks to Elias Boudinot," 38:48;
"Two Letters of David Franks," 22:xiii,
188-91; loyalist, 38:82-83, 96-98; 46:21;
portraits, 41:282-83, 285; 42:416; 43:232,
234-35
Franks, Mrs. David, 27:460
Franks, David (5) (br. Moses Franks), 26:264-
65
Franks, David S., 27:467, 472, 482; 28:xxxviii,
xl; 29:145-46; 31:230; 34:170, 172, 180;
35:253, 286-87; Continental Army pay
claim, 22:195-96; "David S. Franks, an
autobiographical sketch, 1789," 31:xxiv;
diplomat, 49:208-9; The Franks Collection,
30:80; Proclamation, 30:80-81; "When
Did David S. Franks Last Leave Canada?,"
31:234
Franks, David Salisbury (Solebury), 25:113,
142; 38:82, 96; 42:337; 43:237; 46:38-39;
"David Salisbury Franks, a Distinguished
Patriot and Officer of the Revolutionary
War," 26:xiv
Franks (family name), 23:88, 167; 34:176;
38:83
Franks, Hendle, 26:264
Franks, Henry Benjamin, 31:230-31; "The
Will of Henry Benjamin Franks,
December 13, 1758, and Inventory of His
Estate," 25:xii, 125-27

Franks, Isaac (b. Abraham), 25:76-77, 113,
143
Franks, Isaac (Jamaica), 32:62
Franks, Isaac (b. Moses B.), 27:151
Franks, Isaac (br. Moses), 26:264-65
Franks, Isaac (New York), 21:24
Franks, Isaac (Philadelphia), 22:154, 197;
23:88; 28:xxxviii, xl; 29:172; 31:7, 230;
35:133; 37:425; 38:96; 42:337; 47:188;
50:39, 48; business letters, 23:xviii;
"Descendants of Mary Davidson and Col.
Isaac Franks," 23:xvii; portrait, 31:xxxv;
32:xxv; 41:286; 42:417; 43:232, 235
Franks, Jacob (New York), 21:xv, 5-10, 12-
13, 17, 19-26, 32, 38-40, 42, 49-51, 53-55,
60, 62-63, 68, 70-71, 79, 83, 85-89, 91, 93-
94, 97, 99, 101-2, 181, 187, 194-95, 211;
22:39-40, 44, 48-49; 23:150-52, 159;
25:76-79, 90, 125-26; 26:264, 266; 27:1, 5,
29, 39, 70-71, 180, 272, 299, 472; 31:100,
229, 231, 238; 34:119; 35:20-23, 174-75,
182, 186, 286; 37:116, 380; 41:122; 42:433;
43:131; "Genealogical Notes on Jacob
Franks from Official Records," 25:75-80;
"Notes on the Genealogies of Jacob Franks
and Joseph Simson," 22:xiii; portrait,
41:282, 285-87; 42:416; silverware, 42:417;
"Supplemental Notes on the Jacob Franks
Genealogy," 26:260-66
Franks, Jacob (N.C.), 29:141
Franks, Jacob (Philadelphia), 40:120; 50:39
Franks, Mrs. Jacob, 32:xxviii; 35:286; 41:285-
87; 43:232; portrait of, 42:416
Franks, John (Barbados), 32:57
Franks, John (b. David), 37:419
Franks, John (Philadelphia), 26:233-34, 236;
31:42
Franks, Joseph, 29:147
Franks, Major, 25:142
Franks, Mr., 27:385
Franks, Mos, 21:42
Franks, Moses (b. Abraham), 25:76-79
Franks, Moses (b. David), 38:97-98
Franks, Moses (b. Jacob), 22:39, 152; 28:253-
54; 31:229
Franks, Moses (London), 26:236, 264, 266;
34:80, 119; 35:20-22, 186
Franks, Moses (New York), 27:8, 10-11, 362

Franks, Moses (Philadelphia), 37:116-17, 119, 419
Franks, Moses B. (New York), 27:151, 472; 50:48
Franks, Moses B. (Philadelphia), 50:39
Franks, Moses Benjamin (b. Benjamin), 31:230-31
Franks, Moses Benjamin (b. Isaac), 26:265
Franks, Moses Benjamin (New York), 21:47-48, 51, 53, 55, 121; 37:380
Franks, Naphtali, 22:39-40; 37:419
Franks, Naphtali Benjamin, 25:125
Franks, Naphtaly (b. Jacob), 25:78-79; 26:266
Franks, Naphy (New York), 21:128-30, 132, 139; 23:158
Franks, Naphtaly Benjamin, 21:55; 26:265
Franks, Naphtaly Hirsch (Hart), 26:260-66
Franks, Phila, 26:266; 32:xxviii; 40:120; 41:282, 285, 287; 43:131, 232-33; portrait of, 42:416
Franks, Rachel, 29:xlii; 50:48
Franks, Rebecca, 22:55-56; 27:460-61; 31:44; 34:169, 171-72, 176; 38:92, 96; 49:209
Franks, Rebecca, as Janice Merideth, 35:253
Franks, Rebecca (Lady Johnson), 28:xl
Franks, Richa (Ritchie), 22:39-41, 43-46, 49-50; 25:113; 26:265; 30:61
Franks, Samuel D., 22:154; *Minutes of Testimony*, 30:244
Franks, Sara Phila, 26:261-63, 265-66; 29:147
Franks, Simon, 21:60, 63
Frank Sabbath School, Baltimore, 22:215
Franks *v.* Adolphus, 22:xxxiv
Fransen, Cornelis, 32:16
Franson, Jacob, 33:88
Franzblau, Abraham N., 39:353; 40:48, 51
Franzos, Karl Emil, 35:123; 38:247; 39:325
Fraser, "The Conquering Jew," 25:xv
Fraser, John, 31:182, 184
Fraternal Orders, "Jewish Fraternal Orders in the United States," 46:493; Jewish local history, 49:227
Frayne, Hugh, 34:211
Frays, Samuel, 27:79
Frazao, Jacob, 42:279, 394
Frazao, Josseph, 42:278, 394
Frazao, Samuel, 42:237, 241, 254, 258, 279, 281, 290, 390, 394
Frazer, Furness & Hewitt, 41:90

Frazer, James George, 25:182, 191
Frazier (Frazon), 23:80; 26:201, 204-5
Frazon, Joseph, 23:80
Frazon, Joseph Samuel, 42:336
Frazon, Samuel, 23:80
Frazon, *see also*: Frasier
Frébault, député, 41:161
Frece, Benjamin de, 27:515
Frederic, Harold, "Jews and the Jewish Question in the Writings of Harold Frederic," 38:344
Frederick the Great, 28:70, 206; 34:239, 249; 35:122, 231; 37:174, 189; 43:80
Frederick II, King of Denmark, 28:213
Frederick III, 28:167, 207-8; 36:397
Frederick of Prussia, 35:2
Frederick William I, 35:231
Freeborn, Mr., 27:440
Freedman, Gracilah, 27:111
Freedman, Isabella, necrology of, 31:xxix
Free Employment Bureau (Boston), 46:76-78, 81
Freehafer, Edward G., 50:272
Freehof, Solomon B., 40:43; 46:62; executive council, 42:415
Free Library of Philadelphia, 31:vi; 33:19; 42:459
Freeman, Douglas Southall, 46:430, 434
Freeman, Edward Augustus, 28:232
Freeman, Meyer, 36:53-58; 44:136, 140, 142, 189-90, 192
Freemantle, Francis, 35:36
Free Men of Israel, 37:47
Free Religious Association, 42:83-84
Free Sons of Israel, 29:98; 49:17; (New York), 40:166; (Rochester), 40:66
"Free Sons of Zion," 35:58
Free speech, 38:21
Free State Democratic Party (Benton), 23:64
Free Synagogue, New York, 28:xxxviii; 39:335; gift, 32:xxv
Fregaiao, Manuel Perera, 33:119
Fregason, Manuel Perera, 33:116
Fregatje, 48:25
Freiberg, Duffie Workum, 29:161
Freiberg, Julius W., 28:285; 29:161, 163; 39:451; 40:22
Freiberg, J. Walter, 49:199; necrology of, 29:xiv, 161-63

Freiberg, Maurice J., necrology of, 35:x
Freiberg, Stella (Hensheimer), 29:163
Freiberg, Mrs. Walter J., 40:47
Freiberger, S., 29:130
Freiburger, Simon, 41:263
Freidus, Abraham Salomo, 34:190
Freidus, Abraham Solomon, 22:xvi; 23:xii;
  25:137; 28:xiv, xxi; 29:xiv, 151; 33:132,
  141; 35:271; 45:62, 152; "List of Works
  Relating to the History and Condition of
  the Jews in Various Countries," 23:xiii;
  necrology of, 29:xxxvi, 163-65
Freidus Memorial Collection, 45:152
Freie Arbeiter Stimme, Die, 47:228; 48:132-33
Freiheit, Die, 50:251-52
Freimann, Aron, 28:263-64; 34:250; "Dr.
  Aron Freimann Collection," 45:157;
  Necrology of Sigmund Seeligmann,
  37:478; and Max J. Kohler,
  "Communications from the Russian,
  Prussian, Austrian, and English
  Governments to the Senate of Frankfort-
  on-Main in 1816, Probably the Earliest
  Joint Governmental Representation on
  Behalf of the Jews in Modern Times,"
  31:xvii
Freind, Mord., 27:258
Freind, Nahum, 27:259
Freitas, Gasper de Abren de, 25:127-28
Freitman, I., 27:120
Frejka, Ludvik (Freund), 50:112, 115
Frelinghuysen, Frederick T., 25:29; 36:43,
  209-11; 47:99
Fremantile, William Robert, 26:148
Fremont, 34:228
Frémont, John Charles, 42:110; 44:32-33, 40,
  66, 99; 50:383
French, Edwin David, 45:202; 50:394
French, Philip, 23:150
French, William H., 27:506
French Constitutional Assembly, 49:18
French and Indian War, 26:266; "Jewish
  Commissaries to the British and Provincial
  Troops in America during the French and
  Indian War and Pontiac's Conspiracy,"
  42:415; privateers, 23:5, 165-69
French Legion of Honor, 37:475
French National Anti-Semitic League, 41:96
French National Archives, 22:xx

French Revolution, 26:267; 28:66, 79
French Spoliation, 47:187
Frenkel, Eiseman Moses, 32:119
Frenkel, Emil, 32:121; "A Hessian Tax-roll of
  1811," 32:xx; necrology of, 34:ix
Frenkel, Moses Jacob, 32:118-21; 34:xxv
Frenkel-Brunswik, Elsie, *see*: Adorno, T. W.
Frere, David, 21:176
Fresnay, Paul, 41:152
Fresneau, Andrew, 30:33; 35:176; 42:74-75,
  77
Fretos, Antho, de, 33:114
Fretz, R. S., and Brother, 31:137
Freudberg, Leopold, 47:203
Freudenthal, W., 38:73
Freund, Der, 48:195
Freund, Miriam, "Make My Eyes Look to the
  Future—Henrietta Szold Centennial
  Address," 49:159-72, 268
Freund, Robert G., 35:xviii
Frew, Miss, 28:58
Frey, Joseph Samuel Christian Frederick,
  27:205; 45:189-90; *Course of Lectures*,
  30:383; *Essays on the Passover*, 30:294; *The
  Hebrew Messenger*, 30:409; *The Hebrew
  Student's Pocket Companion*, 30:301; *The
  Jewish Intelligencer*, 30:313, 315; *Joseph and
  Benjamin*, 30:301-2, 364, 366; *Judah and
  Israel*, 30:345, 354; *Koul Jacob in Defence of
  the Jewish Religion*, 30:164, 166-67, 174;
  Letter, 30:244; *Narrative*, 30:172-73; *New
  Edition of a Hebrew Grammar*, 30:212, 233,
  269-70, 302; *Report of Agency of Rev.
  J.S.C.F. Frey*, 30:350; *A Short Account of
  Mr. Frey*, 30:129; *Tobit's Letters to Levi*,
  30:170-71
Frey, Samuel, 45:190
Frey, William, 48:89-90, 92
Freyre, Gilberto, 42:305-6
Frezao, Arom Levy, 42:279, 394
Fridenberg, Martin, 32:57
Fried, Jerry, 34:xxvii
Fried, M. J., 33:164
Friedberg, Bernard, 33:132, 137-42; 39:224
Friedberger, Baruch, 41:259
Friedenberg, Albert M., 22:ix, xxiii; 23:vii, ix,
  x, xii; 25:14; 26:xiii; 33:240; 34:165; 50:75;
  "Additional Jewish Grand Masters,"
  22:182; American Academy of Political and

Social Science, 28:xviii; "American Jewish Journalism to the Close of the Civil War," 26:xxxi, 270-73; 33:132; "Anglo-Jewish Legal Cases," 25:134-38; appreciation, 30:vii; "An Austro-Hungarian Movement to Encourage the Migration of Jews to America, 1848," 23:187-89; Battle of Long Island, 28:xxx; by-laws committee, 25:xii; "Calendar of American Jewish Cases," 29:149-53; 34:252; "Charles L. Hallgarten," 31:vii, 187-91; "Columbus and the Jews," 31:234-45; committee on publication, 28:xxix; "The Correspondence of Jews with President Martin Van Buren," 22:xii, 71-100; corresponding secretary, 22:xi, xiv, xvi, xxiv, xxvii; 23:ix, xii; 25:ix, xi; 26:ix, xii, xxiii, xxvi-xxvii, xxx; 28:vi, xiv, xvii, xxi, xxix-xxx, xxxii; 29:xi-xii, xiv, xxvi-xxviii, xxxiii, xxxv; 31:xiii, xv, xix, xxiii, xxvii, xxix; 32:ix-x, xii, xix; 33:xi-xiii, xvi, xx-xxi, xxv; 34:xiii; 35:ix-x, xiv; 37:xxix; "Did Jews Settle in Newport in 1658?," 34:xiv; "Early Jews in Boston," 29:153; early letters, 23:184; 34:75; "Economic Factors in American Jewish History," 25:xiii; "The Economic Interpretation of American Jewish History," 22:xxviii; editing, 22:vii; 23:vii; 25:vii; 26:vii; 28:vii; 29:vii; 31:vii; 32:iv; 33:vi; 34:iv; 35:iv; executive council, 28:xxi; Foreign Archives Committee report, 23:xiv; "Francis Joseph Grund," 26:234-35; "Francis Joseph Grund a Forgotten Journalist and Politician," 22:xxviii; "Further Additions to 'Calendar of American Jewish Cases,' " 26:259-60; "Gabriel of Salamanca," 22:xvii; gifts, 22:xxxii, xxxiii, xxxv; 23:xvii; 25:xv; 26:xxxiii, xxxv; 28:xl-xli, xxxviii; 29:xxxix, xli-xlii; 31:xxxiii, xxxiv, xxxv; 34:xxv; Gratz Papers committee, 25:xiii; "Haym Solomon, and the Revolution," 33:xxxi; *Hebrew Standard*, 34:286; History of Jews, committee on, 29:xxvi; history, writing of, 25:66; 26:30; 39:305; indexing, 34:178; Jewish Historical Society of England, 28:xviii, xix; Jewish Publication Society of America, 22:xxv; "The Jews as American Railroad Financiers, with Special

Reference to Jacob H. Schiff," 29:xv; "The Jews of Dutch Brazil," 29:xxix; "The Jews in the Revolutionary War," 31:xxiv; "Letters of a California Pioneer," 31:vii, xvii, 135-71; loyalists, 38:81; Lyons papers, 21:x, xii; 27:xix; "Memorial Note on Samuel Westheimer," 25:xiii, 124-25; "Miscellanea," 26:242-46; 28:248-52; necrologies of Abe Bloch, 23:xiii, 191; Frank Cundall, 35:x, 311; Georg Caro, 22:xvii, 211-13; Isaac E. Schorsch, 28:xv, 304-6; Johanna Haas Westheimer, 28:xv, 314-15; Julius F. Sachse, 28:xxii, 298-99; Nicholas Darnell Davis, 25:xii, 148-49; necrology of, 37:xi-xii, 461-62; nominating committee, 22:xxvii; 28:xxxii; notes, 34:266-68; Oppenheim library, committee on, 32:xxix; publication committee, 24:lx; 29:xi; recording secretary, 32:ix, xv; 33:xix; "Report of the Foreign Archives Committee," 23:xiv, 91-103; review, 34:248; secretary, 28:xvii, xxv; "A Selected Bibliography of the Writings of Albert M. Friedenberg," 35:xiv, 115-37; "A Selection from the Unedited Correspondence of Aaron Lopez," 23:xiii, 183; "The Simson Trust," 28:246-48; "Some Early Items Relative to New York Jewish History," 28:xxiii; "Some New York Jewish Patriots," 26:237-39; "Stray Notes on Jamaican Jewish History," 22:xviii; "Sunday laws in the U.S.," 26:217; 34:xxv; thirtieth annual meeting, committee on, 29:xi; thirty-first annual meeting, committee on, 29:xxvi; "Thoughts on the Philosophy of American Jewish History," 28:232-36; "Trusts for Jewish Charitable Purposes under the Law of New York," 28:xxiii; "Two Early Letters," 23:xiii, 183-84; "The Value of Old Commercial Letters as a Source of American Jewish History," 28:xv; "Zionist studies," 34:xxv; *see also*: Adler, Cyrus; *see also*: Cundall, Frank

Friedenberg, Samuel, 50:383
Friedenheimer, Bernard, 41:256
Friedenwald, Aaron, 31:226; 37:464; 39:412-13; 45:196; 47:159

Friedenwald, Harry, 28:vii; 31:220; bookplate, 45:178, 196-97; "An Essay on Jewish Physicians in Spain," 29:xxix; gifts, 22:xxxiii; 26:xxxv; gift, 28:xxxviii; 34:xxv; 35:xxi; "Jewish Physicians in Italy: Their Relation to the Papal and Italian States," 28:xxiii, 133-211; necrologies of Julius Levy, 31:xxix, 281-82; Louis Hiram Levin, 29:xxxvi, 176-78; "The Physician's Aphorisms," 28:xxxviii; "Portuguese Jewish Physicians, with an Exhibit of Some of Their Works," 29:xxix; regrets of, 28:xvii; Zionism, 35:60; 39:412

Friedenwald, Herbert, 22:xxviii; 26:xiv; 29:166; 33:8; 36:135; Bucharest Peace Conference, 24:84, 86-89; "Dictionary of American National Biography," 22:x; executive council, 22:xxvii; 23:xii; 25:xi; 26:xii; 28:xxii; 29:xxix; 31:xxiii; 32:xix; 34:xiv; 37:xxxii; gift, 22:xxxiv; International Congress of Americanists, 23:x; Lyons papers, 21:x, xii; 22:xxi; necrology of, 37:xii, 463-66; necrology of A. Howard Clark, 28:xxii, 265-66; "A Note on the Jewish Vestry Bill of Barbados," 22:xiii; presides, 22:ix; recognized, 22:xviii; recording secretary, 22:xii, xvi; regrets of, 28:xvii; thirty-first annual meeting, committee on, 29:xxvi

Friedenwald, Jane (Ahlborn), 37:463; necrology of, 29:xxxvi, 165-67

Friedenwald, Jonas, 37:464

Friedenwald, Jonas S., 45:197

Friedenwald, Julius, death, 37:xii

Friedenwald, Moses, 29:166; 31:225; 37:463

Friedenwald, Rebecca, 23:191

Friedenwald, Rose Diebold, 37:466

Friedl, R. W., 39:83

Friedlaender, David, 43:181

Friedlaender, Michael, 25:180-81

Friedland, Abraham H., 33:147

Friedland, Benjamin L., death, 37:xii

Friedlander, 31:140, 144

Friedlander, Abraham J., 26:283

Friedländer, Alexander, 41:234

Friedländer, Benoni, 26:99

Friedländer, David, 26:47-48, 98-99, 124; 28:73, 79; education, 28:83-84, 92-93, 102-3, 106, 109, 115

Friedlander, Israel, 39:334; "Israel Friedlander's 'Aspects of Historical Judaism,' " 38:342

Friedlander, M. I., 29:132

Friedlander, Rosetta, 32:129

Friedlander, Solomon, 27:509

Friedman, 28:vii; "Elsie T., Sophie M., and Lee Max Friedman: An Appreciation," 48:265

Friedman, Albert M., 34:iv

Friedman, B., 33:153

Friedman Bros., 39:176

Friedman, David, 38:75

Friedman, Elisha, 40:405

Friedman (families), 50:134

Friedman, Harry G., 43:230; Civil War, 50:272, 296, 312, 316, 335, 345; executive council , 46:493; 49:268; Lee Max Friedman Award Medal, 49:271

Friedman, I., 41:142

Friedman, Isaac, 50:197

Friedman, Joseph, 50:197

Friedman, Julian, 39:151

Friedman, L. M. (Utica), 29:135

Friedman, Lee M., 22:229; 30:vi; 34:215; 37:iv; 38:9; 39:114, 176; 41:34; 43:70; "Aaron Lopez' Family Affairs from 'The Commerce of Rhode Island,' " 35:295-304; "Aaron Lopez's Long Deferred 'Hope,' " 37:xxxiii, 103-13; "Abraham Solomon: A Revolutionary Soldier," 40:76-80; "Additional Material on Francisco de Faria," 25:xiii, 127-28; Adler resolutions, 28:xxxv; American Antiquarian Society, 22:xiv; American Historical Association, 22:xiv; 44:245; "American History—the History of Immigrants," 46:194-95; "American Jewish Historical Society: Retrospect and Prospects," 41:217-24; "America's First Jewish Club," 34:xiv; appreciation, 42:415; award, 49:150, 165, 270-71; 50:425; "Baron de Belmonte's Petition," 38:45-46; 42:461; "A Bibliography of the Writings of Lee Max Friedman," 50:427; bookplate, 45:137, 181, 206; book reviews by, 40:199-201; 44:126-28, 248-50; 46:59-60, 125-26; "Boston in American Jewish History," 42:333-40; Civil War, 50:307, 309;

communication from, 26:xxx; "A Contemporary Appraisal of Judah Monis, Harvard's First Instructor in Hebrew," 38:146-47; contributor, 39:206, 336, 477; 40:105, 205, 322; 41:105, 392; 42:112, 331, 467; "The Cordwainers' Case and Moses Levy," 38:342; "Cotton Mather and the Jews," 26:xiv, 201-10; "The de la Penha Family and Its Labrador Grants," 32:xii; "Dr. Hamilton Visits Shearith Israel, 1774," 39:183-85; "Early American Jews," 34:xxv; "Early Jewish Residents in Massachusetts," 22:xiii; 23:vii, 79-90; "1854—Boston and Its Jews," 49:225; "E Pluribus Unum, Unity in Diversity," 40:207-14; executive council, 22:xii, xvi, xxvii; 23:xii; 25:xi; 26:xxx; 28:xxxii; 29:xxxv; 31:xxix; 33:xvii; 35:xiv; 37:xxxiv; "The Farmer's Almanac," 34:xiv; finance committee, 29:xi; "French Colonial Laws relating to Jews in Colonial America," 37:xxx; "Gabriel Milan, the Jewish Governor of St. Thomas, Danish West Indies," 26:xxxi; 28:213-21; 44:115; gifts, 22:xxxv; 26:xxxiv; 28:xxxix; 31:xxxii; 34:xxv; 35:xviii; 44:243; 49:148, 150-51; "A Great Colonial Case and a Great Colonial Lawyer: Solomon de Medina et al v. Rene Het et al," 41:390; 42:71-82, 213; *Growth and Achievement: Temple Israel, 1854-1954*, reviewed, 44:250-51; "Hebrew-Speaking Indians," 39:185-89; history, writing of, 39:239, 288; 42:312; 46:187-89, 255, 270, 431; 49:224; honorary president, 42:414; 43:230; 44:240-41; 45:264; 46:492; index to publications, 44:246; Intercollegiate Menorah Association, 28:xxix; "An Invitation to American Jewish History," 38:12-21, 344; "Jacob Meara and Simon Valentine of Charleston, South Carolina," 41:77-82; "Jewish Colonial Privateersmen," 40:75-76; "Jewish Obituary Notices in the Gentleman's Magazine (1731-1868)," 37:419-20; "Jewish Residents in Massachusetts before 1800," 32:xix; "Jews in the Vice-Admiralty Court of Colonial Rhode Island," 37:xxx, 391-418; "Joseph S. C. F. Frye and the American Society for Meliorating the

Condition of the Jews," 28:xxxiii; "Joshua Montefiore of St. Albans, Vermont," 40:119-34; "Judah Monis, First Instructor in Hebrew at Harvard University," 22:1-24; 30:35; "The Judith Hays-Samuel Myers Marriage Contract," 38:149-50; "Know Thyself—A Program for American Jewish History," 39:337-50; Maurice Jacobs, recognized, 45:264; "A Messenger to George Washington," 37:xxxiii, 115-19; "Miscellanea," 38:45-49; "The Missing Phylactery," 38:49; "Modern American Radanites," 37:xxxv; "Moses Michael Hays," 35:288-92; "Moses Michael Hays' Letter to His Son Judah," 38:150-51; "The Murder at Massena," 49:233; "Mrs. Child's Visit to a New York Synagogue in 1841," 38:173-84; "The Naturalization of Aaron Lopez," 38:342; Necrologies of Albert M. Friedenberg, 37:461-62; Godfrey Morse, 22:xii, 228-30; necrology of, 47:200, 211-15; Newport Synagogue, 37:441; 38:332; newspaper items, 38:46-47; "The New York Synagogue in 1812," 25:xiii, 131-32; nominating committee, 22:xi; 32:xix; "Notes," 31:xxix, 247; 35:293-95; paper, 33:xxxii; "Personal sidelights on Newport Jews from the Rhode Island Commercial Correspondence," 35:xv; "The Phylacteries Found at Pittsfield, Mass.," 23:xiv; 25:vii, 81-85; *Pilgrims in a New Land*, reviewed, 38:249-51; president, 38:344, 346; 39:469; 40:406; 41:387; "President Roosevelt and the Abrogation of the Russian Treaty of 1832," 32:xix; president's address, 40:207-14; 41:387; presides, 38:343-47; 40:405-7; 41:385-90; 42:413; 45:264; 46:493; "The Problems of Nineteenth Century American Jewish Peddlers," 44:1-7; "Robert Grosseteste and the Jews," 33:xxv; "Rowland Gideon, an Early Boston Jew, and his Family," 35:xiv, 27-37; Salo W. Baron recognized, 44:241; "Senator Vance and His Scattered Nation," 43:231; "Sewall's Hebrew Grammar," 38:147-48; "A Side Light on Restrictive Covenants," 41:381-84; "The Significance of American Jewish History," 38:253-59; 345; "Six French Men-of-War

Full of Jews at Louisburg," 26:xiv, 231; "Some Friedman Family Letters," 38:346; "Some Further Notes on Judah Monis," 37:xxx, 121-34; "Some References to Jew in the Sugar Trade," 42:305-9; "Something Additional on General Grant's Order Number 11," 40:184-86; "Synagogues in Fall River, Mass.," 37:421; Taft address publication, 29:xi; vice-president, 37:xxxvi; 38:341; "Washington and Mosaic Law," 39:319-20; "William Davis Robinson's Memoir Addressed to Persons of the Jewish Religion," 38:344; "Wills of Early Jewish Settlers in New York," 22:xiii; 23:vii, 147-61; *Zola and the Dreyfus case*, 35:xxi

Friedman, Ludolph, 50:313

Friedman, M., 29:135

Friedman, Max, 39:177-78, 180; 46:77; 47:211

Friedman, Col. Max (1), 50:291, 307

Friedman, Lieut. Max (2), 50:307

Friedman, Philip, 21:215

Friedman, Samuel, 38:74

Friedman, Sam. N., 37:268

Friedman, Sophie M., 48:265

Friedman, Theodore, 46:63; and Robert Gordis (eds.), *Jewish Life in America*, reviewed, 46:61-64

Friedman, Babette, 39:174

Friedman, Bele (nee Stein), 39:175

Friedmann (family), "Some Friedmann Family Letters," 39:169-76

Friedmann, Felix, 45:137, 168

Friedmann, Isaac, 39:172, 174

Friedmann, J., "Lector M. Friedmann," gift, 33:xxix, xxxii-xxxiii

Friedmann, Jacob, 39:174, 176

Friedmann, Joseph, 39:174-76

Friend, Mrs. Joseph, "Autobiography of Julius Weiss," 33:xxxi

Friedmann, Levi, 39:174

Friedmann, Lob, 39:169, 171-76

Friedmann, Malchen, 39:174

Friedmann, Marianne, 39:174

Friedmann, Max, 39:174, 176

Friedmann, Meir, 25:178-79

Friedmann, Paul, 47:158

Friedmann, Solomon, 39:174, 176

Friedrich (surname), 37:379

Friedrich, Carl J., 46:130

Friend & Adler, Milwaukee, 47:46

Friend & Bros., H., 47:37

Friend, Elias, 47:37

Friend, Henry, 47:37, 42, 46

Friend, Meyer, 47:37, 42

Friend, Meyer M., 25:176

Friend, N. M., 34:289

Friendly (slave), 50:167

Friendship Hebrew Congregation (Baltimore), 23:141

Friends of Zion, New York, 35:xxiii

Fries, Jacob Friedrich, 35:122

Friezner v. Friezner, 29:152

Frink, Samuel, 50:33

Frisch, Benedict, 48:258

Frisch, Ephraim, 39:465

Frisch, J. P., 47:42

Frisch, William, 31:226

Frishbert, Wolf, 33:151

Frishman, David, 40:136

Froes, Manuel Gonsalvos, 33:117

Frogere, Francois de, 33:115

Fröhlich, Leopold, 41:257

Fröhlich, Max, 41:263

Fröhlich, Simon, 41:263

Frohman, Charles, 40:357-58

Frohman, Daniel, 40:357-58

Frois, Abby, 27:293, 298

Frois, Benjamin, 29:22

Frois, Jacob, 32:57

Frois, Joshua, 21:54, 58

Frois, M., 27:105

Frois, Manoel, 29:22

Frois, Mordecai, 27:78, 91, 290, 293, 298

Frois, Morris, 27:291, 293, 298, 303

Frois, Rachel, 27:293-94, 298

Fromkes, Harry, 43:230

Fromonce, S., 39:91

Frontenac, 35:2

Front Page, The, 40:358

Frost & Converse, 31:137

Frost, James, 35:290

Frost, Miller, 35:290

Frothingham, O. B., 42:83

Froude, James Anthony, 33:17

Froys, Abraham, 29:22

Froys, Ishac, 29:22

Froys, Leonor, 29:22
Froys, Ribca, 29:22
Fruhauf, Henry, 50:272
Fruin, R., 22:31n
Fry, Luther C., 34:192
Fry, William, 27:263
Frye, Joseph S. C. F., "Joseph S. C. F. Frye
  and the American Society for Meliorating
  the Condition of the Jews," 28:xxxiii
Fryers, John, 37:168
Fuchs, J., 22:174
Fuchs, Lawrence H., 48:64, 68
Fuchs, Otte, 37:437
Fuchs, Witold, 36:275-76
Fuel Society (N.Y.), 40:163
Fuenleal, Sebastian Ramirez de, 31:17, 23-24
Fuerst, 29:128
Fuerstenberg, Carl, 35:136
Fuerstenberg, Hans, 35:136
Fuerth, Mr., 43:58
Fugitive Slave Law, 23:61; 46:274
Fuld, Felix, 28:xi; 37:455-56; necrologies of
  Abraham Rothschild, 29:xiv, 183-84;
  Rudolph Levi, 29:xiv, 175-76; necrology
  of, 32:xvi
Fuld, Israel, 41:267
Fulds, Martin, 31:148, 159, 168
Fuller, Chief Justice, 25:112
Fuller, Horace S., 37:428
Fuller, Melville W., 36:43
Fuller, R., 30:466

Fulton, 48:172
Fulton, Robert, 35:193; 43:200-201, 222-28;
  48:172
Fulton the First, 48:173
Fundão, Jacob, 42:278, 394; 44:83
Funeral laws, 27:115-16
Funk, Jacob, 26:211
Funk & Wagnalls Co., gift, 32:xxv
Furber, 28:35
Furie, William B., 46:62
Furrer, Dr., 36:310-12, 314, 317-18, 321-22
Fürst, A., 28:84
Fürst, Julius, 28:71-72
Fürst, Livius, 28:172, 186
Fürstenthal, Johann August, 35:122
Furtado, Anna, 29:35
Furtado, Brites, 29:35
Furtado, Gaspar Mendes, 29:35
Furtado, Isaac Henriques, 27:245
Furtado, Izabel, 29:35
Furtado, João, 29:35
Furtado, Luzia (Mendes), 29:35
Furtado, Manuel, 29:35
Furtado, Maria, 29:35
Furtado, Pedro, 29:35
Fürth, Jacob, 37:436; gift, 22:xxxiv
Fürth, Rabbi, 35:68, 105
Fur trade in colonial America, 23:3-8, 10-11,
  13, 16, 21; 35:2, 14-16, 18; 50:128
Fusilier, Capt., 44:108
Fusion Party, 49:9

G

Gabai, Izaque, 42:278, 394
Gabay, Abraham, 23:28
Gabay, Abraham F. de Iahacob, 37:334
Gabay, Isaac, 32:62
Gabay, Jacob, 33:77
Gabay, Joseph Shiprut, 29:26, 29
Gabay, Rybka Myryam, 37:337
Gabay, Salamao, 42:278, 394
Gabay, Samuel, 28:239
Gabay, Sarah Siprut (Seyproot), de, 35:246
Gabay, Sarrah, 23:29
Gabay, Solomon, 23:28; 32:62; 37:337
Gabbai, Abraham de David da Costa
   Andradi, 22:122-23
Gabbot, Ferdinand, 28:68
Gabilho, Daniel, 33:56; 42:239-40
Gabreelow, Joseph, 33:140
Gabriel, Benjamin, 29:147
Gabriel, Benja Rods, 21:55
Gabriel, Nathan, 29:147
Gabriel, Nathaniel, 29:147
Gabriel of Salamanca, 22:xvii, 213
Gabriel, Solomon, 27:43
Gaby, Esther (Bueno), 23:149
Gaby, Isaac, 23:149
Gadelia, Fan., 25:116
Gadje, Hannah Joseph, 37:339-40
Gadje, Joseph Saul, 37:339
Gadsby, John, 47:187
Gaehle, 23:143
Gaffari, Stefano, 28:159
Gage, Billy, 22:40
Gage, Thomas, 35:10, 13-14, 20
Gage, Viscount, 35:36
Gago, Moseh Hamis, 42:394
Gail, Samuel, 27:346
Gaillard, J., 41:162
Gain, John, 25:127

Gajo, Maestro (Isaac ben Mordecai), 28:145-46, 160
Galaxy, The, 38:275; 39:296
Gale, Joseph (ed.), *Eastern Union: The Development of a Community*, 49:228
Gale, Therese, 31:297
Galenson, Walter, book reviewed by, 43:192-94
Gales, Joseph, 48:16
Gales & Seaton, 48:16
Galesburg, Ill., religious observances, mid-nineteenth century, 37:37
Galitzi, Christine A., 34:216
Galitzin, Prince, 26:116, 119, 121, 124; 28:114
Gallagher, Robert H., 27:506
Galland, A., 37:43
Gallatin, Albert, 22:153; 27:495; 43:222-24; 48:4
Gallatin, James, 39:34
Galliner, Arthur, 39:459
Gallois, 32:xxv
Galloway, B. T., 31:202
Galloway, Joseph, 30:77
Galphin, Alexander, 50:176-77
Galphin, Frances, 50:176-77
Galphin, George, 50:176-77
Galphin, James, 50:176-77
Galphin, Nunes, 50:176-77
Galphin, Robert, 50:176-77
Galter, David, 43:238
Galton, Francis, 25:158
Galveston case, 34:181
Galveston, Texas, 50:279; Congregation
   B'nai Israel Sunday School, contribution,
   37:xxxviii; Galveston movement, 42:454;
   religious observances, mid-nineteenth
   century, 37:37; "Some Aspects of the
   Galveston Movement," 37:xxxv; United

Jewish Welfare Association, contribution, 37:xxviii
Galvin, Owen A., 46:76
Gama, Juan Perez de, 31:21, 25
Gambetta, Léon, 41:162
Gambetta Note, 47:88
Gamero in Olinda, Andre, 33:114
Gamma, Abraham de, 33:65
Ganguda, G., 39:100, 104
Gans, David, *Nehmad we-Naim*, 22:116; *Zemah David*, 22:115-16, 119; 28:65-66
Gans, Eduard, 41:12, 227
Gans, Herbert J., 48:66-67
Gans, Isaac, 50:304
Gans, Louis, 40:263
Gans, S. I., 40:141
Gantt, Henry L., 41:43, 45-46, 48, 312; 46:228
Ganzman, Hilda, 28:292
Gaon, Solomon, 42:441
Garacu, Villa de, 47:73
Garay, Francisco de, 31:12
Garcia, Hananiel, 50:123
Garcia, Jacob, 23:175
Gardiner, 29:xxv
Gardner, Mr., 27:316
Gardner, Alexander, 50:300, 361
Gardner, Col., 44:133
Gardner, Job, 35:291
Gardner (photographer), 27:259, 415
Gardner, Rev., 22:24
Gardner, William, 35:291
Gareau, Francois, 23:139
Garey, Francis, 37:400
Garey, John, 37:396
Garfield, James A., 37:71; 43:15; and Simon Wolf, 29:200; 47:82, 84, 95-96
Garfunkel, Aaron, death, 37:xii
Garibaldi, Giuseppe, 28:14
Garland, George, 45:197
Garland, Hamlin, 45:20
Garment trades, 38:18-21; 40:61-62, 65, 67; 41:298, 305-6, 309, 316-17, 320-27; 47:36-37; 48:51; 49:75, 95; Amalgamated Clothing Workers of America, 44:242; 46:241; 49:83; Amalgamated Men's Clothing Workers, 41:323, 327, 332, 344; garment trades unions, 41:332-36; history, writing of, 46:171, 219, 223, 227-32, 236,

241, 248, 255, 257, 395; "The Women's Garment Workers Union," 34:xxvi; *see also:* Clothing industry
Garmidor, M., 39:89
Garner, John Nance, 41:185
Garnet, Henry H., 46:274
Garnett, Alex. Y. P., 33:213, 218, 223
Garnett, D. J., *The Ammi Sought*, 30:452
Garnett, Robert Sheldon, 50:342
Garnett, W., 26:254
Garniss, John P., 22:81
Garrels, Arthur, 36:73
Garrett, T. P., 33:218
Garrett Biblical Institute, 40:51
Garrett, John W., 36:144-45
Garrick, David, 34:273
Garrison, William Lloyd, 42:131-32, 134, 147-48, 151, 356
Garrison & Fretz, 31:137
Garrst, Nathan, 27:105
Garsia, Isaac, 32:57
Garson, M. I., 38:74
Garsteman, George, 33:123
Gartner, Lloyd P., 44:241; "Benjamin Franklin Peixotto, American Consul: The Jewish Question in Roumania and American Jewry (1870-1875)," 47:202; books reviewed by, 46:61-64; 47:121-23; *The Jewish Immigrant in England, 1870-1914*, reviewed, 50:145-46; "Rumania and America, 1873: Leon Horowitz' Rumanian Tour and Its Background," 45:67-92
Garvey, Marcus, 46:275
Garvin, George, gift, 35:xxi
Gary, Hampson, 36:68-69
Gascoyne, Bamber, 31:43, 58
Gasin, I., 39:109
Gaspar Carillo, 23:132
Gasperi, Alcide de, 46:351
Gassner, John, 40:360
Gast, Chayim, 34:101
Gaster, Dr., 39:311
Gaster, Emmanuel, 45:78
Gaster, Moses, 24:82; 28:89; 32:55; 35:64; 42:50, 435, 440; necrology of, 37:xii, 467-68
Gastininer, Yehiel Meir (Lipshitz), 35:275
Gates of Heaven, The (Sha ar ha Shamayim), 22:118

Gates, Christopher, 23:156
Gates, Emanuel, 27:41, 43, 253
Gates, Ephraim, 50:81
Gates, Horatio, 25:143
Gates, Mrs. Horatio, 25:143
Gates, Samson, 21:159
Gates of Prayer Congregation, New York,
    38:75; *Order of Service at Consecration of
    Synagogue "The Gates of Prayer,"* 30:426
Gathright, William, 50:182
Gaubil, Antoine, 49:45
Gaudius, 28:207
Gaulois, Le, 46:89
Gause, Isaac, 50:304
Gautier, Judith, 35:248
Gavalgantij, Antonio, 33:79
Gavalgantij, Manuel, 33:79
Gawler, George, 26:144-47, 149
Gay, Ebenezer, 22:21
Gay, Samuel, 27:246
Gay, Sydney, 42:151
Gaynor, William J., 22:226; 26:287; 31:272
Gay Street Congregation (Baltimore), 23:143
Gaza, Battle of, 26:169
Gazette and Daily Advertiser (Charleston),
    32:41
Gazette of the United States, & Daily Advertiser
    (Philadelphia), 38:132, 134
Gdalen, P., 39:109
Geary, John White, 37:88
Gebhardt, Bruno, 26:102
Gebraude, Jeronimo de Hano, 33:88
Gedulath Shaul, 22:132
Gee, Joshua A., 35:170
Geehr, Peter, 34:77
Geffen, Joel, 43:231; 46:443
Gegiow, Ali, 34:205-6
Geiger, Abraham, 28:72, 76; 31:268-70;
    34:16; 35:xviii; 37:171, 174; 39:452, 454;
    40:18-19; 45:97, 100-103, 108, 110-11,
    114, 117; 50:93
Geiger, Ludwig, 26:46, 96; 28:279, 281;
    34:184; 35:128; Board of Delegates of
    American Israelites, 29:76; "Mendelssohns
    Bart," 22:xviii; necrology of, 28:xxii
Geismar, Alex, 37:266
Geissel, David, 32:120
Geissendorfer, Johanne, 41:259
Gelasius, 28:138

Gelbart, Gershon, *The Essex Story: A History
    of the Jewish Community in Essex County,*
    49:228
Gelber, N. M., 34:243; gift, 29:xliii; "The
    History of the Polish Jewry in the Second
    Half of the Eighteenth Century," 31:xvii
Geliloth ha-Arez, 22:133
Geller, 43:56
Geller, Todros, 45:163, 211
Gellert, Christian F., 35:235
Gelot ha-Arez ha-Hadashah, 22:125
Gelston, David, 38:127
Gemilas Chesed Society, 40:64
Geminder, Bed ich, 50:112, 115
General Assembly of the Lovers and
    Cultivators of the Fine Arts in Rome,
    28:54
General Electric Company, 32:124
General Jewish Colonization Organization,
    42:185-86
General Motors Corp., 41:321
General Society of Merchants & Tradesmen
    of the City of New-York, 38:124
"General Ulysses S. Grant and the Jews,"
    50:293
*Generals in Gray: List of the Confederate
    Commanders,* 50:342
Genessee Valley Club, 40:69
Genesis, 50:388
Genet, Edmond Charles Edouard, 38:111
Geneva Red Cross conference, 33:214
Genizah (Cairo), 25:183-85, 188; 26:21-22;
    39:96-97
Genlis, Stéphanie Felicité Ducrest de Saint
    Aubin, comtesse de, *Sacred Dramas,* 30:112
Gensler, L., 29:132
Gentleman's Magazine, 37:419-20
Gentz, Friedrich von, 26:37, 39, 41, 48-52,
    60-61, 66, 80, 88-89, 101-2
Geofroy *v.* Riggs, 36:234
George I, 31:127
George II, 21:238; 23:91; 27:28, 157, 223,
    472; 35:215-17; 37:369; 40:215-17; 49:37;
    allegiance to, 27:224-26, 486
George III, 25:111; 27:392, 472; 31:58-59;
    40:126; 42:439; 43:235; 46:37, 438
George IV, 31:133
George V, 31:262
George V (Hanover), 26:248

George, Antho, 33:114
George, Henry, 38:285-86, 337; 39:114, 324-25, 327; 43:12; 45:253; 48:40; "The Single-Tax Zionism of Joseph Fels," 46:474-91, 493
George, James Zachariah, 41:211
George, Lloyd, 39:205
George, Prince of Denmark, 26:66; 28:216-17
George, William, 47:54
Georgetown (S.C.), 50:156; "Abraham Cohen: Deputy Postmaster at Georgetown, South Carolina (1789-1800)," 48:177-93
Georgetown Bridge Company, 48:7
Georgetown College, 46:238
Georgia, "Abraham Simons, a Georgia Patriot of the Revolutionary War," 31:xvii; anti-Semitism, 31:223; "Captain Abraham Simons of the Georgia Line in the Revolution," 33:231-36; colonial settlement of Jews, 26:5-6; "The Gratz Papers," 23:3-4; Jewish population (1790), 50:24, 33-34; Jews in law and medicine, 22:148, 152, 158, 164-65; Sheftall family, 31:5-7; Straus family, 22:235-37
Georgia Medical Society, 22:164
Georgia, University of, 40:4; 46:356; 48:12
Geographical Society of Madrid, 22:xxi
Gerant, Baron, Pilgrimage to Jerusalem, 30:345
Gerard (New York), 34:119
Gerard, Sieur, 31:70
Gerber, William, 43:238; 47:203
Gerbier, Baron, 32:16, 18-19
Gerbillon, Jean Francois, 49:44
Gerhard, Friedrich, 35:122
Gericault, 39:63
Germain, Lord, 29:143
Germaine, George, 31:234
German American Bank, 27:402-3
German American Historical Society of Illinois, 32:xxvi
German Benevolent Hebrew Society, New York, 41:229
German Central Committee for the Russian Refugees in Berlin, 40:242; 41:131, 156
German Confederation, 26:38

German Emigrant Aid Society of New York, 49:180
German Hebrew Benevolent Society (Baltimore), 48:210
German Hebrew Society (Philadelphia), 47:205
German Jewish Children, Inc., 34:xix
German Jewish Children's Aid, Inc., 34:245
German Jews, "German Jews and Jewish Journalism in Nineteenth-Century America," 47:202; "German Jews of Prague: A Quest for Self-Realization," 50:98-120; "Hebrew German Society Rodeph Sholom in the City and County of Philadelphia, 1880-1950," 49:235; "A Note on Altenmuhr Jews," 49:53-55; periodization of American Jewish history, 47:127-30, 133
German National Bank of Vincennes, 48:257-58
German Society of Maryland, 34:35
German Union of Jewish Congregations, 24:71
German University of Prague, 50:106
Germania Assembly Rome (New York), 40:151
Germania Judaica, 28:263
Germanic Origins of New England Towns, 46:297
Germansky, Asher L., 35:55
Germany, "American Jewry, the Refugees and Immigration Restriction (1932-1942)," 45:219-47; anti-Semitism, 23:105-8; 33:11-13, 18; 40:200-201; 50:6; "The Congress of Aix-la-Chapelle," 26:82-94; "Congress of Berlin, 1878," 24:40, 42-44, 46, 49, 51, 64, 66, 74-75; Congress of Vienna, 26:34; disabilities, 26:5; "Educational Reforms in Europe in Their Relation to Jewish Emancipation—1778-1919," 28:83-132; "Francis Joseph Grund," 26:234-35; Germany—A Winter's Tale, 45:251; "A Hessian Tax-Roll of 1811," 32:118-21; "The Influence of Lewis Way and Other English Missionaries upon Alexander I's Treatment of the Jews," 26:116-25; Jewish disabilities in Balkans, 24:16, 19, 21-22, 35, 81, 102, 110; Jewish historiography, 26:27, 31; "Jewish Rights at the Congresses of

Vienna (1814-1815), and Aix-la-Chapelle (1818)," 26:vii, xv, 33-125; *Jews from Germany in the United States*, reviewed, 46:59-60; "Regarding the Draft of a Sistem of Legislation for the Jews, July 17, 1809, by Wilhelm von Humboldt," 26:103-15; and Rumanian Jews, 36:105, 109, 115; Russian passports, 46:93, 95, 99; U.S. Intercession for Jews, 36:ix-xii, 348-85; "Wilhelm von Humboldt's Relations to the Jews," 26:95-103

Gerrau, Joseph, 27:392

Gerrits, Captain, 33:99

Gerritsen, Hendrick, 26:247

Gerschel, Mr., 40:275

Gersdorff-Hermsdorf, Count von, 35:36

Gershater, 48:21

Gershberg, 43:54

Gershel, Leopold, 49:186

Gershenfeld, Louis, 39:258; gift, 34:xxv; "The Jew in Science," 34:xxv

Gershom ben Gershom, 38:247

Gershon, Jacob, 27:79

Gershovitz, Amy, 50:435

Gershovitz, David, 50:428

Gershovitz, Jonathan David, 50:435

Gershovitz, Lucy, 50:434

Gershovitz, Rose, 50:428

Gershovitz, Samuel D., 38:346

Gershovitz, Samuel D., 49:149; executive council, 39:470; 41:388; 44:241; 47:201; memorial to, 50:425, 428-35; necrology of Frank Leopold Weil, 47:201, 230-33

Gershovitz, Mrs. Samuel D., 50:425, 434

Gershwin, George. 47:182

Gersoni, Henry, 33:140; 45:70

Gerstäcker, Friedrich, 39:232

Gerstenfeld, Norman, 47:202

Gerster, Arpad G., 42:123

Gerster, Charles, 49:97, 271

Gerstely, Louis, necrology of, 33:xxi

Gerstley, M., 30:421

Gerstley, William, necrology of, 33:xiii

Gerstley, William II, 43:238

Gervais, Claudinia V., 46:103

Gesang-Verein Harmonia, 40:151

Geschichte der Jehudim, 22:126-30

Geschichte der Juden in Schlesien, 28:263

Geschichte der Juden und ihrer Literatur, 28:263

Gesellschaft zur Forderung der Wissenschaft des Judentums, 25:151; 26:284

Gesänge und Gebete, 30:372-73

Gesenius, Heinrich Friedrich Wilhelm, 30:iv; 42:364; *Hebrew and English Lexicon*, 30:308, 383; *Hebrew Grammar*, 30:334, 400

Gest, Morris, 35:273

Getzis, M., gift, 33:xxxiii

Gevits, Leonard, 27:105

Gewirz, Bernard, 47:202

Geyer, Andrew, 41:291

Geymüller, 26:52

Ghent Exhibition, 31:290

Ghent, Treaty of, 26:198; 46:3, 9, 13

Ghika, Gregory, 24:117-19, 122, 125, 127, 138-39, 143-45

Ghulvass, Moses A., book reviewed by, 43:194-97

Giacobbe, 28:191

Giat, Abraham, 40:54

Gib' at Shaul, 22:123

Gibbon, Edward, 23:79; 26:14, 32:5; 33:12; 35:313; 37:188; 39:212; 47:228

Gibbons, Hughes O., 37:191

Gibbons, James, Cardinal, 36:43; 46:269, 272, 283-84; "The Attitude of the Late Cardinal Gibbons toward Problems Affecting Jews," 29:xv; "Cardinal Gibbons and his Attitude Toward Jewish Problems," 31:vii; 219-24

Gibbons, James Sloan, 50:391

Gibbons, Thomas, 25:48

Gibbs, George, 27:447

Gibbs, Josiah Willard, *Manual Hebrew and English Lexicon*, 30:248, 278, 280

Gibbs, Miles H., 27:71

Gibbs, Robert, 37:394

Giberti, Bishop, 28:171

Gibson, C. B., 27:506

Gibson, Chas. B., 43:74

Gibson, Hew, 27:246

Gibson, Hugh, 36:149, 151-55, 157-59

Gibson, John, 23:11, 13, 21; 30:77

Gibson, Mrs., 25:183

Gibson, William, 43:74

Gideon, Barah, 35:32

Gideon, Bathsheba, 35:32

Gideon, Esther, 35:32
Gideon, Jane, 35:35
Gideon, Josef, 41:259
Gideon, Lina, 41:257
Gideon, Lippmann, 41:259
Gideon, Maria, 35:36
Gideon, Moses, 21:27-29, 33-35, 45
Gideon, Roel, 23:29, 35:32
Gideon, Rowland, 23:80; 39:209; 42:335;
    "Rowland Gideon, an Early Boston Jew,
    and his Family," 35:xiv, 27-37
Gideon, Samson, 26:244; 35:34-37, 216-17,
    233; 37:419
Gideon, Sigmund, 41:263
Gidley, John, 40:76
Giers, Nicholas Karlovich de, 36:182, 189,
    201, 213, 216, 221, 223-25, 237; 39:68;
    41:169; 43:63
Giesen, Moses, 27:335
Gikatilla, Joseph, 28:243
Gilbert, Katharine, 46:114
Gilbert, Prentiss B., 36:381-83
Gilbreth, Frank B., 41:44, 48, 58, 312; 46:228
Gilchrist, Agnes Addison, 41:67
Gilder, Mrs., 38:281
Gilead, Jewish colony, 26:154, 156, 159
Gilead Lodge (B'nai B'rith), 47:46-48
Giles, *Heathen Records*, 26:xxxv
Giles, William, 37:168
Gilfillian, G., "Bards of the Bible," 34:xxiii
Gill, Master, 27:337
Gill, William, 26:254
Gillett, Francis, 42:137
Gillett, Frederick H., 45:40
Gillette, Governor, 29:197
Gillhaus, August, 50:231
Gillman, Henry, 36:46-47, 49-50, 53, 55-57
Gilman, Chandler R., 42:117
Gilman, Isaac, 38:250
Gilman, Samuel, 32:36, 42; "Harby's
    Discourse on the Jewish Synagogue,"
    32:49-53
Gilmore, P. S., 50:391
Gilmore, Robert, 28:xxxiv
Gilpin, Judge, 25:137
Gilroy, Mayor, 29:168
Gimbel (store), 38:20
Gimbel, Abraham, 48:258
Gimbel, Adam, 48:257, 261

Gimbel, Amanda, 48:261
Gimbel Brothers, 28:292; 48:257-58
Gimbel, J., Achievement Medal, 48:256, 259
Gimbel, Jake, "Jake Gimbel: Hoosier
    Philanthropist," 48:256-61, 266
Gimbel, Mary Hyman, 48:257
Gimbel, Rose, 48:257
Gimbel Scholarship Loan Fund, 48:260
Gimbel, Seleman, 48:257, 261
Gimpel, Mordecai, 44:141
Ginsberg, Mr., 38:60
Ginsberg, Abraham, 43:65
Ginsberg, H. L., 43:196; 46:130
Ginsberg, Jonah, 44:190, 192
Ginzberg, Louis, 35:120; "Bibliography of
    Prof. Louis Ginzberg," 34:xxv; "Genizah
    Studies," 33:26; "The Jewish Colony at
    Waterview Virginia," 45:265
Ginsburg, Aaron, 23:143-44
Ginsburg, Bernard, necrology of, 33:xiii
Ginsburg, David L., 40:72
Ginsburg, Jekuthiel, 33:166
Ginsburg, M., 38:307
Ginsburg, M. Ph., 28:240
Ginsburg, Michael, 42:467; book reviewed
    by, 42:442-49
Ginsburg, M. S., 39:113
Ginsburg, Saul M., 34:280; 38:242; 43:39;
    "Max Lilienthal's Activities in Russia: New
    Documents," 35:xv, 39-51
Ginzberg, Eli, 41:216; 42:215; 46:246-47;
    book reviewed by, 41:209-14
Ginzberg, Janckel, 39:68
Ginzberg, John, 36:255, 259; 38:331; 39:67;
    41:173-74
Ginzberg, Louis, 43:239, 241, 244, 246;
    47:222; 49:164; *History of the Jews of
    Petersburg (Va.), 1789-1950*, 49:240
Ginzberg, Shimon, 36:255
Ginzburg, Mordecai Aaron, 35:44-51
Ginzburg, Simon, 33:149
Giose, 28:205
Giovanni, Friar, 28:207
Girard, 31:115
Girard College, 46:421
Girbal, Enrique, 28:273
Girlen, Mr., 37:138
Gist, Christopher, 23:13
Gitelson, Joshua, 45:156

Gitelson, M. Leo, 45:143
Gitelson, Nehemiah, Talmudic Library, 45:156
Gitelson, Raphael (1890-1921), Palestine Library, 45:143
Githens, Thomas S., 38:337
Gittelsohn, Roland B., 38:249; *Growth and Achievement: Temple Israel, 1854-1954*, reviewed, 44:250-51
Gittins family, 32:55
Given names, Jewish and non-Jewish, 39:385-87
Gjoe, 28:217
Glacer, Jozef (Glazer), 39:151
Gladstone, William Ewart, 26:157; 35:36
Gladwin, Henry, 35:23; 40:82-83
Glanz, Rudolf, 39:239; 46:122, 418; 47:6, 9; "The German Jews in New York in the 19th Century," 49:230; "The Jews in American Alaska, 1867-1880," 49:217
Glasgow Exhibition, 31:290
Glasgow, University of, 37:473; 50:178
Glasner, Samuel, 49:270
Glass, Montague Marsden, 40:356
Glass (Stiegel glass), 28:255-56
Glassberg, Benjamin, "History of the Jewish Welfare Society of Philadelphia," 31:xxiv
Glassman, Lee, 34:228
Glatzer, Nahum N., book review by, 49:140-42
Glavis, Louis, 47:187
Glazebrook, Otis A., 36:64, 66-67; "Personal Reminiscences of Otis A. Glazebrook, U.S. Consul at Jerusalem," 31:xvii
Glazer, Nathan, *American Judaism*, reviewed, 47:121-23
Glazer, Simon, 37:36; 45:39-40; gift, 29:xli
Gleaner, The, 26:271; 46:117
Gleanings in First Isaiah, 43:196
"Gleanings from a Gathered Harvest," 21:229
Gleason, H., 31:137
Gleason, Russel & Co., 31:137
Gleason, W. J., 39:83
Gleave, Thomas, 34:270-71
Gleaves, Albert, 28:xxxviii
Gleim, Wilhelm Ludwig, 35:121
Glembozki, Moses, 33:145
Glen, James, 49:34

Glenn, Menahem G., books reviewed by, 43:198-99; 48:194-95
Glick, Edward B., *Latin America and the Palestine Problem*, reviewed, 48:136-37
Gliddon, John, 36:3-5
Gliechman, Isaac, 36:53-58
Glion, Abrao, 42:279
Globus, Joseph, 42:129
Glotfelly, J. T., 39:83
Gloucester, Bishop of, 24:16
Glover, John, 40:77
Glover, Wilbur H., 46:161
Gloversville (N.Y.) *Leader-Republican*, 35:xxi
Glowacki, Joseph, 36:231-32
Gluck, Alma, 48:202, 267; 49:70, 143
Glückel, Von Hamelin, 34:106
Glueck, Joseph, 43:196
Glueck, Nelson, 41:91; 43:196; executive council, 38:346; 39:470; 42:414; 45:264; Hebrew Union College, 39:467; 40:48, 51-53
Glushakow, A. D. (ed.), *A Pictorial History of Maryland Jewry*, 49:224
Glyn, Justice, 31:116
Glynn, James, 39:34
Glynn, Martin, 49:10
Gneist, 31:190
"Gnosticism and Judaism," 28:73
Gobineau, Arthur de, 46:309
Gobineau, Joseph Arthur, 47:31
Godefroi, M., 29:90, 127
Godfrey, George, 29:131
Godkin, Edwin L., 43:25
Godlove, Lewis, 37:266, 268, 270-71
Godmannestun, Ralph de, 41:383
Goebbels, Paul Joseph, 36:374
Goelet, Peter P., 27:241, 246
Goethe, Johann Wolfgang von, 28:95; 38:271; 41:68; 45:250, 252, 256
Goetschius, John Henry, 32:113
Goetz, Ella, 27:277
Goetz, Julius, 27:277
Goff, Judge, 25:135
Goforth, William, 27:241
Gohdes, Clarence Louis F., 42:83-84
Going, J. B., 41:48
Goitein, Solomon Dob, 43:197
Gold, Abraham, 35:5, 25
Gold, Elijah, 33:161

Gold, Louis, 45:161, 173
Gold, Mrs. Louis, 45:161, 173
Gold, Michael, 46:436
Gold and Silversmith's Society of New York, 44:207
Goldberg, A., 39:105, 112
Goldberg, Abraham, 33:149, 154; 45:39, 43-44, 164
Goldberg, Mrs. Abraham, 45:164
Goldberg, Arthur, and Gordon, Mrs. Isaac, "The Jew in Norwich: A Century of Jewish Life," 49:219
Goldberg, Benjamin, 36:173
Goldberg, Ber, 45:70
Goldberg, Isaac (Arizona), 37:437
Goldberg, Isaac (author), 43:170; 46:427; "Bibliographical Desiderata in American Jewish History," 43:231; gift, 34:xxvii; Hebrew Union College, 40:53; "A Selected Bibliography of the Writings of David Philipson," 39:445-59, 477
Goldberg, Jacob (Buffalo), 46:164
Goldberg, Jacob A., 46:241
Goldberg, Morris, 29:150
Goldberg, Nathan, book review by, 48:63-68; "Dynamics of the Economic Structure of the Jews in the United States," 46:233-56
Goldberg, Rachel, 29:150
Goldberg, Sam, 41:368
Goldberg v. Kletz, 29:152
Goldblatt family, 48:19
Goldblatt (store), 38:20
Goldburg, H., 27:114
Goldburg, Julius, "A Note on the Military Career of Benjamin Rosenberg," 29:xv
Golden, Harry L., and Martin Rywell, *Jews in American History. Their Contribution to the United States of America*, reviewed, 40:191-92
Goldenberg, Abraham, 39:423
Goldenberg, B., 29:131
Goldenberg, Charles, 37:41
Goldenberg, Samuel Loeb, 22:132
Golden Era, 34:146
"Golden Legend, The," 40:182-83
Golden Links Lodge (I.O.O.F.), 47:46
Goldensky, Elias, 48:222
Goldenstein, Raphael, and Nathan Bibo, "Recollections of Early Days in New

Mexico, and the Beginning of Temple Albert of Albuquerque," 29:xxx
Goldfaden, Abraham, 35:63; 48:201
Goldfaden family, 48:19
Goldfisch, A., 50:313
Goldfogle, Henry M., 24:83; 36:279; 39:428; 40:302; 41:174, 176-77, 185, 378; 50:207, 218-20, 225, 229, 235
Goldin, Judah, 42:331; 43:195; book reviewed by, 42:313-18; "The Historian as Teacher," 45:262; *The Period of the Talmud (135 B.C.E.-1035 C.E.)*, reviewed, 40:194
Goldman, Aaron, 47:203
Goldman, Abraham, 29:62
Goldman, Daniel, 27:105
Goldman, Emma, 48:202, 267; 49:70, 143
Goldman, Henry, 31:203
Goldman, Israel, 49:270
Goldman, Julius, 37:xii; 40:249; 48:114, 116; 49:179-80
Goldman, L. M., 45:261
Goldman, Moses, 33:128, 140
Goldman, R. B., 37:268
Goldman, Solomon, *The Jew and the universe*, 35:xxi
Goldman, Felix, 35:136
Goldmann, 45:107
Goldmann, Jack B., "Pioneer Jews on the Pacific Coast, 1848-1880," 38:342
Goldmann, Nachum, 28:127
Goldmark, Josephine, 34:xxv; "Pilgrims of '48," 34:xxv
Goldmark, Karl, 33:xxxi
Goldrosen family, 48:19
Goldschlager, David, 24:14-15; 36:102-3
Goldschmid, 38:197
Goldschmidt, David, 32:119
Goldschmidt, J., 32:119
Goldschmidt, Lucas, 32:119
Goldschmidt, S. H., 29:77, 127; 38:310; 40:271; 41:132-33, 162; 42:164
Goldschmied, Jonas, 47:53-54
Goldsmid, 31:125
Goldsmid, Abraham, 35:234
Goldsmid, Albert E. W., 34:279; 35:247-48; 43:44, 52, 55-56, 61, 64-65, 68
Goldsmid, Anna Maria (trans.), *The Reformed Israelites*, 30:393-94; *Twelve Sermons*, 30:361-62

Goldsmid, Benjamin, 34:279
Goldsmid, Carmel, 35:248
Goldsmid, Colonel, 43:52
Goldsmid, Francis, 24:2, 16, 22, 24-26;
  26:267; 28:132; 29:77, 92, 95; 35:248;
  41:38
Goldsmid, Julian, 35:248; 40:228; 41:138
Goldsmith, A. L., 29:133
Goldsmith, Belle Maud, 28:271
Goldsmith, Benjamin, 27:246
Goldsmith, Celestina, 27:111
Goldsmith, E. (Richmond, Va.), 29:133
Goldsmith, E. (San Francisco), 37:45
Goldsmith, Harry, *Catechism for Hebrew
  Children*, 30:400
Goldsmith, Henry (New York, 1850s),
  27:514, 516
Goldsmith, Henry (New York, 1920s), 28:xli,
  231, 236
Goldsmith, Henry (Philadelphia), 29:133
Goldsmith, Is., 29:131
Goldsmith, Isaac, 32:127
Goldsmith, J., 27:515
Goldsmith, Judith Peixotto, 29:169
Goldsmith, Leopold, 28:271
Goldsmith, M. J., 37:266, 268, 271
Goldsmith, Oliver, 41:4
Goldsmith, Philip, 50:172
Goldsmith, Samuel, 27:271
Goldsmith, Samuel H., 37:449
Goldsmith, Sophia Heller, 47:52
Goldstein, Benjamin, 37:36
Goldstein family, 48:19; 49:95
Goldstein, Fanny, 33:xxxi; 42:413
Goldstein, Harris, 43:238
Goldstein, Isaac, 22:174-75
Goldstein, Israel, 50:272; "A Century of
  Judaism in New York," 33:xxix, xxxii-xxxiii;
  34:253; "A Chapter on the Founding of
  Congregation B'nai Jeshurun, the Second
  Oldest Synagogue in New York," 31:xvi;
  gift, 32:xxviii
Goldstein, Jacob, 36:227-31
Goldstein, Jennie, 36:227
Goldstein, Leonard J., *see:* Sulman, Esther
Goldstein, Morris, 40:36
Goldstein, Pinchas, 35:49
Goldstein, Sidney, 40:54
Goldstein *v.* Goldstein, 29:149

Goldsticker, A., 29:131
Goldstine, Emanuel, 31:162
Goldstoff, Feivel, *Megillath Damesek*, 22:133
Goldstone, Lafayette A., 34:xx
Goldwasser, I. Edwin, 37:307
Goldwater, Sigismund S., 42:125-26
Goldwyn, Samuel, 46:436
Goldziher, Ignace, 35:124; 43:250
Golesco, Mr., 36:100
Golet, Peter, 27:246
Golijath, Cornelis, 43:130
Gollanez, Hermann, 34:179; 37:2; necrology
  of, 33:xii; "A Plea for a University in
  London, 1647," 22:xviii, xxix
Gollas, Jacob, 42:280, 394
Gollett, Cathrin, 27:246
Gollob *v.* Congregation Ohel Moishe Chevra
  Tehilim, 29:152
Gomara, Francisco Lopes de, *La Historia
  General de las Indias*, 22:111
Gomberg, William, 41:317; 46:230-31
Gomes, Abraham, 32:57
Gomes, David, 32:60
Gomes, Isaac, 23:93
Gomes, Jacob, 32:57
Gomes, Jacob d' Abraham, 29:35
Gomes, Joel, 32:57
Gomes, Joseph da Costa, 44:222, 228-29
Gomes, Miguel, 27:246
Gomes, Sarah, 32:58
Gomes, Semuel de Imanuel da Costa, 44:228
Gomes, Ymanuel, 47:177
Gomez, 21:xv, xvi; 27:386; 35:181
Gomez, Aaron L., 21:169-70; 27:104, 110,
  122, 276, 285, 287, 289-90, 303, 305, 317,
  400, 427, 433, 437, 448; Stephen Gould
  correspondence, 27:432, 438
Gomez, Aaron L. (New York, 1830s), 30:332
Gomez, Aaron Lopez, 31:285
Gomez, Abraham, 50:49
Gomez, Abigail (Mrs. Isaac), 23:89
Gomez, Abigail (Mrs. Isaac, Jr.), 21:190, 193
Gomez, Abigail (nee Lopez), 27:112, 165,
  168, 266, 284, 287, 290, 301, 307
Gomez, Abraham (Barbados), 23:29
Gomez, Abraham (Bordeaux), 27:58-59, 286,
  303
Gomez, Abm. (Curaçao), 22:170

Gomez, Abm. (New York, 1740s), 21:79, 132; 23:153-54; 27:246
Gomez, Abraham (b. Mordecai), 27:41, 43, 51, 253, 289, 291, 298
Gomez, Abraham M., 27:58, 60
Gomez, Alida, 27:289, 293; 38:70
Gomez, Antonio, 37:419
Gomez, B. M., 27:59, 62
Gomez, Benjamin (Barbados), 27:246
Gomez, Benjamin (book dealer), 45:208
Gomez, Benjamin (New York, 1730s), 21:10, 20, 22, 25, 44, 51, 60, 63, 68, 70, 71, 80, 83, 88-91, 93-94, 102-5, 107, 111, 114, 167, 211, 212; 23:154, 156
Gomez, Benjamin (1769-1828), 50:48
Gomez, Benjamin (New York, 1800s), 25:52, 55
Gomez, Benjamin (b. Lewis), 41:109
Gomez, Benjamin (b. Luis Moses), 27:27, 244, 282-83, 288-91, 298
Gomez, Benjamin (b. Matthais), 23:159; 27:41, 51, 61, 72, 83, 122, 242-43, 287-90, 298, 304-6, 309, 314
Gomez, Benjamin (grandson, Benjamin), 23:156
Gomez, Charlotte (nee Hendricks), 27:112, 286-90
Gomez, Charlotte (Miss), 27:110
Gomez, Cristobal, 31:30
Gomez, Cynthia, 27:78, 287-88, 290, 293-94, 298, 303
Gomez, Dacosta, 27:79
Gomez, Daniel (New York), 21:2, 5, 7-8, 10, 15, 19-25, 29, 36-42, 49, 51, 53, 55, 58, 60, 63, 65, 70-71, 84-89, 91, 93-97, 99, 100-105, 107, 111-12, 114, 116, 118-21, 123-24, 126, 128-33, 137-39, 142, 161, 181, 183, 187-88, 211; 29:xxxix; 31:97-99, 101-2; 35:184; 37:373, 377, 386; 38:47, 235; 46:424; 47:224; 49:36; "Daniel Gomez, a Pioneer Merchant in Early New York," 23:xiii; 41:107-25; ledger of, 27:244-50, 297
Gomez, Daniel (b. Luis Moses), 27:1, 3, 5, 38-39, 70-71, 183, 244, 250, 272, 281-83, 289-91, 298-300, 408
Gomez, Daniel (b. Moses), 23:159; 27:282, 284, 287, 290-91, 298

Gomez, Daniel (b. Sinya de Tores), 23:153, 154, 156
Gomez, Daniel da Costa, 27:302
Gomez, David, 21:6, 10-11, 14-15, 19-21, 23-25, 37-38, 42, 49, 51, 53, 60-61, 63, 104, 182, 187; 23:147, 153-56; 27:39, 70, 244, 272, 283, 289, 291, 298-99; 29:xxxix; 31:97-99, 101-2; 37:373, 377, 386; 38:235; 41:109-19
Gomez, Deborah (Mrs. Isaac), 21:108, 161; 23:156, 159
Gomez, Deborah (granddaughter, Benjamin), 23:156, 159
Gomez, Deborah (nee Leon), 27:59, 281-82, 288-90, 298; 50:49
Gomez, Deborah (b. Matthias), 23:159; 27:284, 288-91, 298, 304
Gomez, Diego, 35:27
Gomez, Edwin, 27:289, 293
Gomez, Emeline, 27:287-88, 290, 298
Gomez, Ernest, 27:286, 289, 303
Gomez, Esther, 50:48-49
Gomez, Esther (nee Campos), 27:289
Gomez, Esther (Mrs. Daniel), 27:281, 291
Gomez, Esther (nee Hendricks), 27:111, 276, 285, 287-90, 293-94
Gomez, Esther (d. Isaac), 23:156, 159
Gomez, Esther (nee Lopez), 27:289, 291
Gomez, Esther (nee Marchaze), 27:280, 289, 291
Gomez, Esther (b. Matthias), 27:288, 290-91, 298, 304
Gomez, Esther (b. Mordecai), 27:246, 286-87, 289, 298
Gomez, Esther (Mrs. Moses Mordecai), 23:89
Gomez, Esther (Mrs. Moses Daniel), 27:281, 287-88, 290-91, 298, 310
Gomez, Esther (Mrs. Uriah Hendricks), 27:59, 79; 31:260
Gomez, Esther, see also: Seixas, Esther (Mrs. Solomon)
Gomez, Esther da Costa, 27:302
Gomez, Esther Rachel, 32:126
Gomez, Estter, 27:246
Gomez, Ezekiel, 41:107
Gomez family, 27:xviii; 28:294; 44:214; 45:208; 49:59; 50:28, 37, 48-49, 253; Bible, 27:257, 279, 285-87, 294, 302-17; coat of

arms, 27:279; data relative to, 27:279-317; "The Early Barbados Connections of the Gomez Family of Philadelphia and New York," 29:xxxvii; genealogy, 27:289-90, 298; Oliver Street Cemetery, 27:299-301
Gomez, Gabriel de David da Costa, 22:170; 44:233
Gomez, Gabriel Joseph de Torres, 27:282
Gomez, Guilman, 33:114
Gomez, Mrs. H., gift, 35:xviii
Gomez, Hermione, 27:289, 293
Gomez, Hester (b. Mordecai), 23:153-54
Gomez, Hester (granddaughter, Mordecai), 23:153
Gomez, Hester (Mrs. Mordecai), 23:154
Gomez, Hetty (d. Benjamin), 27:287-88
Gomez, Hetty Miriam, 27:110, 285, 289, 293
Gomez, Horatio, 21:xxvii, 215; 29:113; 38:70; 44:132
Gomez, I. Philip, 27:51
Gomez, Isaac, 21:10, 20-21, 38, 44, 49, 53, 60, 63, 71, 74-75, 77-79, 85-86, 103-4, 107-8, 161, 193, 211; 27:41, 185, 253; 29:xxxix
Gomez, Isaac (1813), 25:34
Gomez, Isaac (grandson, Benjamin), 23:156, 159
Gomez, Isaac (b. Daniel), 27:244
Gomez, Isaac (br. David), 23:154-56
Gomez, Isaac (b. Lewis), 41:109; 43:253
Gomez, Isaac (b. Luis Moses), 27:11, 13, 22, 246, 281-83, 288-89, 298
Gomez, Isaac (b. Matthias), 27:288, 290-91, 298, 304
Gomez, Isaac (b. Mordecai), 23:153-56; 27:289, 298
Gomez, Isaac (b. Moses Daniel), 27:282, 287
Gomez, Isaac (Nevis), 23:93
Gomez, Isaac (Spain), 27:289, 298; 31:284-85; 45:208
Gomez, Isaac, Junr (b. Moses), 21:51, 63, 70, 187-89, 193; 27:58, 61-62, 74, 77-78, 83, 165, 168, 257, 268, 283-84, 287, 290, 294, 297-98, 302-3, 307, 309, 311, 314, 317, 461; 31:100-101; 43:253; 50:37, 49; Benjamin Gomez eulogized, 27:306; family records, 27:285-94, 302-17; "Isaac Gomez, Jr.'s Religious Instruction for His Son," 37:xxx; "John Adams Correspondence,"

37:xxxi, 444-47; "Joshua Hezekiah de Cordova, Isaac Gomez, Jr., and Jacob Mordecai, Apologetes for Judaism," 38:343; Marquis Lafayette letter, 27:308; Oliver Street Cemetery, 27:268-69; prayer-book by, 27:301-2; kosher meat, 25:37-39, 52, 55, 57-59; *Selections in Prose and Verse*, 30:188-90
Gomez, Isaac, Jr., "Selection of a Father," 28:xxxix; 35:xvii
Gomez, Isaac M., 21:160-61, 170; 27:46, 51, 59, 61-64, 69, 83, 86-87, 89-90, 157, 168, 241, 243, 246
Gomez, Isaac Matthias, 50:37, 48
Gomez, Isaac Moses, 23:89
Gomez, Isaac Moses, Jr., literary activity, 22:xxix
Gomez, Isaac de Mordy, 21:23
Gomez, Isaac N., 38:124
Gomez, Jacob (b. Luis Moses), 21:49, 51, 53; 27:289, 291, 298
Gomez, Jacob (Jamaica), 38:47
Gomez, Jacob (b. Mordecai), 21:23; 23:154; 27:244, 289, 298
Gomez, Jacob Valverde, 27:292, 294, 304
Gomez, Joseph, 21:21
Gomez, Joseph (b. Daniel), 27:122, 281, 287, 290
Gomez, Joseph (b. Moses), 27:290
Gomez, Joshua Horatio, 27:285, 289, 294-95, 297
Gomez, Leonora, 27:289
Gomez, Lewis (Luis), 21:7-8, 187, 195; 23:81, 147-49, 151, 158; 26:261; 27:3-4, 39, 70, 268, 272, 280, 288, 289-91, 297-99; 29:148; 31:97-99, 101-2, 238, 284; 41:107-9, 113-20; 43:253; 45:208; 50:164; denization, letter of, 27:150, 295-97
Gomez, Lewis (b. Aaron L.), 27:276, 285, 289, 293, 298, 305
Gomez, Lewis (b. Moses), 27:285, 294, 432
Gomez, Lewis (nephew, Isaac Gomez, Jr.), 27:309, 384
Gomez, Lucilla, 27:289
Gomez, M., 27:95
Gomez, Manuel, 50:123
Gomez, Maria, 27:78, 264, 285, 289, 292, 294, 298, 310

Gomez, Mary Ann, 27:284, 287, 290, 298, 304

Gomez, Matilda, 27:287-88, 290, 298

Gomez, Matthias, 21:88, 101, 103, 107, 114, 117-18, 120-31, 133-38, 140, 183, 212

Gomez, Matthias (b. Benjamin), 27:287-88, 290, 298, 314

Gomez, Matthias (b. Isaac), 23:155-56, 159; 27:283-84, 288, 290-91, 298, 304

Gomez, Mordecai, 21:5, 7-10, 13-14, 17, 19-25, 27, 33, 37-38, 41-42, 46-47, 49-51, 53-54, 60, 62-63, 132, 181, 187, 195, 211; 23:147, 150-51; 29:xxxix; 31:37, 97-99, 101-2; 35:181; 37:373, 377, 386; 38:235; 49:56; will of, 23:153-54

Gomez, Mordecai (b. Isaac Moses, Jr.), 23:156

Gomez, Mordecai (b. Luis Moses), 27:1, 5, 39, 70-71, 246, 272, 280-81, 286-87, 289, 291, 298-99, 384; 41:109, 119

Gomez, Mordecai (b. Moses, Jr.), 27:281

Gomez, Mordecai (N.J.), 33:253

Gomez, Moses, 21:1, 5, 8-13, 16-22, 24-26, 30, 38, 42, 49, 51, 53, 55, 63, 70, 93, 111, 120, 126, 130, 137-39, 142, 144, 157-59, 181, 194, 211; 25:51-52, 61; 26:261; 27:211-12; 29:xxxix; 31:37, 238; 35:141; 41:109; 50:49

Gomez, Moses, Jr., 21:38, 181, 183; 27:43, 51, 185, 253, 281

Gomez, Moses, Sr., 21:5, 146

Gomez, Moses (b. Daniel), 23:156, 159; 27:1, 2, 4-5, 41, 150, 244, 246, 253, 266, 279, 281, 284, 287, 290-91, 297, 298, 462; 41:124

Gomez, Moses (b. Isaac, Jr.), 27:268, 279, 285, 287-88, 290, 295, 297-99, 303, 314

Gomez, Moses (b. Mordecai), 27:51, 54, 58, 60, 63, 65, 72, 74, 78, 83, 122, 150, 276, 281, 285, 289, 291-92, 294, 298, 306, 314

Gomez, Moses (b. Mordecai) (Jamaica), 27:289, 298

Gomez, Moses Daniel, 21:11, 20, 38, 53, 92, 103, 105, 113, 117-21, 123-25, 128-33, 139-40, 145, 147, 149-52, 154-56, 158, 211

Gomez, Moses Lewis (b. Aaron L.), 27:122

Gomez, Moses Mordecai, 21:23, 25, 131-33; 23:89, 153-54; 50:37, 49

Gomez, Mosseh, 21:12

Gomez, Rachel, 27:246

Gomez, Rachel (Mrs. Matthias), 23:156-57; 27:282-83, 288, 290-91, 298, 304

Gomez, Rachel (b. Mordecai), 23:153-54; 27:287, 289-90, 298; 31:37, 55-57

Gomez, Rachel, see also: Judah, Rachel (nee Gomez)

Gomez, Rachel Louise, 27:309

Gomez, Rachel R., 27:168

Gomez, Raphael, 27:292

Gomez, Rebecca (1), 27:281

Gomez, Rebecca (2), 27:310

Gomez, Rebecca (3), 50:37, 49

Gomez, Rebecca (Mrs. Luis Moses), 27:280

Gomez, Rebecca (Mrs. Mordecai), 23:153-54

Gomez, Rebecca (b. Moses), 27:282, 287, 290

Gomez, Roderiques, 27:79

Gomez, Rosalie, 27:166, 285, 289, 293

Gomez, Semuel de Gabriel da Costa, 44:233

Gomez, William, 32:58

Gommes, Alonce, 33:113

Gommes, Alphonse, 33:113

Gommes, Duartes, 33:118

Gommes, Ferdinando, 33:113

Gommes, Louiz, 33:116

Gommes, Mathias, 33:117

Gompers, Samuel, 40:397; 43:32-33; 47:187; 49:107; history, writing of, 46:223-25, 231, 261-62, 299, 302; Jewish unionism, 41:298-302, 311-12, 318, 321, 327-29, 332, 334, 339, 341, 343; and Oscar Straus, 40:9; scientific management, 41:54

Gompers-Strasser experiment, 41:298-99, 318

Gompert, 37:176

Gomperts, 27:79, 312

Gomperts, Barent, 23:155

Gomperts, G., 27:337

Gomperts, Gompert S., 21:161, 163, 169; 25:57; 27:83, 86, 92, 109, 314

Gomperts, Jacob S., 27:74

Gomperts, Sarah, 27:112

Gomperts, Solomon, 27:229; 37:419

Gompertz, 31:112, 125

Gompertz, Elizabeth, 37:419

Gompertz, E. M., 37:341-42

Gompertz, Jack, 45:144

Gompertz, Mordecai, 37:343

Gonsales, Abraham, 32:63
Gonsales, Isaac, 32:63
Gonsales, Isaac Nunes, 28:239
Gonsales, Jacob, 27:246
Gonsales, Jacob Nunes, 37:331, 337
Gonsales, Jahacob de Abm, 21:10, 20
Gonsales, Leah Nunes, 37:331
Gonsales, Louzada, 27:246
Gonsales, Moses, 22:170
Gonsales, Moses Nunes, 32:62
Gonsales, Mosseh, 29:30
Gonsalez, Ishack, 21:10, 20, 60
Gonsalvo, Francisco, 33:117
Gonsalvo, Manuel Lopez en Francisco,
 33:117
Gonsalvos, Josuat, 33:115
Gonzaga family, 28:191
Gonzaga, Francesco, Duke of Mantua,
 28:192
Gonzaga, Federico, Duke of Mantua, 28:192
Gonzaga, Ludovico, Duke of Mantua, 28:192
Gonzago, Jehuda, 28:185
Gonzago, Vincenzo, 28:194
Gonzales, Texas cemetery, 34:xx
Gonzalez, Alvaro, 31:30
Gonzalez, Bartolomé, 31:3, 12, 24
Gonzalez, Simon, 31:29
Goodblatt, Morris S., 43:247
Goode, Alexander D., 45:214-15
Goodell, Nathan, 22:23
Goodenow, L. B., 32:101
Goodhart, Arthur Lehmann, 34:224; 36:160;
 Five Jewish Lawyers of the Common Law,
 reviewed, 40:87-90; "Poland and the
 Minority Races," 28:xli
Goodhart, Howard L., 35:xii
Goodhart, John, Jr., 27:323
Goodhart, Morris, 49:186
Goodhart, Philip J., 37:xii
Goodman, 29:146
Goodman, Abram Vossen, 39:285; 40:414;
 46:389; book reviewed by, 38:249-51;
 executive council, 38:344; 39:470; 45:264;
 48:265; "Jewish Elements in Brown's Early
 History," 37:xxx, 135-45; "The Jews of
 America during the Struggle for
 Independence," 31:xvii
Goodman, Alice W., 26:249
Goodman, H., 29:130

Goodman, Jacob, 31:225
Goodman, Louis, 44:190, 192
Goodman, Morris, 42:419
Goodman, Nathan G., 34:266
Goodman, Paul, 34:xxvii; 42:436
Goodman, Philip, 39:316; 40:205; 41:389;
 42:311; 50:272, 275, 283, 394-96;
 executive council, 42:415; 43:230; 46:493;
 49:268; "American Jewish Bookplates,"
 42:415; 45:129-216; necrologies of
 Benjamin Rabinowitz, 38:335-36; Samuel
 David Gershovitz, 50:428-35; "A Personal
 Tribute to Lincoln by Josephine Phillips,"
 41:204-7; "The Purim Association of the
 City of New York, 1862-1902," 39:470;
 40:135-72; 49:230; Samuel D. Gershovitz
 memorial, 50:425
Goodman, Samuel, 26:183
Goodrich, A. T., 40:188
Goodrich, C. A., *Religious Ceremonies and
 Customs*, 30:322
Goodrich, Grove, 27:304
Goodsby, Simon, 34:267
Goodspeed, 38:25
Goodspeed, George T., 37:129
Goodwin (actor), 33:177
Goodwin, Charles, 29:70
Goodwin, Edward A., *see:* Davidson, Gabriel
Goodwin, Jonathan, *Return and Conversion of
 the Jews*, 30:372
Goodwin, Mathew, 44:97
Goold, Sam, 27:240
Goossen Gerritsen (Van Schayck), 26:247
Gootmann, A. H., 36:303-6
Gorden, Abraham, 23:154
Gordin, Jacob, 39:96; 49:106, 118
Gordis, Robert, 41:105; 43:196; 47:62; "The
 Bible as a Cultural Monument," reviewed,
 40:195; "Mordecai Manuel Noah: A
 Centenary Evaluation," 40:407; 41:1-26;
 see also: Friedman, Theodore
Gordon, Albert I., 39:373, *Jews in Transition*,
 reviewed, 40:196-98
Gordon, Duchess of, 22:40-43
Gordon, George J., 42:13; 50:428
Gordon, H. L., 33:156
Gordon, Mrs. Isaac, 49:219
Gordon, Jakob, 39:146
Gordon, J. G. R., 36:310

Gordon, Judah Loeb, 33:138; 43:39; *Ahoti Ruhamah*, 22;137; *Arez Hadashah*, 22:137
Gordon, Julius, 41:92
Gordon, Lord George, "Lord George Gordon," 26:xxxiv
Gordon, Martin, Jr., 43:105
Gordon, Ruth, 35:274
Gordon, S. T., 50:390
Gordon, William, *Separation of Jewish Tribes*, 30:77, 79
Goremykin, Ivan, 43:66-67
Goren, Louis M., 34:xxv
Gorenstein, Arthur, "A Portrait of Ethnic Politics," 50:202-38
Gorfinke, Joseph I., 40:377
Gorgas, Josiah, 48:153
Gorman, James A., 40:289, 291; 41:184
Gorn, George K., 45:152
Gortschakoff, Prince, 24:62-64, 66, 69, 82, 121, 151; 36:173
Gortchakov, Alexander Mikhailovitch, 41:166
Goslin, Henrietta, 27:111
Goslin, L., 27:110
Goss, Rev., 22:24
Gosse, Edmund William, 46:433
Gotatus, Abraham, 23:81
Gottesman, Mendel, 45:160, 173
Gottesman, Mrs. Samuel David, 45:173
Gottesman Tree of Life Foundation, 45:160
Gotthard, communication from, 26:xxx
Gottheil, Emma, 45:141
Gottheil, Gustave, 29:xli; 34:xviii, 303; 35:64, 121; 37:84, 234, 236; 39:325; 40:72, 277; 42:85; 45:140; Felsenthal correspondence, 45:95-96, 98-99, 109, 121, 125; Hebrew Union College, 40:29, 31-32; Life of Gustave Gottheil, 35:xxi; New York chief rabbi, 44:157, 183; slavery, 31:xxxiii; Zionism, 40:391; 42:100
Gottheil, Richard J. H., 22:xxviii; 25:139-40; 26:xiv; 29:180; 33:132, 135; 35:57-59, 122; 37:474; 39:411-12; 40:391; 47:165; 49:97, 141; acting president, 28:xviii; "The Baron de Belmonte," 22:xii; "The Belmont-Belmonte Family," 26:xxxiii; bookplates, 45:140; communication from, 26:xiv, xxx; Felsenthal correspondence, 45:98-99, 101, 104, 115; Foreign Archives Committee report, 23:xiv; gifts, 29:xli; 31:xxxiii;

History of Jews, committee on, 29:xxvi; Jewish Publications, 43:239; "The Jews in the 'Fueros Leonenses de Salamanca, Zamora, Ledesma y Alba de Tormes,' " 28:xv; *Life of Gustav Gottheil*, 35:xxi; "The Marquis de Schönenberg," 22:xii; Napoleonic Sanhedrin, 26:xxvii; necrology of, 35:ix; necrologies of Abraham Solomon Freidus, 29:xxxvi, 163-65; Adolfo Bonilla y San Martin, 31:xxiii; Morris Jastrow, Jr., 29:xiv, 170-73; Surinam Jewry, 22:26, 30; vice president, 22:xi, xvi, xxvii; 23:xii; 25:xi; 26:xii, xxx; 28:xiv, xxii, xxxii; 29:xiv, xxviii, xxxv; 31:xv, xxiii, xxix; 32:xii, xix; 33:xvi, xxv; 34:xiii; "Zionism," 23:xvii; 42:100
Gotthelf, Bernard Henry, 42:211
Gottheimer, Charlotte, 38:75
Gottheimer, George, 38:75
Gotthold, Florence W., 29:206
Gotthold, N., 29:129
Göttingen University, 36:358
Gottlieb, Gittel, 34:210
Gottlieb, Israel, 34:210
Gottlieb, Samuel, 37:266
Gottschalk, Adelaide, 48:198
Gottschalk, Edward, 48:198
Gottschalk, Louis Moreau, *Where the World Ends: The Life of Louis Moreau Gottschalk*, reviewed, 48:196-99
Goucher College, 25:154
Goudchaux, 29:127
Gougenheim, 42:160
Gould, D., 27:149
Gould, D. J., 27:415, 451
Gould, Edwin, 33:221
Gould, Elias B., 25:6
Gould, Elizabeth P., 45:59
Gould family, 27:xviii
Gould, Isaac, 27:442
Gould, J. E., 50:389
Gould, Jay, 41:32; 48:81
Gould, John, 27:439
Gould, Nathan H., 27:149, 202, 213-14, 409, 413-16, 422, 424, 451, 459; 34:3-9, 38:59; Newport Jews, correspondence concerning, 27:190-91, 215-16, 423-24; Judah Touro portrait, 27:216, 422; Newport, old Jews in, 27:458-59
Gould, Stephen (b. Nathan), 27:423

Gould, Stephen (uncle to Nathan H.), 27:423, 429, 435; correspondence of, 27:425-42; diary quoted, 27:424
Gourevich, M., 39:97
Gouverneur, Margaret, 23:152
Gozani, Jean-Paul, 49:43-45, 47, 50
Grabelsky, Bathsheba, 33:160
Grabfelder, S., 38:30-31
Grace, William R., 40:142
Gracees, Joan, 33:115
Gracel, Isacq, 33:65
Grade, A. I., 35:xxii
Gradis, Abraham, 31:xxxii
Gradis, Moise, 31:xxxii
Gradische, Samuel, "Samuel Gradische, an Eighteenth-Century French Sutler," 25:xiii
Graduate School for Jewish Social Work, 35:324
Graeber, Isacque A., "Self-Studies of the American Jewish Community: A Bibliography," 39:471
Graes, Ortuin de, 35:124
Graetz, Charles, 31:174, 179
Graetz, Heinrich (Hirsh), 26:33; 28:182-83, 262-64, 280; 29:100, 128; 37:96; 38:22; 43:156; 44:65; 45:260; 47:137; 49:164; 50:92; "Gnosticism and Judaism," 28:73; "Heinrich Graetz, The Historian: on the Centenary of his Birth, October 31, 1917," 28:63-81; "The Historian of the Jews," 26:xxx; History of the Jews, 37:483; 45:101, 103; "How to Fill the Gaps in Graetz's History," 28:xxxiii; immigration, 41:140-41; Jewish historiography, 26:12-14, 17, 21, 31; 39:214, 305; Monatsschrift, 26:14; "Sketch of Heinrich Graetz," 28:xxxviii; Zohar, 45:30
Graetz, Leo, 28:77
Graff, Anton, 41:282
Graff, David, 29:69, 73
Graff, Isaac, 41:292
Grafton, N. G., 27:120
Graham, 32:113
Graham, Doctor, 27:42
Graham, General, 29:117
Graham, Gwethalyn, 39:116
Graham, James D., 31:195
Graham, John, 26:277-78
Graham, William Alexander, Judith Bensaddi, 39:115-42

Graham, Winifred, 35:254
Gramophone, 49:64
Granada, Gabriel de, 33:40-41; 34:173; 37:453
Granada, Henriques, 38:236
Granada, Isaac, 23:148
Granados, Fabian, 31:29
Grand Army Gazette and National Guardsman, 50:400
Grand Army of the Republic, 46:162
Grand Island, New York, 21:xx-xxi, 229-52; 22:131; 23:178; 27:236; 34:173, 175-76, 273; 37:441; 40:58, 363; 41:10-15, 21-23, 26, 390; 46:158, 166, 181, 275, 384; 48:100; 50:14-17; Mordecai Manuel Noah's Grand Island address, 21:x, xx-xxi, 229-52; "Noah's Ararat-Jewish State in its Historical Setting," 41:390; 43:170-90
Grand, Samuel, 46:177
Grand Union Hotel, Saratoga, 40:323; 42:348; 47:11-12
Grand Lodge F. & A. M. of Pennsylvania, gift, 26:xxxv
Grande Abreu, Pedro de, 33:122
Grande, Joan ten, 33:116
Granet, député, 41:162
Granison, Abram M., 40:53
Grant, Mr., 31:186
Grant, Asahel, The Nestorians, 30:354, 401
Grant, Hugh J., 25:112; 40:158
Grant, James, 35:7
Grant, James H., 27:506
Grant, Jesse R., 40:185
Grant, Leroy J., 27:506
Grant, Madison, 34:228; 40:324; 45:217; history, writing of, 46:294, 298, 300-302
Grant, Robert, 22:177, 26:268
Grant, Senton, 40:76
Grant, Ulysses S., 21:173; 25:28; 29:xix, 94; 38:37; 46:271, 393; 49:23; 50:131, 289, 293, 309, 343, 386; discrimination, 47:12; expulsion of Jews, 29:104; 34:275; "General Ulysses S. Grant and the Jews," 50:293; Isachar Zacharie, 43:71, 98-99, 101, 112; Joseph Seligman, 41:31-32, 36-37; 42:348; Marcus Otterbourg, 32:73-74; Order #11, 29:76; 35:133; 38:320; 39:236; 40:323; 41:214; 42:110, 133; 47:80, 193; 49:23; 50:293, 407; Otto Mears, 39:346;

Roumania and Jewish disabilities, 24:8-9, 12-13, 110, 112; 36:100-101, 104; Simon Wolf, 29:200-201, 203; 47:76, 78-80; "Something Additional on General Grant's Order Number 11," 40:184-86

Grant, William, 21:18

Granville, Earl, 24:16, 21, 146; 36:109, 207

Grape, Jacob, 31:227

Gras, N. S. B., 23:95-96; 43:205; 46:210

Graslo, David G., 27:274

Graslo, Rachel, 27:274

Graswinckel, Hugo, 33:123

Gratian, 28:138

Grattan, Thomas C., 42:334, 338

Gratz, 26:8; "Two Gratz Documents, 1763 and 1773," 26:xxxi

Gratz, Anderson, 26:xxxiii

Gratz, Ann Boswell, 33:4

Gratz, Barnard (Bernard), 22:xxxi; 25:95; 27:21, 42, 58, 462; 28:xxxviii; 29:142; 33:4, 207, 209; 34:21, 67-69; 37:347-48; 39:215; 41:226; 45:198; 46:377, 424; 50:39, 49, 243; "The Ancestral Background and the Early Youth of Barnard and Michael Gratz," 38:344; day book, 26:232-34; "The Gratz Papers," 23:vii, xiii, 1-23; letters, 34:75-76, 79-85, 97-94, 97-102; papers, 25:113-14; *Sale of Mohawk Valley Lands,* 30:61-63

Gratz, Benjamin, 23:9, 12; 26:181; 29:53; 33:2-5; 39:466

Gratz, Mrs. Benjamin, 29:53, 55-56, 60

Gratz, Elizabeth Twigg (Bearden), 38:30, 40

Gratz family, 22:xxii; 27:465; 29:190; 33:2-3; 34:19; 43:235; 46:387, 421; 49:235; "The Gratz Papers," 23:vii, xiii, 1-23

Gratz, Frances Henriette, 38:40, 42

Gratz, Henriette, 38:41

Gratz, Hyam, 27:83

Gratz, Hyman, 23:12; 29:55, 59; 33:2, 4; 42:398; 48:207, 214, 230; Gratz College, 31:276; 33:22; portrait, 43:232; "The World of Hyman Gratz," 50:241-47

Gratz, Issacher Ber, 34:68, 80

Gratz, Joe, 27:79

Gratz, Joseph, 26:181; 30:133

Gratz, Louis A., "From Peddler to Regimental Commander in Two Years:

the Civil War Career of Major Louis A. Gratz," 38:22-44, 345

Gratz, Louis C., 50:386

Gratz, Mrs. Louis (Fiddler), 38:31

Gratz, Maria Gist, 33:2, 4; letters to, 29:54-60

Gratz, Mary, 48:74

Gratz, Michael (New York), 27:42, 170, 241, 461; 28:xxxiv; 35:xix; 37:347-51; 41:226, 287; 43:233-34, 236; 45:201; 50:39, 49, 242-43, 246; "The Ancestral Background and the Early Youth of Barnard and Michael Gratz," 38:344; "Colonial Merchants: Moses Hayes and Michael Gratz and Their Newport Ventures," 46:493; "Michael Gratz's Interest in Lands in Otsego County, New York, in 1794, and What Came of It. An Unpublished History," 28:xv

Gratz, Michael (Penn.), 21:99; 23:176; 26:181, 233; 29:142; 31:241; 33:5; 34:21; "The Gratz Papers," 23:vii, xiii, 1-23; letter, 34:75-76, 78-102

Gratz, Mrs. Michael, 23:6, 22

Gratz, Miriam, 33:4; 45:201; 50:242

Gratz, Miriam (Simon), 37:348-49; 41:287

Gratz, Missess, 35:197

Gratz Papers, 25:xiii, xv, 119; 34:69, 75

Gratz, Philip, Jr., 36:228

Gratz, Rachel, 27:74; 34:56n; 41:287; portrait of, 42:417

Gratz, Rebecca, 23:144-45; 31:255; 33:xxix; 34:177; 37:65; 45:184; 46:427; 48:202, 229, 233, 267; 49:70, 143; 50:243-45; *Ivanhoe,* 30:219, 408; 35:235-37; 38:15; 39:466; letters, 28:xxxviii; 33:2-5; 34:21; 39:458; 47:180; "Letters of Rebecca Gratz," 33:xxx; "Myth in the Life of Rebecca Gratz," 47:201; "A Note on Rebecca Gratz and Gratz Van Rensselaer," 29:xxix; "The Original of Scott's Rebecca," 22:53-60; 32:xxvlii; 41:280, 287; 43:233, 236; "Rebecca Gratz," 34:xxvi; "Rebecca Gratz and Gratz Van Rensselaer," 31:241; "Rebecca Gratz and her Relation to Rebecca of 'Ivanhoe,' " 22:xvii; "Rebecca Gratz and the Jewish Sunday School Movement in Philadelphia," 48:71-77; 49:235; "Rosa Mordecai's Recollections of

the First Hebrew Sunday School," 42:397-406; slavery, 39:307; "Some Unpublished Papers of Rebecca Gratz," 29:vii, xxxvi, 53-60; Sunday school, 29:5; 30:408; 31:278; 35:133; 42:56, 397
Gratz, Richea, 42:398
Gratz, Simon, 23:12; 27:229; 28:xxxiv; 30:249; 37:346, 348-51; 50:243, 246; War of 1812, 26:181; 33:2
Gratz, Solomon, 23:2
Gratz, Yehiel, 34:91
Gratz College, 23:192; 25:160; 28:xii; 29:190; 31:255, 276, 284; 33:22; 37:291; 38:338; 42:398, 459; 45:196, 207; 48:230-32; 50:241-47
Gratz Correspondence, 33:3
Gratz Fund, 42:16
Gratz v. Cohen, 30:440-41
Grau, M., 38:315
Graubard, Moritz, 50:237-38
Grauman, I., 29:130
Graumann, Max, 47:181
Graves, George, 23:139
Gray, 23:49
Gray, Bessie, 43:118
Gray, John Chipman, 43:118
Gray, John H., 50:272
Gray, Joseph H., 50:275, 341
Gray, Mrs. Samuel, 38:273
Graydon's Memoirs, 28:xxxviii
Grayzel, Solomon, 42:vi, 216, 331; 50:68; "The Attitude of Innocent III Toward the Jews, as Shown in Some of His Letters," 29:xxxvi; book review by, 42:207-10; corresponding secretary, 42:414; 43:230; 44:241; 45:264; 46:492; executive council, 38:346; 39:470; 41:388; history, writing of, 46:404, 414, 419, 445; Lee Max Friedman Award Medal, committee, 49:271; necrologies of Cyrus Adler, 37:451-54; Israel Levi, 37:474-75; presides, 40:407; 43:231; 47:201; 48:266; recording secretary, 47:200; 48:265; 49:268; 50:426
Graziano, Vitale de, 28:155-56
Great Awakening, 45:133
Great Britain, 24:142, 144, 149; 25:128; 26:70, 77-80; 28:216, 246, 248-49, 269, 293; 46:86; 49:33; anti-Semitism, 25:157-58; Balkans and Jewish questions, 24:120-21, 125-26, 128, 132; "British Projects for the Restoration of Jews to Palestine," 26:xv, 127-64; Bucharest Peace Conference, 24:81, 86, 89-91, 93; Bury St. Edmunds, rabbi in, 29:xxiii; civil rights, 22:177-78; 26:35; Congress of Berlin, 1878, 24:40, 43, 45-46, 49, 61-62, 64, 66, 74-75, 77, 79, 108, 115; "The Doctrine that 'Christianity is a Part of the Common Law'; and its Recent Judicial Overthrow in England, with Particular Reference to Jewish Rights," 31:vii, xvi, 103-34; "An Early English Intervention on Behalf of Foreign Jewry," 35:xvi, 213-17; education, 38:85, 87, 89, 120, 124; emancipation, 50:7; immigration, 40:232-33; Jew bill, 26:244; "Jewish Disabilities in Balkans," 24:2, 12, 16, 19-22, 110, 134; *The Jewish Immigrant in England, 1870-1914*, reviewed, 50:145-46; "Jews Interested in Privateering in America During the Eighteenth Century," 23:vii, 163-76; "Jews of Angevin England," 26:31-32; "Memorandum on the Treaty Rights of the Jews of Roumania," 24:137-53; migration, 26:5; naturalization, 26:244; and Palestine, 40:116-18, 40:313-17; 49:200; Palestine, U.S. and Jews, 36:47, 49, 51, 53, 63, 66-68, 70-74, 77-95; Paris Conference, 1876, 34:34, 102, 104; Polish relief, 36:142, 145-47; re-admission of Jews, 31:xviii; religious freedom, 25:114; resettlement, 29:46-49; "The Rightlessness of the Mediaeval English Jewry," 22:xvii; Rumanian Jews, 36:105, 109, 115; Russian passports, 46:86-89, 91-95, 97; Turkey and Jews, 36:7; "Was the Bank of England Protected by a Jew?," 25:111; West Indies trade, 26:243-44
Great Synagogue, "The Rabbinate of the Great Synagogue, London," 28:xl
Greater Federation of Jewish Charities (Boston), 46:82
Great Sanhedrin, 40:2
"Grecian Captive, The," 21:229
Greece, 24:19, 84, 91-93, 110; Rumanian Jews, 36:105
Greef, Richard, 45:197
Greek Catholic Church, 24:85, 87

Greek Orthodox Church, 26:121
Greeley, Horace, 38:51; 39:136; 43:119; 44:99; 50:385
Greely expedition, 47:192
Green, Andrew H., 29:163; 38:50-52
Green, Ashbel, 47:148
Green, D. M., 27:91
Green, Emanuel, 40:54
Green, H. (Providence, R.I.), 29:133; 40:239
Green, H. (St. John, N.B.), 23:98
Green, Henry, 38:71
Green, Mrs. Henry, 22:xxxii
Green, J., 24:19
Green, Jacob, *Inquiry into the Jewish Church*, 30:58, 60
Green, John, 27:175; 38:51
Green, Jonas, 37:124, 128-29
Green, N., 34:244
Green, Samuel A., 37:440
Green, William Chase, 35:257-58
Green Bag, 47:212
Greenbaum, Samuel, 29:168
Greenbaum, Samuel (Judge), 31:257; 37:234, 239, 261, 306-7; necrologies of, Isidor Straus, 22:xvii, 235-39; Seligman J. Strauss, 31:xxiv, 297-98; 33:xii
Greenberg, Abraham S., 43:48
Greenberg, C., 50:117
Greenberg, Chaim, 39:112
Greenberg, Mrs. David J., *Through the Years: A Study of the Richmond Jewish Community*, reviewed, 46:68-69; 49:241
Greenberg, Emanuel, 43:230
Greenberg, Evelyn Levow, "Isaac Polock: Early Settler in Washington, D. C.," 48:1-18
Greenberg, Hank, 48:201
Greenberg, Hayim, 46:130
Greenberg, Isaac, 47:201
Greenberg, Leonard, 42:420; 46:123; "Evidence of Business Discrimination in the Civil War Period," 38:342; "Some American Anti-Semitic Publications of the Late 19th Century," 37:xxxv, 421-25
Greenberg, Meyer, 47:203
Greenberg, Mrs. Meyer, 47:201-3
Greenberg, Simon, 35:xxiii; 43:195
Greenberg *v.* Western Turf Association, 25:136

Greenblatt, Nathan, 33:132, 150, 164
Greenblum, Joseph, 48:67
Greene, Nathanael, 40:79
Greene, Ward, 35:276
Greenebaum, 31:152; 45:109
Greenebaum, Elias, 28:240
Greenebaum, Henriette, 29:159
Greenebaum, Henry, 29:xl; 31:xxxiii
Greenebaum, M. E., 28:240
Greenebaum, Michael, 29:159
Greenebaum, Sarah Spiegel, 29:159
Greenfield, Albert M., 43:236, 238
Greenhalgh, Jo., 33:207
Greenhill, W., 32:30
Greenhut, Joseph B., 31:203; 35:124
Greenleaf, James, 48:2-3
Greenleaf, Thomas, 38:116
Greenleaf's New York Journal & Patriotic Register, 38:116-17
Greenlee, William Brooks, 39:309
Greenly, Edw., 26:249
Greenstein, Henry, 49:270
Greenstone, Julius H., 40:322; 42:26-27; book review by, 40:311-313; (ed.), *Italian Hebrew Literature*, 37:57, 93
Greentree, Mire, 40:59-60, 64; 44:237
Greentree, William B., 40:60
Greenwald, Sam, 41:368-69
Greenwich, Conn., Jewish Welfare Fund, contribution, 37:xxviii
Greenwich Theatre, 33:183
Gregh, Fernand, 35:260
Grégoire, Bishop, 21:241; 26:87
Gregory I, Pope, 28:138
Gregory XIII, 28:175
Gregory IX, 21:241
Gregory X, 28:145
Gregory XII, Pope, 28:154
Gregory XIII, Pope, 28:175
Gregory XIV, 28:179, 193
Gregory XV, 28:193
Gregory the Great, 21:241
Gregory, D. S., 34:171
Gregory, F. H., 39:34, 62
Gregory, G. (trans.), *Lectures of the Sacred Poetry of the Hebrews*, 30:258
Gregory, George, 26:227
Gregory, T. E., 37:473
Greiff, Cecilia, 38:75

Greiff, Raphall, 38:75
Greifswald, University of, 28:77
Grelia, John, Jr., 35:289
Grennell, Henry, 39:35
Grenz, Frederick G., 36:256-58; 41:173
Greppo, député, 41:162
Greppo, J. G. H., *Essay on the Hieroglyphic System*, 30:261
Gresham, W. Q., 36:11, 13-15, 59-62, 230-31, 240-41; 40:306; 41:172
Gretch, V., 38:248
Grew, Joseph C., 46:351
Grey, 28:56
Grey, Edward, 24:89, 93-94; 36:135; 46:97; "Memorandum on the Treaty Rights of the Jews of Roumania," 24:137-53
Grey, Richard, 38:147; *An Hebrew Grammar*, 30:54-55, 121, 127, 149-50
Grier, Robert C., 37:350-51
Grierson, Herbert John Clifford, 35:237; 46:427
Gries, Frances (Hays), 28:276
Gries, Lincoln, 28:276
Gries, Moses J., 26:281; 39:454; gift, 26:xxxiv; necrology of, 28:xv, 274-76
Gries, Robert, 28:276
Grieve, David, 34:235
Griffeth, Root, Jr., 27:250
Griffin, A. P. C., *Bibliography of American Historical Societies*, 49:256
Griffin, Grace G., 46:160
Griffin, president of Williams College, 25:84
Griffith, Mrs. Connie G., 50:271
Griffith, Joshua, 37:104, 107-8, 111
Griffiths, 22:191
Griffiths, Sarah, 23:154
Griffitts, Samuel Powell, 42:191
Grigorieff, V., 36:175-76; 41:167
Grigoriev, Mark, 39:101
Grimani, Cardinal, 28:202
Grimes, Katherine, 25:75, 77
Grimes, Thomas, 25:75
Grimké sisters, 39:307
Grimm, Jacob, 45:33
Grimshaw, Jackson, 44:105
Grimshaw & Williams, 50:350
Grimwade, A. G., 43:5-6; 45:271; 46:11; "Form and Decoration of Silver *Rimonim*," 45:48-53

Grinnell, William, 35:291
Grinnell Expedition, 25:20
Grinsfelder, Mrs. S., 23:145
Grinstein, Hyman B., 33:xxvi; 39:336; 50:270, 276, 385; American Historical Association session, 44:245; "The Americanization of the German Jew in New York City prior to the Civil War," 37:xxxi; "American Jewry and Maimonides," 34:268-70; "American Jewry and Palestine: the Role Played by American Jews in the Establishment of the Jewish State," 38:345; "The American Synagogue and Laxity of Religious Observance, 1750-1850," 34:xiv; book review by, 44:250-51; "The Communal Aspects and Social Aspects of American Jewish History," 38:346; 39:267-82; "The Constitution and by-laws of the *Hebra Hinuch Nearim*, New York, 1825," 35:xv; corresponding secretary, 47:200; 48:265; 49:268; 50:426; "Early Projects for the Formation of a Jewish College or University in the United States," 38:343; "Early Research in American Jewish History," 37:xxxiii; "The Efforts of East European Jewry to Organize Its Own Community in the United States," 48:266; 49:73-89; executive council, 38:346; 39:470; 42:414; "A Haym Solomon Letter to Rabbi David Tevele Schiff, London, 1784," 34:xiv, 107-16; "Hebraists, Talmudists and Jewish Scholars in the United States from the Earliest Times until 1860," 37:xxxiii; "The Hebrew Benevolent Society, Forerunner of the Hebrew Orphan Asylum of New York," 37:xxxv; history, writing of, 46:181, 187; "A Humorist Views the Jewish Community of Old New York," 38:343; "The Jewish Community of New York City, 1654-1860," 37:xxxi; "The Jewish Community of New York City, 1860-1910," 37:xxxiii; "Jewish Immigration Through New York City (1860-1880)," 50:427; Jewish local history, 39:253, 285, 315; 49:262; "Jews and Gentiles in New York: A Study in Inter-Group Relations, 1800-1843," 37:xxxv; "The Jews in New York City Politics, 1860-1880," 39:471;

Judaism, 47:122; "A letter to Saul Lowenstamm, chief rabbi of Amsterdam, from the Mickveh Synagogue of Philadelphia, dated 9 Nissan 5445 (1785)," 35:xv; "The Memoirs and Scrapbooks of the late Dr. Joseph Isaac Bluestone of New York City," 35:xiv, 53-64; recording secretary, 44:241; 45:264; 46:492; "References to the Jewish Village of Shalom in the Minutes of the Anshe Chesed Congregation, New York City," 37:xxxi; "References to Jews in Early New York Weekly Periodicals," 37:xxxv; "Research in American Jewish History, Its Present Status and Its Problems," 38:342; *The Rise of the Jewish Community of New York, 1654-1860*, 49:230; "The Rubinstein Murder Case—Was Pesach Nathan Rubinstein Guilty?," 38:345; "Source Material on the Anshe Chesed School of New York, 1835-1860," 37:xxxi; "Temple Emanu-El of New York and the Chair in Rabbinical Literature at Columbia, 1887," 37:xxxiii; "Thirty Crucial Years in the History of the Jews in the United States," 38:345; "Writing the History of a Large American Jewish Community," 46:170-76
Griscom, Clement A., Jr., 33:221
Griscom, Lloyd C., 36:62-63
Griswold, Rufus W., 39:139
Groce, George C., 50:387
Grocery Bag Manufacturers' Service Bureau, 28:305
Groeneseijn, H., 32:20
Groesbeck, David *v.* William E. Dunscomb and Morgan Dix, 27:382-83
Groghan, George, 30:77
Grolier Club, 35:314
Gronauer, Abraham, 41:255
Gronauer, Louis, 41:257
Groninger family, 48:20
Groot, *see:* Grotius, Hugo
Gropper, Milton Herbert, 40:356
Gropper, William, 47:182
Grosier, Jean-Baptiste-Gabriel-Alexandre, 49:42, 48-52
Gross, Chaim, 40:320
Gross, Charles, 26:xix, 2; 28:266; 33:35; 38:45; 45:102; *Gallia Judaica*, 26:28

Gross, Edward, 37:266, 268
Gross and Wife, 38:202
Gross, Reuben E., "The Bible as Statutory Law in 17th Century New England," 48:266
Gross; State *v.*, 29:152
Grosseteste, Robert, "Robert Grosseteste and the Jews," 33:xxv
Grossman, Hyman, 42:419
Grossman, Louis, 39:457; Hebrew Union College, 40:38, 40, 44; "Louis Grossman Collection," 45:159; necrology of, 31:xxix; necrology of Jacob Ottenheimer, 26:xiv, 282-83; Zionism, 40:371, 392
Grossman, M., 39:110
Grossman, August, 38:203
Grossman, Moses H., 37:xii
Grossman, N., 39:104
Grossman, V., 39:93, 108, 110-11
Grostian, Alexander, 49:39-52
Grote, Count de, 26:62
Groth, Andreas Henry, 23:17
Grothe, Count, 26:43-44
Grotius, Hugo, 34:226; "Hugo Grotius and the Emancipation of the Jews in Holland," 31:xxiv, 173-80
Grotius Society, 31:263
Grotjan, Peter A., 22:90
Grover, Leonard, 50:299
Grover, Wayne C., 47:201
Grover's Theater, 50:299
Groves, Daniel, 41:66
Gruenberg, Louis, 47:182
Gruenewald, Max, "The Attitude toward the Jews as Historical Text," 38:343; "Benjamin Franklin's 'Parable on Brotherly Love,' " 37:xxxv, 147-52; (forw.), *Jews from Germany in the United States*, reviewed, 46:59-60
Gruening, Emil, 42:122
Grünbaum, Elias, 39:151; 45:110
Grund, Francis Joseph, 26:234-35; 35:132; "Francis Joseph Grund, a Forgotten Journalist and Politician," 22:xxviii
Grundman, 39:151
Grunewald, Simon, 31:171
Grunwald, "Graves of Portuguese Jews in Germany," 31:xxxi
Grunwald, Max, 26:267

Grunwalt, Abraham, 50:304
Grusenberg, Oscar, 40:403
Gruss, Louis, 37:436
Gruy, L. V., de, 26:xiv
Guabay, Aron, 42:280, 394
Guadeloupe, "The Gratz Papers," 23:3
Guadelupe, Jacob, 44:227
Guadelupe, Jacob Dias, 44:222
Guardian, The, 33:174, 195
Gubernia, Grodninsky, 38:73
Gubernia, Nahum, 38:73
Gudemann, 28:182
Güedemann, Moritz, 24:47; 26:17; 28:88; 43:250; 45:125; "The 'Magen David,' Its Origin and Significance," 22:xvii; necrology of, 28:xv, 276-81
Guedalla, Haim, 37:214
Guelph Exhibition, 31:290
Guénée, Antoine, *Letters of Certain Jews to M. Voltaire*, 30:104, 401
Guerman, Daniel de Baruch, 29:13
Guerre, de, Mr., 27:304
Guerrero, Juan, 31:25
Guggenheim, Daniel, 31:203; 46:483; necrology of, 33:xii
Guggenheim family, 42:126; 46:213
The Guggenheims, 35:xxii
Guggenheim, Harry F., 47:181
Guggenheim, Meyer, 44:3-4
Guggenheim, Simon, 40:288; 37:xii
Guggenheim, William, 40:65
Guggenheimer, Etta, 31:281
Guggenheimer, Mayer, 41:263
Guggenheimer, Randolph, 38:71
Guggenheimer, Sara, 41:257
Guggenheimer, Salomon, 50:314
Guggenhime, Berthold, 45:144
Guglielmo, Duke of Mantua, 28:193
Gugy, A., 25:121
Guiana, 29:8, 20; 29:46; 34:2; "An Early Jewish Colony in Western Guiana," 32:134; "An Episode in the Jewish Colonization of Guiana, 1660," 32:xiii
Guibert, Archbishop, 41:150
Guichard, Jules, 41:162
"Guide of the Perplexed," 28:69
Guild, Curtis, 36:286-88; 41:188
Guild, Surgeon, 50:323
Guilielmus, son of Dactilus, 28:159

Guillet, Edouard, 23:139
Guimmarais, Luiz, 33:97
Guinzburg, Aaron, 40:63-64
Guiterman, Mrs. Arthur, 32:xxvi
Gulak, Asher, 34:64
Gulhave, 24:102
Gummeré, Samuel, 36:36
Gumpel, R., 25:129
Gumpert, Gompert S., 25:52, 57
Gumpertz, S. G., "The Jewish Legion of Valor," 34:xxiv
Gumpertz Home for the Aged, 31:190
Gumprecht, J. J., 26:36, 46
Gundelfinger, David, 41:267
Gunsburg, Joseph (baron), 28:129
Gunsinhouser, Abraham, 26:183
Gunther, C. G., 40:148
Günzburg, Baron de, 36:292; colony, 39:94; 43:59, 61
Günzburg, David, 28:129
Günzburg family, 28:84, 128
Günzburg, Horace (baron), 28:128-29; 43:40, 64-66
Günzburg, Joseph Yozel, 28:128-29
Günzburg, Mordecai, 28:117-18
Günzberg, Mordecai Aaron, *Gelot ha-Arez ha-Hadashah*, 22:125
Gunzburg Library, St. Petersburg, 22:112
Gurario, 35:221-22
Gurion, Ben, "The Spirit of the New Israel," 46:130
Gurley, Phineas D., 38:320
Gurney, Edmund, 35:248
Gury, A., 25:121
Gusky Orphanage and Home, 28:258
Gustav, Richard, 45:140-41
Gustines, Daniel Vader, 37:414
Gutekunst, F., 48:221
Guteres, Jacob Mendez, 28:239; 37:337
Guterman, Jacob, 44:190, 192
Guterman, Norbert, *Prophets of Deceit*, reviewed, 40:199-201; *see also*: Lowenthal, Leo
Guterus, Joan, 33:115
Gutheim, Emily (Jones), 50:170
Gutheim, James K., 27:524; 28:xxxviii; 37:437; 43:97-98; 44:130; 50:170; Isachar Zacharie, 44:112-13; *Rede gehalten bei der Grundsteinlegung*, 30:409-10; *Sermon*

Delivered at Consecration of Synagogue Adas Israel, 30:445-46; translations, 45:101
Guthman, Sidney, 35:xxiii
Guthrie, Alexander, 45:258
Guthrie, Grace, 38:73
Gutieres, Rachel Gomes, 32:63
Gutierez, Isaque Mendez, 23:27
Gutierez, Jacob Mendez, 23:28
Guitierrez, Manuel, 23:133
Gutmacher, Elijah, 45:209
Gutmacher, Heiman, 41:246
Gutmacher, Regine, 41:246
Gutman, 27:120
Gutman, David, 41:256
Gutman, Ella J., 25:156
Gutman, Joseph, Jr., 39:66
Gutman, Jul., 41:254
Gutman, Leah, 27:111
Gutmann, Abraham, 41:254
Gutmann, Abraham Hirsch, 41:257
Gutmann, Albert, 41:263
Gutmann, Berta, 41:263
Gutmann, Cläre, 41:258
Gutmann, Heinrich, 41:257
Gutmann, Hess, 41:256
Gutmann, Isak, 41:255, 263
Gutmann, Jeanette, 41:258
Gutmann, Jesse, 37:xii
Gutmann, Jonas, 41:258
Gutmann, Joseph, 50:270
Gutmann, Lazarus, 41:263
Gutmann, Lazarus Bär, 41:267
Gutmann, Louis, 41:263
Gutmann, Rieke, 41:263
Gutmann, Samuel, 41:255
Gutmann, Seligmann, 41:263
Gutmann, Simon, 41:259
Gutmann, Solomon, 41:263
Gutmann, Therese, 41:258
Gutsmann, Sigmund, 41:260
Gutstein, Morris A., 35:139; 37:35; 38:57, 63, 65, 332; "A Chassidic Rabbi Visits Newport before the American Revolution," 37:xxx; "A Contribution to the History of the Israelites in Chicago," 44:242; "Descriptive Index of Aaron Lopez Material at the Newport Historical Society," 37:xxxiii, 153-62; 49:236; "The Founding of Kehillath Anshe Mayriv in Chicago and the Building of its First Synagogue," 38:347; gift, 34:xxvi; "Jewish Fraternal Orders in the United States," 46:493; "Jewish Literary Societies in Chicago in the 19th Century," 41:389; "A Newport Ledger, 1760-1770," 37:xxxiii, 163-69; "A Priceless Heritage: The Epic Growth of Nineteenth-Century Chicago Jewry," 49:221; "The Sinai Literary Association in Chicago in 1878," 40:407; "The Touro family of Newport," 34:xxvi; "Touro Street in Newport, Rhode Island," 45:265
Gutterez, Jacob Mendez, 32:62-63
Guttheim, Messr., 40:247
Guttierez, Sarah, 22:178
Guttmacher, Adolf, "History of the Baltimore Hebrew Congregation," 25:152; necrology of, 25:xii, 150-52; "Optimism and Pessimism in the Old and New Testaments," 25:151; "The Perpetual Light—Prayers and Meditations on Death for Home and Burial Ground," 25:152; "A Sabbath School Companion for Jewish Children," 25:152
Guttmacher, Dorothea, 25:150
Guttmacher, Laura (Oppenheimer), 25:152
Guttmacher, Manheim, 25:150
Guttman, *Festschrift, Etwas von der schlesischen Landgemeinde*, 28:264
Guttmann, Alexander, 40:49
Guttmann, Jakob, 35:124
Guttmann, Julius, 35:126
Gutwasser, Johannes Ernestus, 43:134
Gutzkow, 26:46
Guzdorff, Simson, 42:227, 279, 394
Guzman, Nuño de, 31:11, 15
Gwinnett, Button, 32:2

H

Haam, Ahad, 40:43
Haan, Cornelis de, 32:14
Haan, Jakob Israel de, 35:274
Haarburger, 39:172
Haas, Charles, 35:260
Haas, Helena, 28:314
Haas, Jacob, 26:183
Haas, Jacob de, 35:58-59; 49:197; "Jacob de
    Haas, American Zionist Journalist,"
    47:202; "Palestine," 43:xxiv
Haas, Jennie May, 29:180
Haas, Johanna, 25:124
Haas, Levy, 28:314
Haas, Louis S., 37:xii
Haas, Willy, 50:112
Habbeson, 45:201
Habersham, Joseph, 48:179, 181, 190, 192-93
Habilho, Daniel, 33:65
Habilho, Ishac, 23:182
Hack, Jaques, 33:121
Hackenburg, Adeline, 38:72
Hackenburg family, 41:88-90
Hackenburg, I. L., 28:xxxiv
Hackenburg, Judah L., 48:214
Hackenburg, William B., 28:310, 314;
    32:130; Balkan disabilities, 29:106, 111,
    113; gift, 22:xxxv; necrology of, 28:xv, 282-
    84; 29:190; necrology of August B. Loeb,
    25:xii, 173-75; nomination committee,
    26:xxix; Philadelphia, Jews in, 48:208, 226,
    228, 235; Touro Synagogue, 38:72;
    Y.M.H.A., 37:233
Hackett, H. B., *Exercises in Hebrew Grammar*,
    30:423; (trans.), *Grammar of the Chaldee
    Language*, 30:408
Ha-Cohen, Joshua Falk, 48:240
Ha-Cohen, R. Samuel, 34:291, 294
Ha-Dani, Eldad, 34:150

Hadassah, 37:482; 45:38, 198; 49:84, 159-72,
    268; gifts, 34:xxii, xxvi; 35:xxiii
Hadassah-Hebrew University Medical
    Center, 49:167, 171-72
Hadassah Medical Relief Association, 49:167
Hadassah Medical Unit, 49:91
Hadassah Study Group, 49:166-67
Haddon, Captain, 40:76
Hadrassah, The Jewish Orphan, 30:294
Hadrian, 42:317
Haecxs, Hendrick, 44:85
Haes, Andrew Levay de, 45:187
Haeser, 28:138
Haffkins, physician, 28:161
Hafter, L., 29:131
Hagedorn, Fräulein, 35:287
Hager, matter of, 29:150
Hagerstown, Md., religious observances,
    mid-nineteenth century, 37:37
Hagerstown Herald, 50:20
Hagner, Justice, 26:211-13
Ha-Hasid, Judah, 28:243
Hahn, 22:124
Hahn, Caroline, 29:199
Ha-Ibri, 45:72-73, 81-82, 86
Hai Gaon, 47:212
Haight, Benjamin, 26:220
Haight, Henry H., 37:43
Haight, Samuel, 27:319
Hailperin, Herman, necrology of Sol
    Rosenbloom, 31:xxix, 289-90
Haim, Henry Uriah, 21:9, 29, 39, 42-43, 215
Haim, Joseph Abea, 37:333
Haim, Mordecay, Sr., 25:138
Haiman, Miecislaus, 39:152
Ha-Ivri, 44:125
Ha-Karmel, 22:133
Hakhnasat Orhim, 48:127

Hakohen, Joseph, 22:116; *Dibre ha-Yamin*, 22:108-12; *Emek ha-Baka*, 22:112; *Mazzib Gebulot Ammim*, 22:112
Ha-Kohen, Joshua Falk, "Ethics of the fathers," 34:53
Halasz, Nicholas, 45:258
Halbe Emuno, 49:246
Halberstam, Solomon J., 45:154
Halbourne, Haim, 27:43
Halde, Jean-Baptiste, du, 49:41, 44-45
Haldimand, Frederick, 26:257; 27:490; 35:7; 40:85; 50:124
Hale, John Parker, 39:47-50; 42:143
Hale, Matthew, 31:110
Hale, Richard W., Jr., 48:69
Halebanon, 33:128
Ha-leummi, 34:151
Ha-Levi, Abraham, 34:69-71; "A Letter of Abraham ha-Levi of New York to Aaron Lopez, 1770," 34:xv
Halevi, Isaac, 22:120
Halevi, Judah, 26:14; 28:78; 37:257; 38:276, 339
Halevi, Meir, 28:278
Halevi, Menahem Mann ben Salomon, *Sheerit Yisrael (Keter Malkut)*, 22:121-22
Ha-Levi, Samuel Zanwill bar Isaac, 34:60
Halevi, Saul, 22:123
Halevi, Yehudah, 42:297, 299; 43:239
Halevy (missionary), 29:88
Halévy, Daniel, 35:260
Halevy, F., 29:127
Halevy family, 25:70
Halevy, Jehudah, 45:250-51, 255
Haley, John Williams, 38:332
Half-Gods, 40:354
Halfon, Elijah Menahem (Helias), 28:170-71
Halhed, Nathaniel Brassey, *A Calculation on the Commencement of the Millennium*, 30:106; *Testimony of the Authenticity of the Prophecies of Richard Brothers*, 30:106-7, 112
Halifax, "An Early Jewish Merchant of Halifax," 25:xiii; "The Gratz Papers," 23:3-4, 6, 98
Halifax, Lord, 36:95
Halkin, Abraham, 43:196-97
Halkin, Simon, 50:401-2
Hall (Balkan disabilities), 24:96-97
Hall (Oswego), 22:100

Hall, Alfred, 26:147-48
Hall, Aquilla, 34:271
Hall, Benoni, 35:289
Hall, Bolton, 46:486
Hall, Charles, 39:75, 78, 83
Hall, Dr., 42:191
Hall, Edward Hagaman, 25:xvi
Hall, Hubert, 23:95
Hall, Oakley, 42:121
Hall, Prescott, 45:217; 46:127
Hall, Thomas, 48:181-83, 189
Hallam, Lewis, 33:173-74, 183-84
Hallam, Miss, 33:173
Hallam, Mrs. Lewis, 33:173
Hallam, William, 33:173
Hallam and Allen Players, 33:176
Hallam, Hodgkinson & Dunlap, 33:184
Halle, Hiram, 37:268
Halle (store), 38:20
Halleck, General, 29:104
Halleck, H. W., 40:184-86
Haller, General, 36:158
Hallgarten, Adolph, 24:11
Hallgarten, Charles L., 35:135; "Charles L. Hallgarten," 31:vii, xxxii, 187-91
Hallgarten, Elise Mainzer, 31:189-90
Hallgarten, Robert, 31:xxxii
Halliday, S. B., 34:171
Hallo, Rudolph, 35:136
Hallock, Samuel, 27:318
Halper, Benzion, 48:194
Halpern, Ben, *The American Jew: A Zionist Analysis*, reviewed, 47:61-62
Halsbury, Lord, 31:263
Halstead, Christopher, 27:70
Halsted, 25:10
Hamaggid, 33:128; 45:69, 81
Haman, 40:135
Hamberger, B. I., 48:240
Hambroughman, 26:233
Hamburg, Jewish emancipation, 26:35, 37-38, 43-44, 53, 61, 65; Sephardic congregation, 22:xxix
Hamburg-America Line, 45:83
Hamburger Home, 37:296
Hamburger, Isaac, 49:186
Hamburger, Mrs. Merle F., 29:166
Hamburger, Wolf, 23:113
Hamburgo, Daniel de Crasto de, 42:279, 394

Hamburg Temple, 47:123; 50:91
Hameassef, 22:123
Hameassef Be eretz Hachadashah, 33:128
Hamel (Amsterdam), 33:61, 92-93, 97
Hamel, Joseph, 26:117
Hamelin, Augustin, 23:139
Ha-Meliz, 44:151
Hamersley, Andrew, 27:329
Hamersley, Dr., 27:316
Hamevaker, 33:150
Hamilton, Alexander, 25:5; 26:221; 28:xxxiv;
  32:55; 35:253; 44:119; anti-Semitism,
  38:119-20, 130, 136; "Dr. Hamilton Visits
  Shearith Israel, 1774," 39:183-85
Hamilton, Andrew, 23:20; 27:472; 42:77
Hamilton, Captain, 27:304; 28:227
Hamilton, Cosmo, 35:270
Hamilton, James (governor), 23:20
Hamilton, James, 22:35; *The Harp on the
  Willows*, 30:445
Hamilton, James Alexander, 22:87
Hamilton, John C., 22:83
Hamilton, Major, 35:19
Hamilton, Mary Agnes, 50:402
Hamilton, Mr., 22:189
Hamilton, Walter, 23:158
Hamilton, William, 23:20
Hamilton, Canada, religious observances,
  mid-nineteenth century, 37:37
Hamis, Mosseh, 32:58
Hamlin, Hannibal, 25:29; 29:201; 47:81; Civil
  War, 50:289-90, 355
Hamlin, Jabez, 37:108, 110
Hamlin, Talbot F., 46:114
Hammer, Milton, 50:426
Hammerslough, Julius, 50:302
Hammerslough, Mrs. L., 23:145
Hammerstein, Oscar; G. Ricordi and Co. *v.*,
  47:187
Hammet, Charles E., 37:169
Hammett, C. E., Jr., 27:414
Hammond, 39:344
Hammond (actor), 33:179
Hammond, Henry, 37:133
Hammond, Isaac, 27:326
Hammond, James H., 46:271
Hammond, John W., 32:123-24
Hammond, Joseph, Jr., 35:291; 37:167-68
Hammond, States, 27:326

Hamnuna the Elder, 22:103
Hamon, Jonathan, 27:303
Hampton, Wade, 26:180
Hanauer, M., 29:135
Hance, Judge, 29:199
Hancock, Belcher, 30:41
Hancock, John, 23:84; 27:390; 35:143;
  37:115-17, 119; 42:337; 45:59-60
Hancock, John, Sr., 45:59-60
Hancock, Thomas, 38:146
Hand, Learned, 46:435
Handlin, Mary F., 39:234
Handlin, Oscar, 39:234; 40:205, 415; 42:419;
  46:129; 48:245; abolition, 42:137-39;
  *Adventure in Freedom—Three Hundred
  Years of Jewish Life in America*, reviewed,
  44:120-23; "American Views of the Jews at
  the Opening of the Twentieth Century,"
  40:323-44, 405; book review by, 40:191-
  92; executive council, 40:406; 42:414;
  45:264; 48:265; (for.) *Growth and
  Achievement: Temple Israel, 1854-1954*,
  reviewed, 44:250-51; history, writing of,
  46:160, 302, 342, 369, 378; Longfellow
  poetry, 45:32-33; MacIver report, 42:465;
  presides, 50:427; *The Uprooted: The Epic
  Story of the Great Migration that Made the
  American People*, reviewed, 42:207-10
Handy, W. W., 43:74
Hänel, Professor, 36:359
Hanis, W. C., 50:330
Hanna, Mark, 41:321
Hannah Schless Memorial and Jewish
  Institute (Detroit), 37:294, 301
Hanniel, 33:34
Hanover National Bank, 22:238
Hansard, 22:177
Hanseatic towns, "Jewish Rights at the
  Congresses of Vienna (1814-1815), and
  Aix-la-Chapelle (1818)," 26:vii, xv, 33-125
Hansen, Marcus Lee, 46:291, 368-69, 402,
  412; 49:260
Hanson, Thomas, 37:116-17, 119
Hanukkah, 39:367, 374-75; and Christmas,
  39:365-66; 49:163
Hanukkat ha-bayyit, 39:370
Hanway, Judge, 23:69
Hapgood, Hutchins, 43:19, 21-24, 26;
  46:297; 49:106

Hapgood, Norman, 43:12, 19, 25-26; 46:470
Ha-Pisgah, 48:133
Haraszti, Zeltán, 37:189; 45:60
Harburger, Ludwig, 35:xxiii
Harby, Armida, 32:48
Harby, Benjamin, 32:46
Harby, Caroline de Litchfield, 32:39-40, 43, 46
Harby, George Washington, 32:46
Harby, Henry Jefferson, 32:46
Harby, Horace, 32:48
Harby, Isaac, 26:194; 29:139; 32:3, 36, 46; 34:191; 39:229; 40:399; 42:53; 50:193; *Alberti*, 30:179, 182-83; 32:41; "Alexander Severus," 32:41; "Biography of Isaac Harby," 33:xxx; *The Gordian Knot*, 30:129; 32:41; "Harby's Discourse on the Jewish Synagogue," 32:49-53; history, writing of, 46:273, 442; "Isaac Harby, Jewish Religious Leader and Man of Letters," 29:xv; 32:35-53; Reform Judaism, 47:123; *Selection from Miscellaneous Writings*, 30:255-56
Harby, Israel, 32:46
Harby, Julian, 32:48
Harby, Mrs. Lee C., 32:40
Harby, Levi Charles, 39:52
Harby, Levi Myers, 26:194; 32:46; 39:7
Harby, Maria, 32:46
Harby, Marx E., 32:35
Harby, Octavia, 32:48
Harby, Rachael, 32:46-48
Harby, Rebecca, 32:51
Harby, S., 40:127
Harby, Samuel Da Costa, 32:46-47
Harby, Solomon, 32:36, 38, 46-47; 50:42, 49; will of, 32:51-52; 34:191
Hardee, Charles S., 31:6
Hardee, William J., 48:153
Hardee, William Joseph, 50:342
Hardegg, Ernest, 36:53, 55
Harden, Maximilian, 31:291
Hardenberg, C. F. (prince), 26:36-39, 41-46, 51-53, 60, 62, 64-65, 67-69, 75-76, 79, 82, 88, 91-92, 95-96, 101-2, 268; 28:106-8
Hardenberg, Count, 26:39-40
Hardenbrook, 25:56
Hardenbrook, Adolph, 33:252

Hardie, James, "An Account of the Malignant Fever Prevalent in the City of New York," 25:123
Hardie, William, 23:139
Hardin, John R., 37:455
Hardinbrook, Abraham, 27:246
Hardinbrook, Wm., 21:165
Harding, Warren G., 29:xix, xx; 36:84; 45:38-39, 46
Hardwicke, Lord Chancellor, 31:109, 112, 125, 133
Hardy, Thomas, 34:236
Hare, Bishop, *An Hebrew Grammar*, 30:54-55
Hare, Francisci, 30:138-39
Har Elohim, Shreveport, La., 29:134
Hargrave, Robert, 27:71
Haring, 32:xxv
Haris, Juleon, 29:132
Harjes, Hope, 28:57
Harjes, John, 28:57
Harkavy, Alexander, 33:129; 35:55; gifts, 33:xxxiii; 34:xx; Memorial of Bella Harkavy, gift, 33:xxix, xxxii-xxxiii
Harkavy, Bella, 34:xx; gift, 33:xxix, xxxii-xxxiii
Harlan, James S., 41:49-50
Harlem Federation for Jewish Communal Week (New York), 37:295
Harley, Robert, 34:285
Harman, Avraham, 50:435
Harmon, John, 42:309
Harmonic Club, 32:xxvi
Harmony Circle (Baltimore), 25:155
Harmony Club (New York), 22:228; 31:189; 49:76; (Rochester), 40:64, 66
Harmony Hall, 33:177
Harmony Lodge No. 142, 47:46
Har Moriah Hospital, 49:86
Haro, Jehoshuah Jessurun de, 42:253, 280-81, 388, 394
Harper, Joseph B., 33:184
Harper, Lathrop C., 30:vii
Harper, Mr., 27:392
Harper, William Rainey, 46:435
Harper's, 40:413
Harpers Ferry Armory, 48:150
Harper's Weekly, 29:125; 50:343, 385
Harrington, Fred H., 50:378
Harrington, Fred Harvey, 43:72

Harrington, Isaac, *Relics of Ancient Judaism*, 30:322-23
Harrington, James, 35:215-16; 37:186-87
Harrington, Rev., 22:24
Harrington, Richard B., 50:271
Harris, Abraham, 29:129
Harris, Alexander, 27:51, 59-60, 62-64
Harris, Ben E., 38:73
Harris, Daniel Van, 41:211
Harris, E. Knight, 31:259
Harris, Florence Nightingale Knight, necrology of, 31:xxiv, 258-60
Harris, George, 27:246
Harris, George W., 28:31
Harris, H., 29:132
Harris, Isham C., 50:342
Harris, Jacob, 29:132
Harris, Jed, 35:273
Harris, Judith, 26:251
Harris, Leopold, 47:46
Harris, M., 29:133
Harris, M. H., 31:257
Harris, Mr., 33:194
Harris, Maurice H., 29:169
Harris, Moses, 25:113
Harris, Philip, 27:246
Harris, Robert, 23:174
Harris, S. Marcus, 31:259
Harris, Samuel, "Samuel Harris on the Dighton Rock Inscription," 28:xxii
Harris, Samuel J., 34:184
Harris, Thaddeus Mason, 38:146; *Natural History of the Bible*, 30:96-97; *Sephora*, 30:304
Harris, Thomas Lake, "Swedenborgian Background of Thomas Lake Harris's Anti-Semitism," 41:389
Harris, William, *Elements of the Chaldee Language*, 30:212
Harrisburg, Pa., religious observances, mid-nineteenth century, 37:36
Harrison, 28:6
Harrison, Benjamin, 25:112; 26:190; 33:21; 36:42, 225; 38:312; 40:7; Roumanian problem, 24:85, 112-13; Russian disabilities, 40:234; 41:171; 47:158; Russian passports, 46:89; Zionism, 40:363
Harrison, Bernard, 42:420
Harrison, E., 32:30

Harrison, Earl, 39:228
Harrison, Edword, 26:258
Harrison family, 50:244
Harrison, Francis, 41:112-13, 118-19
Harrison, Francis Burton, 40:302
Harrison, Gabriel, 33:194
Harrison, George, 45:134
Harrison, Peter, 27:178, 404; 28:299; 38:332
Harrison, R. M., 27:343
Harrison, William Henry, 23:12; 26:190, 234; 45:56; *Commemoration of Life and Death of William Henry Harrison*, 30:355, 357; death, 21:221; 27:149
Harrisson, Francis, 21:17
Harry, Isaac, 27:278
Har Sinai Booster, 50:382
Har Sinai Congregation (Baltimore), 22:214; 25:155; 26:248; 37:473; 39:464; 40:294; 42:376; 45:120; 49:21; Board of Delegates of American Israelites, 29:79
Har Sinai Lodge, B'nai B'rith, 50:382
Hart, 34:170, "History of the Jews of Canada," 31:xxxiv
Hart, Aaron (Canada), 27:490; 28:xxxviii; 38:86; 43:131; 50:124-26
Hart, Aaron (New York), 23:137, 155
Hart, Aaron Ezekiel, 50:126
Hart, Aaron Philip, 27:76, 493; 30:297
Hart, Abby, 37:217
Hart, Abraham (Newport), 27:246, 450; 37:165, 392, 475; 40:75
Hart, Abraham (New York), 27:277, 397; 21:45, 53, 55
Hart, Abraham (Philadelphia) (1), 27:372; 29:112; 32:3; 37:83; 41:87-88; 42:404; 48:208, 214, 220-21, 226, 237, 239; 49:30; 50:70; "Early Jewish Publishers in America, with Special Reference to Abraham Hart," 31:xvii; "The Lincoln-Hart Correspondence," 38:139-45; "Thomas Carlyle and His American Publisher, Abraham Hart," 26:xxxi
Hart, Abraham (Philadelphia) (2), 41:88
Hart, Abraham Kitzinger, 27:77
Hart, Abram, 28:xxxiv
Hart, Adolphus Mordecai, "Adolphus Mordecai Hart, of Quebec," 25:xiii, 121-22
Hart, Adolphus P., 27:78

Hart, Albert, 37:442
Hart, Alex, 27:79
Hart, Aron, "Further Data on the Hart
Family of Three Rivers, Quebec," 26:xv;
"Two Letters of Aron Hart of Three
Rivers, 1775 and 1776," 26:257-58
Hart, Aron Ezekiel, 26:257; 34:xx; "An
Unpublished Letter of Aron Ezekiel Hart,"
26:xv, 256-57
Hart, Arthur Wellington, 27:490-93;
"Unpublished Correspondence between
Arthur Wellington Hart and Lord John
Russell relating to the Appointment to
Office of the Former's Father, Benjamin
Hart," 26:xxxi
Hart, Asher, 27:491
Hart, B. (Boston), 29:129
Hart, B. (New York), 27:60-61
Hart, Barnet, 27:41
Hart, Barshaba, 23:81
Hart, Bayla, 23:155
Hart, Becky, 37:210
Hart, Benjamin (b. Aaron), 27:51, 74, 76-77,
79, 490-93, 517
Hart, Benjamin (Canada), 28:xxxviii; 30:297;
"Unpublished Canadian State Papers
Relating to Benjamin Hart," 23:vii, 137-
40; "Unpublished References in the
Canadian State Papers to Benjamin and
Samuel B. Hart," 23:xiv; "Unpublished
Correspondence between Arthur
Wellington Hart and Lord John Russell
relating to the Appointment to Office of
the Former's Father, Benjamin Hart,"
26:xxxi
Hart, Benjamin (New York), 32:111
Hart, Benjamin (b. Bernard), 27:164
Hart, Benjamin F., 22:94-96
Hart, Benjamin J., 29:112; 49:30
Hart, Benjamin S., 21:215; 27:119
Hart, Bernard, 21:162, 167, 169, 212; 25:36,
57; 26:178; 27:51, 66-67, 75, 77, 86-87, 89,
96, 109-10, 163-64, 172, 242, 314, 377,
394; 32:xxv; 34:252; "Bret Harte and His
Jewish Ancestor, Bernard Hart," 32:99-111
Hart, Catherine, 27:75
Hart, Charles John, 27:105
Hart, Charlotte, 50:126
Hart, Chava (Catherine), 50:126

Hart, Constance, 27:490
Hart, D., 27:483
Hart, Daniel (b. Bernard), 27:164; 32:111
Hart, Daniel (Newport), 40:76
Hart, Daniel (Georgetown), 50:42, 49
Hart, David (1), 21:49, 51, 53, 61, 64, 167,
169-70, 191-92, 214-15; 27:55, 106-8, 314
Hart, David (2), 23:152
Hart, David (b. Benjamin), 32:111
Hart, David (b. Bernard), 27:164, 400; 34:126
Hart, E., 27:51, 58, 61-62
Hart, E. B., 27:515
Hart, E. J. & Co., 50:169
Hart, Elias, 27:41, 185, 253
Hart, Elizabeth, 25:115
Hart, Emanuel B., 21:215; 26:178; 27:394,
503; 29:xxxix; 32:101, 110-11; Isachar
Zacharie, 43:94, 99; Mt. Sinai Hospital,
42:121
Hart, Eme M., 27:114
Hart, Ephraim (New York), 21:xvi, 163, 166-
67, 169, 212; 27:42-43, 51, 54, 57, 66, 68,
75, 83, 86-88, 274, 278, 397, 490-91;
30:124; 32:102; 50:37, 49; kosher meat,
25:47-48, 51-52, 123
Hart, Ephraim (Philadelphia), 34:114
Hart, Esther, 38:89
Hart, Esther (Mrs. Levy), 27:111
Hart, Esther Eudora, 27:276
Hart, Ezekiel, 23:138, 140; 26:257; 27:76-77,
79, 482; 28:xxxviii; 50:130; "Proceedings
Relating to the Expulsion of Ezekiel Hart
from the House of Assembly of Lower
Canada," 23:xiv, 43-53; "Some
Observations on the Life of Ezekiel Hart
(1770-1843)," 37:xxxv; "An Unpublished
Document in the Case of Thomas Coffin
Against Ezekiel Hart, of Three Rivers,
Province of Quebec," 28:xvi
Hart family, 49:6; (Canada), 27:490-93;
34:xviii; (Easton, Pa.), 42:194; (Newport),
27:212, 455; loyalist claims, 38:83, 86-91
Hart (family name), 37:381-82, 386; 38:236
Hart, Frances (b. Benjamin), 27:493
Hart, Frances (Mrs. Ezekiel), 27:76, 112
Hart, Gerald Ephraim, 32:102
Hart, Grace, 27:348
Hart, Grace Rosa, 27:110, 164
Hart, H., *Jewish Creed*, 30:423

Hart, Hanah, 27:111
Hart, Mrs. Harmon, 32:101
Hart, Harriot Judith, 27:74, 490, 493-94
Hart, Henrietta, 42:59
Hart, Henry (1), 27:164
Hart, Henry (2), 27:277
Hart, Henry (b. Bernard), 32:101, 104-7, 111
Hart, Henry I., 29:85, 112; 49:20, 30; 50:291
Hart, Henry Isaac, 26:264
Hart, Hetty, 27:78
Hart, Hyam, 23:155
Hart, Hymon, 50:41, 50
Hart, Ira James Craig, 27:76
Hart, Isaac (b. Naphtaly), 26:264
Hart, Isaac (Newport), 23:165-67; 34:55;
    37:165, 169; 38:86-88, 91; 46:21
Hart, Isaac (New York), 21:49; 48:11, 18
Hart, J., 35:200
Hart, Jacob (b. Abraham), 26:264
Hart, Jacob (Baltimore), 22:193
Hart, Jacob (Newport), 27:213; 38:87-90
Hart, Jacob (New York) (1), 21:23, 27-29, 31,
    33, 51, 53, 63; 27:51, 54, 57-58, 61-62, 66-
    67, 69-70, 78, 83, 86, 242, 246, 253, 310;
    50:37, 50
Hart, Jacob (New York) (2), 27:55, 83
Hart, Jacob, Sr. (New York) (3), 21:162-64,
    167, 169, 212; 25:48, 51-52; 30:124;
    portrait, 41:277, 280, 287-88, 293; 42:416;
    43:232
Hart, Jacob (Philadelphia), 27:461, 469
Hart, Mrs. Jacob, Sr., 41:288; portrait of,
    42:416; 43:232
Hart, Jacob de (Philadelphia), 23:175
Hart, Capt. Jacob de, 27:246
Hart, Jacob Henry, 26:264
Hart, Joel, 21:161-63; 22:162; 25:52; 27:55,
    114, 314, 491
Hart, John, 27:313, 315
Hart, John I., 21:167; 27:109, 311, 399;
    42:115
Hart, Joseph (Barbados), 26:251, 254
Hart, Joseph (New York), 25:52; 27:315
Hart, Mrs. Joseph, 27:111
Hart, Joseph M., 27:450
Hart, Joshua, 27:162, 388
Hart, Judah, 27:63, 79, 122
Hart, Leah (Mrs. Jacob), 27:112
Hart, Leah (Nathan), 41:288, 293

Hart, Leon, 21:215; 27:91
Hart, Lion (Lyon), 21:142, 145, 148; 27:42,
    253, 314; 38:49; 50:63
Hart, Louisa B., 42:403, 405
Hart, M. de, 27:79
Hart, M. M. de, Jr., 27:144
Hart, Manuel, 27:164
Hart, Maria (nee Gomez), 27:449
Hart, Mathyas, 34:271
Hart, Menahem, 32:102
Hart, Meyer, 34:98-99; 35:286
Hart, Michael (Easton, Pa.), 37:32; 38:15;
    42:193-94; 50:39, 50
Hart, Michael (New York), 27:42, 462
Hart, Miriam, 23:150; 25:78; 34:61
Hart, Mitchel, 27:259
Hart, Mr., 27:105
Hart, Moses (Canada), 27:79
Hart, Moses (England), 31:36, 41, 55
Hart, Moses (R.I.), 23:97, 166; 27:448; 38:89-
    90
Hart, Moses (New York) (1), 21:8, 10, 27-28,
    34, 38, 45, 105; 23:150; 25:78; 34:61
Hart, Moses (New York) (2), 27:55, 83
Hart, Moses (3), *Modern Religion*, 30:179-80;
    34:xvi; "Moses Hart's 'Modern Religion,' "
    38:342
Hart, Moshe, 37:166
Hart, Myer (Easton, Pa.), 42:194; 43:235;
    50:29, 39, 50
Hart, Myer (New York), 27:348; 44:63
Hart, Myer (Philadelphia), 26:233
Hart, Nap, Jr., 27:154
Hart, Napthalai (b. Aaron), 23:155
Hart, Napthali (Newport), 23:165; 27:181-
    83, 350; 37:165-66, 169; 49:236
Hart, Naphtaly (New York), 21:45, 53, 55,
    64, 79
Hart, Naphtaly and Company, 37:163-69
Hart, Naphtaly and Samuel, 27:346
Hart, Nathan (Charleston), 27:519
Hart, Nathan (Newport) (1), 27:154
Hart, Nathan (Newport) (2), 27:348
Hart, Nathan (New York), 27:79
Hart, Nathan (grandson, Aaron L. Gomez),
    27:448
Hart, Nathan (artist), 41:283-84, 288
Hart, Nathan (S.C.), 48:180; 50:42, 164;
    portrait of, 42:416

Hart, Nathan, *Private and Religious Character of Nathan Hart*, 30:347, 349
Hart, Nathaniel (colonel), 23:22
Hart, Nathaniel (Newport), 27:212
Hart, Philip, 27:221; 50:41, 50, 159, 161
Hart, Phoebe Rosa, 27:164
Hart, Rachel (b. Aaron), 23:155
Hart, Rachel (Easton), 35:286
Hart, Raphael, 27:313
Hart, Reba. Bernd., 27:79
Hart, Rebecca (nee Seixas), 27:55, 75, 111, 163-64
Hart, Reinah, 27:110
Hart, Richea, 27:161-62
Hart, S., 27:62
Hart, S., Jr., 27:51, 62
Hart, Samuel (b. Aaron), 23:155
Hart, Samuel (B.W.I.), 25:115
Hart, Samuel (Canada), "Newspaper Comments on the Samuel Hart Case," 25:xiii
Hart, Samuel (Charleston), 29:129
Hart, Samuel (New York) (1), 21:42, 46, 49, 51, 53, 62, 64, 70, 84, 86-87, 93-94, 99, 109, 167, 211; 27:20, 183-84
Hart, Samuel (New York) (2), 27:276
Hart, Samuel (Philadelphia), 22:89-94
Hart, Samuel (R.I.), 23:166
Hart, Samuel (b. Bernard), 27:164
Hart, Samuel (b. Ephraim), 27:274
Hart, Samuel (b. Ezekiel), 27:79
Hart, Samuel (Newport), 27:448; 37:165-66, 169; 38:88
Hart, Samuel, Jr. (B.W.I.), 25:115
Hart, Samuel, Jr. (R.I.), 23:166; 27:448; 38:88
Hart, Samuel, Jr. (New York), 27:51
Hart, Samuel B., 23:140; 30:297; "Unpublished References in the Canadian State Papers to Benjamin and Samuel B. Hart," 23:xiv
Hart, Sarah, 32:62
Hart, Scheina, 50:126
Hart, Seymour, 22:197
Hart, Simon, 50:41
Hart, Solomon (B.W.I.), 32:62
Hart, Solomon (New York) (1), 21:43-47, 51, 213; 31:237
Hart, Solomon (New York) (2), 27:79
Hart, Solomon, Jr., 37:373; 38:235

Hart, Solomon, Sr. (New York), 27:114
Hart, Solomon (R.I.), 37:392
Hart, Theodore (New York), 21:171; 32:111
Hart, Theodore (b. Benjamin), 27:490
Hart, Theodore (b. Bernard), 27:110, 164
Hart, Treinlah, 50:126
Hart, W. C., 23:x; gifts, 23:xviii; 25:xv
Hart, Zipporah (1), 27:110, 164
Hart, Zipporah (2), 31:36, 55
Harte, Bret, 34:252, "Bret Harte and His Jewish Ancestor, Bernard Hart," 32:99-111
Harte, Francis Bret, 26:178; 35:244-45
Harte, W. M., 26:254
Hartford, Conn., religious observances, mid-nineteenth century, 37:36
Hartford Convention, 26:184
Hartford Times, 37:429
Harth & DeCosta, 50:41
Harth, Philip, 50:41
Hartheimer, Lazarus, 41:256
Hartman, 29:128
Hartman, Adriaen, 33:108
Hartman, Capt. J. B., 39:179
Hartmann, Moritz, 38:187, 192, 196
Hartog, Mrs., 30:411
Hartog, P. J., 47:174
Hartogensis, A. E., 38:73
Hartogensis, Benjamin H., 31:219, 226; 37:440; 39:265, 413, 438; 44:208; "Captain John Smith's Reference to a Jew," 32:xiii; "The Earliest Jewish Settler in Maryland," 31:xvii; "An Estimate of Baltimore's Jewish Population," 29:xxix; "Four Early Jewish Cemeteries at Baltimore," 32:xiii; gifts, 25:xvi; 29:xxxix; 32:xxviii; 33:xxxiii; 34:xxvi; necrology of, 37:xii, 469-70; "Notes on Early Jewish Settlers of Baltimore," 22:191-95; "The Price the Jew Dr. Lumbrozo Paid for Maryland's So-Called Toleration," 31:xxx; "The Refusal of a Charter to the Baltimore Hebrew Congregation by the Legislature of Maryland," 32:xiii; "The Russian Night School of Baltimore," 31:vii, xvii, 225-28; "The Sephardic Congregation of Baltimore," 23:vii, xiv, 141-46; "Unequal Religious Rights in Maryland since 1776," 22:xxviii; 25:vii, 93-107
Hartogensis, Frances, 37:470

Hartogensis, Grace, 37:470
Hartogensis, Henry S., 23:146; 37:470
Hart Schaffner & Marx, 38:19; 41:309, 321, 324, 326; 46:231
Hartstein, Jacob I., 33:xxvi; gifts, 34:xxiii; 35:xxiii; "Jewish Parochial Education in New York City," 34:xiv; "The Polonies Talmud Torah of New York," 34:123-41
Hartz, Wilson Tweed, 42:412
Harvard Advocate, 22:228
Harvard, Anne, 35:148
Harvard Business School, 46:210
Harvard Club (Boston), 42:420; 43:22
Harvard College, 23:81; 42:344; 46:180; *Answer to Testimony Against Rev. George Whitefield*, 30:41-42; "Hebrew at Harvard (1636-1760)," 35:xv, 145-70; Julian Mack, 37:476; *Testimony Against Rev. George Whitefield*, 30:38-41
Harvard College Library, 28:243-44; 30:vi; 45:135-38
Harvard Divinity School Library, 45:134-35
Harvard Guide to American History, 49:255
Harvard, John, 35:148; 45:135
Harvard Law Review, 47:212
Harvard Semitic Museum, 28:303
Harvard Theological Review, 47:219
Harvard University, 22:207-9, 238; 25:7, 185; 26:234; 33:30; 34:154; 35:324; 42:336; 44:121, 240; 45:185; 46:211; 49:11; "A Contemporary Appraisal of Judah Monis, Harvard's First Instructor in Hebrew," 38:146-47; discrimination, 34:225; 47:16, 21-22; Hebrew grammar, 38:147-48; "Hebrew and Jews at Harvard," 46:493; Judah Monis, 37:121-25, 442; "Judah Monis, First Instructor in Hebrew at Harvard University," 22:1-24; "Judaica and Hebraica Collection in College Libraries," 45:134-38; Puritanism, 47:147-49; Semitic Department Library, 45:135
Harvard University Press, 35:166
Harvard Yiddish Book Fund Committee, 45:137
Harvey, Gen., 44:56
Harvey, George, 36:81
Harvey, William (1), 40:333
Harvey, William (2), 43:111
Harwell, Richard, 50:271

Harwood, John E., 33:183, 188, 190
Haryon, 22:183
Har Zion Congregation (Baltimore), 45:120; 50:285
Hasadim, Hebra Gemiluth, 42:433
Ha-Sanegor, 48:133
Hašek, Jaroslav, 50:117
Hashiloah, 40:43
Hashmal, Akiba, 45:72-73
Haskalah Literature, "America in Haskalah Literature," 25:xiv
Haskins, Richard O., 27:506
Haskins, William D., 27:506
Haskol, John, 35:182
Hasidism, 43:195; 44:131; "Hasidism, a Revolt of the Masses," 32:xiii
Hassler family, 48:241
Hassler, Isaac, 37:307; necrology of Lewis W. Steinbach, 22:xxviii, 230-35
Hastings, George H., *Illustrations of the Original Use of the Sacred Lyrics*, 30:372, 374
Hastreiter, Helene, 28:24, 26
Hatch, Jabez, 40:77
Hatch, Ozias M., 44:104
Hatchard, Thomas Goodwin, 26:148
Ha-Tekufah, 50:402
Hateret Bahurim u-Malbish Harumim, 44:221
Hatfield, Henry D., 36:368
Hatfield, James T., 45:25
Hathaway, Calvin S., 50:272
Hathaway, H. K., 41:45-46, 48
Hatton, Fanny, 40:357
Hatton, Frederic, 40:357
Hatvany, A., 34:242
Hauff, Wilhelm, 35:120
Haupt, Paul, 33:20-22; "Paul Haupt and the Mesopotamian Project, 1892-1914," 47:154-75; "Paul Haupt's Plan for Settling Russian Jews in Mesopotamia," 44:242
Hauptmann, 43:27
Hauréau, 41:162
Hauschildt, 26:75
Hauser, Hayum, 41:263
Havemeyer, Mayor, 32:97
Haven, 31:152-53
Haverlin, Carl, 50:271
Haviland, John, 41:71

Hawaii, "Henry Obookiah: The First
    Hawaiian Student of Hebrew," 39:190-92
Hawes, Joel, 30:288
Hawkes, James, 36:11-15
Hawkes, Jo, 28:249
Hawkins, Anthony Hope, 35:253-54
Hawkins, Benjamin, 29:145; 34:267
Hawkins, Commodore, 46:103
Hawkins, John, 31:10, 107
Hawthorne, Nathaniel, 34:236; 35:243-44;
    38:282; 39:126; 42:341; 45:20; 46:193
Hay, 35:182
Hay, Colonel, 25:142
Hay, Edward, 31:243
Hay, John, 29:77, 187, 203; 32:xxvi; 33:26-27;
    34:280; 45:250; 46:92, 434; Balkans, 36:62-
    63; "The Hebrew Correspondence
    Between the Reverend Marcus Hillel
    Dubov and Secretary of State John Hay,"
    38:53-56, 342; "Hon. Oscar S. Straus'
    Memoranda Preceding Dispatch of the
    Hay Roumanian Note," 24:108-14; 40:8;
    "Israel," 33:27; Roumanian disabilities,
    24:2, 111, 133-36; 36:x, 119-28; 37:11,
    49:107; Russian disabilities, 36:187, 262,
    264-73, 278; 41:174-75, 178; "Secretary
    Hay's Roumanian Note of 1902 and the
    Peace Conference of Bucharest of 1913,"
    24:80-97
Haydn, Joseph, 39:326
Haydock, Miss, 29:55
Haydon, B. W., 34:267
Hayes, Benjamin, 50:38, 50
Hayes, David, 50:38, 50
Hayes, Hetty, 23:157
Hayes, John, 22:193
Hayes, Rutherford B., 47:81; 50:400; Library,
    50:273, 275, 400; Simon Wolf papers,
    29:xli
Hay(e)s, Sally, 33:205
Hayes, William (Baltimore) (1), 22:193
Hayes, William (Baltimore) (2), 22:193
Hayes, William, Jr., 22:193
Haym, Rudolph, 26:98
Hayman, Moses, 21:53, 55
Haymans, Haym, 27:79
Haymarket Theatre, Boston, 33:183-84, 191
Haymerle, Baron von, 24:121; 36:118
Hayne, Isaac W., 50:317

Haynes & Co., J. C., 50:389
Haynes, Richard, 22:180
Hayom, 33:128
Hays, Abigail, 27:242, 323, 329
Hays, Abraham, 21:27-29, 31, 33-35
Hays, Andrew, 21:94, 104; 27:42; 45:56
Hays, Asher (b. David, Jr.), 27:330
Hays, Asher (b. Isaac), 27:151
Hays, Barah, 27:42
Hays, Barrak, 21:104; 27:349; 43:231;
    bookplate, 45:176, 185-86; 50:26; "Barrak
    Hays: Controversial Loyalist," 45:54-57
Hays, Ben, 27:79
Hays, Benjamin (1), 50:50
Hays, Benjamin (2), 26:181
Hays, Benjamin Etting, 26:250; 27:77, 318,
    321, 323-30; 29:167
Hays, Bertha, 29:158
Hays, Betty Adolphus, 38:339
Hays, Catherine, 27:110, 190, 194
Hays, Charity, 38:339
Hays, Daniel Peixotto, 26:xxi-xxii; 31:257;
    32:130; 37:234, 239, 241, 252-55, 257;
    "Daniel L. M. Peixotto, M.D.," 26:xiv,
    219-29; necrology of, 29:xxxvi, 167-69
Hays, David, 21:6, 10, 16, 20, 23, 27-29, 31,
    40, 44, 48, 51, 53, 60-61, 63, 65, 81, 211;
    23:151; 26:230, 250; 29:167-68; 33:200,
    205-6, 208; 34:122; 37:372-73, 377;
    38:235; 43:253; 50:28, 50
Hays, David (br. Benjamin), 27:42, 77, 83,
    155, 246, 318, 320-28
Hays, David (b. Jacob), 29:167
Hays, David, Jr., 21:51; 27:318, 329-30, 383;
    33:205; 38:339
Hays, Edwin Daniel, 29:169
Hays, Esther Etting, 38:339
Hays family, 27:xviii, 318-30; 43:204-5;
    45:54-57, 187; records, 22:xxiv, xxxiv
Hays (family name), 37:382
Hays, Frances, 28:276
Hays, Gittah, 27:56
Hays, Grace, 33:200
Hays, Hannah, 33:205
Hays, Hetty, 21:123-24, 219
Hays, Hetty (nee Etting), 27:328, 330
Hays, I. Minis, 23:185
Hays, Isaac (New York), 21:48, 51, 53, 55, 63,
    80; 27:151; 37:372-73, 377; 38:235; 42:398

Hays, Isaac (Pa.), 26:226; 44:254
Hays, Jacob (b. Barak), 27:349
Hays, Jacob (Constable), 29:167; 32:xxvi
Hays, Jacob (b. David), 27:155, 321, 323,
329-30, 398; 50:50
Hays, Jacob (b. Michael), 27:154, 243
Hays, Jacob (New York), 21:5-8, 10, 16, 19,
27-29, 34-35, 39-40, 42, 61-64; 25:123;
38:339; 44:63; 45:54
Hays, Jacob (Philadelphia), 35:286
Hays, Jacob (War of 1812), 26:181
Hays, Jane, 45:54
Hays, John, 47:190
Hays, John Jacob, 45:54-56
Hays, Joseph L., 27:91, 258, 314
Hays, Josse, 21:81, 83; 33:201
Hays, Judah (Boston), 23:86; 27:195; 28:xli;
43:204-5; 46:420; "Moses Michael Hays'
Letter to His Son Judah," 38:150-51;
"Receipt Book of Judah and Moses M.
Hays, Commencing January 12, 1763, and
Ending July 18, 1776," 28:xxii, 223-29;
"Receipt Book of Judah Hays," 34:xiv, 117-
22
Hays, Judah (br. David), 33:200-201, 206
Hays, Judah (New York), 21:6, 10, 16, 22, 27-
29, 31, 38, 42, 47, 49, 51, 53, 56, 60-61, 63,
71, 81, 83-84, 87, 167, 182, 211; 27:253,
384-85, 417; 34:xxii; 35:186-88; 37:372-73,
377; 38:235
Hays, Judah (Norfolk), 40:127
Hays, Mrs. Judah, 34:120
Hays, Judith, 31:239; "The Judith Hays-
Samuel Myers Marriage Contract,"
38:149-50
Hays, Judith Salzedo (Peixotto), 29:167
Hays, Kaufman, 29:158
Hays, Lazarus, 29:146
Hays, M., 21:94, 99, 101-3
Hays, M. J., 30:297
Hays, M. S., 27:46
Hays, Michael, 21:51, 149; 27:32, 154-55,
242, 318-22, 328; 33:205; 34:122; 38:339;
45:57; 50:37, 50
Hays, Michael S., 21:113, 143, 213; 27:253
Hays, Moses Judah, 50:132
Hays, Moses Michael (Boston), 23:86-90,
170; 25:113; 27:68, 185, 194-96, 214, 416;
31:273; 34:117-19, 122, 176; 35:133, 141,

288-92; 38:149; 42:337, 418; 43:132, 202-
5; Masonry, 28:298-99; "Moses M. Hays
and the Introduction of 'Sublime Masonry'
in the United Colonies," 23:xiv; *Moses
Michael Hays*, 35:xxii; "Moses Michael
Hays' Letter to His Son Judah," 38:150-
51; "Receipt Book of Judah and Moses M.
Hays, Commencing January 12, 1763, and
Ending July 18, 1776," 28:xxii, 223-29;
Revolutionary War, 28:252-54
Hays, Moses Michael (Newport), 38:63;
"Colonial Merchants: Moses Hayes and
Michael Gratz and Their Newport
Ventures," 46:493; loyalty oath, 46:38, 270
Hays, Moses M. (New York), 21:79, 94, 99,
101-3, 211; 27:240, 323, 329, 330, 383;
28:xli; 50:26, 28, 36, 50, 62
Hays, Moses (Rochester), 50:89
Hays, Rachel (1), 27:67, 83, 112, 242
Hays, Rachel (2), 27:277
Hays, Rachel (Mrs. Barak), 27:349
Hays, Rachel (b. David Jr.), 33:205
Hays, Rachel (b. Judah), 34:121-22
Hays, Rachel (Mrs. Moses Michael), 27:194-
95; 42:418
Hays, Rachel (Newport), 50:26
Hays, Rachel, *see*: Myers, Rachel (nee Hays)
Hays, Rebecca, 28:229
Hays, Rebecca (Mrs. Judah), 33:201; 34:120,
122
Hays, Rebecca (Mrs. Moses), 43:203
Hays, Rebecca Ann, 27:113
Hays, Rebekah, 27:196
Hays, Philip, 25:112
Hays, Sally Minis, 29:55
Hays, Samuel (New York), 27:173, 253, 378
Hays, Samuel (Philadelphia), 30:136, 249;
42:398; 50:39, 51
Hays, Sarah, 29:146
Hays, Simon, 50:95
Hays, Slowey, 27:194; 48:74
Hays, Solomon (New York), 21:6, 38-39, 41-
44, 48-49, 53, 55, 63, 104, 182; 27:246;
45:54, 56, 185-86
Hays, Solomon (N.C.), 29:146
Hays, Solomon M., 27:83, 155
Hays, Widow, 21:70, 72, 116
Hays, William Henry, 29:167
Hays, Yitlah, 27:330

Hayton, Ames, 37:348
Hayward, Gideon, 22:24
Hayyim, Samuel, 35:305
Hazanim, "A Revised List of the Hazanim in New York City in the Eighteenth Century," 25:xiii
Hazard, Dr., 27:442
Hazard, Nathaniel, 27:246
Hazard, Samuel, 27:246
Ha-Zefirah, 44:149, 152, 155
Hazelhurst, Isaac, 37:348-49
Hazelton, Pa., United Jewish Appeal, contribution, 37:xxviii
Ha-Zofeh, 43:198; 44:125; 48:194
Ha-Zofeh ba-Arez ha-Hadashah, 45:71-72, 74
Hazofeh Be etetz Hachadashah, 33:128
Healy, George Peter Alexander, 50:240, 245
Heaps, Porter W., 50:391
Heaps, Willard A., 50:391
Heard, William Allen, 26:117
Heariquez, Lopez, 37:413-14, 416-17
Hearn, Lafcadio, Chinese legends, 35:xxii
Hearst, William R., 41:182, 184; 50:205
Heartman, Charles F., 30:vii; 33:186; 50:186, 287
Heath, William, 28:250; 40:77-80
Heathcote, Gilbert, 28:256
Heber, Israel, 27:515
Heberle, Rudolf, 46:356
Hebra (Burial Society), Curaçao, 26:240-41
Hebra Dorshe Tov Leaman, 35:54
Hebra Gemilut Hasadim Congregation Shearith Israel, 27:252-55, 499; 44:212
Hebra Hased Va Amet, 27:113, 124, 255, 499; 38:52; 44:212
Hebra Hased Va-emet Congregation Shearith Israel, 27:96
Hebra Hinuch Nearim, "The Constitution and by-laws of the Hebra Hinuch Nearim, New York, 1825," 35:xv
Hebra Hovevai Zion, 35:55-56
Hebraeus, Lazarus, 28:190
Hebraeus, Leo (Judah Abravanel), 28:204
Hebrah, Constitution and By-Laws, 30:222-23, 233
Hebrah Bikur Houlam, Constitution and By-Laws, 30:255
Hebraica, 33:20; "Judaica and Hebraica Collections in College Libraries," 45:134-48

Hebraic Union Catalog, 47:184
Hebraism, 42:10-12, 14
Hebra Kadisha Anshe Kalvarie Congregation (New York), 44:136
Hebra-kahal, 39:275-79, 281
Hebra Ziona, 35:63
Hebrat Talmud Torah, 44:215
Hebrat Zion (Baltimore), 49:163
Hebrew, "Hebrew at Harvard (1636-1760)," 35:xv, 145-70; "Hebrew-Speaking Indians," 39:185-89; "Henry Obookiah: The First Hawaiian Student of Hebrew," 39:190-92; "A New York Election Circular in Hebrew of 1867," 34:285-88; "The Status of Hebrew in American Higher Education," 38:346; study of, 40:10-11, 407; teaching of, 40:314-15
Hebrew, The, 26:272
Hebrew Aid Society, 48:84
Hebrew Americana, "Resources on American Jewish History at the Library of Congress," 47:179-85, 201
Hebrew American Typographical Union, gifts, 34:xxvi; 35:xxiii
Hebrew Benevolent Association, 50:302; New Orleans, 26:275
Hebrew Benevolent Congregation (Atlanta, Ga.), 41:369
Hebrew Benevolent Loan Association (Buffalo), 46:163
Hebrew Benevolent and Orphan Society (New York), 37:229, 233
Hebrew Benevolent Society (Albany), 35:322; (Baltimore), 22:214, 217; (Columbia, S.C.), 50:170; (Knoxville), 38:32; (Memphis), 49:239; (Montreal), 40:260; (New Orleans), 49:222; (New York), 42:115; (Philadelphia), 47:188; (Pittsburgh), 28:257; (Rochester), 40:61; (Victoria, B.C.), 50:133-34; "The Hebrew Benevolent Society, Forerunner of the Hebrew Orphan Asylum of New York," 37:xxxv
Hebrew Bible, 30:iv; 34:xvi, xvii; 50:296
Hebrew Charities Building (New York), 25:136
Hebrew Chrestomathy, 28:xxxix
Hebrew College, 31:282
Hebrew Colonization Union, 38:248

Hebrew Congregation (Cincinnati), 43:142; (Madison), 35:xviii; (Washington, D.C.), 50:306
Hebrew Customs, 30:295
Hebrew documents, "Early American Hebrew Documents," 34:51-74
Hebrew Dramatics Club (Rochester, N.Y.), 40:71-72
Hebrew Education, Board of Delegates of American Israelites, 29:106-8; "A Contemporary Appraisal of Judah Monis, Harvard's First Instructor in Hebrew," 38:146-47
Hebrew Educational Fair, autographs, 25:112
Hebrew Educational Institute of South Brooklyn, 25:136
Hebrew Education Society (Baltimore), 25:151; 33:148; 37:470; 42:11; (Brooklyn), 37:295, 323; (Philadelphia), 23:192; 26:290; 28:268; 29:160; 30:435; 31:276; 33:19; 34:270; 37:272-74, 290-91, 295, 324; 38:336; 42:401; 45:207; 48:75, 229, 231; 49:24
Hebrew Female Benevolent Society (New York), 27:123
Hebrew Free and Industrial School (St. Louis), 37:292
Hebrew free school, 29:107, 179; 37:235-36, 288-90; 40:141, 154, 163-64; 42:13, 100; 44:171; 50:297
Hebrew, German and English Institute (Rochester, N.Y.), 40:62, 64
Hebrew General Relief Association (Cincinnati), 28:290
Hebrew German Society Rodeph Sholom (Philadelphia), 40:407; 41:83-93, 227-28; 49:235
Hebrew Grammar, 30:iv; 37:121-34; Stephen Sewall, 38:147-48
Hebrew Home for the Aged (Baltimore), 22:217
Hebrew Hospital (Baltimore), 22:217
Hebrew Immigrant Aid Society, 34:xx; 38:245-47, 310-11, 315; 39:105, 107; 46:360; (Boston), 46:73, 76-78, 82; "The Hebrew Emigrant Aid Society of the United States (1881-1883)," 49:173-87; "The Memoir of Doctor George M. Price," 47:101-10; (New York), 40:225-26,

236-37, 242, 244, 249, 257-59, 272-74, 276-80; Russian Jews in America, 48:35, 37, 39, 41-42, 85-96; (St. Louis), 40:242; *Visas to Freedom: The History of HIAS*, reviewed, 48:137-38
Hebrew Industrial School (Boston), 37:294-95; 46:82
Hebrew Institute (Batushan), 22:133; (Chicago), 37:294; 37:290-93, 298-99; 39:87, 89; (Pittsburgh), 28:258; 31:289; 42:14
Hebrew instructions, 42:10-14
Hebrew Journal, 39:404; 40:234; 42:372, 383; 49:165
Hebrew Kahal Bikkur Cholim, 50:302
Hebrew kindergarten, 42:10
Hebrew Ladies Aid Society (Detroit), 37:47; (Rochester), 40:66
Hebrew Ladies' Benevolent Society (Rochester), 40:63-64
Hebrew Ladies Orphan Society; Easterbrook *v.*, 25:135
Hebrew Ladies' Sewing Society (Baltimore), 23:145; (Boston), 46:79-80, 83
Hebrew language, "A Hebrew-Dakota Dictionary," 42:361-70; "Johnson of Columbia and the Hebrew Language," 25:109-11; Joseph Aaron, "A Key to the Hebrew Language, and the Science of Hebrew Grammar Explained. (With Points) First Part," 25:122-23
Hebrew Leader, The, 26:272; 34:286; 41:210; 46:235
Hebrew Lexicon (*Mahaberet ha-Aruk*), 22:104
Hebrew Literary Association, 45:166, 183; (Cleveland), 37:309, 314
Hebrew Literary Publication Society, 37:231
Hebrew Literary Society (Baltimore), 37:74, 295; 49:162; (Philadelphia), 37:74
Hebrew Literature, 50:271
Hebrew Literature Society (Philadelphia), 37:291, 300
Hebrew Melodies, 45:251
Hebrew Observer, The, 26:271
Hebrew Orphan Asylum, 44:160; (Atlanta), 29:202, 205; 34:xxii; (Baltimore), 22:214, 217; 25:154; (Brooklyn), 22:200; (Newark), 29:183; (New York), 28:36-37; 29:175; 31:189, 296; 34:xxii; 40:12, 141, 155-56,

163-64; 41:33; 42:121; "The Hebrew Benevolent Society, Forerunner of the Hebrew Orphan Asylum of New York," 37:xxxv

Hebrew Orphan Society (Charleston), 32:41; 42:53, 62-67; 49:238; (New York), 40:230, 267

Hebrew Periodical Press, "The History of the Hebrew Periodical Press in America," 23:xiii

Hebrew Philanthropic Society, 50:132; (Canada), 50:131, 134

Hebrew Poultry Butchers Association, 44:165-67, 175

Hebrew Prayer Book, 42:103

Hebrew press, "The Hebrew Periodical Press in America, 1871-1931," 33:127-70

Hebrew Relief Association (St. Louis), 37:292

Hebrew Relief Society (Detroit), 40:232; (New York), 32:110; 44:212

Hebrew Retail Butcher Union, 44:149

Hebrew Sabbath School (Rochester), 40:64

Hebrew Sabbath School Union of America, 39:449; 42:3, 5

Hebrew Sacred Concert, Programme, 30:354

Hebrew Sewing Society, Philadelphia, 41:66

Hebrew Sheltering Guardian Orphan Asylum, 45:210; (New York), 37:233

Hebrew Sheltering Guardian Society (Pleasantville, N.Y.), 50:431

Hebrew Sheltering House in New York City, 48:137

Hebrew Sheltering and Immigrant Aid Society, 29:204

Hebrew Society of Cleveland, 40:238

Hebrew Society for Visitation of the Sick, *Constitution and By-Laws,* 30:284-85, 308, 310-11, 384-85

Hebrew Standard, The, 23:129; 28:xli; 34:286; 35:117, 222; 39:404; 42:101, 375, 384; 44:149; 49:108

Hebrew Sunday School, 32:3; 45:175, 184; 50:243; (Columbia, S.C.), 50:170; (Philadelphia), 23:144; 28:268; 31:278, 287-88, 293; 37:65, 77; 42:35, 397-404; 48:76-79

Hebrew Synagogue of Charleston, 50:13

Hebrew Teachers College (Brookline, Mass.), 45:163-64, 185

Hebrew Teacher's Institute of New York, 39:90

Hebrew Technical Institute, 22:226; 31:275; 48:58, 120; (Haifa), 49:190; (New York), 34:xxii; 35:119; 37:288-89; 40:164

Hebrew Technical School for Girls (New York), 29:179

Hebrew Theological College, 39:262, 300; 43:139; 45:162-63, 183, 185; gift, 35:xxiii

Hebrew tongue, grammar of Judah Monis, 22:1-24

Hebrew Trades, gift, 34:xxvii

Hebrew Union College, 22:216; 25:150-51; 26:283; 28:46-47, 275-76, 284, 290, 297, 302; 29:181, 198; 30:vi; 31:252, 269-70; 33:129; 34:153, 295, 300; 35:322, 327; 37:56-57, 73, 84, 271, 293; 38:306, 333; 39:216, 261-62, 300, 335, 448-49, 455-56, 461-62, 464, 467; 40:43, 51, 201, 214; 42:8-9, 16, 451; 43:139, 250; 45:26, 103, 147-48, 162, 191, 216, 267; 46:276, 465, 488; 47:226; 48:143, 227, 230, 240, 243; 49:30-31; 50:118, 295; gift, 35:xxiii; "The History of the Hebrew Union College," 40:17-55; Jacob Rader Marcus, 50:425; "Studies and Addresses by Rev. Dr. Kaufmann Kohler," 33:xxx; and Zionism, 40:372-80

Hebrew Union College Annual, 31:270; 33:26; 39:468; 40:50; 50:294-95

Hebrew Union College—Jewish Institute of Religion, 39:469; 41:91; 44:252-53; 45:62; 47:233; 49:216; 50:68-69, 270, 272, 275, 292, 300, 393; bookplates, 45:156-60, 185

Hebrew Union College Journal, 40:374

Hebrew Union College Museum, 40:411

Hebrew University of Jerusalem, 31:282; 33:29, 38; 35:225, 324; 37:475, 477; 42:459; 43:197-98; 45:198; 46:434; 47:226; library, 43:143; 50:271

Hebrew Union Veterans Association, 50:312-14, 405

Hebrew Veterans of the War with Spain, 41:370

Hebrew Widows' and Orphans' Association (Milwaukee), 47:45

Hebrew Young Men's Association, 37:237; (Buffalo), 37:226, 309, 313

Hebrew Young Men's Literary Association, 23:142; 37:223-26; (St. Louis), 37:316
Hecateus of Miletus, 47:135
Hechinger, I., 29:131
Hecht, Albert, 27:511-13
Hecht, Arthur, "Abraham Cohen: Deputy Postmaster at Georgetown, South Carolina (1789-1800)," 48:177-93
Hecht, Ben, 35:268-69, 272-73; 40:358
Hecht Bros. (San Francisco), 37:45; 38:20
Hecht, Jacob, 46:74, 76, 79
Hecht, Mrs. Jacob, 46:79
Hecht, Louis, Jr., 46:84
Hecht, Mr., 27:504
Hecht Neighborhood House (Boston), 37:294-95
Hecht, Sigmund, 42:3
Hecker, Friedrich, 38:205
Hecker, Friedrich Karl, 44:104
Heckewelder, John, 23:33; 40:83
Heckheimer, Evelyn, 38:318
Heenan, John C., 34:144
Heenan, Thomas E., 36:229, 231, 257
Hega, Rachek Mendez, 27:476
Hegel, 28:232
He-Haluz, 45:96, 102
Heiberg, Major, 28:56, 61
Heiberg, Mrs., 28:56-57
Heibron, C., 27:145
Heibutt, Nathan, 27:277
Heidelbach, Philip, 47:8
Heidelberger, Sol, 27:154
Heiden, Konrad, 45:238
Heidenheim, M., 29:131
Heidenheim, Wolf, 28:77
Heidenheimer, Isac, 41:260
Heidenrich, Moses, 29:62, 68, 73-74
Heilbern, Eliezer Noah, 35:49
Heilbron, Bertha L., 50:272
Heilbron, Uri, 22:130
Heilbronner, Lazarus, 41:253
Heilbronner, Therese, 41:253
Heilbrooner, 31:151, 154
Heilbrun, Sarah, 23:145
Heilner, L., 23:143
Heilprin, Angelo, 26:287; 39:96
Heilprin, Jechiel, *Seder Haddorot*, 22:119
Heilprin, Jehiel, 28:66
Heilprin, Louis, 26:287

Heilprin, Michael, 26:287; 38:247, 308, 320; 39:158; 40:278; 42:110; 45:70, 155; 50:288; Russian Jews in America, 48:32, 35, 37, 82, 89-90, 97, 121-22; 49:183
Heim, Andries, 33:88
Heimann, M., & Co., 47:37
Heimann, Marcus, 47:37, 39, 41, 46
Heimfurter, Naftali, 41:263
Hein, Piet, 33:46-47, 51
Heine, Heinrich, 29:128; 31:277; 35:118; 38:276-77; 39:324; 40:119; 41:12, 14; 43:184; 44:65; 45:25, 260; Heine collection, 45:137, 139; "The Link Between Heinrich Heine and Emma Lazarus," 45:248-57; "The Rabbi of Bacharach," 28:69
Heineman, David E., 23:vii, xiv, 31-35; necrology of, 34:x
Heinemann, Jeremias, 28:106
Heinsheimer, Edward L., 40:45-46; necrology, 26:xxx; 28:284-85
Heinsheimer, Emma (Goodhart), 28:284-85
Heinsheimer, Lewis, 28:284
Heinsheimer, Norbert, 37:xii
Heinsheimer, Stella, 28:285
Heinzen, K., 42:135
Heishel, Zachial, *The Conversion of Zachial Heishel*, 30:60
Heiter, Simon, 31:151-52, 162, 164
Heitler; United States v., 29:151
Heitner, Rev., 27:504
Helburn, S. & Co., 50:301
Heldelbach, Max, 27:515
Helena *Independent*, 39:69
Helia, 28:156
Hell for the Jews, 37:422
Heller (St. Louis), 38:197
Heller, Edward H., 45:144
Heller, Henry, 50:304
Heller, James G., 34:xxvii
Heller, Joseph, 49:140
Heller, Lipman, 29:177
Heller, Max, 29:xli; 31:xxxii; 37:437; 40:381-82, 391; "Pioneer Types in Louisiana and Mississippi," 29:xxx
Heller, Maximillian, 42:100
Heller and Bros., M. (San Francisco), 37:45
Hellman, Edith C., 28:260
Hellman family, 46:122

Hellman, George S., 33:xxx; 41:105; gift, 33:xxxii; "Joseph Seligman, American Jew," 40:406; 41:27-40
Hellman, Irving, 46:124
Hellman, Irving W., 49:199
Hellman, Isaias Wolf, 39:176; 42:423; 45:144; 46:124
Hellman, Lillian, 40:359
Hellman, Meyer, 37:437
Hellman, Myer, 49:186
Hellsinger, Carl, 38:202
Helme, James, 35:289
Helme, John, 35:291
Helme, Thomas, 35:291
Helmick, William, 47:78
Helms, Arthur, 37:411-18
Helping Hand Temporary Home for Jewish Children (Boston), 46:83-84
Hemenes, Abraham Levi, 31:242-43
Hément, Félix, 41:162
Hemingway, Ernest, 35:269
Hemingway, Friedlander & Co., 50:169
Hemphill, John, 50:318
Henckel, J. B., "Contributions of Adolph S. Ochs to Journalism," 33:xxxi
Henderson, Ebenezer, 26:117
Henderson, Richard, 23:22
Henderson, Robert, 48:180-81
Hendrick, Burton J., 34:187
Hendricks, Aaron (b. Uriah), 27:155
Hendricks, Aaron (father of Uriah), 27:387; 31:260
Hendricks, Mrs. Charles, see: Hendricks, Louise
Hendricks, Cerinna, 27:287, 290
Hendricks, Edgar, 31:261; 49:56
Hendricks, Edmund, 50:309
Hendricks, Eliza, 27:111; 39:62
Hendricks, Emily, 27:286, 290
Hendricks, Emily G., 27:166
Hendricks, Esther, 32:127
Hendricks, Ethel, 32:xxviii; 33:xxxiii
Hendricks family, 27:387, 400; 35:xviii; (Philadelphia), 27:79
Hendricks (family name), 21:xv, xvi
Hendricks, Fanny (Mrs. Harmon), 27:111, 286, 289, 290
Hendricks, Fanny (Mrs. Uriah), 27:111
Hendricks, Frances, 27:110

Hendricks, Francis, 27:389
Hendricks, Frumette, 27:113
Hendricks, Hannah (b. Harmon), 27:287, 290
Hendricks, Hannah (Mrs. Henry), 27:111
Hendricks, Hannah (New York, 1789), 29:xlii
Hendricks, Hannah (b. Uriah), 27:286, 289
Hendricks, Harmon, 21:163, 167, 170, 212; 25:52, 57; 26:191; 27:83, 87, 88, 100-101, 107-10, 142, 155, 276, 286, 289-90, 311-12, 314, 387, 389; 28:293; 31:38, 260; 41:288; 49:59; copper for ships, 48:171-73, 175; and Paul Revere, 43:201-2, 205-15, 217-19, 228
Hendricks, Harmon W., necrology, 32:ix-x
Hendricks, Harriet Tobias, 35:xviii
Hendricks, Helen, 32:xxviii; 33:xxxiii
Hendricks, Henrietta Luna, 27:294
Hendricks, Henry (New York) (1), 31:260
Hendricks, Henry (New York, 1834) (2), 30:298; 39:35
Hendricks, Henry (b. Harmon), 27:286, 290, 311, 314, 344, 399
Hendricks, Henry S., 29:5; 31:261; 50:274, 309; committee on finance, 28:xxix; 29:xi; copper for ships, 48:171; executive council, 39:469; 40:406; 41:388; 42:414; 43:230; 44:241; 46:493; 47:201; gifts, 41:277, 288; Mt. Sinai Hospital, 42:115; necrology of, 49:56-63; nomination committee, 29:xxviii; report of treasurer, 28:xxx-xxxii; 29:xii-xiii, xxvii-xxviii, xxxiv, xxv; 31:xii-xv, xix-xxii, xxvii-xxviii; 32:xi, xvii-xviii; 33:xiii-xvi; xxi-xxv; 34:xiii; 35:x-xiv; 37:xiii-xxviii; thirtieth annual meeting, committee on, 29:xi; treasurer, 28:xxi, xxxii; 29:xiv, xxxix, xxv; 31:xv, xxiii, xxix; 32:xii, xix; 33:xvii, xxv; 34:xiii; 35:xiv; 37:xxix, xxxii, xxxiv; 38:341
Hendricks, Mrs. Henry S., 41:277, 288; 43:202; 50:274, 309
Hendricks, Hermoine, 27:290
Hendricks, Hetty (b. Harmon), see: Gomes, Esther (nee Hendricks)
Hendricks, Hetty (b. Uriah), 27:286, 289; 31:285
Hendricks, I., 27:79
Hendricks, Isaac (1), 21:215
Hendricks, Isaac (2), 27:387
Hendricks, Jacob, 32:127
Hendricks, Joseph, 29:146

Hendricks, Justina L., 31:260
Hendricks, Lebana, 27:110
Hendricks, Lillian Henry, 49:56, 61; gift,
  28:xxxix; necrology of, 31:xxiv, 260-61
Hendricks, Louise S., gifts, 29:xl, xlii;
  31:xxxiii; 32:xxviii; necrology of, 34:ix
Hendricks, Michiel, 33:122-23
Hendricks, Montague M., 21:214; 27:166,
  286, 290; 39:5
Hendricks, Mordecai Gomez, 27:154, 286,
  289
Hendricks, Mortimer, 21:197; 27:123; 29:131
Hendricks, Rachel, 27:111
Hendricks, Rebecca (nee Lopez), 27:113,
  277, 304, 409
Hendricks, Rebecca (Mrs. Solomon), 27:168,
  286, 289, 302, 305
Hendricks, Rebecca (Mrs. Uriah), 23:89
Hendricks, Rebekah, 29:xlii
Hendricks, Richa, 27:286, 289, 303
Hendricks, Rosalie, 27:110, 286, 290
Hendricks, Ruth (Mrs. Hyman A. Schulson),
  49:59
Hendricks, Robbin and Buttenwieser, 49:56
Hendricks, Sally (Mrs. Robert Weber), 49:59
Hendricks, Sarah, 27:79, 286, 289, 306
Hendricks, Selina, 38:70
Hendricks, Solm, 21:171
Hendricks, Solomon, 27:110, 259; 39:62
Hendricks, Sophia Phillips, 38:70
Hendricks, Thomas Andrew, 47:78
Hendricks, Tobias, 29:146
Hendricks, Uriah, 21:73, 79, 142-43, 145,
  171, 212, 216; 23:89; 31:37, 260; 38:49;
  49:59, 62; 50:37, 51; death, 25:123; kosher
  meat, 25:47, 123; non-importation, 26:238
Hendricks, Uriah (b. Harmon), 27:286, 290,
  293, 314, 402, 486; 28:293; 41:288
Hendricks, Uriah (father of Harmon), 27:41,
  43, 51, 59, 61-62, 154-55, 185, 189, 217,
  240, 246, 277, 286, 289, 387-88, 409
Hendricks, Washington, 21:220; 27:107, 277,
  286, 290
Heneriquez, Abraham Baruk, 23:29
Hengstenberg, E. W., *Egypt and the Books of
  Moses*, 30:374
Henle, Salomon, 41:255
Hennessy, Capt., 39:179
Hennig, Helen Kohn, 32:4

Henoch, J. H., 29:130
Henrici, Dr., 36:360
Henricus, I., 27:63
Henricus, Jacob, 27:59, 60
Henrietta Szold Foundation for Child and
  Youth, 49:171
Henriguez, Joshua, 37:394, 407, 409
Henriques, 31:238
Henriques (Philadelphia), 27:462; on Jewish
  marriages, 32:xxvi
Henriques, A. Q., 37:419
Henriques, Ab. Bueno, 42:280, 394
Henriques, Abigail (Mrs. Ebenezer), 27:111
Henriques, Abigail (Mrs. George), 27:111
Henriques, Abigail (Mrs. Joseph), 27:111-12,
  277
Henriques, Abraham, 32:16
Henriques, Abraham Cohen, 29:21
Henriques, Mrs. Abraham D., 27:112
Henriques, Abraham Lopez, 44:234
Henriques, Abraham Nunez, 27:122; 32:126
Henriques, Antonio Vaez, 33:53
Henriques, David, 27:110, 315
Henriques, David (Curaçao), *see*: Henriques,
  Mordy & David
Henriques, Eml, 21:171
Henriques, Ester, 37:339
Henriques, Esther (Mrs. David), 27:112
Henriques, Esther (Mrs. Jacob M.), 27:112
Henriques, Esther Nunez, 27:246
Henriques (family name), 37:382, 386; 48:139
Henriques, Filippa, 29:22
Henriques, Francis, 25:117
Henriques, Gabay David, 32:62
Henriques, Haim Cohen, 27:303
Henriques, Hannah (Mrs. Abraham Blum),
  29:155
Henriques, Hannah (Mrs. Moses), 25:117
Henriques, Henry S. Q., 28:xviii-xx, 246;
  31:105, 111, 116-17, 121, 123, 125;
  40:124; necrology of, 31:xxiii, 261-63
Henriques, Isaac, 25:117; 26:251; 42:253,
  280, 286, 392, 394
Henriques, Isaac Cohen, 29:21
Henriques, Isaac Fernandez, 21:40
Henriques, Isaac Nunes, 21:45, 48, 53, 55;
  27:246
Henriques, Ishac Abrabanel, 32:12

Henriques, Ishac Nunes, 37:373, 377, 386; 38:235
Henriques, Jacob (B.W.I.), 25:117; 42:253, 280, 291, 392, 394
Henriques, Jacob (England), 25:111; "A Note on Jacob Henriques, of London," 32:xix; petition, 32:122-23
Henriques, Jacob (Jamaica), 28:239
Henriques, Jacob (New York), 27:277
Henriques, Jacob Cohen (Curaçao), 29:21; 42:278, 287-89, 392-94
Henriques, Jacob Cohen (New York), 21:176, 178-79; 44:205, 211
Henriques, Jeoshuah, 44:216
Henriques, Joseph, 27:110, 277, 315
Henriques, Joshua Bueno, 32:61
Henriques, Joshua, Jr., 27:246
Henriques, Judah Cohen, 27:91
Henriques, Lopez Abraham, 32:62
Henriques, Mordecai Cohen, 27:79
Henriques, Moseh, 42:280, 394
Henriques, Moseh Cohen (Brazil), 42:278, 394
Henriques, Mosseh Cohen (Hunt's Bay), 37:339
Henriques, Moses (Jamaica), 32:62
Henriques, Moses (1) (New York), 21:42
Henriques, Moses (2) (New York), 25:117; 27:110
Henriques, Mrs. Moses, 27:112
Henriques, Moses Cohen, 27:91
Henriques, Moses Joshua, 28:214
Henriques, N., 27:190
Henriques, Nathaniel, 27:185
Henriques, Nunes, 38:236
Henriques, Rabbi, 39:299
Henriques, Rachel de Menasse Jesurun, 42:214
Henriques, Sarah (Mrs. Emanuel), 27:112
Henriques, Sarah (Mrs. Jacob), 27:277
Henriques, Sarah (Mrs. Moses J.), 27:112
Henriques, Vernon Cohen, 37:329
Henriques, Yeosuah, 27:246
Henriquez, Abigail, 32:58
Henriquez, Abraham, 44:234
Henriqz. Abm. de Binjn. Jesn., 22:170
Henriquez, Abraham Jesurun, 29:30; 44:229
Henriquez, Benjamin, 44:231
Henriquez, Benjamin Lopez, 44:228-29, 231

Henriquez, Benjamin Rephael, 44:231
Henriquez, Cohen, Jr., 27:23
Henriquez, Daniel Cohen, 29:21
Henriquez, David Cohen, 44:234
Henriquez, David d'Isaac Pretto, 29:38
Henriquez, David de Jeudah Cohen, 44:229
Henriquez, David Pretto, 50:148
Henriquez, Eliau Jessurun, 44:228
Henriquez, George, 21:215
Henriquez, Jacob, 27:55
Henriquez, Jacob de Josseph Jesurun, 44:230, 233
Henriquez, Jacob Naar, 44:228
Henriquez, Jeosua de Eleao Israel Jesurun, 44:232-33
Henriquez, Jeosuah, 44:230
Henriquez, Jeosuah de Eliao Jesurun, 44:232-34
Henriquez, Jeosuah Jesurun, 44:232-33
Henriquez, Jeosuah de Mordechay, 44:228
Henriquez, Jeosuah Rephael Lopez, 44:233
Henriquez, Josseph Bueno, 42:280, 394
Henriquez, Josseph Jesurun, 44:229-30, 232
Henriquez, Mordechay de Benjamin Lopez, 44:231
Henriquez, Mordechay de Selo, Lopez, 22:169-70; 29:30
Henriquez, Moses Pretto, 50:148
Henriquez, Mosseh Cohen, 44:232
Henriquis, Rabba, *Reason and Faith*, 30:92-93, 124-25; 34:xvi
Henriquez, Rachel, 50:148
Henriquez, Rebecca, 50:148
Henriquez, Samuel Pretto, 50:148
Henriquez, Selomoh Lopes, 44:229-31
Henriquez Coutinho family, 42:108, 214
Henrriques, Pierre, 28:250
Henry II, 21:238
Henry VI, 28:204
Henry VII of Germany, 28:148
Henry VIII, 28:170-71; 47:151
Henry (slave), 50:161
Henry, A. (New York), 27:63
Henry, A. (Richmond), 29:134
Henry, Aaron, 27:51, 83
Henry Clay Lodge (Free Sons of Israel), 40:166
Henry Cohen Community House (Galveston), 42:451

Henry, Duke of Portland, 34:274
Henry E. Huntington Library and Art
    Gallery, 30:vi; 35:230
Henry family, 22:xxii
Henry, H., *Imrai Shaipher*, 30:322-24
Henry, H. A., 35:xviii; 39:159; 42:57; 43:144
Henry, H. S., 40:249, 275, 277; 49:186
Henry, Henry S., 31:260
Henry, Jacob (Newport), 27:349; 44:63
Henry, Jacob (N.C.), 27:483; 29:140-41, 144,
    190; 43:167; 44:254
Henry, Jacob (Philadelphia), 41:226; 43:234
Henry, John, 33:174, 178
Henry, John, Jr., 37:111
Henry, Justina L., 31:260
Henry, Lilian, 31:261
Henry, Lyon, 27:349; 48:18
Henry, Mrs. Lyon, 48:13
Henry, Patrick, 43:234
Henry, Philip S., necrology of, 33:xxi
Henry, Sarah, 27:349
Henry, Solomon, 23:2-3, 6, 17; 25:113;
    26:233; 31:43, 58-59, 75; 34:76
Henry Street Settlement (New York), 26:260;
    35:323
Henry, William, 22:188
Hens, Abm. Ns., 21:43
Henschel, Albert Edward, "Albert Edward
    Henschel and His Connection with the
    Creation of the Greater New York,"
    38:50-52; gifts, 22:xxxiii; 29:xliii; 31:xxxiii
Henschel, Ernestine, 38:50
Henschel, George, 28:84
Henschel, Joachim, 38:50
Henshel, M., 33:134
Hentschel, Carl, 35:250
Hep-hep movement, 43:178, 182
Herald of Liberty, 38:135
Herberg, Will, 41:298; 46:215; 47:62
Herbert, Edward, "Benjamin Franklin
    Peixotto in Roumania," 22:xvii; gift,
    34:xxvii; "A projected history of the Jews in
    Roumania," 35:xiv; *Roumania as I found it*,
    35:xxi
Herbert, Henry William (trans.), *The
    Wandering Jew*, 30:405, 419
Herbert, Leon Moses, 33:165
Herbst, Fabian, 47:46

Herculanum, "History of the Establishment
    of the Inquisition in Portugal," 31:xxxiv
Hercules, Duke, 22:105
Herder, Johann Gottfried von, 45:25, 29-30,
    34; *Leaves of Antiquity*, 30:421; *Spirit of
    Hebrew Poetry*, 30:286
Hérédia, de, 41:162
Herford, *Pirke Aboth*, 32:xxvi
Herlitz, Georg, 33:132, 164
Herman, A., 21:226
Herman, Albert, 35:268
Herman, D., 29:133
Herman, Henry, 27:515
Herman, Jack J., "The Inner Life of the
    Jewish Community," 49:233
Hermann, Bernard, 47:182
Hermann, Hugo, 29:xliii
Hermann, Isaac, 50:399
Hermann, Joel, 41:263
Hermann, Joseph, 35:306-7
Hermann, Richard J., 45:214
Hermann, S., 49:186
Hernandez and Cheavitean, 25:3
Hernandez, Francisco, 31:30
Hernandez, General, 25:17
Hernandez, Isabel Clara, 31:30
Hernandez, Miguel, 31:29
Hernandez, Pedro, 31:30
Hernando, Alonso, 31:xxix
Herndon, William H., 42:136; 43:122
Hernstadt, I. H., 29:130
Herodotus, 47:135
Herold, David E., 50:380
Herold v. Parish Board of School Directors,
    25:137
Herors, Thomas, 35:291
Herrera, Abraham, *Sha'ar ha-Shamayin (The
    Gate of Heaven)*, 22:118
Herrera, Abraham Cohen, 46:47
Herricksz, Christoffel, 34:265
Herring, Christopher, 34:77
Herring, James, 41:278, 293
Herrmann, G. N., 29:113; 49:20
Herrman, Louis, *History of Jews in South
    Africa*, 35:xx
Hersberg, Dr., 36:58
Herschel, H., 27:521
Herschel, Solomon, 27:233, 521
Herschell, Constance, 50:175

Herschell, Solomon, 31:xviii; 41:12; 45:209
Hershberg, Joseph, 33:132
Hershfeld, Levi, 33:xvi
Hershfield, Atty., 29:168
Hershfield, Levi, 28:xiv; 29:xiv
Hershfield, Rachel, 29:169
Hershman, Abraham M., 43:247
Herskovits, Melville J., 40:196
Herter, Christian A., 42:413; 50:435
Herts, H. B., 27:515
Hertz, Emanuel, 31:xxix, xxxv; 33:249; 37:63; 38:320; 39:455; 41:204; "Abraham Lincoln—The Tribute of the Synagogue," 32:131; Civil War, 50:283, 301, 345, 399, 403; gifts, 32:xxvi; 33:xxix, xxxii-xxxiii; Isachar Zacharie, 43:72; Jonas parole, 42:408
Hertz (family name), 37:381
Hertz, Gerald Berkeley, 26:244
Hertz, Hayman, 27:336
Hertz, Joseph H., 50:399
Hertz, M., 29:132
Hertz, Reyna, 27:336
Hertz, Solom, 27:336
Hertzberg, Arthur (ed.), *The Zionist Idea: A Historical Analysis and Reader*, reviewed, 49:140-42
Herxheimer, S., *Catechism of the Faith*, 30:453-54
Heryon, Mr., 29:141
Herz, 26:37, 49
Herz, Henrietta, 26:38, 96-97, 100-101
Herz, Isak, 41:263
Herz, Jacob, 22:167
Herz, Julius, 41:263
Herz, Leopold, 26:49-50
Herz, Madame, 26:38
Herz, Markus, 26:97-98, 101
Herzberg, Max J., 34:222; necrology of Eugene M. Stern, 31:xvii, 293
Herzfeld, 29:125
Herzl, Sigmund, 23:188; 33:240; 38:194, 232-33
Herzl, Theodor, 26:163-64; 28:281; 31:264; 34:269; 35:54; 58-59, 247, 254-55, 258, 268; 39:203, 411-12; 41:10, 14, 22-23; 43:154, 170, 174; 45:94, 213, 238; 49:84; 50:395; Foundation, 47:61-62; 48:136; history, writing of, 46:164, 184, 371, 477-

78; Mesopotamian project, 47:160-67, 169; "A New York Premiere of Herzl in 1885," 35:287-88; Reform Judaism and Zionism, 40:363, 387-88
Herzl Zion Club, 37:458
Herzliah Teachers' Institute, 45:164, 174
Herzog, A., 29:130
Herzog, Isaac, 49:273, 275
Herzog, Jacob, 22:168
Herzog, Samuel A., 37:xii
Herzogliche Franzschule of Dessau, 28:104
Heschel, Abraham, 40:48-49; 47:62
Heschel, Abraham J., "The Mystical Element in Judaism," reviewed, 40:195
Heslin, James J., 50:272
Hespe, J. E., 50:287
Hess, Alfred F., 26:281
Hess, Captain, 26:183
Hess, David, 41:258
Hess, Ezechiel, 41:263
Hess, Jacob (HIAS), 49:186
Hess, Jacob (War of 1812), 26:186
Hess, Jesse, 26:186
Hess, Moritz, 28:78
Hess, Selmar, necrology of, 26:xiv, 280-81
Hessberg, Albert, 35:320; necrology of, 28:xxxii, 285-86
Hessel, Sidney P., 35:ix
Hessen, Grand Duke of, 26:57-58
Hessen, J., 28:118
Hessen-Homburg, Prince, 26:52
Het, Rene, 30:33; 35:176, 182; "A Great Colonial Case and a Great Colonial Lawyer: Solomon de Medina et al *v.* Rene Het et al," 42:71-82, 213
Heubsch, Dr., 40:277
Heusen, General, 33:92-93, 107
Heuser, Capt., 39:179
Heuvel, Heer Van den, 22:37
Hewitt, E. F., 45:190
Hexter, *Jews in Mexico*, 32:xxvi
Hexter, George, 37:268
Hexter, L., 37:266, 268
Hexter, Meyer, 50:314
Heydeck, "Don" Juan Josef, " 'Don' Juan Josef Heydeck: Missionary Among the Cherokees," 38:347
Heydenfeldt, Elkan, 35:119

Heydenfeldt, Solomon, 29:122; 34:252;
35:118, 124; 50:192; *Communication on
Subject of Slave Immigration*, 30:447
Heyliger, Louis, 35:xix
Heyman, Joseph, 47:46
Heyman, Moses, 27:21; 34:77
Heyman, Rebecca, 34:77
Heyn, Piet Pieterszoon, 47:113
Heywood, James, 27:246
Hiawatha, 22:175
Hibbat Zion, 34:152; 35:54-55
Hibbert Lectures, 25:182
Hickey-Freeman, 38:19
Hicks, Lawrence and Co., 27:345
Hicks, Mr., 21:103
Hicks, Valentine, 37:448
Hicks, Whitehead, 27:28
Higger, Michael, gifts; 33:xxxi, xxxiii; 34:xxvi;
35:xxi
Higgins, William, 37:394
Higginson, Thomas Wentworth, 38:173;
39:325; 42:83
Higham, John, 46:127; "American Anti-
Semitism in the Late Nineteenth Century:
A Re-interpretation," 45:262; "Social
Discrimination Against Jews in America,
1830-1930," 47:1-33; *Strangers in the Land:
Patterns of American Nativism, 1860-1925*,
reviewed, 45:217-18
High German Congregation, Amsterdam,
33:72
Hilb, Emmanuel, 41:263
Hilborn, Walter S., 42:420-22; 46:121
Hildeburn, Charles R., 30:51
Hildesheimer, Israel, 28:78; 29:99; 40:19;
44:137, 141
Hilfman, P. A., 22:26, 30; 25:140; gifts,
23:xviii; 26:xxxiv; 28:xl, xli
Hilfsverein der deutschen Juden, 31:190; 39:99,
197, 433, 439
Hill, Abraham, 38:45-46
Hill, Charles W., 42:411
Hill, David B., 25:112
Hill, David Jayne, 33:228-330
Hill, General, 37:209
Hill, Ira, *Antiquities of America Explained*,
30:270-71
Hill, Jonathan, 35:290
Hillel ben Samuel, 28:146, 188

Hiller *v.* State of Maryland, 25:137
Hillhouse, James Abraham, *Dramas,
Discourses and Pieces*, 30:334; *Hadad*,
30:235; *Scena Quarta di Adad*, 30:235
Hilliard, Mary, 35:273
Hillesum, J. M., 32:21; death, 37:xii
Hillman, Archibald, 35:139
Hillman, Sidney, 38:170; 40:397; 41:309-10,
322, 326, 329-30, 337, 354; 43:193; 46:231
Hillmantel, Louis, 47:41
Hillquit, Morris, 43:193; 50:202-7, 211-18,
220-25, 230
Hillsboro People, 48:252
Hillsborough, Earl of, 31:43, 58
Hilson, Thos., 33:195
Hilton, Amos, 37:105-6, 108
Hilton, Henry, 41:33-34
Hilton, John, 23:158
Hilton-Seligman affair, 39:242; 41:33-34
Hinchman, Benjamin, 27:387
Hindenburg, Paul von, 36:362
Hineman, David E., "The Startling
Experience of a Jewish Trader During
Pontiac's Siege of Detroit in 1763," 23:vii,
xiv, 31-35
Hines, Christian, 48:15
Hingham, Commodore, 40:286
Hinman, 23:55
Hinman, David C., 45:131
Hinreequez, Sarah, 32:58
Hipworth (actor), 33:183
Hiram II, 27:480
Hirsch, Aaron, 50:196
Hirsch, Akiefe, 41:267
Hirsch, Alexander, "The Simson-Hirsch
Letter to the Chinese Jews, 1795," 49:39-
52
Hirsch, Baroness de, 29:155; 31:226; 43:63-
66
Hirsch, B. W., 37:268
Hirsch, Dr., 39:430
Hirsch, Emil G., 28:240; 33:239; 34:xviii,
193; 37:85, 236, 244; 39:102, 430, 465;
40:29, 382, 386; 41:365-66; 45:95, 159;
173
Hirsch, Gisel, 41:258
Hirsch, H., 37:268
Hirsch, Harry B., 37:xii
Hirsch, Hermann, 41:263

Hirsch, Isak Ernst, 41:267
Hirsch, Joseph, *The Mount Sinai Hospital, 1852-1952,* 49:231
Hirsch, Iyda R., "Mears Family and Their Connections, 1696-1824," 33:xvii, 199-210
Hirsch, M. A., 37:40
Hirsch, Maier, 50:346
Hirsch, Martin, 26:187
Hirsch, Maurice de (Baron), 23:109; 28:52, 84, 97, 129, 283; 32:4; 34:xix, 193, 244, 269; 35:248; 36:226, 239, 396; 37:56, 69, 76-77, 86; 38:309, 312; 40:330; 46:77, 81, 483; 49:113, 162, 188; American Baron de Hirsch Fund, 28:130; Balkan disabilities, 24:39; "Baron Maurice de Hirsch, a centenary estimate," 33:xviii; "David Feinberg's Historical Survey of the Colonization of the Russian Jews in Argentina," 43:37-69; European reconstruction, 42:171, 177-78; immigration, 40:241, 250, 254-56; 41:129, 136; Mesopotamian Project, 47:157-58, 160, 165; Oscar Straus, 40:6; Russian Jews, 43:37; 48:30, 97-98, 100, 111-23, 236
Hirsch, Jacob von, 23:110
Hirsch, Meyer, 26:99
Hirsch, Moritz, 41:267
Hirsch, "Moshe," 23:109
Hirsch, Pappenheim, 23:110
Hirsch, Rabbi (Philadelphia), 22:135
Hirsch, Salomon, 41:263
Hirsch, Samson Raphael, 27:71-76; 31:268-69; 47:123; "Nineteen Letters," 28:71
Hirsch, Samuel, 34:xviii; 37:49, 85; Bernhard Felsenthal, 45:95-96, 120, 125; Hebrew Union College, 40:28; necrology of, 31:xvi, 263-65; Reform Judaism and Zionism, 40:364; 43:146
Hirsch, Samuel (1) (Thalheim), 41:263
Hirsch, Samuel (2) (Wankheim), 41:263
Hirsch, Z., 29:133
Hirsch, Zvi, 44:140-42
Hirsch of Ilfeld, *Dibre N'gidim,* 22:124
Hirschel, L., 37:478
Hirschfeld, David, 40:229, 242
Hirschfeld, Hartwig, 37:2
Hirschfeld, Isaiah, 33:161
Hirschfelder, Aaron, 41:260
Hirschfelder, Berta, 41:260

Hirschheimer, Hiedel, 41:255
Hirschheimer, H. J., 38:333
Hirschheimer, Leopold, 41:267
Hirschheimer, Löw, 41:255
Hirschmann, 38:202
Hirschmann, Jachiel, 41:260
Hirschmann, Lazarus, 41:260
Hirshberg, J., 47:46
Hirshler, Eric E. (ed.), *Jews from Germany in the United States,* reviewed, 46:59-60
Hirszenberg, Samuel, 40:319
Hirtz, 42:161
Hisgen, Thomas L., 50:230
Histadruth Ivrith of America, 33:154; 49:85
Historia General de las Indias, La, 22:111
Historian's Conference, 46:133-36, 139-43, 341, 408, 419, 445-46
Historical Essay Award, 43:70
Historical exhibition (New Orleans), 23:x
Historical School of Judaism, 42:92-94, 97, 100, 102, 104
Historical Society of the City of New York, 30:45, 63
Historical Society of Pennsylvania, 22:146, 188; 23:4, 33, 35; 25:113; 28:255; 30:vi; 34:75; 37:185, 193; 39:266; 40:411; 42:459; 43:152, 232-38; 44:244, 247; 45:201; 47:204; 50:245; portraits, 41:277, 289
Historiography, 46:133-34, 147-49, 191-92, 296-97; "Aims and Tasks of Jewish Historiography," 26:xv, 11-32; American Jewish, 46:137-42, 152-57, 170-76, 186-87, 376, 407, 409, 414, 428-46; 47:123, 125-39, 183-84, 214-15; 48:141-46, 199-201; Hebrew, 47:135-37; Jewish, 47:134-37
History of the Destruction of Jerusalem, 30:286
History of the Jews of Richmond from 1769 to 1917, The, 50:316
Hitchcock, Ethan A., 36:256
Hitchcock, Gilbert Monell, 40:296
Hitchcock & Reading, 31:137
Hitler, Adolf, *see*: Nazis and Nazism
Hitzig, Ferdinand, 45:126
Hoag, Jonathan, 27:318
Hoban, James, 48:2
Hobart, John Sloss, 27:38
Hobbs, Thomas, 37:199
Hobby, Elliott, 27:322, 326

Hobby, Wright, 27:327
Hoboken Observer, The, 25:134
Hobson, Laura, 39:116
Hochheimer, H., 23:143
Hochheimer, Henry, 50:301
Hochschild, Max, 31:226
Hochschule für Wissenschaft Judentums,
    40:18-19; 45:100, 267
Hochstadter, Adolph, 28:296
Hochstadter, Albert, 28:296
Hochstadter, David, 28:296
Höchstetter, Seligmann, 41:263
Höchstetter, Simon, 41:263
Hock, Simon, 38:195
Hockett, Homer C., 46:160, 466
Hodge, F. W., 37:443
Hodges, H. C., "The Doctrine of
    Intervention," 24:94-97
Hodgkinson (actor), 33:183-84
Hoeber, Mrs., 28:312
Hoe, R. H., and Co., 44:181
Hoffay, A. A., 34:289
Hoffe, Monckton, 40:354
Hoffheimer, Nathan, 41:250
Hoffman, Charles I., death, 37:xii; Memoir of
    Cornelia Kahn, 33:xxix, xxxii-xxxiii;
    necrology of Leo Stein, 31:xxix, 292; New
    Jersey Historical Society, 26:ix
Hoffman, Mrs. Charles I., 28:xxxix
Hoffman, Col., 42:410
Hoffman, David, 43:244, 246, 249;
    "Chronicles of Carthaphilus the
    Wandering Jews," 33:24
Hoffman family, 22:56-57
Hoffman, Jacob, 34:77
Hoffman, James H., 48:116
Hoffman, John T., 40:150
Hoffman, Lewis, 39:83
Hoffman, Matilda, 22:53, 56-57
Hoffman, Murray, 31:89, 101
Hoffman, Wickham W., 34:214; 36:176, 179-
    82, 203, 208-10
Hoffman, Friedrich, 38:202
Hoffman, Professor, 36:358
Hoffman (sculptor), 28:4
Hofmannsthal, Ignaz von, 23:188; 38:191,
    222-25
Hoffmans, 50:245
Hofheimer, Hirsch, 41:258

Hofstätter, Walter, 37:174, 176-77
Hog, Mr., 39:183
Hogan, John, 41:194
Hogg, John, 33:189-90
Hogg, Mrs., 27:386
Hoheb, Abraham, 50:148
Hoheb, David, 44:227
Hoheb, Mr. (St. Thomas), 44:115
Hoheb, Philipina Gordon, 50:148
Hoheb, Samuel, 50:148
Hoheb, Semuel, 44:229-30
Hohenhausen, Elise von, 45:252
Hohenlohe-Schillingsfurst, Prince of, 24:51,
    121
Hohenstein, Albert, 50:314
Hohler, T. B., 36:72
Hoke, Robert Frederick, 50:333
Holabird, Samuel Beckley, 43:102
Holbrook, 31:106
Holcroft, Thomas (trans.), Sacred Dramas,
    30:112
Holden, John, 50:397
Holdheim, Samuel, 39:451, 454; 40:364;
    45:125; portrait, 35:xviii
Holemes, Reuben, 27:246
Holes, Christian R., 28:290
Holford, George Peter, The Destruction of
    Jerusalem, 30:129-30, 148-49, 152-53, 155,
    157, 261, 264
Holischer, Desider, The Synagogue and Its
    People, reviewed, 46:66-67
Hollaenderski, Leon, 39:159
Holland, anti-Semitism and David Nassy,
    22:25-39; "The Dutch Archives, with
    Special Reference to American Jewish
    History," 32:7-21; education in, 28:87,
    113; emancipation of Jews, 22:124, 126-27;
    26:35, 72-74, 268; "Hugo Grotius and the
    Emancipation of the Jews in Holland,"
    31:xxiv, 173-80; Sephardic Jews, 29:7-38
Holland (family name), 48:19-20
Holland, John C., 39:34
Holland, Lord, 26:268; 31:126, 131-34;
    34:228
Holland, Mr., 31:186
Hollande, Arnout d', 33:114
Hollander, Bertha Hutzler, 37:473
Hollander, David Hutzler, 37:473
Hollander, Ella, 39:467

Hollander, Jacob Henry, 22:158, 191; 23:xii; 25:xi, 93, 114; 31:124; 34:253; 49:195; *The economic library of Jacob H. Hollander*, 35:xxi; executive council, 22:xii, xvi, xxvii; 23:xii; 25:xi; 26:xxx; 28:xxxii; Lopez papers, 26:x; necrology of, 37:xii, 471-73; "The Novel Jew," 26:xxi

Hollander, Meyer, 37:471

Hollander, Rosa (Meyer), 37:471

Hollander, Sidney, 45:242

Hollander, Theresa G. (Mrs. Jacob H.), 25:156

Holländische Steamship Company, 45:85

Hollar, Wenceslaus, 44:10; 45:53

Hollingsworth, Arthur George Harper, "The Holy Land Restored; or an Examination of the Prophetic Evidence for the Restitution of Palestine to the Jews," 26:149; "Remarks upon the Present Condition and Future Prospects of the Jews in Palestine," 26:149

Hollingsworth, Levy, 43:219

Hollins, George N., 50:342

Hollis, Thomas, 22:8; 30:41; 35:166; 37:122-23

Holmes, Abiel, 37:188; 42:341-45

Holmes, David, 42:341

Holmes, David (grandson), 42:341

Holmes, family tradition, 42:341-59, 415

Holmes, John, 42:341

Holmes, John 2d, 42:343

Holmes, Jonathan, 27:175

Holmes, Justin, 46:469

Holmes, N. H., 46:117

Holmes, Oliver Wendell, Jr., 35:127, 161; 38:269, 331; 39:201; 41:218; 46:467; 49:12; history, writing of, 46:469, 471; Holmes tradition, 42:341-59, 415

Holmes, Oliver Wendell, Sr., 36:11-12, 14-15; 42:117, 341-43, 345-50

Holmes, Sarah (Wendell), 42:343

Holmes, Stanley, 21:18, 195

Holmes, T., 21:41

Holmes, Thomas, 43:205

Holstein, Jacob, 29:143

Holt, John, 22:39, 41

Holt, Peter, 35:294

Holy Blossom Temple (Toronto), 50:133

Holyoke, Edward, 22:15; 30:41

Holzmann, 26:77

Homans, J. Smith, 45:270

Homberg family, 22:34

Homberg, Herz, 28:73, 101

Homberg, Moses, 27:43; 35:286

Homberger and Co., M. (San Francisco), 37:45

Home for Aged & Infirm Hebrews (New York), 28:294; 32:110; 40:158, 164; 41:248; gift, 34:xxii

Home for Aged and Infirm Israelites (Philadelphia), 25:174; 28:282, 288

Home of the Daughters of Jacob (New York), gift, 34:xxii

Home for Destitute Jewish Children, 46:84

Home for Incurables of the Jewish Faith (Philadelphia), 28:282

Home, Jewish, 39:368

Home for the Jewish Aged, 48:234

Home News, The, 29:150

Homel program, 49:90

Homen, João de Moraes, 47:69-70

Homer, James, 27:322

Homer, Winslow, 50:341

"Hommage to Manasseh ben Israel," 22:202

Hone, Philip, 27:309

Honen Dalim, 29:15; 44:221, 223

Honesdale, Pa., religious observances, mid-nineteenth century, 37:37

Honest Abe, 50:395

Honeyman, Francis, 23:165

Honor, Leo L., 42:112; "Fifty Years of Jewish Education in the United States," 40:407; "Jewish Elementary Education in the United States (1901-1950)," 42:1-42

Honorius III, 28:143

Honourable Artillery Company, 49:64

Honyman, J., 37:406, 408, 417

Hood, Captain, 22:23

Hooe, George, 39:22

Hooft, 37:199

Hoogstraaten, Diedrick van, 33:84, 86

Hook, Theodore Edward, *The Invisible Girl*, 33:191

Hooker, H. D., 37:443

Hooker, Joseph, 39:148; 50:327

Hooker, Zebulon Vance, 50:384

Hooper, J. J., 50:320

Hooper, Robert Lettis, 30:71

Hoover, Herbert, 36:148, 155, 364; 40:14; 45:220; Benjamin Nathan Cardozo, 49:13-14

Hope of Israel (Mikweh Yisrael), 22:119

Hope, Thomas, 27:97

Hopewell, Daniel, 25:126-27

Hopkins, John, 25:50

Hopkins, Stephen, 35:290

Hopkinson, Joseph, 38:129

Hopkinson, Oliver, 37:350

Hopper, Leopold, 41:260

Hopson, George B., 38:73

Hopson, William Fowler, 45:132

Hordynski, Joseph, 39:147

Horman, Louis, 50:313

Hormanden, Daniel, 45:202

Horn, Henry, 22:90, 94

Horn, William, 38:68

Horne, George, *A Commentary on the Book of Psalms*, 30:95, 200

Horner, Henry, 50:394

Hornesby, Thomas, 27:413

Horowitz, Aaron Judah Loeb, 33:134, "Benjamin Franklin Peixotto, American Consul at the Court of King Charles of Roumania," 22:133-34

Horowitz, George J., 34:xxvii

Horowitz, Harold, 42:419

Horowitz, Israel, 49:105

Horowitz, Jonathan P., 50:328

Horowitz, Lazar, 28:277

Horowitz, Leon Aaron Judah Leib, "Rumania and America, 1873: Leon Horowitz' Rumanian Tour and Its Background," 44:241; 45:67-92

Horowitz, Mr., 40:304-5

Horowitz, Phineas, 23:109

Horta y Pardo, "The True Birthplace of Columbus," 31:xxxi

"Hortensius," 38:118

Horton, Mrs., 48:257

Horwitz, J., 37:449

Horwitz, J., *A Defense of the Cosmogony of Moses*, 30:334-36; 34:xvii

Horwitz, J. A., 42:420

Horwitz, Phillip, 47:54-55

Horwitz, W. (Dov), 39:155

Hosack, David, 26:221; 33:190

Hoschander, Emanuel, 41:296

Hosea, Fanny Polk, "The New South," 28:55, 62

Hosman, Captain, 34:265

Hosmer, James Kendall, 40:352; 46:127

Hospital Relief Association (Rochester, N.Y.), 40:64

Hospital for Women and Children (Syracuse), 22:221-22

Hostovský, Egon, 50:116

Hotchkiss Academy, 47:15

Hotel Universe, 40:357

Houdini, 45:199-200

Houdini, Mrs., 45:200

Houghton, A., 40:129

Houghton Library, Harvard University, 39:319

Hounds, James, 21:17-18

Hourwich, Isaac, 41:320; 43:192; 46:299, 367

Hour With the American Hebrew, 37:422

House, Edward M., 28:259

House of Israel Congregation (New York), 27:509-10; (Philadelphia), 30:443-45; 27:505; 34:xxiv

House Next Door, The, 40:355

House of Peace (Richmond), 29:133

House to be sold, 33:174, 189

Houston, Sam, 48:10

Houston, Texas, religious observances, mid-nineteenth century, 37:37

Houthain, Willem van, 44:81

Hove, Nicholas ten, 33:108, 120, 125

Hovev Zion, 35:55

Hovevai Zion, 35:54-55, 57-58

Hovevei Zion, 49:84

Hovevei Zion Society, 48:114

Hovey, Carl, 43:19-20, 22, 28

How, Ah, 34:196

How, Louie Ah, 34:196

Howard, Sidney Coe, 40:354

Howe, Julia Ward, 40:347

Howe, Richard, 45:55

Howe, Robert, 37:438

Howe, Silas, 45:146

Howe, William, 23:177; 31:39, 57, 61; 38:91, 97; 45:55

Howell, B. C., 26:254

Howells, William Dean, 38:268, 278; 43:10, 12, 20; 50:206

Howland, William, 27:457

Hoxie, Frobert Franklin, 41:55, 316; 46:230
Hoxsey, Lodwick, 37:164
Hoyland, John, *Epitome of the History of the World*, 30:167
Hoyt, Henry, 37:70
Hoyt, J., 22:79-80, 87-88
Hoyt, Jesse, *Lives and Opinions of Benj. Franklin Butler and Jesse Hoyt*, 30:404
Hoyt, Lorenzo, 30:404
Hoyt, Rev. Dr., 44:13
Hubbard, Elbert, 41:125
Hubbard Company, 29:62, 66-73
Hubbard, Frank W., 29:62
Hubbard, Langdon, 29:62
Hubbard, Robert H., 50:272
Hubbart, S., 27:239
Hubbell, Julian B., 33:220
Hübsch, Adolph, 45:98, 125
Hudson, Hendrick, 41:114
Hudson River Aniline Works, 29:193
Hudson River Railroad, 25:145
Hudson, William L., 39:34
Hudson, Winthrop S., 37:187-88
Hudson, N.Y., religious observances, mid-nineteenth century, 37:37
Hudson's Bay Company, 50:128
Huebsch, Adolph, 33:239; 37:84, 89; 40:32
Huett, Thomas, 25:89
Huffman, Mr., 27:327, 473
Huffnagle, George W., 29:172
Huffnagle, Mr., 27:473
Huger, Benjamin, 48:151, 160; 50:342
Hugh of Lucca, 28:169
Hughes, Mr. (New York), 27:241
Hughes (actor), 33:184, 196
Hughes, Charles E., 36:82, 152; 42:356; 45:42; 49:13-14; 50:221, 229
Hughes, John, 43:114; 46:284
Hugo, Countess, "Rome in 1886," 28:28
Hugo, Victor, 37:18; 41:150, 161; 45:71
"Huguenots, The," 40:161
Hugues, Clovis, 41:162
Huhner, Edward, 47:223
Hühner, Leon, 22:vii; 23:88; 25:109; 26:vii; 30:vii; 32:4; 34:3; 37:383; 41:216; 50:285, 335; "Abraham Simons, a Georgia Patriot of the Revolutionary War," 31:xvii; "Additional notes on Francis Salvador," 22:188; Adler resolutions, 28:xxxv; "Albert

Edward Henschel and His Connection with the Creation of the Greater New York," 38:50-52; Battle of Long Island, 28:xxx; "Captain Abraham Simons of The Georgia Line in the Revolution," 33:231-36; "Columbus and the Jews," 29:xxix; curator, 22:xii; xvi, xxvii; 23:xii; 25:xi; 26:xii, xxx; 28:xx, xiv, xxi, xxxii; 29:xiv, xxxix, xxxv; 31:xv, xxiii, xxix; 32:xii, xix; 33:xvii, xxv; 34:xiii; 35:xiv; 37:xxix, xxxii, xxiv; 38:341, 344, 346; 39:469; 40:406; 41:388; 42:414; 43:230; 44:241; 45:264; 46:492; "Daniel Gomez, a Pioneer Merchant in Early New York," 33:xiii; 41:107-25; "David L. Yulee, Florida's First Senator," 25:vii, 1-29; "David Salisbury Franks, a Distinguished Patriot and Officer of the Revolutionary War," 26:xiv; "Existing landmarks in New York State, associated with Jews of Colonial and Revolutionary times," 31:xxiv; Foreign Archives Committee, 23:91; Francis Salvador, 39:97; gifts, 22:xxxii, xxxiii, xxxv; 23:xvii; 25:xvi; 26:xxxiii; 28:xl, xli, xxxix; 29:xxxix, xli, xliii; 31:xxxii, xxxiv, xxxv; 32:xxvi, xxviii; 34:xxiii; 35:xviii; "Gleanings of Jewish Interest in American Colonial and Revolutionary History," 25:xiii; history, writing of, 39:265; 49:244; Jewish bibliographies, committee on, 29:xi; "The Jewish Encyclopedia," 32:35; "Jewish Lawyers and Physicians in America Prior to 1800," 22:xiii; "Jewish Signers to a Patriotic Address to Congress in 1783," 22:196-97; "Jews Interested in Privateering in America During the Eighteenth Century," 23:vii, 163-76; "Jews in the Correspondence of Sir William Johnson," 25:xiii; "Jews in the History of Columbia University," 32:xx; "Jews in the Legal and Medical Professions in America Prior to 1800," 22:147-65; "Jews in North Carolina in Colonial and Revolutionary Times," 22:183; "The Jews of North Carolina Prior to 1800," 29:vii, xxxvi, 137-48; "Jews in the War of 1812," 22:xiii; 26:173-200; Lopez papers, 26:x; Lyons papers, 21:x, xi, xii; 22:xxi; 27:119, 143, 216, 222, 226, 263, 380, 457, 482, 486, 488, 496-97; 35:116;

Max Kohler, 34:253-54; 35:257; Mordecai Manuel Noah, 43:170; Moses Elias Levy, 37:438; necrology of, 47:201, 223-25; necrologies of Joseph C. Levi, 31:xxiv, 280-81; Max James Kohler, 34:295-301; Samuel Oppenheim, 32:xii, 132-34; New Jersey Historical Society, 26:ix; nominating committee, 22:xxvii; 23:xii; 26:xxix; 29:xxxv; "The Participation of Jews in the New York Celebration of the Revolution of 1830 in France," 22:xvii; publication plan, 26:xxvii; "Random Notes in American Jewish History," 22:xvii; report of curator, 22:x, xxv, xxxi-xxxvi; 23:x, xvii, xviii; 25:ix, xv-xvi; 26:x, xxvii, xxxiii-xxxv; 28:xii, xxx, xxxvii-xli; 29:xii, xxvii, xxxiii, xxxix-xliii; 31:xix, xxxi-xxxv; 32:x, xvii, xxv-xxix; 33:vii, xxi, xxvii-xxxiii; 34:x, xvi-xxvii; 35:x, xvii-xxiv; "Sir William Johnson and His Relations to Colonial Jews," 29:xxx; "Some Additional Notes on American Jewish History," 22:xxx; "Some Jewish Associates of John Brown," 23:vii, 55-78; "The struggle for religious liberty in South Carolina," 31:xxiv; thirty-first annual meeting, committee on, 29:xxvi; Touro Synagogue, 38:332

Huhner, Max, 47:223-24

Huhner test, 47:223

Huie, James A., The History of the Jews, 30:366, 374, 384, 409-10, 423-24, 435, 447

Huliel, Jeudah de Mosse, 29:28

Hull, Commodore, 39:59

Hull, Cordell, German persecutions, 34:231; 36:365-66, 370, 373-76; Palestine, 36:90-93; 40:115

Humbert, King of Italy, 36:332, 336

Humboldt, Alexander von, 26:65, 88, 96-97, 99; 33:36

Humboldt, Caroline (von Dacheroden), 26:97, 101

Humboldt, Wilhelm von, 26:36-39, 41, 48, 53-55, 65-68, 70, 88; 28:84, 106; 34:222; 43:178; "Regarding the Draft of a New Sistem of Legislation for the Jews, July 17, 1809, by Wilhelm von Humboldt," 26:103-15; "Wilhelm von Humboldt's Relations to the Jews," 26:95-103

Hume, David, 35:313; 37:188; 38:21

Hume, Joseph, 22:177-78

Hummel, Abraham Henry, 35:272

Humphrey, Commissioner, 46:472

Humphrey, Edward J., "Nationalism and Religion in America," 33:xxix, xxxii-xxxiii

Humphrey, Hubert B., Jr., 46:303

Humphrey, Judge, 29:150

Humphreys, Daniel, A Plain Attempt, 30:119

Humphreys, David, 37:14

Humphries, Richard, 35:234

Hungarian refugee relief, 47:192

Hungary, 24:44, 100; 28:96; 38:186, 190; 50:13, 305; "An Austro-Hungarian Movement to Encourage the Migration of Jews to America, 1848," 23:187-89; "Educational Reforms in Europe in Their Relation to Jewish Emancipation—1778-1919," 28:83-132

Hunt, Barth, 27:175

Hunt, George A., 50:350

Hunt, H., 25:99

Hunt, William, American Biographical Sketch Book, 30:630

Hunt, William Henry, 36:211-12

Hunt, William Holman, 50:352, 360

Hunter College, 47:226

Hunter, Dard, 41:124

Hunter, David, 43:97

Hunter, Henry, 35:290

Hunter, James T., 50:234

Hunter, Mr., 27:104

Hunter, Robert, 50:204, 232-34

Hunter, Robert Mercer Taliaferro, 50:332, 336

Hunter, Sam, 50:272

Hunter, Stephen V. A., 44:111

Hunter, W. F., 21:171

Hunter, William, 36:101, 103

Hunter, William (Newport), 27:428-29

Huntington, Collis P., 43:12

Huntington, Ellsworth, 34:248

Huntington, W. Va., Federated Jewish Charities, contribution, 37:xxviii

Hunt's Bay, Jamaica, cemetery, 37:xxx, 327-44

Huot, 23:49

Hurewitz, J. C., 40:205, The Struggle for Palestine, reviewed, 40:313-17; "United

States Policies on Palestine," 39:469;
40:107-18
Hurlbut, Stephen A., 43:92-93
Huron Indians, 23:32
Hurry, Edmund, 39:35
Hurtz, Abraham, 27:336
Hurwich, Louis, "Jewish Education in
Boston," 49:224
Hurwitz, Abraham Duber, 35:49
Hurwitz, H., 27:521
Hurwitz, Hirsch, 28:118
Hurwitz, Hyman, *Hebrew Tales*, 30:402, 424
Hurwitz, Maxmilian, 34:xxvi; *History of the
Workmen's Circle*, 35:xxii
Hurwitz, Phineas, 33:251
Hurwitz, Shmariah Loeb, 33:164
Hurwitz, S. L., 45:155
Husbands, W., 26:254
Husik, Isaac, 37:92
Husman, George, 37:442
Hutcheson House Boys' Club, 49:64
Hutchinson, Anne, 46:22, 34; 47:144
Hutson, Henry, 22:180
Hutt, I., 45:186
Hutzler, Abram G., 25:153
Hutzler, Albert D., 25:156
Hutzler, David, 37:473; necrology of, 25:xii,
152-56
Hutzler, Ella J., 25:156
Hutzler, Joel G. D., 25:156
Hutzler, Mabel, 25:156
Hutzler, Mrs. Maurice L. (Clare), 50:272
Hutzler, Theresa G., 37:473
Huxley, Thomas Henry, 42:357
Huygens, Mr., 33:109
Huyler, John S., 33:221
Huys, Jacob Janssen, 29:42, 44-45
Hyam, Andrew Israel, 23:151
Hyam, Enoch, 23:151
Hyam, Joseph, 27:154
Hyam, Judah, 27:154
Hyam, Moses, 27:154
Hyam, Robert, 32:58
Hyam, Uriah, 23:147, 151
Hyams, A., 38:63

Hyams, Henry M., 29:122
Hyams, Samuel, 50:164
Hyamson, Albert M., 28:89, 246; 31:119;
33:208; 34:240; 35:12; 37:379, 419-20;
43:254; 44:207; "British Projects for the
Restoration of Jews to Palestine," 26:xv,
127-64; gift, 28:xxxix; *The Sephardim of
England: A History of the Spanish and
Portuguese Jewish Community, 1492-1951*,
reviewed, 42:435-41
Hyatt, James L., 34:239
Hydeman, Edwin M., 37:xii
Hyer, Garett, 23:154
Hyer, Sarah, 23:154
Hyman, 35:10-11
Hyman, Arthur, 42:90
Hyman, B. and Co., 44:36
Hyman, Elsie, 44:55
Hyman, George, 47:203
Hyman, Gershon, 28:286
Hyman, H., 25:52; 27:105
Hyman, Henry (New York), 27:145
Hyman, Henry (Richmond), 46:112; 49:206
Hyman, Louis, 29:133
Hyman, Marks, 47:188
Hyman, Mr., 44:31
Hyman, Moses, 21:61
Hyman, Sam, 44:31, 35-36, 38, 55
Hyman, Samuel I., necrology of, 26:xxx;
28:286-87
Hyman, Samuel L., 31:xxix
Hymens, Henry, 27:75, 79
Hyneman, Adeline Ezekiel, 23:191
Hyneman, Elias L., 37:76
Hyneman family, 41:88-90
Hyneman, Isaac, 23:191
Hyneman, Rebecca, 48:239
Hyneman, S. B., 37:256
Hyneman, Samuel Morais, necrology of,
23:xiii; 191-93
Hynes, John B., 42:413
Hynes, Nathan, 37:268
Hyrcanus b., Alexander, 26:168
Hyrcanus, John, 26:165-69, 171

I

Iavarez, 25:118
Ibanez, Blasco, 33:37
Ibn Daud, Abraham, 39:215
Ibn Ezra, 31:178
Ibn Ezra, Abraham, 47:212
Ibn Ezra, Isaac, 47:212
Ibn Ezra, Moses, 38:276, 338; 43:239; 45:250; 47:199
Ibn Gabirol, Solomon ben Judah, 45:250
Ibn Sa'ud, 40:117
Ibn Shoshanim, I., 33:143
Ibn Tibben, family, 37:74
Ibn Verga, Solomon, 44:65-66
Ibri Anokhi, 45:72, 73, 81-82, 86
Ibsen, Henrik, 34:242
Icazbalceta, 31:2
Icher, I., 39:111
Icher-ver, I., 39:111
Ickes, Secretary, 36:371-72, 383-85
ICOR, 38:242; gift, 34:xxvi
Ida colony, 43:59-60
Idaho, local Jewish history, 49:220
Ida Strauss Day Nursery and Settlement (Los Angeles), 37:296
Idelsohn, Abraham Zevi, 40:48; 47:181; "Music in the American Reform Synagogue," 32:xiii
Iesurun, Binjamin de Abm., 22:170
Iggeret Or'hoth 'Olam, 22:105-8
Ignatieff, Nicholas, 36:209; 43:52
Ilhão, João, *see*: Illan, Jan
Iliowizi, Henry, 35:124; 39:402
Illan, Jan, 29:20
Illinois, 30:iv; "The Gratz Papers," 23:1, 7-9, 13, 17; "The Jewish Historical Society of Illinois," 28:xv, 239-41; Jewish local history, 49:220; "Jewish Merchants in Louisiana and West Florida, and the English Expedition to the Illinois in 1764-

1765," 29:xvi; State Historical Library, 50:273, 275, 302, 347, 367
Illinois and Wabash Company, 33:4
Illinois Centennial Commission, 28:xii, 240
Illinois Company, 23:8
Illinois Land Company, 41:389
Illinois Naval Reserve, 41:365
Illinois State Historical Society, 28:xii; 50:270, 352
Illinois Training School for Nurses, 29:160
Illinois, University of, 50:347
Illoria (consul), 24:19
Illowy, Bernard, 37:45, 63; 42:104; 50:118; "Biography and Works of Rabbi Bernard Illowy," 33:xxix, xxxii-xxxiii
Illoway, Henry, "Biography and Works of Rabbi Bernard Illowy," gift, 33:xxix, xxxii-xxxiii; "Dr. Henry Illoway," 35:xv; necrology of, 33:xxi
Imanuel, Pauline, 41:260
Imber, Naphtali Herz, 35:59, 251
Immanuel of Rome, 28:147
Immigration, 22:xxxii, xxxiii; 31:222; 34:xx, 165, 174, 189, 194-200, 296; 36:119-26, 134-35; 39:286-87; 40:66-67, 324; 41:233, 249; 42:10-16, 114, 137-38, 199-200, 203, 207-211, 219, 233, 242, 265, 339, 454; 43:45, 176-79, 197; 44:1-2, 125, 199-205, 213, 240, 242, 251; 49:29; 50:297-98, 427; Act of 1921, 46:309, 311, 316, 333; Act of 1924, 46:291, 293, 296, 299-300, 309, 311-12, 316, 319-24, 333, 416; Act of 1929, 46:333, 340; Act of 1952, *see*: McCarran-Walter Act; adjustments, 46:366-403; *American Historians and European Immigrants, 1875-1925*, reviewed, 38:325-27; *American Immigration Policy: A Reappraisal*, reviewed, 40:98-100; "The American Immigration Policy: A

Historical and Critical Evaluation," 46:306-36; *American Jewry, The Refugees and Immigration Restrictions (1932-1942)*, 45:219-47; American Jews, attitudes of, 40:98-100, 221, 287, 323; "The Attitude of American Jews to East European Jewish Immigration (1881-1893)," 40:221-80; "Attitudes and Policies on Immigration—An Opportunity for Revision," 46:289-305; Berlin committee, 40:229, 242; Immigration Commission of 1910, 29:205; *Communication on Subject of Slave Immigration*, 30:447; "The Diary of Dr. George Moses Price," 40:173-81; *To Dwell in Safety, The Story of Jewish Migration Since 1800*, reviewed, 39:196-98; "Emigration to America or Reconstruction in Europe (1840-1893)," 41:390; 42:157-88; "The European Aspect of the American-Russian Passport Question," 46:86-100; "The European Attitude to East European Jewish Immigration," 41:127-62; "The Hebrew Emigrant Aid Society of the United States (1881-1883)," 49:173-87; "History of Jewish Immigration to Canada (1947-1957)," 47:202; history, writing of, 46:135, 143, 166, 184, 188, 192-95, 198, 202, 207, 223, 228, 236-37, 246, 260, 264-66, 277, 285, 289-419, 446; "The Impact of Immigration and Philanthropy Upon the Boston Jewish Community (1880-1914)," 46:71-85; Institute on Immigration, 46:317; "Jewish Immigration Through New York City (1860-1880)," 50:427; "Jewish Immigrations to the United States and the Principle of the Right of Asylum Historically Considered," 28:xxxiii; "Jewish Emigration from Württemberg to the United States of America (1848-1855)," 41:225-273; "Jewish Immigration to Mexico as a Result of the World War," 29:xxx; Jewish local history, 49:225, 236; "Jewish Pioneers Along the Mexican Border," 29:xxx; "The Jewish Question in New York City (1902-1903)," 49:90-136, 271; "The Periodization of American Jewish History," 47:125-33, 200; quotas, 46:252-53, 292-93, 311, 313, 318-26, 333-

35, 368; registrations, 50:203, 210, 216-18, 223; reports, 34:xix; Roumania, 45:67-92; Russian Jews, 36:215-27; "The Russian Jews in America," 48:28-62, 78-133; "The Russian Night School of Baltimore," 31:vii, xvii, 225-28; *In Search of Freedom: A History of American Jews from Czechoslovakia*, reviewed, 39:329-31; "Secretary Hay's Roumanian Note of 1902 and the Peace Conference of Bucharest of 1913," 24:80-97; "Social Discrimination Against Jews in America, 1830-1930," 47:1-33; *Strangers in the Land: Patterns of American Nativism, 1860-1925*, reviewed, 45:217; "Too Little and Too Late: A Study of Jewish Attitudes to Immigration in the Light of American Economic Opportunities (1865-1897)," 50:427; *Visas to Freedom: The History of HIAS*, reviewed, 48:137-38; "The Young Men's Hebrew Associations (1854-1913)," 37:xxx, 221, 326; *see also*: McCarran-Walter Act
Immigration and Naturalization Service, 47:191, 194
Immigration Restriction League, 38:326; 45:217; 46:128
Inchbald, Elizabeth S., 33:185-86
Inchiquin, Earl of, 23:26, 28
Incidents of Travel and Adventure in the Far West, 50:383
Indenture, 28:228; "White Labor Servitude," 34:30-49
Independence League, 50:229-34
Independent, The, 39:325; 41:181, 47:32
Independent Chronicle, The, 40:79
Independent Gazetteer, 46:183
Independent Order of Liberty, 38:116
Independent Order of Odd Fellows, 47:45-46
Inderwick, James, 26:242
Index, The, 42:83-84
India, Jews of, 29:xxxix, 38; Trade, 23:3, 6; Palestinian Restoration, 26:142, 146, 149, 152-53; India Company of France, "A Great Colonial Case and a Great Colonial Lawyer: Solomon de Medina et al *v.* Rene Het et al," 42:71-82, 213
Indiana, "The Gratz Papers," 23:1, 7-12, 20
Indiana Broadside, 30:71, 73, 77-78

Indiana High School Basketball Association, 48:258
Indiana University, 48:256, 258, 260
Indianapolis, Ind., religious observances, mid-nineteenth century, 37:37
Indianapolis Conference, 40:365
Indianapolis Water Company, 46:472
Indian depredation cases, 47:187
Indians, 30:270; American indians, 43:189, 191, 234; "Alleged Masonic Symbols and Ritual in Aboriginal America," 28:xxiii; Ararat, 41:12, 15, 26; Cherokee indians, 22:173-74; 23:22 35:7; Chippewa indians, 23:33, 35; "David Franks' Interest in Lands in Virginia in 1774," 25:119-20; *Discourse of Indians Being Descendants of Lost Tribes*, 30:315-17; " 'Don' Juan Josef Heydeck: Missionary Among the Cherokees," 38:347; *Fall of the Spanish American Empire*, reviewed, 38:323-25; "The Hand Symbol in Aboriginal America and Primitive Palestine," 29:xv; "A Hebrew-Dakota Dictionary," 42:361-70; "Hebrew-Speaking Indians," 39:185-89; history, writing of, 46:269, 285, 311, 384; Illinois Nations, 25:120; Indians and traders, 23:32; "Israelites and Indians, a Parallel," 34:xxxiv; Jacob Harry Hollander, 37:472; "A Jew Among the Indians of the Great Lakes," 22:xii, 172-75; *Language of the Nuhbekaneew Indians*, 30:86-87, 120; Lost Tribes, 25:81-85; 27:523; 30:v, 119-20; 34:173; 42:333; 43:189, 191; "Moses Elias Levy's Agricultural Colony in Florida," 25:132-34; "The Phylacteries Found at Pittsfield, Mass.," 25:vii, 81-85; "The Sacred Number Seven in Aboriginal America and the Old Testament Heptad," 28:xxxiii; Seminole indians, 25:8, 13; "The Startling Experience of a Jewish Trader During Pontiac's Siege of Detroit in 1763," 23:vii, xiv, 31-35; "Three Hebrew Epics by American Hebrew Poets on the American Indian," 35:xv; trade with, 35:1-25; 41:114; Treaties and Otto Mears, 39:345-46; Ute indians, 38:322; *see also*: Ten Lost Tribes
Industrial Accident Commission of California, 29:197
Industrial Commission of 1891, 29:205
Industrial Relations Commission, 29:197
Industrial Removal Office, 22:226; 34:181-82; 46:184; (Boston), 46:77; (New York), 49:122-25
Industrial Trade Commission, 49:120, 123-24
Industrial Workers of the World, 41:352-53
Ingalls, Rufus, 50:328
Ingalls, Senator, 23:69
Ingelohe, Johan Abraham, 48:21
Ingersoll, Jared, 38:129; 41:92
Ingersoll, Sturges, 41:92
Ingoldsby, Richard, 23:149
Ingraham, 22:78
Ingraham, Joseph Holt, 39:116-17; 40:336
Ingram, J. H., 35:230
Inman, Henry, 34:xxi; 41:278, 291; 42:416; 43:235
Innis, Mrs., 23:118
Innocent III, 28:142-43, 176; "The Attitude of Innocent III Toward the Jews, as Shown in Some of His Letters," 29:xxxvi
Innocent VII, 28:153, 202
Innocent VIII, 28:161, 204
Innocent X, 28:194
Inns of Court (London), 22:152
Inquisition, 26:6, 243; 27:409, 483-85; 28:160-61, 163, 175, 181, 185-86, 197, 210, 235; 29:8, 11-13, 17, 34-35, 38, 48, 32:xxv; 33:25, 34, 40-41; 46:424; *auto-de-fe*, 23:130-35; 31:10, 15, 19, 21; 35:220; "Auto-de-fe Celebrated by the Mexican Inquisition, 1648," 32:117; Colombia, 29:23; Lisbon (1726), 22:180-82; 29:12; Spain, 35:220; Brazil and inquisition, 33:70; 42:239, 243, 259, 390; 44:83-87, 95, 47:63-75, 113; 50:73; Carthagena, 29:23-25; Evora, 29:17; France, 32:xxvii-xxviii; "History of the Establishment of the Inquisition in Portugal," 31:xxxiv; "History of the Inquisition," 28:xxxix; "Hugo Grotius and the Emancipation of the Jews in Holland," 31:xxiv, 173-80; "Isaac de Castro, Brazilian Jewish Martyr," 47:63-75; *Jews in Colonial Brazil*, reviewed, 50:73-76; Lisbon, 29:11; "Material Relating to the Inquisition and the Jews of Barbados," 32:xx; "Material Relating to the Mexican

Inquisition and the Jews of Barbados,"
32:xx; Medina on American Inquisition,
23:xvii; Mexico, 22:xiii, xxxvi; 23:130-35;
32:xxv; 33:xxxviii, xxxix, 25, 34, 40-41;
37:453; 41:107; "A newspaper Account of
the Auto-de-fe in Lisbon in 1726, in which
a Native of Bahai, South America, was
burned," 22:xviii, 180-82; "A note on
Documents Relating to the Inquisition in
Mexico," 22:xiii; Portugal, 22:117-19, 155-
56, 158, 180-82; 25:72-74; 32:36, 45;
33:44, 52-54, 95-96; 41:2; 44:204-5; 50:73;
"The Portuguese Inquisition of 1730 with
Special Reference to John da Costa,
Sometime Commissary-General of
Portugal," 29:xxxvi; Rule's *History of the
Inquisition*, 32:xxvi; South America, 35:327;
Spain, 22:155-56, 158; 26:22-24, 26;
35:220, 222; 45:112, 155; 46:10, 466
Institute for Advanced Studies, Princeton,
37:457; 50:119
Institute of Arab-American Affairs, 40:117
Institute of Early American History and
Culture, 39:183
Institute on Immigration, 36:317
Institute of Jamaica, 31:243; 35:311
Institute of Labour Management of Great
Britain, 41:323
Institute of Musical Art, 28:308; 35:324
Institute of Physical Medicine and
Rehabilitation of New York University,
Bellevue Medical Center, 50:273, 275, 330,
366
Institution for the Improved Instruction of
Deaf-Mutes, 39:278
Institute of the Novitiate, 28:272
Institution for Young Ladies and Gentlemen,
New York, 42:53
Institutional Synagogue, New York, 37:323
Instructive Visiting Nurses' Association
(Baltimore), 22:217
Intercollegiate Menorah Association, 28:xxix
Intercolonial Railway, 28:270
Interdenominational Society, "A Supposed
Interdenominational Society in 1832,
District of Columbia," 26:211-13
Intergovernmental Committee on Refugees,
36:378-79; 46:353

Intermarriage, 23:148; 27:29-30; 39:293, 300;
41:87; 42:327; 45:124-25; 46:243-44, 402;
47:26, 206; 48:64, 196-97; 49:108, 219,
235, 238, 240, 248-49; 50:25-27, 102-3,
144; David Nassy, 22:34-35; David L.
Yulee, 25:3, 18-19; Jews in Holland,
31:176-77; Portugal, 25:73
Internal Improvement Act, 25:21
Internal Security Act, 46:327, 331
International Art Exhibition in Rome, 28:54
International Association of Machinists,
46:218
International Commission for the Revision of
the Organization of the Mixed Courts,
47:85-86
International Congress of Americanists, 23:x
International Congress of Historical Studies,
22:xiv, xxv
International Congress of Marxists, 50:223
International Court of Peace, 36:270
International Exhibition of St. Petersburg,
31:291
International Exposition at Chicago, 26:2;
37:451; in London, 1883, 28:266
International Geographic Congress at Paris,
1889, 28:266
International Institute of Agriculture at
Rome, 38:250; gift, 34:xxvi; 49:83
International Jewish Committee, 28:132
International Jewish Conference, 29:98;
39:441; (Berlin), 49:177; Board of
Delegates of American Israelites, 29:109-
11; (Brussels), 41:37; (Paris), 24:29-39, 43
International Jewish Conference of
Roumanian Jews, 42:173-74
International Jewish Emigration Conference
in Paris (1890), 42:181
International Ladies' Garment Workers'
Union, 41:317, 323, 326-27, 344; 43:192-
94; 46:230-31
International Law Association, 31:263
International Red Cross, 26:xxv
International Refugee Organizations, 46:313,
353, 364
International Shoe Company of St. Louis,
39:176
International Socialist Congress, 50:216
International Steam Navigation Company,
45:76-77

International Tribunal of Egypt, 36:345
International Typographic Union, 46:219
International Workers Order, 43:192; 50:252; gift, 35:xxiii
International W. W., 41:353
International Zionist Commission, 36:69
In the Shadow of Lincoln's Death, 50:398
Inventory of American Jewish History, An, 46:262
Investigator, The, 32:41
Invisible Girl, The, 33:174, 191
Iollis, I., 38:244
Iowa, Jewish Community Center, 37:440; Jewish local history, 49:222; Masonry, 22:182
Ireland, Jewish relief, 23:122; and Palestine, 26:136
Ireland, John (archbishop), 46:273, 282-84, 288, 407; 49:180
Irene Kaufman Settlement (Pittsburgh), 37:295-96
Irish-Catholic Colonization Association, 49:180
Irrepressible Conflict, The, 50:404
Irvin, Jno J., 21:165
Irving, C., *Catechism of Jewish Antiquities*, 30:222, 226
Irving, Henry, 43:33
Irving, Washington, 28:251; 34:235; 41:120; 45:33; 46:427; Rebecca Gratz, 22:53, 56-59; 35:235-37; 50:245
Irving Place Theatre, 35:287
Irwin, Will, 33:xxx
Isaac, Abraham (N.H.), 50:26, 36
Isaac, Abraham (New York), 21:xvii, 7-8, 10, 19-23, 25, 30, 32, 35-38, 42, 48, 103, 107, 111, 140-44, 148, 169-70, 181, 187, 213; 33:253
Isaac Bar Abram, 27:79, 81
Isaac Bar Levison Hebrew Literary Society, 31:225-26
Isaac, Benjamin, 25:89
Isaac ben Solomon, 32:36
Isaac *v.* Defriez, 28:246
Isaac Elchanan Theological Seminary, New York, 31:282·
Isaac, Ger, 39:97
Isaac *v.* Gumpertz, 31:112, 125
Isaac, Henry, 25:89

Isaac, Jacob (New York), 22:161; 26:245; 27:246
Isaac, Joseph, 35:173
Isaac, Levy (Joel), 21:213
Isaac ben Mordecai (Maestro Gajo), 28:145-46, 160
Isaac, Moses, 25:123
Isaac, Philip, 27:1, 246
Isaac the Scribe, "The Chapters of Isaac the Scribe, a Bibliographical Rarity of 1772," 22:xxviii, 39-51; 30:61
Isaac, Simon, 26:245
Isaac, Solomon, 25:123
Isaac, Yitzhok, 43:192
Isaac Lodge, No 87, B'nai B'rith, 47:47
Isaac Lodge, No. 6, I. O. S. B.; Jacobs *v.*, 25:135
Isaac of York, 29:152
Isaack, John, 32:58
Isaack, Mary, 32:58
Isaacks, Abigail, 33:203
Isaacks, Abraham (1) (New York), 27:74, 371-73; 32:126; 33:202-3
Isaacks, Abraham (2) (New York), 37:373-75, 381, 386; 38:235-36; 48:18
Isaacks, Abraham Mears, 33:202, 206-7; 50:51
Isaacks, Catherine, 33:203
Isaacks, Esther, 33:203
Isaacks, Fanny (Mears), 48:11, 18
Isaacks, Frances, 33:202-3, 206
Issacks, Frances, *see*: Simson, Frances (nee Isaacks)
Isaacks, Frumet, 27:372
Isaacks, Grace, 33:203
Isaacks, Hannah, 32:125-26; 33:202-3
Isaacks, Isaac, 27:416
Isaacks, Iseah, 27:462
Isaacks, Jacob (1), 27:178, 180, 185, 349, 372; 32:125, 126; 33:202-3
Isaacks, Jacob (2), 44:63
Isaacks, Jacob (Newport), 50:26, 36, 51
Isaacks, Jacob (b. Rachel), 27:349
Isaacks, Jochabed, 33:203
Isaacks, Joseph, 25:42
Isaacks, Josey, 33:203
Isaacks, Judah, 27:373; 33:203
Isaacks, Moses, 22:182; 27:349, 372-73, 416; 33:202, 206, 210; 50:37, 51

Isaacks, Mrs., 27:97
Isaacks, Rachel (nee Mears), 22:182; 27:349, 373; 33:206
Isaacks, Rachel (Mrs. Moses), 33:202-3, 210
Isaacks, Rebecca (nee Mears), 27:349, 372
Isaacks, Rebecca (nee Simson), 27:74, 371-72; 33:202-3
Isaacks, Rebecca (b. Sampson), 27:372
Isaacks, Rebecca, see: Simson, Rebecca (nee Isaacks)
Isaacks, Sampson M., 27:83, 150, 314, 337, 372
Isaacks, Samson, 44:63
Isaacks, Samson Mears (1), 27:349; 33:203
Isaacks, Samson Mears (2), 27:349
Isaacks, Samuel M., 27:64, 517
Isaacks, Sarah Lopez, 33:203, 206
Isaacs, Aaron (New York), 21:58; 46:422
Isaacs, Aaron (Jamaica), 23:182
Isaacs, Abraham (Jamaica), 27:483
Isaacs, Abraham (New York) (1), 23:151-52; 27:1, 70, 150, 299; 31:100; 50:37, 51; "Disgraceful Acts of a Mob at a Jewish Funeral in New York, 1743," 31:240-41
Isaacs, Abraham (New York) (2), 27:40, 43, 51, 76, 83, 87-89, 243, 253
Isaacs, Abraham (New York) (3), 27:502
Isaacs, Abraham (N.C.), 29:145, 147
Isaacs, Abraham, Jr., 21:38
Isaacs, Abm. M., 27:59
Isaacs, Abram Samuel, 25:64; 26:1; 37:236, 257; 39:326; 42:100; 45:103; 49:97; communication from, 26:xxx; gift, 22:xxxiii; "Isaac Nordheimer, Orientalist," 28:xvi; necrology of, 31:265-66; nomination committee, 26:xi; 28:xiv
Isaacs, Adelaide Eliza, 25:115
Isaacs, Albert Augustus, 25:115
Isaacs, Barnet, 25:115
Isaacs, Bernard, 33:157
Isaacs, Mrs. Brandley, 27:109
Isaacs, Charles L., 50:313
Isaacs, Colonel (N.C.), 29:143-44
Isaacs, David, 27:323, 329; 50:63, 176
Isaacs, Davy, "Davy Isaacs of Charlottesville," 31:xxx
Isaacs, D. M., 27:521
Isaacs, Elkalah, 27:112
Isaacs family, 38:70; (Newport), 27:211

Isaacs, Fanny (d. Hetty), 27:323, 329
Isaacs, Fanny (Mrs. Michael), 27:373
Isaacs, Fanny, see: Simson, Frances (nee Isaacks)
Isaacs, Frances (Mrs. A. Blolk), 27:76
Isaacs, Frances (Mrs. Harmon Hendricks), 31:260; 41:28; see also: Hendricks, Fanny (Mrs. Harmon)
Isaacs, Mrs. Gitla, 27:112
Isaacs, Gitlah, 27:373
Isaacs, Grace (b. Joshua), 23:152
Isaacs, Grace (sister, S. I. Isaacs), 27:110
Isaacs, Gustavus, 27:393
Isaacs, Gustavus I., 38:58
Isaacs, Hanah (West Indies), 25:115
Isaacs, Hannah (Mrs. Abraham), 23:152
Isaacs, Hannah (Mrs. Jonas), 27:112
Isaacs, Hannah (Mrs. Joshua), 23:152
Isaacs, Hannah (sister, S. I. Isaacs), 27:110
Isaacs, Hannah (Mrs. Tobias Ezekiel), 27:76
Isaacs, Hays, 27:323, 329
Isaacs, Henrietta, 25:115
Isaacs, Henry (b. Barnet), 25:115
Isaacs, Henry (Jamaica, L.I.), 27:152
Isaacs, Hetty (nee Hays), 27:323, 329
Isaacs, I. A., 27:58
Isaacs, I. King, 27:45
Isaacs, Irving, 42:419
Isaacs, Isaac (b. Abraham), 27:373
Isaacs, Isaac (Jamaica, L.I.), 27:51, 152, 372, 387
Isaacs, Isaac (1) (New York), 21:64, 70, 73, 211
Isaacs, Isaac (2) (New York), 27:259
Isaacs, Isaac (Pittsfield, Mass.), 25:85
Isaacs, Isaac (West Indies), 25:115
Isaacs, Isaac A., 27:83, 86-87
Isaacs, Isaac S. (New York), 27:389; 38:72; 40:158, 226
Isaacs, Isaac S. (Oswego), 22:98-100
Isaacs, Isaiah, 27:76
Isaacs, Isiah, 50:30, 63, 161
Isaacs, Isidore, 50:314
Isaacs, Jacob (b. Abraham), 21:25, 45, 49, 51, 53, 55, 64; 23:152
Isaacs, Jacob (Newport), 23:89; 27:447; 37:392
Isaacs, Jane Symmons, 31:265
Isaacs, Joe, 27:338

Isaacs, Jonas, 21:171
Isaacs, Joseph (Jamaica, L.I.), 27:152, 314, 372
Isaacs, Joseph (New York), 21:8, 10, 16, 21, 27, 34, 167, 213; 23:150; 27:122; 31:238
Isaacs, Joshua (Newport), 38:58
Isaacs, Joshua (1) (New York), 21:27-28, 31, 39-40, 44, 48, 148-49, 167, 169, 212; 27:42, 51, 58-60, 62, 66, 72, 83, 242, 246, 253, 393
Isaacs, Joshua (2) (New York), 50:37, 51
Isaacs, Joshua (1) (Philadelphia), 23:84, 151-52
Isaacs, Joshua (2) (Philadelphia), 23:160
Isaacs, J. Stanley, 40:142
Isaacs, Judge, 24:24
Isaacs, Lazarus, 28:255-56
Isaacs, Levi J., 38:72
Isaacs, Levy, 26:233
Isaacs, Lewis M., 25:64; 32:xxvi
Isaacs, Michael (1) (New York), 21:48
Isaacs, Michael (2) (New York), 25:52; 27:79, 83, 86, 373
Isaacs, Mordecai, 26:233
Isaacs, Moses, 35:293
Isaacs, Moses (New York), 27:373
Isaacs, Myer S., 25:64, 112; 26:2, 272; 31:266; 32:130; 37:98, 233; 38:71; 48:116; 50:291; Alliance Israelite, 39:400, 402; Balkan disabilities, 24:24, 31, 33, 39; 36:5-6, 112, 117; Benjamin Butler correspondence, 29:117-228; 34:188; Board of Delegates of American Israelites, 29:77, 81-116; 47:82; 48:236; 49:20, 22, 28-30, 175-76, 183; gifts, 26:xxxiii; 29:xl; 34:xxi; HIAS, 41:131-32, 134-35; 49:186; immigration, 40:227-28, 246, 263-64, 278; Purim Assn., 40:137, 140-42, 147, 158, 169-71; Sampson Simson, 34:253; Y. M. H. A., 37:233
Isaacs, Mr., 27:502
Isaacs, Nathan, death, 37:xii
Isaacs, Nathaniel, 25:123; 27:274
Isaacs, Philip, 21:9, 39, 53, 55; 23:154
Isaacs, Rachel, 29:147
Isaacs, Ralph, 35:188
Isaacs, Rebecca, 22:89
Isaacs, Rebekah, 25:90
Isaacs, Richa, 27:76
Isaacs, Rufus, 40:89

Isaacs, S. I., & Soho Copper Company, 43:223; 48:171
Isaacs, Sampson, 21:170; 25:52
Isaacs, Samson, 27:51, 91
Isaacs, Samuel (1), 25:52
Isaacs, Samuel (2), 48:114
Isaacs, Samuel F., 50:165-66
Isaacs, Samuel H., 35:64
Isaacs, Samuel Myer, 21:xxiv, 141, 223; 26:272; 27:504; 29:105, 109, 112, 131; 31:265; 37:70, 217; 38:75; 39:247; 40:137, 148, 169; 42:104, 115, 120; 43:138-39; 49:16, 18, 20, 30; 50:296; "The Reverend Samuel Myer Isaacs: Forgotten Leader," 44:240
Isaacs, Sarah, 27:76
Isaacs, Solomon (Boston), 23:84, 152, 154
Isaacs, Solomon (N.J.), 35:173-74, 176
Isaacs, Solomon (New York), 21:22, 25, 31, 33-35, 168
Isaacs, Solomon I. (New York), 21:171, 212; 27:110, 114, 120, 174, 314, 344; 30:298; 48:171-72; Paul Revere, 43:202, 214, 217-22, 228
Isaacs, Wm. B. and Co., 47:189
Isaacs, Zeby, 27:372
Isaacson, H. B., 35:62
Isaacson, T., 33:148
Isaaks, Family of, "Genealogical Notes on the Isaaks, Mears and Michels Families of New York and Boston," 22:xiii
Isaaks, Mr., 27:407
Isabella, Queen of Spain, 26:xx; 27:474; 28:34; 33:12, 32; 35:224; see also: Ferdinand and Isabella
Isabel of Castile, 23:30
Isaiah Israel Temple, Chicago, "History of Temple Isaiah Israel, Chicago (1852-1952)," 41:390
Isbart, Charles J., 42:419
Isbitz, Marciaruth R., "The History of the Yiddish Art Theater," 44:240
Isbrants, 33:109-10
Isenbergs, Israel, 32:119
Ishack Bar, Jehudah, 21:11
Ishmael, 46:193
Ishmael, Abraham, 30:425
Isidor, Lazard, 24:29; 41:162

Isidoro, Abraham Gabbai, *Minian Mizwot*, 22:121; Yad Abraham, 22:120-22
Iskander, 38:315; 39:90-92
Israel, 40:118, 136, 313-17, 319, 321, 413; "American Zionism and the Congressional Resolution of 1922 on Palestine," 45:35-47; *Israel: A History of the Jewish People*, reviewed, 39:193-94; *A History of Palestine from 135 A.D. to Modern Times*, reviewed, 39:194-96; history, writing of, 46:199-209, 225, 275, 277, 280, 320, 325, 371, 373, 402-3, 412, 417; "Honeymoons in Ancient Israel," 33:xviii; *Israel: Its Role in Civilization*, reviewed, 46:129-31; *Religion in Israel Today: The Relationship Between State and Religions*, reviewed, 49:272-76; State of, 39:256, 265; *Trial and Error: The Autobiography of Chaim Weizmann*, reviewed, 39:202-5; "Two American Naval Expeditions to Palestine, 1848 and 1854," 40:281-87; "United States Policies on Palestine," 40:107-18
Israel, Abraham Eliezer, 28:xxxiv; 41:88
Israel, Abram, 44:92-93
Israel, Andrew, 23:151
Israel, Bar R., 21:126
Israel Ben Ader, *Chronicle*, 30:41, 43
Israel, Benjamin, 27:42
Israel, Daniel, 26:251
Israel, David (Brazil), 44:92-93
Israel, David (B.W.I.), 32:58
Israel, Davit, 33:65
Israel, Edward, 47:192
Israel, Elias, 21:38
Israel, Eliau, 21:39-40
Israel, Francis, 32:62
Israel, H., 29:132
Israel, Hayyim Abraham, 37:363-67
Israel, Isaac (Barbados), 26:251; 32:58
Israel, Isaac (New York), 27:79
Israel bar Isaac, 27:91
Israel, Isadore, 37:266, 268-69
Israel, Israel, 26:195; 27:68
Israel, Jesse, 29:147
Israel, John, 38:135-36
Israel, John, and Henry Lundt, *Journal of a Cruise*, 30:302
Israel, Joseph (New York), 21:91
Israel, Joseph (N.C.), 29:147

Israel, Joseph (Philadelphia), 22:197; "Midshipman Joseph Israel," 23:xiv
Israel, Joseph (West Indies), 32:62
Israël, Joseph de Abraham, 29:35
Israel, Judah, 21:95-96
Israel, Levy, 21:87, 116, 213
Israel, Menasseh ben, 29:8; 31:xviii, 178; 39:335; 45:62; 47:71
Israel, Michael (New York), 21:45, 48, 55; 23:157; 25:123
Israel, Michael (N.C.), 29:147
Israel, Moses (New York), 21:142, 148-49, 159; 23:161; 27:51, 253
Israel, Mrs., 27:247
Israel, Nancy, 29:147
Israel, Rosey, 23:160
Israel, Samuel (Brazil), 33:95
Israel, Samuel (New York), 21:142, 148-49, 159; 23:161; 27:41, 253; 50:37, 51
Israel, Samuel (Penn.), 26:182
Israel, Sarah, 27:73
Israel, Saul, 22:162
Israel, Simon, 36:350
Israel *v.* Simmons, 31:125
Israel, Solomon (New York), 23:158
Israel, Solomon (N.C.), 29:147
Israel, Solomon (West Indies), 32:64
Israel, Zur, 44:92-93
Israeli-Arab war, 42:203
Israelite, The, 26:271; 34:144-46; 36:317; 38:154, 161; 39:158, 171; 41:360; 45:29, 103, 126; 46:117; 48:216; 49:21; 50:82, 84, 87-90, 280, 293-95; (Longfellow poem), 40:182-83
Israelite Alliance of America, 35:119; 36:360
Israelite Press, 35:xxii
Israelitic Aid Association, 31:190
Israelitische Allianz, 37:98
Israelitische Almanack voor Ned. West Indie 1920, 28:xli
Israelitischer Volksfreund, Der, 26:273
Israelitischer Kreuzerverein of Prague, 38:197
Israel Medical Association, 45:197
Israell, Henry, 35:304
Israelo, Angell, 22:194
Israelo, Ann, 22:194
Israelo, Edward, 22:194
Israelo, Isaac, 22:194

Israelo, Jacob, 22:194
Israelo, Sarah, 22:194
Israel's Advocate, 30:212-13
Israel's Herold, 26:273; 33:240; 38:196-97; 47:8; 48:220
Israels, Israel, 28:253
Israels, Josef, 28:2
Israels, Joseph, 40:318
Israels, Mr., 48:74
Israel Temple, Boston, 22:ix, xii; 44:250-51; 45:270-71; 46:79, 191; *Growth and Achievement: Temple Israel, 1854-1954*, reviewed, 44:250-51; Brooklyn, 22:200, 29:180; New York, 29:169; 37:295; St. Louis, 45:97
Israel Vindicated, 30:190
Isselmuden, I., 33:104
Isserman, Ferdinand M., gift, 34:xxvi; "The Jews in Nazi Germany," 34:xxvi; "Rebels and saints," 34:xxvi
Istrias, d', "Satow on Capo d'Istrias," 29:154
Italy, 45:38; 46:93; Board of Delegates of American Israelites, 29:88-89; "A Celebrated Case among the Italian Jews of the Early Sixteenth Century," 32:xii; education, 28:87-89, 103; Jewish disabilities in Balkans, 24:16-17, 22, 35, 43-44, 49, 81, 102, 110, 121, 125-26, 142,

144; Jewish emancipation, 26:35, 83; "Jewish Physicians in Italy: Their Relation to the Papal and Italian States," 29:xxiii, 133-211; Jewish studies, 26:24; Moses Jacob Ezekiel, 28:21, 52, 136, 158, 171, 279; U.S. diplomatic intercession for rights of Jews, 36:ix, 105, 386-88
Itlas, Judah ben Jonah, *Bikkure ha-Ittim*, 22:130
ITO, 47:167, 169-70, 174
Itzig, Daniel, 26:47, 51; 28:92
Itzig, Isaac Daniel, 28:83, 92
Itzig, Moritz, 26:75
Itzkowitz, Benjamin, 33:159, 161
Iudovic the Moor, 28:196
Ivanhoe, 29:152; 33:174, 196; 38:15; 39:128, 138, 388, 446; 41:280; 42:398; 45:184; "The Original of Scott's Rebecca," 22:53-60
Iverson, Alfred, 23:122; 50:318
Ivo, Saint of Chartres, 28:138-39
Ivri, Lev, 38:245
Ivriah, 33:144
Ivit be-Ivrit, 42:12-14; 49:85
Iwo Jima, 38:249
Izac, Shneur, 49:53
Izarael, Isaque, 42:280, 394
Izidro, Abraham Gabay, 29:13

J

Jablons, Benjamin, 31:210
Jablow, Morris, 34:206
Jabotinsky, Vladimir, 38:239; 39:110, 203; 43:144
Jacie, Henry, see: Jessey, Henry
Jack Drum's Entertainment, 33:172
Jackson, Andrew, 22:80, 84-85, 87; 23:117, 119-20; 26:198-99, 222; 29:xix; 46:148, 150; 48:14; 49:234; David Yulee, 25:4, 10; Mordecai Manuel Noah, 43:191; Russian disabilities, 42:163-64; Uriah Philips Levy, 39:9-10
Jackson, Daniel, 27: 79, 271
Jackson, Eugene J., 27:466; Haym Salomon, 27:227-28
Jackson, Henry, 43:204
Jackson, John, 27:105
Jackson, John B., 36:127-32
Jackson, John M., 27:123; 50:282
Jackson, Joseph (1), 27:105
Jackson, Joseph (2), 41:67
Jackson, Joseph (3), 31:6
Jackson, Rebecca, 41:9
Jackson, Rebecka, Maria, 27:271
Jackson, Sarah Louisa, 27:112
Jackson, Solomon Henry, 26:270; 27:399; 39:299 (trans.), *Form of Daily Prayers*, 30:240-42; *The Jew*, 30:224-26, 235; and E. S. Lazarus, "Prayer-book," 34:xvi
Jackson, Solomon M., 27:99-100
Jackson, Thomas Jonathan "Stonewall," 50:342, 384
Jackson, William A., 38:263
Jackson's Family Almanac, 30:453
Jackson Street Synagogue, Mobile, 46:116
J'Accuse, 45:259
Jacob, 27:22
Jacob, Abraham, 27:155
Jacob b. Abraham, 34:109-11, 113, 116

Jacob, Benjamin, 22:194
Jacob, Esther, 22:194
Jacob, Hart, 27:41
Jacob, Heinrich Eduard, 39:326-37
Jacob ben Immanuel Provinciale, 28:161
Jacob, Isaac, 26:245; 28:255
Jacob ben Isaac, 34:59
Jacob, Joseph, 27:445
Jacob, Joseph (Capt.), 27:450
Jacob, Levi, 27:79
Jacob, Marcus, 27:78
Jacob, Michael, 22:192
Jacob, Mordecai, 22:194
Jacob bar Moshey, 27:114
Jacob, Myer, 27:155
Jacob, Patty, 22:192
Jacob, R., 34:82
Jacob, Simon, 22:192
Jacob, William, 22:192-93
Jacob, Zachariah, 22:193
Jacobi, Abraham, 29:126; 35:64; 42:122, 211; 45:189
Jacobi, Abraham (Dr.), 34:185
Jacobi, Frederick, 47:182
Jacobi, Lotti D., 50:272, 275, 315
Jacobi, Mary Putnam, 42:122
Jacobites, 25:70
Jacobs (B.W.I.), 25:118
Jacobs (Detroit trader), 23:35
Jacobs (London), 26:252
Jacobs (Newport), 26:245
Jacobs (New York) (1), 43:29
Jacobs (New York) (2), 27:91
Jacobs (N.C.), 29:146
Jacobs (stranger), 27:83
Jacobs (Surinam), 28:79
Jacobs, A., 27:97
Jacobs, Aaron, 31:146
Jacobs, A., and Co. (San Francisco), 37:45

Jacobs, Abraham (Barbados), 25:117
Jacobs, Abraham (1) (New York), 27:42, 86, 277, 315, 486
Jacobs, Abraham (2) (New York), 34:124, 130, 135
Jacobs, Abraham (Rye, N.Y.), 50:38, 51
Jacobs, Abraham (b. Raphael), 25:90
Jacobs, Abraham R., 27:84
Jacobs, Alfred, 27:505
Jacobs, Angel, 27:110, 277, 314
Jacobs, Asher, 27:91
Jacobs, B. 27:59
Jacobs, Barnet, 27:87
Jacobs, Bartholomay, 22:192
Jacobs, Belah, 50:36
Jacobs, Bellah, 27:278
Jacobs, Ben (Philadelphia), 43:235
Jacobs, Ben, Sr. (New York), 21:169; 25:48; 27:84
Jacobs, Benjamin (infant), 44:63
Jacobs, Benjamin (Newport), 27:349
Jacobs, Benjamin (New York) (1), 21:8, 142-43, 159, 170, 214; 27:40, 43, 51, 60, 62, 253; 31:238; 37:375; marriage to non-Jewess, 27:29-30
Jacobs, Benjamin (New York) (2), 50:37, 51
Jacobs, Benjamin (b. Raphael), 25:90
Jacobs, Benjamin (War of 1812), 26:188
Jacobs, Benjamin B., 27:84
Jacobs, Benjamin E., 29:129
Jacobs, Benjamin I., 21:143
Jacobs, Benjamin Raphael, 27:241, 278, 329
Jacobs, Bernat, 34:98
Jacobs, Bilhah (Mrs. Joseph), 50:52
Jacobs, Bilhah (Newport), 27:211, 349
Jacobs, Captain, 42:73-74
Jacobs, Colimyer, 29:129
Jacobs, Daniel, 26:238
Jacobs, David, 21:86, 92, 103; 26:238; 27:152-53
Jacobs, Deborah, 25:117
Jacobs, E., *The Doctrine of a Thousand Years Millennium*, 30:384
Jacobs, Eleanor, 23:157
Jacobs, Elinor, 23:157
Jacobs, Ezekiel, 26:183
Jacobs, families, 50:134
Jacobs, Frances (Mrs. Aaron), 27:75
Jacobs, Frances (Miss), 27:110

Jacobs, George (Philadelphia), 29:107, 109, 113, 133; 37:236; 40:33; 48:226
Jacobs, George (Richmond), 38:164
Jacobs, Georgiana, 27:110, 301
Jacobs, Gerrit, 48:20-27, 262-64
Jacobs, Gerson Isaac, 48:22, 24-25
Jacobs, H. L., 23:142
Jacobs, Hart, 21:115, 123-27, 134, 213; 25:47; 27:391
Jacobs, Henry S., 24:39; 29:110-11, 113, 129; 34:xxi; 38:64, 72; 39:400, 404: 42:61
Jacobs, Hetty, 50:167
Jacobs, Isaac (Buffalo), 46:163
Jacobs, Isaac (infant), 44:63
Jacobs, Isaac (New York) (1), 35:181
Jacobs, Isaac (New York) (2), 27:349
Jacobs, Israel (New York) (3), 21:63; 25:52
Jacobs, Israel (Philadelphia) (1), 22:xxxiv
Jacobs, Israel (Philadelphia) (2), 27:462
Jacobs, Israel, portrait, 41:284, 288; 42:416; 43:232; 50:39, 52
Jacobs, Israel B., 27:84
Jacobs, Jacob (Brazil), 33:87
Jacobs, Jacob (Charleston), 50:41, 52, 156, 158
Jacobs, Jacob (New York), 27:152
Jacobs, Jochanan, 31:238
Jacobs, Joel, 23:157
Jacobs, Johanan, 21:79-80, 87
Jacobs, John, 27:79
Jacobs, Jonas, 31:140, 142-43, 147-48, 151-52, 170
Jacobs, Joseph (Baltimore), 22:192
Jacobs, Joseph (Newport), 27:211, 349, 416, 449
Jacobs, Joseph (1) (New York), 21:51, 63, 111; 23:155, 157; 25:90; 27:51, 84, 86, 253, 314, 395, 397, 462; 48:18
Jacobs, Joseph (2) (New York), 50:52
Jacobs, Joseph (3), 23:189; 29:190-91; 33:22; 34:237; 35:127, 236, 249; 43:146, 239; bibliography of, 25:162-73; editing, 22:vii; 23:vii; "Essays and Reviews," 25:157; executive council, 22:xii, xvi, xxvii; 23:xii; "Jewish Ideals," 25:158-59; "The Jewish Race—A Study in National Character," 25:161; "Jews of Angevin England," 26:31-32; "The Mediaeval Status of the Jew," 23:xv; "Mordecai," 25:158; necrology of,

25:xii, 156-73; necrology of Anatole Leroy-Beaulieu, 22:xvii; "The Original of Scott's Rebecca," 22:53-60; "The Persecution of the Jews in Russia," 25:159; "The Philosophy of Jewish History," 25:160; "Plan of projected work," 25:161; "The Radanite Routes: A Description of Jewish Commerce in the Ninth Century," 23:xv; "Rebecca Gratz and her Relation to Rebecca of 'Ivanhoe,' " 22:xvii

Jacobs, Joseph (b. Joseph), 23:157

Jacobs, Joseph R., 27:62

Jacobs, Judah, 21:112

Jacobs, Judith (Kerpels), 48:24, 264

Jacobs, Judith (b. Raphael), 25:90

Jacobs, Julius, 31:141

Jacobs, Lazarus, 26:233-34; 31:44

Jacobs, Levy, 50:172, 175

Jacobs, Louis, 27:91

Jacobs, M., 29:133

Jacobs, Marcus, 27:79; 31:140, 142, 147, 151-52

Jacobs, Maria, 27:110

Jacobs, Mark, 27:29

Jacobs, Maurice, 43:238; 44:66; 46:492; executive council, 43:230; 46:493; 49:268; presides, 49:268; recognition of, 45:264; treasurer, 38:344, 346; 39:469; 40:406; 41:388; 42:414

Jacobs, Michael, 21:117

Jacobs, Morris, 27:395

Jacobs, Moses (Baltimore), 22:192; 50:40, 52

Jacobs, Moses (London), 26:233-34

Jacobs, Moses (New York), 27:84

Jacobs, Moses (b. Myer), 27:156

Jacobs, Myer, 27:156

Jacobs, Mrs., 35:198; 48:10

Jacobs, Oliver, 23:157

Jacobs, Philo, 26:272

Jacobs, Prudence, 23:157

Jacobs, Rachel, 27:112

Jacobs, Ralph, 27:51, 247; 31:237

Jacobs, Raphael (New York) (1), 21:31, 39-40, 42-44, 49, 51, 53, 55, 63, 84, 86-87, 115, 121, 211; 25:90; 34:120

Jacobs, Raphael (New York) (2), 27:22, 55, 57, 59, 61-62; 31:237; 44:63

Jacobs, Raphael (New York) (3), 50:51

Jacobs, Rebecca, gifts, 41:277, 287-88, 293-94, 387

Jacobs, S. (Richmond), 31:xxxv

Jacobs, S. (San Francisco), 37:45

Jacobs, S. J., 50:8

Jacobs, S. R., 31:151

Jacobs, Samuel (Baltimore), 22:192-94

Jacobs, Samuel (Canada), 35:11-12; 46:425; 50:124; "Data on Samuel Jacobs, an Early Canadian Jewish Settler," 28:xxxiii; "Samuel Jacobs, an Early Canadian Jewish Merchant," 23:xiv

Jacobs, Samuel (New York), 27:153, 253

Jacobs, Sarah (Miss), 27:110

Jacobs, Sarah (Simson), 25:90

Jacobs, Solomon (Philadelphia), 23:143-44; *Refutation of Address to Jews of Jamaica,* 30:424

Jacobs, Solomon (Richmond), 50:162, 167

Jacobs, W., 29:134

Jacobs, William, *The Jews' Reasons for Believing in One God Only,* 30:435

Jacobs, Zillah, gifts, 41:277, 287-88, 293-94, 387

Jacobs v. Issac Lodge, No. 6, I. O. S. B., 25:135

Jacobsohn, Herman, 32:124

Jacobsohn, Israel, 26:75; 28:79, 84, 104-5

Jacobson, 40:275

Jacobson, Bertha, 50:272

Jacobson, Gerald, 22:222

Jacobson, Israel, 34:194

Jacobson, J. Mark, 31:xxviii, "Jewish Merchants of Newport in Pre-Revolutionary Days," 31:xxx

Jacobson, Louis, 50:238

Jacobson, Michael, 29:67; 32:62

Jacobson, Minnie, 22:222

Jacobson, Nathan, necrology of, 22:xxviii, 218-22

Jacobson Schule, 28:104

Jacobson, Victor, 36:65

Jacobson, Victor (Fort Wayne), 29:130

Jacobus, David, 27:247

Jacobus, Philip, 27:247

Jacoby, S., 49:186

Jacoby, Victor, 35:269

Jacomo, Sijmon Ferrera, 33:118

Jacquemin, Claude, 49:44

Jacquet, *see*: Leeser
Jacquet, Jean, 34:274
Jadrech Anavim ve-Hozer Dalim, 11:221
Jadwin, Edgar, 36:160, 164
Jaffa, J., 50:403
Jaffa, Nathan, 25:114
Jaffe, A. J., 46:240
Jaffe, Lester A., 40:53
Jaffe, Margolia, 34:149
Jaffrey, George, 45:132
Jahn, Johan, *Biblical Archaeology*, 30:280; 45:24; *History of the Hebrew Commonwealth*, 30:248
Jahoda, Marie, *see*: Ackerman, Nathan W.
Jahrbuch zur Belehrung und Unterhaltung, 28:262
Jakmuss, Minna, 47:223
Jalomstein, Mordecai, 44:158
Jalonick, Issac, 48:224
Jamaica, 25:xv, 43, 114; 26:242; 29:46; 46:125; admiralty court, 46:29; "An Affectionate Address, to the Jews of Jamaica on the Great Subject of Christianity," 23:182; "Baron de Belmonte's Petition," 38:45-46; civil rights, 26:6; DeCordova family, 22:xviii; "Documents Relating to the History of the Jews in Jamaica and Barbados in the Time of William III," 22:xxviii; 23:vii, 25-29; "Extracts from a Jamaica Magazine of 1797 Relating to the Jews," 25:xiv; Hebrew literature, 22:127; historical works, 22:xxxii; "The Hunt's Bay Jewish Cemetery, Kingston Jamaica, British West Indies," 37:xxx, 327-44; "Jamaica under the Spaniards," 28:xl; "Memorial of Solomon and Elias De Paz on the Capture of their Ship in 1728-9 off Jamaica by the Spaniards," 26:248-49; "Michael Leoni," 23:179-80; "The Migration from Surinam to Jamaica," 28:xl; "The Montego Bay Jewish Community, Jamaica, B. W. I.," 38:343; "A Pamphlet on the Subject of Reform, Jamaica, 1848," 26:xv; "A rare work by Israel Lopez Laguna, the first Jamaica author," 31:xxiv; "A Sketch of the Life of David Lindo," 23:vii, 37-41; "Stray Notes on Jamaican Jewish History," 22:xviii; Sephardic Jews, 29:33-37;
Synagogue of Kingston, 23:153; "The Taxation of Jews in Jamaica," 28:xvi, 238-39; "The Taxing of the Jews in Jamaica in the Seventeenth Century," 29:xv; 31:243-47
Jamaica, Institute of, 35:311
James II, King of England, 27:225; 31:122
James, Duke of Ormond, 32:30
James, Abel, 30:77
James of Aragon, 28:143, 207
James, E., *Biography of Adah Isaacs Menken*, 35:xix
James, Ed, 34:147
James, Edward T., 48:202, 267; 49:70
James, F. Wilton, 50:230
James, George S., 50:330
James, Henry, 40:342; 46:127, 433
James, Joseph, *Hebrew and English Lexicon*, 30:242
James, the Pretender, 35:229
James (slave), 50:161
James, William, 42:342; 46:441
Jameson, James F., 42:71
Jameson, John Franklin, 31:231; 32:5; 40:76; necrology of, 35:x
Jameson, William, *A Remembrance of Former Times*, 30:10-11
Jamison, William, 23:151
Janáček, Leoš, 50:117
Jandorf, Isak, 41:263, 267
Jandorf, Löw, 41:263
Jandorf, Merg, 41:267
Jandorf, Moses Hayum, 41:256
Jandorf, Pfeifer, 41:258
Janforf, Rufin, 41:255
Janeway, Edward G., 42:124
Janeway, George, 25:35
Janeway, William, 31:83, 90-100, 102
Janowitz, Morris, *see*: Bettelheim, Bruno
Janowsky, Oscar I., 34:231, 253; 45:245; 46:402; 50:433
Janowsky, S., 39:100, 110-11
Jansen, Marcelis, 26:247
Japan, history, writing of, 46:296, 310, 321, 323, 330, 350-51; Exclusion Act, 46:350-51
Japanese-American Citizens League, 46:285
Japikse, Dr., 32:8, 21n
Jappa, F., 29:132

Jaramilla, Francisco de Leon, 32:117
Jaretzki, Alfred, necrology of, 31:xxiv; 266-68
Jaretzki, Alfred, Jr., 31:268
Jarmulowsky, Sender, 44:136, 142, 146, 149, 189-90, 192
Jartoux, Pierre, 49:44
Jarvis, John Wesley, 31:7; 41:278, 283, 285, 288, 291-92; 43:232; portrait of, 42:417
Jasher, *The Book of Jasher*, 30:341, 343-44
Jasper, 33:220
Jastrow, Helen B., 37:29
Jastrow, Joseph, 37:236
Jastrow, Marcus, 23:88; 26:2; 33:36; 34:xviii; 37:71, 78, 84-86, 236, 257; 45:96, 98, 101, 109, 124-25; 48:226, 230, 240; conservative judaism, 41:90; 42:102; Hebrew Union College, 40:21, 28-29, 32, 35
Jastrow, Morris, Jr., 26:236; 29:107, 109; 33:22; 37:29, 475; 45:101; necrology of, 29:xiv, 170-73; "War and the Coming Peace," 28:xxxviii
Jauncy, James, 26:269
Jaurès, Jean, 46:90
Javneh Talmud Torah (Chicago), 42:13
Javorow, Jacob, 48:32
Jay, John, 24:20; 27:242; 34:121; Danubian disabilities, 29:95; 36:108; treaty, 38:112-13, 119, 128, 136
Jay, Peter A., 22:184; 28:226-28; 34:121
Jechiel, Rabbi, 28:142, 211
Jecutiel, Nathan, 21:42-43, 45
Jeffers, Jonathan, 37:167-68
Jefferson (cadet), 28:2
Jefferson Bank, New York, 22:209
Jefferson Club, 37:228
Jefferson College, Philadelphia, 29:96
Jefferson Literary Association, 37:228, 253, 316
Jefferson Medical College, 22:142-43; 38:336-37; 45:194-95
Jefferson, Joseph, 33:187-88; 42:429; *The Jew and the Papist*, 33:188
Jefferson, Thomas, 22:71, 153, 159; 27:401, 460, 470; 29:xix; 32:1-2; 33:28; 34:168, 186; 35:287; 37:14-15, 345, 347; 38:1, 18; 40:16, 80, 96; 41:18, 62, 84, 330; 43:149; 46:3, 150; 47:140; 48:4, 8-9, 14; 49:50, 104, 131, 139, 208; 50:243, 396; anti-Semitism,

38:111, 130-32; 39:242; Centennial Commission, 35:325; Constitution and Jews, 43:161, 163, 165-66; correspondence, 34:20, 171, 182; Ezekiel Monument, 28:39-43; Isaac Harby, 32:35, 42, 52; Jacob de la Motta letter, 22:xxiii; "Jefferson and the Jews," 33:27; "Life and Morals of Jesus of Nazareth, extracted textually from the Gospels in Greek, Latin, French and English," 33:28; "The Maryland 'Jew Bill': A Footnote to Thomas Jefferson's Work for Freedom of Religion," 37:xxxv; Memorial Foundation, 39:11; religious rights, 25:99; 31:114-15; Samuel B. H. Judah, 26:242-43; "Statute for Religious Liberty," 46:20; Uriah Philips Levy, 39:10-11, 42, 58, 64
Jeffrey, Patrick, 35:142-43
"Jehoash," 22:175
Jehovah's Witnesses, 40:97; 46:405
Jehudah br. Samuel, 21:44
Jehudah bar Simson, 21:10
Jekuthiel, G., 33:160
Jekuthiel b. Samuel, 21:198
Jellinek, Adolf, 25:178, 185; 28:277; 29:126; 45:70; 50:93; "Jellinek and America," 33:xvii, 237-49
Jellinek, Hermann, 33:240, 244, 247
Jellinek, Max Hermann, 33:247
Jenkins, 22:76
Jenks, Jeremiah W., 34:201; 46:298-99
Jenks, W., 30:277
Jenness, Madam La, 40:83
Jennings, John Melville, 50:271
Jenny (slave), 50:159, 162
Jenyns, R. Soame, 44:9
Jeremias, A., 42:314
Jerez, Rodrigo de, 27:474
Jericho, 26:167
Jernegan, Henry, 28:238
Jerningham, Edward, 35:235
Jerome, District Attorney, 35:119
Jerome, Harry, 46:302
Jerome, Jerome Klapka, 35:250
Jerome, Saint, 137
Jersey, Earl of, 38:45
Jerusalem, 50:12, Restoration of Jews to Palestine, 26:132, 135, 138, 148, 150-51, 158, 252; State of Israel, 48:136; "When

Did Jerusalem Surrender to Antiochus Sidetes?," 26:xiv, 165-71; YM-YWHA, 50:433
Jeseron, David, 33:65, 97
Jeshuat Israel Congregation, Newport, 27:180-81, 185, 203-4, 404-12, 417-18, 427-30, 434-37, 440-42, 453-54, 458, 496; 35:317-18; 38:331-32; Shearith Israel correspondence, 27:177-84; see also: Touro Synagogue
Jeshuac Israel Congregation (New York), 27:180-81, 185, 190-91
Jeshurun, 31:237
Jeshurun, Ephim, gift, 34:xxvi; Wilno, 34:xxvi
Jeshurun, Israel, 31:237
Jeshurun, Raphael, 27:4-5
Jessel, George, 31:114
Jessel, Sir George, 40:88-89
Jessey, Henry, 31:117; "The Proposed Scripture Calendar," 32:23-34
Jessop, George Henry, 40:351
Jessurum, Reuel, see: Pina, Paul de,
Jessurum, Sarah, 35:27
Jessurun, Abraham (B.W.I.), 26:252; 29:16; 48:25
Jessurun, Abraham (Curacao), 44:227, 232
Jessurun, Abraham de David, 22:122-23, 170; 44:233
Jessurun, David, 22:123; 44:228-30
Jessurun, David de Jacob, 44:231-33
Jessurun, Jb., 27:264
Jessurun, Moses, 48:25
Jessurun, Moses Benjamin, 27:247
Jessurun, S., 27:515
Jessurun, Solomon, 21:215
Jessy, Henry, 26:242
Jesup, Morris K., 33:221
Jesurun (Curaçao), 22:171
Jesurun, Abraham de Jacob, 44:234
Jesurun, David de Abm., 22:170
Jesurun family, 42:108-214
Jesurun, Israel, 21:24
Jesurun, Jacob, 44:228
Jesurun, Jacob de David, 44:232-33
Jesurun, Moise Abraham, 35:xviii
Jesurun, Raphael, 44:218, 226
Jesurun, Samel, 23:182
Jesus, 30:453; 47:141-42, 147, 149-50
Jesus, Raphael de, 33:44

Jeudah br. Eliezer, 21:45
Jeudah br. Samuel, 21:44
Jew, The, 26:270; 33:173, 182-84; 40:346; 45:63
Jew and the doctor, The, 33:174, 188, 191
Jew and the papist, The, 33:188-89
Jew, At Home and Abroad, The, 30:401
Jew of Malta, 40:346
Jew Bill, Maryland, 25:95-100; 30:182, 184, 258; 31:xviii; 35:216; Niles' Weekly Register, 50:18-22
Jew of Lubeck; or, The heart of a father, The, 33:174, 195
Jewell, Marshall, 36:177, 197, 201; 37:428
Jewish Academy of Arts and Sciences, 47:221
Jewish Advocate, 49:197
Jewish Agency, 35:334; 40:118; 42:454; 45:128; 49:169; for Palestine, 33:19, 29
Jewish Agitation Bureau, 50:222
Jewish Agricultural and Industrial Aid Society, New York, 22:225-26; 26:288; 31:267
Jewish Agricultural Experimental Station, 22:226; 31:203, 205; 49:167
Jewish Agricultural Society, 39:237-38; 40:6; 42:103; 49:122
Jewish Alliance of America, 37:292, 299; 40:237; 48:236; 49:86; (St. Louis), 37:292, 295, 301
Jewish Almanac, 30:iv
Jewish Americana, 34:273-75; 45:206, 265; "An American Jewish Bibliography," 44:252-54
Jewish Apocryphal Literature Series, 47:221
Jewish Archives (Buffalo), 46:162
"Jewish Army Chaplain, A," 50:291
Jewish Artisans and Workers Emigration Society, 45:79
Jewish Artists of the 19th and 20th Centuries, reviewed, 40:317-21
Jewish Art Theatre, 29:151
Jewish Board of Deputies, 31:262; (British), 46:98; (Morocco), 36:19
Jewish Board of Guardians, 41:156-57; 45:199; gift, 34:xxii
Jewish Board for Welfare Work in the United States Army and Navy, 26:xxv, xxvii
Jewish Book Annual, 39:324; 47:220

Jewish Book Council of America, 38:9, 336; 40:412; 47:221, 232; 50:433-34
Jewish Book Fund, 45:152
Jewish Book Month, 45:200
Jewish Calendar for Fifty Years, 50:280
Jewish Center, The, 45:193
Jewish Center (Buffalo), 46:163; (Milwaukee), 37:296, 299, 322; (Stamford, Conn.), 37:326
Jewish Center Activities Association (St. Paul), 37:326
Jewish Center movement, 46:402
Jewish Center Quarterly, 38:336
Jewish Chaplains, 50:292
"Jewish Chaplains During the Civil War," 50:290
Jewish Charitable and Educational Union (St. Louis), 37:292, 301
Jewish Charitable Organization (Paris), 41:158, 160
Jewish Charities Conference, 39:434
Jewish Charities of Chicago, 31:251
Jewish Chautauqua Society, 22:216, 234; 29:157, 160, 180; 31:252; 38:338; 39:98; 42:4; 48:235; gift, 34:xxvi
Jewish Chronicle, The, 22:xxxii; 24:24; 26:147, 152, 258; 28:xxix, 248; 30:386; 39:247; 42:384; 43:137-38; 49:18
Jewish Classics Series, 45:267
Jewish Colonization Association, 28:129-31; 31:190, 206; 36:226; 38:241, 312, 316; 39:413, 418; 40:254; 42:180-86; 43:37-69; 46:480-81, 483; 47:165-66, 168, 170-71
"Jewish Colony at Waterview Virginia, The," 45:265
Jewish Comment, 22:xxxiv; 25:151; 27:143, 216, 263, 407; 29:177; 33:36; 35:117; 39:426, 436; 49:197
Jewish Committee of São Paulo, 46:338
Jewish Committee on Scouting of the Boy Scouts of America, 50:434
Jewish Communal Building (Indianapolis), 37:294, 301-2
Jewish Communal Center (Syracuse), 37:296
"Jewish Community," 39:253
Jewish Community (Buffalo), 46:163
Jewish Community Building (Buffalo), 37:294-95, 302

Jewish Community Center, 37:222-326; 50:431; (Chicago), 37:294, 300; 50:432; (Des Moines), 37:294; (Easton, Pa.), 45:268; (New Haven), 38:335; (Washington), 47:201, 231-32
Jewish Community Center Civic Forum (Des Moines), 47:208
Jewish Community Centers Association (Toronto), 50:431
Jewish Community Council, 50:143, 433; (Easton, Pa.), 42:197-202, 204; (Los Angeles), 46:122; (Utica), 49:232-33
Jewish Community of Greater Miami, 49:220
Jewish Community House (Cincinnati), 37:294
Jewish Community Library (Los Angeles), 46:123
Jewish Congress, 42:3
Jewish Congress Organization Committee, 49:191
Jewish Consistory (Lower Rhine), 42:159-62; (Paris), 41:159-60
Jewish Consumptive Relief Society, 35:274; 45:195; gift, 35:xxiii
Jewish Council of Prague, 50:116
Jewish Criterion, The, 28:xxxviii
Jewish Cultural Council of Eastern Union County, 49:228
Jewish Cultural Foundation, 49:154
Jewish Cultural Reconstruction, 45:184-85
Jewish Culture Foundation, 45:141-42, 169
Jewish Daily Bulletin, 34:193
Jewish Daily Food News, 35:xxi
Jewish Daily Forward, 40:100; 41:209; 43:10, 13-14, 24, 30, 33, 35-36; 44:181; 45:137, 240
Jewish Daily News, 33:129
Jewish Day Nursery and Neighborhood House (Newark), 37:294
Jewish Defense Association, The, 50:213
Jewish Disabilities Removal Act of 1845, England, 31:105, 109
Jewish Education, *The Essex Story: A History of the Jewish Community in Essex County, New Jersey,* reviewed, 46:68-69; 39:263; "Jewish Elementary Education in the United States (1901-1950)," 42:1-42; (Philadelphia), 42:11, 15, 25-26, 35-38

Jewish Educational Alliance, 37:298;
    (Atlanta), 37:294, 301 (Baltimore), 31:282;
    37:294, 319; (Chicago), 37:294;
    (Columbus), 37:294, 301; (Savannah),
    37:294, 302, 326
Jewish Educational Institute, 37:298;
    (Cincinnati), 37:294; (Kansas City),
    37:294, 301
Jewish Educational League (Toledo), 37:294,
    302
Jewish Educational Society, 49:7
Jewish Education Association of New York,
    42:33; gifts, 35:xviii, xxiii
Jewish Education Committee, 39:263; 46:168
Jewish Encyclopedia, The, 25:152; 26:8; 31:269;
    33:19-20, 22, 42; 35:117, 322; 37:452-53,
    483; 39:468; 43:139, 253; 44:238; 45:104,
    195; index to, 22:xiii
Jewish Exponent, The, 25:113, 135, 137;
    31:277; 34:266; 35:ix; 37:57, 470; 41:361;
    42:373, 375; 44:151, 159, 173; 45:121;
    48:126; 49:164, 197, 234
Jewish Expositor, The, 26:117; 49:42
Jewish Family and Child Welfare and
    Vocational Services, 50:141
Jewish Family Service Association, 49:61
Jewish Federation of Charities (Atlanta),
    37:301
Jewish Foster Home and Orphan Asylum of
    Philadelphia, 26:290; 28:268; 37:88;
    42:404; 45:31
Jewish Free Loan Society, 28:258
Jewish Free School, 28:83, 90, 92-93
Jewish Frontier, 47:61
Jewish Gazette, 39:426; 44:181
Jewish Gentleman, The, 33:171
Jewish Girl's Club (Toronto), 37:296
Jewish Guardian, The, 28:xxix
Jewish Hellenistic Literature, 45:102
Jewish Historical Commission for the Civil
    War Centennial, 49:154-55
Jewish Historical and Ethnographical
    Society, 40:402
Jewish Historical Society, England, 22:xxv,
    177, 202-3; 23:ix; 25:111, 162, 189; 26:xii;
    29:xx; 31:249, 261, 263, 290; 43:156, 250;
    44:246; 45:53; 46:354; 49:67; anniversary,
    28:xviii-xx; history of Jews, 29:xx, xxii, xxvi,
    3; records restored, 37:2-4, 11; Illinois,

"The Jewish Historical Society of Illinois,"
    28:xv, 239-41; Israel, American Section,
    41:391; 42:90; Portland, Maine, 49:223
Jewish History Week, 42:311-12; 44:244
Jewish Home for Consumptives (Baltimore),
    25:151
Jewish Home for Convalescents, 49:86
Jewish Home Society for Albany, 29:194;
    35:322
Jewish Hospital (Baltimore), 41:249;
    (Brooklyn), 22:200; (Cincinnati), 26:283;
    (Denver), 37:440; (Philadelphia), 22:232;
    29:189; 48:234
Jewish Hospital and Home for the Aged and
    Infirm of Philadelphia, 25:174
Jewish Hospital Association (Philadelphia),
    25:174; 28:282, 288, 314; 31:276
Jewish Immigrant Aid Society, 50:141
Jewish Immigrant Protective Society (New
    York), 40:237
Jewish Immigrants' Information Bureau,
    34:199; 42:454; 46:484
Jewish Institute Quarterly, 32:xxvi
Jewish Institute of Religion, 33:129; 34:304,
    306; 35:251; 37:477, 480; 39:336; 40:49,
    52-53; 42:451; 45:147-48; 47:219, 233;
    48:243; gifts, 32:xxvi; 34:xxvii
Jewish Labor Committee, 36:367, 375;
    42:320-22, 328; 43:192; (Canada), 50:141;
    and refugees, 45:231-33, 237-38, 244-45,
    247
Jewish Ladies' Benevolent Society of St.
    Joseph, 28:314-15
Jewish League Against Communism, 46:410
Jewish Ledger, 45:145
Jewish Legion in Palestine, 39:441
Jewish Life in America, reviewed, 46:61-64
Jewish Literary Society, 40:402; (Baltimore),
    38:309; (Philadelphia), 38:338
Jewish literature, 39:298-99
Jewish Messenger, The, 25:65, 70-72; 26:1,
    272; 29:77, 128; 31:265; 37:57, 230-31;
    39:326, 391-92, 394; 40:137-38, 141, 145,
    150, 159, 172; 41:361, 371; 42:105, 120;
    43:136; 44:150, 152, 156, 159, 161, 166,
    170; 45:103, 249-50; 46:117; 48:38;
    49:163, 184; 50:280, 297-98, 309
Jewish Miscellany, The, 30:402, 411, 425, 429,
    437, 453, 455

Jewish Mission (Milwaukee), 37:296
Jewish Monthly Magazine, 30:383
Jewish Morning Journal, 33:129; 45:192;
   48:21; "The Jewish Morning Journal
   Observes Its Golden Jubilee," 40:407
Jewish Museum (Cincinnati), 50:270, 275
Jewish Museum (London), 43:6, 9; 44:8; gifts,
   35:xx; 49:61-62, 68
Jewish Museum (New York), 38:345, 347;
   40:321, 405-6, 411; 41:276, 385, 387; 43:4,
   8-9, 243; 44:899; 45:52-53, 61, 128, 260,
   264-65; 49:137, 154; 50:260, 263, 265,
   267, 270, 273, 275, 292, 296-97, 312, 316-
   17, 335, 340, 345, 383, 405, 425-27
Jewish Music Council, 38:9; 40:412
Jewish National Assembly (Turkey), 36:9
Jewish National Council in Palestine, 49:169
Jewish National Fund, 33:162
Jewish National Fund Book, 39:371
Jewish National Home, 42:39
Jewish Occupational Council, 39:237; 46:346
Jewish Old Folks Home (Buffalo), 46:164
Jewish Orphan Asylum (Cleveland), 23:191;
   28:289; (Western New York), 22:222
Jewish Orphan Society (Wilkes-Barre), 31:298
Jewish Orphanage of Providence, 34:xxii
Jewish Orphans' Home Association (New
   Orleans), 26:275
Jewish People's Institute (Boston), 37:294;
   (Chicago), 37:294, 300, 320-21; 45:211;
   50:432
Jewish Pioneers and Patriots, 50:309
Jewish Prayer Book, 30:iv
Jewish Prisoners' Aid Society, 40:164
Jewish Progress, 42:384
Jewish Protective Association, 47:18
Jewish Protectory and Aid Society, 28:261
Jewish Publication Society of America,
   22:233; 25:159, 161; 26:xxv, xxvii; 28:xii,
   32-33, 235, 297, 303-4; 29:166, 180, 190,
   198; 31:227, 252, 258, 269-70, 276, 296,
   298; 32:xvi; 33:4, 19, 25; 34:298; 35:322;
   37:452, 465, 477, 482; 38:249, 338; 39:262,
   290, 467-68; 40:13; 42:100; 43:239-40,
   251; 45:99, 103, 192, 204; 47:204, 216,
   220-21, 226; 48:215, 239-40; 49:17, 24, 39,
   164-66, 168, 230, 234, 247; 50:244;
   American Collection, 45:153; gifts,
   26:xxxiii; 34:xxvi; "The Jews in the Wars of

the United States," 26:x; silver jubilee,
   22:xxv
Jewish Public Library of Montreal, 45:209
Jewish Quarterly Review, 25:184; 29:xlii;
   33:24-25; 35:117; 37:452; 47:219
Jewish question, 46:371; 48:107-14; (New
   York), 49:90-136, 271
Jewish Record, 22:58; 26:272; 28:18; 37:57;
   44:132; 48:239-40
Jewish Reformer, 42:101
Jewish Reform-Verein, Chicago, 45:93
Jewish Refugee Committee, 49:68
Jewish Relief Act, 31:112
Jewish Relief Committee of London, 49:177,
   182
"Jewish Religious and Cultural Life in
   America as Reflected in the Felsenthal
   Collection," 45:93-127
Jewish Religious Education Association,
   Ohio, 28:275
Jewish Religious Education Board, London,
   22:201
Jewish Religious School Union, 42:4
Jewish Religious Union, 31:250, 291
Jewish Review, 41:361
Jewish Seminary, Budapest, 22:203
Jewish Sentinel, The, 28:xxxviii
Jewish Services in Synagogue and Home, 50:345
Jewish Settlement (Cincinnati), 37:294
Jewish Settlement Association (Des Moines),
   37:294
Jewish Social Democratic Party in Russia,
   50:217
Jewish Socialism, "Abraham Cahan and the
   New York *Commercial Advertiser*: A Study
   in Acculturation," 43:10-36
Jewish Socialist Federation, 50:226
Jewish Socialist Party, 42:322
Jewish Socialist Verband, gift, 35:xxiii
Jewish Social Research, Bureau of, 39:253
Jewish Social Service Association, 49:61
Jewish Social Service Bureau (St. Louis),
   37:293
Jewish Social Service Quarterly, The, 39:253;
   50:434
Jewish Social Studies, 40:94-95
Jewish social welfare, 38:336
"Jewish Soldiers in the Union and
   Confederate Armies During the Civil War,

Classified According to States and
Alphabetically Arranged, List of," 50:303
"Jewish South, The," 39:402
Jewish Spectator, 40:404
Jewish Standard, 31:264
Jewish state, 38:2; "American Jewry and
Palestine: the Role Played by American
Jews in the Establishment of the Jewish
State," 38:345; "Noah's Ararat Jewish State
in its Historical Setting," 43:170-91;
"United States Policies on Palestine,"
40:107-18
Jewish State, The, 46:184
Jewish Students' Loan Fund, 29:181
Jewish Teacher's College Fund, 42:16
Jewish Telegraphic Agency, 29:xlii; 34:193
Jewish Tercentenary, 43:151-58; "Raising the
Curtain of History," 43:151-58
Jewish Territorial Organization, history,
writing of, 46:474-75, 477-78, 484-85, 490
Jewish Theatrical Guild, 45:199
Jewish Theological Seminary of America,
22:ix, 122-23, 216-17, 226, 233; 25:161,
185, 187; 26:2, 8, 239; 28:xii, 268, 284,
302; 29:xi, xvii, 4, 166, 169, 190, 192; 30:vi;
31:xviii, 259, 276, 282, 289-90; 32:xvi;
33:18, 20-21, 26, 29, 129; 34:59, 107, 111,
153, 303-4; 35:119-21, 123, 316, 318, 324;
37:xi, xxix, 13, 32, 55-57, 60, 74, 79, 85,
260, 451, 479-80, 482; 38:7, 187, 258, 338,
341; 39:216, 261, 300; 40:36, 44-45, 49,
311; 41:223, 276, 385, 391; 42:8, 15-16, 20,
106; 43:139, 194-96, 242-44, 250; 44:152,
187, 240, 244; 45:62, 103, 117, 136, 138,
142, 147, 151, 185, 198, 260, 262, 264-67;
46:122, 129, 192; 47:218-19, 226, 48:230-
32, 235, 240, 243; 49:31, 61, 105, 137, 151,
165, 216, 263; 50:70, 79, 270, 275, 296,
299, 312, 316-17, 335, 360, 383, 401-2,
425-27; American Jewish Historical
Society, dedication of rooms, 32:xxi-xxiii;
Board of Delegates of American Israelites,
29:77; Jewish bookplates, 45:153-56, 185;
gifts, 28:xl; 34:xxiii; library, 34:286; 39:309;
50:272, 275, 282, 292, 296-97, 299
Jewish Theological Seminary (Breslau),
40:311; 50:88-95
Jewish Theological Seminary and Scientific
Institution of 1852, 22:xxix; 27:159; 49:17

Jewish Tidings, 40:70; 44:152; "The Jewish
Tidings and the Sunday Services
Question," 42:371-85, 415
Jewish Times, 29:xxxix; 39:399; 45:114; "The
Jewish Disabilities in Balkans," 24:6
Jewish Training School (Chicago), 37:294-
95; 39-92
Jewish Tribune, The, 29:153
Jewish Voice, 42:377
Jewish war records, 42:89
Jewish War Relief Committee, Baltimore,
31:221
Jewish war sufferers, 45:211
Jewish War Veterans of America, 42:320-22;
49:137, 154; 50:263, 267, 270-71, 273,
275, 304, 312-314
Jewish Welfare Board, 28:xxxviii-xxxix;
29:160, 180; 33:29; 35:324; 40:15; 43:253;
47:194; 49:12; and American Jewish
Historical Society, 44:243; gifts, 28:xl;
33:xxxiii; "Study of the Social and
Recreational Facilities and Needs of
Rochester, 44:238; war records, 28:xiv
Jewish Welfare Federation, 50:143 (Des
Moines), 49:222
Jewish Welfare Fund, 42:39
Jewish Welfare Society (Palestine), 49:91;
(Philadelphia), 49:91; "History of the
Jewish Welfare Society of Philadelphia,"
31:xxiv
Jewish Widows' & Orphans' Home, New
Orleans, 29:309
Jewish Workers Alliance, 46:222
Jewish Year Book, The, 25:159-60; 29:164
Jewish Young Men's Association (Rochester,
N.Y.), 40:72
*Jews in American History. Their Contributions to
the United States of America,* reviewed,
40:191-92
Jews of Charleston, The, 46:177, 442
Jews' College (England), 22:201; 25:181,
31:263; 49:68; gift, 22:xxxv; (Jerusalem),
23:160
Jews from Germany in the United States,
reviewed, 46:59-60
"Jews Hospital, The," 21:xxiv, *see also*: Mount
Sinai Hospital
Jews and the Mosaic Law, 46:68
Jews' Naturalization Act of 1753, 35:35

"Jews and Negro Slavery in the Old South, 1789-1865," 50:287

Jews: Their History, Culture and Religion, The, reviewed, 40:192-96

Jews of South Carolina from the Earliest Times to the Present Day, The, 50:285

Jews in Transition, 40:196-98

"Jews Who Served in the War Between the States," 50:303-4

Jews Without Money, 46:436

Jezurun, Clara, 32:114

Jezurun, Ischack, 32:114

Jezykowicz, Louis, 39:149

J. Hood Wright Hospital of New York, 22:238

Joachim, Joseph, 28:24; 35:240

Joachimsen, Mrs., 27:113

Joachimsen, Haya Diana, 27:112

Joachimsen, L., 27:114, 399

Joachimsen, L. (Miss), 27:110

Joachimsen, Philip J., 21:215; 27:124, 450, 509, 515, 29:109, 112; 32:130; 34:xxi; 35:124; 44:160, 197; HIAS, 49:27, 30, 186; Palestine, 37:97, 229, 233, 236; president, 29:99; Touro Synagogue, 38:57-58, 63, 67

Joachimsen, Mrs. P. J., 32:35

Joan of Anjou, Queen of Naples, 28:204

João II, 32:36, 46

João of Salerno, 28:205

Joaquin, 44:43

Jochanan bar Kimchi, 21:213; 31:238

Joe William (slave), 50:167

Joel, Benjamin Edgar, 25:113

Joel, Israel, 27:68

Joel, Joseph A., 50:309, 311, 399-400, 406

Joel, M., 28:71

Joel, Manuel, 50:92

Joffe, Joshua A., 34:303

Johalemstein, Mordecai, 35:64

Johanan ben Zakkai, 42:317-18

Johlson, J., 30:264, 367; 42:57; *Johlson's Catechism,* 42:401

John of Capistrano, 28:159

John II (Castile), 45:22

John, King of England, 21:238

John, King of Portugal, 31:174

John II, King of Portugal, 28:214

John IV (Portugal), 33:82-83; 47:117-19

John XXII, 28:148

John XXIII, 28:155

John Chrysostom, Saint, 28:137, 139

John Francis, Duke of Mantua, 28:158

John Holden, Unionist: A Romance of the Days of Destruction and Reconstruction, 50:397

John of Leyden, 28:242

John Marshall Prize, 37:465

"Johnny Reb," 50:323

Johns Hopkins Hospital, 42:122

Johns Hopkins University, 22:216; 25:151, 154; 26:1; 28:34, 251; 31:282; 33:20, 28; 37:465; "Judaica and Hebraica Collection in College Libraries," 45:144

Johnson, Albert, 46:297, 299-300

Johnson (actress), 33:197

Johnson, Allen, 39:285

Johnson, Alvin, 36:371; (foreword), *The Jews in the Soviet Union,* reviewed, 42:442-49

Johnson, Andrew, 25:28; 47:51, 57, 77; 50:293-95, 300, 334-35, 356-57, 380; Marcus Otterbourg, 32:69, 73, 89, 92, 94-95; portrait, 32:xxvi

Johnson, Ben, *Everyman in his humour,* 33:172

Johnson, Charles, 43:94, 99, 106, 109, 115

Johnson, Colonel, 23:177

Johnson, Edward, 25:77

Johnson, Frederick, 22:55

Johnson, Henry, 38:96

Johnson, Henry F. J., 37:419

Johnson, Hiram, 29:197-98

Johnson, Homer H., 36:160, 164

Johnson, Jeromus, 30:404

Johnson, Lady (Rebecca Franks), 22:55; 28:xl

Johnson, Marmaduke, 27:506

Johnson, Mordecai, 47:203

Johnson, Oliver, 42:151

Johnson, Rebecca, 37:419

Johnson, Reverdy, 22:100; 23:124-25; 25:21; 34:192

Johnson, Richard, 23:118, 120

Johnson, Richard M., 40:97

Johnson, Samuel (Columbia), 32:5; 35:158; 42:417; 45:133; 46:180

Johnson, Samuel, "Johnson of Columbia and the Hebrew Language," 25:109-11

Johnson, Samuel (author), 28:235; 33:196; 46:180, 434

Johnson, Solomon Levy, 25:52

Johnson, Thomas, Jr., 37:167-68

Johnson, William, 23:7, 13, 15, 20, 22; 35:15; 37:347, "Jews in the Correspondence of Sir William Johnson," 25:xiii; "Sir William Johnson and His Relations to Colonial Jews," 29:xxx
Johnson v. Auburn, 29:150
Johnson's Fort, 49:34
Johnson's Island, 50:351
Johnston, Albert Sidney, 50:342
Johnston, David, 25:143
Johnston, Governor (Penn.), 27:503
Johnston, John, 35:180
Johnston, James, 27:247
Johnston, Joseph E., 25:27-28
Johnston, Joseph Eggleston, 50:334, 342
Johnston, Moffat, 35:273
Johnston, Samuel, 27:247
Johnstone, Anne Humphreys, 38:279; 39:324
Johnstone, George, 31:47
John Street Theatre, New York, 33:175-76, 178, 182
Joint Board of Cloakmakers Unions, 50:222-23, 225
Joint Board of Sanitary Control, 41:324
Joint Consultative Committee, 45:222-23
Joint Consultative Council, 36:367
Joint Defense Appeal, 42:321
Joint Distribution Committee, 31:214; 33:19; 35:324; 36:69-70, 72; 39:334; 40:15; 43:142; 44:214; 45:38, 196; 50:141; (Paris), 39:219-20, 250; (Poland), 36:141, 143-45, 147, 153, 156, 162
Joint Foreign Committee, 31:262
Joint Palestine Survey Commission, 32:xxvi
Joint Polish American Committee, Society of the, 39:152
Joint University Libraries, "Judaica and Hebraica Collection in College Libraries," 45:147
Jomini, Baron, 36:181-84
Jomtob (Antonio Puigblanch), 26:243
Jonap, Henry, 37:269, necrology of, 32:ix-x
Jonas, A., 23:123-24
Jonas, Abraham, 41:215; 42:407-12; 50:294, 346-51, 367-69; "Abraham Jonas' Role in Lincoln's First Presidential Nomination," 44:98-105; letter to Abraham Lincoln, 50:369; will and testament and records pertaining to the estate of, 50:350-51

Jonas, Mrs. Abraham, 42:408-10; 44:105; 50:350
Jonas, Alexander, 48:90
Jonas, Annie, 42:409-11
Jonas, Benjamin F., 22:195; 35:124; 40:288
Jonas, Charles H., 44:105; 50:351; "New Light on Lincoln's Parole of Charles H. Jonas," 42:407-12
Jonas, Harold J., 39:336; "American Jewish History as Reflected in General American History," 38:346; 39:283-90; Canadian Jewish Congress, 49:265-66; discussant, 50:427; executive council, 44:241; 46:493; 50:426; history, writing of, 46:178-79, 184, 191, 408-9, 417; treasurer, 49:268
Jonas, Jacob, 26:186
Jonas, Joseph, 27:259; 42:110; 48:200
Jonas, Lyon, 21:157-59; 27:253
Jonas, Yecutel, 27:56
Jonaz, Abram, 42:279, 394
Jones, Abraham, 50:41, 52
Jones, Alfred, 21:171
Jones, Alfred T., 27:503; 48:239-40
Jones, Amos, 34:77
Jones, Andrew A., 27:110, 277, 506
Jones, C., 27:425-26
Jones, Charles Marshall, 50:317
Jones, Congressman, 26:216
Jones, D., 31:58, 60
Jones, Daniel, Jr., 25:127
Jones, David S., 26:220
Jones, Dramin, 44:135-36, 140, 142, 146, 149, 166, 189-90, 192
Jones, E. Alfred, 45:52
Jones, Edgar DeWitt, *Lincoln and the Preachers*, reviewed, 38:319-21
Jones, Elias, 23:156
Jones, Emily, 50:170
Jones, Epaphras, *Aborigines of America*, 30:354; *Ten Tribes*, 30:270, 272, 347-48, 354
Jones, George, 26:278-79, *History of Ancient America*, 30:374
Jones, Henry, 43:141, *Auszug aus den Staatsgesetzen von New-York*, 30:336, *Dissertation on the Restoration of Israel*, 30:375
Jones, Howard Mumford, 45:31
Jones, Israel I., 29:112, 131; 49:30; 50:169-70, 184

Jones, Jacob, 39:56
Jones, Jesse, 40:338
Jones, John Beauchamps, 38:164
Jones, John Paul, 23:175; 39:31
Jones, John Richter, 35:242
Jones, Joseph, 21:92; 27:471
Jones, K. K., 44:101-3
Jones, Louis, 27:243
Jones, Miriam, 27:112
Jones, Mr., 27:79; 33:183: 38:151
Jones, Paul, 26:195
Jones, Raphael, 48:15-17
Jones, S. I., 50:169, 184
Jones, Samuel (Charleston), 50:41, 52, 159, 161
Jones, Samuel (New York), 27:299-300
Jones, Thomas A. Catesby, 39:27-28, 34, 51, 63
Jones, Thos. R., 39:83
Jones, William, 30:258; 32:125; 39:35
Jonescu, M. Take, 36:137-38
Joode, Daniel de, 33:74
Joos, Fiedel, 41:253
Jordan, John W., 22:188; 27:503; gift, 22:xxxii; necrology of, 29:xiv; "Original Letters of Moses and Sampson Levy, of Philadelphia," 22:xiii; "Two Letters of David Franks," 22:xiii
Jordon & Osborn, 23:182
Jorge, Os Cristanos Novos, 31:xxxiii
Jorge, Francisco, 31:29
Joselewicz, Berek, 39:151
Joseph (N.Y.), 34:129
Joseph, Emperor of Austria, 48:19
Joseph II, Emperor, 26:73, 93-94, 119; 28:71; 37:174; 50:101, 103, 110; education, 28:84-85, 93, 95-103, 114
Joseph, Aaron, 27:60, 75, 87-88
Joseph, Abraham (New York), 27:60, 62
Joseph, Abm. (Surinam), 48:25
Joseph, Barnet, 25:65
Joseph, Benedict, 25:64-65
Joseph, Benjamin (Solomon), 27:77
Joseph, Ellis, 29:132
Joseph, Emily, 27:112, 276
Joseph, Esther, 28:269
Joseph, Eve, 32:58
Joseph, Fanny, 27:112
Joseph, Frances, 27:113

Joseph, Gertrude, 27:110
Joseph, Goody, 27:113
Joseph ben Gorion, 26:169
Joseph, H., 29:135
Joseph, Harry, 27:77
Joseph, Henry (Canada), 50:125-26
Joseph, Henry (New York), 27:271
Joseph, Henry, 27:376
Joseph, Henry (rabbi), 28:xxxviii, collection of, 46:421
Joseph, I. L., 27:116
Joseph, Isaac, 50:169
Joseph, Israel (1), 44:200
Joseph, Israel (S.C.), 26:233; 27:79, 226; 50:41, 52
Joseph, Jacob (B.W.I.), 32:58
Joseph, Jacob (New York rabbi), 35:63, 120; 39:96; 46:396; 48:129; 49:87, 105, 231; "New York Chooses a Chief Rabbi," 44:129-98
Joseph, Jeshua ben, 35:222
Joseph, Jesse H., Heritage, 35:xxii
Joseph, Joseph L., 21:214
Joseph, Joshua, 25:118
Joseph, L. (New York), 21:165
Joseph, L. (S.C.), 48:180
Joseph, L. I., 29:131
Joseph, Lazarus, 27:79
Joseph, Lazerus, 50:42
Joseph, Lizar, 50:42, 52
Joseph, M. V., 37:266-67, 269
Joseph, Manuel, 26:188, 194; 39:7
Joseph, Martin, 42:407, 411
Joseph bar Nathan, 21:127
Joseph, Nathan, 27:41, 43, 51, 60, 62
Joseph, N. S., 40:226, 236; 41:138
Joseph, O. S. B., 38:73
Joseph, Samuel, 34:209, 254; 39:250, "Jewish Immigration to the United States from 1881 to 1910," 24:82
Joseph, Sol., 27:80
Joseph, Sol I., 21:197, 212, 214
Joseph, Solomon, 25:118
Joseph, Solomon I., 27:116-17, 119, 122, 276
Joseph, son of Deodatus of Nola, 28:169
Joseph, Theodore H., 31:xxxv
Joseph Wheeler: The Man, the Statesman, the Soldier Seen in Semi-Biographic Sketches, 50:397

Josephi, Edward, 29:131
Josephi, Henry, 27:515; 29:112
Josephi, Marcus, 27:271
Josephinian Decree, 50:101-2, 117
Josephs (New Orleans), 34:144
Josephs (Richmond), 27:91
Josephs, A. K., 27:451
Josephs, Aaron, 27:45, 314
Josephs, Abraham Haim, 27:80
Josephs, Annie, 34:144
Josephs, Israel, 21:79
Josephs, Jacob, 48:25
Josephs, Jesse, 28:xxxviii
Josephs, Jos., 27:80
Josephs, Judith (Wolff), 48:25
Josephs, Philip, 48:25
Josephs, Solomon, 27:314
Josephson, Emanuel, 50:39, 53
Josephson, Ester, 34:77, 87, 90
Josephson, Joseph, 34:77, 87
Josephson, M., 38:49
Josephson, Manuel (New York), 21:79, 84-
    86, 104, 113, 211; 26:238; 45:56; 48:144;
    ceremonial customs, 27:185-90, George
    Washington correspondence, 27:221-22
Josephson, Manuel (Philadelphia), 43:232
Josephson, Mayer, 28:255
Josephson, Myer, 26:233; 34:76-78, 81-94,
    96-97, 102, 105
Josephus, 26:127; 165, 167-71; 28:63-65, 69,
    205; 30:iv; 39:218; 41:25; 43:156; 47:136;
    collection, 45:138; Werke, 30:336, 412;
    Works, Vol. I, 30:63-69, 75-77, 95-97, 133,
    138, 140, 143, 214, 236, 255, 257-58, 273,
    286, 437, 477
Josephus Ben Gorion (pseud.), History of the
    Latter Times of the Jews, 30:122; Wonderful
    and Most Deplorable History, 30:182
Joshua I, 50:3-9; inscribed on flag presented
    to Lincoln, 50:351
Josina (slave), 25:141
Josippon, 26:127, 169; 34:xvii; 47:136
Joske, 38:20
Josse, Friederika, 41:253
Jost, B., 39:180
Jost, Isaac Marcus, 22:26; 26:11-13, 33;
    28:66-67, 72-74, 79; 33:239; 39:305;
    43:156, Geschichte der Israeliten, 22:117;
    26:11-12

Jost, M., 29:128
Jourdain, Margaret, 44:9
Journal of the American Oriental Society, 47:219
Journal of Commerce, 38:309
Journal of the Illinois State Historical Society,
    50:352
Journal of Jewish Bibliography, 47:220
Journal of Mount Sinai Hospital, 42:129
Journal of the Society of Oriental Research,
    47:219
Journal of the Southern Jewish Historical Society,
    The, 50:316
Journalism, "American Jewish Journalism to
    the Close of the Civil War," 26:xxxi, 270-
    73; "The American Yiddish Press During
    the First World War," 37:xxxii; Anglo-
    Jewish Press in America, 38:310; Canadian
    Jewish newspapers, 50:137; "Contributions
    of Adolph S. Ochs to Journalism," 33:xxxi;
    Czech journals, 50:106-7; "Early Jewish
    Publishers in America, with Special
    Reference to Abraham Hart," 31:xvii;
    "Francis Joseph Grund a Forgotten
    Journalist and Politician," 22:xxviii;
    "Francis Joseph Grund," 26:234-35;
    "German Jews and Jewish Journalism in
    Nineteenth Century America," 47:202;
    "The Hebrew Periodical Press in America,
    1871-1931," 33:127-70; Hebrew press,
    33:134, 138; 39:105; "Jacob de Haas,
    American Zionist Journalist," 47:202;
    Jewish newspapers, 30:iv; "A List of
    Selected Items of American Jewish Interest
    in the Russian-Jewish Press, 1860-1932,"
    38:239-48, 305-16, 343; 39:87-113;
    "References of Jewish Interest in the
    Newspapers of the American Revolution
    (1761-1789): New York and
    Massachusetts," 23:xiv; "A Spanish-
    American Jewish Periodical," 23:vii, xiv,
    129-35; Yiddish journalism, 38:307;
    39:103, 105, 113; 45:185; 46:122, 192, 203,
    394-95, 397; 48:32-133; 49:92, 99, 110,
    243, 246; 50:137, 208, 403
Juarez, 31:294
Juarez, Ana, 32:117
Juarez, Ana Blanca, 32:117
Juarez, Angela, 23:135

Juarez, Benito, 32:68, 74-76, 78-79, 82, 85, 87, 90, 93, 95-96; 47:52

Jucht, Baer, 40:270

Juda, Jettle, 41:258

Judaens, The, 28:xxx, xxxix; 29:169; 32:133; 34:300; 47:224; gift, 26:xxxv; "The Reception by the Judaens," 26:ix, xv, xvii-xxii

Judah, A., 27:83

Judah, Aaron, 25:52; 27:168, 258, 290, 294, 303, 324, 344, 396

Judah, Aaron Hart, 27:277

Judah, Abigail (nee Seixas), 27:76, 161-62, 164, 170; 35:200

Judah, Abigail (Mrs. Kursheedt), 31:274

Judah, Abraham (Boston), 23:85

Judah, Abraham (Dr.), 27:80

Judah, Abraham (New York), 21:42; 27:555, 278; 31:237

Judah, Abraham (Va.), 50:31, 126

Judah, Abraham (b. Hillel), 27:170

Judah, Adeline, 27:277

Judah, Alfred, 27:114

Judah, Amelia, 27:110, 277, 286, 289, 400

Judah, Andrew, 22:161; 27:22

Judah, Anne, 21:226

Judah, Aron, 26:228; 30:298

Judah b. Asher b. Jehiel, 22:61

Judah, B., 27:51, 58

Judah, B. S., 21:149; 27:62

Judah, Baruch (Germany), 42:433

Judah, Baruch (Newport), 50:64

Judah, Baruch (New York), 21:xvii, 5, 7-8, 10, 19, 21, 24-25, 33, 35, 38-39, 181; 27:56, 170; 37:375; 38:236

Judah, Belah, 27:110, 277, 400

Judah, Benjamin S., 21:142, 212; 25:37-39, 41, 48, 55, 57-60; 27:43, 46, 50-51, 56, 84, 96, 217, 277, 314-17, 395, 461; 45:176, 185, 187-88; 50:37, 53; bookplate of 1761 Prayer Book, 22:xxix

Judah, Bernard, 23:184; 27:51, 60-61, 63, 315; 35:130

Judah, Bernard S., 27:56, 278

Judah, Betsy, 35:201

Judah, Betty S. S. (Elishabang), 27:113

Judah brothers, 50:30

Judah Cary, 21:167-70; 25:52; 27:59, 62, 72, 81, 84, 95-96, 106, 243, 258, 277, 314, 338

Judah, Catherine, 27:113; 50:126

Judah, Celestina, 27:111

Judah, Clinton, 27:286, 289

Judah, David (Baltimore), 23:144

Judah, David (Conn.), 50:27, 169

Judah, David (New York), 27:151

Judah, Dorothea, 27:490

Judah, Dorothy, 50:124, 126

Judah, Edward, 27:114, 315

Judah, Br. Eliezer, 21:42, 45

Judah, Elizabeth, 27:54, 113: 50:37; "Samuel Judah's Bond to His Wife Elizabeth for Additional Marriage Portion and Dowry, March 27, 1775," 26:xxxi

Judah, Esther, 27:112

Judah Ezekiel, 47:197

Judah family, 21:xxvii

Judah, George Fortunatus, 28:238; 31:243, "The deCordova Family in Jamaica," 22:xviii

Judah, Gershom, 27:170; 50:64

Judah, Grace (Newport), 27:213

Judah, Grace (nee Seixas), 27:77, 80; 37:204

Judah, Hannah, 27:111

Judah, Henrietta, 27:286, 289

Judah, Henry, 50:125

Judah, Henry Moses, 29:123

Judah, Henry R., 27:389

Judah, Hillel (Boston), 38:150

Judah, Hillel (Newport), 50:26, 36, 53, 64

Judah, Hillel (Richmond), 27:76, 161, 164, 170, 185

Judah, Hilyard, 21:79, 104

Judah, Huldah, 27:213

Judah, Isaac (New York), 21:38

Judah, Isaac (Richmond), 50:64

Judah, Isaac H., 27:76-77, 170, 340, 462

Judah, Jacob (New York), 21:45; 27:247

Judah, Jacob (Va.), 50:31

Judah, Jacob (b. Hillel), 27:170

Judah, Jacob bar Jacob, 33:95

Judah, Jacob (b. Samuel), 27:153

Judah, Jehutiel, 27:152

Judah, Jessie, 50:53

Judah, Jessy, 27:274

Judah, Jessy Jonas, 45:187

Judah, John, 27:315

Judah, John J., 27:277

Judah, Louisa, 27:111

Judah, Louisa C., 27:277
Judah, M., 43:214
Judah, Maccabee, 28:46
Judah, Manuel (Newport), 50:64
Judah, Manuel (New York), 21:165
Judah, Manuel (Richmond), 27:77, 80, 170;
31:274; 35:191
Judah, Maria, 27:317
Judah, Mical, 38:332
Judah, Michael, 21:47, 55, 150; 27:151, 247;
50:27
Judah, Minky, 27:91, 111
Judah, Miriam, 27:111
Judah, Moses (New York), 21:86, 94, 104;
25:52; 27:306, 398; 34:274, 279
Judah, Moses (Richmond), 27:165, 170
Judah ben Moses (Judah Romano), 28:146-47
Judah br. Myer, 21:106
Judah, Naomi, 27:213
Judah, Naphtali, 21:163-65, 168-69, 190,
192, 212, 226; 25:34, 36, 52; 26:228; 27:62,
84, 86-88, 92, 100-101, 104-5, 107, 142,
243, 286, 289, 314, 338, 394; 38:109, 116,
123-25, 127, 137
Judah, Nissim ben Ezekiel, 47:197
Judah P. Benjamin: Confederate Statesman,
50:287
Judah the physician, 28:205
Judah, R. H., 50:8
Judah, Rachel, 50:65
Judah, Rachel (nee Gomez), 27:113, 277,
287-88, 290, 294, 298, 303
Judah, Rachel (b. Hillel), 27:170
Judah, Rebecca (1), 27:111
Judah, Rebecca (2), 27:277, 400
Judah, Rebekah, *see*: Seixas, Rebecca (Mrs.
Issac B.)
Judah, Riche Ann, 27:286, 289
Judah, Samuel (Canada), 31:184-85; 34:171
Judah, Samuel (b. Naphtalia), 27:286, 289
Judah, Samuel (New York), 21:74, 79, 85, 90-
91, 93, 102, 130, 159-60, 183, 211; 23:184;
25:47; 26:237-38; 27:27, 41, 43-44, 152-
53, 314, 376, 405; 45:187, "Samuel Judah's
Bond to His Wife Elizabeth for Additional
Marriage Portion and Dowry, March 27,
1775," 26:xxxi
Judah, Samuel (Philadelphia), 50:53, 124-26

Judah, Samuel B. H., 26:242-43; 27:314-16;
32:3; 33:197; 45:187; *The Buccaneers*,
30:244, 246-47; *Gotham and the Gothamites*,
30:214-15; *The Maid of Midian*, 30:288-89;
"The Mountain Torrent," 26:xxxv; 30:190-
91; *Odofriede, the Outcast*, 30:200, 202; *The
Rose of Arragon*, 30:202-3; "The Tale of
Lexington," 26:xxxv; 30:216-17
Judah, Samuel Bernard, 37:437, 442
Judah, Samuel N., 27:166, 277; 30:332
Judah, Sarah, 27:170
Judah, Simah, 27:111
Judah, Simon, 35:198
Judah, S. N., 21:168
Judah, Theodore D., 35:128
Judah Touro Ministerial and Cemetery Fund,
38:66
Judah, Uriah, 31:184-85; 50:124-26
Judah, Uriah H., 22:97-98; 27:286, 289;
"Home," 27:501-2
Judah, Walter J., 22:162-63; 37:435
Judah, Walter Jonas, 42:433
Judah, Walter S., 25:123
Judah, Zepy, 27:111
Judaica, 38:331-33; "Judaica and Hebraica
Collection in College Libraries," 45:134-
38; "Resources on American Jewish
History at the Library of Congress,"
47:179-85, 201; "Resources on American
Jewish History in the National Archives,"
47:186-95, 201; "Some Final Words on
Emma Lazarus," 39:321-27; "Some
Judaica in State and Other Regional
Historical Publications," 37:xxx, 435-44
Judaism, 44:121, 124; 50:384; "Adah Isaacs
Menken: A Daughter of Israel," 34:143-47;
"Aims and Tasks of Jewish Historiography,"
26:xv, 11-32; American, 39:291-301, 348,
351-88; *American Judaism*, reviewed,
47:121-23; "American Jewish Journalism to
the Close of the Civil War," 26:xxxi, 270-73;
Brazil, 33:69; "British Projects for the
Restoration of Jews to Palestine," 26:xv,
127-64; Conservative Judaism, 40:361, 401;
"The Contribution of Judaism to World
Ethics," reviewed, 40:195; *Differentiation
Features of Orthodox, Conservative, and
Reform Jewish Groups in Metropolitan*

Philadelphia, reviewed, 49:276-78; "Emma Lazarus' Approach to Renan and Her Essay 'Renan and the Jews,'" 37:xxxiv, 17-29; history, writing of, 46:9, 21, 60-63, 67, 268, 273, 287; "Isaac de Castro, Brazilian Jewish Martyr," 47:63-75; Jewish local history, 49:224, 226, 240, 246; *Jewish Quarterly Review*, 33:24-25; "Judaism and the Democratic Ideal," reviewed, 40:195; "The Mythical Element of Judaism," reviewed, 40:195; Orthodoxy, 40:24, 63, 243, 258; Russia and Jewish education, 35:39-51; "Science and Judaism," reviewed, 40:193: Solomon Schechter, a tribute, 25:177-92; Unitarianism, 38:159; *Yahadut Amerika be-Hitpathutah (The Shaping of American Judaism)*, reviewed, 42:91-107; *The Zionist Idea: A Historical Analysis and Reader*, reviewed, 49:140-42

Judd, Norman B., 44:103

Judean Club (Rochester, N.Y.), 40:72

Judeans, 45:205

Judenstaat, 40:364

Judeo-Christian relations, 39:239, 259-61

Judeo, Gaspar, 42:431

Jüdische Gazetten, 49:88

Jüdische Jugendhilfe, 49:169

Jüdische Volkszeitung, 44:154

Jüdische Zeitschrift für Wissenschaft und Leben, 45:100, 102-3

Jüdische Zeitung, 48:132

Jüdisches Lexikon, 34:xviii, xix

Jüdisches Tageblatt, 44:143, 149, 157, 159, 168; 48:132

Judith, M. S., 27:277

Judson, Roswell, *Two Epistles of Free Stricture*, 30:264

Juedische Rundschau, 45:227

Juellit (slave), 50:160

Juilliard Foundation, 35:325

Jules, Mervin, 47:182

Julian, Moses H., 26:252-53

Julianna Street Synagogue, Philadelphia, 41:85, 90

Juliao, David Henriques, 27:50

Julien (slave), 50:160

Julien, M., 50:148

Julio, David Henriquez, 21:186

Julius II, 28:160, 166-68, 170, 204

Julius III, 28:164, 173, 202-3

Jun, Jacob Ferre, 37:373, 377, 386; 38:235

Jun, Solomon Hart, 37:373, 377, 386; 38:235

Jung, Elias, 41:256

Jung, Lazarus, 41:256

Jung, Leo, 33:xxix, xxxii-xxxiii

Jung, Nanette, 41:267

Junge Maenner Verbruederung (Mil), 47:46

Junior Alliance Israélite Universelle, 39:436

Jurburg, 44:143

Jurewitz, J. C., 40:205

Jury (Ury), John, 27:386

Juster, 26:27; 28:136

Justin II, 28:138

Jusurun, Josef, 32:114-15

Jusurun, Simon, 32:115

Juvenal, 33:41

Juvenile Aid Society, 31:287, 293

Juvenile Miscellany, 38:173

K

Kaal Kadosh Nidhi Israel Congregation, 26:251-54
Kaas, Andrew, necrology of, 35:ix
Kabakoff, Jacob, 46:62; "The Hebrew Correspondence Between the Reverend Marcus Hillel Dubov and Secretary of State John Hay," 38:53-56, 342
Kabatznick, Max, 42:419
Kadden, Aaron, 50:314
Kadden, Jack S., 50:272, 314
Kaddish, 39:373
Kaeglerii (P. Ignatii), 49:42
Kaempf, Saul Isaac, 33:239; 35:211
Kafka, Bruno, 50:111
Kafka, Franz, 35:271; 46:440; 50:109-12, 115-17
Kagan, A., 39:100; *see*: Cahan, Abraham
Kagan, Solomon B., 33:xxxiii
Kagan, Solomon R., 39:258; "Dr. Henry Illoway," 35:xv; gift, 34:xxvi; "Hygiene and Health in the Talmud," 34:xxvi; "Jewish Contributions to Medicine in America," 34:xxvi
Kaganoff, Nathan M., "The Traditional Jewish Sermon in the United States (1763-1915)," 50:427
Kage, Joseph, "History of Jewish Immigration to Canada (1947-1957)," 47:202; "Jewish Immigration and Immigration Aid Efforts in Canada," 49:270
Kahal, 40:335; 43:46, 50; "Communal and Social Aspects of American Jewish History," 39:267-82
Kahal Adath Yeshurun Congregation (New York), 44:136
Kahal Bikkur Cholin (Cholim), 50:302
Kahal Kados Sahar Asamaim, 42:437
Kahal Kados de Talmud Torah, 44:213, 221

Kahal Kadosh, 46:200
Kahal Kadosh Shearith Israel, *Dedication of Synagogue*, 30:177-79
Kahan, Israel Meir, 40:403
Kahana, David, 34:156
Kahane, Hillel, *Geliloth ha-Arez*, 22:133
Kahl Montgomery (Ala.) Congregation, 38:165
Kahn, Aaron, 29:62, 69, 71
Kahn, Abraham, 29:133; 41:255, 260
Kahn, Abram, 28:268
Kahn, Albert, 39:241; 46:255; death, 37:12
Kahn, Aron Judas, 41:258
Kahn, Ber, 50:268n, 297, 359
Kahn, Cora, 40:43
Kahn, Cornelia, gift, 33:xxix, xxxii-xxxiii
Kahn, Doct., 30:421
Kahn, Ed., 47:55
Kahn, Edgar M., 42:420
Kahn, Edward M., 42:420
Kahn, Isaac, 50:375, 385
Kahn, Isadore, 50:314
Kahn, Julius H., 49:199
Kahn, Leon, 28:113
Kahn, Marx, 41:264
Kahn, Mayer, 41:260
Kahn, Mr., 44:47
Kahn, Moses, 41:267
Kahn, Otto, 35:273
Kahn, Peter M., Jr., 46:120
Kahn, Rebecca (Ezekiel), 28:268
Kahn, Zadec, 37:474; 41:134, 150, 153, 162; 42:179; 43:65-66
Kairys, Mrs. Henry, 49:270
Kaiser, Alois, 31:226
Kaiser, Zvi Hirsch, 45:78
Kakeles, 38:197
Kalfe Sedaka Mattan Basether Society, 27:138, 140-42, 255-57; 44:212

Kalisch, Isidor, 26:271; 47:40-41; 50:84; "Studies in Ancient and Modern Judaism," 32:xxvi
Kalisch, Marcus, 22:201
Kalischer, Zvi Hirsch, 45:74-75
Kalish, Max, 50:266, 376, 387
Kalish, Samuel, 27:389; gift, 32:xxvi
Kalisher, D., 29:135
Kallen, Horace M., 46:368; 49:141, 192-93
Kallimachor, Code of, 24:116
Kallman, William, 48:96-97
Kallsall, Johanna, 23:152
Kalm, Peter, 39:293; 40:187
Kalmann, Emmerich, 35:269
Kalnoky, Count, 36:324-25, 327-28, 331-32, 334-36, 338-40, 342
Kalonymos, Marco Calo, 28:170
Kalonymos ben Todros, 35:222
Kals, John William, 32:113
Kaltenborn, H. von, 35:257
Kalussowski, Henryk, 39:154, 157-58, 160, 164
Kamen, Michael, 35:xxiii
Kamenski, A., 50:403
Kamil, Pasha, 47:162
Kaminka, Armand, 39:409
Kamintzky, Moses H., 33:161
Kamp Kohut, 34:303
Kan, Chin Bak, 34:195-96
Kane, George P., 37:448
Kann, M., 24:47, 50-51
Kann, S. E., 41:162
Kann Sons & Company, 48:16
Kanof, Abram, 39:477; 45:260; 46:492; 48:265; 49:137, 155; "The Career of Joseph B. Nones," 42:415; Civil War, 50:260, 270, 274, 282, 308, 312, 323, 383; executive council, 41:388; 42:414; 45:264; Lee Max Friedman Award Medal, 49:270-71; president, 50:426; presides, 49:268; 50:425; "The Role in Medicine," 50:323-31; "Some Remarks on the Career and Character of Commodore Uriah P. Levy," 37:xxxv; treasurer, 47:200; 48:265; "Uriah Phillips Levy: The Story of a Pugnacious Commodore," 39:1-66; vice-president, 49:268; and David Markowitz, "Joseph B. Nones: The Affable Midshipman," 46:1-19

Kansas, 25:25; admission to statehood, 22:141; colonies, 48:87,93; Jewish local history, 49:179, 222; "Some Jewish Associates of John Brown," 23:vii, 55-78; State Board of Charities, 23:76
Kansas Bill Speech of Hon. J. P. Benjamin, of Louisiana, delivered in Senate of United States on Thursday, March 11, 1858. Slavery Protected by the Common Law of the New World. Guaranteed by Constitution. Vindication of the Supreme Court of the United States, 50:287
Kansas-Nebraska Act, 23:58
Kansas State Historical Society, 23:76; 50:273, 275, 285, 354
Kantrowitz, Jacob, 29:132
Kantrowitz, Lazarus, 29:133
Kaplan, Benjamin, The Eternal Stranger: A Study of Jewish Life in the Small Community, reviewed, 48:196-99; 49:223
Kaplan, Benoir, 48:31
Kaplan, Bernard H., 37:92
Kaplan, I., 38:309
Kaplan, Israel, 44:174, 187
Kaplan, J. J., 42:419
Kaplan, Joseph, 42:419
Kaplan, Kivie, 42:419
Kaplan, Leonard, 42:419
Kaplan, Louis L., 49:265, 270
Kaplan, Mitchell M., 45:141, 169
Kaplan, Mordecai M., 46:61, 63; 47:62, 122; "The Contribution of Judaism to World Ethics," reviewed, 40:195; history, writing of, 46:281, 287; Jewish education, 42:26-28; Judaism, 40:198, 312; Mordecai M. Kaplan Jubilee Volume, 43:194-97; Y.M.H.A., 37:307; Zionism, 49:141
Kaplan, Nathan D., 28:240
Kaplan, Paul, 48:92
Kapp, Friedrich, 45:84
Kapparot, 39:370
Kappelman, Mrs. Leroy, 49:270
Kapper, Siegfried, 50:104
Karaites, 43:183, 189
Karbona, 23:28
Karigal, Isaac, 26:245, 251; 27:215; 29:xxxvii, 32; 31:xxxiii; 34:289; 39:299; 42:104; The Salvation of Israel, 30:69-70
Karl Anton, Prince, 24:74-75; 36:116

Karlin, William, 50:237
Karlsruhe Synagogue, 41:68-69
Karolik Collection, 42:418
Karolin, N., 50:403
Karolyi, Baron, 24:121
Karp, Abraham J., 43:231; executive council, 48:265; "New York Chooses a Chief Rabbi," 44:129-98; 49:231; "Simon Tuska Becomes a Rabbi," 50:79-97
Karpeles, "Jews of the Nineteenth Century," 25:xv
Karpeles, Gustav, 45:101, 107
Karpeles, Leopold, 47:191; Civil War, 50:304-6, 362; "Leopold Karpeles: Civil War Hero," 49:268
Karpf, Maurice J., 39:253; "The History of the Graduate School for Jewish Social Work," 37:xxxi
Karpinski, "Dr. L. C. Karpinski Collection," 45:157
Karr, Joseph A., 43:238
Kartak, Mellie Maurer, 37:443
Kaskel, Cesar F., 40:186
Kasovich, Israel Isser, 40:176-77
Kaspe, M., 38:307
Kassel Synagogue, 41:70-71
Kasson, John A., 24:41-43, 71-72, 85; 36:6-7, 113-18, 349
Kassovich, Noah, 43:62-63
Kast, Martin, 34:96
Kastriner and Eiseman, 29:158
Katrin, Yizhak Al, 42:279, 388, 394
Katsh, Abraham I., "The Status of Hebrew in American Higher Education," 38:346
Katty (slave), 23:156
Katz, Albert, *Jews of China*, 31:xxxiii
Katz, A. Raymond, 45:209, 214-15
Katz, Benzion, 33:133
Katz, Irving I., 38:333; 40:105; "Chapman Abraham: An Early Jewish Settler in Detroit," 39:470; 40:81-86; "Jews in Detroit Prior to and Including 1850," 49:226
Katz, M., 39:113
Kätz, Mark J., "The Battleship 'Maine' and the Gunboat 'Scorpion': the part played by Jewish Seamen in United States Marine History," 22:xvii; gifts, 22:xxxii; 29:xliii;

necrology of, 32:ix-x; necrology of Adolph Marix, 28:xxii, 290-92
Katz, Mary, 35:307, 309
Katz, Moses, 35:128
Katz, Robert L., 40:53
Katz, Rosa, 47:53
Katz, Samson, 41:258
Katz, Tobias, "Tobias Katz: a Medical Gyclopaedist of the Seventeenth Century," 25:xiv
Katzenberger, W. M., 37:268
Katzenellenbegen, surname, 37:378
Katzenstein, Emil, 50:313
Katzenstein, Martin, 41:91
Katzer, Friedrich Xavier, 46:284
Kauffman, George, 50:175
Kauffman, Samuel, 50:175
Kauffmann, Sara, 41:267
Kaufman, Abraham, 41:264
Kaufman, Charles H., 27:389
Kaufman, Daniel, 26:188
Kaufman, David, 26:187; 28:262, 264
Kaufman, David S., 50:191
Kaufman, Enit, 48:250
Kaufman, George S., 35:268; 40:354, 357, 359
Kaufman, Isidor, 48:250
Kaufman, J. D., 47:202
Kaufman, Joel S., 47:203
Kaufman, Nathan, 37:266-68, 270
Kaufman, S., 29:129
Kaufman, Samuel, 37:276-77
Kaufman, Sigismund, 49:186; 50:351; "Sigismund Kaufman, An American Jewish Socialist One Hundred Years Ago," 40:406
Kaufman-Mandell, M., 39:438
Kaufmann, David, 39:176
Kaufmann, Isidor, 40:319
Kaufmann, Lene, 41:264
Kaufmann, Renate, 46:162
Kaufmann, Sigismund, 47:77
Kauphman, Hetty, 27:111
Kauphman, Sarah, 27:111
Kautsky, Karl, 41:325
Kavalkanti, Antonio, 33:80
Kavalkanti, Manuel, 33:80
Kay, Abe S., 47:203
Kay, Jacob Teunis de, 31:86n
Kay, Nathaniel, 27:413

Kayser, Alexander, 32:119
Kayser, Asser, 32:110
Kayser, Jacque, 34:230
Kayser, Mrs. Louise, 49:137
Kayser, Louise D., 50:260, 270-71, 281, 285, 303, 313, 340, 351, 353
Kayser, Stephen S., "The American Synagogue of Today: Its Art and Architecture," 44:242; books reviewed by, 46:64-67; Civil War, 50:260, 270; 49:137, 155; Jewish Museum, 38:347; 40:406; 41:385; 43:243; 45:264; 50:425; "Preface," 50:265-66; and Isidore S. Meyer, "Early American Jewish Portraiture," 41:275-96, 387
Kayserling Library, 45:156-57
Kayserling, M., 22:26; 26:xix, 2; 45:102, 111-12, 156-57; "Christopher Columbus," 22:105; ritual slaughtering, 32:xxvi
Kayserling, Meyer, 28:199; 33:xxxi, 238; 34:169, 173, 179; 37:172, 174; 40:12; "Christopher Columbus and the Participation of the Jews in the Spanish-Portuguese Discoveries," 33:35-36, 38; "The Participation of the Jews in the Discovery of America by Christopher Columbus," 28:34
Kazin, Alfred, history, writing of, 46:193, 409-10, 418, 438, 440-41
Kazis, David, 43:57, 59
Kean, Edmund, 33:196-97
Keane, 31:106, 113
Keane, John Joseph, 46:284
Keane, Robert E., 35:272
Kearney, Lawrence, 39:27, 62
Kearny, Michael, 35:180
Keegan, Charles M., 41:361-64
Keene, George, 22:55
Keene, Richard, 41:5
Keese, Abraham Israel, 27:304, 316, 342-43
Keesing, Thomas H., 29:113
Kehal Adath Jeshurun, New York, 49:87
Kehilah Bney Sholem Ubikur Chomim Congregation, Chicago, 29:130
Kehillah, "Isaac Leeser and the Jews of Philadelphia: A Study in National Jewish Influence," 48:207-44
Kehillah, Los Angeles, 42:25; Louisville, 42:25; New York, 28:xxxix; 42:25-29;

43:146, 196; Philadelphia, 28:314; 42:25-26, 35
Kehillath Anshe Maarabh, 28:239
Kehillath Anshe Mayriv, Chicago, "The Founding of Kehillath Anshe Mayriv in Chicago and the Building of its First Synagogue," 38:347
Kehillath Jeshurun Congregation (New York City), 28:286-87
Keiffer, Mrs. Walter B., 28:310
Keiley, Anthony M., 36:51, 323-45
Keim, General, 27:473
Keimer, Samuel, 30:v
Keir, R. Malcolm, 44:5, 7
Keith, Alexander, The Land of Israel, 30:386
Keith, Dr., 22:172
Keith, George, 30:iv, 4, 6-7, 10; 43:237; New England Spirit of Persecution, 30:v, 4, 6-7, 10; Truth Advanced, 30:v, 8-10
Keizer, M. A., 27:144
Kelby, Judge, 25:136
Keller, Count, 26:52
Keller, Naftali, 47:197
Keller, Samuel, 27:91
Keller, Suzanne, 46:250
Kellerman, Jacob, 32:64
Kellert, families, 50:134
Kelley, Copeland, 48:58
Kelley, Florence, 41:308
Kellner, Abraham A., "Jews and the Jewish Question in the Writings of Harold Frederic," 38:344
Kellogg, Stephen Wright, 43:123
Kellor, Frances, 34:242
Kelly, Doctor, 22:220
Kelly, Eben A., 50:391
Kelly, Judge, 25:135-36
Kelly, Lieut., 39:33
Kelly, Mr., 29:105
Kelly, Myra, 38:250
Kelly, R. M., 38:44
Kelonimos Bar Semuel, R., 21:46-47, 213
Kelsohn, 38:202
Kemble, Frances Anne, 38:269
Kemp, Mr., 21:134
Kempe, John, 31:91, 93
Kempe, John Tabor, 31:80-83, 90, 93-94; 45:57
Kempinsky, 36:227

Kempler, Mrs. George W., gift, 34:xxiii
Kempshall, Mrs., 38:31
Kendall, H. P., 41:48
Kendall, John S., 37:438
Kendall, Messmore, 45:200
Keneseth Israel Congregation (Philadelphia),
    28:46, 297; 33:27; 34:xx; 37:77, 91; 41:91,
    361-62, 364; 42:216, 376; 45:120; 46:117;
    48:76, 216, 241; 50:286; (Richmond),
    29:134; 49:19
Kenesseth Israel Temple (Philadelphia), 33:27
Kenna family troupe, 33:176
Kennan collection, 29:xliii
Kennan, William, 37:438
Kennedy, Archibald, 41:113
Kennedy, Captain, 35:6
Kennedy & Foster, 31:137
Kennedy, John P., 25:101
Kennedy (slave), 50:160
Kennedy, Thomas, 25:95, 98, 100-101, 106;
    27:518; 43:167-69, 179; 50:5, 18, 20-21;
    Maryland, Bill Respecting Civil Rights and
    Religious Privileges, 30:216
Kennesset Israel Anshe Russia Congregation
    (New York), 44:136
Kennett, White, 35:161-62
Kenney, James, Ella Rosenberg, 33:174, 191
Kennicott, 25:109
Kennicott, Benjamin, 30:138-39; 49:42, 46
Kenny, 23:4
Kent, Chancellor, 27:273
Kent, James, 26:176; 31:81, 101
Kent, Judge, 22:82
Kent, Robert T., 41:44, 48
Kentucky, 25:24; expulsion of Jews, 1868,
    34:275; "The Gratz Papers," 23:1, 4, 8-9,
    11-12; John Jordan Crittenden, 22:xxiii;
    "References to Jews in the
    Correspondence of John J. Crittenden,"
    23:vii, xiii, 117-27
Keppele, Michael, 40:128
Keratry, Emile de, 32:74-76
Kerekes, Tibor, 47:203
Kerem Hemed, 22:132
Keren Hayesod, 45:38, 40
Kermer, Hendrick, 23:149
Kerpels, Judith, 48:24
Kerr, Charles G., 40:290
Kerr, J. J., 39:83

Kerr-Coolidge Bill, 45:225, 244
Kershner, Edward, 31:195
Kerstein, Solomon, gift, 35:xxii
Kert, James, 31:101
Kertzer, Morris, 46:63
Kesher Israel Charity Fund (W. Chester,
    Pa.), 37:xxviii
Kesher Shel Barzel, 39:279; (Hamilton,
    Canada), 37:34; (Rochester), 40:66
Kesher Shel Barzel Order, 33:xxxiii
Ketcham, Daniel, 35:174
Ketchum, Mrs., 27:73
Ketektas, Petter, 27:247
Keter Malkut (Sheerit Yisrael), 22:121-22
Kettletas, Abraham, 23:149
Ketubah, 39:385
Key, Helena de, 31:95
Key, Jacobus de, 31:94-95
Key, Teunis de, 31:94-95
Key, Thomas J., 34:275
Keyes, Lily, 38:284
Keyl, Philip, 32:113
Keys, Abraham Israel, 26:253; 41:68
Keyserling, Leon, 47:203
Keyworth, 48:17
Keyzer, 21:41
Kibalsky, Lev, 39:104
Kibbe, Isaac, 30:404
Kidd, William, "Benjamin Franks, Merchant,
    and Captain Kidd, Pirate," 29:xxxvi;
    31:229-34
Kidder, Bishop, 37:133
Kidder, D. P., The Jew Among All Nations,
    30:412; Jewish Nation, 30:455
Kief massacre, 36:204, 291-92
Kierkegaard, Søren, 43:149; 50:117
Kielce atrocities, 36:161
Kierski, M., 29:135
Kierski, W., 29:135
Kiersteds, Mr., 27:385
Kiev Committee, 38:244
Kiev, Edward, 40:54
Kiev, I. Edward, 50:270
Kilbourn, J. A., 37:248
Kilby, 35:22
Killian, Ebbinghaus-Killian case, 26:211
Killian, Marcella, 41:248
Kimball, Fiske, 38:332
Kimbert, Rene, 23:139

Kimchi family, 37:74

Kimchi, Maimonides, 21:239

Kimel, Solomon, 39:145

Kimmel, Hans, 45:261

Kimpton, Edward, 30:96

Kind, Morris, necrology of, 33:xxi

King, 25:56

King, Ann, 22:180

King, artist, 26:245

King, Benjamin, 35:291

King, Charles, 22:80; *Letter to Charles King,* 30:216

King, Charlotte, 22:180

King, Cornelius, 25:50

King, Cornelius, Jr., 25:50

King-Crane Commission, 40:114

King, David, 27:404, 422

King David's Lodge (Masonic), 27:416

King, Edward, 35:252

King, Francis, 44:40

King George's War, 23:165; 49:33

King, Harriet, 22:180

King, Henry C., 36:79

King, Jacob, 27:84, 86

King, John, 28:226

King, Judah, 27:274

King, Judge, 22:140

King, Milton, 47:203

King, Mr., 27:215

King, Pendleton, 36:54, 56

King, Richard, 35:184

King, Rufus, 22:73-75, 78-79

King, Samuel, 35:291

King, William H., 36:369

King, William L., 32:40

King, Yee, 34:198

Kinglake, Alexander William, 33:212

King's College, 35:157; 37:135; 40:408-9

Kings County Historical Society, 28:xxx

Kingsland, Edmund, 27:240-41

Kingsland, Richard, 27:338

Kingston, Jamaica, 25:114-16; 26:271; Dutch records, 22:xxxiv; "Michael Leoni," 23:179-80

Kingston, John, 49:37

Kingston, N.Y., religious observances, mid-nineteenth century, 37:37

Kingwood Tunnel, 25:145

Kinsey, Alfred, 48:257

Kinsey, Judge, 23:193

Kip, 41:111

Kip, Isaac, 27:247

Kip, James, 27:242

Kip, Rochd., 27:247

Kipling, Rudyard, 35:255-56

Kipps, James, 27:236

Kippur, *Evening Service of Roshashanah and Kippur,* 30:51-52; *Prayers for Jewish Holidays,* 30:56-59

Kircheisen, 26:101

Kirjath-sanah, 35:151

Kirjath-sepher, 35:151

Kirk, Hyland C., 22:xxi; 33:37; gift, 22:xxxv

Kirkar, Abraham, "The Conversion of Abraham Kirkar, New York, 1848," 33:xvii

Kirkland, John Thornton, 38:123

Kirkley, Joseph W., 50:382

Kirkpatrick, William, 46:8

Kirschbaum, Eliezer Sinai, 43:183-84

Kirschstein, Salli, 45:137; "S. Kirschstein Collection," 45:157

Kisch, Egon Erwin, 50:116

Kisch, Guido, 34:xxiii; 35:211; 40:54; "German Jews in White Labor Servitude in America," 34:xvi, 11-49; "Leopold Waterman, Merchant, Poet, and Lay-Preacher in New Haven (1841-?)," 37:xxxi; "The Revolution of 1848 and the Jewish 'On to America' Movement," 38:185-234, 345; *In Search of Freedom: A History of American Jews from Czechoslovakia,* reviewed, 39:329-31; (ed. intro.), "A Voyage to America Ninety Years Ago," 35:xv, 65-113; "Woodrow Wilson, the Birth of Czechoslovakia and Congressman Sabath," 38:342

Kischineff pogroms, 29:203; 31:220; 33:26-27; 36:261-71; 39:390, 421-28, 436; 40:8; 41:174-76, 303, 306; 46:89-94; 48:143, 145; 49:90; 50:213; "American and British Intervention on Behalf of Kishinev Jews in 1903," 34:280-84; "The Kishineff Pogrom and Jewish Emigration to the United States on the Fiftieth Anniversary," 42:415

Kiser, Miero, 25:88-89

Kiser, Rose, 25:88

Kisselev, Count, 28:119-20

Kissin, J., 45:152

Kitchel, Stanley R., 28:267
Kitchener, Lord, 26:153
Kiwanis, 47:24
Kizer, Rose, 28:247
K.K. Bnai Avrohum, Quincy, Ill., 29:133
Klaber, 38:197
Kladderadatsch, 41:233
Klapper, Sel., 29:131
Klatzkin, Jacob, 49:140
Klauber, Samuel, 29:131
Klausner, Joseph, 34:161-62; 43:196
Klaw, 40:358
Kleber & Bro., H., 50:391
Klee, Max, 28:240
Klee, Mrs. William B., 28:315
Kleeberg, Minna, 32:xxvii
Kleimenhagen, Maurice, gift, 22:xxxv
Klein, Charles, 40:354, 356, 359
Klein, Gustav, 43:238
Klein, H. L., 50:314
Klein, Max D., nomination committee, 25:xi
Klein, Michael, 39:151
Klein, Moses, 48:96, 100
Klein, Mr., 31:223
Klein, Philip, 35:57-59; 43:238
Klein, Samuel, 38:203
Klein, William, 25:36
Kleinberg, Samuel, 50:313
Kleiner, 38:197
Kleinsmith, E., 46:394
Kleinz, Capt., 39:179
Klenze, 41:69
Kletz; Goldberg *v.*, 29:152
Kline and Co. (San Francisco), 37:45
Kline, Priscilla Carrington, 44:5-6
Kloecke, 31:xxxv
Klopfer, Philip, 29:130
Klüber, 26:33, 53, 60-61
Klutznick Exhibit Hall, 50:260, 381; *see*: B'nai B'rith Museum
Klutznick, Philip M., 47:201-2; executive council, 38:344; 39:469; 44:241; 50:426
Knaufft, Eliza C. T. (Harte), 32:101
Knaufft, Ernest, 32:101
Kneeland and Green, 37:128
Knefler, Frederick, 35:125; 50:308, 406
Knefler, Kenneth, 42:211
Kneller, Godfrey, 23:166
Knesset, 49:273-75

Knickerbocker Club, 49:103
Knickerbocker Yacht Club, 49:56
Knight, 31:177
Knight, Emanuel, 31:258
Knight, Jacob, 31:259
Knight, Sarah Micholl, 31:258
Knight, William Beesson, 41:79
Knights of the Golden Circle, 43:111
Knights of Honor, 38:30
Knights of Joseph, 46:164
Knights of Labor, 40:70; 41:300, 302, 334
Knights of Pythias Building and Loan Association, 29:176
Knights of Zion, Order of, 45:183
Know-Nothingism, 42:135-40, 144; 46:294, 303, 309; 50:347-48
Knox, Henry, 35:292
Knox, Israel, book review by, 50:251-52
Knox, John C., 49:14
Knox, John P., 28:216
Knox, Philander, 36:282, 286-88, 290; 40:11; 41:178, 188-89
Knoxville Sentinel, 38:32
Knoxville Water Company, 38:30
Kober Adolf, 39:206; "Aspects of the Influence of Jews from Germany on American Jewish Spiritual Life of the Nineteenth Century," 46:60; "Jewish Culture and Religious Life in America as Reflected in the Felsenthal Collection," 44:242; "Jewish Immigration from Württemberg to the United States of America One Hundred Years Ago," 40:406; 41:225-73; "Jewish Religious and Cultural Life in America as Reflected in the Felsenthal Collection," 45:93-127; "Some Friedmann Family Letters," 38:346; 39:169-76
Koblenzer Anzeiger, 43:172
Kobler, Franz, 39:169; 44:246
Kobler, Louis, 47:46
Kobrin, Leon, 39:103
Koch, Robert, 40:92; 42:122
Kochanowski, 39:152
Koelewijn, J. A., 48:263
Koenen, 31:175
Koeners, Jan, 33:252
Koenig, Samuel, 46:255
Koenigsberg Border Committee, 41:155

Koenigsberg Committee, 29:101-2
Koenigswarter, 29:152
Koenigswarter, Antoine, 41:162
Koestler, Arthur, 50:112
Kogalniceano, *see*: Cogalniceanu
Kogan, Maxim, 43:55-58
Kogan, Michael, 43:62
Kogen, David C., *see*: Babin, Moshe
Kögler, Pere Ignace, 49:47
Kohen, Isaac ha, 28:169
Kohen, Joseph ha-, 29:195
Kohen, Solomon ha, 28:169
Kohler, Babette, 34:178
Kohler, Babette Lowenmeyer, 31:268
Kohler, Edgar J., 31:271; 34:220; 35:xviii;
    death, 37:12
Kohler family, gift, 35:xviii
Kohler, Johanna Einhorn, 31:271
Kohler, Kaufman, 33:35-36; 34:295; 35:64;
    40:397; 42:104; Bible translation, 48:240;
    David Philipson bibliography, 39:450, 452,
    455, 458; gift, 31:xxxii; "Heaven and Hell
    with Special Reference to Dante," 29:xli;
    Hebrew Union College, 40:32-33, 35, 38-
    41, 43-46, 50; Judaism, 43:196; 47:121;
    Max J. Kohler bibliography, 34:178, 182,
    187, 192, 240, 254; necrology of, 31:xxiii,
    268-71; N.Y. chief rabbi, 44:161, 183;
    portrait, 34:xxiv; religious and cultural life,
    45:95-96, 98, 100, 108, 112-15, 126;
    Sabato Morais bibliography, 37:71, 74-75,
    84, 90; "Studies and Addressed by Rev. Dr.
    Kaufmann Kohler," 33:xxx; Sunday
    services, 37:49; Zionism, 40:364, 372-73,
    375-82
Kohler, Mrs. Kaufman, gift, 32:xxviii
Kohler, Lili, 31:271; 34:166, 220; 35:xviii, xx;
    gift, 35:xx; "The Jews in St. Eustatius,
    Dutch West Indies," 31:xvi; and Rose
    Kohler, gift, 34:xxiv
Kohler, Max J., 25:149; 26:30, 211; 30:vii;
    31:271; 32:xv, 4; 33:8, 36; 34:xxi; 35:xviii,
    19; 36:ix; 37:460; 42:211; "The Abrogation
    of the Russian-American Treaty of 1832
    and the Drafting of the Treaties of 1919
    for Protecting Religious and Racial
    Minorities," 32:xix; Alfred Mordecai,
    28:251; "American Contributions Toward
    the Removal of Jewish Disabilities in the

Balkan States," 24:1-153; A. M.
Friedenberg Bibliography, 35:115-16, 125;
"As to the Supposed 18th Century
Translation into Hebrew of Washington's
Correspondence with Hebrew
Congregations," 32:121; "Baron Maurice
de Hirsch, a centenary estimate," 33:xviii;
"A Bibliography of the Writings of Max
James Kohler," 34:xiv, 165-258; "Bismarck
and Beaconsfield in Their Relations to the
Jews," 26:258-59; "The Board of Delegates
of American Israelites, 1859-1878," 28:xv;
29:vii, 75-135; "Charles P. Steinmetz and
His Jewish Descent," 32:123-24;
Disabilities, 36:205, 366; 41:38; "The
Doctrine that 'Christianity is a Part of the
Common Law,' and its Recent Judicial
Overthrow in England, with Particular
Reference to Jewish Rights," 31:vii, xvi,
103-34; "An Early American Hebrew-
Christian Agricultural Colony" (note),
22:184-86; "Educational Reforms in
Europe in Their Relations to Jewish
Emancipation, 1778-1878," 26:xxxi; 28:83-
132; emigration, 34:24-25; 45:221;
executive council, 22:xii, xvi, xxvii; 23:xii;
25:xi; 26:xxx; 28:xxxii; "The Fathers of the
Republic and constitutional establishment
of religious liberty," 31:xxiv; gifts, 22:xxxii,
xxxiii, xxxv; 23:xviii; 25:xvi; 28:xxxix, xl;
29:xxxix, xliii, xli; 31:xxxii, xxxiv; 32:xxvi,
xxviii; 33:xxix, xxxi-xxxiii; 34:xvi, xix; "God
in Freedom," 33:xxx; "Historical Evolution
of the Right of Jews to Own Land in
Europe and the United States," 31:xvii;
"Historical Outline of Anti-Semitism in
the United States," 32:xiii; *Immigration and
Aliens in the United States*, 35:xx; "Influence
of American Precedents and Jewish
Patriotism upon Jewish Emancipation
Abroad," 26:266-68; Intercollegiate
Menorah Association, 28:xxix; "Isaac
Harby, Jewish Religious Leader and Man
of Letters," 29:xv; 32:35-53; "Jacob H.
Schiff and the Immigrant: Some Important
Incidents in the History of the United
States, and of Our Faith," 29:xxxvii; Jewish
bibliographies, committee on, 29:xi; Jewish
history, 39:265, 309; "Jewish Immigration

to the United States and the Principle of
the Right of Asylum Historically
Considered," 28:xxxiii; Jewish patriots,
26:237; Jewish rights, 26:110-13; "Jewish
Rights at the Congresses of Vienna (1814-
1815), and Aix-la-Chapelle (1818)," 26:vii,
xv, 33-125; Jews in Newport, 34:3, 6; "Jews
as a Religious Community Not a Race,"
32:127; "The Jews of Barbados before
1776 and Their Commercial
Connections," 32:xiii; Letter of "German
Jew," 37:172-73; "Lewis Abraham,"
32:117-18; Lyons Collection, 21:x, xi;
22:xxi; 23:xiii, 100; 27:216, 228, 236, 380,
400, 449, 460; "Max J. Kohler Memorial
Collection," 45:166, 175; "Moroccan
Jewish Rights at the Algeciras
Conference," 28:xxxiii; Napoleonic
Sanhedrin, 26:xxvii; necrology of, 34:ix, xv,
295-301; necrologies of Bernard A. Palitz,
29:xiv, 181-83; Isaac Markens, 32:xii, 129-
32; Samuel Fleischman, 31:xvi, 257-58;
Simon Wolf, 29:xxxvi, 198-206; Palestine,
26:149; portrait, 34:xxiv; Mexican War,
37:448; Rebecca Franks, 35:253; religious
and cultural life, 45:55, 98; "Satow on
Capo d'Istrias," 29:154; "Some Notes on
Jewish Incidents during the Second Half of
the Nineteenth Century, with Particular
Reference to Roumania, Russia and
Palestine," 28:xxiii; "Some Recent Light
on Our Pre-War Relations to Russia, with
Particular Reference to the Jews,"
29:xxxvii; Taft address publication, 29:xi;
thirty-first annual meeting, committee on,
29:xxvi; vice-president, 29:xxxv; 31:xv, xxiii,
xxix; 32:xii, xix; 33:xvi, xxv; William
Howard Taft, 28:xxxvii; and Bernard A.
Palitz, "Jean de Bloch (I. S. Blioch),
Champion of International Disarmament,
Advocate of Russian Jewish Emancipation
and Worker for Russian Economic
Development," 29:xv; and Rubin, "Services
rendered by the Seligmans, Rothschilds
and August Belmont to the United States
during the Civil War and the 'Seventies,"
33:xxv; and Simon Wolf, "Jewish
Disabilities in the Balkan States: American
Contributions Toward Their Removal,

with Particular Reference to the Congress
of Berlin," 24:ix, 1-153; 25:xiv; see also:
Bloch, Joshua; Calisch, Edward N.;
Davidson, Gabriel; Freimann, A.
Kohler, Mrs. Max J., "Some American
Litterateurs of the Last Century," 26:xiv
Kohler, Rose, 31:271; 33:xxx; 34:220; 35:xviii;
gift, 35:xx
Kohler, Moritz, 31:268
Kohn, 38:197, 203
Kohn, Abraham, 44:2-3; 46:388-89, 411;
50:351
Kohn, Adler & Company, 28:288
Kohn, August, 23:100; 30:vii; American
Historical Association, 22:xxv; necrology
of, 33:xii; "Notice of Insult," 32:116
Kohn, Edouard, 41:162
Kohn, Eugene (ed.), American Jewry: The
Tercentenary and After, reviewed, 46:61-64;
gift, 34:xxvii
Kohn, Frantz, 49:97
Kohn, Hans, 41:105; 46:427; 50:119; book
reviewed by, 41:95-96
Kohn, Hezekiah, 29:113
Kohn, Isaac, 28:288; 50:313
Kohn, Jacob, 25:182
Kohn, Misch, 47:182
Kohn, Samuel, 29:133; 41:260
Kohn, Simon I., necrology of, 28:xxxii, 288-
89
Kohn, S. Joshua, "The Centennial of Utica's
Jewry," 39:471; "Jacob Mordecai Netter,
World Traveler: His Comments on
American Jewish Life," 47:196-99, 201;
The Jewish Community of Utica, New York,
1847-1948, 49:232-33
Kohn, Sylvan H., The Essex Story: A History of
the Jewish Community in Essex County,
49:228
Kohn, Yetta Techner, 28:288
Kohner, Max, 29:131
Kohns, Irene Dorothy, 31:273
Kohns, Lazarus, 31:271
Kohns, Lee, 22:x, xv, xxv; 23:x; 25:ix;
necrology of, 31:xxix, 271-73; necrologies
of Adolph Werner, 28:xxii, 311-12; Minnie
Dessau Louis, 29:xiv, 178-79; Selmar Hess,
26:xiv, 280-81; regrets of, 28:xvii
Kohns, Paul L., 31:273

Kohns, Robert Lee, 31:273
Kohnstamm family, 29:xl
Kohut, Adolph, 26:96, 258-59
Kohut, Alexander, 26:2; 33:35, 239, 241; 34:xviii, 303; 39:93; 42:102; "Alexander Kohut Memorial Collection of Judaica," 45:138-39; auditor, 31:xiii; bookplates, 45:138; Jewish Theological Seminary, 33:18; 40:35; Judaism, 47:121; N.Y. chief rabbi, 44:183; religious and cultural life, 45:98-99, 101, 103, 115-16; Sabato Morais bibliography, 37:79, 87; Y.M.H.A., 37:236
Kohut, Mrs. Alexander, "As I know them," 34:xxvi; gift, 34:xxvi
Kohut, George Alexander, 22:117, 30:vi; 33:8; 34:51, 253; 35:126; 36:ix; "Adah Isaacs Menken's autograph album," 33:xviii; auditor, 31:xx, xxvii; 32:xi, xvii; 33:xiii, xxii; bibliography, 37:460; bookplates, 45:138-39, 149, 154, 159-60, 165-66; "The Contributions of Cyrus Adler to American Jewish History," 33:xxv, 17-42; Cyrus Adler, 37:453; executive council, 29:xxxv; 31:xxix; 33:xvii; *Ezra Stiles and the Jews*, 31:xxxiii; "George Alexander Kohut Memorial Library," 45:148, 160; gifts, 22:xxxiii; 23:xviii; 33:xxxii; 34:xvi-xviii; "Hebrew Anthology," 33:27; "Heine in America," 33:xviii; Isaac Pinto, 30:58; "Jellinek and America," 33:xvii, 237-49; *Jewish Studies in Memory of George A. Kohut*, 35:xxii; John Hay, 38:53; Lyons Collection, 27:216, 409; necrology of, 34:ix, xv, 303-6; Oppenheim Library, committee, 32:xxix; "A proposal to improve the lotteries of the United States, patented by Jacob I. Cohen and signed by President Monroe and Vice-President Adams, March 3, 1825," 33:xviii; religious and cultural life, 45:99, 104; Sabato Morais bibliography, 37:92; "An unknown Zionist Rhode Island project of Mordecai Manuel Noah," 33:xviii; "An unrecorded pamphlet on the yellow fever epidemic in Philadelphia by David Nassy of Surinam, published November 26, 1793," 33:xviii
Kohut School for Boys, 34:303
Kohut School for Girls, 34:303
Koin, Abraham, 33:80

Kokovtseff, Vladimir, 41:182
Kol Israel Anshe Polin Congregation (New York), 44:136
Kol Mevaser, 50:403
Koller, General, 26:50
Kollowrat, Count, 28:100
Komensky, Jan Amos, 50:100
Kommel, Jacob, 42:420
Kompert, Leopold, 23:188; 24:25; 39:329; "On to America" movement, 38:188-89, 192, 198-201, 203-6, 209-12
Kon, Asher (Oskar), 35:276
Konig, Samuel, 26:187
Königsberg Committee, 42:165-72
Königsberg Conference (1872), 42:175
Königswarter, Moritz von, 24:22
Koning, Jacobus, 34:265
Konovitz, Milton R., 40:105; book review by, 40:94-95; *Judaism and the Democratic Ideal*, reviewed, 40:195
Konowitz, Isidor, gift, 35:xxiii
Koonin, Fanny, 48:26
Koonin, Rebecca, 48:26
Kopeloff, I., *Memoirs of I. Kopeloff*, 35:xxii
Kopeloff, Nicholas, gift, 35:xxii
Kopeman, 27:80
Koplik, Henry, 42:124
Kopp, Harry, 34:212; 50:237
Kopp, John, 41:249
Koppman, Lionel, *A Jewish Guide to the U.S.*, 49:244
Korean War, Jewish war records, 42:89
Koreff, David Ferdinand, 26:101
Korev, L., 39:100
Korff, Arnold, 35:262
Koriat, Abraham, 38:72
Korn, Bertram W., 39:336; 41:392; 42:216; 43:139, 238; 46:117-18; 47:193; 48:266; 50:434; Abraham Lincoln, 41:204; 43:72, 91, 98, 111; American Historical Association sessions, 44:245; 49:213-144; *American Jewry and the Civil War*, reviewed, 41:214-15; books reviewed by, 39:331-33; 42:210-11; Canadian Jewish Congress, 49:265-66; chaplaincy, 38:320; 39:177; Charles H. Jonas, 42:408; Civil War, 42:131-34, 139-44, 154; 50:260, 270, 274, 287-88, 290, 292-95, 299-300, 308, 317-18, 321, 323, 331, 342, 346, 348, 350-

52, 378, 383, 396-98, 400, 403; 49:137; "Epilogue," 405-8; *Eventful Years and Experiences: Studies in Nineteenth Century American Jewish History*, reviewed, 44:251-52; executive council, 38:346; 39:470; 42:414; German emigration, 41:231-32; *Growth and Achievement: Temple Israel, 1854-1954*, reviewed, 44:250-51; Hebrew Union College, 40:53; (ed. and intro.), *Incidents of Travel and Adventure in the Far West*, 44:66; Jacob Rader Marcus awarded Lee M. Friedman Award Medal, 50:425; "Jewish Chaplains during the Civil War," 38:345; Jewish Historical Society of Israel, 42:90; Jewish history, 49:250, 255, 264; Jewish tercentenary, 40:414; "Jewish Welfare Activities for the Military During the Spanish-American War," 41:357-80; "Jewish Welfare Activities for the Military in Spanish American War," 40:406; "Jews and Negro Slavery in the Old South, 1789-1865," 50:151-201, 426; "Judah P. Benjamin as a Jew," 38:153-71; past president, 50:426; "Prelude to Progress," 49:147-56, 265; president, 47:201; 48:265; 49:268; presides, 48:266; "A Proposal to the Membership of the American Jewish Historical Society for a New American Jewish Bibliography," 50:68-72; vice-president, 45:264; 46:492; 47:200; "What Is American Jewish History," 38:347

Korn, Harold, 28:vii; 32:4; committee on finance, 28:xxix, "Documents Relative to the Estate of Aaron Lopez," 35:xv, 139-43; executive council, 28:xxxii; gift, 28:xli; "Gouverneur Morris, father of religion liberty in the states of New York," 33:xxv; "Dr. Nathan Mayer of Hartford, Connecticut: Surgeon, Soldier, Poet, Dramatic and Musical Critic," 37:xxx, 425-29; "Places of Jewish Historical Interest in Old New York," 29:xv; "Receipt Book of Judah Hays," 34:xiv, 117-22; "Receipt Book of Judah and Moses M. Hays, Commencing January 12, 1763, and Ending July 18, 1776," 28:xxii, 223-29; "References of Jewish Interest in the Newspapers of the American Revolution (1761-1789); New York and

Massachusetts," 23:xiv; "Religious and Racial Prejudice in America: An Historical and Psychological Analysis, with Special Reference to the Jews," 29:xxxvi; "A Survey of the Publications of the American Jewish Historical Society, and a Plan Suggested for Future Research," 28:xxxiii; "Three Early Letters, 1769-1782," 28:252-54

Korn, Jack, 43:238

Korn, Jacob, 49:186

Kornfeld, 38:202

Kornfeld, Albert E., death, 37:xii

Kornfeld, Joseph Saul, 36:18

Korobkov, Ch., 39:101, 106

Korolenko, "The Letters of Vladimir Korolenko about Woodbine, New Jersey (1893)," 45:248

Kosciuszko, Thaddeus, 27:467; 39:155, 163

Kosher food, 29:149

Kosher meat, 45:187; 47:195; "Anglo-Jewish Legal Cases," 25:137; exportation of, 27:6-8, 12, 185; "The Question of the Kosher Meat Supply in New York in 1813: with a Sketch of Earlier Conditions," 25:vii, xii, 31-62

Kosloff, General, 36:208

Kossuth, 23:64; 27:509

Kostikoff, Louis, 29:62; 46:290, 350

Kotik, A., 39:96; 50:403

Kotzebue, August F. F. von, 33:174, 185-87

Kovno Conference, 42:175

Kozol, Frank L., executive council, 48:265

Krafft, A. J. C., *Historie on Oude Families Van de Nederlandse Antillen*, reviewed, 42:107-9, 214

Krafft, Charles de, 43:236

Krafft, Herman F., 39:50

Kraft, Louis, 39:336; 50:432; executive council, 38:344; 39:470; "50th Anniversary of the National Conference of Jewish Social Welfare," 39:471; "The Popularization of American Jewish History," 38:347; 39:313-17

Kraines, Oscar, 41:105; 42:467; "Brandeis and Scientific Management," 41:41-60; "The Holmes Tradition," 42:341-59, 415

Kraitsir, Charles B., 39:147

Kramer, Aaron, "The Link Between Heinrich Heine and Emma Lazarus," 45:248-57

Kramer, Adam A., 40:23, 46
Kramer, George, 22:89
Kranz, Philip, *Amerika vor Columbus*, 22:175
Krarup, James Frederick, 44:118; biography of Gabriel Milan, 28:216-21
Krasinski, Zygmunt, 41:389
Kraus, Adolf, 28:240; 39:330; 50:119
Kraus, Marian L., "Rebecca Gratz and Gratz Van Rensselaer," 31:241
Kraus, Mayer & Stein, 29:187
Kraus, Michael, 46:411
Kraus, Walter M., 37:374-75; nominating committee, 33:xvi; "The origin, wives and children of Moses Levy," 33:xvii
Kraus, Mrs. Walter M., "Grace Seixas and Her Descendants," 29:xv; "A Note on Rebecca Gratz and Gratz Van Rensselaer," 29:xxix
Krauskopf, Joseph, 39:100; address by, 33:27; farm school, 29:198; Hebrew Union College, 40:34; Jewish Publication Society, 28:33, 42:100; 48:240; Sabato Morais bibliography, 37:77; Spanish-American War, 41:366-69, 371, 376; Y.M.H.A., 37:236
Krauskopf, Mrs. Joseph, 41:357
Krauss Collection, 45:161
Krauss, Jacob, 45:162
Krause, Mrs. Jacob L., 28:269
Krauss, Samuel, 45:161
Krebs, F., and Son, 34:28
Krehbiel, H. E., 34:239
Kremer, Eugene G., necrology of, 28:xxii
Kreplak, Jacob, gift, 35:xxi
Krepliak, H., gift, 34:xxiv
Kreuter, S., 29:132
Kreuz-Zeitung, 46:93
Kristeller, Samuel, 24:29
Kristeller, Siegfried, 38:71
Krochmal, Abraham, 45:126
Krochmal, Nachman, 43:156
Kroh, Th., 50:301
Kromer, Dorus, 35:72
Kronghaus, S., 39:92
Kropotkin, Peter, 43:32-33
Krug, Mark M., "The Yiddish Schools in Chicago," 49:221
Kruszka, W., 39:156, 161
Krüdener, Mme. de, 26:120

Krummacher, F. W., *Elijah the Tishbite*, 30:337; *Elisha*, 30:347
Kubitschek, Heinrich, 41:258
Kubitschek, Hess, 41:267
Kubitschek, Jacob, 41:264
Kuenen, Abraham, 40:25
Kuh, Dr., 23:116
Kuhn, Arthur K., 34:226; "Dante: His Jewish Connections and Supposed Jewish Origin," 29:xxxvi; "Hugo Grotius and the Emancipation of the Jews in Holland," 31:xxiv, 173-80
Kuhn, Loeb & Co., 35:323
Ku Klux Klan, 40:71, 323-25; 45:218; 46:278, 290, 294, 303; 47:2, 19, 30-32; 49:218
Kulke, Eduard, 33:240
Kulturni Politika, 50:112
Kun, Joseph L., 42:334; 43:254; 44:124
Kundzi, P., 38:309, 313-15
Kunewalder, Jonas, 38:231
Kunha, Gaspar Francisco da, 33:80
Kunitz, M., 22:103
Kunth, 26:97, 99
Kuo, Ping Wen, 34:242
Kuperman, Lawrence, 47:182
Kuppenheimer, 38:19
Kuranda, Igntz, 24:44; 38:186
Kursheedt, A., 37:268
Kursheedt, Alexander, 21:214-15; 27:515; 35:189
Kursheedt, Alphonse, 35:190; 37:203
Kursheedt, Alphonse H., 34:xxi
Kursheedt, Ann Augusta, 27:111
Kursheedt, Asher, 29:131; 31:274; 34:xxi; 37:203, 205; Gershom Mendes Seixas letters, 35:189-90; Lyons Collection, 21:197, 214-15; Touro Synagogue, 38:58, 69
Kursheedt, Edwin, 27:420
Kursheedt, Elkalah, 35:189; 43:202
Kursheedt, Gershom, 27:420; 29:100; 31:274; 34:xxi; 39:333; Isaac Leeser, 48:223; Judah P. Benjamin, 38:163-64; "Some Relations of Gershom Kursheedt and Sir Moses Montefiore," 37:xxxiii, 213-20
Kursheedt, Grace Eloise, 34:xxi
Kursheedt, Hannah, 27:112
Kursheedt, Israel Baer, 31:273-74; 34:xxi; 37:213; 41:227; 42:432; "Gershom Mendes

Seixas' Letters, 1813-1815, to his
Daughter Sarah (Seixas) Kursheedt and
Son-in-Law Israel Baer Kursheedt," 35:xv,
xix, 189-205; Grace Seixas Nathan Letters,
37:203, 205-6, 209; Jewish education,
39:300; kosher meat, 25:48, 51-52; Lyons
Collection, 21:161-63, 168-69, 212; 27:69,
73-74, 83-84, 86-88, 91, 116, 173, 229,
243, 315, 399; marriage contracts, 27:173;
Masonry, 26:228; portrait, 41:289
Kursheedt, J. B., 30:124
Kursheedt, Jeannette, 27:111; 35:189
Kursheedt, Manuel Augustus, 40:225-26,
229, 258, 263, 264-71; 49:182; necrology
of, 31:xvi, 273-75
Kursheedt, Miriam, 27:111

Kursheedt, Moses, 35:189
Kursheedt, Sarah Abigail (nee Seixas), 27:74,
112, 162; "Gershom Mendes Seixas'
Letters, 1813-1815, to his Daughter Sarah
(Seixas) Kursheedt and Son-in-Law Israel
Baer Kursheedt," 35:xv, xix, 189-205
Kursheedt, Sarah Abigail Mendes Seixas,
37:203-11, 213
Kursheedt, Serena, gift, 34:xxi
Kurtzig, Aron, 38:22-23, 26, 33, 43
Kurtzig, Emma Kühlbrand, 38:22-31, 33, 42
Kurtzig, Heinrich, 38:33
Kusiel, Ascher, 41:264
Kussy, Meyer, necrology of, 32:ix-x
Kutner, Adolph, 36:254, 258; 40:303; 41:172
Kyser, Jacob, 21:42

L

Labadie, Monsieur, 40:83
Labat, Jean Baptiste, 44:114
Labatt, Henry J., 42:111
Labe, Jacob, 48:257
La Bésnardière, 26:39
Labor, 39:240; 40:9, 70-71, 222, 275, 339-40;
"Abraham Cahan and the New York
Commercial Advertiser: A Study in
Acculturation," 43:10-36; "American
Jewry, The Refugees and Immigration
Restriction (1932-1942)," 45:219-47;
American labor, history, writing of,
46:215-22, 227, 258-59, 261, 263-65; anti-
Semitism, 39:280; "Brandeis and Scientific
Management," 41:41-60; "German Jews in
White Labor Servitude in America,"
34:xvi, 11-49; history, writing of, 46:185,
204, 209, 398-99; 48:200; "Jewish-
American Unionism, Its Birth Pangs and
Contribution to the General American
Labor Movement," 41:297-337, 387;
Jewish labor, history, writing of, 46:215-
32, 257-63, 266-67, 398; *Jewish Labor in
U.S.A.: An Industrial, Political and Cultural
History of the Jewish Labor Movement, 1882-
1914*, reviewed, 41:209-14; *Jewish Labor in
U.S.A.: An Industrial, Political and Cultural
History of the Jewish Labor Movement, 1914-
1952*, reviewed, 43:192-94; Jewish labor
movement in America, 34:xxvii; "The
Jewish Unions and Their Influence upon
the American Labor Movement," 41:339-
45, 387; "The Political Origins of the
Statement of Principles and Program of
the United Hebrew Trades, 1888," 38:345;
Russian Jews, 48:36, 40-41, 44-52, 83, 105-
6, 122, 132-33; "Some Observations on
Jewish Unionism," 41:347-55, 387; unions,

38:20; unionism, 49:81-83, 112, 250, 262;
50:215-16, 222-23, 226
Labor Bureau, 49:181, 183
Labor Party, 41:328; 49:103, 115
Labor Zionist Organization, 39:202, 371;
48:244; 50:433
Labrador, "The de la Penha Family and Its
Labrador Grants," 32:xii
Laboulaye, 41:162
Labushiner family, 39:159
La Bute, Piero, 40:83
Lachaussee, 43:30
Lachenbruch, Mabel Ray, 29:169
Lachman, Samson, 31:203; 34:193; necrology
of, 33:xxi; necrology of Isaac L. Rice,
25:xii, 175-76
Lachmann, Edward, 43:64-65
Lacon; or, Many things in few words, 35:xvii
Lacôte, docteur A., 41:162
Lacretelle, Henri de, 41:162
Lacy, T. H., 35:233
Lader, Ludwig, gift, 29:xl
Ladies Army Relief, 27:124; 50:281
Ladies Auxiliary and Dispensary (N.Y.),
40:164
Ladies Benevolent Society of New York,
41:289
Ladies Hebrew Benevolent Association (La.),
49:222; (New York), 27:123
Ladies Hebrew Seminary, 37:236
Ladies Helping Hand Society (Boston), 46:83
Ladislaus, King of Naples, 28:156
Ladon, Barnado, 37:401-3
Ladoubles, Mr., 37:408
Lady of the Rose, 40:357
Lafaia, João de, 44:83
Lafargue, Paul, 41:152
LaFayette College, 42:205
Lafayette E. de., 41:162

Lafayette, Ind., religious observances mid-nineteenth century, 37:36
Lafayette, Marquis de, 27:xviii, 308-9, 341, 401; 29:32; 37:345; 39:6, 9; 41:287; 42:346; "Lafayette and the Jews During His Visit to the United States, 1824-1825," 29:xxxvii
Lafever, Minard, 41:71
Laffon (Journalist), 47:91-92
LaFitte, 39:23
LaFollette, Robert, 41:300, 328
LaFont, député, 41:162
Lafont, Mr., 42:79
LaForge, Anatole de, 41:162
Lafosse, Cotrel, 37:394-400
Lafrenaye, Charles, 23:139
Lagarde, Paul de, 45:141
Lagarto, Jacob, 42:228
Lag ba-Omer, 39:366
Lagona, Loper David, 32:62
La Guardia, Fiorello H., 36:372-75; 45:228; 46:258; 49:162-63
Lagumina, Bartolemo and Giuseppe, 26:31
Laguna, Daniel-Israel Lopez, 29:34-35
Laguna, David, 29:34
Laguna, Isaac, 29:34
Laguna, Israel Lopez, 35:311; "A rare work by Israel Lopez Laguna, the first Jamaica author," 31:xxiv
Laguna, Jacob, 29:34
Laguna, Lopez Claron, 32:62
Lahnof, Abraham, 35:49
Laidley, Theodore T. S., 48:152
La Jenness, Madame, 40:83
Lajétchnikoff, *The Heretic*, 30:386
Lake George Steamboat Company, 27:378
Lakewood, N.J., synagogue, 22:217
Lam, Lizzie, 45:184
Lamar, Gazaway B., 48:154-55, 157
Lamar, L. Q. C., 22:141
Lamartine, Alphonse de, *Pilgrimage to the Holy Land*, 30:311, 325
Lamb, Colonel, 25:142-43
Lambe, Harby L., 38:75
Lambert, 29:127
Lambert, Rachel, 50:160
Lambert, Richard S., 50:352
Lambert, W. C., 50:160
Lambert, William, 27:506

Lamberts, Abraham, 31:90
Lambertson, Lambert, 27:326
Lamego, Aaron, 32:63
Lamego, Ester, 32:64
Lamego, Isaac, 32:63
LaMegroa, Aaron, 23:149
Lämel, Leopold Edler von, 38:187
Lämel, Simon Edler von, 26:37, 49
Lämel-Herz, Elise von, 26:49
Lamm, Hans, 44:243, 245; 47:124: book review by, 44:251-52; "The So-Called 'Letter of a German Jew to the President of the Congress of the United States of America' of 1783," 37:xxx, 171-84
Lammfromm, Samuel, 41:264
Lamon, Ward Hill, 43:122; 44:101
Lamont, Daniel S., 50:382
Lampert, Jacob, 22:182
Lamprecht, Karl, 39:257
Lampronti, Isaac ben Samuel, 28:189
Lamsdorff, V. N., 34:281; 36:255, 273
Lamy, Père, 30:145
Lancaster, Joseph, 38:96
Lancaster, Mary Anne, 38:96
Lancaster, Pa., 26:182, 277; religious observances, mid-nineteenth century, 37:36
Lancey, Oliver de, 43:132
Lancy, Stephen de, 28:226
Landa, Joseph De, 23:175
Landa, Myers J., 33:179
Landau, 28:77
Landau, A., 34:106
Landau, Ezekiel, 28:103
Landau, Herman, 40:403
Landau, M. I., 38:187
Landau, Samuel, 40:18
Landauer, Alexander, 41:260
Landauer, Caroline, 41:260
Landauer, Georg, 49:141
Landauer, Israel, 41:264
Landauer, Jakob, 41:267
Landauer, M. H., 35:43
Landauer, Moses, 41:260
Landauer, Salomon, 41:254
Landay, Harry, 49:270
Land Cotton Mills, 28:309
Landis, James M., "Mr. Justice Brandeis: A Law Clerk's View," 46:467-73, 492

Landman, Isaac, 34:258; 39:458; 45:44, 157; gift, 33:xxxi; Reform Judaism, 40:389-90, 393
Lando, M. N., 47:38
Landsberg, Dr., 24:30
Landsberg, M., 41:145; 42:165
Landsberg, Max, 40:65-66, 68-69, 72; 42:371, 383; 44:238; necrology of, 32:ix-x
Landsberg, Mrs. Max, 40:69
Landsberger, Franz, 40:49, 53
Landsdowne, Marquess of, 34:281
Landsmannschaften, 45:232
Landrabbinat, 28:264
Lane (consul), 32:75, 79
Lane, Samuel, 27:247
Laney, Joseph, 22:183; 29:141-42, 144
Lang, Harry, 46:121-22
Lang, Mrs. Harry, 46:122
Langdon, Edwin, 33:221
Langdon, President, 47:147
Langdon, Samuel, *Impartial Examination*, 30:56, 60; *The Republic of the Israelites*, 30:86
Langendijck, Jan Claeszn, 32:16-17
Langhorne, Marshall, 36:143
Lanier, Edmund, 39:31-33, 63
Langley, Samuel Pierpont, 33:20, 24
Langlois, 23:49
Langsdorf, Jacob, 30:421
Langsreths, Mrs., 31:154
Langston, 31:124
Lansberg, J., 29:132
Lansing, Robert, 36:18, 67-69, 72-73, 77-78, 292-93; 40:113; 49:196; Polish problems, 36:141, 143-50, 157, 160
Lanton, John, 27:175
La Parra family, 42:108, 214
LaPayba, Beatriz E., 31:28
Lapidoth, *The Converted Jew*, 30:130-31
Lapidutsohn, Alexander Moses, 44:141
Lapin, Yevsei, 43:57, 62-63
La Porte, Ind., religious observances, mid-nineteenth century, 37:37
Lara, de, 50:130
Lara, Aharon Acohen de, 29:26
Lara, Contessa, 28:35
Lara, Hiya Cohen de, 29:28
Lara, Hiz. Cohen de, 29:28
Lara, Jacob de, 30:33; 35:176; 42:74

Lara, Rebecca Coen de, 29:35
Larah, Aron de, 21:43
Lares, Mr., 32:80
Large City Budgeting Conference, 42:319, 323
Larned, Sylvester, 38:49
Laroche, Hippolyte, 40:307; 46:97
Larrajay, Mr., 38:151
Larremore, W., 25:135
Larsh, Abraham, 22:193
Larson, Harold, 44:119
Las Casas, 31:16
Las Casas, Vicente de, 31:19
Lase, Rabbi, 35:87
Lasker, Abraham, 29:132
Lasker, Bruno, 34:184
Lasker colony, 48:87, 93
Lasker, Eduard, 24:16, 43, 46, 49, 52, 56, 58-61, 64, 66-67, 70, 72, 74-75, 77; 28:71; 29:xliii; 31:xxxiv
Lasker, Edward, 36:239, 351, 359, 397; 37:73; 48:87
Lasker, Florine, 29:xliii
Lasker, Miss, gift, 31:xxxiv
Lasker, Raphael, 46:79
Laski, Harold, 42:354-55
Laski, Samuel M., 37:40
Lasky, Jesse L., 46:123
Lasnier, Monsieur, 47:68-72, 74-75
Lass, H., 44:165
Lassalle, Ferdinand, 35:249; 36:355, 398
Lassalleans, 41:328
Last of the Mohicans, The, 22:175
Last Word, The, 40:351
Latin America and the Palestine Problem, reviewed, 48:136-37
Latour, Count, 39:172
Latrobe, Benjamin, 41:64
Lattes, Bonet de, 28:161, 167-68
Lattes, Immanuel de, 28:168
Lattes, Joseph de, 28:168
Latush, Samuel, 27:247
Latz, A. I., 29:132
Lauchheimer, Abraham, 41:267
Lauchheimer, Babbette Eichberg, 31:193
Lauchheimer, Charles H., "Brigadier General Charles H. Lauchheimer, U. S. M. C.: A Memoir," 28:xxiii; "Charles H. Lauchheimer," 31:vii, 193-96

227

Lauchheimer, Heinrich, 41:258
Lauchheimer, Hirsch, 41:264
Lauchheimer, Isr., 41:264
Lauchheimer, Meyer Henry, 31:193
Lauer, Bernard, 28:125, 127
Laughlin, Homer, China Company, 28:257
Laughlin, Sceva Bright, 37:443
Lauk, W. Jett, 46:298-99
Launay, Count, 24:51, 64, 68-69, 121
Laupheimer, Elias, 41:267
Laureati, Jean, 49:44
Laurens, 39:344
Lauroge, Anthony, 33:114
Lausanne, Treaty of, 36:9
Lausanne, University of, 47:176
Lauterbach, Edward, 36:279; 40:302; 41:145,
   176; 49:183; necrology of, 29:xxix, 173-75;
   necrology of Adolph Mack, 22:xii, 227-28;
   see also: Stern, Louis
Lauterbach, Jacob Z., 40:43, 48
Lauterbach & Spingarn, 29:174
Lavalette, E. A. F., 39:16, 26, 29, 60
Lavanburg, Hannah, 40:10
Lavanburg, Louis, 40:10
Lavanburg, Sarah, 40:10
Lavater, J. C., The Jewish Miscellany, 30:411;
   Letter to Deacon Lavater, 30:193-94
Laveaux, Joseph, 23:139
Lavelaye, Émile de, 38:278
Lavella, Gabriel, 32:19, 20
Lavender, David, The Big Divide, reviewed,
   38:321-22
Lavine, Isaac, 32:55; 37:420
Lavrin, G., 39:88
Lavrov, M., 41:191
Law, "Jews in the Legal and Medical
   Professions in America Prior to 1800,"
   22:147-65
Law of Liquidation (1880), 47:87
Law Quarterly Review, 40:87
Law, Thomas, 48:8
Lawler, Percy E., 30:vii
Lawrence, 22:89; 25:56
Lawrence, Amos, 23:60; 26:200; 42:337, 346
Lawrence, Anna, 27:247
Lawrence, Captain, 27:363
Lawrence, Cornelius W., 30:404
Lawrence, Eugene, 28:85; "The Jews and
   Their Prosecutors," 28:xl

Lawrence and Houseworth, 47:182
Lawrence, Mrs. John, 23:153
Lawrence, Mass., Jewish Community
   Council, contribution, 37:xxviii
Lawrence, P., 25:117
Lawrence, William, 27:247; 33:218, 223
Lawrence, William, Jr., 35:179
Lawson, John Howard, 40:354, 357, 359
Lawson, Thomas, 50:326
Law Student's Helper, 47:212
Lawton, Alexander R., 36:345-46
Lawton, Edward, 27:431-32, 434
Lawton, General, 31:212
Lawyer's Club of Philadelphia, 23:192
Layard, A. H., 26:159
Layard, Henry L., 26:149
Lazar, Jacob, 40:2
Lazar, Jesse, 29:123
Lazard, 31:160, 164
Lazard, Frères, 40:329
Lazard & Goldman, 31:158
Lazare, Jacob, 22:235
Lazarfeld, 38:202
Lazaron, Morris S., 40:369; gifts, 33:xxx,
   xxxiii; 35:xx; "An Unpublished Letter to
   Aaron Lopez," 28:xxxiii
Lazaron, Mrs. S. L., 23:181
Lazarson, M., 39:101-3, 108
Lazarus, Aaron, 27:80; 29:147
Lazarus, B. S., 34:126
Lazarus, Benjamin D., 29:129; 50:166
Lazarus, David, 50:313
Lazarus, Ed., 21:166
Lazarus, Edgar Marks, 50:334-35
Lazarus, Eldon S., 21:168; 30:177; (ed.), Form
   of Daily Prayers, 30:240-42; gift, 35:xviii; see
   also: Jackson, S. H.
Lazarus, Eleazer, 25:52
Lazarus, Eleazer S., 21:212; 27:85, 104, 264,
   337-38
Lazarus, Eliezer, 27:84
Lazarus, Elijah, 27:80
Lazarus, Ella, 27:111
Lazarus, Emma, 28:33; 38:59, 71, 248;
   39:114, 307; 42:434; 45:62; 48:34, 202,
   267; 49:70, 143; history, writing of, 46:410,
   427-29, 440; Purim Association, 40:163-
   64; Sabato Morais, 37:72; "Unpublished
   Letters of Emma Lazarus," 48:266;

"Emma Lazarus' Approach to Renan and Her Essay 'Renan and the Jews,' " 37:xxxiv, 17-29; "Emma Lazarus and Emerson," 38:261-87; "The Jewish Orientation of Emma Lazarus," 38:346; "The Link Between Heinrich Heine and Emma Lazarus," 45:248-57; "New Light on the Religious Development of Emma Lazarus," 42:83-88; "Rosh Hashanah, 5638," 21:xxvii; "Some Final Words on Emma Lazarus," 39:321-27; Y.M.H.A., 37:236, 289

Lazarus (family), 49:6

Lazarus, Miss Fanny, 27:68

Lazarus, Mrs. Fanny, 27:111

Lazarus, Gershom, 27:80

Lazarus, Henry, 23:177

Lazarus, Mrs. Henry, 23:177

Lazarus-Joseph collection, 46:422

Lazarus, Josephine, 39:307-8; 45:251

Lazarus, Joshua, 29:129; 50:334

Lazarus, Levi, 50:313

Lazarus, Liepman, 27:55, 314

Lazarus, Marks, 50:41, 53, 334

Lazarus, Martha, 27:350

Lazarus, Marx E., 50:198

Lazarus, Mary, 38:71

Lazarus, Miriam, 27:111

Lazarus, Moritz, 24:22, 25; 25:158; 28:132; 29:95, 99; 37:98-100; 39:455, 459; 45:102-3; 49:27; Board of Delegates of American Israelites, 29:77, 95, 99

Lazarus, Moses (1), 21:109, 112, 114, 121, 213; 27:28, 42-43, 51, 59, 61-62, 253

Lazarus, Moses (2), 21:215; 27:166, 459

Lazarus of Pavia, 28:196

Lazarus, S., 21:167

Lazarus, Sampson, 21:58, 159; 27:43

Lazarus, Samson, & Co., 26:233

Lazarus, Samuel, 21:159, 169-70, 212-14; 25:123; 27:42-43, 51, 54-55, 58-59, 61-62, 118-19, 121, 174, 242, 253, 274; 50:8, 37, 53

Lazarus, Sarah, 38:282

Lazarus, Sholom, 35:309

Lazarus (store), 38:20

Lazarus, T. H., 21:171

Lazarus, Theodore, 27:277

Lazarus, Zipporah, 27:112

Lazinsky, S., 39:111

Lea, Abraha'de, 37:373, 377, 386; 38:235

Lea, Bunker & Co., 31:137

Lea, Henry C., 22:xx-xxi; 26:6

Lea, Henry Charles, 46:466

Lea, surname, 37:382

Leach, Messer., 40:275, 277

Leaf, Reuben, 45:215

League of Nations, 28:259; 31:296; 33:29: 36:9; 40:14-15, 114; 45:38, 40, 47; 46:299; 50:139; Palestine, 36:80, 85, 87, 89; refugees, 36:369; Zionism, 49:198, 201

League to Enforce Peace, 31:296; 40:14

League for the Restriction of Immigration, 49:131, 135

League of the Rights of Man, 46:97-98

League of Women Voters, New York, 31:259

Leah the Forsaken, 40:350-51

Leake, Isaac Q., 30:404

Leake, Martin, 40:216-17

Lealtad, Abraham, 26:254

Lealtad, Abraham de Mordehay, 29:28

Lealtad, Esther, 29:28

Lealtad, Isaac, 26:254

Lealtad, Moseh, 29:28

Lealtar, Moses, 21:134

Leao, Abraham de, 37:383, 386

Leao, Abraham de Jacob Jeudah, 229-30

Leáo, Dauid Juda, 42:278, 394

Leao, Eliao de Ishac Jeudah, 44:233

Leao, Eliao Jeudah, 44:227

Leao, Eliao de Michael Jeudah, 22:169-70; 29:30

Leao, Ishac de Eliao Jeudah, 44:230-31

Leao, Ishac de Jacob Jeudah, 44:230, 232

Leao, Jacob Jeudah, 44:228

Leao, Michael de Eliao Jeudah, 44:230-31

Leao, Moseh de, 42:278, 394

Leao, Semuel de Eliao Jeudah, 44:230

Learned, Marion D., 23:99, 101

Learsi, Rufus, *Israel: A History of the Jewish People*, reviewed, 39:193-94; *The Jews in America: A History*, reviewed, 44:123-26

Leavenworth City, Kan., religious observances, mid-nineteenth century, 37:37

Leavey, Moses, 50:41

Leavitt, Julian, "The War Record of American Jews," 28:xv

Lebanon Hospital (New York), 29:155; 35:63
Lebensohn, Abraham, 28:118, 125
Leber, Samuel, nominations committee,
  31:xxix
Lebeson, Anita Libman, 34:254, 258; 35:136;
  39:288, 336; 42:211, 467; 46:269-70;
  47:201; 50:272; book review by, 42:425-34;
  executive council, 40:406; 41:388; 44:241;
  50:426; "Jewish Pioneers in America,"
  33:xxx; necrology of Joshua Bloch, 47:201,
  216-22; *Pilgrim People*, reviewed, 40:395-
  98; "Writing American Jewish History,"
  38:347; 39:303-12; "Zionism Comes to
  Chicago," 49:221
LeBland, E., 23:139
Leblond, sénateur, 41:162
Lebman, Mayer, 50:386
LeBoeuf, 23:172
Lebowich, Joseph, 29:76; 34:254; 50:293
Lechford, Thomas, 22:148n
Lecky, William E. H., 39:304; 46:21
Lecky, William H., 44:124
L'École Libre des Sciences Politique, 22:223
Lecompte, Sam'l D., 43:77
Lecompton Constitution, 22:141
Lectures on the Conversion of Jews, 30:412, 414
Lederer, Ephraim, necrology of, 31:xxiv, 275-
  78
Ledermann, Isak, 41:256
Ledesma, Bartolome, 31:21
Ledesma, Francisco Rodriguez de, 31:31
Le Desma, Isaac, 21:45
Ledesma y Aguilar, Leonor de, 23:132
Ledyard, Edwin, 50:397
Lee, 31:72
Lee (privateer), 40:76
Lee, Algernon, 50:237
Lee, Arthur, 27:470-71
Lee, Charles, 27:460
Lee, George Washington Custis, 50:343
Lee, Ivy L., 41:50
Lee, James Fenner, 36:335-36
Lee, Joseph B. de, death, 37:12
Lee, Nancy Curtis, 31:xxxii
Lee, Robert E., 25:27; 28:5-6; 31:xxxii;
  46:430, 434, 467; 50:289, 332, 342-44,
  373-74, 384
Lee, Sidney, 38:113
Lee, surname, 37:382

Lee & Walker, 50:391
Lee, William, 27:353; 37:168
Lees, John, 23:47
Leeser, Isaac, 23:141-45; 27:144, 260, 318,
  420, 516, 519-20, 523; 28:xxiv, xxxix, 78;
  29:133; 30:iv, 425; 32:3; 33:6, 23-24;
  37:217; 38:250; 39:299; 41:88-90, 228;
  42:57, 102-4, 455; 46:68, 276; 50:71, 170;
  296; *Advertisement*, 30:366-67; (ed.),
  American Jewish Advocate, 30:387, 389;
  architecture, 46:64, 116; Board of
  Delegates of American Israelites, 29:78;
  49:16-17, 20-21, 24, 30; *Book of Daily
  Prayers*, 30:438; bookplates, 45:189;
  Catechism for Young Children, 30:337-38,
  402; *Claims of Jews to an Equality of Rights*,
  30:355-56; *Commemoration of Life and
  Death of William Henry Harrison*, 30:355,
  357; David L. Yulee, 25:6; "A Defence of
  the Jews and the Mosaic Law," 28:xxxiv;
  Discourse on the Hope of Israel, 30:367-68;
  Discourses, Argumentative and Devotional,
  30:315; *Discourse Delivered at Consecration of
  New Synagogue*, 30:355, 358-59; *Form of
  Prayers*, 30:313, 415; 34:xxiv; *God Our
  Benefactor*, 30:403; Hebrew education,
  30:302-3; *Hebrew Reader*, 30:325-26;
  history, 48:142, 144; 49:234; *Instruction in
  the Mosaic Religion*, 30:264-65; "Isaac
  Leeser and the Jews of Philadelphia: A
  Study in National Jewish Influence,"
  48:207-44; 49:235; 50:296; Isaac M. Wise,
  35:133; Israel Baer Kursheedt, 35:194; J. B.
  Seixas Funeral, 21:209; *Jews and the Mosaic
  Law*, 30:295; journalism, 26:240, 270-71;
  Judah P. Benjamin, 38:155, 163-64; *The
  Law of God*, 30:403; Maimonides College,
  29:107-8; 40:21; 43:139-40, 148;
  manuscripts, 34:xviii; Mayer Sulzberger,
  29:189-92; Memorial, 37:64; Mordecai M.
  Noah, 41:19; New York chief rabbi,
  44:129-30; (ed.), *The Occident*, 30:387, 389;
  Palestine, 39:333; 40:287; portrait, 43:232;
  44:66; *Review of Controversies Between Rev.
  Isaac Leeser and Congregation Mikve Israel*,
  30:460; Sabbath observance, 37:46; *Sermon
  on Motives of Thankfulness*, 30:386; Simon
  Tuska, 50:79, 82-85; Simon Wolf
  Memorial, 29:201; "Sketch of Isaac

Leeser," 28:xxxviii; slavery, 39:307; *Specimen of Form of Prayers*, 30:355-56; (ed.), *The Spirit of Judaism*, 30:363-64, 477; Sunday School, 42:398-99, 401-3; 48:72-74: Union of Congregations, 44:35, 254; 47:129; Young Men's Hebrew Associations, 37:223, 226
Leeser and Jacquet, "Hebrew Bible," 34:xvi
Leeuw, M. R. de, 29:132
Leeven, Assar, 44:90, 92-93; *see also*: Levy, Asher
Lefanu, Philip (trans.), Guenée, Antoine, *Letters to Monsieur Voltaire*, 30:104, 401
LeFevre, Edwin, 43:19, 21, 28
Lefevre, Samuel, 26:254
Leff, Jacob H., 50:260, 271, 303, 353
Lefkowitz, David, necrology of Martin Zielonka, 35:326-28
Legate, James F., 23:69
Legazpi, Melchor de, 31:25
Legazpi, Miguel Lopez de, 31:18, 25
Leggett, Joseph, 27:320
Leggett, Samuel, 43:170-71, 187
Leghorn, 28:197
Leghorne, 27:247
Lehigh Coal & Navigation Co., 25:146
Lehigh University, 41:29
Lehigh Valley Railroad, 41:50
Lehman, 47:188
Lehman, Abraham & Co., 28:309
Lehman, Arthur, necrology of, 35:ix
Lehman Brothers, 41:232
Lehman, Emanuel, 40:263; 47:8
Lehman family, 50:408
Lehman, Herbert H., 36:142; 40:87, 212, 288, 403; 41:310, 329; 45:198; 46:258, 303; 50:386; Omnibus Immigration Bill, 46:332; "The Search for Ideals, A Program of Action, and Leadership," address by, 45:12-15
Lehman Irving, 25:135; 34:220, 248, 258; 37:307; 40:87; 49:62; death, 37:xii
Lehman, Irving H., 47:231
Lehman, Jacob, 26:187
Lehman, Léonce, 42:164; 43:42
Lehman, Mayer, 47:8
Lehman, Newgass & Company, 28:309
Lehman, Stern & Co., Ltd., 28:309
Lehmann, M., 31:268; 40:158

Lehren, 29:125
Lehren, H., 27:235
Lehrman, Irving, "The Jewish Community of Greater Miami," 49:220
Leib, Judah, 38:236
Leibe, Fritz, New York University, 49:97
Leibnitz, Gottfried Wilhelm Freiherr von, 49:47
Leibowitz, Samuel S., 35:276
Leidersdorf, Bernhard, 47:37
Leidersdorf, Samuel D., 37:456
Leipman, A., 27:45
Leipzig Conference (1869), 42:164, 175-76
Leipziger, Henry M., 26:xvii; 34:184; 35:xviii; "Education among the Jews," 28:87; Y.M.H.A., 37:236, 241
Leitao, Augustius, 33:114
Leitao, George, 33:113
Leite, *The Jew of Brazil*, 31:xxxiii
Leiter, Moses, 33:155
Leitner, Rudolf, 36:370
Leiva, Diego de, 23:134
Lemann, Cecilia, 42:63
Lemberg, 38:191, 216
Lemberg Committee, 41:138, 145
Lemego, Domingo Gonsalvos, 33:115
Lemmertts, Abraham, 27:247
Lemos, Jacob de, 42:258, 278, 283-86, 291-93, 391-92, 394
Lempriere, John, *Bibliotheca Classica*, 30:280, 337
Lems, Adriaen, 33:63
L'Enfant, Pierre, 48:2
Lenghi Jacob, 27:120
Lengyel, Emil, 39:336; book review by, 39:329-31
Lenin, Nikolai, 39:203, 286; 42:443; 46:222, 259, 266
Lenox Foundation, 45:203
Lenox Library, 35:313-14
Leo X, 28:167-68, 170; 31:16
Leo XII, 28:186
Leo XIII, 22:223; 46:282
Leo, Mrs. Ansel, 27:373
Leo, D., 27:521
Leo, the physician, 28:160, 190, 199
Leo, Rev., 27:504
Leo, Sampson Simson, 27:373
Leon, Abraham de (Ga.), 22:165; 26:191, 194

Leon, Abraham de (New York), 27:286, 289
Leon, Abraham Lebeth, 27:30
Leon, Almeiria de, 50:332
Leon, Almira de, 27:286, 289
Leon, B. M. de, 25:113, 116
Leon, Benjamin de, 26:251
Leon, Benjamin Charles Moses de, 50:333
Leon, Benjamin Marache de, 27:247
Leon, Catalina de, 31:26-27, 31
Leon, Charles Moses de, 50:333
Leon, Daniel de, 26:239; 29:xliii; 35:275;
    48:200; 50:217, 231
Leon, David, 27:488
Leon, David Camden de, 32:40; 50:331-32,
    397, 406
Leon, de, family, "Military Records of the
    DeLeon family and of Captain Perry M.
    DeLeon," 50:332-34
Leon, Edward, 27:515
Leon, Edwin de, 32:4, 40; 37:216; 50:193,
    332-33; Position and Duties of "Young
    America," 30:403
Leon, Eleazer, 27:45, 75, 101, 277
Leon, Esther, 27:113
Leon, H. H. de, 50:168
Leon, Harmon Hendricks de, 50:331
Leon, Harry J., 45:146
Leon, Heliahu de, 29:31
Léon, Henri M., "Some Eminent Jewish
    Philologists of Past Ages," 23:xv
Leon, Henrietta de, 27:286, 289; 50:333
Léon, Henry M., "Some Eminent Jewish
    Philolgers of By-gone Ages," 25:xvi
Leon, I., 29:130
Leon, Isaac de, 27:227
Leon, Isabel de, portrait, 22:xxxiv
Leon, Jacob de, 27:51, 60, 62, 286, 289;
    28:239; 29:xlii; 50:332-33
Leon, Jacob Rodriguez de, 37:332, 340
Leon, Luisa de, 27:286, 289
Leon, Mat. Pereira de, 32:10-11
Leon, Miriram de, 50:333
Leon, Mordecai C. de, 50:332
Leon, Mordecai Hendricks de, 50:332
Leon, Mordica de, 27:79, 286, 289
Leon, More de, 33:77
Leon, Morris I., 29:132
Leon, Moseh P. de, 29:19
Leon, Moses, 25:52; 27:45, 84, 86, 91, 314

Leon, Moses de, 22:103; 26:251; 45:30
Leon, Mos. Rod. de, 27:247
Leon, Perry Moses de, 50:332-33
Leon, Ponce de, 31:13
Leon, Rebecca de, 27:286, 289
Leon, Rebecca M. de, 25:116
Leon, Sarah, 27:277
Leon, Simon de, 32:117
Leon, surname, 37:383
Leon, Thomas Cooper de, 50:193; 332-33,
    397-98
Leon, Uriah de, 27:286, 289
Leonard, Benny, 48:201
Leonard, Thomas, 27:73
Leonardo da Vinci, 28:26
Leone, J., 27:95
Leone, Piero, 28:196
Leone, surname, 37:383
Leoni, G. C., 26:188
Leoni, Michael, 22:xxix; 23:179-80
Leopold I of Austria, 35:213
Leopold III, 42:461
Leopold, Moritz, 41:249
Leopold Morse Home for Infirm Hebrews
    and Orphanage, 22:229; 46:83-84
Leov, Moses, 27:278
LeProust, F. J., 23:139
Lerin, Mannie, 41:171-72
Lerin, Mrs. Mannie, 36:235-37, 391
Lerin, Minnie, 40:306
Lerner, Fischel, 40:260
LeRoux, Charles, 42:417
Leroy-Beaulieu, Anatole, necrology of,
    22:xvii, 222-225
Leroy-Beaulieu, M., 35:124
Le Sage, Diable boiteux, 33:176
Lesem, S. J., 29:133
Lesher, John, 34:84, 88
Le Signeur, Tate, 32:52
Lesinsky, Albert R., gift, 32:xxviii
Lesinsky, Henry, 32:xxviii
Lesley, J. P., 38:264
Le Souard, G., 24:19
L'Espée, Abbé, 27:482
Lessah, Gitlah, 27:112
Lesseps, Ferdinand de, 41:162; 47:96
Lesser, Allen F., 33:xxvi; "Adah Isaacs
    Menken: A Daughter of Israel," 34:143-47
Lesser, A. M., 33:217-19, 221, 223

Lessing, 26:96, 100; 31:277

Lessing, Bruno, 35:122

Lessing, Gotthold Ephraim, 35:232-33; 37:186; 45:22; 48:249; *Nathan the wise*, 33:182

Lessing, K. G., 37:186

Lestchinsky, J., 39:107

Lestchinsky, Jacob, 39:105; 40:105, 404; books reviewed by, 38:327-30; 40:98-100; "Jewish Migrations from 1840 to 1946," reviewed, 40:196

L'Estrange, Hamon, "Americans no Jews," 25:81

L'Estrange, Roger, Flavius, *Works of, Vol. I*, 30:63-69, 75-77, 95, 97, 133, 138, 140, 143, 214, 236, 255, 257-58, 273, 286, 437, 477

Lesynsky, Amelia, 38:63

Lesynsky, H. S., 38:63

Lesynsky, William S., 38:63

Letamendi, 25:6

Letellier, A., 41:162

Letob, Benjamin Gabay, 32:58

Letob, Ishac Gabay, 32:58

Letteris, Meir Ha-Levi, 23:187; 33:240; 38:187

Letters, "A Haym Solomon Letter to Rabbi David Tevele Schiff, London, 1784," 34:xiv, 107-16; *Letters From New York*, 38:175; "Some Eighteenth Century American Jewish Letters," 34:75-106

Lettoab, Leah Gabay, 32:58

Leung, Charles H., 34:194

Leusden, Dr., 35:169

Levadi, Solomon S., 45:215

Levaillant, Isaïe, 46:96

Level, Emile, 41:162

Leven, 24:48, 50, 70-71, 73-74

Leven, Narcisse, 24:22, 30, 34; 28:132; 29:84; 36:40; 39:413; 41:162; 42:161, 164, 166-67; 43:42, 52, 64-66; *Cinquante ans d'histoire. L'Alliance Israélite Universelle, 1860-1910*, 24:34; Alliance Israélite Universelle, history of, 25:xvi

Levensohn, Abraham, 28:118

Levenson, L., 29:130

Leventhal, Dr., 38:314

Leventritt, Cook & Nathan, 31:279

Leventritt, David, necrology of, 31:xxiv, 257, 278-80

Leverett, John, 22:2, 5

Leverson, Montague, 26:147

Levey, 35:16

Levey, Augustus A., 49:183

Levey, Augustus S., 40:226, 229, 236, 242, 249

Levey, Hyman, 50:41

Levey, Irving M., 40:48

Levey, Joseph, 35:6-7

Levey, Mr., 27:430

Levey, Moses, 40:75

Levi, 21:198

Levi, A., 38:59

Levi, Aaron, 37:353

Levi, Albert, 41:260

Levi, Alexander, 29:147

Levi, Alfred, 37:475

Levi, Aron, 41:264

Levi, Charles, 37:266, 268, 270

Levi, Charles S., 40:376, 380-81

Levi, Daniel, 26:182

Levi, David, 25:114-18; 28:249-50; 37:76; *A Defence of the Old Testament*, 30:112-14, 116; *Letters to Dr. Priestly*, 30:98-101; (trans.), *Service for Two First Nights of Passover*, 30:318-19

Levi, Eberhard, 41:264

Levi, Eleazer, 29:147

Levi, Elias, 41:260

Levi, Gershon, 40:82

Levi, Gerson B., 45:159

Levi, Mrs. Gerson, B., 45:159, 173

Levi, Grace, 23:89

Levi, H., 29:134

Levi, H. Abraham, 31:242

Levi, H. and Co., 47:187

Levi, Hannah, 28:289

Levi, Harry, 34:255; 44:250; gift, 33:xxxiii; nominations committee, 32:xix

Levi, Henry, 29:147; 31:142, 147, 152, 160, 170; 40:60

Levi, Hyman, 23:89

Levi, Isaac (London), 27:91

Levi, Isaac (Newport), 38:60-61

Levi, Isaak, 41:256

Levi, Isak Hirsch, 41:264

Levi, Israel, necrology of, 37:xii, 474-75

Levi, Israel George, 26:251

Levi, J., 29:134

Levi, Jacob, 29:147
Levi, Jacob George, 26:254
Levi, Jacob Joseph, 22:180
Levi, Jakob, 41:264
Levi, Johanna, 41:267
Levi, Joseph, 25:123
Levi, Joseph C., 31:xxxi; 45:190; 50:395; necrology of, 31:xxiv, 280-81
Levi, Joseph Samuel, 30:129
Levi, Joshua, 26:251; 45:78
Levi, Julia di, gift, 31:xxxi-xxxii; painting, 31:xxxiv
Levi, Kasmir, 41:260
Levi, Leo N., 28:11; 29:202-3; 35:259; 36:270; 39:416; 42:452
Levi, Leopold, 41:260, 264
Levi, Lewis, 26:182
Levi, Louis S., necrology of, 28:xxxii, 289-90
Levi, Malche, 41:253
Levi, Marcus, 50:166
Levi, Meier, 41:268
Levi, Meyer vs. the United States, 47:187
Levi, Miriam, 28:290
Levi, Montefiore, 40:333
Levi, Moritz, 41:260
Levi, Morton, 28:290
Levi, Moses, 21:198; 41:260; 50:36
Levi, Nathan, 39:126, 134-35
Levi, P., 29:134
Levi, Rosette, 41:264
Levi, Rudolph, necrology of, 29:xiv, 175-76
Levi, Ruth, 28:290
Levi, Samuel Zanwill, 34:61
Levi, Sandel, 41:264
Levi, Simon, 28:253
Levi, Solomon, 28:289-90
Levi, Solomon W., 39:451
Levi Strauss and Co. (San Francisco), 37:45
Levi, Sylvania, 39:440
Levi, Walter, 26:251
Levias, Caspar, 33:147; 40:36, 41, 373; 42:100
Levidansky, Ega, 37:42
Levidansky, Jacob, 37:42
Levidansky, Joseph, 37:42
Levidansky, Meier, 37:42
Levidansky, Wolf, 37:42
Levie, Isaac, 35:182
Levie, Joseph, 35:177
Levie, Moses, 35:177, 181-82

Levie, Nathan, 35:186
Levie, Samuel, 35:177
Levin, Benjamin, 42:419
Levin, Bertha Szold, necrology of Henrietta Szold, 37:481-84
Levin, Ernest H., gift, 34:xx
Levin, Gustavus, 50:126
Levin, Hayman, 27:80
Levin, Jacob, 50:169-70
Levin, J. & L. T., 50:169, 185
Levin, Lewis C., 50:69
Levin, Louis Hiram, 31:226: 37:470; necrology of, 29:xxxvi, 176-78; necrologies of Bertha Rayner Frank, 22:xxviii, 213-18; David Hutzler, 25:xii, 152-56
Levin, L. T., 50:169
Levin, Nathaniel, 29:129; 32:130
Levin, P., 40:239
Levin, Shemariah, 33:149; 40:375
Levin, Shmarya, 35:58
Levin, Theodore, 34:219
Levine, Abraham, 50:234
Levine, Ephraim, 34:xxiv
Levine, H., "The Women's Garment Workers Union," 34:xxvi
Levine, Herman J., 35:307-8
Levine, Marcia, 50:434
Levine, Morris, 35:xxi; 42:12
Levine, Nathan, 44:136, 142, 189-90, 192
Levine, Samuel H., 42:419; "Herman Melville's Pilgrimage to the Holy Land," 46:493
Levine, Shmariah, 39:112
Levine, Yitzhak Meir, 49:273
Levinger, Isak, 41:264
Levinger, Lee J., 42:112; "The American Jew in the World War: A Personal and Statistical Study," 29:xxix; "Anti-Semitism in the United States," 33:xxx; 42:112; book reviewed by, 42:109-11; gift, 29:xxxix; nomination committee, 29:xxviii
Levinsohn, Isaac Beer, 28:84, 115-18; 34:159
Levinson, Mr., 31:144
Levinson, A., gift, 26:xxxv; "Tobias Katz: a Medical Cyclopaedist of the Seventeenth Century," 25:xiv
Levinson, Daniel J., see: Adorno, T. W.
Levinson, Elijah, 44:137, 141
Levinson families, 50:134

Levinson, Israel, 29:69
Levinson, J., 29:69
Levinson, Jacob, gift, 35:xxiii
Levinson, L. D., 40:120
Levinthal, B. L., 35:64
Levinthal, Cyrus, 46:122
Levinthal, Helen Hadassah, "Jewish Fraternal Orders in America," 35:xv
Levinthal, Israel H., 47:148
Levinthal, Louis E., 43:238, 240; 46:280; necrology of Julian W. Mack, 37:476-77
Levis, 35:12
Levis, Chevalier de, 34:170
Levis, Richard J., 22:231
Levisohn, Babette, 41:264
Levisohn, Hirsch, 41:264
Levison, Albert, 25:115
Levison, Henry, 25:115
Levison, Jacob, 27:80
Levison, Louis Lehmann, 41:260
Levitan, Solomon, 44:4
Levitas, Irving, "On the Attitude of Some Prominent Reform Jews Towards Zionism," 44:242
Levitate, Isaac, 39:264
Leviticus (Zohar), 22:103
Levitzki, B., 33:162
Levner, J. B., 22:175
Levy, 23:177; 29:127; 38:236; (Montreal), 35:13, 15; (trader), 23:5, 16-17, 21, 23, 32-33
Levy, A., 21:168; 35:200
Levy, Aaron, 21:163, 168-70, 190, 192, 212, 214; 28:xxxiv; 30:177; 33:4; 34:69, 71; 37:347; 42:457; 50:39, 53; *Aaron Levy: Founder of Aaronsburg*, 40:405; bookplates, 45:165; communication from, 26:xxx, 177-78, 180; kosher meat, 25:52, 57; land agreement, 43:235; portrait, 41:280, 284, 289; 43:233; *Proclamation of Aaronsburgh*, 30:83-85; Robert Morris, 33:2; (S.C.), 50:42
Levy, Aaron (b. Hayman), 27:51, 58-59, 63, 83, 86, 96-97, 104-5, 115, 155, 168, 229, 243, 256, 258, 334, 336-40, 345, 394, 398; family records, 27:335-44
Levy, Aaron (b. Meir), 27:151
Levy, Aaron J., 50:232-33, 237-38
Levy, Abigail, 34:61

Levy, Abigail (Bilhah), 42:417, 433
Levy, Abigail (d. Samuel), 23:150
Levy, Abigail Israel, 23:160
Levy, Abner Jacobs, 27:80
Levy, Abner S., 27:80
Levy, Abraham (Amsterdam), 27:76
Levy, Abraham (Curacao), 27:247
Levy, Abraham (father of Moses Albert), 46:101, 109-10
Levy, Abraham (Jamaica), 37:338
Levy, Abraham (London), 23:160-61; 31:36
Levy, Abraham (N.Y.), 27:153, 168, 315, 461; 49:203
Levy, Abraham, Jr., 27:506
Levy, Abraham I., 27:87
Levy, Abm Isaac, 21:125
Levy, Abraham Segal, 34:95
Levy, Affey, 50:175
Levy, A. G., 27:509
Levy, Alexander, 50:160
Levy, Amelia, 38:73
Levy, Andrew, 26:186; 50:40
Levy, Armand, 41:162
Levy, Arthur, 24:29; 40:169
Levy, Arthur L., 29:109
Levy, Asa, 34:xxi
Levy, Ash, 50:169
Levy, Ashel S., 39:61-62, 64-65
Levy, Asher, 21:24, 169; 27:84, 277; 44:67, 90, 92-93; 46:69
Levy, Asher (b. Isaac), 23:160
Levy, Asher (b. Moses), 23:158
Levy, Asser (Conn.), 31:247
Levy, Asser (New York) (1), 23:148; 27:379; 29:52; 31:237; 39:246, 292; 42:109; 44:213; 46:69, 270; civil liberties, 46:28; kosher meat, 25:41-42; "Recorded Transactions of Asser Levy at Albany, N.Y.," 26:246-47; and Stuyvesant, 35:131
Levy, Asser (New York) (2), 28:252
Levy, Augusta, 27:286-89; 35:xix
Levy, B. R., 29:132
Levy, Barnet, 50:39, 53
Levy, Barnet (Bernard Beer), 25:66-68
Levy, Bayla (Hart), 23:155
Levy, Benjamin (b. Moses), 23:158
Levy, Benjamin (Baltimore), 22:194; 28:xxxiv; 34:285; slave trade, 43:235; 50:29, 40, 53

Levy, Benjamin (Brazil), 42:241-42, 254, 258, 279, 281, 291, 390, 394; 44:93

Levy, Benjamin (England), 31:36, 41

Levy, Benjamin (Memphis), 37:270

Levy, Benjamin (negro), 50:174

Levy, Benjamin (New Orleans), 50:70, 160-61

Levy, Benjamin (New York) (1), 25:52; 27:170, 192, 346-47; 33:203; 50:304; "Benjamin Levy," 34:180, 271-72

Levy, Benjamin (New York) (2), 25:143; 26:233, 270

Levy, Benjamin, Sr., 21:45, 53, 63

Levy, Benjamin, Jr., 21:45, 51, 53

Levy, Bernard (Beer), 25:66-68

Levy, Bertha, 41:232

Levy, Betzy, Home, 31:282

Levy, Bilah, 21:20; 27:192, 347; 31:238

Levy, Bilah Abigail, 35:286; 42:433

Levy, C. (Ala.), 22:100

Levy, C. M., 29:133

Levy, Caroline, 27:286, 289

Levy, Chapman (S.C.), 22:154-55; 26:189; 27:483; 40:127; 50:154, 159-60

Levy, Charles C., 50:175

Levy, Charlotte, 50:166

Levy, Cherie M., 50:351-52

Levy, Clifton H., 34:187

Levy Collection, 49:209

Levy, Cornelia Bernard, 46:101; 49:203

Levy, Daniel, 22:154; 39:393

Levy, David, 42:103; *Case on the Contested Seat of David Levy*, 30:364-65; gift, 22:xxxii; *Letter*, 30:226; *see also*: Yulee, David L.

Levy, David (Curacao), 44:228

Levy, David (England), 27:301-2; 31:36

Levy, David (La.), 29:133

Levy, David (New York), 27:55

Levy, David (S.C.), 38:72

Levy, David Jacob, 25:90

Levy, David Jacobs, 27:372

Levy, Deborah (1), 27:168

Levy, Deborah (2), 27:168

Levy, Deborah (3), 31:293

Levy, Dinah, 31:xxxii

Levy, E., 27:163; *The Republican Bank*, 30:337, 339

Levy, E. I., 29:133

Levy, Edward S., 37:266, 268

Levy, Eleazer, 21:183; 27:40, 51, 59, 63, 89, 155, 336, 462; 50:37, 54

Levy, Elias, 25:7

Levy, Emanuel, 32:58

Levy, Esther (1), 27:55

Levy, Esther (2), 27:122

Levy, Esther, cook book, 48:240

Levy, Esther (Mrs. Daniel Gomez), 41:110

Levy, Esther (Henrietta), 23:160

Levy, Esther (d. Isaac), 23:160

Levy, Esther (Mrs. Joseph), 27:271

Levy, Esther (Richmond), 46:102

Levy, Eugene Henry, 50:194

Levy, Ezekiel, 27:462

Levy family (New York), 27:xviii, 331-45; (Newport), 27:455

Levy Ferdinand, 47:56; 49:186

Levy & Franks, 27:247; 46:31

Levy, Gabriel, 44:227

Levy, George, 41:364

Levy, Gershom, 35:19-20

Levy, Gershom, 21:79

Levy, Grace, 27:80

Levy, Grace (Mrs. Hiam), 27:348

Levy, Grace (Mears), 23:159; 41:294

Levy, Grace (Mrs. Moses), 27:161, 169

Levy, Gustave Daniel, 22:182; 26:242

Levy, H., 29:134

Levy, Haim, 27:348; 33:203; 34:71; 50:54

Levy, Hannah, 23:159

Levy, Hannah S., 27:271

Levy, Harry M., 28:31

Levy, Hart, 27:115, 117

Levy, Haya Sara, 27:168

Levy, Hayman, 21:xvi, 51, 60, 63, 70, 73-74, 80-81, 83, 85-91, 93, 94-97, 99-105, 107, 109-14, 116-21, 123-36, 138-48, 150, 161, 183-84, 211; 23:157; 25:47; 26:177, 237-38; 33:204; 34:71; 35:18-20; 37:204; 38:49; 41:291; 45:57; 50:54-55, 60, 332

Levy, Hayman (b. Moses), 27:29-30, 33, 38, 41, 43-44, 150, 153, 155, 157, 168, 186, 240, 243, 347, 353-54, 362, 366, 461, 463; descendants, 27:162-68; Isaac M. Seixas correspondence, 27:171-72

Levy, Hayman (b. Solomon), 27:80, 286, 289

Levy, Henrietta, 37:420

Levy, Henry (Jamaica), 32:62

Levy, Henry (Louisville), 37:270-71

Levy, Hester, 23:158; 50:253
Levy, Hetty, 50:253
Levy, Hetty Grace, 27:286, 289, 291-92, 306
Levy, Howard S., 43:238
Levy, Hyman, 28:225
Levy, Hyman, Jr., 28:225
Levy, I., 29:132
Levy, Is. (Calif.), 28:135
Levy, Isaac (New York) (1), 21:8, 22-23, 25, 30, 38, 55, 170, 214; 23:85, 158-60; 26:233, 236; 27:59, 61, 63, 314; 34:61; 35:184; 39:62; 38:235-36; 50:253; naturalization, 37:373, 377, 386; Tammany, 38:124; will of Nathan Simson, 25:89
Levy, Isaac (New York) (2), 23:150; 27:56, 58-60, 242
Levy, Isaac (New York) (3), 23:152-53
Levy, Isaac (Philadelphia), 22:197; 49:209
Levy, Isaac (Va.), 22:160; 46:102
Levy, Isaac H., 21:142, 148-49, 159, 163, 168; 25:52; 50:37, 54
Levy, Isaac Hayman, 27:39-41, 51, 69, 84, 86, 158, 268, 217, 222, 239, 240-41, 253
Levy, Isaac J., 50:316, 364
Levy, Isaac bar Judah, 21:19
Levy, Isaac S., 47:46
Levy, Isaacs, 33:253
Levy, Isaque, 42:279, 394
Levy, Israel, 28:264: 29:131, 135
Levy, J. (La.), 50:154
Levy, J. A., 47:46
Levy, J. C., 27:496
Levy, J. H., 34:237; executive council, 25:xi
Levy, J. R., 50:175
Levy, Jabica, 23:160
Levy, Jacob (Baltimore), 50:40
Levy, Jacob (Jamaica), 27:84
Levy, Jacob (New Orleans), 50:169
Levy, Jacob (New York) (1), 21:45, 169; 27:84, 277, 312, 314; 28:71; 29:148; 42:280, 394
Levy, Jacob (New York) (2), 27:163
Levy, Jacob (New York) (3), 27:314
Levy, Jacob (New York) (4), 27:462
Levy, Jacob (N.C.), 27:74, 104, 193, 303
Levy, Jacob, Jr., 25:57; 27:75, 84, 92
Levy, Mrs. Jacob, 21:55
Levy, Jacob A., 27:145, 506; 29:133; 46:113, 102; 50:316

Levy, Jacob C., 32:40
Levy, Jahacob Ymanuel, 25:138
Levy, Jefferson Monroe, 39:11, 50, 60
Levy, J. Leonard, 29:198; 41:361-66
Levy, Jochebed, 27:161, 170, 346
Levy, Joh., 27:62
Levy, John, 27:514
Levy, Jonas, 48:243
Levy, Jonas Phillips, 26:213; 27:507, 515; 35:xviii; 36:316; 38:73; 39:52, 62; Sunday legislation, 26:218; Washington Hebrew Congress, 26:213-17
Levy, Joseph (1), 23:150; 26:233; 27:58; 29:132; 34:61; 40:63
Levy, Joseph (2), 23:158; 27:270-71
Levy, Joseph A., 40:140, 151, 169, 171
Levy, Joseph Israel, 23:160
Levy, Joseph M., 39:62
Levy, Joshua, 21:79, 86, 145, 147-52, 154-56, 158-59; 27:43, 51, 60, 72, 75; 50:37, 54
Levy, Judah, 21:131; 27:348; 44:63
Levy, Judah, Jr., 21:60
Levy, Judah Mears, 33:203
Levy, Judith (England), 31:36, 41
Levy, Judith (New York), 27:113
Levy, Judith (d. Benjamin), 33:203
Levy, Judith (Mrs. Benjamin), 27:170, 192, 346-47; 33:203
Levy, Judith (Mrs. Jacob), 27:112
Levy, Julia, 27:78; 46:102
Levy, Juliet, 27:286, 289, 440
Levy, Julian, 50:332
Levy, Julius, necrology of, 31:xxix, 281-82
Levy, Kate, 49:206
Levy, L., 27:486
Levy, Lawrence, 23:150
Levy, Lester S., 49:270; 50:272, 275, 390-91, 393
Levy, Levy Andrew, 23:5, 21, 23; 30:71, 77: 34:99-100; 35:16-18; 37:348; 43:234; 50:54
"The Levy Family of Canada," 25:xiii
Levy, Lewis, 46:102
Levy, Lewis B., 50:165, 184
Levy, Louis, 26:182; 29:131
Levy, Louis Edward, 48:236, necrology of, 28:xxii
Levy, Louis Napoleon, 22:x, xv, xxv; 23:x, xii; 25:ix, xi; 29:xiv; 38:73; Battle of Long

Island, 28:xxx; executive council, 28:xiv; nominating committee, 22:xvi
Levy, Louis Sampter, gift, 31:xxxiv
Levy, Lyon (S.C.), 22:154
Levy & Lyon, 27:247
Levy, Lyon J., 31:281; 37:350
Levy, Lyon J., and wife, paintings, 31:xxxi
Levy, M., 29:131; 48:127
Levy, M. D., 29:133
Levy, M. S., 41:370
Levy, Madame, 26:52
Levy, Manoel, 42:279, 394
Levy, Manuel, 44:229
Levy, Maria (nee Lopez), 27:74, 104, 193, 303
Levy, Maria Bishop, 46:102
Levy, Marks, 29:130
Levy, Martha, 50:316
Levy, Martha Ezekiel, 46:113
Levy, Mary, 46:102; 49:206
Levy, Mary (Solomon), 27:286, 289
Levy, Mary (Mrs. Judah Lyons), 27:74
Levy, Mary Asser, 21:xxiii
Levy, Matje Asser, 27:144
Levy, Maurice, 40:327, 343; 41:162
Levy, Max, 38:61
Levy, Mears, 26:195
Levy, Melvin, 35:244
Levy, Michael (New York), 21:39-40, 43, 45; 29:127; 42:189
Levy, Michael (b. Moses), 23:158-59
Levy, Michael (Philadelphia), 41:87, 280, 290
Levy, Miriam, 23:158; 25:90-91
Levy, Miss, 35:286-87
Levy, Mrs. (New York), 27:95; 34:279
Levy, Mrs. (Philadelphia), 26:233
Levy, Mr. (Canada), 27:80
Levy, Mitchell A. C., 38:73
Levy, Mitchell M., 39:62
Levy, Mordy, 27:462
Levy, Morris, 27:80
Levy, Morris D., 29:130
Levy, Moses (Boston), 40:120
Levy, Moses (Delaware), 43:235
Levy, Moses (Fla.), 50:154
Levy, Moses (Newport), 27:178, 180-81, 184-85, 192, 214, 247, 348, 404, 456; 37:165, 392

Levy, Moses (New York) (1), 21:10, 31, 44, 48, 53, 55, 139; 23:148, 150-51, 158-59; 26:261, 266; 28:xli, 231; 31:239; 33:200, 206, 208; 35:175, 181, 286; 37:373, 377, 386; 38:235, 249; 42:432-33; 46:387-88; 50:253; anti-Semitism, 38:129-30; autograph, 22:xxxi; "The Cordwainers' Case and Moses Levy," 38:342; "The Origin, wives and children of Moses Levy," 33:xvii
Levy, Moses (New York) (2), 23:160; 42:110
Levy, Moses (New York) (3), 23:172; 38:70
Levy, Moses (Philadelphia), 22:152-53, 197; 38:129-30, 137; 50:39, 54; "Original Letters of Moses and Sampson Levy, of Philadelphia," 22:xiii, xxxii, 188-91
Levy, Moses (S.C.), 50:164
Levy, Moses (Spanish Town), 27:161, 169
Levy, Moses (father of Hayman), 27:150, 335
Levy, Mrs. Moses, 41:290, 294
Levy, Moses Albert, "Surgeon Moses Albert Levy, Letters of a Texas Patriot," 45:264; 46:101-13; 49:202-7
Levy, Moses (br. Isaac), 21:29
Levy, Moses Clava, 26:233; 50:41, 55
Levy, Moses Elias, 25:2-12, 19-20, 29; 37:438; 43:177; 49:17; "Moses Elias Levy's Agricultural Colony in Florida," 25:132-34; "Moses Elias Levy (Yulee) of Florida," 25:xii
Levy, Moses H., 33:203; 43:205
Levy, Moses Levy & Co., 23:172
Levy, Moses Raphael, portraits, 41:281-82, 286, 290, 294
Levy, Moshe, 21:8-9, 19
Levy, Myer (1), 21:214; 27:314, 392
Levy, Myer (2), 27:151
Levy, Myer (3), 27:155
Levy, Nathan (D.C.), 48:10
Levy, Nathan (b. Moses), 23:158-59
Levy, Nathan (New York) (1), 21:5, 7-8, 10, 14, 19-21, 23-25, 53, 60, 63, 181, 187; 31:100
Levy, Nathan (New York) (2), 27:70, 272, 299, 483
Levy, Nathan (Philadelphia), 26:235; 34:96, 273; 43:235; 50:53
Levy, Nathan (S.C.), 22:15, 164
Levy, Nathan vs. John Gadsby, 47:187

Levy, Peter, 50:174
Levy, Philadelphia, 34:273
Levy, Philip L., 37:420
Levy, Phillips, 47:188
Levy, Rachael, 32:58
Levy, Rachel (Asher), 34:60-64
Levy, Rachel (Baltimore), 22:194
Levy, Rachel (New York), 21:8, 10, 19, 21;
   27:122; 39:10; portraits, 41:280, 290
Levy, Rachel (Mrs. Benjamin), 34:271; 50:53
Levy, Rachel (Mrs. Isaac Mendes), 37:203
Levy, Mrs. Rachel, 27:75
Levy, Rachel (d. Moses), 23:151, 158; 41:294
Levy, Rachel (Phillips), 41:87
Levy, Rachel (Richmond), 46:102-4, 110-12
Levy, Rachel (Mrs. Samuel), 23:150
Levy, Rachel, see also: Seixas, Rachel Mendes
Levy, Rachel C., 49:202-6
Levy, Raphael Georges, necrology of, 34:ix
Levy, Raphael Moses, 26:261, 266
Levy, Rebecca, 21:191; 46:102
Levy, Rebecka, 27:271
Levy, Reyna, 27:168; 41:291
Levy, Richa, 37:210
Levy, Richa (Mrs. Aaron), 27:112
Levy, Richard, 50:174
Levy, Richea (b. Hayman), 27:168
Levy, Ritzy, 23:152
Levy, Robert, 23:80
Levy, S., 22:177; 23:26; 39:35; gifts, 28:xli;
   31:xxxv
Levy, Salomon, 37:331
Levy, Sam (N.Y.), 38:235-36
Levy, Sampson (b. Moses), 23:158, 160
Levy, Sampson (New York), 21:45, 53, 55;
   27:271
Levy, Sampson (Philadelphia), 22:153;
   26:236; 34:279; 50:54; "Original Letters of
   Moses and Sampson Levy, of
   Philadelphia," 22:xiii, xxxii, 188-91
Levy, Samson (Delaware), 43:235
Levy, Samson (Philadelphia), 27:460; 50:54
Levy, Samuel (N.J.), 33:253
Levy, Samuel (Newport), 27:416
Levy, Samuel (New York) (1), 21:11, 20, 30,
   35, 38, 42, 53, 55, 114, 211; 23:148; 25:87,
   90; 27:156; 29:xxxix; 31:238; 33:200; 34:60;
   35:177; naturalization, 37:373, 377, 386;
   46:387

Levy, Samuel (New York) (2), 23:150; 27:247
Levy, Samuel (Philadelphia), 26:236
Levy, Samuel (S.C.), 50:32, 42, 55
Levy, Samuel Eleazer, 21:113
Levy, Samuel Zanwill, 34:60-64
Levy, Sarah (New York), 27:55
Levy, Sarah (S.C.), 50:159-60
Levy, Sarah (b. Hayman), 27:111, 168, 277
Levy, Sarah (Mrs. Eleazer), 27:336
Levy, Sarah Ann, 27:193
Levy, Saul (Solomon), 50:332
Levy, Simeon, 27:41, 43, 51, 60, 72, 78, 85,
   97, 242, 315, 397; 38:70; Shearith Israel
   School, 27:51-52, 55, 95, 34:124, 136
Levy, Simon, 27:278; 30:51
Levy, Simon (Canada), 31:182
Levy, Simon (Milwaukee), 47:38, 56
Levy, Simon Jonas, 23:155
Levy, Simon M., "Simon M. Levy, Member
   of the First Class to Graduate at the
   United States Military Academy in 1802,"
   23:xiv
Levy, Simson, 21:39-40, 43-44
Levy, Sloe, 50:54
Levy, Solomon (New York), 21:148, 159,
   162, 164, 169, 191; 29:xlii; 50:37, 54;
   kosher meat, 25:52
Levy, Solomon (consul for Venezuela), 38:73
Levy, Solomon (b. Hayman), 27:168, 185,
   286, 289, 292, 305, 314, 336-37
Levy, Solomon (gr.-grandson Hayman),
   27:286, 289
Levy, Solomon (S.C.), 50:41
Levy, Solomons, 35:16
Levy & Summers, 50:169
Levy, surname, 37:383
Levy, Theodore, 41:162
Levy, Thomas, 26:187; 37:420
Levy, Mrs. Thomas, 35:286-87
Levy, Uriah Phillips, 22:xxiii; 23:121-23;
   26:194-95, 242; 27:160, 286, 289, 314,
   400, 402, 483, 515; 28:xl; 29:206; 31:193;
   35:xviii, 133; 39:346; 41:87; 42:110; 47:7;
   50:58; 312; Joseph B. Nones, 46:4, 11-12;
   "Manual of Rules for Men of War,"
   22:xxxiii; Monticello property, 27:401-2;
   portraits, 41:280, 284, 290; 42:416; 43:232;
   Review of Trials of Commander U. P. Levy,
   30:350, 352; "Some Remarks on the

Career and Character of Commodore Uriah P. Levy," 37:xxxv; trial of, 27:518; "Uriah Phillips Levy: The Story of a Pugnacious Commodore," 39:1-66

Levy, Mrs. Uriah P., 22:xxix; 27:160; "The Presentation of a Flag to the Anthon Battalion by Mrs. Commodore Levy," 22:xii

Levy, Vincent, 26:188

Levy, Walter, 27:80

Levy, William, 29:142, necrology of, 33:xiii

Levy, Zipporah, 37:204; 50:60

Levy, see also: Ha-Levi

Levyne, Sidney, A., 49:270

Levyno, L. A., 29:133

Levys, Philip, 37:420

Lewald, 29:127

Lewenberg, Babette, 31:268

Lewenberg, Hyman, 29:62, 73-74

Lewensen, Nancy, 41:249

Lewenstein, M. J., 45:140

Lewes, George H., 35:246-48

Lewi, Isidore, gifts, 22:xxxii; 34:xxi, necrology of Simon W. Rosendale, 35:ix, xvi, 320-22

Lewi, Joseph, 34:xxi

Lewin, A., 28:95

Lewin, Alfred Elkin, 25:118

Lewin, Benjamin F., 27:271

Lewin, Daniel, 39:83

Lewin, Leopold E., 27:271

Lewin, Louis, 50:313

Lewin-Epstein, E. W., 36:69, 72

Lewinson, B., 34:195

Lewinson, Benno, 45:180, 205-6; gift, 33:xxxiii

Lewis, 31:124

Lewis, Andrew, 25:118

Lewis, Capt., 39:179

Lewis, Clarence, gifts, 31:xxxv; 32:xxv

Lewis, David, 26:191

Lewis, Edward Henry, 25:118

Lewis, Harry S., 35:251

Lewis, J. L., 22:79

Lewis, Jacob, 22:193; 29:132

Lewis, J. Hamilton, 36:89, 291, 368

Lewis, John L., 41:336

Lewis, John M., 39:75-78

Lewis, Lloyd, 38:320; 40:184

Lewis, Louis, 25:118

Lewis, Margaret C., gift, 22:xxxii

Lewis, Margaret Sarah, 45:214

Lewis, Mrs., 25:183

Lewis the Ninth, 21:240

Lewis, Rachael, 21:37; 23:151; 31:238

Lewis, Robert M., 39:69-70, 74-78, 80-86

Lewis, Samuel A., 37:234

Lewis, Sarah L., 25:118

Lewis, Theodore N., 40:205; book review by, 40:192-96

Lewis, William, 37:110; 38:129

Lewis, William Berkeley, 22:87

Lewisohn, Adolph, 31:203; 37:234, 307; 45:210; gift, 31:xxxii

Lewisohn, Albert, 38:63

Lewisohn family, 42:126

Lewisohn, Leon, 46:87-88

Lewisohn, Leonard, 35:119; 38:63; 40:158, 263; 49:186

Lewisohn, Lillian, 38:63

Lewisohn, Ludwig, 45:31; 46:279-80; 49:141

Lewisohn, Mr., 36:201-4

Lewisohn, Richard, 42:127-28

Lewkowitz, Albert, 37:172

Lewy, 38:197

Lewy, Israel, 25:179; 28:264

Lewy, Julius, 39:464; 40:49

Lewy, Kathe, 50:271

Lexington Historical Society, 42:339-40

Lexington School for the Deaf, 39:278

Lezare, 27:80

L'Homond, Charles François, Epitome Historlae Sacrae, 30:242

Li, Ng Hong, 34:196

Libel, "Anglo-Jewish Legal Cases," 25:137

Liber Psalmorum, 30:138-39

Liberal Jewish Synagogue of London, 31:250

Liberal Opinions, 33:174, 187-89

Liberal Party, 41:329

Liberator, The, 42:132, 134-36, 145, 148-49

Liberty, N.Y., Congregation Ahavath Israel, contribution, 37:xxviii

Libin, S., 49:105

Libman, Emanuel, 42:125-26

Libowitz, Nehemiah Samuel, 33:139; 45:101, 103, 117, 155; gifts, 34:xxxvi; 35:xxii

Library Club, 42:459

Library Company of Philadelphia, 23:185; 30:vi; 47:204

Library of Congress, 22:xxiii; 23:117; 170; 25:113; 26:266; 30:vi; 34:153; 37:465; 39:309; 40:185, 411; 45:149-50, 185, 200; 47:200; gifts, 35:xx; 37:12; "Resources on American Jewish History at the Library of Congress," 47:179-85, 201

Lichtenauer, Winifred, 34:301

Lichtenberg, Helene, 41:256

Lichtenberg, Karl, 41:268

Lichtenberger, 41:162

Lichtenstein, Amy, 29:206

Lichtenstein, Gaston, 46:68; 49:241; 50:43, 316; "The Virginia Lichtenstein," 22:xxxiii; see also: Ezekiel, Herbert T.

Lichtenstein, Isaac, 45:215

Lichtenstein, Richard C., 45:212

Lichtenstein, S. A., 27:515

Lichthart, Admiral, 33:124

Liebe, Georg H. T., 35:124

Lieben, De, Mrs., 48:13

Lieber, Francis, 26:48; 39:257; 43:140

Lieberman, Gustave, 35:64

Lieberman, J. J., 46:121

Lieberman, Jacob J., 42:420, 422

Lieberman, Morris, 49:270

Lieberman, Max, 40:318, 320

Liebig, Justus von, 46:11

Liebman, Joshua Loth, 44:250-51; 46:280

Liebman, Levi, 41:258

Liebman, Shulamith, 33:154

Liebmann, Gustav, 41:249

Liebmann, Liebmann, 41:260

Liebmann, Rebekka (Einstein), 41:258

Liebmann, Walter H., necrology of, 33:xiii

Liechtenstein, Prince Wentzel, 26:50

Liederkranz Society, 40:167

Lieper, Tom, 31:139, 144, 147, 151, 159, 162

Liesin, A., 45:155

Liessin, Abraham, 43:36

Lieven, Prince, 28:117

Life of Christ, 48:249

Life and Eternity, 30:426

Lifshitz, Hillel, 44:137, 139-41

Lifshitz v. Lifshitz, 29:149

Lifshutz, Emanuel L., 43:238

Lifshutz, Ezekiel, "An English Letter by a Russian Jew Mourning the Death of Abraham Lincoln," 50:248-50

Lightfoot, Dr., 30:15

Lightfoot, John, 35:170

Lighthouse Board, 28:291

Ligier, Leon A., 46:121-22

Ligne, Prince de, 26:38, 52, 73

Ligucius, 28:153

Lilianthal, Charlotte, 38:75

Lilianthal, J., 38:75

Lilien, Ephraim Moses, 40:319; 45:163, 209

Lilienthal, Abraham, 49:54-55

Lilienthal, Benjamin, 49:54-55

Lilienthal, David, 38:170; 48:250

Lilienthal, Howard, 42:122, 127

Lilienthal, Judah, 35:44

Lilienthal, Max, 23:180; 24:11; 25:xvi; 27:516; 37:58; 39:177, 447, 453-54, 456; 41:229-30; 44:130; 45:108, 114, 126; 46:386-87; 47:43; 48:219; educational reform, 28:84, 118-20, 124; Hebrew Union College, 40:27, 29; "Max Lilienthal's Activities in Russia; New Documents," 35:xv, 39-51; Simon Tuska, 50:80, 87-88; Swiss disabilities, 38:167-68; transcendentalism, 42:83, 103; Washington's Correspondence, 32:121; Y.M.H.A., 37:227-31

Lilienthal, Meir Hirsch, 49:55

Lilienthal, Sophie, "The Lilienthal Family," 33:xxx

Lilienthal, Theo., 27:420

Lillendall, 27:120

Lilly, Eli, & Co., 45:197

Lilly, William, The Book of Knowledge, 30:90

Lim, Hom, 34:202

Lima, D. A. de, 38:72; 40:263; 49:186

Lima, David Abinun de, 44:233

Lima, Haim Abinun de, 44:228

Lima, Joseph d'Ishac Mesquita de, 29:38

Limburger, Jeanette, 41:260

Limburger, Joshua Moses, 41:260

Limos, Diegeo de Fonseque, 33:112

Lin, Joseph, 33:133, 135, 139, 145-47, 150, 153, 155-56, 158-63

Lina (slave), 50:180

Lincoln, Abraham, 27:124-25; 29:104-5; 31:xxiv, xxxiv; 32:xxvi, 1-2; 38:2, 25; 39:455; 40:169-70, 191; 41:330; 42:347-48; 43:15; history, writing of, 46:163, 190, 271, 434, 437; 47:224; Civil War, 50:262-63, 266-69, 283-84, 289-90, 294, 300-302,

308, 317, 345-52, 355, 377-82, 395-96, 398-404; abolitionists, 42:136, 142-43; Abraham Jonas, letter to, 50:367; "Abraham Jonas' Role in Lincoln's First Presidential Nomination," 44:98-105; Abraham Jonas warns of plot against, 50:349-50, 368-69; "Abraham Lincoln and the Jews," 32:131; *Abraham Lincoln: His Life and Work (Hebrew Translation)*, 50:402; *Abraham Lincoln, the Liberator of Negro Slaves*, 50:403; *Abraham Lincoln, Liberator of the Slaves: His Life and Social Work*, 50:403; *Abraham Lincoln: A New Portrait*, 50:345; *Abraham Lincoln: The Tribute of the Synagogue*, 50:283, 301, 399; "Abraham Lincoln—The Tribute of the Synagogue," 32:131; Adolph Marix, 28:290; Alfred Mordecai, 48:150-51, 160-61, 165; biblical qualities of, 50:351; bookplates, 45:191, 208; "Chronology," 50:401; David L. Yulee, 25:23-24, 26; death, 47:48-50, 57; Emanuel B. Hart, 32:110; "An English Letter by a Russian Jew Mourning the Death of Abraham Lincoln," 50:248-50; gift, 33:xxix, xxxii-xxxiii; "Isachar Zacharie: Lincoln's Chiropodist," 43:71-126; 44:106-13; Jellinex tribute, 33:247-49; and Jews, 28:xxxix; 29:xix; 35:133; 49:138, 279; 50:267, 345-52, 377-82; Joseph C. Levi, 31:280; Joseph Seligman, 41:27, 32, 36-37, 39:40; *Lincoln for the Ages*, 50:401; *Lincoln: His Life in Photographs*, 50:400; "Lincoln and the Jews," (Bertram W. Korn), 50:352; (Isaac Markens), 50:300, 345-46, 351, 377; *Lincoln, Master of Men*, 50:395; *Lincoln: A Picture Story of His Life*, 50:400; *Lincoln and the Preachers*, reviewed, 38:319-21; *Lincoln and the Russians*, 50:401; Lincoln-Douglas debates, 31:294, 346-47, 350, 367, 380, 404; 50:346; Isachar Zacharie, 50:377-78; "The Lincoln-Hart Correspondence," 38:139-45; "...Man of the Fifteenth Psalm," 38:338; Marcus Otterbourg, 32:66, 68-69; "New Light on Lincoln's Parole of Charles H. Jonas," 42:407-12; Order #11, 29:200; 40:186; "Origin of Famous Lincoln Sayings," 32:132; "A Personal Tribute to Lincoln By Josephine Phillips," 41:204-7; Philadelphia Congregation,

37:15; prayer on death of, 21:14; 27:147-49; "President Lincoln and the Case of John Y. Beall," 32:132; Sabato Morais bibliography, 37:63, 82-83; Simon Wolf, 47:77-78; Solomon's Tribute, 35:xix; "Why President Lincoln Spared Three Lives," 32:132; Lincoln collection of Emanuel Herz, 50:403; Henry Horner, 50:394
Lincoln, Mary Todd, 41:35-37, 39-40; 50:248
Lincoln, Robert Todd, 32:132; 33:213; 38:140; 41:39; collection of, 50:347-50
Lincoln, Thomas ("Tad"), 41:39-40
Lincoln, Willie, 38:320
Lincoln National Bank, Cincinnati, 28:290
Lincolniana, Alfred Whital Stern Collection of, 50:142, 396; Collection of Justin G. Turner, 50:379, 404
Lind, Jenny, 35:240
Lindau, Mr., 38:286
Lindauer, David Hirsch, 41:256, 264
Lindauer, Jette, 41:254
Lindauer, Josef, 41:264
Lindauer, Maier, 41:264
Lindauer, Wolf, 41:254
Linbergh, Charles A., 36:383-84
Lindemann, C., 50:292
Linenmüller Odeon, 33:184
Linder, Mark, 35:268
Lindey, Fanny, 44:243; 50:273
Lindner, Emanuel, 41:264
Lindo, 31:124
Lindo, A. A., 27:519; *A Retrospect of the Past*, 30:438-39
Lindo, Abigail, 22:xxiii
Lindo, Abraham, 32:58
Lindo, Abraham, Jr., 32:58
Lindo, Abraham Alexandre, "Abraham Alexandre Lindo, a Pioneer American Jewish Publicist," 25:xiv
Lindo, Abraham Messiah Isaac, 31:242
Lindo, Alexander, 37:420
Lindo, Alicia, "David Lindo, Bibliography," 22:xxix; "A Sketch of the Life of David Lindo," 23:vii, 37-41
Lindo, David, 32:58; 35:311; "David Lindo, a Biography," 22:xxix; portrait, 22:xxxiv; "A

Sketch of the Life of David Lindo," 23:vii, 37-41
Lindo (family name), 48:139
Lindo, Isaac, 26:251; 31:242
Lindo, Jacob, 26:251
Lindo, Joseph, 27:80
Lindo, Moses, 27:388; 37:137-43; 42:434; 46:31
Lindo, Raphael, 26:251
Lindo, R. H., 23:40-41
Lindsay, Lord, "Letters on Egypt, Edom, and the Holy Land," 26:135, 137
Lindsay, Vachel, 50:268
Lindsay and Wall, 33:176
Lindsey, Theophilus, 35:231
Lines, J., 35:187
Linfield, Harry S., 29:xlii; 39:253; 44:239; "Jewish Population Statistics," 29:xv
Link Belt Company, 41:46
Linton, Captain, 41:292
Linton, Lynn, 40:337-38
Lion, Abrao, 42:279, 394
Lion, Moses de, 33:88
Lions Club, 47:24
Lipchitz, Jacques, 40:320
Lipellt, William, 50:235-36
Lipman, 21:45
Lipman, Jacob, 27:231; 41:88
Lipowsky, Jacob, 29:62
Lippe, C., 24:82
Lippe, Chayyim David, 33:133
Lippincott's Magazine, 37:64
Lippman, A., 28:257
Lippman, Joseph, necrology of, 34:ix
Lippman, M., 29:131
Lippman, Mina, 28:257
Lippmann, Walter, 42:354
Lipschild, Israel, 22:207
Lipschitz, Jacob Halevi, 44:133-34, 140-41
Lipshitz, Rabbi, 29:156
Lipsky, Louis, 32:xxvi; 40:373; 45:43-44; 49:142
Lipson, M., 35:262
Lipson, Max, 33:149
Lipson, Mordecai, 33:133, 153, 156
Liquor, 26:217
Lira, Gonsalvo novo de, 33:118
Lisa, Manuel, 22:xxix
Lisboa, Manuel Gomes de, 33:77

Lisboa, Simon Gomes de, 33:77
Lisbon, *Bibliotheca Nacional de Lisboa*, 25:148
Lishansky, Batya, 49:159
Lisner, A., 23:143
Lispenard, Leonard, 27:45; 32:104, 109
Lispendard & Hart, 32:104
Liss, Mrs. Leonard, 43:238
Lissa, Posen, 50:292
Lissberger, A. K., 38:71
List, Lippman, 29:129
Lister, Joseph, 50:324
Liszt, Franz, 28:24; 35:246
Lit, Samuel D., necrology of, 32:xvi
Litch, Josiah, *Judaism Over-Thrown*, 30:375
Litchfield North Consociation of Congregational Churches, 39:190
Literacy test, 46:294, 310, 333, 393; 49:133-34; 50:210
Literary Chronicle, 50:5
Literary Club of Cincinnati, 39:468
Literary Digest, 41:181-82
Literature, 40:182-83; American and Jewish Problem, 39:115-42; "Henry Wadsworth Longfellow's Presentation of the Spanish Jew," 45:20-34; Jews in, 39:387-88, 446, 454, 465; "The Jew in American Dramatic Literature (1794-1930)," 40:345-60, 406; *On Medieval Hebrew Poetry*, reviewed, 40:195; *The Modern Renaissance of Hebrew Literature*, reviewed, 40:195; "Some American Literateurs of the Last Century," 26:xiv; Yiddish, 39:217
Lithauer, L., 29:132
Litt, Solomon, 50:435
Littauer, Louise, "Louise Littauer her Book," 31:xxxii
Littauer, Lucius Nathan, 24:81; 33:30; 34:154; 45:136, 167; death, 37:xii; gifts, 31:xxxii; 35:xx
Littauer, Nathan, 45:136, 166
Little hunchback; or, A frolic in Bagdad, 33:174, 178
Littlefield, Walter, 34:248
Littlejohn, Abram N., 28:31
Littleworth, Lewis, 30:75
Litvak, David, 35:255
Litvinov, Maxim, 36:294
Litwin, A., 45:155
Liveright, Horace, 35:272, 274

Livermore, H., *Address to the Dispersed of Judah*, 30:448-49
Livermore, Jonathan, 22:23-24
Livingston, Brockholst, 27:67, 242
Livingston, Catha, 42:417
Livingston, Charles L., 30:404
Livingston, Edward, 27:71; 30:404; 32:42, 53
Livingston, James, 26:257-58
Livingston, John, 28:226
Livingston, M., 27:515
Livingston, Mr., 35:296
Livingston, Peter R., 28:226
Livingston, Peter van Burgh, 27:341
Livingston, Robert, 27:318; 31:229; 41:111
Livingston, Robert, Jr., 27:247
Livinson, A. J., "Some Observations on the Life of Ezekiel Hart (1770-1843)," 37:xxxv
Liz, Jose de, 47:63-75
Lloyd, Henry, 23:84
Lloyd's of London, 49:64
Loans, Jacob, 28:167
Löb, Levi, 41:263
Lobanov-Rostovski, Prince Alexis Borisovich, 36:237, 241-43, 247, 250-52, 258; 39:69-70; 41:172
Lobo, Daniel Moses, 26:251, 254-56
Lobo, Isaac, 26:254
Lobo, Isaac Moses, 26:251
Lobo, Jessurun, 38:236
Lobo, Sarah, 26:255
Löbestein, Josua, 41:264
Locke, Alain, 46:279, 288
Locke, John, 29:137; 37:187-88
Locke, Ralph, 35:273
Lockhart, John Gibson, 22:54; 46:434
Lockman, Leonard, 37:393-410
Lockman, Mr., 49:44
Lockroy, E., 41:162
Lockwood, Ezra, 27:323
Lodge, Cornelius, 31:98
Lodge, Henry Cabot, Jr., 46:295
Lodge, Henry Cabot, Sr., 36:84; 40:296; 41:189-91; 46:294; literary test, 46:299; Zionism, 45:40-43, 45
Lodge, Henry Clay, 40:166
Lodge, John Cabot, 46:295
Lodge, Mrs. John Cabot, 46:295
Loeb, 42:227
Loeb, Arthur, 37:xii

Loeb, August B., necrology of, 25:xii, 173-75
Loeb, Babette, 25:173
Loeb, Benjamin, 25:173
Loeb, Carl M., 45:137
Loeb Classical Library Foundation, 45:137
Loeb, Dauid, 42:278, 394
Loeb, Elieser ben Zebi Abraham, 49:178
Loeb, Harold, 35:269
Loeb, Harold S., 45:193, 215
Loëb, Henri, *The Road to Faith*, 30:359
Loeb, Henry, 26:183
Loeb, Isidor, 33:239
Loeb, Isidore, 24:50, 116-17; 40:252, 255, 257, 259; Alliance Israélite Universelle, 42:182-83, 186-88; Carmel Colony, 37:86; Israel Levi, 37:474; *La Situation des Israélites en Turquie, en Serbie et en Roumanie*, 24:30, 34
Loeb, Jacob Moritz, 45:182, 211-12
Loeb, Jacques, 47:15
Loeb, James, 45:137, 168; necrology of, 33:xxi
Loeb, Joseph, 37:44
Loeb, Julius T., 42:103
Loeb, L., 39:395
Loeb, Louis, 45:205
Loeb, Mathilde Adler, dispensary, 25:174
Loeb, Max, 33:33
Loeb, Mayer, 31:149
Loeb, Mr., 47:189
Loeb, Morris, 31:203; 37:306; 45:137-38; 49:119-22, 127, 129-30, 136; "Anglo-Jewish Legal Cases," 25:136; necrology of, 22:xvii, 225-27
Loeb, Sidney, 28:240
Loeb, Solomon, 47:8
Loeb, Solomon and Betty, Home for Convalescents, 22:226; 34:xxii
Loeb, Sophie Irene Simon, 48:202, 267; 49:70, 143; 49:70
Loeb, Wm., Jr., 41:378
Loebl, Lazarus, 29:131
Loesman, Myer, 27:274
Loesmann, Sarah, 27:274
Loevy, Maurice, 41:162
Loewe ben Bezalel, 28:66
Loewe, Heinrich, 34:175
Loewe, L., 27:522; 28:120
Loewe, Louis, 37:214, 219

Loewenberg, Bertha, 31:257
Loewenthal, William, 43:43-44
Loewy, A., 24:22, 30
Loft, Jacob, 46:241
Logan, 23:21
Logan, James, 22:150; 43:236-37
Logan, W. Va., Jewish Community, contribution, 37:xxviii
Loggins, Vernon, *Where the World Ends: The Life of Louis Moreau Gottschalk*, reviewed, 48:196-99
Lohmeyer *v.* Salomon, 25:135
Lombardi, Ltd., 40:357
Lombroso, 33:xxxi
London (slave), 50:159
London, "The Rabbinate of the Great Synagogue, London," 28:xl
London Alliance, 48:96
London Bible Society, 43:172
London, Blanche, "Gertrude Stein, Modernist, her career and influence," 32:xx
London Board of Deputies of British Jews, 24:93; 34:281; 46:97-98
London Committee of Deputies of the British Jews, 24:45; 28:124; 40:232; 41:144; "Memorandum on the Treaty Rights of the Jews of Roumania," 24:137-53
London Courier, 50:11
London Daily Express, 41:249
London Exhibition, 31:290
London Gallery of Fashion, 35:285
London Gazette, The, 46:88
London, Hannah R., 33:210; 38:348; "Colonial Portraits of Jewish Men and Women," 28:xxxiii; "Early American Portraits of Jewish Men and Women, II," 29:xv; "Miniatures of Early American Jews," 38:345; portraits, 41:275-76; "Random Notes in American Jewish History," 37:xxxiii
London hermit; or, Rambles in Dorsetshire, The, 33:174, 184-85
London, Jack, 40:341
London Jewish Shelter, 41:156
London, Joseph, 27:45
London Mansion House Committee (Fund), 26:160; 40:226, 230, 232, 236, 258; 41:128-29, 131-35, 137-38, 141
London, Meyer, 35:57; 50:203, 221-26, 235

London Peace Conference, 24:84-86, 88, 90-91; 44:72
London Poor Jews Shelter, 48:45
London protocol of 1871, 24:40, 120
London Roumanian Committee, 24:24
London Russo-Jewish Committee, 41:156-57; 46:94
London School of Theology, 50:178
London Shorthand Society, 32:133
London Society for Promoting Christianity Among the Jews, 26:82, 116-17, 120-21; 28:114
"London Times," 29:126
London, University of, 25:185; 49:11
Londow, Ezekiel J., necrology of Benjamin Henry Hartegensis, 37:460-70
Long, Barbara, 50:398
Long, E. B., 50:272, 340, 399, 401
Long, Hyman Isaac, 22:162
Long Island, War of 1812, 26:180; 28:xxx
Long, Louis, 37:257
Long, Martin, 34:77
Long, Samuel de, 27:105
Longfellow, Henry Wadsworth, 22:xxxiii, 175; 34:175; 38:269, 276; 39:53, 116; 42:341, 434; "Henry Wadsworth Longfellow's Presentation of the Spanish Jews," 45:20-34; " 'A Simile' Said to Have Been Written by Henry Wadsworth Longfellow for the Israelite: A Correction," 40:182-83
Long Oath, Barbados Synagogue attacked, 22:198
Longstreet, James, 39:341; 50:154
Longworth, David, 35:281-85
Longworth, Nicholas, 40:305
Longworth & Wheeler, 35:285
Lonn, Ella, 50:269; *Foreigners in the Union Army and Navy*, reviewed, 42:210-11
Loockermans, Jacobs, 26:247
Lookstein, Joseph, executive council, 46:493; 49:268
Lopes, Abraham Nunes, 29:28
Lopes, Aharon, 29:32
Lopes, Andre, 33:65
Lopes, Andrea, 33:115
Lopes, Daniel Rodrigues, 29:37
Lopes, Daui, 42:279, 394
Lopes, David, 44:224-25

Lopes, Eliao, 42:214
Lopes, Elias Raphael, 42:214
Lopes, Eliau, 44:218-19, 223
Lopes, Eliau de Aron, 44:224
Lopes, Eliau Rephael, 44:224
Lopes, Esther (d. Abraham), 29:28
Lopes, Esther (Gomez), 50:49
Lopes, Fernandez, 33:112
Lopes, Isaac Nunes, 29:128
Lopes, Manuel, 33:117
Lopes, Mordecai, R., 32:64
Lopes, Moseh, 29:28
Lopes, Moses, Jr., 29:12
Lopes, Moses Henrique, 32:58
Lopes, Moses Paro, 32:62
Lopes, Mosseh de David Rodrigues, 29:37
Lopess, Moses, 32:58
Lopez, 31:4
Lopez (Italy), 28:179
Lopez, Aaron (Newport), 23:84-85, 88-89;
    25:113; 26:8, 244-45; 27:113, 151, 154,
    178, 180, 185, 202, 208-11, 213, 247, 284,
    287, 291, 297, 303, 306, 347, 405, 407,
    409, 427, 447-49, 452, 456; 29:32; 29:148;
    34:70-71, 170, 285; 35:133; 37:164, 392,
    438; 38:51, 70, 83; 39:247; 42:337; 43:142;
    44:204; history, writing of, 46:179, 420-25;
    47:187; 50:49-50; "Aaron Lopez, Colonial
    Merchant," 32:xix; "Aaron Lopez' Long
    Deferred 'Hope,' " 37:xxxiii, 103-13;
    "Calendar of Twenty-one Unprinted
    Letters Relating to Aaron Lopez," 25:xii-
    xiii; civil liberties, 46:31, 39; "Descriptive
    Index of Aaron Lopez Material at the
    Newport Historical Society," 37:xxxiii,
    153-62; 49:236; "Documents Relative to
    the Estate of Aaron Lopez," 35:xv, 139-43;
    "A Letter of Abraham ha-Levi of New
    York to Aaron Lopez, 1770," 34:xv; letters,
    25:xvi; 35:130; Moses M. Hayes, 35:290,
    292; naturalization, 35:xviii; "The
    Naturalization of Aaron Lopez," 38:342;
    portraits, 41:290; 23:xviii; Rhode Island
    Commerce, 35:295-304; "A Selection from
    the Unedited Correspondence of Aaron
    Lopez," 23:xiii, 183; "An Unpublished
    Letter to Aaron Lopez," 28:xxxiii
Lopez, Aaron (New York), 21:130
Lopez, Aaron (b. David), 27:80

Lopez, Aaron (b. Moses), 27:151
Lopez, Aaron (b. Samuel), 27:309, 347
Lopez, Aaron, Jr., 50:41, 55
Lopez, Abigail, 35:140
Lopez, Abigail (b. Aaron), see: Gomez,
    Abigail (nee Lopez)
Lopez, Abigail (Mrs. Aaron), 27:202, 208,
    297
Lopez, Abigail (Mrs. Abraham), 27:207-8
Lopez, Abraham, 30:69; Aaron Lopez,
    35:301-2; slave trade, 34:285
Lopez, Abraham (Boston), 23:88-89
Lopez, Abraham (New York), 27:153, 185,
    207-8, 247
Lopez, Abraham Rodriguez, 37:420
Lopez, Anna, 35:140
Lopez, Antonio, 31:28
Lopez, Catherine, 35:140
Lopez collection, 42:459
Lopez, David (Barbados), 21:11, 20-22, 25
Lopez, David (Boston), 23:88-90
Lopez, David (New York), 21:13, 16, 24;
    27:5, 80, 185, 189, 208, 416, 457; 34:71;
    35:297, 301
Lopez, David (S.C.), 38:70; 50:55
Lopez, David, Jr., 35:302-3; 37:112
Lopez, David Rodriques, 29:36
Lopez, Deborah, 23:89; 27:111
Lopez, Diego, 31:28
Lopez, Edward, 35:140
Lopez, Eliaho, 29:22
Lopez, Eliao, 27:23
Lopez, Elias, 21:11, 20, 49, 55
Lopez family, 23:85, 167; 27:211, 431, 448-
    49, 455; 34:170; "A Genealogical Note on
    the Pimentel, Lopez, Sasportas and Rivera
    Families," 42:303-4; gentleman of the
    Lopez family, portrait of, 42:416; portraits
    of, 41:284, 290
Lopez, Gabriel, 23:81
Lopez, Grace, 23:89; 27:111
Lopez, Hannah, 35:297
Lopez, Isaac (br. David), 23:81
Lopez, Isaac (Hunt's Bay), 37:341-42; "A
    Note on Isaac Lopez, a Jamaican
    Minister," 22:xiii; portrait, 22:xxxiv
Lopez, Isaac (New York) (1), 27:55; 35:311
Lopez, Isaac (New York) (2), 27:151, 203
Lopez, Ishack, 21:11, 20, 22, 51, 194

Lopez, Jacob, 23:89; 35:297-98
Lopez, Jacob (b. Abraham), 27:153, 185, 201, 212, 306, 424, 425
Lopez, Jacob (b. Moses), 27:203, 207
Lopez, Joseph, 21:43; 23:89-90; 27:80, 91, 151, 185, 291, 306, 424, 426-27, 451, 453; Aaron Lopez, 35:141-43; Gould letter, 27:425
Lopez, Joshua, 23:89
Lopez, Joshua (b. Aaron), 37:155
Lopez, Joshua (husband of Mary Ann), 27:284
Lopez, Joshua (husband of Rebecca), 27:154, 207, 214, 284, 417, 427
Lopez, Judith, 23:89; 37:39
Lopez, Judith (Mrs. Samuel), 21:191
Lopez, Judith (nee Seixas), 27:74, 305, 309, 347
Lopez, Julia, 27:212
Lopez, M., 27:59, 61; 50:174
Lopez, Manaseh, 37:420
Lopez, Maria, 29:148
Lopez, Martin, 31:3, 12
Lopez, Mary Ann, 27:449; 38:70
Lopez, Mathias, 27:55; 31:242-43
Lopez, Matthew, 26:251
Lopez, Melchor Rodriguez, 32:117
Lopez, Merriam, 23:89
Lopez, Miss, 27:429
Lopez, Mr., 27:390
Lopez, Mrs. (widow), 27:424
Lopez, Moses (Barbados), 22:179
Lopez, Moses (Newport), 40:75; 50:36, 55
Lopez, Moses (New York) (1), 21:19-20, 25, 31, 49, 51, 53, 163; 23:89; 27:59, 185, 201, 207, 305, 424-25; 37:373, 377, 386, 392, 412; 38:235; Aaron Lopez, 35:141; Gould correspondence, 27:426-27, 430-34, 437-42; lunar calendar, 27:335, 458; 39:299; A Lunar Calendar, 30:127-28, 266
Lopez, Moses (New York) (2), 27:151, 178, 180, 199, 203, 247, 416, 445, 450; letter to Sherith Israel (N.Y.), 27:183-84
Lopez, Moses (New York) (3), 27:153
Lopez, Moses (New York) (4), 27:307
Lopez, Moses (West Indies), 32:58, 34:71
Lopez, Moses, Jr., 31:242-43
Lopez, Priscilla, 27:448; 42:303
Lopez, Rachel (Mrs. David), 27:208

Lopez, Rachel (Mrs. Moses), 27:203
Lopez, Rebecca, 25:116; 35:297
Lopez, Rebecca (Mrs. Mordecai deLeon), 27:289
Lopez, Rebecca (nee Touro), 27:207, 214, 417, 429, 433-34, 439-42
Lopez, Rebecca (nee Touro), petition to R.I. legislature, 27:434-36
Lopez, Rodrigo, 34:181; 42:441
Lopez, Rodringes Abraham, 32:62
Lopez, Rodringes M., 32:62
Lopez, Sally, 35:296-97, 302; 42:56
Lopez, Samuel (New York) (1), 21:191; 27:74, 80, 170, 305, 309, 347, 427, 449, 451
Lopez, Samuel (New York) (2), 27:153
Lopez, Samuel (b. Aaron), 23:89
Lopez, Samuel (Newport), 37:39
Lopez, Samuel A., 27:43
Lopez, Sarah, 23:89
Lopez, Sarah (b. Aaron), 35:140
Lopez, Sarah (Mrs. Aaron), 27:113, 287, 347-48, 452
Lopez, Sarah (granddaughter Aaron), 27:347
Lopez, Sarah (Newport), 50:36, 55
Lopez, Sarah (Rivera), 42:303-4
Lopez, Sarah (West Indies), 32:58
Lopez, surname, 37:384
Lopez, Virginia, 39:53
Lopez, William, 37:106
Lopez Penha family, 44:225
Lopus, 22:198
Lorant, Stefan, 50:400
Loring, Captain, 35:19
Loring, George B., 33:213
Loris-Melikoff, Mikhail, 41:169
Lorwin, Lewis Levitzki, 43:193
Los Alamos, N.M., History of the Los Alamos Jewish Center, 49:228
Los Angeles, 49:264; religious observances, mid-nineteenth century, 37:37
Los Angeles Jewish Community Council, 42:421; 46:124
Loser, Friedrich, 41:260
Lossing, Benson J., 26:175-77; 39:45
Lost Ten Tribes, 21:xxi; 22:119; 25:81; 30:270; 34:173; 39:450, 455; 43:189, 191; "The Phylacteries Found at Pittsfield, Mass.," 25:vii, 81-85

Loth, Moritz, 40:22-23
Lothrop, Mrs. Francis B., 42:418
Lothrop, George V. N., 36:211, 214
Lotteries, 43:235-36; The Aaronsburgh
  Lottery, 30:83-84; Mikve Israel, Scheme of
  a Lottery, 30:133-34; "A proposal to
  improve the lotteries of the United States,
  patented by Jacob I. Cohen and signed by
  President Monroe and Vice-President
  Adams, March 3, 1825," 33:xviii
Lottery of Life, The, 40:348
Loubat Prize, 28:260
Louchheim, Jerome H., death, 37:xii
Louis II, 28:155
Louis XVI, 27:471-72; 31:60
Louis XVIII, 21:241
Louis, A., 29:129
Louis, Adolph H., 29:179
Louis, Mrs. A. H., 25:112
Louis Down-Town Sabbath School, New
  York, 29:179
Louis, Minnie D., 25:112; "America, Thou
  Hope of Nations," 26:xiv; necrology of,
  29:xiv, 178-79
Louis, Thomas, 33:118
Louisburg, "Six French Men-of-War Full of
  Jews at Louisburg," 26:xiv, 231
Louisiana, 25:24; 49:178; agricultural colony,
  37:440; "Anglo-Jewish Legal Cases,"
  25:137; colonization, 48:83-85, 93; *A
  Jewish Agricultural Colony in Louisiana*,
  35:xxii; Jewish local history, 49:222-23;
  "Jewish Merchants in Louisiana and West
  Florida, and the English Expedition to the
  Illinois in 1764-1765," 29:xvi; *The Jews in
  Louisiana*, 35:xxii; Masonry, 22:182;
  "Pioneer Types in Louisiana and
  Mississippi, 29:xxx; Shaare Chesed
  Synagogue, New Orleans, 37:440; "The
  Texel Affair in Louisiana, 44:242
Louisiana Bar Association, 26:276
Louisiana Historical Society, 23:x
Louisiana Purchase, 23:58
Louisiana State Board of Education, 28:309
Louisiana State Museum, gift, 35:xxiii
Louisville, Ky., religious observance, mid-
  nineteenth century, 37:35
Louisville City Hospital, 45:189
Lourie, David A., necrology of, 32:xvi

Lousada, Aaron Baruch, 35:30; 37:338
Lousada, Abigail Baruh, 32:60; 35:31
Lousada, Claude, 31:291
Lousada, Daniel Baruh, 32:64; 35:31
Lousada, Jacob Baruh, 32:63; 35:31
Lousada, Sarah, 32:60
Lousado, Herbert, 43:64-65
Louzada, Aaron, 21:10, 16, 19, 21, 27, 29, 31,
  44, 48, 53, 55, 63, 73; 33:201, 206, 252,
  254
Louzada, Abigel, 33:254
Louzada, Abraham Baruch, 33:252
Louzada, Aron, 31:238; 32:64
Louzada, Bauh (Baruch), 22:179
Louzada, Benjamin, 21:73; 33:254
Louzada, Blume, 33:201, 254
Louzada, Daniel Baruch, 29:10
Louzada, David Baruch, 29:10; 33:252;
  44:229
Louzada, David Baruk, 32:58; 35:31
Louzada, Emanual Baruch, 25:114
Louzada, Hannah, 21:61, 72-73, 89, 91, 93,
  124; 31:237; 33:254
Louzada, Jacob, 21:8, 10, 19; 33:252, 254;
  38:103-4
Louzada, Leah, 32:60
"The Louzada Family of Bound Brook, N.Y.,
  1698-1800," 28:xv
Louzada, Mrs., 21:81
Louzada, Moses, 21:10, 16, 19, 21, 27, 29, 31,
  41, 44, 48, 53, 55; 27:150; 33:252-54
Louzada, Moses Barro (Barruh), 35:30
Louzada, Mosseh Baruh, 29:10; 44:228
Louzada, Rachel, 27:150
Louzada, Rebecca Baruch, 33:252
Louzade, Aaron Baruch, 35:30
Louzado, Aaron, 27:122, 236
Louzado, Aaron Baruch, 26:251
Louzado, Daniel Baruch, 26:251
Louzado, Hannah, 27:21, 247
Louzado, Jacob Baruch, 26:251
Louzado, Jeremiah Baruch, 26:251
Louzado, Moses, 27:236
Louzado, Rebecca, 26:251
Love, Alfred H., 37:86
Love a la mode, 33:174-75
Love, Col., 44:43
"Love in a Village," 23:180
Lovelace, Francis, 31:88-90

Love Laughs at Locksmiths, 33:174, 191
Lovell, Mr., 28:254
Loventhal, Lee, J., 45:147
Lover's vows: or, The natural son, 33:174, 185-86
"Lovers of Zion," 39:237
Low, Cornelia, 21:9
Low, Elizabeth, 40:76
Löw, Leopold, 46:97, 102, 118
Löw, Samuel Hirsch, 41:264
Low, Seth, 36:263
Low, William G., 33:217, 221, 223
Low, Mrs. Wm. G., 33:219
Lowell, Abbot Lawrence, 47:21
Lowell, Amy, 38:281; 45:28
Lowell Institute, 42:352
Lowell, James Russell, 22:1; 34:168, 185; 36:205-7; 40:330; 42:151, 341; 46:128; Emma Lazarus, 38:267, 269, 278; Mrs. Child, 38:174
Löwenberg, David, 41:248, 268
Löwenberg, Josef, 41:258
Löwenberg, Julius, 26:99-100
Löwengart, Elias, 41:264
Löwengart, Samuel, 41:264
Lowenheim, J., 29:130
Löwenhelm, Count, 26:50
Lowenstaff Brothers, 35:177
Lowenstamm, Saul, 34:111, 113, 116; "A Letter to Saul Lowenstamm, chief rabbi of Amsterdam, from the Mickveh Synagogue of Philadelphia, dated 9 Nissan 5445 (1785)," 35:xv
Lowenstein, Hyman, 22:193
Löwenstein, Leopold, 41:264
Lowenstein, Louis C., 32:124
Lowenstein, Moses H., 27:271
Lowenstein, S., 38:333
Lowenstein, Solomon, 34:258
Lowenstein (store), 38:20
Löwenthal, Abraham, 41:260
Löwenthal, Baruch, 41:255
Löwenthal, Carl, 41:246
Löwenthal, Leo, Prophets of Deceit, reviewed, 40:199-201
Löwenthal, Moses, 41:264
Löwenthal, Salomon, 41:265
Löwenthal, Simson, 41:260
Lowenthal, William, 42:178-80

Lower Wall Street Business Men's Association, 23:x
Lowery, Archibald H., 39:35
Lowery, W., 31:247
Lowery, Alexander, 23:4, 13
Lowndes, Thomas, 32:43
Lowrie, Rev., 28:60-61
Lowrie, Walter Macon, The Land of Sinim, 30:403, 455
Lowry, James, 43:234
Lowth, Bishop, 25:109-10
Lowth, Robert, 49:46; Appendix to Lowth's Isaiah, 30:294; Isaiah, 30:98-99, 162, 297; Lectures of the Sacred Poetry of the Hebrews, 30:258
Löwy, Albert, 24:24
Lowyor, Johannes, 27:247
Lowzada, Aaron Baruh, 32:58
Lowzada, Rachel Baruh, 35:31
Loyalists, 23:97-100, 166; 23:166; "Barrak Hays: Controversial Loyalist," 43:231; 45:54-57; Jews among, 40:85; "Some Jewish Loyalists in the War of American Independence," 38:81-107
Loyon, Abraham de, 27:247
Loyson, Hyacinthe, 41:162
Lozado, David Baruh, 32:58; 35:31
Lozowick, Louis, 47:182
Lubarsky, G., 39:108-9
Lübek, Jewish emancipation, 26:35, 37, 43-44, 47-48, 53, 56, 61-62, 64, 80, 84, 89
Lubelsky, Mr., 48:36
Lubin, David, 29:195; 33:xxxi; 34:186; 38:250; portrait, 29:xliii
Lubin, Jeannette, 29:195
Lubin, Rachel, 29:194
Lubomirski, Casimir, 36:149
Lucas, Albert, 34:238; gift, 25:xvi
Lucas, Captain, 26:248
Lucas, Paul, 41:61
Lucas, Phillip, 27:283
Lucas, Sampson, 37:420
Lucena, Abraham d., 21:176, 178-79
Lucena, Abraham de, 21:xiii; 23:149-50; 27:265, 272; 39:292; 44:205, 211; 49:60
Lucena, Abraham Haim de, 49:59-60
Lucena, Esther de, 23:150
Lucena of Georgia, 33:xxxi
Lucena, Isaac de, 37:339

Lucena, Jacob, 31:86; 39:209
Lucena, James, 27:446; 38:94: 46:423-24
Lucena, John Charles, 38:93-96
Lucena, Joseph de, 23:84
Lucena, Judith de, 23:150
Lucena, Manuel de, 31:28-29, 31
Lucena, Matantta, 27:281
Lucena, Moses, 25:42; 31:86
Lucena, Moses de, 23:150
Lucena, Rachel de, 23:150
Lucena, Raphael Carvalho de, 29:28
Lucena, Rebecca de, 27:289, 291; 31:37
Lucena, Samuel de, 21:38, 41, 43-44, 79, 150;
    23:150; 27:41, 247-48, 462
Lucius (b. Angelo), 28:152, 155
Lucius (b. Manuele), 28:152, 155-56
Lucina, Rachel de, 23:154
Luck, George, 50:231
Luckey, Ch. Th., 33:136
Luczynski, Major, 36:162
Lüdering and Company, 38:215
Ludlow, G. S., 27:46
Ludlow, Mr., 27:358
Ludlow, Thomas, Jr., 28:226
Ludlow, William, 27:247
Ludwig, Emil, 46:430
Ludwig, King, 24:100
Luepschuetz, Israel ben Gedaliah, *Mishnah
    Tiferet Yisrael*, 22:131
Luijs, Hans Willem, 33:122
Luis, Antonio, 32:16, 19
Luis, Christovão, 47:64
Luis, Manoel, 44:96
Luis in Pojuca, Anthony, 33:113
Luiza, Rachel, 31:238
Luis, Thomas; 47:63-75; *see also*: Castro, Isaac
    de
Luiza, Rachell, 21:23
Lukens, J., 34:274
Lukens, John, 43:235
Lum, Lum, 34:197
Lumbroso, Mose, 42:279, 394; 44:93
Lumbrozo, Jacob, 22:158, 191, 193; 25:99-
    100; 31:124; 39:209; 46:35-36; "The Price
    the Jew Dr. Lumbrozo Paid for Maryland's
    So-Called Toleration," 31:xxx
Luna, Francisco Ruiz de, 31:27
Luna, Gasalva de, 33:113
Lunar calendar, 27:335, 458

Lundius, Johannes, *Die alten Jüdischen
    Heiligthumer*, 34:xxiv
Lundt, Henry, and John Israel, *Journal of a
    Cruise*, 30:302
Lundy's Lane, 26:182
L'Univers Israélite, 37:474
Lupashku, Prefect, 24:37
Luper, Alfred, 50:271
Lupin, M., 39:88
Lup, Rudolph, 42:420; 46:120
Luria, A., 26:252
Luria, Frank, 44:118
Luria, Solomon, *Shulhan Aruk*, 28:68, 79
Lurie, Aaron, 43:66
Lurie, Harry, 42:465
Lurie, Reuben L., 47:212, "Elsie T., Sophie
    M., and Lee Max Friedman: An
    Appreciation," 48:265
Lurie, S., 43:67
Lurting, Robert, 21:6; 42:80
Lusena, Judith, 37:339
Lusena, Moses de, 37:339
Lush, John, 35:182
Luic, M. M., 34:291
Lusitanus, Amatus (Chabib), *see*: Castel-
    Bianco, Joao Rodrigo de
Lustgarten, Sigismund, 42:124
Luther, Hans, 36:375
Luther, Martin, 27:128; 28:90; 38:325
Lutheran Church, 43:134; 47:146
Lützen, 26:75
Luzado, Solomon, 27:59
Luzena, Jacob, 2nd, 44:227
Luzena, Jacob Hizriahu de, 37:340
Luzern, Chevalier de la, 27:471
Luzzatti, 24:88
Luzzatti, Luigi, 28:21; 34:229, 248; 35:xviii,
    135; 37:76; 40:403; "God in Freedom,"
    33:xxx
Luzzato, 29:128
Luzzatto, Isaiah, 37:70, 88
Luzzatto, Moses Hayyim, 43:239
Luzzatto, Philoxene, 37:68
Luzzatto, Samuel David, 28:72, 34:16; 37:57,
    59, 63-64, 67-70, 79-80; 40:18; 47:123
Lyceum Debating Club, 44:27
Lyceum Theatre, 33:191
Lydenberg, Harry Miller, 35:315; book
    review by, 43:239-40

Lydon, Judge, 29:151-52
Lyell, Charles, 35:178; 42:357
Lynch, William F., 40:281-85; *Narrative of Expedition to River Jordan*, 30:449
Lynd, James, 42:367-68
Lynn, Judge, 25:136
Lynn, Stuart, 50:181
Lyon, 34:101
Lyon, Aaron de, 22:179
Lyon, Abraham (New York), 21:45, 48, 53, 55; 23:154; 37:383
Lyon, Abraham (West Indies), 25:115
Lyon, Abraham de (Ga.), 34:285
Lyon, Abraham de (Lancaster), 27:247
Lyon, Abraham De (Richmond, Va.), 27:488
Lyon, Abraham Henry, 25:177
Lyon, Asher, 25:117
Lyon, Ashur, 25:115
Lyon, Benjamin, 37:420; 40:72, 84
Lyon, Benjamin, Jr., 37:420
Lyon, Benjamin L., 37:420
Lyon, David G., 22:207-8
Lyon, Emanuel, 25:117; 34:266
Lyon, Esther, 25:115, 117
Lyon family, Pennsylvania, 22:xxii
Lyon, Frances, 25:117
Lyon, George, 27:506
Lyon, Hart, 26:251, 254
Lyon, Isaac (New York), 27:80
Lyon, Isaac (Richmond, Va.), 27:506
Lyon, Isaac de, 27:90; 50:41
Lyon, J. J., 50:8
Lyon, J. W., 26:254
Lyon, Lebonah de, 23:155
Lyon, M. I., 27:95
Lyon, Mabel, "Some Pedagogical Aspects of American Jewish History," 25:xiii
Lyon, Mary, 37:420
Lyon, Mordecai, 50:41, 55
Lyon, Robert, 26:271; 27:516; 48:220
Lyon, Sarah A., 26:249
Lyon, Simon, by-laws committee, 25:xii; death, 37:xii; thirty-first annual meeting, committee on, 29:xxvi
Lyon, Solomon, 27:42-43, 253
Lyon, T. Kenton, 27:506
Lyon, surname, 37:383
Lyon-Cahen, Charles, 41:162
Lyons, Alfred J., 21:x; gift, 41:291

Lyons Collection, 21:1ff; 26:xxvii, 9; 27:1ff; 28:xii, 303; 50:274, 283-85
Lyons, Eleazar, 38:58, 65
Lyons, Ellis, 31:84
Lyons, Ellis (Eleazar), 27:266, marriage of J. J. Lyons, 27:146; school of, 27:499-500
Lyons, H., 29:134
Lyons, Henry M., 27:271
Lyons, I. E., 27:144, 236
Lyons, Isaac, 50:154
Lyons, Israel, 38:148; *An Hebrew Grammar*, 30:54-55, 121, 127, 149-50
Lyons, Jacob, 27:144
Lyons, Jacob Judah, 27:105
Lyons, Jacques Judah, 21:xxiii-xxviii; 27:xiii-xv, viii-xix, 78, 113, 115-21, 124, 166, 261, 265, 313, 315, 330, 346, 350, 353, 379, 387, 397, 407, 459-60, 494, 504, 506; 29:131; 31:xvii, 80, 84; 236-40; 33:xxix; 34:xxi, 129-31, 138-41, 291; 35:xix; 37:217, 430; 38:72; 40:148; 42:431; 46:51, 54; 47:125; 50:280, 283-84; biographical sketch, 21:xxiii-xxviii, 193; funeral services for persons married contrary to Jewish law, 27:115-16; Haym, Salomon, correspondence concerning, 27:227-28; Lincoln monument, subscription to, 27:124-25; matters concerning, 27:144-49; Mexican inquisition, 27:485; Newport Jews, history of, 27:190-91, 211-16; pamphlets, 27:518-24; permanent minyan, 27:116; *Rules and Regulations*, 30:403; scrap books, 27:499-517
Lyons, Mrs. Jacques J., 38:72; 50:281
Lyons, James, 27:506
Lyons, Judah, 25:141; 27:74, 84, 86, 158, 229: 31:xxxii
Lyons, Judah Eleazar, 21:xxiii; 27:276; 34:xxi
Lyons, Julius J., 21:x, 215; 41:291
Lyons, Mary, 27:276
Lyons, Mary Asser, 21:xxiii
Lyons, Maxwell, 40:48
Lyons, Sarah, 21:x; 31:xviii; gifts, 31:xxxii; 33:xxix, xxxii; 34:xxi; 35:xviii; 41:291
Lyons, Solomon, 50:39, 55
Lysons, Daniel, 26:263-64
Lyte, Dr., 27:132
Lyte, Ephraim, 27:64, 242
Lyttleton, Governor, 35:7

M

Maarabi, Nahum, 37:59, 68
Maas, Charlotte (Mehlinger), 22:228
Maas, Dr., 37:41
Maas, Mrs. Emil, 35:xviii
Maas, Jacob, 22:228
Maass, Herbert H., 37:456
Maass, Richard, executive council, 44:421;
    45:264
Mabe, Mr., 39:75, 78
McAdoo, William Gibbs, 36:285; 41:184-85
McAgar, Mr., 37:134
McAllister, Mr., 38:156
McAllister, Samuel Ward, 46:167
MacArthur, C. G., 40:358
MacArthur, Charles, 35:273
McArthur, John, 41:68
Macatie, William, 33:252
Macaudo, Solomon, 27:42
McAuley, Charles S., 39:24
Macauley, Thomas B., 22:177; 26:266, 268;
    41:88
Maccabean, The, 46:167
Maccabean Settlement House, 22:217
McCaffrey, Stanley E., 48:259
McCall, John, 26:266
McCarran, Patrick Anthony, 46:301
McCarran-Walter Act, 46:292-96, 302-6,
    309, 312, 315-36, 340, 343, 350-51, 412,
    415-17, 419
McCarter Gallery, 28:xi
McCarthy, Joseph, 46:278
Mccarty, Thaddeus, 45:58
M'Caul, Alexander, 26:149
McCauley, C. L., 39:18
M'Cheyne, Robert Murray, 22:172; 26:134;
    and A. Bonar, *Narrative of a Mission of
    Inquiry to the Jews*, 30:370, 399
McClellan, Captain B., 42:398

McClellan, George Brinton, 25:145; 42:118;
    43:81, 112, 114
McClernand, John A., 32:95; 47:51
McClure, Frank, 40:58
McClure's, 43:34
McCollum, Vashti, 40:97
McComb, John, 27:241-42
McConnel, John Ludlum, 44:6-7
McCord, Ada, 34:143
McCord, James, 34:143
McCord, Mr., 27:376
MacCormack, David, 45:236
McCormack, Richard C., 47:82
McCormick, Anne O'Hare, 39:342
McCormick, Cyrus H., 36:43
McCormick, Robert S., 36:262, 271-73
McCready, N. L., & Co., 31: 137
McCready, William B., 42:116
McCullough, Benjamin, 50:342
McCunn, Judge, 27:383
MacDaniel, Timothy, 26:248-49
McDonald, Alexander, 36:16-18
Macdonald, Arthur N., 50:396
MacDonald, James, 35:16
McDonald, James G., 34:242; 36:369; 39:198
McDonald, John, *Isaiah's Message to the
    American Nation*, 30:157, 226-27
MacDonald, Mr., 36:93
M'Donald, Philip, 39:187-89
McDougall, Brigadier General, 39:319
McDougall, Col., 27:391
McDowell, Irvin, 37:43; 50:326
McDowles, Miss, 31:154
McElwain, William H., 41:43
McEnery, Samuel Douglas, 40:269
McEntire, Walter, "Was Christopher
    Columbus a Jew," 33:37
McEvers, Charles, 35:291-92
McEvoy, C. A., 27:506

McEwan, Frank J., 34:217
McFarland, Henry, 50:307
McFee, William, 35:265
McGee, Anita Newcomb, 33:225, 227-28
McGill University, 38:72; 50:131
Machabeu, Jehudah, 42:278, 394
Machado, Abigail, 37:204
Machado, Antonio, 31:30
Machado, Aron, 21:45
Machado, Binyamin Mendes, 21:11, 20
Machado, David, 21:11, 20, 23, 28, 30, 35-38, 40-41, 47, 54, 56, 172, 208; 23:151; 35:183-84
Machado, David Mendes, 27:262, 267-68, 281; 45:65
Machado, David Mendez, 31:237; 41:288, 292
Machado, David Moses, 35:201
Machado, Mr., 27:384, 386
Machado, Mrs., 21:57
Machado, Nuno Alverres, 33:117
Machado, Rebecca Mendez, 21:172; 50:58
Machado, Sally, 35:201
Machado, Siporah, 21:58; 27:247
Machado, Zipporah Nunez, 41:288, 292
Machazike Talmud Torah (New York), 46:493
Machero, Joshua, 22:179
Machiavelli, Niccolò, 37:186, 199
Machorro, Abraham, 29:17
Machorro, David, 29:17
Machorro, Diogo Fernandes, 29:17
Machorro, Eliau, 29:17
Machorro, Jacob, 29:17
Machorro, Mordehay, 42:279, 394
Machorro, Mosseh, 29:17
Machorro, Salomoh, 29:17
Machudo, David, 33:253
Machzikai Talmud Torah, 35:61
M'Illvaine, William, 30:200
M'Ilvaine, Mrs., 29:55
McIntosh, James, 39:34
MacIver, R. M., Jewish Community Relations: An Analysis of the MacIver Report, reviewed, 42:319-20, 463-66; Report on the Jewish Community Relations Agencies, Section I, reviewed, 42:319-30, 463-66
Mack, Adolph, necrology of, 22:xii, 227-28
Mack, Alexander W., 22:228

Mack Bros. (Milwaukee), 47:37, 42, 45-46
Mack, Clara L., 22:228
Mack, Hermann, 23:112, 116
Mack, Herman S., 47:37, 42, 45-46
Mack, Mr. and Mrs. John J., 50:383
Mack, Julian William, 34:220-21; Agricultural Experiment Station, 31:203, 210; bookplates, 45:136; executive council, 29:xxxv; 31:xxix; 33:xvii; 35:xiv; Henrietta Szold, 49:168; immigration, 39:106; Jewish Historical Society of Illinois, 28:240; necrology of, 37:xii, 476-77; necrology of Sigmund Eisner, 31:xxiii; vice-president, 22:xi, xvi, xxvii; 23:xii; 25:xi; 26:xii, xxx; 28:xiv, xxi, xxxii; 29:xiv, xxviii; Woodrow Wilson, 36:79; Y.M.H.A., 37:306-7; Zionism, 49:192-95, 199-200
Mack, Mrs. Julian W. (Fox), 25:150
Mack, Lewis C., 22:228
Mack, Lewis S., 47:37, 45-46, 48
Mack, Louise (Geldersheimer), 22:227
Mack, Max, 47:37
Mack, Mrs. Millard W. (Fox), 25:150
Mack, Ralph W., 40:47
Mack, Therese (Einstein), 22:228
Mack Trucks, 38:322
Mack, Wolfgang, 22:227
McKaine v. Drake Business School, Inc., 29:150
McKarcher, Jac., 31:147
Mackay, Aeneas, 23:15
Mackay, Clarence, 35:270
McKean, Thomas, 21:xvi; 43:236; 46:3
Mackellar, Thomas, 34:xxiii
McKelvey, Blake, 40:105; "The Jews of Rochester: A Contribution to Their History During the Nineteenth Century," 40:57-73; 49:232
McKenna, S., 29:xliii
McKenney, Samuel T., 45:54, 56
Mackenzie, G. E., 25:114
Mackenzie, Robert, 31:59, 162
Mackenzie, William L., Lives and Opinions of Benj. Franklin Butler and Jesse Hoyt, 30:404
Mackenzie's Catalogue, 26:242
McKesson, John, 37:370
Mackiewicz, Dr., 39:156
McKinley, William, 41:358, 360; 46:228; 50:400; Abraham Cahan, 43:32; Edward

Lauterbach, 29:174; Jacob Harry Hollander, 37:472; Oscar S. Straus, 31:295; 40:7-8; Palestine, 36:43; Red Cross, 33:217-18; Roumanian disabilities, 39:430; Tariff, 40:291
McKinley Industrial Commission, 41:304
McKinney, Billie S., "Cardozo and Brandeis: Modern Sons of Liberty," 44:240
Macklin, Charles, 33:196; *Love a la mode*, 33:174-75
McLachlan, 27:71, 73
McLane, Mr., 36:331, 335, 340
McLaughlin, Chester, 49:10
McLaurin, Anselm J., 36:276
Maclay, Edgar Stanton, 23:170; 26:196-98
McLean, Alexander, 22:180
McLean, Daniel Howes, 22:180
McLean House, 50:343
McLean, Mary (Massiah), 22:180
McLean, Sarah Ann, 22:180
McLean, William, 22:179-80
McLean, William, Sr., 22:180
MacLeish, Archibald, 37:13-14
McLennan, John, 31:98
M'Leod, Alexander, 39:187-89
McLuney, William J., 39:33-34
McMahon, Isaiah, *Hebrew without a Master*, 30:415-16
M'Makin, Andrew, 27:466
McMaster, John Bach, 26:2; 32:5; 37:148, 463; 39:287; necrology of, 33:xx
McMath, Jesse H., 36:20-22
McMath, Mr., 29:87
McMenamy, Hess & Co., 26:280
McMicken University, 40:26
Macmillan's Magazine, 25:158
McMillens, A. J., 39:75, 78
McMorrow, Thomas, 35:272
Macmurde, Charles, 27:506
McNeile, Hugh, *Prospects of the Jews*, 30:347
Macon, Ga., 48:211; religious observances, mid-nineteenth century, 37:37
MacPherson, 28:6
McQuaid, Bernard, 46:284
McReynolds, James Clark, 46:471
McShath, Thomas, 39:35
McWillie, Adam, 26:189
Macy, R. H. & Co., 22:238
Macy (Straus), 38:20

Madariaga, Salvador de, *The Fall of the Spanish American Empire*, reviewed, 38:323-25
Madera, Isaack, 33:116
Madero, Francisco Indalecio, 31:213
Madison Avenue Temple, Baltimore, 26:289
Madison, Dolley, 48:9
Madison, James, 26:185; 29:xix; 34:168, 171; 38:121; 40:96; 43:163-64; 48:9, Haym Salomon, 27:467-70; John Jacob Hays, 45:56; Mordecai Manuel Noah, 41:6-7; 46:10; Uriah Phillips Levy, 39:55
Madison, Wis., Jewish Welfare Fund, contribution, 37:xxviii
Madras, 28:249-50
Madrid Royal Academy of History, 26:23
Madrid, University of, 25:xii; 26:24
Madrin, Sarah, 23:158
Madrin, Thomas, 23:158
Madsen, A. W., 46:487
Maduhy, Haim, 34:289
Madura, Amaro Lopes, 33:115
Madura, Joan Montera, 33:116
Maduro, Abraham de Ishac Levy, 44:229-30
Maduro family, 42:109; 48:139
Maduro, Irmeao de Ishac Levy, 44:229, 231
Maduro, Irmiao Haim Levy, 44:227
Maduro, Isaac Levy, 27:247
Maduro, Ishac Levy, 44:227-29
Maduro, Is. de Jacob Levy, 22:170
Maduro, Ishac de Jacob Levy, 44:230, 232-33
Maduro, Ishac de Jahacob Levy, 25:138
Maduro, J. M. L., 42:214-15, 331; "A Genealogical Note on the Pimental, Lopez, Sasportas and Rivera Families," 42:303-4
Maduro, Jacob Levy, 27:23; 44:228-29, 231
Maduro, Jahacob Levy, 25:138
Maduro, Jossy Levy, 44:118
Maduro, Levi, 29:31
Maduro, Monty D., 44:118
Maduro, Mosseh de Ishac Levy, 44:229-30
Maduro, Samuel Levy, 48:139
Maduro, Selomoh de Is. Levy, 22:169-70; 29:30; 44:229
Maduro, Semuel de Ishac Levy, 44:229
Maduro, Semuel Levy, 44:227
Maduro, Selomoh de Mordy Levy, 22:169-70

Mad Year, "The Revolution of 1848 and the Jewish 'On to America' Movement," 38:185-234, 345

Maens, Francis, 33:108

Maestro, Dauid, 42:279, 394

Magazine of American History, 47:224

Magazine of History with Notes and Queries, The, 50:285

Magaziner, D. Arthur, 41:91, 93

Magee *v.* Nealon, 29:150

Magelhains, Gonsalvo, 33:115

Magen Abraham Congregation of Mauricia, 43:128; 46:43; "The Minute Book of Congregations Zur Israel of Recife and Magen Abraham of Mauricia, Brazil," 42:217-302, 416

Magen David, origin and significance, 22:xvii

Maggie Pepper, 40:356

Maggs Brothers, 28:248

Magnes, Judah L., 43:196; 49:191-93, 195; 50:213; Agricultural Experiment Station, 31:203; Cyrus Adler, 33:29; gift, 35:xxiii; Hebrew Union College, 40:38, 42, 373; Henrietta Szold, 49:166; Joseph Isaac Bluestone, 35:60, 62; Louis Stern, 39:102, 106; Y.M.H.A., 37:306-7; Zionism, 45:99

Magnin, 38:20

Magnin, Edgar, 39:464

Magnin, Edgar F., 46:120-21, 124

Magnus, Charles, 50:342

Magnus, Hermann, 41:144

Magnus, Laurie, 31:291

Magnusson, Eiriker, 25:182

Magpie and the maid, 33:174, 194

Magpye Alley Congregation, London, 33:208

Magrath, A. G., 50:336

Magruder, John Bankhead, 50:332, 342

Mahaberet ha-Aruk (Hebrew Lexicon), 22:104

Maher, Elizabeth, 40:128

Mahler, Gustav, 47:53-54

Mahler, Jacob, 47:48, 56

Mahler, Raphael, "Reverend Gershom Mendes Seixas on the Restoration of Israel," 40:406

Mahmoud Sami, 47:87-88, 91

Mahon, Marion, 28:228-29; 34:120

Mahzike Talmud Torah Mt. Sinai Congregation, N.Y., 44:136

Mai, Jette, 41:268

Maiden Lane Synagogue, London, 35:242

Maier, Samuel, 34:23, 43

Maigne, Jules, 41:162

Mail and Express (New York), 32:129

Mailla, Joseph-Marie-Anne de Moyria de, 49:44

Maimon, Solomon, 35:263

Maimonides, Moses, 26:219; 28:68-69, 163; 31:178; 43:2-3, 195; 44:124; 45:62-63; 50:83; and American Jewry, 34:268-70; "Guide of the Perplexed," 28:69; Letter by Maimonides," 37:59, 68; Maimonides medal, 35:xviii; Mayer Sulzberger, 29:190-91; *Vide e obras de Maimonides*, 35:xxi

Maimonides College, 28:xxxiv; 29:107-8, 190; 34:270; 37:68, 84; 40:21, 28, 35; 42:103; 43:139; 44:252; 48:227, 230-31; 49:24; 50:297

Maimonides Library, New York, 34:270; 41:248

Maimonides Octocentennial Committee, gift, 34:xxi

Maimuni, Abraham, 45:62

Maine, Jewish local history, 49:223-24

"Maine," battleship and role of Jewish seamen, 22:xvii; 29:xliii

Mainz, 50:297-98

Mainzer, Abraham, 41:268

Mainzer Carnival Verein, 40:151

Mainzer, Elise, 31:189

Maison Blanche, 38:20

Majoresco, M., 24:93

Makover, A. B., "Mordecai M. Noah, His Life and Work, from the Jewish Point of View," 26:xv

Makovsky, Donald I., "The Early History of the Jews of St. Louis (1807-1841)," 49:268

Makower, Hermann, 40:242; 41:144-45, 156

Malachi, A. R., 50:271

Malachi, Eliezer Raphael, 33:133-34, 136-39, 141-47

Malak, Muly, 41:4

Malbim, Meir Loeb ben Jehiel Michael, 44:131-32, 151, 188

Malbish Arumim Society, 35:61

Malbone, Edward Greene, 41:278, 287; 42:417; 50:245

Malby, George R., 36:286; 41:186-88

Malcolm, W. A., 27:331

Maldonado, Anton Ruiz, 31:22

Malechowsky, Hillel, 35:62

Malina, Max, "Are there Jews in America, and where are they to be found? A translation from Schudt," 33:xvii; "Captain J. G. Stedman's 'Narrative of a five-year expedition against the revolted negroes of Surinam . . . from the year 1772 to 1777,' and its Jewish interest," 33:xvii; "German Jews in New York after the War," 33:xxx; gift, 35:xxiii; "Jewish references in the will of Eilias Boudinot," 33:xvii; "References to M. M. Noah and A. Phillips, 1821-1822, in 'The theatrical life of Joe Cowell, Comedian, written by himself,' " 33:xvii

Malinoff, Joe, 29:62

Malinoff, Louis, 29:62

Malke, 34:197

Malki, Moses, 34:288

Mallary, C. D., 33:235

Mallary, G., "Israelites and Indian, a parallel," 34:xxiv

Mallorie, John, 44:97

Mallory, Mr., 29:121

Mallory, Stephen Russell, 23:121; 25:21, 26; 43:107; 50:318-19, 365

Malone, Mr., 33:173

Malone, Sylvester, 33:221; 47:96

Malouet (commissioner), 22:26; 25:139

Malric, député, 41:162

Malter, Henry, 40:41, 43, 45, 373-75, 379; 48:194

Maltitz, A., 35:41

Maltos, Joan Tavaros de, 33:116

Malvano, Alessandre, 37:93

Mamelsdorf, Mr. and Mrs. Edward, gift, 32:xxviii; Revue des Etudes Juives, 33:xxxi

Man, Dr., 26:176

"Manassas, an Israelite of Colonial Days," 32:132

Manasse, Albert, 41:265

Manasse, Wolf, 41:265

Manasse, Zion, 41:265

Manasseh ben Israel, 34:9; 37:186, 354, 357-58, 362; 45:62; Mikweh Yisrael, 22:119

Manasses, R., 25:114

Manchester, Nathan, 27:431, 433, 437, 440

Mandel (store), 38:20

Mandelbaum, F. S., 37:428

Mandelkern, Solomon, 35:119

Mandell, Kaufmann, necrology of, 34:ix

Mandells, Joshua H., 27:42

Mandelstamm, Leon, 28:84, 118

Mandeuill, Geoffrey, 41:382-83

Mandeville, William de, 41:383

Mandl, Bernhard, 28:96-97

Mandlebaum, Frederick S., 42:125

Mandlestamm, Leon, 45:151

Mandura, Gaspar Ferdinandes, 33:112

Maney, Anna Marie, 34:215

Manha, Isaac Johannis de la, 33:95

Manhattan Beach, 47:12-13

Manila Pact, 44:71

Manischewitz, Max, death, 37:xii

Manley, James R., 26:225

Manlius Titus, see: Hamilton, Alexander

Mann, 25:56

Mann, Ambrose Dudley, 36:300; 37:441

Mann, Arthur, "Attitudes and Policies on Immigration—An Opportunity for Revision," 46:289-305; book review by, 46:127-29; (ed.), Growth and Achievement: Temple Israel, 1854-1954, reviewed, 44:250-51; 49:224-25; history, writing of, 46:191-92, 408, 412, 415-17; Yankee Reformers in the Urban Age, 49:224

Mann, Frederic R., 43:238

Mann, Horace, 40:96-97; 46:39

Mann, Jacob, 40:48; 45:162; "Texts and Studies in Jewish History and Literature," 33:xxx, 36

Mann, James R., 41:186-88

Mann, Newton N., 40:64

Mann, William P., 50:388

Manners and Customs of the Jews, 30:288, 339, 387

Manners, John Hartley, 40:355

Mannheim (colonel), 41:162

Mannheimer, 29:126

Mannheimer, Eugene, 47:208; 49:222

Mannheimer, Isaac Noah, 28:277; 50:93

Mannheimer, Sigmund, 37:293; 40:36, 43

Mannheimer, V. Fried, 23:188; 38:193, 225-28

Manning, Edward, 22:22

Manning, James, 37:136, 142

Manning, William C., 50:336-37

Manoel, King of Portugal, 31:174

Manozca, Pedro de, 31:31
Mansfield, Lord, 31:107, 110, 132
Mansfield, Ohio, United Jewish Appeal
    Drive, contribution, 37:xxviii
Mansion House Fund and Committee,
    25:159; 46:73; 48:96; 49:177, 181-82, 184
Manso, Alonso, 31:16
Manso (Bishop), 31:20
Mantino, Jacob ben Samuel, 28:164, 170-72,
    199-200
Mantino, Samuel, 28:172
Mantua, 28:158, 181, 190-92
Mantua, Duke of, 28:169, 183, 192-94
Manuchi, Nicolo, 28:250
Manuel, 47:188
Manuel, Antonio, 46:41
Manuel, Captain, 27:486
Manuel, E., 27:80
Manuel, Eugene, 41:162
Manuel, Frank W., *The Realities of American-*
    Palestine Relations, reviewed, 39:331-33
Manuel, Hannah, 33:201; 35:194, 197, 309
Manuel, Katherine, 27:376-77; marriage
    contract, 27:172
Manuel, Professor, 29:84
Manuel ben Solomon, 28:159
Manuele, Angelo di, 28:149-52, 154-55
Manuele di Cesena, 28:178
Manuele, Lucius di, 28:152, 155-56
Manuele, Maestro, 28:149-50
Manuele de Manuele, 28:152, 155
Manuele, son of Vitalucius of Rimini, 28:153
Manufacturing Society of the Dniper Region,
    43:67
Manumition Society (New York), 37:447-48;
    50:285
Mapes, Jonas, 27:316
Map making, "The Gratz Papers," 23:vii, xiii,
    1-23
Mapu, Abraham, 28:118; 34:286
Marache, Benja, 21:58, 63
Marache, Estter, 27:247
Marache family, Philadelphia, 22:34
Marache, Jacob, 21:51
Marache, Judith, 27:111
Marache, Moses, 21:51
Marache, Sol, 22:197
Marache, Solomon (New York), 21:51, 86,
    183; 23:172; 50:55

Marache, Solomon (Philadelphia), 27:461
Maranhaon, Jan Gommes, 33:116
Maranhaon, Michiel, 33:117
Marbois, Consul, 27:471
Marbury, Mr., 48:8
Marbury, H. A., 34:267
Marc, Jacob, 23:99
Marc, Philipp, 23:99
Marcantonio, Vito, 45:228
Marchallech, Joseph, 25:118
Marcgraf, George, 47:116
Marchena (Curaçao), 22:171
Marchena, Abraham, 44:230
Marchena, Abraham de, 44:229-30, 232
Marchena, Abraham and Isaac, 27:248
Marchena family, 42:108, 214
Marchena, Ishac, 44:227
Marchena, Ishac de, 44:227, 231-32
Marchena, Ishac de Abraham de, 44:222, 232
Marchena, Ishac de Ishac de, 44:230
Marchena, Jacob de, 44:227
Marchena, Ishac de, 22:170
Marchman, Watt P., 50:272
Marcin, Max, 40:354
Marco (Surgeon), 22:155
Marcus, Alexander, 33:27
Marcus, Alfred A., 38:62
Marcus, Asa, 35:293
Marcus, Bernard K., 46:175
Marcus, Betsey, 35:293
Marcus, Deborah, 35:293
Marcus, Drusa, 35:293
Marcus, Isaac, 21:123, 125
Marcus, Jacob, 44:252
Marcus, Jacob F., 45:26
Marcus, Jacob Rader, 37:iv; 38:vi, 78, 332,
    347; 40:79; 41:91; 42:467; 43:70; 44:118;
    47:178; 48:12; 50:157; "Address of the
    President," 46:465-66, 492; 47:125-33;
    "Americanization of Isaac M. Wise,"
    33:xxx; (ed.), *An American Jewish
    Bibliography*, reviewed, 44:252-54;
    *American Jewry, Documents Eighteenth
    Century*, reviewed, 49:208-9; Barrak Hays,
    45:55; Bibliography, 42:311; Canadian
    Jewry, 50:122; Civil War Centennial,
    49:137; Civil War History, 50:260, 270,
    332, 386; David Philipson, 39:462; *Early
    American Jewry* (2 vols.), reviewed, 43:131-

32; "From Peddler to Regimental Commander in Two Years: the Civil War Career of Major Louis A. Gratz," 38:22-44, 345; gifts, 34:xxvi; 35:xxiii; Hebrew Union College, 40:44, 48, 53; history, writing of, 39:225; 46:168, 182, 263, 413, 441, 445; 49:216, 247; honorary president, 48:265; 49:268; "Index to Americana in European Jewish Periodicals," 37:57; Jewish bibliography, 50:68-71; Jewish Historical Society of Israel, 41:391; Jewish local history, 49:255-56, 261; Jewish tercentenary, 40:414; Lee Max Friedman Award Medal, 49:271; 50:425; "Letters as a Source of Biography," 46:420, 425; "Light on Early Connecticut Jewry," 49:219; "Moses Hart's 'Modern Religion,' " 38:342; necrology of Henry Cohen, 42:415, 451-55; nomination committee, 49:267-68; 50:426; past president, 50:426; "The Periodization of American History," 47:125-33, 200; president, 45:264; 46:492; 47:200-201; presides, 39:470; 40:406; 41:389; 42:415; 43:231; 44:241-42; 45:260-62; 46:492-93; 48:265; 49:265; "Rise and destiny of the German Jew," 34:xxvi; "The Theme in American Jewish History," 48:141-46, 265; 37:xxxvi; 38:341, 344, 346; 39:469; 40:406; 41:387; 42:414; 43:230; 44:241

Marcus, S. L., 33:135

Marcus, Samuel, 35:293

Marcuse, H., 29:135

Marcuson, Isaac E., "Two Unknown Historic Candelabra from K. K. Beth Elchim of Charleston," 23:xiii, 186-87

Marcy, 22:82, 87

Marcy, Midshipman, 39:33

Marcy, William L., 30:404; 36:305

Marengo (privateer), 26:196

Margalith, Aaron M., 34:230; 36:xiv; 37:11, 453; 47:193; "The Doctrine of Intervention: An Historical Analysis," 37:xxx; Russian disabilities, 39:67, 265; *see also*: Adler, Cyrus

Margles, Mr. and Mrs. Raymond, 50:272, 275, 306

Margolin, Pauline, 38:315

Margolinsky, Julius, 229; *Epitaphs from the Jewish Cemetery in St. Thomas, W.I., 1837-1916, With an Index compiled from Records in the Archives of the Jewish Community in Copenhagen,* reviewed, 48:138-39

Margolies, Moses Z., 44:187

Margolis, Adolph, 35:64

Margolis, Elias, gift, 34:xxi

Margolis, M. S., 35:57

Margolis, Max L., 35:64; 38:315; 40:36, 41-42, 45, 373-81; 43:239; 45:101; 48:194; American Academy of Political and Social Science, delegate to, 29:xii; "The Beginnings of the Egyptian Diaspora," 22:xvii; executive council, 22:xii, xvi, xxviii; 23:xiii; 25:xi; 26:xii; 28:xxi, xxii; 29:xxix; 31:xxiii; 32:xix; History of Jews, committee on, 29:xxvi; "Hyphenated Jews in a Greek Papyrus," 23:xiii; Intercollegiate Menorah Association, 28:xxix; Jewish bibliographies, committee on, 29:xi; "The Jewish Colony of Elephantine," 22:xiii; necrology of, 33:xx; necrology of Harris J. Cohen, 31:xxiii; *Oriental Research in Palestine*, xvii; publication plan, 26:xxvii; Taft address publication, 29:xi; thirty-first annual meeting, committee on, 29:xxvi

Margolis, Mrs. Max L., 43:238

Margoshes, Joseph, *Erinnerungen von mein liben*, 35:xxii

Margoshes, Samuel, 33:133, 137

Margue, député, 41:162

Margulies, Joseph, 47:182

Margulies, Samuel Hirsch, 28:52-53

Maria (slave), 50:160

Maria Theresa, 28:100; 34:14; 35:213, 216; 50:101, 103, 110

Mariano, José, 43:130

Marichal, Josias, 33:123

Marie, Empress, 43:51

Marion, E., 41:162

"Marion or the Hero of Lake George," 21:229

Maris, Davit Gabaij, 33:65

Marix, Admiral, 28:xl

Marix, Adolph, 22:xxv; necrology of, 28:xxii, 290-92; Spanish-American War, 28:290-92

Marix, Frederica, 28:290

Marix, Henry, 28:290

Mariz, Joao Caneiro de, 33:73
Mark, Aaron, 26:188
Mark, J. and P., 47:187
Mark, Jacob, 47:190; necrology of, 32:xvi
Mark, Julius, 50:272
Mark Nathan Home, 42:13
Markell, Samuel, 42:419
Markens, Elias, 32:129
Markens, Isaac, 22:191; 33:202; 42:211;
    50:274, 300; Abraham Lincoln, 38:320;
    American Israelites, 29:75; Charles H.
    Jonas parole, 42:407-10; collection of,
    50:291-92, 345-46, 351, 377; Gershom
    Mendes Seixas, 35:309-10; gifts, 22:xxxii,
    xxxiii, xxxiv; 23:xvii; 26:xxxiv; 28:xxxix;
    29:xli; "Hebrews in America," 32:35-36;
    history, writing of, 39:229, 236; 46:194,
    235-37; Isachar Zacharie, 43:72; Jacob B.
    Nones, 46:3; "Lincoln and the Jews,"
    50:386; Lincoln Tribute, 41:204; "Mayer
    Lehman in Correspondence with General
    U. S. Grant," 50:386; necrology of, 32:xii,
    129-32; 34:191; Uriah Phillips Levy, 39:50
Market Street National Bank, Philadelphia,
    25:174
Markland, Katherine, 28:31
Markoe, Thomas M., 42:118
Markon, I., 39:110
Markowitz, David, see: Kanof, Abram
Markowitz, Moritz (Markson), 39:151, 155
Marks, 27:60, 62
Marks, Alexander, 21:60, 63; 27:78
Marks, Behr, 29:68-69
Marks, Bernhard, 43:231; "A California
    Pioneer: The Letters of Bernhard Marks
    to Jacob Solis-Cohen (1853-1857),"
    44:12-57
Marks, Catherine, 25:115
Marks, D., 29:134
Marks, D. W., 24:24; 27:524
Marks, David, Memoirs of the Life of David
    Marks, 30:417
Marks, Edgar, 41:373
Marks, Elias, 27:78, 310
Marks family, 41:373
Marks, Fanny, 27:460
Marks, Frances, 27:310
Marks, H., 27:173, 378
Marks, H. E., 29:130

Marks, Hannah, 44:12, 15-17, 25, 52-54, 56
Marks, Harry, 36:255
Marks, Harry Hananel, Down with the Jews,
    37:424
Marks, Henry, 27:41, 43, 185, 253, 462
Marks, Hyam, 27:62
Marks, Hyman, 27:80; 33:251
Marks, I., 27:95
Marks, I. A., 29:135
Marks, Isaac, 21:45, 48, 63
Marks, J. W., 39:159
Marks, Jane (Barham), 27:78, 304, 310
Marks, Johaveth, 22:182
Marks, John, 49:20
Marks, Joseph, 26:235; 34:285
Marks, Levy, 34:96
Marks, M., 27:80
Marks, Marilla, Memoirs of the Life of David
    Marks, 30:417
Marks, Mark, 50:164
Marks, Martin A., necrology of, 26:xiv, 281-
    82
Marks, Michael, 22:182; 27:59; 33:203; 50:38,
    56
Marks, Mrs., 27:460
Marks, Moses, 21:64, 107
Marks, M. S., 29:133
Marks, Mordecai, "Notes from the Will of
    Mordecai Marks, Early Connecticut
    Merchant, and Genealogical Data
    Regarding Him and His Family," 29:xvi
Marks, Percy J., gifts, 22:xxv; 26:xxxv
Marks, Phoebe Sarah, 35:246
Marks, Rachel, 26:235; 50:39
Marks, Rebecca, 33:6
Marks, S., 34:xxiv
Marks, Solomon, 25:115; 27:42; 50:56
Marks, Tillie, 47:211
Markson, Aaron David, 33:157
Markson (Markowicz) (Markowitz), Dr. M.,
    39:151, 155
Markwell, Isidor, 47:46
Markwell, Marcus, 47:46
Marlborough, Duke of, 42:72-73
Marlowe, 40:346
Marlowe, Christopher, The Jew of Malta,
    33:171, 174, 196-97
Marmor, Kalmen, 50:252
Marmorek, Alexander, 35:255

Marmorek, Oskar, 35:255
Marone v. Marone, 29:150
Marquand, John P., 46:127
Marques, Esther, 23:149
Marques, Isaac Rodrigues, 23:148-49
Marques, Jacob, 23:149
Marques, Rachel, 23:149
Marques, Rodrigues, 38:236
Marques, Selomoh of The Hague, 29:23
Marquez, Antonio Diaz, 31:30
Marquez, General, 32:80, 82-87, 89-90
Marquez, Jacob, 32:58
Marquez, Manuel, 29:23
Marquise, Rachel Rodriques, 27:122
Marranos, Lisbon, 25:71-74; and migration,
    44:204-5; Ten Tribes, 37:360-63, 366-67
Marren, John, 35:291
Marrero, Marcelina, 27:248
Marret, Abigail, 22:7, 22
Marrett, Amos, 22:22
Marriage, 29:150-52; 41:87; "Anglo-Jewish
    Legal Cases," 25:136; contract of early
    N.Y. Jews, 27:150, 172-73; The Hebrew
    Wife, 30:308; Henriques on Jewish
    Marriages, 32:xxvi; Jewish law, 27:173;
    "The Judith Hays-Samuel Myers Marriage
    Contract," 38:149-50; laws, 44:133, 191-
    95; Maryland Jews, 25:94, 104-5; Shearith
    Israel (N.Y. records), 27:74-78, 96; "Was a
    Civil Marriage ever recognized by Jewish
    Law," 32:xx; wedding ceremony, 39:379-
    83
Marrit, Edward, 22:22-23
Mars, David, "Justice Benjamin Nathan
    Cardozo: His Life and Character," 48:266;
    49:5-15
Marschalk, Isaac, 21:109, 171; 28:229
Marschalk, Peter, 21:171
Marsh, 24:43
Marsh, Benjamin, 27:404
Marsh, Gould, 35:291
Marsh, James (trans.), Spirit of Hebrew Poetry,
    30:286
Marsh, John, An Epitome of General
    Ecclesiastical History, 30:247-49, 280
Marsh, Jonathan, 35:291
Marsh, Thomas, 30:41
Marsh, William, 26:149
Marshalk, Elinor, 27:71

Marshalk, Francois, 27:248
Marshalk, John, 27:248
Marshall, Charles, 50:343
Marshall, H., 26:216
Marshall, James, 34:258; gift, 35:xxiii;
    nominations committee, 28:xxi
Marshall, John, 26:174; 33:24; 46:434, 467-
    68; 49:139
Marshall, Louis, 22:xvii; 31:xxxv; 37:438, 480;
    40:397; 41:205; 47:194; 50:210-11, 299;
    Adolphus S. Solomons, 33:211;
    Agricultural Experiment Station, 31:203;
    Alliance Israelite, 39:408, 411, 419-20,
    429-30, 432, 439; American Jewish
    Committee, 35:322; 49:190, 193-96, 198-
    200; bookplates, 45:204-5; Bucharest
    Peace Conference, 24:83-87; Cyrus Adler,
    33:23; gifts, 32:xxv, xxvi; Jewish Agency,
    35:324; "Louis Marshall," 33:xxx;
    Masonry, 35:135; Max James Kohler
    bibliography, 34:189-90, 193, 200, 203,
    210, 212, 215, 228-29, 248, 298; minority
    treaties, 36:10; necrology of, 32:xvi;
    necrologies of Alfred Jaretzki, 31:xxiv, 266-
    268; David Leventritt, 31:xxiv, 278-80;
    Nathan Jacobson, 22:xxviii, 218-222;
    nominating committee, 22:xvi; Polish
    disabilities, 36:148, 152, 155; portrait,
    33:xxxi; Russian disabilities, 36:278-79,
    285, 290, 293; Russian treaty, 40:302;
    41:176, 179-81; Simon Wolf, 29:203-4;
    Sunday services, 42:378-79; William
    Howard Taft, 36:134-35; Woodrow
    Wilson, 36:79; Y.M.H.A., 37:300, 306-7
Marshall Memorial Home (Syracuse), 37:301
Marshall, Mr., 39:9, 41, 58
Marshall, Mrs. (actress), 33:182
Marston, John, 35:182
Martens, de, 24:97
Martens, F. F., 26:84
Martensen, Direckjen, 26:247
Martí, José Julian, 37:436
Martienzo, Ortiz de, 31:11
Martijn, Sebastiaen, 33:118
Martin, 22:183; 26:256
Martin II, King, 28:210
Martin, King of Messina, 28:208-9
Martin IV, Pope, 28:145
Martin V, Pope, 28:154-58, 208

Martin, Anthony, 33:114
Martin, Esther, 27:112
Martin, G. A., 35:327
Martin, Isaac, 23:4
Martin, John, 33:178-79, 185
Martin, Josiah, 29:143
Martin, Lazarus, 21:215; 27:115
Martin, Percy, 32:88, 91
Martin, Thomas, 35:11
Martin, Thomas S., 22:144
Martineau, 23:48-49
Martineau, Harriet, 28:241; 43:135
Martinez, Isaac N., 26:252
Martinez, Leonor, 32:117
Martinique, 29:46
Martins, Fernão, 44:83
Martov, Julius, 46:266
Martyn, Edward Judah Morris, 22:24
Martyn, John 22:7, 18, 21-24; 28:243-44
Martyn, John Monis, 22:24
Marwick, Lawrence, 47:203
Marx, Abraham, 41:261
Marx, Alexander, 25:63, 161; 26:239; 30:vi;
31:vii; 32:xxi; 33:vi, xxvi, 27, 30-31; 34:iv,
xxiii; 37:461; 38:vi, 78; 43:70; "Aims and
Tasks of Jewish Historiography," 26:xv,
11-32; "The Autobiography of an
Unknown of the Seventeenth Century: a
Picture of the Condition of the Jews of
Bohemia," 25:xiii; bookplates, 45:136, 153;
"A Celebrated Case among the Italian Jews
of the Early Sixteenth Century," 32:xii; "A
Chapter about Banking Affairs in the
Sixteenth Century (from a Hebrew
Code)," 22:xxix; corresponding secretary,
37:xxxii, xxxiv; 38:341, 344; early
documents, 34:69, 74; editing, 22:vii;
23:vii; 25:vii; 26:vii; 28:vii; 29:vii; 31:vii;
32:iv; 33:vi; 34:iv; 35:iv; 37:iv; "Eliezer
Eilenburg, a German Jewish Wanderer of
the Sixteenth Century," 23:xiii; executive
council, 22:xii, xvi, xxviii; 23:xii; 25:xi;
26:xii; 28:xxi, xxii; 29:xxix; 31:xxiii; 32:xix;
34:xiv; 37:xxxii; exhibit, 31:xiii, xviii; Felix
M. Warburg, 34:258; Foreign Archives
Committee, 23:91; George A. Kohut,
34:253; gifts, 26:xxxiv, xxxv; 28:xxxix;
"Glimpses of the Life of an Italian Rabbi
of the First Half of the Sixteenth Century,"

26:xxxi; Gratz Papers Committee, 25:xiii;
history of Jews, committee on, 29:xxvi;
history, writing of, 39:305; 45:62; Jewish
bibliographies, committee on, 29:xi; Jewish
Tercentenary, 40:414; Joshua Bloch,
47:218-19; necrology of, 43:231, 241-52;
necrologies of Marcus Brann, 28:xxxii,
261-65; Mayer Sulzberger, 29:xxxvi, 188-
93; Moritz Gudeman, 28:xv, 276-81;
Moses Baroway, 31:xxiii; Solomon
Schechter, 25:xii, 177-92; Napoleonic
Sanhedrin, 26:xxvii; Oppenheim Library,
committee on, 32:xxix; publication
committee, 24:ix; 26:xxvii; 28:xxix; 29:xi
(pref.), "A Selected Bibliography of the
Writings of Albert M. Friedenberg,"
35:115-37; thirtieth annual meeting,
committee on, 29:xi; thirty-first annual
meeting, committee on, 29:xxvi; vice-
president, 38:346; 39:469; 40:406; 41:387;
42:414; Washington's correspondence,
32:121
Marx, Anschel Marx, 41:256
Marx, Asher, 27:84; 34:267; 35:137; 40:127;
50:64
Marx, Daniel, 41:256
Marx, David, 41:369-70
Marx, Delzel, 41:256
Marx, Dr. (Charleston), 27:80
Marx, Dr. F. (New York), 27:506
Marx, Earl, 39:286
Marx, Esther, 41:265
Marx, Frances, 50:64
Marx, Franklin, 37:254
Marx, Hayum, 41:265
Marx, Isak, 41:268
Marx, Jakob, 41:258
Marx, Joseph, 27:145; 33:205; 50:64
Marx, Karl, 36:398; 41:212; 46:221
Marx, Marie, 41:258
Marx, Marx, 41:265
Marx, Mr. (Peddler), 44:3
Marx, Mordochai, 41:256
Marx, Moses, 29:131; 41:261
Marx, Riches (Myers), 50:64
Marx, Samuel, 27:145; 41:265
Marx, Sol., 40:247
Marxism, 46:221-23, 226, 259, 261, 266;
"Jewish Unionism," 41:297, 301, 307, 320,
337, 347-55

Maryland, 25:24; 46:20, 33, 35, 39; 50:5, 18-22; Bible and schools, 31:221; *Bill Respecting Civil Rights and Religious Privileges*, 30:216; Colonial settlement of Jews, 26:5-6; Council of Maryland for 1742, 22:194; disabilities, 26:193; 31:124; 44:208; "The Earliest Jewish Settler in Maryland," 31:xvii; Jew Bill, 27:518; 30:182, 184; 31:xviii; 32:xxviii; Jewish local history, 49:224; Jewish population (1790), 50:29-30, 34; Jews and civil rights, 49:104; Jews in law and medicine, 22:149, 158; "The Maryland 'Jew Bill': A Footnote to Thomas Jefferson's Work for Freedom of Religion," 37:xxxv; *Maryland tercentenary Jewish book*, 35:xx; Negro disfranchisement, 40:291-92; "The Price the Jew Dr. Lumbrozo Paid for Maryland's So-Called Toleration," 31:xxx; seal of, 26:248; *Speech on Confirmatory Act Abolishing Religious Test*, 30:227; Test Act, 31:xxxii; 29:105; Toleration Act, 43:162, 167; "Unequal Religious Rights in Maryland since 1776," 22:xxviii; 25:vii, 93-107
Maryland Board of State Aid and Charities, 25:154
Maryland Historical Society, 22:194; 25:146; 37:473; 42:417; 45:198
Maryland Ladies' Society, *New Year's Gift*, 30:376-77
Maryland Ladies' Society for Promoting Christianity among the Jews, 27:522
Maryland Prisoners' Aid Association, 25:151
Maryland School for the Blind, 26:289
Maryland Society for the Protection of Children from Cruelty and Immorality, 25:151
Maryland Society for the Relief and Prevention of Tuberculosis, 25:154
Maryland State Convention, 1864, 22:xxxiv
Maryland State Teacher's Association, 49:161
Maryland, University of, 45:198; Medical School, 47:192
Masao, Debora, 29:11
Masaryk, Jan, 50:116; *In Search of Freedom: A History of American Jews from Czechoslovakia*, (foreword), reviewed, 39:329-31
Masaryk, Thomas G., 39:330; 50:108, 116

Mashal ha-Kadmoni, 22:103
Mashbir, Eliezer, 38:245-46, 248, 306, 308
Maskil el Dol Society, 39:91; 49:80
Masliansky, Zvi Hirsch, 35:64; 39:408, 411; 50:213
Mason, 31:148
Mason, Alpheus T., 46:435; 50:345
Mason, George, 43:135
Mason, I. G., 40:282-83
Mason, James Murray, 50:321, 342
Mason, Mrs., 38:173
Mason, Samuel, 28:xl; 38:65
Masonry, 23:130; 28:298-99, 305, 314, 35:128-30, 133, 135; 39:278; 40:342; 41:13, 69, 96; 47:15; 50:44, 170; Abraham Jonas, 44:99; "Additional Grand Masters," 22:182; "Alleged Masonic Symbols and Ritual in Aboriginal America," 28:xxiii; Baltimore, 22:192-94; Charles E. Rosenbaum, 25:114; Charleston, S.C., 50:57; "Freemasonry in Pennsylvania," 28:xl; gifts of, 23:xvii; 26:xxxv; Hunt's Bay Jewish Cemetery, 37:340-42; "A Jewish Masonic Prayer," 48:134-35; and Jews, 27:xviii, 210, 212, 264, 331, 395, 397, 416, 495; "The Jews and Masonry in the United States before 1810," 32:134; Masonic expose and Van Buren, 22:80-81, 89; Milwaukee, 47:45-46; Moses M. Hays, 42:337; "Moses M. Hays and the Introduction of 'Sublime Masonry' in the United Colonies," 23:xiv; Nathan Jaffa, 25:114; New Orleans, 26:242; Newport, R.I., 34:2, 4; 37:166; North Carolina, 29:145-47; *Oriental Antiquities*, 30:88; Paul Revere, 43:141, 202, 204, 239; Pennsylvania, Grand Lodge, 22:142; 28:283, 299, 314; gifts, 26:xxxv; 28:xl; "Old Masonic Lodges, 1730-1800," 22:xxxiv; Rhode Island Grand Lodge, gift, 32:xx; (Rochester, N.Y.), 40:66; Simon Wolf, 29:202; Solomon Etting, 34:68; Spanish America, 38:324; *Washington Lodge, no. 21, F. & A. M.*, 35:xxii
Masquerading in New York (Purim), 40:166-67
Mass, Elinor, 23:153
Massachusetts, 50:25; "Anglo-Jewish Legal Cases," 25:134-36; 42:133-40; "Boston in American Jewish History," 42:333-40;

Colonial constitution, 31:44; Colonial Settlement of Jews, 26:5-6; Democratic State Committee, 22:229; "Early Jewish Residents in Massachusetts," 22:xiii; 23:vii, 79-90; Jewish local history, 49:224-26; "Jewish Residents in Massachusetts before 1800," 32:xix; "References of Jewish Interest in the Newspapers of the American Revolution (1761-1789); New York and Massachusetts," 23:xiv

Massachusetts Bay Colony 40:210; 46:20, 22-25, 34; "The Hebrew Preface to Bradford's History of the Plymouth Plantation," 38:289-303, 346

Massachusetts Board of Charities, 46:74

Massachusetts Body of Liberties of 1641, 46:24, 34

Massachusetts General Hospital, 27:418; 42:417

Massachusetts Historical Society, 22:178; 23:96; 25:112-13; 29:153; 35:139; 40:78; gifts, 23:xviii

Massachusetts Institute of Technology, 46:441

Massachusetts Law Quarterly, 47:212

Massachusetts Mutual Fire Insurance Company, 43:204

Massagan, Domingo Gonsalvo, 33:112

Massarani, Tulle, 37:76

Massarik, Fred, *A Report on the Jewish Population of San Francisco, Marin County and the Peninsula, 1959*, reviewed, 50:143-44

Massena, "The Murder at Massena," 49:233

Masserman, P., 35:136

Massiah, Abigail, 22:180

Massiah, Abraham, 22:178-79; 26:251; 31:242-43

Massiah, Abraham (b. Daniel), 22:178

Massiah, Abraham Howard, 22:180

Massiah, Benjamin (1), 22:178

Massiah, Benjamin (2), 22:179

Massiah, Benjamin (3), 22:179; 32:59

Massiah, Christopher, 22:180

Massiah, Daniel (1), 22:178-79; 32:58

Massiah, Daniel (2), 22:178-79

Massiah, David (1), 22:179; 32:59

Massiah, David (2), 22:179

Massiah, Dorothy Peters, 22:179

Massiah, Elizabeth Rebecca, 22:179

Massiah, Elizabeth Rose, 22:180

Massiah, Esther (1), 22:179; 32:59

Massiah, Esther (2), 22:179-80

Massiah, family of, "Notes from Wills of the Family of Massiah of Barbados," 22:xiii, 178-80

Massiah, Isaac, 32:59

Massiah, Isaac (b. Daniel), 22:178

Massiah, Issac (b. Benjamin), 22:179-80

Massiah, Isaac de Peza, 26:251-53

Massiah, Jacob (1), 22:178, 32:59

Massiah, Jacob (2), 22:180

Massiah, Jacob (b. Benjamin), 22:178-79

Massiah, Jeremiah, 22:178-79

Massiah, John Mitcham, 22:180

Massiah, Judah, 22:179-80

Massiah, Judith, 22:178; 32:58

Massiah, Mary, 22:180

Massiah, Mordecai (1), 22:178-79

Massiah, Mordecai (2), 22:179

Massiah, Mordecai (3), 22:179

Massiah, Mordecay, 22:179

Massiah, Rachel, 22:179

Massiah, Rebecca (1), 22:179-80

Massiah, Rebecca (2), 22:180

Massiah, Samuel, 22:178

Massiah, Sarah (1), 22:180; 32:59

Massiah, Sarah (2), 22:178

Massiah, Sarah (3), 22:179

Massiah, Sarah (Aboab), 22:179

Massiah, Sarah Moore, 22:180

Massiah, Simeon (1), 22:179; 26:251; 32:59

Massiah, Simeon (2), 22:179

Massiah, Simon, 22:178

Massiah, William, 22:180; 32:59

Massiah, William, Sr., 22:179

Massiah, William Benjamin, 22:179

Massiah, William Nesfield, 22:179

Massias, Abraham, 26:192-93

Massias, Benjamin, 26:192

Massias, Joseph, 32:62

Massias, Samuel, Sr., 32:62

Massing, Paul, *Rehearsal for Destruction*, reviewed, 40:199-201

Masson, David, 46:434

Mastbaum, Fanny Ephraim, 28:292

Mastbaum, Hilda (Ganzman), 28:292

Mastbaum, Jules E., necrology of, 31:xxix, 282-83
Mastbaum, Levi, 28:292
Mastbaum, Stanley V., necrology of, 28:xv, 292-93
Mastick, Seabury C., 29:169
Masure, député, 41:162
Matagorda Bulletin, The, 46:103
Matamoras, 46:103-4, 109, 111
Matchet, Gregory, 48:90
Mateles, Mrs. Simon (Jean), 50:272, 276
Mather, Cotton, 23:80; 30:iv; 40:334; 47:148; *American Tears Upon the Ruins of Greek Churches*, 30:13-14; conversion of Jews, 39:260; 42:336; "Cotton Mather and the Jews," 26:xiv, 201-10; *Faith Encouraged*, 30:15-17; *The Faith of the Fathers*, 30:11-12; Hebrew at Harvard, 35:151, 154; Indians, 39:186; Judah Monis, 37:132; *Proposals for Printing "Psalterium Americanum,"* 30:15; *Things to be More Thought Upon*, 30:15; William Bradford, 38:290, 292
Mather, Increase, 22:2, 4; 23:79; 26:206, 210; 30:iv; 23; 46:32; *Dissertation Concerning Future Conversion of the Jewish Nation*, 30:15; *Mystery of Israel's Salvation*, 30:4-5
Mather, John Winthrop, 26:207-8
Mather, Katharine, 26:203
Mather, Richard, 30:3
Mather, Samuel, 26:203; *America*, 30:71-72
Mathews, Colonel, 29:88
Mathews, Felix A., 36:22-31, 33
Mathey, Alfred, 41:162
Mathias, T., 30:247
Mathilda (slave), 50:158
Mathlin, Capt., 21:124
Matienzo, Ortiz de, 31:11
Matlack, Timothy, 23:178; 43:235
Matos, Francisco Rodriguez de, 31:26-30
Matos, Isaquer Rodrigez de, 42:278, 394
Matos, María de, 23:134
Mattauer, John Peter, 43:76
Matte Moshe, 22:133
Matthews, Elias, 23:157
Matthioli of Siena, 28:163
Mathiolus, Peter Andrea, 28:163
Mattos, Abm de, 21:57-58
Mattos, Alexander Teixeira de, 29:xliii

Mattos, Benjamin, 21:45
Mattos, Ben Orobia de, 27:248
Mattos, Ishac de Abraham de, 29:36
Matzel, Dr., 23:188; 38:191, 222-25
Maurel, A., 41:162
Maurera, Jacob de, 50:122
Maurice, Prince of Orange, 29:20
Mauricio colony, 38:314-16; 39:87, 89-94, 96
Maurier, Robert, 43:48-49
Mauritius, Bishop of, 26:149
Maurits, Johan, 33:48, 51-52, 57-61, 65, 68, 70-71, 73, 82, 91; 47:112, 114-17; 50:74-75
Maurois, André, 46:289
Maury, John S., 50:342
Maury, Matthew F., 38:158-59
Maverick, Peter Rushton, 45:188
Maverick, Peter V., 45:134
Mavromatis case record, 31:xxxiii
Mavroyeni Bey, 36:49-51, 56-57
Mawson, G. A., 27:515
Maximilian, 31:294; 32:65, 67, 69, 73, 75-78, 80-93; 33:244-47; 47:50-51
Maximon, Shalom Baer, 33:133, 149, 161, 165; 40:48
Maxwell, 33:220
Maxwell, Mr., 27:316
Maxwell Street Settlement (Chicago), 37:294
May, Edward, 35:307
May, James, 40:86
May, Joseph, 23:90
May, Judge, 29:149
May, Lewis, 27:515; 37:233; 38:68; 40:263
May, Moses, 29:129
May, Samuel Joseph, "Memoirs of Samuel Joseph May," 28:xl
May (store), 38:20
Maya, Pedro de, 31:14
Maybee, John R., 49:266-67
Mayer, *Jews in Vienna*, 31:xxxiii; *Volksbuch*, 30:457
Mayer, Adolph, 29:123
Mayer, Alex, 31:146
Mayer, Alexander, "Letters of a California Pioneer," 31:vii, xvii, 135-71
Mayer, Clinton O., necrology of Edward Wolf, 26:xiv, 289-90
Mayer, Constant, 25:112
Mayer, D., 29:130

Mayer, Elias, 27:259

Mayer, G., Jacobs & Co., 50:168

Mayer, Isaac, 37:429; 40:62-63

Mayer, Isadore, 27:389

Mayer, Julius, 50:175

Mayer, Julius M., 34:221

Mayer, Lazarus, 31:135, 151

Mayer, M., 37:34

Mayer, Maurice, 22:xxxiii; 45:95; 49:20; 50:176

Mayer, Nathan, 34:146; "Dr. Nathan Mayer of Hartford, Connecticut; Surgeon, Soldier, Poet, Dramatic and Musical Critic," 37:xxx, 425-29

Mayer, Sol, 31:154

Mayers, David Campbell, 38:73

Mayers family, 32:55

Mayers, John, 26:254

Mayers, Judah, 33:254

Mayflower Compact, 46:22

Mayflower Descendants, 28:266

Mayflower Tercentenary Medal, 49:271

Mayhew, Johnathan, 24:109

Mayhew, Joseph, 30:41

Mayhoff, Amelia Levy von, 34:xxi; 35:xviii; 41:290

May Laws (Russia), 39:233; 41:22; 49:162

Maynadier, William, 48:163, 165

Maynard, George Henry, 30:95

Maynard, Horace, 24:30-31, 33-34, 36; 36:7-8, 112; 41:38

Mayo, Doctor, 22:220

Mayo, Isaac, 39:30, 33, 51

Mayo-Smith, Richmond, 49:132

Maywood, R. C., 33:196

Mazarin, Cardinal Jules, 28:216-17; 47:68, 74-75

Mazzib, Gebulot Ammin, 22:112

Mazzini, Giuseppe, 37:57

Mazzot, 44:169, 176-77

Mead, Captain, 27:328

Mead, Margaret, 46:298, 301, 412

Mead, Mr., 46:470

Meade, Elwood, 29:197

Meade, George Gordon, 50:387

Meade, Robert Douthat, 50:287

Meader, Captain, 27:366

Meadows, Philip, 38:45-46

Means, Robert, *Considerations Respecting the Genuineness of the Pentateuch*, 30:297-98

Mearns, David C., 50:272, 396, 401

Mears, Abraham, 21:23; 33:209

Mears, Caty, 33:203-4

Mears, Elkalah, 33:209-10

Mears family, 38:70; "Genealogical Notes on the Isaaks, Mears, and Michels Families of New York and Boston," 22:xiii; "Mears Family and Their Connections, 1606-1824," 33:xvii, 199-210

Mears, Grace, 33:203

Mears, Grace (Mrs. Moses R. Levy), 33:200, 203, 205-6, 209; 41:290

Mears, Hannah, 48:18

Mears, Hannah Manuel, 33:201

Mears, Jacob (Jamaica), 33:200

Mears, Jacob (S.C.), 23:159; "Jacob Mears and Simon Valentine of Charleston, South Carolina," 41:77-82

Mears, Jochabed, 33:202-3

Mears, Joyce, 27:372; 33:204

Mears, Judah, 21:6, 8, 19, 42, 48, 51, 55, 63, 81-82, 182, 211; 23:159; 33:200-210

Mears, Mrs. Judah, 33:207

Mears, Judith, 27:248

Mears, Miss, 21:81

Mears, Otto, 38:321-22; 39:345; 49:218

Mears, Rachel (Judith), 33:202

Mears, Rachel (b. Sampson), 33:209-10

Mears, Rebecca (Mrs. Isaiah), 32:126

Mears, Rebecca (Mrs. Jacob Isaacks), 33:202

Mears, Rebecca (Mrs. Mathias Bush), 33:209-10

Mears, Richea, 33:209-10

Mears, Samson (Conn.), 38:332

Mears, Samson (New York), 21:79; 33:199, 202-3, 205, 208-10; 46:422

Mears, Sarah (1768), 33:202

Mease, James, 41:85

Meat, "The Question of the Kosher Meat Supply in New York in 1813; with a Sketch of Earlier Conditions," 25:vii, xii, 31-62

Meatoga, Abraham, 47:64

Meatoga, Sarah, 47:64

Mechado, Matteus de, 33:117

Mecklenburg, 26:89

Mecom, Benjamin, 45:131

Medalie, Hyman Aaron, 35:57

Medem, Vladimir, 40:403
Medford (Mass.), "Why Touro Avenue in Medford, Massachusetts," 46:493
Mediaeval Academy of America, 43:250
Medical College of Virginia, 50:329
Medical Depository, 50:243
Medical Repository, 46:12
Medical Society of the City and County of New York, 26:227-28
Medical Society of the County of New York, 22:162
Medical Society of Lower Canada, 26:226
Medical Society of the State of New York, 26:223, 226
Medici family, 28:196-97
Medici, Giovanni de, 28:169
Medici, Giuliamo de, 28:167
Medici, John de, 28:192
Medici, Lorenzo de, 22:105; 28:196; 32:41
Medici, Maria de, 28:199
Medici, Peter de, 22:105
Medicine, "Jewish Physicians in Italy: Their Relations to the Papal and Italian States," 28:xxiii, 133-211; Jews in, 46:241-42, 252-53; 50:308, 323-31; "Jews in the Legal and Medical Professions in America Prior to 1800," 22:147-65
Medico-Chirurgical College, 29:156
Medigo, Elijah del, 28:202
Medina, Isaac, 21:5, 7-8, 10, 16, 19-20, 23, 28, 181
Medina, J. T., 31:10, 17; gift, 23:xvii
Medina, José Toribio, 42:89-90; 44:64; necrology of, 33:xx
Medina, Moses de, 42:213
Medina, Moses Robles de, 27:229
Medina, Samuel de, 43:247
Medina, Samuel Robles de, "A MS. Hebrew Work of Samuel Robles de Medina, Surinam, 1762," 26:xv
Medina, Solomon, 33:xxviii
Medina, Solomon de, 35:176
Medina, Solomon de (grandfather), 42:213; "A Great Colonial Case and a Great Colonial Lawyer: Solomon de Medina et al v. Rene Het et al," 42:71-82, 213; *Decree in Case of Solomon de Medina, Mosesson and Company*, 30:33-35
Meek, Mary Anne, 40:58

Meeker, Samuel, 30:133
Meeks, Mr., 27:288
Megapolensis, Johannes, 29:41
Megapolensis, John, 44:92, 46:31
Megillath Damesek, 22:133
Mego, Eliauh, 42:280
Megroa, Aaron La, 23:149
Mehemet Ali, 26:133-35, 156, 162
Meier & Franks (store), 38:20
Meier, John H., 27:389
Meighan, Burton Charles, 34:193
Meigs, Henry, 27:467
Meijer, Jacob, 42:461; "Cultural Background of Isaac Aboab da Fonesca: An Analysis of His Library," 45:265; "Notes on Seventeenth Century History of Jewish Settlements in Surinam," 45:265; *Pioneers of Pauroma: Contribution to the Earliest History of the Jewish Colonization of America*, reviewed, 44:248-50
Meindersen, Egbert, 25:42
Meinhard, Henry, memorial, 23:98
Meinheimer, Jacob, 27:80
Meirs, Edward, 37:32
Meisach, Joshua, 22:137
Meisel, 29:xliii, 126
Meisel, Wolf A., 28:102-3, 115, 118
Meisels Beriah, 28:126
Meisels, Elijah Hayyim, 44:137, 139, 140-41
Meisl, J., 28:115
Meissner, 29:128
Meissner, Alfred, 38:196
Meissner, Frank, "A Social Ecology of the German Jews in Prague," 49:268; "German Jews of Prague: A Quest For Self-Realization," 50:98-120
Meister, Wilhelm, 34:235
Meites, Hyman L., 28:239-40; 32:xxv
Mejia, General, 32:82
Mekabetz Nidhe Yisrael Congregation, Barbados, 22:131
Mekommen, Georg, 34:47
Mela Ben Brith, gift, 29:xxxix
Melamed, Samuel Max, 33:149
Melbourne, William Lamb, 2d, 46:434
Meldola, David, 22:xxiii, 131; 27:519-20, 522-23; 37:61; 50:131
Meldola, Raphael, 22:131; 41:12; 42:426
Melegari, 24:35

Melhado, Charles, 37:420
Melhado, D., 37:420
Melhado, Daniel M., 37:420
Melhado, Emanuel, 25:115, 117
Melhado, Jael, 25:117
Melhado, Judith, 37:420
Melhado, Luna, 25:115, 117
Melhado, Sarah, 25:118
Melhado, William Henry, 25:117
Melikoff, Loris, 36:187, 189-90
Melker, Captain, 26:258
Mella, Manuel de, 32:117
Melliah, 32:49
Mello, José Antonio Gonsalves de, 47:112
Melo, Antho. Magelhoins de, 33:113
Melo, Antho. Teixero de, 33:114
Melo, Joan Gommes de, 33:116
Melo, Ledesma y Aguilar, 23:132
Melting Pot, The, 40:356
Meltzer, Samuel James, 49:97
Melville, Herman, 42:457; 46:193; "Herman Melville's Pilgrimage to the Holy Land," 46:493
Memoir of a Veteran who served as a Private in the 60's in the War Between the States: Personal Incidents, Experiences and Observations, 50:399
Memories of Arlington, Vermont, 48:253
Memminger, Christopher G., 43:109
Memminger, Mr., 29:121
Memphis (Tenn.), 49:247; 50:95-97; "The Jews of Memphis, 1860-1865," 49:239; religious observances, mid-nineteenth century, 37:36
Men and Measures, 40:128
Men and Women, 40:359
Menasce, Aharon, 29:16
Menasce, Behor de, 47:89, 98
Menasseh ben Israel, 28:193; 29:7-9, 45, 47-49; 31:xviii; 34:9, 174; 46:382; 47:71-72; Christianity and common law, 31:116-17; *Conciliador*, 33:55; England and Jews, 27;480; Hugo Grotius, 31:178; "Humble Addresses," 33:51; "Life of Menasseh ben Israel," 34:xxvi; *Menasseh ben Israel's mission to Oliver Cromwell*, 35:118; 40:124; 42:428, 437-38, 441; "Which of the Portraits of Menasseh ben Israel Was in the Possession of Ezra Stiles (Illustrated)," 50:427

Mencken, H. L., 39:385
Mendagne, Joan Correa de, 33:116
Mendel, Henriette, 35:125
Mendel, Henry M., 47:48
Mendel, M., 48:96
Mendell, Samuel C., 41:375
Mendelsohn, Erich, 39:241; 46:65
Mendelsohn, Morris J., "The Jewish Veterans of the Wars of the Republic: An Historical Statement," 31:xxx
Mendelsohn, Samuel, 40:21; 42:103; 45:160
Mendelson, L., 39:161
Mendelssohn, 28:279
Mendelssohn celebration, 32:xxvii
Mendelssohn, Dorothea, 26:97-98, 100; 40:119
Mendelssohn, Fanny, 35:240
Mendelssohn, Henrietta, 26:97
Mendelssohn, Joseph, 26:98
Mendelssohn Literary Society, 37:226
Mendelssohn, Moses, 34:16, 25; 35:39, 121, 232, 263; 37:186; 43:181; education, 28:83-84, 86, 90-94, 101-3, 114, 116-17; Heinrich Graetz, 28:77; history, writing of, 39:213, 335; Jewish rights, 26:50, 96-100; *Letter to Deacon Lavater*, 30:193-94; Letter to President and Congress, 37:171-76; *Memoirs of Moses Mendelssohn*, 30:411; portrait, 41:282; "A Sermon by Moses Mendelssohn Printed in Philadelphia 130 years Ago," 30:54
Mendelssohn-Bartholdy, 35:240
Mendes, Abraham, 33:95, 97; 35:141; 50:26
Mendes, Abraham Pereira, 27:191, 414, 522; 34:285; 38:47; Aaron Lopez, 35:295-301, 316-18; Touro Synagogue, 38:57, 59:63, 66, 68-69, 72
Mendes, Benjamin Pereira, 35:316-17
Mendes, Bento, 33:114
Mendes, Brites, 29:35
Mendes, Cajar, 23:175
Mendes, Catulle, 35:287
Mendes, Davi, 42:278, 394
Mendes, David, 50:313
Mendes, David Franco, 29:29; 33:55; 44:89
Mendes, David Pereira, 21:51, 70; 27:274; 35:301
Mendes, David de Sola, 38:72
Mendes family, Leicester, 23:85

Mendes *fils* Cadet, 23:171

Mendes, Frederick de Sola, 37:85, 234, 236, 239, 257; 38:59, 72; 40:35; 44:183

Mendes, Guidon, 44:218

Mendes, Henry Pereira, 21:xxiv, xxvi; 22:xxviii; 27:xix; 35:57; American Israelites, 29:113; 39:404; Bernhard Felsenthal, 45:122; Jewish Theological Seminary, 40:35, 311; 48:231; Moses Montefiore, 25:112; necrology of, 35:x, 316-19; necrology of Abraham H. Nieto, 28:xxii; New York chief rabbi, 44:145, 152-53, 157, 160, 169, 183-84, 186; non-kosher food, 37:39; portrait, 34:xxii; religious observances, 37:53; Sabato Morais bibliography, 37:75, 85, 87, 92; Spanish-American War, 41:377-78; Touro Synagogue, 38:59, 61, 72, 75; Y.M.H.A., 37:239, 257; Zionism, 42:103

Mendes, Isaac (1), 27:248; 44:63

Mendes, Isaac (2), 27:349

Mendes, Isaac (3), 27:349

Mendes, Isaac Jeosherin, 32:59

Mendes, Isaac Pereira, 23:180; 32:130; 35:296; 38:72; "Collection of Isaac P. Mendes," 45:161

Mendes, Mrs. Isaac P., 23:180

Mendez, Israel Levy, 42:278, 394

Mendes, Jacob, 23:182

Mendes, Jacob da Silva, 32:122

Mendes, Jacob Franco, 42:278, 394

Mendes, Joseph, 32:60

Mendes, Joseph H., 45:161

Mendes, Leah, 35:300-1

Mendes, Luzia, 29:35

Mendes, Mary Ann, 25:118

Mendes in Moribeecq, Anthony, 33:114

Mendes, Rachel, 37:336

Mendes, Samuel, 27:348; 44:63

Mendes, Samuel Rodriguez, 32:122

Mendes, Sarah Pereira, 27:349; 50:26

Mendes, Solomon, 37:336

Mendex (s), Moses, 40:75

Mendez, 26:233

Mendez, Abraham, 28:248

Mendez, A. P., Jr., 37:342

Mendez, Eliau, 27:359

Mendez (family), 49:6

Mendez, Isaac (Jamaica), 37:393-410

Mendez, Isaac (New York), 27:6

Mendez, Isaac Pereyra, 27:248

Mendez, Jacob Pereyra, 27:248

Mendez, Joseph, 23:29

Mendez, Joseph Jesurun, 42:278, 287, 392-94

Mendez, Joshua, 27:6

Mendez, Juan, 32:117

Mendez, Justa, 31:29

Mendez, Moses de Solomon, 32:58

Mendez, Rachael, 32:58

Mendez, Rachel, 27:176

Mendez, Symon, 27:176

Mendl, David, 23:188; 38:192-93, 209-12, 228-29

Mendonca, Domingo de, 33:112

Mendosa, Gasper de, 33:114

Mendosa, Joan de, 33:77

Mendoza, Daniel, 35:234

Mends, Isaac Pa, 21:68

Mendus, Michel Rodrigus, 33:47

Menendez, Pedro, 31:247

Menes, Abraham, "The East Side: Matrix of the Jewish Labor Movement," 46:63

Menezes, Francisco Barreto de, 44:80, 82-85

Menihold, Abraham, 41:261

Menihold, Karoline, 41:261

Menken, Adah Isaacs, 35:244; 37:438; 39:258; 48:202, 267; 49:70, 143; 49:70; "Adah Isaacs Menken's autograph album," 33:xviii; "Adah Isaacs Menken: A Daughter of Israel," 34:143-47; *Biography of Adah Isaacs Menken*, 35:xix

Menken, Alexander Isaac, 34:146

Menken, Alice Davis, gifts, 33:xxix, xxxii, 5-6; 34:xxiv; 35:xviii

Menken, Isaacs, 34:xviii

Menken, Jacob, 34:144

Menken, J. Stanwood, 40:263; 49:178, 186-87

Menken, Mortimer M., 35:xviii

Menken, Mrs. Mortimer M., 29:169; 45:178, 198-99

Menkin, Edward, gift, 28:xxxix

Men of Poland and Austria, Congregation of Israel, 44:174

Menorah, The, 24:12

Menorah Journal, 29:181; 37:458

Menorah Monthly, 33:36, 39, 238, 241-42; 37:57; 42:350

Menorah Society, 49:192

Menorat ha-Meor, 33:xxxii
Menschenfreund, Der, 48:132
Mercado, Abraham de, 29:9; 33:55; 42:224, 260, 275, 277, 281-82, 390, 394; 50:76
Mercado, David de, 23:150-53
Mercado, David-Raphael de, 29:9; 32:58
Mercado, Esther de, 25:117
Mercado family, 34:171
Mercado, George de, 25:118
Mercado, Henry de, 25:117
Mercado, Judith, 44:93
Mercado, Luis de, 33:64
Mercado, Manasseh de, 25:117-18
Mercado, Miss de, 25:118
Mercado, Moseh de, 42:278, 394
Mercado, Moses de, 23:150
Mercado, Rafael de, 42:259, 292, 387, 392, 394
Mercado, Samuel d'Israel de, 29:9
Mercantile Library Association, New York, 27:381, 523; 41:15
Mercer, Jesse, 33:233-36
Mercer, John, 48:10
Mercer, John F., 27:470
Mercer, Nancy (Mills), 33:234-35
Mercer University, 33:235-36; 40:192
Merchant of Venice, 29:152; 33:172-74, 189
Merchants Club, Baltimore, 26:289
Merchants' and Manufacturers' Association of Baltimore, 25:153
Merchant Taylors' School, 37:138, 143
Mereda, Judicq de, 44:92-93, 255
Meredith, George, 35:249
Meredith, John, *Short Discourse,* 30:467
Meredith, Mrs., 33:4
Merenberg, Michiel, 33:122
Meriado, Gratia de, 23:29
Merida, Augustine, 37:420
Meridian, Miss., religious observances, mid-nineteenth century, 37:38
Merigot edition, 49:43-44, 47
Meriwether, John, 34:285
Merode, J. de, 33:125; 44:95
Merrett, J. G., 26:218
Merrett, Margery, 31:80-83, 90-99, 102
Merrett, William, 31:80-83, 90-99, 102
Merrick, Captain, 29:141
Merrick, Joseph, 25:82-84
Merrill, Selah, 36:59-60; 40:111-12; 45:138

Merritt, General, 22:174
Merritt, Margary, 27:39
Merritt, William, 27:39
Merry, John, 27:248
Merry, Senor, 36:21
Mersand, Joseph, "Present-day American Jewish drama," 35:xv
Merton of the Movies, 40:354, 357
Merton, Walter, 22:78
Mertz, Isaac, 26:183
Mervine, William, 39:24, 34, 63
Merwin, Henry Childs, 32:100, 102
Merschersky, 48:81
Meserole St. Talmud Torah, 35:62
Meserve, William, 25:50
Meshack (slave), 50:162
Meshullam, 26:148
Mesiah, Selomoh, 29:14, 18
Mesier, 25:56
Mesopotamia, 46:480, 482-83; "Paul Haupt and the Mesopotamian Project, 1892-1914," 47:154-75; "Paul Haupt's Plan for Settling Russian Jews in Mesopotamia," 44:242
Mesquita, Abraham Bueno de, 23:149; 29:16
Mesquita, Benjamin Bueno de, 31:102; 42:280, 394, 426, 428
Mesquita, Bueno de, 38:236
Mesquita, David de Jacob Bueno de, 29:16
Mesquita, Isaque Montissinos, 42:286, 388, 392, 395
Mesquita, Joseph Bueno de, 31:81-83, 90, 93-95, 99, 101-2
Mesquita, Reba Henriques de, 32:64
Mesquita, *see also*: Bueno, Joseph
Messenger, The, 39, 120, 132, 136, 138, 141; 46:117
Messiah, date of coming by G. H. Seixas, 27:128
Messiah, Izaque Mesia, 29:15
Messias, Semuel de Jechiel, 29:18
Messmore-Kendall, 45:200
Mesurier, Paul de, 40:125-26
Metcalf, Edwin, 50:381
Metcalf, Eliab, 50:148
Metcalf, Jesse H., 36:368
Metcalf, Judge, 38:120
Metcalf, Secretary, 34:197

Meth, Jason, "Jews Who Served in the Old Guard of the City of New York," 42:415

Metivier, Joan Baptiste, 41:69

Metropolitan League of Y. W. H. A.'s, 37:284

Metropolitan Life Insurance Company, 46:314

Metropolitan Magazine, 43:20

Metropolitan Museum of Art, 33:204; 42:417; 49:62

Metropolitan Opera House, 40:156-61

Metternich, Prince, 26:37-41, 46, 50, 54, 60-62, 64-66, 68-69, 75-77, 80, 82, 89-91, 93, 125; 38:183; 43:109, 176, 178

Metz, Eleaser, 21:214

Metz, Jacub, 39:151

Metz, Ludwik, 39:151

Metzel, Alexander, 47:53-54, 111

Metzgar, Joseph, 26:183

Metzger, Frances Greenbaum, 37:470

Metzger, Oscher, 41:268

Metzler, Daniel, 26:183

Metzler, David, 26:183

Mexican National Archives, 31:11, 15

Mexican Society of Geography and Statistics, 23:129

Mexican War, 26:7, 194; 34:169; Jews in, 27:502, 505

Mexico, 22:112; 31:213-14; 46:483; "Autos-de-fe Celebrated by the Mexican Inquisition, 1648," 32:117; "Hernando Alonso, a Jewish Conquistador with Cortes in Mexico," 31:xxix, 2-4, 8-31; Inquisition, 32:xxv; 33:xxviii, xxix, 25, 34, 40-41; "Jewish Immigration to Mexico as a Result of the World War," 29:xxx; "Jewish Pioneers Along the Mexican Border," 29:xxx; Jews in, 26:5-6; 31:2-4; 35:326-27; *Jews in Mexico*, 32:xxvi; lost tribes, 25:83; "Marcus Otterbourg, United States Minister in 1867," 32:65-98; "Material relating to the Mexican Inquisition, and the Jews of Barbados," 32:xx; Maximilian, 33:244-47; "Memoir of Marcus Otterbourg, United States Minister to Mexico in 1867," 32:xiii; migration, 35:219; "A Note on Documents relating to the Inquisition in Mexico," 22:xiii, xxxvi;

revolution, 31:213; "A Spanish-American Jewish Periodical," 23:vii, xiv, 129-35

Meyberg, Max, 42:423

Meyer, Adolph, 29:181

Meyer, Alfred, 42:122

Meyer, Annie Nathan, 28:xxxix; 37:203; 41:294; 49:62

Meyer, Arnold, 22:213

Meyer, Arthur, 26:xxxiv

Meyer, Charles, 29:179

Meyer, Eduard, 28:232

Meyer, Edwin Sigmund, 31:147

Meyer, Elias, 35:7-10

Meyer, Eugene, 47:203

Meyer, Eugene, Jr., 49:194

Meyer, George von L., 36:273-75

Meyer, Henry J., 39:237

Meyer, Isidore S., 36:xiv; 37:iv, 12; 38:vi, 9, 78; 39:v-vi; 41:387; 42:415, 459; 43:6, 70; 44:59; 48:202, 267; 50:260, 263, 266-73; California editorial, 45:268-70; Canadian Jewish Congress, 49:265-66; cited, 49:149-52, 155; Civil War centennial, 49:137, 139; conference of historians, 44:247; executive council, 37:xxix; 38:344; 39:470; 40:406; 43:230; 46:493; exhibits, 44:244-45; "Fifty Years of the American Jewish Historical Society," 37:xxxiii; "Hebraic Elements in Early American Culture: Lord North and the Book of Esther; The College of Rhode Island Saves Some Books," 37:xxxv; "Hebrew at Dartmouth," 40:407; "Hebrew at Harvard (1636-1760)," 35:xv, 145-70; "Hebrew at Yale," 38:343; "The Hebrew Oration of Sampson Simson, 1800," 46:51-58; "The Hebrew Preface to Bradford's History of the Plymouth Plantations," 38:289-303, 346; "Hebrew Quotations in Bradford's 'Third Dialogue,'" 39:471; Historical Essay Awards, 45:262; history, writing of, 39:290; 46:136, 168, 179-81, 193, 444-445; 49:216, 255; "Isaac Gomez Jr.'s Religious Instruction for His Sons, 1825," 37:xxx; Jewish biography, 42:312; 50:68, 71-72; Jewish Tercentenary 40:414; "John Adams: Educator," 45:58-60; "John Adams Writes a Letter," 37:xxxv, 185-201; "Jonathan Nathan's Letters to Hamilton Fish, 1847-1857," 37:xxxiii; "Joshua

Hezekiah de Cordova, Isaac Gomez, Jr., and Jacob Mordecai, Apologetes for Judaism," 38:343; "Judaica," 38:331-33; Judah Monis, 37:121; Lee Max Friedman award, 49:265, 270-71; librarian-editor, 37:xi; 42:414; 43:230; 44:241; 45:260, 264; 46:492; 47:200; 48:265; necrologies of Lee M. Friedman, 47:200, 211-15; Samuel Schulman, 45:265; secretary, 37:xxix, xxxii; secretary, 38:341; "The Sheftall Papers," 37:xxxiii; "Towards a Dictionary of American Jewish Biography," 38:343; "200th Anniversary of Easton, Pa.," 41:390; "The Use of the Psalter in Colonial Education," 38:345; see also: Kayser, Stephen S.

Meyer, Jacob, 26:187
Meyer, Jonas Daniel, 26:72
Meyer, Jörgen, 28:219
Meyer (b. Joseph), 27:21; 34:83
Meyer, Julius, 37:270
Meyer, Judah, 27:271
Meyer, Lipman, 50:352
Meyer, Louis A., 48:258
Meyer, Louisa B. (Silberstein), 29:179
Meyer, Louise, 29:181
Meyer, Mariane, 26:51
Meyer, Martin A., "American Jewish Communal Activities in 1860," 29:xv; gift, 26:xxxiv; "Jewish Participation in the Panama-Pacific International Exposition," 25:xiv; necrology of, 29:xxix, 179-81; necrology of Harris Weinstock, 29:xxix, 194-98; "Some Early American Jewish Correspondence with the Jews of the Far East," 28:xxxiii
Meyer, Maximilian, 41:258
Meyer, Minnie, 48:27
Meyer, Miss, 26:245
Meyer, Pieter, 48:21
Meyer, Samuel, 26:183
Meyer, Sara, 26:51
Meyer, Sigmund, 31:140
Meyer, T. A., 27:271
Meyer, W. M., 31:210
Meyer, Wm. and Co. (San Francisco), 37:45
Meyerbeer, 29:127; 33:xxxi
Meyerhoff, Joseph, 49:270
Meyerowitz, Arthur, 34:184

Meyerowitz, Meyer, 34:197
Meyerowitz, William, 47:182
Meyers, Bm. 27:115
Meyers, Frederick, 48:258
Meyers, Hyam, 35:19
Myers, Myer, "The Character and Style of Ritual Silver Made by Myer Myers," 42:413
Meyers, Mordecai, 39:145
Meyers, Philip, 29:144
Meyers, Philip M., executive council, 49:268
Meyers, Rebecca, 22:194
Meyers, S. A., 37:268
Meyerson, Emile, 43:65-66, 68
Meyerstein, E. H. W., 35:230
Meyr, A. de, 27:79
Meyr, Isachar Br. R., 21:14
Meyr, Moses, 23:155
Meza, Abigael, 25:139
Meza, Abraham de, 27:51
Meza, Abraham Hisquiau Mendes, 25:139
Meza, David de, 27:79
Meza, David de Abraham de, 29:24
Meza, David Mendes, 25:138-39
Meza, Ester (Penso), 25:139
Meza, Fonseca de, 32:58
Meza, Isaac de, 26:251
Meza, Ishak de David da, 25:139
Meza, Jacob, 25:139
Meza, Jacob de, 21:32; 27:79
Meza, Jacob de Franco, 26:251
Meza, Jahacob de David de, 25:140
Meza, Jahacob Mendes, 25:138-39
Meza, Lea, 25:139
Meza, Rachel de David de, 25:139
Meza, Rahel (Parra), 25:140
Meza, Raphael de, 27:79
Mezan, Saul, gift, 35:xxiii
Mezel, 39:159
Mezger, Wolf, 41:255
Mezuzah, 39:370
Mezvinsky, Morton, 48:140, book review by, 47:208-9
Mial, Moses, 21:109; 28:215
Miami, 49:264; Indians, 23:32; "The Jewish Community of Greater Miami," 49:220
Miami Medical College, 39:449
Micate, Jacob, 33:55
Michael, Abraham, 27:315

Michael Br Asher, 21:31, 33
Michael, Bernhard, 41:255
Michael, David, 33:95
Michael, Elias, 22:xxiii
Michael, Emanuel, 27:400
Michael, Fany, 41:253
Michael, Jerome, 44:209
Michael, Joseph A., 27:271
Michael, Levy Freres, 29:127
Michael, Morland, 27:105
Michael, Rosa, 27:277
Michaels, Blume, 33:201
Michaels, Catherine, 33:201
Michaels, Mrs. Francis, 28:xxxviii
Michaels, Isaac, 27:253
Michaels, Jochabed, 33:200-201
Michaels, Joseph, 27:253
Michaels, Levi, 27:26
Michaels, Levy, 27:151
Michaels, Michael, 23:151
Michaels, Moses, 23:151; 33:201
Michaels, Myers, 27:151
Michaels, Rachel, 33:201
Michaels, Rebecca, 33:200-201, 205-6
Michaels, Stern & Company, 40:71
Michaelson, B. S., 39:408
Michal, M., 27:315
Michal, Morland, 21:171
Michalls, Michall, 21:8, 25, 36
Michalls, Moses, 21:19-25, 38
Michals, Isaac, 21:159
Michaud, Desire A., 45:259
Michealis, Johanan David, 49:42, 46
Michel-Beer Prix de Rome, 28:7-8, 12
Michel, Charles, 41:146
Michel, Isaac, 27:241
Michelberger, Benedikt, 41:265
Michels, family, "Genealogical Notes on the Isaaks, Mears and Michels Families of New York and Boston," 22:xiii
Michels, Isaac, 27:42
Michel's trusts, 31:113
Michelson, Albert A., 47:192
Michielson, Jan, 26:247
Michigan, 38:333; Jewish local history, 49:226; Michigan superintendency, 47:190; "The Palestine Colony in Michigan," 29:61-74; "The Startling Experience of a

Jewish Trader During Pontiac's Siege of Detroit in 1763," 23:vii, xiv, 31-35
Michigan, University of, 49:11
Mickiewicz, Adam, 39:152
Micholl, Morland, 31:258
Micholl, Rebecca, 31:259
Micholl, Ribka, 27:112
Mickve Israel Congregations, see: Mikve Israel Congregations
Micmac Indians, 22:173-74
Middle East Supply Center, 40:116
Middlemass, R. M., 35:258, 268
Middlesex County (N.J.), "Jews in Middlesex County, New Jersey," 33:251-54
Middleswarth, Captain, 26:183
Middleton, Evan P., 46:153
Midstream, 47:61
Mielziner, Benjamin, 37:266, 268; 40:47
Mielziner, Leo, 33:xxxi; 45:156
Mielziner, Mr. and Mrs. Leo, gift, 33:xxx
Mielziner, Mrs. Leo, gift, 32:xxviii
Mielziner, Moses, 32:xxviii; 33:xxxi; 34:xviii; 45:101, 156; Hebrew Union College, 40:31-32, 38, 46-47; *Introduction to the Talmud*, 47:220
Miers, Gershom, 27:319
Mifflin, Harrison, 27:417
Migdal, David, 22:120
Migration, "An Austro-Hungarian Movement to Encourage the Migration of Jews to America, 1848," 23:187-89; Board of Delegates of American Israelites, 29:79; England, 26:5; "Hon. Oscar S. Straus' Memoranda Preceding Dispatch of the Hay Roumanian Note," 24:108-14; "Jewish Migrations from 1840 to 1946" reviewed, 40:196; Poland, 26:5; "Rumania and America, 1873: Leon Horowitz' Rumanian Tour and Its Background," 45:67-92
Mihanovich, Clement S., 46:416; "The American Immigration Policy: A Historical and Critical Evaluation," 46:306-36
Mikal, Moses, 47:177
Miklaszewiez, Felix, 23:175
Mikra Kodesh Congregation (New York), 44:136
Mikve Israel Association, 31:288

Mikve Israel Congregation, Curaçao, 22:122, 169; 27:5-8, 248, 408; 29:29-31, 51; 42:108, 214, 225; 44:215-36; *Precious Stones of the Jews of Curaçao: Curaçaon Jewry, 1656-1957*, reviewed, 47:176-78; Philadelphia, 21:xvi, xxiv, 172; 22:xxii, 56, 139, 163; 23:171, 173, 192; 27:229, 263, 343, 464, 497, 519, 523; 28:xxxiv, 253, 268-69; 29:xxxiii; 31:181, 255, 276, 284-85, 287; 33:19, 251; 34:67, 112-15, 270; 35:131; 37:345, 347; 38:5, 83, 135, 339; 40:28; 41:2, 83-85, 88-90, 93, 123, 228, 289, 292; 42:15, 102-4, 398; 43:7-8, 231-32, 235-36, 238, 253; 46:183; 47:204-6; 48:195; 49:19, 234; 50:12, 28-29, 241, 296; Abraham Lincoln letter, 37:15; *Act to Enable K. K. Mikve Israel to Lease Ground*, 30:249-50; *Charter and By-Laws of K. K. Mikve Israel*, 30:227-28, 359-61; *Constitution of the K. K. Mikve Israel*, 30:216, 218; "A Description of the Records of the Congregation Mikve Israel of Philadelphia," 32:xii; Egyptian Architecture, 41:63-68, 71-72; *Examination of Sunday School, for Religious Instruction of Israelites*, 30:345-46; *Form of Service at Dedication of K. K. Mikve Israel*, 30:236-38; George Washington, address from, 22:xx; gift, 29:xliii; "The Lincoln-Hart Correspondence," 38:139-45; Lyons collection, material in, 27:519-20; "Rebecca Gratz and the Jewish Sunday School Movement in Philadelphia," 48:71-77; *Review of Controversies Between Rev. Isaac Leeser and Congregation Mikve Israel*, 30:460; "Rosa Mordecai's Recollections of the First Hebrew Sunday School," 42:397-406; Rules and Regulations, 30:152; Sabato Morais, 37:55, 61-63, 70-71, 73, 76, 78-79, 83-84, 89, 91; *Scheme of a Lottery*, 30:133-34; subscribers, 27:461-63; Savannah, 27:488, 520, 523; 29:134; 30:190, 192-93, 359; 38:72; 48:13; 50:33; *Discourse Delivered at Consecration of New Synagogue*, 30:355, 358-59
Mikweh Yisrael (Hope of Israel), 22:119
Milah, "Recent Developments Relating to the Practice of *Milah* in the United States," 50:427

Milan, Ben R., 46:108
Milan, Felix, 28:219
Milan, Ferdinand, 28:220-21
Milan, Gabriel Ferdinand, 28:221; 44:115, 118; 47:193; "Gabriel Milan, the Jewish Governor of St. Thomas, Danish West Indies," 26:xxxi; 28:213-21
Milan, Juliana Regina, 28:218
Milan, Prince, 24:67
Milch, Jacob, *Memoirs*, 35:xxii
Mildenberg, S. H., 50:313
Miles, D. H., 35:229
Military service, 26:7; 38:8-9; Adolph, Marix, 28:290-92; Alfred Mordecai, 28:251; "The American Jew in the World War: A Personal and Statistical Study," 29:xxix; Army chaplains, 29:103-4; 39:437; "The Battleship 'Maine' and the Gunboat 'Scorpion': the part played by Jewish Seamen in United States Marine History, 22:xvii; "Charles H. Lauchheimer," 31:vii, 193-96; Civil War, 29:205; 49:138; 50:267, 269, 303-16, 332-34; "David Salisbury Franks, a Distinguished Patriot and Officer of the Revolutionary War," 26:xiv; "The Diary of Chaplain Michael M. Allen, September, 1861," 39:177-82; Emanuel Woodic, 29:64; expulsion of Jews, 29:104; *Foreigners in the Union Army and Navy*, reviewed, 42:210-11; Frederick Nathan, 28:294; "Hebrew Volunteers" in Maryland, 37:448-49; Jewish war records, 42:89; "Jewish Welfare Activities for the Military During the Spanish-American War," 41:357-80; "Jews in the War of 1812," 22:xiii, 26:173-200; "Jewish Soldiers in Dutch Brazil (1630-1654)," 46:40-50; "The Jews in the Wars of the United States," 26:x; xxv, xxvii; "Joseph B. Nones: The Affable Midshipman," 46:1-19; "Midshipman Joseph Israel," 23:xiv; "A Note on the Military Career of Benjamin Rosenberg," 29:xv; Roumania, 24:99, 104, 106, 117, 124-25, 128, 143, 145, 147, 152; San Dreben, "The Fighting Jew," 31:xiv, 211-17; "Simon M. Levy, Member of the First Class to Graduate at the United States Military Academy in 1802," 23:xiv; "Two Letters of Solomon Bush, A

Revolutionary Soldier," 23:xiii, 177-78;
"Unpublished Canadian State Papers
Relating to Benjamin Hart," 23:vii, 137-
40; war records, 28:xxii; "The War Record
of American Jews," 28:xv
Miliukov, Paul N., 36:292-93
Mill, John Stuart, 40:209
Mill Street Synagogue, New York, 41:121,
123, 286; dedication prayer, 27:99-100;
first congregation, 27:1-2, 89, 260, 299;
second congregation, 27:46, 65, 97, 99-
100, 106, 113, 251, 257-58, 338, 344
Millan, Francisco, 31:10, 26
Millar, Charles C. H., 35:252
Millas y Villacrosa, José María, 37:xii-xiii
Millaud, Edoard, 41:162
Miller, 31:125
Miller (actor), 179, 186
Miller; Botkin v., 25:134
Miller, Charles, 43:204
Miller, George J., 33:xvii; "Early Jews in
Middlesex County, New Jersey," 33:254;
gifts, 33:xxxi; 35:xx; "Isaac Emanuel,"
35:xv; "James Alexander and the Jews,
Especially Isaac Emanuel," 35:171-88;
"Jewish Cases in Essex County, New
Jersey," 38:345
Miller, Grace Gimbel, 48:256
Miller, Henry, see: Bernard, William S.
Miller, Jacob, 26:183
Miller, Jacob L., 47:46
Miller, James, 23:161
Miller, John, 21:xiii; 25:44; 35:291
Miller, Louis H., 46:167; 50:212, 217
Miller, Matthew R., Identity of Judaism and
Christianity, 30:457
Miller v. Miller, 25:135
Miller, Miss, 44:27
Miller, Perry, 47:142-43; "Puritanism and the
Covenant," 46:492
Mills, Nancy, 33:232
Miller, Nathan J., necrology, 32:ix-x
Miller, Samuel, 38:122
Miller, Seth, 27:326
Miller, Silvanus, Report of Trial, Miller vs.
Noah, 30:208-9
Miller, Simon, death, 37:xii; gift, 34:xxvii;
necrology of Morris Newburger, 26:xxx;
28:295-98

Miller, Uri, 49:270
Miller, W. H., 48:97
Miller, William, 27:522; Review of the Doctrine
and Prophetical Chronology of William Miller,
30:393, 395
Miller, William, G., 27:72
Milles, Francis, 27:296
Milliaud, Hippolyte, 41:149
Millikan, J. F., 47:93
Millor, Ludwick, 27:248
Mills, John, 26:147
Mills, Judge, 23:120
Mills, Mr., 39:190
Mills, Robert, 41:71
Milman, Henry Hart, History of the Jews,
30:266, 315
Milner, Henry M., 33:195, The Jew of Lubeck;
or, The heart of a father, 33:174
Milton, John, 46:434
Milwaukee, 47:34; 49:264; 50:202, 224; B'nai
B'rith, 47:47; Masons, 47:45; Milwaukee
Jewish Mission, 37:299; "The Jewish
Community of Milwaukee, Wisconsin,
1860-1870," 47:34-58, 111; 49:242
Milwaukee Committee, 48:42
Milwaukee Daily Atlas, 47:49
Milwaukee Sentinel, 47:39, 41, 48-49
Milwaukee Volunteer Relief Association,
47:52
Mindis, Jacob, 23:85
Mines, Charles, 27:248
Mines, D., gift, 34:xxi
Minhag America, 47:40, 58
Minian Mizwot, 22:121
Mining, New Almaden Mine, 23:124-25
Minis, A., 29:134
Minis, Abigail, 50:66, 154
Minis, Abraham, 21:45; 27:197; 31:239
Minis, Abraham, Jr., 48:170-71
Minis, Mrs. E., 29:129
Minis, Isaac, 26:190; 48:171
Minis, Judith, 26:190; 27:197; 48:170-71
Minis, Philip, 46:37; 48:170-71; 50:66; Aaron
Lopez, 35:301; genealogy, 37:438; War of
1812, 26:190-91
Minis, Mrs. Philip, 48:10, 12-14, 18
Ministers' Conference, New York, 37:84
Minkoff, N. B., 35:xxiii
Minkoff, Nochum, 46:62

Minkowsky, Pinchos, 48:194
Minneapolis, 47:18-19, 24-26; "Unlike Twins: A Study of the Differential Development of St. Paul and Minneapolis," 47:202
Minneapolis Journal, 41:185
Minnesota, Jewish local history, 49:226-27
Minnesota Historical Society, 28:xii; 42:361
Minnesota Jewish Welfare Board, 37:444
Minns, Albert E., Jr., 50:272
Minor, I., 38:309
Minot, George R., 43:204
Minturn, William, 35:291
Mintz, Hannah, 42:63
Mintz, Herman H., 42:419
Mintz, Moses, 35:57
Minzesheimer, Charles, 49:186-87
Mirabeau, Comte de, 26:96; 28:80, 84, 94
Mirabeau, Isac, 41:253
Miramon, General, 32:82
Miranda, Abraham, 21:45; 32:62
Miranda, Abraham de Jahacob Rodriques, 29:28
Miranda, Elias Rodrigs, 27:23
Miranda, Eliau and Isaac Rod., 27:248
Miranda, Isaac, 22:149-50; 29:36; 43:236-37; 50:123
Miranda, Ishac Rodrigz., 22:170
Miranda, Ishac Vaz de, 29:28
Miranda, Mozes Abraham Rodrigues, 38:68, 74
Miranda, Sara Munes de, 29:36
Miranda y Ayala, Francisco de, 23:133
Mirandola, Giovanni Pico di, 28:202
Mircado, Moses, 21:29
Mitchel, Abraham, 26:181, 236
Mitchel, David, 27:394
Mitchell, Abraham, 27:80; 34:xxi
Mitchell, Dr., 27:262; 38:127
Mitchell, Esther Allen, 35:xviii
Mitchell, Hattie, 29:156
Mitchell, Henry, 29:156
Mitchell, John, 41:54, 312
Mitchell, John Purroy, 38:51; 49:9
Mitchell, Jonathan, 35:151
Mitchell, Lewis Allen, 38:70
Mitchell, Max, 46:81
Mitchell, Rachel, 33:6

Mitchell, Rebecca E., 22:182; "Genealogical Notes on the Isaaks, Mears and Michels Families of New York and Boston," 22:xiii
Mitchell, S. W., "Hugh Wynne, Free Quaker," 34:xxiv
Mitchell, Sally, 26:233
Mitchell, Silas W., 35:253
Mitchell, William, 37:277
Mitchell colony, 38:306
Mitchell Hotel, 33:184
Mitchill, Samuel L., 46:12
Mitford, E. L., 26:143-44
Mitnick v. Russian Congregation, 25:135
Mitterwurzer, Friedrich, 35:287-88
Mizpah Congregation of Chattanooga, 28:275
Mizrachi-Hapoel Hamizrachi, 49:273, 275
Mizrachi organization, 35:59-60; 49:84; gift, 35:xxiii
Mizrachi, Solomon J., 42:300-301
Mizrah, 39:370
Mobile (Ala.), 23:6; 50:154; religious observances, mid-nineteenth century, 37:36
Mobile Daily Advertiser and Chronicle, 50:164
Mobile Musical Association, 50:170
Mocat, Isaack, 33:67
Mocata, Abraham, 42:279, 287, 392, 394
Mocata, Jahacob, 42:278, 394
Mocatta, Frederick David, 37:2
Mocatta, Isaac, 28:89
Mocatta Library, 26:xii; 31:291
Mochoro, Yacob, 42:278, 395
Modder, Montagu Frank, 40:346, 352
Model Tenement Houses, 48:58
Modena, Leon, 28:88; 34:13
Modern View, 49:197
Modjeska, Helena, 43:26
Moens, Adriaan, 37:358-59
Moens, Francis, 33:108
Moeribeca, John de Mendonca de, 33:77
Moffatt, John Newland, 39:32-33, 63
Moffit, James, 39:3
Mog, Abraham, 42:279
Mohammad Ali, 26:133
Mohammedanism, Ernest Renan, 37:24; Persian Jews, converts to, 36:11-18
Mohawk Indians, 27:382

Mohegan Indians, "The Phylacteries Found at Pittsfield, Mass.," 25:vii, 81-85
Mohiliwer, Samuel, 35:248, 255
Mohr, Philip, 47:197
Moira, George Lopes de, 33:113
Moira, Manuel da Costa, 33:116
Moïse, Abraham, 32:38, 43; 50:160; "A Selection from the Miscellaneous Writings of the late Isaac Harby," 32:35
Moïse of Bologna, 28:153
Moïse, Charles H., 29:129; 42:68-70
Moïse, Cherry, 32:38, 51
Moïse, Justine, 50:175
Moïse di Lisbona, 28:153
Moïse, Lucius C., 34:255; "Biography of Isaac Harby," 33:xxx
Moïse, Penina, 32:38, 40; 42:56, 60-61; 46:427-29, 442; 48:202, 267; 49:70, 143
Moïse di Tivoli, 28:153
Moiseville colony, 39:92, 95
Moisseiff, Leon S., death, 37:xii
Mol, Abram Lamberts, 31:90
Molasses Act of 1733, 42:75; 46:31
Molcho, David, 29:19
Moldovia, 24:102-4, 112, 115, 117-19, 138-40, 151; 28:132; Jewish disabilities, 24:2, 20, 37, 98
Moldolfi, Angelo, 27:512
Mole Macher, 39:372
Molena, Captain, 27:302
Molho, Mordehay de Selomoh, 29:18
Molijn, Gabriel de, 33:119
Molina, Aron, 44:228
Molina, David de, 27:23
Molina, Joan Tenora de, 33:115
Molina, Moses, 21:23, 25, 29
Moll, Max S., 40:64, 69
Moller, George H., 28:247
Molleschott, Senator, 28:52
Molnar, Ferenc, 35:269-70
Molony, Mrs., 45:39
Mombabo, Jan Ribero da, 33:116
Mominy, Joseph, 23:139
Mommsen, Professor, 36:358, 360
Monachesi, 28:24, 26
Monange, B., 27:105
Monarch Line, 49:184
Monasch, Marie, 28:77
Mondelet, 23:45, 47-49

Monatsschrift, 29:191
Monatsschrift für Geschicte und Wissenschaft des Judentums, 28:262
Moncrieff, William Thomas, 35:241; *Rochester; or, King Charles the Second's merry days*, 33:174, 196
Monheimer, Hayum, 41:265
Monis, Abigail (Marret), 22:7, 22
Monis, Judah, 23:81; 30:iv, 21-22, 41; 37:135, 438; 42:336; "A Cabalistic MS. from the Library of Judah Monis," 28:xv, 242-45; "A Contemporary Appraisal of Judah Monis, Harvard's First Instructor in Hebrew," 38:146-47; conversion, 31:xviii; 37:441; 40:119; Cotton Mather, 26:210; *Dickdook Leshon Gnebreet*, 30:35, 38; *Dissertation Upon the 49th Chapter of Genesis*, 30:38; *Hebrew Grammar*, 27:485; 31:xxxiii; 34:52; 43:237; 45:63; Hebrew at Harvard, 35:146, 161-69; history, writing of, 39:260; "Judah Monis, First Instructor in Hebrew at Harvard University," 22:1-24; "A Note on Monis' MS. Hebrew Grammar in the Library of the Massachusetts Historical Society," 28:xv; Puritans, 44:120-21; "Some Further Notes on Judah Monis," 37:xxx, 121-34; *The Truth, the Whole Truth, and Nothing but the Truth*, 30:23-27
Monize, Alexander, 24:116
Monk, Henry Wentworth, 26:163; 43:71; 50:352, 360
Monk, J., 31:184
Monk, Mary, 22:193
Monod, Th., 41:162
Monomach, Vladimir, 48:118
Monroe, James, 27:401; 32:41; 39:18-19; 41:5-7; 46:10; Monroe Doctrine, Mexico, 32:68; "A proposal to improve the lotteries of the United States, patented by Jacob I. Cohen and signed by President Monroe and Vice-President Adams, March 3, 1825," 33:xviii
Monroe, W. S., "Bulgaria and Her People," 24:79
Monsana, Samuel, 27:80
Monsanta, Isaac Mendes, 27:80
Monsanto, Benjamin, 50:172
Monsanto, Esther M., 32:64
Monsanto, H. M., 27:450

Monsanto, Ishac, 22:170
Monsanto, Ishac Israel, 44:229
Monsanto, Jacob, 50:172
Monsanto, Jacob Mendes, 44:222
Monsanto, Jacob Nunez, 32:58
Monsanto, Joseph Mendes, 50:148
Monsanto, Josiao, 22:170
Monsanto, Louis Mendes, 44:118
Monsanto, Mendes, 44:117
Monsantto, Abraham Israel, and Sasporttas, Abraham Israel, 27:248
Monsheimer, Levi, 49:54
Monsky, Henry, death, 37:xii
Monsky, Mrs. Henry, 46:121-22
Montagsblatt, 50:107
Montagu, Samuel, 31:291; 37:96; 41:141; 43:41
Montagus, 39:204
Montaigne, La, 21:177
Montalto, Elijah, 35:27
Montalto, Filotheo Eliau (Elijah), 28:199, 202
Montana, Jewish local history, 49:227
Montanus, "Hebrew Bible and Dictionary," 27:449; 35:140
Montanye, Jacobus, 27:329
Montcalm, Marquis de, 35:6
Monte, Jacob d'el 33:50
Montefiore, 34:187
Montefiore Agricultural Aid Society, 40:245
Montefiore, Claude, 37:80; 43:64-65, 250; colonization, 47:171; *Jewish Quarterly Review*, 33:25; necrology of Israel Abrahams, 31:xxiii, 249-50; passport issue, 46:98; Solomon Schechter, 25:180-83
Montefiore Colony, 48:87, 93
Montefiore, Eleazar, 26:251
Montefiore Fair, 40:165
Montefiore, Herbert Nathan, 40:132
Montefiore Home, 40:165
Montefiore Home and Aid Society (Boston), 46:83
Montefiore Home for Chronic Invalids, 22:238; 40:164; 42:123
Montefiore, Horatio, 40:132
Montefiore Hospital, 35:318; New York, gift, 34:xxii; Pittsburgh, gift, 34:xxii
Montefiore, J. M., 24:45; 29:86
Montefiore, Jacob, 26:251

Montefiore, John, 37:420
Montefiore, John M., 37:420
Montefiore, Joseph, 40:134
Montefiore, Joseph Elias, 40:123
Montefiore, Joshua, 44:254; "Joshua Montefiore of St. Albans, Vermont," 40:119-34
Montefiore, Judith, 27:147
Montefiore, Lady Moses, 26:132; 37:213-14
Montefiore, Moses, 22:xxxi, 172; 25:67, 112; 27:147, 483; 34:xxi; 35:xviii, 318; 37:82, 84; 40:122, 124, 129, 134; 42:440; 43:48; 49:188; 50:13; Alms House, Jerusalem, 31:274; Board of Delegates of American Israelites, 29:77-78, 86-88, 92, 98-99, 127; 49:26; Balkan disabilities, 41:38; colonization, 48:87; Damascus Affair, 36:3; educational reforms, 28:84, 119-25; etching, 29:xliii; honors, 34:268-69; "Jewish Disabilities in Balkans," 24:2, 22; Lyons collection, material in, 27:521-22; "The Montefiore Testimonial Fund and American Israel," 37:xxx, 95-101; Morocco, 36:19-21; Palestine, Jewish homeland, 26:132-34, 140-41, 146, 150-51, 153, 156, 255; Palestinian aid, 48:242; portrait, 23:xvii; Purim association, 40:165; Russia, 36:239, 396; *Sabbath Visitor*, 34:233; Shearith Israel (N.Y.) Congregation, 27:117-18, 146-47; "Some Relations of Gershom Kursheedt and Sir Moses Montefiore," 37:xxxiii, 213-220; Touro Synagogue, 38:68
Montefiore, Moses Vita, 40:123
Montefiore Testimonial Fund, 49:26; "The Montefiore Testimonial Fund and American Israel," 37:xxxi, 95-101
Monteforo, 27:80
Montégut, Émile, 37:22-23, 28; 38:278
Monteil, E., 41:162
Montesino, Samuel, 33:63
Montesinos, Isaque, 42:253, 257, 280, 286, 288, 395
Montesinos, Ishac, 29:18
Montesinos, Joseph Levi, 29:18
Montesinos, Samuel, 42:280, 395
Montesquieu, 38:324
Montezinos, Antonio de, 34:173; 37:354, 357
Montezinos, Jacob, 29:16, 18

Montezinos, Levy, 38:236
Montezinos Library, 28:xxii
Montgomerie, Gov., 34:122
Montomery, Ala., Jewish Federation, contribution, 37:xxviii; religious observances, mid-nineteenth century, 37:36
Montgomery Advertiser, 34:267
Montgomery, James A., 33:22
Montgomery, John B., 39:62
Montgomery, Thomas Lynch, 30:vi
Monthly Miscellany, 25:114
Monticello, 39:10-11, 45, 64-65
Monticello Farm School, 39:64
Montilla, Jorge Ramirez de, 32:117
Montreal, 26:175-76; 49:264; "History of the Congregation of Spanish and Portuguese Jews Shearith Israel of Montreal, Canada, published at the celebration of its 150th anniversary (1918)," 28:xl; "A Suit at Law Involving the First Jewish Minister in Canada," 31:vii, xvii, 181-86; "Unpublished Documents dealing with 'the petition of Certain Israelites of the City of Montreal for the Benefit of Public Register to Record Births, Deaths, Marriages, etc.,' " 28:xvi
Montreal Federation of Jewish Philanthropic Societies and Canadian Jewish Congress, gift, 35:xxiii
Montreal General Hospital, 28:271
Montreal Jewish Public Library, 34:xxvii
Montufar, Alonso de, 31:21
Monypenny, William Flavelle, 34:224; 35:130, 238; 46:435
Moody, Joshua, 46:21-22
Moore, 22:77; 23:49
Moore, C., "A compendious lexicon of the Hebrew language," 34:xxiii
Moore, Catherine (Mrs. Henry), 22:40-41, 47-48
Moore, Clement C., 30:iv; *Lexicon of the Hebrew Language*, 30:140-41
Moore, Dr., 27:316; 50:332
Moore, E. C. C., 30:247
Moore, George, 45:213
Moore, George F., 28:91
Moore, George Foot, 31:xxxv; 33:21; 37:438, 440; corresponding member, 28:xxii; "A

Cabalistic MS. from the Library of Judah Monis," 28:xv, 242-45; "Judaism in the First Centuries," 33:xxx; necrology of, 33:xii; "A Note on Monis' MS. Hebrew Grammar in the Library of the Massachusetts Historical Society," 28:xv
Moore, George Henry, 35:313
Moore, Hannah, *Sacred Dramas*, 30:83, 86
Moore, Henry, 22:40, 47-48
Moore, Isaac Massiah, 32:59
Moore, J. Hampton, 24:83
Moore, James, 41:78
Moore, John, 27:46, 50, 241, 259
Moore, John Bassett, 24:84, 89-92, 94; 34:186, 242; 36:135
Moore, John W., 39:30-31
Moore, Kathleen M., 42:418
Moore, Nathaniel F., 26:220
Moore, T., 29:130
Moore's Rural New Yorker, 50:90
Moos, H. M., 34:146; 50:293-95, 356-57
Moos, Julius, 41:265
Morache, Solomon, 50:39
Moraes, Pedro Rodrigues de, 29:17
Morais, Abraham, 25:117
Morais, Esther, gift, 28:xli
Morais, Henry, 41:66-67
Morais, Henry S., 29:172; 33:208, 210; 35:309; 38:59, 61-63, 65-66; 48:240
Morais, Henry Samuel, 34:169; 37:80, 91, 93, 236, 345; 46:4; 49:260
Morais, Herbert H., gift, 34:xxvii
Morais, Miss, 37:20
Morais, Nina, 28:268; 37:87
Morais, Sabato, 21:xxiv; 26:2; 27:237; 28:xli, 268; 32:3; 38:65, 339; 41:68; 42:104, 403, 405, 455; 45:125; 50:296, 358; American Israelites, 29:107; Carmel colony, 48:97; Cyrus Adler, 33:18; Emma Lazarus, 39:326; Hebrew Union College, 40:21, 28, 35; honored, 29:xlii; Jewish Theological Seminary, 35:318; 40:311; Jews of Philadelphia, 48:208, 222, 230-32, 238-39; Lincoln-Hart Correspondence, 38:139-45; New York chief rabbi, 44:153-54; Roumanian Jews, 45:85; "Sebato Morais: A Selected and Annotated Bibliography of His Writings," 37:xxxv, 55-93; Y.M.H.A., 37:230, 234, 236, 257

Morais, Samuel, 27:237
Moral, Andres, 31:10
Morales, Ana Maria de, 23:132
Morales, Antonio dc, 31:28
Morales, Bartolomé de, 31:15
Morales, Blanca de, 31:30
Morales, David, 22:170; 29:30
Morales, Gonzalo de, 31:3, 10, 19-24, 26
Morales, Isabel de, 23:132
Morales, Manuel de, 31:27-28, 30
Morales, Moses, 25:116
Moralis (actor), 33:177
Moran, Edmund, 30:77
Moran, Mrs. William, 35:307
Moranda, Mr., 27:261
Morange, 27:315
Morange, Benjamin, 27:80
Moraõ, Abraham de Aron Henriquez, 44:231
Moraõ, Aron Henriquez, 44:230
Moraõ, Aron de Jacob Hz., 22:170
Moraõ, Isaque de Abraham, 29:24
Moraõ, Ishac de Aron Henriques, 29:18
Moraõ, Ishac Henriquez Mora, 29:18
Moraõ, Jacob Hizkiaho, 22:171
Moravia, 26:31; 28:101; 38:190, 192-93
Moravia, Joseph, 27:42
Moravia, Mrs. Martha, 27:201
Morawetz, Moritz, L., 47:37
Mordaunt, Sigismund, 42:169
Mordecai, 40:135
Mordecai, A., 25:xii; 28:xxxiv
Mordecai, Abraham, 34:267; 35:137
Mordecai, Alfred, 23:125; 26:212; 28:251;
    37:438, 442; 42:398; 47:180; 50:196, 198;
    "Divided Loyalties in 1861: The Decision
    of Major Alfred Mordecai," 48:147-69, 266
Mordecai, Alfred, Jr., 42:398; 48:167-68;
    50:308
Mordecai, Augustus, 48:168
Mordecai, B., 50:172-73, 183
Mordecai Bar Baruch, 27:91
Mordecai, Benjamin, 33:205; 38:160-61
Mordecai, Caroline, 48:152-53
Mordecai and Co., 47:189
Mordecai, Elizabeth (Whitlock), 50:63-64
Mordecai, Ellen, 48:166
Mordecai, Emma, 48:162; 50:159, 195
Mordecai family, 22:xxiv, xxxiv; 48:17;
    50:154, 195

Mordecai, Francis, 22:194
Mordecai, Frank, 26:212
Mordecai, Gratz, 29:146
Mordecai, George, 48:149, 151-53, 160-61,
    166, 168
Mordecai, George W., 50:194
Mordecai, Harry, 50:175
Mordecai, Henry, 44:200
Mordecai, Isaac, 22:193
Mordecai, Jacob (1), dispensers of kindness,
    42:430
Mordecai, Jacob (2), 21:147-52, 154-56, 158-
    60; 25:126; 27:41, 253, 461; 33:205;
    42:398; 46:425; 47:205
Mordecai, Jacob (b. Moses Mordecai), 50:64
Mordecai, Jacob (N.C.), 29:146
Mordecai, Jacob (Va.), 33:205
Mordecai, Jacob, "Joshua Hezekiah de
    Cordova, Isaac Gomez, Jr., and Jacob
    Mordecai, Apologetes for Judaism," 38:343
Mordecai, Joseph, 27:42
Mordecai, Laura, 25:xii; 42:398-99, 405;
    48:159
Mordecai, M. C., 29:129; 47:188-89
Mordecai, Major, 22:xxiii, 58
Mordecai, Manuel, 22:194
Mordecai, Miriam, 42:398-99; 45:175, 184
Mordecai, Miss, 22:xxxi, 55-57
Mordecai bar Mordecai, 27:80
Mordecai, Mordecai M. 22:192-93
Mordecai, Mordecai Moses, 50:64
Mordecai, Moses, 25:126-27; 26:233; 27:21;
    50:64
Mordecai, Moses Cohen, 42:64
Mordecai, Myer, 26:183
Mordecai, Rachael, 32:42, 47-48
Mordecai, Rosa, 26:212; 45:184; "Rosa
    Mordecai's Recollections of the First
    Hebrew Sunday School," 42:397-406
Mordecai, Samson, 32:48
Mordecai, Samuel, 32:37, 47-48; 48:150, 159,
    167-68; 50:67, 194
Mordecai, Sara Ann, 35:236
Mordecai, Sarah, 48:148, 151, 158-59, 164,
    167
Mordecai, Sarah (Hays), 42:398
Mordecai, Solomon, 27:231; 48:168
Mordecai, Tobia b. Abraham, 27:235
Mordecai, Zepporah, 22:193; 50:64

Mordechay, Abraham de, Sr. 25:138
Mordell, A., gift, 34:xxvii
Mordell, Albert, 39:336, books reviewed by, 44:120-26; "Some Final Words on Emma Lazarus," 39:321-27
Mordell, Pinchos Phineas ha-Kohen, 48:194
Mordinay, 22:193
Morea, 27:107
Moreah, 22:23
Morehouse, Jabez, 35:188
Moreira, Antonio Joaquin, 47:70
Morena, Anthony, 33:113
Morena, Leah, 27:74
Morena, Manuel, 33:117
Morena, Paulo Perera, 33:118
Moreno, Gabriel, 32:61
Moreno, Gaspar Gonsalvos, 33:113
Moreno, Isaque de Mosseh, 29:16
Moreno, Mathathias, 42:280, 395
Morera, Balthazar Gonsalves, 33:112
Morera, Domingo, 33:112
Morera, Francisco Ferdinando, 33:112
Morera in Goyane, Joan, 33:116
Mores, Marquis de, 41:96
Moresco, Uriel, 50:123
Morgan, 25:12
Morgan affair, Masonic exposé, 22:80-81, 89
Morgan, George, 23:11, 15, 18; 30:77
Morgan, Henry, 32:6; 37:340
Morgan, House of, 47:188
Morgan, John, 28:89; 34:77; 38:27
Morgan, John Pierpont, 33:221; 36:43; 40:332; 46:434, 443
Morgan, Matthew, 39:35
Morgan, Shubal, see: Brown, John
Morgen Freiheit, Die, 50:252
Morgena, Isaac de Isaac de, 22:122
Morgenroth, Maier, 41:265
Morgenroth, Rosa, 41:268
Morgenroth, Sara, 41:268
Morgenstern, Der, 48:132
Morgenstern, Julian, 40:43, 45-54, 214, 379; 45:157; As a Mighty Stream, reviewed, 40:201-4
Morgenstern, Menachem Mendel, 35:263
Morgenthau, Henry, Sr., 36:64-67, 73-77, 293; 39:110, 440; 40:47; 46:431; 47:165, 174, 180; 49:190-91; death, 37:xii; Polish problems, 36:160-61, 163-64

Morgenthau, Henry, Jr., 40:403; 49:191
Morgenthau, M. (San Francisco), 37:45
Morie, Joseph, 27:175
Moriera, Sarah, 27:463
Morina, Paulo Perera, 33:119
Morison, Edward, 27:174
Morison, Henry, 27:174
Morison, Lewis M., 27:166, 174
Morison, Samuel Eliot, 35:169-70; 38:16
Moritz, 28:114
Moritz, Johann C., 26:117
Morley, Christopher, 35:265
Morley, John, 46:434
Mormons, 40:97; 46:268; 49:240; "Joshua Seixas, Alexander Neubauer and the early Mormon church," 33:xxv; "Mormon Petroglyph at Manti, Utah," 28:xxii
Moro, Ab. Querido, 42:278, 395
Moroc, Jacob Gabbay de, 42:280, 389, 394
Morocco, 24:88; 26:143, 252; 28:259; 49:26; Board of Delegates of American Israelites, 29:87-88; "Moroccan Jewish Rights at the Algeciras Conference," 28:xxxiii; U.S. intercession for Jews, 36:ix, 19-41
Morocco Famine Relief Fund, 25:112
Moron, Abm. Hz., 22:170
Moron (family name), 48:139
Morpurgo, Elia, 28:102
Morpurgo, Haim, 21:166
Morpurgo, Moses H., 27:107
Morpurgo, Samson ben Joshua Moses, 28:198
Morrais, Joan Carneiro de, 33:114
Morrais, Manuel Carneiro de, 33:117
Morrell, Jonathan, 23:156
Morricee, O. L., 50:387
Morris, 25:142
Morris, Andrew, 27:241
Morris and Co., 47:189
Morris, Edward Joy, 36:6, 100
Morris, Elena, 27:248
Morris, George P., 26:222
Morris, Gouverneur, 22:196; 27:469-70; "Father of religious liberty in the state of New York," 33:xxv
Morris, Ira Nelson, 36:76-77
Morris, Irving, "Major Lewis Bush: A Correction," 38:346
Morris, J. G., 30:334

Morris, Jastrow, "The First Publication of a Jewish Character Printed in Philadelphia," 30:54
Morris, Joseph, 30:77
Morris, Lewis, 22:40
Morris, Minister, 24:3-4
Morris, Mr., 27:392
Morris, Nelson, 46:436
Morris, Owen, 33:175, 178, 184
Morris, Rachel, 27:112
Morris, Richard, 33:184
Morris, Richard B., 34:244; American Historical Association sessions, 44:245; book reviewed by, 43:131-32; "Civil Liberties and the Jewish Tradition in Early America," 46:20-39; "Jews naturalized in New York colony and serving as jurors," 33:xvii; "Mosaic Law and Common Law in Early New England," 29:xiv
Morris, Robert, 22:196; 23:11, 172-73; 33:1-2; history, writing of, 46:183, 435-36; 48:2-3; Benjamin Levy, 28:xxxiv; 34:271; Gratz Family, 33:4; land company, 30:77; 37:347; 43:235; Moses M. Hays, 28:253-54; "References to Haym Salomon and Other Jews in Robert Morris' 'Diaries in Office of Finance, 1781-84,' " 39:470
Morris, Mrs. Robert, 34:271
Morris, Roland S., 31:277
Morris, Staats (1769), 22:40-43
Morris, William, 22:54; 38:268; 39:324, 327; 45:253; necrology of, 31:xvi, 283-84
Morrison, George Ernest, 46:91
Morrison, Henry, 29:174
Morrison, Hyman, "Charles W. Eliot's Attitude and Expressions of Interest in Jewish Matters," 40:406; gift, 33:xxxiii; "Hebrew and Jews at Harvard," 46:493
Morrison, Isidore, 35:58
Morrison, O., 38:314; 39:88
Morrissey, J. J., 37:428
Morse, 25:56, 32:49
Morse, Godfrey, necrology of, 22:xii, 228-30
Morse, Jacob, 27:91
Morse, Janet Rosenfeld, 22:229
Morse, Jedidiah, 38:128-29
Morse, John, 27:80
Morse, Leopold, 46:83
Morse, Samuel Finley Breese, 42:139

Mortara, 40:150
Mortara Affair, 28:187; 31:189; 34:146; 39:390; 42:152; 48:224-25; 49:16, 18
Mortara, Edgar, 29:77-78, 84, 88-89; 37:218; 48:224-25
Mortara, Marco, 26:99-100; 37:79, 83
Morteira, Saul Levi, 29:21; 44:86, 89, 94, 216; 47:71
Mortimer, Mrs. J., *The Young Jew*, 30:438
Mortman, Mark, 42:417-19
Morton, Eliza Susannah, 34:279
Morton, Gov., 33:218
Morton, I., 25:54, 57, 62
Morton, Jacob, 27:337, 396
Morton, John L., 27:321
Morton, Levi P., 25:112; 32:133; 33:217, 219, 223
Morton, Thomas, *Zorinski*, 33:174, 184
Mosad Szold, Keren lem'aan ha-Yeled veha-No 'ar, 49:171
Mosafia, Solomon, 33:88
Mosaic law, Washington and Mosaic Law, 39:319-20
Mosaicus, 39:101
Moscheles, Felix, 35:252
Moscow Benevolent Society of New York, 39:87
Mose, Abramo di, 28:191
Mose, Jacob, 50:76
Mosely, Myer, 22:100
Mosenson, N., 38:308
Mosenthal, 29:128
Mosenthal, Salomon Hermann von, 40:350
Moser, Jacob, 26:183
Moser, Moses, 41:227
Moses, A. deLeon, 50:333
Moses, A. Monetto, 27:168
Moses, Aaron, 27:80, 314; 29:141
Moses, Aaron I., 29:129
Moses ben Aaron, *Matte Moshe*, 22:133-34
Moses, Abraham, 27:416; 29:144-45, 147; 50:41, 56
Moses, Abraham R. Brandon, 21:215; 27:331-32, 334-35
Moses, Addie, 40:168
Moses, Adolph, 40:29
Moses, Alfred G., 46:116, 118
Moses, Barnett, 21:45, 48; 27:248; 50:41
Moses, Benjamin, 23;175

Moses, Blanche, 33:xxxiii; 50:274, 282
Moses, Brandon, 27:343
Moses, C. S., 21:170-71
Moses, Catherine, 27:112
Moses, Daniel, 27:152
Moses, David, 25:52; 27:84, 258, 314; 29:147
Moses, David Machado, 27:163, 168
Moses, Dr., 41:210
Moses, Edward Aaron, 26:251, 254-56
Moses bar Eleizer, 21:108, 124-25, 213
Moses, Elkin, 25:116
Moses, Esther, 27:113
Moses ben Ezra, 40:163
Moses, Franklin, 39:62
Moses, Franklin J., 37:439
Moses, Franklin J., Jr., 32:37; 37:439; 50:178
Moses, George H., 34:184
Moses, Gertrude, 27:340-41
Moses, Hannah, 26:233
Moses, Hayman, 27:80, 314
Moses, Hayyim, 28:203
Moses, Henry, 40:169; 50:41, 56
Moses, Henry (Zender Falmouth), 25:67-68
Moses, Herbert L., 22:xxxv
Moses, Horace, 50:241
Moses, Horatio, 25:116
Moses, Hortense Guggenheimer, 49:172
Moses, Isaac (Charleston), 27:58, 60; 50:41
Moses, Isaac (Conn.), 33:203
Moses, Isaac (New York), 21:101, 103, 106,
  111, 114, 116-18, 120-31, 133-37, 140-41,
  145-46, 159-60, 163, 168, 170, 183-84,
  212; 23:84, 157, 171-74; 27:xix, 33, 38, 41,
  51, 54-55, 59, 61, 63, 66, 70, 73, 84, 86, 89,
  126-27, 168, 184, 242, 252-53, 255, 328,
  333-34, 337, 383-84, 461-63; 28:xxxiv;
  31:83; 35:19; 42:418; 46:421; 50:37, 56;
  bookplates, 45:187; George Washington,
  address to, 27:217-21; "Isaac Moses and
  his services in the American Revolution,"
  31:xxiv; kosher meat, 25:47; Masonic
  certificate, 27:331; newspaper comment
  on, 27:331-32; New York bank, 38:49;
  portrait, 41:280-81, 291; 42:417; 43:232;
  real property 27:344-45
Moses, Isaac (Philadelphia), 22:197
Moses, Isaac (Pa.), War of 1812, 26:183
Moses, Isaac (captain), 27:390
Moses, Isaac, Robert Morris, 28:253

Moses, Isaac, (rev.), 26:177
Moses, Isaac (shoemaker), 25:123
Moses ben Isaac, 28:158, 160
Moses, Isaac, Jr., 21:214; 23:156; 27:84, 86,
  315, 333, 343-44; kosher meat, 25:52
Moses, Isaac L., 42:101
Moses, Isaiah, 32:127; 50:154
Moses, Israel (1), 21:171
Moses, Israel (2), 27:55, 383, 389
Moses, Israel (3), 42:118-20
Moses, Israel, Civil War, 50:281-82, 324-27
Moses, Israel, "Doctor Israel Moses," 37:xxxii
Moses, J. F., 50:172, 186, 287
Moses, Jacob (Md.), 26:187
Moses, Jacob (New York), 27:154; non-
  importation, 26:237-38
Moses, Jacob (N.C.), 29:147
"Moses Jacob Ezekiel: The Formative Years,"
  article by Zebulon Vance Hooker, 50:384
Moses, Jacob I., 27:515
Moses, James G., 36:208
Moses, John, 32:59
Moses, Joseph (1), 23:152; 27:80
Moses, Joseph (2), 23:175
Moses, Joseph (Texas), 27:237
Moses, Joshua (New York), 21:163, 169-70;
  27:55, 84, 258, 314, 333, 337, 338, 340,
  342-43
Moses, Joshua (N.C.), 29:147
Moses, Joshua, gift, 33:xxxi
Moses, Judah, 27:80; 34:274
Moses, L., 27:277
Moses, Lavinia, 27:343
Moses, Levy, 21:105, 108; 27:152, 154
Moses, Levy and Benjamin, 27:248
Moses, Lionel, 21:215
Moses, Lyon, 27:462; 47:205; 50:41, 56
Moses, M., 27:51
Moses, M. L., 25:36, 57
Moses, Marcus, 33:208
Moses, Max, 27:389
Moses, Michael, 25:113; 26:233
Moses, Minche (Adolphus), 23:157
Moses, Mr., 27:239
Moses, Mont., 27:315
Moses, Mordy, 21:81; 27:462
Moses, Moses, 27:154
Moses, Moses H., 40:140-42, 154, 158, 168-
  70

Moses, Moses L. (New York), 21:161, 167-68, 191-92, 212; 27:59, 61, 63, 84, 86, 89, 97, 102, 105-6, 108, 258-59, 311, 314-15, 338, 343-44; 30:124, 230, 298

Moses, Myer, *Annals of the Revolution in France*, 30:266; *Oration Delivered at Tammany-Hall*, 30:273-74; *Remarks on the Supplementary Vendue Act of 1815*, 30:202

Moses, Myer (S.C.), 26:190; 27:226; 32:36-38, 46, 51; 42:46; 50:169

Moses, Octavia Harby, 32:40, 48

Moses, Oliver Hazard Perry, Jr., 50:333

Moses, Parera, 21:18

Moses, Philip, 27:61, 462; 34:116; 50:41, 56

Moses, Phineas, 27:259, 508

Moses, Rachel, 27:111

Moses, Rachel Gratz, 27:341; 29:55; 42:418

Moses, Raphael J., 39:341; 50:153-54, 159, 201

Moses, Rebecca, 27:111; 32:36, 46

Moses, Rebecca (Mrs. Isaiah), 32:126-27

Moses, Rebecca G., 27:166

Moses, Reyna, 27:80, 111, 343

Moses, Reyna (Levy), 42:418

Moses, Richard, 50:175

Moses, Richea, 27:168

Moses, Samuel, 21:79; 29:147; 34:118, 285

Moses, Sarah, 27:111; 29:55-56, 60; 50:41

Moses, Solomon (Charleston), 50:164

Moses, Solomon (New York), 27:51, 63, 74, 80, 84, 336, 340-41; 41:287; 42:418; 47:206

Moses, Solomon, Jr., 50:164

Mosessohn, David N., necrology of, 33:xiii

Mosessohn, N., 29:153

Moskowitz, Belle Lindner Israels, 48:202, 267; 49:70, 143

Moskowitz, Ira, 47:182

Moskowitz, Sigmond, 50:234

Moskowski, 33:xxxi

Mosler, Henry, 50:385; "Henry Mosler, Pictorial Interpreter of the Civil War," 41:389

Moss, Alfred A., 28:xxxviii

Moss, Annie B., 31:xxxiv

Moss brothers, 48:240

Moss family, 50:244

Moss, Gabriel, 27:95

Moss, Isaac, 27:95

Moss, J. L., 27:503

Moss, John, 27:523; 30:426; 37:350; *Genealogy of the John Moss family*, 35:xx

Moss, Lucien, 28:xxxviii; 48:235; Home for Incurables, 31:276; 48:234

Moss, Lucien Herbert, 37:66

Moss, M., 27:521

Moss, Marion, 30:311

Moss, Mary, 31:xxxiv

Moss, Ralph, 37:229

Moss, Rebecca, 42:402

Moss, Sanford A., 35:xx

Moss, S. D., 29:132

Moss, William, 31:xxxiv; 50:308

Mosseh Br. Michaell, 21:12

Mosseri, Jack, 36:69, 71

Mosses Bar Michaell, 21:10, 12, 13, 194

Mossesson, 42:213

Mota, Mordechay, 44:232

Mothe, Jacques de la, 47:212

Motley, John Lathrop, 42:341

Motovilov, M., 41:191

Mott, Valentine, 42:117-18; 43:78; 46:12

Motta, Abraham and Aron, 27:248

Motta, Aron, 44:229

Motta, Benjamin, 44:218, 228

Motta, Binjamin de Mordy., 22:170

Motta, E. D. L., 32:51

Motta, Emanuel de la, 26:190; 27:120, 264; 32:38; 50:66; prayers, 22:xxxii

Motta, Harris, 27:45

Motta, Ishac, 44:229

Motta, Jacob dela, 22:xxiii, 165; 26:190; 27:258, 338, 398; 32:40; 43:149; 44:252; 50:160, 166; *Discourse at Consecration of Synagogue*, 30:190, 192-93, 359; eulogy of Gershom Mendes Seixas, 27:263, 519, 521; eulogy of Nathan Hart, 27:519; *Funeral Address*, 30:167-68; *Private and Religious Character of Nathan Hart*, 30:347, 349; Savannah synagogue dedication, 27:488, 492, 520

Motta, Mordechay, 22:170; 29:30; 44:232

Motta, Rachel de la, 50:160

Motta, Sarah A., 50:160

Motte, Jacob de la, 21:170

Motte, Jacques de la, 44:87

Moulder, Nicholas, 35:30

Mouley-el-Hassan, 36:39

Mound Street Temple (Cincinnati), 39:450; 40:32
Mountain Meadows Massacre, 29:64
Mount Hope Cemetery Association (Rochester), 44:237
Mount Sinai, New York, 38:24
Mount Sinai, Anshe Emeth Congregation, New York, 45:214
Mount Sinai Cemetery Association, Philadelphia, 28:310
Mount Sinai Dispensary (Boston), 46:82, 85
Mt. Sinai Hospital (New York), 21:xxv; 22:152; 25:87; 26:180; 27:403; 28:294; 29:175; 31:260, 267; 32:110; 33:202; 39:277; 40:155-56, 163-64; 41:19; 42:103; 44:212; 45:189; "The Centennial Anniversary of the Mount Sinai Hospital (1852-1952)," 42:113-30; "History of the Mount Sinai Hospital (1852-1952)," 41:390; *The Mount Sinai Hospital, 1852-1952*, 49:231
Mount Sinai Hospital, Philadelphia, 34:xxii
Mount Sinai Monthly, 49:166
Mount Sinai Society and Ladies' Auxillary (Boston), 46:85
Mt. Sinai Temple, El Paso, 35:326
Mt. Sinai Training School for Nurses, 29:179
Mt. Vernon Community Center (Philadelphia), 41:91
Mount Vernon Theatre, 33:188
Mount Zion Temple (St. Paul), 37:295
Moura, Pedro Morena de, 33:118
Mouradjea D'Ohasson, Ignace de, *Oriental Antiquities*, 30:88
Mourning customs, 39:366, 372; *Compendium of Order of Burial Service and Rules for Mourning, K. K. Shearith Israel*, 30:244-45
Mouton, Alexandre, 44:109
Moynier, Gustav, 33:216, 222, 225, 227-29
Mucata, Abraham de, 21:12-13; 39:246
Mudahai, Moses Judah, 26:252
Mudahy, Haim, 27:18-20
Mueller, Ignatz, 34:xxiii
Muhlenberg, Frederick Augustus, 37:14
Muhlenberg, H. A., 22:88-89, 91-92
Muhlenberg, P., 43:236
Muhlhauser, Sigmund, 36:313
Mulatta, Rose, 50:176-77
Müller, Edward, 28:16

Müller, Frederik, 45:140
Müller, Johann von, 26:84
Müller, W. Max, 33:32
Mul Ohel Temurah, 22:175
Mumford, John I., 22:85-86
Mumford, Peter, 35:290
Mumford, William, 37:418
Mumford, William, Jr., 35:291
Mumfords, P., 35:292
Mundheim, Louis, 50:313
Mundo Judio, gift, 34:xxii
Mundy, Baron, 33:215
Munich, Concordia of, 23:112
Munich Gazette, 50:11
Munich Synagogue, 41:69
Munich, University of, 23:109-10; 28:77
Munick v. City of Durham, 29:152
Municipal Art Society, Baltimore, 25:154
Municipal Civil Service Board of New York, 29:168
Munis, Abraham de Ishac, 29:28
Munis, Sarah de Selomoh, 29:28
Munk (1), 29:xliii
Munk (2), 29:86, 127
Munk, Salomon, 28:264; 35:119
Münster, Count of, 24:121; 26:39-40
Munz, Hirsch, *Jews in South Australia, 1836-1936*, 35:xx
Mupargo, M. M., 34:139-40
Murat, Achille, 50:154
Mure, 23:44-45, 47, 49
Murphy, Francis, 23:18
Murphy, Frank, 42:357
Murpurge, Rachel, 37:79
Murr, Christopher Gottlieb von, 49:42, 46
Murr (Chr. Theoph. de), 49:42
Murray, Alexander, 39:55
Murray, Dominick, 40:349
Murray, James, 35:10-12
Murray, James B., 39:35
Murray, James E., 46:278-79
Murray, John, 35:290
Murray, Joseph, 35:184; 42:80
Murray, Mr., 35:174, 184
Murray, Solicitor General, 31:133
Murray, William, 23:8, 11-21, 23; "David Franks' Interest in Lands in Virginia, in 1774," 25:119-20
Murrow, Edward R., 40:213

Musaphia, Salomon, 42:256-57, 288
Musar movement, 47:220
Musch, Cornelius, 33:104
Museum of the City of New York, 40:411;
   41:277, 289, 291; 42:417; 49:62
Museum of Fine Arts (Boston), 41:296;
   42:416; 43:1
Musher, Sidney, executive council, 50:426
Mustafa Fahmy Pasha, 47:91
Music, 39:380, 383; "Jewish Contributions to
   Music," reviewed, 40:195-96; "Music in
   the American Reform Synagogue," 32:xiii
Musqueto, Jacob, 21:99
Musquita, Abraham Pereira, 40:75
Mussaphia, Benjamin (Dionys), 28:217
Musset, Alfred de, 37:18
Mussey, R. Delavan, 33:213
Mussolini, Benito, 43:134; 46:292
Mutual benefit societies, 239-50
Muzzey, David Saville, 46:269
Myars, Harmon, 29:147
Myars, Jacob, 29:147
Mydans, Max, 42:419
Myer, A., 22:100
Myer, E., 29:133
Myer, Judah Br., 21:106
Myer, Moses, 23:155
Myers, 34:101
Myers, A., 27:51
Myers, Aaron, 33:205
Myers, Abigail, 27:323, 329
Myers, Abraham (S.C.), 22:154; 48:180, 193
Myers, Abraham (New York), 27:58, 253,
   323, 329
Myers, Abraham C., 47:190; 50:314, 397, 406
Myers, Abram (New York), 50:65
Myers, Abram (S.C.), 48:10
Myers, Adelia, 27:111
Myers, Adolph, 37:379
Myers, Algernon, 25:116
Myers, Andrew A., 27:248
Myers, Asher, 21:51, 70, 88-89, 103, 107,
   111-112, 117-118, 120-21, 123-26, 128-
   36, 138-40, 183, 211; 27:151-52, 154, 329,
   462; 33:203-4
Myers, Barnard, 26:188
Myers, Bella, 27:74
Myers, Benjamin (Baltimore), 22:194
Myers, Benjamin (Boston), 33:205

Myers, Benjamin (New York) (1), 27:74, 77-
   78, 84, 253, 330; 50:37, 56
Myers, Benjamin (New York) (2), 27:330
Myers, Benjamin M., 21:214; 27:51
Myers, Captain, 25:113
Myers, Catherine, 22:194
Myers, Caty Mears, 33:204
Myers, Christian, 27:416
Myers, Cosher, 27:91
Myers, Denys, P., 34:222
Myers, D. P., 34:231
Myers, Elkela, 21:61
Myers, Elkalah, 33:210
Myers, E. M., 37:45
Myers, Emanuel, 21:131-32; 50:37, 56
Myers, Esther, 50:42, 56, 156
Myers, Esther A., 26:249
Myers family, 22:xxiii, xxiv, xxxiv; 37:379;
   38:236; 50:32
Myers, Gabriel, 27:154; 33:204
Myers, Gustavus A., 27:145, 506; 33:24
Myers, Haim, 21:61-64, 79-80, 148-49, 170,
   213
Myers, Hannah (Hays), 27:323, 329-30
Myers, Hart, 21:51
Myers, Haym, 27:41, 43, 58-59, 61, 150, 152
Myers, Henry, 27:145
Myers, Horace V., 37:329
Myers, Hyam (New York), 25:47;
   naturalization, 37:373, 377, 386; 38:235-
   36
Myers, Hyam (London), 31:182
Myers, Hyman, 50:30-31
Myers, I., 29:133
Myers, Isaac, 26:183
Myers, Israel (Charleston), 50:41
Myers, Israel (New York), 34:112
Myers, Jacob, 22:191-92, 194
Myers, Jacob (Baltimore), 50:40
Myers, Lieut. Jacob (Md.), War of 1812,
   26:186
Myers, Jacob (N.Y.), non-importation,
   26:237-38
Myers, Jacob (S.C.), 48:180, 193
Myers, Jacob (b. Hyman), 27:152, 461
Myers, Jacob, "Jacob Myers, a Type of
   American Enterprise," 25:xiv
Myers, bar Jacob Levy, 27:80
Myers, Mrs. Jessy, 27:84

Myers, Jochabed, 33:204
Myers, John (New York), 27:80
Myers, John (St. Louis), 29:134
Myers, John (Va.), 34:279
Myers, Joseph (Md.), 22:192; 26:186
Myers, Joseph (New York), 21:63, 79, 85;
 27:43, 151
Myers, Joseph (Va.), 33:203
Myers, Joseph A., 21:142; 27:241, 462
Myers, Joseph M., 27:253
Myers, Josh A., 27:60
Myers, Joyce, 33:205, 209
Myers, Joyce Mears, 33:205, 207
Myers, Judah, 27:51, 58, 84, 153; 50:37, 57;
 Mears family, 33:203, 205-6
Myers, Judith, 21:46-47, 54, 56, 58, 115;
 27:67; 33:204-5
Myers, Judith H., 27:84
Myers, Levy (b. Asher), 33:204
Myers, Levy (New York), 27:51, 84
Myers, Levy (S.C.), 22:164; 27:482
Myers, M. (1), 27:51, 73, 356; 30:124
Myers, M. (2), 27:515
Myers, Manuel, 21:85, 101-5, 111-13, 116,
 118, 121-23, 132, 140, 147-52, 154-56,
 158-59, 168, 211; kosher meat, 25:47;
 27:41, 46, 51, 60-61, 66, 68, 70, 122, 131,
 135, 217, 242; Moses Michael Hays,
 35:291; 38:235; 38:332
Myers, Maria, 22:194
Myers, Mendel, 37:372-74, 377
Myers, Michael, 27:514; 32:127
Myers, Miriam, 27:122; 33:205
Myers, Miss, 27:78
Myers, Mrs., 27:43, 73, 254
Myers, Mordecai (Ga.), 27:483
Myers, Mordecai (New York), 21:162, 168;
 27:51, 84, 86-89, 214, 395, 398, 451;
 Naphtali Phillips correspondence, 27:396-
 97; picture, 28:xl
Myers, Mordecai (S.C.), 50:56
Myers, Mordecai (Va.), 26:174-77, 228
Myers, Moses, 46:421, 425
Myers, Moses (b. Asher), 27:152; 33:203
Myers, Moses (b. Meir), 27:155
Myers, Moses (New York), 21:159-60; 25:5;
 27:41, 61, 394, 462; 28:xxxiv; 40:127
Myers, Moses (S.C.), 22:154; 27:483; 48:10,
 13, 18, 180

Myers, Moses (Va.), 22:xiii; 27:483; 34:279;
 47:190; 50:30
Myers, Mrs. Moses, 48:13, 18
Myers, Moses A., 27:42, 462
Myers, Moses H., 27:80
Myers, Moses M., 27:145
Myers, Moses Mears, 33:205
Myers, Myer, Mears family, 33:203-7, 209-10
Myers, Myer (New York) (1), 21:45, 49, 51,
 53, 63, 70, 79-80, 85-88, 91, 93, 102-3,
 105, 107, 111-12, 116-17, 121, 129-32,
 134, 140-49, 157, 159-60, 184, 211;
 23:152, 157; 26:233; 27:28-29, 33, 38-39,
 41, 51, 55, 59, 61, 63, 71, 153, 155, 180,
 181, 253, 255, 299, 372, 462; 28:225;
 38:332; 50:37, 54, 57, 64; kosher meat,
 25:47
Myers, Myer (New York) (2), 27:323, 329
Myers, Myer (New York) (silversmith),
 27:383-84; 42:413, 417-18; 44:207; 45:50;
 46:420; "A New York Jewish Silversmith
 of the Eighteenth Century," 28:236-38;
 "Ritual Silver Made by Myer Myers,"
 43:1-9; 4:8-11
Myers, N., 26:187
Myers, Naphtali, 25:115
Myers, Naphtali Hart, 31:237
Myers, Naphtaly Hart, 21:49-51, 53, 60, 63,
 70, 81, 83, 88, 211, 220; 27:405, 450
Myers, Nathan, 33:204
Myers, Nathan, 26:181; 27:51
Myers, Rachel (Mrs. Michael Myers), 32:127
Myers, Rachel (nee Hays), 27:74, 112, 323,
 329-30
Myers, Rachel, 50:65
Myers, Rebecca (Mrs. Jacob), 22:194
Myers, Rebecca (b. Myer), 33:205
Myers, Riche, 27:241
Myers, Ritza, 33:205
Myers, Ritzel, 33:205
Myers, S. A., 27:58
Myers, Sally, 27:323, 329
Myers, Salomon, 26:187
Myers, Sam, 25:52
Myers, Samson, 27:51, 61, 152
Myers, Samson (b. Asher), 33:203, 205
Myers, Samson A., 25:123
Myers, Samuel (Charleston), 50:42, 57
Myers, Samuel (Md.), 26:188

Myers, Samuel (New York), 21:16, 20-21, 24, 165, 211; 27:42, 462; 28:xxxiv; 46:421; "The Judith Hays-Samuel Myers Marriage Contract," 38:149-50; (silversmith), 42:418
Myers, Samuel (Va.), 28:224; 34:279
Myers, Samuel H., 27:145
Myers, Sander, 25:117
Myers, Sara, 33:204
Myers, Sarah (Miss), 27:77, 330
Myers, Sarah (Mrs.), 27:112
Myers, Simon, 27:80, 111, 315
Myer, Mrs. Simon, 27:112
Myers, Sloe, 27:150, 162-68; 33:204, 207
Myers, Solomon, Mears family, 33:204-5

Myers, Solomon (New York), 21:8, 21, 27, 29, 31, 38, 40, 46, 56; 27:1, 168; 31:237; 38:235; naturalization, 37:373, 377, 386
Myers, Solomon (West Indies), 25:115-17
Myers, Soln. Aaron, 27:416
Myers, Solomon M., 27:42
Myers, T. Bailey, 27:451
Myers v. United States, 46:471-72
Myers, William, 22:194
Myerson, Goldie, 39:334
Myerston, M., 27:91
Myrdal, Gunnar, 45:9; 46:301
Mysell, Max, 50:237
Mysticism, Jewish historiography, 26:13
Mziat Arez ha-Hadashah, 22:125

N

Naar, Abraham, 44:227-28
Naar, Abraham de Jesouah, 44:230-31
Naar, Benjamin, 27:264; 44:229
Naar, David, 22:xxxiii; 29:122
Naar, Jacob, 44:227
Naar, Jacob de Abraham, 44:230
Naar, Jacob de Jeos, 27:23, 248; 44:231
Naar, Jeiosuah de Jacob, 44:233
Naar, Jeosuah de Jacob de Jeosuah, 44:232
Naar, Joshua, 27:120; 37:341, 343
Naar, Joshua ben Jacob, 22:170-71
Naar, Moses, 27:482
Naar, Sarah, 27:112
Nabaro, David, 21:63
Nabarro, Joseph Nunes, 25:114
Nachbin, Jacob, "The Jews of Portugal and Brazil," 32:xx
Nachman ben Moshe, 34:78, 95-96
Nadelman, Ludwig, 50:272
Nadich, Abraham, "An English Letter by a Russian Jew Mourning the Death of Abraham Lincoln," 50:248-50
Nadic, Judah, "General Dwight D. Eisenhower and the Displaced Jews," 42:415
Naftaly, Me., 27:1
Nagel, Charles, 34:201
Nahamias, Isaac, 42:237, 241, 254, 256, 281, 284, 387, 390, 395
Nahamias, Samuel, 33:96
Nahar, Mosseh de Eliau, 29:16
Nahmanides, Moses, 45:63; "Biographical Material concerning Nahmanides in the Spanish Archives," 28:xxiii
Nahmias, Eliau, 42:259, 278, 284-87, 292, 391, 395
Nahmias, Jacques Bey, 36:9
Nahum, Dr. Hayim, 39:439-40
Namias, Baruch, 23:183

Namias, Daniel, 23:183; 26:251
Namias, Manuel, 32:59
Namias, Moses, 42:259, 278
Namiaz, Daniel, 42:280, 395
"Nancy Lincoln Dreams," 50:268
Naphtali bar Menahem, 27:80
Naphtali, Isaac, 23:150; 25:42
Naphtali, Jacob, 21:198
Naphtalites, 37:355-59, 364, 366
Naphtaly ben Issac Hacohen, see: Jacobs, Gerrit
Naphtaly Bar Isrel a Cohen, see: Jacobs, Gerrit
Naphtaly, Rachel, 21:10, 20
Napoleon I, 25:73; 26:90, 96; 27:140, 333-34; 28:84, 186; 29:xxiv; 31:259; 32:1; 38:23; 39:162; 40:200; 43:50, 80, 176-78; 46:11; anti-Jewish decree, 42:159; "Jewish Rights at the Congresses of Vienna (1814-1815), and Aix-la-Chapelle (1818)," 26:vii, xv, 33-125; John Adams, 37:189, 199; "Napoleon and the Jews," 26:xiv; "Napoleonic Miscellanies," 26:xxxi; Napoleonic Sanhedrin, 22:xx-xxi, 235; 26:xiv, xxvii, 90, 128-29, 131, 268; 27:140, 482; 28:xii, xvii, 105, 108, 113; 29:xliii; 40:2; "The Napoleonic Sanhedrin and the Russian Government," 28:xxiii; 29:xliii; Palestine and Jews, 26:128-32, 156; Poland, 36:140; "A Preliminary Report on 'Napoleon and the Jews,'" 28:xv; and Sunday law, 25:137; synagogue art, 41:61-62, 68, 71
Napoleon III, 22:223; 37:425; 46:8, 97; "Jewish Disabilities in Balkans," 24:2-3; Mexico, 32:67-69, 76, 78, 82
Naquet, Alfred, 41:149, 162
Narai, Mr., 38:151
Narbeus, Issac, 37:340
Nare (family name), 37:384

Nare, Solomon, 37:373, 377, 386; 38:235
Nardoni Listy, 50:107
Narvaez, Panfilo de, 31:11-12
Nasatir, Abraham, 46:121
Nasci, Isaac, 22:26
Nasci, *see*: Nassy
Nash, Abner, 29:145
Nashville (Tenn.), religious observances, mid-nineteenth century, 37:36
Nassau, Johan Maurits van, 46:42-43; 50:74-75
Nassi, *see*: Nassy
Nassy, Blanche, 48:263
Nassy, D. D. J. C., 29:19
Nassy, David, 22:126; 27:481; 29:20; 34:159; 35:286; 42:308; Botany, 23:185; "The Epidemic of Yellow Fever," 23:xiii, 185-86; grant to settle, 32:15-19; *Lettre Politico-theologico-morale sur les Juifs*, 22:xviii, xxix, 25-38; 23:xiii, 185-86; 25:139; "An unrecorded pamphlet on the yellow fever epidemic in Philadelphia by David Nassy of Surinam, published November 26, 1793," 33:xviii
Nassy, David de Isaac, 44:254
Nassy, David Joseph Cohen, 34:xvii, 9
Nassy, Dr. D., 43:238
Nassy, Ishac, 25:138-39
Nassy, Ishak de, 32:9
Nassy, Joseph de Sem. C., 32:10-11
Nassy, Rachel Cotino, 48:263
Nassy, Samuel, 29:16; 42:308
Nassy, Samuel Jacob, 48:263
Nast, Thomas, 43:31
Nathan, Mr., 27:314
Nathan, a stranger, 27:91
Nathan, Mrs. (Canada), 27:80
Nathan, Abot de Rabbi, 25:179-83
Nathan, Abraham, 33:208
Nathan bar Naphtali, 27:80
Nathan, Benjamin, 21:212, 214-15; 27:115, 121, 166, 515; 28:293; 35:xix; 42:115, 121
Nathan Ben Saddi, *Chronicle*, 30:38-39
Nathan, Clara, 27:111, 166
Nathan, Clarence Seixas, 45:208; gifts, 26:xxxiv; 28:xxxix; necrology of, 31:xvi, 284-86; nomination committee, 26:xi
Nathan, Mrs. Clarence S., gift, 32:xxviii
Nathan, Deborah, 27:80, 277

Nathan, Edgar J., necrology of, 32:xvii; necrology of Frederick Nathan, 28:xv, 293-95
Nathan, Edgar J., Jr., 44:240; executive council, 47:200-201; 49:268; gift, 32:xxviii; necrology of Clarence Seixas Nathan, 31:xvi, 284-86
Nathan, Edgar Joshua, 49:59
Nathan, Elvira, 27:111, 166; 43:25
Nathan, Emily, 28:293
Nathan, Emily Grace, 27:112
Nathan, Ernesto, 28:21, 60-61
Nathan, Esther, 27:111, 166
Nathan family, 35:xviii; 43:253; 49:6
Nathan, Frederic, 49:186-87
Nathan, Frederick, necrology of, 28:xv, 293-95
Nathan, Mrs. Frederick, 37:203; gift, 33:xxxiii
Nathan, G., 21:171
Nathan, Geoffrey, 42:419
Nathan, Gershom, 21:215; 27:166; 31:285
Nathan, Grace, 21:xxiv; 31:xxxii; 34:xxi
Nathan, Grace (Miss), 27:111, 166
Nathan, Grace (nee Seixas), 27:122, 161-62, 368-69; "Some Letters of Grace Seixas Nathan, 1814-1821," 37:xxx, 203-11
Nathan, Grace Emily, 35:xix
Nathan, Gratz, 21:215; 27:389
Nathan, H. V., 30:341
Nathan, Henry, 50:133
Nathan, I., 38:49
Nathan, Isaac (Cumberland, Md.), 27:514
Nathan, Isaac (London), 27:518
Nathan, Isaac Mendes Seixas, 27:55, 75, 84, 111, 146, 162-63, 166, 173-74, 314
Nathan, Israel Robert, 27:166
Nathan, J. P., 37:420
Nathan, James, Jerusalem Temple, 27:501
Nathan, John, 27:80
Nathan, Jonathan, 21:213-14; 27:166, 389; 37:435; "Jonathan Nathan's Letters to Hamilton Fish, 1847-1857," 37:xxxiii
Nathan, Joseph, 25:123; 27:59, 253
Nathan, Judah, 31:284
Nathan, Julian, 40:263; gift, 35:xix
Nathan, Justine, 34:xxii
Nathan, Leah, 41:288
Nathan, Levi, 27:80
Nathan, Marks, Jewish Orphan Home (Chicago), 34:xxii

Nathan, Marvin, gift, 33:xxxiii
Nathan, Maud, 28:294; 46:431
Nathan, Mendez, 21:214
Nathan, Miriam, 27:111, 166
Nathan of Montpelier, 28:145
Nathan, Moses, 27:462; 50:39, 57
Nathan, Moses D., 27:253
Nathan, Moses N., 26:271; 27:519; 42:57;
    48:73-74; *Consecration Sermon*, 30:457;
    (ed.), *First Fruits of the West*, 30:383; (ed.),
    Jewish Monthly Magazine, 30:383; receipt
    book, 23:xvii; (trans.), *The Road to Faith*,
    30:359; *Sermon*, 30:376
Nathan br Moses, 21:55
Nathan, Myrtilla, 27:111, 166
Nathan, N., 22:88
Nathan, Paul, 40:403
Nathan, Rachel, 27:166
Nathan, Rachel Gratz, 27:xix
Nathan, Rebecca Washington, 27:111, 166
Nathan, Robert W., 21:215; 28:294; 37:203
Nathan, Rosalie Gomez, 31:285; 49:59; gift,
    35:xviii
Nathan, Rowena, 27:111, 166, 174
Nathan, Seixas, 21:xxiv, 162-63, 165, 168,
    212; 28:293; 37:205, 210; kosher meat,
    25:52, 57
Nathan, Simon, 21:147-52, 154-56, 158-60,
    168-69, 183, 212; 27:41, 51, 54, 61, 63-67,
    72, 75, 84, 86-87, 92, 161-62, 185, 241,
    374, 398, 461; 28:293; 29:145; 31:xxxii,
    285; 34:xxi, 110, 115; 35:xix; 37:203, 206;
    41:280, 291; 43:235; 50:37, 57; portrait of,
    42:416; "Simon Nathan's Important
    Services to the American Cause in the
    Revolution," 31:xvi
Nathan, Mrs. Simon, 41:291; 43:235; portrait
    of, 42:416
Nathan, Simon Mendes, 27:162, 166
Nathan, William N., executive council,
    47:200; 48:265-66
Nathan, Zipporah, 27:166
Nathan the Wise, 33:182; 45:22; 48:249
Nathans, Benja, 21:129, 132
Nathans, Isaac, 50:174
Nathans, Joseph, 21:147; 27:462
Nathans, Levy, 25:52, 57; 27:398
Nathans, Lyon, 21:61, 64; 27:462
Nathans, Nathan, 21:45, 48, 55; 50:154

Nathanson, Edward A., 42:419
Nathanson, Joseph Saul, 25:177
Nathanson, Josephine E., 29:186
Nation, The, 43:25; 45:70; 49:25
National Academy of Fine Arts, Lisbon,
    45:271
National Advisory Committee for the Study
    of Social Work Education, 47:232
National Advocate, 21:173, 229; 30:227, 229-
    30; 41:9, 204, 280, 293; 43:180, 186, 191;
    50:15; *Report of Trial, Miller vs. Noah*,
    30:209-10
National Anti-Slavery Standard, The, 42:131,
    133, 145, 150-53
National Archives, 39:220-21; 40:282; 43:72;
    48:3; Civil War, 50:269, 273-74, 289,
    323n, 325-30, 382; "Resources on
    American Jewish History in the National
    Archives," 47:186-95, 201
National Art Collections Fund, 31:291
National Association for the Advancement of
    Colored People, 46:288
National Association of Jewish Center
    Works, 38:336; 50:434
National Association of Manufacturers,
    41:311; 46:228
National Association of Social Workers,
    50:434
National Board of Trade, 25:153
National Catholic Welfare Conference,
    46:291, 316
National Children's Offering, 33:220
National Citizens Committee, 41:184; gift,
    22:xxxii
National Citizens Committee for United
    Nations, 47:232
National Civic Federation, 29:197; 40:9;
    41:321
National Committee on Foundations and
    Trusts for Community Welfare, 50:434
National Committee for the Relief of
    Sufferers by Russian Massacres, 49:189;
    gift, 31:xxxii
National Community Relations Advisory
    Council, 42:319-20, 322-324, 329; 48:144
National Conference of Catholic Charities,
    46:317
National Conference of Charities and
    Correction, 25:154; 26:282; 29:177; 37:300

National Conference of Christians and Jews, 46:294

National Conference of Jewish Communal Service, 50:434

National Conference of Jewish Social Welfare, 39:250, 253; "50th Anniversary of the National Conference of Jewish Social Welfare," 39:471

National Conference of Jews and Christians, 34:xix

National Conference for Prevention of War, 46:330

National Council of Boy Scouts of America, 50:434

National Council of Churches of Christ in America, 46:291, 350

National Council of Defense, 26:7

National Council of Jewish Federations, 45:242

National Council of Jewish Women, 34:207-9; 37:295-96, 301; 39:92-93; 42:3-4; 45:244; (New York section), 43:253

National Democratic Party (Endeks) (Poland), 39:164

National Farm School, 22:217; 31:293; gift, 34:xxii; "A unique institution; the history of the National Farm School," 34:xxv

National Federation of Temple Brotherhoods, 45:224

National Federation of Temple Sisterhoods, 40:47

National Foundation for Jewish Culture, 49:217

National Gallery of Canada, 50:273, 352, 360

National Gallery (London), 35:325

National Geographic Society, 31:259; 32:xvi

National Guaranty Insurance Co., 31:272

National Hebrew School, 33:157

National Hebrew School for Girls, 42:10

National Hillel Commission, 46:124

National Industrial Recovery Act, 47:195

National Intelligencer, 36:308; 48:16

National Jewish Cemetery, 41:379

National Jewish Hospital for Consumptives (Denver), 23:191; 25:124, 136; 29:157, 162; gifts, 34:xxii; 35:xxiv

National Jewish Immigration Council, 34:205

National Jewish Music Council, 47:232; 50:433-34

National Jewish Welfare Board, 38:7-10, 335-36, 343-44; 39:207-50, 289, 316-17, 386; 40:412; 41:357, 380; 42:89, 311-12; 44:243-44; 45:182, 193, 209-11; 46:167; 47:231; 49:151-52; 50:141, 431-33, 435; American Jewish Historical Society sponsors, 38:7-10; Samuel D. Gershovitz memorial, 50:425

National Jewish Youth Conference, 47:232

National Labor Relations Board, 41:335-36

National Liberal Immigration League, 39:436

National Lincoln Monument Association, 50:302

National Line, 45:89

National Mechanics Bank, Baltimore, 25:153

National Museum, 28:265; 47:85

National News, 50:107

National Origins Act of 1924, 49:73

National Records Management Council, 39:221

National Red Cross Relief, 33:217-18

National Reform Association, 40:96

National Refugee Service, 43:145

National Relief Commission, 41:366

National Relief Society, 33:219

National Religious Party, 49:273, 275

National Security League, 26:xxvii

National Socialist Party, and refugees, 45:221

National Social Welfare, Assembly, 47:232; 50:434

National Steamship Company (Liverpool), 45:83

National Union Catalog, 47:184-85

National Union for Jewish Rights of England, 49:193

National War Labor Board, 37:476

National Youth Administration, 46:161

Native Sons of the Golden West, 47:25

Nativism, 45:235; *Strangers in the Land: Patterns of American Nativism, 1860-1925,* reviewed, 45:217

Naturalization, 26:6; 36:119-26, 134-35; Aaron Lopez, 26:244-45; history, writing of, 46:185, 291, 317-19, 325, 329, 334-35; Isaac Elizur, 26:244-45; Naturalization Act (1740), 35:216; 46:31; (England), 27:482; Naturalization and Alien Acts of 1798, 49:131; "Naturalization Role of Jews of New York (1740-1759)," 37:xxx, 369-89

Nature of the Judicial Process, The, 49:12

Nauarro, Abraham, 26:251

Nauarro, Jaacob, 42:222, 225, 260, 275, 277, 281-83, 289-93, 391, 395

Nauarro, Moseh, 42:278, 395

Naumburg, Lazarus, 35:119

Nautical Almanac, 47:192

Naval Records and Library, office of, 39:2

Navaro, David d'Isaac Nunes, 29:36

Navaro, Israel, 27:394

Navarre, Diego Jose de, 27:471

Navarro, Aaron, 32:59; 33:97; 46:42

Navarro, Abraham, 46:42

Navarro, Daniel Lopes, 32:59

Navarro, Isaac, 21:21-26, 63, 72

Navarro, Jacob, 33:88, 97, 99; 46:42

Navarro, Kathleen, 26:251

Navarro, Manuel Gomez, 31:29

Navarro, Moizes, 33:97

Navarro, Moses, 33:62, 87, 98, 122; 44:83

Navarro, Moyses Moseh Nauarro, 46:41, 44

Navarro, Rebecah, 21:89, 91

Navigation Acts, 31:119; 46:28-31

Navom, Jahacob, 42:222

Navy in the Civil War: The Blockade and the Cruisers, The, 50:298

Navy's Bureau of Medicine and Surgery, 47:194

Nazis and Nazism, 33:11-13, 18; 36:xiv, 362-85; 42:320-322, 351, 446; 45:157-58, 227; 47:2, 176, 195; 49:73, 84, 88; 50:112, 147, 251; "American Jewry, The Refugees and Immigration Restriction (1932-1942)," 45:219-47; "The American Jews' Contribution toward Rescue in the Hitler Period," 45:265; anti-Semitism, 40:200-201; history, writing of, 46:292, 294, 313, 327, 348, 354, 376-77; propaganda, 39:228; "United States Policies on Palestine," 40:107-18

Nealon; Magee *v.*, 29:150

Neander, 28:xxxviii; 31:xxxi; autographs, 26:xxxv

Neanes, 24:19

Neave, Richard, 30:77

Nebraska, 23:58; Jewish local history, 49:227; "Jewish Settlement in Nebraska," 31:xxx

Necarsulmer, Henry, 31:xxxv; 32:xii; 34:258; gift, 32:xxvi

Necarsulmer, Mrs. Henry, gift, 35:xx

Necrology, "Jewish Obituary Notices in the *Gentleman's Magazine* (1731-1868)," 37:419-20

Nefutsoth Jehudah Synagogue (New Orleans), 38:64; 43:97; 44:112; Order of Service at Consecration of, 30:458

Negroes, 40:231, 329; 42:131-35; 45:9; anti-Negro sentiment, 1795-1800, 38:110, 112, 133-34; Hebrew prayer, 27:223-34; history, writing of, 46:268-70, 273-74, 279-81, 286-87, 292, 295-96, 329, 303-7, 424, 442; testimony of, 25:101; *see also*: Slavery

Neighborhood Centre, 31:287

Neighborhood House (Portland, Ore.), 37:296; (Richmond), 37:296; (St. Paul), 37:295

Neighborhood Playhouse, N.Y., 26:260

Neile, Francis, 32:24

Neill, Edward D., 42:368

Neilson, John, 26:257

Neiman & Marcus, 38:20

Neisner, Max, 50:313

Neistad, S., 49:270

Neisuler, Reuben, 29:65

Nell, William C., 46:269

Nelson, B., 29:129

Nelson, Horatio, 46:434

Nelson, M., 29:130

Nelson, Moses, 23:139

Nelto, Phineas, 23:155

Nemoy, Leon, 39:206; 45:139; "Henry Obookiah: The First Hawaiian Student of Hebrew," 39:190-92; "William Gottlieb Schauffler (1798-1883) and his editions of the Old Testament in Ladino," 35:xvi; "William Gottlieb Schauffler," 35:304-6

NEP, 42:445

Ner-Maarabi, 44:125

Nero, 28:135

Nesbit, Louis, "The Jewish Contribution to Argentine Literature," 39:470

Nesbitt, Arnold, 35:20, 22-23

Nesselroade, Count, 26:38, 82, 124; 28:118, 124; 40:299; 41:164

Nesson; Saltman *v.*, 25:135

Netherland-Portuguese-Israelite Congregation in Surinam, 32:10

Netherlands, 26:136, 219; 28:xli, 87, 113,
246; 29:xliii; *The Dutch in Brazil, 1624-
1654*, reviewed, 47:112-20, 209; Jews in
New Netherlands, 29:39, 41, 45-52; Polish
disabilities, 36:143-44; religious freedom,
26:34-35, 70-74
Neto, Ishac, 29:15
Netter, Charles, 37:90; 41:143, 162
Netter, Jacob Mordecai, "Jacob Mordecai
Netter, World Traveler: His Comments
on American Jewish Life," 47:196-99, 201
Netter, M. Charles, 24:30, 35-36, 47, 50, 65,
72-73; 29:84
Netter, Shlomo, 47:196, 199
Nettling, Mr., 27:254
Nettleton, Alfred Bayard, 40:256
Netto, Aharon, 50:76
Netto, Jeosua Nunes, 44:248
Netto, Ladisla, 27:470
Netto, Moseh, 42:279, 395
Netto, Moses, 44:83
Neture Karta, 49:273
Neubauer, Adolf, 25:180; 26:18; 28:274;
37:353-54
Neubauer, Alexander, "Joshua Seixas,
Alexander Neubauer and the early
Mormon church," 33:xxv
Neubauer, Charles, 47:55
Neubauer, F. A., 45:156
Neuberger, L., 29:134
Neuberger, David, 41:256
Neuberger, Mayer, 41:265
Neuberger, Regine, 41:256
Neubert, Caroline, 32:124
Neue Post, Die, 48:132
Neue Warheit, 33:129
Neue Zeitung (Milwaukee), 41:210
Neuhauser, Julius, 41:258
Neuhorne, 39:180
Neuman, Abraham A., 22:vii, xxi; 23:103;
28:128; 37:iv; 40:405-6, 414; 42:90, 467;
43:70, 238, 248; 47:200; 48:194; Adler
biography, 37:452; "Biographical Material
concerning Nahmanides in the Spanish
Archives," 28:xxiii; "A Description of the
Records of the Congregation Mikva Israel
of Philadelphia," 32:xii; "The Economic
Condition of the Jews of Spain," 23:xiv;
"Education Among the Jews in Spain,"

25:xiv; essay contest, 38:vi, 78: 39:vi;
executive council, 29:xiv; 31:xvi; "The
Jewish Courts of Mediaeval Spain,"
22:xxix; *Landmarks and Goals: Historical
Studies and Addresses*, reviewed, 44:64-66;
Mikve Israel Congregation documents,
22:xxii; "Napoleon and the Jews," 26:xiv;
Napoleon and Sanhedrin, 22:xx; 26:xxvii;
"Napoleonic Miscellanies," 26:xxxi;
necrology of Abraham Simon Wolf
Rosenbach, 42:415, 456-60; nomination
committee, 25:xi; 26:xi; "A Note on Haym
Salomon," 37:xxxi; "A Preliminary Report
on 'Napoleon and the Jews,' " 28:xv;
presides, 39:471; "Raising the Curtain of
History," 43:151-58; recording secretary,
32:xii, xix; 33:xi, xvii, xix, xxv; 34:xiii; 35:ix-
xvi; 37:xxix, xxxii, xxxiv, 38:341, 344;
"Some Phases of the Conditions of the
Jews in Spain during the 13th and 14th
Centuries," 22:xviii, 61-70; "The Spanish
Argument for the Jewish Origin of
Columbus," 29:xv; vice-president, 38:346;
39:469; 40:406; 41:387; 42:414; 43:230;
44:241; 45:264; 46:492; 48:265; 49:268;
50:426; "Visions and Visionaries in Jewish
History," 47:134-39, 200
Neuman, Franz L., 46:346
Neuman, J. F., 26:239
Neuman, Lee H., death, 37:xii
Newman, Morris, 45:162
Neuman, Rev., 40:186
Neumann, Alfred, 35:273
Neumann, August, 41:246, 254
Neumann, Emanuel, 33:153; (foreword), *The
Zionist Idea: A Historical Analysis and Reader*,
reviewed, 49:140-42
Neumann, Joshua N., "Some Eighteenth
Century American Jewish Letters," 34:75-
106
Neumann, Rudolf, 38:42
Neumark, David, 39:451, 465; 40:43, 45, 48,
50; "Philosophy of the Bible," 28:xxxviii
Neumark, S. E., 38:73
Neurath, Konstantin von, 36:375
Neusner, J. Jacob, "Anglo-Jewish Influence in
the Development of American Jewish
Life," 44:242; books reviewed by, 47:60;
50:145-46; "The Impact of Immigration

and Philanthropy Upon the Boston Jewish
Community (1880-1914)," 46:71-85;
49:225; "Philanthropy and the Rise of the
Jewish Community of Boston, 1880-1914,"
44:240
Neustadt, Isaac Elchanan, 42:13
Neustadt, Max, 50:314
Neustadtel, 38:197
Neustadtl, Isaac, 47:48, 50
Neustadtl, Nathan E., 47:53, 111
Neutra, Richard, 46:114
Neuzeit, 33:240
Nevada, Jewish local history, 49:227
Nevay Shalem Congregation (Surinam),
27:408, centennial, 27:228
Neve Salom Congregation (Amsterdam),
42:225; (Paramaribo), 48:262, 264
Neve Sedek u Mehil Sedaca, 44:222
Nevie Shalom Congregation (Surinam),
21:xxiii
Nevin, John W., *Summary of Biblical
Antiquities*, 30:449
Nevins, Allan, 46:126; 49:137, 155, 216, 263-
64; Civil War, 50:260, 268, 270, 401; "The
Essence of Biography—Character Study,"
46:433-39; "The Future of Israel," 46:130;
"History of the Bank of New York,"
34:xxv; history, writing of, 46:150, 210,
442-43, 445
Nevis, 23:149, 157-58; Sephardic Jews,
29:37-38
New Almaden case, 38:155-56
New Almaden Company, 23:124-25
New Amsterdam, 29:31, 39, 41-42, 45, 47,
51; 44:205, 211, 213; "The Exodus from
Brasil and Arrival in New Amsterdam of
the Jewish Pilgrim Fathers, 1654," 44:80-
97, 255; Jews in, 26:5, 9; 31:4; records,
29:xl
New Amsterdam Eye and Ear Infirmary,
40:164
Newark (N.J.), religious observances, mid-
nineteenth century, 37:37
Newark Institute of Arts and Sciences, 29:183
Newark Museum, 37:456; gift, 34:xxxvi;
"Louis Bamberger," 34:xxvi
Newark Museum Association, 29:183
Newberger, G., 27:514
Newberry, Library of Chicago, 39:309

Newbold, 22:82, 85
Newbold, John, 27:248
New Bowery burial ground, 38:52; 40:409;
44:76; "What We Learn from the
Tombstones in the New Bowery
Cemetery," 32:xiii
New Brunswick (N.J.), religious observances,
mid-nineteenth century, 37:37
New Brunswick-Highland Park, N.J., United
Jewish Appeal, contribution, 37:xxviii
Newburger, Carrie, 26:283
Newburger, Frank L., death, 37:xii
Newburger, Hannah, gift, 34:xxi
Newburger, Henderson & Loeb, 28:297
Newburger, Joseph E., 34:xxi; necrology of,
33:xii
Newburger, Morris, necrology, 26:xxx;
28:295-98
Newburgh (N.Y.), religious observances,
mid-nineteenth century, 37:37
"New Colossus, The," 39:325
Newcorn, William, 34:229
New Deal, 41:298, 308-10, 325, 329-30, 354
New England, *Ancestors and Immigrants: A
Changing New England Tradition*, reviewed,
46:127-29; "The Hebraic Background of
Puritanism," 47:140-53, 200; Jewish
population (1790), 50:25-27, 34, 36;
"Mosaic Law and Common Law in Early
New England," 29:xiv
New England Commonwealth, 40:4
New Era Club (New York), 37:294-95
New Era Illustrated Magazine, The, 33:26-27
Newfield, Morris, death, 37:xii
Newgass, Benjamin, 28:309
New Hampshire, emancipation, 47:128
New Haven Colony Code, 46:23
New Haven (Conn.), Jewish Welfare Fund,
contribution, 37:xxviii; religious
observances, mid-nineteenth century,
37:36
Newhouse, Grace, 31:277
Newhouse, Henry, 29:133
Newhouse, Joseph, 31:170
New Jersey, 25:134; colonies, 48:92-99;
disabilities, "Anglo-Jewish Legal Cases,"
25:134-38; Jewish local history, 49:228;
Jews in law and medicine, 22:147; "Jews in
Middlesex County, New Jersey," 33:251-54

New Jersey Federation of Y. W. H. A.'s, 37:284, 306
New Jersey Historical Society, 26:ix; 37:456
New Leader, 41:330
New Light Congregational churches, 47:152
New London (Conn.), *A Goodly Heritage: The Story of the Jewish Community of New London, 1860-1955*, 49:219; United Jewish Appeal, contribution, 37:xxviii
New London River Company, 48:172
Newman Bros., 40:247
Newman, Harriet, 22:194
Newman, Ignatz, 35:307
Newman, Jacob, 37:307
Newman, Joshua, 25:113
Newman, Leopold C., 29:123
Newman, Louis I., 29:169; 34:231; 35:234; 39:336; "Albert M. Bender and Fine Printing in Northern California," 39:470; "The Body of Liberties," 29:xiv; books reviewed by, 39:333-35; 44:64-66; "The Cornerstone Box of the Old Temple Emanu-El of San Francisco; New Light on Pacific Coast Jewry, 1849-1864," 32:xiii-xiv; executive council, 41:388; 44:241; "Hebraic Aspects of the Legislation of Puritan New England," 28:xxxiii; "Jewish Items in 'Select Cases of the Mayor's Court of New York City, 1674-1784,' " 34:xiv; "The Jewish University Idea in Early American Jewish Education," 29:xxix; "The Life of David Eckstein, American Consul at Amsterdam, 1878-1890," 34:xiv; "Moses His Judicials," 29:xiv; necrology of Daniel Peixotto Hays, 29:xxxvi, 167-69; necrology of Martin A. Meyer, 29:xxix, 179-81; "Solomon Roubin, Cataloguer of the Sutro Hebrew MSS. in the San Francisco Public Library," 32:xiii; "The True Origin of the Phrase: 'Hebraic Mortar Cemented the Foundation of American Democracy,' " 39:470
Newman, Miss, 48:27
Newman, Ralph C., Civil War, 50:270-71, 275, 340, 399, 401
Newman, Selig, *The Challenge Accepted*, 30:457-58
Newmark, Abraham, 31:289
Newmark, Celie, 31:289

Newmark, Harris, 42:423; "References to Jews in Harris Newmark's 'Sixty Years in Southern California,' " 26:xiv
Newmark, Marco, 42:420-22; 46:120-22
Newmarket, battle of, 28:2
New Mexico, 25:22; Jewish local history, 49:228; Masonry, 25:114; "Recollections of Early Days in New Mexico, and the Beginning of Temple Albert of Albuquerque," 29:xxx
Newmin, Augustus, 38:90
New Netherland, Jewish migration, 29:39-52
New Odessa colony, 38:246, 307-8; 40:245, 247-48, 259; 48:89-93
New Orleans, 23:5, 18, 88; 26:198-99, 275; Battle of, 23:x; 25:xv; Civil War, 50:279, 317, 320, 349-50, 368-69; "Early Jewish Philanthropy in New Orleans," 49:222; "Home Rule," 26:275; "A Note on the Early History of the Touro Synagogue in New Orleans," 32:xiii; Proceedings of the New-Orleans Commercial Library Society, 30:312; public library, 50:273; religious observances, mid-nineteenth century, 37:35
New Orleans committee, 40:247
New Orleans Cotton Exchange, 28:309
New Orleans Dry Dock and Shipbuilding Company, 28:309
New Orleans Grays, 46:102, 108
New Orleans Railway & Light Co., 28:309
New Orleans, Shanari-Chasset, 30:252-53
New Orleans Times, 47:56
New Orleans Times-Democrat, 41:185
New Orleans Times-Picayune, 31:294
New Palestine Book Service, gift, 32:xxvi
New Park Theatre, New York, 33:185, 191
Newport (R.I.), 26:174, 177, 192, 244, 245; address to George Washington, 27:xvi, 217-20; cemetery at, 22:xxxiii; 31:77; colonial congregations, 28:xxvi; 32:xxv; "Descriptive Index of Aaron Lopez Material at the Newport Historical Society," 49:236; early Jews, 25:131; "The First Settlement of the Jews in Newport," 34:1-10; George Washington address to, 22:xx; Jewish Community Fund, contribution, 37:xxviii; "Jewish Merchants of Newport in Pre-Revolutionary Days,"

31:xxx; "A Jewish Shipowner of Newport, R. I., in 1705," 26:xxxi; religious observances, mid-nineteenth century, 37:35; synagogue, 22:127-28; 23:90, 166, 172; 28:237, 299; 39:246-47; 43:5; "Touro Street in Newport, Rhode Island," 45:265; "The Touro Synagogue: Aspects of the Missing Half-Century of its History (1850-1900), 38:57-76; 49:236

Newport Historical Society, 37:153-69; 38:57; 46:420

Newport Mercury, 38:47

Newspapers, Canadian Jewish, 50:137; Czech, 50:106-7; Jewish, 30:iv; "References of Jewish Interest in the Newspapers of the American Revolution (1761-1789): New York and Massachusetts," 23:xiv; Yiddish, 45:185; 49:92

Newstadt, Louis, 29:134

New Theatre, Philadelphia, 33:182

Newton, A. Edward, 35:266

Newton, John, 35:266

Newton, Simon, 35:291

New West End Synagogue, 31:291

New York, "Albert Edward Henschel and His Connection with the Creation of the Greater New York," 38:50-52; "Anglo-Jewish Legal Cases," 25:135-36, 138; Board of Education, 22:226; colonial congregations, 28:xxvi; colonial settlement of Jews, 26:5-6; Common Council, 27:395-96; early Jewish cemeteries, 27:265-78; early Jews, 25:131; emancipation, 47:128; "The Exodus From Brazil and Arrival in New Amsterdam of the Jewish Pilgrim Fathers, 1654," 44:80-97, 255; 49:229; "The Gratz Papers," 23:3-4; "History of the State of New York," 34:xix; Jewish cemetery, 22:162; Jewish community, 31:257; Jewish population (1790), 50:27-28, 34; "The Jewish Question in New York City (1902-1903)," 49:90-136, 271; Jewish local history, 49:229-33, 260, 262; Jews in law and medicine, 22:150-52, 157, 160-62; "Jews Who Died of Yellow Fever in the Epidemic in New York in 1798," 25:xii, 123; Masonry, 22:182; "The Minutes of the Common Council of the City of New York,

1784-1831," 33:xxxii; Negro conspiracy, 27:384-86; "New York Chooses a Chief Rabbi," 44:129-98; "The New York Synagogue in 1812," 25:xiii, 131-32; oath by magistracy of, 27:379; "A Portrait of Ethnic Politics," 50:202-38; "The Question of the Kosher Meat Supply in New York in 1813: with a Sketch of Earlier Conditions," 25:vii, xii, 31-62; "References of Jewish Interest in the Newspapers of the American Revolution (1761-1789): New York and Massachusetts," 23:xiv; religious observances, mid-nineteenth century, 37:35; religious societies, incorporation, 30:300; "A Revised List of the Hazanim in New York City in the Eighteenth Century," 25:xiii; "Some New York Jewish Patriots," 26:237-39; "Wills of Early Jewish Settlers in New York," 23:vii, 147-61

New York Academy of Medicine, 32:xxvi; 42:116, 118; 45:189

New York Academy of Political Sciences, 28:308

New York Academy of Sciences, 22:225

New York Aid Society, 40:238

New York Almanack, 30:387-88

New York American, 26:278

New York and New Jersey Bridge Commission, 38:51

New York Athletic Club, 49:103

New York Atlas, 43:77

New York Board of Jewish Ministers, 29:156; 35:318

New York Board of Rabbis, 47:221

New York Board of Trade & Transportation, 31:272

New York Central Railroad, 49:184

New York Chamber of Commerce, 21:xvi; 23:84, 174; 28:307; 45:65

New York Chapter of the Daughters of Zion, 49:167

New York City Dispensary, 26:223; 27:344

New York Federation of Women's Clubs, 31:259

New York City Jewish Theatre of the Air, 47:192

New York City Young Women's Hebrew Association, 37:274, 277

New York College, 22:129

New York College of Physicians and
Surgeons, 22:162; 45:188
New York Commercial Advertiser, 32:129
New York commercial tercentenary (1914),
23:x
New York Committee, 40:247; 48:45, 96
New York Committee of the Alliance
Israelite, 47:82
New York Congregation (1795), 22:162
New York Cotton Exchange, 32:129
New York County Lawyer's Association,
26:288; 45:191, 205; 47:223; 49:56
New York County Medical Society, 26:222-
23, 225-26
New York Critic, 39:325
New York Daily Tribune, 41:48; 43:25-26;
45:250-51; 46:161; 50:288, 302, 341, 385
New York Educational Alliance, 37:299
New York Electoral College, 50:345
New York Electric Society, 22:225
New York Enquirer, 27:158
New York Evening Call, 50:204, 206-7
New York Evening Journal, 39:421
New York Evening Post, 29:200; 32:39, 41, 43;
39:428; 40:150; 43:11-13, 23, 25, 28, 30,
33, 35, 78, 80, 186; 44:161; 48:155; 50:391
New York Evening Star, 39:48
New York Express, 49:25
New York Factory Commission, 40:173
New York Federation, 43:146
New York Free School, 27:92-94
New York Gazette, 22:161; 38:47
New York Gazette and Weekly Post Boy, 26:237
New York Health Department, 40:173
New York Hebrew Aid Society, 40:226
New York Hebrew Benevolent Society,
38:182
New York Hebrew Emigrant Aid Society,
31:274; 41:127-35, 137, 139, 145-46, 153,
155; 46:73
New York Hebrew Institute, 37:274
New York *Hebrew Leader*, 46:10
New York Hebrew Sheltering Guardian
Society, 37:233
New York Hebrew Technical Institute,
37:288
New York Herald, 21:229; 28:4; 33:216;
34:147; 40:233-34; 41:19; 43:81-82, 108-

12; 44:131, 150-51, 153, 155, 173; 45:251;
47:4; 49:25; 50:17, 400
New-York Historical Society, 23:147; 26:221,
237; 28:251; 29:xliii; 34:267; 35:172, 314;
38:51; 40:405, 411; 41:35; 45:57, 63-64,
128, 260; 50:285; *Dictionary of Artists in
America*, 50:387; *Quarterly Bulletin*, 34:270
New York Hospital, 42:114; 45:188
New York Illustrated News, 34:144, 147
New York Inquirer, The, 21:229
New York Journal, 26:278; 35:309-10; 39:428
New York Journal or General Advertiser, 22:39,
41
New York Law Journal, The, 29:149-53
New York Ledger, 46:7
New York Magazine or Literary Repository,
49:52
New York Mayor's Committee on National
Defense, 47:223
New York Medical College, 45:189
New York Medical and Physical Journal, The,
26:221-222, 227
New York Mercury, 42:77
New York Mirror, 32:44; 39:136
New York Oratorio Society, 28:308
New York Public Library, 23:19, 97, 176,
185; 25:112; 26:176, 236, 242, 268;
29:163-64; 30:vi; 33:131; 34:153; 35:313;
37:12, 57, 225; 38:187; 39:309; 45:61-63,
93, 151-53, 185, 199; 47:216-17, 219-22,
226; 50:70, 269, 271, 273, 275, 312; gifts,
22:xxxv; 33:xxxii; 34:xxiv; 35:xx
New York Public Service Commission, 40:9
New York Red Cross, 33:216
New York Relief Association, 38:247
New York Relief Society, 39:111
New York Republican County Committee,
29:174
New York Samaritan Society, 22:97
New York Society for the Information and
Assistance of Persons Emigrating from
Foreign Countries, 38:116
New York Star, 32:129
New York State Bar Association, 28:285;
49:56
New York State Commission Against
Discrimination, 47:233
New York State Department of Mental
Hygiene, 47:216

New York State Historical Association, 32:133; 34:xix
New York State Library, 28:252; 46:186
New York Stock Exchange, 21:xvi; 23:171; 28:294; 32:102, 105, 109
New York Sun, 33:217; 34:267; 39:241, 325; 41:211; 42:429; 43:11, 13-14, 18, 34-35; 44:154, 156, 159; 48:124-25; 49:25
New York Supreme Court, 37:479
New York Symphony Society, 28:308
New York Teachers' Association, 28:311
New York Theater Club, 31:259
New York Times, The, 26:278; 28:xii; 31:294; 33:18; 38:32; 39:164, 461; 40:70; 41:182, 185; 42:119, 371; 45:28, 191, 220; 46:9, 161; 47:51, 151, 223; 49:10, 199-200; 50:204, 206-7; Zionism, 45:41, 43, 45
New York Times Review of Books, The, 33:30
New York Tribune, 41:182; 43:119; 44:99; 45:28, 185; 47:11; 49:25
New York United Hebrew Charities, 37:233; 49:61
New York University, 22:225; 28:252; 31:265-66; 41:19; 45:169, 185; 46:210; 47:21, 219; 49:11, 25; 50:275, 330, 366; "Judaica and Hebraica Collection in College Libraries," 45:141-42
New York Weekly Journal, 22:161; 42:77
New York Welcome House, 37:294
New York World, 34:281; 40:185; 43:93, 117; 49:25, 181; 50:385
New Yorke, 25:44
New-Yorker, The, 39:136
New-Yorker Staats-Zeitung, 35:287; 44:149
New Yorker Yiddisher Zeitung, 35:55
New York's Gold and Silversmiths' Society, 43:1
New Zealand Exhibition, 31:290
Neyman, Clinton, 46:124
Neyra, Joseph Attias de, 27:248
Ngar, Fong Ping, 34:207
Nhul, Jacob Moses Aaron, 50:76
Nicaragua, 31:212, 294; 46:483
Nicator, 26:169
Nicolai, 26:96, 100; 28:92
Nicholas I, 28:119; 29:182; 35:39-40, 43; 36:394, 401; 39:155; 41:164, 196; 46:197; "The Upward Struggle of the Cause of Secular Education in Russian Jewry in the Reigns of Alexander I and Nicholas I," 28:xv
Nicholas II (czar), 34:282; 36:274; 41:151, 175-76
Nicholas II (pope), 21:241; 28:142
Nicholas IV (pope), 28:145-46
Nicholas V (pope), 28:158-59
Nicholas, Richard, 21:9, 17
Nicolay, John George, 46:434
Nicolay, M., 43:119
Nichols, 37:133
Nichols, Anne, 40:357
Nichols, Charles L., 32:30
Nichols Engineering Hall, 50:384
Nichols, John, 35:34
Nichols, Richard, 23:151, 159
Nicholson, John, 33:2; 48:2-3
Nidhe Israel Congregation (Baltimore), 48:210, 242
Nidhi Israel Congregation (Barbados), 26:251, 254-55; 27:463; 31:243; 34:275-76; 42:225; *Consecration Service*, 30:284
Niebuhr, Reinhold, 22:53
Niedielnaya Khronika Voskhoda, 38:242
Niedlander, F., 29:135
Nierel, Izydor, 39:151
Nies, Maniel Gonsaluns de, 33:47
Nieto, Abraham H., 35:319; 38:67; necrology of, 28:xxii
Nieto, David, 27:482; 42:440
Nieto, David H., 38:72
Nieto, Isaac, 35:230
Nieto, Rev., 21:77
Nieuburgh, 33:110-11
Nieuhoff, John, 44:9-10; 46:46
Nieuport, 29:48
Niger, Samuel, 46:397
Nightingale, Florence, 33:212
Nihell, Edmund, 23:160
Nijhoff, Martinus, 26:243
Nijs, Isaac Jan, 33:50
Niles, Hezekiah, *Niles' Weekly Register on the Jews*, 50:3-22
Niles' Weekly Register, "American Jewish Items in *Niles Weekly Register*, 1811-1849," 49:268
Nilus, Saint, 28:140-41
"Nineteen Letters", 28:71
Nineteenth Century Club, 43:33

Nissan, Abraham, 47:196, 198
Nissan, David, 27:60
Nissan, Touroff, 33:161
Nissen, Johan Peter, 44:115-16, 118
Nitchie, 25:56
Niverville, Joseph, 23:139
Niwicki, Ladislas, 41:146
Noah Benevolent Society, 37:47
Noah, Catherine Glosenger, 27:277
Noah, Daniel, 41:9
Noah, Daniel Jackson, 27:277
Noah, E., 27:60
Noah, Elias, 27:42, 45, 51, 67, 84, 87
Noah, Frances, 27:491
Noah, Jacob J., 27:509
Noah, L., 26:188
Noah, Manl, 21:142
Noah, Manuel (Manos), 27:43, 253, 491
Noah, Manuel M., 22:158; 32:102; 35:137; 39:242; 41:2; 42:434; 50:39, 57
Noah, Mrs. Manuel, 42:434
Noah, Mary A., 40:58
Noah, Michael William, 46:164
Noah, Miss, 32:102
Noah, Mordecai Manuel, 21:xi, xx, 166-71, 200, 204, 207, 214; 22:xxiii, 81, 83; 23:120, 178; 26:180, 229, 270; 27:xiii, 55, 107, 119, 158, 236, 257, 275, 277, 306, 314, 394, 400-401, 483, 499, 504, 509; 28:xxxiv, xxxviii; 29:206; 30:404; 32:3, 40; 33:xxix, 24, 197; 34:126-28, 173, 175-76, 273, 279; 35:128, 284; 37:208-9, 387; 40:58, 405; 41:87, 227, 277, 280, 283, 292; 42:152, 434; 46:6, 10; 48:200; 50:57, 69; Ararat, 40:363; 48:100-101; assault, 30:249, 251; autograph letter, 22:xxxv; "Barn-Burners," 30:440; Broadside, 30:249, 251; Correspondence, 30:167, 169-70; correspondence with President Martin Van Buren, 22:71-73; Discourse of Indians Being Descendants of Lost Tribes, 30:315-17; Discourse on the Restoration of the Jews, 30:405-6; "The Fortress of Sorrento," 26:xxxv: 30:136-37; "Gleanings from a Gathered Harvest," 29:xli; 30:405, 407; Grand Island Address, 21:x, xx-xxi, 229-52; Grand Island project, 22:131; "The Grecian Captive," 26:xxxv; 30:202, 204; history, writing of, 46:158, 161, 166, 181,

275, 383-84, 440-42; John Adams, 36:42; K. K. Shearith Israel, dedication, 30:179, 181; A Letter Addressed to Southern Delegates, 30:440; letters, 23:xviii; Lyons collection, 27:522-23; Marion, 30:205-6; "Mordecai Manuel Noah: A Centenary Evaluation," 40:407; 41:1-26; "Mordecai M. Noah, His Life and Work, from the Jewish Point of View," 26:xv; "New Light on the Diplomatic Career of Major Mordecai M. Noah," 44:242; Niles' Weekly Register, 50:8, 12, 14-17; "Noah's Ararat-Jewish State in its Historical Setting," 41:390; 43:170-91; Oration, 30:174-75; origin of Indians, 22:xxxv; Polish emigrants, 39:145; Port of New York, 22:xxxiii; portrait, 43:232; "References to M. M. Noah and A. Phillips, 1821-1822, in 'The theatrical life of Joe Cowell, Comedian, written by himself,' " 33:xvii; Report of Trial, Miller vs. Noah, 30:208-9; She Would Be a Soldier, 30:185-86; Statement Relative to Henry Eckford, 30:227, 229-30; Travels in England, France, Etc., 30:185, 187; "An unknown Zionist Rhode Island project of Mordecai Manuel Noah," 33:xviii; Uriah Phillips Levy, 39:3, 58; The Wandering Boys, 30:193, 195
Noah, Rebecca, 27:112, 277
Noah, Robert L., gift, 33:xxxi
Noah, Samuel, 26:180-81
Noah, Uriah, 27:55, 57
Noah, Mrs. William, 27:112
Noah, William Glosenger, 27:277; 40:58
Noah's Weekly Messenger, 27:159
Nobel, Shlomo, 48:266; 49:137; Civil War, 50:260, 268, 270-71, 298
Noble, Thomas S., 28:31
Noble Women of the North, 50:396
Nobles, Milton, 40:351-52
Noel, Madame, 27:401
Noemi, A., 39:101-2
Nogueira, Ishac Pinheiro, 29:35
Noiret, Jeronimias, 33:50
Noiseux, François, 23:138
Nolde, 40:320
Nöldeke, Theodor, 33:238
Nones, Aaron, 27:45
Nones, A. B., 21:171

Nones, Abraham, 26:182; 46:10
Nones, Abraham B., 26:182
Nones, B., 27:58
Nones, Benjamin, 27:42, 80, 229, 253, 494-
95; 30:136; 37:345; 43:236; 44:254; 46:2;
50:29, 332; anti-Semitism, 38:109, 132-34,
137
Nones, Benjamin, & Co., 47:205
Nones, Catherine Kilah, 27:112
Nones, Cohen, 46:10
Nones, David, 27:120
Nones (family name), 43:253
Nones, Hava, 27:112
Nones, I. B., 27:494
Nones, Jacob, 27:80
Nones, Jean Batiste, 46:10
Nones, Joseph, 21:xxvii
Nones, Joseph B., 26:185, 194; 27:495-96;
32:xxviii, 4; 39:34; "Joseph B. Nones: The
Affable Midshipman," 46:1-19; "The
Career of Joseph B. Nones," 42:415
Nones, Moses, 27:45
Nones, Raphael, 46:10
Nones, Raphael de, 46:2
Non-Governmental Organizations of the
United Nations, 50:434
Non-importation resolutions (1765), 22:xxxv,
139, 152; 23:5-6, 11; 28:294; 29:5; 31:284;
34:273; 37:209, 348; 38:96; 39:3; 41:292;
42:434; 45:65; "The Jewish Signers of the
Non-Importation Agreement of 1765,"
26:236-37; "Some New York Jewish
Patriots," 26:237-39
Noot, M., 38:68; 40:239
Noot, Rev., 27:504
Noot, S. C., 38:68
Nordamerikanische Kolonisationsgesellschaft, Die,
43:177
Nordau, Max, 35:58-59; 39:203; 40:388;
47:167
Norden, Frederick L., 41:61
Norden, Margaret Kanof, "A Bibliography of
the Writings of Lee Max Friedman,"
50:427
Nordheimer, "The Nordheimers of
Toronto," 26:xxxi
Nordheimer, Isaac, 30:341; A Critical
Grammar of the Hebrew Language, 27:215;
30:325, 327-28, 367, 369; Grammatical

Analysis, 30:328; "Isaac Nordheimer,
Orientalist," 28:xvi
Nördlinger, Fredrick, 29:130
Nördlinger, Isaac, 41:246
Nördlinger, Isak, 41:254, 256
Nördlinger, Isak Hirsch, 41:265
Nördlinger, Jakob, 41:258
Nördlinger, Lazarus, 41:258
Nordman, M., 36:316, 319
Norfolk, Duke of, 35:36
Norfolk (Va.), 26:185-86; Moses Myers,
22:xiii, religious observances, mid-
nineteenth century, 37:36
Norfolk Hebrew & English Literary
Institute, 29:133
Norfolk Herald, 39:48
Norman (surgeon), 22:163
Norris, Matthew, 42:80-81
Norris, Sarah P., 50:159
North, Lord Frederick, 28:254; 31:44; 38:98-
99; "Hebraic Elements in Early American
Culture: a) Lord North and the Book of
Esther; b) The College of Rhode Island
Saves Some Books," 37:xxxv
North American, 50:246
North American Phalanx, 50:198
North American Relief Society, 47:224
North American Review, The, 29:139; 32:37;
45:22-23, 25; 50:210
North Carolina, 46:33; Civil War, 50:280,
295, 304, 357, 378; disabilities, 29:76;
49:23; Jews in law and medicine, 22:149;
"Jews in North Carolina in Colonial and
Revolutionary Times" (note), 22:183, 188;
"The Jews of North Carolina Prior to
1800," 29:vii, xxxvi, 137-48; religious
disability, 29:105; Religious Liberty and
Board of Delegates of American Israelites,
29:81-82
North Carolina, University of, 37:471
North London Synagogue, 42:441
Northwest Side Branch of the Jewish People's
Institute (Chicago), 37:294
North River Steamboat, 48:172
Northwest Territory, 43:162
Northwestern Bible Institute, 47:25
Northwestern University, 37:476; 46:210
Norton, A. O., 35:156, 169
Norton, Charles Eliot, 35:169

Norton, Joshua Abraham, 37:439
Norton, M., 29:130
Norton, Martha, 27:71
Norton, S. Tilden, 42:422; 46:121-22
Norwich (Conn.), "The Jew in Norwich: A
Century of Jewish Life," 49:219; religious
observances, mid-nineteenth century,
37:37
Nossing, Alfred, 47:171
Notable American Women, 1607-1950, 48:202,
267
*Note on Solomon Nunes Carvalho and His
Portrait of Abraham Lincoln, A*, 50:383
Nothangel, 33:238
Notkin, Nathan, 28:114
Nott, Josiah C., *Chronology, Ancient and
Scriptural*, 30:458; *Physical History of the
Jewish Race*, 30:458; *Two Lectures*, 30:449
Noveno, Aaron, 33:96
Novoye Vremya, 41:181-82, 192; 46:92
Novogrodsky, Irving, 33:161
Noyes, 25:109
Noyes, Mr. (Calif.), 44:47
Noyes, Eli, *A Hebrew Reader*, 30:417-18
Noyes, George Rapell, *New Translation of the
Book of Job*, 30:328; *New Translation of the
Book of Psalms*, 30:417; *A New Translation of
the Hebrew Prophets*, 30:288, 317
Nugée, George, 26:163
Nugent, John, 44:32
Numismatic and Antiquarian Society of
Philadelphia, 31:256
Numpo, Rabi, 27:91
Nunes, 22:189
Nunes, A. J., 21:164
Nunes, Abraham, 27:296; 28:239; 37:336
Nunes, Abraham Israel, 32:59
Nunes, Abm. de Leaõ, 22:170
Nunes, Benjamin (1), 25:116
Nunes, Benjamin (2), 25:116; 32:59
Nunes, Cordozo Isaac, 32:62
Nunes, David, 27:80
Nunes, David Hayim, 37:337
Nunes, David Nunnes, 33:68
Nunes, Doctor, 21:44-45
Nunes, Esther (Mrs. Benjamin Gomez),
25:116; 27:289; 29:11
Nunes, Esther (Mrs. Isaac Gomez), 27:290

Nunes (family name), 37:384
Nunes, Francisco, 33:113
Nunes, Hetty, 27:289, 296
Nunes, Isaac, 42:461
Nunes, Isaac R., 32:64
Nunes, Jahacob de Gabriel, 29:14
Nunes, James, 50:177
Nunes, Joseph, 50:177
Nunes, Moses, 50:176-77
Nunes, Moshe, 42:280, 395; 44:93
Nunes, Phillip, 27:274
Nunes, Pinhas, 26:251
Nunes, Rachel, 32:60
Nunes, Ricke, 44:90, 92-93
Nunes, Rosa, 25:118
Nunes, Samuel, 39:2
Nunes, Sarah (Mrs. Abraham), 37:336
Nunes, Sarah (West Indies), 25:115
Nunes, Torres, 38:236
Nunes, William George, 37:420
Nunes, Zipporah, 50:52
Nuñez, Abraham, 32:59
Nuñez, Alvaro (Brazil), 22:156
Nuñez, Ana, 32:117
Nuñez, Andres, 31:30
Nuñez, Antonio, 32:117
Nuñez, Clara, 32:117
Nuñez, Daniel (Del.), 26:236
Nuñez, Daniel (N.J.), 33:253
Nuñez, Dr. (N.Y.), 22:160; 41:2
Nuñez, Enriquez Alvarez, 23:135
Nuñez, Fernandez, 23:29
Nuñez, Isaque, 23:27
Nuñez, Jacob Israel, 32:59
Nuñez, Joseph, 21:5, 7-8, 10, 19, 22-23, 28,
181; 23:148
Nuñez, Judith, 32:59
Nuñez, Mariana, 31:27, 29
Nuñez, Mosseh, 42:278, 395
Nuñez, Rebecca, 32:59; 41:2
Nuñez, William, 32:59
Nununs, Louwies, 33:47
Nuremberg racial laws, 44:209; 50:107
Nurtling (Netting), Solomon, 27:51, 58, 60-
62, 84, 86, 253
Nusbaum, 31:149, 152
Nussbaum, C., 27:109
Nuys, Gaspar, 33:88

O

Oaths, 25:134; of abjuration, 37:370-89;
allegiance, 50:315, 334; (England), 50:130;
(Maryland), 50:20; "Proceedings Relating
to the Expulsion of Ezekiel Hart from the
House of Assembly of Lower Canada,"
23:xiv, 43-53
Obediante, Benjamin, 37:336
Obediante, Joseph, 37:336
Obediente, Laodrel, 26:251
Obenheimer, Abraham, 41:261
Oberdorfer, Jette, 41:255
Oberholtzer, Ellis Paxton, 39:287; 46:269
Obermayer, Herrman, 45:206-7; 50:314-15
Obermayer, Leon Jacob, 43:238; 45:206-7;
48:265; Civil War, 50:260, 270, 275, 314-
15, 395; Civil War centennial commission,
49:137; executive council, 38:346; 39:470;
41:388; 44:241; 47:201; planning
committee, 49:153; vice-president, 49:268;
50:426
Obituaries, "Jewish Obituary Notices in the
Gentleman's Magazine (1731-1868),"
37:419-20
*Obligations of Christians to Attempt the
Conversion of the Jews*, 30:196, 205
Obolenski, Prince, 42:163
Obookiah, Henry, "Henry Obookiah: The
First Hawaiian Student of Hebrew,"
39:190-92
Obragero, Julian Castellanos, 31:27
O'Brien, Anthony, 23:161
Obser, K., 23:101
Ocaña, Diego de, 31:10-11, 13, 24, 26
"O Captain, My Captain" (Hebrew
translation), 50:401
Occident, The, 23:141-42, 144; 27:237, 318,
420, 464; 29:77, 190; 30:387, 389; 37:57,
233; 38:155, 163-64, 169; 39:307, 333;
41:18-20, 89; 42:378; 44:12, 28, 34, 48,

130; 45:111; 46:68, 117-18; 47:35; 48:218-
20, 225, 237, 241; 50:82-84, 280, 296
Occident and American Jewish Advocate, The,
26:270; 50:170
Ocean & Inland Transportation Company,
28:270
Ocean Steamship Company of Canada,
28:270
Ochs, Adolph S., 29:169; 37:244; 38:32, 44;
40:47; 45:41, 157; 46:436; 49:199;
"Contributions of Adolph S. Ochs to
Journalism," 33:xxxi; gifts, 32:xxvi;
33:xxxiii; necrology of, 34:ix
Ochs, Mrs. Adolph S., 35:322
Ochs, Judas, 41:265
Ochs, Julius, 38:32-34
Ochs, Milton B., 38:32
Ochs, Naftali, 41:261
Ochs, Nannie, 35:322
O'Connell, Daniel, 26:268
O'Connell, Denis J., 46:282, 284
O'Connor, Harvey, *The Guggenheims*, 35:xxii
Odd Fellows, Independent Order of, 26:283;
47:45-46; 48:200; 50:179
Odell, Benjamin B., Jr., 29:174
Odell, George C. D., 33:184, 190, 196
Oder, Irwin, "American Zionism and the
Congressional Resolution of 1922 on
Palestine," 44:242; 45:35-47; book review
by, 46:129-31
Odessa pogrom, 50:248
Odler, Ezekiel, 27:55
Odler, Meyer, 27:45, 80
Odler, Simon, 27:41, 51, 59, 61, 63; 50:37, 57
Odler, Solomon, 21:159; 27:253
Oeb, Binyamin, 29:16
Oesterlein, Justus, necrology of, 35:x
*Oesterreichisches Central-Organ für
Glaubensfreiheit, Cultur, Geschichte und
Literatur der Juden*, 38:187-234

Oettinger, Moses, 41:265
O'Farrell, Capt. J., 39:179
Offerman, Philip, 37:416-17
Office of Indian Trade, 47:190
Office of Public Opinion Research, 46:242
Office of War Information, 40:116
Ogden, Abraham, 27:320
Ogden, C. R., 23:139
Ogden, Robert, 27:329
Ogden, Robert C., 33:222
Ogdon, Mr., 35:177
Oglethorpe, James E., 22:158-59; 41:2;
   46:178; 48:170; 50:52
O'Grady, John, "Immigration and Basic
   Religious Ideals," 46:337-40
Ohab Sholom, "History of Congregation
   Ohab Sholom," 33:xxx
Ohab Shalom Congregation (Baltimore),
   45:121
Ohab Zedek Congregation (New York),
   29:xliii; 43:250
Ohabai Shalom Congregation (San
   Francisco), 37:43
Ohabei Sholom Congregation (Boston),
   29:129; 38:71; 42:338; 45:270; 46:79;
   47:60; 49:19, 225; "History of the
   Congregation Ohabei Shalom," 32:xix
Ohave Emuno, 49:246
Oheb Israel Congregation (Baltimore),
   50:301
Oheb Shalom Congregation (Baltimore),
   37:482; (Hartford), 49:19; (Newark),
   31:292
Ohel Moishe Chevra Tehilim; Gollob v.,
   29:152
Ohel-Tom, 50:402
Ohev Sholom Congregation (Harrisburg),
   41:373
Ohio, 26:225; 30:iv; Bible and schools,
   31:222; Civil War, 50:278, 280, 304, 346-
   47, 387, 399; "The Black Hand Rock near
   Newark, Ohio," 28:xxiii; "Dr. Abraham
   Bettmann, a Pioneer Physician of
   Cincinnati," 23:vii, 105-16; "The Gratz
   Papers," 23:1, 7; Jewish local history,
   49:233
Ohio Company, 25:xvi
Ohio Company of Virginia, 23:7
Ohio Land Company, 22:xxxiv

Ohio & Mississippi Railroad, 25:146
Ohole Shem Association, 33:144
Ohole Shem Society of New York, 35:120;
   39:93
O'Horan, General, 32:96; 47:52
Oil, "United States Policies on Palestine,"
   40:107-18
Oil City (Pa.), religious observances, mid-
   nineteenth century, 37:38
O'Keefe, John, Little hunchback; or, A frolic in
   Bagdad, 33:174, 178; The London hermit; or,
   Rambles in Dorsetshire, 33:184; The Young
   Quaker, 33:179
O'Keeffe (Miss), Patriarchal Times, 30:205,
   426, 437
Okesen, John, 35:174
Oklahoma, Jewish local history, 49:234
Oko, Adolph S., 30:vi; 40:43, 47-48; 45:156
Olarowsky, A. E., 36:236, 246-47
Olcott, 22:82
Old Allen Street Synagogue, New York City,
   28:286
Old Country Store, The, 46:167
Old Dominion, 39:32, 48
Old Faith in the New World; Portrait of
   Shearith Israel, 1654-1954, An, 50:281, 290
Old First Church Evangelical and Reformed
   (Philadelphia), 41:92
Old First Presbyterian Church of New York,
   33:204
Old Jewish Burial Ground (New York), 38:52
Old Jewish Cemetery (Milwaukee), 47:54
Old People's Home (Chicago), 42:12
Old Pine St. Presbyterian Church
   (Philadelphia), 41:92
Old Pretender, 42:76
Olde Ulster, 23:178
Oleveira (Curacao), 22:171
Olgin, Moissay, 50:252
Oliphant, Laurence, 26:151, 154-63; 35:63;
   36:43-44; 38:278
Olin, Stephen, Travels in Egypt, Etc., 30:450
Oliueira, Mose de, 42:284-86
Oliver, Dr., 49:67
Oliver, R., 22:100
Oliver, Vere Langford, 32:55; 34:277;
   "Monumental Inscriptions of Barbados,"
   33:xxxii
Olivera, de, 23:175

Olivera, Henriques Vas de, 27:248
Olivera, Jacob de, 49:37
Olivera, Leah de, 49:37
Olivera, Policarpio Ester de, 32:61
Oliver Street Cemetery, 27:46, 162, 265-74, 278, 299, 305-7, 310, 312, 330, 340, 343, 372, 491; burial records of internments, 27:121-22; Gomez family, 27:299-301
Oliveyra, Aron Iesurun de, 22:170
Oliveyra, Solomon de, 47:71; *Ayyelet Ahabim*, 22:120; *Sharshot Gablut*, 22:118
Oliviera, Abraham d', 43:6
Oliviera, Antonio de, 33:79
Oliviera, de, family, 42:108, 214
Oliviera, Moses d', 33:88
Olmsted, Frederick Law, 50:164
Olney, Richard, 36:246; 39:71, 82, 85
Omichund, 31:111, 124, 133
Ominium gentium more leges et ritus, 22:111
Ommeren, 33:125
Once Upon a Time and Today, 46:431
O'Neal, Henry, 22:188
Oneg Shabbat, 39:372
Oneida community, 41:21
Oneida Indians, 22:173-74
O'Neil, Henry, 29:143
O'Neill, James M., 46:279
O'Neill, John Belton, 22:154-55; 26:189
Onet, Emile, 45:258
Ontario, "The Jews of Northern Ontario," 25:xiii; "Newman L. Steiner, the First Jewish Justice of the Peace in Ontario," 26:xv
"On to America" movement, 42:159; "The Revolution of 1848 and the Jewish 'On to America' Movement," 38:185-234, 345
Opatoshu, Joseph, 35:262-63
Opdyke, George, 40:145
Opera, "Michael Leoni," 23:179-80
Opert, 29:127
Ophir, "The Old Fancy That Ophir Was in the New World," 29:xxix
Opinione Nationale, 29:127
Oppenheim, Abraham, 26:259
Oppenheim, Alexander W., 34:273; gift, 34:xxi
Oppenheim, Charlotte Esther, 35:323
Oppenheim, H. B., 28:80
Oppenheim, I., 29:133

Oppenheim, Isaac, 32:132
Oppenheim, Louis K., 37:266; gift, 33:xxxiii
Oppenheim, Melia, 32:132
Oppenheim, Moritz, 40:319
Oppenheim, R., 32:119
Oppenheim, Samuel, 22:vii, xxvii, 182, 192; 24:95-97; 26:xiv, 237; 27:xix, 236, 354, 423; 30:vii; 31:vii, 4; 32:15; 33:xxxiii; 34:255; 42:223, 299; 44:88-90, 210, 248; 46:193; 50:44; "Benjamin Franks, Merchant, and Captain Kidd, Pirate," 29:xxxvi; 31:229-34; "Calendar of Twenty-one Unprinted Letters Relating to Aaron Lopez," 25:xii-xiii; "The Chapters of Isaac the Scribe, a Bibliographical Rarity, of 1772," 22:xxviii, 39-51; 30:61; communication from, 26:xxx; "The Congressional Debates and Reporters (1889)," 32:134; "A contemporary account of how the Jews came to arrive in New Netherland in 1654," 31:xxiv; "David S. Franks, an autobiographical sketch, 1789," 31:xxiv; "David Franks as an Insurance Broker, 1757 and 1758," 26:xxxi, 268-70; "David Franks and George Washington," 31:235-36; "David Franks' Interest in Lands in Virginia in 1774," 25:xiii, 119-20; "Disgraceful Acts of a Mob at a Jewish Funeral in New York, 1743," 31:240-41; "Early History of the Jews in New York," 32:134; "An Early Jewish Colony in Western Guiana," 32:134; "The First Settlement of the Jews in Newport," 34:1-10; "Genealogical Notes on Jacob Franks from Official Records," 25:75-80; gifts, 22:xxxiv; xxxv; 25:xv; 26:xxxiii, xxxv; 28:xxxix, xl; 29:xxxix, xliii; 31:xxxiv; 34:xxiv; "Isaac Moses and his services in the American Revolution," 31:xxiv; "Is the Cemetery in the New Bowery on the Site Granted by the Dutch in New York in 1656?," 29:xv; "The Jewish Burial Ground on New Bowery, New York, Acquired in 1682, Not 1656," 31:vii, 77-103; "Jewish Owners of Ships Registered at the Port of Philadelphia, 1730-1775," 22:xviii; 26:235-36; Jewish Publication Society of America, 22:xxv; "A Jewish Shipowner of Newport, R. I., in 1705," 26:xxxi; "The Jewish

Signers of the Non-Importation Agreement of 1765," 26:236-37; "The Jews in Barbados in 1739. An Attack Upon Their Synagogue. Their Long Oath," 22:197-98; "The Jews and Masonry in the United States before 1810," 32:134; "The Jews, the Protestant Episcopal Minister and the Poor in Colonial New York," 29:xv; "Jews Who Died of Yellow Fever in the Epidemic in New York in 1798," 25:xii, 123; "Jews Who Helped to Finance the New or Park Theatre, New York, in 1794 and 1795," 28:xv; "A Letter of David S. Franks," 22:195-96; "A Letter of David Franks, dated 1778, as Commissary of Prisoners, etc.," 26:xxxi; "A Letter of David Nassy, of Surinam," 23:xiii, 185-86; "Letter of Jonas Phillips, July 28, 1776, Mentioning the American Revolution and the Declaration of Independence," 25:xiii, 128-31; library of, 32:xxvii; "A List of Wills of Jews in the British West Indies, Proved Before 1800," 29:xxx; 32:55-64; "The Louzada Family of Bound Brook, N.J., 1698-1800," 28:xv; "Memorial of Solomon and Elieas De Paz on the Capture of their Ship in 1728-9 off Jamaica by the Spaniards," 26:248-49; "Michael Gratz's Interest in Lands in Otsego County, New York, in 1794, and What Came of it. An Unpublished History," 28:xv; "More About Jacob Barsimson, The First Jewish Settler in New York," 29:vii, xiv, 39-52; necrology of, 32:xii, 132-34; "A Newspaper Account of an Auto-da-Fe in Lisbon in 1726, in which a Native of Bahia, South America was burned," 22:xviii, 180-82; "Newspaper Notices of and by Jews of Philadelphia, 1735-1760," 22:xxviii; "A Note on Documents relating to the Inquisition in Mexico," 22:xiii; "Notes on the Genealogies of Jacob Franks and Joseph Simson," 22:xiii; "A Philadelphia Jewish Merchant's Day Book, 1755-1761," 22:xiii; 26:231-235; "The Question of the Kosher Meat Supply in New York in 1813: with a Sketch of Earlier Conditions," 25:vii, xii, 31-62; recording secretary 23:xii; 25:xi;

26:xii, xxx; 28:xi, xiv, xxi, xxxii; 29:xi, xiv, xix, xxix, xxxiii, xxxv; 31:xv, xix, xxiii, xvii, xxix; "Rodrigo Pacheco, a Leading Jewish Merchant in Colonial New York," 29:xxix; "Samuel Judah's Bond to His Wife Elizabeth for Additional Marriage Portion and Dowry, March 27, 1775," 26:xxxi; "Simon Nathan's Important Services to the American Cause in the Revolution," 31:xvi; "Solomon Bush's Patriotic Action in London in 1789," 31:xvi; "Some Items relating to the Jews in New York after 1734," 22:xiii; "Some Revolutionary Letters," 25:142-43; "A Study of Brazilian Jewish History, 1623-1654, Based Chiefly Upon the Findings of the Late Samuel Oppenheim," 33:xxvi, 43-125; "Supplemental Notes on the Jacob Franks Genealogy," 26:260-66; "The Supposed Disfranchisement of the Jews in New York After the Contested Election for Representative in 1737: A History," 29:xxx; "Three Pre-Revolutionary Items," 28:255-56; "The True Story of the Relation of the Jews to the Contested Election for Representative in New York in 1737," 29:xxxvii; "Two Gratz Documents, 1763 and 1773," 26:xxxi; "Two Letters of Aron Hart of Three Rivers, 1775 and 1776," 26:257-58; "Two Letters of Solomon Bush, a Revolutionary Soldier," 23:xiii, 177-78; "Was the Bank of England Protected by a Jew?," 25:111; "The Will of Henry Benjamin Franks, December 13, 1758 and Inventory of His Estate," 25:xii, 125-27; "Will of Nathan Simson, a Jewish Merchant in New York before 1722, and Genealogical Note Concerning him and Joseph Simson," 22:xxviii; 25:vii, 87-91
Oppenheim, W., 32:119
Oppenheimer, Cora R. (Mrs. Henry), 25:156
Oppenheimer, David, 31:226; "Rabbi David Oppenheimer (1664-1736), and the Acquisition of his Books and MSS. by the Bodleian Library, Oxford," 31:xvi
Oppenheimer, George, 35:273-74
Oppenheimer, Jacob, 26:47-48, 90
Oppenheimer, Laura, 25:152
Oppenheimer, Wilhelm G. G., 50:148

Oppert, Jules, 35:253; 41:162
Oracees, Sebastian, 33:118
Orach Chaim Congregation (New York), 43:250
Orah Hayim Congregation (New York), 31:289
Oraked, John Harris, 28:253
Orange, Joan d', 33:116
Orange, Prince of, 26:71-72
Oration on the Character of Jesus Christ, 30:328-29
Orb, Susskind von, 39:327
Orbanski (Orbansky), David, 50:304-6, 362
Orcherd, Emery de, 41:383
Orchestral Association of Chicago, 31:251
Ordaz, Beatriz, 31:11, 24
Ordaz, Diego de, 31:11
Order of the Free Sons of Israel, 49:17
Order of Isabella, 50:7
Order of Kesher Shel Barzel, 29:202
Order of the Knights of Zion, 45:183
Order of St. Francis, 28:157
Order of St. Michael and St. George, 31:290
Order of Sons of Zion, 35:58, 60; 48:194; gift, 35:xxiii
Order of the United American, 46:2
Order Zion, 24:22-23
Ordinaire, Dionys, 41:162
Ordroneaux, John, 26:196-98
Ordway, Judge, 26:260
Oregon, Civil War, 50:278, 280, 326, 346; colonization, 48:89-92
O'Reilly, George S., 45:259
Orenstein, Hirsch, 22:136
Organization for Health among Jews, 50:141
Organization for Rehabilitation and Training, 50:141
Orient, Der, 28:72; 50:11
Oriental Club, Philadelphia, 33:22
Original Mr. Jacobs: A Startling Exposé, 37:422-24
Or Jacob, 22:136
Orlans, Abraham Sholom, 33:133, 146
Orlemann, Clinton, 50:385-86
Orlik, Emil, 45:200
Orlinsky, Harry M., 40:54
Orloff, Prince, 24:35
Orlov family, 40:175, 177
Ormond, Duke of, 32:30

Ormsby, John, 30:77
Ornitz, Samuel B., 35:264
Orozco, 31:213
Orphan Asylum (Baltimore), 29:202
Orphan Home (Baltimore), 29:178
Orphan Society of Lexington, 29:55
Orphan's Fund, 44:218
Orphans of the Rhine, The, 21:229
Orr, Alexander E., 33:217, 219, 221, 223
Orr, Mrs. Alexander E., 33:219
Orsini, Nicholas, 28:165
Orth, Godlove Steiner, 47:77-78
Orth, Samuel P., 39:285-86
Orthodox Congregation (Easton, Pa.), 42:201
Orthodox Federation (Chicago), 42:33-34
Orthodox Greek Church, 24:85, 87
Orthodox Home for Aged Jews (Chicago), 29:157
Orthodox Jewish Congregational Union, 41:377-78
Orthodox Judaism, 39:259, 297-98, 370-72, 379-80, 383; 40:24, 63, 243, 258; 41:90; 42:33-34, 50, 58-59, 61, 68, 91-101, 104-7, 114-15, 196-97, 200-201, 326-37, 372; 43:136-37, 146, 250; 45:192, 239, 267; 46:61, 63, 65; 47:122, 130-31, 208; 48:63, 67-68, 119, 195, 224-25, 229, 231; 50:91, 93, 103, 110, 118, 243; *Differentiation Features of Orthodox, Conservative, and Reform Jewish Groups in Metropolitan Philadelphia,* reviewed, 49:276-78; history, writing of, 46:156, 163, 181, 187, 191, 386-87, 396; "New York Chooses a Chief Rabbi," 44:129-98; observances, 39:239, 264, 292; "The Question of the Kosher Meat Supply in New York in 1813; with a Sketch of Earlier Conditions," 25:vii, xii, 31-62; Rabbis, 41:214-15; and Reform Jews, Alliance Israélite Universelle, 39:394; Russia and Jewish education, 35:39-51
Orthodox Talmud Torahs (Chicago), 42:34
Or Torah, 44:222
Osawatomie, 62-63; battle of, 23:75
Osborn Case, 29:150
Osborne, 31:125
Osceola, 25:8
Osgood, Rev. Dr., 27:516
Osgood, Samuel, 48:181
O'Shaughnessy, M. T., 28:236

Osimov, 48:78, 80-81

Osler, William, 25:154; 46:434

Osofsky, Gilbert, "The Hebrew Emigrant Aid Society of the United States (1881-1883)," 49:173-87

Osten-Sacken, Baron, 36:242-45, 247-50, 253, 256; 39:70-72, 79; 41:172

Osterman, Moses, 50:314

Osterweis, Rollin G., 35:236-37; 46:441; gift, 34:xxvi; "The Problems of Literary Biography in Relation to American Jewish History," 46:426-32; "Rebecca Gratz," 34:xxvi

Ostrander, Elizabeth Rebecca, 32:101, 106

Ostrander, Henry Philip, 32:106

Ostro, Bertram, 45:214

Ostrover Ladies' Society, 26:260

Ostrovsky, Igarion, 43:54-55

Ostrow, Jacob, 33:163

Ostwald, Wilhelm, 28:233

Oswald, Eleazer, 46:183

Oswego (N.Y.), religious observances, mid-nineteenth century, 37:38

Otis, James, 24:109

Otis, Sam A., 37:14

Otry, William de, 41:383

Ottawa, "The First Jewish Settler of Ottawa, Canada," 23:xiv

Ottenberg, Reuben, 42:127

Ottendorfer, 38:50

Ottendorfer, Oswald, 32:97; 48:58

Ottenheimer, Clara, 41:253

Ottenheimer, Emanuel, 41:261

Ottenheimer, Henry (1), 26:282

Ottenheimer, Henry (2), 26:283

Ottenheimer, Hirsch, 41:253

Ottenheimer, Jacob, 40:381; necrology of, 26:xiv, 282-83

Ottenheimer, Jette, 41:261

Ottenheimer, Julian Robert, 26:283

Ottenheimer, Julius, 41:265

Ottenheimer, Karoline, 41:265

Ottenheimer, Sophie (Levi), 26:282

Ottensoser, David, Geschichte der Jehudim, 22:126-30

Ottensoser, Eleazer, 23:108

Otterbourg, Eugene, 32:66, 98

Otterbourg, George, 32:66

Otterbourg, Marcus, 47:42, 49-52; "Marcus Otterbourg, United States Minister to Mexico in 1867," 32:65-98; "Memoir of Marcus Otterbourg, United States Minister to Mexico in 1867," 31:xxiv; 32:xiii

Otterbourg, Mathilde (Bruno), 32:66

Otterbourg, Solomon Jonas, 32:65; 47:49

Ottinger, Max, 45:154

Ottinger, Moses, 45:154

Ottinger, Nathan, 45:154

Ottolenghe, Joseph, 43:237

Ottolenghi, 28:21

Ottolengui, A., vs. G. V. Ancker, 30:390

Ottolengui, Jacob, 50:168-69, 184

Ottoman Empire, 36:5; 43:155, 247; 46:482; 47:83, 161; Bucharest Peace Conference and Jews, 24:80-97; civil rights, 24:30; see also: Turkey

Ottoman Porte, 21:232, 237

Oubril, Paul d', 24:121

Ouelozo, Israel Levy, 42:278

Ouelozo, Izrael Isra, 42:278, 395

Ouray, Chief, 38:322

"Our Living World," 26:280

Outlet (Samuels), 38:20

Outlook, 41:180-81

Outre-Mer, 45:23

"Outside the Church," 42:83

Overing, Henry John, 27:447

Overseas American Red Cross, 29:180

Overseas relief, 48:217

Overstreet, Harry A., 39:206; book review by, 39:199-201

Owen, Dr., 37:132

Owen, Hugh, 26:147

Owen, Robert, 39:66

Owen, Robert Dale, 42:83

Owens, Catherine, 50:180

Oxford calendars, 31:xviii

Oxford University, 22:202

Oxlee, John, 27:519; Three Letters, 30:376, 379-80

Oxley, W., 26:254

Oxnam, Bromley, 41:92

Ozrai Ovdai Adama, 35:63

Ozeley, Joseph, 27:242

P

Paca, William, 37:111
Pachao, Hester, 26:251
Pacheckoe, 27:413
Pacheckoe, Moses, 29:31; 34:8-10
Pacheco, Aaron, 29:19
Pacheco, Abraham, 26:251
Pacheco, Benjamin Mendez, 21:2, 5, 8-9, 12, 19-24, 181, 194
Pacheco, Benjamin Mendes, Jr., 27:1, 4, 169, 486
Pacheco, Binjamin Mendez, 21:12
Pacheco, David, 32:61
Pacheco, Eliau de Mosseh, 29:19
Pacheco, Emanuel, 34:10
Pacheco, Ester, 32:59
Pacheco, Isacq, 33:65
Pacheco, Mendes, 38:236
Pacheco, Moseh, 29:19·
Pacheco, Rodrigo (New York), 21:7, 39; 26:265; 27:1, 3, 5-6, 39, 70-71, 248, 299, 350-52; 30:33; 33:253; 35:176-77, 181-87; 42:74-75, 79, 81; "Rodrigo Pacheco, a Leading Jewish Merchant in Colonial New York," 29:xxix
Pacheco, Sebastian, 33:118
Pacheco, Thomas, 33:118
Pacheco & Tavares, 27:248; 35:186
Pacific, 48:172
Pacific Charter, 44:71
Pacific Messenger, The, 26:272
Packard, Kate E. R., 50:197
Packer, Asa, 41:29
Packwood, Theodore, 50:153
Paderewski, Ignace, 36:149, 165
Padgett, James A., 37:438
Padthuysen, Pieter, 32:14-15, 20; 33:63
Padua, University of, 28:201-2
Paducah, "History of the Settlement of Jews in Paducah and in the Lower Ohio Valley," 22:xviii

Padula, Marquis di la, 28:167
Pagan, Mr., 28:253
Page, Thomas Nelson, 23:103; 28:58-61
Page, Mrs. Thomas Nelson, 28:57
Page, Walter Hines, 36:73, 78; 36:146; 40:14
Paiba, Mr., 26:233
Paine, Charles, 23:90
Paine, Nathaniel, 35:141
Paine, Thomas, 22:196; 30:112, 114, 129; 38:124; 46:289
Painted Woods colony, 38:306; 40:239; 48:87, 93
Paiva, Antonio Ribeiro de, 29:34
Paix et Droit, 32:127
Paiz, Abrao Aboab, 42:278, 395
Palache, Abraham de Joseph, 29:28
Palache, Alexander, 27:389
Palache, David, 29:9, 28
Palache, Samuel, 29:10
Palacký, Frantisek, 39:329
Palasios, Jos de, 27:248
Pale of Settlement, 36:175, 214, 274
Paleske, 22:191
Palestine, 39:93, 205, 322, 325, 352, 393-94, 410-12, 415, 440; "Aaron Aaronsohn, Agricultural Explorer," 31:vii, 197-210; American Israelites, 49:26-27; American Jewish appeal, 27:233-35; "American Zionism and the Congressional Resolution of 1922 on Palestine," 45:35-47; Board of Delegates of American Israelites, 29:98-101; "British Projects for the Restoration of Jews to Palestine," 26:xv, 127-64; *A History of Palestine from 135 A. D. to Modern Times*, reviewed, 39:194-96; Jewish incidents during the second half of the nineteenth century, 28:xxiii; Joseph Fels, 46:483; *Latin America and the Palestine Problem*, reviewed, 48:136-37;

Mesopotamian Project, 47:161, 163-65, 167; migration, 45:225; Mordecai M. Noah, 21:xi; New York Congregation, 27:xvi, 12, 19-20, 103, 146-47; *Niles' Weekly Register*, 50:11-12, 14-17; "The Palestine Colony in Michigan," 29:61-74; *The Realities of American-Palestine Relations*, reviewed, 39:331-33; *The Struggle for Palestine*, reviewed, 40:313-17; "Two American Naval Expeditions to Palestine, 1848 and 1854," 39:470; 40:281-87; U.S. intercession for Jews, 36:ix, 42-95; "United States Policies on Palestine," 40:107-18

Palestine Colonization Fund, 26:149
Palestine Development Council, 40:393
Palestine Economic Corporation, 35:324
Palestine Electric Corporation, 37:477
Palestine Endowment Fund, 37:477
Palestine Exploration Fund, 26:153
Palestine Foundation Fund, 45:38
Palestine Potash Company, 37:477
Palestine Resolution, 29:xli
Palestine Restoration Fund, 29:181
Palestine Survey Commission, 35:324
Palestinian Concession, 31:xxxiii
Palfrey, John Gorham, *Academical Lectures on the Jewish Scriptures*, 30:329; *Elements of Chaldee...and Rabbinical Grammar*, 30:304
Palisades Commission, 29:168
Palitz, Bernard A., 34:188, 249; necrology of, 28:xiv, 181-83; "The Upward Struggle of the Cause of Secular Education in Russian Jewry in the Reigns of Alexander I and Nicholas I," 28:xv; *see also*: Kohler, Max J.
Pallacio, Pedro, 43:43
Pallard, Joseph, 23:161
Palma, 31:22
Palmella, Count, 26:50
Palmer, 25:56
Palmer, Benjamin Franklin, 39:6
Palmer, Henry (Newport), 27:175
Palmer, Henry (Pa.), 31:297
Palmers, Sylvanus, 35:182
Palmerston, Lord, 26:138, 151, 162
Paltsits, V. H., 28:255; 34:274; 35:314
Panama Canal, 28:307; 41:32
Panama issue, 22:79
Panama-Pacific International Exposition, 28:309; "Jewish Participation in the

Panama-Pacific International Exposition," 25:xiv
Pan American Union, 42:89
Panitz, David H., 47:202, and Esther L. Panitz, "Simon Wolf as United States Consul to Egypt," 46:493; 47:76-100
Panitz, Esther L., "Too Little and Too Late: A Study of Jewish Attitudes to Immigration in the Light of American Economic Opportunities (1865-1897)," 50:427; *see also*: Panitz, David H.
Panken, Jacob, 50:215
Pantorro, Diago Ferdinandes, 33:112
Papal States, 36:330
Paparrobalos, Antonio Dias, 45:40
Papé, G., 27:505
Papé, Gabriel, 41:72
Pape, L. G., 37:266, 268-70
Papineau, 23:49
Papineau Rebellion, 50:129
Papini, Giovanni, 48:249-50
Pappenheim, Bertha, 40:403
Pappenheim, Frau, 23:110
Para, la, 27:80
Para, Semuel de Selomoh de la, 25:138-40
Paragon, 48:172
Paramaribo, 26:243
Parara, Mordy, 27:248
Parcelyns, Natanl. Levy, 48:24
Parchon, Salomon, 28:205; Hebrew Lexicon, 22:104
Pardes Binah, 22:133
Pardes Hakmah, 22:133
Pardo, Abraham (Surinam), 32:64; 48:25; portrait, 50:148
Pardo, David (Amsterdam), 29:15, 21; 44:216-17, 221
Pardo, David ben Joseph, *Shulhan Tahor*, 22:120
Pardo, Hannah, 27:169
Pardo, Joseph (Rotterdam), 29:15
Pardo, Josiau de David, 44:216-17, 221
Pardo, Judith, 50:148
Pardo, Saul, 47:178
Pardo, Yeosiahu, 29:21, 34
Parennin, Dominique, 49:44
Parente, Joan, 33:77
Paris Committee, 41:129-30, 132-33, 138-39, 144, 148-53; 49:177

Paris Conference, 29:98, 102, 109-11, 114-16; 41:37

Paris Consistoire Israélite, 41:148

Paris, Convention of 1858, 24:98, 102-3, 106-7, 119, 122, 127, 132, 136-41, 145, 150-51

Paris, Council of, 1225, 28:144

Paris Exposition of 1899, 28:266

Paris, Gaston, 41:162

Paris memorial, 24:30-31, 34-35, 102-5

Paris Peace Conference, 37:476; 40:113-14; 49:198, 200

Paris Royal Library, 27:482

Paris, widow, 27:80

Parish Board of School Directors; Harold v., "Anglo-Jewish Legal Cases," 25:137

Parisian Jewish Philanthropic Committee, 41:152

Parizen, Philip, 43:232; portrait of, 42:416

Park, Lawrence, 41:294

Park, Robert E., 46:300

Park Theatre, New York, 33:185-86, 188-89, 191, 194-96; "Jews Who Helped to Finance the New or Park Theatre, New York, in 1794 and 1795," 28:xv

Parker, Donald Dean, 46:445

Parker, Dorothy (Rothschild), 35:274

Parker, Eli, 50:343

Parker, Elisha, 35:186

Parker, Ely Samuel, 47:78

Parker, H. T., 35:257

Parker, John, 27:175

Parker, Lord, 31:106, 111, 113, 133

Parker, Mr., 44:26

Parker, Theodore, 22:1; 34:265; 38:159; 42:83, 131, 138, 145-47; 46:212

Parker, Ursilla, 27:248

Parker, Willard, 42:118

Parkersburg, W. Va., Congregation B'nai Israel, contribution, 37:xxviii

Parkes, James, A History of Palestine from 135 A. D. to Modern Times, reviewed, 39:194-96

Parkman, Ebenezer, 22:24

Parkman, Francis, 35:14; 38:254

Park Street Theatre, New York, 35:285

Parma, Duke of, 28:191

Parnassus, 38:269-71, 275, 277-79; 39:324, 327

Parochial schools, Cornerstones of Religious Freedom in America, reviewed, 40:96-98

Parra, David de la, 25:140

Parra, Ester de la, 25:140

Parra, Isaac de la, 29:19

Parra, Rachel (Meza), 25:139

Parra, Rahel (1), 25:140

Parra, Rahel (2), 25:140

Parra, Ribca (Arrias), 25:139

Parra, S. H. de la, 29:19

Parra, Samuel de la, 25:140

Parra, Selomoh de la, 25:139-40

Parrara, Jacob de Mordy, 27:248

Parrish, Mr., 43:28

Parry, Peter, 44:96

Parry, William, 40:160

Parsley, Robert, 48:193

Parson, Eugene, 37:440

Parson, Herbert, 36:285; 41:180

Parsons, James, 23:156

Parsons, Levi, Dereliction and Restoration of the Jews, 30:185, 188

Parsons, Mosby Monroe, 50:342

Parson, William, 43:204

Parelow, Isaac, 27:326

Partelow, Silas, 27:326

Parton, James, 26:199

Parzen, Herbert, 39:206; 40:105, 205, 415; 41:105; 42:331; books reviewed by, 39:193-94; 40:101-4; 201-4; 395-98; 41:97-104; 42:319-20; 49:272-76; "Communications," 42:463-66

Pas, Daniel, 26:254

Pas de, 27:91

Pas, Duarte Dias de, 32:20

Pas, Jan Nunes de, 33:115

Pascal, Blaise, 50:117

Pascalis, Felix, 26:222

Pascoe, Isaac, 32:55

Pasha, Djemal, 31:207

Pasha, Eliakim, 33:147

Paskevich, Countess, 43:48-49

Pasmanik, Daniel, 39:101

Pasos, Kosmo de Krasto, 33:80

Pasquale of Catane, 28:208

Pass, Abraham de, 25:117; 50:66

Pass, Albert de, 25:115

Pass, Isaac Garcia de, 25:116

Pass, Jacob de, 25:115; 27:483

Pass, James Henry de, 25:117

Pass, Jane de, 25:117

Pass, Joseph de, 27:185; 35:142
Pass, Maria de, 25:116
Pass, Moses de, 25:116
Pass, Rachel de, 25:115
Pass, Ralph de, 25:115; 50:169
Pass, Raphael de, 50:66
Pass, Rebecca de, 50:66
Pass, Sarah de (1), 25:116
Pass, Sarah de (2), 25:117
Passaic, New Jersey, *Jewish Roots, A History of the Jewish Community of Passaic and Environs*, 49:228
Passi, Nahman, "Nahman Passi, a Sixteenth-Century Turkish Statesman," 29:xxxvi
Passo, Issac, 27:61
Passover, "Passover in Camp (1862)," 50:309-11, 400; *Service for Two First Nights of Passover*, 30:318-19
Passover Relief Association, 40:164
Passports, "The European Aspect of the American-Russian Passport Question," 46:86-100; Passport Question, 39:67-86, 426-28; 41:163-94; 42:415; 50:219, 221; Russia and Isidor Rayner (1850-1912), 40:288-310
Pasteur, Louis, 40:92; 42:122; 50:324
Pastor Britos colony, 39:93
Pastore, John O., 46:293-94
Patai, Raphael, book review by, 50:146-47
Pate, Captain, 23:71-74
Patek, Jacob, 47:71
Pater, *The Book of Knowledge*, 30:90
Paterson, John, 26:116-17, 123
Paterson, N.J., religious observances, mid-nineteenth century, 37:37; United Jewish Appeal, contribution, 37:xxviii
Pathscoe, Jacob, 32:59
Patience (slave), 50:177
Pato, Haim Jeudah Gomes, 34:293
Patriotic League of America, 39:437
Patten, James H., 34:204
Patten, Joseph H., 39:35, 65
Patterson, Alfred Nash, 46:492
Patterson, C. Stuart, 28:313
Patterson, John W., 29:201
Pattison, Gov., 33:218
Patton, Robert, 48:192
Paukorue, Dr., 27:329

Paul, *Review of Paul's Letter to the Hebrews*, 30:393, 396
Paul II, 28:160
Paul III, 21:241; 28:171-73
Paul IV, 28:164-65, 174-75, 177, 197
Paul V, 28:180-81
"Paul and Alexis," 21:229
Paul, Asher Michells de, 33:199-201
Paulding, James Kirke, 39:12
Pauper Bill, 49:79
Pauroma, *Pioneers of Pauroma: Contribution to the Earliest History of the Jewish Colonization of America*, reviewed, 44:248-50
Pavias, Mr., 21:54
Pavlovich, Constantin, 28:117
Pawle, Lennox, 35:270
Pawling & Burrel, 40:86
Paxton, J. D., *No Future Return of Jews Called for by Prophecy*, 30:390-91
Payba, Beatriz Enriquez la, 31:28, 31
Payba, Simon, 31:28, 31
Payne, John Howard, 33:186, 194; *Maid and magpie*, 33:194
Payne, Judge, 21:190
Payva, Daniel Ribeyro de, 29:34
Paz, de, 31:109, 111-113, 125
Paz, Aron Dorta de, 42:279, 394
Paz, Izabel de, 47:64
Paz, Manuel de la, 23:135
Paz, Mord. Garcia de, 22:170
Paz, Rodrigo de, 31:14
Peabody College, 45:147
Peabody, David, *The Patriarch of Hebron*, 30:290
Peabody, Elizabeth Palmer, *Key to History*, 30:361
Peabody, George Foster, 35:322
Peabody Institute, Baltimore, 25:147
Peabody Museum, Baltimore, 28:31
Peace Conference (1901) (1907), 25:155; (1919), 43:231; 47:202; Bucharest of 1913, 24:2; Paris, 28:xvii, 258-60; Versailles, 33:29
Peace of Westphalia, 46:384; 47:118
Peale, Charles Willson, 31:7; 41:278, 292
Pearsall, Thomas, 23:156
Peartree, William, 23:149
Pease, Roger W., 22:219
Pease, Simon, 35:291

Pecare, Jacob, 27:514
Peck, Geo., 27:72
Peck, Harry Thurston, 43:19
Peck, Miss, 34:279
Peck, William, 34:279
Peckham, Rosendale & Hessberg, 28:285
Peckham, Rufus W., 35:320
Peddlers, "The Problems of Nineteenth Century American Jewish Peddlers," 44:1-7
Pedro, Don, 39:31
Peekskill Conference, "The Writing of American Jewish History," 49:215
Peel, Robert, 28:124
Peel, Viscount, 36:85
Peers, Henry, Jr., 27:319
Peers, John, 27:322
Peers, Miriam, Jr., 27:322
Peggy (slave), 50:176
Peirce, Charles, 42:342
Peirce, Franklin, 23:62
Peirce, Herbert A. D., 36:241-43, 245-46, 255; 41:172, 180-81
Peirce, Herbert H., 39:70-72, 82
Peiser, Jacob, 35:137
Peister, Abraham de, 27:6
Peister, Isaac and Abraham de, 27:350-56, 358
Peixotto, Abraham, 32:59
Peixotto, Abm. Cohen, 27:80
Peixotto, Benjamin Franklin, 24:82; 25:112; 26:230; 27:167; 32:130; 38:72, 243; 45:100; 46:394; 49:28; American Israelites, 29:77, 86, 94-96, 98; "Benjamin Franklin Peixotto, American Consul at the Court of King Charles of Roumania," 22:xvii, 133; "Benjamin Franklin Peixotto, American Consul: The Jewish Question in Roumania and American Jewry (1870-1875)," 47:202; B'nai B'rith, 43:141; Brussels Conference 1872, 24:25-29; disabilities, 47:35, 40, 47, 81, 83, 98; education, 28:132; immigration, 40:234-35; 42:172-73; International Jewish Conference, 24:32, 39; Joseph Seligman, 41:37-38; Paris Conference, 29:109-10; Roumania, 24:1-24; 36:100-7, 110-11; 45:67-69, 73-74, 78, 80, 85; Simon Wolf, 29:199, 201, 203; Y. M. H. A., 37:236

Peixotto, Daniel L. M., 25:4, 11; 26:219-30, 249; 27:158, 163, 167, 264-65, 277, 314, 389, 518; 33:6; *Address Before Medical Society of New York*, 30:273, 275-76; *Anniversary Discourse*, 30:266-68; sermons of father, 27:312-13
Peixotto (family), 49:6
Peixotto, Grace, 27:111, 264
Peixotto, Hetty, 27:289, 294, 310
Peixotto, Isaac Moses Cohen, 27:271
Peixotto, Jacob Cohen, 29:35
Peixotto, Judith, 27:167, 507; 32:59
Peixotto, Judith Salzedo, 26:229, 249-50; 29:167
Peixotto, Leah, 27:264
Peixotto, Levi Maduro, 21:198
Peixotto, Luisa Hetty, 27:285, 289, 294
Peixotto, Lunah, 27:112
Peixotto, Miriam, 27:167
Peixotto, Mr., 40:189
Peixotto, Moses, 27:285, 289, 291-92, 294; 42:228
Peixotto, Moses Levy Maduro, 21:166, 198, 209, 215; 26:219, 230; 27:77-78, 103-5, 107, 109-10, 122, 167, 235, 264-65, 276, 303-4, 310-13, 315-16, 338, 342-43; 30:177; 35:200; 37:207-8; 40:189; 41:68
Peixotto, Mosseh Coen, 29:35
Peixotto, Mosseh de Jacob Acohen, 29:35
Peixotto, Rachel (Miss), 27:111
Peixotto, Rachel (Barbados), 32:59
Peixotto, Rachel (Louisa), 27:294, 310
Peixotto, Mrs. Rachel (nee Seixas), 27:112, 163, 167, 264; 33:6
Peixotto, Raphael, 26:230
Peixotto, Raphael (b. Daniel L. M.), 27:167
Peixotto, Raphael (b. Moses L. M. M.), 27:264
Pcixotto, Rebecca (d. Daniel L. M.), 27:167
Peixotto, Rebecca (d. Samuel), 27:111, 285, 289, 294, 310
Peixotto, Samuel, 27:78, 264, 285, 289, 292, 294, 310, 314
Peixotto, Sarah (Mrs. Abraham H. Cardozo), 26:230, 249
Peixotto, Sarah (b. Daniel L. M.), 27:167
Peixotto, Sarah (b. Moses L. M.), 27:264
Peixotto, Simba C., 30:367; 42:57, 401-2; 48:74

Peixotto, Zipporah, 26:230, 249; 27:167
Peiza, Emanuel de, 26:251
Peiza, Isaac de, 26:251
Peiza, Moses de, 26:251
Pelcovitz, Nathan, 47:203
Pelham, 25:67
Pelham, W., 26:245
Pell, 25:56
Pell, Evert, 23:154
Pell & Ferris, 32:108
Pell, Roger, 38:47
Pelletan, Camille, 41:162
Pelletan, Eugène, 41:162
Pemberton, John Clifford, 43:98; 44:113
Pemberton, Murdock, 35:272-73
Peña, Abm. Lopez, 27:23
Peña, Daniel Lopes, 39:28, 30
Peña, Esther, 26:116
Peña, Isaac Lopez, 22:170
Peña, Maria dela, 23:133
Peña, Mose Israel, 42:253, 288, 387, 392, 395
Peña, Nicolás Géronimo de la, 23:135
Pendarves, J., 32:30
Pendleton, Edmund, 27:471
Pendleton, Judge, 25:138
Pene Shabath v Shahare Sedek, 44:221
Penfield, Josiah, 33:235
Penfield & Penfield, 40:305
Penha, Daniel Lopes, 22:169-70; 44:225
Penha, Eliao Lopez, 22:170
Penha family, "The de la Penha Family and Its Labrador Grants," 32:xii
Penha, Jb. Zu. Abm. Lopez, 22:170
Penha, Moshe Lopez, 44:225
Penington, Edward, 30:77
Penley, Samson, 33:196
Penn Club, 31:256
Penn, Governor, 22:194
Penn, William, 22:147; 38:1; 40:96-97; 46:144
Pennock, Thomas, "An Affectionate Address, to the Jews of Jamaica on the Great Subject of Christianity," 23:182; 30:429
Pennsylvania, 26:181-82; 46:20-21; "Anglo-Jewish Legal Cases," 25:137; Board of Law Examiners, 23:192; colonial settlement of Jews, 26:5-6; constitution of, 29:189; Grand Lodge F. & A.M., gifts, 23:xvii; 26:xxxv; "The Gratz Papers," 23:vii, xii, 1-

23; Jewish-German pioneers, 22:xxii; Jewish local history, 49:234-36; Jewish population (1790), 50:28-29, 34; Jews in law and medicine, 22:147, 149-50, 152-54, 163; "Old Masonic Lodges of Pennsylvania," 22:xxxiv; 23:xvii; pioneers, 29:xxxi
Pennsylvania Academy of Fine Arts, 31:7; 42:417; 50:246-47
Pennsylvania Avenue Talmud Torah (Brooklyn), 35:62
Pennsylvania Central Railroad, 27:402
Pennsylvania College, 43:74
Pennsylvania Company for Insurance on Lives and Granting Annuities, 22:145-46; 50:243, 245-46
Pennsylvania Federation of Y. M. H. A.'s, 37:306
Pennsylvania Gazette, 25:126
Pennsylvania German Society, 28:299
Pennsylvania Historical and Museum Commission, 46:151
Pennsylvania Historical Society, 22:51; 25:113; 44:244
Pennsylvania Hospital, 22:231
Pennsylvania Insurance Company, 28:257
Pennsylvania Institution for the Deaf and Dumb, Dismissal of David G. Seixas, 30:198-201
Pennsylvania Packet and Daily Advertiser, 27:228; 29:xlii
Pennsylvania Railroad, 28:301; 41:50; 45:75-76, 86
Pennsylvania Railroad Company, 22:144-45
Pennsylvania Society to Protect Children from Cruelty, 28:268
Pennsylvania State Anatomical Board, 22:232
Pennsylvania State Board of Public Charities, 47:192
Pennsylvania State Constitution, 47:193
Pennsylvania, University of, 23:xvii, 99; 25:162; 28:310, 313; 29:172; 31:296; 33:20; 37:85, 91, 451, 453; 40:8; 42:457; 45:197; 46:149-50, 210; 47:22; 49:11
Penrose, Boies, 38:337
Penso, Abigail (de Britto), 25:139
Penso, Abraham, 44:234
Penso, Daniel Messias, 25:138-40
Penso, Eliao, 22:170

Penso, Elias, 44:232
Penso, Ester, 25:139
Penso, Ishac, 44:229
Penso, Jahacob Messiah, 25:139
Penso, Moses, 27:248
Penso, Mosseh, 44:229, 232
Penso, Rephael, 44:232-33
Pentecost, Dorsey, 23:11-12, 21
People's Institute, 28:308
People's Relief Committee, 33:xxxii; 36:155;
    49:88
Pepys, Samuel, 37:340; 42:439
Pera, David, 42:279, 395
Perada, Immanuel, 23:79
Perahim ve-Shoshanim, 22:137
Perara, Rodrigues, 27:45
Pereboom, de (The Peartree), 29:39, 42:44, 51
Pereferkovich, M., 39:96
Pereira (Curacao), 22:171
Pereira (Jamaica), 25:113
Pereira (Portugal), 25:73
Pereira, Privateer, 23:175
Pereira, Aaron, 32:59, 62
Pereira, Abigail, 32:64
Pereira, Benjamin, 21:45, 48, 55, 57-58, 74-
    75, 84, 171, 208; 27:17-18, 26-27; 31:237;
    37:420
Pereira, Benjamin M., 27:150, 168, 262
Pereira, Daniel, 32:62
Pereira, David, 25:116
Pereira, Ephraim Lopez, 27:20
Pereira family, 42:108, 214; 48:139; inter-
    marriage, Portugal, 25:73
Pereira, Isaac M., 32:64
Pereira, Isaque, 42:279, 395
Pereira, Ishac, 29:36
Pereira, Jacob de Eliao, 44:229-31
Pereira, Jacob de Mordechay, 44:231
Pereira, Jacob Levi, 33:65
Pereira, Joseph, 32:62; 44:248
Pereira, Lopes Samuel, 32:62
Pereira, Manaseh, 21:45
Pereira, Menassah, 32:62
Pereira, Moses, 32:62
Pereira, Nuño Alvarez, 23:134
Pereira, Pedro Alvarez, 23:134
Pereira, Ralph, 25:116
Pereira, Rephael, 29:36
Pereira, Rynia, 32:59

Pereira, Sarah, 32:62
Pereira, Simon, 29:36
Pereira, S. Rodrigues, 43:254
Péreire, Alfred, 37:474
Péreire, Eugene, 41:162
Péreire family, 29:125, 127
Péreire, Rodrigues, 29:12
Pereirra, Eliao Haim, 44:232
Pereirra, Jacob de Mordechay, 44:232
Pereirra, Mordechay, 44:229
Pereles, Nathan, 47:38, 42, 48
Perera, Antho., 33:114
Perera, Bras, 33:114
Perera, Francisco de Britto, 33:112
Perera, George de Barros, 33:113
Perera, Gonsalvo, 33:112
Perera, Michiel Soaris, 33:117
Perera, Phillipo, 33:118
Perera, Sijmon Berboza, 33:117
Peres, Daniel, 29:37
Peres, Hardwig, 37:268-69
Peres, Jean, 33:115
Peres, Mose, 42:278, 395
Peres, Sara, 29:37
Pereyra, 33:73
Pereyra, Aharon Israel, 21:11, 20
Pereyra, Esther de Abraham Rodrigues, 29:12
Pereyra, Jacob, 27:248
Pereyra, Jacob Haim Rods., 22:170
Pereyra, Joseph Rodrigues, 29:12
Pereyra, Madame, 26:38, 52
Perez, Isaac Loeb, 43:239
Perez, Isabell, 31:28
Perez, Jizchak Lejb, 34:24
Perez, Mr., 26:252
Perez, Marco, 38:325
Perezhitoye, 38:242
Pergaus, 33:125
Pergeno, Jacob, 33:108
Périer, Paul-Casimir, 41:162
Périgneux, Synod of, 28:148
Periodicals, "The Hebrew Periodical Press in
    America, 1871-1931," 33:127-70; "A List
    of Selected Items of American Jewish
    Interest in the Russian-Jewish Press, 1860-
    1932," 38:239-48, 305-16, 343; 39:87-113;
    "A Spanish-American Jewish Periodical,"
    23:vii, xiv, 129-35

"Periodization of American Jewish History, The," 47:125-33, 200
Perira, M. J., 27:482
Perira, Moses, Lopez, 27:9
Perkins, G. C., 36:254, 258
Perkins, Mr., 39:190
Perkins, Thomas H. and Asyd, 43:216
Perl, Josef, 28:84, 115-16
Perles, Felix, *Jüdische Skizzen*, xvii
Perlewitz, Herman, 47:55
Perlman, Harold B., "Dr. Nicholas Murray Butler on Columbia's Jewish Graduates," 37:435; "Sampson Simson's Bequest to Columbia," 37:xxxiii, 434
Perlman, Max, 50:233-34
Perlman, Nathan, 45:222
Perlman, Selig, 41:339-45, 392; 42:215; 47:190; "America and the Jewish Labor Movement—A Case of Mutual Illumination," 46:221-32; history, writing of, 46:257-61, 265-66; "Jewish-American Unionism, Its Birth Pangs and Contributions to the General American Labor Movement," 41:297-37, 387
Perlmann, Moshe, "Paul Haupt and the Mesopotamian Project, 1892-1914," 47:154-75; "Paul Haupt's Plan for Settling Russian Jews in Mesopotamia," 44:242
Perlstein, Meyer, 41:316; 46:230
Permanent Court of International Arbitration, 31:295
Pernambuco, "The Classis of Pernambuco," 32:xiii
Perreau, Peter, 37:72
Perrera, Louis da Costa, 33:116
Perrin, W., *Hebrew Canticles*, 30:198
Perry, 31:124
Perry, Belmont, 50:322
Perry, Betsy, 27:437, 439, 442
Perry, Captain, 27:442
Perry, Leslie J., 50:382
Perry, Matthew C., 26:173, 177; 27:214, 456; 39:24
Perry, Miss, 27:432
Perry, Mr., 27:433
Persecution of Jews in the East, 30:350-51
Pershing, John J., 31:213, 215

Persia, U.S. Intercession for Jews, 36:xi, 11-18; Board of Delegates of American Israelites, 29:88; 49:27; 24:122
Persky, Daniel, 33:133, 142, 144-54, 156-60, 162, 166
Peru, 22:111, 114-16; lost tribes, 25:83
Pesera, Louis Bras, 33:116
Pesoa, 21:xxvii
Pesoa, Cynthia, 27:293
Pesoa, Gustavus I., 21:171; 27:115, 290, 292-93, 298
Pesoa, Isaac Gomez, 27:293, 297-98
Pesoa, Judith, 27:112
Pesoa, Juliet, 27:287-88, 291, 293, 297-98
Pesoa, Oscar, 27:293
Pesoa, Rosina, 27:293
Pesoa, Samuel, 27:293
Pessca, Joao, 33:79
Pessoa, Joan, 33:80
Petachiah of Regensburg, 34:150
Peter I, Czar, 23:166
Peter of Fonesca, Cardinal, 28:155
Peter, King, 28:207
Peter the Great, 36:401; 46:2
Peterkin, Julia, *Roll Jordan, Roll*, 35:xx
Peters, "Jews in America," 28:xxxviii
Peters, Margaret E., 50:272
Peters, Mr., 35:187
Peters, Mrs., 23:20-21
Peters, Richard, 23:19
Peters, Richard, Jr., 23:19
Peters, William, 23:19, 21
Petersburg, Va., 50:162; *History of the Jews of Petersburg 1789-1950*, 49:240; religious observances, mid-nineteenth century, 37:38
Peterson, C. G., 36:247
Peterson, Dan, 48:259
Peterson, Frank A., 34:166; 37:459; gift, 33:xxxiii
Peterson, M. L., 50:272
Peterson, P. Edward, 34:3-4, 7, 9
Petit (family name), 48:139
Petrikofsky, J., 38:245-46, 248, 306, 310
Pettenkofer, Max Joseph von, 46:11
Petterson, George, 27:246
Pettit, John, 47:78
Peyre, Henri, 46:347
Peyser, J., 29:134

Peyster, Arent Schuyler de, 40:85
Peyster, John de, 27:245; 41:111
Peyster, Maria de, 42:77
Peytral (deputy), 41:162
Pfefferkorn, 28:168
Pfiester, Durst, 34:77
Phagan, Mary, 31:223; 35:276
Phanix, Alexander, 27:248
Pharisees, Philadelphia, 31:276
Phelps, John S., 22:141
Phelps, Thaddeus, 30:404
Phenix Bank (New York), 27:398
Phi Epsilon Pi Fraternity, gift, 34:xxii
Philadelphia, Academy of Music, 22:144;
"Additional Data on the History of
Congregation Rodeph Shalom of
Philadelphia," 28:xxxiii; Board of City
Trusts, 22:144; Chamber of Commerce,
31:256; "Colonel Myer Asch and the
Centennial Exposition at Philadelphia,
1876," 26:xv; colonial congregations,
28:xxvi; Court of Common Pleas, 23:192;
Democratic Club, 22:89-90; *Differentiation
Features of Orthodox, Conservative, and
Reform Jewish Groups in Metropolitan
Philadelphia*, reviewed, 49:276-78; early
Jews, 25:131; Exposition (1876), 28:12, 14;
Fairmount Park commissioners, 22:143-
44; Female Hebrew Benevolent Society,
Constitution, 30:233-34, 308-9, 320-21;
"The Gratz Papers," 23:vii, xiii, 1-23;
Hebra, Constitution and By-Laws, 30:222-
23, 233; Hebrew-English school, 22:xxii-
xxiii; "Hebrew German Society Rodeph
Sholom in the City and County of
Philadelphia, 1880-1950," 49:235; Hebrew
Society for Visitation of the Sick, 30:284-
85, 308, 310-11, 384-85; Henry M.
Phillips, 22:139-46; *The History of the Jews
of Philadelphia from Colonial Times to the Age
of Jackson*, 49:234-35; reviewed, 47:204-7;
"Isaac Leeser and the Jews of Philadelphia:
A Study in National Jewish Influence,"
48:207-44; 49:235; Jewish local history,
49:260-61; "Jewish Owners of Ships
registered at the Port of Philadelphia
1730-1755," 22:xviii; 26:235-36; Jews in,
27:460-65; *Kehillah*, Philadelphia, 22:233;
Masonry, 22:182; "Newspaper Notices of

and by Jews of Philadelphia, 1735-1760,"
22:xxviii; "Original Letters of Moses and
Sampson Levy, of Philadelphia," 22:xiii; "A
Philadelphia Jewish Merchant's Day Book,
1755-1761," 22:xviii; "Rebecca Gratz and
the Jewish Sunday School Movement in
Philadelphia," 49:235; religious
observances, mid-nineteenth century,
37:35; "The Revolutionary Soldiers Buried
in the Spruce Street Cemetery,
Philadelphia, Pa.," 44:242; Spruce Street
Cemetery, 22:xxxii; United Hebrew
Beneficent Society, 30:261-62; Young
Men's Hebrew Association, 23:192;
"Zionism Comes to Philadelphia," 49:235
Philadelphia Academy of Surgery, 22:232
Philadelphia Board of Election, 33:19
Philadelphia Board of Jewish Ministers, 37:46
Philadelphia Charity Hospital, 22:231
Philadelphia Club, 50:244
Philadelphia College of Pharmacy and
Sciences, 38:337
Philadelphia Committee, 48:96
Philadelphia Conference, 40:364-65
Philadelphia Dancing Assembly, 27:460
Philadelphia Fountain Society, 31:256
Philadelphia General Hospital, 22:232
Philadelphia Hebrew Education Society,
37:273-74
Philadelphia Larynological Society, 45:194
Philadelphia Lawyer's Club, 23:192
Philadelphia Ledger, 35:281; 37:58
Philadelphia Municipal League, 38:337
Philadelphia Museum of Art, 41:91-92;
42:459
Philadelphia National Relief Association,
33:217-18
Philadelphia Polyclinical and School for
Graduates in Medicine, 22:231-32; 38:337
Philadelphia Post, 25:143
Philadelphia Press, 40:253; 42:148
Philadelphia Psychiatric Hospital, 48:234
Philadelphia Public Ledger, 41:89
Philadelphia Rapid Transit Company, 25:174
Philadelphia Reading Railroad, 25:146
Philadelphia Sunday and Adult School
Union, 48:71
Philadelphia, Jacob, 23:100; 28:298; 34:249;
35:131

Philanthropin, 28:104
Philanthropy, 48:232; "The Impact of Immigration and Philanthropy Upon the Boston Jewish Community (1880-1914)," 46:71-85; "Jake Gimbel: Hoosier Philanthropist," 48:256-61, 266; Jewish local history, 49:221-22, 225; "Trusts for Jewish Charitable Purposes under the Law of New York," 28:xxiii
Philip II, 29:33; 31:18
Philip V, 27:487
Philip the Fair, 21:240
Philip, Hays, 25:112
Philip, Hoffman, 36:67, 73
Philip Neri, Oratory of St., 23:103
Philip & Solomons, 50:299-300, 361
Philip the Tall, 21:240
Philippe de Tubières de Caylus, 41:61
Philippine Islands, 31:212; 34:227; 40:8; Jews in, 26:5-6
Philippson, Ludwig, 26:284; 28:67, 73-74; 29:128; 35:41, 43; 39:455; 42:159, *Allgemeine Zeitung des Judentums*, 33:36
Philips, David, 27:60
Philips, G., 29:129
Philips, Mrs. G., 27:64
Philips, Henry, 27:61
Philips, Isaac, 50:8
Philips, Israel, 27:278
Philips, Jacob, 21:148-49
Philips, Jonas, 28:225
Philips, Jonas B., 50:8
Philips, Miriam Eugenia, 27:277
Philips, Philip, 22:xxxiii
Philips, Rachel, 27:278
Philipse, Adolph, 46:31
Philipse, Philip, 27:318
Philipson, David, 28:vii, 118; 35:250; 38:73; 50:295; bookplates, 45:176, 191-92; "Centenary papers and others," 34:xxvi; communication from, 26:xxx; "An Early Confirmation Certificate from St. Thomas, B.W.I.," 22:xxviii, 23:180-82; editor, 32:3-4; gifts, 25:xvi; 34:xxvi; Hebrew Union College, 40:33-34, 38, 42, 45; "The Hebrew Words on the Tombstone of William Bradford," 22:xiii, 186-87; history, writing of, 39:259, 46:427, 431; Isaac Harby, 32:41; "Letters of

Rebecca Gratz," 33:xxx; "Midshipman Joseph Israel," 23:xiv; "Moses Jacob Ezekiel," 28:xxii, 1-62; necrology of, 39:461-68, 471; necrologies of Edward L. Heinsheimer, 26:xxx; 28:284-85; J. Walter Freiberg, 29:xiv, 161-63; Kaufmann Kohler, 31:xxiii, 268-71; Louis S. Levi, 28:xxxii, 389-90; Martin Phillipson, 26:xiv, 283-86; Moses J. Gries, 28:xv, 274-76; Solomon Fox, 25:xii, 149-50; Ohio pioneers, 34:174; paper by, 22:xxviii; "Reform Movement in Judaism," 32:35; "A Selected Bibliography of the Writings of David Philipson," 39:445-59; "Simon M. Levy, Member of the First Class to Graduate at the United States Military Academy in 1802," 23:xiv; Simon Wolf, 34:247; "Sir Moses Ezekiel: A Memoir," 28:xvi; "Some Unpublished Papers of Rebecca Gratz," 29:vii, xxxvi, 53-60; Sunday services, 42:378-79; vice-president, 22:xi, xvi, xxvii; 23:xii; 25:xi; 26:xii, xxx; 28:xiv, xxxi, xxxii; 29:xiv, xxviii, xxxv; 31:xv, xxiii, xxix; 32:xix; 33:xvi, xxv; 34:xiii; 35:xiv; 37:xxxix, xxxii, xxxiv; 38:341, 344, 346; Y. M. H. A., 37:266, 268-70; Zionism, 40:366, 371, 381, 389-90; 45:44; 49:193, 199
Philipson, Ella Hollander, 38:73, 39:467
Philipson, Joseph, 39:464
Philipson, Louisa Freudenthal, 39:464
Philipson, Rabbi, 27:91
Phillips, 21:xvi; 29:146
Phillips, A. W., 27:231
Phillips, Aaron, 27:80, 314
Phillips, Aaron Jonas, 41:292
Phillips, Abigail (nee Seixas), 27:74, 113, 163, 165
Phillips, Abraham, "Abraham Phillips, U. S. N.," 32:xx, 125-27
Phillips, Abram, 26:195
Phillips, Abm. L., 27:76, 84
Phillips Academy, 42:344
Phillips, Alfred A. (ed.), *The Forget-Me-Not*, 30:433
Phillips, A. Moratto, 27:166
Phillips, Arabella, 33:207
Phillips, Augustus, 21:240
Phillips, B. B., 27:315

Phillips, Barnet, 39:325
Phillips, Barzila, 25:112
Phillips, Beatrice, 32:xxviii
Phillips, Benjamin, 27:165; 50:42, 58
Phillips, Benjamin I., 27:74, 84, 163, 165, 315
Phillips, Catherine, 27:111
Phillips, Charles, 30:196
Phillips, Daniel, 27:416
Phillips, David, 21:197, 213; 27:42, 111, 259; 38:70
Phillips, David Machado, 27:153
Phillips, Dinah, 27:111
Phillips, Eleazar, 27:398
Phillips, Elias H., 37:268, 270
Phillips, Ella, 27:111, 269, 496; 39:63
Phillips, Ellen, 37:77; 42:405
Phillips, Esther, 38:70
Phillips, Esther (Mrs. Jacob Hendrick), 32:127
Phillips, Esther (nee Seixas), 27:112, 163, 166
Phillips, Eugenia, 27:165
Phillips, Fanny, 32:127; 41:256
Phillips, George, 28:xxxiv
Phillips, Gitlah, 27:112
Phillips, Hannah Issaacks, 32:125
Phillips, Henry (1), 27:84
Phillips, Henry (2), 27:165
Phillips, Henry M., 29:122; 34:266; "Henry Phillips on the Yarmouth Petroglyph," 28:xxii-xxiii; "Life of Hon. Henry M. Phillips," 22:xiii, 139-46
Phillips, Hetty, 27:165
Phillips, I., 47:188
Phillips, I. B., 27:173
Phillips, Isaac (Baltimore), 22:192; 26:187-88
Phillips, Isaac (New York), 22:xxvii, 197, 212, 214; 27:119, 124, 388, 515; 29:131; 38:51-52; 41:207; 45:64-66; Mt. Sinai Hospital, 42:115; Simon Gratz, 37:350
Phillips, Isaac, Jr., 26:187
Phillips, Isaac B., 37:350
Phillips, Isadore, 50:315
Phillips, Israel, 27:165
Phillips, J. Altamont, 22:xxxiv, 142; 39:35
Phillips, J. Campbell, 50:329, 366
Phillips, Jacob, 27:43, 185, 253; 32:125-26; 33:203; 50:42, 58
Phillips, Jacob D., 21:213
Phillips, Jane, 27:111

Phillips, John D., 42:115
Phillips, John S., 43:34
Phillips, Jonas (b. Benjamin L.), 27:165
Phillips, Jonas (father of Benjamin I.), 27:42, 152-53, 335, 350, 388, 460; freeman, certification, 27:156-57
Phillips, Jonas (New York), 21:90, 94, 99-100, 106-7, 170, 172, 213; 26:179, 181, 237-38; 34:170; 35:xviii; 38:83; 39:3; 41:2-3, 204, 227, 280, 284, 292-93; 42:189, 191, 434; 45:64-65; 46:423; "Letter of Jonas Phillips, July 28, 1776, Mentioning the American Revolution and the Declaration of Independence," 25:xiii, 128-31; letters, 34:75; Moses Hays, 28:253-54; portrait, 22:xxxvi; 43:232
Phillips, Jonas (Philadelphia), 22:xxxiv, 139, 153, 163, 197; 47:193; 50:39, 58
Phillips, Mrs. Jonas, 41:292; portrait, 43:232
Phillips, Jonas B., 32:108; 33:197; *Camillus*, 30:290; *The Evil Eye*, 30:276; *Zamira*, 30:304-5
Phillips, Jonas N., 21:197, 214; 27:113, 123, 157, 258; 38:70
Phillips, Jonas W., 29:131
Phillips, Joseph (1), 27:84; (War of 1812), 26:181
Phillips, Joseph (2), 27:451
Phillips, Josephine, 27:111; 50:283; "A Personal Tribute to Lincoln by Josephine Phillips," 41:204-7
Phillips, Joshua, 21:xxvii, 166; 22:75; 27:314, 346, 388, 393
Phillips, L., 29:135; 47:46
Phillips, Lavinia, 27:111
Phillips, Leah (Simon), 37:349-50
Phillips, Levi, 37:349, 351
Phillips, Levy, 27:64, 378; 50:39, 58
Phillips, Manuel (Pa.), 22:163
Phillips, Manuel (1), 26:179, 195
Phillips, Manuel (2), 27:231-32, 394
Phillips, Mical, 27:445
Phillips, Mr., 27:461
Phillips, Morton, 39:62
Phillips, Moses, 27:314, 390; portrait, 41:293
Phillips, Mrs. Moses, 41:293
Phillips, Moses I., 21:169
Phillips, Moses N., 27:80

Phillips, Naphtali, 21:xi, xix, xx, xxvii, 140, 162-63, 165-66, 168-70, 190-92, 208, 212, 214; 27:xiii, 81, 83-84, 86, 96-97, 102-4, 106, 111, 118-19, 143, 146, 163, 166, 214, 229, 231-32, 236, 243, 258-59, 261, 265, 267, 314, 338, 350, 465; 30:298, 445; 31:80; 33:207; 34:291; 38:69-70; 41:204; 45:64-66; Eulogium, 30:170; Historical Sketch of Shearith Israel Congregation, N.Y., 21:172-228; kosher meat, 25:51-52; Mordecai Myers correspondence, 27:396-97; portraiture, 41:280, 293-94; 42:417; Van Buren papers, 22:75; War of 1812, 26:179

Phillips, Mrs. Naphtali, 27:340; 41:294

Phillips, Naphtali J., 27:211

Phillips, Nathaniel, 27:416

Phillips, N. Taylor, 21:xx; 25:ix, 33; 27:143, 216, 252, 268, 285; 31:82, 257; 33:xiii, xxii, xxxi, 8; 35:xii, 309; 38:51-52, 61-62; 43:2; 44:58-63; 50:274, 300; Adler resolutions, 28:xxxv; auditor, 34:x; Battle of Long Island, 28:xxx; by-laws committee, 25:xii; communication from, 26:xxx; on David Mendes Machado, 27:267-68; executive council, 43:230; 44:241; finance committee, 26:x, xxvii; gifts, 32:xxix; 33:xxix; 35:xix; 41:285, 385-86; Lyons papers, 21:x, xii; 22:xxi; necrology of, 45:64-66; necrology of Clarence I. De Sola, 28:xxxii, 269-72; portraiture, 41:276, 286-88, 290, 292-94; "References to M. M. Noah and A. Phillips 1821-1822, in 'The theatrical life of Joe Cowell Comedian, written by himself,' " 33:xvii; regrets of, 28:xvii; Sampson Simson, 34:253; Sampson Simson Oration, 46:51, 54; thirtieth annual meeting, committee on, 29:xi; treasurer and reports, 22:x-xii, xv, xxv-xxvii; 23:x, xii; 25:ix-xi; 26:x-xii, xvii-xix, xxx; 28:xiii-xiv, xx-xxi, xxxi-xxxii; vice-president, 28:xxi, xxxii; 29:xiv, xxviii, xxxv; 31:xv, xxiii, xxix; 32:xii, xix; 33:xvi, xxv; 34:xiii; 35:xiv; 37:xxix, xxxii, xxxiv; 38:341, 344; 39:469; 40:406; 41:387; 42:414

Phillips, Mrs. N. Taylor, 32:xxv

Phillips, Peter, 27:447

Phillips, Philip, 50:192; "Sketch of Philip Phillips," 28:xxxix

Phillips, P. Lee, gift, 28:xxxix

Phillips, R., 47:188

Phillips, Rachel (b. David), 27:111

Phillips, Rachel (b. Jonas), 35:xviii; 50:58

Phillips, Rachel (Mrs. Micael Levy), 42:189-92

Phillips, Rachel (Mrs. Michael Myers), 32:127

Phillips, Rachel (b. Moses Seixas), 38:70

Phillips, Rachel (b. Napthali), 27:111, 166

Phillips, Rachel Hannah (Mendes Seixas), 41:293

Phillips, Rebecca, 39:63

Phillips, Rebecca (b. Benjamin), 27:165

Phillips, Rebecca (Mrs. Isaiah Moses), 32:127

Phillips, Rebecca (Mrs. Jonas), 27:350; 42:434

Phillips, Rebecca Machado, 22:xxxiv

Phillips, Rebecca (Mendez Machado), 41:201, 292-93

Phillips, Rebecca (Mrs. Moses S.), 27:112

Phillips, Rebecca (b. Naphtali), 27:111; 38:70

Phillips, Rosalie (Mrs. N. Taylor), 50:300

Phillips, Ruben, 27:166

Phillips, Sam, 44:239

Phillips, Samuel, 26:183

Phillips, Sarah, 27:111, 166; 28:xxxiv

Phillips, Simon, 25:113

Phillips, Stephen, 35:121

Phillips, Uriah, 27:152

Phillips, W. Alison, 26:82

Phillips, Wendell, 42:131, 137, 155

Phillips, William, 36:70, 75, 142, 145, 149, 151-52, 159, 366-67, 386-88; 45:222

Phillips, Zalegman, 22:139, 153; 27:84; 30:249; 33:207; 34:266

Phillips, Zipporah, 41:2-3

Phillips, Zipporah (b. Benjamin), 27:165

Phillips, Zipporah (b. Jonas), 42:434

Phillips, Zipporah (b. Naphtali), 27:111, 166

Phillipse, Frederick, 27:320

Phillipson, Franz, 43:64

Phillipson, Martin, Geschicte Heinrichs des Lowen, 26:285; necrology of, 26:xiv, 283-86; Neueste Geschicte des Jüdischen Volkes, 26:285

Phillipson, Samuel, 28:240

Philobiblon Club, 42:459

Philolexian Society, 26:220

Philology, "Some Eminent Jewish
    Philologists of Past Ages," 23:xv
Philosophical and Medical Society of
    Würzburg, 23:111
Phineas, Elias, 27:43
Phineas, Isaac, 23:139
Phinsy, Rabbi, 27:91
Phipps, John, 37:128
Phoenix, Ariz., Jewish Community Council,
    contribution, 37:xxviii
Phoenix, The, 40:351, 353
Phoenix Club (Baltimore), 25:155;
    (Cincinnati), 22:227; (Rochester), 40:66-67
Phoenix Hose Company, 42:399, 401-2;
    48:75
Phoenix Trust Company, 31:284
Photocopied Historical Materials, Guide to,
    48:69
Photographic Sketchbook of the War of the
    Rebellion, 50:300
Phylacteries, "The Phylacteries Found at
    Pittsfield, Mass.," 23:xiv; 25:vii, 81-85
Physicians, "Jewish Physicians in Italy: Their
    Relation to the Papal and Italian States,"
    28:xxiii, 133-211
Picard, 27:97
Picard, Hart, 27:84, 103
Picard, Mrs., 27:103
Picciotto, 34:171
Picciotto, James, 42:435
Pichon, Stephen Jean Marie, 46:97
Pichot, Daniel, 37:394-95, 399, 407-9
Piciotto, Cohen, 38:237
Pick (immigrant), 38:202
Pickens, 25:12
Pickering, Timothy, 38:120, 130-31; 46:438;
    48:179, 183-84
Pickert, Lehmann, 46:75-76, 84
Pickup, Alice, 46:161
Pickus, Manuel, History of the Beckley Jewish
    Community (Beckley, West Virginia) and of
    Congregation Beth El (The Beckley Hebrew
    Association) (including Raleigh and Fayette
    Counties, West Virginia) (1895-1955),
    49:241-42
Picquart, Georges, 45:258-59
Pidyhon ha-ben, 39:369
Pierce, Clother, Jr., 35:291
Pierce, Edward L., 42:141

Pierce, Franklin, 25:16, 27; 38:160; 39:52;
    50:332
Pierce, John, 25:131-32; 37:442
Pierce, Stephen, 23:157
Pierce, Thomas, 27:326
Pierce, Ulysses G. B., 40:293
Pierpont Morgan Library, 37:12; 45:62
Pierson, 22:76
Pierson, Johnson, The Judaid, 30:390, 392-93;
    34:xvi
Pieterez, Joseph L., see: Gundall, Frank
Pietersen, Solomon, 22:151
Pietersz, Salomon, 44:87, 92-94
Pietschmann, 28:10, 28
Piety, T., 49:44
Pietz, A., 45:206
Pikard, H., 27:95
Pike, 27:315
Pike, Boas Israel, 27:277
Pike, M. S., 27:399
Pike, Samuel, Compendious Hebrew Lexicon,
    30:120, 147
Pilcher, Joseph Mitchell, 37:436
Pilcher, Lewis F., 41:68
Pile, R. P., 26:254
Piles, B. M., 27:105
Pilgrim People, 40:395-98
Pilgrims in a New Land, reviewed, 38:249-51
Pillet, H., 27:400
Pillow, Gideon Johnson, 50:342
Pilsudski, Josef, 36:148, 156-57
Pimenta, David Dias (Abraham), 29:23-24
Pimentel, Abraham, 42:303-4
Pimentel family, "A Genealogical Note on
    the Pimentel, Lopez, Sasportas and Rivera
    Families," 42:303-4
Pimentel, Hannah, 42:303-4
Pimentel, Rodrigo de Borras, 33:118
Pimentel, Samuel Rodriguez, 42:303-4
Pimento, Jan, 33:116
Pimontel, Aaron, 27:42
Pina, Aaron de, 33:99
Pina, Benjamin de, 42:225, 260, 283-84, 388
Pina, David Sarfaty de, 29:13
Pina, Jacob de, 29:14
Pina, Manoel de, 29:14
Pina, Paul de, 35:27
Pina, Ribqa de, 29:14
Pina, Sarah de, 35:27-28

Pina, Yosua Sarfatti, 29:13
Pinah, 42:388
Pinah, Benjamin de, 44:83
Pinanaki, Samuel, 42:419
Pinchas, 42:193
Pinchion, William, 43:237
Pinchot, Gifford, 47:187
Pinckney, Charles C., 38:4, 119
Pinckney, Henry L., 32:43
Pincus, Adolph, 50:314
Pinder, J. H., 26:254
Piné, David Sarfaty de, 26:252
Pine, Max, 50:215, 233
Pine, Robert Edge, 41:278, 289; 43:233
Pine, Samson, 35:125-26
Pinedo, Gabriel, 21:70; 27:248; 44:231-32
Pinedo, Jacob, 27:248
Pinedo, Jacob de Gabriel, 44:233-34
Ping, Chan, 34:197
Pinhas, Ishak, 27:122
Pinheiro, Aaron, 26:251; 32:60
Pinheiro, Abraham (b. Abraham), 23:158
Pinheiro, Abraham (Barbados), 26:251; 32:59
Pinheiro, Abraham (Brazil), 42:280, 395
Pinheiro, Abraham (father of Isaho), 23:157
Pinheiro, Benjamin, 26:251
Pinheiro, David, 26:251; 32:59
Pinheiro, Elizabeth (Esther), 23:158
Pinheiro, Isaac (Barbados), 26:251; 32:60
Pinheiro, Isaac (New York), 23:149, 157-58
Pinheiro, Jacob, 23:157-58; 26:251
Pinheiro, Jael, 32:59
Pinheiro, Judith, 23:157
Pinheiro, Lunah, 32:59
Pinheiro, Manuel, 29:35
Pinheiro, Moses, 23:157-58; 26:251
Pinheiro, Rachel, 23:157
Pinheiro, Rebekah, 23:157
Pinheiro, Sarah, 23:157
Pinheiro, Robert, 26:117
Pinkey, William, 25:95
Pinkos, Henry, 36:179-85, 187, 189, 192, 195, 197-98; 41:168
Pinkus, Lazar F., 35:123
Pinna, David Larfaty de, 32:57
Pinney, Azariah, 32:64
Pino, Benjamin de, 33:62
Pinsker, Leo, 43:48, 174; 46:371
Pinson, Koppel S., 49:137; 50:260, 270

Pinto, Aaron, 21:91
Pinto, Abraham (br. Jacob), 38:92
Pinto, Abraham (New York) (1), 21:45-48, 54, 56-58, 61, 63, 213
Pinto, Abraham (New York) (2), 27:122; 27:64-65, 248
Pinto, Abraham (West Indies), 25:116
Pinto, Abraham, Jr., 25:116
Pinto, Aris, 33:114
Pinto, Bento Teixeira, 50:74-75
Pinto, David, 27:241; 32:10
Pinto, D. R. Joseph Yesurun, 22:51; 39:299
Pinto, Esther, 25:116
Pinto family, 50:28
Pinto, Ferdinand Mendez, 35:229
Pinto, George Rodrigus, 33:115
Pinto, Isaac (Barbados), 32:62
Pinto, Isaac (Conn.), 38:92
Pinto, Isaac (New York) (1), 21:44, 53, 55, 63; 25:47; 27:41, 43; non-importation, 22:50-51; 26:238; *Prayers for Jewish Holidays*, 30:56-59; 34:54
Pinto, Isaac (West Indies), 25:116
Pinto, Isaac de, 42:440; 47:224
Pinto, Is. de Seml. Jesurun, 22:169; 29:30
Pinto, Jacob, 27:241; 50:27, 36, 58
Pinto, Jacob (Conn.), 38:92
Pinto, Jacob (New York), 21:45, 53; 23:152
Pinto, Jacob and Solomon, 27:248
Pinto, Johacob de, 33:50
Pinto, Jorge Homen, 33:58, 76-78, 81, 97, 118; 47:113, 209; 50:75
Pinto, Joseph, 35:291
Pinto, Joseph (Barbados), 32:62
Pinto, Joseph (New York), 21:79, 94, 140, 145, 148; 27:41:43, 51, 59, 253; 28:237; 50:37, 58
Pinto, Joseph Jessurun, 21:79, 86, 91-92, 208; 27:11, 23, 26-27, 262-63, 330, 361; 31:237; Shearith Israel correspondence, 27:13-17, 24-25
Pinto, Joseph Yesurun, "Form of Prayer Performed at Jews Synagogue," 30:48, 50
Pinto, Joshua, 27:62
Pinto, Josiah (b. Joseph), 45:63
Pinto, Moses, 27:80
Pinto, Rachel (Conn.), 38:92-93
Pinto, Rachel (Hunt's Bay), 37:334

Pinto, Rachel (New York), 27:41, 43, 58-59, 61, 84, 96, 158; 34:134, 140; 45:187; 50:37, 58

Pinto, Salomon, 21:53, 55, 61

Pinto, Samuel, 21:60-61, 63; 23:152; 44:228

Pinto, Sarah, 42:430

Pinto, Semuel, 44:228

Pinto, Semuel Jesurun, 44:232

Pinto, Solomon, 38:92; 50:58

Pinto, William, 38:92

Pioda, Mr., 36:311

Pioneer of Freedom, 44:175

Pioneers (St. Louis), 37:281-82

Pionier (Boston), 42:135

Pious, see: Antiochus VII

Piperno, Abraham Baruch, 37:63, 73, 83

Pipernuter, der, 48:132

Pique, Rabbi, 34:124, 136, 140

Piquis, Rabbi, 27:95

Pirates, 28:219; "Benjamin Franks, Merchant and Captain Kidd, Pirate," 31:229-34

Piso, William, 47:116

Pissaro (family name), 48:139

Pissarro, Camille, 40:318; 44:119

Pitman, Frank W., 35:294

Pitman, J. T., 50:381

Pitt, Thomas, 28:250

Pitt, William, 25:81; 35:2, 17; 38:113

Pittsburgh, 47:34; The Early Migration and Settlement of Jews in Pittsburgh, 1754-1894, 49:235-36; religious observances, mid-nineteenth century, 37:36

Pittsburgh Conference, 34:187; 40:365; 42:105, 376, 379, 385

Pittsburgh & Connellsville Railroad, 25:146

Pittsburgh Gazette, 38:136

"Pittsburgh Platform," 39:467; 44:251; 45:266; 48:228

Pittsburgh, University of, 46:151

Pittsfield (Mass.), "The Phylacteries Found at Pittsfield, Mass.," 23:xiv; 25:vii, 81-85

Pius II, 28:158

Pius IV, 28:165, 175, 211

Pius V, 28:175-76, 177, 179

Pius VIII, 28:186

Pius XII, 46:258

Pius, King of Greece, 26:169

Pixotto, Abraham, 26:251

Piza, Abram Ysrael de, 42:278, 395; 44:92

Piza, David, 21:43; 50:131

Piza, David M., 39:403-4

Piza, Emanuel de, 22:179-80

Piza (family name), 48:139

Piza, Jacob Fonseca de, 22:178

Piza, Jeudah, 29:26

Pizarro, Francisco, 31:4

Pizarro, Jacob, 44:119

Pizarro, Rachel Pomier, Petit, 44:119

Pizzarro, Abraham, 44:119

Placide, Alexander, 33:178, 190; 34:143

Placquea, Guilliemo de, 33:122

Plante, 23:49

Platke, T., 29:130

Platt, Thomas C., 29:174

Plattsburg, N.Y., religious observances, mid-nineteenth century, 37:37

Platzek, M. Warley, bequest, 33:xx; necrology, 33:xxi

Plaut, W. Gunther, 42:467; "A Hebrew-Dakota Dictionary," 42:361-70; *The Jews in Minnesota; The First Seventy Five Years*, 49:226-27; "Unlike Twins: A Study of the Differential Development of St. Paul and Minneapolis," 47:202

Players, New York City, 37:473

Plehve, Viatcheslaf K. von, 34:281; 36:263; 46:91-93

Plessen, von, 26:88

Plesur, Milton, 46:162

Plont, Grace, 25:88

Plont, Samuel, 25:88

Plotke, Julius, 43:64-65

Plotnik, Sh., 39:94

Plumb, Edward L., 32:91-92, 94

Plumptre, Anne, 33:185-86

Plumsted (Philadelphia), 35:20, 22-23

Plum Street Temple (Cincinnati), 40:32-33

Plymouth Code, 46:23

Plymouth Colony, "The Hebrew Preface to Bradford's History of the Plymouth Plantation," 38:289-303, 346; "The Hebrew Words on the Tombstone of William Bradford" (note), 22:186-87

Plymouth Plantation, 43:198

Po'ale Agudat Israel, 49:273

Poale Zion, 48:244

Poalei Zion Organization, gift, 33:xxxiii

Pobiedonostzev, Constantine, 43:38, 46

Pocahontas, 32:6
Pocock, Isaac, 33:194
Pococke, John, 27:175
Pococke, Richard, 41:61
Podell, David L., gift, 34:xxiv
Poe Amendment, 40:291
Poe, Edgar Allan, 28:55, 56; 33:24; 38:277; 42:457
Poel Zedek Congregation (New York City), 50:301
Poems and Translations, 38:261; 45:248
"Poet Heine, The," 45:255
Poets of America, 45:251
Poets and Poetry of Europe, The, 45:21
Poincaré, Raymond, 46:98
Poindexter, 46:470
Poindexter, Miles, 24:83
Pointel, W., 43:216
Point Petre, 26:192-93
Polache, Mrs. Alexander, 27:112
Polache, Eliza, 27:112
Polachek, Solomon, 33:162
Polack, Friederika, 41:261
Polack, Maier, 41:261
Polack, Mr., 27:407
Polack, William N., 23:179
Polack, Zachariah, 21:21-25, 31, 40, 42, 48
Polak, Abraham, 41:268
Polak, Gabriel, 22:121
Polak, Jacob, 35:208
Polak, Meyer, 27:199
Poland, 24:14; "American Jews and the Polish Insurrection of 1863," 37:xxx; Board of Delegates of American Israelites, 29:91; education, 28:83, 87, 106, 110-12, 114, 119-20, 123, 125-27; "Efforts of Polish Jews in America in behalf of Poland's Independence before and during the Polish Revolution of 1863," 37:xxxii; family names, 48:19; *Gedulath Shaul*, 22:132; "The History of Polish Jewry in the Second Half of the Eighteenth Century," 31:xvii; "The Influence of Lewis Way and Other English Missionaries upon Alexander I's Treatment of the Jews," 26:116-25; insurrection, 41:196-97; Jewish rights, 26:38, 83, 94; 34:xix, 222-23; migration, 26:5; 42:162-64, 170, 175; "Poland and the Minority Races," 28:xli;

"Polish Alliance of All Religious Faiths," 39:160; "Polish Political Emigree in the United States and the Jews, 1833-1865," 39:143-67; and refugees, 45:232-33; Russian Poland, 36:208-14; "Some Remarks on the Shabbethai-Zebi Movement in Poland and Ukrania," 28:xxxiii; Treaty of 1919, 28:83, 127; U.S. intercession for Jews, 36:ix; 140-67, 389-402
Polanke, Mr., 37:402
Polano, Hyman, 48:240
Polhemius, Johannes, 44:90-91, 93-94
Poliakoff, Jacob, 43:65
Poliakoff, Lazar, 43:65-66
Poliakoff, S. de, 42:178
Polier, Justine Wise, 39:334
Polignac, Prince, 25:70
Poling, Clark W., 45:215
Polish Central Committee, 39:156
Polish Committee in Paris, 39:154
Polish National Committee, 36:149-50; 39:156, 158, 165-67
Polish Jews, 45:232
Polish Relief Committee, 36:147
Politianus, Angelus, 28:196
Political Action Committee, 41:329
Polk, Frank L., 36:71, 142, 150, 152-53, 158-59
Polk, James Knox, 25:16-17; 50:10
Polk, Leonidas, 29:121; 50:342
Polk, Mr., 36:75
Pollack, William N., 35:307
Pollack, Celia Heilprin, 26:286
Pollak, Francis Déak, necrology of, 26:xiv, 286-88
Pollak, Gustav, 26:286
Pollak, Max, 39:462; 45:192
Pollard, William, 30:77
Poller, Leonard, 49:270
Pollexfen, John, 38:45-46
Pollock, Abigail, 50:36, 59
Pollock, Abm., 27:416
Pollick, Asher, 38:15
Pollock, Benjamin F., 26:188
Pollock, Channing, 40:354
Pollock family (Newport), 27:212, 455; 38:83-85, 91
Pollock, Frederick, 31:179; 42:354

Pollock, I., 22:100
Pollock, Jacob, 27:213
Pollock, Solomon, 50:42
Pollock, the Tory, 46:21
Pollock, William, 40:75
Pollock, Zachariah, 21:21-25, 31, 40, 42; 37:392
Polly (slave) (1), 50:161
Polly (slave) (2), 50:163
Polock, Abigail, 27:348
Polock, Mrs. Abigail, 48:12-14
Polock, Abraham, 48:11-12, 18
Polock, Ann, 48:13
Polock, Bilhah, 48:11, 18
Polock, Cushman, 27:461; 50:67
Polock, David, 27:348; 44:63; 48:6-8, 12-14, 18
Polock, Eitlah, 27:74
Polock, Esther, 35:291
Polock, Fanny (Isaacks), 48:11, 18
Polock, Francis, 35:291
Polock, Hannah (b. Isaac), 48:11, 18
Polock, Hannah (d. Myer), 48:11-12, 18
Polock, Hyman, 47:204-6
Polock, Isaac (1), 21:15, 24, 38-39, 42, 48, 53, 55
Polock, Isaac (2), 27:178, 180, 185, 199; 48:11, 18; 50:52; "Isaac Polock: Early Settler in Washington, D.C.," 47:201; 48:1-18
Polock, Isaac (b. Myer) (R.I.), 27:153
Polock, Isaac (N.J.), 33:254
Polock, Isaachar (1), 27:180
Polock, Isaachar (2), 37:392
Polock, Isachar Junr, 21:53
Polock, Izachar, 21:11, 14, 64
Polock, Jacob (b. Isaac), 48:11, 18
Polock, Jacob (b. Myer), 27:348; 44:62; 48:11, 18
Polock, Judith, 48:10-12, 18
Polock, M., 31:159
Polock, Moses, 35:282; 42:457; 47:204
Polock, Myer (New York), 50:59
Polock, Myer (rabbi), 48:18
Polock, Myer (R.I.), 27:153, 213, 348, 350, 413, 448; 35:288-92; 48:11, 13, 18; Moses M. Hays, 28:225
Polock, Myra, 48:19
Polock, Rachel, 48:11-12, 14, 18

Polock, Rebecca, 27:199
Polock, Sarah, 48:13, 18
Polock, Solomon, 50:154
Polock, Zephaniah, 27:199
Polok, Isaac Jacob, 27:193
Polonies, Myer, 27:xvii
Polonies Talmud, 34:xxiv
Polonies Talmud Torah, 42:110
Polonies Talmud Torah School, 21:xxvi; 27:81-83, 95, 115, 137, 140, 146, 243, 397-98
Polony, Meyer, "Polonies Talmud Torah of New York," 34:123-41
Polsky, Howard W., 48:67-68
Poluck, Isacher, 27:392
Polyclinic Hospital, Philadelphia, 29:157
Polygamy, 43:165
Pombal, Marquis de, 37:360-61; 38:94
Pomegranates, 43:3
Pomeroy, George, 47:99
Pomis, David ben Isaac de, 28:165
Pomis, Vitale (Jehiel Rehabiah), Alatino di, 28:173, 179
Pompey (slave), 50:176
Pomrenze, Seymour J., 47:203; book review by, 48:136-37
Ponce, Luis, 31:13
Pond, Charles F., 39:10
Pond, Gideon, 42:361, 363-64, 366
Pond, Samuel W., 42:361; "A Hebrew-Dakota Dictionary," 42:361-70
Ponet, John, 37:187
Pongoski, Stanisles, 41:166
Poniatowski, Stanislaus, 41:196
Pontchartrain, Comte de, 40:81
Ponte, L. L. de, 30:284
Ponte, Lorenzo da, 29:xliii; 34:175, 179; 50:69; *Almachide*, 30:268; *Apologetical Discourse on Italy*, 30:196; (ed.), *Economia della Vita Umana*, 30:232-33; (trans.), *Hadad*, 30:235; *Il Don Giovanni*, 30:243; *Il Mezenzio*, 30:298; *L'Ape Musicale*, 30:268; *La Profezia di Dante*, 30:198; *Le Nozze Di Figaro, Il Don Giovanni, e l'Assure Re d'Ormus*, 30:242-43; "Memoirs," 32:xxvii; 34:xvii; *Memorie*, 30:216, 219, 258-60; *Sketch of His Life*, 30:369; *Storia Compendiosa*, 30:130, 132; *Storia della*

Lingua e letterature italiana, 30:247-48; *Versi*, 30:281

Pontiac, chief, 35:3, 16, 18-19; 40:82; "Jewish Commissaries to the British and Provincial Troops in America during the French and Indian War and Pontiac's Conspiracy," 42:415; "The Startling Experience of a Jewish Trader During Pontiac's Siege of Detroit in 1763," 23:vii, xiv, 31-35

Pool, David de Sola, 37:385; 39:206, 336; 40:205, 414-15; books reviewed by, 38:323-25; 47:176-78; 50:252-53; "The Burial Society in Curacao in 1783," 22:xii; "By-Laws of Congregation Shearith Israel, New York, 1761," 31:xxx; Civil War, 50:272, 281, 290; "Colonel Myer Asch and the Centennial Exposition at Philadelphia, 1876," 26:xv; "Committee Report on the Building of a New Synagogue and List of Promised Donations, New York, 1817, including letters from Curacao and Baltimore Supporting the Synagogue, 1818," 22:xxx; "The Conversion of Abraham Kirkar, New York, 1848," 33:xvii; "David G. Seixas and the Pennsylvania Institution for the Deaf and Dumb," 22:xxix; "Descriptions of the Synagogue in New York in 1776 and 1828," 40:187-89; "The Diary of Chaplain Michael M. Allen, September, 1861," 38:347; 39:177-82; *The Earliest Jewish Prayer Book Printed in America*, 30:51; "Early Jewish Residents in Massachusetts," 23:vii, 79-80; "An Early Zionist Project," 25:xiii; executive council, 38:344; 39:470; 46:493; 47:201; 48:266; "The First Hebrew and English Prayer-Book Printed in the United States," 32:xii; "Gershom Mendes Seixas' Letters, 1813-1815, to his Daughter Sarah (Seixas) Kursheedt and Son-in-Law Israel Baer Kursheedt," 35:xv, xix, 189-205, 22:xxxii; 33:xxxi, xxxiii; 34:xxi, xxvi; 35:xix, xxiii; "The Hebra Gemiluth Hasadim, New York, 1784-1790," 33:xvii; Hebrew Learning, 38:202; history, writing of, 39:313; 46:193, 413; "A Jew Among the Indians of the Great Lakes," 22:xii; "The Jewish Colony of Sholem, Ulster County, New York, 1838,"

23:178-79; Jewish Tercentenary, 40:408-14; "The Jewish Theological Seminary and Scientific Institution of 1852," 22:xxix; "J. Seixas, Hebraist," 22:xxix; Lee Max Friedman Award Medal, 49:271; "The Literary Activity of Isaac Moses Gomez, Jr.," 22:xxix; Lyons papers, 21:x, xii; 22:xxi; 31:236-40; "A MS. Hebrew Work of Samuel Robles de Medina, Surinam, 1762," 26:xv; "The Missing Half-Century of Jewish Story in Newport, R.I., 1850-1900," 38:343; "The Mohelim of Curacao and Surinam, and Other Notes," 25:xiii, 138-41; "Moses Cohen Dazavedo: sermon preached by him on the Revolution in London, December 13, 1776," 33:xvii; naturalization, 38:235-37; necrologies of: Elvira Nathan Solis, 43:231, 253; Florence Nightingale Knight Harris, 31:xxiv, 258-60; Henry Pereira Mendes, 35:x, 316-19; Henry S. Hendricks, 49:56-63; Hermann Adler, 22:xii, 200-203; Leon Huhner, 47:201, 223-225; Lilian H. Hendricks, 31:xxiv, 260-61; Manuel Augustus Kursheedt, 31:xvi, 273-275; Moses Gaster, 37:467-68; N. Taylor Phillips, 45:64-66; Solomon Solis-Cohen, 38:336-40; nominations, 32:xii; "A Note on the Early History of the Touro Synagogue in New Orleans," 32:xiii; "Note on the Jewish Colony of Sholam, Ulster County, N.Y., 1838," 22:xxix; notes on American Jewish History, 22:167-75; "Notes on the Jewish Community in St. Thomas, 1841-1846," 31:xxx; "Notes on the Lyons Collection," 31:xvii; orthodoxy, 39:264; Palestine, 34:288-89; "A Pamphlet on the Subject of Reform, Jamaica, 1848," 26:xv; "A Passover Tray from Easton, Pa., 1843," 34:xiv; past president, 50:426; *Portraits Etched in Stone / Early Jewish Settlers, 1682-1831*, reviewed, 42:425-34; 49:229; prayer book, 49:60; "The Prayer Book of 1761, including a Note on the Bookplate of Benjamin S. Judah," 22:xxix; "The Presentation of a Flag to the Anthon Battalion by Mrs. Commodore Levy," 22:xii; president, 44:241; presidential message, 45:260-62; presides, 41:390;

44:242; Puritans, 22:186; "A Real Estate Record of the Sholam Colony," 25:xiii; "The Refutation of Rabbi B. C. Carillon, Jamaica, 1847," 26:xv; "Religious and Cultural Phases of American Jewish History," 38:346; 39:291-301; "A Revised List of the Hazanim in New York City in the Eighteenth Century," 25:xiii; "Saul Brown, the First Hazan in North America, and Benjamin Wolf, the Third Recorded Hazan," 32:xix; "The Sermon Preached in London, 1776, by Rabbi Moses Cohen D'Azevedo on the American Revolution," 31:xxx; "Shemah Israel, A Magazine of the Reform Movement in Curacao, 1864-1865," 26:xv, 239-41; "A Slave Proclamation of De Witt Clinton," 25:xiii; "Some Business Relations of Jacob L. Seixas," 29:xxxvi; "Some Early Relations between Palestine and American Jewry," 32:xiii; "Some Further Notes on Mrs. Commodore U. P. Levy," 22:xxxix; "Some Letters of Grace Seixas Nathan, 1814-1821," 37:xxx, 203-11; "Some Relations of Gershom Kursheedt and Sir Moses Montefiore," 37:xxxiii, 213-20; "The threat to the Chatham Square Cemetery in the eighteenth century," 33:xvii; "The Touro Synagogue: Aspects of the Missing Half-Century of its History (1850-1900)," 38:57-76; 49:236; "Two Visitors to Congregation Shearith Israel," 39:471; vice-president, 40:406; 41:387; 42:414; 43:230; "Warder Cresson's 'The Key of David,' 1852," 26:xv; "What We Learn from the Tombstones in the New Bowery Cemetery," 32:xiii; William H. Taft wedding anniversary, 22:x; and Tamar de Sola, *An Old Faith in the New World: Highlights of Three Hundred Years*, 44:210-14; 49:230; review, 46:125-26

Pool, Tamar de Sola, 50:281, 290; *see also*: Pool, David de Sola

Pope, 25:14

Pope, Joseph, 43:204

Pope, Liston, 46:242

Popish Plot, "Additional Material on Francisco de Faria," 25:xiii, 127-28

Popkin, Zelda F., "The Synagogue in the Wilderness," 32:xx

Popolo Romani, 28:14, 37

Poppa, 40:358

Popper, Alice I., 32:xxxvi

Popper (family name), 38:197

Popper, William, 26:241; 33:132, 135

Popple, Mr., 26:231

Popple, Secretary, 35:294

Porcupine, Peter, 38:129

Porcupine's Gazette, 38:121

"Porotergus Gimbeli," 48:258

Porphyry, 26:167, 171

Portaleone, Abraham di, 28:179, 183

Portaleone, Abraham Arje, 28:192

Portaleone, Abram, II, 28:183, 192-93

Portaleone, Abram, III, 28:193

Portaleone, Benjamin (1), 28:168, 191-92, 204

Portaleone, Benjamin (2), 28:193

Portaleone, David, 28:192

Portaleone, David, II, 28:193

Portaleone, Eleazar (Lazzaro), 28:192

Portaleone, Guglielmo de, 28:168

Portaleone, Leon, 28:193

Portaleone, Lucius, 28:193

Port Books, 23:92-96

Port Chester, N.Y., "The Economic Life of the Jews of Port Chester, N.Y.," 45:262

Porte, Dr., 33:214

Portello, Moses, 36:62

Porter, David, 34:174; 39:8

Porter, David Dixon, 44:112-13

Porter, Fitz John, 50:398

Porter, Horace, 48:162-64

Porter, Jack, *Differentiating Features of Orthodox, Conservative, and Reform Jewish Groups in Metropolitan Philadelphia*, reviewed, 49:276-78

Porter, Joseph, 39:18, 29

Portheim family, 38:187

Portland, Maine, 49:251; *Portland Jewry: Its Growth and Development*, 49:223; religious observances, mid-nineteenth century, 37:38

Portland Ore., religious observances, mid-nineteenth century, 37:37

Portland, Society for Promoting Christianity among the Jews, 30:219

Porto, 21:115
Porto, Esther do, 35:32
Porto, Samuel do, 29:28
Portraiture, "Early American Jewish
    Portraiture," 41:275-96, 387
Portugal, anti-Semitism, 22:112-14, 117-19,
    126, 131-32, 155-56, 158, 180-82; *The
    Dutch in Brazil, 1624-1654*, reviewed,
    47:112-20, 209; expulsion of Jews, 22:112-
    14; 26:5; 44:204; "History of the
    Establishment of the Inquisition in
    Portugal," 31:xxxiv; inquisition, 22:117-19,
    131-32, 155-56, 158, 180-82; 32:36, 45;
    33:44, 52-54, 95-96; 41:2; 44:204-5; 50:73;
    "Isaac de Castro, Brazilian Jewish Martyr,"
    47:63-75; Israel Solomon, 25:70-74; Jews
    and Colonial America, 26:xviii; Jews in
    New Netherlands, 29:39-42; "The Jews of
    Portugal and Brazil," 32:xx; "A Newspaper
    Account of an Auto-da-Fe in Lisbon in
    1726, in which a Native of Bahia, South
    America, was burned," 22:xviii, 180-82;
    "The Portuguese Inquisition of 1730 with
    Special Reference to John da Costa,
    Sometime Commissary-General of
    Portugal," 29:xxxvi; "Portuguese Jewish
    Physicians, with an Exhibit of Some of
    Their Works," 29:xxix; readmission of
    Jews, 37:359-63
"Portuguese Art, 800-1800," 45:271
Portuguese Congregation, London, 26;252
Portuguese Jewish Congregation of
    Hamburg, "Extracts From the Minute-
    Book of the Portuguese-Jewish
    Congregation of Hamburg," 23:182-83
Portuguese Congregation Talmud Torah
    (Venice), 42:225-26
Portuguese Hebrew Congregation
    (Philadelphia), 39:46, 65; (Richmond),
    39:46, 65
Portuguese Hebrew Hospital (N.Y.), 39, 45,
    65
Portuguese Jewish Community (Amsterdam),
    42:220-21, 226
Portuguese Jewish Society (N.Y.), 39:63
Portuguese Jews, "Hugo Grotius and the
    Emancipation of the Jews in Holland,"
    31:xxiv, 173-80

Portuguese Jews' Societies in London,
    22:178-79
Posegate, F. M., 25:124
Posener, S., 35:136
Posnanski, Gedalia, 27:344
Posner, Stanley I., 47:203
Posner, Zalman, 35:263
Post, Frans, 47:116
Postal, Bernard, *A Jewish Guide to the U. S.*,
    49:244
Postal Service, 47:188; "Abraham Cohen:
    Deputy Postmaster at Georgetown, South
    Carolina (1789-1800)," 48:177-93; of the
    Confederate States of America, 50:381
Postlethwait, Samuel, 30:77
Potash and Perlmutter, 40:356
Potomac Canal Company, 48:10
Potsdamer & Rosenboum, 31:158
Pottawatomie Massacre, 23:67, 69
Potter, Captain, 35:298
Potter, Henry Codman, 33:212, 217, 221-23,
    228-29; 43:32-33
Potter, Marion E., 46:160
Potter, Paul M., 35:252
Potter, Stephen, 35:290
Pottsville, Pa., religious observances, mid-
    nineteenth century, 37:36
Poughkeepsie, N.Y., religious observances,
    mid-nineteenth century, 37:37
Pound, Cuthbert W., 49:15
Pound, Roscoe, 34:244
Pouren, Jan Janoff, 41:176-77
Pouzzner, Benjamin S., "Benjamin S.
    Pouzzner," 32:xx
Pouzzner, Bessie London, "Benjamin S.
    Pouzzner," 32:xx; "The Jewish Women of
    the German Salons," 32:xiii
Powderly, T. V., 24:109
Powel, John, 35:174
Powell, Charles S., 33:183
Powell, Frederick York, 35:127
Powell, J. H., 37:185
Powell, L. M., 39:29, 33
Powell, Lazarus Whitehead, 42:141, 143
Powell, Mrs. (actress), 33:193
Powell, Rep., 34:275
Powell, Thomas, 22:20
Powell, Thomas Reed, 46:471
Powell, William, 31:182

Power, Hersh, 27:335-36

Power, Hiram, 28:62

Powers, Mary V., 40:322; "The Salvador Grant of Arms," 40:215-20

Powers, Mr., 27:91

Pozanski, Gustavus, 21:168, 214; 42:47, 57-58, 62

Pozo y Cordova, Ana Maria del, 23:133

Prado, Abraham, 38:103-5

Prado, Abraham Rodrigues, 32:16, 19

Prado, Isaac Rodriguez del, 37:338

Prado, Samuel, 38:104-5

Prager (family name), 38:197

Prager, Mark, 50:59

Prager, Michael, 50:39, 59

Prager Tagblatt, 50:107

Prague, "German Jews of Prague: A Quest For Self-Realization," 50:98-120; Jewish emancipation, 26:37

Prall, 22:78

Prateau, Mr., 37:402

Pratt, Fred A., 27:459

Pratt, Harry E., 42:409; 50:401

Pratt, Marion Dolores, 50:379, 401

Pratte, Claude, 23:139

Pratte, Joseph, 23:139

Pratte, M. D., 23:139

Pratte, Noel, 23:139

Pravitelvstvenyi Viestnik, 43:53

Prayer, "Form of Prayer Performed at Jews Synagogue," 30:48, 50; *Prayer for Jewish Holidays*, 30:56-59; "Prayers for Private Devotion," 25:152

Prayer Book, "A Pocket Edition Prayer Book for German Jewish Emigrants to America, 1842," 35:xvi, 207-12; 1761 and Benjamin S. Judah, 22:xxix

Preble, Edward, 45:22

Preble, Ned, 45:22

Preil, Gabriel, 50:268

Preiss, Hirsh, 23:143

Prentice, W. F., 39:83

Prentiss, Benjamin M., 44:104-5

Presbyterian Board of Publication, 22:172

Presbyterian Conference, state religion, 29:104

Presbyterians, 47:144-45, 148

Presbyter Judaeorum, 22:203

Prescott, William H., 45:24, 33

Present (negro), 48:25

President's Committee for Hungarian Refugee Relief, 47:192

President's Committee on Religion and Welfare in the Armed Forces, 47:232

President's Council on Fitness for Youth, 50:434

Pressburger, Nathan, 41:265

Pressensé, de (pastor), 41:162

Pressensé, Francis de, 46:97-99

Preston, Ebenezer, 27:318

Preterre, Louis Dias, 33:116

Preto, Francisco de sa, 33:113

Preto, Isaque, 42:280, 395

Preto, Izaia, 42:280, 395

Pretto, Eliau, 42:279, 395

Pretto, Gordon, 43:105

Prevost, Augustine, 23:15, 22

Prevost, George, 23:137-40

Přibram, (Dr. Emanuel?), 38:187, 197

Price, Benjamin, 31:99-100

Price, George M., 38:310-14, 316; 41:324, "Leaves from the Diary of Dr. George M. Price," 38:347; "The Memoir of Doctor George M. Price," 47:101-10; "The Russian Jews in America," 48:28-62, 78-133; 49:91; "The Diary of Dr. George Moses Price," 40:173-81

Price, John, 27:318

Price, Julius J., 23:vii; "Adolphus Mordecai Hart, of Quebec," 25:xiii, 121-22; "The Ashers of Toronto," 26:xv; "Data on Samuel Jacobs, an Early Canadian Jewish Settler," 28:xxxiii; "An Early Jewish Merchant of Halifax," 25:xiii; "Esther Brandeur, an Early Canadian Jewish Convert," 26:xv; "The First Jewish Settler of Ottawa, Canada," 23:xiv; "Further Data on the Hart Family of Three Rivers, Quebec," 26:xv; "The Jews of Northern Ontario," 25:xiii; "The Levy Family of Canada," 25:xiii; "Newman L. Steiner, the First Jewish Justice of the Peace in Ontario," 26:xv; "Newspaper Comments on the Samuel Hart Case," 25:xiii; "The Nordheimers of Toronto," 26:xxxi; "Proceedings Relating to the Expulsion of Ezekiel Hart from the House of Assembly of Lower Canada," 23:xiv, 43-53; "The

Rossin Brothers of Toronto, Canada," 28:xvi; "Samuel Gradische, and Eighteenth Century French Sutler," 25:xiii; "Samuel Jacobs, an Early Canadian Jewish Merchant," 23:xiv; "Unpublished Correspondence between Arthur Wellington Hart and Lord John Russell relating to the Appointment to Office of the Former's Father, Benjamin Hart," 26:xxxi; "An Unpublished Document in the Case of Thomas Coffin against Ezekiel Hart, of Three Rivers, Province of Quebec," 28:xvi; "Unpublished Documents dealing with 'the Petition of Certain Israelites of the City of Montreal for the Benefit of Public Register to Record Births, Deaths, Marriages, etc.,' " 28:xvi; "An Unpublished Letter of Aron Ezekiel Hart," 26:xv, 256-57; "Unpublished References in the Canadian State Papers to Benjamin and Samuel B. Hart," 23:xiv, 137-40

Price, R. M., 39:34

Price, Sterling, 50:342

Priebatsch, Felix, 37:177

Priest, Albert, 27:515

Priestley, Joseph, 28:252; 35:203; 37:186, 188, 199-200; *Letters to the Jews*, 30:98-101

Prigmore (actor), 33:182

Prillio (family name), 38:151

Prim, General, 29:89

Prime, Nathaniel, 43:207

Primrose, Neil, 35:254

Prince, Charles Edward, 35:217

Prince Charles of Brandenburg, 34:265

Prince, Emma, 28:285

Prince, Mr., 37:133

Prince *v.* Prince, 29:149

Prince, Thomas, 35:150

Prince Edward Island Railway Company, 28:270

Princeton College, 47:145, 148

Princeton University, 37:135, 471; 47:16; 49:11

Princeton University Library, 45:62

Prins, Abm. 27:235; Dutch intervention on behalf of alien Jews, 31:xxxiii

Priscilla (slave), 50:162

Pritchard, James, 33:195

Pritchard, Mrs., 28:57

Privateering, 26:195-98; 38:47; "Aaron Lopez' Long Deferred 'Hope,' " 37:xxxiii, 103-13; "Benjamin Franks, Merchant, and Captain Kidd, Pirate," 31:229-34; "Jewish Colonial Privateersmen," 40:75-76; "Jewish Owners of Ships Registered at the Port of Philadelphia, 1730-1775," 26:235-36; "Jews Interested in Privateering in America During the Eighteenth Century," 23:vii, 10-11, 163-76; "Jews in the Vice-Admiralty Court of Colonial Rhode Island," 37:xxx, 391-418; "Uriah Phillips Levy: The Story of a Pugnacious Commodore," 39:1-66

Probst, Mendel, 33:132-33, 135, 139, 145-48, 154-56, 164

Proceedings of the Bar Association of New Hampshire, 47:212

Proctor, John Clagett, 48:7; gift, 23:xvii

Proctor, Redfield, 50:382

Proctor, Samuel, "Jewish Life in New Orleans from 1719 to 1860," 40:406; "Pioneers of Jewish Settlement in Florida, 1765-1900," 49:220

Professional League, 50:225

Professional Women's League, 31:259

Progressive movement, 49:83

Progressive Party, 40:11-12

Prolo, 37:401, 405-6

Prologue to the *Rabbi of Bacharach*, 45:255

Prophecy, *Evidence of Prophecy*, 30:344

Prophecy Interpreted, 30:380

Prophets of Deceit, reviewed, 40:199-201

Proskauer, Adolph, 38:26; 50:315

Proskauer, Joseph, 50:315

Proskauer, Joseph M., 38:332; 46:116

Prostitution, 49:114-16

Protestantism, 50:100, 102; "The Hebraic Background of Puritanism," 47:140-53, 200; *Jews in Colonial Brazil*, reviewed, 50:73-76

Protestant Reformation, 47:151

Protocols of the Elders of Zion, 46:37

Protocol of Peace, 41:309, 319-20, 324

Protocols of Zion, 40:323, 340

Proust, Marcel, 35:260; 46:441

Providence, R.I., religious observances, mid-nineteenth century, 37:36; United Jewish Appeal, contribution, 37:xxviii

Provident Association (Boston), 45:73-74
Provincetown Banner, 42:136
Provisional Executive Committee for General Zionist Affairs, 36:70, 72; 49:168, 191, 193, 200
Provoost, John, 35:186
Provoost, Mary, 35:172, 175, 181-82, 185
Provoost, Samuel, 35:172; 42:77
Provosst, D., 34:121
Provost, David, 21:26
Provost, David William, 27:249
Provost, General, 22:xxxi
Provost Prison, 29:xlii
Prussia, 26:89, 96, 124, 136, 284; civil rights, 26:36, 39, 41-44, 46-47, 54; "The Congress of Aix-la-Chapelle," 26:82-94; "Educational Reforms in Europe in Their Relation to Jewish Emancipation—1778-1919," 28:83-132; Heinrich Graetz, 28:70-81; "Jewish Rights at the Congresses of Vienna (1814-1815), and Aix-la-Chapelle (1818)," 26:vii, xv, 33:125
Prynne, William, 37:187
Prys, Joseph, 35:136
Pschorr (brewer), 39:172
Public Archives, Ottawa, 45:55
Public Archives Commission, 49:257
Public Record Office, London, 23:26, 93-96; 35:1, 173; 38:82, 84, 101-2
Puccini, Giacomo, 47:187
Puck's Pictorial History, 39:48
Pue, Elizabeth, 23:160
Puigblanch (Natanael Jomtob), 26:243
Puigcerver, Francisco Rivas, "Francisco Rivas," 35:219-225; *Los Judios y el Nuevo Mundo*, 33:35
Pulaski, Casimir, 27:467, 494-95
Pulis, William, 25:50

Punch, 29:126
Punch, Joan, 48:181
Punch, John, Jr., 48:184, 187-88
Purchas, Samuel, 49:42
Purdy, Elijah, 30:404
Purim Associations, 32:xxvi; 39:470; collection, 39:400-2; "The Purim Association of the City of New York (1862-1902)," 40:135-72
Purim Gazette, 40:148, 154, 158, 169-72
Purim Reformatory, 40:165
Puritan College at Cambridge (Eng.), 47:152
Puritans, 40:408; 46:22-25, 32; "Cotton Mather and the Jews," 26:xiv, 201-10; "Hebraic Aspects of the Legislation of Puritan New England," 28:xxxiii; "The Hebraic Background of Puritanism," 47:140-53, 200; "The Proposed Scripture Calendar," 32:23-24; "Puritanism and the Covenant," 46:492
Purse; or Benevolent Tar, The, 26:245
Pusey, Nathan M., "America and Jerusalem," address by, 45:1-5
Putland, George, 35:185
Putland, Penthisilia, 35:185
Putman, Frank, 46:122
Putman, Genl., 39:319
Putnam, Georgiana Lowell, 35:169
Putnam, Herbert, 30:vi
Putnam's Magazine, 22:xxxiii; 45:27
Puttawattamee Indians, 23:33
Putzel, Michael, 42:195
Pye, Henry James, 38:113-14; *The Democrat*, 38:113-14
Pye, Joseph, 27:329
Pyke, C. & E., 42:57
Pyke's Catechism, 42:400, 402
Pyner, Captain, 35:297

Q

Quakers, 46:186, 268, 295; 47:143-44, 146; *New England's Spirit of Persecution*, 30:4, 6-7, 10; North Carolina, 29:140; Some Considerations, 30:80; "Unequal Religious Rights in Maryland Since 1776," 25:vii, 93-107

Quaritch, Bernard, 28:249

Quarterly Review, 26:136-37

Quarterly Sentinel, The, 37:423

Quasimodo (A. D. Straus), 31:293-95

Quebec, 35:2, 6, 11-12; "Adolphus Mordecai Hart, of Quebec," 25:xiii, 121-22; "Archives de la Province de Quebec," 31:xxxiii; civil rights, 30:295-97; "Further Data on the Hart Family of Three Rivers, Quebec," 26:xv; suffrage, 30:295-97; "Two Letters of Aron Hart of Three Rivers, 1775 and 1776," 26:257-58; "An Unpublished Document in the Case of Thomas Coffin against Ezekiel Hart, of Three Rivers, Province of Quebec," 28:xvi; "An Unpublished Letter of Aron Ezekiel Hart," 26:xv, 256-57

Quebec Gazette, 26:257

Queen Anne's War, 49:59

Queen Esther Ladies Society, 40:166

Queenstown, Battle of, 26:182

Queirrios, Manuel de, 33:117

Quello, Rebecca, 25:116

Querido, Abraham, 42:277, 395

Quincy, B., 37:134

Quincy, Josiah, 37:117-18; 43:223-24

Quincy, Quatremère de, A. C., 41:62, 71

Quincy (Ill.), religious observances, mid-nineteenth century, 37:36; United Jewish Appeal, contribution, 37:xxviii

Quincy Whig, 44:105

Quinet, Edgar, 38:278

Quinisext Oecumenical Council, 28:138-39

Quinn, Arthur H., 33:182, 194; 35:232

Quiros, Benjamin Mendes, 29:24

Quiver, 32:41

Quixano, Abraham Henriques, 27:249

Quixano, Mendes David, 32:63

Quixano, Mendez Abraham, 32:63

Quotas, educational, 46:252-53; immigration, 46:292-93, 311, 313, 318-26, 333-35, 368

R

Raabe, Jacob, 47:120
Rabb, George, 42:419
Rabb, Maxwell, 42:419; 47:203
Rabb, Sidney R., 42:419
Rabbi Isaac Elchanan Theological Seminary, 31:289; 48:231; 49:89; bookplates, 45:160, 173
Rabbi of Bacharach, 45:253, 255
Rabbi, Jacob, 33:98
Rabbiner Seminar, 43:243
Rabbinical Assembly of America, 39:296; 42:20
Rabbinical Assembly of the Jewish Theological Seminary, gift, 33:xxxiii
Rabbinical Conference (Breslau), 39:450; (Cleveland), 45:94; (1844), 41:24; (Frankfort), 39:450; (Pittsburgh), 39:456-57
Rabbinical Council of America, 39:296
Rabbinical literature, 43:244, 248; 45:136, 140-41, 145-47, 160, 163, 169
Rabbinical schools, 40:17-55
Rabbinical Seminary, 29:84
Rabina, 22:67
Rabinovich Zvi Hirsch, 44:141
Rabinovitz, Saul Pinchas, 26:14
Rabinowicz, Iskar, 42:213
Rabinowitz, Benjamin, 39:255; 50:280; necrology of, 38:335-36; "The Young Men's Hebrew Associations (1854-1913)," 37:xxx, 221-326
Rabinowitz, Louis M., 43:230; 44:243; 45:262; 47:124, 222; bookplates, 45:139, 152; *Dictionary of American Jewish Biography*, 44:247; executive council, 45:264; 46:492; gift, 45:168; Historical Essay Awards, 44:240, 245; history, writing of, 46:133-36, 192, 419; Memorial Fund, 47:124; necrology of, 47:201, 226-29;

Louis M. Rabinowitz Foundation, 45:61; vice-president, 44:241
Rabinowitz, Mary, 38:335
Rabinowitz, Myron, 38:336
Rabinowitz, Samuel, 33:148; 38:335
Rabinowitz, Sarah (Prigot), 38:336
Racah, Esther, 40:123
Race Congress (London), 47:173
Rachel (slave), 50:161
Rachel colony, 43:59
Rachel Goldberg Home for Jewish Female Minors, 29:150
Racket, The, 40:358
Rackman, Emanuel, 33:157; 46:63
Radbill, Samuel X., 45:197-98
Radcliffe College, 48:202, 267
Radin, Adolph M., 35:64; 42:100
Radin, Adolph Moses, 33:140
Radin, H., 39:408
Radin, Max, 43:239; "The Pursuit of Gain," 33:xxx
Radovsky, H. William, 48:266; executive council, 44:241; 45:264; 48:266
Raffaeli, Samuel, 34:160
Rafinesque, C. S., *Genius and Spirit of the Hebrew Bible*, 30:330-31
Ragensdorfer, 38:203
Railroads, Baltimore & Ohio Railroad, 25:145; "Brandeis and Scientific Management," 41:41-60; Hudson River Railroad, 25:145; "The Jews as American Railroad Financiers, with Special Reference to Jacob H. Schiff," 29:xv; Ohio & Mississippi Railroad, 25:146; Philadelphia & Reading Railroad, 25:146; Pittsburgh & Connellsville Railroad, 25:146; Reading Railroad, 22:55; regulation of, 45:203; Wilmington and Weldon Railroad, 29:147

"Rainbow-Bible," 33:20
Rains, Claude, 35:276
Raisin, Jacob J., 28:115, 118; 33:xxvi; gift, 31:xxxiv; "Lafayette and the Jews During His Visit to the United States, 1824-1825," 29:xxxvii
Raisin, M. S., 32:121
Raisin, Max, 33:134-37, 140
Raisin, Mordecai Max, 48:195
Rakocz v. Rakocz, 25:135
Rakonitz, Anastasia, 35:267
Ramage (artist), 27:373
Ramapo Valley Chapter, D.A.R., 31:xxxiii
Ramos, Moses, 21:55
Ramos, Moses Lopez, 21:44-45; 27:249
Ramsay, 32:49
Ramsay, Allan R., 33:22
Ramsay Case, 31:107, 113
Ramsey, Elizabeth, 25:75-76
Ranallo, Emanuel, 27:249
Ranc, A., 41:162
Randall, 32:95
Randolph, Edmund, 27:227, 466, 468, 471; 35:xix
Randolph, George Wythe, 50:322
Randolph, Miss, 33:27
Ranger, Gustav, 49:186
Ranke, Leopold von, 44:252; 46:153
Ransohoff, Joseph, "Under the Northern Lights," 29:xli
Ransohoff, Mrs. Joseph, gift, 29:xli
Raouf Pasha, 36:46
Rapaport, Solomon Judah Löb, 40:19
Rapaport; Woklovsky v., "Anglo-Jewish Legal Cases," 25:136
Rapely, Richard A., 29:143
Rapeport, Osher Noah, 44:174, 180
Raphael, Alexander, 35:xix
Raphael Bar Benjamin, 31:237
Raphael, Benjamin, 50:395
Raphael, Benjamin I., 45:185, 188-89
Raphael, Clarissa, 45:188
Raphael family (Richmond), 27:337
Raphael, Isaac (New York), 27:80
Raphael, Isaac (Richmond), 45:188-89
Raphael bar Natan, 27:80
Raphael, Solomon (Pa.), 47:205; 50:39, 59
Raphael, Solomon (Richmond), 50:162
Raphaelson, Samson, 40:359

Raphall, Morris Jacob, 27:160, 505, 514, 516; 34:xviii; 35:xix; 37:217; 38:58, 65, 68, 75; 42:102-4, 110, 152-53; 46:21; 50:287-88; The Constancy of Israel, 30:460-63
Rapley, Richard A., 22:188
Rapoport, Grigori, 43:52, 54-55, 58-60
Rapoport, Judah Löb, 45:209
Rapoport, S., 38:310; 39:100, 107
Rapoport, Solomon Judah Loeb, 22:103, 201; 34:16; 37:64; 50:93
Rappaport, Aaron, 45:142-43
Rappaport, Joseph, 46:192, 412; "The Relation of Jewish and General Institutional Development," 49:233
Rapperswyl Ms., 39:165-67
Raritan Woolen Mills, 22:227
Rash, Irwin, 34:219
Rasiere, Isaac de, 33:123
Raskin, Saul, 45:141, 164; 47:182
Raspail, Benjamin, 41:162
Raspe, Rudolph E., 35:232
Ratcliffe, Dorothy Una, 35:264
Rath, Ernst von, 36:380-81
Rathenau, Walther, 35:273
Rathier, député, 41:162
Ratisbonne, Archile, 42:161
Ratner, M. B., 39:108
Rau, John, 40:255
Raubenheimer, Albert, 46:124
Ravel, Maurice, 38:317
Raven, Cornelius, 37:413-17
Ravenna, Mario, 33:38
Ravenna, Synod of, 28:148
Rawicz, Joseph, 36:208-9
Rawidowicz, 43:195
Rawidowicz, Simon, 49:141; The Chicago Pinkas, 49:220
Rawinsky, Hans, 50:260, 271, 303, 353, 376, 387
Rawlins, John Aaron, 50:293
Raw Material, 48:252
Ray, J. M., 35:281
Ray, Robert, 27:392
Rayim, Ben F., 34:286
Raymond, Lord, 31:121, 125
Raynal, 38:324
Raynal, D., 41:162
Rayner, Albert W., 22:218; 31:226
Rayner, Amalie, 22:213

Rayner, George W., 22:213
Rayner, Isidor, 22:213; "Isidor Rayner (1850-1912)," 40:288-310
Rayner, William S., 22:213; Scholarship, 22:216
Razek, M., 29:68
Razsviet, 38:240, 242
Read, Charles, 25:126-27
Read, Deborah, 25:65
Read, George C., 46:4, 6
Read, John, 22:190-91
Read, Keith, manuscript collection, 48:12
Read, Mr., 34:88
Reade, Laurence, 26:270
Reader's Digest, 40:413
Reading, Earl of, 28:xviii, xxxix
Reading, Lord, 36:72; 40:403
Reading, Pa., religious observances, mid-nineteenth century, 37:38
Reading Railroad, 22:55
Real Motive, The, 48:250-52
Real, Sijmon Rodrigus Villa, 33:118
Real Estate Trust Company (Philadelphia), 25:174
Reaume, Hyacinth, 40:83
Reaume, Piero, 40:83
"Rebecca Franks," 27:460
Rechberg, Count, 26:55, 65
Recife in Pernambuco, 29:9, 39, 45
Reckendorfer, Joseph, 40:249, 263, 279; 49:186
Reckendorfer, Mrs. B., 40:279
Reconstruction Act of 1866, religious disability, 29:105
Recreation Rooms and Settlement (New York), 37:296
Redcliffe, Stratford de, 26:140, 150
Red Cross, 26:xxv; 41:366; 45:44; "The Relation of Adolphus S. Solomons to the Red Cross," 28:xv
Red Cross Association, 29:202
Red Cross Relief Committee, 26:xxv
Reddick, David, 38:136
Redelsheimer, Henry, 29:130
Redfield, Amasa A., 22:150, 151
Redondo, Selomoh, 29:23
Redpath, James, 23:71-72
Redwood, Abraham, Jr., 35:290
Redwood, Jonas S., 35:290-91

Redwood, William, Jr., 35:290
Redwood Library (Newport), 27:213, 215-16, 404, 449-51, 453; 35:140; 37:165-66; 42:417
Ree, Jacobus van der, 32:14
Reeb, M., 29:135
Reed, Mr., 44:111
Reed and Forde, 22:191
Reed, E. B., 45:43-44
Reed, Harriet L., 33:225-26
Reed, Joseph, 22:196; 23:173; 27:470
Reed, Thomas B., 36:43; 40:291
Reeder, 23:60
Reefer, Mrs. E. J., 31:253
Reeks, 31:xxxi
Reely, Mary K., 34:205
Rees, Mr., 45:145
Rees, Elfan, 46:359
Reese, Michael, 45:143
Reese, Samuel, 50:169
Reeve, Mr., 26:245
Reform Advocate, The, 32:124; 35:117; 40:386, 388; 42:101, 384
Reform Church of American Israelites, 40:384-85
Reform Club of New York, 22:238; 26:288
Reform Jews of America, 44:143
Reform Jews and Orthodox Jews, Alliance Israélite Universelle, 39:394
Reform Judaism, 26:286; 28:xl; 29:204; 30:iv; 34:286; 38:20, 184; 39:92, 98, 109, 259, 274, 279, 292, 297-98, 368, 449-51, 454, 455; 40:36, 159-60, 168; 43:136-37, 146; 46:60, 63, 118; 47:40-41, 43, 58, 129, 208, 233; 48:143, 195; 50:82, 84, 91, 93, 96-97, 118, 286, 297; *American Judaism*, 47:121-23; *As a Mighty Stream*, 40:201-4; Bernhard Felsenthal, 45:94, 118-27; Board of Delegates of American Israelites, 29:78; 49:16-32; (Canada), 50:133; (Charleston), 32:50; communal and social aspects, 39:275-79; confirmation of girls, 39:371-72; *Differentiation Features of Orthodox, Conservative, and Reform Jewish Groups in Metropolitan Philadelphia*, reviewed, 49:276-78; *Growth and Achievement: Temple Israel, 1854-1954*, reviewed, 44:250-51; Hebra-Kahal, 39:277; Hebrew Union College, 40:34-55; Heinrich Graetz, 28:72-81;

history, writing of, 46:171, 187, 191, 197, 271, 388-90, 401-2; *Introduction to Reform Judaism at Charleston, S. C.*, 31:xxxiv; "Isaac Harby, Jewish Religious Leader and Man of Letters," 32:35-53; "Isaac Leeser and the Jews of Philadelphia: A Study in National Jewish Influence," 48:207-44; *The Israelite*, 26:271; Jewish local history, 49:218, 221, 231-32, 238, 241, 249-50, 258; "Jewish Religious and Cultural Life in America as Reflected in the Felsenthal Collection," 45:93-127; journalism, 26:271-73; Kashrut, 39:375-78; Mordecai Manuel Noah," 41:24; "Music in the American Reform Synagogue," 32:xiii; "New York Chooses a Chief Rabbi," 44:129-98; Philipson on, 39:461-68; radical reform, 49:249-50; "The Reaction of Reform Judaism in America to Political Zionism," 40:361-94; (Rochester), 40:68; Samuel Schulman, 45:266-67; "*Shemah Israel*, a Magazine of the Reform Movement in Curaçao, 1864-1865," 26:xv, 239-41; Temple Israel (Boston), 45:270-71; Temple Ohabei Shalom (Boston), 45:270-71; "The Trend in Jewish Religious Observance in Mid-Nineteenth-Century America," 37:xxxiv, 31-53; *Yahadut Amerika be-Hitpathutah (The Shaping of American Judaism)*, reviewed, 42:91-107; and Zionism, 49:193-200

Reform Society of the Israelites in Charleston, 50:12

Reformed Israelites, The, 30:393-94

Reformed Society of Israelites, 40:399; (Charleston), 27:518; 42:49, 54; constitution, 30:238-39, 243, 268; service and miscellaneous prayers adopted by, 30:268

Refugees, "American Jewry, The Refugees and Immigration Restriction (1932-1942)," 45:219-47; Refugee Relief Act (1953), 46:315-16, 333, 343, 357

Regalon, Diego Lopez, 31:30

Regelson, Abraham, 50:402

Regensburg, Myer, 21:159; 27:41, 43, 253

Reggio, Isaac Samuel, 34:16; 40:18

Regina, 31:113

Regnier, Ad., 41:162

Rehabiah, Jehiel (Vitale Alatina di Pomis), 28:173, 179

Rehearsal for Destruction, reviewed, 40:199-201

Rehfish, "S. Rehfish Collection," 45:157

Rehiné, Rachel (Judah), 50:65

Rehiné, Zalma, 48:218; 50:65

Reich, Nathan, 41:392; "The Economic Structure of Modern Jewry," reviewed, 40:196; "Some Observations on Jewish Unionism," 41:347-55, 387

Reichenberger, Nathan, 41:268

Reichersohn, Moses, 33:140

Reichert, Irving F., 45:144; gift, 33:xxxiii

Reichert, Jonathan, 39:463

Reichert, Victor E., 39:477; 45:192; necrology of David Philipson, 39:461-68, 471

Reichman, Jacob, 36:53-58

Reichow, Arthur, 48:31, 60, 117, 120

Reid, Mrs. C. A., 25:29

Reid, Elizabeth Mills, 33:222

Reid, Mayne, 43:15

Reid, Robert W., Washington Lodge, No. 21 F.&A.M., 35:xxii

Reid, Robert R., 25:8

Reider, Joseph, 30:vi; "Secular Currents in the Synagogal Chant in America," 26:xxxii

Reid's Tavern, 41:86

Reiff, Conrad, 34:85

Reijnst, Jacobus, 33:108

Re'im, Seudat, 33:164

Reinach, Salomon, 39:438; 43:64-65

Reinach, Theodore, 26:28; 34:243; 35:213

Reinagle, 33:182-83

Reinert, Paul C., 46:317

Reines, Isaac Jacob, 35:58; 40:403

Reinganum, Maximilian, 38:185

Reingold, Nathan, 47:201, 203; "Resources on American Jewish History in the National Archives," 47:186-95, 201

Reinhardt, Max, 45:199; "Max Reinhardt Theatre Collection," 45:200

Reinheimer *v.* Standard Scale & Supply Co., 25:136

Reinstein, S., 29:129

Reintzel, D., 26:212

Reisen, Abraham, 43:36

Reisen, Zalman, 33:135

Reiser, Koppel, 45:85

Reiss, F., 29:131

Reizchen, 42:432

Reizenstein, 31:226

Relandus, Hadrianus, 37:186

Relief Committee for Suffers from the War, 26:276

Relief Fund for Jewish War Sufferers, 28:309

Reis, Carl, 22:168

Religion, *Darkhei ha-Yahadut ba-Amerika (Jewish Religious Life and Institutions in America: An Historical Study)*, reviewed, 43:197-98; and Jewish American history, 39:290-301; "Jews as a Religious Community Not a Race," 32:127; *Religion in Israel Today: The Relationship Between State and Religion*, reviewed, 49:272-76

Religious Bodies, "A Side Light on Restrictive Covenants," 41:381-84

Religious Disabilities Act of 1846, England, 31:105, 109

Religious freedom, 28:135; 34:165; 36:178; 38:1-6, 18, 200-225; 40:4-5, 16; "American Jewish Communal Pioneering," 43:133-50; army chaplain, 29:103-4; Brazil, 33:43-125; "Civil Liberties and the Jewish Tradition in Early America," 46:20-39; Civil War, liberty, 50:295, 356-57; conference of Israelites, 24:102-5; "The Congress of Aix-la-Chapelle," 26:82-94; "Congress of Berlin, 1878," 24:40-79; *Cornerstones of Religious Freedom in America*, reviewed, 40:96-98; "The Doctrine that 'Christianity is a Part of the Common Law,' and its Recent Judicial Overthrow in England, with Particular Reference to Jewish Rights," 31:vii, xvi, 103-34; *The Dutch in Brazil, 1624-1654*, reviewed, 47:112-20, 209; England, 25:114; "The Exodus from Brazil and Arrival in New Amsterdam of the Jewish Pilgrim Fathers, 1654," 44:80-97, 255; Ezekiel statue, 29:106; "Hon. Oscar S. Straus' Memoranda Preceding Dispatch of the Hay Roumanian Note," 24:108-14; "The Impact of the American Constitution Upon the Jews of the United States," 43:159-69; "The Influence of Lewis Way and Other English Missionaries Upon

Alexander I's Treatment of the Jews," 26:116-25; "Jewish Disabilities in the Balkan States: American Contributions Toward Their Removal, with Particular Reference to the Congress of Berlin," 24:ix, 1-153; 25:xiv; "Jewish Elements in Brown's Early History," 37:xxx, 135-45; "Jewish Rights at the Congresses of Vienna (1814-1815), and Aix-la-Chapelle (1818)," 26:vii, xv, 33-125; Maryland, 29:105; "Memorandum on the Treaty Rights of the Jews of Roumania," 24:137-53; "Moses Jacob Ezekiel," 28:xxii, 1-62; North Carolina, 29:81-82, 105, 137-48; Paris Conference, 29:110-11, 114-16; "Petition of Pennsylvania Jews to Council of Censors regarding a Religious Test," 31:xxix; "Petition of the Roumanian Jews to the Chamber of Deputies, 1872," 24:98-101; Reconstruction Act of 1866, 29:105; "Regarding the Draft of a Sistem of Legislation for the Jews, July 17, 1809, by Wilhelm von Humboldt," 26:103-15; "Religious liberty," statue of, 50:384; Rumania, 36:6; "Secretary Hay's Roumanian Note of 1902 and the Peace Conference of Bucharest of 1913," 24:80-97; Serbia, 36:6; "Unequal Religious Rights in Maryland since 1776," 22:xxviii; U.S. Constitution and Christianity, 29:104; "Wilhelm von Humboldt's Relations to the Jews," 26:95-103; *see also*: Board of Delegates of American Israelites

Religious observance, "The Trend in Jewish Religious Observance in Mid-Nineteenth-Century America," 37:xxxiv, 31-53

Religious societies, *Act to Provide for Incorporation of Religious Societies, Etc.*, 30:300

Remas, Esther, 27:112

Rembert, Pedro, 49:34

Rembrantdt Harmenszoon van Rijn, 46:374

Remedios, J. Mendes dos, 42:221-22; "The Portuguese Jews in Amsterdam," 31:xxxi

Reminiscences, 50:295

Remoiville, député, 41:162

Remon, Peter, 23:14

Remos, David, 27:120

Remsen & Val Alstyn, 27:329

Remson, Henry, 27:392
Remusat, M. de, 24:21, 30
Rémusat, Paul de, 41:162
Renan, Ernest, 38:278; 39:321-23; 41:162;
"Emma Lazarus' Approach to Renan and
Her Essay 'Renan and the Jews,' " 37:xxxiv,
17-29
Renan, Joseph Ernest, 28:63
Rendon, Francisco, 27:471
Renshaw, James, 37:439
Rensselaerswyck, Colony of, 28:252
Rephael Br Benjamin, 21:29, 34
Rephoel, Ben, 39:94-95
Republikanischer Katechismus, 41:233
Resartus, Sartor, 38:182
Reschid Pasha, 26:138
Resen, Mr., 33:120
Resio, Gaspar Francisco, 33:115
Resorts, "Social Discrimination Against Jews
in America, 1830-1930," 47:1-33
Responsa, index, 22:xvii; and Jewish
historiography, 26:25
Restricted Commercial Intercourse, records,
47:189
Restrictive covenants, 45:218; "A Side Light
on Restrictive Covenants," 41:381-84
Retch, 41:192
Return of the Jews, The, 30:174, 176
Reuben, Asher bar Reuben, 21:45, 53;
31:238
Reuchlin, Johann von, 28:167-68
Reutel, Henricus, 22:115-16
Revera, Jacob Rods, 21:81
Revere, Edward H. Warren, 43:202
Revere, Joseph Warren, 48:172; "Paul Revere
and Son and Their Jewish
Correspondents," 43:199-229
Revere, Paul, 37:117; 42:337, 418; 48:172;
"Paul Revere and His Jewish
Correspondents," 42:415; "Paul Revere
and Son and Their Jewish
Correspondents," 43:199-229; 49:62
Reviewers Reviewed: A Challenge to Historical
Critics, 50:398
Revolutionary War Prize Cases, 47:187
Revue des Etudes Juives, 43:156; 45:108
Reyes, Diego Garcia de los, 23:135
Reyneau, député, 41:162
Reynell, John, 30:77

Reynolds, Grindall S., 45:97
Reynolds, James G., 21:165
Reynolds, John Fulton, 50:387
Reynolds, Joshua, 27:401
Reynolds, Robert R., 45:230
Rezio, Gaspar Correa, 33:115
Rezio, Moseh Levy, 42:278
Reznikoff, Charles, 39:254; 46:441-42; 49:39,
260; "The Jewish Community of
Charleston, S.C., 1750-1950," 39:471; The
Jews of Charleston: A History of an American
Jewish Community, 49:237-38; and Uriah
Z. Engelman (collab.), The Jews of
Charleston, 40:398-401
Rhees, J. L., Scriptural View of the Restoration
of the Jews, 30:397
Rhees, Rush, Library, 43:72
Rheindorf, David Ben Moses, 22:115
Rheinhold, Hanoch, 49:170
Rheinstrom, Mr., 31:144, 147
Rhett, N. Barnwell, 50:342
Rhine, Abraham B., 45:162, 174
Rhinelander, William, 27:227, 466
Rhinewine, Abraham, gift, 33:xxxiii;
necrology of, 33:xxi
Rhode Island, 35:293; 46:22, 29-30, 32-33,
39; Aaron Lopez, 25:113; Bank of, 27:210-
11, 369, 456; Civil War, 50:279, 304, 372,
381-82; colonial settlement of Jews, 26:5-
6; "Commerce of Rhode Island, 1726-
1800," 25:113; history, writing of, 46:152,
179, 270, 293, 423; Jewish local history,
49:236-37; Jewish population, 50:25-27,
45, 48-49, 55, 59-60, 62, 65; Moses
Michael Hays, 25:113; oath of allegiance
act, 27:184, 443-44
Rhode Island Hospital, 38:68
Rhode Island Jewish Historical Association,
49:152, 237
Rhode Island Jewish Historical Notes, 46:184-85;
49:237
Rhode Island State Charity Board, 22:209
Rhodes, 29:145
Rhodes, Isle of, 36:4
Rhodes, James Ford, 23:56-57, 59-61, 67, 70,
76; 38:14; 39:287; 46:466; 49:254
Rhodes, Simon, 27:450
Ribalenko, Michael, 41:174
Ribalow, Menachem, 33:156, 160

Ribero, Francisco, 33:112
Ribero, Isaac, 32:63
Ribiero, Samuel Nunez, 22:158-59; 33:253
Ricardo, Benjamin Israel, 23:187
Ricardo, Sarah, 23:187
Rice, Abraham, 23:141; 44:130; "Abraham
Rice, First Traditionally Ordained Rabbi
in the United States," 44:242
Rice, Charles, 49:106
Rice, Elmer L., 40:358-59
Rice, Henry, 24:39; 29:72, 111; 40:226;
49:186; 50:377
Rice Institute, 22:xiv
Rice, Isaac L., necrology of, 25:xii, 175-76
Rice, Titus C., 27:506
Rich and Boyer, 28:313
Rich (dept. store), 38:20
Rich, George L., 50:314
Rich, L., 29:134
Richard I, 26:128; 29:xxiii
Richard, C. B., 36:227
Richard, Paul, 25:78-79
Richard, S., 29:131
Richard, Stephen C., 27:317
Richards, Bernard G., 34:257; 35:121; 36:79;
46:63; 49:199
Richards, David, 37:393
Richards, J. E., 39:70
Richards, Morris, 41:375
Richards, William, 25:143; 35:186
Richardson, Asa M., 50:307
Richardson, Ebenezer, 35:291
Richardson, George, 32:64
Richardson, Joseph, Jr., 42:418
Richardson, Thomas, 35:291
Richardson, Tracey, 31:213
Richardson, William A., 44:102, 104
Riche, Aaron, 46:120
Richelieu, 26:82
Richepin, Jean, 35:250
Richman, Julia, 37:248, 282, 288; 50:213
Richmond (Va.), 22:130; 47:23, 53, 128, 189;
50:162-63; Civil War, 50:279, 321, 378,
383-86, 397, 407; "The History of the Jews
of Richmond from 1769 to 1917," 26:xxiv;
Jewish Congregation, 22:193; 25:50;
28:xxvi; Mordecai Myers, 26:174; religious
observances, mid-nineteenth century,
37:35; *Through the Years: A Study of the*

Richmond Jewish Community, reviewed,
46:68-69; 49:241
Richmond Compiler, The, 39:137
Richmond Dispatch, 50:385
Richmond Enquirer, 50:370
Richmond News Leader, 50:385
Richmond Times Dispatch, 50:385
Richmond Whig, The, 39:138; 50:385
Richter, Mr., 36:359; 44:136, 140, 146, 161-
62, 177
Richter, John, 39:159
Richtmann, Leopold, 38:203
Richtmann, S., 38:203
Rickert, 31:190
Ricordi, G. and Company, 47:187
Ricout, Mr., 31:119
Ridana, Joseph, 23:28
Riddell, engraver, 30:69
Ridder, Jean De, 26:70-72
Ridder, Nicholaes de, 33:121-22
Riddle, J. W., 36:132-33
Ridgely, Commodore, 27:497
Ridpath, John Clark, 40:334
Ridvaz, Jacob David, 44:187
Rief, Judah Leib, 44:141
Riega, Garcia de la, 22:xxi; 33:37
Rieger, Paul, 28:88
Rienzi, 28:148; 41:88
Rierson, George, 25:50
Rieser, Samuel, 41:261
Riesser, Gabriel, 26:81; 28:264; 29:126
Riez, Marx, 41:256
Rifkind, Simon, 50:79
Rigg, J. M., 34:239; "Calendar of the Plea
Rolls," 34:xxiii
Riggs, Elies, *A Manual of the Chaldes
Language*, 30:281
Riggs; Geofroy v., 36:234
Riggs, Lawrence J., 34:230
Riggs National Bank, 47:187
Riggs, Rev. Dr., 50:88
Riggs, Stephen, 42:365, 370
Rights, Mathew, 35:290
Riis, Jacob A., 43:14, 17-18; 46:297
Riker, I. L., 37:434
Riker, Richard, 27:317
Riklis, Levi Isaac, 33:161
Rimonim, "The Form and Decoration of
Silver Rimonim," 45:48-53

Rimos, Moses, 28:209
Rimson, 43:222
Rinder, Irwin D., 48:68
Rindskopf, Morris, 40:263
Ringel, Hedge, 35:307
Ringel, Mosher R., "Further information concerning the Jewish colony 'Shalom' at Yageville, in Ulster County, N.Y.," 35:xv, 306-9
Rios, Pedro de los, 31:24
Ripin, Benjamin, necrology of, 32:xvii
Ripley, Edward Hastings, 50:399
Ripley, James W., 48:161-64
Ripon, Dean of, 26:148
Rirning, Abraham, 23:151
Rischin, Moses, 46:413, 418; "Abraham Cahan and the New York *Commercial Advertiser*: A Study in Acculturation," 43:10-36; "The Early Attitude of the American Jewish Committee to Zionism (1906-1922)," 49:199-201; *Growth and Achievement: Temple Israel, 1854-1954,* reviewed, 44:250-51; "The Human Element and Jewish Labor," 46:260-62
Rison, Izaque, 42:280, 395
Ristitch, 24:52, 67, 72
Ritchie, Thomas, 22:83-85
Ritchie, William F., 27:506
"Rites of the Hebrews," 28:xxxix
Ritner, 22:89
Ritteman, I., 29:134
Rittenberg, Louis, 34:257
Rittenhouse, David, 21:xvi; 27:471; 43:236
Ritter, Joseph E., 46:317
Ritterband, Benveneda, 27:112
Ritterband, L., 27:115
Ritual bath, 39:371
Ritual murder, 40:325; 45:25; 47:4, 128; 49:233; Damascus Affair, 36:3-5; Kishineff, 36:261-71
Ritualistic slaughtering, 31:223; 37:31-39; 49:87
Ritual silverware, 45:270; "Chinese Influence in Seventeenth-Century Jewish Silver," 44:8-11; "The Form and Decoration of Silver Rimonim," 45:48-53; "The Ritual Silver Made by Myer Myers," 43:1-9
Rivard, Alexis, 23:139

Rivas, Francisco, 23:129; 35:327; "Francisco Rivas," 34:xv; 35:219-25
Rivas, Maria, 35:225
Riveira, Abraham, 22:182
Rivera, Mr., 27:187, 297; 34:139; 35:296-97, 302
Rivera, Mrs., 27:212
Rivera, Aaron, 29:148
Rivera, Abraham, 35:296
Rivera, Abraham R., 50:59
Rivera, Abraham Rodriguez, 21:5, 8, 10, 15-16, 19-20, 27-28, 30, 38, 42, 44, 49-51, 53-54, 58, 63, 181, 211; 23:89; 25:43; 31:239; 37:373, 377, 386; 38:235
Rivera, Abraham Rodriques (b. Jacob), 27:59, 152, 303, 306, 307, 349, 408, 451
Rivera, Abram, 50:36
Rivera, Daniel Rs De, 21:44
Rivera family, 34:170; 37:384; "A Genealogical Note on the Pimentel, Lopez, Sasportas and Rivera Families," 42:303-4; (Leicester), 23:85; (Newport), 27:211, 455
Rivera, Hannah (Mrs. Abraham), 23:89; 27:307, 439; 50:59
Rivera, Hannah (Mrs. Jacob), 27:210-11, 307, 424
Rivera, Isaac Rs De, 21:44-45, 53, 63
Rivera, Jacob, 27:349, 439
Rivera, Jacob Rodriguez, 21:45-46, 49, 51, 53, 58, 60, 63, 81, 130, 131; 27:152, 178, 180-81, 185, 200, 212-13, 249, 287, 307, 347, 404, 406-8, 451-52, 457; 34:71, 285; 37:165, 373-74, 377, 386; 38:235; 42:303-4; 44:63; 50:59; portrait of, 42:417
Rivera, Jacob Rodriguez (b. Jacob), 27:59, 152, 303, 306-7, 349, 408, 451
Rivera, Manuel, 27:349
Rivera, Rachel Rodriquez, 27:203; 31:239
Rivera, Rodrigues, 37:165, 374, 377, 386
Rivera, Samuel, 44:63
Rivera, Sarah Rodriguez, 27:122, 307
Rives, G. L., 36:55-57
Rives, Thomas, 27:436
Rivington, James, 38:113, 117-18
Rivington, James, Jr., 38:114
Rivington, John, 38:114
Rivington's Gazette, 23:167
Rivington's New-York Gazetteer, 38:113

Rivkin, Ellis, 40:53
Rivkin, William, 45:166
Rivkind, Isaac, 34:xx, 286; 35:282; "The
    Correct Date of Gershom Mendes Seixas'
    Second Marriage," 35:309-10; "Early
    American Hebrew Documents," 34:51-74;
    "(a) A New York Tosefeth-Ketubah of the
    Year 1718; (b) A Shechitah Certificate
    Issued to Solomon Etting in Lancaster,
    1782; (c) A Letter of Abraham ha-Levi of
    New York to Aaron Lopez, 1770," 34:xiv-
    xv; gifts, 33:xxxi; 34:xxiv; 35:xxiii; "A Letter
    of Abraham ha-Levi of New York to Aaron
    Lopez, 1770," 34:xv; necrology of Edward
    Davidson Coleman, 37:458-60; "A Pocket
    Edition Prayer Book for German Jewish
    Emigrants to America, 1842," 35:xvi, 207-
    12; "A Posen Letter of Introduction,
    1854," 37:xxxi; "On Printing and Printers,"
    37:xxxi; "A Shechitah Certificate Issued to
    Solomon Etting in Lancaster, 1782,"
    34:xiv-xv; "Some Remarks about
    Messengers from Palestine to America,"
    34:288-94; "The Yeshiva of Volozhin and
    American Jewry," 35:xvi
Riza Bey, Ahmed, 47:172
Rizio, Sarah, 32:60
Roades, Walter, 27:175
Roak, John C., 41:92
Roback, A. A., 45:138
Robbins, C. E., 27:436
Robbins, M. J., gift, 34:xxvii
Robbins, R. D. C., 30:374
Robbins, Walter Raleigh, "War Record and
    Personal Experiences of Walter Raleigh
    Robbins, 1861-1865," 31:xxxii
Robbins, Mrs. W. R., gift, 31:xxxii
Robbins, Willet, 37:448
Robeley, 31:124
Roberts, Dr., 23:117-18
Roberts, Edmund, 23:171
Roberts, Elijah J., 30:249
Roberts, Gustave R., 50:272, 274, 375, 385
Roberts, Major, 23:32-33
Robertson (actor), 33:191
Robertson, Captain, 40:82
Robertson, John, 23:173
Robespierre, 38:112
Robinet, doct., 41:162

Robinson, Aaron G., nominations committee,
    31:xxix
Robinson, Bernard, 50:232
Robinson, Beverly, 28:226
Robinson, Charles, 23:60, 69
Robinson, Douglas, 33:221, 223
Robinson, Dr., 50:85-86, 88
Robinson, Edward, 30:iv, (trans.), Hebrew and
    English Lexicon, 30:383
Robinson, G., 37:199
Robinson, Hercules George, 48:26
Robinson, Jackie, 48:201
Robinson, James Harvey, 39:290
Robinson, Joseph T., 36:368
Robinson, Leonard G., 22:186; 31:210
Robinson, Poitaiux, 27:506
Robinson, William Davis, 27:520; Jewish
    State, 43:172, 174-76, 179-81, 183;
    "William Davis Robinson's Memoir
    Addressed to Persons of the Jewish
    Religion," 38:344
Robinson, Aaron G., 31:xxix
Robison, Mr. and Mrs. Adolph, 50:272
Robison, Sophia M., 39:237; 47:25
Robitaille, 23:48-49
Robitschek, 38:197
Robitscher, 38:203
Robles, Antonio Rodrigues, 42:437
Robles, Mrs., 33:202
Roblez, Jacob David de, 23:27
Robsen, David, 50:232
Robson, J., 37:199
Robyn & Co., 45:188
Rochambeau, Count, 31:74
Roche, Captain De La, 32:125; 39:3, 34
Rochefort, Henri, 46:90
Rochelau, T., 23:139
Rochell, Mr., 27:91
Rochester (N.Y.), 46:172, 284; 49:249; The
    Jewish Community in Rochester, 1845-1925,
    44:246; 49:231-32; "Jewish Population
    Growth in Rochester, 1843-1938," 44:237-
    39; Jewish local history, 49:250-51, 256,
    260-61; "The Jews of Rochester: A
    Contribution to Their History During the
    Nineteenth Century," 40:57-73; religious
    observances, mid-nineteenth century,
    37:36; "Simon Tuska Becomes a Rabbi,"
    50:79-97; "Study of the Social and

Recreational Facilities and Needs of
Rochester," 44:238
Rochester Catholic Journal, 42:383
Rochester Daily Advertiser, 50:81
Rochester Daily Democrat, The, 50:81-82
Rochester Democrat and Chronicle, 42:383;
44:238
Rochester Historical Society, 45:205
Rochester Post-Express, 40:70; 42:371
*Rochester; or, King Charles the Second's merry
days*, 33:174, 196
Rochester Union and Advertiser, 50:95
Rochester, University of, 43:72; 44:106;
50:81-82
Rock, R. W., 50:382
Rock Creek Cemetery (Baltimore), 40:293
Rockdale Avenue Temple (Cincinnati),
39:454, 463, 467, 471; 45:214
Rockefeller Foundation, 46:149-50
Rockefeller Institute of Medical Research,
49:97, 271
Rockefeller, John D., 33:221; 36:43; 46:435,
437-38
Rockhill, William W., 36:282; 39:86; 41:178
Rockwell, John A., 23:124-25
Rödelheimer, Abraham, 41:261
Rödelsheimer, Hans, 41:255
Rodelsheimer, Jette, 41:255
Rodeph Shalom Congregation (New York),
27:504; 41:229; 49:19; *Gesange und Gebete*,
30:372-73; (Philadelphia), 26:289; 28:xl,
269, 310; 31:252-53; 37:78; 39:249;
41:228; 42:95, 438; 43:136; 46:387;
47:204-6; 48:76, 209, 235, 241, 243; 49:19;
50:12-13, 292; "Additional Data on the
History of Congregation Rodeph Shalom
of Philadelphia," 28:xxxiii; dedication,
34:xvi; gift, 32:xxviii; "Hebrew German
Society Rodeph Shalom in the City and
County of Philadelphia," 40:407; 41:83-93;
*Order of Service at Consecration of Synagogue
Rodeph Sholum*, 30:374, 378, 426;
(Pittsburgh), 28:258; 39:453
Roderige, Joseph, 37:396-97
Rodez, Jehuda di, 28:168
Rodgers, John, 46:15; 48:173
Rodgers, Richard, 47:182
Rodkinson, M. L., 44:125
Rodman, Mr., 27:432, 441

Rodman, Elias, 35:307
Rodman, Samuel, 27:442
Rodney, Admiral, 28:216; 31:48; 34:273
Rodney, George Brydges, 38:91
Rodondo, Abraham, 33:87
Rodrick, Isaac de, 27:249
Rodriges, Isaac Raphael, 21:45; 27:249
Rodrigo, Juan, 35:222, 224
Rodrigo de Porto, Francisco, 33:119
Rodrigos, Franco, 33:65
Rodrigues, Abraham, 32:63
Rodrigues, Abraham Jacob, 33:87
Rodrigues, Aron Cohen, 44:227
Rodrigues, Bartholomeus, 33:77
Rodrigues, Daniel, 32:63
Rodrigues, David, 33:87
Rodrigues (family name), 37:385
Rodrigues, Hester, 26:251; 33:87
Rodrigues, Imanuel, 29:35
Rodrigues, Israel, 33:87
Rodrigues, Rebecca, 26:251
Rodrigues, Sarafine Hester, 33:87
Rodriguez, Aaron, 37:339
Rodriguez, Andres, 31:28
Rodriguez, Antonio, 31:28
Rodriguez, Beatriz, 23:134
Rodriguez, Blanca Maria, 23:134
Rodriguez, Domingo, 31:28
Rodriguez, Francisco (shoemaker), 31:30
Rodriguez, Francisco (Francisco Rodrigez de
Cea) (silversmith), 31:29
Rodriguez, Gabriel, 31:27
Rodriguez, Inés Francisco, 23:134
Rodriguez, Jorge, 31:30
Rodriguez, José Honorio, 42:224
Rodriguez, Juan, 31:30
Rodriguez, Leonor María, 23:134
Rodriguez, Manuel, 31:29
Rodriguez, Maria Alejandra, 23:134
Rodriguez, Miguel, 31:21, 27-28
Rodriguez, Pedro, 31:29
Rodriguez, Simon, 31:31
Rodriguez, Violante, 31:29
Rodrigus, Bento, 33:114
Rodrigus, Domingo, 33:112
Rodrigus, Francisco, 33:117
Rodrigus, Ignatio, 33:116
Rodrigus, Jacob, 33:50
Rodrigus, Joan, 33:116

Rodrigus, Moses, 33:117
Rodrigus, Moses Nunes, 33:50
Rodrigus, Vincent, 33:118
Rodrigus de Lixboa, Francisco, 33:113
Rodriques, Is. Rapl., 21:182; 27:6, 249
Rodriquez, Pedro, 27:485
Rodriquez, Rachel, 50:148
Roeder, L., 29:131
Roeloffsen, Jan, 26:247
Roger II, 28:206
Roger, Duke of Salerno, 28:205
Rogers, Isaiah, 41:71
Rogers, James E. Thorold, 34:234
Rogers, John Thomas, 22:180
Rogers, Moses, 48:175
Rogers, Robert, 35:19; 40:81
Rogers, Robert Emmons, 35:257-58
Rogers, Stephen, 23:157
Rogers, Will, 43:140
Rogers, William, Jr., 22:96-97
Rogers, Zephaniah, 23:157
Roget, Moses, 27:91
Roget, Mr., 27:62
Rogoff, Hillel, 50:218
Rohrbacher, Leopold, 41:258
Rohrbacher, Ulrich, 41:265
Roi, F., 23:49
Roi, L., 23:49
Roland of Parma, 28:169
Rolland, Romain, 41:96
Rollin, 31:72; 35:313
Rolph, Mr., 35:177
Rolvaag, Ole, 46:127
Romaine, 22:79
Roman, 49:84
Roman Catholicism, 47:142, 146, 148, 150-52
Romancero, 45:251
Romanelli, Luigi, *Elisa e Claudio*, 30:282, 290
Romano, Anthony, 34:216
Romano, Judah (Judah ben Moses), 28:146-47
Romanoff, Paul, gift, 35:xxiii
Roman rule, Jewish historiography, 26:27
Romberg, Sigmund, 47:182
Rombout, Catharyna, 32:104
Rombro, J., 38:244; 39:95, 107
Rome, 28:5; "The Ghetto and the Jews of Rome," 28:18; Jewish physicians, 28:135-87; "Moses Jacob Ezekiel," 28:xxii, 1-62

Rome, Charles A., 42:419
Rome, Mr., 27:390
Rome Exhibition, 31:290
Rome, University of, 28:172
Romer, Henry, 27:326
Romer, Joseph, 27:321, 326
Romer, Sally, 27:321
Romig, E. F., gift, 34:xxvi; "William the Silent," 34:xxvi
Ron, Philip de, 33:119
Rondout (N.Y.), religious observances, mid-nineteenth century, 37:36
Ronsheim, Nelson, 45:215
Roos, Gerrit Jansen, 25:42
Roos, Hyman J., 36:59-60
Roos, J. S., 25:139
Roos, Marten, 33:108
Roos, Moritz, necrology of, 32:xvii
Roosevelt, Cornelius, 27:45
Roosevelt, Franklin Delano, 37:9, 454; 38:5, 318; 39:243; 45:220; 49:14; history, writing of, 46:224, 258, 437, 472; Jewish disabilities, 36:xii, 90, 294, 365, 370-71, 377-79, 381; labor, 41:298-310, 325, 329-30, 354; Library, 49:257; Palestine, 40:115-17
Roosevelt, Franklin Delano, Jr., 46:303
Roosevelt, Isaac, 27:70, 329
Roosevelt, John, 42:428
Roosevelt, Theodore, 28:307; 29:xix, 203; 31:209, 272, 295; 34:xxi, 185; 35:214, 321; 39:428; 42:353; 43:31-33; 46:90, 93, 228; 47:195; 50:221; Balkan disabilities, 23:111-14; Cyrus Adler, 33:26-27; Isidor Rayner, 40:288, 292-93; labor, 41:310, 330; Oscar Straus, 40:8-9, 11-13, 409; Russian passports, 41:175-77, 181; war with Spain, 41:368, 369, 378
Root, Elihu, 33:27; 40:299, 302; Jewish disabilities, 36:36-37, 39, 273, 279, 281; Russian treaty, 41:176-77
Roques, de Fillol, 41:162
Rosa, J. S. da Silva, 31:172; 32:21; 42:222; corresponding member, 28:xxii; death, 37:xii; gifts, 26:xxxiv; 35:xxi; "The Mohelbook of Juda ben Michael de Vires, 1799-1818, in Surinam," 35:xvi; "A volume of Ketubahs of K. K. Berachah Vesalom,

Surinam, Nissan 20, 5537-Adar I, 17, 5543 (June 25, 1777-Feb. 19, 1783)," 35:xvi
Rosa, Mateo de la, 23:134
Rosalie, Phillips, 45:64
Roscher, Wilhelm, 26:15; 34:249
Rose (slave), 50:160
Rose, Cornelius, 29:129
Rose, Elizabeth, 22:180
Rose, Ernestine L., 38:250; 42:110; 48:199-200, 202, 267; 49:70, 143; "A Refutation of Anti-Semitism Among American Atheists, 1864: An Episode in the Life of Ernestine L. Rose," 49:268
Rose, Fred, 49:151
Rose, George, 26:120
Rose, Morris W., 27:506
Rose, de; Clement v., 25:135
Rose of Dutcher's Coolly, 45:20
Rose of Killarney, 32:xxviii
Rosebery, Lord, 35:254
Rosebom, John, 27:249
Rosecrans, William Starke, 38:27, 37-38
Roselli-Mollet, député, 41:162
Rosen, Abraham, 40:72
Rosen, Anna, 38:63
Rosen, Ben, 42:36
Rosen, Bernard C., 48:67
Rosen, Joseph A., 39:113
Rosen, Joseph B., 40:403
Rosen, Morris, 38:59-60, 63
Rosen, Theodore, death, 37:xii
Rosenau, Milton J., 31:vii, 203
Rosenau, William, 33:21; 40:366; "The Attitude of the Late Cardinal Gibbons toward Problems Affecting Jews," 29:xv; "Brigadier General Charles H. Lauchheimer, U.S.M.C.: A Memoir," 28:xxiii; *Call for Readjustment*, 32:xxvi; "Cardinal Gibbons and his Attitude Toward Jewish Problems," 31:vii, 219-24; "Charles H. Lauchheimer," 31:vii, 193-96; "History of Congregation Ohab Sholom," 33:xxx; necrology of, 37:xii, 92; necrology of Adolf Guttmacher, 25:xii, 150-52
Rosenbach, A. S. W., 26:vii; 30:83; 31:vii; 33:xxix, xxxii, 21; 34:53, 72, 255; 35:134, 264-67; 37:185, 460; 38:139; 39:vi, 288, 299; 41:67, 276; 46:1; 47:205; 48:235; 50:68-71, 254; address, dedication of

society rooms, 32:xxi-xxiii; address of president, 29:xix-xxii, 1-6; 31:1-7; 32:1-6; 33:xi, xix, 1-9, 11-16; 34:ix; 35:ix; 37:xxix, 1-5, 7-10, 10-25; 38:1-6, 7-11, 343; Adler resolutions, 28:xxxv; American Academy of Political and Social Science, delegate to, 29:xii; American Jewish Committee, delegate, 29:xii; "In Appreciation," 42:i-ii; bibliography, 28:xxx; 39:224; *A bookhunter's holiday*, 35:xvii; bookplates, 45:152, 164-65, 175; Early American children's books, 35:xvii; "Early Jewish Publishers in America, with Special Reference to Abraham Hart," 31:xvii; editing, 23:vii; 25:vii; 28:vii; 31:vii; 32:iv; 33:vi; executive council, 22:xii, xvi, xxviii; 23:xiii; 25:xi; 26:xxx; foreword, 36:ix-x; gifts, 22:xxxiv; 25:xvi; 32:xxviii; 33:xi, xxvii-xxviii, xxx; 34:xvi, xxii, xxiv, 117, 266, 271; 35:xvii; honorary president, 38:343, 346; 39:469; 40:406; 41:387; Jewish Americana, 32:xxi; 44:252-54; "Jewish Bibliography, 1640-1850," 30:iii-486; "Jewish Merchants in Louisiana and West Florida, and the English Expedition to the Illinois in 1764-1765," 29:xvi; "Jewish Participation in the Discovery and Settlement of the West in the Eighteenth Century," 28:xxxiii; "Jewish Portraits Painted by Gilbert Stuart and Thomas Sully," 22:xxix; *Jews of Philadelphia*, 31:xxxiii; letters, 31:135; "A List of Books and Pamphlets by or relating to Jews Printed in America, from the Establishment of the Press in the Colonies until 1850," 26:xxxi; Lopez papers, 26:x; necrology of, 42:415, 456-60; necrology of Mrs. Abraham S. Wolf, 28:xxii; necrology of Samuel Morais Hyneman, 23:xiii, 191-93; nomination committee, 25:xl; 28:xxi; president, 28:xxxii; 29:xiv, xxviii, xxxv; 31:xv, xxiii, xxix; 32:xii, xix; 33:xvi, xxv; 34:xiii; 35:xiv; 37:xxix, xxxii, xxxiv; 38:341; presides, 29:xi-xvii, xix-xxxi, xxxiii-xxxvii; 31:xiii-xviii; xix-xxv, xxvii-xxx; 32:ix, xv, xv-xx; 33:xi-xviii, xix-xxvi; 34:ix-xv; 35:ix-xvi; 37:xxix-xxxiv; 38:341-43; publication committee, 24:ix; 28:xxix; "Some Notes on the Participation of Jews in the American Revolution, 1775-1783," 31:xxx; "Thomas

Carlyle and His American Publisher, Abraham Hart," 26:xxxi; "The Use of Hebrew Type in American Colonial Publication," 29:xxx

Rosenbach Foundation Museum, 43:234-35, 237

Rosenbach, Henry, 27:514

Rosenbach, Hyman Pollock, 32:130; 37:256-58; 41:85; 42:456; 50:45

Rosenbach, Isabella H., 30:83; 33:xi, xii, xxvii; 35:xvii; bookplates, 45:165, 175

Rosenbach, Isabella Polock, 31:287; 42:ii, 456

Rosenbach, Morris, 31:287; 42:456

Rosenbach papers, 39:309

Rosenbach, Philip, 42:456

Rosenbach, Rebecca, necrology of, 31:xxiv, 287-88; memorial, 31:288

Rosenbaum, 38:197

Rosenbaum, Arnold, 47:53-54

Rosenbaum, Bernhard, 35:68

Rosenbaum, Charles E., 25:114

Rosenbaum, David, necrology of, 35:ix

Rosenbaum, E., 35:67

Rosenbaum, Furth, 35:68

Rosenbaum, J. H., 49:187

Rosenbaum, Jeanette W., 41:105; 50:57; "Hebrew German Society Rodeph Shalom in the City and County of Philadelphia," 40:407; 41:83-93; 49:235

Rosenbaum, Moriz, 35:67

Rosenbaum, Morris, necrology of, 33:xiii

Rosenbaum, Robert, 41:91

Rosenbaum, Mrs. Robert, 43:1, 7, 238; 45:57

Rosenbaum, S., 47:46

Rosenbaum, S. E., "A Voyage to America Ninety Years Ago," 35:xv, 65-113

Rosenberg, 43:52, 54

Rosenberg, A. H., 35:64

Rosenberg, Abraham Hayyim, 33:140, 142

Rosenberg, Adam, 35:56-57

Rosenberg, Benjamin, "A Note on the Military Career of Benjamin Rosenberg," 29:xv

Rosenberg, Betty, 50:175

Rosenberg, Lester, 42:419

Rosenberg, Louis J., 28:xvii; 49:266-67; "Some Aspects of the Historical Development of the Canadian Jewish Community," Canada, 49:270; 50:121-42

Rosenberg, M. D., 34:217

Rosenberg, M. L., 29:134

Rosenberg, Morris, 46:249

Rosenberg, Moses, 29:62

Rosenberg, Mrs. Moses, 27:112

Rosenberg, S., 39:408

Rosenburg, Samuel, 50:313

Rosenberg, Sigmund, 40:59-60; 44:237

Rosenberg, Stuart E., 42:468; 46:172; 49:256; The Jewish Community in Rochester, 1845-1925, 44:246; 49:231-32; Jewish local history, 49:261; "Jewish Population Growth in Rochester, 1843-1938," 44:237-39; "The Jewish Tidings and the Sunday Services Question," 42:371-85, 415

Rosenberger, Gabriel, 41:265

Rosenberger, Isak, 41:258

Rosenberger, Lipmann, 41:265

Rosenberger, Mandel, 41:258

Rosenberger, Samuel, 41:265

Rosenberg's Fashion Park, 38:19

Rosenblatt, Asher, 27:514

Rosenblatt Brothers, 29:158

Rosenblatt, Levy, 37:40

Rosenblatt, Samuel, 47:203

Rosenblatt, Samuel, 49:270

Rosenbloom, Arthur, 31:289

Rosenbloom, Charles, 31:289

Rosenbloom, Estelle, 31:289

Rosenbloom, Joseph R., 47:201; "Myth in the Life of Rebecca Gratz," 47:201; "Rebecca Gratz and the Jewish Sunday School Movement in Philadelphia," 48:71-77; A Biographical Dictionary of Early American Jews, reviewed by, 50:252-53

Rosenbloom, Meyer, 31:289

Rosenbloom, Sol, 42:13; necrology of, 31:xxix, 289-90

Rosenblum, A., 43:66-67

Rosendale, Helen C., 29:xxxiii; 35:321

Rosendale, Samuel, 38:71

Rosendale, Simon W., 22:xviii; 25:ix, 33:xix-xxvi; 34:255, 299; 37:236, 245, 263; 47:78; communication from, 26:xxx; felicitations, 22:xiv; finance committee, 26:x, xxvii; gifts, 28:xxxix; 29:xxxiii; 34:xxiv; Jewish Publication Society of America, 22:xxv; necrology of, 35:ix, xvi, 320-22; necrology of Abraham Abraham, 22:xii, 199-200;

necrology of Albert Hessberg, 28:xxxii, 285-86; necrology of Louis I. Waldman, 29:xxxvi, 193-94; necrology of Max Schlesinger, 28:xxii, 304; presides, 26:ix; "Recorded Transactions of Asser Levy at Albany, N.Y.," 26:246-47; regrets of, 28:xvii; vice-president, 22:xi, xvi, xxvii; 23:xii; 25:xi; 26:xii, xxx; 28:xiv, xxi, xxxii; 29:xiv, xxviii, xxxv; 31:xv, xxiii, xxix; 32:xii, xix; 33:xvi, xxv; 34:xiii

Rosenfeld, Abraham, 41:265

Rosenfeld, Büssle, 41:258

Rosenfeld, Feisel, 41:254

Rosenfeld, Hanne, 41:268

Rosenfeld, Harry N., 46:404, 415-17, 419; 47:203; "Historical Research as a Tool for Immigration Policy," 46:341-65

Rosenfeld, Immanuel, 41:265

Rosenfeld, Isaac, 29:134

Rosenfeld, Jacob, *Discourse*, 30:429

Rosenfeld, Jakob, 41:261

Rosenfeld, Lazarus, 24:11; 40:263; 49:186

Rosenfeld, Ludwik, 39:145

Rosenfeld, Marie, 41:258

Rosenfeld, Morris, 28:12

Rosenfeld, Samuel, 33:161, 164

Rosenfeldt, Louis, 27:515

Rosenfield, Leonora Cohen, 47:124

Rosenfield, Morris, 43:23

Rosengarten, Albert, 41:70-71

Rosengarten, E., 29:135

Rosengarten family, 50:244

Rosenhayn colony, 38:310; 48:92, 98-99, 118

Rosenheim, David, 41:257

Rosenheim, Jettle, 41:256

Rosenheim, Moritz Moses, 41:257

Rosenheim, Moses, 41:255, 261

Rosenheim, Therese, 41:265

Rosenheim, Ulrich, 41:26, 258

Rosenman, Yehuda, 49:270

Rosenmann, M., 33:237, 239, 244, 247

Rosensteel, Jacob, 26:183

Rosenstein, Barney, 48:27

Rosenstein, Mrs. Barney, 48:26-27

Rosenstein, Edwin, 27:191

Rosenstein, Julius, 41:255

Rosenstein, Leo, 27:191

Rosenstein, Matilda, 27:191

Rosenstock and Price (San Francisco), 37:45

Rosenstraus, Herman, 36:176-77, 195, 197-98; 41:167-68

Rosenstraus, Theodore, 36:177, 197, 232; 41:167

Rosenstrauss, David Theodor, 41:265

Rosenstrauss, Fanny, 41:265

Rosenstrauss, Herman, 41:266

Rosenswaike, Ira, "An Estimate and Analysis of the Jewish Population of the United States in 1790," 50:23-67

Rosental, Abraham Hirsch, 41:266

Rosenthal, 31:149, 152

Rosenthal, Abraham, 41:254

Rosenthal, Albert, 41:195-96

Rosenthal, Arndt, 40:63

Rosenthal, Babeth, 41:254

Rosenthal, Mrs. Ben, 46:120-21

Rosenthal, Berta, 41:254

Rosenthal, C., 29:135

Rosenthal, Ephraim, 41:261

Rosenthal, F., 28:264

Rosenthal, Frank, 48:140; *The Jews of Des Moines: The First Century*, 49:222; reviewed, 47:207-9

Rosenthal, Franz, 40:49; 47:217

Rosenthal, Gilbert, "New Light on the Diplomatic Career of Major Mordecai M. Noah," 44:242

Rosenthal, Helene, 41:254

Rosenthal, Herman, 33:142-43; 35:57, 64; 38:239; 40:246-47; 48:83-85, 117

Rosenthal, I., 29:130

Rosenthal, Isak, 41:254

Rosenthal, Judah M., 41:216; "Philadelphian Rosenthaliana," 39:471; 41:195-203

Rosenthal, Julius, 45:100

Rosenthal, Lazarus, 41:254

Rosenthal, Leon, 28:128

Rosenthal, Lessing, 28:240

Rosenthal, Lipman, 35:248

Rosenthal, Louis, 41:195-203

Rosenthal, Louis Naphtali, 48:241; 50:387-88

Rosenthal, Luise, 41:254

Rosenthal, Marx, 41:254

Rosenthal, Max, 41:195, 198; 50:387

Rosenthal, Morris, 41:195-203

Rosenthal, N., 38:306

Rosenthal, Nathan, 41:268

Rosenthal, Rebecca, 46:120

Rosenthal, Regine, 41:268
Rosenthal, Salomon, 41:258
Rosenthal, Sam, 44:17, 55
Rosenthal, Simon, 41:195, 198
Rosenthal, Solomon, 45:142, 169
Rosenthal, Sophie, 41:254
Rosenthal, Theresia, 41:254
Rosenthal, William, 45:142
Rosenthal, Mrs. William, 45:142
Rosenthal, Wolf, 41:196-97, 203
Rosenwald, I., 40:158
Rosenwald, Julius, 28:240; 29:158; 31:203,
    205-6; 36:293; 37:306; 40:47; 42:12;
    46:436; bookplates, 45:136, 156-57; gift,
    32:xxv; necrology of, 33:xxi
Rosenwald, Lessing J., 37:12; 43:238; 45:144;
    48:254-55; executive council, 29:xxxv;
    31:xxix; 33:xvii; 35:xiv; 37:xxxiv; 38:346;
    39:470; 41:388; 42:414; 43:230; 44:241;
    gift, 32:xxv
Rosenzweig, Gerson, 33:138-39
Rosenzweig, Joseph, 29:169
Rosenzweig, Louis, 50:232
Rosetta, Abm., 21:64
Rosetta, Elkanah, 21:51, 64
Rosetti, M., 24:128-29, 150
Rosevelt, John, 21:22-23
Rosewalt, Mr., 21:145
Roshashanah, *Evening Service of Roshashanah
    and Kippur*, 30:51-52; *Prayers for Jewish
    Holidays*, 30:56-59
Rosh Pinah colony, 43:59-60
Rosin, M., 39:113
Ross, Alexander, 23:17
Ross, Arthur A., 34:2-4, 7
Ross, Edward A., 46:297
Ross, General, 26:186
Ross, John, 34:88
Ross, Mr., 27:470
Rossale, Christopher de, 42:71
Rosseau, 35:203
Rossell, Zachariah, Jr., 25:127
Rossi, 29:xliii, 190
Rossi, Azariah de', *Meor Enaim*, 22:114, 116,
    121
Rossin, "The Rossin Brothers of Toronto,
    Canada," 28:xvi
Rossin, Samuel, 49:186
Rosskopf, Isidore, 50:313

Rosso, Moseh Levy, 42:278
Rotcha, Francisco de, 33:113
Rotcha, Jeronimo de, 33:115
Rotcha, Joseph da, 33:116
Rotcha, Pedro de, 33:117
Roth, A., 43:44
Roth, Cecil, 37:2-4, 11; 39:185, 308; 42:223,
    413, 436; 43:195; 46:354; 49:67; 50:71;
    bibliography, 39:224; corresponding
    member, 31:xix; " 'Don' Juan Josef
    Heydeck: Missionary Among the
    Cherokees," 38:347; *The European Age in
    Jewish History*, reviewed, 40:194; "History
    of the Maranos," 34:xxvi; *The Jews of
    Western Europe*, reviewed, 40:194; "Life of
    Menasseh ben Israel," 34:xxvi; "A Jewish
    Voice for Peace in the War of American
    Independence, The Life and Writings of
    Abraham Wagg, 1719-1803," 31:xiv, 33-
    75; "Marranos of Guyenne," 33:xxxii; ritual
    silver, 43:4-5; "The Sephardic Archives of
    Europe," 31:xxix; "Some Jewish Loyalists
    in the War of Independence," 31:xxiv;
    38:81-107
Roth, Heinrich, 47:55-56
Roth, Mathilde, 25:181-82
Rothafel, Samuel Lionel, 35:274
Rothe, Emil, 41:249
Rothenberg, Morris, 39:206; book review by,
    39:202-5
Rothenheim, Wolf, 26:271
Rothman, Walter, 40:48
Rothschild, 26:37, 46-47, 80, 84, 259; 34:250;
    38:189, 200; 40:231, 329, 334; 47:188;
    50:12, 14; Mesopotamian Projects, 47:157,
    165, 168; "Services rendered by the
    Seligmans, Rothschilds and August
    Belmont to the United States during the
    Civil War and the 'seventies," 33:xxv
Rothschild, Abraham, necrology of, 29:xiv,
    183-84
Rothschild, Albert de, 36:345-46; 41:139
Rothschild, Alfred de, 35:238; 40:333
Rothschild, Alonzo, 34:183; 50:395;
    photograph of, 25:xvi
Rothschild, Alphonse de, 41:148; 42:160;
    49:176
Rothschild, Amschel de, 37:214
Rothschild, Baron, 34:xxii; 39:53; 45:268-69

Rothschild, Bettie de, 37:219
Rothschild, Edmund de, 25:67; 26:160; 31:198; 34:xxv; 35:57; 36:21; 41:133, 138-39; 49:188
Rothschild, Gustave de, 27:512
Rothschild, Hannah, 35:254
Rothschild, Hester, 42:103
Rothschild, Herz, 41:258
Rothschild, Imanuel, 41:261
Rothschild, Isak Low, 41:266
Rothschild, Jacob M., 41:358
Rothschild, James de, 27:511; 35:240; 36:21, 239, 396; 37:214
Rothschild, Lionel de, 24:45; 26:254; 27:483, 518
Rothschild, Lionel Nathan de, 35:239; 37:444
Rothschild, Lord, 36:78
Rothschild, Mrs. Louis P., 28:315
Rothschild, M. A. von, 29:125
Rothschild, Marx, 41:266
Rothschild, Mayer de, 37:219
Rothschild, Mayer Amschel, 26:46
Rothschild, Moses, 41:258
Rothschild, N. M. de, 27:483
Rothschild, Nathan, 34:245; 36:239, 396
Rothschild, Nathan Mayer, 46:481; 47:97-98, 165, 168
Rothschild, Salomo, 41:261
Rothschild, Salomon de, 50:200
Rothschild, Sam, 50:167
Rothschild, Samuel, 41:255
Rothschild, Simon, 41:253
Rothschild, Mrs. Stanford Z., 49:270
Rothschild-Hadassah-University Hospital, 37:482
Rothschild Memorial (Beth-El) Congregation, Philadelphia, 31:276
Rothstein, Arnold, 35:268; 43:192-94
Rothstein, Joshua, 44:136, 140, 146, 161-62, 177
Roubin, Solomon, "Solomon Roubin, Cataloguer of the Sutro Hebrew MSS. in the San Francisco Public Library," 32:xiii
Rouen, Synod of, 28:147
Roumania, 26:159-60; 29:201, 203; 35:119; 36:348-49; 37:11; 46:94; 49:28-29, 73, 78, 90, 93, 107, 135; anti-Semitism, 38:53-56; "Benjamin Franklin Peixotto, American Consul at the Court of the King Charles of

Roumania," 22:xvii, 133; "Benjamin Franklin Peixotto, American Consul: The Jewish Question in Roumania and American Jewry (1870-1875)," 47:202; "Benjamin F. Peixotto's Mission to Roumania," 24:1-24; "Bismarck and Beaconsfield in Their Relations to the Jews," 26:258-59; Board of Delegates of American Israelites, 29:79, 85-86, 92-97, 101-2; Brussels Conference 1872, 24:25-29; civil liberties, 24:102-7; 36:6; "Congress of Berlin, 1878," 24:40-79; disabilities, 26:8; education, 28:83, 86, 131-32; history, writing of, 46:201, 312, 321, 325, 417; "Jewish Disabilities in the Balkan States: American Contributions Toward Their Removal, with Particular Reference to the Congress of Berlin," 24:ix, 1-24; Jewish incidents during the second half of the nineteenth century, 28:xxiii; Jews, 42:172-75; "The Jews of Roumania and the Treaty of Berlin," 24:114-37; "Memorandum on the Treaty Rights of the Jews of Roumania," 24:137-53; Paris Conference 1876, 24:29-39; persecutions, 31:190; "Petition of the Roumanian Jews to the Chamber of Deputies, 1872," 24:98-101; "A projected history of the Jews in Roumania," 35:xiv; public schools, 28:83; religious freedom, 36:6; "Rumania and America, 1873: Leon Horowitz' Rumanian Tour and Its Background," 45:67-92; *Roumania as I found it*, 35:xxi; "Secretary Hay's Roumanian Note of 1902 and the Peace Conference of Bucharest of 1913," 24:80-97; Sublime Porte, 36:8-9; U.S. Intercession for Jews, 36:ix, 99-139
Roumanian Committee in Berlin, 45:84-85
Roumanian Emigration Society, 24:26; 45:77, 81
Roumelia, 24:42, 55-56, 58-61, 73, 79, 107
Round Table, The, 28:260
Rousseau, Jean Jacques, 37:188; 38:324
Rouville, Hertel de, 31:182, 184-85
Rowell, Joseph C., 45:143
Rowland, E. A., 39:179
Rowland, Peter S., 27:509

Rowson, Susanna Haswell, 33:195; 40:347; *Charlotte Temple*, 33:180, 193; *Slaves in Algiers; or, A struggle for freedom*, 33:174, 180-82

Roy, William L., *Complete Hebrew and English Dictionary*, 30:317-18, 419; *Defense of Roy's Hebrew Dictionary*, 30:320

Royal Academies of History, of Language and Fine Arts, 28:272

Royal Academy of Arts (London), 45:271

Royal Academy of Fine Arts, Berlin, 28:4, 7

Royal Academy of History (Madrid), 25:159, 162

Royal Academy of Medicine (Paris), 22:165

Royal American Order of Isabella, 31:294

Royal American Regiment, 35:7-10

Royal Arch Masons (Milwaukee Chapter No. 1), 47:45

Royal Canadian Archives, 26:256

Royal College of Physicians (London), 33:176

Royal College of Surgery, 22:162

Royal Colonial Institute, 25:149

Royal Commission on Palestine, 40:315

Royal Economic Society, 37:473

Royal Family, The, 40:357

Royal Library of Berlin, 22:112

Royal Pavilion (Brighton, Eng.), 44:9

Royal Society, London, 28:261

Royal Victorian Order, 22:202

Royce, Josiah, 28:47; 40:208

Royer, Maximilien, 49:44

Rozenberg, Anthonie Corneille, 48:23

Rozenfeld, 39:151

Rosenzwig, Gershon, 44:125

Rozsa *v.* Rozsa, 29:151

Ruben, George, 27:277

Rubens, Alfred, 35:230; *Anglo-Jewish portraits*, 35:xx

Rubens, Harold, 49:270

Rubens, S. B., 27:235

Rubenstein, Charles A., gift, 28:xxxix

Rubenstein, Pesach N., 34:xxiii

Rubenstein, Philip, 42:419

Rubin, 29:xliii

Rubin, Amsel, 21:42; 31:238

Rubin, Howard, 42:419

Rubin, Isidore C., 42:128

Rubin, Joseph H., death, 37:xii

Rubin, Joseph L., 34:250; "Joshua Seixas, Alexander Neubauer and the early Mormon church," 33:xxv

Rubin, Maurice, 42:419

Rubinow, Isaac Max, 36:366; 39:95-100; "The Jewish Question in New York City (1902-1903)," 49:90-136, 271

Rubinson *v.* Rubinson, 29:150

Rubinstein, Anton, 35:251

Rubinstein, Esther, 40:403

Rubinstein, Leon J., gift, 33:xxxi

Rubinstein, Pesach Nathan, "The Rubinstein Murder Case--Was Pesach Nathan Rubinstein Guilty?," 38:345

Rublee, George, 36:379

Ruchames, Louis, 42:216; "Abolitionists and the Jews," 41:389; 42:131-55; "New Light on the Religious Development of Emma Lazarus," 42:83-88

Ruchames, Luis, 42:112

Rudavsky, David, *The Essex Story: A History of the Jewish Community in Essex County*, 49:228

Rudd & Carleton, 50:288

Ruden, Alexander, 21:163; 25:52; 27:105

Ruden, Fanny, 27:112-13

Ruden, Harriet, 34:139

Ruden, Jacques, 21:168, 212; 25:36; 27:84, 86, 89, 256, 336

Rudewitz, Christian, 41:177

Rudgers, Peter, 27:249

Rudin, Alexander, 27:314

Rudolfi, 28:24, 26

Rudolph II, Emperor, 28:66

Rudy, Jacob, Steerhead's Inn, 41:86

Ruehl, Franz, 43:243

Ruetgets, Helena, 27:249

Ruffin, Edmund, 50:194

Ruffner, Henry, 38:331, "Judith Bensaddi and the Reverend Doctor Henry Ruffner," 39:115-42; *Seclusaval*, 39:136-37, 139

Rufus, William, 21:238

Rugg, Henry W., *History of Freemasonry in Rhode Island*, 35:xx

Ruggels (Ruggles), Rev., 22:24

Ruhl, Julius Eugen, 41:71

Ruhman, Joseph Wolf, 29:132

Ruijch, N., 33:125

Ruijs, Pedro, 33:117

Ruiz, Maldonado Anton, 31:22, 27

Rule, "History of the Inquisitions," 28:xxxix; 32:xxvi

Rülf, Isaac, 42:163-64, 166-68, 181; 45:99

Rumanische Poste, 24:22

Rumsey, James, 23:15-18

Runyan, Damon, 31:212; "A Jew," 31:215-16

Rupp, I. Daniel, 50:71; *He Pasa Ekklesia*, 30:397

Ruppin, Arthur, 40:401; 46:248

Rural Credit Commission (California), 29:197

Rusel, Philip, 27:462

Rush, Mr., 39:56

Rush, Benjamin, 37:197; 38:129-30, 133; 46:21; 49:209; "A Philadelphia Wedding, 1787," 42:189-92

Rush, Mrs. Benjamin (Julia), 42:189-92

Rush, Richard, 33:24; 48:9

Rush-Light, The, 38:129

Rushworth, 47:140

Rusk, Ralph L., 39:324

Rusle, Abraham, 27:315

Russel, Charles P., 37:43

Russel, Israel, 43:144

Russel, Morris, 26:194; 39:7

Russel, Samuel, 45:132

Russell, Benjamin F., 32:97

Russell, Charles Edward, 35:136; 50:206, 220, 235; "Haym Solomon and the Revolution," 33:xxxi

Russell, Earl, 36:21

Russell, G. E. W., 34:242

Russell, Gordon W., 37:428

Russell, James, 23:139

Russell, John, 40:134, "Unpublished Correspondence between Arthur Wellington Hart and Lord John Russell relating to the Appointment to Office of the Former's Father, Benjamin Hart," 26:xxxi

Russell, Jonathan, 46:13

Russell, Lord, 24:51, 121

Russell, Michael, *Palestine or the Holy Land*, 30:290, 311

Russell, Milton C., 50:271

Russell, Philip Moses, 22:163-64; 50:29

Russia, 26:69-70, 77, 82, 84-87, 93, 137, 157-61; 28:86; 29:187; 34:222; 40:294, 296-310; 50:219; "The Abrogation of the Russian-American Treaty of 1832 and the Drafting of the Treaties of 1919 for Protecting Religious and Racial Minorities," 32:xix; American diplomatic relations during the Civil War, 50:401; anti-Semitic May Laws of 1882, 49:162; anti-Semitism, 23:98; 50:6; "The Attitude of American Jews to East European Jewish Immigration (1881-1893)," 40:221-80; Balkan disabilities, 24:14, 16, 35, 40, 46, 49-50, 52, 58, 61-64, 67, 81, 96, 113, 115, 120, 134, 136; Board of Delegates of American Israelites, 29:79, 86, 90-92, 96, 101-2; civil rights, 26:35; The Diary of Dr. George Moses Price, 40:173-81; 32:xvi; "Educational Reforms in Europe in Their Relation to Jewish Emancipation—1778-1919," 28:83-132; emancipation, 26:7; "The European Aspect of the American-Russian Passport Question," 46:86-100; "The European Attitude to East European Jewish Immigration," 41:127-62; famine, 24:9; "The History of the Jews in Russia in the 19th Century," 22:xviii; history, writing of, 46:197-98, 201, 224, 228, 308, 312, 391, 392, 396; "The Influence of Lewis Way and Other English Missionaries upon Alexander I's Treatment of the Jews," 26:116-25; "The Influence of the Russo-American Treaty of 1832 on the Rights of American Jewish Citizens," 41:163-94; "Jean de Bloch (I. S. Blioch), Champion of International Disarmament, Advocate of Russian Jewish Emancipation and Worker for Russian Economic Development," 29:xv; Jewish emigration, 33:7, 12; 42:162-78, 180-88; Jewish incidents during the second half of the nineteenth century, 28:xxiii; Jewish state, 43:172, 176, 182; *Justice for the Russian Jew*, 32:xxvi; Kishineff outrages, 33:26-27; "Max Lilienthal's Activities in Russia: New Documents," 35:xv, 39-51; "The Memoir of Doctor George M. Price," 47:101-10; "The Napoleonic Sanhedrin and the Russian Government," 28:xxiii; 29:xliii; Paris Conference 1876, 24:30-32, 35-36; passport issue, 22:178;

29:189; 37:464-65; Passport Treaty, 29:203; persecution, 25:158-59; 37:19, 86, 440; "President Roosevelt and the Abrogation of the Russian Treaty of 1832," 32:xix; refugees, 29:205; Rumanian disabilities, 36:102-3, 106, 109-10, 112; "A Russian Incident: 1894-1897," 38:347; 39:67-86; "Some Recent Light on Our Pre-War Relations to Russia, with Particular Reference to the Jews," 29:xxxvii; treatment of Jews, 36:42-44, 46; U.S. intercession for Jews, 36:xi, 171-295, 389-402

.ussian-American League, 48:132

.ussian Bible Society, 26:116-17, 121-22, 124-25

*ussian Correspondence, 46:95

.ussian Emigrant Relief Committee, 49:175

.ussian Emigrant Relief Fund, 40:164, 223-24, 229, 243, 251, 261-71; 49:175

.ussian-Jewish press, 39:87-113; "A List of Selected Items of American Jewish Interest in the Russian-Jewish Press, 1860-1932," 38:239-49, 305-16, 343; 39:87-113

.ussian-Jewish Union, 48:40

.ussian Jews, 50:281, 402; "An English Letter by a Russian Jew Mourning the Death of Abraham Lincoln," 50:248-50; "The Hebrew Emigrant Aid Society of the United States (1881-1883)," 49:173-87; "The Jewish Question in New York City (1902-1903)," 49:90-136, 271; "Paul Haupt and the Mesopotamian Project, 1892-1914," 47:154-75; "Periodization of American Jewish History," 47:127-33; "The Russian Jews in America," 48:28-62, 78-133

Russian Labor Lyceum, 48:131
Russian Labor Union, 48:40, 131
Russian Relief Committee, 49:174-75
Russian treaty, 22:xxxii; 29:190; 34:180; 37:465; (1832) 45:262; "The Influence of the Russo-American Treaty of 1832 on the Rights of American Jewish Citizens," 41:163-94; Isidor Rayner (1850-1912), 40:288-310
Russian Zionist Organization, 35:254
Russki Yevrei, 38:242
Russo-American Jewish Association, 39:91
Russo-Jewish Committee, 31:291
Russo-Turkish War, 26:155-56; 29:97
Rustice, Mr., 37:396
Ruter, Martin, *Easy Entrance into the Sacred Language*, 30:230-31
Rutgers, 41:110
Rutgers, Colonel, 27:50
Rutgers, Henry, 38:127
Rutgers University, 34:229; 45:262
Rutledge, 39:344; 42:357
Ruttenber, E. M., 41:114
Rüttlinger, Johann Jacob, 35:72, 78
Ruyter, Michel de, 42:461
Ruyven, Cornelis van, 34:274
Ryan, Denis, 33:175-77
Ryan, John, 29:68
Ryan, Monsignor, 46:470
Ryckman, John, 23:154
Ryder, Dudley, 27:352-53
Ryder, Robert, 31:93
Ryhim Ahavim, Stockton, California, 29:135
Rypins, I. L., 45:259
Ryttenberg, C. M., 29:153
Rywell, Martin, *see*: Golden, Harry L.

S

Sa, Francisco Rodriguez de, 31:28
Sa, Michiel Ferdinando de, 33:117
Saa, Aaron, 21:186; 27:50
Saadia, 44:64, 125
Saadya, 25:180, 184
Saalburg, William, 26:271
Saalshuetz, Joseph Lewin, 50:87
Saar Asamaim Congregation, London, 42:43-44, 220, 225, 258, 300
Saarbach, Emily, 31:294
Saar Ha Samayim Congregation, 21:73, 186
Saba, Abraham, *Rabbi Abraham Saba*, 35:xxii
Sabado Secreto, El, 23:129
Sabaldachio, Salomo de, 28:150, 153
Sabath, Adolph Joseph, 39:330; 50:119; "Woodrow Wilson, the Birth of Czechoslovakia and Congressman Sabath," 38:342
Sabbath, 39:367, 447, 457; discourse, 30:467-68; *Naked Truth*, 30:467; 37:44-52; 41:134; 44:132, 249; 46:389, 395, 425; and "Anglo-Jewish Legal Cases," 25:136; "The Jewish Tidings and the Sunday Services Question," 42:371-95, 415; *Prayers for Jewish Holidays*, 30:56-59; "Religious and Cultural Phases of American Jewish History," 39:291-301
Sabbathai, Hayyim, Torat Hayyim, 22:117
Sabbathai Zevi, 26:128
Sabbath Delight, 39:372
Sabbath School Union, 39:468
Sabbato, Elijah de (Elijah Be'er Fonte ben Shabbathai), 28:152-53, 155-56
Sabin, Joseph, 35:314
Sabsovich, H. L., 29:182
Sabsovich, Professor, 22:211
Sacco-Vanzetti, 46:128
Sacerdote, Moses Vitta, 32:63

Sacerdotibus, Theodorus de (Elieser Ha-Cohen de Viterbo), 28:173
Sachar, Abram L., 46:492; 47:201; executive council, 38:346; 39:470; 41:388; 44:241; 47:201; 50:426
Sachar, Howard, 46:121-23
Sachs, Bernard, 42:124; death, 37:xii
Sachs and Co., L. & M. (San Francisco), 37:45
Sachs, Leon, 49:270
Sachs, Ludwik, 39:151
Sachs, Michael, 22:201
Sachs, Morris, 37:266, 268, 270
Sachs, Raphael, gifts, 34:xxii; 35:xix
Sachs, Senior, 45:70
Sachse, Julius F., gift, 23:xviii; "Moses M. Hays and the Introduction of 'Sublime Masonry' in the United Colonies," 23:xiv; necrology of, 28:xxii, 298-99; 35:134; "Old Masonic Lodges of Pennsylvania," 23:xvii
Sack, Benjamin G., 35:12; "Early Beginnings of Canadian Jewish History," 29:xxxvii; gift, 31:xxxii; "A Suit at Law Involving the First Jewish Minister in Canada," 31:vii, xvii, 181-86; "When Did David S. Franks Last Leave Canada?," 31:234
Sack, C., 28:118
Sackett, Henry W., 38:52
Sacks, 28:109
Sacks, Samuel I., gift, 34:xxiv
Saco, Sara & Abm., 27:249
Sacramento, Cal., religious observances, mid-nineteenth century, 37:38
Sacred Music Press, 47:181
Sacy, Sylvestre de, 38:278
Sadi, Subhi Mustafa, 34:217; 37:147
Sadler, John, 35:148
Sadoks, Haija, 48:24-25
Sadolet, Cardinal, 28:172

Sadowski, Edmund R., "A Jewish Masonic Prayer," 48:134-35
Sadullah Bey, 24:121
Saeta, Maurice, 46:121
Safian, Samuel, 35:49
Saffi, imprisonment, 29:87
Sage, Russell, 36:43; 43:32
Saginaw, Mich., Jewish Welfare Federation, contribution, 37:xxviii
Sagonof, Mr., 36:394
Sagua de Tancano Land Company, 28:309
Sahm, Hirsch, 41:266
Sahnd, William H., 45:163
Sahroni, Charles A., 35:307
Sahula, Isaac ben Solomon, *Mashal ha-Kadmoni*, 22:103
Saïd Pasha, 36:51, 54, 61
St. Albans Transcript, 40:134
St.-Cère, Jacques, 46:89
St. Clair, Captain, 23:21
St. Crosse, Dr., 27:80
Saint Elizabeth Hospital (Boston), 46:83
St. Etienne, Rabout de, 22:38
St. Eustatius, "The Jews in St. Eustatius, Dutch West Indies," 31:xvi
St. Francis, Order of, 28:157
St. George's Methodist Church, Philadelphia, 41:92
St. George Society, 32:108
St. Jago, Domingo de, 33:112
St. John's College, 25:157
St. John's Guild, 28:308
St. John's Lodge of Masons (Boston), 22:229; (New York), 27:495; 37:67; (Newport), 27:369, 416
St. Joseph (Mo.), Congregation Adath Joseph, 25:124; Federated Jewish Charities, contribution, 37:xxviii; "Memorial Note on Samuel Westheimer," 25:xiii, 124-25
St. Joseph Gazette, The, 25:124
St. Joseph Observer, The, 25:124
St. Lewis, Monsieur, 40:82-83
St. Louis, Mo., "The Early History of the Jews of St. Louis (1807-1841)," 49:268; religious observances, mid-nineteenth century, 37:35; United Hebrew Congregation Minute Book, 1841-1859, 22:xxxiv
St. Luke's Hospital (New York), 42:114

Saint-Martin, député, 41:162
Saint-Maurice, Count de, 46:93
St. Michael's and Zion Evangelical Lutheran Church, Philadelphia, 41:92
St. Olave's Church (London), 37:340
St. Paijo, Manuel Pais de, 33:117
St. Paul, Minn., religious observances, mid-nineteenth century, 37:36; "Unlike Twins: A Study of the Differential Development of St. Paul and Minneapolis," 47:202
St. Paul Dispatch, 45:258
St. Paul's Church, Baltimore, 22:192-94
St. Peter's Episcopal Church, Philadelphia, 41:92
Saint-Saëns, 28:57
Saint-Simonism, 45:253
St. Tammany's Society, 38:116, 124
St. Thomas, B.W.I., 22:xxxiii, 112-14; "An Early Confirmation Certificate from the Island of St. Thomas, Danish West Indies," 23:180-82; *Epitaphs from the Jewish Cemetery in St. Thomas, W.I., 1837-1916. With an Index compiled from Records in the Archives of the Jewish Community in Copenhagen*, reviewed, 48:138-39; "Gabriel Milan, the Jewish Governor of St. Thomas, Danish West Indies," 26:xxxi; 28:213-21; "Notes on the Jewish Community in St. Thomas, 1841-1846," 31:xxx; "The Preservation of the Sephardic Records of the Island of St. Thomas, Virgin Islands," 44:114-19
St. Vallier de, 24:50, 70, 121
Saint Vincent de Paul Hospital, 50:333
St. Vincent's Hospital (New York), 42:114
Saks (store), 38:20
Saks, Isadore, necrology of, 33:xxi
Salamanca, Gabriel von, 22:xiii; "Gabriel of Salamanca," 22:xvii
Salamon, Frederick, 47:55
Salamon, Joseph, 32:60
Salamons, E. T., 23:175
Salant, Samuel, 37:219
Salanter, Israel, 44:143
Salas, Guidon, 22:170
Salas, Moseh, 29:16
Salazar, Inez, 31:213
Sale, Lee, 37:270
Sale, Samuel, 37:271

Salem, Morris, 50:230-31
Salem, Selomo, 44:224
Salerno, 28:204-10
Salewski, Jakob, 39:151
Salinger, Rev., 27:504
Salisbury, Lord, 26:157, 159
Salisbury, Marquis of, 24:30, 46, 49, 58-62, 67-68, 71, 77, 121; 41:38
Salisbury, Samuel, 43:204
Salit, Joseph ben Joshua Netef, 27:96
Salkind, Solomon, 28:118
Sallomans, Joseph, 21:49, 53
Salm, Felix, 32:87
Salmon, Horatio, 25:117
Salmon, Philip, 25:118
Salmon, Rachel, 25:117-18
Salmon, Robert, 25:117-18
Salom, Aaron, 27:17
Salom, David, 33:95
Salom, Isaiah, 42:279, 395
Salomon, A., 34:119
Salomon, B. F., 27:399
Salomon, Barnett L., 24:11
Salomon, David (Mobile), 28:300
Salomon, David (New York), 27:402-3, 473
Salomon, Deborah, 27:74
Salomon, Debby, 27:111
Salomon, Edward, 29:122
Salomon, Edward S., 38:15; 42:211; 50:309
Salomon, Ezekiel, 27:156, 473
Salomon, Gotthold, *The Reformed Israelites*, 30:393-94; *Twelve Sermons*, 30:361-62
Salomon, Haym (Philadelphia), 22:197; 27:227-28, 461, 463, 466-73; 28:225-26, 253, 300; 29:xl, 145; 31:xxxiii, 231; 32:xxvii-xxviii, 134; 33:1-2; 34:69; 35:136, 139, 242-43; 37:425; 38:16, 249; 39:105, 215; 41:7; 42:109; 49:235; 50:48
Salomon, Haym M., 43:202, 234, 236; 47:205; bibliography, 34:191-92, 253; "Facts Relating to Haym Salomon," 29:xli; "Haym Salomon's Address in the Synagogue," 38:344; "A Haym Salomon Letter to Rabbi David Tevele Schiff, London, 1784," 34:xiv, 107-16; history, writing of, 46:183, 386-87, 435-36; "Is Haym Salomon Mentioned in the Responsa of Aryeh Loeb Ben Hayyim Breslau?," 33:251; "A Note on Haym

Salomon," 31:xvii; 37:xxxi; Paul Revere, 43:212, 214-17; "Reference to Haym Salomon and Other Jews in Robert Morris' 'Diaries in Office of Finance, 1781-1784,' " 39:470
Salomon, Haym, Jr., 21:212, 214
Salomon, Haym M., 22:xxiii; 23:127; 26:179; 27:84, 109, 111, 315, 398, 466-67, 469, 472-73; 43:202; 50:285; kosher meat, 25:41, 52, 55, 59, 62
Salomon, Hendla, 27:112
Salomon, Isaac A., 27:271
Salomon, Louis, *The Mosaic System*, 30:361
Salomon, Rachel, 27:111
Salomon, S., 27:145
Salomon, Samuel, 27:400
Salomon, Sarah, 27:111
Salomon, William, 31:xxxiii; 32:130; gifts, 31:7; 41:286; necrology of, 28:xxii, 300-301
Salomons, 31:125
Salomons, Abigail, 26:264
Salomons, Alex., 27:145
Salomons, Anne, 26:264
Salomons, Collman, 21:21
Salomons, D., 27:483
Salomons, F. M., 27:80
Salomons, Filagh, 26:264
Salomons, Haym, 21:145, 148-49, 159
Salomons, Hester, 26:264
Salomons, Miryam, 26:264
Salomons, Moses, 21:45
Salomons, Philip, 27:342
Salomons, Sarah, 26:264
Salomons, Widow, 27:22
Salonica, 24:84, 87
Salter, William D., 39:34
Salt Lake City Tribune, 41:135
Saltman v. Nesson, 25:135
Salvador, 29:127
Salvador family, 26:193
Salvador, Francis, 27:497; 29:142-43; 35:131; 38:83, 104; 39:97, 344; 46:33; "Additional note on Francis Salvador," 22:188; "The Salvador Grant of Arms," 40:215-20
Salvador, Francisco, 28:250
Salvador, Jacob, 38:104; 40:217
Salvador, Joseph, 37:420; 38:278; 40:217-18
Salvadore, Mr., 28:250

Salwen, Asher, 44:140
Salzedo, David Lopez, 29:23
Salzedo, Joseph Cohen, 27:45
Salzedo, Juan, 31:31
Salzedo, Judith Lopez, 26:219; 27:264
Salzedo, Pedro de, 31:25
Sam (slave), 22:189; 50:166
Samelson, Solomon, 35:307
Samfield, M., 37:266, 268, 271
Saminsky, Lazare, 47:181-82
Sam'l of Posen, 40:351-52
Sampson, Aaron, 25:116
Sampson, Augustus, 25:116
Sampson, Isaac, 29:145
Sampson, Rebecca, 25:116
Sampson, Rosalind Stella, 25:116
Sampter, Jessie E., 31:197, 210; "Modern
    Palestine," 34:xxvi
Samson, David, 27:515
Samson, Gideon, 23:171
Samson, Gumpel, 25:128-31; letter, 25:xvi
Samson, Isaac Herz, 28:106
Samson, Philip Abraham, 48:262-63; "A
    Jewish Religious Problem in Surinam,
    1795," 39:471
Samsonische Freischule, 28:104
Samuel, Barnett, 49:64
Samuel, Bunford, 30:vi
Samuel, Ellen Phillips, 22:xxiv; 41:292;
    bequest, 22:xxv
Samuel family, 50:244; "The Samuel Family,"
    22:xxxiii; "A Synopsis of the Records of the
    Samuel Family," 22:xviii
Samuel, Frank, 31:xxxiv
Samuel, Herbert, 31:263; 39:205; 40:403
Samuel, Hyman, 22:192; 50:31
Samuel, Isaac, 23:148; 27:241
Samuel Bar Isaac, 21:123-28
Samuel, J. Bunford, 22:vii; 34:266; executive
    council, 22:xii, xvi; gifts, 22:xxxii, xxxiii;
    "Henry M. Phillips, a Biographical
    Sketch," 22:xiii, 139-46; "Historical Sketch
    of the Dalmbert Brothers," 23:xiv;
    necrology of, 32:xvii; "The Samuel
    Family," 22:xxxiii; "A Synopsis of the
    Records of the Samuel Family," 22:xviii
Samuel the Jew, 23:80
Samuel, Judah, 21:38, 42
Samuel, Judah (New York), 23:148

Samuel, Judah B., 21:42
Samuel, Levy (New York), 37:373, 377, 385-
    86; 38:235-36
Samuel, Levy & Lipmon, Lymon, 27:249
Samuel, Matilda, 31:255
Samuel, Maurice, 40:211-12, 214
Samuel Bar Meyr Cohen, 31:236
Samuel, Philip, 23:83; 25:71-73; 44:200
Samuel the Pole, 25:73
Samuel, Sampson, 26:254; 49:64
Samuel, Stuart, 36:160
Samuel, Wilfred S., 35:242; 42:436;
    Bridgetown, Barbados, Jews in, 34:275-78;
    "The Early Barbados Connections of the
    Gomez Family of Philadelphia and New
    York," 29:xxxvii; *The Jewish colonists in
    Barbados*, 35:xxii; "The Last Will of Rabbi
    Haim Carregal, 1777," 29:xxxvii; 31:242-
    43; necrology of, 49:64-69; "Note on
    Mordecai Campanell," 29:xxix
Samuel, Wolf, 34:23-25, 27-30, 35-49; 35:69
Samuels, Charles, 27:120; 32:63
Samuels, Esther, 28:50
Samuels, Esther (Adolphus), 23:157
Samuels, Helen L., gift, 33:xxx
Samuels, Joseph, 21:214; 27:91, 109
Samuels, Judge, 29:122
Samuels, Levy, 21:45
Samuels, Mrs. Louis, 49:270
Samuels, M., *The Jewish Miscellany*, 30:411
Samuels, Seymour, 28:50
Samuels, Sifrah, 27:112-13
Samuels, William, 26:188
Samuelson, Myron I., "Early Town
    Proprietors in Vermont," 45:265
Samuelson, S., 27:399, 504
Samulson, S., 29:132
Sanabria, Diego & Marrero, Marcelina,
    27:249
San Antonio colony, 39:91, 95
Sanborn, Franklin B., 23:55, 65, 67, 69
Sanborn, Herbert J., 50:272
Sanborn, Mr. and Mrs., 38:274
Sanches, Jacob, 29:22
Sanches, Lopo, 33:116
Sanchez, Gabriel, 23:103; 26:xx; 38:442
Sanchez, Prudencia Otero, 29:xl; 33:37
"Sandalphon," 45:28
Sandburg, Carl, 40:186; 46:438

Sandeman, Robert, *Impartial Examination,* 30:60; *Some Thoughts on Christianity,* 30:54
Sander, Charles, 27:515
Sanders, 39:151
Sanders, Robert, 26:247; 27:249
Sanders, Wm., 21:65
Sanderson, T. H., 34:281
Sandford, Thomas B., 34:139
Sandmel, Rebecca, 45:147
Sandmel, Samuel, 45:147
Sandoval, Francisco Tello de, 31:18
Sandoval, Gonzalo de, 31:13
Sandrow, Edward T., book review by, 38:317-19
Sands, Mr., 27:391
Sandys, 31:117
Sanford, 22:80
Sanford, John, 27:175
Sanford, R. Nevitt, *see*: Adorno, T. W.
San Francisco, "The Cornerstone Box of the Old Temple Emanu-El of San Francisco: New Light on Pacific Coast Jewry, 1849-1864," 32:xiii-xiv; "Jewish Contributions to the Economic Life of San Francisco," 39:471; Jews in, 33:xxxviii; religious observances, mid-nineteenth century, 37:36; *A Report on the Jewish Population of San Francisco, Marin County and the Peninsula, 1959,* reviewed, 50:143-44
San Francisco Chronicle, The, 38:318; 41:183-85; 44:46, 49-50
San Francisco Economic Club, 29:197
San Francisco Examiner, 41:182
San Francisco Hebrew, 47:9
San Francisco Herald, 44:33
San Francisco Sun, 45:268
Sang, Elsie O., 50:270, 272, 274, 294-95, 300, 302, 312, 314, 319-22, 331, 336-40, 342, 347, 350, 356-57, 365, 370, 380-81, 399, 404
Sang, Philip D., 37:200; 49:137; Civil War, 50:260, 270, 274, 294-95, 300, 302, 312, 314, 319-22, 331, 336-40, 342, 347, 350, 356-57, 365, 370, 380-81, 399, 404; curator, 49:268; 50:426; executive council, 48:266
Sang, Mrs. Philip D., *see:* Sang, Elsie O.
Sanger, Adolph L., 29:113; 36:29-31; immigration, 40:246, 263; Purim

Association, 40:140-41, 151, 169-70; Y.M.H.A., 37:234, 236, 261
Sanger, Joseph, 40:169
Sanger, Lina, 41:259
Sanguinete, J. J., 27:483
Sanhedrin of 1806, 22:xx-xxi, 235; 28:xii, xvii, 105, 108, 113; "Napoleon and the Jews," 26:xiv; "The Napoleonic Sanhedrin and the Russian Government," 28:xxiii; 29:xliii
Sanhedrin, 26:90
Sanitary Aid Society of the Tenth Ward, 48:31, 54, 57
Sanitary Commission of the Tenth Ward, 48:57-58
Sanitary Commission (U.S.), 50:286, 299, 323
San Remo Declaration, 40:362, 366, 382, 392-94; 49:200
San Stefano, Treaty of, 24:40-41, 46, 52, 61, 120-21
Santa Anna, Antonio Lopez, 39:12
Santa Barbara (Cal.) Morning Press, 35:327
Santa Companhia of Amsterdam, 29:10, 14, 21, 37
Santa Maris, Vicente de, 31:17-22, 25
Santander, Francisco Paula de, 34:280
Santangel, Luis de, 26:xx; 31:235; 33:32; 34:175; 35:223; 37:442; 45:63
Santangel, Sanchez, 37:442
Santob, Rabbi, 45:22
Santos, Antonio Dias dos, 23:175
Santos, Reynaldo Dos, "Portuguese Art, 800-1800," 45:271
Sanxay, Richard, 49:203, 206-7
Saperstein, Jacob, 35:64
Saperstone *v.* Saperstone, 29:153
Saphir, 29:128
Sapienza University, 28:185
Sapinsky, Alvin T., "The History of American Jewish College Fraternities," 23:xv
Saquis, Abm., 22:170
Sarah (slave), 50:180
Sarahson, Kasriel, 49:88
Saraiva, Diego, 33:118
Saraiva, Duarte, 44:83
Saraiva, George, 33:118
Saramento, Jacob de Castro, 35:230
Sararus, Joshua, 26:254
Sarasohn family, 44:180

Sarasohn, Kathriel, 35:64
Sarasohn, Kathriel Hirsch, 45:70, 85
Sarayer Synagogue, 44:175
Sarazal, Esther, 37:20
Sarazal, Esther, *see*: Lazarus, Emma
Sarfatti, Aron, 42:338, 392, 395
Sarfatti, Beinjamy, 42:225, 275, 277, 282-84, 388, 395
Sarna, Nahum M., 50:270
Sarnaiva, Duarte, 33:121
Sarner, Ferdinand Leopold, 40:63; 42:211; 50:292
Sarner, S., 29:134
Saroni, Abraham S., 40:222
Saroni, Alexander S., 29:101, 113; 49:30
Saroni, Simon, 27:271
Sarphati, David, 29:13
Sarphatine, Rachel, 23:148
Sartorius, Philip, 50:167
Saruya; People *v.*, "Anglo-Jewish Legal Cases," 25:136
Sarzados, Abraham, 34:121-22
Sarzados, Rachel, 34:121-22
Sarzedas, Abigail, 48:11-14, 18
Sarzedas, Abm., 21:51, 63, 79; 28:225; 48:18; 50:59
Sarzedas family, 50:32
Sarzedas, physician, 22:164
Sarzedas, Rebecca, 50:47
Saso, Moseh Ha Mir, 42:279
Saso, Zara, 29:32
Sasportas, Abraham, 23:172; 27:462; 29:32; 42:303-4; 50:42, 59
Sasportas, Augustus, 27:304
Sasportas, Charlotte, 27:304
Sasportas family, "A Genealogical Note on the Pimental, Lopez, Sasportas and Rivera Families," 42:303-4
Sasportas, Jacob, 28:243; 29:25
Sasportas, Jacob Jesurun, 44:233
Sasportas and LeBoeuf, 23:172
Sasportas, Mosseh Issurun, 22:170
Sasportas, Raphael Issurun, 22:170
Sasportas, Samuel, 28:89
Sasportas, Simha, 42:303-4
Sasportas, T. K., 50:175
Sasportes, Catherine, 50:175
Sassatelli, Giovanni, 28:192
Sasso (family name), 48:139

Sasso, Reuben, 22:169-70; 29:30
Sassoon, David, 47:197
Sassoon, David, and Company, 37:88
Sassoon, Reuben, 47:197
Sassoon, Siegfried, 35:274
Satinsky, Sol, 43:238
Satow, Capo d'Istrias, 34:226
Satow, Ernest, "Satow on Capo d'Istrias," 29:154
Sattellis, Manuel, 33:117
Sattur, Jacob, 23:158
Sattur, Mary, 23:158
Saturday Courier, 29:xlii
Saturday Review of Literature, 41:332
Satz *v.* Sherman, 29:149
Saul, Joseph, 47:190
Saunders, Lawrence, 35:273
Saunders, Lewis, 23:120
Sauer, Emil, 27:403
Saur's German Grammar, 43:237
Saurez, Lorenzo, 28:199
Savage, E. G., 38:26, 36
Savage, M. J., 45:97
Savage, Richard, 46:434
Savage, Samuel, 40:78
Savannah (Ga.), 22:130; colonial congregations, 28:xxvi; early Jews, 25:131; George Washington address to congregation, 22:xx; Jews in law and medicine, 22:158-59, 165; Mikva Israel, 30:190, 192-93, 359; *Discourse Delivered at Consecration of New Synagogue*, 30:355, 358-59; religious observances, mid-nineteenth century, 37:36
Savannah, "Copper for the *Savannah* of 1818," 48:170-76
Savannah National Republican, 50:337
Savannah Steamship Company, 48:171
Saveth, Edward N., 46:412, 415; *American Historians and European Immigrants, 1875-1925*, reviewed, 38:325-27
Savitz, Harry A., 42:419
Savry (slave), 50:174
Sawyer, Adolph L., 44:154
Sawyer, Professor, 46:211
Saxe, Marshall, 34:236
Saxe, Sig., death, 37:xii
Saye & Sele, Lord, 35:36
Sazanoff, 36:288-89

Sazanov, Sergey Dmitrievich, 41:186, 188

Scank, Abraham, 27:249

Scaramanga, General, 50:249

Scarrit College, 45:147

Scattered of Israel Congregation, 25:99

Schaar, Sophia, 49:160

Schabaalja, Pedro, 32:14

Schachter *v.* Schachter, 29:150

Schaeffer, Baron, 36:51, 323-31, 335, 338-40

Schaeffer, Samuel, 37:440

Schafer, Simon, 40:141

Schafier, H., 40:224, 270

Schafler, Samuel, 41:391

Schaick, John Van, Jr., 45:31

Schaikewitz, Nahum Meir, 33:140; 40:329; 48:132

Schamberg, Jay F., necrology, 34:ix

Schamberg, Mrs. Lewis M., 29:186

Schapiro, Israel, 33:147; 35:64; "Ephraim Deinard," 34:xiv, 149-63; gift, 34:xxvi

Schapiro, J., 32:121

Schappes, Morris U., 39:321, 324-26; 42:211; 50:288; "Anti-Semitism and Reaction, 1795-1800," 38:109-37, 343; "The Background of the Founding of the Amalgamated Clothing Workers of America in 1914," 44:242; *Documentary History of the Jews in the United States*, 42:109-11; history, writing of, 46:183-85, 412, 414; "Jewish Participation in the Anti-Imperialist Movement in the United States, 1898-1905," 41:390; *The Jews in the United States: A Pictorial History, 1654 to the Present*, reviewed, 48:199-201; "New Light on the Struggle to Change the 1850 Swiss Treaty with the United States," 38:347; "The Political Origins of the Statement of Principles and Program of the United Hebrew Trades, 1888," 38:345; "References to Haym Solomon and Other Jews in Robert Morris' 'Diaries in Office of Finance, 1781-1784,'" 38:470; "A Refutation of Anti-Semitism among American Atheists, 1864: An Episode in the Life of Ernestine L. Rose," 49:268; "Sigismund Kaufmann, An American Jewish Socialist One Hundred Years Ago," 40:406; "Unpublished Letters of Emma Lazarus," 48:266

Scharfstein, Zevi, 33:152; "At the Crossroads," 43:195

Scharps, David, necrology, 32:ix-x

Schatz, Brois, 40:319

Schauffler, William Gottlieb, 35:304-6; "William Gottlieb Schauffler (1798-1883) and his editions of the Testament in Ladino," 35:xvi

Schaumburg-Lippe, 26:57-58

Schechter, Abraham I. S., 45:146

Schechter, Dr., 35:117

Schechter, Frank I., gift, 22:xxxv; "The Rightlessness of the Mediaeval English Jewry," 22:xvii; "Some Biographical Material Relating to Solomon Schechter," 29:xv; "An Unfamiliar Aspect of Anglo-Jewish History," 25:vii, 63-74

Schechter, Ida, 34:215

Schechter, Mathilde (Roth), 25:181-82

Schechter, S., 22:216, 218; necrology of Wilhelm Bacher, 22:xxviii, 203-6

Schechter, Solomon, 24:82; 26:21; 28:87, 235; 33:18, 22-26; 35:64, 119-20; 39:96, 110; 40:397; 42:455; 45:103, 155; 47:122, 222; 49:141; 50:401; addresses and other papers, 50:401; Adolph Jellinek, 33:239; "Aspects of Rabbinic Theology," 25:185; 43:239, 244, 246, 249; "The Chassidim," 25:181; "Documents of Jewish Sectaries," 25:185; "Epistles to the Jews of England," 25:187; Hebrew Union College, 40:44-45; Isaac Leeser, 48:230, 232, 240; Jewish Theological Seminary, 37:451-52; 40:311; necrology of, 25:xii, 177-92; "Seminary Addresses," 25:xv; "Some Biographical Material Relating to Solomon Schechter," 29:xv; "Studies in Judaism," 25:180, 185; "Talmud," 25:188; Y.M.H.A., 37:306; Zionism, 40:386

Schechter, Mrs. Solomon, 45:155

Schell, Augustus, 39:35

Schenck, Robert C., 24:21; 36:109

Schenthal, Hermine, Center (Columbus, Ohio), 37:301

Scher, Sola, 21:169

Scherb, Emmanuel Vitalis, 45:23-24, 28

Scherbel, Dr., 34:223

Scherer, 26:27

Schereschewsky, Samuel I., 38:72

Schermerhorn, F. Augustus, 33:222
Schernbacher, Joel, 41:266
Scheurer-Kestner, A., 41:162
Scheyer, David, necrology, 33:xii
Schick, Bela, 42:128
Schickler, Baron, 31:118
Schiele, Salomon Levi, 41:266
Schiff *v.* Adler, 25:135
Schiff, David Tevle, 22:115; 33:251; "A Haym
    Solomon Letter to Rabbi David Tevle
    Schiff, London, 1784," 34:xiv, 107-16
Schiff family, 26:48
Schiff, Frieda, 35:323
Schiff, Jacob H., 24:39, 81; 28:284; 29:66, 97,
    164, 203-4; 31:116, 203; 32:xxv; 35:61,
    122, 258, 323-24; 37:453; 40:7, 397; 42:16;
    43:247; 45:109; 46:443; 47:104, 221-22;
    50:213; Alliance Israelite, 39:408, 418-20,
    429-30, 432, 439; bookplates, 45:135, 137,
    149, 151-52, 154, 171, 205, 210; Cyrus
    Adler, 33:18-19, 23, 29, 31; Deinard
    Collection, 34:153; 41:178; disabilities,
    U.S. diplomacy, 36:36-38, 64, 152; "Hon.
    Oscar S. Straus' Memoranda Preceding
    Dispatch of the Hay Roumanian Note,"
    24:108-14; immigrant aid society, 49:175-
    76, 180, 186; immigration, 40:228, 338;
    48:35, 37, 114, 116; "Jacob H. Schiff,"
    33:31; "Jacob H. Schiff, His Life and
    Letters," 32:6; "Jacob H. Schiff and the
    Immigrant: Some Important Incidents in
    the History of the United States, and of
    Our Faith," 29:xxxvii; Jewish Theological
    Seminary, 40:44; "The Jews as American
    Railroad Financiers, with Special
    Reference to Jacob H. Schiff," 29:xv;
    Joseph Fels, 46:483-84; Max James Kohler
    bibliography, 34:179, 185-86, 190, 201,
    209; memorial library building, 32:xxi;
    Mesopotamian project, 47:165-72;
    necrology of, 28:xxxii, 301-4; 33:xiii;
    necrology of William Salomon, 28:xxii,
    300-301; Purim Association, 40:158, 162;
    Red Cross, 33:220-21; regrets of, 28:xvii;
    "Steinschneider Collection Presented by
    Jacob H. Schiff," 45:154; views of, 39:100,
    102, 111; Y.M.H.A., 37:233, 263-64, 274,
    289, 300-301, 304, 307; Zionism, 49:190-
    91, 193-95

Schiff, Mrs. Jacob H., 33:31; gift, 32:xxv
Schiff, Jacob R., Fund, 40:44; 47:204
Schiff, Mortimer L., 33:31; 45:154-55, 210-
    11; necrology of, 33:xiii
Schiff, Mortimer M., 35:62
Schiff, Philip, 47:203
Schiffer, Gabriel, 40:169
Schiffer, Louis G., 40:140, 169
Schiffer, S., 27:515
Schiffman, M., 33:161
Schifter, Charles, 50:233
Schiller, Mrs. Daniel (ed.), *Through the Years:
    A Study of the Richmond Jewish Community,*
    reviewed, 46:68-69
Schiller-Szinessy, Simon, 25:180
Schiller-Szinessy, Solomon M., 45:151
Schilling, Baron, 36:230
Schilt, Hendrick, 33:122
Schindler, Solomon, 42:378, 380, 393;
    44:250-51; 46:79, 81; 47:59; 49:224
Schinzler, Abraham, 38:63
Schinzler, Mark, 38:63
Schitz, Mayer, 40:169
Schkoppe, Margarida van, 44:82
Schkoppe, Sigismond van, 44:82
Schlachter, Abraham, 41:266
Schlechta, 24:19
Schlegel, Dorothea, 22:55; 26:97, 100
Schlegel, Friedrich, 45:33
Schlesinger, Arthur M., Jr., 38:15
Schlesinger, Arthur M., Sr., 39:287; 43:140;
    46:149; 48:202, 267
Schlesinger, Daniel, *Biographical Notices,*
    30:339-40
Schlesinger, Humboldt M., 35:321
Schlesinger (immigrant), 38:203
Schlesinger, Max, 35:321; 40:242; necrology
    of, 28:xxii, 304
Schlesinger, Nathan, 41:259
Schlesinger, Samuel, 42:453
Schlesinger, Walter, 38:68
Schley, Winfield Scott, 40:288, 291; 43:29
Schley-Sampson, trial, 40:288
Schloessinger, Max, 40:42; 373-76, 379
Schloss, Alex, 38:71
Schloss, Gustav, 38:71
Schloss, H. B., 37:270
Schloss, Henry, 37:46
Schloss, Martin, 50:313

Schloss, Moses, 37:263
Schloss, Phillip, 38:71
Schlossberg, Joseph, 50:234
Schlosser, 28:95
Schlottman, Professor, 27:479
Schlusstein, B., 49:186
Schlüter, Hermann, 46:261
Schmerler, Elias, 33:134
Schmidt, 28:77
Schmidt, Abram, 40:63-64
Schmidt, Otto L., 28:240
Schmidt, Professor, 36:310
Schmidt, Wilhelm A., 26:53
Schmiedl, Abraham, 23:188; 38:192-93, 217-21
Schnabel, Charles, 38:73
Schnabel, Louis, 33:36; 40:31; 45:70
Schnapper-Arndt, Gottlieb, 31:190
Schnatz, Isidor, 41:253
Schneeberger, Henry Williams, 37:85
Schneider, Herbert W., 35:146-48
Schneider, Irving, 42:420
Schneider, Lippman, 34:96
Schneiderman, Henry, 31:xxxiv; 36:xiii-xiv;
    gifts, 31:xxxv; 34:xxiv; immigration law,
    34:220; necrology of Herbert Friedenwald,
    37:463-66
Schneiderman, Rose, 48:250
Schnitzer; People v., 29:151
Schoelcher, Victor, 41:162
Schoen, Isaac L., 37:270
Schoenberg, Arnold, 47:182
Schoenberger, Guido, 40:322; book review
    by, 40:317-21; "The Character and Style
    of Ritual Silver Made by Myer Myers,"
    42:413; "The Ritual Silver Made by Myer
    Myers," 43:1-9; 44:8-11
Schoenhof, Mrs., 28:312
Scholefield, Harry B., 41:92
Scholem, Gerhard G., 40:195
Scholes, Frances V., 37:443
Scholle Bros. (San Francisco), 37:45
Schömberg, Alexander, 34:273; 35:4
Schomberg, Isaac, 33:176
Schomberg, Meyer Löw, 33:176
Schomberg, Solomon, 31:58
Schomburgk, "History of Barbados," 26:255-
    56
Schomer, Nahum Meir, 22:207
Schon, Solomon, 38:65

Schonberg, August, see: Belmont, August
Schonenberg, Marquis de, 22:xii
Schonerer, Georg von, 50:114
Schoney, L., 38:71
Schonthal Jewish Community Center
    (Columbus), 37:294
School of Mines, 35:326
School for Prejudice, 33:187-89
School of Philanthropy, New York, 22:210
Schoonenborch, Wouter van, 44:85
Schoonmaker, Joachim, 35:307
Schor, Ilya, 45:164, 215
Schor, Jacob L., 38:73
Schorey, 27:247
Schorr, Osias H., 45:96, 101-3, 117, 123
Schorsch, Babette (Hirsch), 28:305
Schorsch, Emanuel, 28:305
Schorsch, Isaac E., 35:134; necrology of,
    28:xv, 304-6
Schorsch, Moses, 28:305
Schorsch, Ricka, 28:305
Schorsch, Sophie, 28:305
Schot, Guilliam, 33:121
Schott, 28:105
Schouvaloff, Count, 24:56, 58, 61, 64, 67, 121
Schoyer, Abraham S., 27:313
Schoyer, R., 27:115
Schoyer, Raphael, 27:493
Schram, Louis B., 40:238, 242
Schreiber, E., 34:xxiii; 37:268
Schreier, Eugene, 38:60-66, 74
Schreiner, Martin, 34:303
Schrier, Louis, 50:271
Schriftgiesser, Ph. L., 39:161
Schriver, Isaac, 27:506; 29:133
Schroeder, Henry, 27:413
Schrötter, von, 28:110
Schubin, Ossip, 35:251
Schuchardt, August, 41:70-71
Schudt, 28:133; "Are there Jews in America,
    and where are they to be found? A
    translation from Schudt," 33:xvii
Schuhl, Henry, 39:398
Schulman, Rabbi, 34:238
Schulman, Samuel, 37:306; necrology of,
    45:265-67; necrology of Ludwig Geiger,
    28:xxii; regrets of, 28:xvii
Schulson, Mrs. Hyman A., 49:59

Schulveis, Harold M., 46:61-63; "American Influences on Jewish Religion," 46:61
Schuman, Moses, 50:314
Schuman, William, 47:182
Schumpeter, Joseph A., 46:211
Schur, William, 33:136; 44:125
Schürer, 26:31
Schurz, Carl, 24:11; 29:201; 32:66; 34:185; 47:49, 78, 81; 48:34; Joseph Seligman, 41:35-36, 39-40; migration, 41:233, 249; slavery, 42:136-37; Y.M.H.A., 37:234
Schütz, 38:197
Schutz, A. Henry, 40:140, 142, 169
Schuyler, Eliza, 27:249
Schuyler, Eugene, 36:109, 131, 174-76; 41:66
Schuyler, Harmanus, 31:241
Schuyler, Henrietta Ann, 31:241
Schuyler, John Harmanus, 31:241
Schuyler Mansion, 28:285
Schuyler, Mindert, 27:249; 41:111
Schuyler, Nicholas (1), 31:241
Schuyler, Nicholas (2) (doctor), 31:241
Schuyler, Peter B., 26:174
Schwab, B., 50:89
Schwab, Benjamin Wolf bar Jahacob, 21:5; 37:375
Schwab, Gustav H., 33:221-23
Schwab, Moïse, 26:23, 26; 34:176
Schwartz, Esther I., 49:236
Schwartz, Hugh, "Oscar S. Straus: An American Jew," Historical Essay Award, 44:240
Schwartz, Maurice, 35:277
Schwartz, Minnie, 22:221
Schwartz, Mrs. Samuel, 47:200-201; 48:266; executive council, 48:266; treasurer, 50:426
Schwartzman, 42:128
Schwarz, Adolf, 45:117
Schwarz, J. E., 22:100
Schwarz, Joseph, 48:223, 239; Descriptive Geography, 30:464
Schwarz, Karl, Jewish Artists of the 19th and 20th Centuries, reviewed, 40:317-21
Schwarz, Lippmann, 41:261
Schwarz, Solomon M., The Jews in the Soviet Union, reviewed, 42:442-49
Schwarz, Veit, 41:261
Schwarzberg, Samuel Benjamin, 33:140
Schwarzchild, Heinrich, 41:234

Schwarzchild and Sulzberger, 47:189
Schwarzenberg, M. H., 47:43, 46, 48
Schwarzfeld, Benjamin, 28:84, 131
Schwarzfeld, Élie, 82
Schwarzkopf, A., 29:131
Schweich Lectures, 31:249
Schwellenbach, Louis B., 45:242-43
Schwimmer, I., 29:133
Schwinfurth, 31:199-200
Schwötz, Dr., 31:155
Scientific management, 41:311-14, 322, 351-52; 46:223, 228; "Brandeis and Scientific Management," 41:41-60
Scofield, Ebenezer, 27:321
Scofield, Ebenezer, Jr., 27:326
Scorpion, USS, 29:xliii; gunboat and role of Jewish seamen, 22:xvii
Scot, Gabriel, 35:183
Scotch rebellion, 25:70
Scotland, Church of, 26:134
Scotsman, The, 28:36
Scott, Andrew, 26:268-69
Scott, Charles S., 34:281
Scott, Geoffrey, 46:114
Scott, Joe, 46:122
Scott, Mr., 27:391
Scott, Robert, 23:79
Scott, Sarah, 48:250
Scott, Saul, 39:180
Scott, Vivian, 48:250
Scott, Walter, 29:152; 34:243; 39:128, 138, 388, 466; 40:337; 41:280; 42:398; 46:427, 434; Ivanhoe, 30:219-20, 311; 33:196; 38:15; Jewish prototypes, 35:232, 235-37; "The Original of Scott's Rebecca," 22:53-60
Scott, William, 31:121
Scott, Winfield, 26:180, 182; 28:251; 34:252; 47:54; 48:157; 50:326; "Memoirs of General Scott," 28:xl
Scovil, Captain, 39:4
Scoville, 32:108
Scranton, Pa., religious observances, mid-nineteenth century, 37:37
Screven, William, 48:180
Scribner's, 46:300
Scribner's Monthly, 39:326
Scull, John, 38:136
Sculpture, "Moses Jacob Ezekiel," 28:xxii, 1-62
Seager, Samuel, 37:107

Seal of the United States, 41:62
Seals Opened, The, 30:353
Seaman, William, "A Catechism of the
  Christian Religion," 34:xvii; Catechesis,
  30:196
Seamon, 27:120
Searchfield, Will, 44:97
Searle, Addison, 41:13
Sears, Isaac, 23:170; 41:111
Sears, Roebuck and Company, 46:210
Seasoned Timber, 48:246-50
Seasongood, Alfred, 37:269
Seasongood, Lewis, 40:7; 47:8
Seattle, Wash., Federated Jewish Fund,
  contribution, 37:xxviii
Sebag, A. Montefiore, 38:72
Sebag-Montefiore, Joseph, 31:291
Seboff, 42:227
Seboff, Izaque, 42:280, 395
Secker, Archbishop, 25:109
Seclusaval, 39:136-40, 142
Second Adventist "colonies," 40:108
Second Industrial Revolution, 46:223, 229-30
Secrétan, Charles, 38:278
Secular society, 31:106, 113
Seddon, James A., 43:107; 50:336
Seder Haddorot, 22:119
Sedgwick, Major, 44:96-97
See (modern capitalism), 32:xxv
See, Abraham, 27:323
See, John, 27:326
Sée, Germain, 41:162
Seefahrer (immigrant), 38:203
Seelig, S., 29:132, 134
Seeligmann, Sigmund, 22:vii; "The Classis of
  Pernambuco and the Jews," 32:xiii; "David
  Nassy of Surinam and his 'Lettre Politico-
  theologico-morale sur les Juifs,' " 22:xviii,
  xxix, 25-38; 23:185; gift, 35:xxii; necrology
  of, 37:xii, 478
Sefer ha-Yashar, 41:25
Sefer Toledot Ya-akob Yosef be-New York,
  44:172
Seforim, Mendele Mocher, 44:164
Segal, Abraham, 34:95
Segal, Bernard, 43:238
Segal, Charles M., 42:468; 50:46, 378;
  "Abraham Jonas' Role in Lincoln's First
  Presidential Nomination," 44:98-105;

"Isachar Zacharie: Lincoln's Chiropodist,"
  43:71-126; 44:106-13; "Isachar Zacharie:
  Union Spy," 50:427; "New Light on
  Lincoln's Parole of Charles H. Jonas,"
  42:407-12
Segal, Johua, 44:165, 173-74
Segel, Jacob, 35:293
Segment of My Times, A, 50:315
Segre, Esther, 27:112
Segree, M., 27:115
Seguredo, Sijmon de, 33:118
Seide, Salomon, 50:314
Seidel, Herman, 49:270
Seidenbach, Löb, 39:172
Seidenbachs, Louis, 39:174-76
Seidenbachs, Martin, 39:174-76
Seidman, Joel Isaac, 43:193
Seigneur, Tate Le, 32:52
Seignor, Abraham, 27:80
Seilhamer, George Overcash, 33:175, 177, 182
Seixas, Aaron, 27:163, 314
Seixas, A. B., 50:15
Seixas, Abigail (1), 27:55
Seixas, Abigail (b. Abraham M.), 27:169
Seixas, Abigail (b. Benjamin), 27:163
Seixas, Abigail (b. Benjamin M.), *see:* Philips,
  Abigail (nee Seixas)
Seixas, Abigail (b. Isaac), *see:* Judah Abigail
  (nee Seixas)
Seixas, Abigail (b. Moses), 27:111, 170, 347
Seixas, Abigail (b. Moses B.), 27:111, 164
Seixas, Abigail (b. Solomon B.), 27:111
Seixas, Abigail (Mrs. Hyman L.), 27:112
Seixas, Abigail Mendes (Mrs. Abraham M.),
  27:161, 169
Seixas, Abraham, 26:179-80; 27:55, 87-88
Seixas, Abraham (b. Benjamin), 27:163, 165
Seixas, Abraham (b. Hyman L.), 27:167
Seixas, Abraham (b. Isaac M. and Rachel),
  27:161
Seixas, Abraham Mendes, 23:154; 42:74;
  50:42, 59, 169-71
Seixas, Abraham Mendes (b. Isaac M. and
  Hannah), 27:168-69
Seixas, Abraham Mendes (b. Isaac M. and
  Rachel), 27:161-62, 348
Seixas, Abraham Mendes (Miguel Pacheco da
  Silva), 27:6, 161, 169, 350, 352-53

Seixas, Anne (nee Manuel), 27:97, 103-4, 161-62, 370
Seixas, Arch McIntyre, 27:164
Seixas, Archibald, 27:278
Seixas, Asser, 31:274
Seixas, B., 27:51, 58, 60-61
Seixas, Bellah, 27:111, 170, 347
Seixas, Ben I., 21:170
Seixas, Ben L., 27:259
Seixas, Benjamin (New York) (1), 35:141; 45:57; 49:5-6, 11; circumcision, 44:58-63; kosher meat, 25:34-35, 52
Seixas, Benjamin (New York) (2), 26:230
Seixas, Benjamin (b. Abraham of Benjamin), 27:165
Seixas, Benjamin (b. Abraham M. of Isaac), 27:169
Seixas, Benjamin (b. Gershom M.), 27:102
Seixas, Benjamin (b. Hyman L.), 27:167
Seixas, Benjamin (b. Isaac B.), 27:164
Seixas, Benjamin (b. Isaac M.), 27:169
Seixas, Benjamin (b. Moses), 27:170, 348, 461
Seixas, Benjamin (b. Moses B.), 27:163
Seixas, Benjamin (b. Solomon), 27:165, 290, 292, 298, 314
Seixas, Benjamin Mendez, 21:xvi, 103, 111, 116, 121, 129-30, 140-41, 147-48, 150, 153, 156-57, 159-60, 168-69, 173, 183, 212, 214; 26:229; 27:38, 40, 51, 54-56, 72, 75, 86-88, 111, 115, 161-62, 168, 172, 241, 377, 397, 398; 28:294; 31:284; 32:107; 37:203-4, 209; 41:293-94; 42:430; 50:37, 60; descendants of, 27:162-68; Hayman Levy letter, 27:171-72
Seixas, Benjamin S., 27:115, 258-59
Seixas, Caroline, 27:169
Seixas, Daniel, 27:163, 314
Seixas, Daniel Brandon, 27:169, 360, 368
Seixas, Daniel Mendes, 27:9, 169, 350-54, 486; Isaac Mendes Seixas correspondence, 27:355-58
Seixas, David, 35:191-92, 197, 204
Seixas, David C., 50:333
Seixas, David G., 21:166-67; 26:181-82; 27:96, 162, 165, 223, 235, 243, 370; *Dismissal of David G. Seixas*, 30:198-201; Pennsylvania Institution for the Deaf and Dumb, 22:xxix
Seixas, deLeon, 50:333

Seixas, Elias, 50:122
Seixas, Elkalah, 35:191, 196-97
Seixas, Elkalah (Cohen), 41:289
Seixas, Elkalah Myers (Cohen), 35:189
Seixas, Elkalah, *see also*: Solomons, Elkala (nee Seixas)
Seixas, Emily (b. Abraham M.), 27:169
Seixas, Emily (b. Moses B.), 27:111, 164
Seixas, Esther, 21:173; 33:207
Seixas, Esther (b. Moses), 27:170, 347
Seixas, Esther (b. Moses B.), 27:111, 163
Seixas, Esther (Mrs. Solomon), 27:77, 112, 163, 165, 287-88, 290, 292, 298
Seixas, Esther B., *see*: Phillips, Esther (nee Seixas)
Seixas, Esther Mendez, 41:293-94
Seixas, Eugene, 27:167
Seixas family, 26:177; 27:xviii, 211, 431; 37:385-86; 48:210; 50:28, 45, 253; DePeister litigation, 27:350-56, 358; items relating to, 27:161-274, 346-70; genealogical records, 27:161-70; records in family Bible, 27:346-48
Seixas, Gershom, 22:128, 130; 26:182, 184-85; 44:58-63
Seixas, Mrs. Gershom, 21:166
Seixas, Gershom (b. Isaac B.), 27:164
Seixas, Gershom (b. Moses), 27:347, 349
Seixas, Gershom Mendes, 21:xvi, 100, 103, 133, 135-37, 142, 144, 146-48, 158, 161-63, 165, 173, 183-84, 186, 195, 208-9, 226; 23:171; 25:44, 47-48, 51; 26:220; 27:xvii, 41, 43, 45, 50, 66-67, 69, 71, 73-77, 84, 87, 89-90, 95-96, 104, 161-62, 170-72, 216, 223, 241, 252, 262-63, 273, 309, 310, 338, 346, 370, 372, 374, 377, 389, 397, 418, 461; 30:iv, 127; 31:237, 274, 285; 32:3, 37; 34:xxi; 37:203, 207-9, 213, 430, 435; 39:299; 40:187, 189, 406; 41:66, 227; 42:430, 432, 439; 43:235; 46:51, 382-84, 421; 47:205; 49:5-6, 11; 50:13, 37, 59, 171; anti-Semitism, 38:109, 122-27, 137; bookplates, 45:187, 208; 45:198; Bret Harte, 32:102, 107; Congregation Shearith Israel School, 27:52-55, 57, 71; "The Correct Date of Gershom Mendes Seixas' Second Marriage," 35:309-10; *A Discourse*, 30:116-17; discourses by, 27:133-34, 137-43, 256; eulogized, 27:143, 263, 519, 521;

Funeral Sermon, 30:164-65, 167-68; "Gershom Mendes Seixas' Letters, 1813-1815, to his Daughter Sarah (Seixas) Kursheedt and Son-in-law Israel Baer Kursheedt," 35:xv, xix, 189-205; items relating to, 27:126-43; London Congregation letter, 27:46-50; Mears family, 33:201, 207; Polonies Talmud Torah, 34:124; portraiture, 41:280, 289, 290-91, 294; post-Revolutionary War address, 27:129-30; *Religious Discourse*, 30:88-89; salary discussions, 27:129-32, 134-37

Seixas, Gershom Mendes (b. Solomon), 27:165, 290, 292, 298

Seixas, G. I., 27:259

Seixas, Grace, 31:274, 285; "Grace Seixas and Her Descendants," 29:xv

Seixas, Grace (Mrs. Manuel Judah), 35:191, 196-97

Seixas, Grace (b. Gershom Mendes), *see*: Judah, Grace (nee Seixas)

Seixas, Grace (b. Isaac), *see*: Nathan, Grace (nee Seixas)

Seixas, Grace (b. Jacob), 27:163-64, 167

Seixas, Grace (b. Moses), 27:111, 170, 347

Seixas, Grace Mendez, 41:291

Seixas, Hannah (Manuel), 35:194, 197, 309-10

Seixas, Hannah (Nancy) Mendez, 27:113

Seixas, Hayman, 27:164

Seixas, Henrietta, 50:333

Seixas, Henry, 27:162; 35:191, 197

Seixas, Hetty, 37:204-5; *see also*: Seixas, Esther (b. Moses)

Seixas, Hillel, 27:124, 164, 258

Seixas, Hillel M., 21:215

Seixas, Hortensia, 27:112

Seixas, Hyman, 27:111, 163, 167

Seixas, Hyman L., 21:214

Seixas, I. L., 29:131

Seixas, Isaac, 23:160; 26:237-38; 27:55, 115; 43:253; 44:63; 50:59; naturalization, 37:373, 377, 386; 38:124; Y.M.H.A., 38:235

Seixas, Isaac (b. Hyman L.), 27:167

Seixas, Isaac (b. Moses B.), 27:163, 274

Seixas, Isaac (b. Solomon), 27:165, 290, 292, 298

Seixas, Mrs. Isaac, 43:232

Seixas, Isaac B., 27:76, 84, 86-87, 110, 114, 163-65, 258-59, 265, 277, 315, 340, 343-44, 417, 499; Polonies Talmud Torah, 34:125, 129-30, 135

Seixas, Isaac Benjamin, 21:203, 209-10

Seixas, Isaac Cardoso, 27:167

Seixas, Isaac M., 27:168-69

Seixas, Isaac Mendes (b. Abraham), 27:6, 161-62, 169, 209, 249, 347; correspondence, 27:170-72, 354-68; descendants of, 27:161-68, 170; litigation, 27:350-51, 353-56, 358

Seixas, Isaac Mendes (b. Moses), 27:170, 193, 347, 349

Seixas, Isaac Mendez, 21:xxiv, 42, 45, 49-51, 60, 63, 65, 71, 94, 130; 26:229; 28:294; 31:239, 284; 37:203; 41:294

Seixas, Mrs. Isaac Mendez, 41:290, 294; portrait of, 42:417

Seixas, J., 22:xxix

Seixas, Jacob, 27:51, 61

Seixas, Jacob B., 21:170; 27:163

Seixas, Jacob L., 21:197, 213; 27:115, 199, 123, 147, 163; "Some Business Relations of Jacob L. Seixas," 29:xxxvi

Seixas, Jacob Mendez, 27:56, 75, 168

Seixas, James, 34:xxi; *Manual Hebrew Grammar*, 30:291-92, 298-99

Seixas, Jeannet, 27:169

Seixas, John B. Yates, 27:164

Seixas, Joseph, 27:164

Seixas, Joseph G., 27:243

Seixas, Joshua, 27:162; 35:197; 42:147; "Joshua Seixas, Alexander Neubauer and the Early Mormon Church," 33:xxv

Seixas, Judith (Mrs. Benjamin), 27:75, 112, 163-64, 274

Seixas, Judith (b. Moses), 27:170

Seixas, Judith, *see*: Lopez, Judith (nee Seixas)

Seixas, Judith Mendes, 27:161, 169

Seixas, Leah, 27:111, 163

Seixas, Lucia Orah, 35:197

Seixas, Lucy, 27:162

Seixas, M., 27:150

Seixas, M. B., 21:167-70

Seixas, Madison, 27:165

Seixas, Mendez, 27:6; 31:285; 38:236

Seixas, Miriam (b. Abraham), 27:165

Seixas, Miriam (b. Benjamin), 27:163, 168

Seixas, Moise, 27:56
Seixas, Moses, 27:51, 62; 35:302-4; 37:103; 38:70; 43:2; 44:58-63; 50:36, 60
Seixas, Moses (New York), 27:55, 314; 30:298
Seixas, Moses (b. Hyman L.), 27:167
Seixas, Moses (b. Solomon), 27:298
Seixas, Moses B., 26:179-80; 27:75, 84, 86, 99-101, 107, 111, 163-64, 258-59, 268, 274, 338, 344
Seixas, Moses Mendez, 21:173; 27:111, 161-62, 170, 210-12, 214, 305, 348, 362-63, 367, 410, 416, 451, 456, 462; 38:70; 41:293; 49:5-6, 11; circumcision records, 27:348-49; family records, 27:346-48, 350; George Washington, address to, 27:217-20; Grace Nathan letter, 27:368-69; Manuel Josephson letter, 27:185-90; Newport records, 27:185; obituary notice, 27:369-70
Seixas, Myer L., 27:277
Seixas, Myra, 27:164
Seixas, Myrtilla, 35:197
Seixas, Pedro, 27:366
Seixas, Rabbi, 37:435
Seixas, Rachel, 35:197; 38:70
Seixas, Rachel (Mrs. Abraham), 27:163, 165
Seixas, Rachel (b. Benjamin), see: Peixotto, Rachel (nee Seixas)
Seixas, Rachel (b. Benjamin Mendez Seixas), 26:229
Seixas, Rachel (b. Isaac B.), 27:164
Seixas, Rachel (Levy), 23:160; 38:203
Seixas, Rachel (b. Moses), 27:170, 214, 350
Seixas, Rachel (b. Solomon), 27:111
Seixas, Rachel Hannah, 21:173
Seixas, Rachel Hannah Mendez, 41:293
Seixas, Rachel Mendez, 27:161, 169-70, 348; 41:280
Seixas, Raphael, 27:161
Seixas, Rebecca, 27:111
Seixas, Rebecca (Mrs. Daniel B.), 27:169
Seixas, Rebecca (b. Gershom M.), 27:162; 35:196
Seixas, Rebecca (Mrs. Isaac B.), 27:76, 112, 163-64
Seixas, Rebecca B., 32:102, 105, 107-9, see also: Hart, Rebecca (nee Seixas)
Seixas, Rebecca Mendes (Mrs. Daniel M.), 27:161, 169; Isaac Mendes Seixas correspondence, 27:354-55, 358-68

Seixas, Samuel, 27:162; 35:197
Seixas, Sara (b. Moses B.), 27:164
Seixas, Sarah (b. Abraham), 27:169
Seixas, Sarah (b. Benjamin), 27:75, 162-63, 166
Seixas, Sarah (b. Gershom M.), 35:189; 37:203
Seixas, Sarah (b. Hyman L.), 27:111, 167
Seixas, Sarah (b. Isaac M.), 27:169
Seixas, Sarah Abigail, 31:273-74, see also: Kursheedt, Sarah Abigail (nee Seixas)
Seixas, Sarah Abigail Mendez, 41:289
Seixas, Sarah Mendes, 21:xxiv
Seixas, Seixas Lawrence, 50:333
Seixas, Selina, 35:197, see also: Solomons, Selina (nee Seixas)
Seixas, Solomon (New York), 25:41, 52, 55-57, 59; 26:179-80; 35:200
Seixas, Solomon (b. Benjamin), 27:55, 77, 87-88, 96, 115, 163, 165, 258-59, 290, 292, 298, 314
Seixas, Solomon (b. Hyman L.), 27:167
Seixas, Solomon (b. Moses B.), 27:164
Seixas, Solomon B., 27:111
Seixas, Theodore, 27:162; 35:197
Seixas, Theodore I., 38:58, 69
Seixas, Theodore J., 21:226; 27:258; 42:115
Seixas, Theodore L., 27:173
Seixas, Zipporah (b. Isaac B.), 27:164-65
Seixas, Zipporah (b. Hyman L.), 27:111, 167
Seixas, Zipporah (Levy), 27:168, 171-72, 336; 38:204; descendants of, 27:162-68
Seixas, Zipporah (b. Moses B.), 27:111, 163
Seixas, Zipporah (Peixotto), 26:230
Seixas, Zipporah (b. Solomon), 27:111
Seixas, Zipporah Virginia, 27:165
Seixas, Company, War of 1812, 26:179
Sekretter, J., 39:151
Selective Service System, 47:194
Self-immolation, 33:174, 187
Seligman, Abraham, 35:xix; 50:386
Seligman, Arthur, 37:439
Seligman, Mrs. Arthur R., 29:186
Seligman, Babet, 41:28, 31, 33
Seligman, Ben B., 39:230
Seligman, Deborah, 26:275
Seligman, de Witt, 48:34
Seligman, Edward, 48:34, 37, 114, 116
Seligman, Edwin, 37:435

Seligman, Edwin R. A., 36:398; 49:97
Seligman, Eustace, 31:268
Seligman family, 34:xix, 250; 44:4; "Services rendered by the Seligmans, Rothschilds and August Belmont to the United States during the Civil War and the 'seventies," 33:xxv
Seligman, George, 48:114
Seligman, Henry, 35:xix; 41:31, 33, 35-36, 39-40
Seligman, Mrs. Henry, "The Seligman Family Register," 33:xxx
Seligman, Isaac, 33:xxxii; 35:xix; 40:231; 41:33, 37; 42:173
Seligman, Isaac Newton, 29:109; 34:194; 50:395; Agricultural Experiment Station, 31:203; Brussels Conference 1872, 24:25-26; Cyrus Adler, 33:27; necrology of, 26:xxx; 28:306-8
Seligman, J., 50:386
Seligman, J., and Co. (San Francisco), 37:45
Seligman, J. and W., 47:188
Seligman, J. and W., & Company, 28:306; 50:386
Seligman, Jacob, 40:263; 49:186
Seligman, James, 35:xix; 41:30-31, 33
Seligman, Jesse, 24:11; 28:36-39, 306; 34:194; 35:xix; 40:7, 158, 228; 41:30-32, 37-38; 48:58
Seligman, Joseph, 24:11; 27:515; 28:306; 34:194; 35:xix; 40:323, 406; 42:120, 348; 47:8, 11, 188; "Joseph Seligman, American Jew," 41:27-40
Seligman, Leopold, 35:xix
Seligman, Louis, 47:55-56
Seligman, N., 29:134
Seligman, Theodore, 47:13
Seligman, W., 50:386
Seligman, Walter, gift, 35:xix
Seligman, William, 24:29-31; 29:109; 35:xix; 41:30-31, 33, 37-38; migration, 41:128, 134-35, 148, 162
Seligmann, Emanuel, 41:259
Seligmann, Moritz, 41:261
Seligmann, Simon, 41:259
Seligsberg, Alice, 36:69
Seligson, Isaac, 49:149, 151; executive director, 49:265
Selihot, 39:383

Selikowitz, Getzel, 35:64; 44:154, 164, 166
Selling, Ben, 45:157; necrology of, 33:xiii
Selomo bar Meyr, 21:10, 13, 16, 26-28, 41
Selomoh Jehuda Leão, Templo, 29:31
Selomon, Haym, 34:56n
Seltzer, Julius, 42:339-40
Selz, Emanuel F., 28:240
Selz, J. Harry, gift, 22:xxxv
Seman, Philip L., 28:240; 34:209; 46:120-24; 50:432
Seminary of the B'nai Jeshurun Educational Institute in New York City, 39:43
Seminole Indians, 25:8, 13; 26:194; 37:15; *Sketch of the Seminole War*, 30:306
Semitic Museum, 28:303
Semmedo, Alvaro, 49:41, 43
Semmelweis, 42:117
Semo Bey, Santo, 47:169
Senior, Abraham, 44:228
Senior, Abraham de David, 44:229
Senior, Abraham de Ishac, 44:222, 229-30
Senior, Abraham de Ishac Haim, 231-32
Senior, Abraham de Mordechay, 25:138; 44:232-33
Senior, Abraham de Mordechay Haim, 44:231
Senior, David, 44:22, 225, 227
Senior, David de Ishac, 44:228-29
Senior, David de Jacob, 44:231
Senior, David, Jr., 26:240
Senior, Jaacob, 42:278, 395
Senior, Jacob, 44:228-30
Senior, Leah, 35:xviii
Senior, Max, 36:143-44; 49:199
Senior, Mr., 27:91
Senior, Mordechay Haim, 22:169; 25:138; 29:30
Senior, Mordochaj, 42:279, 395
Senior, Selomoh de Mordechay, 33:231
Sentinel, Milwaukee, 47:39, 41, 48-49
Senyor, Philip, 35:294
Sephardic Congregation (Barbados), 43:6; 41:226
Sephardic Jews, "Henry Wadsworth Longfellow's Presentation of the Spanish Jews," 45:20-34; history, writing of, 46:190, 376-77, 381-84, 386-88, 401, 412, 413, 421; "Hugo Grotius and the Emancipation of the Jews in Holland,"

31:xxiv, 173-80; "Items from the Old Minute Book of the Sephardic Congregation, of Hamburg, Relating to the Jews of Barbados," 32:114-16; "Notes on the Spanish and Portuguese Jews in the United States, Guiana, and the Dutch and British West Indies During the Seventeenth and Eighteenth Centuries," 29:7-38; periodization of American Jewish history, 47:125, 127-30, 133; prayer-book, 31:xviii; *Precious Stones of the Jews of Curacao: Curacaon Jewry, 1656-1957,* reviewed, 47:176-78; "The Sephardic Archives of Europe," 31:xxix; "The Sephardic Congregation of Baltimore," 23:vii, xiv, 141-46; *The Sephardim of England: A History of the Spanish and Portuguese Jewish Community, 1492-1951,* reviewed, 42:435; "A Spanish-American Jewish Periodical," 23:vii, xiv, 129-35

Sequeira, David Machado de, 29:17

Sequerra, Solomon, 26:147

Serafatim, Aron, 42:258, 275, 277-78, 284, 291-93, 358, 388, 392, 395

Serane, Manuel Rodrigus, 33:117

Serbia, 24:29, 34-35, 49-50, 52, 61-65, 67-68, 70-74, 79, 91-93, 120, 122, 135, 152; civil liberties, 24:102-7; "Jewish Disabilities in Balkans," 24:203; Jews of, 42:161-62; proscription, 36:5-6

Sereno, Mrs., 25:118

Sermons, "The Traditional Jewish Sermon in the United States (1763-1915)," 50:427

Serra, Isaque da, 42:279, 395

Serra, Moses Gomes, 27:9

Serra, Widow, and family, 21:60

Serrana, Jacob, 33:87

Serrano y Sanz, Manuel, 31:235

Servat, D., 37:394, 399

Sesquicentennial Exposition at Philadelphia, 40:16

Sessa, 26:75

Sestieri, A., 27:512

Settlement House (Seattle), 37:296

Settlement House and Center (Norfolk), 37:296

Setzer, S. H., Das "Wort" Bibliothek, 35:xxii

Seuenok, Richard de, 41:383

Seventeenth of Tammuz, 39:366

Seventh Day Adventists, 46:414

Seventh-Day Baptist, 25:104

Sevy, Mos B., 21:16

Sewall, Jonathan, 35:232

Sewall, Mr., 37:133

Sewall, Samuel, 26:203, 206-10; 30:iv; 37:440; 42:336; *Phaenomena Quaedam Apocalyptica,* 30:11, 33

Sewall, Stephen, 22:18; 30:iv; 38:146-49; *An Hebrew Grammar,* 30:54-55, 121, 127, 149-50

Seward, Frederick W., 32:72, 74, 86; 50:335

Seward, William H., 24:3; 27:148; 29:87-88, 90, 92; 38:141; 41:121, 166, 206-7; 43:72; 46:276; 47:50-51, 77; 48:10; 50:284, 377; disabilities, U.S. diplomacy, 36:5, 100, 172-73, 322; Isachar Zacharie, 43:72, 81, 83, 94-96, 98, 101-2, 104-11, 116, 123; Lincoln's nomination, 44:100-102, 106-10; Marcus Otterbourg, 32:71-74, 80-81, 83-87, 89-92, 94-95; Morocco, persecutions in, 36:20-21

Sewell, J., 23:50-53

Seybolt, Robert Francis, "Hebrew in the Schools of Colonial America," 32:113-14

Seymour, Horatio, 26:177

Seymour, Ralph Fletcher, 50:396

Sforno, Obadja (or Servadeus) de, 28:168

Sforza family, 28:165

Sforza, Galleazzo, Duke of Milan, 28:192

Sgambati, 28:24, 26

Shaar Hashamayim Congregation (London), 27:xv, 8-11, 18, 46-50, 519-23; (Montreal), 50:132

Shaar Hashamoyem Synagogue (New York), 21:223-26

Shaarai Shomayim Congregation (Mobile), 46:117; 50:170

Shaarai Tefilla Congregation (New York), 21:xxiv; 27:504, 517; 38:59, 75; 45:190-91; 49:18-19; 50:297

Shaarai Torah Congregation (New York), 44:136, 168

Shaaray Berocho Congregation (New York), 49:19

Shaaray Rachamim Congregation (New York), 49:19

Shaaray Shomayim Congregation (New York), 27:504; 49:19; (Schenectady), 29:134; 49:19

Shaaray Tefila Congregation (New York City), 29:131

Shaaray Zedek Congregation (New York), 49:19

Shaare Binah Congregation (New York), 44:136

Shaare Chesed Synagogue (New Orleans), 38:440; 41:228

Shaare Hoshomayim Congregation (New York), 41:229

Sha'are Shamayim Congregation (Mobile), 31:252

Shaare Shomaim Congregation (Madison, Wisc.), 29:131

Shaare Torah Congregation (Brooklyn), 38:336

Shaarey Zedek Congregation (New York), 27:504; 50:118

Shaarey Emeth Congregation (St. Louis), 45:97

Shaari Zedek Congregation (New York City), 29:132

Shaary Tefiloh Congregation (New Orleans), 29:131

Sha'atnez, 39:370

Shabbetai, Sevi, 43:155

Shabbethai, Hayim, 34:51

Shabbethai-Zebi, "Some Remarks on the Shabbethai-Zebi Movement in Poland and Ukrainia," 28:xxxiii

Shadkhan, 39:381

Shadwell, Chancellor, 31:125

Shaffer *v.* Temple Beth Emeth of Flatbush, 29:151

Shafter, William, 43:29

Shaftesbury, Earl of, 24:16, 112; 26:137-40, 153; 29:137; 31:129

Shagan, Rebecca, 48:26

Shaikewitz, Nahum Meir, 22:207

Shake, Curtis G., 48:258

Shakespeare-Gallery, 35:282, 285

Shakespeare, William, 40:337, 346; 46:342; *The Merchant of Venice*, 30:220, 440; 33:172

Shakman Bros., 47:37

Shaler, 22:78

Shaler, William, 46:13

Shalom colony, *see*: Sholom colony

Shalom, Solomon, "Book of Prayers for Dew and Rain," 22:122-23

Shalome Ben Shalomoh, 30:13-14

Shalom Zakhar, 39:369

Shanarai-Chasset, constitution and by-laws, 30:252-53

Shanger Hashamayim Congregation (Jamaica), 27:408, 519

Shangarai Chesed Congregation (New Orleans), 35:xvii; 49:19

Shangare Lamud, Barbados, Sunday school, 26:255-56

Shannon, David, 50:216, 223

Shannon, Joseph, 27:80

Shannon, Julia, 27:112

Shannon, Sampson, 26:251, 254

Shannon's Sharp Shooters, 23:71

Shapira, Moshe, 49:273

Shapira, M. W., 45:151

Shapiro, Alfred L., 45:152

Shapiro, Anshel, 35:49

Shapiro, Barnet, 29:184

Shapiro, Charles Hillison, necrology of, 29:184-85; "Notes from the Will of Mordecai Marks, Early Connecticut Merchant, and Genealogical Date Regarding Him and His Family," 29:xvi

Shapiro, Esther, 29:184

Shapiro, Harry L., *The Jewish People: A Biological History*, reviewed, 50:146-47

Shapiro, Joseph, 33:164

Shapiro, Judah J., 49:154; executive council, 49:268

Shapiro, Morris, 45:152

Shapiro, Samuel, 33:166

Shapiro, Solomon, 44:141

Shapter (actor), 33:191

Sharay Shamayim Congregation (Mobile), 29:131

Sharay Tefila Congregation (New York), 48:243

Sharff, 31:159

Sharfman, Israel H., "Abraham Rice, First Traditionally Ordained Rabbi in the United States," 44:242

Sharp, 29:145

Sharp, Peter, 27:467

Sharp, Samuel, 47:203

Sharp, William G., 36:150

Sharpas, Wm., 21:8-9, 17; 25:79

Sharpe, 22:78-80; 27:72

Sharpe, Governor, 22:194

Sharpe, H. E., 26:254
Sharshot Gablut, 22:118
Sharswood, Chief Justice, 22:141
Shartenberg, Jacob, 45:145, 170
Shatara, Fuad, 45:43-44
Shatz, Abraham, 26:183
Shatzel, 22:98
Shatzky, Jacob, 39:224
Shauffler, W. C., *Sermon at the Ordination of the Rev. W. G. Shauffler*, 30:276, 405
Shaw, Abraham, 49:270
Shaw, Frank W., 28:267
Shaw, Irwin, 39:116
Shaw, Paul V., 33:44
Shaw, Thomas B. (trans.), *The Heretic*, 30:386
Shcherbakov, 42:446
Shearit Israel Congregation (Cincinnati), 40:23
Shearith Israel Congregation (New York), 21:xxiii-xxviii; 22:128, 160-61; 25:112, 125; 26:184, 220, 229, 237, 265; 28:215, 236, 294; 29:50; 30:445; 31:259-60, 274, 285-86; 32:3, 102, 108, 110, 126; 33:199-200, 204, 206, 209, 253; 34:xxi, 288, 291; 35:xix, 176, 286, 316; 37:43, 80-81, 166, 295, 374, 383, 385; 38:57, 59, 61-62, 67, 72, 115-16, 122, 124; 39:43, 46, 245, 249; 40:408, 410-11; 41:65, 68, 121-23, 204-7, 277, 280, 282, 289, 291-94; 42:74, 95, 115-16, 225, 371-85, 415, 417, 425, 430, 438; 43:1-9, 135, 142, 171-72, 179-80; 44:93, 132, 145, 248; 45:50, 56, 64-66, 186-87, 208; 46:2; 47:125, 128, 197, 205, 224; 48:141, 209, 217, 233, 241; 49:6-7, 19, 22, 37, 59-61; 50:7-8, 27, 124, 272, 276, 280, 283-85; Abraham ben Isaac, 22:xxii; American Jewish Historical Society annual meeting, 44:240-47; burial grounds, 27:2, 39-40, 70, 85, 95, 103-5, 120-22, 265-78; 31:80, 91; 37:211; "By-Laws of Congregation Shearith Israel, New York, 1761," 31:xxx; Cohen *vs.*, 35:124; Chicago congregation correspondence, 27:5-8; *Committee Reports*, 30:230; *Compendium of Order of Burial Service and Rules for Mourning, K.K. Shearith Israel*, 30:244-45; constitution, 30:124, 126, 304; Crosby Street Synagogue, 27:99, 251-52, 258-60, 344, 503-4; "Dr. Hamilton Visits Shearith

Israel, 1744," 39:183-85; education, 27:xvi, 8, 10, 17-18, 51-55, 57, 71, 81-83, 92, 95, 115, 137, 140, 146, 243, 397-98; Eleventh Street Cemetery, 27:120, 267, 277-78, 313-14, 491; finances, 27:6, 8, 28, 40-46, 55, 58-63, 68-70, 72-73, 81, 89, 95-96, 104-6, 114, 124; *Form of Service at Dedication of New Synagogue*, 30:298, 300; German members, 27:3-4; Governor George Clinton address, 27:32-34; Greenwich school fund, 27:87-88; Hebrew documents, 34:57, 59-61; Hebrew teacher, 30:332; "History of the Congregation of Spanish and Portuguese Jews Shearith Israel of Montreal, Canada, published at the celebration of its 150th anniversary (1918)," 28:xl; history, writing of, 46:193, 382-84, 387-88, 421; intermarriage and proselytes, 27:20-30, 41; Jamaica congregation correspondence, 27:xvi, 2-3, 12-13; kosher meat exports, 27:6-8, 12-13; London congregation correspondence with, 27:8-11, 18, 46-50; Lyons collection, 22:xxi-xxii; 31:236-40; Mark Solomons, 23:179; members and seatholders, 27:51, 78-81, 83-84, 90-91, 105, 110-15, 258-59, 314-15; "Mrs. Child's Visit to a New York Synagogue in 1841," 38:173-84; Mordecai Manuel Noah, 41:7, 10, 15; Naphtali Phillips Historical Sketch, 21:172-228; *An Old Faith in the New World; Highlights of Three Hundred Years*, 44:210-14, 240; 49:230; reviewed, 46:125-26; Palestinian Jews, 27:19-20, 103, 146-47, 157, 503-4; patriotic occasions, 27:xvi-xvii, 31-32, 34-37, 99-101, 104, 107, 117, 120, 129-30, 132-34, 137, 147-49, 338, 342; "The Polonies Talmud Torah of New York," 34:123-41; *Portraits Etched in Stone; Early Jewish Settlers, 1682-1831*, 49:229; "The Question of the Kosher Meat Supply in New York in 1813; with a Sketch of Earlier Conditions," 25:vii, xii, 31-62; school, conduct of, 27:xvi, 8, 10, 17-18, 51 55, 57, 71, 81-83, 95, 115, 137, 140, 146; seal of congregation, 27:67; seating arrangements, 27:28, 50-51, 56, 65-67, 70, 97-99, 114; Society of the Sons of Tammany, 46:3; Spanish prayer for royal

family, 27:392-93; "Two Visitors to Congregation Shearith Israel," 39:471; Synagogues, 27:1-5, 97, 99, 100, 113, 123-24, 251-52, 257-61, 344; wills, 23:147, 151-54, 156-57

Shearith Israel Congregation (Montreal), 49:269; 50:123-214, 126, 130-31, 133

Shearith Israel Synagogue (Charleston, S.C.), 42:58-59, 61-62, 68

Shearith Israel's Junior League, 49:59

Shearith Jacob Congregation (New York), 27:2, 4

Shearman, Benjamin, 35:141

Shearn, Clarence J., 50:230-31

Shearn, Judge, 26:278

Shebile ha-Hinnukh, 39:263

Shee, Walter, 23:160

Sheel, Henry V., 41:44, 48

Sheerit Israel Congregation (Cincinnati), 50:118

Sheerit Yisrael (Keter Malkut), 22:121-22

Sheftal, Mordy, 27:461

Sheftall, Abraham, 26:189

Sheftall, Benjamin, 34:58; 39:209; 50:67

Sheftall family, 27:80; 32:xxviii; 37:439; 46:37, 387, 420; "The Sheftall Papers," 33:xviii, 37:xxxiii, 8; 42:459; 46:180

Sheftall, Levi, 47:190; 48:12, 14

Sheftall, Levy, 50:67

Sheftall, Mordecai, 22:164; 31:5; 34:170; 39:209; 43:132; 50:67, 164

Sheftall, Moses, 22:164; 27:488; 49:209

Sheftall, Sheftall, 27:91, 488; 31:xxxiv, 5-7; 50:67

Sheil, Bernard J., 46:278-79

Shelburne, Lord, 31:43, 49, 58, 67

Shelby, Evan, 30:77

Shelby-Friedman Company, 39:176

Shelby, General, 23:69

Sheldon, Benjamin, 37:167

Sheldon, Edward B., 35:257

Sheldon, Joseph, 33:214-15

Shelley, 34:235

Shelley, Percy Bysshe, 38:267, 277

Shelomoh ben Zebi Bluch, 25:113

Shelly, 32:1

Sheltering Home (New York), 49:80

Shelton, Daniel, 42:418

Shemoel bar Moshe, 27:408

Shem Tob ibn Gaon, 28:68

Shemuel, Reb, 43:27

Shenberg, M., 39:94

Shepaninski, J., 29:69

Shepherd, Rezin Davis, 27:214, 417, 420-21, 450

Shepherd, Rezin M., 26:199

Sheppard, Elizabeth S., 35:240

Sher, Jack, 45:268

Sherbow, Joseph, 44:208; 49:270; "The Impact of the American Constitution Upon the Jews of the United States," 43:159-69

Sheridan, Philip Henry, 32:73, 86; 47:79

Sheridan, Richard Brinsley, *The Duenna*, 23:179; 33:174, 176; *The School for Scandal*, 33:177

Sherif Pasha, 47:89

Sherira, 39:215; *Epistle of Sherira Gaon*, 28:65

Sherman brothers, 23:63, 66, 69

Sherman, Charles, 39:206

Sherman, Charles Bezalel, 40:403; 46:264-65; 48:266; book reviewed by, 39:196-98; "Secularism and Religion in the Jewish Labor Movement," 46:63

Sherman, J. H., 27:143, 263

Sherman, John, 22:142; 23:61; 41:173; disabilities, U.S. diplomacy, 36:16-18, 255-59

Sherman; Satz v., 29:149

Sherman, William Tecumseh, 32:71, 74-75, 77-79; 38:28, 40; 40:185; 42:118; 43:125; 50:289, 334, 340

Sherman-Campbell expedition, 32:71

Sherman Silver Act, 40:289

Sherwood, Robert E., 40:354

Sherwood, Solomon, 37:412, 417

Shevitch, Serge, 48:90

Sheyreth Israel Congregation (Charleston), 29:129

Shields, Abraham, 27:514

Shientag, Bernard L., 40:105; book review by, 40:87-90

Shiffner, 37:420

Shifris, M., gift, 35:xxiii

Shilman v. Shilman, 29:149

Shilstone, Eustace M., 34:276-78; 37:459-60; 49:67; *Monumental Inscriptions of Barbados*, 44:246

Shimkin, N., 39:103

Shinedling, Abraham I., *History of the Beckley Jewish Community (Beckley, West Virginia), and of Congregation Beth El (The Beckley Hebrew Association) (including Raleigh and Fayette Counties, West Virginia), (1895-1955)*, 49:241-42; *History of the Los Alamos Jewish Center*, 49:228

Shipping, "Gabriel Milan, the Jewish Governor of St. Thomas," 28:213-21; "The Gratz Papers," 23:vii, xiii, 1-23; "Jewish Owners of Ships Registered at the Port of Philadelphia, 1730-1755," 22:xviii; 26:235-36

Shipton, Clifford K., "The Hebraic Background of Puritanism," 47:140-53, 200

Shire, Tillie, 31:267

Shir ha-ma 'alot, 39:368

Shir Hillulim, 22:120

Shirley, William, Governor of Mass., 22:17, 19

Shiva, 39:373

Shiver, C., 50:331

Shloss, Simon, 31:158-60

Shmi, 39:100, 105

Shnirer, Sara, 40:403

Shochareh Sefat Eber, 33:128

Shoenfeld, Abraham H., 35:270-71

Shoharai Sefat Eber, 35:63

Shohet, Raphael, 33:161

Sholom colony, 38:xxxi; "Further Information Concerning the Colony 'Sholam' on Yageville Hill, Ulster County, New York," 35:306-9; "The Jewish Colony of Sholam, Ulster County, New York, 1838," 23:178-79; "A Real Estate Record of the Sholam Colony," 25:xiii

Shore, Captain, 23:72

Short, Luther, 36:60

Short, R. F., 23:138

Shosteck, Robert, 47:202; 49:137, 155; Civil War, 50:260, 270-71, 275, 299, 378; history, writing of, 46:240-41, 244; "Leopold Karpeles: Civil War Hero," 49:268

Shosteck, Mrs. Robert, 50:272, 275, 299, 378

Shotwell, John B., 39:449

Shovai Zion, 35:57

Show Shop, The, 40:357

Shoyer, Charles C., 47:38

Shoyer, Gabriel, 47:48

Shpall, Leo, 33:xxvii, 167; 34:258; 37:437-40; 39:477; 40:205; book review by, 48:196-97; "The Diary of Dr. George Moses Price," 40:173-81; "David Feinberg's Historical Survey of the Colonization of the Russian Jews in Argentina," 43:37-69; "Early Jewish Philanthropy in New Orleans," 49:222; "An Immigrant's Trip to the United States in 1882," 41:390; *A Jewish agricultural colony in Louisiana*, 35:xxii; "Jewish Agricultural Colonies in the United States," 38:345; "Jewish Americana in Yiddish Periodicals of Russia and Poland, 1862-1940," 39:470; "Jewish Emigration from Russia-Poland in the Eighties in European Jewish Periodicals," 40:406; "The Jewish Question in New York City (1902-1903)," 49:90-136, 271; *The Jews in Louisiana*, 35:xxii; "Kishineff Pogrom and Jewish Emigration to the United States on the Fiftieth Anniversary," 42:415; "Leaves from the Diary of Dr. George M. Price," 38:347; "The Letters of Vladimir Korolenko about Woodbine, New Jersey (1893)," 45:265; "A List of Selected Items of American Jewish Interest in the Russian-Jewish Press, 1860-1932," 38:239-48; 305-16, 343; 39:87-113; "The Memoir of Doctor George M. Price," 47:101-10; "The Minute Book of the Machazike Talmud Torah, New York (1890-1902)," 46:493; Russian-Jewish press, 39:87-113; "The Russian Jews in America," 48:28-62, 78-133; "Some Aspects of the Galveston Movement," 37:xxxv; "Some Judaica in State and Other Regional Historical Publications," 37:xxx, 435-44; "The Texel Affair in Louisiana," 44:242

Shrady, George F., 33:217-21, 223

Shreveport, La., Jewish Federation, contribution, 37:xxviii

Shroder, Jacob, 37:269

Shubow, Leo, 43:231; "Jacob de Haas, American Zionist Journalist," 47:202; "Why Touro Avenue in Medford, Massachusetts," 46:493

Shubricke, William B., 23:122; 39:13, 24
Shulamith, 35:55
Shulamith School of Music, Tel Aviv, 45:198
Shulhan Aruk, 28:68, 79
Shulhan Tahor, 22:120
Shulman, Isaac, 29:71
Shulman, Max, 28:240
Shulman, Samuel, 39:408
Shulvass, Moses A., book review by, 43:197
Shund, 49:84
Shurman, Jacob Gould, 41:184
Shuster, W. Morgan, 41:183
Shusterman, Abraham, 49:270
Shutz, Mayer, 40:169
Shuvalov, Count, 24:121
Shylock, 40:327-29, 334
Si, 39:101
Sibley, Henry, 42:367
Siccary, Dr., 22:159
Sichel, Simon, necrology of, 33:xxi
Sichelgarti, Duchess, 28:205
Sicily Island colony, 37:245-46, 305; 38:245-46, 305, 440; 40:246-47; 49:178
Sickles, 42:118
Side, Isaque Gabai, 42:279, 395
Sidney, Algernon, 37:186-87
Sidney, George, 35:259
Siege of Algiers, The, 40:347
"Siege of Tripoli, The," 21:229; 41:26
Siegel, 38:20
Siegel, Mrs. Benjamin M., 41:275-76
Siegel, Hannah London, 31:7; "Anglo-Jewish Portraits," 33:xxx; "Early American Jewish Portraits," 32:xix; *Jewish Portraits*, 31:xxxiv; "Notes on Silhouettes of American Jews by August Edouart and Other Silhouettists," 34:xiv
Siegel, Max, 40:356
Siegler, Joseph, 34:229
Siemering, Rudolf, 28:4
Siena, Aron de Jacob de, 29:11
Sigel, Franz, 47:55
Sigilman, Samuel, death, 37:xii
Sigismund, Emperor, 28:66
Sigorgnes, Mrs., 29:55
Silber, Mendel, 22:vii; "America in Hebrew Literature," 22:xii, 101-37; Louisiana Historical Society, 23:x
Silber, Saul, 28:240

Silberberg, Mendel B., 42:421
Silberman, H. S., 22:136
Silberman, Jacob, 22:136; 24:14-15; 36:102-4
Silberman, Mr., 27:145
Silberman, S., 21:226
Silberna, Manuel Gomez, 31:31
Silk, Benjamin Nachum, 33:149
Silkiner, B. N., 50:267-68; *Mul Ohel Temurah*, 22:175
Sille, Nicassius de, 21:176-77; 29:44-45
Silua, Isaque da, 42:279, 286-88, 391, 395
Silua, Jahacob da, 42:279, 283, 392, 395
Silva, Abraham A. Cohen da, 29:28
Silva, Alberto Carlos da, necrology of, 22:xxviii; 25:148
Silva, Aron da, 42:257, 289, 387, 392, 395
Silva, Duarte da, 47:118
Silva, Ebyatar Cohen da, 29:32
Silva, Fernando Martins da, 33:99
Silva, Francisco Arthur da, 25:148
Silva, Francisco Maldonado de (Peru), 22:156
Silva, Fr. Meld. da, 27:484
Silva, Gasper de, 33:114
Silva, George da, 33:119
Silva, Gomes Daniel, 32:63
Silva, Isaac Cohen de, 21:92, 100, 208; 27:27, 262-63; 31:237
Silva, Isaac Joao da, 27:157
Silva, Jacob Gomez da, 29:25
Silva, Jan Baptista da, 33:115
Silva, Joseph da, 32:57, 64
Silva, Joshua de, 23:153; 32:61
Silva, Josiah de, 23:153
Silva, Juan Rodriguez de, 31:29
Silva, Mordechay de, 32:61; 37:339
Silva, Moses Gomes, 37:420
Silva, Pedro da, 47:63-64
Silva, Rachel de, 23:153; 27:289
Silva, Rev. de, 27:262
Silva, Rosa da, *Portuguese Jews in Holland*, 31:xxxiii
Silva, Samuel de, 23:153
Silva, Sinya de, 23:153
Silva, Telles da, 33:85
Silva in Pariba, Manuel da, 33:114
Silver, Abba Hillel, 39:463
Silver, Harold, 40:231
Silver, Henry H., 50:238
Silver, Lewis, 27:277

Silver, Louis, "The Jews in Albany, New York, 1655-1914," 49:229
Silvera, Manuel, 23:132
Silvera, Sarah, 32:63
Silverman, Henry P., "The Hunt's Bay Jewish Cemetery, Kingston, Jamaica, British West Indies," 37:xxx, 327-344; "The Montego Bay Jewish Community, Jamaica, B. W. I.," 38:343
Silverman, Joseph, 37:266-67; 42:350, 378-79; necrology of, 33:xii; necrology of Abraham Blum, 29:xiv, 155-56
Silverman, Lion, 47:56
Silversmith, Julius, 42:378
Silversmiths, 43:1-9, 200, 203-4; "A New York Jewish Silversmith of the Eighteenth Century," 28:236-38; "Notes on Jewish silversmiths at the time of the Revolution," 31:xxiv
Silverware: "Chinese Influence in Seventeenth-Century Jewish Silver," 44:8-11; "The Form and Decoration of Silver *Rimonim*," 45:48-53
Silverstein, Joseph, New York chief rabbi, 44:151-52, 157, 165, 169, 185
Silveyra, Abraham Gomez, 29:25
Simeon Ben Johauy, 28:243
Simhat Torah, 39:366
Simitière, Du, 23:166
Simmons, 31:125
Simmons, Ann Marie, 50:160
Simmons, Augustus, 50:160
Simmons, Maurice, Jewish Publication Society of America, 22:xxv
Simon, 26:165-67; 40:119; 43:91
Simon, Abraham, 29:131; 32:121
Simon, Abraham H., 39:408, 427-29
Simon, Abram, 34:255; gifts, 26:xxxv; 34:xxvii; 35:xix; "Notes of Jewish Interest in the District of Columbia," 26:xiv, 211-18; "A Supposed Interdenominational Society in 1832," 26:211-13; thirty-first annual meeting, committee on, 29:xxvi
Simon, A. M., 41:130
Simon, Bilah, 37:349
Simon and Campbell, 23:21
Simon, Ernst, "Philanthropism and Jewish Education," 43:194
Simon and Etting, 34:67

Simon, Henry G., 50:272, 274, 287
Simon, James, 40:403
Simon, Joseph, 22:xxix
Simon, Joseph (Lancaster, Pa.), 22:188-89; 23:4-7, 13, 15-17, 19-23; 25:113; 26:8, 233, 236; 27:20, 462; 31:241; 33:4; 34:67; 35:16-18; 37:347-49; 40:288; 43:234-35; 50:29, 39, 60, 287; "David Franks and Joseph Simon, Commissaries," 39:470; letters, 34:78, 99-103
Simon, Joseph Cohen, 37:346, 349
Simon ben Kamhit, 28:69
Simon, Kaufman, 27:389
Simon, Leah, 37:349-50
Simon, Levy and Company, 23:13
Simon, Miriam, 23:6; 31:241; 37:348
Simon, Rachel, 34:67
Simon, Shinah, 31:241
Simon the Asmonean, 25:165, 167
Simon of Trent, 28:160
Simon, Victor, 48:258
Simonds, Samuel, 27:249
Simons (Pa.), 23:177
Simons (Va.), 27:60, 62
Simons, Abraham, 40:192; 47:224; "Abraham Simons, a Georgia Patriot of the Revolutionary War," 31:xvii; "Captain Abraham Simons of The Georgia Line in the Revolution," 33:231-36
Simons, Benjamin, 42:419
Simons, Benjamin Benneau (S.C.), 22:164
Simons, Hananel, 27:156
Simons, Hart, 27:120
Simons, Joseph (N.Y.), 155-56
Simons, Joseph, Indiana Land, 30:63, 71, 77
Simons, Levy, 21:142
Simons, Nancy (Mills), 33:222-35
Simons, Sampson, 50:42, 60
Simons, Samuel, 50:176
Simons, Simcha, 27:155
Simons, Sol, 21:148-49, 159
Simons, Solomon, 27:253
Simonson, Lee, 35:257
Simonson, M. H., 27:518
Simpson, 29:146
Simpson, Daniel L., 27:277
Simpson, Edmund, 33:196
Simpson, Edward, 23:154
Simpson, Henry, 22:90

Simpson, Jacob, 22:197
Simpson, Jerucham Zevi, 35:57
Simpson, Joseph, 37:449
Simpson, Judith (Mrs. B. L.), 27:112
Simpson, Judith (Mrs. M. L.), 27:112
Simpson, S., 27:416
Simpson, Sampson, 40:76; 45:57; "The Hebrew Oration of Sampson Simpson, 1800," 46:51-58
Simpson, Samuel, 35:291
Simpson, Solomon, 38:109, 115, 125, 127-28, 137, 332; 50:37, 60
Simpson, William Brooks, 35:291-92
Simson, Dyfie, 25:88-89; 28:247
Simson, Ellen (Helena), 27:371-72; 33:202
Simson family, 27:xviii, 371-75; 37:385
Simson, Frances, 25:90-91
Simson, Frances (nee Isacks), 27:74-75, 112, 372-73
Simson, Frumet, 27:371; 33:202
Simson, Mrs. Frumet, 27:371
Simson, H., 30:421
Simson, Helena, 33:202
Simson, Jacob, 44:211
Simson, Jochabed, 33:202
Simson, Joice, 27:372
Simson, Jochebed, 27:371
Simson, Joseph (New York), 21:8, 10, 16, 21, 27, 29, 31, 33, 40, 48-49, 51, 53, 55-56, 58, 60, 63, 70-72, 81, 83, 85, 88-89, 91, 93, 96-97, 99-103, 105, 107, 111-12, 114, 116, 118, 130, 132, 136, 211, 213; 23:151-52; 33:202-3, 206; 42:433, 46:424; naturalization, 37:373, 377, 385-86; 38:235
Simson, Joseph (1), 26:180; 33:202
Simson, Joseph (2), "Notes on the Genealogies of Jacob Franks and Joseph Simson," 22:xiii; "Will of Nathan Simson, a Jewish Merchant in New York before 1722, and Genealogical Note Concerning him and Joseph Simson," 25:vii, 87-91
Simson, Joseph (b. Solomon), 27:74-75, 84, 86, 371-72
Simson, Joseph (father of Solomon), 27:8, 28-29, 39, 42, 71, 183, 299, 371, 373
Simson, Joseph S., 27:277
Simson, Martin Edward, 36:239, 397
Simson, Matthew, 23:150

Simson, Nathan, 33:253; 35:174-75, 182; "The Simson Trust," 28:246-48; "The Will of Nathan Simson, a Jewish Merchant in New York before 1772, Proved in London in 1725," 22:xxviii; "Will of Nathan Simson, a Jewish Merchant in New York before 1722, and Genealogical Note Concerning him and Joseph Simson," 25:vii, 87-91
Simson, Rebecca (Mrs. Abraham Mears Isaacks), 33:202, 206
Simson, Rebecca (nee Isacks), 27:371
Simson, Rebecca Isaacs (Mrs. Joseph), 33:202
Simson, Rebecca, see: Isaacks, Rebecca (nee Simson)
Simson, Rebekah (Isaacs), 25:90
Simson, Richa, 25:90
Simson, Sampson (New York) (1), 21:xv, 45, 48-49, 51, 53, 62-63, 74, 77-79, 85, 88-89, 93, 102-3, 105, 107, 111-12, 114, 116, 211; 22:152; 25:52, 56-57, 87; 29:100; 37:137, 143-44; 42:115, 418, 433-34; 43:212; 49:17; "Sampson Simson's Bequest to Columbia," 37:xxxiii, 434; "Sampson Simson's Hebrew Oration, 1800," 37:430-33
Simson, Sampson (New York) (2), 21:xxv, 163, 168, 215; 25:87; 26:180; 34:253; 35:55; 47:224
Simson, Sampson (b. Joseph), 27:11, 13, 371
Simson, Sampson (grandson of Joseph), 27:84, 86, 92, 142, 372-75
Simson, Sampson, Jr., 25:90
Simson, Samson, 33:202, 207, 254; 44:212
Simson, Samuel, 25:90
Simson, Sarah (1), 25:90
Simson, Sarah (2), 25:90
Simson, Sarah, see: Jacobs, Sarah (nee Simson)
Simson, Sarah (nee Mears), 27:371-72; 33:102
Simson, Solomon, 21:79, 90, 103, 111-12, 116-23, 129-31, 140-41, 145-50, 157, 159-60, 168, 211; 23:161; 25:47, 52, 90; 28:225; 33:202, 204, 206; 37:137, 143-44; 38:332; 42:433
Simson, Solomon (father of Joseph), 27:28-29, 38, 40, 41, 43, 46, 51, 60-61, 70, 253,

371-73; George Washington, address to, 27:217-22

Simson, Solomon (b. Joseph), 27:75, 372

Simson, Solomon Joseph, "The Simson-Hirsch Letter to the Chinese Jews, 1795," 49:39-52

Simsons, Ritcha, 27:372

Simsons, Samuel, 27:372

Sinai, 42:101; 45:95, 103

Sinai. Ein Organ für Erkenntniss und Veredlung des Judenthums, 26:273

Sinai, "The Sinai Literary Association in Chicago in 1878," 40:407

Sinai Temple, Chicago, 31:251, 269; 37:49, 294; 40:68; 41:365; 42:376; 45:93-94; gift, 35:xxiii

Sinai Temple, New Orleans, 28:309; "Jubilee Souvenir of Temple Sinai of New Orleans," 29:xli; 31:xxxii

Sinclair, Lieutenant, 35:19

Sinclair, Upton, 41:54

Sing, Yee, 34:198

Singer, Abraham, 50:402

Singer, B., 24:30

Singer, Charles, "Science and Judaism," 40:193

Singer, I. J., 43:36

Singer, Isaac, 32:55

Singer, Isidore, 25:160; 33:19; 35:120; 39:97; 45:104

Singer, Israel J., 35:276-77

Singer, Jacob, 37:257

Singer, L., 39:113

Singer, Paul, 41:211

Singing Sixties: the Spirit of Civil War Days Drawn from Music of the Times, The, 50:391

Single tax, 38:337; 41:328; 42:103; 43:29; "The Single-Tax Zionism of Joseph Fels," 46:474-91, 493

Singular Revelations, 30:464-65

Sinton, David, 28:10

Sion, 38:242

Sionnet (L'Abbé), 49:42

Sirovich, William I., death, 37:xii

Sisme, Anne de, 27:329

Sismondi, Jean Charles Leonard Simdonde de, 45:25-26

Sisson, Gideon, 23:165

Sisson, John, 27:175

Sisterhood of the Spanish and Portuguese Synagogue, 45:198-99

Sisterhood of Zion (Buffalo), 37:295

Six-Nation Confederacy, 46:285

Sixtus IV, 28:160, 204

Sixtus V, 28:165, 178; 37:199; 38:117

Sizoo, Joseph R., 47:203

Skawinski, "Citizen," 39:150

Skene, James, 22:54

Skimer, Captain, 27:355

Skinner, 22:77

Skinner, Charles W., 39:3

Skinner, Richard, 22:178

Skinner, Roger, 30:404

Sklare, Marshall, 47:122; book review by, 47:62; (ed.), *The Jews: Social Patterns of an American Group*, reviewed, 48:63

Skuratowski, Hersch, 34:199

Skuy v. United States, 29:150

Slamm, Levi D., 39:34

Slánský, Rudolph, 50:98, 112, 115

Slansky trials, 50:98, 112

Slasson, William, 31:81

Slaton, John M., 42:356

Slaughter, Kayserling on ritual slaughtering, 32:xxvi

Slavery, 22:189; 23:126; 25:7, 14, 20, 22; 26:35, 273; 28:228; 29:125, 200; 30:466; 31:xxxiii, 45, 189; 32:11-12; 36:ix; 37:57, 82; 38:47, 111-12, 173; 39:307; 41:20; 42:102, 108, 110; 46:21; 48:21, 24-25, 199-200; 49:37, 138, 250; 50:267, 379, 402; abolitionists, 48:148-49; 50:288-90, 355; "Abolitionists and the Jews," 41:389; 42:131-55; Brazil, 33:45, 48-49, 59, 63-64, 76; 47:113-15; chattel slavery, 31:106; *Communication on Subject of Slave Immigration*, 30:447; "Haym M. Solomon Frees His Slave," 37:xxxi, 447-48; Henry Ruffner, 39:122, 126, 132; Henry Wadsworth Longfellow, 45:37; Jamaica, 28:238; "Jewish Merchants and Colonial Slave Trade," 34:285; Jews, anti-slavery, 34:171, 174-75; "Jews and Negro Slavery in the Old South, 1789-1865," 50:151-201 426; Judah P. Benjamin, 22:xxxiii; *Liberty Tract*, 30:375; Russia, 26:119; "The Sale of a Negro Slave in Brooklyn in 1683," 49:229; "A Slave Proclamation of De Witt

Clinton," 25:xiii; "Slavery Protected by the Common Law of the New World," 50:287; "Some Jewish Associates of John Brown," 23:vii, 55-78; "White Labor Servitude," 34:30-49; "Wills of Early Jewish Settlers in New York," 23:147-49, 151-54, 156-57, 160

aves in Algiers; or, A struggle for freedom, 33:174, 180-82; 40:347

avinsky, Gregory, 48:90

avonic Society of Garfield, Ohio, 41:190

eath, Gabriel, 43:5, 9

echt, Simon, 46:45

idell, John, 50:318, 321, 342

iosberg, Heinrich, 43:39

iosberg, Henry, 40:403

ocum, Giles, 27:175

oman, Charles, 35:241

oman, Henry, 35:241

onimsky, Henry, 40:48, 54

onimsky, Leon, 45:148

onimsky, Nicolas, 47:182

oss, Marcus C., 37:307; 49:199

osson, William, 21:187

ough, 34:101-2

ouschz, Nahum, 38:316; 39:441

ilow and Easy," 38:117-18

utski, Aaron, 46:77

uys, *German Jews in Amsterdam*, 31:xxxiii

nall & McGill, 31:137

nall Oriental Club, 47:159

nallman, 23:32

nallman, Thomas, 23:15; 30:77

nart, Nicholas, 25:32-33, 37

nidt, Johann, 26:41-42, 53-55, 58, 60, 102

niley, Alexander, 23:170

nith (New York), 22:83; 25:56

nith, Abraham, 50:173

nith, Absalom, 27:319

nith, Alfred E., 34:228; 46:269, 278, 291; 50:237

nith, Arthur, 27:249

nith, C. F., 26:254

nith, Charles, 36:288

nith, Charles Emory, 24:113; 36:216-26; 37:86

nith, Charles Stewart, 33:221

nith, Colonel, 25:142

nith, Doctor, 22:189; 26:222

Smith, Edgar F., gift, 23:xvii

Smith, Ethan, 31:xxxiv; 39:186, "View of the Hebrew," 25:84; 30:220-21, 238

Smith, F. Hopkinson, 35:258-59

Smith, General, 28:56-57

Smith, George, *The Hebrew People*, 30:450, 464, 466

Smith, Harry, 43:204; and Col. J. H. Tatsch, *Moses Michael Hays*, 35:xxii

Smith, Hezekiah, 37:136-39, 143-44

Smith, J., *Slavery*, 30:466

Smith, Jacob, 27:424, 425

Smith, Ja., 35:180

Smith, John, 27:447; 30:iv; 31:xxxiv; 32:1, 6; *A Hebrew Grammar*, 30:122-23, 143-44; "A Treatise on the Prophets," 30:98; "Captain John Smith's Reference to a Jew," 32:xiii

Smith, John (R.I.), 32:126

Smith, John Cotton, 48:1

Smith, Jonathan, 43:216

Smith, Jonathan S., 40:347

Smith, Joseph, 34:270-71

Smith, Joshua Toulmin, *Comparative View of Ancient History*, 30:341-42

Smith, Karl M., 50:271

Smith, Leslie, 50:307

Smith, Mary, 34:120

Smith, Mr., 43:210

Smith, Moses, 23:156

Smith, N. R., 43:74

Smith, Nathaniel, 28:xli, 231

Smith, P. S., 25:11

Smith, Philip, 27:175

Smith, Mrs. Pogson, *Zerah, the Believing Jew*, 30:318

Smith, Richmond Mayo, 46:127-28

Smith, Robert, 35:291

Smith, Robertson, 37:71, 89

Smith, Russell F., 50:307

Smith, S. Hosford, 40:285

Smith, Sidney, 26:128

Smith, Timothy G., 50:248-50

Smith, W. Robertson, 40:25

Smith, William (Canada), 42:76-77

Smith, William (Dr., New York), 23:157; 34:122

Smith, William (N.Y.) (1737), 46:32

Smith, William (S.C.), 41:77-78

Smith, William (Va.), 43:75

Smither, Harriet, 37:441
Smithsonian Institution, 28:265-66; 33:22; 37:451; 40:6, 11; 47:156; 50:273
Smollett, Tobias George, 34:243; 35:235
Smolyar, Baer, 33:134-35, 137
Smuts, General, 34:228
Smyrna Railroad, 47:170
Snedicor, Abraham, 21:193
Sneersohn, Haim, 45:74
Sneersohn, Hyman L., 36:7-8
Snellenburg, Joseph J., 29:185; 41:364
Snellenburg, Morton E., 29:186
Snellenburg, N., & Co., 29:185
Snellenburg, Nathan, 29:185
Snellenburg, Samuel, necrology of, 29:xxxvi, 185-86
Snoek, Jan, 32:14
Snyder, Charles R., 48:68
Snyder, Louis L., 40:105; book review by, 40:91-93
Soares, Batho., 33:114
Soares, Domingo Botelho, 33:112
Soares, Gabriel, 33:113
Soares, Joan, 33:116
Soares, Sebastian Falcao, 33:118
Soares da Cunha, Andreas, 33:113
Soarez, Aron Jacob, 23:27
Soarez, David, 25:117
Soarez, Isaac, 25:117
Soarez, Rebecca (1), 25:117
Soarez, Rebecca (2), 25:117
Soarez, Samuel Carvalho, 25:117
Soaris, Ferdinand, 33:113
Soaris, Manuel Dias, 33:119
Sobel, Jacob, 35:64
Sobel, Jacob Zebi, 45:63
Sobeloff, Simon E., 49:270
Soble, Nathan W., 40:66
Sobremonte, Rafael de, 32:117
Sobremonte, Tomas Tebino de, 33:41
Sochen, Fraeda, "The Jews and the Russo-American Treaty of 1832" essay award, 45:262
Socher, A., 38:245
Social Center (Nashville), 37:296
Social clubs, Jewish local history, 49:222, 225, 239
Social Democratic Workers Party, 50:105
Social Insurance, 49:90

Socialism, 39:100, 102, 104; 41:209, 211, 318, 351; 41:307-8, 328; 43:13, 29, 34-35, 146; 49:81-84; history, writing of, 46:223, 258-59, 261, 391; "A Portrait of Ethnic Politics," 50:202-38
Socialist Labor Party, 50:217
Socialist-Zionists, 50:223-24
Social Legislation Information Service, 50:434
Social Security, 41:324-25
Société des Amis des Noirs, 38:111
Société des Etudes Juives, 26:28; 43:156
Society of Antiquaries, 49:68
Society for Biblical Literature and Exegesis, 40:51
Society of Chemical Industry, 22:225
Society of Colonial Wars, 28:266
Society of Concord, Syracuse, New York, 22:221
Society for Dispensing Kindness to the Dead, 42:430
Society for the Dissemination of Culture among Russian Jewry, 43:67
Society for the Dissemination of Knowledge of Jewish Art, 31:190
Society for Education, 34:126-28, 130
Society for the Education of Orphan Children and the Relief of Indigent Persons of the Jewish Persuasion, 26:228; 27:311-12, 518; 30:266-68; 44:212
Society for Ethical Culture, 41:33; 45:96, 105; 46:477
Society of Ezrath Orchim (Philadelphia), 43:236
Society of Friends of a Jewish Palestine, 45:46
Society of Hebrew Literature, 25:158
Society of Israelitish Christians, 37:183
Society for Jewish Emigration to the United States of America, 37:191
Society for Jewish Scientific Publications in St. Petersburg, 40:403
Society for Jewish Social Workers, 22:211
Society of the Joint Polish American Committee, 39:152
Society for Offerings, Constitution and Bye-Laws, 30:282-83
Society of Poles in America, 39:149
Society to Promote the Science of Management, 41:50

Society for the Promotion of Culture among the Jews of Russia, 28:128-29; 43:156
Society for the Promotion of Jewish Agricultural Labour in the Holy Land, 26:147-48
Society for the Relief of Distressed Jews, 26:140
Society for Relief of Poor in Palestine, 41:289
Society Rodeph Shalom, 41:288
Society of Russian Jews, 37:245
Society for Self-Education, 48:132
Society of the Sons of St. Tammany, 46:3
Sociology, "American Jewish Sociology," 48:215; history, writing of, 46:177, 204-5, 233, 297-98, 367, 369, 372, 407, 416, 418
Soden, Thomas, 35:181-82
Soesman, Maria, 27:74
Soesman, Sarah, 27:120
Sofer, Moses, 34:16
Soher, Miriam, 27:112
Sohr, Solomon, 21:214
Sokobin, Samuel, 43:231; 45:271; 50:68; "Chinese influence in Seventeenth-Century Jewish Silver," 44:8-11; 45:48, 50, 52-53; "The Simson-Hirsch Letter to the Chinese Jews, 1795," 49:39-52
Sokolofsky, S., 38:246, 248, 305-7
Sokolofsky, Saul, 48:86
Sokolow, Nahum, 35:254-55; 42:222; 49:140; Zionism, 28:xxxix
Sokolsky, George, 45:224
Sola, A. D. Meldola de, 37:72
Sola, Abraham de, 37:72; 50:126, 131-32, 280
Sola, Arthur de, 44:118
Sola, B. de, 37:72
Sola, Clarence de, 50:122
Sola, D. A. de, 42:426
Sola, Francisco de, 44:116-18
Sola, Gershon de, 37:72
Sola, Herbert de, 50:148
Sola, Jacob de, 50:148
Sola, Meldola de, 42:378, 380
Solam, Abraham, 33:65
Solas, Aaron Mendez, 21:31; 29:28
Solas, Daniel Mendes de, 29:25
Solas, David de, 29:25
Solas, Ishac de, 44:219
Solas, Mosseh de, 29:25
Solas, Semuel Mendes de, 44:219, 223

Soldado, Abraham de Daniel Rodrigues, 29:19
Solem, Cor, 33:253
Soley, James Russell, 50:298
Solins, Jacob, 41:370
Solis, Abraham, 23:86; 50:36, 60
Solis, Binjamin de, 42:280, 395
Solis, Charity (nee Hays), 27:113, 277, 321, 323, 329
Solis, Miss Charity, 27:111
Solis, Mrs. Charity, 27:111
Solis, Daniel, 25:52; 27:80
Solis, David H., 27:166, 515
Solis, David Hays, 31:285; 43:253
Solis, David Hays da Silva, 38:338
Solis, Elvira N., 34:256; 38:338
Solis, Esther, 44:56
Solis family, 22:34; 43:253
Solis, Jacob da Silva, 38:339
Solis, Jacob Fenseca da Silva, 37:239
Solis, Jacob S., 27:84, 120, 277, 321, 327-28; Calendar of Festivals, 30:252, 254
Solis, Judith Simha de Silva, 38:338
Solis, Mr., 44:25, 34-35, 41, 52, 57
Solis, Sarah, 49:59
Solis-Cohen, Effie Cowen, 34:220
Solis-Cohen, Elfrida C., 35:240; "An Interesting Reference to Warder Cresson," 28:241-42
Solis-Cohen, Elinor, 43:238
Solis-Cohen, Emily, 33:23; 43:239; gifts, 22:xxxii; 33:xxxiii; necrology of Rebecca Rosenbach, 31:287-88
Solis-Cohen, Emily Grace Nathan, 38:338
Solis-Cohen family, 48:235
Solis-Cohen, J., 42:382
Solis-Cohen, J. Jr., 41:93; 43:238; 45:194; 50:272, 275, 329; "Barrak Hays: Controversial Loyalist," 45:54-57; book review by, 47:204-7; executive council, 37:xxxiv; 38:344; 39:470; 40:406; 43:230-31; 46:493; 49:268; "A Famous Family Fight About Real Estate: Gratz vs. Cohen," 37:xxxiii, 345-52; "Jake Gimbel: Hoosier Philanthropist," 48:256-61, 266; "The World of Hyman Gratz," 50:241-47
Solis-Cohen, Jacob, 43:231; "A California Pioneer: The Letters of Bernhard Marks to Jacob Solis-Cohen (1853-1857)," 44:12-57

Solis-Cohen, Jacob, Jr., "A California
 Pioneer: The Letters of Bernhard Marks to
 Jacob Solis-Cohen (1853-1857)," 44:12-57
Solis-Cohen, Jacob da Silva, 45:194-95;
 50:329, 395
Solis-Cohen, Mrs. Leon, 30:vii
Solis-Cohen, Meyer, "The Revolutionary
 Soldiers Buried in the Spruce Street
 Cemetery, Philadelphia, Pa.," 44:242
Solis-Cohen, Solomon, 34:xx; 37:19-21, 86-
 87, 92-93; 38:73; 39:321, 325; 48:208, 230,
 232, 240, 244; 50:241; gifts, 31:xxxii; 45:54;
 46:489-90; 33:xxxiii; necrology of, 38: 336-
 40; Y.M.H.A., 37:234, 236, 238-39, 252,
 254, 257-59, 263
Soliviera, Gaspar, 33:114
Solla, Ishac Mendes de, 29:27
Solla, Jacob, 29:25
Solla, Joseph, 29:25
Solla, Samuel Mendes de, 27:6-8; 29:24-27
Sollas, Jacob de, 44:232
Sollee's Charleston Company, 33:179, 183
Solms, Count, 26:52
Soloman, Abraham, 50:39
Soloman, H., 29:133
Soloman, Nathan, 23:155
Solomans, Isaac, 50:37
Solomon, 23:28; 28:148
Solomon ("Ye Malata Jew"), 42:335
Solomon, Abraham, 26:182; 40:76-80
Solomon, Abraham (Boston), 46:21
Solomon b. Abraham b. Adret, 22:61, 63-66,
 69
Solomon, Angelo (1), 28:153
Solomon, Angelo (2), 28:153
Solomon, Barbara Miller, *Ancestors and
 Immigrants: A Changing New England
 Tradition*, reviewed, 46:127-29; book
 review by, 48:137-38; *Pioneers in Service:
 The History of the Associated Jewish
 Philanthropies of Boston*, reviewed, 47:59-60;
 49:225
Solomon, Barnes, 29:146
Solomon, Barnet L., 25:63-64
Solomon, Barnett, 40:169
Solomon, Bernard, 35:281
Solomon, Benjamin, 22:193; 50:164
Solomon, Benjamin N., 26:117, 119
Solomon, B. L., 27:515

Solomon, Captain, 35:4
Solomon, Caroline, 49:64
Solomon, Colonel, 29:123
Solomon, E., 37:34
Solomon, Elizabeth, 23:82
Solomon, Elkin, 50:40
Solomon ben Ephraim, 35:120
Solomon, Ezekiel, 26:195; 38:333
Solomon, Gertrude, 27:277
Solomon, Goodwin, 29:146
Solomon, Gotthold, 50:91
Solomon, Hannah G., 29:xl
Solomon, Hart, 27:84
Solomon, Haym, 26:179; 40:79; 32:xxviii;
 33:xxx; "Haym Solomon and the
 Revolution," 33:xxxi
Solomon, Haym M., 21:212; 26:179; "Haym
 M. Solomon Frees His Slave," 37:xxxi,
 447-48
Solomon, Hayman, 26:179
Solomon, Hetty, 27:113
Solomon, Hyam, 27:xviii, 40, 43, 51, 156,
 253, 392
Solomon, Hyman, 50:37, 61
Solomon, I. (New York), 29:132
Solomon, Isaac (Boston), 23:82, 86; 29:153;
 42:336
Solomon, Issac (New York), 21:60; 26:239
Solomon, Isaac (N.C.), 29:144
Solomon, Isaac, 50:40, 60
Solomon, Isham, 29:146
Solomon, Israel, "Records of My Family,"
 25:63; "An Unfamiliar Aspect of Anglo-
 Jewish History," 25:vii, 63-74
Solomon, Israel, Sr., 25:71
Solomon, J. P., 37:229; 44:132
Solomon ben Jacob, 33:95
Solomon, Jacob, 49:64
Solomon, Jacob P., 27:389
Solomon, Jacob Philip, 34:286
Solomon, James, 29:146
Solomon, John, 27:78; 29:146
Solomon, Jonas, 35:307
Solomon, Joseph, 21:53; 50:60
Solomon, Josephine, 26:280
Solomon, King, 22:115, 116, 185
Solomon, Lazarus, 29:145
Solomon, Levi, 27:28
Solomon, Levy, 48:180; 50:33, 42, 61

Solomon, Louis, 30:367
Solomon, Maestro, 28:160
Solomon, Marcus, 48:263
Solomon, Mark, 27:315
Solomon de Medina, Mosesson and
    Company, 35:176
Solomon, Mela, 28:153
Solomon Bar Meyr, 31:236
Solomon, Miss, 26:245
Solomon, Mrs., 26:245
Solomon, Moses, 41:287; 50:164
Solomon, Myer, 50:39, 61
Solomon le Petit, 28:69
Solomon, physician (S.C.), 22:164
Solomon, Rabi, 27:81
Solomon in Rimini, 28:169
Solomon, Samuel, 26:188
Solomon, Samuel S., 26:182
Solomon, Seligman, 49:186
Solomon, Shinah, 50:60
Solomon, Siegfried, 26:184
Solomon, Solomon B., 25:64; gift, 32:xxvi;
    Purim Association, 40:140, 142, 151, 158,
    169
Solomon, William, 29:144, 146
Solomons, 35:201
Solomons, Adolphus S., 26:2; 27:278; 33:27;
    34:xx; 35:xix; 37:241, 263-64; 38:70;
    41:205-7; 45:64; 46:236; 48:117, 119;
    49:189; "Adolphus S. Solomons and the
    Red Cross," 33:211-30; 26:xxv; American
    Israelites, 39:404, 406, 408, 419, 421-22;
    Civil War, 50:283, 299-300, 360-61;
    disabilities, U.S. diplomacy, 36:177-78;
    immigration, 40:250; Michael M. Allen,
    37:178-79; Mt. Sinai Hospital, 42:115;
    Order #11, 29:104; Red Cross, 50:299;
    "The Relation of Adolphus S. Solomons to
    the Red Cross," 28:xv
Solomons, Alexander, 28:266
Solomons, Aline, 50:299, 360
Solomons, Benedict, 27:91
Solomons, Benjamin Samuel, 27:77, 376
Solomons, Catherine (Miss), 27:376
Solomons, Catherine (Mrs.), 27:113
Solomons, D., 27:107
Solomons, Dav, 21:170
Solomons, David, 27:81, 259
Solomons, Elias, 21:63, 69, 213

Solomons, Elizabeth, 27:376
Solomons, Elkala (Seixas), 27:77, 81
Solomons, Ezekiel, 27:84; 40:82
Solomons family, 27:xviii, 376-78
Solomons, Gedaliah, 27:151
Solomons, Gertrude, 27:112
Solomons, H. M., 21:168; 27:258
Solomons, Hendrick, 27:97
Solomons, Hyam, 25:47; 50:42, 61
Solomons, Hyman, 50:42, 61
Solomons, I. M., 29:134
Solomons, Isaac (1), 21:24, 79; 26:239;
    27:151; 50:37, 61
Solomons, Isaac (2), 27:156
Solomons, Israel, 22:39-40; 25:114, 127;
    26:242, 261-62, 264, 266; 28:xxxix;
    bookplates, 45:155, 216; collection,
    31:xviii; elected member, 22:xiv; "Lord
    George Gordon," 26:xxxiv
Solomons, Jessica, 27:376
Solomons, John (1), 25:52
Solomons, John (2), 27:105
Solomons, John (3), 27:395
Solomons, Jonas, 23:179
Solomons, Joseph, 21:48; 27:249; 50:42, 61
Solomons, Lazar, 31:5
Solomons, Lazarus, 29:147
Solomons, Levi, 40:81
Solomons, Levy, 25:113; 35:16; "A Suit at
    Law Involving the First Jewish Minister in
    Canada," 31:vii, xvii, 181-86
Solomons, Levy, Jr., 27:81, 235, 278, 313,
    376-77; marriage contract, 27:172
Solomons, Levy, Sr., 27:376
Solomons, Lucius Levi, 27:235, 377-78;
    44:13; marriage contract, 27:172-73
Solomons, M. Abrahams, 21:51
Solomons, Mark, 21:170, 214; 23:179; 27:64-
    65, 67, 73, 78, 84, 95, 109, 242, 338;
    31:238; kosher meat, 25:39, 46, 51-52
Solomons, Mary (Polly), 27:376
Solomons, Mrs., 27:235
Solomons, Mrs. Mordecai, 27:257, 286-87,
    302, 312
Solomons, Moses, 27:216, 346, 378, 399
Solomons, Perla Sheftall, 31:5
Solomons, Rachel, 21;89; 27:376
Solomons, Raymond, 29:144
Solomons, Rebecca (Mrs. Levy), 27:376

Solomons, Rebecca (Mrs. Simon Nathan), 27:111, 166
Solomons, Rosa, 25:115
Solomons, Rosalie, 41:294
Solomons, S., 27:399
Solomons, Samson M., 21:215
Solomons, Samuel David, 27:235
Solomons, Seixas, 27:378; 44:13
Solomons, Selina (nee Seixas), 27:113, 162, 377-78; marriage contract, 27:172-73
Solomons, Solomon, 27:156
Solomons, Widow, 21:86, 88
Solomons, Wolfe, 27:81
Soloveitchik, Hayyim, 40:403
Soltes, Mordecai, "The Jewish *Morning Journal* Observes Its Golden Jubilee," 40:407
Solvera, Moses, 32:61
Sombart, Werner, 22:ix; 26:xxvi; 28:233; "The Jews in the Economic History of Modern Times," 22:xxxi; sugar trade, 42:306-7
Somers, John, *The Judgment of Whole Kingdoms*, 30:71, 74-75
Somerset Manufacturing Company, 22:227
Sommerfeld, Rose, 31:227
Sommerfield, Adolph W., 37:266
Sommerfield, J. E., 37:266
Sommers, E., 29:129
Soncino, Gerson, 22:103
Sondheim, Nathan, 27:515
Songs of a Semite, 38:278, 280
Songs for the Times, 45:251
"Song, Venus," 45:254
Sonmans, Peter, 35:182
Sonne, Isaiah, 40:49; "An Italian Letter," 37:xxx; "Jewish Settlement in the West Indies," 37:353-67
Sonnebaum, A., 27:514
Sonnebaum, I., 27:514
Sonneborn, H. B. Paul F., 38:348
Sonneborn, Siegmund B., death, 37:xii
Sonnenfeld, J., 42:181-82
Sonnenfeld, Sigismund, 43:57-60, 63, 65
Sonnenfels, Joseph von, 28:101
Sonneschein, Solomon H., 37:73, 75-76, 87; 42:104; 45:97

Sonora and Columbia Hebrew Benevolent Society, Sonora and Columbia California, 29:135
Sons of the American Revolution, 28:266; 31:286; 45:65, 208; California, gift, 26:xxxv
Sons of Cincinnati, 39:123
Sons of Israel and David Congregation, Providence, R. I., 22:208; 29:133; 38:71
Sons of Israel Congregation, Toronto, 50:132-33
Sons of Liberty, 38:113
"Sons of the Prophet," 35:151
Sontheimer, Göz, 41:266
Sontheimer, Jacob, 41:254
Soosman, Jacob, 27:45
Sopher (Lewis Abraham), 32:117
Sophie Amalie, Queen of Denmark, 28:217
Sophie Wirth Camp, 50:431
Sorbonne, 31:272
Sorea, Aaron, 21:170; 31:258
Sorea, Isaac, 21:171
Sorenson *v.* Sorenson, 29:153
Soria, Aaron, 27:111, 277, 315, 475-79
Soria, Esther, 27:112
Soria, Isaac, 27:81, 84, 115, 258, 315, 475
Soria, Jacob, 27:91; 50:169
Soria, Joseph, 21:197; 27:123; 29:131
Soria, Judith, 27:476
Soria, Martin, 50:148
Soria, Rachel (Mrs. Aaron), 27:112, 277
Soria, Zipporah, 27:112
Sosa, Abraham de, 26:251
Sosa, Augustina de, 23:133
Soskin, S., 31:199, 203
Soulage, A., Jr., 22:31
Soule, George Henry, 43:193
Soulé, N. O., 44:49-50
Soule, Mr., 27:510-11
Soumaine, Simeon, 28:237
Sousa, Gonsalvo de, 33:114
Sousa, Isaque Rodriguez de, 23:27
Sousa, Louis Rodriguez de, 33:50, 67
Sousa, Manuel de, 33:117
Sousa, Marcus de, 33:117
Sousa, Mathias, 34:34
Sousa, Simon de, 33:50, 67
South African Jewish Board of Deputies, gift, 35:xx; 38:348

South African Jewish Sociological and Historical Society, 38:348; 45:261

South America, "A Newspaper Account of an Auto-da-Fe in Lisbon in 1726, in which a Native of Bahia, South America, was burned," 22:xviii

South Carolina, 22:129; 46:31, 33; colonial settlement of Jews, 26:5-6; Constitutional Convention of 1868, 50:178; Jewish local history, 49:237-39; Jewish population (1790), 50:26, 31-34; Jews in law and medicine, 22:152, 154-55, 161-62, 164-65; "Joseph Tobias of Charles Town: 'Linguister,' " 49:33-38; Provincial Congress, 22:188; slavery, 50:189; "The Struggle for religious liberty in South Carolina," 31:xxiv

South Carolina College, 50:178

South Carolina Conference of the Methodist Episcopal Church, 50:175

South Carolina Gazette, 49:36

South Carolina Historical Society, 42:46

South Carolina State Council of Union Leagues, 50:178

South Carolina, University of, 50:178

South Chester Tube Company, 25:174

South Dakota colonies, 48:85-87, 93

South End House (Boston), 46:297

Southern California Jewish Historical Society, 42:420-23; "The Third Annual Meeting of the Southern California Jewish Historical Society," 46:120-22

Southern California, University of, 45:200; 46:123

Southern Historical Association, 49:155

Southern Historical Society Papers, 50:381

Southern Israelite, *100 years of Southern Jewry*, 35:xxii

Southern Jewish Historical Society, 50:273, 316, 364

Southern Jewry, "David L. Yulee, Florida's First Senator," 25:vii, 1-29; *100 years of Southern Jewry*, 35:xxii

Southern Literary Messenger, The, 39:119-20, 124, 130, 132, 136, 138, 141

Southern Pacific Railroad Company, 44:13

Southern Patriot and Commercial Advertiser, 32:41; 39:42

Southern Quarterly Review, 27:518; 32:40; 39:121; "The Reformed Israelites," 30:393-94

Southern Star, The, 39:139

Southern States Land & Timber Company, 28:309

Southey, Robert, 35:282-84; 46:434; "Chronological History of the West Indies," 33:36

South Sea Bubble, 31:37; 35:34

South Sea Company of Great Britain, 25:88

South Shore Temple, Chicago, 35:xx

South Shore Temple Year Book for 1926, 35:xx

South Side Neighborhood House, Minneapolis, 50:428

Southwark Theatre, 33:173, 175, 178-79

Southwestern Bell Telephone Case, 46:472

Southwick, Solomon, 35:290

Soutine, Chaim, 40:319-20

Souvenir, The, 39:118, 136, 142

Souza, Antonio de, 42:436

Souza, Samuel, 27:120

Sovereignty Convention, 25:24

Soviet Union, 40:118, 194, 313-14, 404; 46:371; *The Jews in the Soviet Union*, reviewed, 42:442-49

Sowerby, Miss E. M., 30:vii

Sp, Robert, 21:171

Spafford, Tiliston & Co., 44:111

Spagnoletto, The, 38:269, 271-72; 45:250

Spaight, Richard D., 29:145

Spalding, John L., 49:180

Spain, anti-Semitism, 23:130; Board of Delegates of American Israelites, 29:89; "The Economic Condition of the Jews of Spain," 23:xiv; "Education Among the Jews in Spain," 25:xiv; "An Essay on Jewish Physicians in Spain," 29:xxix; expulsion of Jews and America, 22:132; 23:130; 26:5, 22; 28:33-34; 29:89; 33:11-12; 35:220, 222; *Fall of the Spanish American Empire*, reviewed, 38:323-25; "Hugo Grotius and the Emancipation of the Jews in Holland," 31:xxiv, 173-80; inquisition, 22:155-56, 158; 26:22-24, 26; "The Jewish Court of Mediaeval Spain," 22:xxix; Jews in Christian Spain, 32:xxvii; Jews and Colonial America, 26:xviii; "Some Phases of the Condition of the Jews in Spain

during the 13th and 14th Centuries,"
22:xviii, 61-70
Spalding, John Lancaster, 46:283-84
Spanish-American War, 23:xvii; 25:xv;
28:290-91; 40:406; "The Battleship
'Maine' and the Gunboat 'Scorpion': and
the part played by Jewish Seamen in
United States Marine History," 22:xvii;
"Jewish Welfare Activities for the Military
during the Spanish-American War,"
41:357-80; news clippings, 26:xxxiii, 7;
reports, 22:xxxi
Spanish and Portuguese Congregation,
London, 35:230; 42:102; 49:67
Spanish and Portuguese Congregation, New
York, see: Shearith Israel Congregation,
New York
Spanish and Portuguese Jews' Hospital,
London, 27:480
Spanish and Portuguese Synagogue of
Montreal, 28:269, 271-72
Sparber, Max, gift 33:xxxi
Sparks, Doctor, 27:469
Spatz, A. T. Jones, 39:180
Spatz, Bernard, 29:133; 31:270
Spatz & New House, 31:148, 152, 170
Spatz & Roggenburger, 31:143
Spaulding, Doctor, 27:237
Spaulding, Mr., 44:2
Special Committee for the Relief of Jews in
Palestine, 36:68-69
Spectator, The, 26:146
Spector, Isaac Elechanan, 43:48, 55
Spector, Yizhak Elhanan, 40:403
Speier, J. and Bro. (San Francisco), 37:45
Speiser, E. A., 39:206; book review by,
39:194-96
Spektor, Isaac Elhanan, 44:133, 137, 139-41
Spektor, Zvi Hirsch, 44:133, 137, 139-41
Spencer, 22:79
Spencer, Herbert, 25:175
Spencer, John, 37:186
Spencer, Richard Irving, 34:143
Spencer, Selden, 45:40
Spencer (slave), 50:162
Spencer, William A., 39:20
Sperry, *Liberalism in Contemporary Religion*,
32:xxvi
Sperry, Jacob, 30:133

Spertner, Rev., 37:42
Spewack, Bella, 40:358
Spewack, Samuel, 40:358
Speyer, Albert, 47:188
Speyer & Co., 28:300-301
Speyer, James, 33:220-21
Spicehandler, Abraham, 33:156
Spicer, Peter W., 30:404
Spiegel, Adolph, 41:370
Spiegel, Hans W., "An Early English
Intervention on Behalf of Foreign Jewry,"
35:xvi, 213-17
Spiegel, Shalom, 43:196; *On Medieval Hebrew
Poetry*, reviewed, 40:195
Spiegelberg, Betty, 47:188
Spiegelberg, Flora, gifts, 32:xxvi; 34:xxii;
"Reminiscences of a Bride of the Santa Fe
Trail," 34:xiv
Spiegelberg, Frederick, necrology of, 35:x
Spiegelberg, Lehman, 47:188
Spiegelberg, Levi, 47:188
Spiegelberg, Mrs. Willy, gift, 32:xxviii
Spielman, Isidor, 46:94; necrology of, 31:xiii,
290-91
Spielman, M. A., 47:174
Spielmann, Harold, 31:291
Spier, Robert, 27:45
Spindler, C., *The Jew*, 30:380, 397
Spingarn, Sigmund, 49:186
Spink, Walter, 37:133; 50:272
"Spinners, The," 45:255-56
Spinoza, Baruch, 31:179; 33:xxxii; 34:269;
35:203, 247; 36:239, 397; 37:72; 42:440;
44:75; 47:177
Spiro, Herzl Robert, 50:395
Spiro, Saul, 50:395
Spitz, Abraham P., "History of the
Congregation Ohabei Shalom," 32:xix
Spitz, Admiral de, 36:68
Spitz, Leon, 33:164; gift, 34:xxvii
Spitz, Moritz, 45:126
Spitzer, Barend, 50:42, 61
Spitzstein (immigrant), 38:202
Spivak, Chaim, 38:306
Spivak, Charles David, 35:274; 45:177, 195-
96; "The Jewish Physicians of Colorado,
Biographic and Bibliographic," 31:xviii;
necrology of, 32:ix-x
Spivak, Charles M., 49:218

Spofford, Prescott, 38:269
Spondre, Henry, 26:259-60
Sprague, William B., *Sermon*, 30:429
Springfield, Ill., Jewish Federation, contribution, 37:xxviii
Springfield, Ohio, United Jewish Welfare Fund, contribution, 37:xxviii
Spring-Rice, Cecil, 36:70-72, 142
Spuller, E., 41:162
Squires, Edward, 22:180
Staats-Zeitung (New York), 48:58
Stachel, Jack, 50:252
Stachhouwer, Jacob, 33:121-22
Stack, Jacques, 33:73
Stadler, 38:197
Staempfli, Mr., 36:310-12
Stag, 22:79
Stage Children's Fund, 31:259
Stägemann, 26:42
Stagg, Peter, 27:467
Stair, Earl of, 42:77
Stalin, Joseph, 42:443; 46:293
Stalin-Hitler pact, 50:251
Stalling, Leonard, 40:357
Stamp Act, 26:236
Stanbury, Josiah, 33:254
Standard Club, Chicago, 50:431
Standard Oil of New Jersey, 46:210
Standard Scale & Supply Co.; Reinheimer *v.*, 25:136
Standard Oil Company, 36:64
Standard Union (Brooklyn), 44:182
Stanford, John, 23:81
Stanford, Leland, 48:256
Stanford University, 46:300
Stanley, Lord, 24:104, 112; 29:92
Stannard, Robert C., 27:506
Stanton, Capt. (1769), 22:40
Stanton, Edwin M., 25:20-21, 28; 43:81, 83, 92-93, 113, 118-19; 50:308, 351-52
Stanton, F. P., 39:35, 41
Stanton, Frederick Perry, 47:77
Staple, Job, 23:153
Stark, J. H., 26:255
Starkie, Serjeant, 31:108, 125
Star of David, The, 45:261
Starr, Harry, 46:492; 47:201; executive council, 41:388; 44:241; 50:426; nominating committee, 44:241

Star Theatre (New York), 35:287
State Archives of Israel, 50:271, 273
State Board of Horticulture, California, 29:197
State College, Pa., United Jewish Fund, contribution, 37:xxviii
State religion, 29:104
Stavenisse, 33:110-11
Steckelmacher, M., 34:241
Stedman, Edmund Clarence, 37:281; 38:275-76, 281, 286-87; 39:114, 324-25; 45:250
Stedman, Griffin A., 37:426
Stedman, J. G., "Captain J. G. Stedman's 'Narrative of a five-year expedition against the revolted negroes of Surinam . . . from the year 1772 to 1777,' and its Jewish interest," 33:xvii
Steeg, Jules, 41:162
Steel, Baron, 31:116
Steel, Nicholas, 25:50
Stefan III, 24:100
Steffens, Lincoln, 43:11-14, 18-19, 21-22, 24-25, 30, 33-35; 46:297, 490-91; 50:206, 211
Stegman, Lewis R., 50:399
Stehelin, John Peter, 45:25, 28-29
Stein, 38:197
Stein, A., 30:421
Stein, Abrams, 31:139, 147, 149
Stein & Adler, 40:65
Stein, Albert, 31:292
Stein, Block, & Company, 40:71
Stein, Edith, 46:441
Stein, Freiherr von, 26:38, 68-70
Stein, Gertrude, "Gertrude Stein, Modernist, her career and influence," 32:xx
Stein, Harold C., gift, 33:xxxiii
Stein, Herman D., 48:66
Stein, Joseph, 29:131
Stein, Julius, 41:233
Stein, L., *Die Pessach-Hagada*, 30:466
Stein, L. M., gifts, 34:xxvii; 35:xxii
Stein, Leo, necrology of, 31:xxix, 292
Stein, Louis, 50:313
Stein, Meyer, 32:119
Stein, Nathan, 41:233, 268
Stein, Nathaniel E., 50:270-71, 275, 342-44, 373, 380; "From a Collector's Vantage," 50:427

Stein, Philip, 22:197; necrology of, 29:xxix, 186-88
Stein, Rose G., 36:xiv
Stein, Solomon, 40:263
Steinbach, Lewis W., 38:73; necrology of, 22:xxviii, 230-35
Steinbach, Rosalie (Weiskopf), 22:230
Steinbach, Simon, 22:230
Steinberg, Dorothy, 47:202
Steinberg, M., 39:95
Stein-Bloch, 38:19
Steinborn, Sam, 29:62
Steinborn, Uriah, 29:62
Steiner, Joseph H., 50:314
Steiner, Löw, 41:266
Steiner, Newman L., "Newman L. Steiner, the First Jewish Justice of the Peace in Ontario," 26:xv
Steinhardt, Isak, 41:259
Steinhardt, Menachim, 28:106
Steinhardt, W. & I. (San Francisco), 37:45
Steinhausen, Georg, 34:12
Steinmetz, Carl, 32:124
Steinmetz, Carl Heinrich, 32:124
Steinmetz, Charles P., 34:191; "Charles P. Steinmetz and His Jewish Descent," 32:123-24
Steinschneider, Moritz, 25:158, 179; 28:72, 140-41, 205; 33:239; 34:303; 43:244, 246; 45:102, 127, 154; 47:222
Steinthal, Hermann, 34:303
Stengel and Rothschild, 29:183
Stephany, M., 28:248
Stephen, Justice, 31:107
Stephen, Leslie, 35:248
Stephen, Mr., 27:429
Stephens, Alexander H., 43:105; 50:342
Stephens, Governor, 29:197
Stephens, John, 23:153
Stephens, John Lloyd, 40:283
Stephens, Philip, 30:106
Stephens, W. Hudson, 23:125
Stephenson, John, 22:142
Stepney, George, 38:45-46
Sterling, James, 40:81
Sterling Library at Yale, 45:139
Stern, 26:31
Stern, A., 29:133
Stern, Aaron, 41:253

Stern, Abraham, 41:266; 50:174
Stern, Adolf, 24:12, 27, 36-38, 82; 34:243; 50:232
Stern, Alfred, 26:92; 28:108
Stern, Alfred Whital, 50:396, 404
Stern, Arnold E., 41:370
Stern, Baruch, 41:268
Stern, Bezalel, 28:118
Stern, Charles S., 37:428
Stern College for Women, 48:265-66
Stern, David, 45:96-97
Stern (dept. store), 38:20
Stern, E. A., 27:515
Stern, Edgar B., 28:310
Stern, Elizabeth, 31:293
Stern, Emanuel, 50:158
Stern, Eugene M., necrology of, 31:xvi, 292-93
Stern, Gladys G., 35:267
Stern, H. A., "Wanderings among Falashas in Abyssinia," 34:xxiii
Stern, H., Jr. & Bro., 47:37
Stern, Hanna (Bloom), 28:310
Stern, Henry, 47:37, 42, 52
Stern, Horace, 31:293; 34:218; 43:238; 44:64; necrologies of Oscar B. Teller, 28:xxii, 310-11; Simon I. Kohn, 28:xxxii, 288-89
Stern, Israel, 41:268
Stern, James L., 31:293
Stern, Johanna, 41:266
Stern, Joseph, 29:133; 41:261
Stern, Julius, 48:215-16
Stern, Karoline, 41:268
Stern, Lafayette, 31:293
Stern, Louis, 32:130; 39:102; and Edward Lauterbach, In Memoriam Volumes, 31:xxxiv
Stern, Malcolm, 48:12; 50:156, 332
Stern, Malcolm H., 50:253
Stern, Maurice, necrology of, 28:xxii, 308-10
Stern, Milton C., death, 37:12
Stern, Mr., 29:102
Stern, Morris, 31:293
Stern, Morris L., 34:212
Stern, Morton L., 31:293
Stern, Moses, 29:145
Stern, Myer, 24:39; 29:110-11, 113; 37:229, 233; 40:263; 49:30
Stern, Natan, 41:261

Stern, Nathan, 41:268
Stern, Rösle, 41:253
Stern, Ross, 23:145
Stern, S., 29:129; 32:119
Stern, S. Walter, 28:310
Stern, Samuel, 23:126; 41:254
Stern, Sidney M., 31:293
Sternberg, I., 29:134
Sternberger, Mayer, 29:113
Sterne, Adolphus, 37:439, 441
Sterne, Simon, 32:132; 45:180, 203; "Life of Simon Sterne," 28:xxxix
Sternheimer, Sigmund, 40:65
Sterns, Dr., 26:222
Stern-Taeubler, Selma, 46:59
Stetson, Ebenz, 37:167
Stettenheimer, I., 32:121
Stettenheimer, Jacob, 40:169
Stettheimer, Herman H., 40:140, 169
Stettheimer, Jakob, 41:266
Stettheimer, Sigmund, 40:65
Steuben, Baron, 25:142
Steuben Society, 34:232
Steubenville, Ohio, Jewish Community Council, contribution, 37:xxviii
Steuer, Max D., death, 37:xii
Stevens, J., 25:89
Stevens, James, 27:433
Stevens, John A., 23:174
Stevens, Major, 42:337
Stevens, Mr., 28:238
Stevens, Sylvester K., history, writing of, 46:178, 181, 183, 185-87, 190, 361-62, 444-45; "Voluntarism in Community Life in the United States in Relations to Local History," 46:143-51
Stevens, Walter H., 50:343-44
Stevens, William, 27:450
Stevenson, Adlai E., "Address By the Honorable Adlai E. Stevenson," 45:16-19
Stevenson, John W., 22:141
Steward, Thomas S., 41:71
Stewart, 22:85
Stewart, A. T., 41:34
Stewart, Charles, 32:125; Uriah Philips Levy, 39:7, 18, 27-28, 33, 55
Stewart, Commodore, 27:473
Stewart-Hilton-Seligman, incident, 34:178
Stewart, John, 22:180

Stewart, Walter, 43:235
Stewart, Widow, 27:342
Stewart, William H., 43:113
Stewart, Wm. R., 33:221
Stichtenhorst, Gerrit, 26:247
Stiefel, Colonel, 29:123
Stieffel, Joseph, 40:60
Stiegel, William, 28:255-56
Stieglitz, 29:125
Stile, George, 26:187
Stiles, Ezra, 22:127-28; 23:166, 172; 26:244-45; 27:418, 449; 29:172; 34:55, 70; 34:288; 35:140, 302; 37:440, 443; 39:260; 40:96; 42:342-43; 43:143; 45:138; 46:25, 37-38, 181; 47:149; 49:236; 50:25; *Discourses on Saving Knowledge,* 30:61; "Ezra Stiles and the Jews," 31:xxxiii; Rabbi Carigal, 31:242; "Which of the Portraits of Menasseh ben Israel Was in the Possession of Ezra Stiles (Illustrated)," 50:427
Still, Peter, 50:197
Stille, Cornelius Jacobson, 31:102
Stillers, Cornelijs Jacobs, 31:89, 91, 102
Stillman, James, 46:443
Stimers, A. C., 50:312
Stimson, Daniel M., 42:123
Stimson, Henry L., 40:115; 50:236
Stirling, Earl of, 42:76
Stirnberg, Jakob (Szternberg), 39:151
Stivelman, S., 39:113
Stix Baer & Fuller, 38:20
Stix, Louis, 50:195
Stobbe, 26:27; 28:280
Stoch, Peter, 28:178
Stock, Joseph and Michael Dodson, *Appendix to Lowth's Isaiah,* 30:294
Stocker, Adolf, 36:348, 354-57, 359-60
Stockmeyer, C., 45:90
Stockton, Robert, 42:192
Stockwell (actor), 33:193
Stodard, The, 37:407
Stoddard, Colonel, 30:408
Stoddard, Jonathan, 35:290-91
Stoddard, Lothrop, 40:324; 46:300
Stoddert, Benjamin, 48:9, 14
Stoecker, Adolphe, 40:325
Stokes, Henry Paine, 25:110; elected corresponding member, 23:ix; necrology of, 33:xxi

Stokes, James Graham Phelps, 50:203, 233
Stokes, Phelps, 41:308
Stokes, Rose Harriet Pastor, 48:202, 267;
  49:70, 143
Stolberg, Benjamin, 43:193; 46:258
Stolberg-Wernigerode, Count, 36:359
Stollard, Elizabeth, 25:78-79
Stolypin, Petr Arkadyevich, 41:175-76, 182
Stolypin, Premier, 36:274
Stolz, Joseph, 28:240; 40:381; American
  Historical Association, 23:x; Congress of
  National Service, 26:xxvii; gifts, 29:xxxix;
  34:xxiv; "The Jewish Historical Society of
  Illinois," 28:xv, 239-41
Stone, A. J., 45:258
Stone, Charles P., 47:88
Stone, Eliphalet, 22:23
Stone, Harlan Fiske, 49:13
Stone, Irving, 46:121
Stone, Mrs. Julius, 28:240
Stone, Rev., 22:24
Stone, William J., 36:77
Stoneman, Genl., 39:182
Storer, Mrs. Bellamy, 28:28
Stork, Aaron, 41:93
Storman, Mr., 44:136, 140, 146, 161-62, 177
Story, Isaac, 40:76
Story, Joseph, 26:200; 43:164
Story, Justice, 31:115
Story, William Wetmore, 39:325
Stout, John, 34:85
Stoutenburgh, Isaac, 27:320
Stovall, Pleasant A., 36:159
Stowarzyszenie Polskich Wygnancow w
  Ameryce (Association of Polish Exiles in
  America), 39:150
Stowe, Calvin E., 30:258, (trans.), *History of
  the Hebrew Commonwealth*, 30:248
Stowe, Harriet Beecher, 39:307; 50:173, 193,
  402-3
Strachan, J. M., 26:149
Strack, Hermann L., 34:303
Stradivarius Quartette, 35:325
Strange, John, 23:183; 35:130
Stranger in the Synagogue, 50:83
Strangthfield, William, 37:411-18
Strashun, Matthias, 28:118
Strashun, Simon, 44:177
Strassburg, 26:37

Strassburg, Fanner, 41:266
Strassburg University, gift, 22:xxxv
Strassburger, 28:118
Strassburger, Mina, 41:266
Strassburger, Moses, 41:255, 257
Strasser, Adolph G., 41:298, 318; 46:231
Straton, Betsey, 27:431, 437
Stratton, 31:124
Stratton, Elipalet, 27:429
Stratton, Henry, 27:506
Straubenmuller, Gustave, 43:11
Straus, Abraham, 31:125
Straus, Adolph Delisle, necrology of, 31:xxiv,
  293-95
Straus family, 50:408
Straus & Goldman, 31:158
Straus, Herbert N., 37:307
Straus, Hermine, 31:271
Straus, Ida (Blün), 22:237-39
Straus, Isidor, 31:203, 272; 39:419; 40:3, 158;
  41:232; 43:231; necrology of, 22:xvii, 235-
  39
Straus, Jacob, 22:235
Straus, Jesse Isidor, necrology of, 35:ix;
  necrology of David Blaustein, 22:xvii, 206-
  11
Straus, L. and Sons, 22:237; 31:272, 295
Straus, Lazarus, 22:235, 237; 31:271-72; 40:2;
  45:102; 50:196
Straus, Lina Gutherz, 34:190
Straus, Nathan, 22:237-8; 31:272; 34:187,
  192; 34:269; 40:3; 47:15; 49:190;
  agricultural experiment station, 31:203,
  205; portrait, 35:xix
Straus, Oscar S., 22:xvii; 25:ix; 24:81-82; 26:2;
  31:1, 272; 32:130, 132; 33:16; 34:153, 174,
  267; 38:72, 253-54; 39:104; 40:409;
  41:221, 367; 42:100; 44:124; 45:102-3;
  46:194, 483; 47:190; 48:115; 49:189;
  50:196, 200, 256; address, 26:xvii-xx; Cyrus
  Adler, 33:18, 23, 27, 33, 35-38; 37:453;
  disabilities, U.S. diplomacy, 36:xiii, 46-54,
  56-58, 61, 126, 155; 40:306-7; 41:194;
  finance committee, 26:x, xxvii; 28:xxix;
  29:xi; gifts, 28:xxxviii, xl; history, writing
  of, 39:314; "Hon. Oscar S. Straus'
  Memoranda Preceding Dispatch of the
  Hay Roumanian Note," 24:108-14; labor
  unions, 41:310, 321; Louisiana Historical

Society, 23:x; Max James Kohler, 34:298-99; Mesopotamian Project, 47:159-60, 163-64, 168-69, 171, 173; Napoleon and Sanhedrin, 22:xx-xxi; 26:xxvii; necrology of, 31:xxiii, 295-97; necrology of Benjamin Franklin Einstein, 26:xiv, 277-79; "Oscar S. Straus: An American Jew," 44:240; "Oscar S. Straus: An Appreciation," 39:469; 40:1-16; Palestine, 40:111; papers, 47:180; "The Pilgrims and the Hebrew Spirit," 28:xxx; Roger Williams, 34:169; Y.M.H.A., 37:234

Straus, Percy S., death, 27:xii

Straus, Raphael, 35:136

Straus, Roger W., necrology of Lee Kohns, 31:xxix, 271-73

Straus, Sara, 31:271

Straus, Sarah, 22:235

Straus, Solomon, 22:235

Strause, Nathan, 31:151, 154

Strauss, Abraham, 31:297

Strauss, Albert (Cleveland), 37:265-69

Strauss, Benet, 41:268

Strauss, Corlatine, 41:266

Strauss, David, 41:261

Strauss, Emilie, 31:297

Strauss, Frank, 31:297

Strauss, Frederick, Helon's Pilgrimage, 30:238, 306

Strauss, Georg Michael, 41:261

Strauss, H., 29:135

Strauss, H. C. Henri, 40:253-54, 271

Strauss, Hohna, 41:257

Strauss, J. Henry, gift, 29:xliii

Strauss, Jakob, 41:268

Strauss, Johann, 39:326

Strauss, Mrs. Joseph L., 22:218

Strauss, Karoline, 41:253

Strauss, Kauffmann, 41:266

Strauss, Lämmlein, 41:254

Strauss, Lazarus, 41:232, 261

Strauss, Leon, 42:65

Strauss, Lewis, 34:218

Strauss, Lewis L., 36:148; 40:105, 212; 47:203; "Oscar Straus: An Appreciation," 39:469; 40:1-16

Strauss, Lewis L., Jr., 34:x; executive council, 29:xxix; 31:xvi; 32:xii; 33:xxv; 37:xxix; 38:342; 39:470

Strauss, Ludwig, 41:266

Strauss, Moses, 41:266, 268

Strauss, Paul, 46:88

Strauss, Samuel, 41:266

Strauss, Seligman J., necrology of, 31:xxiv, 297-98

Strauss, Sigmund, 41:257

Strauss, William, 49:186

Strebeck, Professor, 26:220

Street Scene, 40:358

Strengthfield, S., 37:400

Streusand, N., "Rabbi N. Streusand and His Anti-Reform Tract," 37:xxxv

Stribling, 23:122

Strickland, William, 41:63-68, 71-74, 89

Stringham, 39:179

Stringhan, Silus H., 39:24

Strohmeier, Augusta, 32:66, 70

Strong, Martin, 37:400

Stroock, Alan M., 45:155

Stroock, Joseph, death, 37:xii

Stroock, Moses Jesse, 34:192; necrology of, 33:xiii

Stroock, Solomon M., 26:213; 36:ix; 45:155; Board of Delegates of American Israelites, 29:76; gift, 32:xxv; "How Economic Freedom Came to the Jews in Switzerland," 32:xiv; necrology of, 37:xii, 479-80; "Switzerland and Jewish Emancipation," 28:xxii; 34:256

Strouse, Eliza, 26:289

Strouse, Goldena, 26:289

Strouse, Isaac, 37:263

Strouse, Leopold, 31:154, 226; 45:144

Strouse, Levi, 26:289

Strouse, Myer, 29:123

Struck, Hermann, 40:320

Struggle for Palestine, The, reviewed, 40:313-17

Stuart, Gilbert, 27:xix, 420; 31:7; 41:275, 286; 43:232; 48:9; exhibition, 31:290; Jewish portraits, 22:xxix; portrait of, 42:417

Stuart, Math, 27:249

Stuart, Moses, 30:iv; 45:24; Course of Hebrew Study, 30:268; Defence of Roy's Hebrew Dictionary, 30:320; Grammar of the Hebrew Language, 30:252, 276, 306, 330, 430; Hebrew Chrestomathy, 30:252, 255, 259, 282, 330, 332; Hebrew Grammar,

30:152, 154, 198, 220; *Sermon at the Ordination of the Rev. W. G. Shauffler*, 30:276, 405
Stuart, Robert W., 23:112, 116
Snuermer collection, 45:185
Stump, John F., 22:90
Sturdza, 36:130-31
Stuttgard, Joseph, 27:277
Stuyvesant, Gr., 21:17, 23
Stuyvesant Neighborhood House, New York City, 38:335
Stuyvesant, Peter, 21:xiv, xx, 176-77; 22:151; 34:3, 274; 35:133; 42:109; 43:144-45, 155; 44:75, 78-89, 205, 211; 46:26-28, 35; 47:127; early settlers, 29:39-45, 47, 49-50, 52
Stuyvesant, Petrus, 31:88-89, 91, 102
Suares, Jacob de Abraham, 44:229
Suares, Jacob de Ishac, 44:233
Suarez, Joseph, 49:43
Suarez, Lorenzo, 28:199
Suasso, Antonio Lopes, 33:50
Subado, Campa, 34:5-6
Success Story, 40:354, 357
Suckley, Rutsen, 39:34
Sudam, John, 27:249
Sue, Eugene, 40:336; 45:20; *The Wandering Jew*, 30:405, 419
Suez Canal, 26:153; 47:87-88, 91, 95-96
Suffrage, "The Supposed Disfranchisement of the Jews in New York After the Contested Election for Representative in 1737: A History," 29:xxx; "The True Story of the Relation of the Jews to the Contested Election for Representative in New York in 1737," 29:xxxvii
Sugar, 38:17-18; sugar trade, 42:244-45, 275-76, 305-9
Sukenikov, M., 39:99
Sulamith, 28:106
Suliotis, M., 24:128, 150
Sullivan & Cromwell, 26:286; 31:266
Sullivan, George, 27:173
Sullivan, Harry R., 31:195
Sullivan, James, 43:204
Sullivan, Timothy (Big Tim), 50:206
Sully, 29:54
Sully, Thomas, 31:7; 32:xxviii; 41:278, 287; 50:245; Jewish portraits, 22:xxix

Sulman, Esther, *A Goodly Heritage: The Story of the Jewish Community of New London, 1860-1955*, 49:219
Sulzberger, Arthur Hays, 34:247; 41:232; 48:250; 49:62; gift, 32:xxix
Sulzberger, Cyrus L., 35:58; 49:122; necrology of, 33:xxi; necrology of Morris Loeb, 22:xvii, 225-27; Y.M.H.A., 37:234, 236, 238-39, 255-59
Sulzberger, David, 25:44; 45:181, 207-8
Sulzberger family, 41:236
Sulzberger, Joseph E., 29:xxx; necrology of, 33:xiii
Sulzberger, Leopold, 37:32
Sulzberger, Mayer, 22:xxv; 26:271; 28:265, 313; 29:111, 113; 32:122; 34:75, 286; 38:73; 41:88, 178; 42:102; 43:250; 45:154; 49:31, 194-95; bookplates, 45:193, 203-5, 207; "A Catalogue of the Mayer Sulzberger Papers in the Dropsie College for Hebrew and Cognate Learning," 38:342; Cyrus Adler, 33:18, 23, 27, 30; death of, 29:xxi; disabilities, U.S. diplomacy, 36:278, 281-85; executive council, 22:xii, xvi, xxvii; 23:xii; 25:xi; 28:xiv; Fels collection, 45:99, 107-8, 122; gift, 25:xv; Hebrew Library, 34:153, 157; Hebrew Union College, 40:29; honored, 28:xii; Mesopotamian Project, 47:159-50, 163-65, 167, 169-70; necrology of, 29:xxxvi, 188-93; necrologies of Henry N. Wessel, 28:xxxii, 313-14; Joseph Jacobs, 25:xii, 156-73; William B. Hackenburg, 28:xv, 282-84; Pennsylvania Jewish families, 22:xxii; Philadelphia Jewry, 48:208, 226, 228, 231-32, 235-36; Purim associations, 40:166; tribute to, 29:xxx; Y.M.H.A., 37:233, 236, 257, 259, 263
Sulzberger, Solomon, 38:71
Sulzer, 33:237
Sulzer, Salomon, 50:93
Sulzer, William, 36:285; 41:184-91; 47:16; gift, 22:xxxii
Sumberg, Alfred D., "Notes on the History of the Jews of Wisconsin," 44:242
Summerfield, M., 37:266, 268-69, 271
Sumner, Charles, 24:8, 11, 94; 29:104; 38:174; abolition and Jews, 42:131, 136-37, 140-41, 143-45; Mary Todd Lincoln, 41:35-37

Sumner, Lord, 31:106-11
Sumpter, General, 32:37
Sunday laws, 29:151, 187; 34:xxv; 35:121, 123, 127; 39:265; 46:406; 49:238; 50:166; "Anglo-Jewish Legal Cases," 25:134-38; *Cornerstone of Religious Freedom in America*, reviewed, 40:96-98; "Court Decisions on the Sunday laws," 45:264; District of Columbia, 26:217-18; Jewish local history, 49:238-39, 248; Kentucky, 26:260; Maryland, 25:94, 101, 103; Napoleon, 25:137; (New York), 49:209; New York theater, 26:260
Sunday Lecture Association, 45:96
Sunday school, 46:166; 48:229, 244; "Rebecca Gratz and the Jewish Sunday School Movement in Philadelphia," 48:71-77; 49:235; "Rosa Mordecai's Recollections of the First Hebrew Sunday School," 42:397-406
Sunsheimer, Abe, 29:131
Sun Yat-sen, 44:126-27
Superior, Wis., Jewish Federation, contribution, 37:xxviii
Supino, David de Haim, 20:124
Supino, Esther, 40:124
Supino, Raphael, 40:124
Supple, Barry E., "A Business Elite: Some Successful German-Jewish Investment Bankers in Nineteenth-Century New York," 46:493
Surinam, 26:243, 265; 29:xl; 32:8-9, 20; Berachah we-Shalom Congregation, 22:27; "Captain J. G. Stedman's 'Narrative of a five-year expedition against the revolted negroes of Surinam . . . from the year 1772 to 1777,' and its Jewish interest," 33:xvii; "David Nassy of Surinam and his 'Lettre Politico-theologico-morale sur les Juifs,' " 22:xviii, xxix, 25-28; Hebrew literature, 22:120-21, 126-27, 130; "Jamaica under the Spaniards," 28:xl; "A Letter of David Nassy, of Surinam," 23:xiii, 185-86; "The Migration from Surinam to Jamaica," 28:xl; "The Mohelim of Curacao and Surinam, and Other Notes," 25:xiii, 138-41; "The Name of the Country Surinam as a Family Name: The Biography of a Surinam Planter of the Eighteenth

Century," 48:19-27, 262-64; "Notes on Seventeenth-Century History of Jewish Settlements in Surinam," 45:265; Sephardic Jews, 29:14-19; Neweh Shalom Synagogue, 22:130
Surinamer, Ahron Zoddek, 48:263
Surinamer, Behr Wulf, 48:263
Surinamer (family name), 48:20, 27
Surinamer, Jacob, 48:23
Surinamer, L. H., 48:263
Surinamer, Selina, 48:263
Surinamer, Zire Gotlieb, 48:263
Surinamer-Nassy, Blanche, 48:263
Surratt, John, 50:380
Suryu, 27:59, 61-62
Suse, R. Moses, 34:291
Susman, Magnus, 38:73
Susman, Sara, 38:73
Süssfeld, Lazarus, 41:266
Süsskind of Trimberg, 35:117-18, 121, 126
Sutherland, Duchess of, 36:401
Sutker, Solomon, 48:66
Sutro, Adolph, 34:153; 46:436
Sutro, Adolph Henry Joseph, 45:150-51, 171
Sutro Hebrew MSS., "Solomon Roubin, Cataloguer of the Sutro Hebrew MSS. in the San Francisco Public Library," 32:xiii
Suvorin, 48:78
Sviet, 41:191
Swados, 39:230
Swart, Emanuel M., 27:514
Swarthwort, John, 26:174
Swartwout, Samuel, 30:404
Swartzberg, M. N., 44:149
Swaythling, Lord, 31:291
Sweden, 26:74, 136
Swedish Metal Workers' Union, 43:193
Sweers, Solomon, 33:108-9
Sweerts, Jacob de, 44:90
Sweerts, Paulus de, 44:90
Sweetser, John, 43:204
Swellem, Asser Levy van, 46:50
Swichkow, Louis J., "The Jewish Community of Milwaukee, Wisconsin, 1860-1870," 47:34-58, 111; 49:242
Swick, Moses, 42:128
Swift, John, 26:181
Swinburne, Algernon Charles, 35:244; 38:277; 46:433

Swingle, Robert, 31:204, 210
Swiren, David B., 33:xxvi; "Honeymoons in ancient Israel," 33:xviii; "The Jewish Woman," 29:xv; "A Note on the background of the American national colors," 35:xv; "Our Young," 29:xxix; "Was a Civil Marriage ever recognized by Jewish Law," 32:xx; "The White and the Blue—the Colors of the Jew," 28:xxxiii
Swiss question, 49:27
Swiss treaty, 26:213; 48:224, 226, 243
Switz, Abraham J., 27:339
Switzerland, 26:137; 39:392; Board of Delegates of American Israelites, 29:76, 89-90; disabilities, 49:16; "How Economic Freedom Came to the Jews in Switzerland," 32:xiv; "Switzerland and Jewish Emancipation," 28:xxii; 32:xxv; "New Light on the Struggle to Change the 1850 Swiss Treaty with the United States," 38:347; treaty with, 27:507-8; U.S. intercession for the Jews, 36:xi, 299-322
Sydebothom & Co., 35:185
Sydney's Jewish Community, 45:261
Sylvester, Harry, 41:373
Sylvester, James Joseph, 28:251
Sylvester, William F., 46:163
Sylvia (slave), 50:162, 166
Sylvia, Rebecca, 21:21, 23
Symes, Lancaster, 23:149
Symmons, Jane, 31:265
Symonds, Aaron, 27:45
Symons, Joseph, 31:241
Synagogue Council of America, 39:296; 40:194
Synagogue and housing, 25:135
Synagogue-*kahal*, 39:270-74
Synagogues, "Descriptions of the Synagogues in New York in 1776 and 1828," 40:187-89

Syracuse, N.Y., Jewish Welfare Federation, contribution, 37:xxviii
Syracuse University, 22:219-21
Syria, 40:110, 285-86; 41:16; restoration of Jews to Palestine, 26:135-36, 140-41, 144, 146-48, 150, 156, 158, 162
Syrian Colonization Fund, 26:140
Syrkin, Nachman, 49:84
Szajkowski, Zosa, 39:477; 40:322; 41:216; 42:216; "The Alliance Israélite Universelle in the United States, 1860-1949," 39:389-443; "The Attitude of American Jews to East European Jewish Immigration (1881-1893)," 40:221-80; "Emigration to America or Reconstruction in Europe (1840-1893)," 41:390; 42:157-58; "European Aspect of the Passport," 42:415; 46:86-100; "The European Attitude to East European Jewish Immigration," 41:127-62
Szanto, Simon, 28:188; 33:240; 38:191, 207-8
Szögyenyi, Mr., 36:331, 338-40
Szold, Benjamin, 29:178; 31:225; 34:xviii; 37:84, 236, 481; 40:28, 33, 35; 42:100, 102; 49:160, 162, 165; 50:79, 92-93; Felsenthal Collection, 45:96, 98-99, 119-20, 124-25
Szold, Bertha, 29:178; 45:122
Szold, Henrietta, 22:191; 33:22; 37:452; 39:334; 40:158; 49:147; Agricultural Experiment Station, 31:203, 208-10; bookplates, 45:193; Felsenthal Collection, 45:99, 103, 121-23; gift, 22:xxxv; "Make My Eyes Look to the Future—Henrietta Szold Centennial Address," 49:159-72, 268; night school, 31:225-26; Y.M.H.A., 37:226, 236, 295
Szold, Misses, 38:60
Szold, Sophie Schaar, 37:481

T

Tabares, Benjamin, 21:45
Tabera, General, 32:90
Tabor Manufacturing Company, 41:45
Tachau, William G., 41:68
Tacitus, 49:41, 45-47
Taft, William H., 22:x; 24:84, 86, 89; 28:291;
  29:203; 31:295; 34:190, 248; 36:134, 281-
  82, 290; 46:98, 333, 471-72; 50:220, 229;
  address by, 29:xi; honorary member, 29:xii;
  Isidor Rayner, 40:292-93; necrology of,
  32:xvi; Oscar S. Straus, 40:11, 14;
  "Progressive World Struggle of the Jews
  for Civil Equality," 28:xxxvii; Russian
  treaty, 41:163, 178-80, 184, 186, 188-89,
  191
Taft, Mrs. William Howard, 22:x; 40:293
Tageblatt, 47:228; 49:88; 50:211, 214-16, 218
Tahl, Samuel, 31:226
Tai, Lee Yen, 34:195-96
Taine, Hippolyte, 38:263
Talaat Pasha, 36:65, 74
Talbot, Mr., 31:107
Talbot, James M., 27:506
Tales of the Wayside Inn, The, 45:21, 30-33
Talheimer, Abraham, 41:266
Talheimer, Salomon, 41:266
Talheimer, Samuel, 41:266
Tall, Tobias, 22:130
Talleyrand, 26:38, 50, 73; 38:119
Tallit (*Arba kanfet*), 39:370, 375
Talmon, Jacob, 46:434
Talmud, burning of, 28:148, "The Criticism
  of Historical Sources in the Talmud,"
  22:xviii
Talmud Torah, 42:10-20, 31-36; (Canada),
  50:137; (Minneapolis), 42:13; 50:428; "The
  Polonies Talmud Torah of New York,"
  34:123-41; (Recife), 43:128

Talmud Torah Anshe Augustov
  Congregation (New York), 44:136
Talmud Torah Community (Amsterdam),
  44:234-36
Talmud Torah Congregation (Venice),
  42:225
Talmudical Academy, 45:160
Tamari, Guiseppe, 28:199
Tammany Hall, 32:97, 110; 41:8, 329; 43:12,
  31; 49:114; 50:203, 205-8, 218-20; *Myer
  Moses, Oration Delivered at Tammany-Hall*,
  30:273-74
Tammany Society, 21:174; 27:523
Tancred, 34:234
Taney, Alice, 45:201
Taney, Roger Brooke, 37:350; 45:201
Tangier, 36:19-20; murders, 29:87-88
Tannhauser, 45:249, 252
Tantzunder, Paul, 27:393
Tappan, David, *Lectures on Jewish Antiquities*,
  30:132
Tappan, Frederick D., 33:221, 223
Tapper, Abraham, 33:79-80, 97
Tarazao, Semuel, 33:55
Tarbell, Ida M., 32:132
Tarbourieck, député, 41:162
Tares, *Exposition of the Parable of the Tares and
  Wheat*, 30:370, 372
Targee, 22:76
Tarkington, Booth, 40:328
Tarner, Samuel H., 30:341
Tarshish, Allan, "The Board of Delegates of
  the American Israelites," 48:266; 49:16-32;
  gift, 33:xxxiii
Tartakower, Arieh, 40:194, "The Problem of
  Bi-Culturalism," 43:197
Tartas, *see*: Castro, Isaac de
Tartas, Aron de Mosseh, 29:34
Tartas, Isaac de Castro, 22:119; 29:34

Tasch, William L., nominations committee, 31:xv

Taryag, 39:371

Tassel, 31:124

Tatsch, J. Hugo, 35:xx; 43:204; *see also*: Smith, Harry

Tauares, Abraham, 27:244

Taubes, Isaac, 45:69, 80, 82

Tauebler, Eugen, 40:49

Taussig, 38:197

Tavares, Mr., 27:355

Tavares, Benjamin, 27:358

Tavares, Manuel, 31:31

Taverez, 35:186

Tavarez, David, 27:358; 32:63

Tavarus, Antonio Roderigus, 33:47

Tavarus, Maniel Roderigus, 33:47

Tavel, Henry, 45:157-58

Taxation, "A Hessian Tax-Roll of 1811," 32:118-21; "The Taxation of Jews in Jamaica," 28:238-39; "The Taxing of the Jews in Jamaica in the Sevententh Century," 29:xv; 31:243-47; *see also*: Non-importation Agreement

Taxil, Leo, 41:96

Tayler, John, 35:130

Tayler, Robert, 27:175

Taylor (1), 31:110

Taylor (2), 37:132

Taylor, Bayard, 24:42; 37:234

Taylor, Benjamin Oglie, 39:29, 35

Taylor, Charles, 25:182, 184-85

Taylor, Col. (Kentucky), 50:397

Taylor family, 40:120

Taylor, Fredrick Winslow, 41:43, 48, 50-51, 53, 56, 312; 46:228

Taylor, Jacob, 30:29; *A Compleat Ephemeris, Containing Hebrew Alphabet*, 30:v, 29-30

Taylor, James, 35:291

Taylor, Jeremy, 37:147

Taylor, John, 23:184; 34:266

Taylor, Mary Agnes, 28:48

Taylor, Mr. and Mrs. Milton S., 50:272

Taylor, Myron C., 36:378-79

Taylor, Randal, 25:127

Taylor, Richard, 44:108

Taylor, Samuel H., 41:374

Taylor Society, 41:50, 315; 46:229

Taylor, William, 35:233

Taylor, Zachary, 37:448; 46:276

Tcherikover, Elias, 39:110

Tchernichowski, Saul, 33:163, 165

Tchetchik, Leiser, 39:68

Tea Act, 46:21

Teachers College at Columbia University, 35:323

Teachers Institute, 35:324; 42:20; (Yeshiva University), 45:160; 50:270

Teachers' and Parents' Assistant, The, 30:408

Tebel, David, 28:103

Tebo, Joseph, 35:30

Tebrich, Jacob, 29:131

Techenbach, L., 50:89

Tecumseh, 45:56

Tedeschi, Moses, 37:71

Tehuantepec Isthmus railroad project, 38:160

Teitlebaum, Henry, 45:147

Teitlebaum, Mrs. Henry, 45:147

Tejada, Lerdo de, 32:85, 96

Telegraph, Der, 48:132

Telephon, Der, 48:132

Telesinus, 28:138

Teller, David, 28:310

Teller, Oscar B., necrology of, 28:xxii, 310-11

Teller, Rebecca, 28:310

Temine Darex of Amsterdam, 29:10

Temmink, 37:199

Temperance, 26:217

Temperley, H. W. V., 34:226

Temple Bar, 29:126; 50:322

Templeman, John, 48:8, 14

Temple Street Congregational Church (New Haven, Conn.), 50:178

Templeton and Stewart (auctioneers), 28:255

Templo, Selomoh Jehuda Leão, 29:31

Temps, Le, 46:93

Tena'im, 39:379

Ten Broeck, Christina, 31:241

Tenbrook, Cornelius, 27:249; 41:111

Tendlan, Ab. M., 45:26

Tendler, Max, 47:202

Tenedo, Abraham, 27:249

Tenement House Building Company, 45:202

Tenenbaum, Aaron, 46:191

Tenenbaum, Joseph, "The American Jews' Contribution toward Rescue in the Hitler Period," 45:265; "The Anti-Nazi Boycott Movement in the United States," 44:242;

"Peace Conference in 1919 Discusses the Yiddish Language," 47:202

Tener, John K., 23:192

Ten Hove, Michiel, 33:120

Ten Hove, Nicholaes, 33:108, 120, 125

Ten Lost Tribes and American Indians, 21:xxi; 22:119; 39:450, 455; 42:333; 43:189, 234; Ararat, 41:12, 15, 26; *Discourse of Indians Being Descendants of Lost Tribes,* 30:315-17; "Hebrew-Speaking Indians," 39:185-89; "Jewish Settlement in the West Indies," 37:353-67; "Several Unnoted Writings on the Vagary of the Ten Tribes in America," 28:xxiii; *Ten Tribes,* 30:270, 272, 347-48, 354

Tennessee, Civil War, 50:279-80, 304; Jewish local history, 49:239

Tenney, Josiah, 22:24

Tennyson, Alfred, 38:268

Tentyra, Temple, 41:63

Tenzer family, *10th jubilee volume of the Michael Tenzer family,* 35:xxii

Tepfer, John J., 40:54

Teplitzky, J., 39:107

Tercentenary, American Jewish, 46:139-40, 143, 158, 196, 411, 445; British Jews, 49:147, 271; "An Old Faith in the New World: Highlights of Three Hundred Years," 44:210-14, 240; "Some of the Tercentenary's Historic Lessons," 44:199-209, 240

Tercero, Gonsalve, 33:113

Terkheim, Isaac, Gib' at Shaul, 22:123

Terman, Lewis M., 46:254-55

Terraresi, Professor, 28:60

Terrell, A. W., 36:60-61

Teschner, Rosebud Lotta, "The Portuguese Inquisition of 1730 with Special Reference to John da Costa, Sometime Commissary-General of Portugal," 29:xxxvi

Testa, Dauid David, 46:41

Teunissen, Gerrit, 26:247

Teunissen, Jacob, 26:247

Tewfik, Pasha, 47:84, 87-88

Texas, 25:24; Civil War, 50:279-80, 293-95, 304, 326; Jewish local history, 49:239; *One hundred years of Jewry in Texas,* 35:xxi; "Social Service Endeavor for Jewish Soldiers, El Paso, 1916," 26:xxxi; "Surgeon

Moses Albert Levy: Letters of a Texas Patriot," 46:101-13; 49:202-7

Texas, University of, "Judaica and Hebraica Collection in College Libraries," 45:146-47

"The Texel Affair in Louisiana," 44:242

Texero, Alvaro, 33:113

Texero, Jan Cornero, 33:112

Thacher, James, 22:159

Thackeray, William Makepeace, 28:241; 32:3, 103; 35:240-42

Thalheimer, Alvin, 49:270

Thalheimer, Walter, 50:166

Thalheimer, William, 27:506; 29:133

Thalmessinger, Maier Mosses, 41:255

Thalmessinger, Meyer Moses, 41:247-48; 49:186

Thanksgiving Day, 42:439; 43:191; 46:271; (Brazil), 42:240, 273-74; District of Columbia, 26:217; sermon, 50:286, 296, 358; Shearith Israel Congregation observing, 27:101, 104, 120, 132, 137-38, 503

Thannhauser, Salomin, 41:266

Thatcher, John, 23:158

Thayer, *Life of Hay,* 32:xxvi

Thayer, W. E., 50:391

Theater, 38:308, 311, 318-19; 46:145; 47:182; 50:397; bookplates, 45:199-200; "The History of the Yiddish Art Theater," 44:240; Jewish, 48:132; "Jews Who Helped to Finance the New or Park Theatre, New York, in 1794 and 1795," 28:xv; Yiddish, 43:25; 46:203; 47:192; 48:133; 49:99, 101, 105-6; *see also:* Drama

Theatre Royal, 33:175

Theodatus, 28:203

Theodore, Adah Bertha, 34:144

Theodoric, 28:203

Theodosius, 28:137-38

Theological Seminary College, "College Bookplates With Hebrew Inscriptions," 45:131, 134

Theosophic Lodge (Masons), 28:60-61

Theriault, J. Edward, 42:413

"Thesaurus of Mediaeval Hebrew Poetry," 33:26

Thidan, 24:19

Thielmans, Joachim, 32:14

Tile, Baron, 36:350
Third Degree, The, 40:354, 359
Third Lantern Council, 28:69
Third Seder, 39:371
Thirty years ago, 33:190
This is New York, 40:354
Thomas, 33:27
Thomas, Annibal Fernandes, 22:30
Thomas, Archbishop of Canterbury, 23:154
Thomas, Augustus, 40:354-55
Thomas, Charles, 23:139
Thomas, Gabriel, 22:147
Thomas, Henry L., 38:53
Thomas, John P., 22:179
Thomas, Robert, 50:342
Thomas, T. Gallard, 33:221
Thomas, William Isaac, 46:368, 374
Thomason, George, 32:23
Thompson (New York) (1819), 22:73, 76
Thompson (Pa.) (1789), 189
Thompson, Cephas Giovanni, 41:278, 289
Thompson, George, 36:401, *A View of the Holy Land*, 30:466
Thompson, Henry, 32:91
Thompson, John, 39:20, 38-39, 46, 49
Thompson, John Reuben, 39:138
Thompson, Jonathan, 27:467
Thompson, Mr., 43:221
Thompson, W. (General), 25:8
Thompson, Wm., 21:165; 30:77
Thomsen, Hans, 36:374, 383-85
Thomsen, Laur., 34:41
Thomson, Acheson, 23:155
Thomson College, 44:26
Thoreau, Henry D., 23:55, 77; 38:262, 267; 42:341, 356; 45:33; 46:212
Thorne, Herman, 46:6
Thornton, Jeremiah, 27:318
Thornton, William, 48:2, 8-9
Thornton, Mrs. William, 48:8-10, 14
Thoroughman, Thomas, 44:105
Thorowgood, Thomas, 39:186; 43:234; "Jews in America," 25:81
Thorpe, John, 28:226
Throckmorton, Captain, 38:69
Throop, Enos T., 30:404
Thrush, Captain, 25:6
Thucydides, 47:135
Thun, Franz von, 50:108

Thurloe, 34:8
Thurloe, John, 27:480
Thurlow, Lord, 31:112
Thurston, Edward, 35:290
Thwing, Annie Haven, 29:153
Thwing, Walter Eliot, "Judah Touro," 31:xxx
Thwing, Supply C., 38:64
Tiberias, 26:148, 151; 29:99
Tiberias, Lake, 40:282
Ticknor, Elisha, 43:204
Ticknor, Mary Agnes, 35:250, "The Jewel in the Lotus," 28:27
Ticktinsky, Hayyim Judah, 44:141
Ticonderoga, 35:6
Tid, Andrew, 35:188
Tierney, Judge, 25:136; 29:149
Tiferes Israel Community Center (Morristown, Pa.), 37:324
Tiferet Israel Anshe Neustadt Congregation (New York), 44:136
Tifereth Israel Congregation (Des Moines), 47:208; 48:140
Tiferet Mizrachi, 35:59
Tiferet Yisrael, 22:131
Tiffele, L. Y. Van, 45:213
Tiffereth Israel Congregation of Cleveland, 28:275
Tiktin, Solomon, 45:209
Tilden Centenary Commission, 38:51
Tilden Foundation, 45:203
Tilden, Samuel J., 38:50
Tilden, Thomas G., 46:4
Tilghman, William, 40:127
Tillinghast, Mr., 27:438
Timayenik, Telemachus T., *The Original Mr. Jacobs: A Startling Expose*, 37:422-24
Time Piece, The, 38:123, 126-27
Times of India, The, 47:169
Times, The (London), 25:158; 26:135-37; 46:91, 98
Times and Messenger, The, 21:229
Times-Democrat (New Orleans), 40:225
Times-Star (Cincinnati), 39:462
Timm, Bernhardt L., 27:399
Timothy, 28:138
Timrod, 38:269
Tindal, 35:203
Tingey, Thomas, 48:9
Tirado, Juan, 31:11

Tiraspolsky, I., 39:99
Tisdale, 22:183
Tishbi, A., 33:154
Titanic disaster, 43:231
Tites, Mr., 30:63
Titian, 28:26
Titus Vespesianous, 21:241
T. J. B., Literary Society (St. Louis), 37:243, 253
T'minim, Zovchei, 44:134
Tob, Joseph Ibn Shem, 34:159
Tobacco industry, 48:46-47, 51-52, 124
Tobago, David Fernandez, 29:37
Tobago, Sephardic Jews, 29:37
Tobath Mareh, 44:222
Tobias, Mr., 27:60, 107
Tobias, Abraham, 50:174, 187
Tobias, Alfred, 21:215
Tobias, Frances, 27:293
Tobias, Harriet, 27:112; 31:260
Tobias, Henry, 27:277
Tobias, Jacob, 27:226-27
Tobias, John, 22:193
Tobias, Joseph (Charleston), 27:249; 42:59; 50:42, 61, 162; "Joseph Tobias of Charles Town: 'Linguister,' "49:33-38
Tobias, Joseph (New York), 21:45
Tobias, Myer, 27:277
Tobias, Myer Isaac, 27:276
Tobias, S., 27:314
Tobias, S., Jr., 21:171
Tobias, Samuel, 27:81
Tobias, Samuel L., 27:277
Tobias, T. I., 21:168
Tobias, Thomas Jefferson, 40:215; 42:59; 47:201; 50:187; Civil War, 50:272, 276, 286-87, 316, 334-35; executive council, 50:426; *The Hebrew Orphan Society of Charleston, S. C. Founded 1801: An Historical Sketch*, 49:238; "Joseph Tobias of Charles Town: 'Linguister,' " 49:33-38; presides, 39:471
Tobias, Tob, 27:81, 314
Tobias, Tobias I. (1), 30:332
Tobias, Mrs. Tobias, 27:112
Tobias, Tobias I. (2), 27:111, 120
Tobin, John, *The Guardian*, 33:195
Tobit, *Letters to Levi*, 30:170-71
Tobiyah, Riby, 21:116

Toby, Jackson, "Hoodlum or Business Man," 48:67-68
Toch, Ernest, 47:182
Toch, Leopold, 21:215
Tochman, Casper, 39:147
Tod, Robert E., 34:212
Today's Health (Magazine), 50:340
Todd, Colonel, 27:467
To Dwell in Safety, The Story of Jewish Migration since 1800, reviewed, 39:196-98
Tog, Der, 33:129; 48:21
Toggart, William, 35:291
Toinel, Anthony, 26:247
Toiro, Moses, 28:239
Toizé, M., 24:51
Toklas, Wise and Co. (San Francisco), 37:45
Toland, 35:203
Toledano (family name), 48:139
Toleration Act, 46:20
Tolner, 33:59
Tolochko, J. G., gift, 34:xxvii
Tolstoi, Demetrius, 43:38
Tolstoy, Leo, 34:223; 43:21; 48:90; 50:115, 117
Tom (slave), 50:159
Tomas, Diego, 33:112
Tomashoff, Moses Benjamin, 33:151
"Tombstones That Tell a Story: Charleston's Historic Coming Street Cemetery," 50:316
Tompkins, Governor (N.Y.), 22:73-74; 26:179-80
Tompkins papers, 32:xxix
Tomson, Robert, 31:10, 21
Toner, Joseph N., 22:163
Tong, Toy, 34:197
Tonge, Mark, 50:42
Tonkin, Felsh *v.*, "Anglo-Jewish Legal Cases," 25:137
Tonna, Charlotte Elizabeth Browne Phelan, 30:425; *Israel's Ordinances*, 30:398; *Judaea Capta*, 30:420; *Judah's Lion*, 30:380-81; *Meditorial Reign of Christ on Earth*, 30:387
Tonna, Mrs., 30:425
Tonnancour, J. G. de, 23:139
Tonneman, Peter, 29:44-45
Tooker, 22:76
Toombs, Mr., 25:23

Torah, Machazike Talmud, "The Minute Book of the Machazike Talmud Torah, New York (1890-1902)," 46:493
Torah, Umersorah, 45:185
Tores, B., 27:62
Tores, Daniel Gomez, 23:153
Tores, Moses Gomez, 23:153
Tores, Sinya de, 23:147, 153
Torez, Lopez Sarah, 32:63
Toronto, "The Ashers of Toronto," 26:xv; "The Nordheimers of Toronto," 26:xxxi; religious observances, mid-nineteenth century, 37:37; "The Rossin Brothers of Toronto, Canada," 28:xvi
Torre, Conda da, 46:44
Torre, Hillel Hakohen Della, 40:18
Torres, Ana de Galarza de, 23:134
Torres, Antonio de, 27:475
Torres, Daniel, 21:79, 93, 103
Torres, Daniel Aluares de, 42:280, 395
Torres, Daniel Lopes, 37:337
Torres, David Aluares de, 42:253, 257, 280, 289, 392, 395
Torres, David Alvares, 29:10
Torres, David Lopes, 37:336
Torres, Francisco de, 32:117
Torres, Gabriela de, 23:134
Torres, Hester, 33:68
Torres, Jacob de, 27:279
Torres, Jacob Lopez, 28:239; 37:333, 336-37
Torres, Jan de, 33:115
Torres, João de, 33:65
Torres, Joseph de, 27:279-81
Torres, Louis de, 33:36
Torres, Luis de, 27:474-75; 35:223-24
Torres, Mordecai de, 27:280
Torres, Moses, 27:122
Torres, Rachel, 29:10
Torres, Rebecca de, 41:109
Torres, Rebecca de (Mrs. Daniel Gomez), 27:289-90
Torres, Rebecca de (Mrs. Joseph), 27:279
Torres, Sarah Lopez (1), 32:64; 37:333
Torres, Sarah Lopez (2), 37:337
Torres, Sarah Lopez (3), 37:337
Torres, Simha de, 21:8, 45, 51, 55; 27:122, 249, 280-81
Tortosa, Cardinal, 31:16
Toscano, Samuel, 27:512-13

Totah, Selim, 45:43-44
Totten, Daniel, 27:318-19
Totten, James, 27:320
Totten, James Wallace, 34:234
Totten, Peter, 27:319
Touaer, Abraham de, 33:77
Tougaloo University, 50:179
Toulouse, Council of, 28:144
Tounnensan, Pieter, 21:180
Toupin, Francois, 23:139
Touro, Mr., 35:197
Touro, Abraham b. Rev. Isaac, 21:166, 220; 27:107, 204-5, 214, 406, 410, 417, 420, 427-28, 435; 31:xxxv, 239; 38:60, 64-65; 50:62; gift to Shearith Israel Congregation, 27:100-101, 103, 107; obituary, 27:418-19; portrait of, 42:417; Stephen Gould letter, 27:425-26
Touro, Abraham, 23:88, 90; 42:337
Touro, Aharon, 29:16-17
Touro family, 23:88; 42:108, 214; (Newport), 27:xviii, 417, 422
Touro Infirmary (New Orleans), 26:275; 28:309; 31:257
Touro, Isaac, 21:209; 27:156, 203-7, 252, 417-18; 29:35; 33:201; 34:71; 38:87-88; 50:62
Touro, Ishac, 44:227-28, 230
Touro, Jacob de Eliau, 29:17
Touro, Jeoshuah, 44:219
Touro, Jeudah de Haim, 44:228
Touro, Judah, 21:166, 216; 23:x, 88, 170; 26:xxxiv, 150, 199-200; 27:121, 194, 206-7, 212, 214, 216, 413-15, 417, 420, 424, 450-51; 28:235; 29:5, 35, 100, 124; 31:274; 32:4; 34:131, 134, 172, 178, 269; 35:129, 133; 36:239, 396; 37:439; 39:333; 40:192; 42:110, 116, 337, 346; 44:30; 45:208; 46:431; 47:214, 224; 48:223; 50:7, 62, 196; data on, 27:420-22; "Judah Touro," 23:xvii; 31:xxx; legacy, Palestinian aid, 37:213-20; synagogue history, 38:64-65, 68-69, 332
Touro, Manuel de Ieuda, 29:24
Touro Memorial Cemetery (Newport), 41:71, 373
Touro, Nathan, 27:156, 417
Touro, Rebecca, 21:166; 50:62

Touro, Reyna, 27:204-5, 214-15, 417-18; 50:62

Touro Synagogue (Newport), 35:318; 38:278, 331; 40:408, 411; 41:373; 42:417-18; 46:115; 49:60; "A Note on the Early History of the Touro Synagogue in New Orleans," 32:xiii; restoration, 47:201; "The Touro Synagogue: Aspects of the Missing Half-Century of its History (1850-1900)," 38:57-76; 49:236

Touron, Aaron, 37:392, 397-98, 402-3

Tourow, Lea, 27:249

Tovey, Captain, 27:303

Towanda, Pa., religious observances, mid-nineteenth century, 37:37

Towarzystwo Demokratyczne Wygnancow Polskich w Ameryce (Democratic Society of Polish Exiles in America), 39:150-51

Towarzystwo Polakow w Ameryce (Society of Poles in America), 39:149

Towne, Mrs. Burton (Alice), 29:196

Towne, H. R. 41:48

Towro, Moses, 32:63

Townsend, David, 43:204

Townsend, Dyett & Einstein, 26:278

Townsend, Dyett & Morrison, 29:174

Townsend, Howard, 33:221-23

Townsend, Joseph, 27:318-19

Townshead, Charles, 34:273

Townsley, 23:68

Toynbee, Arnold Joseph, 40:193; 46:155

Tractenberg, A., 39:94

Trachtenberg, Joshua, 39:253; 40:415; 42:216, "An American Jewish Community, Easton, Pennsylvania, on its Two Hundredth Anniversary," 42:193-206; 49:234; book review by, 40:398-401; 41:390

Trachtenberg, Y., 39:89-91, 93-94

Tracy, Benjamin V., 43:13, 26

Tradesmen's Bank (New York), 21:166; 27:266, 301; 31:101

Tradesmen's National Bank (Philadelphia), 25:173

Trade unions, history, writing of, 46:185, 203, 215-20, 230-31, 257-61, 398; Jewish, 43:192-94

Trade Union Sponsoring Committee, 43:194

Trade Union Unity League, 48:200

"Trail Blazers of the Trans-Mississippi West," 49:217

Trani, Baruch, 45:74

Transcendentalism, "New Light on the Religious Development of Emma Lazarus," 42:83-88

Transcontinental Choral Library, 50:393

Transcontinental Music Corporation, 50:393

Transformation; or, Love and law, 33:174, 194-95

Transylvania Company, 23:22

Trask, Spencer, 33:222

Trauenfels, Dr., 42:165, 174

Trauttmansdorff, Prince, 26:52

Trautwein, Joseph, 50:398

"Travels," 21:229

Tray, Van Wike, 27:316

Treadwell, Thomas, 35:5

Tream, John, 22:81

Treasurer, report of, 26:x-xi, xxvii-xxix; 28:xiii-xiv, xx-xxi, xxxi-xxxii; 32:xi, xvii-xviii; 33:xiii-xvi, xxi-xxv; 34:x, xiii; 35:x-xiv; 37:xiii-xxviii

Treaty of Belin (1878), 28:83; 41:38

Treaty of Commerce and Navigation, 50:219

Treaty of 1832, 36:171-72, 176, 179, 190, 192-94, 198-202, 233-35, 251, 277, 281, 285-90

Treaty of Paris (1763), 35:2; (1856), 24:40, 102, 120-21; 38:4

Treaty of Sevres, 45:38

Treaty of Utrecht (1579), 50:74-75

Tredwell, Captain, 27:391

Tree of Liberty, 38:135-36

Tree of Life Congregation (Pittsburgh), 31:289

Treidel, I., 31:199

Treitschke, Heinrich, 28:80; 36:356-57, 360

Trelawny, Edward, 35:295

Trenholm, G. A., 50:336

Trent, Council of, 28:211

Trent (Pa.), 22:189

Trent, William, 23:4, 7, 11, 13, 15, 19; 30:71, 77; 37:347-49

Trenton, N.J., religious observances, mid-nineteenth century, 37:37

Trseria, Anna Maria, 37:109

Trestler, 23:47

Treue Zions-Wachter, Der, 49:54

Trevelyan, George Macaulay, 28:235; 34:235
Treves, Bishop of (Nicholas Franco), 28:200
Treves, Council of, 28:143, 148
Treves, David, 37:420
Treves, Eliezer, 28:65
Treves, Jacob T., 37:420
Treves, Synod of, 28:144
Trevor, Thomas, 28:249
Triana, Rodrigo de, 33:34-35; 35:224
Tribuna, La, 28:35; 38:242
"Tribute to Lincoln by Josephine Phillips, A," 50:283
Tri-City Jewish Chronicle, The, 28:xxxviii
Triest and Friedlander (San Francisco), 37:45
Trietsch, Davis, 35:64
Trigault, Nicolas, 49:41-43
Trinidad, W., 34:227
Trinidade, Adelaide Elisa, 25:148
Trinity Cemetery (New York), 27:502
Trinity Church (Newport), 27:212; (New York), 21:xv; 27:382-83; 41:108, 286, 290; 42:433; 49:59
Trinity College (England), 47:149
Trip, Benjamin, 37:394
Triplett, R., 23:120
Tripoli, 26:194
Tripolitan War, 33:180, 192
Tripp, Stephen, 35:291
Tristaon, Manuel, 33:112
Trivulce, Theodore, 28:171
Troileo, Professor, 28:59
Trollope, Anthony, 35:246
Trollope, Mrs., 39:121
Trommer, Marie, "Henry Mosler, Pictorial Interpreter of the Civil War," 41:389
Trompetler, Abraham Levy, 27:277
Trotsky, Leon, 39:203, 286; 46:266, 441
Trott, Nicholas, 41:81-82
Trotter, R., 26:149
Troubetsky, Amelie (Rives), 34:233
Trowbridge, 38:269
Trowbridge, Edm., 22:22
Troy (N.Y.), religious observances, mid-nineteenth century, 37:38
Truby, Asher, 21:16
True American, 26:222
True Craftsman Lodge, No. 651 (Masonic), 45:191
True Sisters, Benevolent Society of, 47:44

Trujillo, Rafael L., 45:233
Truman, Harry S., 38:5; 39:342; 40:118; 41:357; 47:232; history, writing of, 46:258, 291, 317, 332; Library, 49:271
Trumbull, 29:104; 22:148; 44:102
Trumbull, Lyman, 41:39
Trumpet, The, 32:124
Truscutt, J. S., 39:78
Trustman, Benjamin, 42:419
Trusts, "The Simson Trust," 28:246-48; "Trusts for Jewish Charitable Purposes under the law of New York," 28:xxiii
Tryon, William, 31:58-59
Tschasky, Mayor, 43:48-49
Tszur Yisroel Congregation, Recief, 33:55-56
Tu Bishevat, 39:366
Tubman, Harriet, 41:75
Tuck, Gustav, gift, 34:xxiv
Tuckerman, Edward, 43:204
Tucson, Arizona, Jewish Community Council, contribution, 37:xxviii
Tudesca, Judith, 26:251
Tudor Exhibition, 31:290
Tufts College, 22:228-29
Tuggle, W. O., 39:341
Tulane University, 26:275; 31:257
Tunis, 21:229; Board of Delegates of American Israelites, 29:88
Tunnicliffe's Tavern, 48:8
Turcot, Joseph, 23:139
Turgenev, Ivan Sergeevich, 38:271; 43:15, 20-21
Turgeon, Joseph, 23:43, 47, 49
Turin Exhibition, 31:290
Turkey, 24:40, 46, 49-50, 58-61, 64, 66-68, 74, 78; 26:137-39, 142, 144-46, 148-50, 153, 155-59, 161-62; 29:96-97; 31:295; 36:3-10; 40:306-7; 45:38; 47:170, 172; Balkan states and Jewish disabilities, 24:21, 31, 81, 115, 120-21, 134, 149-50; Bucharest Peace Conference, 24:84-93; civil liberties, 24:102-7; custom revenue, 26:243-44; Damascus Affair, 36:3-5; education, 28:86, 129; Jewish homeland, 36:42-78; Jewish National Assembly, 36:9; Mesopotamian project, 47:160-64; migration from, 48:43; "Naham Passi, a Sixteenth-Century Turkish Statesman," 29:xxxvi; naturalized American Jews,

36:44-46; Oscar S. Straus, 40:7-8, 11; Paris
Conference 1876, 24:30-36, 39; Sneersohn
case, 36:7-8; U.S. intercession for Jews,
36:xi, 3-10; "United States Policies on
Palestine," 40:107-18
Turnbull, Lawrence, 22:231
Turner, 39:290
Turner, Alfred E., 47:174
Turner-Baker papers, 47:189
Turner, C. C., 40:286-87
Turner, Frederick Jackson, 41:330; 46:367
Turner, Peter, 39:30, 33, 63
Turner, John, 21:17
Turner, Justin G., 42:420-23; 46:120-23;
48:266; 49:137, 155; Civil War, 50:260,
263, 270, 273, 275, 288, 290, 296, 301,
341, 355, 379, 383, 396, 400-401, 404;
executive council, 42:414-15; 45:264;
48:266; presides, "The Civil War: The
Resurgent Interest of Collectors and
Writers," 50:427; "Re: The Affairs
Dreyfus," 45:258-59
Turner, Mrs. Justin G., 46:122; 50:383
Turner, Mr. and Mrs. Maurice, 50:383
Turner, Lawrence, 27:175
Turner, Samuel B., *Biographical Notices*,
30:430

Turner, Samuel H., *The Claims of the Hebrew
Language*, 30:277
Turover, I. S., 47:203
Tur-Sinai, H. H., 43:195
Tuska, Marcus, 40:61-62
Tuska, Mordecai, 50:80-81, 89
Tuska, Moritz, 49:186
Tuska, Morris, 48:35
Tuska, Simon, 40:61; 45:63; 49:239; "Simon
Tuska Becomes a Rabbi," 50:79-97
Tut-ankh-Amen, 33:14
Tuxeira, Samuel, 32:60
Twain, Mark, 41:220; 42:348; 47:224
Twaites, William, 33:191
Tweedy, William, 26:269; 35:291
21st Street Cemetery (New York), 27:120-22,
266-67, 273, 275-78, 284, 493
Twining, Nathaniel, 48:180
Tydings, Millard E., 36:368-69
Tygel, Z., *Gestalten*, 35:xxii; gift, 33:xxxiii
Tyler (New York) (1831), 22:85
Tyler, Mr. (actor), 33:188
Tyler, John, 21:221; 25:15-16, 18, 23; 30:339;
36:11-16; 39:21; 42:346
Tyler, John S., 33:183
Tyndale, William, 28:90
Tyson, John S., 30:258
Tzioni, 39:93

U

Uchill, Ida Libert, "Pioneers, Peddlers, and Tzadikim," 49:218
Ucko, Henry Z., "The Integration of the Dominican Sephardim," 45:264
U. C. L. A. Daily Bruin, 48:259
Ueiga, Eliahu, 42:280, 395
Uffenheim, G. G., 26:36, 45
Uganda project, 46:477
Uhl, Byron H., 34:205-6
Uhl, Edward (Edwin), 36:242; 39:70
Uhlfelder and Cahn (San Francisco), 37:45
Uhlman, Salomon, 41:268
Uhlmann, Mayer, 41:266
Uhlmann, Moses Isak, 41:266
Uhlmann, Simon, 41:268
Uilareal, Abram Gabay, 42:280, 395
Ukrainia, "Some Remarks on the Shabbethai-Zebi Movement in Poland and Ukrainia," 28:xxxiii
Ukrainian Jews, 46:290
Ullman, Bertha, 26:289
Ullman, Mrs. David, 43:238
Ullman, Nathan, 37:254, 256
Ullman, Samuel, 37:266
Ullmann, Abraham, 41:266
Ullmann, Isak, 41:266
Ullmann, Salomon, 31:174
Ulloa, Abraham Hisquiao, 44:228
Ulloa, Daniel, 32:60
Ulloa, Esther, 32:60
Ulloa, Luis, 33:37
Ulloa, Solomon, 32:60
Ulman, Amalia, 29:199
Ulman, Henry, 37:34
Ulmann, Abraham, widow of, 41:259
Ulmann, Albert, 34:172
Ulmann, Doris, 35:xx
Ulshoeffer, Henry, 22:77, 79; 30:404

Ulster County, 25:140-41; "The Jewish Colony of Sholam, Ulster County, New York, 1838," 23:178-79
Umstadter, Miriam, 22:210
Umstetter, Mr., 37:32
Uncle Tom's Cabin, 50:268; (Hebrew translation), 50:402; (Yiddish translation), 50:403
Underhill, Abraham, 27:321
Une Folie, Capt. Beldare, 33:191
Unfailing Light: Memoirs of an American Rabbi, Bernard Drachman, reviewed, 40:311-13
Ungar, 38:202
Unger, Joseph, 50:314
Uniform Law Commission, 38:51
Union Club (New York), 28:294
Union of American Hebrew Congregations, 22:xxxii, 200; 23:129; 25:150; 26:xxvii, 282; 28:46, 283-84, 309; 29:xli, 162, 169, 181, 200, 202; 31:xxxv; 32:xxviii, 117; 34:183, 188, 199, 214; 35:321; 37:84, 90, 234, 245, 251; 39:108, 296, 335, 396, 400, 453, 455, 462; 40:383-84, 390; 42:5, 7, 320-23; 45:271; 46:276; 47:83; 48:35, 39, 143-44, 227-29; 49:26, 30-32, 188-89; 50:118; "As to the Supposed 18th Century Translation into Hebrew of Washington's Correspondence with Hebrew Congregations," 32:121; Board of Delegates of American Israelites, 1859-1878, 29:75, 79, 111-16; Board of Delegates on Civil Rights, 24:81; Disabilities, 36:29-30, 177-78, 285; "The First Attempt to Form a Union of American Jewish Congregations," 37:xxxiii; gifts, 33:xxxiii; 34:xxiii; 35:xxiv; Hebrew Union College, 40:22-24, 28-31, 33-35, 44, 47; immigration, 40:222-23, 262; Jewish statistics, 29:106; Serbia, 36:6

Union of American Israelites, 37:262
Union College (Cincinnati), 29:108
Union of German Jewish Congregations, 28:81
"Union Hagadah," 25:152
Union Health Center, 40:173
Union League Club (New York), 41:32-33; 47:13
Union Lodge (Masons) (New York), 27:331
Union of Orthodox Jewish Congregations, 35:318; 39:296, 378; 44:186; 45:199; 49:86
Union of Orthodox Rabbis, 49:89
Union Prayer Book, 31:270; 41:367; 42:102
Union of Sephardic Congregations, 42:467; 49:60-61
Union Technological Institute of America, 37:267, 269, 293
Union Theological Seminary, 40:51; 50:88
Union University (Albany), 35:321
Unionism, 46:221-32, 258; "Jewish-American Unionism, Its Birth Pangs and Contributions to the General American Labor Movement," 41:297-337, 387; "The Jewish Unions and Their Influence upon the American Labor Movement," 41:339-45, 387; "Some Observations on Jewish Unionism," 41:347-55, 387
Unitarianism, 42:83, 341, 344-45; 47:142-43, 145, 149; 50:20; and Judaism, 38:159; S. H. Sonneschein, 45:97
United Brethren, 23:33
United Committee for the Taxation of Land Values, 46:487
United Company of Spermaċeti Candlers, 37:165
United Congregation B'nai Sholom, "History of Temple Isaiah Israel, Chicago (1852-1952)," 41:390
United Daughters of the Confederacy, 28:54
United Drive (Chicago), 45:211
United Hebrew Beneficent Fuel Society (Philadelphia), constitution and by-laws, 30:398
United Hebrew Beneficent Society (Philadelphia), constitution and by-laws, 30:261-62
United Hebrew Benevolent Association (Boston), 46:72-81; 47:60

United Hebrew Charities, 24:113; 28:308; 31:275; 38:309, 311-12; 39:88, 277; 43:145; 49:61, 111, 174-75, 184; (Newark), 29:183; (New York), 29:111; 37:288; 40:141, 152-53, 164, 226, 241, 243, 255, 259, 263; 42:123, 394-95; 48:31-33, 35, 38-42, 45, 53, 55-56, 60, 83, 86, 88-90, 100, 107-108, 112-13, 118, 120; (Philadelphia), 37:291; 46:394
United Hebrew Congretations (British Empire), 22:201; (St. Louis), 29:134; minute book (1841-59), 22:xxxiv
United Hebrew Orthodox Association, 44:129-98
United Hebrew Orthodox Congregations, 44:129-98
United Hebrew Relief Association (Chicago), 40:268; (Pittsburgh), 28:257; (St. Louis), 40:268
United Hebrew Trades, 41:343-44; 48:133, 200; 49:82; 50:215; gift, 35:xxiv; (Philadelphia), 48:238
United HIAS Service, 48:138
United Hospital Fund, 31:271
United Jewish Appeal, 39:248; 42:199; 43:147; 44:214; 48:66
United Jewish Charities (Cincinnati), 26:283; 28:289; (St. Louis), 37:292; (Rochester), 40:67, 71, 232
United Jewish Federation (Buffalo), 46:158-59, 163; (Pittsburgh), 49:236
United Jewish Social Agencies, Cincinnati, 28:289
United Jewish Welfare Fund, 46:124
United Mine Workers, 46:218
United Nations, 40:108, 116, 118; 44:73; 48:136-37; 50:434; Relief and Rehabilitation Administration, 46:353; *Struggle for Palestine*, reviewed, 40:313-17
United Nations Conference, 38:319
United Nations Educational, Scientific and Cultural Organization, 47:232
United Nations Food and Agriculture Organization, 38:250
United Orthodox Synagogue, 35:59
United Palestine Appeal, 36:371; 42:454; 43:144
United Press Association, 32:129

United Services Organizations, 38:335; 41:366; 42:340; 47:231-32; 50:431-33
United States, 24:75; 26:137, 271, 286; Algeciras Conference, 24:88-89; "American Zionism and the Congressional Resolution of 1922 on Palestine," 45:35-47; anti-Semitism, 40:323-60; Austria, commission for, 48:136; Balkan States and Jewish diabilities, 24:1-3, 6-21, 30-34, 36-38, 41-42, 71-72, 75, 79-80, 93, 110-14, 133-36, 149; "Benjamin F. Peixotto's Mission to Roumania," 24:1-24; Brussels Conference 1872, 24:25-29; Bucharest Conference, 24:92-93; diplomatic intercession for rights of Jews in Austria, 36:323-47; Germany, 36:348-85; Italy, 36:386-88; Morocco, 36:19-41; Palestine, 36:42-95; Persia, 36:11-18; Poland, 36:140-67, 389-402; Rumania, 36:99-139; Russia, 36:171-295, 389-402; Switzerland, 36:299-322; Turkey, 36:3-10; "The European Aspect of the American-Russian Passport Question," 46:86-100; Great War and Jews, 26:xxiv, xxv, xxvii; Holy Land naval expedition, 40:281-87; immigration, 40:221-80, 404; Information Agency in Israel, 50:271, 273; Information Service, 50:404; Meyer Levi vs., 47:187; Morocco and Jews, 24:88; and Palestine, 40:107-18, 361, 367-68, 370-72, 374, 384, 389-90; religious liberty, 24:ix, 1-6, 8, 13, 18, 20, 30, 42, 80, 86, 88-89, 94, 102, 112-13, 132; and Russia, 40:294, 296-310; "Secretary Hay's Roumanian Note of 1902 and the Peace Conference of Bucharest of 1913," 24:80-97; Sephardic Jews, 29:31-33; "Simon M. Levy, Member of the First Class to Graduate at the United States Consul to Egypt," 47:76-100
United States v. Castillero, 38:154
U.S. Catholic Historical Society, 23:xviii
United States Christian Commission, 37:231
United States Commerce Court, 37:476
United States Commission on Industrial Relations, 41:55, 320; 47:190
United States Commission to UNESCO, 47:232
U.S. Democratic Review, 29:xxxix
United States Export Association, 34:197

United States Fish Commission, 28:265
United States Gazette, 32:121; 50:246
U.S. George Washington Bi-Centennial Commission, gift, 34:xxvii
United States Military Academy, 48:147, 167
United States National Museum, 33:21, 27
United States Naval Academy, 28:290; 39:41
United States Navy, 28:291-92, 306; 39:1-66; 50:329; see also: Levy, Uriah P.
United States Pharmacopoeia, 38:340
United States Potters' Association, 28:258
United States Sanitary Commission, 50:299
U.S. Senate, "David L. Yulee, Florida's First Senator," 25:vii, 1-29
United States Sesqui-Centennial Commission, gift, 35:xxiv
U.S. Steel, 41:311; 46:228
United Synagogue of America, 39:296; 42:20, 331; 43:250
United Young Men's Hebrew Association, 37:265-71, 276, 282-88, 293, 299, 319
United Zionists, 35:58-59
Unity House, 41:327
Universal Alliance, 37:261
Universal Asylum, The, 49:52
Universal Jewish Encyclopedia, 39:468, 47:219
Universalists, 47:148-49
Universidad Central, 28:272
Universities, see: specific university
University Club (Baltimore), 26:289; (Cincinnati), 47:13
University-in-Exile, 36:370
University of Judaism, 42:422
University Settlement Society (New York), 37:287; 45:193, 202
Unsworth, 31:124
Unterberg, Israel, necrology of, 34:ix; necrology of Samuel I. Hyman, 26:xxx
Unterberg, Mrs. Israel, 37:306-7
Untermeyer, Samuel, 47:187
Unus, 39:98
Updike, Mr., 37:417
Upham, Thomas Cogswell, 45:24; (trans.), Biblical Archaeology, 30:280
Uprooted, The, 46:302, 369
Upshur, Abel Parker, 39:21
Uptown Talmud Torah, 35:62; (Harlem), 42:10-11
Urban VIII, 28:194

Urbino, 28:198

"Uriah Phillips Levy: The Story of a Pugnacious Commodore," 50:312

Uris, Leon, 50:116

Ursinus College, 28:292

Urussov, Prince, 36:275

Ury, John, 27:386

Ury, Lesser, 40:318

Urzidil, Johannes, 50:99, 106

Usen, Irving, 42:419

Usher, Esther, 44:106

Usque, Samuel, 44:64

Usselinx, Willem, 33:45-46, 51; 47:113-114

Ussishkin, M. M., 35:258

Utah, 38:333; 50:279; "The Earliest Jewish Settlers in Utah," 29:xxxvi; Jewish local history, 49:239-40; Masonic Grand Lodge, 22:182; "Mormon Petroglyph at Manit, Utah," 28:xxii

Ute Indians, 38:322

Utica (N.Y.), 50:278; "The Centennial of Utica's Jewry," 39:471; The Jewish Community of Utica, New York, 1847-1948, 49:232-33; Jewish local history, 49:261-62; religious observances, mid-nineteenth century, 37:36; Workmen's Circle Branch in Utica, 49:246

Utica Public Library, gift, 33:xxxiii

Utrecht, Treaty of, 50:74-75

Uvarov, S., 35:39-41

Uvarow, Count, 28:119-20, 123

Uz, Johann Peter, 35:121

Uziel, Ben-Zion Meir Hai, 49:274

V

Vaad Leumi, 37:483; 49:169, 171
Vaas, Hieronimus, 33:115
Vaca, Alvaro Nuñez Cabeza de, 38:11
Vacant Lots Cultivation Association, 46:477
Vadna-Vel, 38:244
Vaez, Francisco, 31:29
Vaez, Jorge, 31:29
Vail, R. W. G., 35:283; 40:405; 45:260; book
  review by, 45:61-63
Vail, Stephen, 48:175
Vajda, Erno, 35:270
Valabrega, Jacob, 29:18
Valabrega, Rachel, 29:18
Valcao, Vaico Marino, 33:118
Valcaon, Pedro Marinho, 33:118
Valdes, Diego, 31:24
Valdivieso, Juan de, 31:13
Vale, Symon de, 33:77
Valencia, Abigail, 27:168-69
Valencia (family name), 48:139
Valencia, Judith, 48:139
Valencia, Martin de, 31:16-17
Valensi, Brahim, 38:75
Valensi, Clement, 38:72
Valenti, Louis da Costa, 33:116
Valentine, 27:315
Valentine, David, 27:68, 72
Valentine, David H., 21:213
Valentine, David Henriques, 27:75, 120, 258,
  315
Valentine, David T., 27:380-81
Valentine, Elias Henriques, 27:313
Valentine, Isaac (1), 27:87
Valentine, Isaac (2), 27:390
Valentine, Isaac (3), 27:390
Valentine, Isaac H., 27:84
Valentine, Kitty, 27:111
Valentine, M., 27:243
Valentine, Mitchell and Company, 43:9

Valentine, Rebekah, 27:75
Valentine, Robert G., 41:315; 46:229
Valentine, S., 29:129
Valentine, Simon, "Jacob Mears and Simon
  Valentine of Charleston, South Carolina,"
  41:77-82
Valentine's "Manual," 25:45
Valkenbrugh, S. M., 38:72
Vallabrega, Manuel, 29:17
Valladolid, Synod of, 28:147
Valle, Jacob de Franco, 26:251
Valle, Marquis del, 31;24
Vallenberg, Abraham, 27:249
Vallenbergh family, 41:111
Valo, Ferdinando, 33:118
Valori, 28:196
Valuerde, Abraham, 42:279, 395
Valuerde, Jacob, 27:249; 42:225, 258, 260,
  275, 277, 284-87, 291-93, 391, 395
Valvarde, Aaron, 32:60
Valvarde, Abraham, 22:180; 26:251; 32:60
Valvarde, David, 32:60
Valvarde, David, Jr., 32:60
Valvarde, Elias, 32:60
Valvarde, Hester, 32:60
Valvarde, Isaac, 32:60
Valvarde, Jacob, 32:60
Valvarde, Lunah, 32:60
Valvarde, Moses, 32:60
Valverde, David, 22:179; 26:251
Van Campen, M. H., 37:478
Vance, Zebulon Baird, 43:231
Van Coerland, Abraham S., 27:144
Van Cortland, John, 27:426
Van Cortland, Philip, 27:320
Van Cortland, Pierre, 27:391
Van Cortland, Stephen, 27:249
Van Cortland, Catherine, 31:241
Van Cortland family, 41:110

Van Cortlandt, Frederick, 23:150
Van Cortlandt, J., 23:150
Van Cortlandt, Jacobus, 34:270
Van Cott, Joshua, 31:280
Van Daelen, Francisco, 32:17
Vandalia colony, 23:18-19
Van Dam, 26:247
Van Dam, Rip, 23:149-50, 158
Vandenburg, Galeb, 25:33-37
Vanderbilt, 25:56
Vanderbilt, Alice Gwynne, 30:3
Vanderbilt University, 45:147
Van der Contre, Martinus, 33:122
Van der Elst, Jacob, 33:110-11
Vanderheul, John, 21:18
Van der Hooght, Everardo, 30:140, 142, 157-58
Van der Kemp, Francis Adrian, 43:237; "John Adams Writes a Letter," 37:xxxv, 185-201
Van der Ley, Gaspar Nihof, 33:122
Van der Mesen, Jeronimo Correa, 33:116
Van der Nesen, Antho Correa, 33:113
Van der Nesen, Sijmon, 33:118
Van der Nezen, Diego Mendez, 33:112
Vanderpool, Aaron, 39:35
Van der Veen, H. R. S., 35:230, 235
Vander-Wilden, see: Valentine, Simon
Van Deussen, Abraham, 28:226
Van Doren, Carl, 38:332
Van Dorn, Nicholas, 27:329
Van Dyck, E. A., 47:92-93, 95
Van Eass, Hendrick, 27:249
Van Eckelen, Jan, 26:247
Van Gansbeek, T., Jr., 25:141
Van Gansevoort, Herman, 26:247
Van Gelden, 27:110
Van Gelderen, Marcus, 21:197, 214; 23:179; 25:140-41; 35:307
Van Heyden, Dirk, 26:269
Van Hook, Aaron, 27:249
Van Hook, Colonel, 26:179
Van Hoorne, Melchior, 33:108
Van Horn, Abraham, 35:184
Van Horne, Cornelius, 21:32
Vanier, Abr., 48:21
Van Kirk, Walter W., 46:350-51
Vanlew, John N., 27:506
Van Nassau, Johan Maurits, 42:253; 46:42-43
Van Ness, 22:75

Van Oettingen, Hendla-Iehochanan, 27:34
Van Olen, Cornelis, 33:123
Van Olen, Jan, 33:123
Van Olen, John, 27:249
Van Ottinger, A. A., 21:149, 155, 170, 214; 27:41, 240, 253
Van Pauw, Reinier, 31:175-76, 178
Van Pelt, Peter I., The Happiness of Israel and America, 35:xvii
Van Praag, A. S., 27:514
Van Praag, Morris, 27:271
Van Praag, Solomon, 27:271
Van Rensselaer, Gratz, 22:58-59; "A Note on Rebecca Gratz and Gratz Van Rensselaer," 29:xxix; "Rebecca Gratz and Gratz Van Rensselaer," 31:241
Van Rensselaer, James, 31:241
Van Rensselaer, Philip, 31:241
Van Rensselaer, Stephen (1), 22:184
Van Rensselaer, Stephen (2), 27:376
Van Ruyven, Cornelis, 34:274
Van Schaack, Cornelius, 27:249
Van Schaick, Sybrant G., 27:156-57
Van Schayck, 26:247
Van Shank, M., 27:119
Van Schoppe, Sigis Mundus, 33:121
Van Sickle, James, 31:227
Van Swellen, Asser Levy, 21:xiv; 22:151
Van Tienhoven, Cornelis, 34:274
Van Tiffele, L. Y., 45:213
Van Tuyl, Otter, 34:271
Van Walbeeck, Johannes, 42:108
Van Weazle, Alexan, 21:171
Van Wyck, Abraham, 27:249
Van Wyck, Augustus, 43:31
Van Wyck family, 41:110
Van Wyck, Pierre C., 25:56
Van Wyck, Theodore, 28:226
Van Wyck, Theodorus, 27:249
Van Wyck, Mrs. William P., gift, 35:xix
Van Wyckersloot, Sophia, 26:247
Vargas, Antonia de (Nunes), 29:11
Vargas, Izabel de (Nunes), 29:11
Vargas, Luis Mendes, 29:12
Vargas, Maria de, 29:11-12
Varian, Michl, 21:112
Varick, Henry, 27:241
Varick, John, 27:242
Varick, Richard, 27:158; 46:38-39

Varnhagen, Francisco Adolfo de, 42:240
Varnhagen, Rachel, 40:119
Varon, David J., 39:442
Varrick, 21:170
Vas, Abraham, 44:227
Vasall, Johannes, 37:417
Vashti McCollum case, 40:97
Vass, Emanuel, 28:215
Vatican, 45:38; library, *I Manoscritti Palatini Ebraici*, 35:xxii
Vaughan, Benjamin, 37:151
Vaughan, Lord, 23:26
Vaux, Richard, 146
Vavelberg, Ippolit A., 43:58, 65
Vaxer, Menasseh, "Clippings from New York Papers, 1814-1854," 37:xxxi; "Haym M. Solomon Frees His Slave," 37:xxxi, 447-48; "Hebrew Volunteers" in Maryland, 37:448-49; "H. M. Solomon's Emancipation of His Slave," 37:xxxi; "Isaac Gomez Jr.-John Adams Correspondence," 37:xxxi, 444-47; naturalization, 38:235-237; "Naturalization Role of Jews of New York (1740-1759)," 37:xxx, 369-89; 49:230
Vaz, Aharon Nunes, 29:28
Vaz, Antonio, 33:56
Vaz, Antonio Rodriguez, 29:11
Vaz, David, 44:249
Vaz, Diogo, 29:22
Vaz, Isaac, 25:115
Vaz, Isaac Nunes, 25:115
Vaz, Jacob, 25:116
Vaz, Leah, 25:115-16
Vaz, Maria Franca, 29:11-12
Vaz, Phenias, 25:115-16
Vaz, Rafael, 29:22
Veail, John, 27:249
Veblen, Thorstein, 42:342
Veer, Abraham de, 22:130
Vehu, Manuel Vaaz, 33:117
Veiga, Samuel da, 42:220, 258, 285
Veit, David, 26:100
Veit, Dorothea, 26:97
Veit, Moritz, 41:268
Veits, Esther, 26:209
Veits, Guttel, 26:209
Veits, Isaac, 26:209
Veits, Sophia (Moses), 26:209
Veits, Sprintz, 26:209

Velho, Samuel, 33:95, 97
Vellosino, Jacob de Andrade (Brazil), 22:156
Velosino, Jeosua, 42:279, 390, 395
Velozinos, Jehosua, 33:55; 42:237, 254, 279, 281, 290, 390, 395
Vendig, Sol, 31:150
Veneziani, Emanuel, 37:56, 69, 76, 86, 88; 41:129, 135-37, 144-47, 153; 42:178; 43:41; 48:97
Veneziani, F., 24:30, 39, 47, 50
Veneziani, M., 29:97
Venir, Samuel, 27:45
Venning, R., 32:30
Venor, Manuel, 27:81
"Venus of the Louvre," 45:256-57
Vera, Pedro Lopes de, 33:117
Vera Cruz Affair, 1914, 28:xli
Verband der Vereine für jüdische Geschichte und Literatur in Deutschland, 26:285
Verbeeck, Jan, 26:247
Verde, Maria de Cabo, 33:117
Verdi Club, 31:259
Verdier, Captain, 27:494
Verdugo, Aaron, 32:63
Vere Beau Clerk, Lord, 49:33-34
Verein für Kultur und Wissenschaft der Juden, 41:12; 43:183-85
Verein zur Abwehr des Antisemitismus, 31:190
Verga, Ibn, 44:64-65
Verga, Solomon Ben, *Shebet Yehudah*, 22:112-14
Vergara, Pedro Vasquez de, 31:21-24
Vermeulen, Poulus, 33:121
Vermon, Widow, 30:63
Vermont, 50:304; "Early Town Proprietors in Vermont," 45:265
Vermont Chronicle, 40:133
Vermont General: The Unusual War Experiences of Edward Hastings Ripley, 1862-1865, 50:399
Vermont Record, The, 40:134
Vermont Tradition, 48:253
Vermont Transcript, 40:134
Vermont, University of, 48:255
Vernon, Thomas, 27:454; 37:418
Vernon, William, 27:447
Veroli, S. de, 27:512
Verplanck, 22:78
Verrend, William Samuel, *see*: Samuel, Wolf

Verrichtungen der Special Conferenz, 30:179
Versailles Peace Conference, 50:139
Versailles, Treaty of, 31:296; 40:114; 47:131
Verse, Aron, 27:176
Verspreet, Anthony, 33:108
Verster, J. F. L. de Balbian, 42:461
Vervelen, Joannes, 44:27
Vesey's Reports, 28:246
Vespasian, War of, 26:165
Vespucci, 32:xxii, 1
Vetzler, 27:91
Vice-Admiralty Court, "Jews in the Vice-Admiralty Court of Colonial Rhode Island," 37:xxx, 391-418
Vicksburg (Miss.), religious observances, mid-nineteenth century, 37:37
Vicksburg (Miss.), *Plain Dealer*, 50:179
Victor Emmanuel I, 28:13; 36:330, 334
Victor Emmanuel II, 28:187
Victor Emmanuel III, 23:103
Victoria, Queen, 31:105, 109, 125; 32:4; 46:25, 434
Victoria and Albert Museum, 31:291
Victorian Order of Nurses, 28:271
Vidal, 31:115
Vidal, André, 33:86
Vidaver, Henry, 37:64; 45:71-72, 82
Vieira, Antonio, 47:117-18
Vieira, João Fernando, 33:79-81, 100, 116; 43:129; 47:117
Viele, 23:142, 146
Vielska, Princess, 43:51
Viener, Saul, 43:231; 50:272; "Surgeon Moses Albert Levy, Letters of a Texas Patriot," 45:264; 46:101-13; 49:202-7
Vienna, 26:33-81, 91, 234; Congress of, 1814-1815 and Jewish emancipation, 26:33-81, 95-115
Vienna Academic Legion, 23:64
Vienna Alliance, 41:139, 146, 154
Vienna *Allianz*, 29:78, 86, 99
Vienna Committee, 29:109; 41:139, 143
Vienna, Council of, 1267, 28:144
Vienna Ministerial Conference of 1820, 26:90
Vienna, Treaty, 1815, 24:42; 26:71, 82
Viera aenda Caep, Antho., 33:115
Vieyra, D., 34:265
Vige, 23:46

Viger, 25:121
Vignaud, Henry, 22:xxi
Vigodsky, L., 39:97-99, 102
Vilace, Sid, 39:75
Vilcov, Roumania, 24:19; 36:102-6, 110
Villa, Pancho, 31:213
Villar, Francisco Perera, 33:113
Villas, Gaspa R. Gonzalvos, 33:112
Villiers (actor), 33:183
Vilman, S., 38:316
Vincennes University, 48:258
Vincent, Lady, "To Ezekiel's Status of Columbus," 28:36
Vincenzo I, Duke of Mantua, 28:193
Vincenzo Gonzago, Duke of Mantua, 28:194
Vincze, Paul, 49:150, 271
Vineberg, families, 50:134
Vineland Colony, 40:164, 273, 275, 280; 46:192; 47:109; 48:92; 49:178-79, 264
Vinera (family name), 37:385
Vinera, Daniel Rodrigues, 37:373, 386; 38:235
Vingboons, Johannes, 43:130
Vinson, Frederick Moore, 41:381
Violet, Thomas, 27:480
Viox, Camille, 41:162
Virchow, Professor, 36:358-59
Virdimura, 28:208
Vires, Juda ben Michael de, "The Mohelbook of Juda ben Michael de Vires, 1799-1818, in Surinam," 35:xvi
Virginia, 25:24, 145; 46:20; 48:152, 161; 50:24; Civil War, 50:279-80, 304, 315, 332, 343-44, 378, 383-87, 395; colonial settlement of Jews, 26:5-6; "David Franks' Interest in Lands in Virginia, in 1774," 25:119-20; Hebrew literature, 22:130; "The Gratz Papers," 23:6, 8, 12, 21-22; Jewish local history, 49:240-41; Jewish population (1790), 50:30-31, 34; Jews in law and medicine, 22:159-60, 162-63; Ordinance of Secession, 50:384-85
Virginia Historical Library, 28:xli
Virginia Historical Society, 28:223, 253; 34:117; 50:273
Virginia Magazine of History and Biography, 50:384
Virginia Medical College, 28:3

Virginia Military Institute, 28:2-3; 50:273, 276, 383-84
Virginia Military Institute and Battle of New Market, 50:384
Virginia State Library, 50:385
Virginia, University of, 28:43, 251; alumni bulletin, 28:47-48
Viscarilla, Professor, 28:274
Vischer, Claes Ians, 43:130
Visconti, Duke of, 28:196
Vishengradsky, Alexander, 43:51
Vita, 39:109
Vital, Hayyim, 43:236-37
Vitale, Dr., 28:173
Vitalucius of Rimini, 28:153
Viterbo, Elieser Ha-Cohen de (Theodorus de Sacerdotibus), 28:173
Vivas, David de Ishac Bueno, 44:230
Vivas, Ishac Bueno, 44:227-28
Vivas, Joseph Bueno, 44:222
Vivas, Josseph Haim Bueno, 44:230
Vladeck, B. Charney, gift, 35:xxiv
Voe, Thomas F. de, 25:37, 50
Vogelstein, 28:88
Vogelstein, Heinemann, 39:452
Vogelstein, Hermann, 39:457
Vogelstein, Ludwig, 34:247, 258; 45:152; gift, 29:xlii; "Ludwig Vogelstein Memorial Collection," 45:152; necrology of, 34:ix
Voice of Jacob, The, 23:181-82; 26:146
Volcao, Francisco Camelho, 33:118
Volk, Leonard Wells, 50:380
Volkland (actor), 33:184
Volksadvokat, Der, 44:154, 164, 166-67, 175, 185; 48:132
Volkszeitung, Die, 44:166; 48:90
Volney, Constantin Franscois Chaseboeuf, 37:188
Volta Bureau of Washington, 31:259
Voltaire, 35:203; 37:189, 198-200; 38:324; 39:212; 40:283; *Letters of Certain Jews to M. Voltaire*, 30:104, 401
Volterra, Professor, 28:59
Voluntary umpire system, 41:322-24
Volunteer Army of Texas, 46:102
Von Arnstein, Fanny, 26:38, 51-52, 66-67
Von Arnstein, Nathan, 26:51-52
Von Berg, 26:58
Von Boppard, Simon, 31:55

Von Bühl, Weil, 41:233
Von Donniges, Helena, 35:249
Von Eggert, M., 41:191
Von Elderen, Count, 22:29
Von Ense, Karl Varnhagen, 26:46, 51, 74-75, 97, 100-101
Von Ense, Rahel Varnhagen, 22:55; 26:38, 46, 51, 66-67, 73-74, 100
Von Eskeles, Cecilie, 26:38, 51
Von Eybenburg, Mariane (Meyer), 26:51
Von Gagern, 26:38
Von Gernsbach, Weil, 41:233
Von Gökingk, Leopold Friedrich Gunther, 37:176
Von Gorsdorff-Hermsdorf, Count, 35:36
Von Grotthus, Sara (Meyer), 26:51
Von Hohenlohe, Gustav, 28:51-52
Von Knonau, Gerold Meyer, 22:213
Von Ottingen, A. A., 25:47
Von Papen, 36:365
Von Raaben, Lieutenant-General, 36:263
Von Racowitza, Helena, 35:249
Von Russbach, Mayer, 38:201-2
Von Schkegel, Wilhelm, 26:97
Von Schlegel, Dorothea Mendelssohn, 26:38, 50, 98
Von Schlegel, Friedrich, 26:50, 76
Von Schmid, Anton Edler, 33:239
Von Schrotter, 26:267
Von Struve, Gustav, 38:205
Von Werthheimer, Ritter Josef, 24:22; 28:132
Vonk, Nicolass, 32:14
Voorhees, Philip Falkerson, 39:30, 33
Voorsanger, Jacob, 29:179-80; 37:47-48, 86, 257; 38:72; 40:241; 41:370; 45:143
Vorhaus, David, 50:272
Vorontzov-Dashkov, Ivan, 43:49
Vorspan, Max, 46:121
Vosburg, John R., 40:63
Vosch, Hans, 26:247
Voskhod, 38:242; 47:101; 48:29, 112; 49:91, 108, 116, 123
Vosmaer, Carel, 35:250; "The Amazon," 28:27
Voss, von, 28:110
Vossius, Isaac, 31:178
Vrede, Abraham de, 26:251
Vries, Abraham de, 33:65

W

Waad Hakolel (Rochester), 40:72
Waag, Moses, 32:63
Waage, Abraham, 27:156, 287, 289-90
Waage, Amelia Ziporah, 27:287, 290
Waage, M. G., 26:191
Waage, Mordecai, 27:156, 287, 290
Waage, Ziporah, 27:290
Waage, *see also*: Wagg
Wabash Land Company, 41:389
Wachsman, Henry, 50:313
Wachstein, Bernhard, 34:13
Waco, Texas, ritual slaughtering, 37:39
Waddington, M., 24:151; 26:159
Waddington, William Henry, 24:53, 56-60, 62-66, 70, 72, 121, 151
Wadsworth, Benjamin, 22:11-12; 35:150, 162, 164, 168; 37:134
Wadsworth, James, 22:184
Wagenseil, J. C., 28:193
Wager, Charles, 49:33-34
Wagg, Abraham, 31:36-37; 38:106; "A Jewish Voice for Peace in the War of American Independence, The Life and Writings of Abraham Wagg, 1719-1803," 31:xiv, 33-75
Wagg, David, 31:36, 42, 44
Wagg, Elkan, 31:34, 55
Wagg, Gumprecht (Ephraim), 31:34, 55
Wagg, Hart, 31:55-56
Wagg, Hart (Herman), 13:36, 55
Wagg, Judith, 31:55-56
Wagg, Margoles, 31:55-56
Wagg, Matthias, 31:42, 55
Wagg, Meir, 31:35-37, 55
Wagg, Meyer, 31:55
Wagg, Minky, 31:55-56
Wagg, Mordecai, 31:39, 42, 55
Wagg, Moses Benedict, 31:34-36, 55
Wagg, Myer (1773), 31:55-56
Wagg, Myer (1783), 31:55-56

Wagg, Phaibush, 31:34-36, 55
Wagg, Rachel, 31:57
Wagg, Uri Phoebus, 31:36
Wagg, Uriah, 21:55
Wagg, Zipporah, 31:55-56
Wagg, *see also*: Wagge
Wagge, M. G., 31:42
Wagman, Mr., 44:166
Wagner, Robert F., 36:368; 38:51; "Address by Mayor Robert F. Wagner," 44:78-79
Wagner-Rogers Bill, 45:230
Wah, Quan, 34:202
Wahl, Lutz, 31:212
Wahl, Saul, 22:132
"Wahrheit," 39:434
Wahrmann, Moritz, 24:44
Wainor, M., 38:307
Wainright, Miss, 33:174
Wais, 39:151
Waist, Silk Suits and Children's Dressmakers Union Loc. 15, Philadelphia, 45:183
Waite, Arthur E., 35:135
Waite, Morrison Remick, 43:165
Waix, Maior, 36:246-47; 41:172
Wakefield, John, 23:82
Wald, Lillian D., 41:308; 48:202, 267; 49:70, 143; "The House on Henry Street," 25:xv
Waldeck, 26:57
Waldeck-Rousseau, député, 41:162
Waldenberg, David, 36:231
Waldenberg, Jacob, 36:231
Waldman, Louis I., necrology of, 29:xxxvi, 193-94
Waldman, Szejwa, 34:212, 214
Waldron, Mr., 25:56
Waldron, Captain, 38:47
Waley, Professor, 29:86
Walker, B., 26:156
Walker, Francis A., 46:128, 367

Walker, Francis Eugene, 46:295, 316-17
Walker, Guy Warren, Jr., 42:418
Walker in the City, A, 46:316, 438, 444
Walker, James, 35:169
Walker, John, 31:182, 184-85, 229
Walker, Leroy Pope, 50:322
Walker, Norman, 31:214
Walker, Robert, 32:126
Walker, Robert I., 43:94
Walker, William, 23:139
Wall (actor), 33:175
Wall and Lindsay, 33:176
Wall Street Church (New York), 27:92
Wallace, Mr., 27:239
Wallace, David, 50:387
Wallace, Edwin S., 36:60
Wallace, Judge, 44:155
Wallace, Lewis, 36:43-45; 39:116; 40:336
Wallace, Louis, 47:84
Wallace, McKenzie, 36:394, 399
Wallace, William S., 38:331; 39:477; "A
   Russian Incident: 1894-1897," 38:347;
   39:67-86
Wallach, Moses Abraham, 23:86; 40:120
Wallach family (Philadelphia), 22:34
Wallachia, Roumania, 24:20, 98, 102-4, 112,
   115, 117-19, 138-40, 151
Wallack, H., 27:120
Wallack, J. W., Jr., 50:299
Wallack, Moses, 50:26
Wallas, Graham, 39:303
Wallenrod, Reuben, 33:159
Wallenstein, Carrie Baumgarten, "Selig
   Baumgarten," 26:xv, 248
Wallenstein, Henry, necrology of, 35:x
Wallerstein (family name), 38:197
Wallis, S. Teackle, 26:288
Walls, Gamaliel, 27:250
Walpole Galleries, 28:236
Walpole, Robert, 31:37
Walrond, Benjamin, 26:254
Walsh, David I., 36:368
Walt, Abraham, 45:155
Walter, Josephine, 42:122
Walter, Mr., 40:177
Walter, Moses R., 23:145; 31:226; necrology
   of, 26:xiv, 288-89
Walter, R., & Sons, 26:285
Walter, Raphael, 26:288

Walter, Regina, 26:288
Walter, Thomas Ustick, 41:71, 73-74; 46:116
Walton, Clyde C., 50:272
Walton, Jacob, 23:152
Walton, John, 32:113
Walton, William, 23:152
Walton, William, Jr., 23:152
Wamser, Samuel, 26:184
Wanamaker, John, 41:34, 363
Wandering Jew, The, 30:51; 33:174, 185;
   45:21
Wangenheim, 26:89
Wanhope, Joshua, 50:230
Wanton, John (Gov.), 27:416
Wanton, Joseph, Jr., 23:165-66
Wanton, Stephen, 21:81
Wanton, William, 23:166
Warburg, Felix M., 33:21; 37:480; 40:397;
   Alliance Israelite, 39:440; Jewish
   education, 35:62; Max J. Kohler, 34:258;
   necrology of, 35:x, 323-25; necrology of
   Arnold W. Brunner, 31:xxiii, 253-55;
   Y.M.H.A., 37:306-7
Warburg, Mrs. Felix M., gift, 35:xix; 37:12
Warburg, Frederick, 25:134; 43:177
Warburg, M. M. and Company, 36:141
Warburg, Moritz, 35:323
Warburg, Otto, 31:199, 203
Warburg, Paul M., 22:238; 31:203; necrology
   of, 33:xxi
Ward, 44:43-44
Ward, Adjutant, 38:48
Ward, Adolphus, 26:37-38
Ward, Edward, 23:7
Ward, Elizabeth Stuart Phelps, 42:350
Ward, Henry Dana, *Israel and the Holy Land*,
   30:381
Ward, Mrs. Humphrey, 34:233-36
Ward, John (1), 34:234
Ward, John (2), 38:274-75
Ward, Mr., 37:408, 417
Ward, Mrs., 38:273
Ward, Samuel Gray, 38:261, 273
Ward, Thomas, 38:273, 275, 282-84
Wardell, William T., 33:216-19, 221, 223
Ward's Island Refuge, 49:180, 184
Ware, Edith Ellen, 42:134
Ware, William, *Julian, Or Scenes in Judes*,
   30:361

Warfield, David, 26:187
Warheit, 33:129; 50:212, 214, 217-18
War Between the States, *see*: Civil War
"War in Books: A Basic Civil War Diary,
The," 50:401
War Industries Board, 47:190
Warinsky, Israel, 29:132
War Labor Policies Board of World War I,
47:190
Warner, Benjamin, 35:282
Warner, Ezra J., 50:342
Warner, George H., 35:125
Warner, Jane (nee Hart), 27:77, 112
Warner, Richard, 28:250
Warner, William, 25:52; 27:77, 85, 314
War of 1812, 22:155, 163, 165; 26:7; 27:337,
464, 495; 46:269; 50:13; "Jews in the War
of 1812," 22:xiii, xxix; 26:173-200; "The
Jews in the Wars of the United States,"
26:xxiv, xxv, xxvii
War of Vespasian, 26:165
War of Independence, *see*: Revolutionary
War
War records, 28:xxii
War Refugee Board, 47:195
War Relief Board, 46:354
Warren, Admiral, 49:59
Warren, Charles, 26:153
Warren, Fiske, 35:36
Warren, Israel, 46:168
Warren, James, 37:115-17; 40:80
Warren, John, 35:291-92
Warren, Joseph, 43:201
Warren, Rev., 44:155
Warren, Thomas, 31:232
Warrensky, Israel, 46:168
Warsaw massacres, 36:208, 212, 274
Warsaw, N.Y., religious observances, mid-
nineteenth century, 37:38
Warschauer, A., 28:110
Washburn, Emory, 23:85
Washburn, Israel, 22:141
Washburne, Elihu B., 24:20-21, 30; 36:190;
40:185; 43:122
Warsower, S., 29:132
Warszawski, Szymon, 39:151
Washington Academy of Science, 33:22
Washington and Lee University, 31:296;
39:118, 120, 122; 40:8

Washington Bi-centenary Commission, gift,
33:xxxiii
Washington, Bishop, 50:89
Washington, Booker T., 46:274
Washington College, 39:120, 122, 126
Washington (D.C.), Civil War, 50:260, 279-
80, 289, 293, 299-300, 306, 317, 328, 349,
351-52, 371, 381, 405; "Isaac Polock: Early
Settler in Washington, D.C.," 48:1-18;
religious observances, mid-nineteenth
century, 37:36
Washington, George, 21:172-73; 22:71;
26:221; 27:36, 126, 482; 28:xxxiv, 5, 300;
29:xix; 33:4, 173; 34:xxi, xxv, 168; 35:133,
135, 143; 37:32, 196; 38:15, 338; 39:9;
40:77; 41:83; 42:429; 43:15, 163; 46:3;
addresses to Jewish congregations, 22:xx,
xxxi; 38:18; American Israelites, 49:17;
anti-Semitism, 38:120, 133; bookplates,
50:395-96; "Calendar of the
Correspondence of George Washington,
Commander in Chief of the Continental
Army, with the Continental Congress,"
25:113; census, 50:23-24, 35; church-state,
43:135; civil liberties, 46:39;
correspondence with, 27:xvi, xvii, 217-22,
496-97; 32:xxv; 34:20, 191; 38:5; 39:210;
42:109; 43:236-37; 45:65; 48:144; 49:5; "As
to the Supposed 18th Century Translation
into Hebrew of Washington's
Correspondence with Hebrew
Congregations," 32:121; "David Franks
and George Washington," 31:235-36;
Graetz *v.* Cohen, 37:345, 347; Isaac
Polock, 48:2, 4, 8; Jewish physicians,
22:163; and Jews, 28:xxii; 33:7; Masonry,
23:xvii, 4, 7; 28:299; "A Messenger to
George Washington," 37:xxxiii, 115-19;
pay for troops, 22:196; Philadelphia, 22:56;
religious tolerance, 46:270, 272;
"Washington and Mosaic Law," 39:319-20
Washington Hebrew Congregation, 26:213;
29:202; 39:43; 41:373; 48:242
Washington Hebrew Congress,
Congressional Charter, 26:213-17
Washington Heights Hospital, 31:259
Washington Host Committee, 47:200, 202-3
Washington Jewish Tercentenary, 48:10
Washington, John P., 45:215

Washington Literacy and Dramatic
Association, 29:201
Washington Market, 25:45
Washington Monument, 37:74
Washington, Peter G., 39:35
Washington Post, 33:214-15, 223, 225
Washington Republican, 22:78
Washington Star, The, 26:218; 33:225, 227
Wassermann, Aron, 41:267
Wassermann, David, 23:100; 34:252; 41:257
Wassermann, Karl, 41:268
Wassermann, Löw, 41:261
Wassermann, M., "Judah Touro," 23:xvii;
29:xlii
Wassermann, Moses, 35:129; 46:431
Wasson, David, 42:83
Wastell, Samuel, 43:9; 45:53
Watchmaker, David M., 42:419
Watchorn, Robert, 24:109, 111
Waterhouse, Benjamin, 42:345
Waterman, Hannah, 28:5
Waterman, James, *The Legend of Louise: The
Life Story of Mrs. Stephen S. Wise*, reviewed,
39:333-35
Waterman, Leopold, "Leopold Waterman,
Merchant, Poet, and Lay-Preacher in New
Haven (1841-?)," 37:xxxi
Waterson, William, 25:77
Watertown, Weltbürger, 41:249
Waterview (Va.), "The Jewish Colony at
Waterview, Virginia," 45:265
Watervliet Arsenal, 48:147-66
Wätjen, Herman J. E., 35:134; 47:112; 50:75;
Brazilian Jewish history, 33:44; "Colonial
Empire of Holland in Brazil," 29:xliii;
Dutch in Brazil, 31:xxxi
Watkins Institute, 45:147
Watkins *v.* Watkins, 29:151
Watson, 29:172
Watson, Elkanah, 25:82-83
Watson, Jacob, 35:290
Watson, Lieutenant, 23:122
Watson, P. H., 43:106
Watson, Richard, *Biblical and Theological
Dictionary*, 30:363
Watson, Thomas Edward, 40:324
Watson, Tom, 47:32
Watt, 32:30

Watters, Leon L., 38:333; book review by,
44:66; "Davy Isaacs of Charlottesville,"
31:xxx; "The Earliest Jewish Settlers in
Utah," 29:xxxvi; "Early Jews in the Far
West: Random Notes," 45:265; "Early
Jews of Utah," 40:407; *The Pioneer Jews of
Utah*, 49:239-40
Watters, Thomas, 27:319
Watts, Isaac, 37:441; 42:399-400; *Short View
of the Whole Scripture History*, 30:114
Watts, John, 50:352
Watts, Jr. (Dr.), 26:222
Watts, T. H., 50:386
Watts, W. W., 45:53
Waud, Alfred R., 50:343, 373
Waugh, Julia M., "Castroville and Henry
Castro," 34:xxvii; gift, 34:xxvii
Wax, Bernard, 50:272
Wax, James A., 47:201; 50:407; executive
council, 50:426; "The Jews of Memphis,
1860-1865," 49:239
Waxman, Meyer, 33:149; 44:125
Way, Drusilla, 26:120
Way, Lewis, 26:82-85, 88, 91-93; 28:84, 114;
29:154; 34:222; 43:172-73; "The Influence
of Lewis Way and Other English
Missionaries upon Alexander I's
Treatment of the Jews," 26:116-25
Wayland, Dr., 30:466
Wayne, Caleb P., 38:132, 134
We Americans, 40:356
"We Are Coming Father Abra'am," 50:389-
91
Weather Bureau, 47:192
Weaver, William A., 39:19
Webb, Alexander Stewart, 47:78
Webb, Beatrice, 41:305, 337
Webb; Cohen *v.*, 26:260
Webb, James Watson, 22:82, 85-87
Webb, Joseph, 27:250
Webb, P. Cartaret, 31:121
Webber, 22:205
Webber, Aernout, 31:90
Webber, Anneken, 31:89-90
Webber, Wolphert, 31:88-91, 93, 95, 99,
102-3
Weber, J. C., 36:390
Weber, Max, 37:148; 46:261
Weberblum, Herman, 41:374

Webster, Daniel, 25:16; 26:184, 200, 271; 27:400; 34:176; 42:346; 46:276; Joseph Abraham correspondence, 21:507-8; Judah P. Benjamin, 38:158-60, 166; Swiss Treaty, 36:300

Webster, John, *The Devil's law case,* 33:178

Webster, Noah, 42:457; 43:12

Wechsler, Albert, 42:419

Wechsler colony, 38:306-7

Wechsler, Dr. J., 38:307

Wechsler, Joseph, 48:87

Wechsler, Judah, 40:239

Weddings, 39:379-83, 385

Wedeles (family name), 38:197

Wedum, A. J., 39:83

Weed, Thurlow, 43:115

Weekday Religious Education Association, 38:337

Weekly Gleaner, The, 38:154-56, 158-61, 164

Weekly Register, The, 50:3-22

Weems, Mason L., 32:6

Wegelin, Oscar, 30:60

Weglein, David, 31:227

Wehle (family name), 38:195

Weigel (family name), 38:197

Weil, 35:68

Weil, A. Leo, 37:307; 49:195; necrology of Louis I. Aaron, 28:xxxii, 257-58

Weil, Mrs. Benjamin F., 28:315

Weil, Bernard S., 47:42

Weil, Clara Esther, 27:237

Weil, E., 29:131

Weil, Frank Leopold, 38:7, 343; awards, 47:232; executive council, 38:344; 39:470; 46:493; necrology of, 47:201, 230-33

Weil, Gotshal and Manges, 47:230

Weil, Gustave, 45:26; *The Bible, the Koran and the Talmud,* 30:420

Weil, Henri, 41:162

Weil, Henry Isaac, 27:237

Weil, Isak, 41:257

Weil, Leopold, 47:230

Weil, M. S., 40:239

Weil, Maier, 41:262

Weil, Majer, 41:142

Weil, Marx, 41:267

Weil, Rebecca, 47:230

Weil, Richard, 50:396

Weil, Simone, 46:441

Weil, Sol, 38:72

Weil, W. H., 28:xxxviii

Weill, Aaron, 36:352-54

Weill, Felix, 40:169

Weill, Isidore, 41:370, 373

Weill, Jeanne, 35:260

Weill, Julien, 37:475

Weill, Louis, 35:260

Weill, Solomon, 40:140, 151, 169

Wein, Hyman, 45:162

Wein, Susan, 45:162

Weinberg, Gabriel, 29:129

Weinberg, Jacob, 50:393

Weinberg, Walter, 39:151

Weinberger, B. W., gifts, 32:xxvi; 33:xxxiii

Weinberger, Moses, 44:134-35; 46:387-87

Weinbrenner, Friedrich, 41:68-69

Weiner, Theodore, 23:63-73, 75

Weiner, Zeeb, 33:161

Weingart, Isaac, 34:182-83

Weingart, Lena B., 34:186

Weinrich, Max, 46:265-67, 409; "Yidishkayt and Yiddish," 43:197

Weinryb, Bernard, 37:172; 46:186-89, 404, 408-11, 413, 417-18; "Jewish Immigration and Accommodations in America, Research, Trends, Problems," 46:366-403; 48:66; "Noah's Ararat-Jewish State in its Historical Setting," 41:390; 43:170-91; "Yiddish and Hebrew Fiction as a Source of American Jewish History," 44:242

Weinstein, Lewis, 42:419

Weinstein, W., 29:130

Weinstock, A., 29:134

Weinstock, Barbara Felsenthal, 29:195-96

Weinstock, Harris, necrology of, 29:xxix, 194-98

Weinstock, Harry C., 41:374

Weinstock, Robert, 29:196

Weinstock, Solomon, 29:194

Weinstock, Walter, 29:196

Weinstock and Lubin Company, 29:195

Weinstock-Lubin Real Estate Company, 29:196

Weinstock-Nicholas, 29:196

Weintal, Edward, 34:230

Weis, 39:151

Weis, Josef, 41:255

Weis, Julius, 40:247; 50:195

Weisberg, William, 29:68
Weisberger, Rosamond Hutzler, 37:473;
  necrology of Jacob Harry Hollander,
  37:471-73
Weisberger, Siegfried, 37:473
Weisblum, Eliezer Lipa, 33:154
Weisen, Naphtali, 33:159
Weisl, Edwin L., executive council, 37:xxxvi;
  38:342; 39:470; 40:406; 43:231
Weisman, Mordecai, 47:197
Weiss, A., 39:104, 106
Weiss, B., 33:186
Weiss, Charles, "Recent Developments
  Relating to the Practice of Milah in the
  United States," 50:427
Weiss, Eric, 45:200
Weiss, H. B., 40:47
Weiss, Harry, 45:179, 199, see also: Houdini
Weiss, Isaac Hirsch, 25:178-79; 28:72; 45:70
Weiss, John, 42:83
Weiss, Julius, "Autobiography of Julius
  Weiss," 33:xxxi
Weiss, Louise, 34:242
Weiss, M. (San Francisco), 37:45
Weiss, Miriam, 31:297
Weiss, Moritz, 40:69
Weiss, Phineas, 33:159
Weiss, S., 44:165
Weiss, Samuel, 26:184; 41:254
Weisskopf, F. C., 50:112, 115, 120
Weissman, Henry, 34:xxiii
Weiszäcker, Ernst, 36:382
Weitzman (Russian Jew), 47:108; 48:36
Weizmann, Chaim, 36:69, 71, 74-75; 39:333;
  45:37; 46:184; Trial and Error: The
  Autobiography of Chaim Weizmann,
  reviewed, 39:202-5
Welch, G., 29:131
Welch, William H., 42:122
Welcome, Haim, 27:120
Weld, William, 42:352
Welfare, "Jewish Welfare Activities for the
  Military During the Spanish-American
  War," 41:357-80
Weller, 25:14
Welles, Gideon, 32:95
Welles, Sumner, 36:383-85; 39:333
Welles, Titus, 27:428-30, 436-37
Wellford, Mrs. J. McDonald, 42:418

Wellhausen, Julius, 40:25
Wellhoff Bros. (San Francisco), 37:45
Wellington, Duke of, 26:38, 50-51, 82, 267
Wells, 31:121
Wells & Fargo Banking Office, 44:47
Wells, Herbert George, 35:261; 38:12
Wells, Linton, 41:34-35
Wells, Mrs. T. B., 50:347
Weltbürger und Anzeiger, 41:249
Weltsch, Felix, 50:116
Weltsch, Robert, 49:141
Wendell, Sarah, 42:343
Wendell, W. G., 35:257
Wendover, Mr., 22:79; 25:56
Wentz, Jacob, 26:183
Wenzel, King of Bohemia, 28:156
Werber, Baruch, 45:72, 81
Werfel, Franz, 39:330; 45:199; 50:112, 116-
  17
Werne, Isaac, 33:142
Werner, Adolph, necrology of, 28:xxii, 311-
  12
Werner, Edward, 28:311
Werner, Eric, 40:49; 47:181; Jewish
  Contribution to Music, reviewed, 40:195-96
Werner, Ida, 28:312
Werner, Julian, 44:132
Werner, Maurice, 29:131
Wertenbaker, Thomas Jefferson, 39:283-85
Werth, Léon, 42:160
Wertheim, A., 27:68
Wertheim, Maurice, 49:190
Wertheimer, Baron von, 29:77, 86, 95
Wertheimer, Bela, 41:262
Wertheimer, Henriette, 41:262
Wertheimer, Immanuel, 41:259
Wertheimer, Isaac, 29:132
Wertheimer, Joseph von, 28:132; 41:139, 142
Wertheimer, M., 29:130
Wertheimer, Moses, 41:262
Wertheimer, Samson, 34:14
Wertheimer, Samuel, 41:259
Wertheimer, Wolf, 34:14
Wesleyan University, 37:471
Wessel, Bessie Bloom, 40:205; book review
  by, 40:196-98
Wessel, Henry N., necrology of, 28:xxxii,
  313-14
Wessel, M. J., 23:98

Wesseley, Wolfgang, 22:201
Wessels, L. W., 50:387
Wessels, Peter, 34:271
Wessely, Naphtali Hartwig, 28:84, 91, 102-3, 118; 37:359
Wessenberg, Baron von, 26:37, 39-40, 65
West, Mr., 35:175
West, Mrs., 40:78
West, Benjamin (1769), 22:47
West, Nancy, 50:176
West, Syshorus, 27:320
West, T. S., 47:53
West, Thomas, 35:184
Westchester, 29:169
Westchester County, 29:168-69
Westchester County Commission on County Government, 29:168
Westchester Historical Society, 29:169
Westchester State Normal School, 29:168
West Chester (Pa.), Kesher Israel Charity Fund, contribution, 37:xxviii
Westcott, James D., 25:16-17
Westcott, Thompson, 29:172
West End Educational Union (Boston), 46:78
West End Synagogue (New York), 45:190-91
Wester, Gasper, 27:300
Westergaard, Waldemar, 28:216; 44:114
Western New York Jewish Orphan Asylum Society, 40:68
Western Steam Tobacco Works, 47:37
Western Synagogue, "Records of the Western Synagogue 1761-1832," 33:xxxii
Westheimer, Benjamin S., 28:315
Westheimer, Duffie (Heinsheimer), 28:285
Westheimer family, gift, 25:xvi
Westheimer, Johanna (Haas), 25:124; 35:134; necrology of, 28:xv, 314-15
Westheimer, Samuel, 28:314; 35:131; "Memorial Note on Samuel Westheimer," 25:xiii, 124-25
West India Committee (London), 25:149
West India Company, 21:175-81; 22:126; 28:246; 32:8-9, 12, 15, 17; 33:43-125; 42:108, 217, 245; 47:127
West Indian archives, 32:xxvii
West Indies, 25:43, 149; 28:214-16, 218-19; 32:xxiii; civil rights, 26:6; "Extracts from Various Records of the Early Settlement of the Jews in Barbados, W.I.," 26:xxxiii, 250-

56; "Gabriel Milan, the Jewish Governor of St. Thomas, Danish West Indies," 26:xxxi; "The Gratz Papers," 23:2, 5; history, writing of, 46:188, 292, 381, 422; "Jewish Settlement in the West Indies," 37:353-67; Jews in, 26:5-6; "List of Wills of Jews in the British West Indies Prior to 1800," 32:55-64; Lost Ten Tribes, 37:353-67; "Records of a West Indian Mohel," 25:114; trade, 26:243-44
West Indies Company for the Exploitation of Culture-Enterprises, 48:23
Westkett, John, 31:44
Westliche Monatsschrift, 41:249
West London Synagogue of British Jews, 27:524; 31:262; 42:440
Westmann, Mr., 36:109-10
Westminister Assembly, 47:144
Westminister, Marquess of, 26:267
Westminister Review, The, 38:268
Weston, Charles, 23:161
West 134th Street Realty Co.; Commonwealth Securities Co. v., "Anglo-Jewish Legal Cases," 25:138
Westphalia, 26:35; Westphalian Jewish Consistory, 28:104-5
West Point, "Simon M. Levy, Member of the First Class to Graduate at the United States Military Academy of 1802," 23:xiv
West Virginia, Civil War, 50:279, 304, 310-11; "The Gratz Papers," 23:1, 11; Jewish local history, 49:241-42
Westwood, N.J., Temple Emanuel, contributions, 37:xxviii
Wetherill, Thomas, 35:182
Wetmore, Prosper M., 30:404; 39:35
Wetterhahn, M., 29:130
Wetterhon, Levy, 42:63
Wetumpka Daily Stateguard, 50:192
We Who Built America, 46:302
Wexler, Joseph, 35:6
Wexley, John, 35:276
Weyl, Monsieur, 36:74
Weyler, R., 38:65
Weyman, W., 22:50-51, 161
Wharton, Edith, 35:262; 40:341
Wharton, Samuel, 23:20, 23; 30:77
Wharton, Thomas, 23:20, 23; 30:77
Wharton, William F., 36:236-37

Whately, Archbishop, 26:268
What Price Glory, 40:357
Wheat, *Exposition of the Parable of the Tares and Wheat*, 30:370, 372
Wheaton, 22:80
Wheelan, Albertine Randall, 45:143
Wheeler, Joseph, 41:368-69; 43:29; 50:397-98
Wheeler, Rev., 22:24
Wheelock, Eleazer, 45:133
Wheelock, John Hall, 35:257
Wheelright, George, 46:103
Whelpley, James D., 41:193-94
"When Lilacs Last in the Dooryard Bloom'd" (Hebrew translations), 50:401-2
When We Were Twenty-one, 40:354
Whimster, David, 27:68
Whiskey Insurrection, 38:136
Whistler, Henry, 35:294
Whiston, *Josephus*, 31:xxxiii
Whiston, William, 30:97
White, Alfred T., 30:3
White, Andrew D., 28:26, 41-43; 33:27; 36:185-88, 229-30, 232, 237-41, 352-63, 389-402; 41:184-85
White, Mrs. Andrew D., 28:26, 41
White, Anthony, 23:152
White, Arnold, 36:226; 43:37-39, 44-53, 55
White, Bernard S., 32:64; 47:202
White, Campbell P., 22:82; 30:404
White Caps, 40:71
White, George, 26:193
White, H. W., 39:83
White, Henry, 36:36-37, 39-40
White, James, 43:204
White, John, 32:86
White, Philo, 39:32
White, Richard, 50:160
White, Samuel, 22:192-93
White, T., 28:248
White, Thomas W., 39:132
White, William (Dublin), 27:250
White, William (rev.), 37:189; 41:68
White, William A., 24:124, 142; 36:49
White, William Allen, 40:342-43
Whitefield, George, 22:15; *Answer to Testimony Against Rev. George Whitefield*, 30:41-42; *Testimony Against Rev. George Whitefield*, 30:38-41
Whitehall Conference, 27:480; 31:116-17

Whitehead, Alfred North, 39:304
Whitehead Report, 36:93
Whitehorne, Samuel, 35:290
White House Conference on Aging, 50:434
White Labor Servitude, Pennsylvania, 34:30-49
Whitelock, Hohn, 37:412
Whiteman, Kolmon, 33:155-56
Whiteman, Maxwell, 43:238; 49:62, 209; 50:70; books reviewed by, 46:68-69; 48:199-201; Civil War, 50:270-71, 296, 382; "David Franks, Jew, Merchant and Suspected Tory," 44:242; executive council, 46:493; 49:268; "German Jews and Jewish Journalism in Nineteenth-Century America," 47:202; "The History of the Jews of Philadelphia from Colonial Times to the Age of Jackson," 49:234-35; history, writing of, 46:178, 182, 411-12; "Isaac Leeser and the Jews of Philadelphia: A Study in National Jewish Influence," 48:207-44; 49:235; presides, 49:268; "The Role and Efforts of Isaac Leeser and Philadelphia in Organizing the American Jewish Community," 48:266; "Zionism Comes to Philadelphia," 49:235; *see also*: Wolf, Edwin II
Whitfield, Charles, 27:211
Whitfield, Sally, 27:426
Whitlock, Elizabeth, 50:64
Whitman, Charles Seymour, 40:9; 49:10
Whitman, Edward B., 23:74
Whitman, Walt, 38:262; 45:16, 34; 46:289, 477; 50:268, 401-2
Whitney Bank, 28:309
Whitney Central National Bank, 28:309
Whitney, James W., 44:98
Whitridge, John, 43:74
Whittaker, B., 34:267
Whittaker, Samuel, 31:162
Whittier, John Greenleaf, 38:174; 39:116; 42:341
Whom Shall We Welcome, 46:291-92, 296, 300-305, 314-15
Who's Who in American Jewry, 50:394
Why the Civil War?, 50:399
Why Was Lincoln Murdered?, 50:398
Wice, David, 41:89, 91
Wichers, J. G., 22:27

Wickham, Benjamin, 27:450
Wickham, William C., 27:506
Wickliffe, Governor (Ky.), 25:18
Wickliffe, Mr. (N.Y.), 23:119
Wickliffe, Miss (Mrs. David L. Yulee), 25:18-19, 26-29
Widener Library, 42:459
Wiener, Leo, 45:137
Wiener, M., 29:127
Wiener, Max, 40:49
Wiernik, Peter, 28:155, 125; 29:75; 34:182, 223, 256; 45:161; 47:125; bookplates, 45:166, 176, 191-92; "History of the Jews in America," 33:xxx; necrology of, 35:ix
Wiesl, L., 29:133
Wigfall, Louis T., 50:318
Wigglesworth, Edward, 22:11; 30:41; 35:167-68
Wigglesworth, Michael, 22:1, 6; 47:143
Wight, Isle of, 29:43, 50-51
Wightman, William, 31:108
Wigington, Henry, 41:77-80
Wignell, T., 33:177, 183
Wihl, 29:127
Wijmants, Jan, 33:112, 123
Wijnties, Balthazar, 33:123
Wilansky, D., Sinai to Cincinnati, 35:xix
Wilberforce, William, 26:119-20
Wilbor, Constant, 35:291
Wilbore, William, 27:175
Wilbour, Job, 27:437, 439
Wilburn, Cora, 22:xii
Wilcox, Samuel, 22:191
Wilczynski, Max, 36:179, 184-88, 192, 198, 203
Wilde, de, 32:14
Wilden, David Valentine van der, 25:42
Wilden, Symon van der, 25:42
Wildey, Edward, 27:326
Wilds, Samuel, 48:181, 188-90
Wile, Brickner & Wile, 40:70-71
Wile Brothers, 40:65
Wile, Frederic William, 29:xix; nomination committee, 29:xxviii; thirty-first annual meeting, committee on, 29:xxvi
Wile, Gabriel, 40:59
Wile, Isaac A., 40:58, 65
Wile, Joseph, 40:59
Wile, Solomon, 40:65

Wilensky, Joseph, 46:191
Wilensky, Michael, 40:49
Wilensky, Mordecai L., 46:191
Wiley, Louis, 40:70; 42:371, 374
Wilhelm I, 24:75
Wilhelm II, 34:243
Wilhelm, Kurt, book review by, 48:138-39
Wilhelm School of Breslau, 28:104
Wilhelmina, Queen, 42:467
Wilkes, Mr., 31:129-30, 133
Wilkes, George, 34:144
Wilkes' Spirit of the Times, 34:143
Wilkins, Mr., 22:89
Wilkins, Charles, 38:264
Wilkins, John, 23:14, 18
Wilkins, Major, 35:13-14, 16
Wilkinson brothers, 23:63, 69
Wilkinson, Dorothy (Massiah), 22:180
Wilkinson, General, 26:174
Wilkinson, James, 48:9
Wilkinson, Senator, 27:466
Wilkinson, William, 22:180
Will, William, 41:291
Willard, Joseph, 37:442
Willard, Joseph E., 36:74-75, 141
Willard, Samuel, 30:iv; The Fountain Opened, 30:11, 13, 26, 28-29, 32-33
Willard, Sidney, "Hebrew Grammar," 26:xxxv; 30:177
Willcocks, Schemes, 47:166
Willemsen, Cornelis, 26:247
Willen, Joseph, executive council, 41:388
Willes, Lord, 31:110
Willet, Abraham, 27:250
Willet, Dr., 32:31
Willet family, 41:110
Willet, Isaac, 27:250
Willet, John, 27:250
Willet, Thomas, 27:250
Willett, Henry, 27:71
Willey, Noy, 27:39, 46, 70, 299; 31:94-97, 98-100, 102
William I (Holland), 22:35; 26:72
William I (Kaiser), 26:284; 36:348
William II (England), 35:130
William III (England), 27:482; 31:121; 42:72; "Documents Relating to the History of the Jews in Jamaica and Barbados in the Time of William III," 23:vii, 25-29

William IV (England), 27:521; 26:255-56
William the Conqueror, 21:238; 41:383
William the Silent, 47:114
William (slave), 50:161
William and Mary, 23:26
William of Norwich, 34:xxiii
William, Prince of Orange, 29:27; 42:438
William Rufus, King of England, 21:238
Williams (1), 27:437
Williams (2), 31:106
Williams, Archibald, 44:99, 102
Williams, Caroline R., 28:251
Williams College, 25:84; 28:266; 49:11, 56
Williams, Commissioner, 34:199
Williams, D., 27:432
Williams, David, 27:427
Williams, E., 27:73
Williams, E. C., 38:26, 36
Williams, Ezekiel (1), 27:71
Williams, Ezekiel (2), 37:111, 113
Williams, Frank M., 50:229, 236
Williams, G. W., 34:190
Williams, George H., 41:36
Williams, H. H., 23:67
Williams, Mrs. Henry J., 23:181
Williams, J. A., 27:415, 459
Williams, J. H., 41:48
Williams, Jenkin, 23:49-50
Williams, John, 27:432-33
Williams, Jonathan, 43:235
Williams, Lydia, 50:177
Williams, Lyman J., 50:272, 275, 306, 362
Williams, Mat. J., 43:75
Williams, Obadiah, 27:439
Williams, R. Norris 2d, 43:238
Williams, Roger, 27:453; 31:296; 34:5-6, 169,
    190, 192; 37:140; 38:1, 18, 76; 40:4, 16, 96;
    44:65, 46:20, 24; 47:144
Williams, S., 26:193
Williams, Solomon, 47:147
Williams, Stanley, 35:237; 46:427
Williams, Thomas (1), 27:432-33; 35:174-75,
    178-79
Williams, Thomas (2), 40:86
Williams, William, 39:109
Williamson, 26:183
Williamson (actor), 33:183-84
Williamson, Henry, 35:274
Williamson, Hugh, 25:82-83

Williamson, Jonathan-Drayton, 39:19, 29
Williamson, Major, 39:344-45
Williamson, Thomas, 42:370
Williamson (W. Va.), Congregation B'nai
    Israel, contribution, 37:xxviii; United
    Jewish Charities, contribution, 37:xxviii
Williamsport (Pa.), religious observances,
    mid-nineteenth century, 37:38
Willing, Mr., 23:11
Willing, Morris & Co., 25:131; 26:270
Willis, 38:269
Willis, H., 27:75
Willis, Nathaniel P., 26:222
Willner, Wolf, 22:xiv
Willoughby College (Ohio), 26:255, 227
Willoughby, Governor, 46:34
Wilmerdonex, Abraham, 33:108-9, 120
Wills, "A List of Wills of Jews in the British
    West Indies, Proved Before 1800," 29:xxx;
    32:55-64; "The Last Will of Rabbi Haim
    Carregal, 1777," 29:xxxvii; "Notes from
    Wills of the Family of Massiah of
    Barbados," 22:xiii, 178-80; "Notes from
    the Will of Mordecai Marks, Early
    Connecticut Merchant, and Genealogical
    Data Regarding Him and His Family,"
    29:xvi; "The Simson Trust," 28:246-48;
    Solomon Harby, 32:51-52; "The Will of
    Henry Benjamin Franks, December 13,
    1758, and Inventory of His Estate," 25:xii,
    125-27; "The Will of Nathan Simson, a
    Jewish Merchant of New York before
    1722, Proved in London in 1725,"
    22:xxviii; 25:vii, 87-91; "Wills of Early
    Jewish Settlers in New York," 22:xiii;
    23:vii, 147-61; "Wills of Rabbi Carigal,"
    31:242-43
Willson, 27:470
Willson, Ebenezer, 23:149
Willson, J. G., 29:100-101
Wilmington (N.C.), religious observances,
    mid-nineteenth century, 37:38
Wilmington and Weldon Railroad, 29:147
Wilmot, Eardley, 35:36
Wilmot, John, 38:101
Wilmot, John Eardley, 35:36
Wilmot Proviso, 25:22
Wilmslow, 26:151
Wilner, Morton H., 47:203

Wilson, Beckles, 49:127
Wilson, Capt. (Civil War), 39:179
Wilson, Captain (War of 1812), 26:184
Wilson, Charles, 26:153
Wilson, Charles S., 36:120-28, 133-34
Wilson & Co., W. W., 46:160
Wilson, Henry, 38:174; 42:131, 133, 136-41, 143-45
Wilson, Hugh R., 36:376, 381
Wilson, J., *Our Israelitish Origin*, 30:467
Wilson, James (Canada), 23:139
Wilson, James (Congress), 22:141
Wilson, James (Pa.), 28:xxxiv
Wilson, James (1778), 37:110
Wilson, James Patriot, *Easy Introduction to the Knowledge of the Hebrew Language*, 30:149, 151
Wilson, Judge (1898), 40:288
Wilson, P., 30:282
Wilson, Robert, 42:418
Wilson, Romer, 35:264
Wilson, William, 23:21
Wilson, Woodrow, 26:10; 28:259; 31:277, 285-96; Balkan disabilities, 24:84, 86, 89; 29:203; 36:xii, 135; 38:51, 326; 40:8, 14-15, 89, 173, 288; Brandeis, 41:49; 42:353; Ezekiel Monument, 28:54; Harris Weinstock, 29:197; history, writing of, 46:333, 368, 434; labor, 41:308, 330; Poland and Jewish disabilities, 36:147-49, 153, 160; Russian Treaty, 41:184; U.S. diplomacy and Jewish disabilities, 36:73-74, 79, 84, 91; "Woodrow Wilson, the Birth of Czechoslovakia and Congressman Sabath," 38:342; "Woodrow Wilson in His Relation to Jewish Problems," 31:xvii; Zionism, 45:37; 49:199
Wilson's "Memorial History of New York," 23:174
Wiltshire, W., 37:340
Winans, Ross, 25:145
Winawer, Maxim, 40:403
Winchell, Walter, 35:273
Winchester (congressman), 24:8
Winchester, Boyd, 36:100
Winchevsky, Morris, 39:113
Winder, John H., 43:107
Windsor, Lord, 23:26
Windsor, Solomon, 27:45, 84

Wineman, Laura L., 42:68-70
Wineman, Philip, 29:129
Winer, George B., 30:281; *Grammar of the Chaldee Language*, 30:408
Winer, Mrs. Herman L., gift, 35:xxi
Winestine, Norman, book review by, 38:321-22
Wing, Abraham, 27:318
Wingate, Andrew, 47:167, 170
Wingate, Judge, 22:15
Winkeroy, Ernest, 42:180
Winkler, Helen, 34:209
Winn, Isaac Lascelles (1769), 22:40, 49
Winnebago Indians, 22:173-74
Winship, George Parker, 30:vi
Winslow, Josias, 38:292
Winslow, Warren, 48:152
Winsor, Benjamin, 35:291
Winsor, J., 34:173
Winsor, Justin, 26:xvii, 2
Winston, Richard, 25:120
Winter, Carl George, 41:216; "The Influence of the Russo-American Treaty of 1832 on the Rights of American Jewish Citizens," 41:163-94
Winterbotham, W., "An Historical, Geographical, Commercial and Philosophical View of the United States of America," 25:131
Winter & Bottom, 21:165
Winterton, Lord, 36:379
Winthrop, John, 23:96; 25:19; 26:207; 30:41; 34:274; 46:22; Judah Touro portrait, 27:214, 216, 422
Winyah Indigo Society, 48:177
Winz, Leo, 45:163
Winzingerode, Count, 26:40
Wirkham, Samuel, 35:290
Wischnitzer, Mark, 40:415; 46:66, 360; books reviewed by, 38:325-27; 40:401-4; *To Dwell in Safety, The Story of Jewish-Migration since 1800*, reviewed, 39:196-98; *Visas to Freedom: The History of HIAS*, reviewed, 48:137-38
Wischnitzer, Rachel, 41:105; 43:137; "The Egyptian Revival in Synagogue Architecture," 41:61-75; "The Source of the Architectural Historian," 45:265; 46:114-19; *Synagogue Architecture in the*

United States: History and Interpretation, reviewed, 46:64-66; "Which of the Portraits of Menasseh ben Israel Was in the Possession of Ezra Stiles (Illustrated)," 50:427

Wisconsin, Civil War, 50:279-80, 304; Jewish local history, 49:242-43; "Notes on the History of the Jews of Wisconsin," 44:242

Wisconsin State Historical Society, 46:149, 151

Wisconsin, University of, 23:103; 46:149, 151; 49:192

Wise, Aaron, 35:57; 40:35; 44:183; 45:159

Wise, Edward H., 31:226

Wise, Henry Alexander, 38:173; 50:342

Wise, Isaac Mayer, 28:275, 284; 31:270; 32:121, 130; 34:xviii, xxi, 146, 175, 193; 35:133, 320, 326; 38:250; 39:171, 454-58; 41:91; 42:455; 44:1, 252; 45:28, 96, 103, 126; 48:261; 49:76; American Israelites, 49:16-18, 21, 31; "Americanization of Isaac M. Wise," 33:xxx; Bernhard Marks, 44:12, 34-35; Board of Delegates American Israelites, 29:79; chaplaincy, 40:186; 41:358, 360; Civil War, 42:131-34, 139, 142, 144; 50:293-96; David Philipson, 39:462, 467; emigration, 41:230; Emma Lazarus, 42:83; Hebrew press, 33:134, 138; Hebrew Union College, 40:19-21, 23-41, 46-47; history, writing of, 39:239, 258; 46:167, 271, 276, 281, 283, 388, 431; "Isaac M. Wise on the Jewish Community of Cincinnati in 1872," 37:xxxii; *Israelite,* 26:271-73, 283; Jewish history, 48:142-44; Judah P. Benjamin, 38:154-56, 158-61, 164; Milwaukee Jewry, 47:36, 42-43, 46-47; Moses Jacob Ezekiel, 28:44-47; New York chief rabbi, 44:132, 151; Philadelphia Jewry, 49:219, 223-25, 227, 230, 243; Reform Judaism, 39:330, 403; 40:364-65, 368, 370, 372, 382-83, 386, 394; 42:101; 43:138, 146; 50:118-19; Sabato Morais bibliography, 37:62, 67, 73, 75-77, 84, 90; Sabbath closing, 37:45; Simon Tuska, 50:79-82, 84-96; Union American Hebrew Congregation, 29:202; Y.M.H. Associations, 37:227-28, 250

Wise, Isador, 28:46

Wise, James Waterman, *The Legend of Louise: The Life of Mrs. Stephen Wise,* reviewed, 39:333-35

Wise, Jonah B., 37:58; 41:91

Wise Legion, 50:315

Wise, M. S., 37:275

Wise, Stephen S., 29:169; 31:257; 34:162; 38:63; 39:111; 48:243; Adolph Jellinek, 33:238, 244; *Challenging Years: The Autobiography of Stephen Wise,* reviewed, 39:333-35; disabilities, 36:79; George A. Kohut, 34:306; Hebrew Union College, 40:52-53, 381, 391; 45:158; Justice Cardozo, 49:7, 13; National Socialist Party, 45:221, 230-31, 233-35, 238, 241-42; sermons, 32:xxv; "Woodrow Wilson in His Relation to Jewish Problems," 31:xvii; Zionism, 35:57-59; 42:100-101; 45:99; 47:165; 49:141, 199

Wise, Mrs. Stephen S., 36:374-75; *The Legend of Louise: The Life Story of Mrs. Stephen S. Wise,* reviewed, 39:333-35

Wise, Therese Bloch, 50:296

Wiseman, Emma (Jacobson), 22:222

Wiseman, Heim, 40:284

Wiseman, Joseph, 22:222

Wissig, Eduard, 33:184

Wister family, 50:244

Wister, Owen, 50:244

Wit, Gisbert de, 33:110-11

Witchcraft, 46:22

With, Witte Corneliszoon de, 47:117-19

Witherby, Thomas, 26:129-31

Withers, R. F., 39:42

Withers, Reuben, 39:35

Witherspoon, John, 37:188; 46:181

Withington, 28:163, 169

Witkowsky, S. D., 29:130

Witnesses, disabilities of Jews as, 25:94, 101, 103; "Anglo-Jewish Legal Cases," 25:134-38

Witt, Bernard, gifts, 33:xxxiii; 35:xxii

Witt, Susannah, 22:22

Witte, Serge Julievich, 41:175

Witte, Sergius de, 36:264-68, 275; 39:100; 40:9; 43:67

Wittke, Carl F., 45:2; 46:302

Wittkowsky, B., 29:130

Wiznitzer, Arnold, 42:331, 468; 47:115, 119-20, 209; "The Exodus from Brazil and

Arrival in New Amsterdam of the Jewish Pilgrim Fathers, 1654," 44:80-97, 255; 49:229; "Isaac de Castro, Brazilian Jewish Martyr," 47:63-75; "Jewish Soldiers in Dutch Brazil (1630-1654)," 46:40-50; *Jews in Colonial Brazil*, reviewed, 50:73-76; "The Members of the Brazilian Jewish Community (1648-1653)," 42:387-95, 416; "The Minute Book of Congregations Zur Israel of Recife and Magen Abraham of Mauricia, Brazil," 42:217-302, 416; "The Records of the Earliest Jewish Community in the New World," 44:246; "The Synagogue and Cemetery of the Jewish Community in Recife, Brazil (1630-1654)," 43:127-32

Woelfflin, Heinrich, 46:114

Wohl, J. J., 33:167

Wohlfarth, Michael, *The Naked Truth*, 30:467

Wohlgemuth, Ephraim, 29:130

Wolcott, Francis Metcalfe, 46:166-67

Wolcott, Oliver, 46:438

Wolcott, Oliver, Jr., 38:128

Wolcott, Roger, 38:289

Woldman, Albert A., 50:401

Wolf, 49:209

Wolf, A., 39:101

Wolf, Abraham, 29:199

Wolf, Mrs. Abraham S., necrology of, 28:xxii

Wolf, Adolph Grant, 29:206

Wolf, Albert, necrology of, 33:xiii

Wolf, Benjamin, 29:199; "Saul Brown, the First Hazan in North America, and Benjamin Wolf, the Third Recorded Hazan," 32:xix

Wolf, Colonel, 43:66

Wolf, D., 27:95

Wolf, Edward, necrology of, 26:xiv, 289-90

Wolf, Edwin, 47:204; necrology of, 34:ix

Wolf, Edwin II, 43:238; 48:266; 50:427; books reviewed by, 44:252-54; 49:208-9; executive council, 40:406; 41:388; 44:241; 47:201; 50:426; history, writing of, 46:181-83, 185, 189-90, 404, 410-11; Jewish bibliography, 50:69-71; "The Pollocks: American Pioneers and Adventures, 1833-1853," 43:231; Whiteman, Maxwell, *History of the Jews of Philadelphia from Colonial Times to the Age of Jackson*, 47:134;

49:234-35; reviewed, 47:204-7; Jewish local history, 49:260-61

Wolf, Elias, 21:215; 29:199

Wolf, Emanuel, 50:314

Wolf, Esther, 41:257

Wolf, Gerson, 28:96, 100-101

Wolf, Henry (Md.), 26:188

Wolf, Henry (Pa.), 23:175

Wolf, Horace J., 28:290

Wolf, Isaac, 26:188

Wolf, Isaac, Jr., 26:289

Wolf, Jacob (Canada), 35:6

Wolf, Jacob (Ky.), 28:269

Wolf, Jacob (Md.), 22:193; 26:184

Wolf, Jacob (Pa.), 26:188

Wolf, James (General), 22:91

Wolf, Joseph, *Missionary Journal and Memoir*, 30:230

Wolf, Levi, 29:199

Wolf, L. S., 39:404

Wolf, Lucien, 31:56; 35:36; 37:2; 38:17; 49:67; Christianity and common law, 31:117, 119-21; 35:118; gift, 25:xvi; historical exhibition, 25:159; 42:435-36; Joshua Montefiore, 28:120, 123; 29:78; 40:123-24; Kohler bibliography, 34:173-74, 225; necrology of, 33:xii; Zionism, 47:168, 172, 174

Wolf, Louis, death, 37:xii

Wolf, May V., 29:206

Wolf, Michael, 26:184, 187

Wolf, Morris, 43:238; executive council, 29:xxxvi; 31:xvi; 32:xii; 33:xxv; 37:xxix; 38:342; 39:470; nominations committee, 31:xxiii

Wolf, Moses de, 21:215

Wolf, R., 27:1

Wolf, Rebecca, 22:193

Wolf, Ruth (Levi), 28:290

Wolf, S., 29:131

Wolf, Samuel, 26:188

Wolf, Simon, 25:xii; 26:7, 30; 32:121; 35:131; 36:ix; 37:169; 39:1; 41:38, 205, 378; 42:211, 452; 47:195; Alliance Israelite, 39:418, 426-28, 436; "American Contributions Toward the Removal of Jewish Disabilities in the Balkan States," 24:1-153; 25:xiv; American Israelites, 49:30-31; B'nai B'rith, 45:99; Board of

Delegates of American Israelites, 29:76, 78-79, 91, 93, 96, 111-13; civil and religious rights, 36:177-78, 271; Civil War, 50:269, 303-4, 307-9, 315, 406; communication from, 26:xxx; executive council, 22:xii, xvi, xxvii; 23:xii; 25:xi; 28:xiv; 29:xiv; "Extracts from a Diary of the First Five Months of 1865," 22:xxix; gifts, 23:xviii; 29:xli, xliii; HIAS, 49:186; history, writing of, 39:210; 40:230-31, 252, 257; International Congress of Americanists, 23:x; "Jewish Disabilities in the Balkan States: American Contributions Toward Their Removal, with Particular Reference to the Congress of Berlin," 24:ix, 1-153; 25:xiv; Kohler bibliography, 34:170-71, 181, 183, 185-89, 205, 211, 226, 247, 256; Milwaukee, 47:53, 58, 111; necrology of, 29:xxxvi, 198-206; necrology of Martin A. Marks, 26:xiv, 281-82; papers, 31:xxxi, xxxv; Red Cross, 33:227-28; "Simon Wolf an United States Consul to Egypt," 46:493; 47:76-100; thirty-first annual meeting, committee on, 29:xxvi; War of 1812, 26:181, 183; Y.M.H.A., 37:229, 236, 241, 263-64; Zionism, 48:189, 199; *see also*: Kohler, Max J.

Wolf, Mrs. Simon, gift, 31:xxxi
Wolf, Solomon B., 50:329
Wolf, Sussel, 41:253
Wolf, widow, 27:95
Wolf, William, 26:194; 39:7
Wolfe, Albert B., 34:203
Wolfe, B., 22:193
Wolfe, Benjamin, 22:193; 50:65, 164
Wolfe, Daniel, 25:118
Wolfe, David, 25:118
Wolfe, Frederick, 50:329
Wolfe, James, 35:2, 4, 6
Wolfe, Lucien, memorial lecture, 40:87
Wolfe, M., 27:120
Wolfe, Michael B., 27:145
Wolfe, Rachel, 27:112
Wolfe, Simon, 27:81
Wolfe of London, 27:81
Wolfenbüttel, Gumpel, 33:251; 34:109-10, 112
Wolfenson, Louis B., 40:48
Wolfenstein, S., 40:28
Wolff, Aaron, 50:148

Wolff, Albert, 28:4, 16
Wolff, B., 37:266, 268
Wolff, Frances N., gift, 34:xxii
Wolff, Joseph, 26:117; 33:24; *Narrative of a Mission to Bokhars*, 30:408; *Researches and Missionary Labours among the Jews*, 30:318-19
Wolff, Judith, 48:25
Wolff, M. (San Francisco), 37:45
Wolff, Rachel Cappé, 50:148
Wolff, Samuel, 29:131
Wolford Forwarding Company, 28:270
Wolfsohn, Joel D., 47:203
Wolfson, Harry A., 35:169; 37:459; 43:195; 44:121; 45:136; 47:221; gift, 35:xxii; vice-president, 43:230; 44:241; 45:264; 46:492
Wolfson, Michael, 29:132
Wolfstein, Florine, 46:122
Wolk, Isadore, 46:164
Wolkonsky, Sergius, 36:398
Wolkovisky v. Rapaport, "Anglo-Jewish Legal Cases," 25:136
Wollaston, John, 41:294; 43:232; portrait of, 42:417
Wollenberger, Judas, 41:267
Wollenberger, Paul, 41:375
Wollf, Abram E., 40:70
Wollman, Maurice, 35:238
Wolman, Leo, 41:321
Wolsey, Louis, 41:90-92
Woman in the Case, The, 40:354
Women's rights, 38:250; Convention in 1852, 42:110
Women's Zionist Organization of America, 49:159
Wood, Anthony, 32:24
Wood v. Baker, 29:150
Wood, Charles, 40:293
Wood, Fernando, 27:121
Wood, John, 44:102
Wood, John H., 38:72
Wood, Thomas W., 27:177; *The Mosaic History of the Creation of the World*, 30:277
Wood, William, 35:294-95
Woodbine, N.J., 29:181-82; 38:311; 39:89, 95; "The Letters of Vladimir Korolenko about Woodbine, New Jersey (1893)," 45:265
Woodbridge, Alderman, 23:169

Woodbury, Levi, 30:404
Woodic, Emanuel, 29:64-69
Woodly, John, 23:158
Woods, Al, 35:268
Woods, Frederick A., 28:233
Woods, Robert A., 39:241
Woodson, Carter, 46:269
Woodsville, Mississippi, cemetery, 34:xx
Woodward, 31:159, 169
Woodworth, Samuel, "Poems, odes and songs," 34:xxiv
Wool, John E., 48:155-58
Woolf, Cairis, 27:97
Woolf, Rachel, 50:42, 62
Woolf, Edward, 40:147
Woolf, H., 29:130
Woolf, I., 29:132
Woolf, L., 29:134
Woolin, Elias, 21:45, 47-48; 22:160-61
Woolsey, C. Meech, 41:118-19
Woolsey, Richard, 41:119
Woolverton, Samuel, 33:222
Woonsocket, R. I., United Jewish Appeal, contribution, 37:xxviii
Worcester Auxiliary Society, 30:222
Worcester Convention of 1850, 38:250
Wordsworth, William, 35:239; 38:267
Working Girls' Home, Baltimore, 22:216
Workman, I., 29:135
Workman, Jacob, 27:105
Workman's Circle, 39:371; 45:233, 245; 46:164, 400; 50:252; (Utica), 49:246; gifts, 34:xxiii; 35:xxiii; *History of the Workmen's Circle*, 35:xxii
Works of Julius Bien: An Exhibition of Original Maps and Engravings, The, 50:381
Works Progress Administration, 46:161, 186; 47:192
Workum, Hanah E., 28:55-61
World Council of Churches, 41:92
World Court, 46:299
World Exposition, St. Louis, 31:290
World Federation of YMHAs and Jewish Community Centers, 47:232; 50:433
World Jewish Congress, 50:139
World Parliament of Religions, 42:3-4; 49:165
World's Fair, Chicago, 29:187
"World's Great Nations, The," 26:280

World's Own, The, 40:347
World's Work, 43:23
World Union for the Protection of Health among Jews, 50:141
World War II, 28:259-60, 270
World Youth Aliyah Organization, 49:170
World Zionist Organizations, 38:399; 49:200-201
Worms, Baron de, 24:46, 77; 29:86, 95
Worms, Hannah (Adolphus), 23:157
Worms, Henry de, 24:29-30, 45
Worth, General, 25:17
Worthington, Colonel, 50:21
Worthington, H. P. C., *Hell for the Jews*, 37:422
Worthington, W. G. D., 30:258; 31:xxxii; *Speech on Confirmatory Act Abolishing Religious Test*, 30:227
Worman, Tunis, 25:36
Wotton, William, 25:111
Woytywimmer, Hubert, 45:193
W. R., *Three Ladies of London*, 33:171
Wrede, Prince, 26:39
Wren, Christopher, 27:178; 45:50, 53
Wrenbury, Lord, 31:113
Wreschner, Abisch, 28:71
Wright, Bened., 27:367
Wright, Benjamin, 35:295, 298-300, 302; 37:105, 109
Wright, Carroll D., 48:31
Wright, Hary J., 43:12-13, 19, 26, 34
Wright, I. C., 22:100
Wright, James, 43:132; 46:37
Wright, P. T., 39:2, 55-60
Wright, Silas, 30:404
Writing, art of, 29:xl; Jewish, "An Evaluation of Achievement in American Jewish Local Historical Writing," 49:214-53
Writings on American History, 46:160; 49:255
Wroth, Lawrence C., 30:vi
Wunder, Richard P., 50:271
Wunderlich, George, 47:181
Wurts, George W., 36:109
Wurts, Mr., 36:225-26
Württemberg, 26:39-40, 89, 136; "Jewish Emigration from Württemberg to the United States of America (1848-1855)," 41:225-73
Wyatts, Lemuel, 35:297

X

Xenophobia, *see:* Discrimination
Ximenes, Abraham Levy, 27:30-31; 31:242-43
Ximenes, David, 27:250

"X Plan," 46:231
Xuarez, Violante, 32:117
XYZ affair, 38:119:20

Y

Ya'ari, Abraham, 49:55
Yad Abraham, 22:120-22
Yagdil Thora, 44:221
Yahai, Gedaliah ibn, 22:114
Yahrzeit, 39:373-74
Yahuda, Abraham S., 22:xxv; 25:xii, 26:24;
  gift, 26:xxxiv
Yakubov, Alexander, 38:314-16; 39:87
Yale College, 23:166; 26:245; 29:172; 32:113;
  34:70; 35:140; 42:342; 46:181, 429, 431;
  "College Bookplates With Hebrew
  Inscriptions," 45:131-32, 167-68; "Hebrew
  at Yale," 38:343
Yale, Elihu, 28:249-50
Yale University, 23:92; 34:304; 37:135;
  39:190; 40:51; 45:131-32; 46:426; 47:16,
  147, 149; 48:257; 49:11-12, 90;
  Congregationalism, 47:143, 145; "Judaica
  and Hebraica Collection in College
  Libraries," 45:138-40
Yale Law Journal, 47:212
Yale University Art Gallery, 42:417
Yale University Library, 35:305; 45:132, 138-
  40, 167-68, 185, 268
Yalta Conference, 40:117
Yamins, Nathan, 42:419
Yampolskaya, E., 38:244
Yancey, William L., 50:342
Yanai, 33:161
Yancy, 23:126
Yankee City, 46:398-99
Yankees (baseball team), 46:400
Yanow, Albert, 45:271
Yanow, H. C., 39:178
Yarmolinsky, 29:xliii
Yarmouth, "Henry Phillips on the Yarmouth
  Petroglyph," 28:xii-xxiii
Yarmouth, Countess of, 31:41
Yarnell, John J., 46:7, 10

Yaroslavsky, Jacob, 45:75-76, 86
Yashar, Book of, 21:229
Yates, George S., 49:181-82
Yates and Cahoon, 37:167-68
Yavorov (Galician Jew), 47:108
Ydana, Isaac, 32:63
Ydana, Joseph, 32:63
Ydana, Moses, 32:63
Yeamans, John, 29:138
Yearwood, H. G., 34:277
Yeates & Cahoone, 35:291
Yedidyah Bar Baruch alevy, 21:33
Yehiel b. R. Joseph, 34:291
Yellin, David, 39:449, 465; "Personal
  Reminiscences of Otis A. Glazebrook, U.
  S. Consul at Jerusalem," 31:xvii
Yellow badge, 28:69
Yellow fever, 43:238; "The Epidemic of
  Yellow Fever," 23:185; "The Jewish Dead
  During the 1793 Yellow Fever," 35:285-
  87; "Jews Who Died of Yellow Fever in
  the Epidemic in New York, in 1798,"
  25:xii, 123
Yeomans, William, 35:183
Yerk, John, 27:326
Yerk, William, 27:326
Yeshibah Minhat Areb, 44:212
Yeshibat Minhat Areb, 34:123
Yeshibot, 46:396-97
Yeshiva Endowment Foundation, 45:160
Yeshiva University, 39:216, 261, 300; 43:139;
  45:160-61, 185; 48:265; 50:70; Civil War,
  50:270, 273, 385
Yeshivah College, gift, 35:xxiii
Yeshuat Israel Congregation (Newport),
  32:126; 37:165-66; 42:225, 302
Yeshurun, I., 39:112
Yesiba de los Pintos, 44:217, 223
Yeshiba of Ros David Senior, 44:221

433

Yevreiskaya Biblioteka, 38:242
Yevreiskaya Mysl, 38:242
Yevreiskaya Niedielya, 38:243
Yevreiskaya Zhizn, 38:243
Yevreiski Krestianin, 38:243
Yevreiski Mir, 38:243
Yevreiski Viestnik, 38:243
Yevreiskoya Obozrenie, 38:243
Yidden Un Andere Etnische Grupes In Die Fareinigte Shtaten (Jew and Other Ethnic Groups in the United States), reviewed, 38:327-30
Yiddish Americana, "Resources on American Jewish History at the Library of Congress," 47:179-85, 201
Yiddish Culture Society, 45:240
Yiddish Labor Verein, 48:131
Yiddish Language, "Peace Conference in 1919 Discusses the Yiddish Language," 47:202
Yiddish literature, 50:267-68, 271
Yiddish press, 46:122, 192, 203, 394-95, 397; 48:32-133; 49:92, 99, 110, 243, 246; 50:137, 208, 402-3; "The American Yiddish Press during the First World War," 37:xxxii; in New York, 38:307
Yiddish theater, 39:257, 362, 367-68, 383-84, 388; 47:192; 49:99, 101, 105-6
Yiddesher Tageblatt, Der, 38:54
Yiddish Scientific Institute, 39:226, 240; 40:173; 42:209; 45:185; 46:164, 168, 215-16, 265, 372, 400
Yiddishe Welt, 45:224-25, 234
Yidishkeit, 46:387, 391
Yihkes, 46:387, 391
Ying, Chin, 34:195
YIVO Institute for Jewish Research, 49:137, 152, 154; 50:70; Civil War, 50:263, 267, 271, 273, 276, 297-98, 359, 403
Yonkers (N.Y.), religious observances, mid-nineteenth century, 37:38
Yonkers Historical Society, 23:xviii
York, Duke of, 44:76; 47:127
York, Lord Chancellor, 25:119-20
York (Pa.), Jewish Organized Charities, contribution, 37:xxviii
York (Pa.), Recorder, 34:39
Yorzeit, 46:424

Young, Alfred, "Attitudes to the Jew in Rural New York (1790-1800)," 41:390
Young, Brigham, 44:56
Young, Edward, 45:84
Young, Edward J., 42:348
Young, George Malcolm, 46:441
Young, Isaac de, 26:182
Young Israel, 33:36; 39:296; gift, 34:xxiii
Young, John (Canada), 23:49-50
Young, John (New York), 27:331
Young Judah, 49:84
Young Ladies Charitable Union, 37:288
Young Ladies' Hebrew Social Club (Rochester), 40:72
Young, Lublinck de, 22:124
Young, M. de, 27:114
Young Men's Association of Temple Ahavath Chesed (New York), 37:253; Temple Anshe Chesed (New York), 37:256; Temple Beth-El (New York), 37:252
Young Men's Christian Associations, 37:223, 225, 228, 231-32
Young Men's Committee (New York), 42:115
Young Men's Hebrew Association, 35:324; 39:255; 44:211; 49:31, 262; 50:280; (Albany, N.Y.), 37:245, 311, 313; (Alexandria, La.), 37:246, 311, 313; (Altoona, Pa.), 37:245, 251, 311, 313; (Appleton, Wis.), 37:249, 322-23; (Atlanta, Ga.), 37:245, 249, 251, 266, 274, 301, 311-13; (Augusta, Ga.), 37:226, 248, 309, 312-13; (Baltimore, Md.), 37:226, 228-30, 240, 242, 249, 251, 268, 272, 276, 309-13; (Birmingham, Ala.), 37:248, 265-69, 271-72, 283, 312-13; (Boston, Mass.), 37:240, 244, 246, 260, 272, 276, 278, 286, 309-11, 313, 320; (Bradford, Pa.), 37:245, 311, 313; (Brooklyn, N.Y.), 37:241, 243, 247-48, 253, 310-11, 313; (Buffalo, N.Y.), 37:226, 245-46, 251, 253, 255, 309, 311, 313; 46:163; (Canton, Miss.), 37:248, 312-13; (Charleston, S.C.), 37:242-43, 247, 272, 310, 312-13; (Chattanooga, Tenn.), 37:243-44, 310, 313; (Chelsea, Mass.), 37:320; (Chicago, Ill.), 37:242-43, 245, 281, 310, 313; (Cincinnati, Ohio), 37:227-28, 230, 242, 253, 265-70, 272, 276, 272, 281-82, 293, 309-10, 313-14; (Cleveland,

Ohio), 37:226, 228, 240, 245-46, 248, 265-70, 272, 276, 278, 309-11, 314; (Columbus, Ohio), 37:247, 283, 311, 314; (Cumberland, Md.), 37:245, 311, 314; (Dallas, Tex.), 37:244, 255-56, 273, 310, 314; (Danville, Va.), 37:245, 311, 314; (Denver, Colo.), 37:247, 272, 283, 312, 314; (Detroit, Mich.), 37:272; (Donaldson, La.), 37:245, 251, 311, 314; (Elizabeth, N.J.), 37:247, 282, 311, 314; (Fort Scott, Kan.), 37:248, 312, 314; (Fort Worth, Tex.), 37:248, 312, 314; (Gainesville, Tex.), 37:249, 312, 314; (Galveston, Tex.), 37:243, 257, 305, 310, 314; (Grand Rapids, Mich.), 37:246, 311, 314; (Greenville, Miss.), 37:249, 266, 268-71, 312, 314; (Hackensack, N.J.), 37:321; (Hamilton, Ont.), 37:249, 266, 312, 314; (Hartford, Conn.), 37:243, 251, 310, 314; (Henderson, Ky.), 37:229, 309, 314; (Hoboken, N.J.), 37:246, 311, 314; (Horrellsville, N.Y.), 37:311, 314; (Houston, Tex.), 37:247, 311, 314; (Indianapolis, Ind.), 37:242, 310, 314; (Jackson, Miss.), 37:247, 312, 314; (Jacksonville, Fla.), 37:240, 246, 257, 311, 314, 321; (Jersey City, N.J.), 37:240, 310, 314; juniors, 37:280-86; (Lafayette, Ind.), 37:228, 247, 309, 312, 314; (Leavenworth, Kan.), 37:241, 310, 314; (Little Rock, Ark.), 37:247, 268, 270, 312; (Los Angeles, Cal.), 37:248, 312, 314; (Louisville, Ky.), 29:182; 37:226, 228-29, 243-44, 249, 251, 253, 255, 258, 266, 268-74, 276, 279, 283, 309-10, 312, 314, 322; (Lynn, Mass.), 37:322; (Macon, Ga.), 37:243-44, 251, 253, 256, 272, 281, 310, 314; (Madison, Ind.), 37:228-29, 251, 253, 256-57, 281, 309, 314; (Marion, S.C.), 37:240, 310, 315; (Memphis, Tenn.), 37:246, 255, 266, 268-71, 311, 315; (Milford, Mass.), 37:305; (Milwaukee, Wis.), 37:247, 311, 315; (Minneapolis, Minn.), 37:247, 311, 315; (Mobile, Ala.), 37:246-47, 282, 311, 315; (Montgomery, Ala.), 37:228-29, 248, 266, 268, 270, 272, 309, 312, 315; (Montreal, Que.), 37:322; (Mount Vernon, Ind.), 37:245-46, 311, 315; (Nashville, Tenn.), 37:246, 255, 311, 315; (Newark, N.J.),

31:292; 37:241-43, 251, 253-55, 266, 268, 270, 272, 279, 282, 310, 315, 456; (New Orleans, La.), 26:276; 37:227, 242-43, 251, 253, 255, 272, 274, 283, 286, 309-10, 315; (New York), 22:211; 27:275; 29:169; 31:275, 296; 37:225, 229-30, 232-44, 246-48, 250-64, 266-68, 272, 274-85, 289-90, 304, 306, 309, 311, 315, 324; 40:134, 141, 164; 41:376; 45:191; (Oakland, Cal.), 37:244, 252-53, 255, 310, 315; (Olean, N.Y.), 37:247, 312, 315; (Omaha, Neb.), 37:247, 312, 315; (Opelousas, La.), 37:243, 310, 315; (Parkersburg, W. Va.), 37:228, 309, 315; (Paterson, N.J.), 37:242, 310, 315; (Perth Amboy, N.J.), 37:324; (Petersburg, Va.), 37:246, 311, 315; (Philadelphia), 22:231, 233, 235; 23:192; 28:266, 310; 29:189; 31:255, 276; 37:19-21, 225-26, 230, 232-40, 243, 250-59, 262-63, 272, 274-76, 278, 280-81, 283, 285, 290-91, 309-10, 315; 38:338; 39:321; 40:166; 45:203-4; (Pittsburgh, Pa.), 37:242-43, 251, 266, 268-70, 286, 310, 315; (Portland, Ore.), 37:244, 251, 253, 255, 257, 310, 315; (Pottsville, Pa.), 37:244, 310, 315; (Providence, R.I.), 37:245, 249, 311-12, 315; 38:73; (Quincy, Ill.), 37:227, 245, 281, 309, 311, 315; (Richmond, Va.), 37:226, 228-29, 309, 316; (Rochester, N.Y.), 37:247, 312, 316; (Rome, Ga.), 37:244, 248, 310, 312, 316; Russian-Jewish immigration, 37:286-97; (St. Louis, Mo.), 37:228, 242-43, 245, 247-48, 251, 253, 260, 266-68, 270-71, 275, 278-79, 281-82, 285-86, 292-93, 304, 311, 312, 316; (St. Paul, Minn.), 37:247, 311, 316; (San Antonio, Tex.), 37:244, 310, 316; (San Francisco, Cal.), 37:242, 246, 251-55, 274, 310-11, 316; (Savannah, Ga.), 37:240, 271-72, 274, 276, 309, 312, 316; (Scranton, Pa.), 37:246, 248, 311-12, 316, 326; (Selma, Ala.), 37:248, 266, 268, 272, 312, 316; (Syracuse, N.Y.), 37:226, 247, 309, 312, 316; (Tampa, Fla.), 37:326; (Tarboro, N.C.), 37:242, 310, 316; (Texarkana, Tex.), 37:248, 312, 316; (Trenton, N.Y.), 37:326; (Trinidad, Colo.), 37:249, 312, 316; (Troy, N.Y.), 37:244-45, 251, 253, 310, 316; (Vicksburg, Va.), 37:249, 268, 312, 316;

(Waco, Tex.), 37:248, 312, 316; (Waltham, Mass.), 37:305; (Washington, D.C.), 37:241, 245, 272, 283, 310-11, 316; 41:205; (Wheeling, W. Va.), 37:228, 244, 311, 316; (Wichita, Kan.), 37:248, 312, 316; (Wilkes-Barre, Pa.), 31:298; 37:242, 251, 253, 255-57, 310, 316; (Williamsport, Pa.), 37:242, 310, 316; (Wilmington, N.C.), 37:246, 311, 316; women in, 37:280-86; (Yonkers, N.Y.), 37:249, 312, 316; "The Young Men's Hebrew Association (1854-1913)," 37:xxx, 221-326
Young Men's Hebrew Benevolent Society (Montreal), 50:135
Young Men's Hebrew Literary Associations, 37:223-26, 271-72, 277, 280; (Baltimore, Md.), 37:224, 226, 295; (Chicago, Ill.), 37:224; (Cleveland, Ohio), 37:224, 228, 309; (Davenport, Iowa), 37:224; (New Orleans, La.), 37:224; (New York City), 37:224; (Philadelphia, Pa.), 37:223-26, 258, 284, 300; 43:140; (Richmond, Va.), 37:224; Rock Island, Ill.), 37:224; (St. Louis, Mo.), 37:224, 242-43, 253, 310; (San Francisco), 37:224
Young Men's Hebrew Literary Society (Cleveland), 29:199
Young Men's Hebrew Union (Philadelphia), 37:291
Young Men's Jewish Association (Rochester), 40:69-70, 72
Young Men's Literary Association (Philadelphia), 48:234
Young Men's Philanthropic League (New York), gift, 35:xxiv

Young Men's Sir Moses Montefiore Association of Providence, 38:64-65
Young Men's and Young Women's Hebrew Associations (Brooklyn, N.Y.), 50:431; (Lawrence, Mass.), 50:431; (New York), 47:230-31; (Philadelphia), 45:206
Young People's Hebrew Association (Quincy, Ill.), 37:281
Young, Pierce M. B., 50:397
Young Poale Zion Alliance, gift, 35:xxii
Young Quaker, The, 33:174, 179-80
Young, Samuel, 30:404
Young Turks, 47:169
Young Women's Hebrew Association, 35:318; 37:306; (Newark), 31:292; 37:456; (New Orleans), 37:296; (New York), gift, 34:xxiii
Young Women's Hebrew Association v. Sanders, 25:136
Young Women's Union, 31:287
Youth Aliyah, 49:170-71
Ysrael, Abraham, 44:92-93
Yudelson, A. B., 28:240
Yuells, Florence, 27:xix
Yulee, C. Wickliffe, 25;1-2, 29; 37:440
Yulee, David Levy, 22:xxxi, 100; 32:xxvi; 37:440; 38:160-61, 167; 40:288; 44:254; 47:224; 49:17; 50:69, 191, Civil War, 50:317-18, 335-38, 340; "David L. Yulee, Florida's First Senator," 25:vii, 1-29; portrait, 26:xxxiv; 29:xli
Yulee, Elias, 25:7
Yulee, Mary, 25:29
Yuxsheimer, Abraham, 26:184

Z

Zach, Captain, 23:64

Zacharie, Isachar, 38:320; 41:215; Civil War, 50:352, 377-78; "Isachar Zacharie: Lincoln's Chiropodist," 43:71-126; 44:106-13; "Isachar Zacharie: Union Spy," 50:427

Zacharie, Samuel, 43:107

Zacuto, Abraham, 35:133; 39:215

Zacutto, Jacob, 42:279, 395

Zacutto, Moseh, 42:279, 395

Zacutto, Moses, 44:83

Zaddocks, E., 27:45

Zadok (Hungarian Jew), 47:105, 107; 48:36

Zafren, Herbert C., 50:270

Zahalon, Jacob ben Isaac, 28:183-84

Zak, Alexander, 43:59

Zak, I., 39:111

Zak, V., 39:103

Zakkai, Ben, 39:104-7

Zakynthus (Zante) and Kephalonia, Bishop of, 28:181

Zalinski, Edmund Louis Grey, 35:255-56

Zand, Walter P., "The Economic Life of the Jews of Port Chester, N.Y.," essay award, 45:262

Zangwill, Israel, 25:162; 35:124, 250-51; 39:103; 40:346-47, 353, 356; 43:23, 26-28, 239; 45:205; 46:474-75, 477-86; Mesopotamian Project, 47:160, 163, 166-75

Zangwill, Mrs. Israel, 35:246

Zaphet (Safed), 27:19

Zarchin, Michael, 33:167, "Jewish Contributions to the Economic Life of San Francisco," 39:471

Zarfati, Isaac, 28:168

Zarfati, Joseph, 28:166, 170, 199

Zarfati, Samuel, 28:166-67, 170, 199

Zarikoew, Sabas, 34:206-7

Zaritzky, Max, 41:336, 354

Zausmer, Jacob, *Be Ikebei ha Dor: Reshimot, Masot ve Zikronot*, reviewed, 48:194-95

Zausner, Philip, 43:192-93

Zebi ben Mordecai, kosher meat, 22:xxii

Zedler, Johann Heinrich, 37:379-80

Zeeby, Hiya, 34:293

Zeichek, Naftali, 47:208

Zeifert, M., 38:307-8, 310

Zeiger, Arthur, 39:326

Zeimer, Joseph, 50:314

Zeisler, Fannie Bloomfield, 48:202, 267; 49:70, 143

Zeitgeist, 35:xvii; 42:101

Zeitlin, Jacob, 42:420-22; 46:120

Zeitlin, M., 39:100

Zeitlin, Solomon, 32:121; 44:64; 48:194; gift, 28:xxxix; 29:xliii; "Hasidism, a Revolt of the Masses," 32:xiii; "The Napoleonic Sanhedrin and the Russian Government," 28:xxiii; nominations committee, 31:xxiii; "Some Remarks on the Shabbetha-Zebi Movement in Poland and Ukrainia," 28:xxxiii; "The Struggle between the Sects in the Last Days of Jerusalem," 26:xxxi; "When Did Jerusalem Surrender to Antiochus Sidetes?," 26:xiv, 165-71

Zeitschrift für Hebraische Bibliographie, 45:102-3

Zeitung für das Wahre Judenthum, 22:136

Zeleny, Carolyn, *see*: Bernard, William S.

Zeller, Jacob Hirsch, 49:54

Zellner, Benjamin, 47:36

Zellner & Bonbs, 47:37

Zelman, Samuel V., 37:79

Zelter, 35:240

Zemah David, 28:65-66

Zenger, John Peter, 22:161; 35:172; 42:77

Zerahiah ben Shealtiel Hen, 28:146

Zerin, Edward, 42:420
Zevi, Shabbetai, 43:155; 46:383
Zewi, Ben, 38:315
Zeydel, H. E., 34:189
Zhitlowsky, Chaim, 39:441; 45:240
Zichy, Charles, 26:50
Zieber, George, 26:183-84
Ziegler, Aloysius K., 47:203
Zielenziger, Kurt, 35:136
Zielonka, David, 35:327-28
Zielonka, Dora Schatzky, 35:328
Zielonka, Martin, "The Fighting Jew," 31:xiv,
    211-17; "Francisco Rivas," 34:xv; 35:219-
    25; "Jewish Immigration to Mexico as a
    Result of the World War," 29:xxx; "Jewish
    Pioneers Along the Mexican Border,"
    29:xxx; necrology of, 35:326-28; "Social
    Service Endeavor for Jewish Soldiers, El
    Paso, 1916," 26:xxxi; "A Spanish-American
    Jewish Periodical," 23:vii, xiv, 129-35
Zilenziger, Solomon, 48:241
Zimmerman, Charles S., 43:194
Zimmerman, Frank, "A Letter and
    Memorandum on Ritual Circumcision,
    1772," 44:58-63
Zimmerman, Jules, "The Reverend Samuel
    Myer Isaacs: Forgotten Leader," Historical
    Essay Award, 44:240
Zinberg, S., 33:134
Zinsler, Leopold, 44:166
Zinzendorf, Count, 28:103
Zion, 41:391
Zion, Ben, 40:320
Zion College (Cincinnati), 40:21
Zion Congregation (Chicago), 45:94
Zion House (Buffalo), 37:294
Zionism, 29:204; 31:262-63; 33:17, 29;
    34:xxxiii, 173, 226; 35:117-18, 122-23, 135;
    38:2, 280, 330, 339; 39:194, 265, 359, 463;
    40:340, 402, 404; 42:100, 321-22; 43:154;
    44:122, 124; 47:122, 131-32; 48:145, 243,
    254-55; 49:81-82, 84, 245; and Alliance
    Israélite Universelle, 39:409-13, 440-42;
    The American Jew: A Zionist Analysis,
    reviewed, 47:61-62; and American Jewish
    historical writing, 49:216; "American
    Zionism and the Congressional Resolution
    of 1922 on Palestine," 44:242; 45:35-47;
    anti-Zionism, 40:361-94; "British Projects

for the Restoration of Jews to Palestine,"
    26:xv, 127-64; Canada, 50:138; "The Early
    Attitude of the American Jewish
    Committee to Zionism (1906-1922),"
    49:188-201; "The Early History of
    Zionism in America," 45:128; 49:215; "An
    Early Zionist Project," 25:xiii; English
    Federation, 31:264; Ephraim Deinard,
    34:152; Hebrew periodicals, 33:129;
    Hebrew Union College, 40:41, 43, 50;
    Henrietta Szold, 49:163, 165-69; history,
    writing of, 46:269, 275, 277, 280-81, 286,
    373, 383-84, 391, 402, 409-10, 412; "Jacob
    de Haas, American Zionist Journalist,"
    47:202; and Jewish education, 42:10, 14;
    Jewish local history, 49:219, 221-22, 227,
    232-33, 235, 245, 248, 251, 256; "Jewish
    Religious and Cultural Life in America as
    Reflected in the Felsenthal Collection,"
    45:93-127; Joseph Isaac Bluestone, 35:53-
    61; *Latin America and the Palestine Problem*,
    reviewed, 48:136-37; Mordecai Manuel
    Noah, 21:x, xx-xxi, 229-52; 41:7, 10-16, 18,
    21-23, 26; *Niles' Weekly Register*, 50:11-12,
    14-17; "Noah's Ararat Jewish State in its
    Historical Setting," 43:170-91; "On the
    Attitude of Some Prominent Reform Jews
    Towards Zionism," 44:242; "Paul Haupt
    and the Mesopotamian Project, 1892-
    1914," 47:154-75; Philipson on, 39:461-62;
    "The Reaction of Reform Judaism in
    America to Political Zionism," 40:361-94;
    The Realities of American-Palestine Relations,
    reviewed, 39:331-33; and refugees, 45:234-
    35, 239, 241-42, 247; "Rumanian Jews,"
    45:74; Samuel Schulman, 45:267; "The
    Single-Tax Zionism of Joseph Fels,"
    46:474-91, 493; Sokolow's history,
    28:xxxix; *The Struggle for Palestine*,
    reviewed, 40:313-17; *Trial and Error: The
    Autobiography of Chaim Weizmann*,
    reviewed, 39:202-5; U.S. and Palestine,
    40:113-14, 117-18; "An unknown Zionist
    Rhode Island project of Mordecai Manuel
    Noah," 33:xviii; "the World Significance
    of a Jewish State," 28:xl; "Zionism,"
    23:xvii; *The Zionist Idea: A Historical
    Analysis and Reader*, reviewed, 49:140-42
Zionist Actions Committee, 37:483

Zionist Congress, 45:194; 47:163; 48:194; 49:169; (6th), 46:477-78; (7th), 46:478; of 1913, minutes, 23:xvii
Zionist Library and Archives, 46:167
Zionist Organization of America, 29:177; 31:206; 37:476; 39:332; 40:393; 42:202; 45:37-39, 196; 46:280; 47:163, 170; 49:91, 191; 50:395; gift, 33:xxxiii
Zionist Record, 48:20-23
Zirndorf, H., 40:28, 36
Zitt, Hersch L., 49:208, "An Attempted Jewish Land Company in Colonial Carolina," 44:242; "Naturalization of Jews in Colonial Rhode Island—A Re-Examination," 41:390
Zlotow, Yankel, *see*: Goldstein, Jacob
Znaniecki, Florian, 46:368, 374
Zoddek, Arnold, 48:263
Zohar, 22:103
Zola, Émile, 26:96; 41:96; 45:258-59; *Zola and the Dreyfus case*, 35:xxi
Zolotkoff, Leon, 33:137
Zommer, Herman, 39:151
Zonnestein, Johannes, 32:14
Zorach, William, 40:320
Zorinski, Morton, 33:174, 184
Zoutman, Admiral, 22:29
Zuber, W., 37:439
Zubo, Cardoso Abraham, 32:63
Zucker, Adolf E., 41:231-32; 47:203
Zuckerman, Baruch, 36:155
Zuckerman, Benedict, 28:262, 50:92
Zuckerman, Esther, 37:iv
Zukor, Adolph, "Biography of Will Irwin," 33:xxx
Zukunft, 35:xvii; 45:155; 46:397; 47:228
Zumárraga, Juan, 31:15, 18, 25
Zundel, Enoch, 34:289
Zunser, Eliakim, 43:22
Zunsser, biography, 31:xxxiii
Zuntz, Mr., 35:200
Zuntz, A., 21:166
Zuntz, Abraham, 27:55
Zuntz, Alexander, 21:141-46, 148-49, 168, 184, 212; 27:32, 38-40, 43, 51, 54-55, 58, 60-62, 64, 66-67, 70, 72, 78, 84, 86, 88, 241-42, 253; 31:83; 38:49, 83; 50:37, 62
Zuntz, Ellen, 27:111

Zuntz, Grace, 27:78
Zuntz, Jacob, 21:167
Zuntz, Judah, 21:161, 168-69; 27:55, 69, 86-88, 95, 105, 107, 122, 314; 30:124, 230
Zuntz, Moses, 27:55
Zuntz, Rachel, 27:113
Zuntz, Uriah, 27:55
Zunz, Adelheid, 33:238
Zunz, Leopold, 26:11; 28:72, 264; 29:128; 33:238-39; 34:16; 39:169, 208; 41:12, 227, 241; 44:65; 45:100, 126
Zupbeiler, Meyer, 50:253
Zurbrick, John L., 34:219
Zürich, University of, 22:211, 213
Zur Israel Congregation of Recife, 43:128; 46:42-43; "The Minute Book of Congregations Zur Israel of Recife and Magen Abraham of Mauricia, Brazil," 42:217-302, 416
Zurnamer (family name), 48:20-22, 26
Zurnamer, Fanny, 48:26
Zurnamer, Gatze Solomon, 48:26:27, 263
Zurnamer, Harry, 48:26
Zurnamer, Jack, 48:26
Zurnamer, Jacob, 48:26
Zurnamer, Joey, 48:27
Zurnamer, Kalie, 48:26
Zurnamer, Mrs. Kalie (Newman), 48:27
Zurnamer, Lenie, 48:26-27
Zurnamer, Leonie, 48:27
Zurnamer, Marcus, 48:26
Zurnamer, Meyer, 48:26, 263
Zurnamer, Minnie, 48:27
Zurnamer, Rachel Collitz, 48:26
Zurnamer, Rebecca (Mrs. Jacobs), 48:26
Zurnamer, Rebecca (Shagan), 48:26
Zurnamer, Rose, 48:26
Zurnamer, Samuel, 48:26
Zurnamer, Shinke (Jane), 48:26
Zurnamer, Zalman, 48:27
Zurne (family name), 48:20, 26
Zurne, Harry, 48:26
Zuzorffe, Dauid, 42:227, 279, 395
Zwarts, Jacob, "An Episode in the Jewish Colonization of Guiana, 1660," 32:xiii; gift, 28:xli; 29:xliii
Zweig, Arnold, 35:135, 274
Zychlinski, Ludwik, 39:148